Economics, 7e *offers a powerful collec* *of innovative student resources.*

ECONOMICS IN THE MOVIES

Bring economic topics to life in a context that students will really relate to. *Economics in the Movies,* by Professor G. Dirk Mateer of The Pennsylvania State University, is a supplement that consists of clips from recent popular films and classic movies that show economic elements playing a "role" in the story. Students can access these clips over the Internet. A DVD with the clips will be provided to adopting professors. (0-324-32323-9)

MARKETSIM

MarketSim (http://marketsim.swlearning.com) is an online microeconomics simulation designed to help students understand how markets work by allowing them to take on the roles of consumers and producers in a simulated economy. This innovative program helps students master microeconomics concepts by producing and trading with one another in both barter and monetary economies, concurrently having fun while gaining a thorough understanding of real-world concepts such as opportunity cost, price determination, and more. (0-324-22205-X)

Economics

A Contemporary Introduction

7|e

William A. McEachern

Professor of Economics
University of Connecticut

THOMSON

SOUTH-WESTERN

Australia · Canada · Mexico · Singapore · Spain · United Kingdom · United States

THOMSON
SOUTH-WESTERN

Economics: A Contemporary Introduction, 7e

William A. McEachern

VP/Editorial Director:
Jack W. Calhoun

VP/Editor-in-Chief:
Dave Shaut

Sr. Acquisitions Editor:
Michael W. Worls

Sr. Developmental Editor:
Susanna C. Smart

Sr. Marketing Manager:
John Carey

Sr. Production Editor:
Elizabeth A. Shipp

Sr. Technology Project Editor:
Peggy Buskey

Web Coordinator:
Karen L. Schaffer

Sr. Manufacturing Coordinator:
Sandee Milewski

Photography Manager:
John Hill

Photography Researchers:
Sam Marshall & Rose Alcorn

Art Director:
Michelle Kunkler

Internal Designer:
Chris Miller

Cover Designer:
Diane Gliebe/Design Matters
Cincinnati, Ohio

Cover Image:
© Digital Vision, Inc.

Production House:
Pre-Press Company, Inc.

Printer:
CTPS

For permission to use material from
this text or product, contact us by
Tel (800) 730-2214
Fax (800) 730-2215
http://www.thomsonrights.com

For more information
contact South-Western,
5191 Natorp Boulevard,
Mason, Ohio, 45040.
Or you can visit our Internet site at:
http://www.swlearning.com

William A. McEachern began teaching large sections of economic principles when he joined the University of Connecticut in 1973. In 1980, he began offering teaching workshops around the country, and, in 1990, he created *The Teaching Economist*, a newsletter that focuses on making teaching more effective and more fun.

His research in public finance, public policy, and industrial organization has appeared in a variety of journals, including *Economic Inquiry, National Tax Journal, Journal of Industrial Economics, Quarterly Review of Economics and Finance, Southern Economic Journal, Kyklos,* and *Public Choice.* His books and monographs include *Managerial Control and Performance, School Finance Reform,* and *Tax-Exempt Property and Tax Capitalization in Metropolitan Areas.* He has also contributed chapters to edited volumes such as *Rethinking Economic Principles, Federal Trade Commission Vertical Restraint Cases,* and *Issues in Financing Connecticut Governments.*

Professor McEachern has advised federal, state, and local governments on policy matters and directed a bipartisan commission examining Connecticut's finances. He has been quoted in or written for publications such as the *New York Times, London Times, Wall Street Journal, Christian Science Monitor, Boston Globe, USA Today, Challenge Magazine, Connection, CBS MarketWatch.com,* and *Reader's Digest.* He has also appeared on *Now with Bill Moyers,* Voice of America, and National Public Radio.

In 1984, Professor McEachern won the University of Connecticut Alumni Association's Faculty Award for Distinguished Public Service and in 2000 won the Association's Faculty Excellence in Teaching Award. He is the only person in the university's history to receive both awards.

He was born in Portsmouth, N.H., earned an undergraduate degree with honors from College of the Holy Cross, served three years as an Army officer, and earned an M.A. and Ph.D. from the University of Virginia.

To Pat

Brief Contents

Contents

Part 2

Introduction to the Market System

Part **3**

Market Structure and Pricing

Part 4

Resource Markets

Part **5**

Market Failure and Public Policy

Part **8**

Fiscal and Monetary Policy

Part 9

International Macroeconomics

The Leader in Technology

McEachern's *Economics: A Contemporary Introduction, 7e* has once again raised the bar for Economics resources and builds upon its tradition of innovation by again focusing its newest edition around technological integration. Year after year, this text has consistently been recognized as a leader in technological advances in the Economics classroom by utilizing the most current high-tech resources. Previously, in the Fourth Edition of this text, McEachern integrated the World Wide Web for the very first time, and in the Fifth Edition he introduced multimedia graphing exercises, thus proving the effectiveness and necessity of technology in the classroom. The Sixth Edition took the market by storm, introducing *Xtra!*, a program that assessed students' strengths and provided a unique tutorial system based upon each individual student's needs. Most recently, in the new Seventh Edition, we are proud to introduce the latest innovation in Economics instruction: *Homework Xpress!*, a program that simplifies the process of assigning and grading homework and increases students' comprehension of material through additional review and hands-on learning with practice questions and exercises.

Beyond this, a variety of Economic programs and Web exercises are integrated throughout this updated text, enhancing its effectiveness by engaging today's technologically savvy students with the most up-to-date methods of instruction. This consistent technological integration results in a deeper and richer understanding of the material that comes not just from reading the text, but also from seeing, from hearing, and from doing.

Would you like to be able to assign homework directly from your textbook and have it graded and downloaded to your grade book automatically?

McEachern once again leads the pack in innovation — with this edition he provides a complete homework management solution with **Homework Xpress!**. And, although this beneficial technology is fully integrated into the text, its use is completely optional for those who prefer a more traditional style of instruction.

Homework Management Solution!

Finally, there is a tool to cut the inefficiencies out of homework — for both instructors and students! Instructors realize the value of assigned homework, but with increasingly demanding schedules, they have little time to grade it — especially frequent assignments. Students, in turn, are also pulling heavy loads and often require concrete incentives like graded assignments to encourage them to invest extra time in studying. **Homework Xpress!** helps both instructors and students make the most efficient use of their time. This easy-to-use, text-specific homework management system allows students to complete end-of-chapter exercises via the Internet. This innovative program alleviates the administrative burden of assigning and grading homework, and makes it simple to give assignments as frequently as you like, while tracking students' results in an integrated grade book. **Homework Xpress!** allows instructors to easily assess whether students have adequately prepared for class, identify potential problem areas to cover in class, and—with students well grounded in the basics—spend more class time covering higher-level or abstract concepts.

Assignment Material

Includes *text-specific* problems and exercises that are derived from and correlate closely with the book's end-of-chapter material. Instructors may pick and choose the assignments they wish to use, and student results are automatically recorded in a grade book.

Concept Practice and Review Activities

Students can access a wide range of practice and review material from a multimedia library of both book-specific and generic elements to build a customized teaching and learning solution. Students can go through a complete review of the material and get feedback on their preparation before they try to do the graded assignments.

Graphing Tools

Homework Xpress! offers graphing problems without the grading hassles through its unique "Sketch It" tool, which gives students freehand graphing problems and checks them automatically. Sketch It problems are provided both as Assignment and as Concept Practice and Review exercises.

Current Events

To help you easily incorporate current events into your classroom without having to devote time to searching for the most relevant and timely articles, links to South-Western's EconNews, EconDebates, and EconData Online features are included in **Homework Xpress!**.

Customizable

You can tailor **Homework Xpress!** to your individualized course needs—pick and choose the assignments you want to give, decide when and for how long to make them available to your students, and use only the features and/or chapters of your choice, or use them all. It's up to you!

Economics in the Movies

Bring economic topics to life in a context that students will really relate to. *Economics in the Movies,* by Professor G. Dirk Mateer of The Pennsylvania State University, is a supplement that consists of clips from recent popular films and classic movies that show economic elements playing a "role" in the story. Students can access these clips on the Internet. A DVD with the clips will be provided to adopting professors.

In addition, a student workbook provides economic background and exercises for each movie clip. The exercises are designed to help students explore the meaning of the economic elements presented and how they might affect people and situations. This is truly an exciting way to showcase economics to a receptive audience!

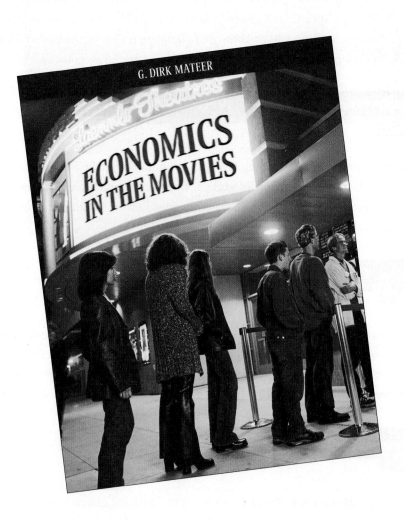

MarketSim

MarketSim is an online microeconomics simulation designed to help students understand how markets work by allowing them to take on the roles of consumers and producers in a simulated economy. This innovative program helps students master microeconomics concepts by producing and trading with one another in both barter and monetary economies, concurrently having fun and gaining a thorough understanding of real-world concepts such as opportunity cost, price determination, and more.

Instructors value this teaching tool for the way it engages students' interest as classroom instruction alone cannot, and its simple set-up, customizable settings, and user-friendly instruction manuals make it the perfect solution for any section. Perhaps the most valuable aspects of the program, though, are its many benefits for students: Its hands-on method brings abstract economic concepts to life and teaches students to make sound economic decisions through trial-and-error in the simulated environment. Also, its interactive structure allows students to engage in friendly competition with their fellow students and to see the results of their actions almost instantly — and, as a result, they become eager to understand the economic concepts they will need to succeed.

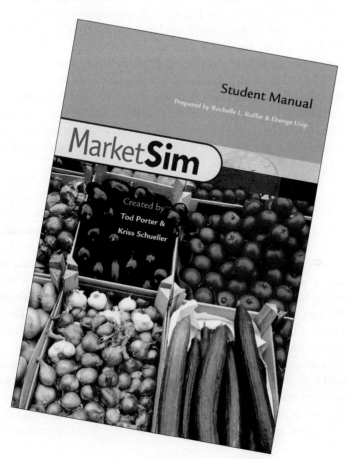

Economics has a short history but a long past. As a distinct discipline, economics has been studied for only a few hundred years, yet civilizations have confronted the economic problem of scarce resources but unlimited wants for millennia. Economics, the discipline, may be centuries old, but it's renewed every day by fresh evidence that reshapes and extends economic theory. In *Economics: A Contemporary Introduction*, I draw on more than 25 years of teaching and research to convey the vitality, timeliness, and evolving nature of economics.

Leading by Example

Remember the last time you were in unfamiliar parts and had to ask for directions? Along with the directions came the standard comment, "You can't miss it!" So how come you missed it? Because the "landmark," so obvious to locals, was invisible to you, a stranger. Writing a principles textbook is much like giving directions. The author must be familiar with the material, but that very familiarity can cloud the author's ability to see the material through the fresh eyes of a new student. Some authors revert to a tell-all approach, which can overwhelm students who find absorbing so much information like trying to drink from a fire hose. Opting for the minimalist approach, some other authors write abstractly about good x and good y, units of labor and units of capital, or the proverbial widget. But this turns economics into a foreign language.

Good directions rely on landmarks familiar to us all—a stoplight, a fork in the road, a white picket fence. Likewise, a good textbook builds bridges from the familiar to the new. That's what I try to do—*lead by example*. By beginning with examples that draw on common experience, I create graphic images that need little explanation, thereby eliciting from the reader that light of recognition, that "Aha!" I believe that the shortest distance between an economic principle and student comprehension is a lively example. Examples should be self-explanatory to convey the point quickly and directly. Having to explain an example is like having to explain a joke—the point gets lost. Throughout the book, I provide just enough intuition and institutional detail to get the point across without overwhelming students with information. The emphasis is on economic ideas, not economic jargon.

Students show up the first day of class with at least 18 years of experience with economic choices, economic institutions, and economic events. Each grew up in a household—the most important economic institution in a market economy. As consumers, students are familiar with fast-food outlets, cineplexes, car dealerships, online retailers, and scores of stores at the mall. Most students have supplied labor to the job market—more than half held jobs in high school. Students also have ongoing contact with government—they know about taxes, driver's licenses, speed limits, and public education. And students have a growing familiarity with the rest of the world. Thus, students have abundant experience with the stuff of economics. Yet some principles books neglect this rich lode of personal experience and instead try to create for students a new world of economics—a new way of thinking. Such an approach fails to connect economics with what Alfred Marshall called "the ordinary business of life."

Because instructors can cover only a portion of the textbook in class, material should be self-explanatory, thereby providing instructors the flexibility to focus on topics of special interest. This book starts where students are, not where instructors would like them to be. For example, to explain the division of labor, rather than discuss Adam Smith's pin factory, I begin with McDonald's. And to explain resource substitution, rather than rely on abstract units of labor and capital, I begin with washing a car, where the mix can vary from a drive-through car wash (much capital and little labor) to a Saturday morning charity car wash (much labor and little capital). This edition is filled with similar down-to-earth examples that turn the abstract into the concrete to help students learn.

SEVENTH Edition Content and Changes

This edition builds on the success of previous editions to make the material even more student-friendly through additional examples, more questions along the way, and frequent summaries as a chapter unfolds. By making the material both more natural and more personal, I try to draw students into a collaborative discussion. Chapters have been streamlined for a clearer, more intuitive presentation, with fresh examples, new or revised case studies, and added exhibits that crystalize key points.

Introductory Chapters Topics common to both macro- and microeconomics are covered in the first four chapters. Limiting introductory material to four chapters saves precious class time, particularly at institutions where students can take macro and micro courses in either order (and so must cover introductory chapters twice). For this edition, the order of Chapters 3 and 4 have been reversed for a better flow of topics, moving from an introduction to economics in the first three chapters, to an examination of market theory in Chapter 4.

Microeconomics My approach to microeconomics underscores the role of time and information in production and consumption. The presentation also reflects the growing interest in the economic institutions that underpin impersonal market activity. More generally, I try to convey the idea that most microeconomic principles operate like gravity: Market forces work, whether or not individual economic actors understand them.

At every opportunity, I try to turn the abstract into the concrete. For example, rather than describing an abstract monopolist, the monopoly chapter focuses on the De Beers diamond monopoly. New microeconomic material in this edition includes added coverage of labor issues, more about government regulation in other countries, more emphasis on the role of technological change in undermining monopoly power, additional discussion of public choice around the world, a new section entitled "Pollution Rights and Public Choice," a state-by-state examination of poverty levels, and a broader comparison of U.S. and world poverty levels.

Instructors who prefer to present macroeconomics first can easily do so by jumping from the final introductory chapter, Chapter 4, to the first macro chapter, Chapter 20.

Macroeconomics Rather than focus on the differences among competing schools of thought, I use the aggregate demand and aggregate supply model to underscore the fundamental distinction between the *active approach,* which views the economy as unstable and in need of government intervention when it gets off track, and the *passive approach,* which views the economy as essentially stable and self-correcting.

Wherever possible, I rely on student experience and intuition to help explain the theory behind macroeconomic abstractions such as aggregate demand and aggregate supply. For example, to explain how employment can temporarily exceed its natural rate, I note how students, as the term draws to a close, can temporarily shift into high gear, studying for exams and finishing term papers. And to reinforce the link between income and consumption, I point out how easy it is to figure out the relative income of a neighborhood just by driving through it.

This edition includes added emphasis on the differences between aggregate demand and market demand, more about developing countries, technological change, and cost-of-living adjustment, more on how banks work and how they create money, a new section entitled "Credit Cards and Debit Cards: What's the Difference," updated coverage of the Bush tax cuts and federal deficits for 2003 and 2004, and a discussion of federal deficits since the adoption of the U.S. Constitution rather than just since 1980. There is also more focus on differences in unemployment rates and in inflation rates across U.S. metropolitan areas.

International This edition reflects the growing impact of the world economy on U.S. economic welfare. International issues are introduced early and discussed often. For example, the rest of the world is introduced in Chapter 1 and profiled in Chapter 3. Comparative advantage and the production possibilities frontier are discussed from a global perspective in Chapter 2.

International coverage is woven throughout the text. By comparing the U.S. experience with that of other countries around the world, students gain a better perspective about such topics as unionization trends, antitrust laws, pollution, conservation, environmental laws, tax rates, the distribution of income, economic growth, productivity, unemployment, inflation, central bank independence, and government deficits. Exhibits have been added to show comparisons across countries of various economic measures—everything from the percentage of paper that gets recycled to public outlays relative to GDP. International references are scattered throughout the book, including a number of relevant case studies. This edition reflects additional coverage of international trade and trade barriers—including the Doha Round of WTO negotiations and the Central American Free Trade Agreement (CAFTA), and places more emphasis on the role of technological change in international trade, especially with regard to outsourcing.

Case Studies Some books use case studies as boxed asides to cover material that otherwise doesn't quite fit. I use case studies as real-world applications to reinforce ideas in the chapter and to demonstrate the relevance of economic theory. My case studies are different enough to offer variety in the presentation yet are integrated enough into the flow of the chapter to let students know they should be read. The four categories of case studies in this textbook are as follows: (1) *Bringing Theory to Life* draws on student experience to reinforce economic theory, (2) *Public Policy* highlights trade-offs in the public sector, (3) *The World of Business* offers students a feel for the range of choices confronting business decision makers today, and (4) *The Information Economy* underscores the critical role of information in the economy. All case studies have been either revised or replaced.

In addition, the book features an even tighter integration of text and technology. For example, all case studies include relevant Web addresses and end-of-chapter questions for further analysis. These links plus navigation tips and other information can also be accessed through the McEachern Interactive Study Center at http://mceachern.swlearning.com/.

Clarity by Design

In many principles textbooks, chapters are broken up by boxed material, qualifying footnotes, and other distractions that disrupt the flow of the material. Students aren't sure when or if they should read such segregated elements. But this book has a natural flow. Each chapter opens with a few stimulating questions and then follows with a logical narrative. As noted already, case studies appear in the natural sequence of the chapter, not in separate boxes. Students can thus read each chapter from the opening questions to the conclusion and summary. I also adhere to a "just-in-time" philosophy, introducing material just as it is needed to build an argument. Footnotes are used sparingly and then only to cite sources, not to qualify or extend material in the text.

This edition is more visual than its predecessors, with more exhibits to reinforce key findings. Exhibit titles are also more descriptive to convey the central points, and more exhibits now have summary captions. The idea is to make the exhibits more self-contained. Additional summary paragraphs have been added throughout the chapter, and economics jargon has been cut down. Although the number of terms defined in the margin has increased, definitions have been pared to make them clearer, more concise, and less like entries from a dictionary.

In short, economic principles are now more transparent (a textbook should not be like some giant Easter egg hunt, where it's up to the student to figure out what the author is trying to say). Overall, the seventh edition is a cleaner presentation, a straighter shot into the student's brain. It omits needless words without tightening things too much. Despite the addition of fresh examples, new topics, additional summaries, and new exhibits, this edition contains about 4 percent fewer words of text than the previous one had.

Form Follows Function In most textbooks, the page design—the layout of the page and the use of color—is an afterthought, chosen with little regard for how students learn. No element in the design of this book has been wasted, and all work together for the maximum pedagogical value. By design, all elements of each chapter have been carefully integrated. Every effort has been made to present students with an open, readable page design. The size of the font, the length of the text line, and the amount of white space were all chosen to make learning easier. Graphs are uncluttered and are accompanied by captions explaining the key points. These features are optimal for students encountering college textbooks for the first time.

Color Coordinated Color is used systematically within graphs, charts, and tables to ensure that students can quickly and easily see what's going on. Throughout the book, demand curves are blue and supply curves are red. In each comparative statics example, the curves determining the final equilibrium point are lighter than the initial curves. Color shading distinguishes key areas of many graphs, such as measures of economic profit or loss, tax incidence, consumer and producer surplus, output above or below the economy's potential, and the welfare effects of tariffs and quotas. Graphical areas identifying positive outcomes such as economic profit, consumer surplus, or output exceeding the economy's potential are shaded blue. Areas identifying negative outcomes, such as economic loss, deadweight loss, or output falling below the economy's potential are shaded pink. In short, color is more than mere eye entertainment—it is coordinated consistently and with forethought to help students learn. Students benefit from these visual cues (a dyslexic student has told me that she finds the book's color guide quite helpful).

Net Bookmarks Each chapter includes a Net Bookmark. These margin notes identify interesting Web sites that illustrate real-world examples, giving students a chance to develop their research skills. And these bookmarks are extended at our Web site with additional information on resources as well as step-by-step navigation hints. They can be accessed through the McEachern Interactive Study Center at http://mceachern.swlearning.com/.

Reading It Right Each chapter contains special pedagogical features to facilitate classroom use of *The Wall Street Journal*. "Reading It Right" margin notes ask students to explain the relevance of statements drawn from *The Wall Street Journal*. There are also end-of-chapter questions asking students to read and analyze information from *The Wall Street Journal*.

Experiential Exercises Some end-of-chapter questions encourage students to develop their research and critical-thinking skills. These experiential exercises ask students to apply what they have learned to real-world, hands-on economic analysis. Most of these exercises involve the Internet, *The Wall Street Journal*, or other media resources.

Homework Xpress! Exercises New end-of-chapter exercises tie in to the *Homework Xpress!* (http://homeworkxpress.swlearning.com) supplement available for packaging with the textbook. The exercises afford additional practice in applying chapter graphing concepts.

The Internet

As mentioned already, we devoted careful attention to capitalizing on the vast array of economic resources and alternative learning technologies the Internet can deliver. I gave much thought to two basic questions: What can this technology do that a textbook cannot do? And how can Web-based enhancements be employed to bring the greatest value to teaching and learning?

It's clear that students learn more when they are involved and engaged. The Internet provides a way to heighten student involvement while keeping the introductory economics course as current as today's news. With these ideas in mind, we have designed the textbook's supporting Web site to tightly integrate the book and the Internet. We have done this in a way that exploits the comparative advantage of each medium and in a structure that optimizes both teaching and learning experiences. Each chapter opener presents a HomeworkXpress! icon to remind students to check the site for problems, information, videos, news, debates, and graphing that will enhance their understanding of the chapter. In addition, graphs throughout the textbook that are enhanced in HomeworkXpress! Graphing are identified with the HomeworkXpress! icon.

The McEachern Interactive Study Center (http://mceachern.swlearning.com/) The Web site designed to be used with this textbook provides a comprehensive chapter-by-chapter online study guide that includes interactive quizzing, a glossary, updated and extended applications from the book, and numerous other features. Some of the highlights include:

> ***Quizzes*** Interactive quizzes help students test their understanding of the chapter's concepts. Multiple-choice questions include detailed feedback for each answer. Students can email the results of a quiz to themselves and/or their instructor.

> ***Key Terms Glossary*** A convenient, online glossary enables students to use the point-and-click flashcard functionality of the glossary to test themselves on key terminology.

> ***Extensions of In-Text Web Features*** To streamline navigation, the Study Center links directly to Web sites discussed in the Internet-enhanced in-text features for each chapter—Net Bookmarks, e-Activities, and end-of-chapter experiential exercises. These applications provide students with opportunities to interact with the material by performing real-world analyses. Their comments and answers to the questions posed in these features can be emailed to the instructor.

McEachern HomeworkXpress! Web Site (http:// homeworkxpress.swlearning.com) This new Web-based product allows professors to assign end-of-chapter graphing problems for student completion as well as tests and quizzes. The program grades the assignments and tests and transfers the grades to a gradebook. The students not only get immediate feedback, but can access extensive Review and Tutorial materials. Problems that can be completed using Homework Xpress! Are identified with an icon.

McEachern Xtra! Web Site (http://mceachernxtra.swlearning.com/) Each student has an individual learning style, and different learning styles require different tools. By tapping into today's technology, this textbook can reach out to a variety of students with a variety of learning styles and can help instructors ensure that they address the needs of all students. The McEachern Xtra! available to be packaged with the textbook provides access to a robust set of additional online learning tools. McEachern Xtra! contains these key features:

Master the Learning Objectives This element is the central navigational tool for McEachern Xtra! Step-by-step instructions associated with each learning objective systematically guide students through all available text and Xtra! multimedia tools to deepen their understanding of that particular concept. Each tool is accompanied by icons that identify the learning styles (print, aural, tactile, haptic, interactive, visual) for which it is most appropriate. Students can thus choose the most appropriate tools to support their own learning styles.

Graphing Workshop The Graphing Workshop is a one-stop learning resource for help in mastering the logic of graphs, one of the more difficult aspects of an economics course for many students. It enables students to explore important economic concepts through a unique learning system made up of tutorials, interactive drawing tools, and exercises that teach how to interpret, reproduce, and explain graphs.

CNN Online Video segments from the Cable News Network (CNN) bring the real world right to your desktop. The accompanying exercises illustrate how economics is an important part of daily life and how the material applies to current events.

Ask the Instructor Video Clips Streaming video explains and illustrates difficult concepts from each chapter. These video clips are extremely helpful review and clarification tools if a student has trouble understanding an in-class lecture or is a visual learner.

Xtra! Quizzing In addition to the open-access chapter-by-chapter quizzes found at the McEachern Product Support Web site (http://mceachern.swlearning.com), *McEachern Xtra!* offers students the opportunity to practice by taking interactive quizzes.

e-con @pps Economic Applications. EconNews Online, EconDebate Online, Econ-Data Online, and EconLinks Online help to deepen students' understanding of theoretical concepts through hands-on exploration and analysis of the latest economic news stories, policy debates, and data.

None of these features requires detailed knowledge of the Internet. Nor are they required for a successful classroom experience if an instructor wants to assign only the materials contained within the textbook. The online enhancements simply offer optional paths for further study and exploration—new ways for students to use their individual learning styles and new ways for instructors to experiment with technology and a wider range of assignment materials.

The Support Package

The teaching and learning support package that accompanies *Economics: A Contemporary Introduction* provides instructors and students with focused, accurate, and innovative supplements to the textbook.

Study Guides Written by John Lunn of Hope College, study guides are available for the full textbook, as well as for the micro and macro "split" versions. Every chapter of each study guide corresponds to a chapter in the text and offers (1) an introduction; (2) a chapter outline, with definitions of all terms; (3) a discussion of the chapter's main points; (4) a *lagniappe*, or bonus, which supplements material in the chapter and includes a "Question to Think About"; (5) a list of key terms; (6) a variety of true-false, multiple-choice, and discussion questions; and (7) answers to all the questions. Visit the McEachern Interactive Study Center at http://mceachern. swlearning.com/ for more details.

Instructor's Manual The *Instructor's Manual*, revised by Christy Vineyard of Southwestern Tennessee Community College, is keyed to the text. For each textbook chapter, it includes (1) a detailed lecture outline and brief overview, (2) a summary of main points, (3) pedagogical tips that expand on points raised in the chapter and indicate use of PowerPoint slides, and (4) suggested answers to all end-of-chapter questions and problems. Tina Mosleh of Ohlone College revised each classroom economics experiment to include an abstract, an overview, a clear set of instructions for running the experiment, and forms for recording the results.

Teaching Assistance Manual I have revised the *Teaching Assistance Manual* to provide additional support beyond the *Instructor's Manual*. It is especially useful to new instructors, graduate assistants, and teachers interested in generating more class discussion. This manual offers (1) overviews and outlines of each chapter, (2) chapter objectives and quiz material, (3) material for class discussion, (4) topics warranting special attention, (5) supplementary examples, and (6) "What if?" discussion questions. Appendices provide guidance on (1) presenting material; (2) generating and sustaining class discussion; (3) preparing, administering, and grading quizzes; and (4) coping with the special problems confronting foreign graduate assistants.

Test Banks Thoroughly revised for currency and accuracy by Dennis Hanseman of the University of Cincinnati, the microeconomics and macroeconomics test banks contain over 6,600 questions in multiple-choice and true-false formats. All multiple-choice questions have five possible responses, and each is rated by degree of difficulty.

ExamView—Computerized Testing Software *ExamView* is an easy-to-use test-creation software package available in versions compatible with Microsoft Windows and Apple Macintosh. It contains all the questions in the printed test banks. Instructors can add or edit questions, instructions, and answers; select questions by previewing them on the screen; and then choose them by number or at random. Instructors can also create and administer quizzes online, either over the Internet, through a local area network (LAN), or through a wide area network (WAN).

Microsoft PowerPoint Lecture Slides Lecture slides, created by Dale Bails of Christian Brothers University, contain tables and graphs from the textbook, as well as additional instructional materials, and are intended to enhance lectures and help integrate technology into the classroom.

Microsoft PowerPoint Figure Slides These PowerPoint slides contain key figures from the text. Instructors who prefer to prepare their own lecture slides can use these figures as an alternative to the PowerPoint lecture slides.

Transparency Acetates Many of the key tables and graphs from this textbook are reproduced as full-color transparency acetates.

Economics in the Movies This edition now features a tie-in to Thomson's *Economics in the Movies*. The guide, created by G. Dirk Mateer of The Pennsylvania State University, borrows from feature films in a way that enhances core economics content. Concepts are visualized by utilizing short film scenes, including *Out of Sight, Seabuscuit, Erin Brockovich, Waterworld, Being John Malkovich,* and many others. Icons direct professors to where they can use this guide to tie economic concepts to scenes in popular films.

CNN Economics Video The *CNN Economics Video* provides a variety of brief video clips, taken from Cable News Network (CNN) programs, that illustrate various aspects of economics.

Market Sim Markets come alive in this new microeconomic simulation product. Students can participate in a barter or a monetary economy while competing with their classmates and learning how markets work with this Web-based program.

Online learning is growing at a rapid pace. Whether instructors are looking to offer courses at a distance or to offer a Web-enhanced classroom, South-Western/Thomson Learning offers them a solution with WebTutor. WebTutor provides instructors with text-specific content that interacts with the two leading systems of higher education course management—WebCT and Blackboard. WebTutor is a turnkey solution for instructors who want to begin using technology like Blackboard or WebCT but do not have Web-ready content available or do not want to be burdened with developing their own content. South-Western offers two levels of WebTutor:

Web Tutor Toolbox WebTutor uses the Internet to turn everyone in your class into a front-row student. WebTutor offers interactive study guide features such as quizzes, concept reviews, flashcards, discussion forums, and more. Instructor tools are also provided to facilitate communication between students and faculty. Preloaded with content, *WebTutor ToolBox* pairs all the content of the book's support Web site with all the sophisticated course management functionality of either course management platform.

Web Tutor Advantage More than just an interactive study guide, *WebTutor Advantage* delivers innovative learning aids that actively engage students. Benefits include automatic and immediate feedback from quizzes; interactive, multimedia-rich explanations of concepts, such as flash-animated graphing tutorials and graphing exercises that use an online graph-drawing tool; streaming video applications; online exercises; flashcards; and interaction and involvement through online discussion forums. Powerful instructor tools are also provided to facilitate communication and collaboration between students and faculty.

The Teaching Economist For more than a dozen years, I have edited *The Teaching Economist,* a newsletter aimed at making teaching more interesting and more fun. The newsletter discusses imaginative ways to present topics—for example, how to "sensationalize" economic concepts, useful resources on the Internet, economic applications from science fiction, recent research in teaching and learning, and more generally, ways to teach just for the fun of it. A regular feature of *The Teaching Economist,* "The Grapevine," offers teaching ideas suggested by colleagues from across the country.

The latest issue—and back issues—of *The Teaching Economist* are available online at http://economics.swlearning.com/.

Acknowledgments

Many people contributed to this book's development. I gratefully acknowledge the insightful comments of those who have reviewed the book for this and previous editions. Their suggestions expanded my thinking and improved the book.

Steve Abid
Grand Rapids Community College

Polly Reynolds Allen
University of Connecticut

Hassan Y. Aly
Ohio State University

Ted Amato
University of North Carolina, Charlotte

Donna Anderson
University of Wisconsin, La Crosse

Richard Anderson
Texas A&M University

Kyriacos Aristotelous
Otterbein College

James Aylesworth
Lakeland Community College

Mohsen Bahmani Mohsen Bahmani-Oskooee
University of Wisconsin, Milwaukee

Dale Bails
Christian Brothers College

Benjamin Balak
Rollins College

Andy Barnett
Auburn University

Bharati Basu
Central Michigan University

Klaus Becker
Texas Tech University

Charles Bennett
Gannon University

Trisha L. Bezmen
Old Dominion University

Jay Bhattacharya
Okaloosa Walton Community College

Gerald W. Bialka
University of North Florida

William Bogart
Case Western Reserve University

Kenneth Boyer
Michigan State University

David Brasfield
Murray State University

Jurgen Brauer
Augusta College

Taggert Brooks
University of Wisconsin, La Crosse

Gardner Brown, Jr.
University of Washington

Eric Brunner
Morehead State University

Francine Butler
Grand View College

Judy Butler
Baylor University

Charles Callahan III
SUNY College at Brockport

Giorgio Canarella
California State University, Los Angeles

Shirley Cassing
University of Pittsburgh

Shi-fan Chu
University of Nevada–Reno

Ronald Cipcic
Kalamazoo Valley Community College

Larry Clarke
Brookhaven College

Rebecca Cline
Middle Georgia College

Stephen Cobb
Xavier University

Doug Conway
Mesa Community College

Mary E. Cookingham
Michigan State University

James P. Cover
University of Alabama

James Cox
DeKalb College

Jerry Crawford
Arkansas State University

Thomas Creahan
Morehead State University

Joseph Daniels
Marquette University

Carl Davidson
Michigan State University

Elynor Davis
Georgia Southern University

Susan Davis
SUNY College at Buffalo

A. Edward Day
University of Central Florida

David Dean
University of Richmond

Janet Deans
Chestnut Hill College

Dennis Debrecht
Carroll College

David Denslow
University of Florida

Gary Dymski
University of California–Riverside

John Edgren
Eastern Michigan University

Ron D. Elkins
Central Washington University

Donald Elliott, Jr.
Southern Illinois University

G. Rod Erfani
Transylvania University

Gisela Meyer Escoe
University of Cincinnati

Mark Evans
California State University, Bakersfield

Gregory Falls
Central Michigan University

Eleanor Fapohunda
SUNY College at Farmingdale

Mohsen Fardmanesh
Temple University

Paul Farnham
Georgia State University

Rudy Fichtenbaum
Wright State University

T. Windsor Fields
James Madison University

Rodney Fort
Washington State University

Richard Fowles
University of Utah

Roger Frantz
San Diego State University

Julie Gallaway
Southwest Montana State University

Gary Galles
Pepperdine University

Edward Gamber
Lafayette College

Adam Gifford
California State University, Northridge

J. P. Gilbert
MiraCosta College

Robert Gillette
University of Kentucky

Art Goldsmith
Washington and Lee University

Rae Jean Goodman
U.S. Naval Academy

Robert Gordon
San Diego State University

Fred Graham
American University

Philip Graves
University of Colorado, Boulder

Harpal S. Grewal
Claflin College

Carolyn Grin
Grand Rapids Community College

Daniel Gropper
Auburn University

Simon Hakim
Temple University

Robert Halvorsen
University of Washington

Nathan Eric Hampton
St. Cloud State University

Mehdi Haririan
Bloomsburg University

William Hart
Miami University

Baban Hasnat
SUNY College at Brockport

Julia Heath
University of Memphis

James Heisler
Hope College

James Henderson
Baylor University

James R. Hill
Central Michigan University

Jane Smith Himarios
University of Texas, Arlington

Calvin Hoerneman
Delta College

Tracy Hofer
University of Wisconsin, Stevens Point

George E. Hoffer
Virginia Commonwealth University

Dennis Hoffman
Arizona State University

Bruce Horning
Fordham University

Calvin Hoy
County College of Morris

Jennifer Imazeki
San Diego State University

Beth Ingram
University of Iowa

Paul Isley
Grand Valley State University

Joyce Jacobsen
Wesleyan University

Nancy Jianakoplos
Colorado State University

Claude Michael Jonnard
Fairleigh Dickinson University

Nake Kamrany
University of Southern California

Bryce Kanago
Miami University

John Kane
SUNY College at Oswego

David Kennett
Vassar College

William Kern
Western Michigan University

Robert Kleinhenz
California State University, Fullerton

Faik Koray
Louisiana State University

Joseph Kotaska
Monroe Community College

Barry Kotlove
Edmonds Community College

Marie Kratochvil
Nassau Community College

Joseph Lammert
Raymond Walters College

Christopher Lee
Saint Ambrose University, Davenport

J. Franklin Lee
Pitt Community College

Jim Lee
Fort Hays State University

Dennis Leyden
University of North Carolina, Greensboro

Carl Liedholm
Michigan State University

Hyoung-Seok Lim
Ohio State University

C. Richard Long
Georgia State University

Ken Long
New River Community College

Michael Magura
University of Toledo

Thomas Maloy
Muskegon Community College

Gabriel Manrique
Winona State University

Barbara Marcus
Davenport College

Robert Margo
Vanderbilt University

Nelson Mark
Ohio State University

Richard Martin
Agnes Scott College

Peter Mavrokordatos
Tarrant County College

Wolfgang Mayer
University of Cincinnati

Bruce McCrea
Lansing Community College

John McDowell
Arizona State University

KimMarie McGoldrick
University of Richmond

David McKee
Kent State University

James McLain
University of New Orleans

Mark McNeil
Irvine Valley College

Michael A. McPherson
University of North Texas

Scott Eric Merryman
University of Oregon

Michael Metzger
University of Central Oklahoma

Art Meyer
Lincoln Land Community College

Carrie Meyer
George Mason University

Martin Milkman
Murray State University

Green R. Miller
Morehead State University

Bruce D. Mills
Troy State University, Montgomery

Milton Mitchell
University of Wisconsin, Oshkosh

Shannon Mitchell
Virginia Commonwealth University

Barry Morris
University of North Alabama

Tina Mosleh
Ohlone College

Kathryn Nantz
Fairfield University

Paul Natke
Central Michigan University

Rick Nelson
Lansing Community College

Heather Newsome
Baylor University

Farrokh Nourzad
Marquette University

Maureen O'Brien
University of Minnesota, Duluth

Norman P. Obst
Michigan State University

Jeffrey Phillips
Thomas College

Jeffrey D. Prager
East Central College

Fernando Quijano
Dickinson State University

Jaishankar Raman
Valparaiso University

Reza Ramazani
St. Michael's University

Carol Rankin
Xavier University

Mitch Redlo
Monroe Community College

Kevin Rogers
Mississippi State University

Scanlon Romer
Delta College

Duane Rosa
West Texas A&M University

Robert Rossana
Wayne State University

Mark Rush
University of Florida

Richard Saba
Auburn University

Simran Sahi
University of Minnesota, Twin Cities

Richard Salvucci
Trinity University

Rexford Santerre
University of Connecticut

George D. Santopietro
Radford University

Sue Lynn Sasser
University of Central Oklahoma

Ward Sayre
Kenyon College

Ted Scheinman
Mt. Hood Community College

Peter Schwartz
University of North Carolina, Charlotte

Carol A. Scotese
Virginia Commonwealth University

Shahrokh Shahrokhi
San Diego State University

Roger Sherman
University of Houston

Michael Shields
Central Michigan University

Alden Shiers
California Polytechnic State University

Frederica Shockley
California State University, Chico

William Shughart II
University of Mississippi

Paul Sicilian
Grand Valley State University

Charles Sicotte
Rock Valley College

Calvin Siebert
University of Iowa

Gerald P. W. Simons
Grand Valley State University

Phillip Smith
DeKalb College

V. Kerry Smith
Duke University

David Spencer
Brigham Young University

Jane Speyrer
University of New Orleans

Joanne Spitz
University of Massachusetts

Mark Stegeman
Virginia Polytechnic Institute

Houston Stokes
University of Illinois, Chicago

Robert Stonebreaker
Indiana University of Pennsylvania

Michael Stroup
Stephen Austin State University

William Swift
Pace University

James Swofford
University of South Alabama

Linghui Tang
Drexel University

Donna Thompson
Brookdale Community College

John Tribble
Russell Sage College

Lee J. Van Scyoc
University of Wisconsin, Oshkosh

Percy Vera
Sinclair Community College

Han X. Vo
Winthrop University

Jin Wang
University of Wisconsin, Stevens Point

Gregory Wassall
Northeastern University

William Weber
Eastern Illinois University

David Weinberg
Xavier University

Bernard Weinrich
St. Louis Community College

Donald Wells
University of Arizona

Robert Whaples
Wake Forest University

Mark Wheeler
Western Michigan University

Michael White
St. Cloud State University

Richard Winkelman
Arizona State University

Stephan Woodbury
Michigan State University

Kenneth Woodward
Saddleback College

Patricia Wyatt
Bossier Parish Community College

Peter Wyman
Spokane Falls Community College

Mesghena Yasin
Morehead State University

Edward Young
University of Wisconsin, Eau Claire

Michael J. Youngblood
Rock Valley College

William Zeis
Bucks Community College

To practice what I preach, I relied on the division of labor based on comparative advantage to help put together the most complete teaching package on the market today. John Lunn of Hope College authored the study guides, which have become quite popular. Christy Vineyard of Southwestern Tennessee Community College carefully revised the instructor's manual. Dennis Hanseman of the University of Cincinnati undertook a thorough revision of the test banks. And Dale Bails of Christian Brothers University revised the PowerPoint lecture slides. I thank them for their imagination and their discipline.

The talented staff at Thomson Business & Professional Publishing provided invaluable editorial, administrative, and sales support. I owe a special debt to Susan Smart, senior developmental editor, who nurtured the manuscript throughout the revision and production. I also appreciate very much the smooth project coordination by senior production editor Libby Shipp, the exciting design created by Chris Miller, the imaginative photography management of John Hill, the patient production assistance of Jan Turner of Pre-Press Company, and the thoughtful copyediting of Cheryl Hauser. Peggy Buskey, Pam Wallace, and Karen Schaffer have been particularly helpful in developing the *McEachern Xtra!* and *Homework Xpress!* Web sites.

In addition, I am most grateful to Jack Calhoun, vice president and editorial director; Dave Shaut, vice president and editor-in-chief; Michael Worls, senior acquisitions editor and problem solver; and John Carey, the senior marketing manager, whose knowledge of the book dates back to the first edition. As good as the book may be, all our efforts would be wasted unless students get to read it. To that end, I greatly appreciate Thomson's dedicated service and sales force, who have contributed in a substantial way to the book's success.

Finally, I owe an abiding debt to my wife, Pat, who provided abundant encouragement and support along the way.

William A. McEachern

The Art and Science of Economic Analysis

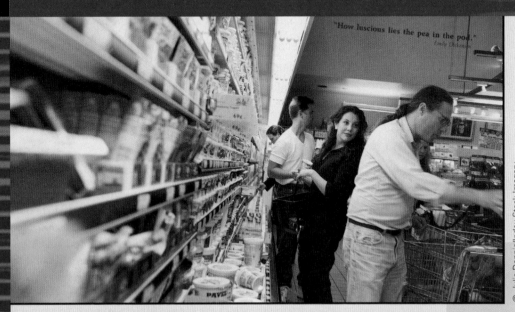

"How luscious lies the pea in the pod."

© Julie Dennis/Index Stock Imagery

hy are comic-strip characters like Hagar the Horrible, Hi and Lois, Cathy, Monty, and FoxTrot missing a finger on each hand? And where is Dilbert's mouth? Why does Japan have twice as many vending machines per capita as the United States? In what way are people who pound on vending machines relying on a theory? What's the big idea with economics? Finally, how can it be said in economics that "what goes around comes around"? These and other questions are answered in this chapter, which introduces the art and science of economic analysis.

You have been reading and hearing about economic issues for years—unemployment, inflation, poverty, federal deficits, college tuition, airfares, stock prices, computer prices, gas prices. When explanations of these issues go into any depth, your eyes may glaze over and you may tune out, the same way you do when a weather forecaster tries to provide an in-depth analysis of high-pressure fronts colliding with moisture carried in from the coast.

What many people fail to realize is that economics is livelier than the dry accounts offered by the news media. Economics is about making choices, and you make economic choices every day—choices about whether to get a part-time job or focus on your studies, live in a dorm or off campus, take a course in accounting or one in history, pack a lunch or grab a sandwich. You already know much more about economics than you realize. You bring to the subject a rich personal experience, an experience that will be tapped throughout the book to reinforce your understanding of the basic ideas. Topics discussed include:

- The economic problem
- Marginal analysis
- Rational self-interest

- Scientific method
- Normative versus positive analysis
- Pitfalls of economic thinking

The Economic Problem: Scarce Resources, Unlimited Wants

Would you like a new car, a nicer home, better meals, more free time, a more interesting social life, more spending money, more sleep? Who wouldn't? But even if you can satisfy some of these desires, others will pop up. *The problem is that, although your wants, or desires, are virtually unlimited, the resources available to satisfy these wants are scarce.* A resource is *scarce* when it is not freely available—that is, when its price exceeds zero. Because resources are scarce, you must choose from among your many wants and, whenever you choose, you must forgo satisfying some other wants. The problem of scarce resources but unlimited wants exists to a greater or lesser extent for each of the more than 6 billion people around the world. Everybody—taxicab driver, farmer, brain surgeon, shepherd, student, politician—faces the problem.

Economics examines how people use their scarce resources to satisfy their unlimited wants. The taxicab driver uses the cab and other scarce resources, such as knowledge of the city, driving skills, gasoline, and time, to earn income. The income, in turn, buys housing, groceries, clothing, trips to Disney World, and thousands of other goods and services that help satisfy some of the driver's unlimited wants.

Let's pick apart the definition of economics, beginning with resources, then examining goods and services, and finally focusing on the heart of the matter—economic choice, which arises from scarcity.

Resources

Resources are the inputs, or factors of production, used to produce the goods and services that people want. *Goods and services are scarce because resources are scarce.* Resources sort into four broad categories: labor, capital, natural resources, and entrepreneurial ability. **Labor** is human effort, both physical and mental. It includes the effort of the cab driver and the brain surgeon. Labor itself comes from a more fundamental resource: *time.* Without time we can accomplish nothing. We allocate our time to alternative uses: we can *sell* our time as labor, or we can *spend* our time doing other things, like sleeping, eating, studying, playing sports, going online, watching TV, or just relaxing with friends.

Capital includes all human creations used to produce goods and services. Economists often distinguish between physical capital and human capital. *Physical capital* consists of facto-

ECONOMICS
The study of how people use their scarce resources to satisfy their unlimited wants

RESOURCES
The inputs, or factors of production, used to produce the goods and services that people want; resources consist of labor, capital, natural resources, and entrepreneurial ability

LABOR
The physical and mental effort used to produce goods and services

CAPITAL
The buildings, equipment, and human skill used to produce goods and services

ries, machines, tools, buildings, airports, highways, and other human creations employed to produce goods and services. Physical capital includes the taxi driver's cab, the surgeon's scalpel, the farmer's tractor, the interstate highway system, and the building where your economics class meets. *Human capital* consists of the knowledge and skill people acquire to enhance their productivity, such as the taxi driver's knowledge of city streets, the surgeon's knowledge of human biology, and your knowledge of economics.

Natural resources are all so-called *gifts of nature,* including bodies of water, trees, oil reserves, minerals, and even animals. Natural resources can be divided into renewable resources and exhaustible resources. A *renewable resource* can be drawn on indefinitely if used conservatively. Thus, timber is a renewable resource if felled trees are replaced to provide a steady supply. The air and rivers are renewable resources if they are allowed to clean themselves of pollutants. More generally, biological resources like fish, game, livestock, forests, rivers, groundwater, grasslands, and soil are renewable if managed properly. An *exhaustible resource*— such as oil, coal, or copper ore—does not renew itself and so is available in a limited amount. Once burned, each barrel of oil and each ton of coal are gone forever. The world's oil reserves and coal mines are exhaustible.

A special kind of human skill called **entrepreneurial ability** is the talent required to dream up a new product or find a better way to produce an existing one. The *entrepreneur* tries to discover and act on profitable opportunities by hiring resources and assuming the risk of business success or failure. Every large firm in the world today, such as Ford, Microsoft, and Dell, began as an idea in the mind of an entrepreneur.

Resource owners are paid **wages** for their labor, **interest** for the use of their capital, and **rent** for the use of their natural resources. The entrepreneur's effort is rewarded by **profit,** which equals the *revenue* from items sold minus the *cost* of the resources employed to make those items. The entrepreneur claims what's left over after paying other resource suppliers. Sometimes the entrepreneur suffers a loss. Resource earnings are usually based on the *time* these resources are employed. Resource payments therefore have a time dimension, as in a wage of $10 *per hour,* interest of 6 percent *per year,* rent of $600 *per month,* or profit of $10,000 *per year.*

Goods and Services

Resources are combined in a variety of ways to produce goods and services. A farmer, a tractor, 50 acres of land, seeds, and fertilizer combine to grow the good: corn. One hundred musicians, musical instruments, chairs, a conductor, a musical score, and a music hall combine to produce the service: Beethoven's Fifth Symphony. Corn is a **good** because it is something you can see, feel, and touch; it requires scarce resources to produce; and it satisfies human wants. The book you are now holding, the chair you are sitting in, the clothes you are wearing, and your next meal are all goods. The performance of the Fifth Symphony is a **service** because it is intangible, yet it uses scarce resources to satisfy human wants. Lectures, movies, concerts, phone calls, broadband connections, yoga lessons, dry cleaning, and haircuts are all services.

Because goods and services are produced using scarce resources, they are themselves scarce. *A good or service is scarce if the amount people desire exceeds the amount available at a zero price.* Because we cannot have all the goods and services we would like, we must continually choose among them. We must choose among more pleasant living quarters, better meals, nicer clothes, more reliable transportation, faster computers, and so on. Making choices in a world of **scarcity** means we must pass up some goods and services.

A few goods and services seem *free* because the amount available at a zero price exceeds

NATURAL RESOURCES

So-called gifts of nature used to produce goods and services; includes renewable and exhaustible resources

ENTREPRENEURIAL ABILITY

Managerial and organizational skills needed to start a firm, combined with the willingness to take risks

WAGES

Payment to resource owners for their labor

INTEREST

Payment to resource owners for the use of their capital

RENT

Payment to resource owners for the use of their natural resources

PROFIT

The reward for entrepreneurial ability; the revenue from sales minus the cost of resources used by the entrepreneur

GOOD

A tangible item used to satisfy human wants

SERVICE

An activity used to satisfy human wants

SCARCITY

Occurs when the amount people desire exceeds the amount available at a zero price the amount people want. For example, air and seawater often seem free because we can breathe all the air we want and have all the seawater we can haul away. Yet, despite the old saying "The best things in life are free," most goods and services are scarce, not free, and even those that appear to be free come with strings attached. For example, *clean* air and *clean* seawater have become scarce. *Goods and services that are truly free are not the subject matter of economics. Without scarcity, there would be no economic problem and no need for prices.*

Sometimes we mistakenly think of certain goods as free because they involve no apparent cost to us. Subscription cards that fall out of magazines appear to be free. At least it seems we would have little difficulty rounding up about three thousand if necessary! Producing the cards, however, absorbs scarce resources, resources drawn away from competing uses, such as producing higher-quality magazines. You may have heard the expression "There is no such thing as a free lunch." There is no free lunch because all goods and services involve a cost to someone. The lunch may seem free to us, but it draws scarce resources away from the production of other goods and services, and whoever provides a free lunch often expects something in return. A Russian proverb makes a similar point but with a bit more bite: "The only place you find free cheese is in a mousetrap." And Albert Einstein said, "Sometimes one pays the most for things one gets for nothing."

Economic Decision Makers

There are four types of decision makers, or participants, in the economy: households, firms, governments, and the rest of the world. Their interaction determines how an economy's resources are allocated. *Households* play the leading role. As consumers, households demand the goods and services produced. As resource owners, households supply labor, capital, natural resources, and entrepreneurial ability to firms, governments, and the rest of the world. *Firms, governments,* and *the rest of the world* demand the resources that households supply and then use these resources to supply the goods and services that households demand. The rest of the world includes foreign households, firms, and governments that supply resources and products to U.S. markets and demand resources and products from U.S. markets.

Markets are the means by which buyers and sellers carry out exchange. Bringing together the two sides of exchange, demand and supply, markets determine price and quantity. Markets are often physical places, such as supermarkets, department stores, shopping malls, or flea markets. But markets also include other mechanisms by which buyers and sellers communicate, like classified ads, radio and television ads, telephones, bulletin boards, the Internet, and face-to-face bargaining. These market mechanisms provide information about the quantity, quality, and price of products offered for sale. Goods and services are bought and sold in **product markets.** Resources are bought and sold in **resource markets.** The most important resource market is the labor, or job, market. Think of your own experience looking for a job, and you get some idea of that market.

A Simple Circular-Flow Model

Now that you have learned a bit about economic decision makers, consider how they interact. Such a picture is conveyed by the **circular-flow model,** which describes the flow of resources, products, income, and revenue among economic decision makers. The simple circular-flow model focuses on the primary interaction in a market economy—that between households and firms. Exhibit 1 shows households on the left and firms on the right; please take a look.

Households supply labor, capital, natural resources, and entrepreneurial ability to firms through resource markets, shown in the lower portion of the exhibit. In return, households

MARKET

A set of arrangements through which buyers and sellers carry out exchange at mutually agreeable terms

PRODUCT MARKET

A market in which a good or service is bought and sold

RESOURCE MARKET

A market in which a resource is bought and sold

HOMEWORK
Xpress!
econ-apps news

CIRCULAR-FLOW MODEL

A diagram that outlines the flow of resources, products, income, and revenue among economic decision makers demand goods and services from firms through product markets, shown on the upper portion of the exhibit. Viewed from the business end, firms demand labor, capital, natural resources, and entrepreneurial ability from households through resource markets, and firms supply goods and services to households through product markets.

The flows of resources and products are supported by the flows of income and expenditure—that is, by the flow of money. So let's add money. The demand and supply of resources come together in resource markets to determine resource prices, which flow as *income* to households. The demand and supply of products come together in product markets to determine the prices of goods and services, which flow as *revenue* to firms. Resources and products flow in one direction—in this case, counterclockwise—and the corresponding payments flow in the other direction—clockwise. What goes around comes around. Take a little time now to trace the circular flows.

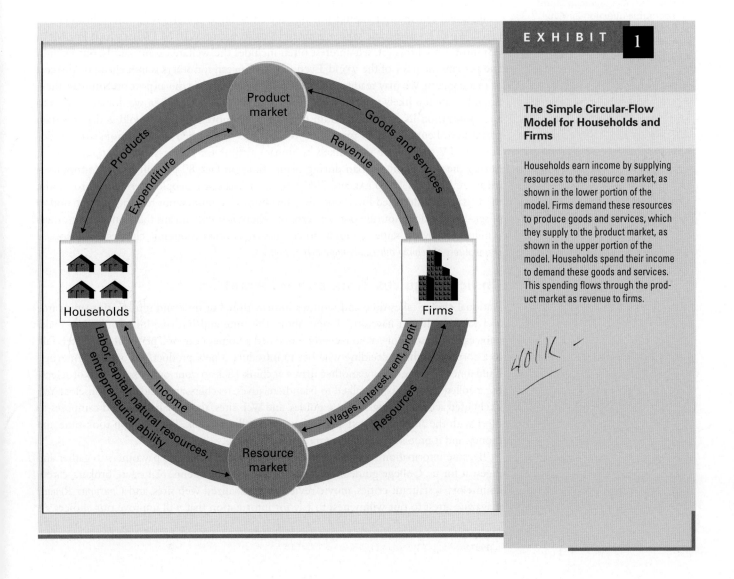

EXHIBIT 1

The Simple Circular-Flow Model for Households and Firms

Households earn income by supplying resources to the resource market, as shown in the lower portion of the model. Firms demand these resources to produce goods and services, which they supply to the product market, as shown in the upper portion of the model. Households spend their income to demand these goods and services. This spending flows through the product market as revenue to firms.

The Art of Economic Analysis

An economy results from the choices that millions of individuals make in attempting to satisfy their unlimited wants. Because these choices lie at the very heart of the economic problem—coping with scarce resources but unlimited wants—they deserve a closer look. Learning about the forces that shape economic choice is the first step toward mastering the art of economic analysis.

Rational Self-Interest

A key economic assumption is that individuals, in making choices, rationally select alternatives they perceive to be in their best interests. By *rational,* economists mean simply that people try to make the best choices they can, given the available information. People may not know with certainty which alternative will turn out to be the best. They simply select the alternatives they *expect* will yield the most satisfaction and happiness. *In general, rational self-interest means that individuals try to maximize the expected benefit achieved with a given cost or to minimize the expected cost of achieving a given benefit.*

Rational self-interest should not be viewed as blind materialism, pure selfishness, or greed. We all know people who are tuned to radio station WIIFM (What's In It For Me?). For most of us, however, self-interest often includes the welfare of our family, our friends, and perhaps the poor of the world. Even so, our concern for others is influenced by the cost of that concern. We may readily volunteer to drive a friend to the airport on Saturday afternoon but are less likely to offer if the plane leaves at 6:00 A.M. When we donate clothes to an organization like Goodwill Industries, they are more likely to be old and worn than brand new. People tend to give more to charities when their contributions are tax deductible. TV stations are more likely to donate airtime for public-service announcements during the dead of night than during prime time (in fact, 80 percent of such announcements air between 11:00 P.M. and 7:00 A.M.[1]). In Asia some people burn money to soothe the passage of a departed loved one. But they burn fake money, not real money. The notion of self-interest does not rule out concern for others; it simply means that concern for others is influenced by the same economic forces that affect other economic choices. *The lower the personal cost of helping others, the more help we offer.*

Choice Requires Time and Information

Rational choice takes time and requires information, but time and information are scarce and valuable. If you have any doubts about the time and information required to make choices, talk to someone who recently purchased a home, a car, or a personal computer. Talk to a corporate official deciding whether to introduce a new product, sell over the Internet, build a new factory, or buy another firm. Or think back to your own experience of selecting a college. You probably talked to friends, relatives, teachers, and guidance counselors. You likely used school catalogs, college guides, and Web sites. You may have visited campuses to meet with the admissions staff and anyone else willing to talk. The decision took time and money, and it probably involved aggravation and anxiety.

Because information is costly to acquire, we are often willing to pay others to gather and digest it for us. College guidebooks, stock analysts, travel agents, real estate brokers, career counselors, restaurant critics, movie reviewers, specialized Web sites, and *Consumer Reports* magazine attest to our willingness to pay for information that will improve our choices. As

1. Sally Goll Beatty, "Media and Agencies Brawl Over Do-Good Advertising," *Wall Street Journal,* 29 September 1997.

we'll see next, *rational decision makers will continue to acquire information as long as the additional benefit expected from that information exceeds the additional cost of gathering it.*

Economic Analysis Is Marginal Analysis

Economic choice usually involves some adjustment to the existing situation, or status quo. Amazon.com must decide whether to add an additional line of products. The school superintendent must decide whether to hire another teacher. Your favorite jeans are on sale, and you must decide whether to buy another pair. You are wondering whether you should carry an extra course next term. You have just finished dinner at a restaurant and are deciding whether to have dessert.

Economic choice is based on a comparison of the *expected marginal benefit* and the *expected marginal cost* of the action under consideration. **Marginal** means incremental, additional, or extra. Marginal refers to a change in an economic variable, a change in the status quo. *You, as a rational decision maker, will change the status quo as long as your expected marginal benefit from the change exceeds your expected marginal cost.* For example, Amazon.com compares the marginal benefit expected from adding a new line of products (the added sales revenue) with the marginal cost (the added cost of the resources required). Likewise, you compare the marginal benefit you expect from eating dessert (the added pleasure and satisfaction) with its marginal cost (the added money, time, and calories).

Typically, the change under consideration is small, but a marginal choice can involve a major economic adjustment, as in the decision to quit school and get a job. For a firm, a marginal choice might mean building a plant in Mexico or even filing for bankruptcy. By focusing on the effect of a marginal adjustment to the status quo, the economist is able to cut the analysis of economic choice down to a manageable size. Rather than confront a bewildering economic reality head-on, the economist begins with a marginal choice to see how this choice affects a particular market and shapes the economic system as a whole. Incidentally, to the noneconomist, *marginal* usually means relatively inferior, as in "a movie of marginal quality." Forget that meaning for this course and instead think of *marginal* as meaning incremental, additional, or extra.

MARGINAL

Incremental, additional, or extra; used to describe a change in an economic variable

Microeconomics and Macroeconomics

Although you have made thousands of economic choices, you probably have seldom thought about your own economic behavior. For example, why are you reading this book right now rather than doing something else? **Microeconomics** is the study of your economic behavior and the economic behavior of others who make choices about such matters as how much to study and how much to play, how much to borrow and how much to save, what to buy and what to sell. Microeconomics examines the factors that influence individual economic choices and how markets coordinate the choices of various decision makers. Microeconomics explains how price and quantity are determined in individual markets—for breakfast cereal, sports equipment, or used cars, for instance.

You have probably given little thought to what influences your own economic choices. You have likely given even less thought to how your choices link up with those made by millions of others in the U.S. economy to determine economy-wide measures such as total production, employment, and economic growth. **Macroeconomics** studies the performance of the economy as a whole. Whereas microeconomics studies the individual pieces of the economic puzzle, as reflected in particular markets, macroeconomics puts all the pieces together to focus on the big picture.

MICROECONOMICS

The study of the economic behavior in particular markets, such as that for computers or unskilled labor

MACROECONOMICS

The study of the economic behavior of entire economies

To review: The art of economic analysis focuses on how individuals use their scarce resources in an attempt to satisfy their unlimited wants. Rational self-interest guides individual choice. Choice requires time and information, and choice involves a comparison of the marginal cost and marginal benefit of alternative actions. Microeconomics looks at the individual pieces of the economic puzzle; macroeconomics fits the pieces together to shape the big picture.

The Science of Economic Analysis

ECONOMIC THEORY, OR ECONOMIC MODEL

A simplification of reality used to make predictions about cause and effect in the real world

Economists use scientific analysis to develop theories, or models, that help explain economic behavior. An **economic theory,** or **economic model,** is a simplification of economic reality that *is used to make predictions about the real world.* A theory, or model, such as the circular-flow model, captures the important elements of the problem under study; it need not spell out every detail and interrelation. In fact, adding more details may make a theory more unwieldy and less useful. The world is so complex that we must simplify if we want to make sense of things, just as comic strips simplify characters—leaving out fingers or a mouth, for instance. You might think of economic theory as a stripped-down, or streamlined, version of economic reality.

The Role of Theory

Many people don't understand the role of theory. Perhaps you have heard, "Oh, that's fine in theory, but in practice it's another matter." The implication is that the theory provides little aid in practical matters. People who say this fail to realize that they are merely substituting their own theory for a theory they either do not believe or do not understand. They are really saying, "I have my own theory that works better."

All of us employ theories, however poorly defined or understood. Someone who pounds on the Pepsi machine that just ate a quarter has a crude theory about how that machine works and what went wrong. One version of that theory might be "The quarter drops through a series of whatchamacallits, but sometimes it gets stuck. *If* I pound on the machine, *then* I can free up the quarter and send it on its way." Evidently, this theory is pervasive enough that many people continue to pound on machines that fail to perform (a real problem for the vending machine industry and one reason newer machines are fronted with glass). Yet, if you were to ask these mad pounders to explain their "theory" about how the machine operates, they would look at you as if you were crazy.

The Scientific Method

To study economic problems, economists employ a process of theoretical investigation called the *scientific method,* which consists of four steps, as outlined in Exhibit 2.

Step One: Identify the Question and Define Relevant Variables

VARIABLE

A measure, such as price or quantity, that can take on different values

The first step is to identify the economic question and define the variables that are relevant to the solution. For example, the question might be "What is the relationship between the price of Pepsi and the quantity of Pepsi purchased?" In this case, the relevant variables are price and quantity. A **variable** is a measure that can take on different values. The variables of concern become the elements of the theory, so they must be selected with care.

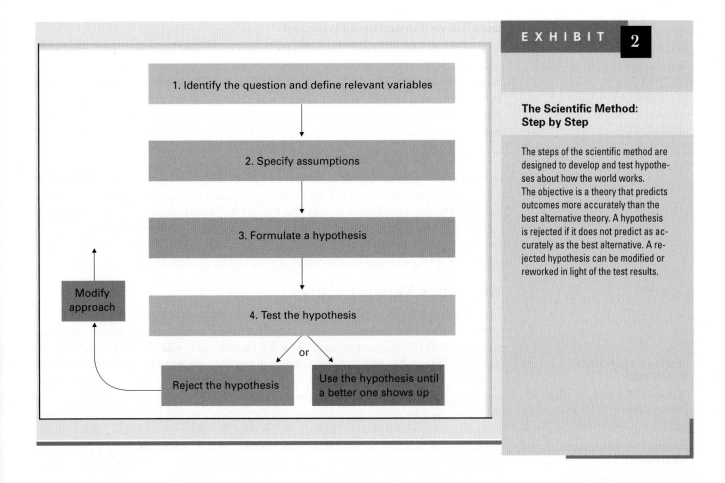

EXHIBIT 2

The Scientific Method: Step by Step

The steps of the scientific method are designed to develop and test hypotheses about how the world works. The objective is a theory that predicts outcomes more accurately than the best alternative theory. A hypothesis is rejected if it does not predict as accurately as the best alternative. A rejected hypothesis can be modified or reworked in light of the test results.

Step Two: Specify Assumptions

The second step is to specify the assumptions under which the theory is to apply. One major category of assumptions is the **other-things-constant assumption**—in Latin, the ceteris paribus assumption. The idea is to identify the variables of interest and then focus exclusively on the relationships among them, assuming that nothing else of importance will change—that other things will remain constant. Again, suppose we are interested in how the price of Pepsi influences the amount purchased. To isolate the relation between these two variables, we assume that there are no changes in other relevant variables such as consumer income, the average temperature, or the price of Coke.

We also make assumptions about how people will behave; these we call **behavioral assumptions.** The primary behavioral assumption is rational self-interest. Earlier we assumed that individual decision makers pursue self-interest rationally and make choices accordingly. Rationality implies that each consumer buys the products expected to maximize his or her level of satisfaction. Rationality also implies that a firm supplies the products expected to maximize profit. These kinds of assumptions are called behavioral assumptions because they specify how we expect economic decision makers to behave—what makes them tick, so to speak.

OTHER-THINGS-CONSTANT ASSUMPTION

The assumption, when focusing on the relation among key economic variables, that other variables remain unchanged

BEHAVIORAL ASSUMPTION

An assumption that describes the expected behavior of economic decision makers, what motivates them

Step Three: Formulate a Hypothesis

The third step is to formulate a **hypothesis,** which is a theory about how key variables relate to each other. For example, one hypothesis holds that if the price of Pepsi goes up, other things constant, then the quantity purchased will decline. The hypothesis becomes a prediction of what will happen to the quantity purchased if the price goes up. *The purpose of this hypothesis, like that of any theory, is to help make predictions about cause and effect in the real world.*

Step Four: Test the Hypothesis

In the fourth step, by comparing its predictions with evidence, we test the validity of a hypothesis. To test a hypothesis, we must focus on the variables in question, while carefully controlling for other effects assumed not to change. The test will lead us either to (1) reject the hypothesis, or theory, if it predicts worse than the best alternative theory or (2) use the hypothesis, or theory, until a better one comes along. If we reject it, we can go back and modify our approach in light of the results. Please spend a moment now reviewing the steps in Exhibit 2.

Normative Versus Positive

Economists usually try to explain how the economy works. Sometimes they concern themselves not with how the economy *does* work but how it *should* work. Compare these two statements: "The U.S. unemployment rate is 5.7 percent" and "The U.S. unemployment rate should be lower." The first, called a **positive economic statement**, is an assertion about economic reality that can be supported or rejected by reference to the facts. The second, called a **normative economic statement,** reflects an opinion. And an opinion is merely that—it cannot be shown to be true or false by reference to the facts. Positive statements concern what *is;* normative statements concern what, in someone's opinion, *should be.* Positive statements need not necessarily be true, but they must be subject to verification or refutation by reference to the facts. Theories are expressed as positive statements such as "If the price of Pepsi increases, then the quantity demanded will decrease."

Most of the disagreement among economists involves normative debates—for example, the appropriate role of government—rather than statements of positive analysis. To be sure, many theoretical issues remain unresolved, but economists generally agree on most fundamental theoretical principles—that is, about positive economic analysis. For example, in a survey of 464 U.S. economists, only 6.5 percent disagreed with the statement "A ceiling on rents reduces the quantity and quality of housing available." This is a positive statement because it can be shown to be consistent or inconsistent with the evidence. In contrast, there was much less agreement on normative statements such as "The distribution of income in the United States should be more equal." Half the economists surveyed "generally agreed," a quarter "generally disagreed," and a quarter "agreed with provisos."[2]

Normative statements, or value judgments, have a place in a policy debate such as the proper role of government, provided that statements of opinion are distinguished from statements of fact. In such policy debates, you are entitled to your own opinion, but you are not entitled to your own facts.

Economists Tell Stories

Despite economists' reliance on the scientific method for developing and evaluating theories, economic analysis is as much art as science. Formulating a question, isolating the key

---

2. Richard M. Alston, et al., "Is There a Consensus Among Economists in the 1990s?" *American Economic Review* 82 (May 1992): pp. 203–209, Table 1.

variables, specifying the assumptions, proposing a theory to answer the question, and devising a way to test the predictions all involve more than simply an understanding of economics and the scientific method. Carrying out these steps requires good intuition and the imagination of a storyteller. Economists explain their theories by telling stories about how they think the economy works. To tell a compelling story, an economist relies on case studies, anecdotes, parables, the personal experience of the listener, and supporting data. Throughout this book, you will hear stories that bring you closer to the ideas under consideration. The stories, such as the one about the Pepsi machine, breathe life into economic theory and help you personalize abstract ideas. As another example, here is a case study about the popularity of vending machines in Japan.

A Yen for Vending Machines

© Paul Chesley/Stone/Getty Images

Japan faces a steady drop in the number of working-age people. Here are three reasons why: (1) Japan's birthrate has reached a record low, (2) Japan allows virtually no immigration—only 2 of every 1,000 workers in Japan are foreigners, and (3) Japan's population is aging. As a result, unemployment has usually been lower in Japan than in other countries. Because labor is relatively scarce there, it is relatively costly. To sell products, Japanese retailers rely on capital, particularly vending machines, which obviously eliminate the need for sales clerks.

Japan has more vending machines per capita than any other country on the planet—twice as many as the United States and nearly ten times as many as Europe. And vending machines in Japan sell a wider range of products than elsewhere, including beer, sake, whiskey, rice, eggs, vegetables, pizza, entire meals, fresh flowers, clothes, video games, DVDs, even X-rated comic books. Japan's vending machines are also more sophisticated. The newer models come with video monitors and touch-pad screens. Wireless chips alert vendors when supplies are running low. Machines selling cigarettes or alcohol require a driver's license, which is used to verify the buyer's age (and the machines can spot fake IDs).

Some cold-drink dispensers automatically raise prices in hot weather. Coca-Cola machines allow mobile phone users to pay for drinks by pressing a few buttons on their mobiles. Sanyo makes a giant machine that sells up to 200 different items at three different temperatures. Perhaps the ultimate vending machine is Robo Shop Super 24, a totally automated convenience store in Tokyo. After browsing long display cases, a customer can make selections by punching product numbers on a keyboard. A bucket whirs around the store, collecting the selections.

As noted earlier, it is common practice in the United States to shake down vending machines that malfunction. Such abuse increases the probability the machines will fail again, leading to a cycle of abuse. Vending machines in Japan are less abused, in part because they are more sophisticated and more reliable and in part because the Japanese generally have greater respect for property and, consequently, a lower crime rate (for example, Japan's theft rate is only about half the U.S. rate).

Japanese consumers use vending machines with great frequency. For example, 40 percent of all soft-drink sales in Japan are through vending machines, compared to only 12 percent of

U.S. sales. Japanese sales per machine are double the U.S. rate. Research shows that most Japanese consumers prefer an anonymous machine to a salesperson (Robo Shop 24's Web site notes, "Grumpy, nervous store clerks have been replaced by the cheery little Robo"). Despite the abundance of vending machines in Japan, more growth is forecast, spurred on by a shrinking labor pool, technological innovations, and wide acceptance of machines there.

Sources: Ginny Parker, "Vending the Rules," *Time*, 25 August 2003; and "In 2001 Japanese Spent $87.5 Billion on Vending Machines," *The Food Industry Report*, 3 March 2003; pictures and descriptions of Robo Shop 24 can be found at http://www.theimageworks.com/Robo/roboftur.htm.

This case study makes two points. First, producers combine resources in a way that conserves, or economizes on, the resource that is more costly—in this case, labor. Second, the customs and conventions of the marketplace can differ across countries, and this variance can result in different types of economic arrangements, such as the more extensive use of vending machines in Japan.

Predicting Average Behavior

The goal of an economic theory is to predict the impact of an economic event on economic choices and, in turn, the effect of these choices on particular markets or on the economy as a whole. Does this mean that economists try to predict the behavior of particular consumers or producers? Not necessarily, because a specific individual may behave in an unpredictable way. But the unpredictable actions of numerous individuals tend to cancel one another out, so the *average behavior* of groups can be predicted more accurately. For example, if the federal government cuts personal income taxes, certain households may decide to save the entire tax cut. On average, however, household spending will increase. Likewise, if Burger King cuts the price of Whoppers, the manager can better predict how much sales will increase than how a specific customer will respond. *The random actions of individuals tend to offset one another, so the average behavior of a large group can be predicted more accurately than the behavior of a particular individual.* Consequently, economists tend to focus on the average, or typical, behavior of people in groups—for example, as average taxpayers or average Whopper consumers—rather than on the behavior of a specific individual.

Some Pitfalls of Faulty Economic Analysis

Economic analysis, like other forms of scientific inquiry, is subject to common mistakes in reasoning that can lead to faulty conclusions. We will discuss three possible sources of confusion.

The Fallacy That Association Is Causation

In the last two decades, the number of physicians specializing in cancer treatment increased sharply. At the same time, the incidence of most cancers increased. Can we conclude that physicians cause cancer? No. To assume that event A caused event B simply because the two are associated in time is to commit the **association-is-causation fallacy,** a common error. The fact that one event precedes another or that the two events occur simultaneously does not necessarily mean that one causes the other. Remember: Association is not necessarily causation.

The Fallacy of Composition

Standing up at a football game to get a better view of the action does not work if others stand as well. Arriving early to buy concert tickets does not work if many others have the

ASSOCIATION-IS-CAUSATION FALLACY

The incorrect idea that if two variables are associated in time, one must necessarily cause the other same idea. These are examples of the **fallacy of composition,** which is an erroneous belief that what is true for the individual, or the part, is also true for the group, or the whole.

The Mistake of Ignoring the Secondary Effects

In many cities, public officials have imposed rent controls on apartments. The primary effect of this policy, the effect on which policy makers focus, is to keep rents from rising. Over time, however, fewer new apartments get built because renting becomes less profitable. Moreover, existing rental units deteriorate because owners have no incentive to pay for maintenance since they have plenty of customers anyway. Thus, the quantity and quality of housing may decline as a result of what appears to be a reasonable measure to keep rents from rising. The mistake was to ignore the **secondary effects,** or the unintended consequences, of the policy. Economic actions have secondary effects that often turn out to be more important than the primary effects. Secondary effects may develop more slowly and may not be obvious, but good economic analysis takes them into account.

If Economists Are So Smart, Why Aren't They Rich?

Why aren't economists rich? Well, some are, earning over $25,000 per appearance on the lecture circuit. Others earn thousands a day as consultants. Economists have been appointed to cabinet positions, such as Secretaries of Commerce, Defense, Labor, State, and Treasury, and to head the Federal Reserve System. Economics is the only social science and the only business discipline for which the prestigious Nobel Prize is awarded, and pronouncements by economists are reported in the media daily. *The Economist,* a widely respected news weekly from London, argues that economic ideas have influenced policy "to a degree that would make other social scientists drool."[3]

The economics profession thrives because its models usually do a better job of making economic sense out of a confusing world than do alternative approaches. But not all economists are wealthy, nor is personal wealth the goal of the discipline. In a similar vein, not all doctors are healthy (some even smoke), not all carpenters live in perfectly built homes, not all marriage counselors are happily married, and not all child psychologists have well-adjusted children. Still, those who study economics do reap financial rewards, as discussed in this closing case study, which looks at the link between earnings and the choice of a college major.

College Major and Career Earnings

Earlier in the chapter, you learned that economic choice is based on a comparison of expected marginal benefit and expected marginal cost. Surveys show that students go to college because they believe a college diploma is the ticket to better jobs and higher pay. Put another way, for about two-thirds of U.S. high school graduates, the expected marginal benefit of college apparently exceeds the expected marginal cost. The cost of college will be discussed in the next chapter; the focus here is on the benefits of college, particularly expected earnings.

3. "The Puzzling Failure of Economics," *The Economist,* 23 August 1997, p. 11.

FALLACY OF COMPOSITION

The incorrect belief that what is true for the individual, or part, must necessarily be true for the group, or whole

SECONDARY EFFECTS

Unintended consequences of economic actions that may develop slowly over time as people react to events

HOMEWORK Xpress!
Ask the Instructor Video

Case **Study**

The Information Economy

*e*Activity

The Federal Reserve Bank of Minneapolis asked some Nobel Prize winners how they became interested in economics. Their stories can be found at http://woodrow.mpls.frb.fed.us/pubs/region/98-12/quotes.cfm.

WALL STREET JOURNAL

Reading It **Right**

What's the relevance of the following statement from the Wall Street Journal: *"With economics the most popular undergraduate major at many top colleges, demand for economics professors has led to a bidding war for the most highly-regarded candidates."*

Among college graduates, all kinds of factors affect earnings, such as general ability, occupation, college attended, college major, and highest degree earned. To isolate the effects of college major on earnings, a National Science Foundation study surveyed people in specific age groups who worked full time and had earned a bachelor's as their highest degree. Exhibit 3 shows the median earnings by major for men and women ages 35 to 44. As a point of reference, the *median* annual earnings for men was $43,199 (half earned more and half earned less). The median earnings for women was $32,155, only 74 percent of the median for men. Among men, the top median pay was the $53,286 earned by engineering majors; that pay was 23 percent above the median for all men surveyed. Among women, the top median pay was the $49,170 earned by economics majors; that pay was 53 percent above the median for all women surveyed.

Incidentally, men who majored in economics earned a median of $49,377, ranking them seventh among 27 majors and 14 percent above the median for all men surveyed. Thus, even though the median pay for all women was only 74 percent of the median pay for all men, women who majored in economics earned about the same as men who majored in economics. We can say that economics majors earned more than most, and they experienced no pay difference based on gender.

Notice that among both men and women, the majors ranked toward the top of the list tend to be more quantitative and analytical. According to the study's author, "Employers may view certain majors as more difficult and may assume that graduates in these fields are more able and hard working, whereupon they offer them higher salaries."[4] The selection of a relatively more challenging major such as economics sends a favorable signal to future employers.

The study also examined the kinds of jobs different majors actually found. Those who majored in economics became mid- and top-level managers, executives, and administrators. They also worked in sales, computer fields, financial analysis, and economic analysis. Remember, the survey was limited to those whose highest degree was the baccalaureate, so it excluded the many economics majors who went on to pursue graduate studies in law, business administration, economics, public administration, journalism, and other fields (a separate study showed that lawyers with undergraduate degrees in economics earned more than other lawyers).

A number of world leaders majored in economics, including three of the last six U.S. presidents, Supreme Court Justice Sandra Day O'Connor, and Philippines President Gloria Macapagal-Arroyo, who earned a Ph.D. in the subject. Other well-known economics majors include eBay President Meg Whitman, Intel President Paul Otellini, Governor Arnold Schwarzenegger, aging rocker Mick Jagger, high-tech guru Esther Dyson, and Scott Adams, creator of Dilbert, the mouthless wonder.

Source: R. Kim Craft and Joe Baker, "Do Economists Make Better Lawyers? Undergraduate Degree Fields and Lawyer Earnings," *Journal of Economic Education,*" Summer 2003; and Daniel E. Hecker, "Earnings of College Graduates, 1993," *Monthly Labor Review,* December 1995. For a survey of employment opportunities, go to the U.S. Labor Department's Occupational Outlook Handbook at http://www.bls.gov/oco/.

4. Daniel E. Hecker, "Earnings of College Graduates, 1993," *Monthly Labor Review* (December 1995): p. 15.

EXHIBIT 3

Median Annual Earnings of 35- to 44-Year-Olds with Bachelor's as Highest Degree by Major

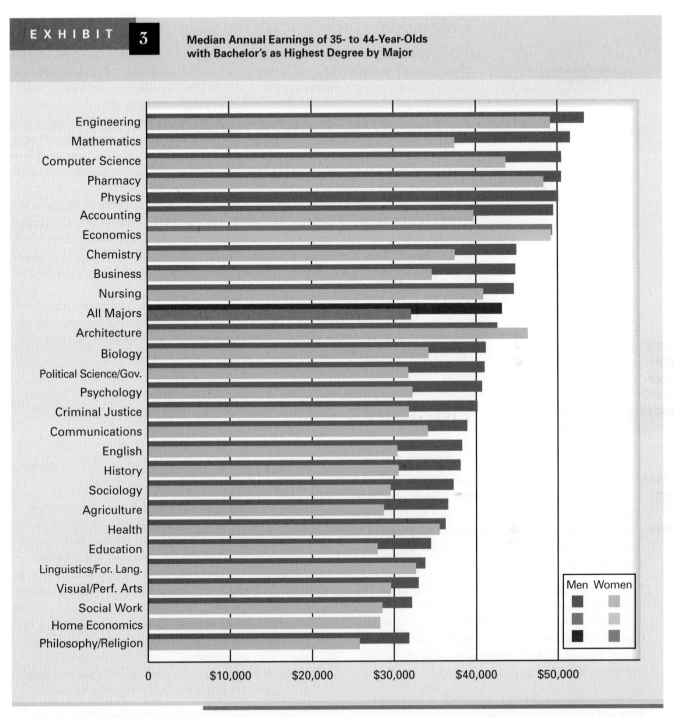

Source: Earnings are for 1993 based on figures reported by Daniel Hecker in "Earnings of College Graduates, 1993," *Monthly Labor Review* (December 1995): 3–17.

Conclusion

This textbook describes how economic factors affect individual choices and how all these choices come together to shape the economic system. Economics is not the whole story, and economic factors are not always the most important. But economic considerations have important and predictable effects on individual choices, and these choices affect the way we live.

Sure, economics is a challenging discipline, but it is also an exciting and rewarding one. The good news is that you already know a lot about economics. To use this knowledge, however, you must cultivate the art and science of economic analysis. You must be able to simplify the world to formulate questions, isolate the relevant variables, and then tell a persuasive story about how these variables relate.

An economic relation can be expressed in words, represented as a table of quantities, described by a mathematical equation, or illustrated as a graph. The appendix to this chapter provides an introduction to graphs. You may find this information unnecessary. If you are already familiar with relations among variables, slopes, tangents, and the like, you can probably just browse. But if you have little recent experience with graphs, you might benefit from a more careful reading with pencil and paper in hand.

The next chapter will introduce key tools of economic analysis. Subsequent chapters will use these ideas to explore economic problems and to explain economic behavior that may otherwise seem puzzling. You must walk before you can run, however, and in the next chapter, you will take your first wobbly steps.

SUMMARY

1. Economics is the study of how people choose to use their scarce resources to produce, exchange, and consume goods and services in an attempt to satisfy unlimited wants. The economic problem arises from the conflict between scarce resources and unlimited wants. If wants were limited or if resources were not scarce, there would be no need to study economics.

2. Economic resources are combined in a variety of ways to produce goods and services. Major categories of resources include labor, capital, natural resources, and entrepreneurial ability. Because economic resources are scarce, only a limited number of goods and services can be produced with them; therefore, choices must be made.

3. Microeconomics focuses on choices made in households, firms, and governments and how these choices affect particular markets, such as the market for used cars. Choice is guided by rational self-interest. Choice typically requires time and information, both of which are scarce and valuable.

4. Whereas microeconomics examines the individual pieces of the puzzle, macroeconomics steps back to look at the big picture—the performance of the economy as a whole as reflected by such measures as total production, employment, the price level, and economic growth.

5. Economists use theories, or models, to help understand the effects of economic changes, such as changes in price and income, on individual choices and how these choices affect particular markets and the economy as a whole. Economists employ the scientific method to study an economic problem by (a) formulating the question and isolating relevant variables, (b) specifying the assumptions under which the theory operates, (c) developing a theory, or hypothesis, about how the variables relate, and (d) testing that theory by comparing its predictions with the evidence. A theory might not work perfectly, but it is useful as long as it predicts better than competing theories do.

6. Positive economics aims to discover how the economy works. Normative economics is concerned more with how, in someone's opinion, the economy should work. Those who are not careful can fall victim to the fallacy that association is causation, to the fallacy of composition, and to the mistake of ignoring secondary effects.

QUESTIONS FOR REVIEW

1. *(Definition of Economics)* What determines whether or not a resource is scarce? Why is the concept of scarcity important to the definition of economics?

2. *(Resources)* To which category of resources does each of the following belong?

   a. A taxicab
   b. Computer software
   c. One hour of legal counsel
   d. A parking lot
   e. A forest
   f. The Mississippi River
   g. An individual introducing a new way to market products on the Internet

3. *(Goods and Services)* Explain why each of the following would *not* be considered "free" for the economy as a whole:

   a. Food stamps
   b. U.S. aid to developing countries
   c. Corporate charitable contributions
   d. Noncable television programs
   e. Public high school education

4. *(Economic Decision Makers)* Which group of economic decision makers plays the leading role in the economic system? Which groups play supporting roles? In what sense are they supporting actors?

5. *(Micro Versus Macro)* Determine whether each of the following is primarily a microeconomic or a macroeconomic issue:

   a. Determining the price to charge for an automobile
   b. Measuring the impact of tax policies on total consumption spending in the economy
   c. A household's decisions about how to allocate its disposable income among various goods and services
   d. A worker's decision regarding how many hours to work each week
   e. Designing a government policy to affect the level of employment

6. *(Micro Versus Macro)* Some economists believe that to really understand macroeconomics, you must fully understand microeconomics. How does microeconomics relate to macroeconomics?

7. *(Normative Versus Positive Analysis)* Determine whether each of the following statements is normative or positive:

   a. The U.S. unemployment rate was below 6.0 percent in 2003.
   b. The inflation rate in the United States is too high.
   c. The U.S. government should increase the minimum wage.
   d. U.S. trade restrictions cost consumers $20 billion annually.

8. *(Role of Theory)* What good is economic theory if it cannot predict the behavior of a specific individual?

PROBLEMS AND EXERCISES

9. *(Rational Self-Interest)* Discuss the impact of rational self-interest on each of the following decisions:

   a. Whether to attend college full time or enter the workforce full time
   b. Whether to buy a new textbook or a used textbook
   c. Whether to attend a local college or an out-of-town college

10. *(Rational Self-Interest)* If behavior is governed by rational self-interest, why do people make charitable contributions?

11. *(Marginal Analysis)* The owner of a small pizzeria is deciding whether to increase the radius of its delivery area by one mile. What considerations must be taken into account if such a decision is to contribute to profitability?

12. *(Time and Information)* It is often costly to obtain the information necessary to make good decisions. Yet your own interests can be best served by rationally weighing all options available to you. This requires informed decision making. Does this mean that making uninformed decisions is irrational? How do you determine how much information is the right amount?

13. *(C a s e **S t u d y**: A Yen for Vending Machines)* Do vending machines conserve on any resources other than labor? Does your answer offer any additional insight into the widespread use of vending machines in Japan?

14. *(C a s e **S t u d y**: A Yen for Vending Machines)* Suppose you had the choice of purchasing identically priced lunches from a vending machine or at a cafeteria. Which would you choose? Why?

15. *(Pitfalls of Economic Analysis)* Review the discussion of pitfalls in economic thinking in this chapter. Then identify the fallacy or mistake in thinking in each of the following statements:

    a. Raising taxes will always increase government revenues.
    b. Whenever there is a recession, imports decrease. Therefore, to stop a recession, we should increase imports.
    c. Raising the tariff on imported steel will help the U.S. steel industry. Therefore, the entire economy will be helped.
    d. Gold sells for about $400 per ounce. Therefore, the U.S. government could sell all the gold in Fort Knox at $400 per ounce and eliminate the national debt.

16. *(Association Versus Causation)* Suppose I observe that communities with lots of doctors tend to have relatively high rates of illness. I conclude that doctors cause illness. What's wrong with this reasoning?

EXPERIENTIAL EXERCISES

17. *(Micro Versus Macro)* Go to the Bank of Sweden's page on the Nobel Prize in economic science at http://www.nobel.se/economics/. Review the descriptions of some recent awards, and try to determine whether those particular awards were primarily for work in macroeconomics or in microeconomics.

18. *(C a s e **S t u d y**: College Major and Career Earnings)* The Bureau of Labor Statistics maintains online copies of articles from its *Monthly Labor Review*. Go to the site http://stats.bls.gov/opub/mlr/mlrhome.htm, click on "Archives" and find the article by Daniel Hecker entitled "Earnings of College Graduates: Women Compared with Men" (March 1998). What can you learn about the payoff to college education for both women and men? (Note: You will need Adobe Acrobat Reader to get the full text of this article. You can download a copy of Reader at http://www.adobe.com/prodindex/acrobat/readstep.html.

19. *(Wall Street Journal)* Detecting economic fallacies is an important skill. Review the section titled "Some Pitfalls of Faulty Economic Analysis" in this chapter. Then use the *Wall Street Journal* to find at least one example of faulty reasoning. (Hint: Begin with the "Markets Diary" column in the "Money & Investing" section.)

HOMEWORK XPRESS! EXERCISES

These exercises require access to McEachern Homework Xpress! If Homework Xpress! did not come with your book, visit **http://homeworkxpress.swlearning.com** *to purchase.*

1. The price for a basic cheese pizza at Giorgio's is $5. Each additional topping is $1. Sketch a graph to illustrate the relationship between the price of a pizza and the number of toppings for up to 5 toppings.

2. Reproductions of the National Gallery of Art's *Girl with a Watering Can* by Renoir are offered for sale in the gift shop. The manager finds that if she sets the price at $20, no reproductions are sold. For every dollar she reduces the price, 10 additional copies are sold each week. Sketch a graph showing the relationship between the price of a reproduction and the number sold each week.

3. Economists studying consumption of pizza notice that households buy more pizzas per month as income increases, but only up to an income of $3,000 per month. At this income level, the average household consumes 10 pizzas per month. As income increases beyond this level, household consumption of pizzas declines. Sketch a graph showing a curvilinear relationship between household income and the number of pizzas consumed per month.

4. Nicer Pants Inc. found that at a price of $50 per pair, no one bought its product. For every dollar less it charged, it sold an additional 200 pairs of pants per month. Draw a graph to illustrate the relationship between the price of the pants and the quantity purchased per month. Label this as D for consumer demand.

   Due to an economics recession, the firm now finds that it has no sales at prices about $40 per pair. However, for each dollar it reduces the prices, it still sells an additional 200 pairs per month. Sketch a graph to illustrate this new relationship between the price of the pants and the quantity purchased each month. Label this as D1.

Appendix

Understanding Graphs

Take out a pencil and a blank piece of paper. Go ahead. Put a point in the middle of the paper. This is your point of departure, called the **origin.** With your pencil at the origin, draw a straight line off to the right. This line is called the **horizontal axis.** The value of the variable x measured along the horizontal axis increases as you move to the right of the origin. Now mark off this line from 0 to 20, in increments of 5 units each. Returning to the origin, draw another line, this one straight up. This line is called the **vertical axis.** The value of the variable y measured along the vertical axis increases as you move upward. Mark off this line from 0 to 20, in increments of 5 units each.

Within the space framed by the two axes, you can plot possible combinations of the variables measured along each axis. Each point identifies a value measured along the horizontal, or x, axis *and a* value measured along the vertical, or y, axis. For example, place point a in your graph to reflect the combination where x equals 5 units and y equals 15 units. Likewise, place point b in your graph to reflect 10 units of x and 5 units of y. Now compare your results with points shown in Exhibit 4.

A **graph** is a picture showing how variables relate, and a picture can be worth a thousand words. Take a look at Exhibit 5, which shows the U.S. annual unemployment rate since 1900. The year is measured along the horizontal axis and the unemployment rate along the vertical axis. Exhibit 5 is a *time-series graph,* which shows the value of a variable, in this case the unemployment rate, over time. If you had to describe the information presented in Exhibit 5 in words, the explanation could take many words. The picture shows not only how one year compares to the next but also how one decade compares to another and how the rate trends over time. The sharply higher unemployment rate during the Great Depression of the 1930s is unmistakable. *Graphs convey information in a compact and efficient way.*

This appendix shows how graphs express a variety of possible relations among variables. Most graphs of interest in this book reflect the relationship between two economic variables, such as the unemployment rate and the year, the price of a product and the quantity demanded, or the price of production and the quantity supplied. Because we focus on just two variables at a time, we usually assume that other relevant variables remain constant.

One variable often depends on another. The time it takes you to drive home depends on your average speed. Your weight depends on how much you eat. The amount of Pepsi people buy depends on its price. A *functional relation* exists between two variables when the value of one variable *depends* on the value of another variable. The value of the **dependent variable** depends on the value of the **independent variable**. The task of the economist is to isolate economic relations and determine the direction of causality, if

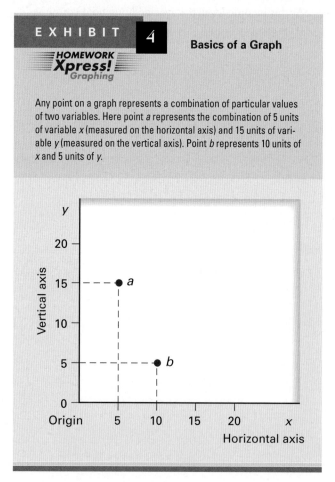

EXHIBIT   **4**   **Basics of a Graph**

HOMEWORK Xpress! *Graphing*

Any point on a graph represents a combination of particular values of two variables. Here point *a* represents the combination of 5 units of variable *x* (measured on the horizontal axis) and 15 units of variable *y* (measured on the vertical axis). Point *b* represents 10 units of *x* and 5 units of *y*.

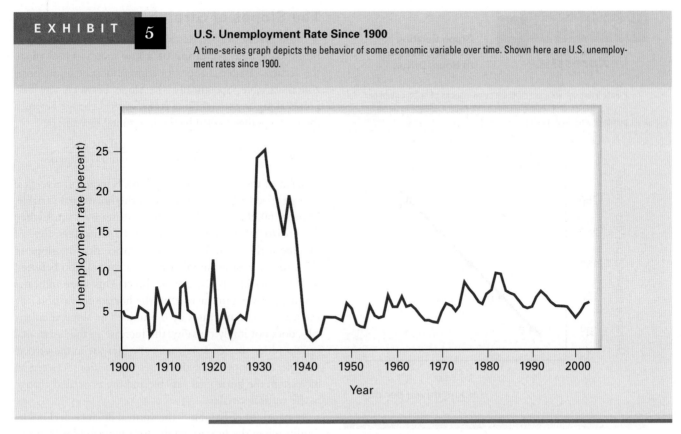

Sources: *Historical Statistics of the United States,* 1970, and *Economic Report of the President,* February 2004.

any. Recall that one of the pitfalls of economic thinking is the erroneous belief that association is causation. We cannot conclude that, simply because two events relate in time, one causes the other. There may be no relation between the two events.

Drawing Graphs

Let's begin with a simple relation. Suppose you are planning to drive across country and want to determine how far you will travel each day. You plan to average 50 miles per hour. Possible combinations of driving time and distance traveled appear in Exhibit 6. One column lists the hours driven per day, and the next column lists the number of miles traveled per day, assuming an average speed of 50 miles per hour. The distance traveled, the *dependent* variable, depends on the number of hours driven, the *independent* variable. Combinations of hours driven and distance traveled are shown as *a, b, c, d,* and *e.* Each combination of hours driven and distance

---

E X H I B I T   **6**

Schedule Relating Distance Traveled to Hours Driven

	Hours Driven per Day	Distance Traveled per Day (miles)
a	1	50
b	2	100
c	3	150
d	4	200
e	5	250

EXHIBIT 5 — U.S. Unemployment Rate Since 1900

A time-series graph depicts the behavior of some economic variable over time. Shown here are U.S. unemployment rates since 1900.

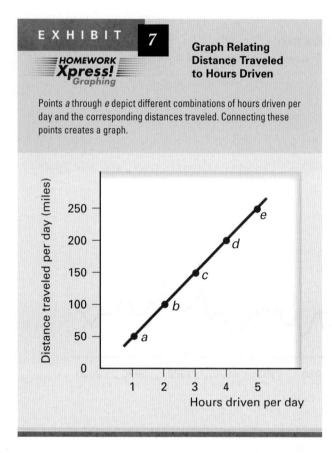

**Graph Relating
Distance Traveled
to Hours Driven**

Points *a* through *e* depict different combinations of hours driven per day and the corresponding distances traveled. Connecting these points creates a graph.

The Slopes of Straight Lines

A more precise way to describe the shape of a curve is to measure its slope. The **slope of a line** indicates how much the vertical variable changes for a given increase in the horizontal variable. Specifically, the slope between any two points along any straight line is the vertical change between these two points divided by the horizontal increase, or

$$\text{Slope} = \frac{\text{Change in the vertical distance}}{\text{Increase in the horizontal distance}}$$

Each of the four panels in Exhibit 8 indicates a vertical change, given a 10-unit increase in the horizontal variable. In panel (a), the vertical distance increases by 5 units when the horizontal distance increases by 10 units. The slope of the line is therefore 5/10, or 0.5. Notice that the slope in this case is a positive number because the relation between the two variables is positive, or direct. This slope indicates that for every 1-unit increase in the horizontal variable, the vertical variable increases by 0.5 units. The slope, incidentally, does not imply causality; the increase in the horizontal variable does not necessarily *cause* the increase in the vertical variable. The slope simply measures the relation between an increase in the horizontal variable and the associated change in the vertical variable.

In panel (b) of Exhibit 8, the vertical distance declines by 7 units when the horizontal distance increases by 10 units, so the slope equals −7/10, or −0.7. The slope in this case is a negative number because the two variables have a negative, or inverse, relation. In panel (c), the vertical variable remains unchanged as the horizontal variable increases by 10, so the slope equals 0/10, or 0. These two variables are unrelated. Finally, in panel (d), the vertical variable can take on any value, although the horizontal variable remains unchanged. Again, the two variables are unrelated. In this case, any change in the vertical measure, for example a 10-unit change, is divided by 0, because the horizontal value does not change. Any change divided by 0 is infinitely large, so we say that the slope of a vertical line is infinite.

The Slope, Units of Measurement, and Marginal Analysis

The mathematical value of the slope depends on the units measured on the graph. For example, suppose copper tubing costs $1 a foot to make. Graphs depicting the relation between output and total cost are shown in Exhibit 9. In panel (a), the total cost of production increases by $1 for each

traveled is represented by a point in Exhibit 7. For example, point *a* shows that if you drive for 1 hour, you travel 50 miles. Point *b* indicates that if you drive for 2 hours, you travel 100 miles. By connecting the points, or combinations, we create a line running upward and to the right. This makes sense, because the longer you drive, the farther you travel. Assumed constant along this line is your average speed of 50 miles per hour.

Types of relations between variables include the following:

1. As one variable increases, the other increases—as in Exhibit 7; this is called a **positive,** or **direct, relation** between the variables.

2. As one variable increases, the other decreases; this is called a **negative,** or **inverse, relation.**

3. As one variable increases, the other remains unchanged; the two variables are said to be *independent,* or *unrelated.* One of the advantages of graphs is that they easily convey the relation between variables. We do not need to examine the particular combinations of numbers; we need only focus on the shape of the curve.

EXHIBIT   8

Alternative Slopes for Straight Lines

The slope of a line indicates how much the vertically measured variable changes for a given increase in the variable measured along the horizontal axis. Panel (a) shows a positive relation between two variables; the slope is 0.5, a positive number. Panel (b) depicts a negative, or inverse, relation. When the *x* variable increases, the *y* variable decreases; the slope is –0.7, a negative number. Panels (c) and (d) represent situations in which two variables are unrelated. In panel (c), the *y* variable always takes on the same value; the slope is 0. In panel (d), the *x* variable always takes on the same value; the slope is infinite.

(a) Positive relation

(b) Negative relation

(c) No relation: zero slope

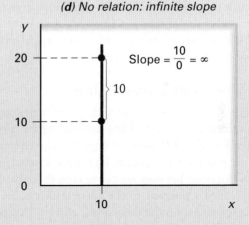

(d) No relation: infinite slope

1-foot increase in the amount of tubing produced. Thus, the slope equals 1/1, or 1. If the cost per foot remains the same but the unit of measurement is not *feet* but *yards,* the relation between output and total cost is as depicted in panel (b). Now total cost increases by $3 for each 1-*yard* increase in output, so the slope equals 3/1, or 3. Because different units are used to measure the copper tubing, the two panels reflect different slopes, even though the cost of tubing is $1 per foot

in each panel. Keep in mind that *the slope will depend in part on the units of measurement.*

Economic analysis usually involves *marginal analysis,* such as the marginal cost of producing one more unit of output. The slope is a convenient device for measuring marginal effects because it reflects the change in total cost along the vertical axis for each 1-unit change in output along the horizontal axis. For example, in panel (a) of Exhibit 9, the

EXHIBIT 9

Slope Depends on the Unit of Measure

The value of the slope depends on the units of measure. In panel (a), output is measured in feet of copper tubing; in panel (b), output is measured in yards. Although the cost of production is $1 per foot in each panel, the slope is different in the two panels because copper tubing is measured using different units.

(a) Measured in feet

Slope $= \dfrac{1}{1} = 1$

Feet of copper tubing

(b) Measured in yards

Slope $= \dfrac{3}{1} = 3$

Yards of copper tubing

marginal cost of another *foot* of copper tubing is $1, which also equals the slope of the line. In panel (b), the marginal cost of another *yard* of tubing is $3, which again is the slope of that line. Because of its applicability to marginal analysis, the slope has special relevance in economics.

The Slopes of Curved Lines

The slope of a straight line is the same everywhere along the line, but the slope of a curved line differs along the curve, as shown in Exhibit 10. To find the slope of a curved line at a particular point, draw a straight line that just touches the curve at that point but does not cut or cross the curve. Such a line is called a **tangent** to the curve at that point. The slope of the tangent is the slope of the curve at that point. Look at the line *A,* which is tangent to the curve at point *a.* As the horizontal value increases from 0 to 10, the vertical value drops along *A* from 40 to 0. Thus, the vertical change divided by the horizontal change equals −40/10, or −4, which is the slope of the curve at point *a.* This slope is negative because the curve slopes downward at that point. Line *B,* a line tangent to the curve at point *b,* has the slope −10/30, or −0.33. As you can see, the curve depicted in Exhibit 10 gets flatter as the horizontal variable increases, so the value of its slope approaches zero.

Other curves, of course, will reflect different slopes as well as different changes in the slope along the curve.

Downward-sloping curves have a negative slope, and upward-sloping curves, a positive slope. Sometimes curves, such as those in Exhibit 11, are more complex, having both

EXHIBIT 10

HOMEWORK
Xpress!
Graphing

Slope at Different Points on a Curved Line

The slope of a curved line varies from point to point. At a given point, such as *a* or *b,* the slope of the curve is equal to the slope of the straight line that is tangent to the curve at that point.

Curves with Both Positive and Negative Slopes

Some curves have both positive and negative slopes. The hill-shaped curve has a positive slope to the left of point *a*, a slope of 0 at point *a*, and a negative slope to the right of that point. The U-shaped curve starts off with a negative slope, has a slope of 0 at point *b*, and has a positive slope to the right of that point.

Shift in Line Relating Distance Traveled to Hours Driven

Line *T* appeared originally in Exhibit 7 to show the relation between hours driven per day and distance traveled per day, assuming an average speed of 50 miles per hour. If the average speed is only 40 miles per hour, the entire relation shifts to the right to *T'*, indicating that each distance traveled requires more driving time. For example, 200 miles traveled takes 4 hours of driving at 50 miles per hour but 5 hours at 40 miles per hour. This figure shows how a change in assumptions, in this case, the average speed assumed, can shift the entire relationship between two variables.

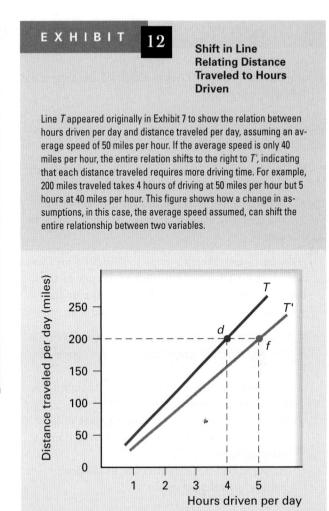

positive and negative ranges. In the hill-shaped curve, for small values of *x*, there is a positive relation between *x* and *y*, so the slope is positive. As the value of *x* increases, however, the slope declines and eventually becomes negative. We can divide the curve into two segments: (1) the segment between the origin and point *a*, where the slope is positive; and (2) the segment of the curve to the right of point *a*, where the slope is negative. The slope of the curve at point *a* is 0. The U-shaped curve in Exhibit 11 represents the opposite relation: *x* and *y* are negatively related until point *b* is reached; thereafter, they are positively related. The slope equals 0 at point *b*.

Line Shifts

Let's go back to the example of your cross-country trip, where we were trying to determine how many miles you traveled per day. Recall that we measured hours driven per day on the horizontal axis and miles traveled per day on the vertical axis, assuming an average speed of 50 miles per hour. That same relation is shown as line *T* in Exhibit 12. What if the average speed is 40 miles per hour? The entire relation

between hours driven and distance traveled would change, as shown by the shift to the right of line *T* to *T'*. With a slower average speed, any distance traveled per day now requires more driving time. For example, 200 miles traveled requires 4 hours of driving when the average speed is 50 miles per hour (as shown by point *d* on curve *T*), but 200 miles takes 5 hours when your speed averages 40 miles per hour (as shown by point *f* on curve *T'*). Thus, *a change in the assumption about average speed changes the relationship between the two variables observed*. This changed relationship is expressed by a shift of the line that shows how the two variables relate.

That ends our once-over of graphs. Return to this appendix when you need a review.

APPENDIX QUESTIONS

1. *(Understanding Graphs)* Look at Exhibit 5 and answer the following questions:

   a. In what year (approximately) was the unemployment rate the highest? In what year was it the lowest?
   b. In what decade, on average, was the unemployment rate highest? In what decade was it lowest?
   c. Between 1950 and 1980, did the unemployment rate generally increase, decrease, or remain about the same?

2. *(Drawing Graphs)* Sketch a graph to illustrate your idea of each of the following relationships. Be sure to label both axes appropriately. In each case, explain under what circumstances, if any, the curve could shift:

   a. The relationship between a person's age and height
   b. Average monthly temperature over the course of a year
   c. A person's income and the number of hamburgers consumed per month
   d. The amount of fertilizer added to an acre of land and the amount of corn grown on that land in one growing season
   e. An automobile's horsepower and its gasoline mileage (in miles per gallon)

3. *(Slope)* Suppose you are given the following data on wage rates and number of hours worked:

Point	Hourly Wage	Hours Worked per Week
a	$0	0
b	5	0
c	10	30
d	15	35
e	20	45
f	25	50

   a. Construct and label a set of axes and plot these six points. Label each point. Which variable do you think should be measured on the vertical axis, and which variable should be measured on the horizontal axis?
   b. Connect the points. Describe the curve you find. Does it make sense to you?
   c. Compute the slope of the curve between points *a* and *b*. Between points *b* and *c*. Between points *c* and *d*. Between points *d* and *e*. Between points *e* and *f*. What happens to the slope as you move from point *a* to point *f*?

Some Tools of Economic Analysis

© Digital Vision/Getty Images

Why are you reading this book right now rather than doing something else?

What is college costing you? Why will you eventually major in one sub-

ject rather than continue to take courses in different ones? Why is fast food so fast?

Why is there no sense crying over spilt milk? These and other questions are ad-

dressed in this chapter, which introduces some tools of economics—some tools of

the trade.

Chapter 1 introduced the idea that scarcity forces us to make choices, but the

chapter said little about how to make economic choices. This chapter develops a

framework for evaluating economic alternatives. First, we consider the cost involved

in selecting one alternative over others. Next, we develop tools to explore the

choices available to individuals and to the economy as a whole. Finally, we examine the questions that different economies must answer—questions about what goods and services to produce, how to produce them, and for whom to produce them. Topics discussed include:

- Opportunity cost
- Division of labor
- Comparative advantage
- Specialization

- Production possibilities frontier
- Three economic questions
- Economic systems

HOMEWORK **Xpress!** *Pre-test*

Choice and Opportunity Cost

Think about a decision you just made: the decision to read this chapter right now rather than use your time to study for another course, play sports, watch TV, go online, get some sleep, hang with friends, or do something else. Suppose your best alternative to reading right now is getting some sleep. The cost of reading is passing up the opportunity of sleep. Because of scarcity, whenever you make a choice, you must pass up another opportunity; you must incur an *opportunity cost.*

Opportunity Cost

OPPORTUNITY COST

The value of the best alternative forgone when an item or activity is chosen

Economics in the Movies

What do we mean when we talk about the cost of something? Isn't it what we must give up—must forgo—to get that thing? The **opportunity cost** of the chosen item or activity is *the value of the* best *alternative that is forgone.* You can think of opportunity cost as the *opportunity lost.* Sometimes opportunity cost can be measured in terms of money, although, as we shall see, money is usually only part of opportunity cost.

How many times have you heard people say they did something because they "had nothing better to do"? They actually mean they had no alternatives as attractive as the choice they selected. Yet, according to the idea of opportunity cost, people *always* do what they do because they have nothing better to do. The choice selected seems, at the time, preferable to any other possible choice. You are reading this chapter right now because you have nothing better to do. In fact, you are attending college for the same reason: College appears more attractive than your best alternative, as discussed in the following case study.

The Opportunity Cost of College

Case Study

Bringing Theory to Life

eActivity

Is college a sensible investment for you? Find out by reading "Sure You Should Go to College?" by Marty Nemko from the *Princeton Review* at http://www.princetonreview.com/college/research/articles/find/shouldyougo.asp.

What is your opportunity cost of attending college full time this year? What was the best alternative you gave up? If you held a full-time job, you have some idea of the income you gave up to attend college. Suppose you expected to earn $16,000 a year, after taxes, from a full-time job. As a full-time college student, you plan to work part time during the academic year and full time during the summer, earning a total of $7,000 after taxes. Thus, by attending college this year, you gave up after-tax earnings of $9,000 (= $16,000 − $7,000).

There is also the direct cost of college itself. Suppose you are paying $5,000 this year for in-state tuition, fees, and books at a public college (paying out-of-state rates would add another $5,000 to that, and attending a private college would add about $13,000). The opportunity cost of paying for tuition, fees, and books is what you and your family could otherwise have purchased with that money.

How about room and board? Expenses for room and board are not necessarily an opportunity cost because, even if you were not attending college, you would still need to live somewhere and eat something, though these could cost more in college. Likewise, whether or not you attended college, you would still buy items such as DVDs, CDs, clothes, toiletries, and laundry. These items are not an opportunity cost of attending college; they are personal upkeep costs that arise regardless of what you do. So for simplicity, assume that room, board, and personal expenses are the same whether or not you attend college. The forgone earnings of $9,000 plus the $5,000 for tuition, fees, and books yield an opportunity cost of $14,000 this year for a student paying in-state rates at a public college. Opportunity cost jumps to about $19,000 for students paying out-of-state rates and to about $27,000 for those at private colleges. Scholarships, but not loans, would reduce your opportunity cost (why not loans?).

This analysis assumes that other things remain constant. But if, in your view, attending college is more of a pain than you expected your next best alternative to be, then the opportunity cost of attending college is even higher. In other words, if you are one of those people who find college difficult, often boring, and in most ways more unpleasant than a full-time job, then the cost in money terms understates your opportunity cost. Not only are you incurring the expense of college, but you are also forgoing a more pleasant quality of life. If, on the other hand, you believe the wild and crazy life of a college student is more enjoyable than a full-time job would be, then the above figures overstate your opportunity cost, because the next best alternative involves a less satisfying quality of life.

Apparently, you view college as a wise investment in your future, even though it's costly and maybe even painful. College graduates on average earn about twice as much per year as high school graduates, a difference that exceeds $1 million over a lifetime. These pay gains from college encourage a growing fraction of college students to pile up debts to finance their education.

Still, college is not for everyone. Some find the opportunity cost too high. For example, Tiger Woods, once an economics major at Stanford, dropped out after two years to earn a fortune in professional golf. Some high school seniors who believe they are ready for professional basketball skip college altogether, as do most pro tennis players and many singers and actors. Some would-be actors even drop out of high school to pursue their careers, including Drew Barrymore, Tom Cruise, Cameron Diaz, Matt Dillon, Nicole Kidman, Demi Moore, Keanu Reeves, Kiefer Sutherland, and Catherine Zeta-Jones.

Sources: "College Tuition 101," *Wall Street Journal*, 15 September 2003; and Mary Beth Marklein, "College Braces for Bigger Classes and Less Bang for More Buck," *USA Today*, 27 August 2003; Greg Winter and Jennifer Medina, "More Students Line Up at Financial Aid Office," *New York Times*, 10 March 2003; and "2002–2003 College Costs," http://www.collegeboard.com/.

Opportunity Cost Is Subjective

Like beauty, opportunity cost is in the eye of the beholder. It is subjective. Only the individual making the choice can identify the most attractive alternative. But the chooser seldom knows the actual value of the best alternative forgone, because that alternative is "the road not taken." If you give up an evening of pizza and conversation with friends to work on a term paper, you will never know the exact value of what you gave up. You know only what you *expected*. Evidently, you expected the value of working on that paper to exceed the value of the best alternative. (Incidentally, focusing on the best alternative forgone makes all other alternatives irrelevant.)

Calculating Opportunity Cost Requires Time and Information

Economists assume that people rationally choose the most valued alternative. The idea of choosing rationally does not mean people exhaustively calculate the value of all possibilities. Because acquiring information about alternatives is costly and time consuming, people usually make choices based on limited or even incorrect information. Indeed, some choices may turn out to be poor ones (you went for a picnic but it rained; the DVD you rented stunk; your new shoes pinch; the exercise equipment you bought gets no exercise). Regret about lost opportunities is captured in the common expression "coulda, woulda, shoulda." At the time you made the choice, however, you thought you were making the best use of all your scarce resources, including the time required to gather and evaluate information about your alternatives.

Time Is the Ultimate Constraint

The sultan of Brunei is among the world's richest people, with wealth estimated at over $10 billion based on huge oil revenues that flow into his tiny country. He has two palaces, one for each wife (though he divorced one in 2003). The larger palace has 1,788 rooms, with walls of fine Italian marble and a throne room the size of a football field. The royal family owns hundreds of cars, including dozens of Rolls-Royces. Supported by such wealth, the sultan appears to have overcome the economic problem caused by scarcity. But though he can buy just about whatever he wants, he lacks the time to enjoy his stuff. If he pursues one activity, he cannot at the same time do something else, so each activity he undertakes has an opportunity cost. Consequently, the sultan must choose from among the competing uses of his scarcest resource, time. Although your alternatives are less exotic, you too face time constraints, especially toward the end of the college term.

Opportunity Cost May Vary with Circumstance

Opportunity cost depends on the value of your alternatives. This is why you are more likely to study on a Tuesday night than on a Saturday night. On a Tuesday night, the opportunity cost of studying is lower because your alternatives are less attractive than on a Saturday night, when more is happening. Suppose you go to a movie on Saturday night. Your opportunity cost is the value of your best alternative forgone, which might be attending a college game. For some of you, studying on Saturday night may be well down the list of alternatives—perhaps ahead of reorganizing your closet but behind doing your laundry.

Opportunity cost is subjective, but in some cases, money paid for goods and services is a reasonable approximation. For example, the opportunity cost of the new DVD player you bought is the value of spending that $100 on the best forgone alternative. The money measure may leave out some important elements, however, particularly the value of the time involved. For example, renting a movie costs you not just the $4 rental fee but the time and travel required to get it, watch it, and return it.

Sunk Cost and Choice

Suppose you have just finished shopping for groceries and are wheeling your grocery cart toward the checkout counters. How do you decide which line to join? You pick the shortest one. Suppose, after waiting 10 minutes in a line that barely moves, you notice that a cashier has opened another cash register and invites you to check out. Do you switch to the open line, or do you think, "Since I've already spent 10 minutes in this line, I'm staying put"? The 10 minutes you waited represents a **sunk cost,** which is a cost that has already been incurred and cannot be recovered, regardless of what you do now. You should ignore sunk cost in making economic choices. Hence, you should switch to the newly opened register. *Economic decision makers should consider only those costs that are affected by the choice. Sunk costs have already been incurred and are not affected by the choice, so they are irrelevant.* Likewise, you should walk out on a bad movie, even if it cost you $10 to get in. That $10 is gone and sitting through that stinker only makes you worse off. The irrelevance of sunk costs is underscored by the proverb "There's no sense crying over spilt milk." The milk has already spilled, so whatever you do now cannot change that.

Now that you have some idea about opportunity cost, you are ready to consider applying this idea to how best to use scarce resources to help satisfy unlimited wants.

Comparative Advantage, Specialization, and Exchange

Suppose you live in a dormitory. You and your roommate have such tight schedules that you each can spare only about an hour a week for mundane tasks like ironing shirts and typing papers (granted, in reality you may not iron shirts or type papers, but this example will help you understand some important points). Each of you must turn in a typed three-page paper every week, and you each prefer to have your shirts ironed when you have the time. Let's say it takes you a half hour to type your handwritten paper. Your roommate is from the hunt-and-peck school and takes about an hour to type a handwritten paper. But your roommate is a talented ironer and can iron a shirt in 5 minutes flat (or should that be, iron it flat in 5 minutes?). You take twice as long, or 10 minutes, to iron a shirt.

During the hour set aside each week for typing and ironing, typing takes priority. If you each do your own typing and ironing, you type your paper in a half hour and iron three shirts in the remaining half hour. Your roommate takes the entire hour typing the paper, leaving no time for ironing. Thus, if you each do your own, the combined output is two typed papers and three ironed shirts.

The Law of Comparative Advantage

Before long, you each realize that total output would increase if you did all the typing and your roommate did all the ironing. In the hour available for these tasks, you type both papers and your roommate irons 12 shirts. As a result of specialization, total output increases by 9 shirts! You strike a deal to exchange your typing for your roommate's ironing, so you each end up with a typed paper and 6 ironed shirts. Thus, *each of you is better off as a result of specialization and exchange.* By specializing in the task that you each do best, you are using the **law of comparative advantage,** which states that the individual with the lowest opportunity cost of producing a particular output should specialize in producing that output. You face a lower opportunity cost of typing than does your roommate, because in the time it takes to type a paper, you could iron 3 shirts whereas your roommate could iron 12 shirts. And if you face a lower opportunity cost of typing, your roommate must face a lower opportunity cost of ironing (try working that out).

Absolute Advantage Versus Comparative Advantage

The gains from specialization and exchange so far are obvious. A more interesting case is if you are faster at both tasks. Suppose the example changes in one way: your roommate takes

SUNK COST

A cost that has already been incurred in the past, cannot be recovered, and thus is irrelevant for present and future economic decisions

LAW OF COMPARATIVE ADVANTAGE

The individual, firm, region, or country with the lowest opportunity cost of producing a particular good should specialize in that good

12 minutes to iron a shirt compared with your 10 minutes. You now have an *absolute advantage* in both tasks, meaning each task takes you less time than it does your roommate. More generally, having an **absolute advantage** means making something using fewer resources than other producers require.

Does your absolute advantage in both activities mean specialization is no longer a good idea? Recall that the law of comparative advantage states that the individual with *the lower opportunity cost* of producing a particular good should specialize in that good. You still take 30 minutes to type a paper and 10 minutes to iron a shirt, so your opportunity cost of typing the paper remains at three ironed shirts. Your roommate takes an hour to type a paper and 12 minutes to iron a shirt, so your roommate could iron five shirts in the time it takes to type a paper. Your opportunity cost of typing a paper is ironing three shirts; for your roommate it's ironing five shirts. *Because your opportunity cost of typing is lower than your roommate's, you still have a comparative advantage in typing.* Consequently, your roommate must have a comparative advantage in ironing (again, try working this out to your satisfaction). Therefore, you should do all the typing and your roommate, all the ironing. Although you have an absolute advantage in both tasks, your **comparative advantage** calls for specializing in the task for which you have the lower opportunity cost—in this case, typing.

If neither of you specialized, you could type one paper and iron three shirts. Your roommate could still type just the one paper. Your combined output would be two papers and three shirts. If you each specialized according to comparative advantage, in an hour you could type both papers and your roommate could iron five shirts. Thus, specialization increases total output by two ironed shirts. Even though you are better at both tasks than your roommate, you are comparatively better at typing. Put another way, your roommate, although worse at both tasks, is not quite as bad at ironing as at typing.

Don't think that this is simply common sense. Common sense would lead you to do your own ironing and typing, because you are better at both. *Absolute advantage focuses on who uses the fewest resources, but comparative advantage focuses on what else those resources could have produced—that is, on the opportunity cost of those resources.* Comparative advantage is the better guide to who should do what.

The law of comparative advantage applies not only to individuals but also to firms, regions of a country, and entire nations. Individuals, firms, regions, or countries with the lowest opportunity cost of producing a particular good should specialize in producing that good. Because of such factors as climate, workforce skills, natural resources, and capital stock, certain parts of the country and certain parts of the world have a comparative advantage in producing particular goods. From Washington State apples to Florida oranges, from software in India to hardware in Taiwan—*resources are allocated most efficiently across the country and around the world when production and trade conform to the law of comparative advantage.*

Specialization and Exchange

In the previous example, you and your roommate specialized and then exchanged output. No money was involved. In other words, you engaged in **barter,** where products are traded directly for other products. Barter works best in simple economies with little specialization and few traded goods. But for economies with greater specialization, *money* facilitates exchange. Money—coins, bills, and checks—is a *medium of exchange* because it is the one thing that everyone accepts in return for goods and services.

Because of specialization and comparative advantage, most people consume little of what they produce and produce little of what they consume. Each individual specializes then exchanges that product for money, which in turn is exchanged for goods and services. Did you make anything you are wearing? Probably not. Think about the degree of specialization that went into your cotton shirt. A farmer in a warm climate grew the cotton and sold it to someone who spun it into thread, who sold it to someone who wove it into fabric, who sold it to someone who sewed the shirt, who sold it to a wholesaler, who sold it to a retailer, who sold it to you. Your shirt was produced by many specialists.

Division of Labor and Gains from Specialization

Picture a visit to McDonald's: "Let's see, I'll have a Big Mac, an order of fries, and a chocolate shake." Less than a minute later your order is ready. It would take you much longer to make a homemade version of this meal. Why is the McDonald's meal faster, cheaper, and—for some people—tastier than one you could make yourself? Why is fast food so fast? McDonald's takes advantage of the gains resulting from the **division of labor.** Each worker, rather than preparing an entire meal, specializes in separate tasks. This division of labor allows the group to produce much more.

How is this increase in productivity possible? First, the manager can assign tasks according to *individual preferences and abilities*—that is, according to the law of comparative advantage. The worker with the toothy smile and pleasant personality can handle the customers up front; the one with the strong back but few social graces can handle the heavy lifting out back. Second, a worker who performs the same task again and again gets better at it (experience is a good teacher). The worker filling orders at the drive-through, for example, learns to deal with special problems that arise. Third, no time is lost in moving from one task to another. Finally, and perhaps most importantly, the **specialization of labor** allows for the introduction of more sophisticated production techniques—techniques that would not make sense on a smaller scale. For example, McDonald's large shake machine would be impractical in the home. Specialized machines make workers more productive.

To review: The specialization of labor takes advantage of individual preferences and natural abilities, allows workers to develop more experience at a particular task, reduces the time required to shift between different tasks, and permits the introduction of laborsaving machinery. Specialization and the division of labor occur not only among individuals but also among firms, regions, and indeed entire countries. The cotton shirt mentioned earlier might involve growing cotton in one country, turning it into cloth in another, making the shirt in a third, and selling it in a fourth.

We should also acknowledge the downside of specialization. Doing the same thing all day can become tedious. Consider, for example, the assembly-line worker whose sole task is to tighten a particular bolt. Such a job could drive that worker bonkers or lead to repetitive motion injury. Thus, the gains from dividing production into individual tasks must be weighed against the problems caused by assigning workers to repetitive and tedious jobs.

Specialization is discussed in the following case study.

Specialization Abounds

Evidence of specialization is all around us. Look at the extent of specialization in higher education. A large university may house a dozen or more schools and colleges—agriculture, architecture, business, drama, education, engineering, law, fine arts, liberal arts and sciences, medicine, music, nursing, pharmacy, social work, and more. Some of these include a dozen or more departments. And each department may offer courses in a dozen or more specialties. Economics, for example, offers courses in micro, macro, development, econometrics, economic history, health, industrial organization, international finance, international trade, labor, law and economics, money and banking, poverty, public finance, regulation, urban and

DIVISION OF LABOR

Organizing production of a good into its separate tasks

SPECIALIZATION OF LABOR

Focusing work effort on a particular product or a single task

Case **Study**

Bringing Theory to Life

eActivity

Economics is a subject that has benefited from specialization and the division of labor. To get a feel for the many different subjects that economists investigate, take a look at the *Journal of Economic Literature*'s classification system at http://www.aeaweb.org/journal/jel_class_system.html.

regional, and more. Altogether, a university may offer courses in thousands of specialized fields.

How about a trip to the mall? Specialty shops range from luggage to lingerie. Restaurants can be quite specialized—from subs to sushi. Or let your fingers do the walking through the *Yellow Pages,* where you find thousands of specializations. Under "Physicians" alone, you uncover dozens of medical specialties. Without moving a muscle, you can witness the division of labor within a single industry as the credits roll at the end of a movie. There you will see scores of specialists—from gaffer (lighting electrician) to assistant location scout. TV is no different. An episode of *The Sopranos,* for example, requires contributions from about three hundred people.

Magazines also offer fine degrees of specialization, with tens of thousands to choose from. Fans of the Chevy Corvette, for example, can subscribe to *Corvette Enthusiast, Corvette Fever,* or *Vette.* The extent of specialization is perhaps most obvious on the Web, where the pool of potential customers is so vast that individual sites become sharply focused. For example, you can find sites for each of the following: miniature furniture, paper airplanes, musical bowls, prosthetic noses, tongue studs, toe rings, brass knuckles, mouth harps, ferret toys, cat bandannas, juggling equipment, and bug visors (for motorcycle helmets)—just to name a few of the hundreds of thousands of specialty sites. You won't find such specialists at the mall, but they can find their niche in the virtual world. Adam Smith said the degree of specialization is limited by the extent of the market. Sellers on the Web face the broadest customer base in the world.

Source: You can find online versions of the *Yellow Pages* at http://www.yellowpages.com/ and http://www.superpages.com/. Any search engine will turn up the specialty sites reported above.

The Economy's Production Possibilities

The focus to this point has been on how individuals choose to use their scarce resources to satisfy their unlimited wants or, more specifically, how they specialize based on comparative advantage. This emphasis on the individual has been appropriate because the economy is shaped by the choices of individual decision makers, whether they are consumers, producers, or public officials. Just as resources are scarce for the individual, they are also scarce for the economy as a whole (no fallacy of composition here). An economy has millions of different resources that can be combined in all kinds of ways to produce millions of different goods and services. This section steps back from the immense complexity of the real economy to develop our second model, which explores the economy's production options.

Efficiency and the Production Possibilities Frontier

Let's develop a model to get some idea of how much an economy can produce with the resources available. What are the economy's production capabilities? Here are the model's simplifying assumptions:

1. To simplify matters, output is limited to just two broad classes of products: consumer goods, such as pizzas and haircuts, and capital goods—physical capital, such as a pizza ovens, and human capital, such as higher education.

2. The focus is on production during a given period—in this case, a year.

3. The economy's resources are fixed in both quantity and quality during that period.

4. Society's knowledge about how these resources combine to produce output—that is, the available *technology*—does not change during the year.

The point of these assumptions is to freeze the economy's resources and technology in time so we can focus on the economy's production alternatives.

Given the resources and the technology available in the economy, the **production possibilities frontier,** or **PPF,** identifies possible combinations of the two types of goods that can be produced when all available resources are employed fully and efficiently. *Resources are employed fully and efficiently when there is no change that could increase the production of one good without decreasing the production of the other good.* **Efficiency** involves getting the maximum possible output from available resources.

The economy's PPF for consumer goods and capital goods is shown by the curve *AF* in Exhibit 1. Point *A* identifies the amount of consumer goods produced per year if all the economy's resources are used efficiently to produce consumer goods. Point *F* identifies the amount of capital goods produced per year if all the economy's resources are used efficiently to produce capital goods. Points along the curve between *A* and *F* identify possible combinations of the two goods that can be produced when *all* the economy's resources *are used efficiently*.

PRODUCTION POSSIBILITIES FRONTIER (PPF)

A curve showing alternative combinations of goods that can be produced when available resources are used fully and efficiently; a boundary between inefficient and unattainable combinations

EFFICIENCY

The condition that exists when there is no way resources can be reallocated to increase the production of one good without decreasing the production of another

Inefficient and Unattainable Production

Points inside the PPF, such as *I* in Exhibit 1, represent combinations that do not employ resources fully, employ them inefficiently, or both. Note that point *C* yields more consumer goods and no fewer capital goods than *I*. And point *E* yields more capital goods and no fewer consumer goods than *I*. Indeed, any point along the PPF between *C* and *E*, such as point *D*, yields both more consumer goods and more capital goods than *I*. Hence, point *I* is *inefficient*. By using resources more efficiently or by using previously idle resources, the economy can produce more of at least one good without reducing the production of the other good. Points outside the PPF, such as *U* in Exhibit 1, represent *unattainable* combinations, given the resources and the technology available. Thus, *the PPF not only shows efficient combinations of production but also serves as the boundary between inefficient combinations inside the frontier and unattainable combinations outside the frontier.*

The Shape of the Production Possibilities Frontier

Focus again on point *A* in Exhibit 1. Any movement along the PPF involves giving up some of one good to get more of the other. Movement down along the curve indicates that the opportunity cost of more capital goods is fewer consumer goods. For example, moving from point *A* to point *B increases* the amount of capital goods produced from none to 10 million units but *reduces* production of consumer goods from 50 million to 48 million units. Increasing production of capital goods to 10 million units reduces consumer goods only a little. Capital production initially employs resources (such as heavy machinery used to build factories) that add little to production of consumer goods but are quite productive in making capital goods.

As shown by the dashed lines in Exhibit 1, each additional 10 million units of capital goods reduces consumer goods by successively larger amounts. As more capital goods are produced, the resources drawn away from consumer goods are those that are increasingly better suited to producing consumer goods. *Opportunity cost increases as the economy produces*

The Economy's Production Possibilities Frontier

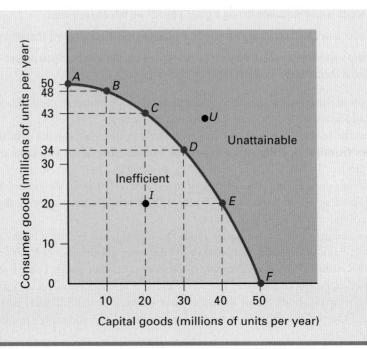

If the economy uses its available resources and technology fully and efficiently in producing consumer goods and capital goods, that economy is on its production possibilities frontier, *AF.* The PPF is bowed out to illustrate the law of increasing opportunity cost: additional units of capital goods require the economy to sacrifice more and more units of consumer goods. Note that more consumer goods must be given up in moving from *E* to *F* than in moving from *A* to *B,* although in each case the gain in capital goods is 10 million units. Points inside the PPF, such as *I,* represent inefficient use of resources. Points outside the PPF, such as *U,* represent unattainable combinations.

LAW OF INCREASING OPPORTUNITY COST

To produce each additional increment of a good, a successively larger increment of an alternative good must be sacrificed if the economy's resources are already being used efficiently

---

ECONOMIC GROWTH

An increase in the economy's ability to produce goods and services; an outward shift of the production possibilities frontier

---

more capital goods, because the resources in the economy are not all perfectly adaptable to the production of both types of goods. The shape of the production possibilities frontier reflects the **law of increasing opportunity cost.** If the economy uses all resources efficiently, the law of increasing opportunity cost states that each additional increment of one good requires the economy to sacrifice successively larger and larger increments of the other good.

The PPF derives its bowed-out shape from the law of increasing opportunity cost. For example, whereas the first 10 million units of capital goods have an opportunity cost of only 2 million units of consumer goods, the final 10 million—that is, the increase from point *E* to point *F*—have an opportunity cost of 20 million units of consumer goods. Notice that the slope of the PPF shows the opportunity cost of an increment of capital. As the economy moves down the curve, the curve becomes steeper, reflecting the higher opportunity cost of capital goods in terms of forgone consumer goods. The law of increasing opportunity cost also applies when moving from the production of capital goods to the production of consumer goods. If resources were perfectly adaptable to alternative uses, the PPF would be a straight line, reflecting a constant opportunity cost along the PPF.

What Can Shift the Production Possibilities Frontier?

Any production possibilities frontier assumes the economy's resources and technology are fixed. Over time, however, the PPF may shift if resources or technology change. **Economic growth** is an expansion in the economy's production possibilities and is reflected by an outward shift of the PPF.

Changes in Resource Availability

If people decide to work longer hours, the PPF shifts outward, as shown in panel (a) of Exhibit 2. An increase in the size or health of the labor force, an increase in the skills of the labor force, or an increase in the availability of other resources, such as new oil discoveries, also shifts the PPF outward. In contrast, a decrease in the availability or quality of resources shifts the PPF inward, as depicted in panel (b). For example, in 1990 Iraq invaded Kuwait, setting oil fields ablaze and destroying much of Kuwait's physical capital, thereby shifting Kuwait's PPF inward. In West Africa, the encroaching sands of the Sahara cover and destroy thousands of square miles of productive farmland each year, shifting the PPF of that economy inward.

The new PPFs in panels (a) and (b) appear to be parallel to the original ones, indicating that the resources that changed could produce both capital goods and consumer goods. For example, an increase in electrical power can enhance the production of both. If a resource such as farmland benefits just consumer goods, then increased availability or productivity of that resource shifts the PPF more along the consumer goods axis, as shown in panel (c). Panel (d) shows the effect of an increase in a resource such as construction equipment that is suited only to capital goods.

Increases in the Capital Stock

An economy's PPF depends in part on the stock of human and physical capital. The more capital an economy produces during one period, the more output can be produced in the next period. Thus, producing more capital goods this period (for example, more machines in the case of physical capital or better education in the case of human capital) shifts the economy's PPF outward the next period. The choice between consumer goods and capital goods is really the choice between present consumption and future production. Again, the more capital goods produced this period, the greater the economy's production possibilities next period.

Technological Change

A technological discovery that employs resources more efficiently could shift the economy's PPF outward. Some discoveries enhance the production of both capital goods and consumer goods, as shown in panel (a) of Exhibit 2. For example, the Internet has increased each firm's ability to identify available resources. A technological discovery that benefits consumer goods only, such as more disease resistant seeds, is reflected by a rotation outward of the PPF along the consumer goods axis, as shown in panel (c). Note that point F remains unchanged because the technological breakthrough does not affect the production of capital goods. Panel (d) shows a technological advance in the production of capital goods, such as improved software for designing heavy machinery.

What Can We Learn from the PPF?

The PPF demonstrates several ideas introduced so far. The first is *efficiency:* The PPF describes the efficient combinations of outputs, given the economy's resources and technology. The second idea is *scarcity:* Given the stock of resources and technology, the economy can produce only so much. The PPF slopes downward, indicating that, as the economy produces more of one good, it must produce less of the other good, thus demonstrating *opportunity cost.* The PPF's bowed-out shape reflects the *law of increasing opportunity cost,* which arises because some resources are not perfectly adaptable to the production of each good. And a shift outward in the PPF reflects *economic growth.*

Finally, because society must somehow select a specific combination of output—a single point—along the PPF, the PPF also underscores the need for *choice.* Selecting a particular combination determines not only current consumption but also the capital stock available next period. One thing the PPF does not tell us is which combination to choose. The PPF tells us only about the costs, not the benefits, of the two goods. To make a selection, we need

EXHIBIT 2

Shifts in the Economy's Production Possibilities Frontier

When the resources available to an economy change, the PPF shifts. If more resources become available or if technology improves, the PPF shifts outward, as in panel (a), indicating that more output can be produced. A decrease in available resources causes the PPF to shift inward, as in panel (b). Panel (c) shows a change affecting consumer goods production. More consumer goods can now be produced at any given level of capital goods. Panel (d) shows a change affecting capital goods production.

(a) Increase in available resources

(b) Decrease in available resources

(c) Increase in resources or technological advance that benefits consumer goods

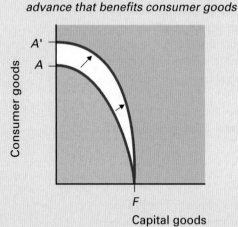

(d) Increase in resources or technological advance that benefits capital goods

information on both costs *and* benefits. How society goes about choosing a particular combination depends on the nature of the economic system, as you will see shortly.

Three Questions Every Economic System Must Answer

Each point along the economy's production possibilities frontier is an efficient combination of outputs. Whether the economy produces efficiently and how the economy selects the most preferred combination depends on the decision-making rules employed. Regardless of how decisions are made, each economy must answer three fundamental questions: What goods and services are to be produced? How are they to be produced? And for whom are they to be produced? An **economic system** is the set of mechanisms and institutions that resolve the *what, how,* and *for whom* questions. Some criteria used to distinguish among economic systems are (1) who owns the resources, (2) what decision-making process is used to allocate resources and products, and (3) what types of incentives guide economic decision makers.

What Goods and Services Will Be Produced?

Most of us take for granted the incredible number of choices that go into deciding what gets produced—everything from which new kitchen appliances are introduced and to which roads get built and which movies get made (for example, movie studios pay for about 10,000 scripts a year but make only about 500 movies[1]). Although different economies resolve these and millions of other questions using different decision-making rules and mechanisms, all economies must somehow make such choices.

How Will Goods and Services Be Produced?

The economic system must determine how output gets produced. Which resources should be used, and how should they be combined to produce each product? How much labor should be used and at what skill levels? What kinds of machines should be used? What new technology should be incorporated into the latest video games? Should the factory be built in the city or closer to the interstate highway? Millions of individual decisions determine which resources are employed and how these resources are combined.

For Whom Will Goods and Services Be Produced?

Who will actually consume the goods and services produced? The economic system must determine how to allocate the fruits of production among the population. Should everyone receive equal shares? Should the weak and the sick get more? Should those willing to wait in line get more? Should goods be allocated according to height? Weight? Religion? Age? Gender? Race? Looks? Strength? Political connections? The value of resources supplied? The question "For whom will goods and services be produced?" is often referred to as the distribution question.

Economic Systems

Although the three economic questions were discussed separately, they are closely interwoven. The answer to one depends very much on the answers to the others. For example, an economy that distributes goods and services uniformly to all will, no doubt, answer the what-will-be-produced question differently than an economy that somehow allows personal choice. Laws about resource ownership and the role of government determine the "rules of the game"—the set of conditions that shape individual incentives and constraints. Along a spectrum ranging from the freest to the most regimented types of economic systems, *capitalism* would be at one end and the *command system* at the other.

Pure Capitalism

Under **pure capitalism,** the rules of the game include the private ownership of resources and the market allocation of products. Owners have *property rights* to the use of their resources and are therefore free to supply those resources to the highest bidder. **Private property rights** allow individuals to use resources or to charge others for their use. Any

1. As reported in Ian Parker, "The Real McKee," *New Yorker*, 20 October 2003.

ECONOMIC SYSTEM

The set of mechanisms and institutions that resolve the what, how, and for whom questions

WALL STREET JOURNAL

Reading It **Right**

What's the relevance of the following statement from the Wall Street Journal*: "Capitalism is supposed to be the one economic system that puts consumers at the center."*

PURE CAPITALISM

An economic system characterized by the private ownership of resources and the use of prices to coordinate economic activity in unregulated markets

PRIVATE PROPERTY RIGHTS

An owner's right to use, rent, or sell resources or property income derived from supplying labor, capital, natural resources, or entrepreneurial ability goes to the individual resources owners. Producers are free to make and sell whatever they think will be profitable. Consumers are free to buy whatever goods they can afford. All this voluntary buying and selling is coordinated by unrestricted markets, where buyers and sellers make their intentions known. Market prices guide resources to their most productive use and channel goods and services to the consumers who value them the most.

Under pure capitalism, markets answer the what, how, and for whom questions. That's why capitalism is also referred to as *market system*. Markets transmit information about relative scarcity, provide individual incentives, and distribute income among resource suppliers. No individual or small group coordinates these activities. Rather, it is the voluntary choices of many buyers and sellers responding only to their individual incentives and constraints that direct resources and products to those who value them the most. According to Adam Smith (1723–1790), market forces allocate resources as if by an "invisible hand"—an unseen force that harnesses the pursuit of self-interest to direct resources where they earn the greatest payoff. According to Smith, *although each individual pursues his or her self-interest, the "invisible hand" of markets promotes the general welfare.* Capitalism is sometimes called *laissez-faire;* translated from the French, this phrase means "to let do," or to let people do as they choose without government intervention. Thus, under capitalism, voluntary choices based on rational self-interest are made in unrestricted markets to answer the questions what, how, and for whom.

As we will see in later chapters, pure capitalism has its flaws. The most notable market failures are:

1. No central authority protects property rights, enforces contracts, and otherwise ensures that the rules of the game are followed.

2. People with no resources to sell could starve.

3. Some producers may try to monopolize markets by eliminating the competition.

4. The production or consumption of some goods involves harmful side effects, such as pollution, that affect people not involved in the market transaction.

5. Private firms have no incentive to produce so-called *public goods,* such as national defense, because private firms cannot prevent nonpayers from enjoying the benefits of public goods.

Because of these limitations, countries have modified pure capitalism to allow a role for government. Even Adam Smith believed government should play a role. The United States is one of the most market-oriented economies in the world today.

Pure Command System

PURE COMMAND SYSTEM

An economic system characterized by the public ownership of resources and centralized planning

In a **pure command system,** resources are directed and production is coordinated not by market forces but by the "command," or central plan, of government. In theory at least, instead of private property, there is public, or communal, ownership of property. That's why central planning is sometimes called *communism.* Government planners, as representatives of all the people, answer such questions through *central plans* spelling out how much steel, how many cars, and how many homes to produce. They also decide how to produce these goods and who gets them.

In theory, the pure command system incorporates individual choices into collective choices, which, in turn, are reflected in central plans. In practice, the pure command system also has flaws, most notably:

1. Running an economy is so complicated that some resources are used inefficiently.

2. Because nobody in particular owns resources, people have less incentive to employ them in their highest-valued use, so some resources are wasted.

3. Central plans may reflect more the preferences of central planners than those of society.

4. Because government is responsible for all production, the variety of products tends to be more limited than in a capitalist economy.

5. Each individual has less personal freedom in making economic choices.

Because of these limitations, countries have modified the pure command system to allow a role for markets. North Korea is perhaps the most centrally planned economy in the world today.

Mixed and Transitional Economies

No country on earth exemplifies either type of economic system in its pure form. Economic systems have grown more alike over time, with the role of government increasing in capitalist economies and the role of markets increasing in command economies. The United States represents a **mixed system,** with government directly accounting for about one-third of all economic activity. What's more, government regulates the private sector in a variety of ways. For example, local zoning boards determine lot sizes, home sizes, and the types of industries allowed. Federal bodies regulate workplace safety, environmental quality, competitive fairness, food and drug quality, and many other activities.

Although both ends of the spectrum have moved toward the center, capitalism has gained more converts in recent decades. Perhaps the benefits of markets are no better illustrated than where countries were divided by ideology into capitalist economies and command economies, such as Taiwan and China or South Korea and North Korea. In each case, the economies began with similar human and physical resources, but income per capita diverged sharply, with the capitalist economies outperforming the command economies. For example, Taiwan's production per capita in 2003 was 4 times that of China's, and South Korea's production per capita was 13 times that of North Korea's.

Recognizing the incentive power of markets, some of the most die-hard central planners now reluctantly accept some free-market activity. For example, about 20 percent of the world's population lives in China, which grows more market oriented each day, even going so far as to give private property constitutional protection. More than a decade ago, the former Soviet Union dissolved into 15 independent republics; most are trying to convert state-owned enterprises into private firms. From Hungary to Mongolia, the transition to mixed economies now under way in former command economies will shape economies of this new century.

MIXED SYSTEM

An economic system characterized by the private ownership of some resources and the public ownership of other resources; some markets are unregulated and others are regulated

Economies Based on Custom or Religion

Finally, some economic systems are molded largely by custom or religion. For example, caste systems in India and elsewhere restrict occupational choice. Family relations also play significant roles in organizing and coordinating economic activity. Even in the United States, some occupations are still dominated by women, others by men, largely because of tradition. Your own pattern of consumption and choice of occupation may be influenced by some of these factors.

Conclusion

Although economies can answer the three economic questions in a variety of ways, this book will focus primarily on the mixed market system, such as exists in the United States. This type of economy blends *private choice,* guided by the price system in competitive markets, with *public choice,* guided by democracy in political markets. The study of mixed market systems grows more relevant as former command economies try to develop markets. The next chapter focuses on the economic actors in a mixed economy and explains why government gets into the act.

SUMMARY

1. Resources are scarce, but human wants are unlimited. Because you cannot satisfy all your wants, you must choose, and choice involves an opportunity cost. The opportunity cost of the selected option is the value of the best alternative forgone.

2. The law of comparative advantage says that the individual, firm, region, or country with the lowest opportunity cost of producing a particular good should specialize in that good. Specialization according to the law of comparative advantage promotes the most efficient use of resources.

3. The specialization of labor increases efficiency by (a) taking advantage of individual preferences and natural abilities, (b) allowing each worker to develop expertise and experience at a particular task, (c) reducing the time required to move between different tasks, and (d) allowing for the introduction of more specialized capital and large-scale production techniques.

4. The production possibilities frontier, or PPF, shows the productive capabilities of an economy when all resources are used fully and efficiently. The frontier's bowed-out shape reflects the law of increasing opportunity cost, which arises because some resources are not perfectly adaptable to the production of different goods. Over time, the frontier can shift in or out as a result of changes in the availability of resources and in technology. The frontier demonstrates several economic concepts, including efficiency, scarcity, opportunity cost, the law of increasing opportunity cost, economic growth, and the need for choice.

5. All economic systems, regardless of their decision-making processes, must answer three fundamental questions: What will be produced? How will it be produced? And for whom will it be produced? Economies answer the questions differently, depending on who owns the resources and how economic activity is coordinated. Economies can be directed by market forces, by the central plans of government, or by a mix of the two.

QUESTIONS FOR REVIEW

1. *(Opportunity Cost)* Discuss the ways in which the following conditions might affect the opportunity cost of going to a movie tonight:

   a. You have a final exam tomorrow.
   b. School will be out for one month starting tomorrow.
   c. The same movie will be on TV next week.

2. *(Opportunity Cost)* Determine whether each of the following statements is true, false, or uncertain. Explain your answers:

   a. The opportunity cost of an activity is the total value of all the alternatives passed up.
   b. Opportunity cost is an objective measure of cost.

c. When making choices, people gather all available information about the costs and benefits of alternative choices.

d. A decision maker seldom knows the actual value of a forgone alternative and must base decisions on expected values.

3. *(Comparative Advantage)* "You should never buy precooked frozen foods because you are paying for the labor costs of preparing food." Is this conclusion always valid, or can it be invalidated by the law of comparative advantage?

4. *(Specialization and Exchange)* Explain how the specialization of labor can lead to increased productivity.

5. *(Production Possibilities)* Under what conditions is it possible to increase production of one good without decreasing production of another good?

6. *(Production Possibilities)* Under what conditions would an economy be operating inside its PPF? Outside its PPF?

7. *(Shifting Production Possibilities)* In response to an influx of illegal aliens, Congress made it a federal offense to hire

them. How do you think this measure affected the U.S. production possibilities frontier? Do you think all industries were affected equally?

8. *(Production Possibilities)* "If society decides to use its resources fully and efficiently (that is, to produce *on* its production possibilities frontier), then future generations will be worse off because they will not be able to use these resources." If this assertion is true, full employment of resources may not be a good thing. Comment on the validity of this assertion.

9. *(Economic Questions)* What basic economic questions must be answered in a barter economy? In a primitive economy? In a pure capitalist economy? In a command economy?

10. *(Economic Systems)* What are the major differences between a pure capitalist system and a pure command system? Is the United States more like a pure capitalist system or more like a pure command system?

PROBLEMS AND EXERCISES

11. (*C a s e* **S t u d y** : The Opportunity Cost of College) During the Vietnam War, colleges and universities were overflowing with students. Was this bumper crop of students caused by a greater expected return on a college education or by a change in the opportunity cost of attending college? Explain.

12. *(Sunk Cost and Choice)* You go to a restaurant and buy an expensive meal. Halfway through, despite feeling quite full, you decide to clean your plate. After all, you think, you paid for the meal, so you are going to eat all of it. What's wrong with this thinking?

13. *(Opportunity Cost)* You can either spend spring break working at home for $80 per day or go to Florida for the week. If you stay home, your expenses will total about $100. If you go to Florida, the airfare, hotel, food, and miscellaneous expenses will total about $700. What's your opportunity cost of going to Florida?

14. *(Absolute and Comparative Advantage)* You have the following information concerning the production of wheat and cloth in the United States and the United Kingdom:

Labor Hours Required to Produce One Unit

	United Kingdom	United States
Wheat	2	1
Cloth	6	5

a. What is the opportunity cost of producing a unit of wheat in the United Kingdom? In the United States?

b. Which country has an absolute advantage in producing wheat? In producing cloth?

c. Which country has a comparative advantage in producing wheat? In producing cloth?

d. Which country should specialize in producing wheat? In producing cloth?

15. (*C a s e* **S t u d y** : Specialization Abounds) Provide some examples of specialized markets or retail outlets. What makes the Web conducive to specialization?

16. *(Shape of the PPF)* Suppose a production possibilities frontier includes the following combinations:

Cars	Washing Machines
0	1,000
100	600
200	0

a. Graph the PPF, assuming that it has no curved segments.

b. What is the cost of producing an additional car when 50 cars are being produced?

c. What is the cost of producing an additional car when 150 cars are being produced?

d. What is the cost of producing an additional washing machine when 50 cars are being produced? When 150 cars are being produced?

e. What do your answers tell you about opportunity costs?

17. *(Production Possibilities)* Suppose an economy uses two resources (labor and capital) to produce two goods (wheat and cloth). Capital is relatively more useful in producing cloth, and labor is relatively more useful in producing wheat. If the supply of capital falls by 10 percent and the supply of labor increases by 10 percent, how will the PPF for wheat and cloth change?

18. *(Production Possibilities)* There's no reason why a production possibilities frontier could not be used to represent the situation facing an individual. Imagine your own PPF. Right now—today—you have certain resources—your time, your skills, perhaps some capital. And you can produce various outputs. Suppose you can produce combinations of two outputs, call them studying and partying.

a. Draw your PPF for studying and partying. Be sure to label the axes of the diagram appropriately. Label the points where the PPF intersects the axes, as well as several other points along the frontier.

b. Explain what it would mean for you to move upward and to the left along your personal PPF. What kinds of adjustments would you have to make in your life to make such a movement along the frontier?

c. Under what circumstances would your personal PPF shift outward? Do you think the shift would be a "parallel" one? Why, or why not?

19. *(Shifting Production Possibilities)* Determine whether each of the following would cause the economy's PPF to shift inward, outward, or not at all:

a. An increase in average length of annual vacations

b. An increase in immigration

c. A decrease in the average retirement age

d. The migration of skilled workers to other countries

20. *(Economic Systems)* The United States is best described as having a mixed economic system. What are some elements of command in the U.S. economy? What are some elements of tradition?

EXPERIENTIAL EXERCISES

21. *(Production Possibilities Frontier)* Here are some data on the U.S. economy taken from the *Economic Report of the President* at http://www.access.gpo.gov/eop/.

Year	Unemployment Rate	Real Government Spending (billions)	Real Civilian Spending (billions)
1982	9.7%	$ 947.7	$3,672.6
1983	9.6	960.1	3,843.6
1996	5.4	1,257.9	5,670.5
1997	4.9	1,270.6	5,920.8

a. Sketch a production possibilities frontier for the years 1982 and 1983, showing the trade-off between public-sector (government) and private-sector (civilian) spending. Assume that resource availability and technology were the same in both years, but notice that the unemployment rate was relatively high.

b. Sketch a PPF for the years 1996 and 1997. Assume that resource availability and technology were the same in both years but higher than in 1982 and 1983. Note that the unemployment rate in the late 1990s was much lower than in the early 1980s.

c. What lessons did you learn about the U.S. economy of the past 20 years?

22. *(Economic Systems)* The transitional economies of Eastern Europe are frequently in the news because they provide testing grounds for the transition from socialist central

planning to freer, more market-oriented economies. Take a look at the World Bank's Transition Newsletter at http://www.worldbank.org/html/prddr/trans/recent.htm. Click on "Recent Issues," open an issue, and choose a particular country. Try to determine how smoothly the transition is proceeding. What problems is that nation encountering?

23. *(Wall Street Journal)* The ability to measure the true (opportunity) cost of a choice is a skill that will pay you great dividends. Use any issue of the *Wall Street Journal,* and find an article that discusses a decision some firm has made. (Try the "Business Bulletin" column on the front page of Thursday's issue.) Then review this chapter's section titled "Choice and Opportunity Cost." Finally, make a list of the kinds of opportunity costs involved in the firm's decision.

HOMEWORK XPRESS! EXERCISES

These exercises require access to McEachern Homework Xpress! If Homework Xpress! did not come with your book, visit **http://homeworkxpress.swlearning.com** *to purchase.*

An economy producing only two goods—silver and potatoes—faces a bowed-out production possibility frontier. Draw one in the diagram and label it.

1. Suppose plant biologists develop a new type of potato that increases the quantity of potatoes produced without any additional resources. Show how the new production possibilities curve would differ from the original.

2. Suppose mining engineers find a new technique that results in extracting more silver from the mines than previously without using additional resources. Show how the new production possibilities curve differs from the original.

3. Suppose that immigrants arrive seeking work in both potato production and silver mining. Show how the new production possibilities curve will differ from the original.

Economic Decision Makers

© Royalty-Free/Corbis

I f we live in the age of specialization, then why haven't specialists taken over all production? For example, why do most of us still do our own laundry and perform dozens of other tasks for ourselves? In what sense has production moved from the household to the firm and then back to the household? If the "invisible hand" of competitive markets is so efficient, why does government get into the act? Answers to these and other questions are addressed in this chapter, which examines the four economic decision makers: households, firms, governments, and the rest of the world.

To develop a better feel for how the economy works, you must get more acquainted with these key players. You already know more about them than you may realize. You grew up in a household. You have dealt with firms all your life, from

Sony to Subway. You know a lot about governments, from taxes to public schools. And you have a growing awareness of the rest of the world, from international Web sites to foreign travel. This chapter will draw on your abundant personal experience with economic decision makers to consider their makeup and objectives. Topics discussed include:

- Evolution of the household
- Evolution of the firm
- Types of firms
- Market failures and government remedies
- Taxing and public spending
- International trade and finance

The Household

Households play the starring role in a market economy. Their demand for goods and services determines what gets produced. And their supplies of labor, capital, natural resources, and entrepreneurial ability produce that output. As demanders of goods and services and suppliers of resources, households make all kinds of choices, such as what to buy, how much to save, where to live, and where to work. Although a household usually consists of several individuals, we will view each household as acting like a single decision maker.

The Evolution of the Household

In earlier times, when the economy was primarily agricultural, a farm household was largely self-sufficient. Each family member specialized in a specific farm task—cooking, making clothes, tending livestock, planting crops, and so on. These early households produced what they consumed and consumed what they produced. With the introduction of new seed varieties, better fertilizers, and laborsaving machinery, farm productivity increased sharply. Fewer farmers were needed to grow enough food to feed a nation. Simultaneously, the growth of urban factories increased the demand for factory labor. As a result, many people moved from farms to cities, where they became more specialized but less self-sufficient.

Households evolved in other ways. For example, in 1950, only about 15 percent of married women with young children were in the labor force. Since then, higher levels of education among married women and a growing demand for labor increased women's earnings, thus raising their opportunity cost of working in the home. This higher opportunity cost contributed to their growing labor force participation. Today more than half of married women with young children are in the labor force.

The rise of two-earner households has affected the family as an economic unit. Households produce less for themselves and demand more from the market. For example, child-care services and fast-food restaurants have displaced some household production. Most people eat at least one meal a day away from home. The rise in two-earner families has reduced specialization within the household—a central feature of the farm family. Nonetheless, some production still occurs in the home, as we'll explore later.

Households Maximize Utility

There are more than 110 million U.S. households. All those who live under one roof are considered part of the same household. What exactly do households attempt to accomplish in making decisions? Economists assume that people attempt to maximize their level of satisfaction, sense of well-being, or overall welfare. In short, households attempt to maximize **utility.** Households, like other economic decision makers, are viewed as rational, meaning that they try to act in their best interests and do not deliberately make themselves worse off. Utility maximization depends on each household's subjective goals, not on some objective

UTILITY

The satisfaction or sense of well-being received from consumption standard. For example, some households maintain neat homes with well-groomed lawns; others pay little attention to their homes and use their lawns as junkyards.

Households as Resource Suppliers

Households use their limited resources—labor, capital, natural resources, and entrepreneurial ability—in an attempt to satisfy their unlimited wants. They can use these resources to produce goods and services in their homes. For example, they can prepare meals, mow the lawn, and fix a leaky faucet. They can also sell these resources in the resource market and use the income to buy goods and services in the product market. The most valuable resource sold by most households is labor.

Panel (a) of Exhibit 1 shows the sources of personal income received by U.S. households in 2003, when personal income totaled $9.2 trillion. As you can see, 63 percent of personal income came from wages, salaries, and other labor income. A distant second was transfer payments (to be discussed shortly), at 13 percent of personal income, followed by personal interest at 10 percent, and proprietors' income at 8 percent each. *Proprietors* are people who work for themselves rather than for employers; farmers, plumbers, and doctors are often self-employed. Proprietors' income could also be considered a form of labor income. *Over two-thirds of personal income in the United States comes from labor earnings rather than from the ownership of other resources such as capital or natural resources.*

HOMEWORK
Xpress!
econ-apps news

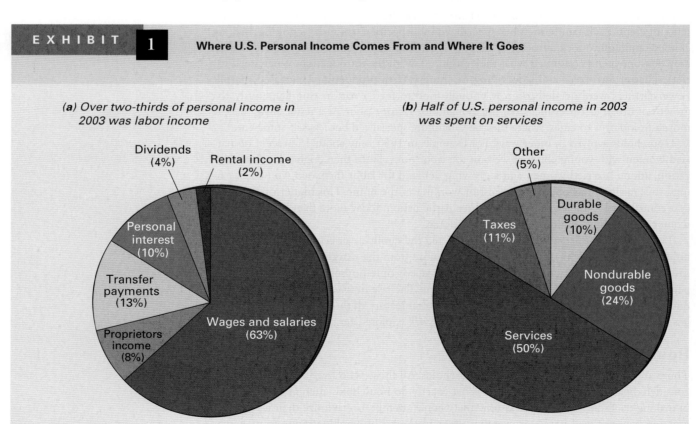

EXHIBIT 1   **Where U.S. Personal Income Comes From and Where It Goes**

(a) *Over two-thirds of personal income in 2003 was labor income*

Dividends (4%)
Rental income (2%)
Personal interest (10%)
Transfer payments (13%)
Proprietors income (8%)
Wages and salaries (63%)

(b) *Half of U.S. personal income in 2003 was spent on services*

Other (5%)
Durable goods (10%)
Taxes (11%)
Nondurable goods (24%)
Services (50%)

Source: Based on figures from *Survey of Current Business*, Bureau of Economic Analysis, April 2004, Table B-1. For the latest figures, go to http://www.bea.doc.gov/bea/pubs.htm.

Because of a poor education, disability, discrimination, time demands of caring for small children, or bad luck, some households have few resources that are valued in the market. Society has made the political decision that individuals in such circumstances should receive short-term public assistance. Consequently, the government gives some households **transfer payments,** which are outright grants. *Cash transfers* are monetary payments, such as welfare benefits, Social Security, unemployment compensation, and disability benefits. *In-kind* transfers provide for specific goods and services, such food stamps, health care, and housing.

TRANSFER PAYMENTS

Cash or in-kind benefits given to individuals as outright grants from the government

Households as Demanders of Goods and Services

What happens to personal income once it comes into the household? Most goes to personal consumption, which sorts into three broad spending categories: (1) *durable goods*—that is, goods expected to last three or more years—such as an automobile or a refrigerator; (2) *nondurable goods,* such as food, clothing, and gasoline; and (3) *services,* such as haircuts, plane trips, and medical care. As you can see from panel (b) of Exhibit 1, durable goods in 2003 claimed 10 percent of U.S. personal income; nondurables, 24 percent; and services, 50 percent. Taxes claimed 11 percent, and all other categories, including savings, claimed just 5 percent. So half of all personal income went for services—the fastest growing sector, since many services, such as child care, are shifting from home production to market production.

The Firm

Households members once built their own homes, made their own clothes and furniture, grew their own food, and amused themselves with books, games, and hobbies. Over time, however, the efficiency arising from comparative advantage resulted in a greater specialization among resource suppliers. This section takes a look at firms, beginning with their evolution.

The Evolution of the Firm

Specialization and comparative advantage explain why households are no longer self-sufficient. But why is a firm the natural result? For example, rather than make a woolen sweater from scratch, couldn't a consumer take advantage of specialization by negotiating with someone who produced the wool, another who spun the wool into yarn, and a third who knit the yarn into a sweater? Here's the problem with that model: If the consumer had to visit each of these specialists and strike an agreement, the resulting *transaction costs* could easily erase the gains from specialization. Instead of visiting and bargaining with each specialist, the consumer can pay someone to do the bargaining—an entrepreneur, who hires all the resources necessary to make the sweater. *An entrepreneur, by contracting for many sweaters rather than just one, is able to reduce the transaction costs per sweater.*

For about two hundred years, profit-seeking entrepreneurs relied on "putting out" raw material, like wool and cotton, to rural households that turned it into finished products, like woolen goods made from yarn. The system developed in the British Isles, where workers' cottages served as tiny factories. This approach, which came to be known as the *cottage industry system,* still exists in some parts of the world. You might think of this system as halfway between household self-sufficiency and the modern firm.

As the British economy expanded in the 18th century, entrepreneurs began organizing the stages of production under one roof. Technological developments, such as waterpower and later steam power, increased the productivity of each worker and contributed to the shift of employment from rural areas to urban factories. *Work, therefore, became organized in large, centrally powered factories that (1) promoted a more efficient division of labor, (2) allowed for the direct supervision of production, (3) reduced transportation costs, and (4) facilitated the use of machines far bigger than anything used in the home.* The development of large-scale factory production, known as the **Industrial Revolution,** began in Great Britain around 1750 and spread to the rest of Europe, North America, and Australia.

Production, then, evolved from self-sufficient rural households to the cottage industry system, where specialized production occurred in the household, to the current system of production in a firm. Today, entrepreneurs combine resources in firms such as factories, mills, offices, stores, and restaurants. **Firms** are economic units formed by profit-seeking entrepreneurs who combine labor, capital, and natural resources to produce goods and services. Just as we assume that households try to maximize utility, we assume that firms try to *maximize profit.* Profit, the entrepreneur's reward, equals sales revenue minus the cost of production.

Types of Firms

There are about 25 million for-profit businesses in the United States. Two-thirds are small retail businesses, small service operations, part-time home-based businesses, and small farms. Each year more than a million new businesses start up and almost as many fail. Entrepreneurs organize a firm in one of three ways: as a sole proprietorship, as a partnership, or as a corporation.

Sole Proprietorships

The simplest form of business organization is the **sole proprietorship,** a single-owner firm. Examples are self-employed plumbers, farmers, and dentists. Most sole proprietorships consist of just the self-employed proprietor—there are no hired employees. To organize a sole proprietorship, the proprietor simply opens for business by, for example, taking out a classified ad announcing availability for plumbing, or whatever. The owner is in complete control. But he or she faces unlimited liability and could lose everything, including a home and other assets, as a result of debts or claims against the business. Also, since the sole proprietor has no partners or other financial backers, raising enough money to get the business going can be challenging. One final disadvantage is that a sole proprietorship usually goes out of business when the proprietor dies. Still, a sole proprietorship is the most common type of business, accounting most recently for 72 percent of all U.S. businesses. Nonetheless, because this type of firm is typically small, proprietorships generate just a tiny portion of all U.S. business sales—only 4 percent.

Partnerships

A more complicated form of business is the **partnership,** which involves two or more individuals who agree to contribute resources to the business in return for a share of the profit or loss. Law, accounting, and medical partnerships typify this business form. Partners have strength in numbers and often find it easier than sole proprietors to raise sufficient funds to get the business going. But partners may not always agree. Also, each partner usually faces unlimited liability for any debts or claims against the partnership, so one partner could lose everything because of another's mistake. Finally, the death or departure of one partner can disrupt the firm's continuity and prompt a complete reorganization. The partnership is the least common form of U.S. business, making up only 8 percent of all firms and 10 percent of all business sales.

Corporations

By far the most influential form of business is the corporation. A **corporation** is a legal entity established through articles of incorporation. Shares of stock confer corporate ownership, thereby entitling stockholders to a claim on any profit. A major advantage of the corporate form is that many investors—hundreds, thousands, even millions—can pool their

---

INDUSTRIAL REVOLUTION

Development of large-scale factory production that began in Great Britain around 1750 and spread to the rest of Europe, North America, and Australia

FIRMS

Economic units formed by profit-seeking entrepreneurs who use resources to produce goods and services for sale

SOLE PROPRIETORSHIP

A firm with a single owner who has the right to all profits and who bears unlimited liability for the firm's debts

PARTNERSHIP

A firm with multiple owners who share the firm's profits and bear unlimited liability for the firm's debts

CORPORATION

A legal entity owned by stockholders whose liability is limited to the value of their stock funds, so incorporating represents the easiest way to amass large sums of money to finance the business. Also, stockholder liability for any loss is limited to the value of their stock, meaning stockholders enjoy limited liability. A final advantage of this form of organization is that the corporation has a life apart from its owners. The corporation survives even if ownership changes hands, and it can be taxed and sued as if it were a person.

The corporate form has some disadvantages as well. A stockholder's ability to influence corporate policy is limited to voting for a board of directors, which oversees the operation of the firm. Each share of stock usually carries with it one vote. The typical stockholder of a large corporation owns only a tiny fraction of the shares and thus has little say. Whereas the income from sole proprietorships and partnerships is taxed only once, corporate income gets whacked twice—first as corporate profits and second as stockholder income, either as corporate dividends or as realized capital gains. A *realized capital gain* is any increase in the market value of a share that occurs between the time the share is purchased and the time it is sold.

A hybrid type of corporation has evolved to take advantage of the limited liability feature of the corporate structure while reducing the impact of double taxation. The *S corporation* provides owners with limited liability, but profits are taxed only once—as income on each shareholder's personal income tax return. To qualify as an S corporation, a firm must have no more than 75 stockholders and must have no foreign or corporate stockholders.

Corporations make up only 20 percent of all U.S. businesses, but because they tend to be much larger than the other two business forms, they account for 86 percent of all business sales. Exhibit 2 shows, by business type, the percentage of U.S. firms and the percentage of U.S. sales. *The sole proprietorship is the most important form in the sheer number of firms, but the corporation is the most important in terms of total sales.*

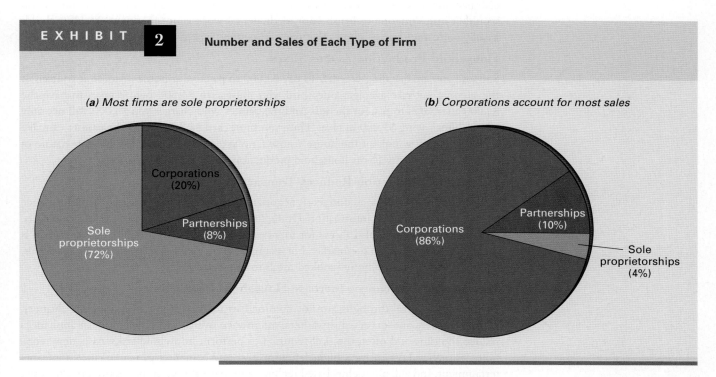

E X H I B I T   2   **Number and Sales of Each Type of Firm**

(a) Most firms are sole proprietorships

Corporations (20%)

Sole proprietorships (72%)

Partnerships (8%)

(b) Corporations account for most sales

Corporations (86%)

Partnerships (10%)

Sole proprietorships (4%)

Source: U.S. Census Bureau, *Statistical Abstract of the United States: 2003*, U.S. Bureau of the Census, Table No. 731. For the latest figures, go to http://www.census.gov/statab/www/.

Nonprofit Institutions

To this point we have considered firms that maximize profit. Some institutions, such as museums, ballet companies, nonprofit hospitals, the Red Cross, the Salvation Army, churches, synagogues, mosques, and perhaps the college you attend, are private organizations that do not have profit as an explicit goal. Yet even nonprofit institutions must somehow pay the bills. Revenue sources typically include some combination of voluntary contributions and service charges, such as college tuition and hospital bills. According to the U.S. Internal Revenue Service, there were 1.6 million tax-exempt organizations in the United States in 2001 and they controlled assets totaling $2.4 trillion. So the average tax-exempt organization controlled assets worth $1.5 million. Although the nonprofit sector is important, the *firms* discussed in this book will have profit as their goal.

Why Does Household Production Still Exist?

If firms are so great at reducing transaction and production costs, why don't they make everything? Why do households still perform some tasks, such as cooking and cleaning? *If a household's opportunity cost of performing a task is below the market price, then the household usually performs that task.* People with a lower opportunity cost of time will do more for themselves. For example, janitors are more likely to mow their lawns than are physicians. Let's look at some reasons for household production.

No Skills or Special Resources Are Required

Some activities require so few skills or special resources that householders find it cheaper to do the jobs themselves. Sweeping the floor requires only a broom and some time so it's usually performed by household members. Sanding a wooden floor, however, involves special machinery and expertise, so this service is left to professionals. Similarly, although you wouldn't hire someone to brush your teeth, dental work is not for amateurs. Households usually perform domestic chores that demand neither expertise nor special machinery.

Household Production Avoids Taxes

Suppose you are deciding whether to pay $3,000 to paint your house or to do it yourself. If the income tax rate averages one-third, you must earn $4,500 before taxes to have the $3,000 after taxes to pay for the job. And the painter who charges you $3,000 will net only $2,000 after paying $1,000 in taxes. Thus, you must earn $4,500 so that the painter can take home $2,000. If you paint the house yourself, no taxes are collected. The tax-free nature of do-it-yourself activity favors household production over market transactions.

Household Production Reduces Transaction Costs

Getting estimates, hiring a contractor, negotiating terms, and monitoring job performance all take time and require information. Doing the job yourself reduces these transaction costs. Household production also allows for more personal control over the final product than is usually available through the market. For example, some people prefer home-cooked meals, because they can season home-cooked meals to individual tastes.

Technological Advances Increase Household Productivity

Technological breakthroughs are not confined to market production. Vacuum cleaners, clothes washers and dryers, dishwashers, microwave ovens, and other modern appliances reduce the time and often the skill required to perform household tasks. Also, new technologies such as DVD players, high-definition TVs, and computer games enhance home entertainment. Indeed, microchip-based technologies have shifted some production from the firm back to the household, as discussed in the following case study.

The Electronic Cottage

The Industrial Revolution shifted production from rural cottages to large urban factories. But the **Information Revolution** spawned by the microchip and the Internet is decentralizing the acquisition, analysis, and transmission of information. These days, someone who claims to work at a home office is usually referring not to a corporate headquarters but to a spare bedroom. According to one recent survey, in the last decade the number of telecommuters more than doubled. Worsening traffic in major cities and wider access to broadband is pushing the trend. Nearly half the white-collar employees at AT&T work at home at least part of the time.

From home, people can write a document with coworkers scattered throughout the world, then discuss the project online in real time or have a videoconference (McDonald's saves millions in travel costs by videoconferencing). Software allows thousands of employees to share electronic files. When Accenture moved its headquarters from Boston to a suburb, the company replaced 120 tons of paper records with a huge online database accessible anytime from anywhere in the world.

To support those who work at home, an entire industry has sprung up, with magazines, newsletters, Web sites, and national conferences. In fact, an office need not even be in a specific place. Some people now work in *virtual offices,* which have no permanent locations. With mobile phones and other handhelds, people can conduct business on the road—literally, "deals on wheels." Accountants at Ernst & Young spend most of their time in the field. When returning to company headquarters, they call a few hours ahead to reserve an office. IBM is developing "Butler in a Dashboard" to help people work on the road. Speech recognition software allows the driver to dictate and send emails as well as send and receive voicemails. If traffic is too noisy, a tiny camera mounted on the visor reads the driver's lips. This Butler also provides directions and weather conditions, and warns of traffic tie-ups and flight delays. The model is expected to reach the market in 2005.

Chip technology is decentralizing production, shifting work from a central place either back to the household or to no place in particular. More generally, the Internet has reduced the transaction costs, whether it's a market report authored jointly by researchers from around the world or a new computer system assembled from parts ordered over the Internet. Easier communication has even increased contact among distant research scholars. For example, economists living in distant cities were four times more likely to collaborate on research during the 1990s than during the 1970s.

Sources: "IBM Envisions Butler in a Dashboard," *USA Today*, 25 June 2003; Jonathan Glater, "Telecommuting's Big Experiment," *New York Times*, 9 May 2001; and Daniel Hamermesh and Sharon Oster, "Tools or Toys? The Impact of High Technology on Scholarly Productivity," *Economic Inquiry*, October 2002. For a discussion of the virtual office, go to http://www.office.com/.

The Government

You might think that production by households and firms could satisfy all consumer wants. Why must yet another economic decision maker get into the act?

Case **Study**

The Information Economy

*e*Activity

Economists have begun to study the economic implications of the virtual office and other virtual phenomena. Try visiting Google (http://www.google.com) and Excite (http://www.excite.com/). Search for the words *virtual* and *economics,* and see what you find.

WALL STREET JOURNAL

Reading It **Right**

What's the relevance of the following statement from the Wall Street Journal*: "The rise of factories took work out of the home, and only now are we . . . rediscovering how to work and live in the same buildings."*

INFORMATION REVOLUTION

Technological change spawned by the invention of the microchip and the Internet that enhanced the acquisition, analysis, and transmission of information

The Role of Government

Sometimes the unrestrained operation of markets yields undesirable results. Too many of some goods and too few of other goods get produced. This section discusses the sources of **market failure** and how society's overall welfare may be improved through government intervention.

Establishing and Enforcing the Rules of the Game

Market efficiency depends on people like you using your resources to maximize your utility. But what if you were repeatedly robbed of your paycheck on your way home from work? Or what if, after you worked two weeks in a new job, your boss called you a sucker and said you wouldn't get paid? Why bother working? The system of private markets would break down if you could not safeguard your private property or if you could not enforce contracts. Governments safeguard private property through police protection and enforce contracts through a judicial system. More generally, governments try to make sure that market participants abide by the "rules of the game." These rules are established through laws and through the customs and conventions of the marketplace.

Promoting Competition

Although the "invisible hand" of competition usually promotes an efficient allocation of resources, some firms try to avoid competition through collusion, which is an agreement among firms to divide the market and fix the price. Or an individual firm may try to eliminate the competition by using unfair business practices. For example, to drive out local competitors, a large firm may temporarily sell at a price below cost. Government antitrust laws try to promote competition by prohibiting collusion and other anticompetitive practices.

Regulating Natural Monopolies

Competition usually keeps the product price below what it would be without competition—that is below the price charged by a **monopoly,** a sole supplier to the market. In rare instances, however, a monopoly can produce and sell the product for less than could competing firms. For example, electricity is delivered more efficiently by a single firm that wires the community than by competing firms each stringing its own wires. When it is cheaper for one firm to serve the market than for two or more firms to do so, that one firm is called a **natural monopoly.** Since a natural monopoly faces no competition, it maximizes profit by charging a higher price than would be optimal from society's point of view. Therefore, the government usually regulates the natural monopoly, forcing it to lower its price.

Providing Public Goods

So far this book has been talking about private goods, which have two important features. First, private goods are *rival* in consumption, meaning that the amount consumed by one person is unavailable for others to consume. For example, when you and some friends share a pizza, each slice they eat is one less available for you. Second, the supplier of a private good can easily exclude those who fail to pay. Only paying customers get pizza. Thus, private goods are said to be *exclusive*. So **private goods** are both rival in consumption and exclusive, such as pizza. In contrast, **public goods,** such as reducing terrorism, providing national defense, and administering a system of justice, are *nonrival* in consumption. One person's benefit from the good does not diminish the amount available to others. Your family's benefit from a safer neighborhood does not reduce your neighbor's benefit. What's more, once produced, public goods are available to all. Suppliers cannot easily prevent consumption by those who fail to pay. For example, reducing terrorism is *nonexclusive*. It benefits all in the

---

MARKET FAILURE

A condition that arises when the unregulated operation of markets yields socially undesirable results

MONOPOLY

A sole producer of a product for which there are no close substitutes

NATURAL MONOPOLY

One firm that can serve the entire market at a lower per-unit cost than can two or more firms

PRIVATE GOOD

A good that is both rival in consumption and exclusive, such as pizza

PUBLIC GOOD

A good that, once produced, is available for all to consume, regardless of who pays and who doesn't; such a good is nonrival and nonexclusive, such as national defense community, regardless of who pays for it and who doesn't. Because public goods are *nonrival* and *nonexclusive*, private firms cannot sell them profitably. The government, however, has the authority to collect taxes for public goods.

Dealing with Externalities

Market prices reflect the private costs and private benefits of producers and consumers. But sometimes production or consumption imposes costs or benefits on third parties—on those who are neither suppliers nor demanders in a market transaction. For example, a paper mill fouls the air breathed by nearby residents, but the market price of paper fails to reflect such costs. Because these pollution costs are outside, or external to, the market, they are called externalities. An **externality** is a cost or a benefit that falls on a third party. A negative externality imposes an external cost, such as factory pollution or auto emissions. A positive externality confers an external benefit, such as driving carefully or beautifying your property. Because market prices do not reflect externalities, governments often use taxes, subsidies, and regulations to discourage negative externalities and encourage positive externalities. For example, because education generates positive externalities (educated people can read road signs and have better paying options other than crime as sources of income), governments try to encourage education with free public schools, subsidized higher education, and keeping people in school until their 16th birthdays.

A More Equal Distribution of Income

As mentioned earlier, some people, because of poor education, mental or physical disabilities, or perhaps the need to care for small children, are unable to support themselves and their families. Because resource markets do not guarantee even a minimum level of income, transfer payments reflect society's attempt to provide a basic standard of living to all households. Nearly all citizens agree that government should redistribute income to the poor (note the normative nature of this statement). Opinions differ about how much should be redistributed, what form it should take, who should receive benefits, and how long benefits should last.

Full Employment, Price Stability, and Economic Growth

Perhaps the most important responsibility of government is fostering a healthy economy, which benefits just about everyone. The government—through its ability to tax, to spend, and to control the money supply—attempts to promote full employment, price stability, and economic growth. Pursuing these objectives by taxing and spending is called **fiscal policy.** Pursuing them by regulating the money supply is called **monetary policy.** Macroeconomics examines both policies.

Government's Structure and Objectives

The United States has a *federal system* of government, meaning that responsibilities are shared across levels of government. State governments grant some powers to local governments and surrender some powers to the national, or federal, government. As the system has evolved, the federal government has assumed primary responsibility for national security, economic stability, and market competition. State governments fund public higher education, prisons, and—with aid from the federal government—highways and welfare. Local governments provide primary and secondary education with aid from the state, plus police and fire protection. Here are some distinguishing features of government.

Difficulty in Defining Government Objectives

We assume that households try to maximize utility and firms try to maximize profit, but what about governments—or, more specifically, what about government decision makers?

EXTERNALITY

A cost or a benefit that falls on a third party and is therefore ignored by the two parties to the market transaction

N e t B o o k m a r k

The annual Economic Report of the President is an invaluable source of information on current economic policy. It also contains many useful data tables. You can find it online at http://w3. access.gpo.gov/eop/index.html.

FISCAL POLICY

The use of government purchases, transfer payments, taxes, and borrowing to influence economy-wide activity such as inflation, employment, and economic growth

MONETARY POLICY

Regulation of the money supply to influence economy-wide activity such as inflation, employment, and economic growth

What do they try to maximize? One problem is that our federal system consists of not one but many governments—more than 87,000 separate jurisdictions in all. What's more, because the federal government relies on offsetting, or countervailing, powers across the executive, legislative, and judicial branches, government does not act as a single, consistent decision maker. Even within the federal executive branch, there are so many agencies and bureaus that at times they seem to work at cross-purposes. For example, at the same time as the U.S. Surgeon General requires health warnings on cigarettes, the U.S. Department of Agriculture pursues policies to benefit tobacco growers. Given this thicket of jurisdictions, branches, and bureaus, one useful theory of government behavior is that elected officials try to maximize the number of votes they receive in the next election. So let's assume that elected officials try to maximize votes. In this theory, vote maximization guides the decisions of elected officials who, in turn, control government employees.

Voluntary Exchange Versus Coercion

Market exchange relies on the voluntary behavior of buyers and sellers. Don't like tofu? No problem—don't buy any. But in political markets, the situation is different. Any voting rule except unanimous consent must involve some government coercion. Public choices are enforced by the police power of the state. Those who fail to pay their taxes could go to jail, even though they may object to some programs those taxes support.

No Market Prices

Another distinguishing feature of governments is that the selling price of public output is usually either zero or below the cost. If you are now paying in-state tuition at a public college or university, your tuition probably covers only about half the state's cost of providing your education. Because the revenue side of the government budget is usually separate from the expenditure side, there is no necessary link between the cost and the benefit of a public program. In the private sector, the expected marginal benefit is at least as great as marginal cost; otherwise, market exchange would not occur.

The Size and Growth of Government

One way to track the impact of government over time is by measuring government outlays relative to the U.S. *gross domestic product,* or *GDP,* which is the total value of all final goods and services produced in the United States. In 1929, the year the Great Depression began, government outlays, mostly by state and local governments, totaled about 10 percent of GDP. At the time, the federal government played a minor role. In fact, during the nation's first 150 years, federal outlays, except during wars, never exceeded 3 percent relative to GDP.

The Great Depression, World War II, and a change in macroeconomic thinking boosted the share of government outlays to 36 percent of GDP in 2004, with about two-thirds of that by the federal government. In comparison, government outlays relative to GDP were 38 percent in Japan, 40 percent in Canada, 43 percent in the United Kingdom, 48 percent in Germany and Italy, and 54 percent in France. Government outlays by the 24 largest industrial economies averaged 40 percent of GDP in 2004.[1] Thus, government outlays in the United States represent a relatively small share of GDP compared to other advanced economies.

Let's look briefly at the composition of federal outlays. Since 1960, defense spending has declined from over half of federal outlays to one-fifth by 2004, as shown in Exhibit 3.

---

1. The Organization of Economic Cooperation and Development, *OECD Economic Outlook* (June 2004), Annex Table 26.

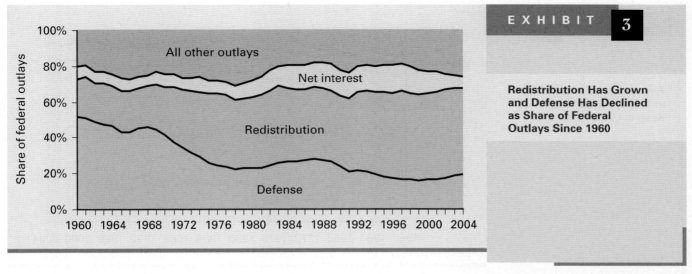

Source: Computed based on figures from the *Economic Report of the President*, February 2004, Table B-80. For the latest figures, go to http://w3.access.gpo.gov/eop.

Redistribution—Social Security, Medicare, and welfare programs—is the mirror image of defense spending, jumping from only about one-fifth of federal outlays in 1960 to nearly half by 2004.

Sources of Government Revenue

Taxes provide the bulk of revenue at all levels of government. The federal government relies primarily on the individual income tax, state governments rely on income and sales taxes, and local governments rely on the property tax. In addition to taxes, other revenue sources include user charges, such as highway tolls, and borrowing. To make money, some states monopolize certain markets, such as for lottery tickets and liquor.

Exhibit 4 focuses on the composition of federal revenue since 1960. The share made up by the individual income tax has remained relatively constant, ranging from a low of 42 percent in the mid-1960s to a high of 50 percent in 2000. The share from payroll taxes more than doubled from 15 percent in 1960 to 40 percent in 2004. *Payroll taxes* are deducted from paychecks to support Social Security and Medicare, which funds medical care for the elderly. Corporate taxes and revenue from other sources, such as excise (sales) taxes and user charges, have declined as a share of the total since 1960.

Tax Principles and Tax Incidence

The structure of a tax is often justified on the basis of one of two general principles. First, a tax could relate to the individual's ability to pay, so those with a greater ability pay more taxes. Income or property taxes often rely on this **ability-to-pay tax principle.** Alternatively, the **benefits-received tax principle** relates taxes to the benefits taxpayers receive from the government activity funded by the tax. For example, the tax on gasoline funds highway construction and maintenance, thereby linking tax payment to road use, since the more people drive, the more gas tax they pay.

Tax incidence indicates who actually bears the burden of the tax. One way to evaluate tax incidence is by measuring the tax as a percentage of income. Under **proportional taxation,** taxpayers at all income levels pay the same percentage of their income in taxes. A

ABILITY-TO-PAY TAX PRINCIPLE

Those with a greater ability to pay, such as those with a higher income or those who own more property, should pay more taxes

BENEFITS-RECEIVED TAX PRINCIPLE

Those who receive more benefits from the government program funded by a tax should pay more taxes

TAX INCIDENCE

The distribution of tax burden among taxpayers; who ultimately pays the tax

PROPORTIONAL TAXATION

The tax as a percentage of income remains constant as income increases; also called a flat tax

EXHIBIT   4

Payroll Taxes Have Grown as a Share of Federal Revenue Since 1960

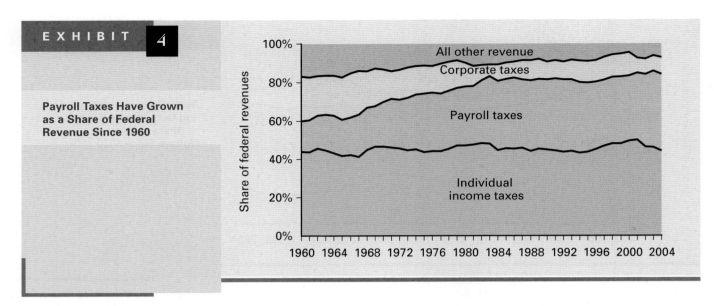

Source: Computed based on figures from the *Economic Report of the President*, February 2004, Tables B-81 and B-84. For the latest figures, go to http://w3.access.gpo.gov/eop.

PROGRESSIVE TAXATION

The tax as a percentage of income increases as income increases

MARGINAL TAX RATE

The percentage of each additional dollar of income that goes to the tax

REGRESSIVE TAXATION

The tax as a percentage of income decreases as income increases

proportional income tax is also called a flat tax, since the tax as a percentage of income remains constant, or flat, as income increases. Under **progressive taxation,** the percentage of income paid in taxes increases as income increases.

The **marginal tax rate** indicates the percentage of each additional dollar of income that goes to taxes. Because high marginal rates reduce the after-tax return from working or investing, they can reduce people's incentives to work and invest. As of 2004, the six marginal rates range from 10 to 35 percent, down from a range of 15 to 39.6 percent in 2000. The top marginal tax bracket each year during the history of the personal income tax is shown by Exhibit 5. Although the top marginal rate in 2004 was lower than it was during most other years, high income households still pay most of the federal income tax collected. For example, the top 1 percent of tax filers, based on income, pay about 33 percent of all income taxes collected. The bottom 50 percent pay less than 5 percent of all income taxes collected. So the U.S. income tax is progressive, and high-income filers pay the overwhelming share of the total.

Finally, under **regressive taxation,** the percentage of income paid in taxes decreases as income increases, so the marginal tax rate declines as income increases. Most U.S. *payroll taxes* are regressive, because they impose a flat rate up to a certain level of income, above which the marginal rate drops to zero. For example, Social Security taxes were levied on the first $87,900 of workers' pay in 2004. Half the 12.4 percent tax is paid by employers and half by employees (the self-employed pay the entire amount).

This discussion of revenue sources brings to a close, for now, our examination of the role of government in the U.S. economy. Government has a pervasive influence on the economy, and its role is discussed throughout the book.

The Rest of the World

So far, the focus has been on institutions within the United States—that is, on *domestic* households, firms, and governments. This focus is appropriate because our primary objective

HOMEWORK
Xpress!
Ask the Instructor Video

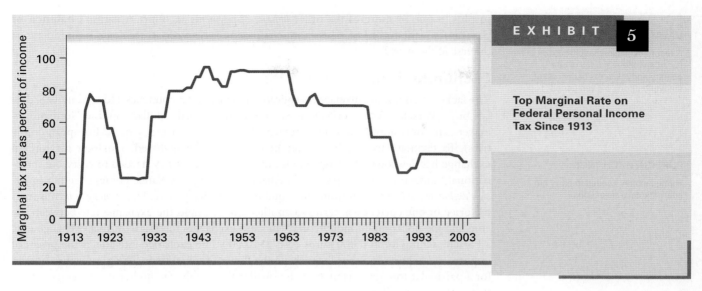

EXHIBIT 5

Top Marginal Rate on
Federal Personal Income
Tax Since 1913

Source: U.S. Internal Revenue Service. For the latest figures on the personal income tax go to http://www.irs.gov/individuals/index.html.

is to understand the workings of the U.S. economy, by far the largest in the world. But the rest of the world affects what U.S. households consume and what U.S. firms produce. For example, Japan and China supply U.S. markets with all kinds of manufactured goods, thereby affecting U.S. prices, wages, and profits. Likewise, political events in the Persian Gulf can affect what Americans pay for oil. Foreign decision makers, therefore, have a significant effect on the U.S. economy—on what we consume and what we produce. The *rest of the world* consists of the households, firms, and governments in the two hundred or so sovereign nations throughout the world.

International Trade

Economics in
the Movies

In the previous chapter, you learned about comparative advantage and the gains from specialization. These gains explain why householders stopped doing everything for themselves and began to specialize. International trade arises for the same reasons. *International trade occurs because the opportunity cost of producing specific goods differs across countries.* Americans import raw materials like crude oil, diamonds, and coffee beans and finished goods like cameras, DVD players, and automobiles. U.S. producers export sophisticated products like computer hardware and software, aircraft, and movies, as well as agricultural products like wheat and corn.

International trade between the United States and the rest of the world has increased in recent decades. In 1970, U.S. exports of goods and services amounted to only 6 percent of the gross domestic product. That percentage has since nearly doubled. Chief destinations for U.S. exports in order of importance are Canada, Japan, Mexico, the United Kingdom Germany, France, South Korea, and Taiwan.

The **merchandise trade balance** equals the value of exported goods minus the value of imported goods. Goods in this case are distinguished from services, which show up in another trade account. For the last two decades, the United States has imported more goods than it has exported, so there has been a merchandise trade deficit. Just as a household must pay for its spending, so too must a nation. The merchandise trade deficit must be offset by a

HOMEWORK
Xpress!
econ-apps debate

**MERCHANDISE TRADE
BALANCE**

The value of a country's exported goods minus the value of its imported goods during a given period

BALANCE OF PAYMENTS

A record of all economic transactions between residents of one country and residents of the rest of the world during a given period

FOREIGN EXCHANGE

Foreign money needed to carry out international transactions

TARIFF

A tax on imports

QUOTA

A legal limit on the quantity of a particular product that can be imported or exported

surplus in one or more of the other *balance-of-payments* accounts. A nation's **balance of payments** is the record of all economic transactions between its residents and residents of the rest of the world.

Exchange Rates

The lack of a common currency complicates trade between countries. How many U.S. dollars buy a Porsche? An American buyer cares only about the dollar cost; the German carmaker cares only about the *euros* received (the common currency of 12 European countries). To facilitate trade when different currencies are involved, a market for foreign exchange has developed. **Foreign exchange** is foreign currency needed to carry out international transactions. The supply and demand for foreign exchange comes together in *foreign exchange markets* to determine the equilibrium exchange rate. The *exchange rate* measures the price of one currency in terms of another. For example, the exchange rate between the euro and the dollar might indicate that one euro exchanges for $1.10. At that exchange rate, a Porsche selling for 100,000 euros costs $110,000. The exchange rate affects the prices of imports and exports and thus helps shape the flow of foreign trade. The greater the demand for a particular foreign currency or the smaller the supply, the higher its exchange rate—that is, the more dollars it costs.

Trade Restrictions

Although there are clear gains from international specialization and exchange, nearly all nations restrict trade to some extent. These restrictions can take the form of (1) **tariffs,** which are taxes on imports; (2) **quotas,** which are limits on the quantity of a particular good that can be imported from a country; and (3) other trade restrictions. If specialization according to comparative advantage is so beneficial, why do most countries restrict trade? Restrictions benefit certain domestic producers that lobby their governments for these benefits. For example, U.S. textile manufacturers have benefited from legislation restricting textile imports, thereby raising U.S. textile prices. These higher prices hurt domestic consumers, but consumers are usually unaware of this harm. Trade restrictions interfere with the free flow of products across borders and tend to hurt the overall economy. International trade in the auto industry is discussed in the following case study.

Case **Study**

World of Business

*e*Activity

The International Motor Vehicle Program at MIT maintains a Web site rich with links and other useful information about automobile production worldwide. You can find it at http://web.mit.edu/ctpid/www/impv.html.

Wheels of Fortune

The U.S. auto industry is huge, with annual sales of about $300 billion a year, an amount exceeding the gross domestic product of 90 percent of the world's economies. There are over 200 million motor vehicles in the United States alone, about two for every three people. In the decade following World War II, imports accounted for just 0.4 percent of U.S. auto sales. In 1973, however, the suddenly powerful Organization of Petroleum Exporting Countries (OPEC) more than tripled

© Stewart Cohen/Index Stock Imagery

oil prices. In response, Americans scrambled for more fuel-efficient cars, which at the time were primarily by foreign makers. As a result, imports jumped to 21 percent of U.S. auto sales by 1980.

In the early 1980s, at the urging of the so-called Big Three automakers (General Motors, Ford, and, at the time, Chrysler), the Reagan administration persuaded Japanese producers to adopt "voluntary" quotas limiting the number of automobiles they exported to the United States. The quotas, or supply restrictions, drove up the price of Japanese imports. U.S. automakers used this as an opportunity to raise their own prices. Experts estimate that reduced foreign competition cost U.S. consumers over $15 billion.

The quotas had two effects on Japanese producers. First, faced with a strict limit on the number of cars they could export to the United States, they began shipping more upscale models instead of subcompacts. Second, Japanese firms built factories in the United States. Making autos here also reduced complications caused by fluctuations in yen-dollar exchange rates. Japanese-owned auto plants in the United States now account for more than one-quarter of auto production in the United States. Imports still make up about one-quarter of U.S. car sales, with Japan accounting for most of that. Imports include cars produced abroad by foreign firms but sold under the names of U.S. firms. U.S. automakers also produce around the world. In fact, Ford is the largest automaker in Australia, the United Kingdom, Mexico, and Argentina.

In China, India, and Latin America, the potential car market is enormous. Here's something to consider: There are more people in China under age of 26 than the combined population of the United States, Japan, Germany, the United Kingdom, and Canada. For years private car ownership was banned in China by Chairman Mao. Now car ownership there is on a roll. Passenger car sales grew from 0.5 million in 1998 to 1.2 million in 2002, for an average annual growth of 24 percent. Because of high tariffs in China, less than 10 percent of cars sold are imports. As a condition for entry into the World Trade Organization, a group that streamlines world trade, China has agreed to reduce tariffs. So China's auto market should gradually open up.

Sources: "Ford to Triple China Production," *South China Morning Post,* 24 September 2003; "China Goes Car Crazy," *Fortune,* 8 September 2003; Micheline Maynard, "Foreign Automakers Unleash a New Wave of Luxury," *New York Times,* 27 September 2003; and Walter Adams and James Brock, "Automobiles," in *The Structure of American Industry,* 9th ed. (New York: Prentice-Hall, 1995), 65–92. For the latest in the auto industry, go to http://www.autocentral.com/.

Conclusion

This chapter examined the four economic decision makers: households, firms, governments, and the rest of the world. Domestic households are by far the most important, for they, along with foreign households, supply the resources and demand the goods and services produced. In recent years, the U.S. economy has come to depend more on the rest of the world as a market for U.S. goods and as a source of products.

If you were to stop reading right now, you would already know more economics than most people. But to understand market economies, you must learn how markets work. The next chapter introduces demand and supply.

SUMMARY

1. Most household income arises from the sale of labor, and most household income is spent on personal consumption, primarily services.

2. Household members once built their own homes, made their own clothes and furniture, grew their own food, and supplied their own entertainment. Over time, however, the efficiency arising from comparative advantage resulted in a greater specialization among resource suppliers.

3. Firms bring together specialized resources and reduce the transaction costs of bargaining with all these resource

providers. Firms can be organized in three different ways: as sole proprietorships, partnerships, or corporations. Because corporations are typically large, they account for the bulk of sales.

4. When private markets yield undesirable results, government may intervene to address these market failures. Government programs are designed to (a) protect private property and enforce contracts; (b) promote competition; (c) regulate natural monopolies; (d) provide public goods; (e) discourage negative externalities and encourage positive externalities; (f) promote equality in the distribution of income; and (g) promote full employment, price stability, and economic growth.

5. In the United States, the federal government has primary responsibility for providing national defense, ensuring market competition, and promoting stability of the economy. State governments fund public higher education, prisons, and—with aid from the federal government—

highways and welfare. And local governments fund police and fire protection, and, with aid from the state, provide primary and secondary education.

6. The federal government relies primarily on the personal income tax, states rely on income and sales taxes, and localities rely on the property tax. A tax is often justified based on (a) the individual's ability to pay or (b) the benefits the taxpayer receives from the activities financed by the tax.

7. The rest of the world is also populated by households, firms, and governments. International trade creates gains that arise from comparative advantage. The balance of payments summarizes transactions between the residents of one country and the residents of the rest of the world. Despite the benefits from comparative advantage, nearly all countries impose trade restrictions to protect specific domestic industries.

QUESTIONS FOR REVIEW

1. *(Households as Demanders of Goods and Services)* Classify each of the following as a durable good, a nondurable good, or a service:
   a. A gallon of milk
   b. A lawn mower
   c. A DVD player
   d. A manicure
   e. A pair of shoes
   f. An eye exam
   g. A personal computer
   h. A neighborhood teenager mowing a lawn

2. (*C a s e* **S t u d y :** The Electronic Cottage) How has the development of personal computer hardware and software reversed some of the trends brought on by the Industrial Revolution?

3. *(Evolution of the Firm)* Explain how production after the Industrial Revolution differed from production under the cottage industry system.

4. *(Household Production)* What factors does a householder consider when deciding whether to produce a good or service at home or buy it in the marketplace?

5. *(Corporations)* Why did the institution of the firm appear after the advent of the Industrial Revolution? What type of business organization existed before this?

6. *(Sole Proprietorships)* What are the disadvantages of the sole proprietorship form of business?

7. *(Government)* Often it is said that government is necessary when private markets fail to work effectively and fairly. Based on your reading of the text, discuss how private markets might break down.

8. *(Externalities)* Suppose there is an external cost associated with production of a certain good. What's wrong with letting the market determine how much of this good will be produced?

9. *(Government Revenue)* What are the sources of government revenue in the United States? Which types of taxes are most important at each level of government? Which two taxes provide the most revenue to the federal government?

10. *(Objectives of the Economic Decision Makers)* In economic analysis, what are the assumed objectives of households, firms, and the government?

11. *(International Trade)* Why does international trade occur? What does it mean to run a deficit in the merchandise trade balance?

12. *(International Trade)* Distinguish between a tariff and a quota. Who benefits from and who is harmed by such restrictions on imports?

13. (*C a s e* **S t u d y :** Wheel of Fortune) What factors led Japanese auto producers to build factories in the United States?

PROBLEMS AND EXERCISES

14. *(Evolution of the Household)* Determine whether each of the following would increase or decrease the opportunity costs for mothers who choose not to work outside the home. Explain your answers.

    a. Higher levels of education for women
    b. Higher unemployment rates for women
    c. Higher average pay levels for women
    d. Lower demand for labor in industries that traditionally employ large numbers of women

15. *(Household Production)* Many households supplement their food budget by cultivating small vegetable gardens. Explain how each of the following might influence this kind of household production:

    a. Both husband and wife are professionals who earn high salaries.
    b. The household is located in a city rather than in a rural area.
    c. The household is located in a region where there is a high sales tax on food.
    d. The household is located in a region that has a high property tax rate.

16. *(Government)* Complete each of the following sentences:
    a. When the private operation of a market leads to over-production or underproduction of some good, this is known as a(n) _____.
    b. Goods that are nonrival and nonexcludable are known as _____.
    c. _____ are cash or in-kind benefits given to individuals as outright grants from the government.
    d. A(n) _____ confers an external benefit on third parties that are not directly involved in a market transaction.
    e. _____ refers to the government's pursuit of full employment and price stability through variations in taxes and government spending.

17. *(Tax Rates)* Suppose taxes are related to income level as follows:

Income	Taxes
$1,000	$200
$2,000	$350
$3,000	$450

    a. What percentage of income is paid in taxes at each level?
    b. Is the tax rate progressive, proportional, or regressive?
    c. What is the marginal tax rate on the first $1,000 of income? The second $1,000? The third $1,000?

EXPERIENTIAL EXERCISES

18. *(The Evolution of the Firm)* Get a library copy of *The Wealth and Poverty of Nations,* by David Landes, and read pages 207–210. How would you interpret Landes's story about mechanization using the ideas developed in this chapter?

19. *(The Evolution of the Firm)* The Contracting and Organizations Research Institute at the University of Missouri maintains lots of interesting information about the evolution of the firm. Visit the institute's Web site at http://cori.missouri.edu/index.htm to familiarize yourself with the kinds of issues economists are studying.

20. *(International Trade)* Visit McEachern Xtra! at http://mceachernxtra.swlearning.com and go to Econ-Debate Online. Review the materials on "Does the U.S. economy benefit from foreign trade?" in the "International Trade" section. What are some of the benefits of international trade—not just to the United States, but to all nations?

21. *(Wall Street Journal)* The household is the most important decision-making unit in our economy. Look through the rotating columns (e.g., "Work and Family" and "Personal Technology") in the *Wall Street Journal* this week. Find a description of some technological change that might affect household production. Explain how production would be affected.

Demand and Supply Analysis

© Connie Coleman/Stone/Getty Images

W hy do roses cost more on Valentine's Day than during the rest of the year? Why do TV ads cost more during the Super Bowl ($2.3 million for 30 seconds in 2004) than during *Nick at Nite* reruns? Why do hotel rooms in Phoenix cost more in February than in August? Why do surgeons earn more than butchers? Why do pro basketball players earn more than pro hockey players? Why do economics majors earn more than most other majors? Answers to these and most economic questions boil down to the workings of demand and supply—the subject of this chapter.

This chapter introduces demand and supply and shows how they interact in competitive markets. *Demand and supply are the most fundamental and the most powerful of all economic tools*—important enough to warrant their own chapter. Indeed, some believe that if you program a computer to answer "demand and supply" to every economic question, you could put many economists out of work. An understanding of the two ideas will take you far in mastering the art and science of economic analysis. This chapter uses graphs, so you may need to review the Chapter 1 appendix as a refresher. Topics discussed include:

- Demand and quantity demanded
- Movement along a demand curve
- Shift of a demand curve
- Supply and quantity supplied

- Movement along a supply curve
- Shift of a supply curve
- Markets and equilibrium
- Disequilibrium

Demand

How many six packs of Pepsi will people buy each month if the price is $3? What if the price is $2? What if it's $4? The answers reveal the relationship between the price of Pepsi and the quantity purchased. Such a relationship is called the *demand* for Pepsi. **Demand** indicates how much of a good consumers are both *willing* and *able* to buy at each possible price during a given period, other things remaining constant. Because demand pertains to a specific period—a day, a week, a month—think of demand as the *planned rate of purchase per period* at each possible price. Also, notice the emphasis on *willing* and *able*. You may be *able* to buy a new Harley-Davidson for $5,000 because you can afford one, but you may not be *willing* to buy one if motorcycles don't interest you.

DEMAND

A relation between the price of a good and the quantity that consumers are willing and able to buy during a given period, other things constant

The Law of Demand

In 1962, Sam Walton opened his first store in Rogers, Arkansas, with a sign that read: "Wal-Mart Discount City. We sell for less." Wal-Mart now sells more than any other retailer in the world because its prices are among the lowest around. As a consumer, you understand why people buy more at a lower price. Sell for less, and the world will beat a path to your door. Wal-Mart, for example, sells on average over 20,000 pairs of shoes *an hour.* This relation between the price and the quantity demanded is an economic law. The **law of demand** says that quantity demanded varies inversely with price, other things constant. Thus, the higher the price, the smaller the quantity demanded; the lower the price, the greater the quantity demanded.

LAW OF DEMAND

The quantity of a good demanded during a given period relates inversely to its price, other things constant

Demand, Wants, and Needs

Consumer demand and consumer wants are not the same. As we have seen, wants are unlimited. You may want a new Mercedes SL600 convertible, but the $130,000 price tag is likely beyond your budget (that is, the quantity you demand at that price is zero). Nor is demand the same as need. You may need a new muffler for your car, but if the price is $200, you decide, "I am not going to pay a lot for this muffler." Apparently, you have better uses for your money. If, however, the price drops enough—say, to $100—then you become both willing and able to buy one.

The Substitution Effect of a Price Change

What explains the law of demand? Why, for example, is more demanded when the price is lower? The explanation begins with unlimited wants confronting scarce resources. Many goods and services could satisfy particular wants. For example, you can satisfy your hunger with pizza, tacos, burgers, chicken, or hundreds of other goodies. Similarly, you can satisfy your desire for warmth in the winter with warm clothing, a home-heating system, a trip to Hawaii, or in many other ways. Clearly, some alternatives have more appeal than others (a trip to Hawaii is more fun than warm clothing). In a world without scarcity, everything would be free, so you would always choose the most attractive alternative. Scarcity, however, is a reality, and the degree of scarcity of one good relative to another helps determine each good's relative price.

Notice that the definition of *demand* includes the other-things-constant assumption. Among the "other things" assumed to remain constant are the prices of other goods. For example, if the price of pizza declines while other prices remain constant, pizza becomes relatively cheaper. Some consumers are more *willing* to purchase pizza when its relative price falls; they substitute pizza for other goods. This principle is called the **substitution effect of a price change**. On the other hand, an increase in the price of pizza, other things constant, causes some consumers to substitute other goods for the now higher-priced pizza, thus reducing their quantity of pizza demanded. Remember that *it is the change in the relative price—the price of one good relative to the prices of other goods—that causes the substitution effect*. If all prices changed by the same percentage, there would be no change in relative prices and no substitution effect.

The Income Effect of a Price Change

A fall in the price of a product increases the quantity demanded for a second reason. Suppose you clear $30 a week from a part-time job, so that's your money income. **Money income** is simply the number of dollars received per period, in this case, $30 per week. Suppose you spend all your income on pizza, buying three a week at $10 each. What if the price drops to $6? At the lower price you can now afford five pizzas a week. Your money income remains at $30 per week, but the decrease in the price has increased your **real income**—that is, your income measured in terms of what it can buy. The price reduction, other things constant, increases the purchasing power of your income, thereby increasing your ability to buy pizza. The quantity of pizza you demand will likely increase because of this **income effect of a price change.** You may not increase your quantity demanded to five pizzas, but you could. If you decide to purchase four pizzas a week when the price drops to $6, you have $6 remaining to buy other goods.

Thus, the income effect of a lower price increases your real income and thereby increases your ability to purchase all goods. Because of the income effect of a price decrease, other things constant, consumers typically increase their quantity demanded. Conversely, an increase in the price of a good, other things constant, reduces real income, thereby reducing the *ability* to purchase all goods. Because of the income effect of a price increase, consumers typically reduce their quantity demanded as price increases. Again, note that money income, not real income, is assumed to remain constant along a demand curve.

The Demand Schedule and Demand Curve

Demand can be expressed as a *demand schedule* or as a *demand curve*. Panel (a) of Exhibit 1 shows a hypothetical demand schedule for pizza. In describing demand, we must specify the units measured and the period considered. In our example, the unit is a 12-inch regular pizza and the period is a week. The schedule lists possible prices, along with the quantity demanded at each price. At a price of $15, for example, consumers demand 8 million pizzas per week. As you can see, the lower the price, other things constant, the greater the quantity demanded. Consumers substitute pizza for other foods. And as the price falls, real income increases, causing consumers to increase the quantity of pizza they demand. If the price drops as low as $3, consumers demand 32 million per week.

The demand schedule in panel (a) appears as a **demand curve** in panel (b), with price on the vertical axis and the quantity demanded per week on the horizontal axis. Each price-quantity combination listed in the demand schedule in the left panel becomes a point in the right panel. Point *a,* for example, indicates that if the price is $15, consumers demand 8 million pizzas per week. These points connect to form the demand curve for pizza, labeled *D.* (By the way, some demand curves are straight lines, some are curved lines, and some are even jagged lines, but all are called demand *curves.*)

The demand curve slopes downward, reflecting the *law of demand:* Price and quantity demanded are inversely related, other things constant. Assumed constant along the demand curve are the prices of other goods. Thus, along the demand curve for pizza, the price of pizza changes *relative to the prices of other goods.* The demand curve shows the effect of a change in the *relative price* of pizza—that is, relative to other prices, which do not change.

Take care to distinguish between *demand* and *quantity demanded.* The *demand* for pizza is not a specific amount, but rather the *entire relationship* between price and quantity demanded—represented by the demand schedule or the demand curve. An individual point on the demand curve indicates the **quantity demanded** at a particular price. For example, at a price of $12, the quantity demanded is 14 million pizzas per week. If the price drops to, say, $9, this drop is shown in Exhibit 1 by *a movement along the demand curve*—in this case from point *b* to point *c.* Any movement along a demand curve reflects a *change in quantity demanded,* not a change in demand.

DEMAND CURVE

A curve showing the relation between the price of a good and the quantity demanded during a given period, other things constant

QUANTITY DEMANDED

The amount demanded at a particular price, as reflected by a point on a given demand curve

---

EXHIBIT	1	**The Demand Schedule and Demand Curve for Pizza**

The market demand curve *D* shows the quantity of pizza demanded, at various prices, by all consumers. Price and quantity demanded are inversely related.

(a) Demand schedule

	Price per Pizza	Quantity Demanded per Week (millions)
a	$15	8
b	12	14
c	9	20
d	6	26
e	3	32

(b) Demand curve

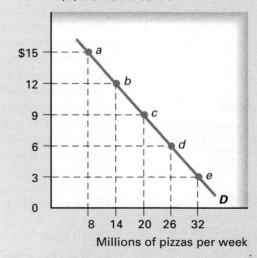

The law of demand applies to the millions of products sold in grocery stores, department stores, clothing stores, drugstores, music stores, bookstores, travel agencies, and restaurants, as well as through mail-order catalogs, the *Yellow Pages,* classified ads, Internet sites, stock markets, real estate markets, job markets, flea markets, and all other markets. The law of demand applies even to choices that seem more personal than economic, such as whether or not to own a pet. For example, after New York City passed an anti-dog-litter law, owners had to follow their dogs around the city with scoopers, plastic bags—whatever would do the job. Because the law raised the personal cost of owning a dog, the quantity demanded decreased. Some owners simply abandoned their dogs, raising the number of strays in the city. The number of dogs left at animal shelters doubled. The law of demand predicts this inverse relation between cost, or price, and quantity demanded.

It is useful to distinguish between **individual demand,** which is the demand of an individual consumer, and **market demand,** which is the sum of the individual demands of all consumers in the market. In most markets, there are many consumers, sometimes millions. Unless otherwise noted, when we talk about demand, we are referring to market demand, as in Exhibit 1.

INDIVIDUAL DEMAND

The demand of an individual consumer

MARKET DEMAND

Sum of the individual demands of all consumers in the market

Shifts of the Demand Curve

A demand curve isolates the relation between prices of a good and quantities demanded when other factors that could affect demand remain unchanged. What are those other factors, and how do changes in them affect demand? Variables that can affect market demand are (1) the money income of consumers, (2) prices of related goods, (3) consumer expectations, (4) the number or composition of consumers in the market, and (5) consumer tastes. How do changes in each affect demand?

Changes in Consumer Income

Exhibit 2 shows the market demand curve D for pizza. This demand curve assumes a given level of money income. Suppose consumer income increases. Some consumers will then be willing and able to buy more pizza at each price, so market demand increases. The demand curve shifts to the right from D to D'. For example, at a price of $12, the amount of pizza demanded increases from 14 million to 20 million per week, as indicated by the movement from point *b* on demand curve D to point *f* on demand curve D'. In short, *an increase in demand—that is, a rightward shift of the demand curve—means that consumers are willing and able to buy more pizza at each price.*

Goods are classified into two broad categories, depending on how demand responds to changes in money income. The demand for a **normal good** increases as money income increases. Because pizza is a normal good, its demand curve shifts rightward when consumer income increases. Most goods are normal. In contrast, demand for an **inferior good** actually decreases as money income increases, so the demand curve shifts leftward. Examples of inferior goods include bologna sandwiches, used furniture, and used clothing. As money income increases, consumers tend to switch from consuming these inferior goods to consuming normal goods (like roast beef sandwiches, new furniture, and new clothing).

NORMAL GOOD

A good, such as new clothes, for which demand increases, or shifts rightward, as consumer incomes rise

INFERIOR GOOD

A good, such as used clothes, for which demand decreases, or shifts leftward, as consumer incomes rise

Changes in the Prices of Related Goods

Again, the prices of other goods are assumed to remain constant along a given demand curve. Now let's bring these other prices into the picture. There are various ways of addressing any particular want. Consumers choose among substitutes based on relative prices. For example,

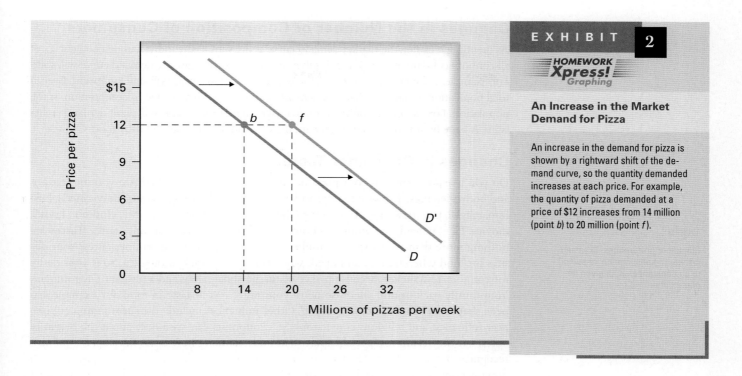

EXHIBIT 2

HOMEWORK
Xpress!
Graphing

An Increase in the Market Demand for Pizza

An increase in the demand for pizza is shown by a rightward shift of the demand curve, so the quantity demanded increases at each price. For example, the quantity of pizza demanded at a price of $12 increases from 14 million (point *b*) to 20 million (point *f*).

pizza and tacos are substitutes, though not perfect ones. An increase in the price of tacos, other things constant, reduces the quantity of tacos demanded along a given taco demand curve. An increase in the price of tacos also shifts the demand curve for pizza to the right. Two goods are considered **substitutes** if a price increase of one shifts the demand for the other rightward and, conversely, if a price decrease of one shifts demand for the other leftward.

Two goods used in combination are called *complements*. Examples include Coke and pizza, milk and cookies, computer software and hardware, and airline tickets and rental cars. Two goods are considered **complements** if a price increase of one shifts the demand for the other leftward. For example, an increase in the price of pizza shifts the demand curve for Coke leftward. But most pairs of goods selected at random are *unrelated*—for example, pizza and socks, or milk and gasoline.

Changes in Consumer Expectations

Another factor assumed constant along a given demand curve is consumer expectations about factors that influence demand, such as income or prices. A change in consumers' *income expectations* can shift the demand curve. For example, a consumer who learns about a pay raise might increase demand well before the raise takes effect. A college senior who lands that first real job may buy a new car even before graduation. Likewise, a change in consumers' *price expectations* can shift the demand curve. For example, if you expect the price of pizza to jump next week, you may buy an extra one today for the freezer, shifting this week's demand for pizza rightward. Or if consumers come to believe that home prices will climb next month, some will increase their demand for housing now, shifting this month's demand for housing rightward. On the other hand, if housing prices are expected to fall next month, some consumers will postpone purchases, thereby shifting this month's housing demand leftward.

SUBSTITUTES

Goods, such as Coke and Pepsi, that are related in such a way that an increase in the price of one shifts the demand for the other rightward

COMPLEMENTS

Goods, such as milk and cookies, that are related in such a way that an increase in the price of one shifts the demand for the other leftward

Changes in the Number or Composition of Consumers

As mentioned earlier, the market demand curve is the sum of the individual demand curves of all consumers in the market. If the number of consumers changes, the demand curve will shift. For example, if the population grows, the demand curve for pizza will shift rightward. Even if total population remains unchanged, demand could shift with a change in composition of the population. For example, a bulge in the teenage population could shift pizza demand rightward. A baby boom would shift rightward the demand for car seats and baby food.

Changes in Consumer Tastes

Do you like anchovies on your pizza or sauerkraut on your hot dog? Are you into tattoos and body piercings? Is music to your ears more likely to be rock, country, heavy metal, hip-hop, reggae, jazz, new age, or classical? Choices in food, body art, music, clothing, books, movies, TV—indeed, all consumer choices—are influenced by consumer tastes. **Tastes** are nothing more than your likes and dislikes as a consumer. What determines tastes? Your desires for food when hungry and drink when thirsty are largely biological. So is your desire for comfort, rest, shelter, friendship, love, status, personal safety, and a pleasant environment. Your family background affects some of your tastes—your taste in food, for example, has been shaped by years of home cooking. Other influences include the surrounding culture, peer influence, and religious convictions. So economists can say a little about the origin of tastes, but they claim no special expertise in understanding how tastes develop. Economists recognize, however, that tastes have an important impact on demand. For example, although pizza is popular, some people just don't like it and those who are lactose intolerant can't stomach the cheese topping. Thus, some people like pizza and some don't.

In our analysis of consumer demand, *we will assume that tastes are given and are relatively stable.* Tastes are assumed to remain constant along a demand curve. A change in the tastes for a particular good shifts the demand curve. For example, a discovery that the tomato sauce and cheese combination on pizza promotes overall health could change consumer tastes, shifting the demand curve for pizza to the right. But because a change in tastes is so difficult to isolate from other economic changes, we should be reluctant to attribute a shift of the demand curve to a change in tastes.

That wraps up our look at changes in demand. Before we turn to supply, you should remember the distinction between a **movement along a given demand curve** and a **shift of a demand curve.** A change in *price,* other things constant, causes a *movement along a demand curve,* changing the quantity demanded. A change in one of the determinants of demand other than price causes a *shift of a demand curve,* changing demand.

Supply

Just as demand is a relation between price and quantity demanded, supply is a relation between price and quantity supplied. **Supply** indicates how much producers are *willing* and *able* to offer for sale per period at each possible price, other things constant. The **law of supply** states that the quantity supplied is usually directly related to its price, other things constant. Thus, the lower the price, the smaller the quantity supplied; the higher the price, the greater the quantity supplied.

TASTES

Consumer preferences; likes and dislikes in consumption; assumed to be constant along a given demand curve

MOVEMENT ALONG A DEMAND CURVE

Change in quantity demanded resulting from a change in the price of the good, other things constant

SHIFT OF A DEMAND CURVE

Movement of a demand curve right or left resulting from a change in one of the determinants of demand other than the price of the good

SUPPLY

A relation between the price of a good and the quantity that producers are willing and able to sell during a given period, other things constant

LAW OF SUPPLY

The quantity of a good supplied during a given period is usually directly related to its price, other things constant

The Supply Schedule and Supply Curve

Exhibit 3 presents the market *supply schedule* and market **supply curve** S for pizza. Both show the quantities of pizza supplied per week at various possible prices by the thousands of pizza makers in the economy. As you can see, price and quantity supplied are directly, or positively, related. Producers offer more at a higher price than at a lower price, so the supply curve slopes upward.

There are two reasons producers offer more for sale when the price rises. First, as the price increases, other things constant, a producer becomes more *willing* to supply the good. Prices act as signals to existing and potential suppliers about the rewards for producing various goods. An increase in the price of pizza, with other prices constant, provides suppliers a profit incentive to shift some resources from producing other goods, for which the price is now relatively lower, and into pizza, for which the price is now relatively higher. *A higher pizza price attracts resources from lower-valued uses.*

Higher prices also increase the producer's *ability* to supply the good. The law of increasing opportunity cost, as noted in Chapter 2, states that the opportunity cost of producing more of a particular good rises as output increases—that is, the *marginal cost* of production increases as output increases. Because producers face a higher marginal cost for additional output, they must receive a higher price for that output to be *able* to increase the quantity supplied. *A higher price makes producers more able to increase quantity supplied.* As a case in point, a higher price for gasoline increases oil companies' ability to drill deeper and to explore in

SUPPLY CURVE

A curve showing the relation between price of a good and the quantity supplied during a given period, other things constant

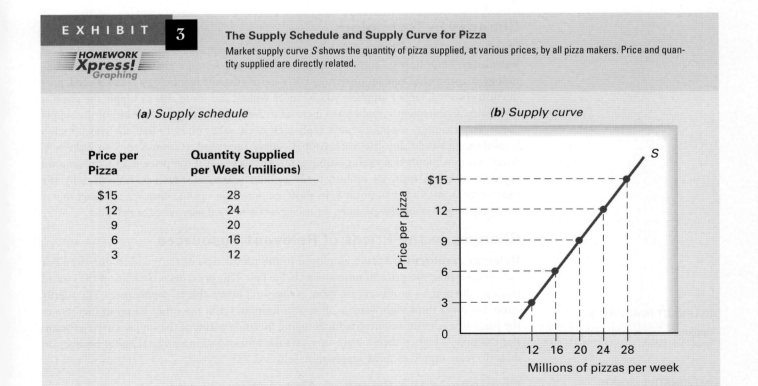

EXHIBIT 3 **The Supply Schedule and Supply Curve for Pizza**

Market supply curve *S* shows the quantity of pizza supplied, at various prices, by all pizza makers. Price and quantity supplied are directly related.

less accessible areas, such as the remote jungles of the Amazon, the stormy waters of the North Sea, and the frozen tundra above the Arctic Circle. On the other hand, the price of gold today is only half what it was decades ago so miners are less able to prospect for gold or to refine ore with lower gold content.

Thus, a higher price makes producers more *willing* and more *able* to increase quantity supplied. Producers are more *willing* because production becomes more profitable than the alternative uses of the resources involved. The higher price also *enables* producers to cover the higher marginal cost that typically results from a greater rate of output.

As with demand, we distinguish between *supply* and **quantity supplied.** *Supply* is the entire relationship between prices and quantities supplied, as reflected by the supply schedule or supply curve. *Quantity supplied* refers to a particular amount offered for sale at a particular price, as reflected by a point on a given supply curve. We also distinguish between **individual supply,** the supply of an individual producer, and **market supply,** the sum of individual supplies of all producers in the market. Unless otherwise noted the term supply refers to market supply.

Shifts of the Supply Curve

The supply curve isolates the relation between the price of a good and the quantity supplied, other things constant. Assumed constant along a supply curve are the determinants of supply other than the price of the good, including (1) the state of technology, (2) the prices of relevant resources, (3) the prices of alternative goods, (4) producer expectations, and (5) the number of producers in the market. Let's see how a change in each affects the supply curve.

Changes in Technology

Recall from Chapter 2 that the state of technology represents the economy's stock of knowledge about how to combine resources efficiently. Along a given supply curve, technology is assumed to remain unchanged. If a more efficient technology is discovered, production costs will fall; so suppliers will be more willing and more able to supply the good at each price. Consequently, supply will increase, as reflected by a rightward shift of the supply curve. For example, suppose a new high-tech oven bakes pizza in half the time. Such a breakthrough would shift the market supply curve rightward, as from S to S' in Exhibit 4, where more is supplied at each possible price. For example, if the price is $12, the amount supplied increases from 24 million to 28 million pizzas, as shown in Exhibit 4 by the movement from point *g* to point *h*. In short, *an increase in supply—that is, a rightward shift of the supply curve—means that producers are willing and able to sell more pizza at each price.*

Changes in the Prices of Relevant Resources

Relevant resources are those employed in the production of the good in question. For example, suppose the price of mozzarella cheese falls. This price decrease reduces the cost of pizza production, so producers are more willing and better able to supply pizza. The supply curve for pizza shifts rightward, as shown in Exhibit 4. On the other hand, an increase in the price of a relevant resource reduces supply, meaning a shift of the supply curve leftward. For example, a higher cheese price increases the cost of making pizzas. Higher production costs decrease supply, so pizza supply shifts leftward.

Changes in the Prices of Alternative Goods

Nearly all resources have alternative uses. The labor, building, machinery, ingredients, and knowledge needed to run a pizza business could produce other baked goods. **Alternative**

QUANTITY SUPPLIED
The amount offered for sale at a particular price, as reflected by a point on a given supply curve

INDIVIDUAL SUPPLY
The supply of an individual producer

MARKET SUPPLY
The sum of individual supplies of all producers in the market

RELEVANT RESOURCES
Resources used to produce the good in question

ALTERNATIVE GOODS
Other goods that use some or all of the same resources as the good in question

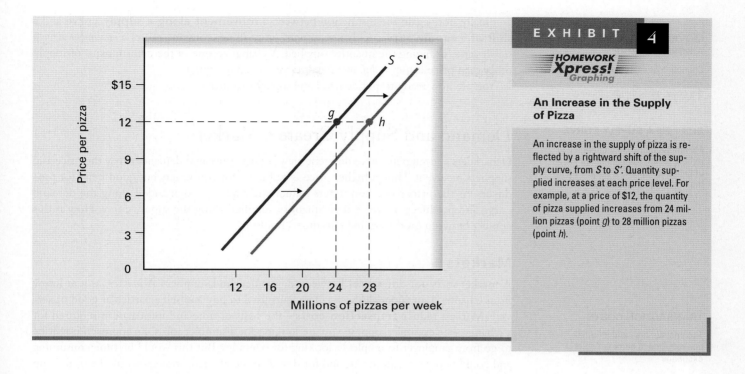

goods are those that use some of the same resources employed to produce the good under consideration. For example, a decrease in the price of Italian bread reduces the opportunity cost of making pizza. As a result, some bread makers become pizza makers so the supply of pizza increases, shifting the supply curve rightward as in Exhibit 3. On the other hand, if the price of an alternative good, such as Italian bread, increases, supplying pizza becomes relatively less attractive compared to supplying Italian bread. As resources shift into bread making, the supply of pizza decreases, or shifts to the left.

Changes in Producer Expectations

Changes in producer expectations can shift the supply curve. For example, a pizza maker expecting higher pizza prices in the future may expand his or her pizzeria now, thereby shifting the supply of pizza rightward. When a good can be easily stored (crude oil, for example, can be left in the ground), expecting higher prices in the future might prompt some producers to *reduce* their current supply while awaiting the higher price. Thus, an expectation of higher prices in the future could either increase or decrease current supply, depending on the good. More generally, any change expected to affect future profitability, such as a change in business taxes, could shift the supply curve now.

Changes in the Number of Producers

Because market supply sums the amounts supplied at each price by all producers, market supply depends on the number of producers in the market. If that number increases, supply will increase, shifting supply to the right. If the number of producers decreases, supply will decrease, shifting supply to the left. As an example of increased supply, the number of gourmet coffee bars more than quadrupled in the United States during the last decade (think Starbucks), shifting the supply curve of gourmet coffee to the right.

Finally, note again the distinction between a **movement along a supply curve** and a **shift of a supply curve.** A change in *price,* other things constant, causes *a movement along a supply curve,* changing the quantity supplied. A change in one of the determinants of supply other than price causes a *shift of a supply curve,* changing supply.

You are now ready to put demand and supply together.

Demand and Supply Create a Market

Demanders and suppliers have different views of price, because demanders pay the price and suppliers receive it. Thus, a higher price is bad news for consumers but good news for producers. As the price rises, consumers reduce their quantity demanded along the demand curve and producers increase their quantity supplied along the supply curve. How is this conflict between producers and consumers resolved?

Markets

A market sorts out differences between demanders and suppliers. A *market,* as you know from Chapter 1, includes all the arrangements used to buy and sell a particular good or service. Markets reduce **transaction costs**—the costs of time and information required for exchange. For example, suppose you are looking for a summer job. One approach might be to go from employer to employer looking for openings. But this would be time consuming and could have you running around for days. A more efficient strategy would be to pick up a copy of the local newspaper and read through the help-wanted ads or go online and look for openings. Classified ads and Web sites, which are elements of the job market, reduce the transaction costs of bringing workers and employers together.

The coordination that occurs through markets takes place not because of some central plan but because of Adam Smith's "invisible hand." For example, the auto dealers in your community tend to locate together, usually on the outskirts of town, where land is cheaper. The dealers congregate not because someone told them to or because they like one another's company but because together they become a more attractive destination for car buyers. Similarly, stores group together so that more shoppers will be drawn by the call of the mall. From Orlando theme parks to Broadway theaters to Las Vegas casinos, suppliers congregate to attract demanders. Some gatherings of suppliers can be quite specialized. For example, shops selling dress mannequins cluster along Austin Road in Hong Kong.

Market Equilibrium

To see how a market works, let's bring together market demand and supply. Exhibit 5 shows the market for pizza, using schedules in panel (a) and curves in panel (b). Suppose the price initially is $12. At that price, producers supply 24 million pizzas per week, but consumers demand only 14 million, resulting in an *excess quantity supplied,* or a **surplus,** of 10 million pizzas per week. Producers' desire to eliminate this surplus puts downward pressure on the price, as shown by the arrow pointing down in the graph. As the price falls, producers reduce their quantity supplied and consumers increase their quantity demanded. The price continues to fall as long as quantity supplied exceeds quantity demanded.

Alternatively, suppose the price initially is $6 per pizza. You can see from Exhibit 5 that at that price, consumers demand 26 million pizzas but producers supply only 16 million, resulting in an *excess quantity demanded,* or a **shortage,** of 10 million pizzas per week. Producers quickly notice that their quantity supplied has sold out and those customers still demanding pizzas are grumbling. Profit-maximizing producers and frustrated consumers create market pressure for a higher price, as shown by the arrow pointing up in the graph. As the price rises, producers increase their quantity supplied and consumers reduce their quantity demanded. The price continues to rise as long as quantity demanded exceeds quantity supplied.

Thus, *a surplus creates downward pressure on the price, and a shortage creates upward pressure.* As long as quantity demanded differs from quantity supplied, this difference forces a price change. Note that a shortage or a surplus depends on the price. There is no such thing as a general shortage or a general surplus.

A market reaches equilibrium when the quantity demanded equals quantity supplied. In **equilibrium,** the independent plans of both buyers and sellers exactly match, so market forces exert no pressure to change price or quantity. In Exhibit 5, the demand and supply curves intersect at the *equilibrium point,* identified as point *c*. The *equilibrium price* is $9 per pizza, and the *equilibrium quantity* is 20 million per week. At that price and quantity,

EQUILIBRIUM

The condition that exists in a market when the plans of buyers match those of sellers, so quantity demanded equals quantity supplied and the market clears

---

(a) Market schedules

Millions of Pizzas per Week

Price per Pizza	Quantity Demanded	Quantity Supplied	Surplus or Shortage	Effect on Price
$15	8	28	Surplus of 20	Falls
12	14	24	Surplus of 10	Falls
9	20	20	Equilibrium	Remains the same
6	26	16	Shortage of 10	Rises
3	32	12	Shortage of 20	Rises

(b) Market curves

E X H I B I T 5

HOMEWORK **Xpress!** *Graphing*

Equilibrium in the Pizza Market

Market equilibrium occurs at the price where quantity demanded equals quantity supplied. This is shown at point *c*. Above the equilibrium price, quantity supplied exceeds quantity demanded. This creates a surplus, which puts downward pressure on the price. Below the equilibrium price, quantity demanded exceeds quantity supplied. The resulting shortage puts upward pressure on the price.

the market *clears*. Because there is no shortage or surplus, there is no pressure for a price change.

A market finds equilibrium through the independent actions of thousands, or even millions, of buyers and sellers. In one sense, the market is personal because each consumer and each producer makes a personal decision regarding how much to buy or sell at a given price. In another sense, the market is impersonal because it requires no conscious coordination among consumers or producers. *Impersonal market forces synchronize the personal and independent decisions of many individual buyers and sellers to achieve equilibrium price and quantity.*

Changes in Equilibrium Price and Quantity

Equilibrium is the combination of price and quantity at which the intentions of demanders and suppliers exactly match. Once a market reaches equilibrium, that price and quantity will prevail until one of the determinants of demand or supply changes. A change in any one of these determinants usually changes equilibrium price and quantity in a predictable way, as you'll see.

Shifts of the Demand Curve

In Exhibit 6, demand curve *D* and supply curve *S* intersect at point *c* to yield the initial equilibrium price of $9 and the initial equilibrium quantity of 20 million 12-inch regular pizzas per week. Now suppose that one of the determinants of demand changes in a way that increases demand, shifting the demand curve to the right from *D* to *D'*. Any of the following could shift the demand for pizza rightward: (1) an increase in the money income of consumers (because pizza is a normal good); (2) an increase in the price of a substitute, such as tacos, or a decrease in the price of a complement, such as Coke; (3) a change in consumer

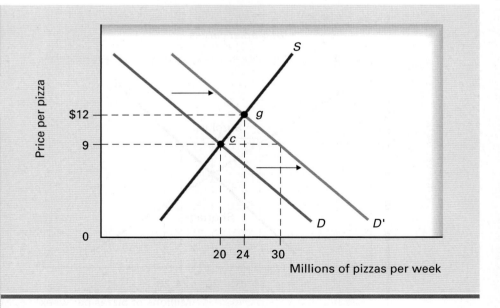

**Effects of an
Increase in Demand**

An increase in demand is shown by a shift of the demand curve rightward from *D* to *D'*. Quantity demanded exceeds quantity supplied at the original price of $9 per pizza, putting upward pressure on the price. As the price rises, quantity supplied increases along supply curve *S*, and quantity demanded decreases along demand curve *D'*. When the new equilibrium price of $12 is reached at point *g*, quantity demanded once again equals quantity supplied. Both price and quantity are higher following the rightward shift of the demand curve.

expectations that encourages them to demand more pizzas now; (4) a growth in the number of pizza consumers; or (5) a change in consumer tastes—based, for example, on a discovery that the tomato sauce on pizza has antioxidant properties that improve overall health.

After the demand curve shifts rightward to *D'* in Exhibit 6, the amount demanded at the initial price of $9 is 30 million pizzas, which exceeds the amount supplied of 20 million by 10 million pizzas. This shortage puts upward pressure on the price. As the price increases, the quantity demanded decreases along the new demand curve *D'*, and the quantity supplied increases along the existing supply curve *S* until the two quantities are equal once again at equilibrium point *g*. The new equilibrium price is $12, and the new equilibrium quantity is 24 million pizzas per week. Thus, given an upward-sloping supply curve, an increase in demand, meaning a rightward shift of the demand curve, increases both equilibrium price and quantity. A decrease in demand, meaning a leftward shift of the demand curve, would lower both equilibrium price and quantity. These results can be summarized as follows: *Given an upward-sloping supply curve, a rightward shift of the demand curve increases both equilibrium price and quantity and a leftward shift of the demand curve decreases both equilibrium price and quantity.*

Shifts of the Supply Curve

Let's consider shifts of the supply curve. In Exhibit 7, as before, we begin with demand curve *D* and supply curve *S* intersecting at point *c* to yield an equilibrium price of $9 and an equilibrium quantity of 20 million pizzas per week. Suppose one of the determinants of supply changes, increasing supply from *S* to *S'*. Changes that could shift the supply curve rightward include (1) a technological breakthrough in pizza ovens; (2) a reduction in the price of a relevant resource, such as mozzarella cheese; (3) a decline in the price of an alternative good,

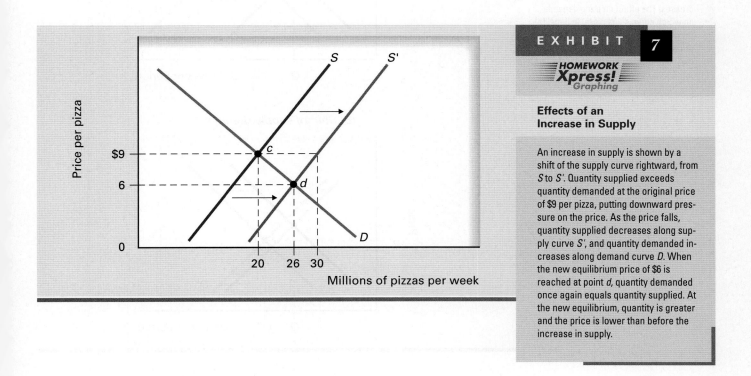

EXHIBIT 7

HOMEWORK
Xpress!
Graphing

Effects of an Increase in Supply

An increase in supply is shown by a shift of the supply curve rightward, from *S* to *S'*. Quantity supplied exceeds quantity demanded at the original price of $9 per pizza, putting downward pressure on the price. As the price falls, quantity supplied decreases along supply curve *S'*, and quantity demanded increases along demand curve *D*. When the new equilibrium price of $6 is reached at point *d*, quantity demanded once again equals quantity supplied. At the new equilibrium, quantity is greater and the price is lower than before the increase in supply.

such as Italian bread; (4) a change in expectations that encourages pizza makers to expand production now; or (5) an increase in the number of pizzerias.

    After the supply curve shifts rightward in Exhibit 7, the amount supplied at the initial price of $9 increases from 20 million to 30 million, so producers now supply 10 million more pizzas than consumers demand. This surplus forces the price down. As the price falls, the quantity supplied declines along the new supply curve and the quantity demanded increases along the existing demand curve until a new equilibrium point *d* is established. The new equilibrium price is $6, and the new equilibrium quantity is 26 million pizzas per week. In short, an increase in supply reduces the price and increases the quantity. On the other hand, a decrease in supply increases the price but decreases the quantity. Thus, *given a downward-sloping demand curve, a rightward shift of the supply curve decreases price but increases quantity, and a leftward shift increases price but decreases quantity.*

EXHIBIT 8

Indeterminate Effect of an Increase in Both Demand and Supply

When both demand and supply increase, the equilibrium quantity also increases. The effect on price depends on which curve shifts more. In panel (a), the demand curve shifts more, so the price rises. In panel (b), the supply curve shifts more, so the price falls.

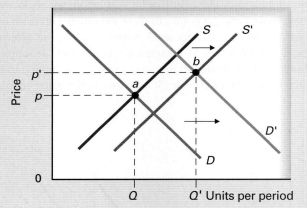

(a) Shift of demand dominates

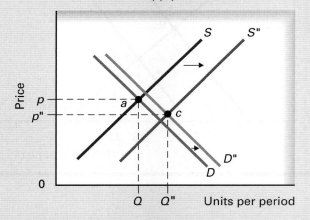

(b) Shift of supply dominates

Simultaneous Shifts of Demand and Supply Curves

As long as only one curve shifts, we can say for sure how equilibrium price and quantity will change. If both curves shift, however, the outcome is less obvious. For example, suppose both demand and supply increase, or shift rightward, as in Exhibit 8. Note that in panel (a), demand shifts more than supply, and in panel (b), supply shifts more than demand. In both panels, equilibrium quantity increases. The change in equilibrium price, however, depends on which curve shifts more. If demand shifts more, as in panel (a), equilibrium price increases. For example, in the last decade, the demand for housing has increased more than the supply, so both price and quantity have increased. But if supply shifts more, as in panel (b), equilibrium price decreases. For example, in the last decade, the supply of personal computers has increased more than the demand, so price has decreased and quantity increased.

Conversely, if both demand and supply decrease, or shift leftward, equilibrium quantity decreases. But, again, we cannot say what will happen to equilibrium price unless we examine relative shifts. (You can use Exhibit 8 to consider decreases in demand and supply by viewing D' and S' as the initial curves.) If demand shifts more, the price will fall. If supply shifts more, the price will rise.

If demand and supply shift in opposite directions, we can say what will happen to equilibrium price. Equilibrium price will increase if demand increases and supply decreases. Equilibrium price will decrease if demand decreases and supply increases. Without reference to particular shifts, however, we cannot say what will happen to equilibrium quantity.

These results are no doubt confusing, but Exhibit 9 summarizes the four possible combinations of changes. Using Exhibit 9 as a reference, please take the time right now to work through some changes in demand and supply to develop an intuitive understanding of the results. Then, in the following case study, evaluate changes in the market for professional basketball.

WALL STREET JOURNAL
Reading It **Right**

What's the relevance of the following statement from the Wall Street Journal*: "California officials attribute generally lower electricity prices to relatively mild weather in recent days, conservation efforts in the state, and the return of some power plants to full operation."*

EXHIBIT　9

Effects of Shifts of Both Demand and Supply

When the demand and supply curves shift in the same direction, equilibrium quantity also shifts in that direction. The effect on equilibrium price depends on which curve shifts more. If the curves shift in opposite directions, equilibrium price will move in the same direction as demand. The effect on equilibrium quantity depends on which curve shifts more.

C a s e **S t u d y**

World of Business

*e***Activity**
InsideHoops hosts a current salary
list for top NBA players at
http://www.insidehoops.com/
nbasalaries.shtml.

The Market for Professional Basketball

Toward the end of the 1970s, the National Basketball Association (NBA) seemed on the verge of collapse. Attendance had sunk to little more than half
capacity. Some teams were nearly bankrupt. Cham-
pionship games didn't even get prime-time television coverage. But in the 1980s, three superstars
turned things around. Michael Jordan, Larry Bird,
and Magic Johnson attracted millions of new fans
and breathed new life into the sagging league. Now
a generation of new stars, including Allen Iverson,
Tracy McGrady, and LeBron James, continue to fuel
interest.

© Mike Cassese/Reuters/Corbis

Since 1980, game attendance has doubled, and
the league expanded from 22 to 29 teams. New
franchises sold for record amounts. More importantly, league revenue from broadcast rights jumped
more than *40-fold* from $19 million per year during the 1978–1982 contract to $785 million per year during the 2002–2008 contract. Popularity also increased around the world as
international players, such as Yao Ming, joined the league (basketball is now the most widely
played team sport among young people in China). NBA rosters in 2003 included 80 international players from 36 countries. The NBA formed marketing alliances with global companies such as Coca-Cola and McDonald's, and league playoffs are now televised around the
world.

What's the key resource in the production of NBA games? Talented players. Exhibit 10
shows the market for NBA players, with demand and supply in 1980 as D_{1980} and S_{1980}. The
intersection of these two curves generated an average pay in 1980 of $170,000, or $0.17
million, for the 300 or so players in the league. Since 1980, the talent pool expanded somewhat, shifting the supply curve a bit rightward from S_{1980} to S_{2003} (almost by definition,
the supply of the top few hundred players in the world is limited). But demand exploded
from D_{1980} to D_{2003}. With supply relatively fixed, the greater demand boosted average pay to
$4.1 million by 2003 for the 400 or so players in the league. Such pay attracts younger and
younger players. For example, Kevin Garnett, whose $28 million annual salary topped the
league in 2003, entered the NBA in 1995 right out of high school. LeBron James, the top
pick in the 2003 NBA draft, and heir apparent to Michael Jordan, also had just graduated
from high school.

But rare talent alone does not command high pay. For example, top rodeo riders, top
bowlers, and top women basketball players also possess rare talent, but the demand for their
talent is not enough to support pay anywhere near NBA levels. Demand is also critical. Some
sports aren't even popular enough to support professional leagues (for example, the U.S.
women's pro soccer league folded in 2003). NBA players are now the highest-paid team athletes in the world—earning 60 percent more than pro baseball's average and at least double
that for pro football and pro hockey. Both demand *and* supply determine average pay.

Sources: Brian Straus, "Women's Pro Soccer League Forced to Fold," *Washington Post,* 16 September 2003; Allen
Cheng, "Basketball Shoots to Top Sport for Young Chinese," *South China Morning Post,* 25 September 2003;
"Salary Cap for 2003–04 Set at $43.8 million," http://www.nba.com/; "NBA TV Deal Moves to ABC, ESPN,"
http://espn.go.com/nba/news/2002/0122/1315389.html; and U.S. Census Bureau, *Statistical Abstract of the
United States: 2003,* http://www.census.gov/prod/www/statistical-abstract-02.html.

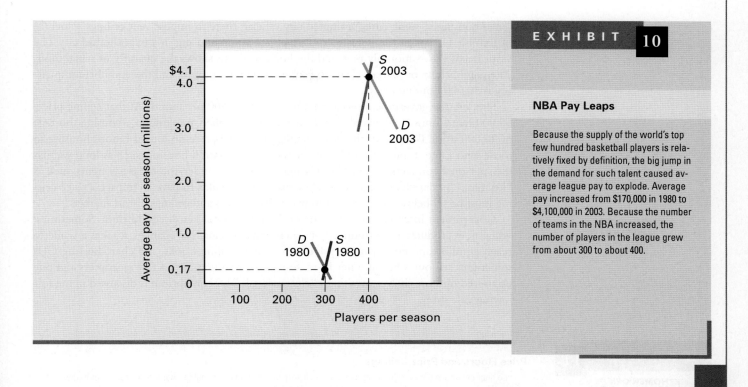

EXHIBIT 10

NBA Pay Leaps

Because the supply of the world's top few hundred basketball players is relatively fixed by definition, the big jump in the demand for such talent caused average league pay to explode. Average pay increased from $170,000 in 1980 to $4,100,000 in 2003. Because the number of teams in the NBA increased, the number of players in the league grew from about 300 to about 400.

Disequilibrium

A surplus exerts downward pressure on the price, and a shortage exerts upward pressure. Markets, however, do not always reach equilibrium quickly. During the time required to adjust, the market is said to be in disequilibrium. **Disequilibrium** is usually temporary as the market gropes for equilibrium. But sometimes, often as a result of government intervention, disequilibrium can last a while, as we will see next.

Price Floors

Sometimes public officials set prices above their equilibrium levels. For example, the federal government regulates some agriculture prices in an attempt to ensure farmers a higher and more stable income than they would otherwise earn. To achieve higher prices, the federal government sets a **price floor,** or a *minimum* selling price that is above the equilibrium price. Panel (a) of Exhibit 11 shows the effect of a $2.50 per gallon price floor for milk. At that price, farmers supply 24 million gallons per week, but consumers demand only 14 million gallons, yielding a surplus of 10 million gallons. This surplus milk will pile up on store shelves, eventually souring. To take it off the market, the government usually agrees to buy the surplus milk. The federal government, in fact, spends billions buying and storing surplus agricultural products. Note, to have an impact, a price floor must be set above the equilibrium price. A floor set below the equilibrium price would be irrelevant (how come?).

Price Ceilings

Sometimes public officials try to keep prices below their equilibrium levels by establishing a **price ceiling,** or a *maximum* selling price. For example, concern about the rising cost of

DISEQUILIBRIUM

The condition that exists in a market when the plans of buyers do not match those of sellers; a temporary mismatch between quantity supplied and quantity demanded as the market seeks equilibrium

PRICE FLOOR

A minimum legal price below which a good or service cannot be sold; to have an impact, a price floor must be set above the equilibrium price

PRICE CEILING

A maximum legal price above which a good or service cannot be sold; to have an impact, a price ceiling must be set below the equilibrium price rental housing in some cities prompted city officials there to impose rent ceilings. Panel (b) of Exhibit 11 depicts the demand and supply of rental housing in a hypothetical city. The vertical axis shows monthly rent, and the horizontal axis shows the quantity of rental units. The equilibrium, or market-clearing, rent is $1,000 per month, and the equilibrium quantity is 50,000 housing units.

Suppose the government sets a maximum rent of $600 per month. At that ceiling price, 60,000 rental units are demanded, but only 40,000 supplied, resulting in a housing shortage of 20,000 units. Because of the price ceiling, the rental price no longer rations housing to those who value it the most. Other devices emerge to ration housing, such as long waiting lists, personal connections, and the willingness to make under-the-table payments, such as "key fees," "finder's fees," high security deposits, and the like. To have an impact, a price ceiling must be set below the equilibrium price. Price floors and ceilings distort markets.

Government intervention is not the only source of market disequilibrium. Sometimes, when new products are introduced or when demand suddenly changes, it takes a while to reach equilibrium. For example, popular toys, best-selling books, and chart-busting CDs sometimes sell out. On the other hand, some new products attract few customers and pile up unsold on store shelves, awaiting a "clearance sale." Disequilibrium is discussed in the following case study.

EXHIBIT 11 Price Floors and Price Ceilings

A price floor set above the equilibrium price results in a surplus, as shown in panel (a). A price floor set at or below equilibrium price has no effect. A price ceiling set below the equilibrium price results in a shortage, as shown panel (b). A price ceiling set at or above the equilibrium price has no effect.

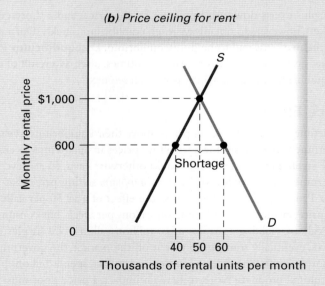

The Toy Business Is Not Child's Play

U.S. toy sales exceeded $25 billion a year in 2003, but the business is not much fun for toy makers. Most toys don't make it from one season to the next, turning out to be costly duds. A few have staying power, like G.I. Joe, who could retire after 40 years of military service; Barbie, who is now over 40; and the Wiffle Ball, still a hit after 50 years. Because toy factories, which are mostly in China, need time to gear up, most retailers must order in February for Christmas delivery. Can you imagine the uncertainty of this market? Who, for example, could have anticipated the success of Chicken Dance Elmo, Beanie Babies, Teletubbies, FurReal Friends, or Yu-Gi-Oh trading cards?

© Photodisc/Getty Images

A few years ago, the Mighty Morphin Power Rangers were the rage. Within a year, the manufacturer increased production 10-fold, with 11 new factories churning out nearly $1 billion in Rangers. Still, at $13 each, quantity demanded exceeded quantity supplied. Why don't toy makers simply let the price find its equilibrium level? Suppose, for example, that the market-clearing price for Power Rangers was $26, twice the actual price. First, it's hard for toymakers to anticipate demand well enough to boost the price before supplies run out. Second, suppliers who hope to retain customers over the long haul may want to avoid appearing greedy. That may be why Home Depot doesn't raise the price of snow shovels after the first winter storm, why Wal-Mart doesn't boost air conditioner prices during the dog days of summer, and why DaimlerChrysler preferred long waiting lists to raising prices still higher for its Mercedes SUV.

To sum up, uncertainty abounds in the market for new products. Suppliers can only guess what the demand will be, so they must feel their way in deciding what price to charge and how much to produce. Eventually, markets do achieve equilibrium. For example, Daimler-Chrysler doubled production of its SUV, eventually erasing the shortage. Because finding the market-clearing price takes time, some markets are temporarily in disequilibrium. But even when hot toys are sold out at retailers, they are usually available on the Internet at a higher price. For example, just before one recent Christmas, the hot toy that year, Spider-Man Web Blaster, was sold out most everywhere. But the toy was still available on eBay for $135, or nine times its $15 retail price.

Sources: Alexander Coolidge, "Hot Toys Are Hard to Come By for Those Who Wait," *Sarasota Herald Tribune*, 21 December 2002; "Hot Toys," *BusinessWeek*, 9 December 2002; Raymond Gorman and James Kehr, "Fairness as a Constraint on Profit Seeking," *American Economic Review*, March 1992; the Official Yu-Gi-Oh site at http://www.yugiohkingofgames.com; and the Toy Industry Association site at http://www.toy-tia.org/.

Conclusion

Demand and supply are the building blocks of a market economy. Although a market usually involves the interaction of many buyers and sellers, few markets are consciously designed. Just as the law of gravity works whether or not we understand Newton's principles, market forces operate whether or not participants understand demand and supply. These forces arise naturally, much the way car dealers cluster on the outskirts of town.

Markets have their critics. Some observers may be troubled, for example, that NBA star Kevin Garnett's annual salary could fund a thousand new schoolteachers, or that U.S. consumers spend billions each year on pet food when some people lack enough to eat. On your next trip to the supermarket, notice how much shelf space goes to pet products—often an entire aisle. Petsmart, a chain store, sells over 12,000 pet items. Veterinarians offer cancer treatment, cataract removal, and root canals for pets. Kidney dialysis for a pet can cost $55,000 per year.

SUMMARY

1. Demand is a relationship between the price and the quantity consumers are willing and able to buy per period, other things constant. According to the law of demand, quantity demanded varies inversely with its price, so the demand curve slopes downward.

2. A demand curve slopes downward for two reasons. A price decrease makes consumers (a) more *willing* to substitute this good for other goods and (b) more *able* to buy the good because the lower price increases real income.

3. Assumed to be constant along a demand curve are (a) money income, (b) prices of related goods, (c) consumer expectations, (d) the number and composition of consumers in the market, and (e) consumer tastes. A change in any one of these will shift the demand curve.

4. Supply is a relationship between the price of a good and the quantity producers are willing and able to sell per period, other things constant. According to the law of supply, price and quantity supplied are usually directly related, so the supply curve typically slopes upward. The supply curve slopes upward because higher prices make producers (a) more *willing* to supply this good rather than supply other goods that use the same resources and (b) more *able* to cover the higher marginal cost associated with greater output rates.

5. Assumed to be constant along a supply curve are (a) the state of technology; (b) the prices of resources used to produce the good; (c) the prices of other goods that could be produced with these resources; (d) supplier expectations; and (e) the number of producers in this market. A change in any one of these will shift the supply curve.

6. Demand and supply come together in the market for the good. Markets provide information about the price, quantity, and quality of the good. In doing so, markets reduce the transaction costs of exchange—the costs of time and information required for buyers and sellers to make a deal. The interaction of demand and supply guides resources and products to their highest-valued use.

7. Impersonal market forces reconcile the personal and independent intentions of buyers and sellers. Market equilibrium, once established, will continue unless there is a change in factor that shapes demand or supply. Disequilibrium is usually temporary while markets seek equilibrium, but sometimes disequilibrium lasts a while, such as when government regulates the price or when new products are introduced.

8. A price floor is the minimum legal price below which a particular good or service cannot be sold. The federal government imposes price floors on some agricultural products to help farmers achieve a higher and more stable income than would be possible with freer markets. If the floor price is set above the market clearing price, quantity supplied exceeds quantity demanded. Policy makers must figure out some way to prevent this surplus from pushing the price down.

9. A price ceiling is a maximum legal price above which a particular good or service cannot be sold. Governments impose price ceilings to reduce the price of some consumer goods such as rental housing. If the ceiling price is below the market clearing price, quantity demanded exceeds the quantity supplied, creating a shortage. Because the price system is not allowed to clear the market, other mechanisms arise to ration the product among demanders.

QUESTIONS FOR REVIEW

1. *(Law of Demand)* What is the law of demand? Give two examples of how you have observed the law of demand at work in the "real world." How is the law of demand related to the demand curve?

2. *(Changes in Demand)* What variables influence the demand for a normal good? Explain why a reduction in the price of a normal good does not increase the demand for that good.

3. *(Substitution and Income Effects)* Distinguish between the substitution effect and income effect of a price change. If a good's price increases, does each effect have a positive or a negative impact on the quantity demanded?

4. *(Demand)* Explain the effect of an increase in consumer income on the demand for a good.

5. *(Income Effects)* When moving along the demand curve, income must be assumed constant. Yet one factor that can cause a change in the quantity demanded is the "income effect." Reconcile these seemingly contradictory facts.

6. *(Demand)* If chocolate is found to have positive health benefits, would this lead to a shift of the demand curve or a movement along the demand curve?

7. *(Supply)* What is the law of supply? Give an example of how you have observed the law of supply at work. What is the relationship between the law of supply and the supply curve?

8. *(Changes in Supply)* What kinds of changes in underlying conditions can cause the supply curve to shift? Give some examples and explain the direction in which the curve shifts.

9. *(Supply)* If a severe frost destroys some of Florida's citrus crop, would this lead to a shift of the supply curve or a movement along the supply curve?

10. *(Markets)* How do markets coordinate the independent decisions of buyers and sellers?

11. (**C a s e S t u d y:** The Market for Professional Basketball) In what sense can we speak of a market for professional basketball? Who are the demanders and who are the suppliers? What are some examples of how changes in supply or demand conditions have affected this market?

PROBLEMS AND EXERCISES

12. *(Shifting Demand)* Using demand and supply curves, show the effect of each of the following on the market for cigarettes:

   a. A cure for lung cancer is found.
   b. The price of cigars increases.
   c. Wages increase substantially in states that grow tobacco.
   d. A fertilizer that increases the yield per acre of tobacco is discovered.
   e. There is a sharp increase in the price of matches, lighters, and lighter fluid.
   f. More states pass laws restricting smoking in public places.

13. *(Substitutes and Complements)* For each of the following pair of goods, determine whether the goods are substitutes, complements, or unrelated:

   a. Peanut butter and jelly
   b. Private and public transportation
   c. Coke and Pepsi
   d. Alarm clocks and automobiles
   e. Golf clubs and golf balls

14. *(Equilibrium)* "If a price is not an equilibrium price, there is a tendency for it to move to its equilibrium value. Regardless of whether the price is too high or too low to begin with, the adjustment process will increase the quantity of the good purchased." Explain, using a demand and supply diagram.

15. *(Market Equilibrium)* Determine whether each of the following statements is true, false, or uncertain. Then briefly explain each answer.

    a. In equilibrium, all sellers can find buyers.
    b. In equilibrium, there is no pressure on the market to produce or consume more than is being sold.
    c. At prices above equilibrium, the quantity exchanged exceeds the quantity demanded.
    d. At prices below equilibrium, the quantity exchanged is equal to the quantity supplied.

16. *(Equilibrium)* Assume the market for corn is depicted as in the table that appears below.
    a. Complete the table.
    b. What market pressure occurs when quantity demanded exceeds quantity supplied? Explain.
    c. What market pressure occurs when quantity supplied exceeds quantity demanded? Explain.
    d. What is the equilibrium price?
    e. What could change the equilibrium price?
    f. At each price in the first column of Exhibit 12, how much is sold?

17. *(Demand and Supply)* How do you think each of the following affected the world price of oil? (Use basic demand and supply analysis.)

    a. Tax credits were offered for expenditures on home insulation.
    b. The Alaskan oil pipeline was completed.
    c. The ceiling on the price of oil was removed.
    d. Oil was discovered in the North Sea.
    e. Sport utility vehicles and minivans became popular.
    f. The use of nuclear power decreased.

18. *(Demand and Supply)* What happens to the equilibrium price and quantity of ice cream in response to each of the following? Explain your answers.

    a. The price of dairy cow fodder increases.
    b. The price of beef decreases.
    c. Concerns arise about the fat content of ice cream. Simultaneously, the price of sugar (used to produce ice cream) increases.

19. *(Equilibrium)* Consider the following graph in which demand and supply are initially D and S, respectively. What are the equilibrium price and quantity? If demand increases to D', what are the new equilibrium price and quantity? What happens if the government does not allow the price to change when demand increases?

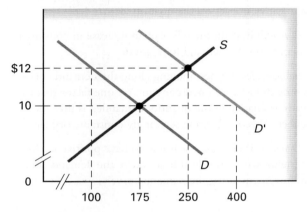

20. *(Changes in Equilibrium)* What are the effects on the equilibrium price and quantity of steel if the wages of steelworkers rise and, simultaneously, the price of aluminum rises?

Price per Bushel	Quantity Demanded (millions of bushels)	Quantity Supplied (millions of bushels)	Surplus/ Shortage	Will Price Rise or Fall?
$1.80	320	200	_____	_____
2.00	300	230	_____	_____
2.20	270	270	_____	_____
2.40	230	300	_____	_____
2.60	200	330	_____	_____
2.80	180	350	_____	_____

21. *(Price Floor)* There is considerable interest in whether the minimum wage rate contributes to teenage unemployment. Draw a demand and supply diagram for the unskilled labor market, and discuss the effects of a minimum wage. Who is helped and who is hurt by the minimum wage?

22. *(Price Ceilings)* Suppose the demand and supply curves for rental housing units have the typical shapes and that the rental housing market is in equilibrium. Then, government establishes a rent ceiling below the equilibrium level.

    a. What happens to the quantity of housing consumed?
    b. Who benefits from rent control?
    c. Who loses from rent control?

23. *(C a s e* **S t u d y :** The Toy Business Is Not Child's Play) Use a demand and supply graph to describe developments in the market for Mighty Morphin Power Rangers toys. Keep in mind the shortage at the $13 selling price, the development of new factories, and the continued shortage.

EXPERIENTIAL EXERCISES

24. *(Market Demand)* With some other students in your class, determine your market demand for gasoline. Make up a chart listing a variety of prices per gallon of gasoline—$1.00, $1.25, $1.50, $1.75, $2.00, $2.25. Ask each student—and yourself—how many gallons per week they would purchase at each possible price. Then:

    a. Plot each student's demand curve. Check to see whether each student's responses are consistent with the law of demand.
    b. Derive the "market" demand curve by adding the quantities demanded by all students at each possible price.
    c. What do you think will happen to that market demand curve after your class graduates and your incomes rise?

25. *(Price Floors)* The minimum wage is a price floor in a market for labor. The government sets a minimum price per

hour of labor in certain markets, and no employer is permitted to pay a wage lower than that. Go to the Department of Labor's minimum wage Web page to learn more about the mechanics of the program: http://www.dol.gov/esa/whd/flsa. Then use a demand and supply diagram to illustrate the effect of imposing an above-equilibrium minimum wage on a particular labor market. What happens to quantity demanded and quantity supplied as a result of the minimum wage?

26. *(Wall Street Journal)* After reading this chapter, you have a basic understanding of how demand and supply determine market price and quantity. Find an article in the "first section" of today's *Wall Street Journal* and interpret the article, using a demand and supply diagram. Explain at least one case in which a curve shifts. What caused the shift, and how did it affect price and quantity?

HOMEWORK XPRESS! EXERCISES

These exercises require access to McEachern Homework Xpress! If Homework Xpress! did not come with your book, visit **http://homeworkxpress.swlearning.com** *to purchase.*

1. Ice cream sellers recognize that demand for ice cream is seasonal: high in the summer, lower in the winter. Draw a demand curve for ice cream in the winter months. Draw a demand curve for ice cream in the summer months.

2. The major ingredients in ice cream are dairy products derived from milk. This summer the price of milk is expected to rise significantly. Draw a supply curve for ice cream before the price increase in milk is known. Draw a supply curve for ice cream in the summer months following the increase in the price of milk.

3. The increasing popularity of sports utility vehicles, SUVs, has led auto dealers to keep a large quantity of them in stock. With the increase in the price of gasoline, however, demand has been falling. Draw demand and supply curves in the diagram for SUVs before the increase in the price of gasoline. Show the equilibrium price and quantity. Illustrate the effect of the increase in the price of gasoline in the market for SUVs. Indicate the effect of this on equilibrium price and quantity.

4. Innovations in materials engineering allow automakers to substitute lower cost materials in their production of sports utility vehicles, SUVs, without reducing the safety of the vehicles. Draw demand and supply curves in the diagram for SUVs before the innovations in materials and show the equilibrium price and quantity. Illustrate the effect of the cost reducing innovations in the market for SUVs. Indicate the effect of this on equilibrium price and quantity.

Elasticity of Demand and Supply

© Frank Siteman Studio

W hy did visits to Microsoft's online magazine, *Slate*, drop 95 percent when the access charge increased from zero to $20 a year? Why did total online usage explode when AOL switched from an hourly charge to a flat monthly fee? Why do higher cigarette taxes cut smoking by teenagers more than by other age groups? Why does a good harvest often spell trouble for farmers? Answers to these and other questions are explored in this chapter, which takes a closer look at demand and supply.

As you learned in Chapter 1, macroeconomics concentrates on aggregate markets—on the big picture. But the big picture is a mosaic pieced together from individual decisions made by households, firms, governments, and the rest of the world. To understand how a market economy works, you must take a closer look at these individual decisions, especially at the role of prices. In a market economy, prices inform producers and consumers about the relative scarcity of products and resources.

A downward-sloping demand curve and an upward-sloping supply curve combine to form a powerful analytical tool. But to use this tool, you must learn more about demand and supply curves. The more you know, the better you can predict the effects of a change in the price on quantity demanded and on quantity supplied. Decision makers are willing to pay dearly for such knowledge. For example, Taco Bell would like to know what happens to sales if taco prices change. Governments would like to know how cigarette taxes affect teenage smoking. Colleges would like to know how tuition increases affect enrollments. And subway officials would like to know how price changes affect ridership. To answer such questions, we must learn how responsive consumers and producers are to price changes. This chapter introduces the idea of *elasticity*, a measure of *responsiveness*. Topics discussed include:

- Price elasticity of demand
- Determinants of price elasticity
- Price elasticity and total revenue
- Price elasticity of supply
- Income elasticity of demand
- Cross-price elasticity of demand

Price Elasticity of Demand

To fill more seats just before a recent Thanksgiving weekend, Delta Airlines cut fares up to 50 percent. Was that a good idea? A firm's success or failure often depends on how much it knows about the demand for its product. For Delta's total revenue to increase, the gain in ticket sales would have to more than make up for the decline in ticket prices. Likewise, the operators of Taco Bell would like to know what happens to sales if its price drops, say, from $1.10 to $0.90 per taco. The law of demand says a lower price increases quantity demanded, but by how much? How sensitive is quantity demanded to a change in price? After all, if quantity demanded increases enough, a price cut could be a profitable move for Taco Bell.

Calculating Price Elasticity of Demand

Let's get more specific about how sensitive changes in quantity demanded are to changes in price. Take a look at the demand curve in Exhibit 1. At the initial price of $1.10 per taco, consumers demand 95,000 per day. If the price drops to $0.90, quantity demanded increases to 105,000. Is such a response a little or a lot? The *price elasticity of demand* measures in a standardized way how responsive consumers are to a change in price. *Elasticity* is another word for *responsiveness*. In simplest terms, the **price elasticity of demand** measures the percentage change in quantity demanded divided by the percentage change in price, or:

PRICE ELASTICITY OF DEMAND

Measures how responsive quantity demanded is to a price change; the percentage change in quantity demanded divided by the percentage change in price

$$\text{Price elasticity of demand} = \frac{\text{Percentage change in quantity demanded}}{\text{Percentage change in price}}$$

So what's the price elasticity of demand when the price of tacos falls from $1.10 to $0.90—that is, what's the price elasticity of demand between points *a* and *b* in Exhibit 1? For price elasticity to be a clear and reliable measure, we should come up with the same result between points *a* and *b* as we get between points *b* and *a*. To ensure that consistency, we must take the average of the initial price and the new price and use that as the base for computing the percentage change in price. For example, in Exhibit 1, the base used to calculate the percentage change in price is the average of $1.10 and $0.90, which is $1.00. The per-

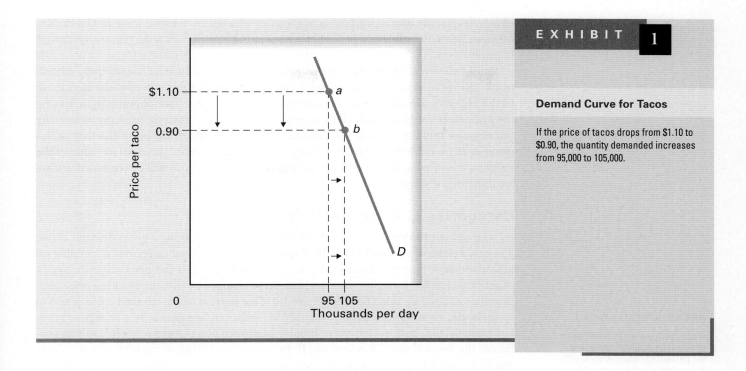

E X H I B I T   1

Demand Curve for Tacos

If the price of tacos drops from $1.10 to $0.90, the quantity demanded increases from 95,000 to 105,000.

centage change in price is therefore the change in price, −$0.20, divided by $1.00, which works out to be −20 percent.

The same holds for changes in quantity demanded. In Exhibit 1, the base used for computing the percentage change in quantity demanded is the average of 95,000 and 105,000, which is 100,000. So the percentage increase in quantity demanded is the change in quantity demanded, 10,000, divided by 100,000, which works out to be 10 percent. So the resulting price elasticity of demand between points *a* and *b* is the percentage increase in quantity demanded, 10 percent, divided by the percentage decrease in price, −20 percent, which is −0.5 (=10%/−20%).

Let's generalize the **price elasticity formula**. If the price changes from p to p', other things constant, the quantity demanded changes from q to q'. The change in price can be represented as Δp and the change in quantity as Δq. The formula for calculating the price elasticity of demand, E_D, between the two points is the percentage change in quantity demanded divided by the percentage change in price, or:

$$E_D = \frac{\Delta q}{(q + q')/2} \div \frac{\Delta p}{(p + p')/2}$$

Again, because the average quantity and average price are used as the bases for computing percentage change, the same elasticity results whether going from the higher price to the lower price or the other way around.

Elasticity expresses a relationship between two amounts: the percentage change in quantity demanded and the percentage change in price. Because the focus is on the *percentage change*, we need not be concerned with how output or price is measured. For example, suppose the good in question is apples. It makes no difference in the elasticity formula whether we measure apples in pounds, bushels, or even tons. All that matters is the percentage

PRICE ELASTICITY FORMULA

Percentage change in quantity demanded divided by the percentage change in price; the average quantity and the average price are used as bases for computing percentage changes in quantity and in price change in quantity demanded. Nor does it matter whether we measure price in U.S. dollars, Mexican pesos, French francs, or Zambian kwacha. All that matters is the percentage change in price.

Finally, the law of demand states that price and quantity demanded are inversely related, so the change in price and the change in quantity demanded move in opposite directions. In the elasticity formula, the numerator and the denominator have opposite signs, leaving the price elasticity of demand with a negative sign. Because constantly referring to elasticity as a negative number gets old fast, from here on we will discuss the price elasticity of demand as an absolute value, or as a positive number. For example, the absolute value of the elasticity measured in Exhibit 1 is 0.5. Still, from time to time, you will be reminded that we are discussing absolute values.

Categories of Price Elasticity of Demand

As you will see, the price elasticity of demand usually varies along a given demand curve. The price elasticity of demand can be divided into three general categories, depending on how responsive quantity demanded is to a change in price. If the percentage change in quantity demanded is smaller than the percentage change in price, the resulting price elasticity has an absolute value between 0 and 1.0. That portion of the demand curve is said to be **inelastic,** meaning that quantity demanded is relatively *unresponsive* to a change in price. For example, the elasticity derived in Exhibit 1 between points *a* and *b* was 0.5, so that portion of the demand curve was inelastic. If the percentage change in quantity demanded just equals the percentage change in price, the resulting price elasticity has an absolute value of 1.0, and that portion of a demand curve has **unit–elastic demand.** Finally, if the percentage change in quantity demanded exceeds the percentage change in price, the resulting price elasticity has an absolute value exceeding 1.0, and that portion of a demand curve is said to be **elastic.** In summary, *the price elasticity of demand is inelastic if its absolute value is between 0 and 1.0, unit elastic if equal to 1.0, and elastic if greater than 1.0.*

Elasticity and Total Revenue

Knowledge of price elasticity is especially valuable to producers, because it indicates the effect of a price change on total revenue. **Total revenue** (*TR*) is the price (*p*) multiplied by the quantity demanded (*q*) at that price, or $TR = p \times q$. What happens to total revenue when price decreases? Well, according to the law of demand, a lower price increases quantity demanded, which tends to increase total revenue. But, a lower price means producers get less for each unit sold, which tends to decrease total revenue. The overall impact of a lower price on total revenue depends on the net result of these opposite effects. *If the positive effect of greater quantity demanded more than offsets the negative effect of a lower price, then total revenue will rise.* More specifically, if demand is *elastic,* the percentage increase in quantity demanded exceeds the percentage decrease in price, so total revenue increases. If demand is *unit elastic,* the percentage increase in quantity demanded just equals the percentage decrease in price, so total revenue remains unchanged. Finally, if demand is *inelastic,* the percentage increase in quantity demanded is more than offset by the percentage decrease in price, so total revenue decreases.

Price Elasticity and the Linear Demand Curve

A look at elasticity along a particular type of demand curve, the linear demand curve, will tie together the ideas discussed so far. A **linear demand curve** is simply a straight-line demand curve, as in panel (a) of Exhibit 2. Panel (b) shows the total revenue generated by each

---

INELASTIC DEMAND

A change in price has relatively little effect on quantity demanded; the percentage change in quantity demanded is less than the percentage change in price; the resulting price elasticity has an absolute value less than 1.0

UNIT-ELASTIC DEMAND

The percentage change in quantity demanded equals the percentage change in price; the resulting price elasticity has an absolute value of 1.0

ELASTIC DEMAND

A change in price has a relatively large effect on quantity demanded; the percentage change in quantity demanded exceeds the percentage change in price; the resulting price elasticity has an absolute value exceeding 1.0

TOTAL REVENUE

Price multiplied by the quantity demanded at that price

LINEAR DEMAND CURVE

A straight-line demand curve; such a demand curve has a constant slope but usually has a varying price elasticity

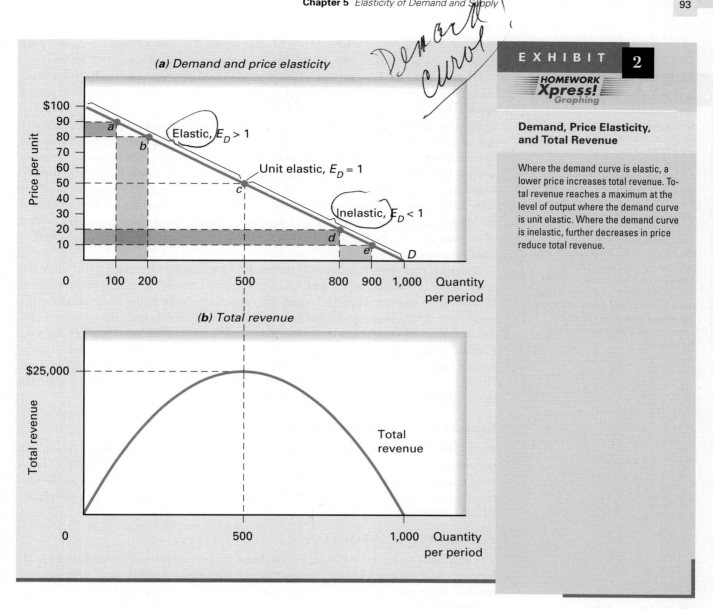

(a) Demand and price elasticity

Elastic, $E_D > 1$

Unit elastic, $E_D = 1$

Inelastic, $E_D < 1$

(b) Total revenue

Total revenue

price-quantity combination along the demand curve in panel (a). Recall that total revenue equals price times quantity.

Because the demand curve is linear, its slope is constant, so a given decrease in price always causes the same unit increase in quantity demanded. For example, along the demand curve in Exhibit 2, a $10 drop in price always increases quantity demanded by 100 units. But the price elasticity of demand is larger on the higher-price end of the demand curve than on the lower-price end. Here's why. Consider a movement from point *a* to point *b* on the upper end of the demand curve in Exhibit 2. The 100-unit increase in quantity demanded is a percentage change of 100/150, or 67 percent. The $10 price drop is a percentage change of 10/85, or 12 percent. Therefore, the price elasticity of demand between points *a* and *b* is 67%/12%, which equals 5.6. Between points *d* and *e* on the lower end, however, the 100-unit quantity increase is a percentage change of 100/850, or only 12 percent, and the $10 price decrease is a percentage change of 10/15, or 67 percent. The price

PERFECTLY ELASTIC DEMAND CURVE

A horizontal line reflecting a situation in which any price increase reduces quantity demanded to zero; the elasticity has an absolute value of infinity

elasticity of demand is 12%/67%, or 0.2. In other words, *if the demand curve is linear, consumers are more responsive to a given price change when the initial price is high than when it's low.*

Demand becomes less elastic as we move down the curve. At a point halfway down the linear demand curve in Exhibit 2, the elasticity equals 1.0. *This halfway point divides a linear demand curve into an elastic upper half and an inelastic lower half.* You can observe a clear relationship between the elasticity of demand in panel (a) and total revenue in panel (b). Notice that where demand is elastic, a decrease in price increases total revenue because the gain in revenue from selling more units (represented by the large blue rectangle) exceeds the loss in revenue from selling all units at the lower price (the small red rectangle). But where demand is inelastic, a price decrease reduces total revenue because the gain in revenue from selling more units (the small blue rectangle) is less than the loss in revenue from selling all units at the lower price (the large red rectangle). And where demand is unit elastic, the gain and loss of revenue exactly cancel each other out, so total revenue at that point remains constant (thus, total revenue "peaks" in the lower panel).

To review, total revenue increases as the price declines until the midpoint of the linear demand curve is reached, where total revenue peaks. In Exhibit 2, total revenue peaks at $25,000 when quantity demanded equals 500 units. To the right of the midpoint of the demand curve, total revenue declines as the price falls. More generally, regardless of whether the demand curve is a straight line or a curve, there is a consistent relationship between the price elasticity of demand and total revenue: *A price decline increases total revenue if demand is elastic, decreases total revenue if demand is inelastic, and has no effect on total revenue if demand is unit elastic.* Finally, note that a downward-sloping linear demand curve has a constant slope but a varying elasticity, so *the slope of a demand curve is not the same as the price elasticity of demand.*

Constant-Elasticity Demand Curves

Again, price elasticity measures the responsiveness of consumers to a change in price. This responsiveness varies along a linear demand curve unless the demand curve is horizontal or vertical, as in panels (a) and (b) of Exhibit 3. These two demand curves, along with the special demand curve in panel (c), are called *constant-elasticity demand curves* because the elasticity does not change along the curves.

Perfectly Elastic Demand Curve

The horizontal demand curve in panel (a) indicates that consumers will demand all that is offered for sale at the given price *p* (the quantity actually demanded will depend on the amount supplied at that price). If the price rises above *p*, however, quantity demanded drops to zero. It is a **perfectly elastic demand curve,** and its elasticity value is infinity, a number too large to be defined. You may think it is an odd sort of demand curve: Consumers, as a result of a small increase in price, go from demanding as much as is supplied to demanding none of the good. Consumers are so sensitive to price changes that they will tolerate no price increase. As you will see in a later chapter, this behavior reflects the demand for the output of any individual producer when many producers sell identical products. The shape of the demand curve for a firm's product is an important element in the pricing and output decision.

Perfectly Inelastic Demand Curve

Along the vertical demand curve in panel (b) of Exhibit 3, quantity demanded does not vary when the price changes. This demand curve expresses consumer sentiment when "price is no object." For example, if you are extremely rich and need insulin injections to survive, price would be no object. No matter how high the price, you would continue to demand whatever it takes. And if the price of insulin should drop, you would not increase your quan-

EXHIBIT 3

Constant-Elasticity Demand Curves

The three panels show constant-elasticity demand curves, so named because the elasticity value does not change along the demand curve. Along the perfectly elastic, or horizontal, demand curve of panel (a), consumers will demand all that is offered for sale at price *p*, but will demand nothing at a price above *p*. Along the perfectly inelastic, or vertical, demand curve of panel (b), consumers will demand amount *Q* regardless of price. Along the unit-elastic demand curve of panel (c), total revenue is the same for each price-quantity combination.

tity demanded. Because the percentage change in quantity demanded is zero for any given percentage change in price, the numerical value of the price elasticity is zero. A vertical demand curve is called a **perfectly inelastic demand curve** because price changes do not affect quantity demanded.

Unit-Elastic Demand Curve

Panel (c) in Exhibit 3 presents a demand curve that is unit elastic everywhere. Along a **unit-elastic demand curve,** any percentage change in price results in an identical and offsetting percentage change in quantity demanded. Because percentage changes in price and in quantity are equal and offsetting, total revenue remains constant for every price-quantity combination along the curve. For example, when the price falls from $10 to $6, the quantity demanded increases from 60 to 100 units. The pink shaded rectangle shows the loss in total revenue because units are sold at the lower price; the blue shaded rectangle shows the gain in total revenue because more units are sold when the price drops. Because the demand curve is unit elastic, the revenue gained from selling more units just equals the revenue lost from lowering the price on all units, so total revenue is unchanged at $600.

Each demand curve in Exhibit 3 is called a **constant–elasticity demand curve** because the elasticity is the same all along the curve. In contrast, the downward–sloping linear demand curve examined earlier had a different elasticity value at each point along the curve. Exhibit 4 lists the absolute values for the five categories of price elasticity we have discussed, summarizing the effects of a 10 percent price increase on quantity demanded and on total

PERFECTLY INELASTIC DEMAND CURVE

A vertical line reflecting a situation in which any price change has no effect on the quantity demanded; the elasticity value equals zero

UNIT-ELASTIC DEMAND CURVE

Everywhere along the demand curve, the percentage change in price causes an equal but offsetting percentage change in quantity demanded, so total revenue remains the same; the elasticity has an absolute value of 1.0

CONSTANT-ELASTICITY DEMAND CURVE

The type of demand that exists when price elasticity is the same everywhere along the curve; the elasticity value is constant revenue. Give this exhibit some thought now, and see if you can draw a demand curve for each type of elasticity.

Determinants of the Price Elasticity of Demand

So far we have explored the technical properties of demand elasticity and discussed why price elasticity varies along a downward-sloping demand curve. But we have yet to consider why price elasticities of demand are different for different goods. Several characteristics influence the price elasticity of demand for a good.

Availability of Substitutes

As we saw in Chapter 4, your particular wants can be satisfied in a variety of ways. A rise in the price of pizza makes other food relatively cheaper. If close substitutes are available, an increase in the price of pizza will prompt some consumers to shift to substitutes. But if nothing else satisfies like pizza, the quantity of pizza demanded will not decline as much. *The greater the availability of substitutes and the more similar the substitutes are to the good in question, the greater the good's price elasticity of demand.*

The number and similarity of substitutes depend on how the good is defined. *The more broadly defined a good is, the fewer substitutes there are and the less elastic the demand.* For example, the demand for shoes is less elastic than the demand for running shoes because there are few substitutes for shoes but several substitutes for running shoes, such as sneakers, tennis shoes, cross-trainers, and so on. The demand for running shoes, however, is less elastic than the demand for Nike running shoes because the consumer has more substitutes for the Nike brand, including Reebok, New Balance, Fila, and so on. Finally, the demand for Nike running shoes is less elastic than the demand for a specific Nike model, because Nike has dozens of models.

E X H I B I T	**4**	**Summary of Price Elasticity of Demand**

Effects of a 10 Percent Increase in Price

Absolute Value of Price Elasticity	Type of Demand	What Happens to Quantity Demanded	What Happens to Total Revenue
$E_D = 0$	Perfectly inelastic	No change	Increases by 10 percent
$0 < E_D < 1$	Inelastic	Drops by less than 10 percent	Increases by less than 10 percent
$E_D = 1$	Unit elastic	Drops by 10 percent	No change
$1 < E_D < \infty$	Elastic	Drops by more than 10 percent	Decreases
$E_D = \infty$	Perfectly elastic	Drops to 0	Drops to 0

Certain goods—some prescription drugs, for instance—have no close substitutes. The demand for such goods tends to be less elastic than for goods with close substitutes, such as Bayer aspirin. Much advertising is aimed at establishing in the consumer's mind the uniqueness of a particular product—an effort to convince consumers "to accept no substitutes." Why might a firm want to make the demand for its product less elastic?

As an example of the impact of substitutes on price elasticity, consider the pattern of commercial breaks during network TV movies. When the movie begins, viewers have several substitutes for it, including other shows and perhaps movies on other networks. To keep viewers from switching channels, the first movie segment is longer than usual, perhaps 20 or 25 minutes before a commercial break. But once viewers get interested in the movie, shows on other channels are no longer close substitutes, so broadcasters inject commercials with greater frequency without fear of losing many viewers.

Proportion of the Consumer's Budget Spent on the Good

Recall that a higher price reduces quantity demanded in part because a higher price reduces the real spending power of consumer income. Because spending on some goods claims a large share of the consumer's budget, a change in the price of such a good has a substantial impact on the consumer's *ability* to buy it. An increase in the price of housing, for example, reduces consumers' ability to buy housing. The income effect of a higher price reduces the quantity demanded. In contrast, the income effect of an increase in the price of, say, paper towels is trivial because paper towels represent such a tiny share of any budget. *The more important the item is as a share of the consumer's budget, other things constant, the greater is the income effect of a change in price, so the more price elastic is the demand for the item.* Hence, the quantity of housing demanded is more responsive to a given percentage change in price than is the quantity of paper towels demanded.

A Matter of Time

Consumers can substitute lower-priced goods for higher-priced goods, but finding substitutes usually takes time. Suppose your college announces a significant increase in room and board fees, effective next term. Some students will move off campus before the next term begins; others may wait until the next academic year. Over time, more incoming students will choose off-campus housing. The longer the adjustment period, the greater the consumers' ability to substitute away from relatively higher-priced products toward lower-priced substitutes. Thus, *the longer the period of adjustment, the more responsive the change in quantity demanded is to a given change in price.* Here's another example: Between 1973 and 1974, the OPEC cartel raised the price of oil sharply. The result was a 45 percent increase in the price of gasoline, but the quantity demanded decreased only 8 percent. As more time passed, however, people purchased smaller cars and made greater use of public transportation. Because the price of oil used to generate electricity and to heat homes increased as well, people bought more energy-efficient appliances and added more insulation to their homes. Again, the change in the amount of oil demanded was greater as consumers adjusted to the price hike.

Exhibit 5 demonstrates how demand becomes more elastic over time. Given an initial price of $1.00 at point *e*, let D_w be the demand curve one week after a price change; D_m, one month after; and D_y, one year after. Suppose the price increases to $1.25. The more time consumers have to respond to the price increase, the greater the reduction in quantity demanded. The demand curve D_w shows that one week after the price increase, the quantity demanded has not declined much—in this case, from 100 to 95 per day. The demand curve D_m indicates a reduction to 75 per day after one month, and demand curve D_y shows a re-

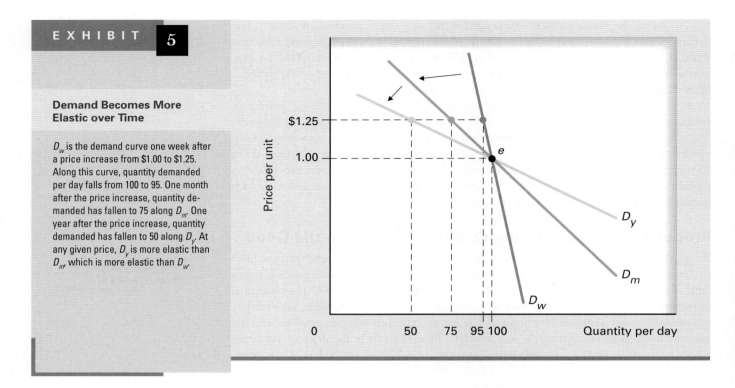

EXHIBIT 5

Demand Becomes More Elastic over Time

D_w is the demand curve one week after a price increase from $1.00 to $1.25. Along this curve, quantity demanded per day falls from 100 to 95. One month after the price increase, quantity demanded has fallen to 75 along D_m. One year after the price increase, quantity demanded has fallen to 50 along D_y. At any given price, D_y is more elastic than D_m, which is more elastic than D_w.

duction to 50 per day after one year. Notice that among these demand curves and over the range starting from point *e*, the flatter the demand curve, the more price elastic the demand. Here, elasticity seems linked to the slope because we begin from a common point—the same price-quantity combination.

Elasticity Estimates

Let's look at some estimates of the price elasticity of demand for particular goods and services. As we have noted, finding substitutes when the price increases takes time. Thus, when estimating price elasticity, economists often distinguish between a period during which consumers have little time to adjust—let's call it the *short run*—and a period during which consumers can more fully adjust to a price change—let's call it the *long run*. Exhibit 6 provides some short-run and long-run price elasticity estimates for selected products.

The price elasticity of demand is greater in the long run because consumers have more time to adjust. For example, if the price of electricity rose today, consumers in the short run might cut back a bit in their use of electrical appliances, and those in homes with electric heat might lower the thermostat in winter. Over time, however, consumers would switch to more energy-efficient appliances and might convert from electric heat to oil or natural gas. So the demand for electricity is more elastic in the long run than in the short run, as shown in Exhibit 6. In fact, in every instance where values for both the short run and the long run are listed, the long run is more elastic than the short run. Notice also that the long-run price elasticity of demand for Chevrolets exceeds that for automobiles in general. There are many more substitutes for Chevrolets than for automobiles in general. There are no close substitutes for cigarettes, even in the long run, so the demand for cigarettes among adults is price inelastic. Such elasticity measures are of more than just academic interest, as discussed in the following case study.

Product	Short Run	Long Run	EXHIBIT 6
Cigarettes (among adults)	—	0.4	
Electricity (residential)	0.1	1.9	**Selected Price Elasticities of Demand (absolute values)**
Air travel	0.1	2.4	
Medical care and hospitalization	0.3	0.9	
Gasoline	0.4	1.5	
Milk	0.4	—	
Fish (cod)	0.5	—	
Wine	0.7	1.2	
Movies	0.9	3.7	
Natural gas (residential)	1.4	2.1	
Automobiles	1.9	2.2	
Chevrolets	—	4.0	

Sources: F. Chaloupka, "Rational Addictive Behavior and Cigarette Smoking," *Journal of Political Economy* (August 1991); Hsaing-tai Cheng and Oral Capps, Jr., "Demand for Fish," *American Journal of Agricultural Economics* (August 1998); J. Johnson et al., "Short-Run and Long-Run Elasticities for Canadian Consumption of Alcoholic Beverages," *Review of Economics and Statistics* (February 1992); Douglas Young, et al., "Alcohol Consumption, Measurement Error, and Beverage Prices," *Journal of Studies on Alcohol* (March 2003); J. Griffin, *Energy Conservation in the OECD, 1980–2000* (Cambridge, Mass.: Balinger, 1979); H. Houthakker and L. Taylor, *Consumer Demand in the United States: Analysis and Projections,* 2nd ed. (Cambridge, Mass.: Harvard University Press, 1970); and G. Lakshmanan and W. Anderson, "Residential Energy Demand in the United States," *Regional Science and Urban Economics* 10 (August 1980).

Deterring Young Smokers

As the U.S. Surgeon General warns on each pack of cigarettes, smoking can be hazardous to your health. Researchers estimate that smoking kills 440,000 Americans a year, ten times the deaths from traffic accidents. Lung cancer is now the top cancer killer among women, and 9 of 10 lung cancers are smoking related. Smoking is also the leading cause of heart disease, emphysema, and stroke.

According to the U.S. Centers for Disease Control and Prevention, each pack of cigarettes sold in the United States results in $7.18 in added health care costs and in lost worker productivity. The total cost exceeds $150 billion a year, divided roughly between health care and productivity losses. This amount works out to be about $3,400 per smoker per year. Health-related issues have created a growing public-policy concern about smoking, especially smoking by teenagers, which jumped by one-third during the 1990s. A federal study of 16,000 U.S. high school students found cigarette smoking rose from 27.5 percent of those surveyed in 1991 to 36.4 percent in 1997. Among black youths, the rate nearly doubled from 12.6 percent to 22.7 percent. Reasons behind these jumps include stable prices for cigarettes (prices didn't increase between 1992 and 1997), advertising aimed at young people (such as Joe Camel), and glamorization of smoking in movies and television (for exam-

Case **Study**

Public Policy

eActivity

In 2003, only 1 in 5 high school students smoked. The CDC stated that anti-smoking efforts targeting high school teens have been successful—including TV ads, school campaigns, and higher cost per pack. Read more at http://166.70.44.66/2004/Jun/06182004/nation_w/176579.asp. Also read about the Mayo Clinic's smoking cessation study at http://www.mayoclinic.org/checkup-2003/march-teens.html, or visit the Web site of the CDC at http://www.cdc.gov for their studies and findings.

ple, in the hit movie of the decade, *Titanic,* the two young, attractive leading characters smoked cigarettes). In one study, teens indicated that they were more likely to try smoking if they saw their favorite characters smoke in movies. Each day, about 3,000 U.S. teens under 18 become regular smokers. Worldwide, an estimated 100,000 teens become regular smokers each day.

One way to reduce youth smoking is to prohibit the sale of cigarettes to minors. A second way is to raise the price through higher cigarette taxes. The amount by which a given price increase reduces teen smoking depends on the price elasticity of demand. This elasticity is higher for teens than for adults. Why are teenagers more sensitive to price changes than adults? First, recall that one of the factors affecting elasticity is the importance of the item in the consumer's budget. Because teen income is relatively low, the share spent on cigarettes usually exceeds the share for adult smokers. Second, peer pressure is more influential in a young person's decision to smoke than in an adult's decision to continue smoking (if anything, adults face negative peer pressure for smoking). The impact of a higher price gets multiplied among young smokers because it reduces smoking by peers. With fewer peers smoking, teens receive less pressure to smoke. And third, young people not yet hooked are more sensitive to price increases than are adult smokers, who are more likely to be addicted. The experience from other countries supports the effectiveness of higher prices in reducing teen smoking. For example, a large tax increase on cigarettes in Canada cut youth smoking by two-thirds.

Another way to reduce smoking is to change consumer tastes through health warnings on packages. The Canadian government has proposed putting pictures of cancerous tongues and lips on cigarette packs and publicizing the link between smoking and male impotence (so much for the Marlboro man). In California, a combination of higher cigarette taxes and an ambitious awareness program has contributed to a 5 percent decline in lung cancer among women there, even as it rose 13 percent in the rest of the country.

In a 1997 U.S. court settlement, tobacco companies agreed to pay $368 billion in health-related damages, tear down billboards, and retire Joe Camel. A federal study reported a slight decline in teenage smoking, dropping from 36.4 percent of those surveyed in 1997 to 34.8 percent in 1999.

Sources: "Annual Smoking-Attributable Mortality, Years of Potential Life Lost, and Economic Costs," Centers for Disease Control and Prevention, 12 April 2002; Hana Ross and Frank Chaloupka, "The Effects of Public Policies and Prices on Youth Smoking," *Southern Economic Journal* (April 2004); and Madeline Dalton, et al., "Effect of Viewing Smoking in Movies on Adolescent Smoking Initiative," *The Lancet,* Vol. 362, Issue 9380 (2003). For background on the tobacco settlement, go to http://www.pbs.org/wgbh/pages/frontline/shows/settlement/.

Price Elasticity of Supply

Prices are signals to both sides of the market about the relative scarcity of products. Higher prices discourage consumption but encourage production. The price elasticity of demand measures how responsive consumers are to a price change. Likewise, the **price elasticity of supply** measures how responsive producers are to a price change. This elasticity is calculated in the same way as price elasticity of demand. In simplest terms, the price elasticity of supply equals the percentage change in quantity supplied divided by the percentage change in price. Because the higher price usually results in an increased quantity supplied, the percentage change in price and the percentage change in quantity supplied move in the same direction, so the price elasticity of supply is usually a positive number.

Exhibit 7 depicts a typical upward-sloping supply curve. As you can see, if the price increases from p to p', the quantity supplied increases from q to q'. Price and quantity supplied

PRICE ELASTICITY OF SUPPLY

A measure of the responsiveness of quantity supplied to a price change; the percentage change in quantity supplied divided by the percentage change in price move in the same direction. Let's look at the elasticity formula for the supply curve. The price elasticity of supply is:

$$E_S = \frac{\Delta q}{(q + q')/2} \div \frac{\Delta p}{(p + p')/2}$$

where Δq is the change in quantity supplied and Δp is the change in price. This is the same formula used to compute the price elasticity of demand except that q here is quantity supplied, not quantity demanded. The terminology for supply elasticity is the same as for demand elasticity: If supply elasticity is less than 1.0, supply is **inelastic;** if it equals 1.0, supply is **unit elastic;** and if it exceeds 1.0, supply is **elastic.**

Constant Elasticity Supply Curves

Again, price elasticity of supply measures the responsiveness of producers to a change in price. This responsiveness varies along a linear supply curve unless it's horizontal or vertical, as in panels (a) and (b) of Exhibit 8, or passes through the origin, as in panel (c). These three supply curves are called *constant-elasticity supply curves* because the elasticity does not change along the curves.

Perfectly Elastic Supply Curve

At one extreme is the horizontal supply curve, such as supply curve S in panel (a) of Exhibit 8. In this case, producers will supply none of the good at a price below p but will supply any

INELASTIC SUPPLY

A change in price has relatively little effect on quantity supplied; the percentage change in quantity supplied is less than the percentage change in price; the price elasticity of supply has a value less than 1.0

UNIT-ELASTIC SUPPLY

The percentage change in quantity supplied equals the percentage change in price; the resulting price elasticity of supply equals 1.0

ELASTIC SUPPLY

A change in price has a relatively large effect on quantity supplied; the percentage change in quantity supplied exceeds the percentage change in price; the resulting price elasticity of supply exceeds 1.0

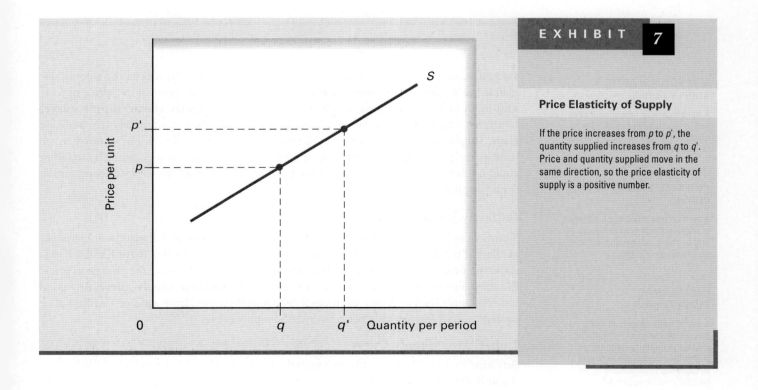

E X H I B I T 7

Price Elasticity of Supply

If the price increases from p to p', the quantity supplied increases from q to q'. Price and quantity supplied move in the same direction, so the price elasticity of supply is a positive number.

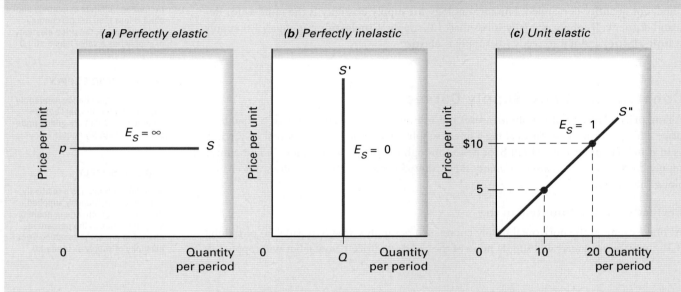

EXHIBIT 8

Constant-Elasticity Supply Curves

In each of the three panels is a constant-elasticity supply curve, so named because the elasticity value does not change along the curve. Supply curve *S* in panel (a) is perfectly elastic, or horizontal. Along *S*, firms will supply any amount of output demanded at price *p*, but will supply none at prices below *p*. Supply curve *S'* is perfectly inelastic, or vertical. *S'* shows that the quantity supplied is independent of the price. In panel (c), *S"*, a straight line from the origin, is a unit-elastic supply curve. Any percentage change in price results in the same percentage change in quantity supplied.

PERFECTLY ELASTIC SUPPLY CURVE

A horizontal line reflecting a situation in which any price decrease drops the quantity supplied to zero; the elasticity value is infinity

PERFECTLY INELASTIC SUPPLY CURVE

A vertical line reflecting a situation in which a price change has no effect on the quantity supplied; the elasticity value is zero

UNIT-ELASTIC SUPPLY CURVE

A percentage change in price causes an identical percentage change in quantity supplied; depicted by a supply curve that is a straight line from the origin; the elasticity value equals 1.0

amount at price *p* (the quantity actually supplied at price *p* will depend on the amount demanded at that price). Because a tiny increase from a price just below *p* to a price of *p* results in an unlimited quantity supplied, this is called a **perfectly elastic supply curve,** which has a numerical value of infinity. As individual consumers, we typically face perfectly elastic supply curves. When we go to the supermarket, we usually can buy as much as we want at the prevailing price but none at a lower price. Obviously all consumers together could not buy an unlimited amount at the prevailing price (recall the fallacy of composition from Chapter 1).

Perfectly Inelastic Supply Curve

The most unresponsive relationship is where there is no change in the quantity supplied regardless of the price, as shown by the vertical supply curve *S'* in panel (b) of Exhibit 8. Because the percentage change in quantity supplied is zero, regardless of the change in price, the price elasticity of supply is zero. This is a **perfectly inelastic supply curve.** Any good in fixed supply, such as Picasso paintings, 1995 Dom Perignon champagne, or Cadillacs once owned by Elvis Presley, has a perfectly inelastic supply curve.

Unit-Elastic Supply Curve

Any supply curve that is a straight line from the origin—such as *S"* in panel (c) of Exhibit 8— is a **unit-elastic supply curve.** This means a percentage change in price will always generate an identical percentage change in quantity supplied. For example, along S'' a doubling of the price results in a doubling of the quantity supplied. Note that unit elasticity is based not on the slope of the line but on the fact that the linear supply curve emanates from the origin.

Determinants of Supply Elasticity

The elasticity of supply indicates how responsive producers are to a change in price. Their responsiveness depends on how easy it is to alter quantity supplied when the price changes. If the cost of supplying additional units rises sharply as output expands, then a higher price will elicit little increase in quantity supplied, so supply will tend to be inelastic. But if the marginal cost rises slowly as output expands, the lure of a higher price will prompt a large increase in quantity supplied. In this case, supply will be more elastic.

One determinant of supply elasticity is the length of the adjustment period under consideration. Just as demand becomes more elastic over time as consumers adjust to price changes, supply also becomes more elastic over time as producers adjust to price changes. The longer the time period under consideration, the more able producers are to adjust to changes in relative prices. Exhibit 9 presents a different supply curve for each of three periods. S_w is the supply curve when the period of adjustment is a week. As you can see, a higher price will not elicit much of a response in quantity supplied because firms have little time to adjust. This supply curve is inelastic if the price increases from $1.00 to $1.25.

S_m is the supply curve when the adjustment period under consideration is a month. Firms have a greater ability to vary output in a month than they do in a week. Thus, supply is more elastic when the adjustment period is a month than when it's a week. Supply is even more elastic when the adjustment period is a year, as is shown by S_y. So a given price increase elicits a greater quantity supplied as the adjustment period lengthens. For example, if

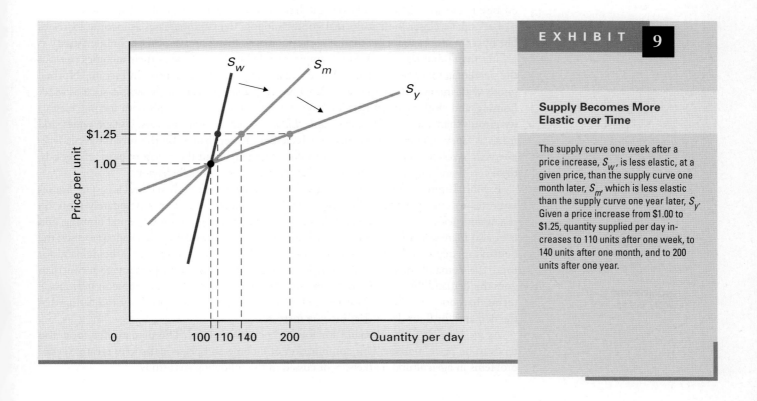

EXHIBIT 9

Supply Becomes More Elastic over Time

The supply curve one week after a price increase, S_w, is less elastic, at a given price, than the supply curve one month later, S_m, which is less elastic than the supply curve one year later, S_y. Given a price increase from $1.00 to $1.25, quantity supplied per day increases to 110 units after one week, to 140 units after one month, and to 200 units after one year.

the price of oil increases, oil producers in the short run can try to pump more from existing wells, but in the long run, a higher price stimulates more exploration. Research confirms the positive link between the price elasticity of supply and the length of the adjustment period. *The elasticity of supply is typically greater the longer the period of adjustment.*

The ease of increasing quantity supplied in response to a higher price differs across industries. The response time will be slower for producers of electricity, oil, and timber (where expansion may take years) than for window washing, lawn maintenance, and hot-dog vending (where expansion may take only days).

Other Elasticity Measures

Price elasticities of demand and supply are frequently used in economic analysis, but two other elasticity measures also provide useful information.

Income Elasticity of Demand

What happens to the demand for new cars, fresh vegetables, or computer software if consumer income increases by, say, 10 percent? The answer is of great interest to producers because it helps them predict the effect of changing consumer income on quantity sold and on total revenue. The **income elasticity of demand** measures how responsive demand is to a change in consumer income. Specifically, *the income elasticity of demand measures the percentage change in demand divided by the percentage change in income that caused it.*

As noted in Chapter 4, the demand for some products, such as used furniture and used clothing, actually declines, or shifts leftward, as income increases. Thus, the income elasticity of demand for such products is negative. Goods with income elasticities less than zero are called *inferior goods*. The demand for most goods increases, or shifts rightward, as income increases. These are called *normal goods* and have income elasticities greater than zero.

Let's take a closer look at normal goods. Suppose demand increases as income increases but by a smaller percentage than income increases. In such cases, the income elasticity is greater than 0 but less than 1. For example, people buy more food as their incomes rise, but the percentage increase in demand is less than the percentage increase in income. Normal goods with income elasticities less than 1 are called *income inelastic*. Necessities such as food, housing, and clothing often have income elasticities less than 1. Goods with income elasticity greater than 1 are called *income elastic*. Luxuries such as high-end cars, vintage wines, and meals at fancy restaurants have income elasticities greater than 1. By the way, the terms *inferior goods, necessities,* and *luxuries* are not value judgment about the merits of particular goods; these terms are simply convenient ways of classifying economic behavior.

Exhibit 10 presents income elasticity estimates for some goods and services. The figures indicate, for example, that as income increases, consumers spend proportionately more on restaurant meals, owner-occupied housing, and wine. Spending on food, rental housing, and beer also increases as income increases, but less than proportionately. So as income rises, the demand for restaurant meals increases more in percentage terms than does the demand for food, the demand for owner-occupied housing increases more in percentage terms than does the demand for rental housing, and the demand for wine increases more in percentage terms than does the demand for beer. Flour has negative income elasticity, indicating that the demand for flour declines as income increases.

As we have seen, the demand for food is income inelastic. The demand for food also tends to be price inelastic. This combination of income and price inelasticity creates special problems in agricultural markets, as discussed in the following case study.

INCOME ELASTICITY OF DEMAND

The percentage change in demand divided by the percentage change in consumer income; the value is positive for normal goods and negative for inferior goods

EXHIBIT 10	Selected Income Elasticities of Demand			

Product	Income Elasticity	Product	Income Elasticity
Private education	2.46	Physicians' services	0.75
Automobiles	2.45	Coca-Cola	0.68
Wine	2.19	Beef	0.62
Owner-occupied housing	1.49	Food	0.51
Furniture	1.48	Coffee	0.51
Dental service	1.42	Cigarettes	0.50
Restaurant meals	1.40	Gasoline and oil	0.48
Shoes	1.10	Rental housing	0.43
Chicken	1.06	Beer	0.27
Spirits ("hard" liquor)	1.02	Pork	0.18
Clothing	0.92	Flour	−0.36

Sources: Ivan Bloor, "Food for Thought," *Economic Review* (September 1999); F. Gasmi et al., "Econometric Analysis of Collusive Behavior in a Soft-Drink Market," *Journal of Economics and Management Strategy* (Summer 1992); J. Johnson et al., "Short-Run and Long-Run Elasticities for Canadian Consumption of Alcoholic Beverages," *Review of Economics and Statistics* (February 1992); H. Houthakker and L. Taylor, *Consumer Demand in the United States: Analyses and Projections*, 2nd ed. (Cambridge, Mass.: Harvard University Press, 1970); C. Huang et al., "The Demand for Coffee in the United States, 1963–77," *Quarterly Review of Economics and Business* (Summer 1980); and G. Brester and M. Wohlgenant, "Estimating Interrelated Demands for Meats Using New Measures for Ground and Table Cut Beef," *American Journal of Agricultural Economics* (November 1991).

The Market for Food and "The Farm Problem"

© Photodisc/Getty Images

Case Study

Public Policy

eActivity
What are the forces shaping U.S. agriculture today? The Economic Research Service of the U.S. Department of Agriculture provides some answers with its briefing book at http://www.ers.usda. gov/Emphases/Competitive/. Find out what the latest edition says about the current state of the American farm family. How have farm size and the number of family farms been changing? How does farm family income compare to average household income? What percent of farm income is a result of government farm support policies?

Despite decades of federal support and billions of tax dollars spent on various farm-assistance programs, the number of American farmers continues its long slide, dropping from 10 million in 1950 to under 3 million today. The demise of the family farm can be traced to the price and income elasticities of demand for farm products and to technological breakthroughs that increased supply.

Many of the forces that determine farm production are beyond a farmer's control. Temperature, rainfall, insects, and other natural forces affect crop size and quality. For example, favorable weather boosted crop production 16 percent in one recent year. Such jumps in production create special problems for farmers because the demand for most farm crops, such as milk, eggs, corn, potatoes, oats, sugar, and beef, is price inelastic.

The effect of inelastic demand on farm revenue is illustrated in Exhibit 11. Suppose that in a normal year, farmers supply 10 billion bushels of grain at a market price of $5 a bushel. Annual farm revenue, which is price times quantity, totals $50 billion in our example. What if favorable weather raises grain production to 11 billion bushels, an increase of 10 percent? Because demand is price inelastic, the average price in our example must fall by more than 10 percent to, say, $4 per bushel to sell the extra billion bushels. Thus, the 10 percent increase in farm production gets sold only if the price drops by 20 percent.

Because, in percentage terms, the drop in price exceeds the increase in quantity demanded, total revenue declines from $50 billion to $44 billion. So total revenue drops by over 10 percent, despite the 10 percent rise in production. *Because demand is price inelastic, total revenue falls when the price falls.* Of course, for farmers, the upside of inelastic demand is that a lower-than-normal crop results in a higher total revenue. For example, one recent drought sent corn prices up 50 percent, increasing farm revenue in the process. So weather-generated changes in farm production create year-to-year swings in farm revenue.

Fluctuations in farm revenue are compounded in the long run by the *income inelasticity* of demand for grain and, more generally, for food. As household incomes grow over time, spending on food may increase because consumers substitute prepared foods and restaurant meals for home cooking. But this switch has little effect on the total demand for farm products. Thus, as the economy grows over time and incomes rise, the demand for farm products tends to increase but by less than the increase in income. This modest increase in demand from *D* to *D'* is reflected in Exhibit 12.

Because of technological improvements in production, however, the supply of farm products has increased sharply. Farm output per hour of labor is about *eight times* greater now than in 1950 because of such developments as more sophisticated machines, better fertilizers, and healthier seed strains. For example, farmers can seed at night using a 32-row planter and global positioning satellites. With new strains of pest-resistant plants, farmers have cut insecticide applications from seven per season to one or none.

Exhibit 12 shows a big increase in the supply of grain from *S* to *S'*. Because the increase in supply exceeds the increase in demand, the price declines. And because the demand for

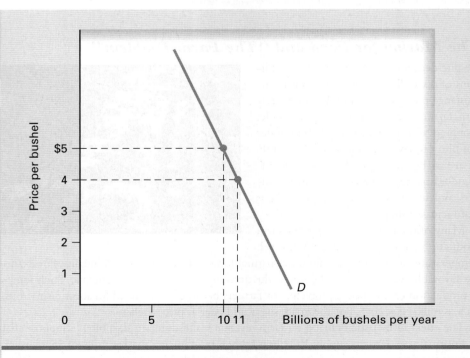

EXHIBIT   11

The Demand for Grain

The demand for grain tends to be price inelastic. As the market price falls, so does total revenue.

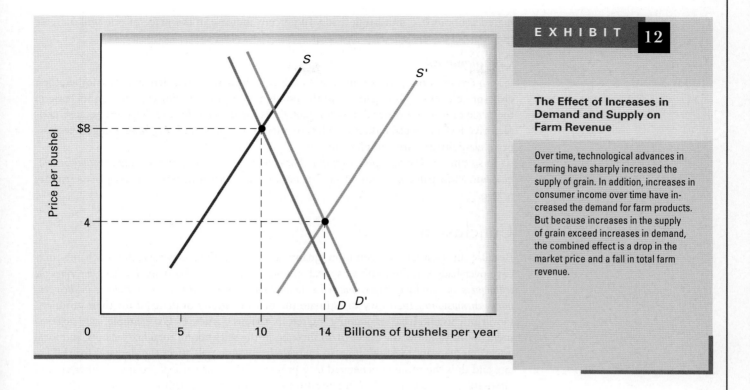

The Effect of Increases in Demand and Supply on Farm Revenue

Over time, technological advances in farming have sharply increased the supply of grain. In addition, increases in consumer income over time have increased the demand for farm products. But because increases in the supply of grain exceed increases in demand, the combined effect is a drop in the market price and a fall in total farm revenue.

grain is price inelastic, the percentage drop in price exceeds the percentage increase in output. The combined effect in our example is lower total revenue. In fact, net income (adjusted for inflation) to all U.S. farmers in 2003 was 20 percent below what it was in 1960.

Sources: Bruce L. Gardner, "Changing Economic Perspective on the Farm Problem," *Journal of Economic Literature* 30 (March 1992): 62–105; and *Economic Report of the President*, February 2004, Tables B-97 at http://www.gpoaccess.gov/eop/index.html. For current economic research at the U.S. Department of Agriculture, go to http://www.ers.usda.gov/.

Cross-Price Elasticity of Demand

Because a firm often produces an entire line of products, it has a special interest in how a change in the price of one product will affect the demand for another. For example, the Coca-Cola Company needs to know how changing the price of Lemon Coke will affect sales of Classic Coke. The company also needs to know the relationship between the price of Coke and the demand for Pepsi and vice versa. The responsiveness of the demand for one good to changes in the price of another good is called the **cross–price elasticity of demand.** It is defined as the percentage change in the demand of one good divided by the percentage change in the price of another good. Its numerical value can be positive, negative, or zero, depending on whether the two goods in question are substitutes, complements, or unrelated, respectively.

Substitutes

If an increase in the price of one good leads to an increase in the demand for another good, their cross-price elasticity is positive and the two goods are *substitutes*. For example, an increase in the price of Coke, other things constant, shifts the demand for Pepsi rightward, so the two are substitutes. The cross-price elasticity between Coke and Pepsi has been esti-

CROSS-PRICE ELASTICITY OF DEMAND

The percentage change in the demand of one good divided by the percentage change in the price of another good mated at about 0.7, indicating that a 10 percent increase in the price of one will increase the demand for the other by 7 percent.[1]

Complements

If an increase in the price of one good leads to a decrease in the demand for another, their cross-price elasticity is negative and the goods are *complements*. For example, an increase in the price of gasoline, other things constant, shifts the demand for tires leftward because people drive less and replace their tires less frequently. Gasoline and tires have a negative cross-price elasticity and are complements.

In summary: *The cross-price elasticity of demand is positive for substitutes and negative for complements.* Most pairs of goods selected at random are *unrelated,* so their cross-price elasticity is zero.

Conclusion

Because this chapter has been more quantitative than earlier ones have, the mechanics may have overshadowed the intuitive appeal and neat simplicity of elasticity. *Elasticity measures the willingness and ability of buyers and sellers to alter their behavior in response to changes in their economic circumstances.* Firms try to estimate the price elasticity of demand for their products. Governments also have an ongoing interest in various elasticities. For example, state governments want to know the effect of an increase in the sales tax on total tax receipts, and local governments want to know how an increase in income will affect the demand for real estate and thus the revenue generated by a property tax. International groups are interested in elasticities; for example, the Organization of Petroleum Exporting Countries (OPEC) is concerned about the price elasticity of demand for oil—in the short run and in the long run. Because a corporation often produces an entire line of products, it also has a special interest in certain cross-price elasticities. Some corporate economists estimate elasticities for a living. The appendix to this chapter shows how price elasticities of demand and supply shed light on who ultimately pays a tax.

SUMMARY

1. The price elasticities of demand and supply show how responsive buyers and sellers are to changes in the price of a good. More elastic means more responsive.

2. When the percentage change in quantity demanded exceeds the percentage change in price, demand is price elastic. If demand is price elastic, a price increase reduces total revenue and a price decrease increases total revenue. When the percentage change in quantity demanded is less than the percentage change in price, demand is price inelastic. If demand is price inelastic, a higher price increases total revenue and a lower price reduces total revenue. When the percentage change in quantity demanded equals the percentage change in price, demand is unit elastic; a price change does not affect total revenue.

3. Along a linear, or straight-line, downward-sloping demand curve, the elasticity of demand falls steadily as the price falls. But a constant-elasticity demand curve has the same elasticity everywhere.

4. Demand is more elastic (a) the greater the availability of substitutes and the more similar they are to the good in question; (b) the more narrowly the good is defined; (c) the larger the proportion of the consumer's budget spent on the good; and (d) the longer the time allowed for adjustment to a change in price.

1. F. Gasmi, J. Laffont, and Q. Vuong, "Econometric Analysis of Collusive Behavior in a Soft-Drink Market," *Journal of Economics and Management Strategy* (Summer 1992).

5. The price elasticity of supply uses a similar approach to the price elasticity of demand. Price elasticity of supply depends on how much the marginal cost of production changes as output changes. If marginal cost rises sharply as output expands, quantity supplied is less responsive to price increases and is thus less elastic. Also, the longer the time producers have to adjust to price changes, other things constant, the more elastic the supply.

6. Income elasticity of demand measures the responsiveness of demand to changes in consumer income. Income elasticity is positive for normal goods and negative for inferior goods.

7. The cross-price elasticity of demand measures the impact of a change in the price of one good on the demand for another good. Two goods are defined as substitutes, complements, or unrelated, depending on whether their cross-price elasticity of demand is positive, negative, or zero, respectively.

QUESTIONS FOR REVIEW

1. *(Categories of Price Elasticity of Demand)* For each of the following values of price elasticity of demand, indicate whether demand is elastic, inelastic, perfectly elastic, perfectly inelastic, or unit elastic. In addition, determine what would happen to total revenue if a firm raised its price in each elasticity range identified.

   a. $E_D = 2.5$
   b. $E_D = 1.0$
   c. $E_D = \infty$
   d. $E_D = 0.8$

2. *(Elasticity and Total Revenue)* Explain the relationship between the price elasticity of demand and total revenue.

3. *(Price Elasticity and the Linear Demand Curve)* How is it possible for many price elasticities to be associated with a single demand curve?

4. *(Determinants of Price Elasticity)* Why is the price elasticity of demand for Coca-Cola greater than the price elasticity of demand for soft drinks generally?

5. *(Determinants of Price Elasticity)* Would the price elasticity of demand for electricity be more elastic over a shorter or a longer period of time?

6. *(Determinants of Price Elasticity)* What factors help determine the price elasticity of demand? What factors help determine the price elasticity of supply?

7. *(Cross-Price Elasticity)* Using demand and supply curves, predict the impact on the price and quantity demanded of Good 1 of an increase in the price of Good 2 if the two goods are substitutes. What if the two goods are complements?

8. *(Other Elasticity Measures)* Complete each of the following sentences:

   a. The income elasticity of demand measures, for a given price, the _____ in quantity demanded divided by the _____ income from which it resulted.
   b. If a decrease in the price of one good causes a decrease in demand for another good, the two goods are _____.
   c. If the value of the cross-price elasticity of demand between two goods is approximately zero, they are considered _____.

PROBLEMS AND EXERCISES

9. *(Calculating Price Elasticity of Demand)* Suppose that 50 units of a good are demanded at a price of $1 per unit. A reduction in price to $0.20 results in an increase in quantity demanded to 70 units. Show that these data yield a price elasticity of 0.25. By what percentage would a 10 percent rise in the price reduce the quantity demanded, assuming price elasticity remains constant along the demand curve?

10. *(Price Elasticity and Total Revenue)* Fill in values for each price-quantity combination listed in the following table. What relationship have you depicted?

P	Q	Price Elasticity	Total Revenue
$8	2	_____	_____
7	3	_____	_____
6	4	_____	_____
5	5	_____	_____
4	6	_____	_____
3	7	_____	_____
2	8	_____	_____

11. *(Income Elasticity of Demand)* Calculate the income elasticity of demand for each of the following goods:

	Quantity Demanded When Income Is $10,000	Quantity Demanded When Income Is $20,000
Good 1	10	25
Good 2	4	5
Good 3	3	2

12. *(Price Elasticity of Supply)* Calculate the price elasticity of supply for each of the following combinations of price and quantity supplied. In each case, determine whether supply is elastic, inelastic, perfectly elastic, perfectly inelastic, or unit elastic.

   a. Price falls from $2.25 to $1.75; quantity supplied falls from 600 units to 400 units.
   b. Price falls from $2.25 to $1.75; quantity supplied falls from 600 units to 500 units.
   c. Price falls from $2.25 to $1.75; quantity supplied remains at 600 units.
   d. Price increases from $1.75 to $2.25; quantity supplied increases from 466.67 units to 600 units.

Use the following diagram to answer the next two questions.

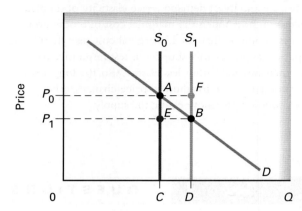

13. (*C a s e* **S t u d y :** The Market for Food and "the Farm Problem") Interpret this diagram as showing the market demand and supply curves for agricultural products. Suppose that demand is inelastic over the relevant range of prices and supply increased from S_0 to S_1. What areas in the figure would you use to illustrate the net change in farmers' total revenue as a result of the increase in supply?

14. (*C a s e* **S t u d y :** The Market for Food and "the Farm Problem") Again suppose that this diagram represents the market for agricultural products and that supply has increased from S_0 to S_1. To aid farmers, the federal government decides to stabilize the price at P_0 by buying up surplus farm products. Show on the diagram how much this would cost the government. By how much would farm income change compared to what it would have been without government intervention?

15. *(Cross-Price Elasticity)* Rank the following in order of increasing (from negative to positive) cross-price elasticity of demand with coffee. Explain your reasoning.

   Bleach
   Tea
   Cream
   Cola

EXPERIENTIAL EXERCISES

16. (*C a s e* **S t u d y :** Deterring Young Smokers) The Campaign for Tobacco Free Kids maintains a Web site with a page devoted to articles on the economics of tobacco policy at http://tobaccofreekids.org/campaign/global/worldconference.shtml. For additional background infor- mation in the form of the transcript of a five-part television series, check *The Tobacco Wars,* by Walter Adams and James Brock (Cincinnati, OH: South-Western College Publishing Co., 1999).

17. (*C a s e* **S t u d y**: The Market for Food and "the Farm Problem") Farm problems are not unique to the United States. Alan Matthews at Trinity College, Dublin, has an interesting Web page devoted to "The Farm Problem and Farm Policy Objectives" at http://econserv2.bess.tcd.ie/amtthews/FoodCourse/LectureTopics/Topics.htm. Review the material presented there and determine to what extent agricultural issues in the European Union (EU) are similar to those experienced in the United States. What role does economics play in the analysis of EU farm policy?

18. *(Wall Street Journal)* In the computer industry, cross-elasticities of demand are quite important. For example, we know that computers and computer software are complements, and the cross-elasticity of demand would tell us how strong that relationship is. Read the "Personal Technology" column in Thursday's Wall Street Journal and find a story that describes pricing of computer hardware or software. Based on what you know about the relationships among different types of computers, among different types of software, and between computers and software, try to predict the effects of the price change. How will the change affect the quantity demanded of the item described? How will it affect the demand for substitutes and complements to that item?

HOMEWORK XPRESS! EXERCISES

These exercises require access to McEachern Homework Xpress! If Homework Xpress! did not come with your book, visit **http://homeworkxpress.swlearning.com** *to purchase.*

1. Sellers of personal computers, PCs, to households quickly notice changes in consumer sensitivity to price because most are made to order. Draw and label a demand curve for PCs that is relatively insensitive to changes in price. Identify an initial price as P, and the quantity that would be demanded at this price as Q. Identify a lower price as P1 and show the quantity that would be demanded as Q1.

   Illustrate the effect of an increase in consumer sensitivity to price by drawing in a new demand curve, D1, that passes through P but is more elastic than D at lower prices. Show the quantity that would be purchased along this demand curve if the price were to fall to P1. Label this as Q2.

2. Most PCs sold to households now come equipped with DVD players. When DVD players were first introduced several years ago, they were very expensive, so the supply of PCs with DVD players was very inelastic. Now that the cost of DVD players has fallen significantly, supply is much more elastic. Draw and label a supply curve for DVD-equipped PCs that is relatively insensitive to changes in price. Identify an initial price as P, and the quantity that would be supplied at this price as Q. Identify a higher price as P1 and show the quantity that would be supplied as Q1.

   Illustrate the effect of an increase in the elasticity of supply by drawing in a new supply curve, S1, that passes through P but is more elastic than S. Show the quantity that would be offered for sale along this supply curve if the price were to rise to P1. Label this as Q2.

3. Innovations in seed corn have dramatically increased the productivity of U.S. corn producers. Nonetheless, revenues for corn farmers do not seem to increase. Draw and label a demand and supply diagram for corn in which both curves are relatively inelastic before the innovations in seed. Show the equilibrium price and quantity. Illustrate the effect on supply of the innovations in corn seed, the effect of a small population increase on the demand for corn, and the resulting effects on equilibrium price and quantity.

4. Government officials are debating whether to impose a 50-cent per pound tax on coffee or carrots. They are wondering which would be more effective at raising revenue. Draw a supply curve that represents the quantity supplied per pound for coffee. Let this supply curve also represent the supply for carrots.

   Draw in a new supply curve representing supply for both with the tax.

   Draw in a relatively inelastic demand curve for coffee, D, and indicate the pretax price and quantity as P and Q.

   Draw in a relatively elastic demand curve, D1, for carrots so that the pretax price and quantity are identical.

   Illustrate the effects of the tax on the price and quantity of carrots, labeling the new values as P1 and Q1.

   Illustrate the effects of the tax on the price and quantity of coffee, labeling the new values as P2 and Q2.

Price Elasticity and Tax Incidence

A contributing factor to the Revolutionary War was a British tax on tea imported by the American Colonies. The tea tax led to the Boston Tea Party, during which colonists dumped tea leaves into Boston Harbor. There was confusion about who would ultimately pay such a tax: Would it be paid by suppliers, demanders, or both? As you will see, tax incidence—that is, who pays a tax—depends on the price elasticities of demand and supply.

Demand Elasticity and Tax Incidence

Panel (a) of Exhibit 13 depicts the market for tea leaves, with demand D and supply S. Before the tax is imposed, the intersection of demand and supply yields a market price of $1.00 per ounce and a market quantity of 10 million ounces per day. Now suppose a tax of $0.20 is imposed on each ounce sold. Recall that the supply curve represents the amount that producers are willing and able to supply at each

---

EXHIBIT 13

Effects of Price Elasticity of Demand on Tax Incidence

The imposition of a $0.20-per-ounce tax on tea shifts the supply curve leftward from S to S_t. In panel (a), which has a less elastic demand curve, the market price rises from $1.00 to $1.15 per ounce and the market quantity falls from 10 million to 9 million ounces. In panel (b), which has a more elastic demand curve, the same tax leads to an increase in price from $1.00 to $1.05; market quantity falls from 10 million to 7 million ounces. The more elastic the demand curve, the more the tax is paid by producers in the form of a lower net-of-tax receipt.

(a) Less elastic demand

(b) More elastic demand

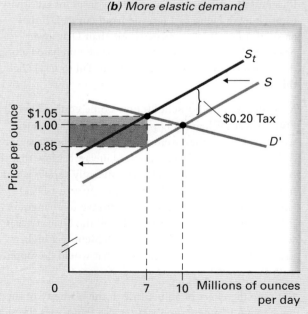

price. Because the government now gets $0.20 for each ounce sold, that amount must be added to the original supply curve to get a supply curve that includes the tax. Thus, the shift of the supply curve from S to S_t reflects the decrease in supply resulting from the tax. *The effect of a tax on tea is to decrease the supply by the amount of the tax.* The demand curve remains the same because nothing happened to demand; only the quantity demanded changes.

The result of the tax in panel (a) is to raise the equilibrium price from $1.00 to $1.15 and to decrease the equilibrium quantity from 10 million to 9 million ounces. As a result of the tax, consumers pay $1.15, or $0.15 more per ounce, and producers receive $0.95 after the tax, or $0.05 less per ounce. Thus, consumers pay $0.15 of the $0.20 tax as a higher price, and producers pay $0.05 as a lower receipt.

The shaded area of panel (a) shows the total tax collected, which equals the tax per ounce of $0.20 times the 9 million ounces sold, for a total of $1.8 million in tax revenue per day. You can see that the original price line at $1 divides the shaded area into two portions—an upper portion showing the tax paid by consumers through a higher price and a lower portion showing the tax paid by producers through a lower net-of-tax receipt.

The same situation is depicted in panel (b) of Exhibit 13, except that demand is more elastic than in the left panel. Consumers in panel (b) cut their quantity demanded more sharply in response to a price change, so producers cannot as easily pass the tax along as a higher price. The tax increases the price by $0.05, to $1.05, and the net-of-tax receipt to suppliers declines by $0.15 to $0.85. Total tax revenue equals $0.20 per ounce times 7 million ounces sold, or $1.4 million per day. Again, the upper rectangle of the shaded area shows the portion of the tax paid by consumers through a higher price, and the lower rectangle shows the portion paid by producers through a lower net-of-tax receipt. The tax is the difference between the amount consumers pay and the amount producers receive.

More generally, as long as the supply curve slopes upward, the more price elastic the demand, the more tax producers pay as a lower net-of-tax receipt and the less consumers bear as a higher price. Also notice that the amount sold decreases more in panel (b) than in panel (a): Other things constant, the total tax revenue declines more when demand is more elastic. Because tax revenue falls as the price elasticity of demand increases, governments around the world tend to tax products with inelastic demand, such as cigarettes, liquor, gasoline, gambling, coffee, tea, and salt.

Supply Elasticity and Tax Incidence

The effect of the elasticity of supply on tax incidence is shown in Exhibit 14. The same demand curve appears in both panels, but the supply curve is more elastic in panel (a). Again we begin with an equilibrium price of $1.00 per ounce and an equilibrium quantity of 10 million ounces of tea leaves per day. Once the sales tax of $0.20 per ounce is imposed, supply decreases in both panels to reflect the tax. Notice that in panel (a), the price rises to $1.15, or $0.15 above the pretax price of $1.00, while in panel (b), the price increases by only $0.05. Thus, more of the tax is passed on to consumers in panel (a), where supply is more elastic. The more easily suppliers can cut production in response to a newly imposed tax, the more of the tax consumers will pay. More generally, as long as the demand curve slopes downward, *the more elastic the supply, the less tax producers pay and the more consumers pay.*

We conclude that *the less elastic the demand and the more elastic the supply, the greater the share of the tax paid by consumers.* The side of the market that's more nimble (that is, more price elastic) in adjusting to a price increase is more able to stick the other side of the market with most of the tax.

EXHIBIT 14   **Effects of Price Elasticity of Supply on Tax Incidence**

The imposition of a $0.20-per-ounce tax on tea shifts leftward both the more elastic supply curve in panel (a) and the less elastic curve of panel (b). In panel (a) the market price rises from $1.00 to $1.15 per ounce. In panel (b), the price rises only to $1.05 per ounce. Thus, the more elastic the supply curve, the more the tax is paid by consumers as a higher price.

(a) More elastic supply

(b) Less elastic supply

APPENDIX QUESTIONS

1. The claim is often made that a tax on a specific good will simply be passed on to consumers. Under what conditions of demand and supply elasticities will this occur? Under what conditions will little of the tax be passed on to consumers?

2. Suppose a tax is imposed on a good with a perfectly elastic supply curve.

   a. Who pays the tax?
   b. Using demand and supply curves, show how much tax is collected.

   c. How would this tax revenue change if the supply curve becomes less elastic?

3. During the 1980s, the U.S. Congress imposed a high sales tax on yachts, figuring that the rich could afford to pay for this luxury. But so many jobs were lost in the boat–building industry that the measure was finally re-pealed. What did Congress get wrong in imposing this luxury tax?

Consumer Choice and Demand

© Gary Houlder/Corbis

Why are newspapers sold in vending machines that allow you to take more than one copy? How much do you eat when you can eat all you want? Why don't restaurants allow doggie bags with their all-you-can-eat specials? What's a cure for spring fever? Why is water cheaper than diamonds even though water is essential to life and diamonds are mere baubles? To answer these and other questions, we take a closer look at consumer demand, a key building block in economics.

You have already learned two reasons why demand curves slope downward. The first is the *substitution effect* of a price change. When the price of a good falls, consumers substitute that now-cheaper good for other goods. The second is the *income effect* of a price change. When the price of a good falls, real incomes increase, boosting consumers' ability to buy more.

Demand is so important that you must learn more about it. This chapter develops the law of demand based on the utility, or satisfaction, derived from consumption. As usual, the assumption is that you and other consumers try to maximize utility, or satisfaction. The point of this chapter is not to teach you how to maximize utility—that comes naturally. But understanding the theory behind your behavior will help you understand the implications of that behavior, making predictions more accurate. Topics discussed include:

- Total and marginal utility
- Law of diminishing marginal utility
- Measuring utility

- Utility-maximizing condition
- Consumer surplus
- Role of time in demand
- Time price of goods

Utility Analysis

Suppose you and a friend dine out together. After dinner, your friend asks how you liked your meal. You wouldn't say, "I liked mine twice as much as you liked yours." Nor would you say, "It deserves a rating of 86 on the U.S. Consumer Satisfaction Index." The utility, or satisfaction, you derive from that meal cannot be compared with another person's experience, nor can you measure your utility objectively. But you might say, "I liked it better than my last meal here" or "I liked it better than campus food." More generally, you can say whether one of your experiences was more satisfying than another. Even if you say nothing about your likes and dislikes, we can draw conclusions by observing your behavior. For example, we can conclude that you prefer apples to oranges if, when the two are priced the same, you always buy apples.

Tastes and Preferences

As was mentioned in Chapter 3, *utility* is the sense of pleasure, or satisfaction, that comes from consumption. Utility is subjective. The utility you derive from consuming a particular good depends on your *tastes*, which are your preferences for different goods and services— your likes and dislikes in consumption. Some goods are extremely appealing to you and others are not. You may not understand, for example, why someone would pay good money for sharks' fin soup, calves' brains, polka music, or martial arts movies. Why are nearly all baby carriages sold in the United States navy blue, whereas they are yellow in Italy and chartreuse in Germany? And why do Australians favor chicken-flavored potato chips and chicken-flavored salt?

Economics in the Movies

Economists actually have little to say about why tastes differ across individuals, across households, across regions, and across countries. *Economists assume simply that tastes are given and are relatively stable—that is, different people may have different tastes, but an individual's tastes are not constantly in flux.* To be sure, tastes for some products do change over time. Here are two examples: (1) during the last two decades, hiking and work boots replaced running shoes as everyday footwear among college students, and (2) Americans began consuming leaner cuts of beef after a 1982 report linked the fat in red meat to a greater risk of cancer. Still, economists believe tastes are stable enough to allow us to examine relationships such as that between price and quantity demanded. If tastes were not relatively stable, then we could not reasonably make the other-things-constant assumption in demand analysis. We could not even draw a demand curve.

The Law of Diminishing Marginal Utility

Suppose it's a hot summer day and you are extremely thirsty after jogging four miles. You pour yourself an eight-ounce glass of ice water. That first glass is wonderful, and it puts a serious dent in your thirst. The next glass is not quite as wonderful, but it is still pretty good. The third one is just fair; and the fourth glass you barely finish. Let's talk about the *utility*, or satisfaction, you get from water.

It's important to distinguish between total utility and marginal utility. **Total utility** is the total satisfaction you derive from consumption. For example, total utility is the total satisfaction you get from consuming four glasses of water. **Marginal utility** is the change in total utility resulting from a one-unit change in consumption of a good. For example, the marginal utility of a third glass of water is the change in total utility resulting from consuming that third glass of water.

Your experience with water reflects an economic law—the **law of diminishing marginal utility.** This law states that the more of a good a person consumes per period, other things constant, the smaller the increase in total utility from additional consumption—that is, the smaller the marginal utility of each additional unit consumed. The marginal utility you derive from each additional glass of water declines as your consumption increases. You enjoy the first glass a lot, but each additional glass provides less and less marginal utility. If forced to drink a fifth glass, you wouldn't enjoy it; your marginal utility would be negative. Diminishing marginal utility is a feature of all consumption. A second foot-long Subway sandwich at one meal, for most people, would provide little or no marginal utility. You might still enjoy a second movie on Friday night, but a third would probably be too much to take.

After a long winter, that first warm day of spring is something special and is the cause of "spring fever." The fever is "cured" by many warm days like the first. By the time August rolls around, you attach much less marginal utility to yet another warm day. For some goods, the drop in marginal utility with additional consumption is more pronounced. A second copy of the same daily newspaper would likely provide no marginal utility (in fact, the design of newspaper vending machines relies on the fact that people will take no more than one).[1] Likewise, a second viewing of the same movie at one sitting usually yields no additional utility. More generally, expressions such as "Been there, done that" and "Same old, same old" conveys the idea that, for many activities, things start to get old after the first time. Restaurants depend on the law of diminishing marginal utility when they hold all-you-can-eat specials—and no doggie bags allowed, because the deal is all you can eat now, not now and the next few days.

Measuring Utility

So far, the description of utility has used such words as *wonderful, good,* and *fair.* The analysis cannot be pushed very far with such subjective language. To predict consumption behavior, we must develop a consistent way of viewing utility.

Units of Utility

Let's go back to the water example. Although there really is no objective way of measuring utility, if pressed, you could be more specific about how much you enjoyed each glass of water. For example, you might say the second glass was half as good as the first, the third was half as good as the second, the fourth was half as good as the third, and you passed up a fifth

---

1. This example appears in Marshall Jevons, *The Fatal Equilibrium* (Cambridge, Mass.: MIT Press, 1985).

HOMEWORK
Xpress!
Ask the Instructor
Video

glass because you expected no positive utility. To get a handle on this, let's assign arbitrary numbers to the amount of utility you derived from each quantity consumed, so the pattern of numbers reflects your expressed level of satisfaction. Let's say the first glass of water provides you with 40 units of utility, the second glass with 20, the third with 10, and the fourth with 5. A fifth glass, if you were forced to drink it, would yield negative utility, in this case, say, −2 units of utility. *Developing numerical values for utility allows us to be more specific about the utility derived from consumption.* If it would help, you could think of units of utility more playfully as thrills, kicks, or jollies—as in, getting your kicks from consumption.

By attaching a numerical measure to utility, we can compare the total utility a particular consumer gets from different goods as well as the marginal utility that consumer gets from additional consumption. Thus, we can employ units of utility to evaluate a consumer's preferences for additional units of a particular good or even additional units of different goods. Note, however, that we cannot compare utility levels across consumers. *Each person has a uniquely subjective utility scale.*

The first column of Exhibit 1 lists possible quantities of water you might consume after running 4 miles on a hot day. The second column presents the total utility derived from that consumption, and the third column shows the marginal utility of each additional glass of water consumed. Recall that marginal utility is the change in total utility from consuming an additional unit of the good. You can see from the second column that total utility increases with each of the first four glasses but by smaller and smaller amounts. The third column shows that the first glass of water yields 40 units of utility, the second glass yields an additional 20 units, and so on. Marginal utility declines after the first glass of water, becoming negative with the fifth glass. *At any level of consumption, marginal utilities sum to total utility.* Total utility is graphed in panel (a) of Exhibit 2. Again, because of diminishing marginal utility, each glass adds less to total utility, so total utility increases for the first four glasses but at a decreasing rate. Marginal utility appears in panel (b).

Utility Maximization in a World Without Scarcity

Economists assume that your purpose for drinking water, as with all consumption, is to *maximize your total utility.* So how much water do you consume? If the price of water is zero, you drink water as long as doing so increases total utility; so you consume four glasses of water. *If a good is free, you increase consumption as long as additional units add utility.* Let's extend the analysis to discuss the consumption of two goods—pizza and video rentals. We will continue to translate the satisfaction you receive from consumption into units of utility. Based on your tastes and preferences, suppose your total utility and marginal utility from con-

EXHIBIT 1	Units of Water Consumed (8-ounce glasses)	Total Utility	Marginal Utility
	0	0	—
Utility You Derive from Water After Jogging Four Miles	1	40	40
	2	60	20
	3	70	10
	4	75	5
	5	73	−2

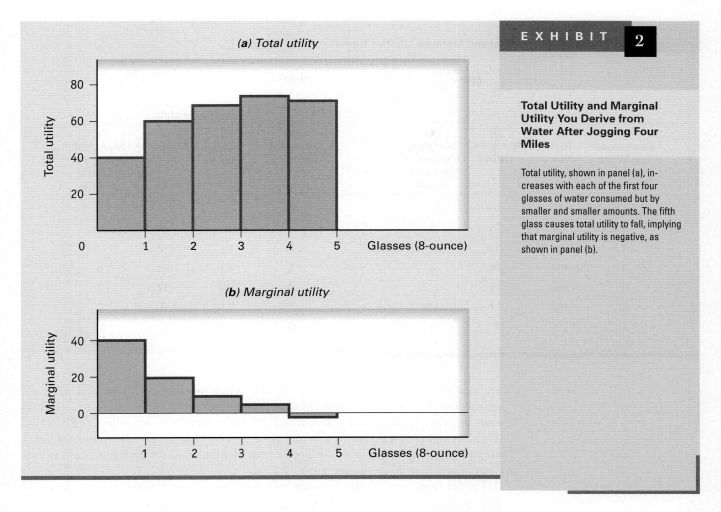

EXHIBIT 2

Total Utility and Marginal Utility You Derive from Water After Jogging Four Miles

Total utility, shown in panel (a), increases with each of the first four glasses of water consumed but by smaller and smaller amounts. The fifth glass causes total utility to fall, implying that marginal utility is negative, as shown in panel (b).

sumption are as presented in Exhibit 3. The first four columns apply to pizza and the second four to video rentals. Please take a little time right now with each column.

Notice from columns (3) and (7) that each good shows diminishing marginal utility. Given this set of preferences, how much of each good would you consume per week? At a zero price, you would increase consumption as long as marginal utility is positive. Thus, you would consume at least the first six pizzas and first six videos because the sixth unit of each good yields marginal utility. Did you ever go to a party where the food and drinks were free to you? How much did you eat and drink? You ate and drank until you didn't want any more—that is, until the marginal utility of each additional bite and each additional sip fell to zero. Your consumption was determined not by prices or income but simply by your tastes.

Utility Maximization in a World of Scarcity

Alas, goods are usually scarce, not free. Suppose the price of a pizza is $8, the rental price of a video is $4, and your after-tax income from a part-time job is $40 per week. Your utility is still based on your tastes, but you now must pay for the goods with your limited income. How do you allocate your income between the two goods to maximize utility? To get the ball rolling, suppose you start off spending your entire budget of $40 on pizza, purchasing five pizzas a week, which yields a total of 142 units of utility. You soon realize that if you

| EXHIBIT | 3 | Total and Marginal Utilities from Pizza and Videos |

Pizza					Video Rentals			
(1) Consumed per Week	(2) Total Utility	(3) Marginal Utility	(4) Marginal Utility per Dollar if $p = \$8$		(5) Viewed per Week	(6) Total Utility	(7) Marginal Utility	(8) Marginal Utility per Dollar if $p = \$4$
0	0	—	—		0	0	—	—
1	56	56	7		1	40	40	10
2	88	32	4		2	68	28	7
3	**112**	**24**	3		3	88	20	5
4	130	18	$2\frac{1}{4}$		**4**	**100**	**12**	3
5	142	12	$1\frac{1}{2}$		5	108	8	2
6	150	8	1		6	114	6	$1\frac{1}{2}$

buy one less pizza, you free up enough money to rent two movies. Would total utility increase? Sure. You give up 12 units of utility, the marginal utility of the fifth pizza, to get 68 units of utility from the first two videos. Total utility thereby increases from 142 to 198. Then you notice that if you reduce purchases to three pizzas, you give up 18 units of utility from the fourth pizza but gain a total of 32 units of utility from the third and fourth videos. This is another utility-increasing move.

Further reductions in pizza, however, would reduce your total utility because you would give up 24 units of utility from the third pizza but gain only 14 units from the fifth and sixth videos. Thus, you quickly find that the utility-maximizing equilibrium combination is three pizzas and four videos per week, for a total utility of 212. This combination involves an outlay of $24 on pizza and $16 on videos. *You are in equilibrium when consuming this combination because any affordable change would reduce your total utility.* Note that you demand fewer pizzas and videos now than when their price was zero.

Utility-Maximizing Conditions

Once equilibrium has been achieved, any change in your consumption pattern will decrease utility. *Once a consumer is in equilibrium, there is no way to increase utility by reallocating the budget.* But we can say more: *In equilibrium, the last dollar spent on each good yields the same marginal utility.* Let's see how this works. Column (4) shows the marginal utility of pizza divided by its price of $8. Column (8) shows the marginal utility of videos divided by its price of $4. The equilibrium choice of three pizzas and four videos exhausts the $40 budget and adds 3 units of utility for the last dollar spent on each good. **Consumer equilibrium** is achieved when the budget is completely spent and the last dollar spent on each good yields the same amount of marginal utility. In equilibrium, pizza's marginal utility divided by its price equals video's marginal utility divided by its price. In short, the consumer gets the same bang per last buck spent on each good. This equality can be expressed as:

CONSUMER EQUILIBRIUM

The condition in which an individual consumer's budget is spent and the last dollar spent on each good yields the same marginal utility; therefore, utility is maximized

$$\frac{MU_p}{p_p} = \frac{MU_v}{p_v}$$

where MU_p is the marginal utility of pizza, p_p is the price of pizza, MU_v is the marginal utility of videos, and p_v is the rental price. The consumer will reallocate spending until the last dollar spent on each product yields the same marginal utility. Although this example considers only two goods, the logic of utility maximization applies to any number of goods.

In equilibrium, higher-priced goods must yield more marginal utility than lower-priced goods—enough additional utility to compensate for their higher price. Because a pizza costs twice as much as a video rental, the marginal utility of the final pizza purchased must, in equilibrium, be twice that of the final video rented. Indeed, the marginal utility of the third pizza, 24, is twice that of the fourth video, 12. Economists do not claim that you consciously equate the ratios of marginal utility to price, but they do claim that you act as if you had made such calculations. *Thus, you decide how much of each good to purchase by considering your tastes, market prices, and your income. Consumers maximize utility by equalizing the marginal utility per dollar of expenditure across goods.* This approach resolved what had been an economic puzzle, as discussed in the following case study.

Water, Water, Everywhere

Centuries ago, economists puzzled over the price of diamonds relative to the price of water. Diamonds are mere baubles—certainly not a necessity of life in any sense. Water is essential to life and has hundreds of valuable uses. Yet diamonds are expensive, while water is cheap. For example, the $10,000 spent on a one-carat diamond could instead buy about 10,000 bottles of water or about 4 million gallons

of municipally supplied water (which typically sells for about 25 cents per 100 gallons). However measured, diamonds are extremely expensive relative to water. For the price of a one-carat diamond, you could buy enough water to last a lifetime.

How can the price of something as useful as water be so much lower than something of such limited use as diamonds? In 1776, Adam Smith discussed what has come to be called the *diamonds-water paradox.* Because water is essential to life, the total utility derived from water greatly exceeds the total utility derived from diamonds. Yet the market value of a good is based not on its total utility but on what consumers are willing and able to pay for an additional unit—that is, on its marginal utility. Because water is so abundant in nature, we consume water to the point where the marginal utility of the last gallon purchased is relatively low. Because diamonds are relatively scarce compared to water, the marginal utility of the last diamond purchased is relatively high. Thus, water is cheap and diamonds expensive. As Ben Franklin said "We will only know the worth of water when the well is dry."

Speaking of water, sales of bottled water doubled in the United States between 1997 and 2002—growing faster than any other beverage category—creating an $8.5 billion industry. The United States offers the world's largest market for bottled water—importing water from places such as Italy, France, Sweden, Wales, even Fiji. "Water bars" in Boston, New York, and Los Angeles offer bottled water as the main attraction.

Why would consumers pay a premium for bottled water when they can drink from the tap for virtually nothing? First, many people do not view the two as good substitutes. Some people have concerns about the safety of tap water, and they consider bottled water a healthy alternative (about half those surveyed in a Gallup Poll said they won't drink water straight from the tap). Second, even those who drink tap water find bottled water a convenient option away from home. According to the theory of utility maximization, people who buy bottled water apparently feel the additional benefit offsets the additional cost.

Bottled-water sales threaten the soft-drink industry. Fast food restaurants now offer bottled water as a healthy alternative to soft drinks. McDonald's, for example, is test marketing a "Go Active Happy Meal" that includes a bottle of water. But if you can't fight 'em, join 'em: Pepsi's Aquafina is the top-selling U.S. brand of bottled water, and Coke also has its own brand, Dasani.

Sources: "Bottled Water Continues Double-Digit Growth," *Beverage Aisle*, 15 August 2003; and "Wendy's Joins Rival Chains in Offering Healthier Foods," *Wall Street Journal*, 24 September 2003. The Definitive Bottled Water site is http://www.bottledwaterweb.com/ and the International Bottled Water Association site is http://www.bottledwater.org/.

The Law of Demand and Marginal Utility

How does utility analysis relate to your demand for pizza? The previous analysis yields a single point on your demand curve for pizza: At a price of $8, you demand three pizzas per week. This point is based on income of $40 per week, a price of $4 per video, and your tastes reflected by the utility tables in Exhibit 3. This single point, in itself, offers no clue about the shape of your demand curve for pizza. To generate another point, let's see what happens to quantity demanded if the price of pizza changes, while keeping other things constant (such as tastes, income, and the price of video rentals). Suppose the price of a pizza drops from $8 to $6.

Exhibit 4 is the same as Exhibit 3, except the price per pizza is $6. Your original choice was three pizzas and four video rentals. At that combination and with the price of pizza now $6, the marginal utility per dollar expended on the third pizza is 4, but the marginal utility per dollar on the fourth video remains at 3. The marginal utilities of the last dollar spent on each good are no longer equal. What's more, the original combination leaves $6 unspent. So you could still buy your original combination but have $6 to spend (this, incidentally, shows the income effect of a lower price of pizza). You can increase your utility by consuming a different bundle. Take a moment now to see if you can figure out what the new equilibrium should be.

In light of your utility schedules in Exhibit 4, you would increase your consumption to four pizzas per week. This strategy exhausts your budget and equates the marginal utilities of the last dollar expended on each good. Your video rentals remain the same (although they could have changed due to the income effect of the price change). But as your consumption increases to four pizzas, the marginal utility of the fourth pizza, 18, divided by the price of $6 yields 3 units of utility per dollar of expenditure, which is the same as for the fourth video. You are in equilibrium once again. Your total utility increases by the 18 units you derive from the fourth pizza. Thus, you are clearly better off as a result of the price decrease.

We now have a second point on your demand curve for pizza—if the price of pizza is $6, your quantity demanded is four pizzas. The two points are presented as *a* and *b* in Exhibit 5. We could continue to change the price of pizza and thereby generate additional points on the demand curve, but you can get some idea of the demand curve's downward slope from these two points. The shape of the demand curve for pizza conforms to our expectations based on the law of demand: Price and quantity demanded are inversely related.

EXHIBIT 4				**Total and Marginal Utilities from Pizza and Videos After the Price of Pizza Decreases from \$8 to \$6 Each**			

Pizza				Video Rentals			
(1) Consumed per Week	(2) Total Utility	(3) Marginal Utility	(4) Marginal Utility per Dollar if $p = \$6$	(5) Viewed per Week	(6) Total Utility	(7) Marginal Utility	(8) Marginal Utility per Dollar if $p = \$4$
0	0	—	—	0	0	—	—
1	56	56	9⅓	1	40	40	10
2	88	32	5⅓	2	68	28	7
3	112	24	4	3	88	20	5
4	**130**	**18**	**3**	**4**	**100**	**12**	**3**
5	142	12	2	5	108	8	2
6	150	8	1⅓	6	114	6	1½

EXHIBIT 5

Demand for Pizza Generated from Marginal Utility

At a price of \$8 per pizza, the consumer is in equilibrium when consuming three pizzas (point *a*). Marginal utility per dollar is the same for all goods consumed. If the price falls to \$6, the consumer will increase consumption to four pizzas (point *b*). Points *a* and *b* are two points on this consumer's demand curve for pizza.

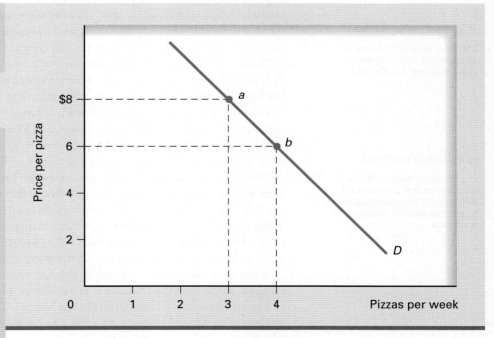

(Try estimating the price elasticity of demand between points *a* and *b*. Hint: What does total spending on pizza tell you?)

We have gone to some length to see how you (or any consumer) maximizes utility. Given prices and your income, your tastes and preferences naturally guide you to the most preferred bundle. You are not even conscious of your behavior. The urge to maximize utility is like the force of gravity—both work whether or not you understand them. Even animal behavior seems consistent with the law of demand. Wolves, for example, exhibit no territorial concerns when game is plentiful. But when game becomes scarce, wolves carefully mark their territory and defend it against intruders. Thus, wolves appear to value game more when it is scarce.

Now that you have some idea of utility, let's consider an application of utility analysis.

Consumer Surplus

In our earlier example, total utility increased when the price of pizza fell from $8 to $6. In this section, we take a closer look at how consumers benefit from a lower price. Suppose your demand for foot-long Subway sandwiches is as shown in Exhibit 6. Recall that in constructing an individual's demand curve, we hold tastes, income, and the prices of related goods constant. Only the price varies. At a price of $8 or above, you find that the marginal utility of other goods that you could buy for $8 is higher than the marginal utility of a Subway. Consequently, you buy no Subways. At a price of $7, you are willing and able to buy one per month, so the marginal utility of that first Subway exceeds the marginal utility you expected from spending that $7 on your best alternative—say, a movie ticket. A price of $6 prompts you to buy two Subways a month. The second is worth at least $6 to you. At a price of $5, you buy three Subways, and at $4, you buy four. *In each case, the value of the last Subway purchased must at least equal the price; otherwise, you wouldn't buy it.* Along the demand curve, therefore, the price reflects your **marginal valuation** of the good, or the dollar value of the marginal utility derived from consuming each additional unit.

MARGINAL VALUATION

The dollar value of the marginal utility derived from consuming each additional unit of a good

Notice that if the price is $4, you can purchase each of the four Subways for $4 each, even though you would have been willing to pay more than $4 for each of the first three Subways. The first sandwich provides marginal utility that you valued at $7; the second you valued at $6; and the third you valued at $5. In fact, if you had to, you would have been willing to pay $7 for the first, $6 for the second, and $5 for the third. The dollar value of the total utility of the first four sandwiches is $7 + $6 + $5 + $4 = $22 per month. But when the price is $4, you get all four for $16. Thus, a price of $4 confers a **consumer surplus,** or a consumer bonus, equal to the difference between the maximum amount you would have been willing to pay ($22) rather than go without Subways altogether and what you actually pay ($16). When the price is $4, your consumer surplus is $6, as approximated by the six darker shaded blocks in Exhibit 6. Consumer surplus equals the value of the total utility you receive from consuming the sandwiches minus your total spending on them. Consumer surplus is reflected by the area under the demand curve but above the price.

CONSUMER SURPLUS

The difference between the maximum amount that a consumer is willing to pay for a given quantity of a good and what the consumer actually pays

If the price falls to $3, you purchase five Subways a month. Apparently, you feel that the marginal utility from the fifth one is worth at least $3. The lower price means that you get all five for $3 each, even though all but the fifth are worth more to you than $3. Your consumer surplus when the price is $3 is the value of the total utility conferred by the first five, which is $7 + $6 + $5 + $4 + $3 = $25, minus your cost, which is $3 × 5 = $15. Thus, your consumer surplus totals $25 − $15 = $10, as indicated by both the dark and the light shaded blocks in Exhibit 6. So if the price declines to $3, your consumer surplus increases by $4, as reflected by the four lighter-shaded blocks in Exhibit 6. You can see how consumers benefit from lower prices.

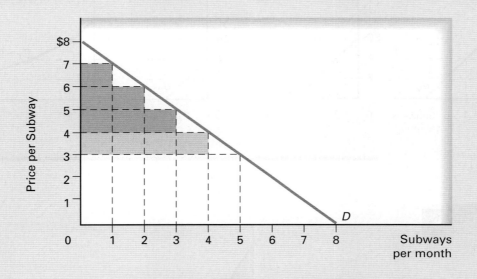

EXHIBIT 6

HOMEWORK Xpress!
Graphing

Consumer Surplus from Subway Sandwiches

At a given quantity of Subway sandwiches, the height of the demand curve shows the value of the last one purchased. The area under the demand curve for a specific quantity shows the total value a consumer attaches to that quantity. At a price of $4, the consumer purchases four Subways. The first one is valued at $7, the second at $6, the third at $5, and the fourth at $4. The consumer values four at $22. Because the consumer pays $4 per Subway, all four can be purchased for $16. The difference between what the consumer would have been willing to pay ($22) and what the consumer actually pays ($16) is called consumer surplus. When the price is $4, the consumer surplus is $6, as represented by the dark shaded area under the demand curve above $4. When the price of Subways falls to $3, consumer surplus increases by $4, as reflected by the lighter shaded area.

Market Demand and Consumer Surplus

Let's talk now about the market demand for a good, assuming the market consists of you and two other consumers. *The market demand curve is simply the horizontal sum of the individual demand curves for all consumers in the market.* Exhibit 7 shows how the demand curves for three consumers in the market for Subway sandwiches sum horizontally to yield the market demand. At a price of $4, for example, you demand four Subways per month, Brittany demands two, and Chris demands none. The market demand at a price of $4 is therefore six sandwiches. At a price of $2, you demand six per month, Brittany four, and Chris two, for a market demand of 12. *The market demand curve shows the total quantity demanded per period by all consumers at various prices.* Consumer surplus can be used to examine market demand as well as individual demand. *At a given price, consumer surplus for the market is the difference between the most consumers are willing to pay for that quantity and the total amount they do pay.*

Instead of just three consumers in the market, suppose there are many. Exhibit 8 presents market demand for a good with millions of consumers. If the price is $2 per unit, each person adjusts his or her quantity demanded until the marginal valuation of the last unit purchased equals $2. But each consumer gets to buy all other units for $2 each as well. In Exhibit 8, the dark shading, bounded above by the demand curve and below by the price of $2, depicts the consumer surplus when the price is $2. The light shading shows the increase

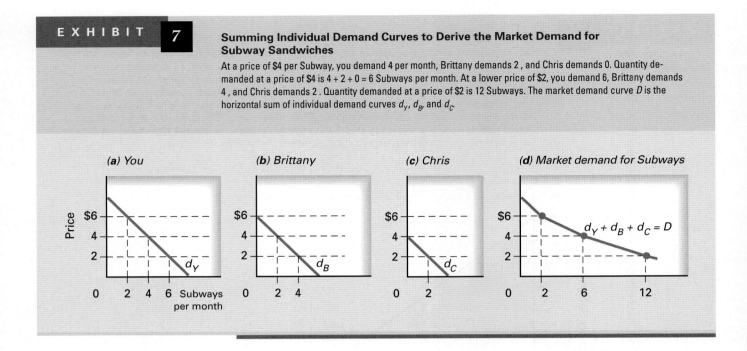

EXHIBIT 7

Summing Individual Demand Curves to Derive the Market Demand for Subway Sandwiches

At a price of $4 per Subway, you demand 4 per month, Brittany demands 2, and Chris demands 0. Quantity demanded at a price of $4 is 4 + 2 + 0 = 6 Subways per month. At a lower price of $2, you demand 6, Brittany demands 4, and Chris demands 2. Quantity demanded at a price of $2 is 12 Subways. The market demand curve D is the horizontal sum of individual demand curves d_Y, d_B, and d_C.

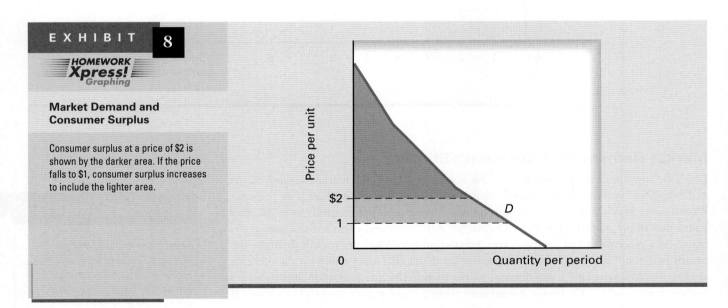

EXHIBIT 8

HOMEWORK Xpress! Graphing

Market Demand and Consumer Surplus

Consumer surplus at a price of $2 is shown by the darker area. If the price falls to $1, consumer surplus increases to include the lighter area.

in consumer surplus if the price drops to $1. Notice that if this good were given away, the consumer surplus would not be significantly greater than when the price is $1.

Consumer surplus is the net benefit consumers get from market exchange. It can be used to measure economic welfare and to compare the effects of different market structures, different tax structures, and different public expenditure programs, such as for medical care, as discussed in the following case study.

The Marginal Value of Free Medical Care

Certain Americans, such as the elderly and those on welfare, receive government-subsidized medical care. State and federal taxpayers spend over $420 billion a year providing medical care to 75 million Medicare and Medicaid recipients, for an average annual cost of about $5,600 per beneficiary. The dollar cost to most beneficiaries is usually little or nothing. The problem with giving something away is that beneficiaries consume it to the point where their marginal valuation is zero, although the marginal cost to taxpayers can be sizeable.

© Ed Kashi/Corbis

Case Study

Public Policy

*e*Activity
This case study points out that patients have little incentive to monitor physician behavior when they do not pay the bill. In an attempt to control costs, Medicare reduces the reimbursement rate for services provided by physicians. How do you suppose physicians respond? Auditors with the Health Care Financing Administration (HCFA) examined physician behavior and found that they increase the volume and intensity of work in response to declining prices to maintain revenue. HCFA's easy-to-read report on physician response, which includes several real examples, can be found at http://www.cms.hhs.gov/statistics/actuary/physicianresponse/.

This is not to say that beneficiaries derive no benefit from free medical care. Although they may attach little or no value to the final unit, they likely derive a substantial consumer surplus from all the other units they consume. For example, suppose that Exhibit 8 represents the demand for medical care by Medicaid beneficiaries. Because the price to them is zero, they consume to the point where the demand curve intersects the horizontal axis, where their marginal valuation is zero. Their consumer surplus is the entire area under the demand curve.

One way to reduce the cost to taxpayers of such programs without significantly harming beneficiaries is to charge a small amount—say, $1 per physician visit. Beneficiaries would eliminate visits they value less than $1. This practice would yield significant savings to taxpayers but would still leave beneficiaries with excellent health care and a considerable consumer surplus (measured in Exhibit 8 as the area under the demand curve but above the $1 price). As a case in point, one Medicaid experiment in California required some beneficiaries to pay $1 per visit for their first two office visits per month (after two visits, the price of additional visits reverted to zero). A control group continued to receive free medical care. The $1 charge reduced office visits by 8 percent compared to the control group.

Medical care, like other goods and services, is also sensitive to its time cost (a topic discussed in the next section). For example, a 10 percent increase in the average travel time to a free outpatient clinic reduced visits by 10 percent. Similarly, when the relocation of a free clinic at one college campus increased students' walking time by 10 minutes, visits dropped 40 percent.

Another problem with giving something away is that beneficiaries are less vigilant about getting honest value, which may increase the possibility of fraud and abuse. According to a study by the U.S. General Accounting Office, about 1 in 7 Medicare dollars is wasted because of padded bills and fake claims that recipients would not tolerate if they paid their own bills. For example, in one case, the government was billed for round-the-clock cardiac monitoring when the patient was in fact monitored only 30 minutes a month.

These findings do not mean that certain groups do not deserve low-cost medical care. The point is that when something is free, people consume it until their marginal valuation is zero and they pay less attention to getting honest value. Some Medicare beneficiaries, for example, visit one or more medical specialists most days of the week. Does all this medical attention improve their health care? Maybe not. Researchers have found no apparent medical benefit from so many visits. As one doctor told the *New York Times*, "The system is broken. I'm not being a mean ogre, but when you give something away for free, there is nothing to keep utilization down."[2] Even a modest money cost or time cost would reduce utilization, yet would still leave beneficiaries with quality health care and a substantial consumer surplus.

Sources: Elliot Fisher, et al., "The Implications of Regional Variation in Medicare Spending," *Annals of Internal Medicine*, 18 February 2003; Gina Kolata, "Patients in Florida Lining Up for All That Medicare Covers," *New York Times*, 13 September 2003; and Steven Rhoads, "Marginalism," in *The Fortune Encyclopedia of Economics*, edited by D. R. Henderson (New York: Warner Books, 1993), pp. 31–33. For more on Medicare and Medicaid, go to the Centers for Medicare & Medicaid Services site at http://www.cms.hhs.gov/.

The Role of Time in Demand

Because consumption does not occur instantaneously, time also plays an important role in demand analysis. Consumption takes time and, as Ben Franklin said, time is money—time has a positive value for most people. Consequently, the cost of consumption has two components: the *money price* of the good and the *time price* of the good. Goods are demanded because of the benefits they offer. Thus, you may be willing to pay more for medicine that works faster. Similarly, it is not the microwave oven, personal computer, or airline trip that you value but the benefits they provide. Other things constant, you are willing to pay more to get the same benefit in less time, as with faster ovens, computers, and airline trips. Likewise, you are willing to pay more for seedless grapes, seedless oranges, and seedless watermelon.

Your willingness to pay a premium for time-saving goods and services depends on the opportunity cost of your time. Differences in the value of time among consumers help explain differences in the consumption patterns observed in the economy. For example, a retired couple has more leisure time than a working couple and may clip coupons and search the newspapers for bargains, sometimes going from store to store for particular grocery items on sale that week. The working couple tends to ignore the coupons and sales and will eat out more often or buy more at convenience stores, where they pay extra for the "convenience." The retired couple will be more inclined to drive across the country on vacation, whereas the working couple will fly to a vacation destination.

Just inside the gates at Disneyland, Disney World, and Universal Studios are signs posting the waiting times of each attraction and ride. At that point, the dollar cost of admission has already been paid, so the marginal dollar cost of each ride and attraction is zero. The waiting times offer a menu of the marginal *time costs* of each ride or attraction. Incidentally, people who are willing to pay up to $55 an hour at Disney World and $60 an hour at Disneyland (plus the price of admission) until recently could take VIP tours that bypass the lines.[3] How much would you pay to avoid the lines?

Differences in the opportunity cost of time among consumers shape consumption patterns and add another dimension to our analysis of demand.

Conclusion

This chapter has analyzed consumer choice by focusing on utility, or satisfaction. We assumed that utility could be measured in some systematic way for a particular individual, even though utility could not be compared across individuals. The ultimate goal is to predict how consumer choice is affected by such variables as a change in price. We judge a theory not by the realism of its assumptions but by the accuracy of its predictions. Based on this criterion, the theory of consumer choice presented in this chapter has proven to be quite useful.

2. As reported by Gina Kolata, "Patients in Florida Lining Up for All That Medicare Covers," *New York Times*, 13 September 2003.
3. Nancy Keates, "Tourists Learn How to Mouse Around Disney's Long Lines," *Wall Street Journal*, 27 March 1998.

N e t Bookmark

Go to http://www.freechess.org, where you can play chess online with people around the world. (There are many other similar sites, just do a search in Yahoo! or Google.) Suppose you play 50 games of chess in the next two years in each of two settings. In setting X, you always play chess with the same person, and in setting Y, you always play each game with a different person. In which setting, X or Y, do you think the marginal utility of the 40th game of chess will be higher? What can you conclude about the marginal utility of playing chess?

Again, to maximize utility, you or any other consumer need not understand the material presented in this chapter. Economists assume that rational consumers seek to maximize utility naturally and instinctively. In this chapter, we simply tried to analyze that process. A more general approach to consumer choice, one that does not require a specific measure of utility, is developed in the appendix to this chapter.

SUMMARY

1. Utility is the sense of pleasure or satisfaction that comes from consumption; it is the want-satisfying power of goods, services, and activities. The utility you receive from consuming a particular good depends on your tastes. The law of diminishing marginal utility says that the more of a particular good consumed per period, other things constant, the smaller the increase in total utility received from each additional unit consumed. The total utility derived from consuming a good is the sum of the marginal utilities derived from consuming each additional unit of the good.

2. Utility is subjective. Each consumer makes a personal assessment of the want-satisfying power of consumption. By translating an individual's subjective measure of satisfaction into units of utility, we can predict the quantity demanded at a given price as well as the effect of a change in price on quantity demanded.

3. The consumer's objective is to maximize utility within the limits imposed by income and prices. In a world without scarcity, utility is maximized by consuming each good until its marginal utility reaches zero. In the real world—a

world shaped by scarcity as reflected by prices—utility is maximized when the budget is spent and the marginal utility for the final unit consumed divided by that good's price is identical for each different good.

4. Utility analysis can be used to construct an individual consumer's demand curve. By changing the price and observing the change in consumption, we can generate points along a demand curve.

5. When the price of a good declines, other things constant, a consumer is able to buy all units of the good at the lower price. Consumers typically receive a surplus, or a bonus, from consumption, and this surplus increases as the price declines. Consumer surplus is the difference between the maximum amount consumers would pay for a given quantity of the good and the amount they actually pay.

6. There are two components to the cost of consumption: the money price of the good and the time price of the good. People are willing to pay a higher money price for goods and services that save time.

QUESTIONS FOR REVIEW

1. *(Law of Diminishing Marginal Utility)* Some restaurants offer "all you can eat" meals. How is this practice related to diminishing marginal utility? What restrictions must the restaurant impose on the customer to make a profit?

2. *(Law of Diminishing Marginal Utility)* Complete each of the following sentences:

   a. Your tastes determine the _____ you derive from consuming a particular good.
   b. _____ utility is the change in _____ utility resulting from a _____ change in the consumption of a good.
   c. As long as marginal utility is positive, total utility is _____.

   d. The law of diminishing marginal utility states that as an individual consumes more of a good during a given time period, other things constant, total utility _____.

3. *(Marginal Utility)* Is it possible for marginal utility to be negative while total utility is positive? If yes, under what circumstances is it possible?

4. *(Utility-Maximizing Conditions)* For a particular consumer, the marginal utility of cookies equals the marginal utility of candy. If the price of a cookie is less than the price of candy, is the consumer in equilibrium? Why or why not? If not, what should the consumer do to attain equilibrium?

5. *(Utility-Maximizing Conditions)* Suppose that marginal utility of Good $X = 100$, the price of X is $10 per unit, and the price of Y is $5 per unit. Assuming that the consumer is in equilibrium and is consuming both X and Y, what must the marginal utility of Y be?

6. *(Utility-Maximizing Conditions)* Suppose that the price of X is twice the price of Y. You are a utility maximizer who allocates your budget between the two goods. What must be true about the equilibrium relationship between the marginal utility levels of the last unit consumed of each good? What must be true about the equilibrium relationship between the marginal utility levels of the last dollar spent on each good?

7. *(Consumer Surplus)* The height of the demand curve at a given quantity reflects the marginal valuation of the last unit of that good consumed. For a normal good, an increase in income shifts the demand curve to the right and therefore increases its height at any quantity. Does this mean that consumers get greater marginal utility from each unit of this good than they did before? Explain.

8. *(Consumer Surplus)* Suppose supply of a good is perfectly elastic at a price of $5. The market demand curve for this good is linear, with zero quantity demanded at a price of $25. Given that the slope of this linear demand curve is -0.25, draw a supply and demand graph to illustrate the consumer surplus that occurs when the market is in equilibrium.

9. *(**C a s e Study:** The Marginal Value of Free Medical Care)* Medicare recipients pay a monthly premium for coverage, must meet an annual deductible, and have a co-payment for doctors' office visits. President George W. Bush introduced some coverage of prescription medications (prior to that, there was none). What impact would an increase in the monthly premium have on their consumer surplus? What would be the impact of a reduction in co-payments? What is the impact on consumer surplus of offering some coverage for prescription medication?

10. *(Role of Time in Demand)* In many amusement parks, you pay an admission fee to the park but you do not need to pay for individual rides. How do people choose which rides to go on?

11. *(**C a s e Study:** Water, Water Everywhere)* What is the diamonds–water paradox, and how is it explained? Use the same reasoning to explain why bottled water costs so much more than tap water.

PROBLEMS AND EXERCISES

12. *(Utility Maximization)* The following tables illustrate Eileen's utilities from watching first-run movies in a theater and from renting movies from a video store. Suppose that she has a monthly movie budget of $36, each movie ticket costs $6, and each video rental costs $3.

Movies in a Theater

Q	TU	MU	MU/P
0	0	——	——
1	200	——	——
2	290	——	——
3	370	——	——
4	440	——	——
5	500	——	——
6	550	——	——
7	590	——	——

Movies from a Video Store

Q	TU	MU	MU/P
0	0	——	——
1	250	——	——
2	295	——	——
3	335	——	——
4	370	——	——
5	400	——	——
6	425	——	——
—	——	——	——

a. Complete the tables.

b. Do these tables show that Eileen's preferences obey the law of diminishing marginal utility? Explain your answer.

c. How much of each good will Eileen consume in equilibrium?

d. Suppose the prices of both types of movies drop to $1 while Eileen's movie budget shrinks to $10. How much of each good will she consume in equilibrium?

13. *(Utility Maximization)* Suppose that a consumer has a choice between two goods, X and Y. If the price of X is $2 and the price of Y is $3, how much of X and Y will the consumer purchase, given an income of $17? Use the following information about marginal utility:

Units	MU_X	MU_Y
1	10	5
2	8	4
3	2	3
4	2	2
5	1	2

14. *(The Law of Demand and Marginal Utility)* Daniel allocates his budget of $24 per week among three goods. Use the following table of marginal utilities for good A, good B, and good C to answer the questions below:

Q_A	MU_A	Q_B	MU_B	Q_C	MU_C
1	50	1	75	1	25
2	40	2	60	2	20
3	30	3	40	3	15
4	20	4	30	4	10
5	15	5	20	5	7.5

a. If the price of A is $2, the price of B is $3, and the price of C is $1, how much of each will Daniel purchase in equilibrium?

b. If the price of A rises to $4 while other prices and Daniel's budget remain unchanged, how much of each will he purchase in equilibrium?

c. Using the information from parts (a) and (b), draw the demand curve for good A. Be sure to indicate the price and quantity demanded for each point on the curve.

15. *(Consumer Surplus)* Suppose the linear demand curve for shirts slopes downward and that consumers buy 500 shirts per year when the price is $30 and 1,000 shirts per year when the price is $25.

a. Compared to the prices of $30 and $25, what can you say about the marginal valuation that consumers place on the 300th shirt, the 700th shirt, and the 1,200th shirt they might buy each year?

b. With diminishing marginal utility, are consumers deriving any consumer surplus if the price is $25 per shirt? Explain.

c. Use a market demand curve to illustrate the change in consumer surplus if the price drops from $30 to $25.

EXPERIENTIAL EXERCISES

16. *(Consumer Surplus)* Access a copy of "Creating Value and Destroying Profit? Three Measures of Information Technology's Contributions," by Loren Hitt and Erik Brynjolfsson at http://ccs.mit.edu/papers/CCSWP183.html. Use your browser's Edit/Find function to search for the words *consumer surplus* in this paper. How do Hitt and Brynjolfsson use the concept of consumer surplus to measure the value of information technology?

17. **(C a s e S t u d y:** The Marginal Value of Free Medical Care) To learn more about economic issues related to health care, visit McEachern Xtra!, http://mceachernxtra.swlearning.com, go to EconDebate Online, and find the debate "Is there a need for health-care reform?" in the Government and the Economics section. What are some economic issues related to health-care reform?

18. *(The Role of Time in Demand)* To learn more about the economics of consumption, read Jane Katz's "The Joy of Consumption: We Are What We Buy," in the Federal Reserve Bank of Boston's *Regional Review* at http://www.bos.frb.org/nerr/rr1997/winter/katz97_1/htm. What evidence does Katz cite about how the rising value of time has affected consumer spending patterns?

19. *(Wall Street Journal)* In this chapter, you learned that the cost of consumption involves both a money price and a time price. Turn to the Wednesday *Wall Street Journal* and find the "Work and Family" column. See if you can find some examples of changes in new goods, services, government policies, or institutional arrangements that work by reducing the time price of a product. How do you think that change will affect the demand for the product? Will demand for any related products be affected?

*These exercises require access to McEachern Homework Xpress! If Homework Xpress! did not come with your book, visit **http://homeworkxpress.swlearning.com** to purchase.*

1. Would another topping on a pizza always increase the utility derived from eating it? Consider Maria's total utility curve for pizza toppings as shown in the table. Find the marginal utility for each additional topping and draw a diagram indicating the corresponding marginal utility curve.

Number of toppings	Total utility
0	0
1	10
2	22
3	32
4	39
5	43
6	42

2. Demand curves for movie tickets per month for Rene, Eddie, and Mary are shown in the table. Sketch the market demand curves for movie tickets for each of them, labeling them as D1, D2, and D3, respectively. Find the market demand when the market consists only of these three people. Label the market demand curve D4.

Price per movie ticket	Rene	Eddie	Mary
$10	1	0	0
9	2	0	0
7	3	0	1
6	4	1	2
5	5	2	3

Indifference Curves and Utility Maximization

The approach used in the body of the chapter, marginal utility analysis, requires some numerical measure of utility to determine optimal consumption. Economists have developed another, more general, approach to consumer behavior, one that does not rely on a numerical measure of utility. All this new approach requires is that consumers be able to indicate their preferences for various combinations of goods. For example, the consumer should be able to say whether combination A is preferred to combination B, combination B is preferred to combination A, or both combinations are equally preferred. This approach is more general and more flexible than the one developed in the body of the chapter. But it's also a little more complicated.

Consumer Preferences

An **indifference curve** shows all combinations of goods that provide the consumer with the same satisfaction, or the same utility. Thus, the consumer finds all combinations on a curve equally preferred. Because each bundle of goods yields the same level of utility, the consumer is *indifferent* about which combination is actually consumed. We can best understand the use of indifference curves through the following example.

In reality, consumers choose among thousands of goods and services, but to keep the analysis manageable, suppose only two goods are available: pizzas and video rentals. In Exhibit 9, the horizontal axis measures the number of pizzas you buy per week, and the vertical axis measures the number of videos you rent per week. Point *a*, for example, consists of one pizza and eight video rentals. Suppose you are given a choice of combination *a* or some combination with more pizza. The question is: Holding your total utility constant, how many video rentals would you be willing to give up to get a second pizza? As you can see, in moving from point *a* to point *b*, you are willing to give up four videos to get a second pizza. Total utility is the same at points *a* and *b*. The marginal utility of that additional pizza per week is just sufficient to compensate you for the utility lost from decreasing your videos by four movies per week. Thus, at point *b*, you are eating two pizzas and watching four movies a week.

In moving from point *b* to point *c*, again total utility is constant; you are now willing to give up only one video for another pizza. At point *c*, your consumption bundle consists of three pizzas and three videos. Once at point *c*, you are willing to give up another video only if you get two more pizzas in return. Combination *d*, therefore, consists of five pizzas and two videos.

Points *a*, *b*, *c*, and *d* connect to form indifference curve *I*, which represents possible combinations of pizza and video rentals that would provide you the same level of total utility. Because points on the curve offer the same total utility, you are indifferent about which you choose—hence the name *indifference curve*. Note that we don't know, nor do we need to know, the value you attach to the utility reflected by the

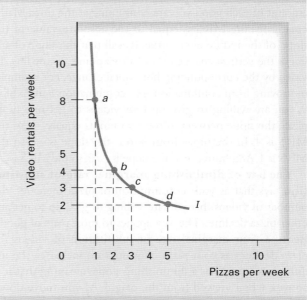

EXHIBIT 9   **An Indifference Curve**

An indifference curve, such as *I*, shows all combinations of two goods that provide a consumer with the same total utility. Points *a* through *d* depict four such combinations. Indifference curves have negative slopes and are convex to the origin.

indifference curve—that is, there is no particular number attached to the total utility along *I. Combinations of goods along an indifference curve reflect some constant, though unspecified, level of total utility.* So unlike the approach adopted in the body of the chapter, indifference curves need not be measured in units of utility.

For you to remain indifferent among consumption combinations, the increase in your utility from eating more pizza must just offset the decrease in your utility from watching fewer videos. Thus, along an indifference curve, there is an inverse relationship between the quantity of one good consumed and the quantity of another consumed. Because of this inverse relationship, *indifference curves slope downward.*

Indifference curves are also *convex to the origin,* which means they are bowed inward toward the origin. The curve gets flatter as you move down it. Here's why. Your willingness to substitute pizza for videos depends on how much of each you already consume. At combination *a,* for example, you watch eight videos and eat only one pizza a week. Because there are many videos relative to pizza, you are willing to give up four movies to get another pizza. Once you reach point *b,* your pizza consumption has doubled, so you are not quite so willing to give up movies to get a third pizza. In fact, you will forgo only one video to get one more pizza. This moves you from point *b* to point *c.*

The **marginal rate of substitution,** or **MRS,** between pizza and videos indicates the number of videos that you are willing to give up to get one more pizza, neither gaining nor losing utility in the process. Because the MRS measures your willingness to trade videos for pizza, it depends on the amount of each good you are consuming at the time. Mathematically, the MRS is equal to the absolute value of the slope of the indifference curve. Recall that the slope of any line is the vertical change between two points on the line divided by the corresponding horizontal change. For example, in moving from combination *a* to combination *b* in Exhibit 9, you are willing to give up four videos to get one more pizza; the slope between those two points equals −4, so the MRS is 4. In the move from *b* to *c,* the slope is −1, so the MRS is 1. And from *c* to *d,* the slope is −¹/₂?, so the MRS is ¹/₂.

The **law of diminishing marginal rate of substitution** says that as your consumption of pizza increases, the number of videos that you are willing to give up to get another pizza declines. This law applies to most pairs of goods. Because your marginal rate of substitution of videos for pizza declines as your pizza consumption increases, the indifference curve has a diminishing slope, meaning that it is convex when viewed from the origin. As you move down the indifference curve, your pizza consumption increases, so

the marginal utility of additional pizza decreases. Conversely, the number of movies you rent decreases, so the marginal utility of movies increases. Thus, in moving down the indifference curve, you require more pizza to offset the loss of each video.

We have focused on a single indifference curve, which indicates some constant but unspecified level of utility. We can use the same approach to generate a series of indifference curves, called an **indifference map.** An indifference map is a graphical representation of a consumer's tastes. Each curve reflects a different level of utility. Part of such a map is shown in Exhibit 10, where indifference curves for a particular consumer, in this case you, are labeled I_1, I_2, I_3, and I_4. Each consumer has a unique indifference map based on his or her preferences.

Because both goods yield marginal utility, you, the consumer, prefer more of each, rather than less. Curves farther from the origin represent greater consumption levels and, therefore, higher levels of utility. The utility level along I_2 is higher than that along I_1. I_3 reflects a higher level of utility

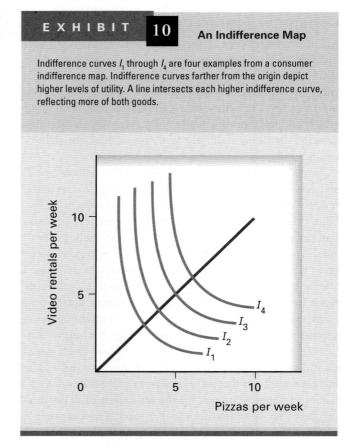

E X H I B I T   10   An Indifference Map

Indifference curves I_1 through I_4 are four examples from a consumer indifference map. Indifference curves farther from the origin depict higher levels of utility. A line intersects each higher indifference curve, reflecting more of both goods.

than I_2, and so on. We can show this best by drawing a line from the origin and following it to higher indifference curves. Such a line has been included in Exhibit 10. By following that line to higher and higher indifference curves, you can see that the combination on each successive indifference curve reflects greater amounts of *both* goods. Because you value both goods, the greater amounts of each reflected on higher indifference curves represent higher levels of utility.

Indifference curves in a consumer's indifference map do not intersect. Exhibit 11 shows why. If indifference curves did cross, as at point *i*, then every point on indifference curve *I* and every point on curve *I'* would have to reflect the same level of utility as at point *i*. But because point *k* in Exhibit 11 is a combination with more pizza and more videos than point *j*, it must represent a higher level of utility. This contradiction means that indifference curves cannot intersect.

Let's summarize the properties of indifference curves:

1. A particular indifference curve reflects a constant level of utility, so *the consumer is indifferent about all consumption combinations along a given curve.* Combinations are equally attractive.

2. If total utility is to remain constant, an increase in the consumption of one good must be offset by a decrease in the consumption of the other good, so *each indifference curve slopes downward.*

3. Because of the law of diminishing marginal rate of substitution, *indifference curves bow in toward the origin.*

4. Higher indifference curves represent higher levels of utility.

5. Indifference curves do not intersect.

An indifference map is a graphical representation of a consumer's tastes for the two goods. Given a consumer's indifference map, how much of each good will be consumed? To determine that, we must consider the relative prices of the goods and the consumer's income. In the next section, we focus on the consumer's budget.

The Budget Line

The **budget line** depicts all possible combinations of videos and pizzas, given their prices and your budget. Suppose videos rent for $4, pizza sells for $8, and your budget is $40 per week. If you spend the entire $40 on videos, you can afford 10 per week. Alternatively, if you spend the entire $40 on pizzas, you can afford 5 per week. In Exhibit 12, your budget line meets the vertical axis at 10 video rentals and meets the horizontal axis at 5 pizzas. We connect the intercepts to form the budget line. You can purchase any combi-

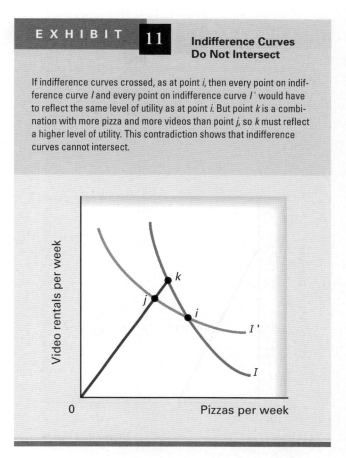

EXHIBIT 11   **Indifference Curves Do Not Intersect**

If indifference curves crossed, as at point *i*, then every point on indifference curve *I* and every point on indifference curve *I'* would have to reflect the same level of utility as at point *i*. But point *k* is a combination with more pizza and more videos than point *j*, so *k* must reflect a higher level of utility. This contradiction shows that indifference curves cannot intersect.

nation on your budget line, or your budget constraint. You might think of the budget line as your *consumption possibilities frontier.*

Let's find the slope of the budget line. At the point where the budget line meets the vertical axis, the maximum number of videos you can rent equals your income (I) divided by the video rental price (p_v), or I/p_v. At the point where the budget line meets the horizontal axis, the maximum quantity of pizzas that you can purchase equals your income divided by the price of a pizza (p_p), or I/p_p. The slope of the budget line between the vertical intercept in Exhibit 12 and the horizontal intercept equals the vertical change, or $-I/p_v$, divided by the horizontal change, or I/p_p:

$$\text{Slope of budget line} = -\frac{I/p_v}{I/p_p} = -\frac{p_p}{p_v}$$

Note that the income term cancels out, so the slope of a budget line depends only on relative prices, not on the level of income. In our example the slope is $-\$8/\$4$, which equals -2. The slope of the budget line indicates the cost of another

EXHIBIT   **12**   **A Budget Line**

A budget line shows all combinations of pizza and videos that can be purchased at fixed prices with a given amount of income. If all income is spent on videos, 10 can be purchased. If all income is spent on pizzas, 5 can be purchased. Points between the vertical intercept and the horizontal intercept show combinations of pizzas and videos. The slope of this budget line is –2, illustrating that the price of 1 pizza is 2 videos.

$$\text{Slope} = -\frac{p_p}{p_v} = -\frac{\$8}{\$4} = -2$$

pizza in terms of forgone videos. You must give up two videos for each additional pizza.

The indifference curve indicates what you are *willing* to buy. The budget line shows what you are *able* to buy. We must therefore bring together the indifference curve and the budget line to find out what quantities of each good you are both *willing* and *able* to buy.

Consumer Equilibrium at the Tangency

As always, the objective of consumption is to maximize utility. We know that indifference curves farther from the origin represent higher levels of utility. You, as a utility-maximizing consumer, will select a combination along the budget line in Exhibit 13 that lies on the highest attainable indifference curve. Given prices and income, you maximize utility at the combination of pizza and videos depicted by point *e* in Exhibit 13, where indifference curve I_2 just touches, or *is tangent to,* your budget line. At point *e,* you buy 3 pizzas at $8

each and rent 4 videos at $4 each, exhausting your budget of $40 per week. Other attainable combinations along the budget line reflect lower levels of utility. For example, point *a* is on the budget line, making it a combination you are *able* to purchase, but *a* is on a lower indifference curve, I_1. Other "better" indifference curves, such as I_3, lie completely above the budget line and are thus unattainable.

Because you maximize your utility at point *e,* that combination is an equilibrium outcome. Note that the indifference curve is tangent to the budget line at the equilibrium point, and at the point of tangency, the slope of a curve equals the slope of a line drawn tangent to that curve. At point *e,* the slope of the indifference curve equals the slope of the budget line. Recall that the absolute value of the slope of the indifference curve is your marginal rate of substitution, and the absolute value of the slope of the budget line equals the price ratio. In equilibrium, therefore, your marginal rate of substitution between videos and pizza, MRS, must equal the ratio of the price of pizza to the price of video rentals:

$$MRS = \frac{p_p}{p_v}$$

The marginal rate of substitution of pizza for video rentals can also be found from the marginal utilities of pizza and

EXHIBIT   **13**   **Utility Maximization**

A consumer's utility is maximized at point *e,* where indifference curve I_2 is just tangent to the budget line.

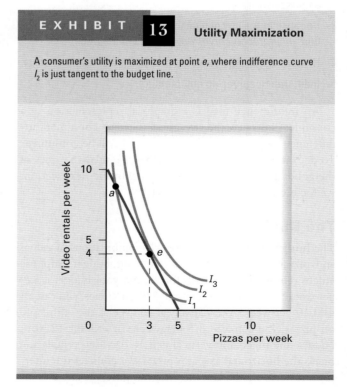

videos presented in the chapter. Exhibit 3 indicated that, at the consumer equilibrium, the marginal utility you derived from the third pizza was 24 and the marginal utility you derived by the fourth video was 12. Because the marginal utility of pizza (MU_p) is 24 and the marginal utility of videos (MU_v) is 12, in moving to that equilibrium, you were willing to give up two videos to get one more pizza. Thus, the marginal rate of substitution of pizza for videos equals the ratio of pizza's marginal utility (MU_p) to video's marginal utility (MU_v), or

$$MRS = \frac{MU_p}{MU_v}$$

In fact, the absolute value of the slope of the indifference curve equals MU_p/MU_v. Because the absolute value of the slope of the budget line equals p_p/p_v, the equilibrium condition for the indifference curve approach can be written as

$$\frac{MU_p}{p_p} = \frac{MU_v}{p_v}$$

This equation is the same equilibrium condition for utility maximization presented in the chapter using marginal utility analysis. The equality says that in equilibrium—that is, when the consumer maximizes utility—the last dollar spent on each good yields the same marginal utility. If this equality did not hold, the consumer could increase utility by adjusting consumption until the equality occurs.

Effects of a Change in Price

What happens to your equilibrium consumption when there is a change in price? The answer can be found by deriving the demand curve. We begin at point *e*, our initial equilibrium, in panel (a) of Exhibit 14. At point *e*, you eat 3 pizzas and watch 4 videos per week. Suppose that the price of pizzas falls from $8 to $6 per unit, other things constant. The price drop means that if the entire budget were devoted to pizza, you could purchase 6.67 pizzas (= $40/$6). Your money income remains at $40 per week, but your real income has increased because of the lower pizza price. Because the rental price of videos has not changed, however, 10 remains the maximum number you can rent. Thus, the budget line's vertical intercept remains fixed at 10 videos, but the lower end of the budget line rotates to the right from 5 to 6.67.

After the price of pizza changes, the new equilibrium occurs at *e"*, where pizza purchases increase from 3 to 4 and, as it happens, video rentals remains at 4. Thus, price and the quantity of pizza demanded are inversely related. The demand curve in panel (b) of Exhibit 14 shows how price and quan-

tity demanded are related. Specifically, if the price of pizza falls from $8 per unit to $6 per unit, other things constant, your quantity demanded increases from 3 to 4. Because you are on a higher indifference curve at *e"*, you are clearly better off after the price reduction (your consumer surplus has increased).

Income and Substitution Effects

The law of demand was initially explained in terms of an income effect and a substitution effect of a price change. You

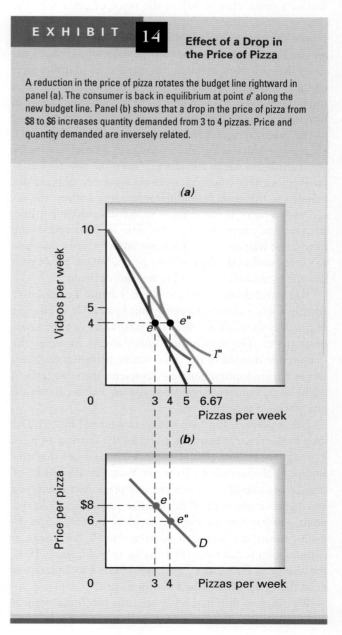

EXHIBIT 14

Effect of a Drop in the Price of Pizza

A reduction in the price of pizza rotates the budget line rightward in panel (a). The consumer is back in equilibrium at point *e"* along the new budget line. Panel (b) shows that a drop in the price of pizza from $8 to $6 increases quantity demanded from 3 to 4 pizzas. Price and quantity demanded are inversely related.

now have the tools to examine these two effects more precisely. Suppose the price of a pizza falls from $8 to $4, other things constant. You can now purchase a maximum of 10 pizzas with a budget of $40 per week. As shown in Exhibit 15, the budget-line intercept rotates out from 5 to 10 pizzas. After the price change, the quantity of pizzas demanded increases from 3 to 5. The increase in utility shows how you benefit from the price decrease.

The increase in the quantity of pizzas demanded can be broken down into the substitution effect and the income effect of a price change. When the price of pizza falls, the change in the ratio of the price of pizza to the price of video rentals shows up through the change in the slope of the budget line. To derive the substitution effect, let's initially assume that you must maintain the same level of utility after the price change as before. In other words, let's suppose your utility level has not yet changed, but the relative prices you face have changed. We want to learn how you would adjust to the price change. A new budget line reflecting just the change in relative prices, not a change in utility, is shown by the dashed line, *CF*, in Exhibit 15. Given the new set of relative prices, you would increase the quantity of pizza demanded to the point on indifference curve *I* where the indifference curve is just tangent to the dashed budget line. That tangency keeps utility at the initial level but reflects the new set of relative prices. Thus, we adjust your budget line to correspond to the new relative prices, but we adjust your income level so that your utility remains unchanged.

You move down along indifference curve *I* to point *e'*, renting fewer videos but buying more pizza. These changes in quantity demanded reflect the *substitution effect* of lower pizza prices. The substitution effect always increases the quantity demanded of the good whose price has dropped. Because consumption bundle *e'* represents the same level of utility as consumption bundle *e,* you are neither better off nor worse off at point *e'*.

But at point *e'*, you have not spent your full budget. The drop in the price of pizza has increased the quantity of pizza you can buy, as shown by the expanded budget line that runs from 10 video rentals to 10 pizzas. Your *real income* has increased because of the lower price of pizza. As a result, you are able to attain point *e** on indifference curve *I**. At this point, you buy 5 pizzas and rent 5 videos. Because prices remain constant during the move from *e'* to *e**, the change in consumption is due solely to a change in real income. Thus, the change in the quantity demanded from 4 to 5 pizzas reflects the *income effect* of the lower pizza price.

We can now distinguish between the substitution effect and the income effect of a drop in the price of pizza. The

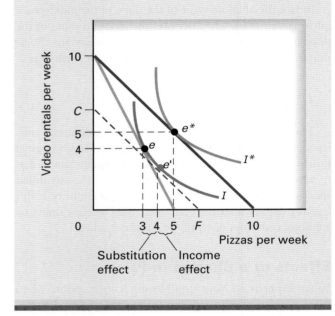

EXHIBIT 15   Substitution and Income Effects of a Drop in the Price of Pizza from $8 to $4

A reduction in the price of pizza moves the consumer from point *e* to point *e**. This movement can be decomposed into a substitution effect and an income effect. The substitution effect, shown from *e* to *e'*, reflects the consumer's reaction to a change in relative prices along the original indifference curve. The income effect, shown from *e'* to *e**, moves the consumer to a higher indifference curve at the new relative price ratio.

substitution effect is shown by the move from point *e* to point *e'* in response to a change in the relative price of pizza, with your utility held constant along *I*. The income effect is shown by the move from *e'* to *e** in response to an increase in your real income, with relative prices held constant.

The overall effect of a change in the price of pizza is the sum of the substitution effect and the income effect. In our example, the substitution effect accounts for a one-unit increase in the quantity of pizza demanded, as does the income effect. Thus, the income and substitution effects combine to increase the quantity of pizza demanded by two units when the price falls from $8 to $4. The income effect is not always positive. For inferior goods, the income effect is negative; so as the price falls, the income effect can cause consumption to fall, offsetting part or even all the substitution effect. Incidentally, notice that as a result of the increase in your real income, video rentals increase as well—from 4 to 5 rentals per week in our example, though it will not always be the case that the income effect is positive.

Conclusion

Indifference curve analysis does not require us to attach numerical values to particular levels of utility, as marginal utility theory does. The results of indifference curve analysis confirm the conclusions drawn from our simpler models. Indifference curves provide a logical way of viewing consumer choice, but consumers need not be aware of this approach to make rational choices. The purpose of the analysis in this chapter is to predict consumer behavior—not to advise consumers how to maximize utility.

APPENDIX QUESTIONS

1. *(Consumer Preferences)* The absolute value of the slope of the indifference curve equals the marginal rate of substitution. If two goods were *perfect* substitutes, what would the indifference curves look like? Explain.

2. *(Effects of a Change in Price)* Chris has an income of $90 per month to allocate between Goods A and B. Initially the price of A is $3 and the price of B is $4.

   a. Draw Chris's budget line, indicating its slope if units of A are measured on the horizontal axis and units of B are on the vertical axis.

   b. Add an indifference curve to your graph and label the point of consumer equilibrium. Indicate Chris's consumption level of A and B. Explain why this is a consumer equilibrium. What can you say about Chris's total utility at this equilibrium?

   c. Now suppose the price of A rises to $4. Draw the new budget line, a new point of equilibrium, and the consumption level of Goods A and B. What is Chris's marginal rate of substitution at the new equilibrium point?

   d. Draw the demand curve for Good A, labeling the different price-quantity combinations determined in parts (b) and (c).

Production and Cost in the Firm

W hy do too many cooks spoil the broth? Why do movie theaters have so many screens? Why don't they add even more? If you go into business for yourself, how much must you earn just to break even? Why might your grade average fall even though you improved from the previous term? Answers to these and other questions are discovered in this chapter, which introduces production and cost in the firm.

The previous chapter explored the consumer behavior shaping the demand curve. This chapter examines the producer behavior shaping the supply curve. A firm's operation is background for an analysis of supply. In the previous chapter, you were asked to think like a consumer, or demander. In this chapter, you must think like a producer, or supplier. You may feel more natural as a consumer (after all, you *are* one), but you already know more about producers than you may realize. You have been around them all your life—Wal-Mart, Blockbuster, Starbucks, Exxon, Barnes & Noble, McDonald's, Pizza Hut, FedEx Kinko's, Ford, The Gap, and hundreds more. So you already have a crude idea how businesses operate. They all have the same goal—they try to maximize profit, which is revenue minus cost. This chapter introduces the cost side of the profit equation. Topics discussed include:

- Explicit and implicit costs
- Economic and normal profit
- Increasing and diminishing returns
- Short-run costs
- Long-run costs
- Economies and diseconomies of scale

Cost and Profit

With demand, we assume that consumers try to maximize utility, a goal that motivates their behavior. With supply, we assume that producers try to maximize *profit,* and this goal motivates their behavior. *Firms transform resources into products to earn a profit.* Over time, firms that survive and grow are those that are more profitable. Unprofitable firms eventually fail. Each year, millions of new firms enter the marketplace and almost as many leave. The firm's decision makers must choose what goods and services to produce and what resources to employ. They must make plans while confronting uncertainty about consumer demand, resource availability, and the intentions of other firms in the market. *The lure of profit is so strong, however, that eager entrepreneurs are always ready to pursue their dreams.*

Explicit and Implicit Costs

To hire a resource, a firm must pay at least the resource's *opportunity cost*—that is, at least what the resource could earn in its best alternative use. For most resources, a cash payment approximates the opportunity cost. For example, the $3 per pound that Domino's Pizza pays for cheese must at least equal the cheese producer's opportunity cost of supplying it. Some firms (or firm owners) own their resources, so they make no direct cash payments. For example, a firm pays no rent to operate in a company-owned building. Similarly, small-business owners usually don't pay themselves an hourly wage. Yet these resources are not free. *Whether hired in resource markets or owned by the firm, all resources have an opportunity cost.* Company-owned buildings can be rented or sold; small-business owners can find other jobs.

A firm's **explicit costs** are its actual cash payments for resources: wages, rent, interest, insurance, taxes, and the like. In addition to these direct cash outlays, or explicit costs, the firm also incurs **implicit costs,** which are the opportunity costs of using resources owned by the firm or provided by the firm's owners. Examples include the use of a company-owned building, use of company funds, or the time of the firm's owners. Like explicit costs, implicit costs are opportunity costs. But unlike explicit costs, implicit costs require no cash payment and no entry in the firm's *accounting statement,* which records its revenues, explicit costs, and accounting profit.

Alternative Measures of Profit

An example may help clarify the distinction between explicit and implicit costs. Wanda Wheeler earns $50,000 a year as an aeronautical engineer with the Skyhigh Aircraft Corporation. On her way home from work one day, she gets an idea for a rounder, more friction-resistant airplane wheel. She decides to quit her job and start a business, which she calls Wheeler Dealer. To buy the necessary machines and equipment, she withdraws $20,000

EXPLICIT COST

Opportunity cost of resources employed by a firm that takes the form of cash payments

IMPLICIT COST

A firm's opportunity cost of using its own resources or those provided by its owners without a corresponding cash payment from her savings account, where it was earning interest of $1,000 a year. She hires an assistant and starts producing the wheel using the spare bay in her condominium's parking garage that she had been renting to a neighbor for $100 a month.

Sales are slow at first—people keep telling her she is just trying to reinvent the wheel—but her wheel eventually gets rolling. When Wanda and her accountant examine the firm's performance after the first year, they are quite pleased. As you can see in the top portion of Exhibit 1, company revenue in 2004 totaled $105,000. After paying her assistant and for materials and equipment, the firm shows an accounting profit of $64,000. **Accounting profit** equals total revenue minus explicit costs. Accountants use this profit to determine a firm's taxable income.

But accounting profit ignores the opportunity cost of Wanda's own resources used in the firm. First is the opportunity cost of her time. Remember, she quit a $50,000-a-year job to work full time on her business, thereby forgoing that salary. Second is the $1,000 annual interest she passes up by funding the operation with her own savings. And third, by using the spare bay in the garage for the business, she forgoes $1,200 per year in rental income. The forgone salary, interest, and rental income are implicit costs because she no longer earns income generated from their best alternative uses.

Economic profit equals total revenue minus all costs, both implicit and explicit; *economic profit takes into account the opportunity cost of all resources used in production.* In Exhibit 1, accounting profit of $64,000 less implicit costs of $52,200 equals economic profit of $11,800. What would happen to the accounting statement if Wanda decided to pay herself a salary of $50,000 per year? Explicit costs would increase by $50,000, and implicit costs would decrease by $50,000 (because her salary would no longer be forgone). Thus, accounting profit would decrease by $50,000, but economic profit would not change because it reflects both implicit and explicit costs.

There is one other profit measure to consider. The accounting profit just sufficient to ensure that *all* resources used by the firm earn their opportunity cost is called a **normal profit.** Wheeler Dealer earns a normal profit when accounting profit equals implicit costs—the sum of the salary Wanda gave up at her regular job ($50,000), the interest she gave up by using her own savings ($1,000), and the rent she gave up on her garage ($1,200). Thus, if the accounting profit is $52,200 per year—the opportunity cost of resources Wanda

ACCOUNTING PROFIT

A firm's total revenue minus its explicit costs

ECONOMIC PROFIT

A firm's total revenue minus its explicit and implicit costs

NORMAL PROFIT

The accounting profit earned when all resources earn their opportunity cost

EXHIBIT 1			
Accounts of Wheeler Dealer, 2004	Total revenue		$105,000
	Less explicit costs:		
	Assistant's salary	−$21,000	
	Material and equipment	−$20,000	
	Equals accounting profit		$64,000
	Less implicit costs:		
	Wanda's forgone salary	−$50,000	
	Forgone interest on savings	−$1,000	
	Forgone garage rental	−$1,200	
	Equals economic profit		$11,800

supplies to the firm—the company earns a normal profit. *Any accounting profit in excess of a normal profit is economic profit.* If accounting profit is large enough, it can be divided into normal profit and economic profit. The $64,000 in accounting profit earned by Wanda's firm consists of (1) a normal profit of $52,200, which covers her implicit costs—the opportunity cost of resources she supplies the firm, and (2) an economic profit of $11,800, which is over and above what these resources, including Wanda's time, could earn in their best alternative use.

As long as economic profit is positive, Wanda is better off running her own firm than working for Skyhigh Aircraft. If total revenue had been only $50,000, an accounting profit of only $9,000 would cover less than one-fifth of her salary, to say nothing of her forgone rent and interest. Because Wanda would not have covered her implicit costs, she would not be earning even a normal profit and would be better off back in her old job.

To understand profit maximization, you must develop a feel for both revenue and cost. In this chapter, you will begin learning about the cost of production, starting with the relationship between inputs and outputs.

Production in the Short Run

We shift now from a discussion of profit, which is why firms exist, to a discussion of how firms operate. Suppose a new McDonald's has just opened in your neighborhood and business is booming far beyond expectations. The manager responds to the unexpected demand by quickly hiring more workers. But cars are still backed up into the street waiting for a parking space. The solution is to add a drive-through window, but such an expansion takes time.

Fixed and Variable Resources

Some resources, such as labor, are called **variable resources** because they can be varied quickly to change the output rate. But adjustments in some other resources take more time. Resources that cannot be altered easily—the size of the building, for example—are called **fixed resources.** When considering the time required to change the quantity of resources employed, economists distinguish between the short run and the long run. In the **short run,** at least one resource is fixed. In the **long run,** no resource is fixed.

Output can be changed in the short run by adjusting variable resources, but the size, or *scale,* of the firm is fixed in the short run. In the long run, all resources can be varied. The length of the long run differs from industry to industry because the nature of production differs. For example, the size of a McDonald's outlet can be increased more quickly than can the size of an auto plant. Thus, the long run for that McDonald's is shorter than the long run for an automaker.

The Law of Diminishing Marginal Returns

Let's focus on the short-run link between resource use and the rate of output by considering a hypothetical moving company called Smoother Mover. Suppose the company's fixed resources are already in place and consist of a warehouse, a moving van, and moving equipment. In this example, labor is the only variable resource. Exhibit 2 relates the amount of labor employed to the amount of output produced. Labor is measured in worker-days, which is one worker for one day, and output is measured in tons of furniture moved per day. The first column shows the amount of labor employed, which ranges from 0 to 8 worker-days. The second column shows the tons of furniture moved, or the **total product,** at each level of employment. The relationship between the amount of resources employed and total product is called the firm's **production function.** The third column shows the **marginal product** of each worker—that is, the amount by which the total product changes with each

VARIABLE RESOURCE

Any resource that can be varied in the short run to increase or decrease production

FIXED RESOURCE

Any resource that cannot be varied in the short run

SHORT RUN

A period during which at least one of a firm's resources is fixed

LONG RUN

A period during which all resources under the firm's control are variable

TOTAL PRODUCT

The total output produced by a firm

PRODUCTION FUNCTION

The relationship between the amount of resources employed and a firm's total product

MARGINAL PRODUCT

The change in total product that occurs when the use of a particular resource increases by one unit, all other resources constant

E X H I B I T   **2**

Units of the Variable Resource (worker-days)	Total Product (tons moved per day)	Marginal Product (tons moved per day)
0	0	—
1	2	2
2	5	3
3	9	4
4	12	3
5	14	2
6	15	1
7	15	0
8	14	−1

The Short-Run Relationship Between Units of Labor and Tons of Furniture Moved

Marginal product increases as the firm hires the first three workers, reflecting increasing marginal returns. Then marginal product declines, reflecting diminishing marginal returns. Adding more workers may, at some point, actually reduce total product (as occurs here with an eighth worker) because workers start getting in each other's way.

INCREASING MARGINAL RETURNS

The marginal product of a variable resource increases as each additional unit of that resource is employed

LAW OF DIMINISHING MARGINAL RETURNS

As more of a variable resource is added to a given amount of a fixed resource, marginal product eventually declines and could become negative

N *et* **B o o k m a r k**

Unit labor cost is the term used to describe the cost of labor per unit of output. Because labor costs generally represent the largest share of costs, this value is closely watched by business-people and analysts at the Federal Reserve. Look at the most recent data on unit labor costs at http://stats.bls.gov/news. release/prod2.toc.htm from the Bureau of Labor Statistics. What is the current trend? What forces may be pushing unit labor costs downward? What does this mean for the profitability of firms?

additional unit of labor, assuming other resources remain unchanged. Spend a little time now getting acquainted with each column.

Increasing Marginal Returns

Without labor, nothing gets moved, so total product is 0. If one worker is hired, that worker must do all the driving, packing, crating, and moving. Some of the larger items, such as couches and major appliances, cannot easily be moved by a single worker. Still, in our example one worker moves 2 tons of furniture per day. When a second worker is hired, some division of labor occurs, and two can move the big stuff more easily, so production more than doubles to 5 tons per day. The marginal product of the second worker is 3 tons per day. Adding a third worker allows for a finer division of labor. For example, one can pack fragile items while the other two do the heavy lifting. Total product is 9 tons per day, 4 tons more than with two workers. Because the marginal product increases, the firm experiences **increasing marginal returns** from labor as each of the first three workers is hired.

Diminishing Marginal Returns

A fourth worker's marginal product is less than that of a third worker. Hiring still more workers increases total product by successively smaller amounts, so the marginal product declines after three workers. With that fourth worker, the **law of diminishing marginal returns** takes hold. This law states that as more of a variable resource is combined with a given amount of a fixed resource, marginal product eventually declines. *The law of diminishing marginal returns is the most important feature of production in the short run.* As additional units of labor are added, marginal product could turn negative, so total product declines. For example, when Smoother Mover hires an eighth worker, workers start getting in each other's way, and workers take up valuable space in the moving van. As a result, the eighth worker actually subtracts from total output, yielding a negative marginal product. Likewise, a McDonald's outlet can hire only so many workers before congestion and confusion in the work area cut total product ("too many cooks spoil the broth").

The Total and Marginal Product Curves

Exhibit 3 illustrates the relationship between total product and marginal product, using data from Exhibit 2. Note that because of increasing marginal returns, marginal product in

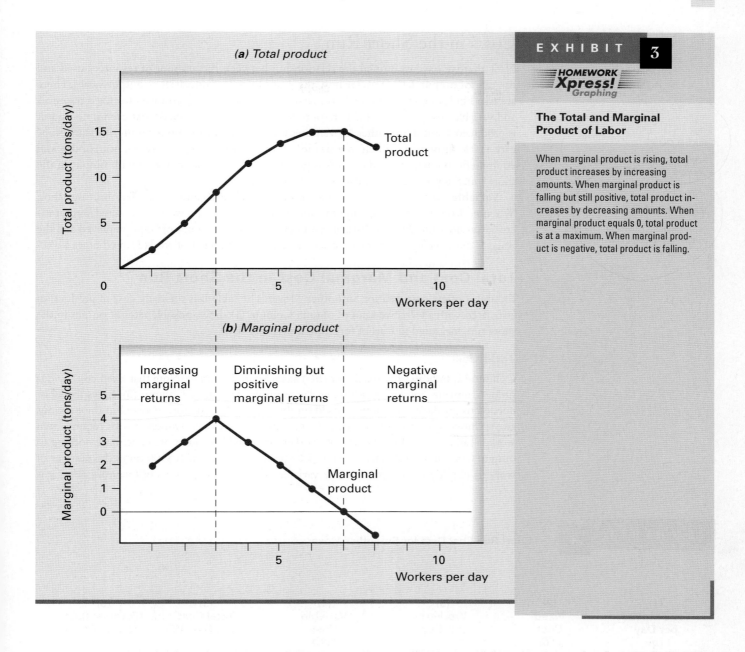

EXHIBIT 3

HOMEWORK
Xpress!
Graphing

(a) Total product

Total product

(b) Marginal product

Increasing marginal returns

Diminishing but positive marginal returns

Negative marginal returns

Marginal product

The Total and Marginal Product of Labor

When marginal product is rising, total product increases by increasing amounts. When marginal product is falling but still positive, total product increases by decreasing amounts. When marginal product equals 0, total product is at a maximum. When marginal product is negative, total product is falling.

panel (b) increases with each of the first three workers. With marginal product increasing, total product in panel (a) increases at an increasing rate (although this is hard to see in Exhibit 3). But once decreasing marginal returns set in, which begins with the fourth worker, marginal product declines. Total product continues to increase but at a decreasing rate. As long as marginal product is positive, total product increases. Where marginal product turns negative, total product starts to fall. Exhibit 3 summarizes all this by sorting production into three ranges: (1) increasing marginal returns, (2) diminishing but positive marginal returns, and (3) negative marginal returns. These ranges for marginal product correspond with total product that (1) increases at an increasing rate, (2) increases at a decreasing rate, and (3) declines.

Costs in the Short Run

Now that we have examined the relationship between the amount of resources used and the rate of output, let's consider how the cost of production varies as output varies. There are two kinds of costs in the short run: fixed and variable. Fixed cost pays for fixed resources and variable cost pays for variable resources. A firm must pay a **fixed cost** even if no output is produced. Even if Smoother Mover hires no labor and moves no furniture, it incurs property taxes, insurance, vehicle registration, plus any opportunity cost for warehouse and equipment. By definition, fixed cost is just that: fixed—it does not vary with output in the short run. Suppose the firm's *fixed cost* is $200 per day.

Variable cost, as the name implies, is the cost of variable resources—in this case, labor. When no labor is employed, output is zero, as is variable cost. As workers are hired, output increases, as does variable cost. Variable cost depends on the amount of labor employed and the wage. If the wage is $100 per day, *variable cost* equals the number of workers hired times $100.

Total Cost and Marginal Cost in the Short Run

Exhibit 4 offers cost data for Smoother Mover. The table lists the daily cost of production associated with alternative rates of output. Column (1) shows possible rates of output in the short run, measured in tons of furniture moved per day.

Total Cost

Column (2) indicates the fixed cost (*FC*) at each rate of output. Note that fixed cost, by definition, remains constant at $200 per day regardless of output. Column (3) shows the labor needed to produce each output based on the productivity figures reported in the previous two exhibits. For example, moving 2 tons a day requires one worker, 5 tons requires two workers, and so on. Only the first six workers are listed because more contribute nothing to output. Column (4) lists variable cost (*VC*) per day, which equals $100 times the number of workers employed. For example, the variable cost of moving 9 tons of furniture per day is

HOMEWORK
Xpress!
Ask the Instructor
Video

FIXED COST

Any production cost that is independent of the firm's rate of output

VARIABLE COST

Any production cost that changes as the rate of output changes

EXHIBIT 4   **Short-Run Cost Data for Smoother Mover**

(1) Tons Moved per Day (*q*)	(2) Fixed Cost (*FC*)	(3) Workers per Day	(4) Variable Cost (*VC*)	(5) Total Cost (*TC = FC + VC*)	(6) Marginal Cost (*MC=ΔTC/Δq*)
0	$200	0	0	$200	—
2	200	1	$100	300	$ 50.00
5	200	2	200	400	33.33
9	200	3	300	500	25.00
12	200	4	400	600	33.33
14	200	5	500	700	50.00
15	200	6	600	800	100.00

$300 because this output requires three workers. Column (5) lists the **total cost** (*TC*), the sum of fixed cost and variable cost: *TC* = *FC* + *VC*. As you can see, when output is zero, variable cost is zero, so total cost consists entirely of the fixed cost of $200. Incidentally, because total cost is the opportunity cost of all resources used by the firm, total cost includes a normal profit but not an economic profit. Think about that.

Marginal Cost

Of special interest to the firm is how total cost changes as output changes. In particular, what is the marginal cost of producing another unit? The **marginal cost** (*MC*) of production listed in column (6) of Exhibit 4 is simply the change in total cost divided by the change in output, or $MC = \Delta TC/\Delta q$, where Δ means "change in." For example, increasing output from 0 to 2 tons increases total cost by $100 (= $300 − $200). The marginal cost of each of the first 2 tons is the change in total cost, $100, divided by the change in output, 2 tons, or $100/2, which equals $50. The marginal cost of each of the next 3 tons is $100/3, or $33.33.

Notice in column (6) that marginal cost first decreases and then increases. *Changes in marginal cost reflect changes in the marginal productivity of the variable resource employed.* Because of increasing marginal returns, each of the first three workers produces more than the last. This greater productivity results in a falling marginal cost for the first 9 tons moved. Beginning with the fourth worker, the firm experiences diminishing marginal returns from labor, so the marginal cost of output increases. *When the firm experiences increasing marginal returns, the marginal cost of output falls; when the firm experiences diminishing marginal returns, the marginal cost of output increases.* Thus, marginal cost in Exhibit 4 first falls and then rises, because marginal returns from labor first increase and then diminish.

Total and Marginal Cost Curves

Exhibit 5 shows cost curves for the data in Exhibit 4. Because fixed cost does not vary with output, the fixed cost curve is a horizontal line at the $200 level in panel (a). Variable cost is zero when output is zero, so the *variable cost curve* starts from the origin. The *total cost curve* sums the fixed cost curve and the variable cost curve. Because a constant fixed cost is added to variable cost, the total cost curve is just the variable cost curve shifted vertically by the amount of fixed cost.

In panel (b) of Exhibit 5, marginal cost declines until the ninth unit of output and then increases, reflecting labor's increasing and then diminishing marginal returns. There is a relationship between the two panels because the change in total cost resulting from a one-unit change in production equals the marginal cost. With each successive unit of output, total cost increases by the marginal cost of that unit. Thus, *the slope of the total cost curve at each rate of output equals the marginal cost at that rate of output.* The total cost curve can be divided into two sections, based on what happens to marginal cost:

1. Because of increasing marginal returns from labor, marginal cost at first declines, so total cost initially increases by successively smaller amounts and the total cost curve becomes less steep.

2. Because of diminishing marginal returns from labor, marginal cost starts increasing after the ninth unit of output, leading to a steeper total cost curve.

Notice that the total cost curve has a backward S shape, the result of combining the two sections discussed above. Keep in mind that economic analysis is marginal analysis. Marginal cost is the key to economic decisions firms make. *Marginal cost indicates how much total cost will increase if one more unit is produced or how much total cost will drop if production declines by one unit.*

EXHIBIT **5**

Total and Marginal Cost Curves for Smoother Mover

In panel (a), fixed cost is $200 at all levels of output. Variable cost starts from the origin and increases slowly at first as output increases. When the variable resource generates diminishing marginal returns, variable cost begins to increase more rapidly. Total cost is the vertical sum of fixed cost and variable cost. In panel (b), marginal cost first declines, reflecting increasing marginal returns, and then increases, reflecting diminishing marginal returns.

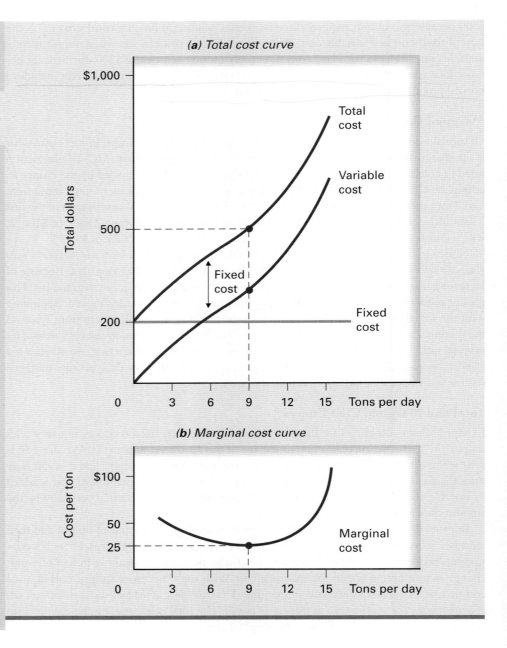

AVERAGE VARIABLE COST

Variable cost divided by output, or $AVC = VC/q$

AVERAGE TOTAL COST

Total cost divided by output, or $ATC = TC/q$; the sum of average fixed cost and average variable cost, or $ATC = AFC + AVC$

Average Cost in the Short Run

Although marginal cost is of most interest, the average cost per unit of output is also useful. Average cost measures correspond to variable cost and to total cost. These measures appear in columns (5) and (6) of Exhibit 6. Column (5) lists **average variable cost,** or *AVC,* which equals variable cost divided by output, or $AVC = VC/q$. The final column lists **average total cost,** or *ATC,* which equals total cost divided by output, or $ATC = TC/q$. Average cost first declines as output expands and then increases.

EXHIBIT	6	Short-Run Cost Data for Smoother Mover

Because of increasing marginal returns from labor, marginal cost at first declines, as shown in column (4). Because of diminishing marginal returns from labor, marginal cost starts increasing after the 9 tons are moved per day. Average costs first decline then increase, reflecting increasing and diminishing marginal returns.

(1) Tons Moved per Day (q)	(2) Variable Cost (VC)	(3) Total Cost (TC = FC + VC)	(4) Marginal Cost (MC = ΔTC/Δq)	(5) Average Variable Cost (AVC = VC/q)	(6) Average Total Cost (ATC = TC/q)
0	$ 0	$200	0	—	∞
2	100	300	$50.00	$ 50.00	$150.00
5	200	400	33.33	40.00	80.00
9	300	500	25.00	33.33	55.55
12	400	600	33.33	33.33	50.00
14	500	700	50.00	35.71	50.00
15	600	800	100.00	40.00	53.33

The Relationship Between Marginal Cost and Average Cost

To understand the relationship between marginal cost and average cost, let's begin with an example of college grades. Think about how your grades each term affect your grade point average (GPA). Suppose you do well your first term, starting your college career with a 3.4. Your grades for the second term drop to 2.8, reducing your GPA to 3.1. You slip again in the third term to a 2.2, lowering your GPA to 2.8. Your fourth-term grades improve a bit to 2.4, but your GPA continues to slide to 2.7. In the fifth term, your grades improve to 2.7, leaving your GPA unchanged at 2.7. And in the sixth term, you get 3.3, pulling your GPA up to 2.8. Notice that when your term grades are below your GPA, your GPA falls. Even when your term performance improves, your GPA does not improve until your term grades *exceed* your GPA. Your term grades first pull down your GPA and then eventually pull it up.

Let's now take a look at the relationship between marginal cost and average cost. In Exhibit 6, marginal cost has the same relationship to average cost as your term grades have to your GPA. You can observe this marginal-average relationship in columns (4) and (5). Because of increasing marginal returns from the first three workers, the marginal cost falls for the first 9 tons of furniture moved. If marginal cost is below average cost, marginal cost pulls down average cost. Marginal cost and average cost are equal when output equals 12 tons, and marginal cost exceeds average cost when output exceeds 12 tons, so marginal cost pulls up average cost.

Exhibit 7 shows the same marginal cost curve first presented in Exhibit 5, along with average cost curves based on data in Exhibit 6. At low rates of output, marginal cost declines as output expands because of increasing marginal returns from labor. As long as marginal cost is below average cost, average cost falls as output expands. At higher rates of output, marginal cost increases because of diminishing marginal returns from labor. Once marginal cost exceeds average cost, marginal cost pulls up the average. The fact that marginal cost first pulls average cost down and then pulls it up explains why the average cost curves have a U shape. The shapes of the average variable cost curve and the average total cost curve are determined by the shape of the marginal cost curve, so each is shaped by increasing and diminishing marginal returns.

E X H I B I T   **7**

≡HOMEWORK≡
Xpress!≡
Graphing

Average and Marginal Cost Curves for Smoother Mover

Average variable cost and average total cost curves first decline, reach low points, and then rise. Overall, they have U shapes. When marginal cost is below average variable cost, average variable cost is falling. When marginal cost equals average variable cost, average variable cost is at its minimum. When marginal cost is above average variable cost, average variable cost is increasing. The same relationship holds between marginal cost and average total cost.

≡HOMEWORK≡
Xpress!≡
econ-apps news

Notice also that the rising marginal cost curve intersects both the average variable cost curve and the average total cost curve where these average curves are at their minimum. This occurs because the marginal pulls down the average where the marginal is below the average and pulls up the average where the marginal is above the average. One more thing: The distance between the average variable cost curve and the average total cost curve is *average fixed cost,* which gets smaller as the rate of output increases. (Why does average fixed cost get smaller?)

The law of diminishing marginal returns determines the shapes of short-run cost curves. When the marginal product of labor increases, the marginal cost of output falls. Once diminishing marginal returns take hold, the marginal cost of output rises. Thus, marginal cost first falls and then rises. And the marginal cost curve dictates the shapes of the average cost curves. When marginal cost is less than average cost, average cost declines. When marginal cost is above average cost, average cost increases. Got it? If not, please reread this paragraph.

Costs in the Long Run

So far, the analysis has focused on how costs vary as the rate of output expands in the short run for a firm of a given size. In the long run, all inputs that are under the firm's control can be varied, so there is no fixed cost. The long run is not just a succession of short runs. The long run is best thought of as a *planning horizon.* In the long run, the choice of input combinations is flexible. But once the size of the plant has been selected and the concrete has been poured, the firm has fixed costs and is operating in the short run. Firms plan for the long run, but they produce in the short run. We turn now to long-run costs.

The Long-Run Average Cost Curve

Because of the special nature of technology in the industry, suppose a firm must choose from among three possible plant sizes: small, medium, and large. Exhibit 8 presents this simple case. The average cost curves for the three sizes are *SS'*, *MM'*, and *LL'*. Which size

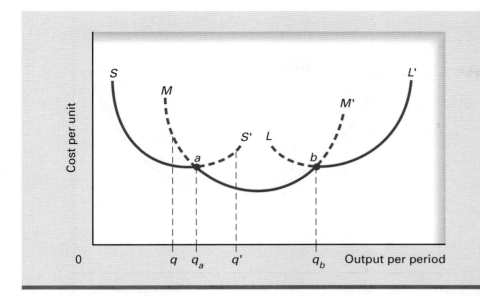

EXHIBIT 8

Short-Run Average Total Cost Curves Form the Long-Run Average Cost Curve, or Planning Curve

Curves *SS'*, *MM'*, and *LL'* show short-run average total costs for small, medium, and large plants, respectively. For output less than q_a, average cost is lowest when the plant is small. Between q_a and q_b, average cost is lowest with a medium-size plant. If output exceeds q_b, the large plant offers the lowest average cost. The long-run average-cost curve is *SabL'*.

should the firm build to minimize average cost? The appropriate size, *or scale,* for the firm depends on how much the firm wants to produce. For example, if q is the desired output, average cost will be lowest with a small plant size. If the desired output is q', the medium plant size offers the lowest average cost.

More generally, for any output less than q_a, average cost is lowest when the plant is small. For output between q_a and q_b, average cost is lowest for the plant of medium size. And for output that exceeds q_b average cost is lowest when the plant is large. The **long-run average cost curve,** sometimes called the firm's *planning curve,* connects portions of the three short-run average cost curves that are lowest for each output rate. In Exhibit 8, that curve consists of the line segments connecting *S, a, b,* and *L'*.

Now suppose there are many possible plant sizes. Exhibit 9 presents a sample of short-run cost curves shown in *pink.* The long-run average cost curve, shown in *red,* is formed by connecting the points on the various short-run average cost curves that represent the lowest per-unit cost for each rate of output. Each of the short-run average cost curves is tangent to the long-run average cost curve, or *planning curve.* If we could display enough short-run cost curves, we would have a different plant size for each rate of output. *These points of tangency represent the least-cost way of producing each particular rate of output, given the technology and resource prices.* For example, the short-run average total cost curve ATC_1 is tangent to the long-run average cost curve at point *a,* where $11 is the lowest average cost of producing output q. Note, however, that other output rates along ATC_1 have a lower average cost. For example, the average cost of producing q' is only $10, as identified at point *b*. Point *b* depicts the lowest average cost along ATC_1. So, while the point of tangency reflects the least-cost way of producing a particular rate of output, that tangency point does not reflect the minimum average cost for this particular plant size.

If the firm decides to produce q', which size plant should it choose to minimize the average cost of production? Output rate q' could be produced at point *b,* which represents the minimum average cost along ATC_1. But average cost is lower with a larger plant. With the plant size associated with ATC_2, the average cost of producing q' would be minimized at $9 per unit at point *c*. *Each point of tangency between a short-run average cost curve and the long-run average cost curve represents the least-cost way of producing that particular rate of output.*

LONG-RUN AVERAGE COST CURVE

A curve that indicates the lowest average cost of production at each rate of output when the size, or scale, of the firm varies; also called the planning curve

EXHIBIT 9

Many Short-Run Average Total Cost Curves Form a Firm's Long-Run Average Cost Curve, or Planning Curve

With many possible plant sizes, the long-run average cost curve is the envelope of portions of the short-run average cost curves. Each short-run curve is tangent to the long-run average cost curve. Each point of tangency represents the least-cost way of producing that level of output.

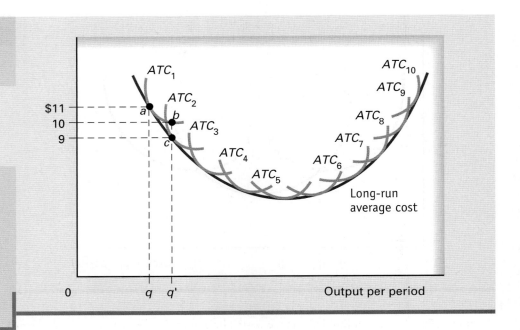

WALL STREET JOURNAL
Reading It **Right**

What's the relevance of the following statement from the Wall Street Journal: *"As with any new technology, the early OLED [organic light-emitting diode] display screens are expensive, perhaps six times more than liquid-crystal-display screens. But OLED backers say that problem will in part be addressed once mass production gears up and economies of scale are reached."*

ECONOMIES OF SCALE

Forces that reduce a firm's average cost as the scale of operation increases in the long run

DISECONOMIES OF SCALE

Forces that may eventually increase a firm's average cost as the scale of operation increases in the long run

Economies of Scale

Like short-run average cost curves, the long-run average cost curve is U-shaped. Recall that the shape of the short-run average total cost curve is determined primarily by increasing and diminishing marginal returns of the variable resource. A different principle shapes the long-run cost curve. If a firm experiences **economies of scale,** long-run average cost falls as output expands. Consider some sources of economies of scale. *A larger size often allows for larger, more specialized machines and greater specialization of labor.* For example, compare the household-size kitchen of a small restaurant with the kitchen at a McDonald's. At low rates of output, the smaller kitchen produces meals at a lower average cost than does McDonald's. But if production in the smaller kitchen increases beyond, say, 100 meals per day, a kitchen on the scale of McDonald's would produce at a lower average cost. Thus, because of economies of scale, the long-run average cost for a restaurant may fall as size increases.

A larger scale of operation allows a firm to use larger, more efficient machines and to assign workers to more specialized tasks. Production techniques such as the assembly line can be introduced only if the rate of output is great enough. Typically, as the scale of firm increases, capital substitutes for labor and complex machines substitute for simpler machines. As an extreme example of capital substituting for labor, some Japanese auto factories are automated enough to operate in the dark.

Diseconomies of Scale

Often another force, called **diseconomies of scale,** eventually takes over as a firm expands its plant size, increasing long-run average cost as output expands. As the amount and variety of resources employed increase, so does the *task of coordinating all these inputs.* As the workforce grows, additional layers of management are needed to monitor production. In the thicket of bureaucracy that develops, communications may get mangled. Top executives have more difficulty keeping in touch with the factory floor because information is distorted as it moves up and down the chain of command. Indeed, in very large organizations, rumors may become a primary source of information, reducing the efficiency of the organization and increasing average cost. Note that *diseconomies of scale result from a larger firm size, whereas diminishing marginal returns result from using more variable resources in a firm of a given size.*

In the long run, a firm can vary the inputs under its control. Some resources, however, are not under the firm's control, and the inability to vary them may contribute to diseconomies of scale. Let's look at economies and diseconomies of scale at movie theaters in the following case study.

At the Movies

Movie theaters experience both economies and diseconomies of scale. A theater with one screen needs someone to sell tickets, someone to sell popcorn (concession stand sales account for well over half the profit at most theaters), and someone to operate the projector. If another screen is added, the same staff can perform these tasks for both screens. Thus, the ticket seller becomes more productive by selling tickets to both movies. Furthermore, construction costs per screen are reduced because only one lobby and one set of rest rooms are required. The theater can run bigger, more noticeable newspaper ads and can spread the cost over more films. These are the reasons why we see theater owners adding more and more screens at the same location; they are taking advantage of economies of scale. From 1990 to 2000, the number of screens in the United States grew faster than the number of theaters, so the average number of screens per theater increased. Europe experienced similar growth.

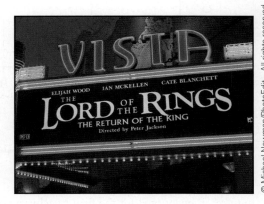

But why stop at, say, 10 or even 20 screens per theater? Why not 30 screens, particularly in thickly populated areas with sufficient demand? One problem with expanding the number of screens is that the public roads leading to the theater are a resource the theater cannot control. The congestion around the theater grows with the number of screens at that location. Also, the supply of popular films may not be large enough to fill so many screens.

Finally, time itself is a resource that the firm cannot easily control. Only certain hours are popular with moviegoers. Scheduling becomes more difficult because the manager must space out starting and ending times to avoid the congestion that occurs when too many customers come and go at the same time. No more "prime time" can be created. Thus, theater owners lack control over such inputs as the public roads, the supply of films, and the amount of "prime time" in the day. These factors contribute to diseconomies of scale.

Sources: "Not-So-Special Effects," *Daily Variety*, 2 July 2003; "AMC Will Build Megaplex in Virginia," *Business Journal*, 14 May 2003; and *Statistical Abstract of the United States: 2002*, U.S. Census Bureau, http://www.census.gov/prod/www/statistical-abstract-us.html.

Case **Study**

World of Business

eActivity
With substantial economies of scale in the movie theater industry, a few chains now operate thousands of theaters. Their corporate Web sites provide information on current plans and include histories of how they grew to be so large. Browse through the following sites: AMC theatres at http://www.amctheatres.com/aboutamc/ourhistory.html and Regal Cinemas at http://www.uatc.com/corporate/about.html. Can you find the average number of screens per theater for each corporation? What is a megaplex? Where can megaplexes be found?

It is possible for average cost to neither increase nor decrease with changes in firm size. If neither economies of scale nor diseconomies of scale are apparent over some range of output, a firm experiences **constant long-run average cost.** Perhaps economies and diseconomies of scale exist simultaneously in the firm but have offsetting effects. Exhibit 10 presents a firm's long-run average cost curve, which is divided into output segments reflecting economies of scale, constant long-run average costs, and diseconomies of scale. Output

CONSTANT LONG-RUN AVERAGE COST

A cost that occurs when, over some range of output, long-run average cost neither increases nor decreases with changes in firm size

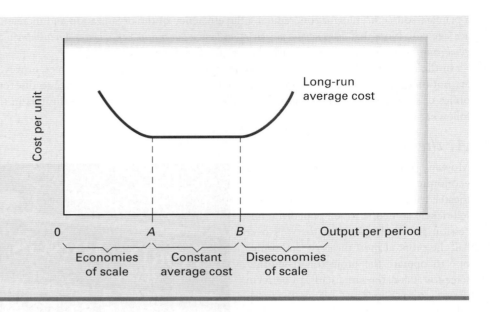

EXHIBIT 10

A Firm's Long-Run Average Cost Curve

Up to output level *A*, long-run average cost falls as the firm experiences economies of scale. Output level *A* is the minimum efficient scale—the lowest rate of output at which the firm takes full advantage of economies of scale. Between *A* and *B*, the average cost is constant. Beyond output level *B*, long-run average cost increases as the firm experiences diseconomies of scale.

MINIMUM EFFICIENT SCALE

The lowest rate of output at which a firm takes full advantage of economies of scale

must reach quantity *A* for the firm to achieve the **minimum efficient scale,** which is the lowest rate of output at which long-run average cost is at a minimum.

Economies and Diseconomies of Scale at the Firm Level

Our discussion so far has referred to a particular plant—a movie theater or a restaurant, for example. But a firm could also be a collection of plants, such as the hundreds of movie theaters in a chain or the thousands of McDonald's restaurants. More generally, we can distinguish between economies and diseconomies of scale at the *plant level*—that is, at a particular location—and at the *firm level,* where the firm is a collection of plants. The following case study explores issues of multiplant scale economies and diseconomies.

Billions and Billions of Burgers

McDonald's experiences economies of scale at the plant, or restaurant, level because of its specialization of labor and machines, but it also benefits from economies of scale at the firm level. Experience gained from decades of selling hamburgers can be shared with new managers through centralized training programs. Costly research and efficient production techniques can also be shared across thousands of locations. For example, McDonald's took three years to decide on the exact temper-

ature of the holding cabinets for its hamburger patties and took seven years to develop Chicken McNuggets. What's more, the cost of advertising and promoting McDonald's through sponsorship of world events such as the Olympics can be spread across its 29,000 restaurants in 121 countries.

Some diseconomies may also arise in such large-scale operations. The fact that the menu must be reasonably uniform across thousands of locations means that if customers in some parts of the country or the world do not like a product, it may not get on the menu, even though it might be popular elsewhere. Another problem with a uniform menu is that the ingredients must be available around the world and cannot be subject to droughts or sharp swings in price. For example, one chain decided not to top its burgers with bacon strips because the price of bacon fluctuates too much.

Because McDonald's has moved aggressively overseas (10 percent of the beef sold in Japan is in McDonald's hamburgers, and McDonald's is the third largest corporate employer in Brazil), planning has grown increasingly complex. For example, McDonald's is kosher in Israel, closes five times a day for Muslim prayer in Saudi Arabia, and serves mutton burgers in India, where cows are worshiped, not eaten. Running a worldwide operation also opens the company to global risks, such as mad-cow disease in Europe and terrorism worldwide.

Change usually comes slowly in large corporations, but it does come. McDonald's recently reorganized its U.S. operation into five regions, allowing managers in each region more leeway in pricing and promotion. McDonald's has also become more flexible by putting mini-restaurants in airports, gas stations, and Wal-Marts. These so-called satellite restaurants recently accounted for half of the company's new U.S. openings. McDonald's has also begun closing unprofitable restaurants. This greater flexibility across regions and in restaurant structure is an effort by McDonald's to address diseconomies of scale.

Sources: Erin White and Shirley Leung, "McDonald's Germany: Little Mac?", *Wall Street Journal*, 23 September 2003; Pallavi Gogoi and Michael Arndt, "Hamburger Hell: McDonald's Aims to Save Itself by Going Back to Basics," *Business Week*, 3 March 2003; James L. Watson, ed., *Golden Arches East: McDonald's in East Asia* (Palo Alto, Calif.: Stanford University Press, 1998); and McDonald's Web site at http://www.mcdonalds.com/.

serves the Rhode Island McFeast Menu? If you can read a foreign language, try to find a McDonald's page for a country where it is spoken.

Other large firms do what they can to reduce diseconomies of scale at the firm level. For example, IBM undertook a massive restructuring program to decentralize into six smaller decision-making groups. Some big corporations have spun off parts of their operation to form new corporations. For example, Hewlett-Packard split off Agilent Technologies, and AT&T created Lucent Technologies.

Conclusion

By considering the relationship between production and cost, we have developed the foundation for a theory of firm behavior. Despite what may appear to be a tangle of short-run and long-run cost curves, *only two relationships between resources and output underlie all the curves. In the short run, it's increasing and diminishing returns from the variable resource. In the long run, it's economies and diseconomies of scale.* If you understand the sources of these two phenomena, you grasp the central ideas of the chapter. Our examination of production and cost in the short run and long run lays the groundwork for a firm's supply curve, to be covered in the next chapter. But before that, the appendix develops a more sophisticated approach to production and cost.

SUMMARY

1. Explicit costs are opportunity costs of resources employed by a firm that take the form of cash payments. Implicit costs are the opportunity costs of using resources owned by the firm. A firm earns a normal profit when total revenue covers all implicit and explicit costs. Economic profit equals total revenue minus both explicit and implicit costs.

2. Resources that can quickly be varied to increase or decrease output are called variable resources. In the short run, at least one resource is fixed. In the long run, all resources are variable.

3. A firm may initially experience increased marginal returns as it takes advantage of increased specialization of the variable resource. But the law of diminishing marginal returns indicates that the firm will eventually reach a point where additional units of the variable resource yield an ever-smaller marginal product.

4. The law of diminishing marginal returns from the variable resource is the most important feature of production in the short run and explains why marginal cost and average cost eventually increase as output expands.

5. In the long run, all inputs under the firm's control are variable, so there is no fixed cost. The firm's long-run average cost curve, also called its planning curve, is an envelope formed by a series of short-run average total cost curves. The long run is best thought of as a planning horizon.

6. In the long run, a firm selects the most efficient size for the desired rate of output. Once the firm's size is chosen, some resources become fixed, so the firm is back operating in the short run. Thus, the firm plans for the long run but produces in the short run.

7. A firm's long-run average cost curve, like its short-run average cost curves, is U-shaped. As output expands, average cost at first declines because of economies of scale—a larger plant size allows for bigger and more specialized machinery and a more extensive division of labor. Eventually, average cost stops falling. Average cost may be constant over some range. If output expands still further, the plant may encounter diseconomies of scale as the cost of coordinating resources grows. Economies and diseconomies of scale can occur at the plant level and at the firm level.

QUESTIONS FOR REVIEW

1. *(Explicit and Implicit Costs)* Amos McCoy is currently raising corn on his 100-acre farm and earning an accounting profit of $100 per acre. However, if he raised soybeans, he could earn $200 per acre. Is he currently earning an economic profit? Why or why not?

2. *(Explicit and Implicit Costs)* Determine whether each of the following is an explicit cost or an implicit cost:

   a. Payments for labor purchased in the labor market
   b. A firm's use of a warehouse that it owns and could rent to another firm
   c. Rent paid for the use of a warehouse not owned by the firm
   d. The wages that owners could earn if they did not work for themselves

3. *(Alternative Measures of Profit)* Calculate the accounting profit or loss as well as the economic profit or loss in each of the following situations:

   a. A firm with total revenues of $150 million, explicit costs of $90 million, and implicit costs of $40 million
   b. A firm with total revenues of $125 million, explicit costs of $100 million, and implicit costs of $30 million
   c. A firm with total revenues of $100 million, explicit costs of $90 million, and implicit costs of $20 million
   d. A firm with total revenues of $250,000, explicit costs of $275,000, and implicit costs of $50,000

4. *(Alternative Measures of Profit)* Why is it reasonable to think of normal profit as a type of cost to the firm?

5. *(Short Run Versus Long Run)* What distinguishes a firm's short-run period from its long-run period?

6. *(Law of Diminishing Marginal Returns)* As a farmer, you must decide how many times during the year you will plant a new crop. Also, you must decide how far apart to space the plants. Will diminishing returns be a factor in your decision making? If so, how will it affect your decisions?

7. *(Marginal Cost)* What is the difference between fixed cost and variable cost? Does each type of cost affect short-run marginal cost? If yes, explain how each affects marginal cost. If no, explain why each does or does not affect marginal cost.

8. *(Marginal Cost)* Explain why the marginal cost of production *must* increase if the marginal product of the variable resource is decreasing.

9. *(Costs in the Short Run)* What effect would each of the following have on a firm's short-run marginal cost curve and its total fixed cost curve?

   a. An increase in the wage rate
   b. A decrease in property taxes
   c. A rise in the purchase price of new capital
   d. A rise in energy prices

10. *(Costs in the Short Run)* Identify each of the curves in the following graph:

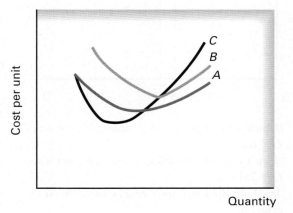

11. *(Marginal Cost and Average* cost curve must intersect the average variable cost Why do the average tot curves get closer to on

12. *(Marginal Cost and Ave* ter, the output level w mum is greater than the able cost is at a minimum. Why?

13. *(Long-Run Average Cost Curve)* What types of changes could shift the long-run average cost curve? How would these changes also affect the short-run average total cost curve?

14. *(Long-Run Average Cost Curve)* Explain the shape of the long-run average cost curve. What does "minimum efficient scale" mean?

15. *(Case **Study**: At the Movies)* The case study notes that the concession stand accounts for well over half the profits at most theaters. Given this, what are the benefits of the staggered movie times allowed by multiple screens? What is the benefit to a multiscreen theater of locating at a shopping mall?

16. *(Case **Study**: Billions and Billions of Burgers)* How does having a menu that is uniform around the country provide McDonald's with economies of scale? How is menu planning made more complex by expanding into other countries?

PROBLEMS AND EXERCISES

17. *(Production in the Short Run)* Complete the following table. At what point does diminishing marginal returns set in?

Units of the Variable Resource	Total Product	Marginal Product
0	0	—
1	10	_____
2	22	_____
3	_____	9
4	_____	4
5	34	_____

18. *(Total Cost and Marginal Cost)* Complete the following table, assuming that each unit of labor costs $75 per day.

Quantity of Labor per Day	Output per Day	Fixed Cost	Variable Cost	Total Cost	Marginal Cost
0	_____	$300	$_____	$_____	$_____
1	5	_____	75	_____	15
2	11	_____	150	450	12.5
3	15	_____	_____	525	_____
4	18	_____	300	600	25
5	20	_____	_____	_____	37.5

e fixed cost, variable cost, and total cost
s for these data.
at is the marginal product of going from two to
three units of labor?
What is average total cost when output is 18 units per
day?

19. *(Total Cost and Marginal Cost)* Complete the following
table, where *L* is units of labor, *Q* is units of output, and
MP is the marginal product of labor.

L	Q	MP	VC	TC	MC	ATC
0	0	___	$ 0	$12	___	___
1	6	___	3	15	___	___
2	15	___	6		___	___
3	21	___	9		___	___
4	24	___	12		___	___
5	26	___	15		___	___

a. At what level of labor input do the marginal returns
   to labor begin to diminish?
b. What is the average variable cost when *Q* = 24?
c. What is this firm's fixed cost?
d. What is the wage rate per day?

20. *(Relationship Between Marginal Cost and Average Cost)* Assume that labor and capital are the only inputs used by a
firm. Capital is fixed at 5 units, which cost $100 each.
Workers can be hired for $200 each. Complete the fol-
lowing table to show average variable cost (*AVC*), average
total cost (*ATC*), and marginal cost (*MC*).

Quantity of Labor	Total Output	AVC	ATC	MC
0	0	___	___	___
1	100	___	___	___
2	250	___	___	___
3	350	___	___	___
4	400	___	___	___
5	425	___	___	___

21. *(Long-Run Costs)* Suppose the firm has only three possible
scales of production as shown below:

a. Which scale of production is most efficient when
   Q = 65?
b. Which scale of production is most efficient when
   Q = 75?
c. Trace out the long-run average cost curve on the
   diagram.

EXPERIENTIAL EXERCISES

22. *(Short- and Long-Run Costs)* The terms "diminishing returns" and "economies of scale" are often referred to in
everyday discussions and in the popular press. Using an
Internet search engine, search for diminishing returns or
economies of scale. Check the first five sites you find and,
in each case, decide whether the term is being used correctly or incorrectly. If the latter, see if you can determine
the nature of the writer's confusion. For example, check
"The Concepts of Increasing and Diminishing Returns"
(http://www.useit.com/alertbox/increasingreturns.html),
in which the author manages to compare a short-run
concept—diminishing (marginal) returns—with a long-
run concept—increasing returns (to scale).

23. *(Costs in the Long Run)* Find Erik Brynjolfsson and
Shinkyu Yang's "Information Technology and Productivity: A Review of the Literature," available online at
http://ccs.mit.edu/papers/ccswp202/. Using the concepts
you learned in this chapter, try to explain the expected
long-run impact of information technology on productivity and costs.

24. *(Wall Street Journal)* A firm's cost curves are based on the
prices of the inputs it uses and on the firm's technology.
Technology is the way the inputs are combined to produce a product. The "Technology" column in the Marketplace section of the *Wall Street Journal* describes many in-

teresting technological innovations. Pick one and see if you can determine how it might affect a firm's cost curves. Will it cause one resource to be substituted for

another? Try to guess both the short-run and long-run effects.

HOMEWORK XPRESS! EXERCISES

These exercises require access to McEachern Homework Xpress! If Homework Xpress! did not come with your book, visit **http://homeworkxpress.swlearning.com** *to purchase.*

1. The total product of workers added to the production line at Charles Cobbler, maker of fine shoes, is shown in the table. Find the marginal product for each additional worker. Plot the points indicating increasing marginal returns and identify. Then plot the points representing diminishing but positive marginal returns and identify, and plot the points representing negative marginal returns and identify them. Include any border points in each section.

Workers per day	Total product
0	0
1	3
2	7
3	12
4	16
5	19
6	21
7	22
8	22
9	21

2. Charles Cobbler faces typical short-run cost functions. The firm's fixed costs are $200 per day, and workers cost $100 per day. Draw a line to represent fixed costs. Then draw in curves to represent variable cost and total cost.

3. Charles Cobbler, who continues to make fine shoes, faces typical short-run cost curves. Draw a curve that would represent marginal cost of production for this firm. Then draw in curves that would represent average total cost and average variable cost of production for this firm.

4. Industries in which small, medium, and large firms all compete are usually characterized by economies of scale initially, followed by a long range of constant returns to scale before eventually running into diseconomies of scale. In the diagram draw in a long-run average cost curve for such an industry where economies of scale are exhausted at a quantity of 100 and diseconomies of scale begin at quantities greater than 1,000.

A Closer Look at Production and Costs

This appendix develops a model for determining how a profit-maximizing firm will combine resources to produce a particular rate of output. The quantity of output that can be produced with a given amount of resources depends on the existing *state of technology,* which is the prevailing knowledge of how resources can be combined. Therefore, let's begin by considering the technological possibilities available to the firm.

The Production Function and Efficiency

The ways in which resources can be combined to produce output are summarized by a firm's production function. The *production function* identifies the maximum quantities of a particular good or service that can be produced per time period with various combinations of resources, for a given level of technology. The production function can be presented as an equation, a graph, or a table.

The production function summarized in Exhibit 11 reflects, for a hypothetical firm, the output resulting from particular combinations of resources. This firm uses only two resources: capital and labor. The amount of capital used is listed down the left side of the table, and the amount of labor employed is listed across the top. For example, if 1 unit of capital is combined with 7 units of labor, the firm can produce 290 units of output per month. The firm produces the maximum possible output given the combination of resources used; that same output could not be produced with fewer resources. Because the production function combines resources efficiently, 290 units are the most that can be produced with 7 units of labor and 1 unit of capital. Thus, we say that production is **technologically efficient.**

We can examine the effects of adding labor to an existing amount of capital by starting with any level of capital and reading across the table. For example, when the firm uses 1 unit of capital and 1 unit of labor, it produces 40 units of output per month. If the amount of labor increases by 1 unit and the amount of capital remains constant, output increases to 90 units, so the marginal product of labor is 50 units. If the amount of labor employed increases from 2 to 3 units, other things constant, output goes to 150 units, yielding a marginal product of 60 units. By reading across the table, you will discover that the marginal product of labor first

EXHIBIT	11	A Firm's Production Function Using Labor and Capital: Production per Month

Units of Capital Employed per Month	Units of Labor Employed per Month						
	1	2	3	4	5	6	7
1	40	90	150	200	240	270	290
2	90	140	200	250	290	315	335
3	150	195	260	310	345	370	390
4	200	250	310	350	385	415	440
5	240	290	345	385	420	450	475
6	270	320	375	415	450	475	495
7	290	330	390	435	470	495	510

rises, showing increasing marginal returns from labor, and then declines, showing diminishing marginal returns. Similarly, by holding the amount of labor constant and following down the column, you will find that the marginal product of capital also reflects first increasing marginal returns and then diminishing marginal returns.

Isoquants

Notice from the tabular presentation of the production function in Exhibit 11 that different combinations of resources yield the same rate of output. For example, several combinations of labor and capital yield 290 units of output per month (try to find the four combinations). Some of the information provided in Exhibit 11 can be presented more clearly in graphical form. In Exhibit 12, labor is measured along the horizontal axis and capital along the vertical axis. Combinations that yield 290 units of output are presented in Exhibit 12 as points *a, b, c,* and *d.* These points can be connected to form an *isoquant,* Q_1, a curve that shows the possible combinations of the two resources that produce 290 units of output per month. Likewise, Q_2 shows combinations of inputs that yield 415 units of output, and Q_3, 475 units of output. (The isoquant colors match those of the corresponding entries in the production function table in Exhibit 11.)

An **isoquant,** such as Q_1 in Exhibit 12, is a curve that shows all the technologically efficient combinations of two resources, such as labor and capital, that produce a certain rate of output. *Iso* is from the Greek word meaning "equal," and *quant* is short for "quantity"; so *isoquant* means "equal quantity." Along a particular isoquant, such as Q_1, the rate of output produced remains constant—in this case, 290 units per month—but the combination of resources varies. To produce a particular rate of output, the firm can use resource combinations ranging from much capital and little labor to little capital and much labor. For example, a paving contractor can put in a new driveway with 10 workers using shovels, wheelbarrows, and hand rollers; the same job can also be done with only 2 workers, a road grader, and a paving machine. A charity car wash is labor intensive, involving many workers per car, plus buckets, sponges, and hose. In contrast, a professional car wash is fully automated, requiring only

one worker to turn on the machine and collect the money. An isoquant depicts alternative combinations of resources that produce the same rate of output. Although we have included only three isoquants in Exhibit 12, there is a different isoquant for every quantity of output listed in Exhibit 11. Indeed, there is a different isoquant for every output rate the firm could possibly produce. Let's consider some properties of isoquants:

1. Isoquants farther from the origin represent greater output rates.

2. *Isoquants have negative slopes* because along a given isoquant, the quantity of labor employed inversely relates to the quantity of capital employed.

3. *Isoquants do not intersect* because each isoquant refers to a specific rate of output. An intersection would indicate that the same combination of resources could, with equal efficiency, produce two different amounts of output.

4. *Isoquants are usually convex to the origin,* which means that any isoquant becomes flatter as you move down along the curve.

The slope of an isoquant measures the ability of additional units of one resource—in this case, labor—to substitute in production for another—in this case, capital. As noted already, the isoquant has a negative slope. The absolute value of the slope of the isoquant is the **marginal rate of technical substitution,** or **MRTS,** between two resources. The MRTS is the rate at which labor substitutes for capital without affecting output. When much capital and little labor are used, the marginal productivity of labor is relatively great and the marginal productivity of capital relatively small, so one unit of labor will substitute for a relatively large amount of capital. For example, in moving from point *a* to *b* along isoquant Q_1 in Exhibit 12, one unit of labor substitutes for two units of capital, so the MRTS between points *a* and *b* equals 2. But as more labor and less capital are employed, the marginal product of labor declines and the marginal product of capital increases, so it takes more labor to make up for a one-unit reduction in capital. For example, in moving from point *c* to point *d,* two units of labor substitute for one unit of capital; thus, the MRTS between points *c* and *d* equals $1/2$.

The extent to which one input substitutes for another, as measured by the marginal rate of technical substitution, is directly linked to the marginal productivity of each input. For example, between points *a* and *b,* one unit of labor replaces two units of capital, yet output remains constant. So labor's marginal product, MP_L—that is, the additional out-

---

E X H I B I T | **12** | **A Firm's Isoquants**

Isoquant Q_1 shows all technologically efficient combinations of labor and capital that can be used to produce 290 units of output. Isoquant Q_2 reflects 415 units, and Q_3 reflects 475 units. Each isoquant has a negative slope and is convex to the origin.

put resulting from an additional unit of labor—must be twice as large as capital's marginal product, MP_C. In fact, *anywhere along the isoquant, the marginal rate of technical substitution of labor for capital equals the marginal product of labor divided by the marginal product of capital, which also equals the absolute value of the slope of the isoquant,* or:

$$|\text{Slope of isoquant}| = MRTS = MP_L/MP_C$$

where the vertical lines on either side of "Slope of isoquant" indicate the absolute value. For example, the slope between points *a* and *b* equals −2 and has an absolute value of 2, which equals both the marginal rate of substitution of labor for capital and the ratio of marginal productivities. Between points *b* and *c,* three units of labor substitute for three units of capital, while output is constant at 290. Thus, the slope between *b* and *c* is −3/3, for an absolute value of 1. Note that the absolute value of the isoquant's slope declines as we move down the curve because larger increases in labor are required to offset each one-unit decline in capital. Put another way, as less capital is employed, its marginal product increases, and as more labor is employed, its marginal product decreases.

If labor and capital were perfect substitutes in production, the rate at which labor substituted for capital would remain fixed along the isoquant, so the isoquant would be a downward-sloping straight line. Because most resources are *not* perfect substitutes, however, the rate at which one substitutes for another changes along an isoquant. As we move down along an isoquant, more labor is required to offset each one-unit decline in capital, so the isoquant becomes flatter and is convex to the origin.

Isocost Lines

Isoquants graphically illustrate a firm's production function for all quantities of output the firm could possibly produce. We turn now to the question of what combination of resources to employ to minimize the cost of producing a given rate of output. The answer, as we'll see, depends on the cost of resources.

Suppose a unit of labor costs the firm $1,500 per month, and a unit of capital costs $2,500 per month. The total cost (*TC*) of production per month is

$$TC = (w \times L) + (r \times C)$$
$$= \$1,500L + \$2,500C$$

where *w* is the monthly wage rate, *L* is the quantity of labor employed, *r* is the monthly cost of capital, and *C* is the quantity of capital employed. An **isocost line** identifies all combinations of capital and labor the firm can hire for a given total cost. Again, *iso* is Greek for "equal," so an isocost line is a line representing resource combinations of equal cost. In Exhibit 13, for example, the line *TC* = $15,000 identifies all combinations of labor and capital that cost the firm $15,000 per month. The entire $15,000 could pay for either 6 units of capital or 10 units of labor per month. Or the firm could employ any other combination of resources along the isocost line.

Recall that the slope of any line is the vertical change between two points on the line divided by the corresponding horizontal change. At the point where the isocost line meets the vertical axis, the quantity of capital that can be purchased equals the total cost divided by the monthly cost of a unit of capital, or *TC/r*. At the point where the isocost line meets the horizontal axis, the quantity of labor that can be hired equals the firm's total cost divided by the monthly wage, or *TC/w*. The slope of any isocost line in Exhibit 13 can be calculated by considering a movement from the vertical intercept to the horizontal intercept. That is, we divide the vertical change (−*TC/r*) by the horizontal change (*TC/w*), as follows:

$$\text{Slope of isocost line} = -\frac{TC/r}{TC/w} = -\frac{w}{r}$$

EXHIBIT   13   A Firm's Isocost Lines

Each isocost line shows combinations of labor and capital that can be purchased for a given amount of total cost. The slope of each equals the negative of the monthly wage rate divided by the rental cost of capital per month. Higher costs are represented by isocost lines farther from the origin.

The slope of the isocost line is the negative of the price of labor divided by the price of capital, or $-w/r$, which indicates the relative prices of the inputs. In our example, the absolute value of the slope of the isocost line equals w/r, or

$$|\text{Slope of isocost line}| = w/r$$
$$= \$1,500/\$2,500$$
$$= 0.6$$

The monthly wage is 0.6, or six-tenths, of the monthly cost of a unit of capital, so hiring one more unit of labor, without changing total cost, implies that the firm must employ 0.6 fewer units of capital.

A firm is not confined to a particular isocost line. This is why Exhibit 13 includes three of them, each corresponding to a different total budget. In fact, there is a different isocost line for every possible budget. *These isocost lines are parallel because each reflects the same relative resource prices.* Resource prices in our example are assumed to be constant regardless of the amount of each resource the firm employs.

The Choice of Input Combinations

Exhibit 14 brings together the isoquants and the isocost lines. Suppose the firm has decided to produce 415 units of output and wants to minimize the cost of doing so. The firm could select point *f*, where 6 units of capital combine with 4 units of labor to produce 415 units. This combination, however, would cost $21,000 at prevailing prices. Because the profit-maximizing firm wants to produce its chosen output at the minimum cost, it tries to find the isocost line closest to the origin that still touches the isoquant. The isoquant for 415 units of output is tangent to the isocost line at point *e*. From that point of tangency, any movement in either direction along an isoquant increases the cost. So *the tangency between the isocost line and the isoquant shows the minimum cost required to produce a given output.*

Look at what's going on at the point of tangency. At point *e* in Exhibit 14, the isoquant and the isocost line have the same slope. As mentioned already, the absolute value of the slope of an isoquant equals the *marginal rate of technical substitution* between labor and capital, and the absolute value of the slope of the isocost line equals the *ratio of the input prices*. So when a firm produces output in the least costly way, the marginal rate of technical substitution must equal the ratio of the resource prices, or:

$$\text{MRTS} = w/r = \$1,500/\$2,500 = 0.6$$

This equality shows that the firm adjusts resource use so that the rate at which one input substitutes for another in production—that is, the marginal rate of technical substitution—equals the rate at

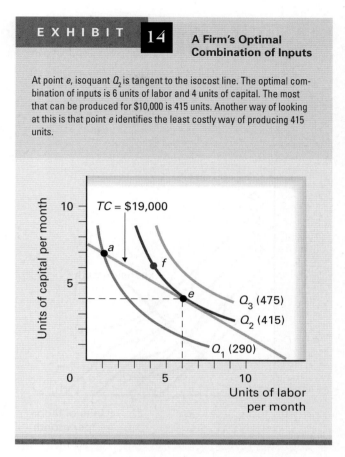

EXHIBIT   14   **A Firm's Optimal Combination of Inputs**

At point *e*, isoquant Q_2 is tangent to the isocost line. The optimal combination of inputs is 6 units of labor and 4 units of capital. The most that can be produced for $10,000 is 415 units. Another way of looking at this is that point *e* identifies the least costly way of producing 415 units.

which one resource exchanges for another in resource markets, which is w/r. If this equality does not hold, the firm could adjust its input mix to produce the same output for a lower cost.

The Expansion Path

Imagine a set of isoquants representing each possible rate of output. Given the relative cost of resources, we could then draw isocost lines to determine the optimal combination of resources for producing each rate of output. The points of tangency in Exhibit 15 show the least-cost input combinations for producing several output rates. For example, output rate Q_2 can be produced most cheaply using *C* units of capital and *L* units of labor. The line formed by connecting these tangency points is the firm's **expansion path.** The expansion path need not be a straight line, although it will generally slope upward, indicating that the firm will expand the use of both resources in the long run as output increases. Note that we have assumed that the prices of inputs remain constant as the firm varies output along the expansion path, so the isocost lines at the points of tangency are parallel—that is, they have the same slope.

EXHIBIT **15**   **A Firm's Expansion Path**

Points of tangency between isoquants and isocost lines identify the least costly resource combination of producing each particular quantity of output. Connecting these tangency points traces out the firm's expansion path.

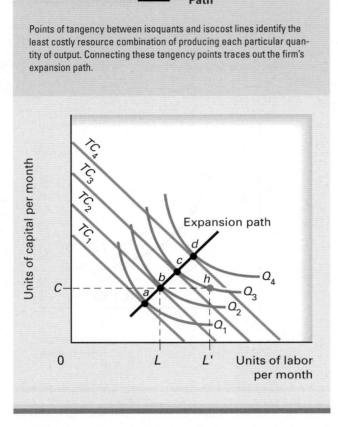

The expansion path indicates the lowest long-run total cost for each rate of output. For example, the firm can produce output rate Q_2 for TC_2, output rate Q_3 for TC_3, and so on. Similarly, the firm's long-run average cost curve indicates, at each rate of output, the total cost divided by the rate of output. The firm's expansion path and the firm's long-run average cost curve represent alternative ways of portraying costs in the long run, given resource prices and technology.

We can use Exhibit 15 to distinguish between short-run and long-run adjustments in output. Let's begin with the firm producing Q_2 at point b, which requires C units of capital and L units of labor. Now suppose that in the short run, the firm wants to increase output to Q_3. Because capital is fixed in the short run, the only way to produce Q_3 is by increasing the quantity of labor employed to L', which requires moving to point h in Exhibit 15. Point h is not the cheapest way to produce Q_3 in the long run because it is not a tangency point. In the long run, capital is variable, and if the firm wishes to produce Q_3, it should minimize total cost by adjusting from point h to point c.

One final point: If the relative prices of resources change, the least-cost resource combination will also change, so the firm's expansion path will change. For example, if the price of labor increases, capital becomes cheaper relative to labor. The efficient production of any given rate of output will therefore call for less labor and more capital. With the cost of labor higher, the firm's total cost for each rate of output rises. Such a cost increase would also be reflected by an upward shift of the average total cost curve.

Summary

A firm's *production function* specifies the relationship between resource use and output, given prevailing technology. An *isoquant* is a curve that illustrates the possible combinations of resources that will produce a particular rate of output. An *isocost* line presents the combinations of resources the firm can employ, given resource prices and the firm's total budget. For a given rate of output—that is, for a given isoquant—the firm minimizes total cost by choosing the lowest isocost line that just touches, or is tangent to, the isoquant. The least-cost combination of resources depends on the productivity of resources and their relative cost. Economists believe that although firm owners may not understand the material in this appendix, they must act as if they do to maximize profit.

APPENDIX QUESTIONS

1. *(Choice of Input Combinations)* Suppose that a firm's cost per unit of labor is $100 per day and its cost per unit of capital is $400 per day.

   a. Draw the isocost line for a total cost per day of $2,000. Label the axes.
   b. If the firm is producing efficiently, what is the mar-

ginal rate of technical substitution between labor and capital?

   c. Demonstrate your answer to part (b) using isocost lines and isoquant curves.

2. *(The Expansion Path)* How are the expansion path and the long-run average cost curve related?

Perfect Competition

© Photodisc/Getty Images

W hat does a bushel of wheat have in common with a share of Microsoft stock? Why might a firm continue to operate even though it's losing money? Why do many firms fail to earn an economic profit? In what sense can it be said that the more competitive the industry, the less individual firms compete with each other? What's the difference between making stuff right and making the right stuff? And what's so perfect about perfect competition? To answer these and other questions, we examine our first market structure—perfect competition.

The previous chapter developed cost curves for an individual firm in the short run and in the long run. In light of these costs, how much should a firm produce and what price should it charge? To discover the firm's profit-maximizing output and price, we revisit an old friend—demand. Demand and supply, together, guide the firm to maximum economic profit. In the next few chapters, we will examine how firms respond to their economic environments in deciding what to supply, in what quantities, and at what price. We continue to assume that firms try to maximize profit. Topics discussed include:

- Market structure
- Price takers
- Marginal revenue
- Golden rule of profit maximization
- Loss minimization

- Short-run supply curve
- Long-run supply curve
- Competition and efficiency
- Producer surplus
- Gains from exchange

An Introduction to Perfect Competition

Market structure describes the important features of a market, such as the number of suppliers (are there many or few?), the product's degree of uniformity (do firms in the market supply identical products, or are there differences across firms?), the ease of entry into the market (can new firms enter easily or is entry blocked?), and the forms of competition among firms (do firms compete only based on price, or do they also compete through advertising and product differences?). The various features will become clearer as we examine each market structure in the next few chapters. *A firm's decisions about how much to produce or what price to charge depend on the structure of the market.*

Before we get started, a few words about terminology. An *industry* consists of all firms that supply output to a particular *market*, such as the auto market, the shoe market, or the wheat market. The terms *industry* and *market* are used interchangeably throughout this chapter.

Perfectly Competitive Market Structure

We begin with **perfect competition,** in some ways the most basic of market structures. A *perfectly competitive* market is characterized by (1) many buyers and sellers—so many that each buys or sells only a tiny fraction of the total amount exchanged in the market; (2) firms sell a **commodity,** which is a standardized product, such as a bushel of wheat or an ounce of gold; such a product does not differ across producers; (3) buyers and sellers that are fully informed about the price and availability of all resources and products; and (4) firms and resources that are freely mobile—that is, over time they can easily enter or leave the industry without facing obstacles like patents, licenses, high capital costs, or ignorance about available technology.

If these conditions exist in a market, an individual buyer or seller has no control over the price. Price is determined by market demand and supply. Once the market establishes the price, each firm is free to produce whatever quantity maximizes profit. *A perfectly competitive firm is so small relative to the size of the market that the firm's choice about how much to produce has no effect on the market price.* Examples of perfectly competitive markets include those for most agricultural products, such as wheat, corn, and livestock; markets for basic commodities, such as gold, silver, and copper; markets for widely traded stock, such as Microsoft, Citibank, and General Electric; and markets for foreign exchange, such as yen, euros, and pesos. Again, there are so many buyers and sellers that the actions of any one cannot influence the market price. For example, about 150,000 farmers in the United States raise hogs, and tens of millions of U.S. households buy pork products.

MARKET STRUCTURE

Important features of a market, such as the number of firms, product uniformity across firms, firms' ease of entry and exit, and forms of competition

HOMEWORK
Xpress!
Ask the Instructor
Video

PERFECT COMPETITION

A market structure with many fully informed buyers and sellers of a standardized product and no obstacles to entry or exit of firms in the long run

COMMODITY

A standardized product, a product that does not differ across producers, such as bushels of wheat or an ounce of gold

The model of perfect competition allows us to make a number of predictions that hold up well when compared to the real world. Perfect competition is also an important bench-mark for evaluating the efficiency of other types of markets. Let's look at demand under perfect competition.

Demand Under Perfect Competition

Suppose the market in question is the world market for wheat and the firm in question is a wheat farm. In the world market for wheat, there are tens of thousands of farms, so any one supplies only a tiny fraction of market output. For example, the thousands of wheat farmers in Kansas together produce less than 3 percent of the world's supply of wheat. In Exhibit 1, the market price of wheat of $5 per bushel is determined in panel (a) by the intersection of the market demand curve *D* and the market supply curve *S*. Once the market determines the price, any farmer can sell all he or she wants to at that market price.

Each farm is so small relative to the market that each has no impact on the market price. Because all farmers produce an identical product—bushels of wheat, in this case—anyone who charges more than the market price sells no wheat. For example, a farmer charging $5.05 per bushel would find no buyers. Of course, any farmer is free to charge less than the market price, but why do that when all wheat can be sold at the market price? Farmers aren't stupid (or if they are, they don't last long). *The demand curve facing an individual farmer is, therefore, a horizontal line drawn at the market price.* In our example, the demand curve facing an individual farmer, identified as *d* in panel (b), is drawn at the market price of $5 per

EXHIBIT	1	**Market Equilibrium and a Firm's Demand Curve in Perfect Competition**

In panel (a), the market price of $5 is determined by the intersection of the market demand and market supply curves. A perfectly competitive firm can sell any amount at that price. The demand curve facing the perfectly competitive firm is horizontal at the market price, as shown by demand curve *d* in panel (b).

(a) Market equilibrium

(b) Firm's demand

PRICE TAKER

A firm that faces a given market price and whose quantity supplied has no effect on that price; a perfectly competitive firm

bushel. Thus, each farmer faces a horizontal, or a *perfectly elastic,* demand curve. A perfectly competitive firm is called a **price taker** because that firm must "take," or accept, the market price—as in "take it or leave it."

It has been said, "In perfect competition there is no competition." Ironically, two neighboring wheat farmers in perfect competition are not really rivals. They both can sell all they want at the market price. The amount one sells has no effect on the market price or amount the other can sell.

Short-Run Profit Maximization

Each firm tries to maximize economic profit. Firms that ignore this strategy don't survive. Economic profit equals total revenue minus total cost, including both explicit and implicit costs. Implicit cost, you will recall, is the opportunity cost of resources owned by the firm and includes a normal profit. Economic profit is any profit above normal profit. How do firms maximize profit? You have already learned that the perfectly competitive firm has no control over price. What the firm does control is the rate of output—the quantity. The question the wheat farmer asks boils down to: *How much should I produce to earn the most profit?*

Total Revenue Minus Total Cost

The firm maximizes economic profit by finding the quantity at which total revenue exceeds total cost by the greatest amount. The firm's total revenue is simply its output times the price per unit. Column (1) in Exhibit 2 shows an individual farmer's output possibilities measured in bushels of wheat per day. Column (2) shows the market price per bushel of $5, a price that does not vary with the farmer's output. Column (3) shows total revenue, which is output times price, or column (1) times column (2). And column (4) shows the total cost of production. Total cost already includes a normal profit, so total cost includes all opportunity costs. Although the table does not distinguish between fixed and variable costs, fixed cost must equal $15 per day, because total cost is $15 when output is zero. The presence of fixed cost tells us that at least one resource is fixed, so the farm must be operating in the short run.

Total revenue in column (3) minus total cost in column (4) yields the farmer's economic profit or economic loss in column (7). As you can see, total revenue exceeds total cost when 7 to 14 bushels are produced, so the farm earns an *economic profit* at those output rates. Economic profit is maximized at $12 per day when the farm produces 12 bushels of wheat per day (the $12 and 12 bushels combination is just a coincidence).

These results are graphed in panel (a) of Exhibit 3, which shows the total revenue and total cost curves. As output increases by 1 bushel, total revenue increases by $5, so the farm's total revenue curve is a straight line emanating from the origin, with a slope of 5. The short-run total cost curve has the backward S shape introduced in the previous chapter, showing increasing and then diminishing marginal returns from the variable resource. Total cost always increases as more output is produced.

Subtracting total cost from total revenue is one way to find the profit-maximizing output. For output less than 7 bushels and greater than 14 bushels, total cost exceeds total revenue. The economic loss is measured by the vertical distance between the two curves. Between 7 and 14 bushels per day, total revenue exceeds total cost. The economic profit, again, is measured by the distance between the two curves. *Profit is maximized at the rate of output where total revenue exceeds total cost by the greatest amount.* Profit is greatest when 12 bushels are produced per day.

(1) Bushels of Wheat per Day (q)	(2) Marginal Revenue (Price) (p)	(3) Total Revenue (TR = q x p)	(4) Total Cost (TC)	(5) Marginal Cost (MC = ΔTC/Δq)	(6) Average Total Cost (ATC = TC/q)	(7) Economic Profit or Loss = TR – TC
0	—	$ 0	$15.00	—	—	-$15.00
1	$5	5	19.75	$4.75	$19.75	-14.75
2	5	10	23.50	3.75	11.75	-13.50
3	5	15	26.50	3.00	8.83	-11.50
4	5	20	29.00	2.50	7.25	-9.00
5	5	25	31.00	2.00	6.20	-6.00
6	5	30	32.50	1.50	5.42	-2.50
7	5	35	33.75	1.25	4.82	1.25
8	5	40	35.25	1.50	4.41	4.75
9	5	45	37.25	2.00	4.14	7.75
10	5	50	40.00	2.75	4.00	10.00
11	5	55	43.25	3.25	3.93	11.75
12	**5**	**60**	**48.00**	**4.75**	**4.00**	**12.00**
13	5	65	54.50	6.50	4.19	10.50
14	5	70	64.00	9.50	4.57	6.00
15	5	75	77.50	13.50	5.17	-2.50
16	5	80	96.00	18.50	6.00	-16.00

Short-Run Costs and Revenues for a Perfectly Competitive Firm

Marginal Revenue Equals Marginal Cost

Another way to find the profit-maximizing rate of output is to focus on marginal revenue and marginal cost. **Marginal revenue,** or **MR,** is the change in total revenue from selling another unit of output. In perfect competition, each firm is a price taker, so selling one more unit increases total revenue by the market price. Thus, *in perfect competition, marginal revenue is the market price*—in this example, $5. Column (2) of Exhibit 2 presents the farm's marginal revenue for each bushel of wheat.

In the previous chapter, you learned that *marginal cost* is the change in total cost from producing another unit of output. Column (5) of Exhibit 2 shows the farm's marginal cost for each bushel of wheat. Marginal cost first declines, reflecting increasing marginal returns in the short run as more of the variable resource is employed. Marginal cost then increases, reflecting diminishing marginal returns from the variable resource.

The firm will increase production as long as each additional unit adds more to total revenue than to total cost—that is, as long as marginal revenue exceeds marginal cost. Comparing columns (2) and (5) in Exhibit 2, we see that marginal revenue exceeds marginal cost for each of the first 12 bushels of wheat. The marginal cost of bushel 13, however, is $6.50, compared with its marginal revenue of $5. Therefore, producing bushel 13 would reduce economic profit by $1.50. The farmer, as a profit maximizer, will limit output to 12 bushels per day. More

MARGINAL REVENUE

The change in total revenue from selling an additional unit; in perfect competition, marginal revenue is also the market price

EXHIBIT 3

Short-Run Profit Maximization

In panel (a), the total revenue curve for a competitive firm is a straight line with a slope of 5, the market price. Total cost increases with output, first at a decreasing rate and then at an increasing rate. Economic profit is maximized where total revenue exceeds total cost by the greatest amount, which occurs at 12 bushels of wheat per day. In panel (b), marginal revenue is a horizontal line at the market price of $5. Economic profit is maximized at 12 bushels of wheat per day, where marginal revenue equals marginal cost (point *e*). That profit equals 12 bushels multiplied by the amount by which the market price of $5 exceeds the average total cost of $4. Economic profit is identified by the shaded rectangle.

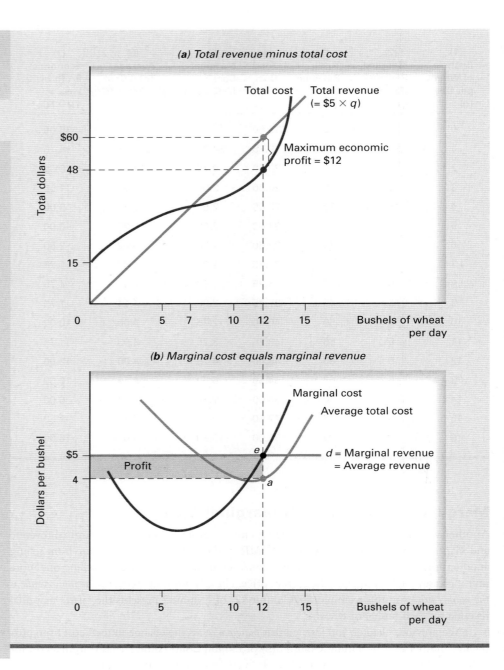

GOLDEN RULE OF PROFIT MAXIMIZATION

To maximize profit or minimize loss, a firm should produce the quantity at which marginal revenue equals marginal cost; this rule holds for all market structures

generally, a firm will expand output as long as marginal revenue exceeds marginal cost and will stop expanding before marginal cost exceeds marginal revenue. A shorthand expression for this approach is the **golden rule of profit maximization,** which says that a profit-maximizing firm produces the quantity where *marginal revenue equals marginal cost.*

Economic Profit in the Short Run

Per-unit revenue and cost data from Exhibit 2 are graphed in panel (b) of Exhibit 3. Because marginal revenue in perfect competition equals the market price, the marginal revenue curve is a horizontal line at the market price of $5, which is also the perfectly competitive firm's demand curve. At any quantity measured along the demand curve, marginal revenue is the price. Because the perfectly competitive firm can sell any quantity for the same price per unit, marginal revenue is also **average revenue,** or *AR*. Average revenue equals total revenue divided by quantity, or $AR = TR/q$. Regardless of the output rate, therefore, the following equality holds along a perfectly competitive firm's demand curve:

AVERAGE REVENUE

Total revenue divided by output, or $AR = TR/q$; in all market structures, average revenue equals the market price

$$\text{Market price} = \text{Marginal revenue} = \text{Average revenue}$$

The marginal cost curve intersects the marginal revenue curve at point *e,* where output is about 12 bushels per day. At lower rates of output, marginal revenue exceeds marginal cost, so the farm could increase profit by expanding output. At higher rates of output, marginal cost exceeds marginal revenue, so the farm could increase profit by reducing output. Profit itself appears as the shaded rectangle. The height of that rectangle, *ae,* equals the price (or average revenue) of $5 minus the average total cost of $4. Price minus average total cost yields an average profit of $1 per bushel. Profit per day, $12, equals the average profit per bushel, $1 (denoted by *ae*), times the 12 bushels produced.

Note that with the total cost and total revenue curves, we measure economic profit by the vertical *distance* between the two curves, as shown in panel (a). But with the per-unit curves of panel (b), we measure economic profit by an *area*—that is, by multiplying the average profit of $1 per bushel times the 12 bushels sold.

Minimizing Short-Run Losses

An individual firm in perfect competition has no control over the market price. Sometimes that price may be so low that a firm loses money no matter how much it produces. Such a firm can either continue to produce at a loss or temporarily shut down. But even if the firm shuts down, it cannot, *in the short run,* go out of business or produce something else. The short run is by definition a period too short to allow existing firms to leave the industry. In a sense, firms are stuck in their industry in the short run.

Fixed Cost and Minimizing Losses

So should a firm produce at a loss or temporarily shut down? Intuition suggests the firm should shut down. But it's not that simple. Keep in mind that the firm faces two types of cost in the short run: fixed cost, such as property taxes and fire insurance, which must be paid in the short run even if the firm produces nothing, and variable cost, such as labor, which depends on the amount of output the firm wants to produce. A firm that shuts down in the short run must still pay its fixed cost. But, by producing, a firm's revenue may pay variable cost and also cover a portion of fixed cost. What this boils down to is that *a firm will produce rather than shut down if total revenue exceeds the variable cost of production.* After all, if total revenue exceeds variable cost, that excess can go toward covering at least a portion of fixed cost.

Let's look at the same cost data presented in Exhibit 2, but now suppose the market price of wheat is $3 a bushel, not $5. This new situation is presented in Exhibit 4. Because of the lower price, total revenue is less than total cost at all output rates. Each quantity thus results in a loss, as indicated by Column (8). If the firm produces nothing, it loses the fixed cost of $15 per day. But, by producing anywhere from 6 and 12 bushels, the firm can reduce that

...izing Short-Run Losses

171

		(3) Revenue $= q \times p$	(4) Total Cost (TC)	(5) Marginal Cost $(MC = \Delta TC/\Delta q)$	(6) Average Total Cost $(ATC = TC/q)$	(7) Average Variable Cost $(AVC = VC/q)$	(8) Economic Profit or Loss $= TR - TC$
0			$15.00	—	—	—	−$15.00
		3	19.75	$4.75	$19.75	$4.75	−16.75
2	3	6	23.50	3.75	11.75	4.25	−17.50
3	3	9	26.50	3.00	8.83	3.83	−17.50
4	3	12	29.00	2.50	7.25	3.50	−17.00
5	3	15	31.00	2.00	6.20	3.20	−16.00
6	3	18	32.50	1.50	5.42	2.92	−14.50
7	3	21	33.75	1.25	4.82	2.68	−12.75
8	3	24	35.25	1.50	4.41	2.53	−11.25
9	3	27	37.25	2.00	4.14	2.47	−10.25
10	**3**	**30**	**40.00**	**2.75**	**4.00**	**2.50**	**−10.00**
11	3	33	43.25	3.25	3.93	2.57	−10.25
12	3	36	48.00	4.75	4.00	2.75	−12.00
13	3	39	54.50	6.50	4.19	3.04	−15.50
14	3	42	64.00	9.50	4.57	3.50	−22.00
15	3	45	77.50	13.50	5.17	4.17	−32.50
16	3	48	96.00	18.50	6.00	5.06	−48.00

loss. From column (8), you can see that the loss is minimized at $10 per day where 10 bushels are produced. Producing that amount adds $25 to total cost but adds $30 to total revenue. The net gain of $5 can pay some of the firm's fixed cost.

Panel (a) of Exhibit 5 presents the firm's total cost and total revenue curves for data in Exhibit 4. The total cost curve remains as before in Exhibit 3. Because the price is $3, the total revenue curve now has a slope of 3, so it's flatter than at a price of $5. The total revenue curve now lies below the total cost curve at all quantities. The vertical distance between the two curves measures the loss at each quantity. If the farmer produces nothing, the loss is the fixed cost of $15 per day. The vertical distance between the two curves is minimized at 10 bushels, where the loss is $10 per day.

Marginal Revenue Equals Marginal Cost

We get the same result using marginal analysis. The per-unit data from Exhibit 4 are presented in panel (b) of Exhibit 5. First we find the rate of output where marginal revenue

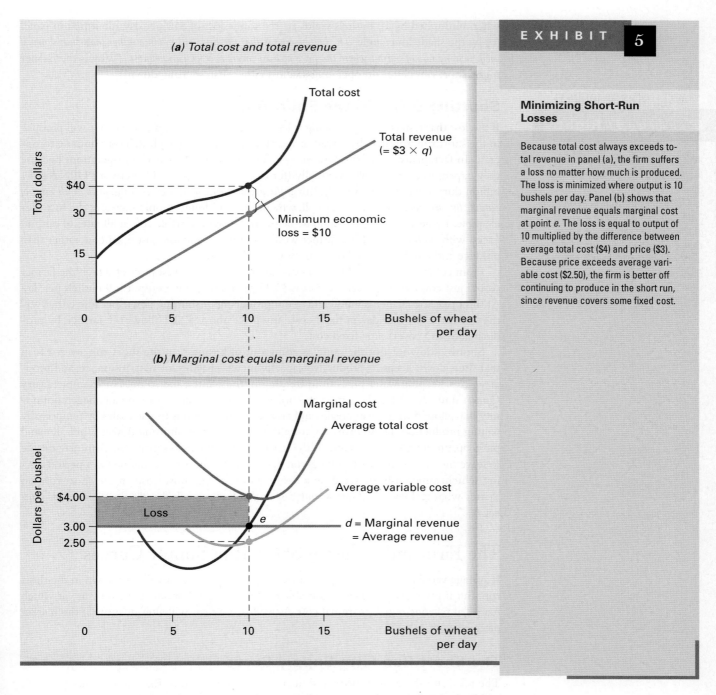

(a) Total cost and total revenue

Total cost

Total revenue
(= $3 × q)

Total dollars

$40

30

15

Minimum economic
loss = $10

0   5   10   15   Bushels of wheat
per day

(b) Marginal cost equals marginal revenue

Marginal cost

Average total cost

Average variable cost

Dollars per bushel

$4.00

Loss

3.00   e

2.50

d = Marginal revenue
= Average revenue

0   5   10   15   Bushels of wheat
per day

EXHIBIT 5

**Minimizing Short-Run
Losses**

Because total cost always exceeds total revenue in panel (a), the firm suffers
a loss no matter how much is produced.
The loss is minimized where output is 10
bushels per day. Panel (b) shows that
marginal revenue equals marginal cost
at point *e*. The loss is equal to output of
10 multiplied by the difference between
average total cost ($4) and price ($3).
Because price exceeds average variable cost ($2.50), the firm is better off
continuing to produce in the short run,
since revenue covers some fixed cost.

equals marginal cost. Marginal revenue equals marginal cost at an output of 10 bushels per
day. At that output, the market price of $3 exceeds the average variable cost of $2.50. Because price exceeds average variable cost, total revenue covers variable cost plus a portion of
fixed cost. Specifically, $2.50 of the price pays the average variable cost, and the remaining
$0.50 helps pay some of average fixed cost (average fixed cost equals average total cost of
$4.00 minus average variable cost of $2.50). This still leaves a loss of $1 per bushel, which

when multiplied by 10 bushels yields an economic loss of $10 per day, identified in panel (b) by the shaded rectangle. *The bottom line is that the firm will produce rather than shut down if there is some rate of output where the price at least covers average variable cost.* (Why is the farmer in the short run better off operating at a loss rather than shutting down?)

Shutting Down in the Short Run

If the loss that results from producing is less than the shutdown loss, the farmer will produce in the short run. You may have read or heard of firms reporting a loss; most continue to operate. In fact, many new firms lose money during the first few years of operations because they expect to be profitable eventually (for example, the upstart TV network UPN lost $1 billion during its first five years[1]). But *if the average variable cost exceeds the price at all rates of output, the firm will shut down.* After all, why produce if doing so only increases the loss? For example, a wheat price of $2 would be below the average variable cost at all rates of output. Faced with such a low price, a farmer would shut down and lose just fixed cost, rather than produce and lose both fixed cost plus some variable cost.

From column (7) of Exhibit 4, you can also see that the lowest price at which the farmer would just cover average variable cost is $2.47 per bushel, when output is 9 bushels per day. At this price, the farmer is indifferent about producing or shutting down, because either way the loss is the $15 per day in fixed cost. Any price above $2.47 allows the farmer, by producing, to also cover some fixed cost.

Shutting down is not the same as going out of business. In the short run, even a firm that shuts down keeps its productive capacity intact—paying for rent, insurance, and property taxes, keeping water pipes from freezing in the winter, and so on. For example, Dairy Queen shuts down for the winter in cooler climates, a business serving a college community may close during term breaks, and an auto plant responds to slack sales by temporarily halting production. These firms do not escape fixed cost by shutting down. When demand picks up, production will resume. If the market outlook remains grim, the firm may decide to leave the market, but that's a long-run decision. The short run is defined as a period during which some costs are fixed, so a firm cannot escape those costs in the short run, no matter what it does. *Fixed cost is sunk cost in the short run, whether the firm produces or shuts down.*

The Firm and Industry Short-Run Supply Curves

If average variable cost exceeds price at all output rates, the firm will shut down in the short run. But if price exceeds average variable cost, the firm will produce the quantity at which marginal revenue equals marginal cost. As we'll see, a firm will alter quantity if the market price changes.

The Short-Run Firm Supply Curve

The relationship between price and quantity is summarized in Exhibit 6. Points 1, 2, 3, 4, and 5 identify where the marginal cost curve intersects various marginal revenue, or demand, curves. At a price as low as p_1, the firm will shut down rather than produce at point 1 because that price is below average variable cost. So the loss-minimizing output rate at price p_1 is zero, as identified by q_1. At price p_2, that price just equals average variable cost, so the

---

1. Joe Flint, "Will Viacom's Big Bet on 'Buffy' Become UPN's Savior or Slayer," *Wall Street Journal,* 12 July 2001.

firm will be indifferent about producing q_2 or shutting down; either way the firm loses fixed cost. Point 2 is called the *shutdown point*. If the price is p_3, the firm will produce q_3 to minimize its loss (see if you can identify that loss in the diagram). At p_4, the firm will produce q_4 to earn just a normal profit, because price equals average total cost. Point 4 is called the *break-even point*. If the price rises to p_5, the firm will earn short-run economic profit by producing q_5 (see if you can identify that economic profit).

As long as the price covers average variable cost, the firm will supply the quantity at which the upward-sloping marginal cost curve intersects the marginal revenue, or demand, curve. Thus, that portion of the firm's marginal cost curve that intersects and rises above the lowest point on its average variable cost curve becomes the **short-run firm supply curve.** In Exhibit 6, the short-run supply curve is the upward-sloping portion of the marginal cost curve, beginning at point 2, the shutdown point. The solid portion of the short-run supply curve indicates the quantity the firm offers for sale at each price. The quantity supplied when the price is p_2 or higher is determined by the intersection of the firm's marginal cost curve and its demand, or marginal revenue, curve. At prices below p_2, the firm shuts down in the short run.

The Short-Run Industry Supply Curve

Exhibit 7 presents examples of how supply curves for three firms with identical marginal cost curves can be summed *horizontally* to form the short-run industry supply curve (in perfect competition, there will be many more firms). The **short-run industry supply curve** is the horizontal sum of all firms' short-run supply curves. At a price below p, no

SHORT-RUN FIRM SUPPLY CURVE

A curve that shows the quantity a firm supplies at each price in the short run; in perfect competition, that portion of a firm's marginal cost curve that intersects and rises above the low point on its average variable cost curve

SHORT-RUN INDUSTRY SUPPLY CURVE

A curve that indicates the quantity supplied by the industry at each price in the short run; in perfect competition, the horizontal sum of each firm's short-run supply curve

E X H I B I T 6

HOMEWORK *Xpress!* *Graphing*

Summary of Short-Run Output Decisions

At price p_1, the firm produces nothing because p_1 is less than the firm's average variable cost. At price p_2, the firm is indifferent about shutting down or producing q_2 units of output, because in either case, the firm suffers a loss equal to its fixed cost. At p_3, it produces q_3 units and suffers a loss that is less than its fixed cost. At p_4, the firm produces q_4 and just breaks even, earning a normal profit, because p_4 equals average total cost. Finally, at p_5, the firm produces q_5 and earns an economic profit. The firm's short-run supply curve is that portion of its marginal cost curve at or rising above the minimum point of average variable cost (point 2).

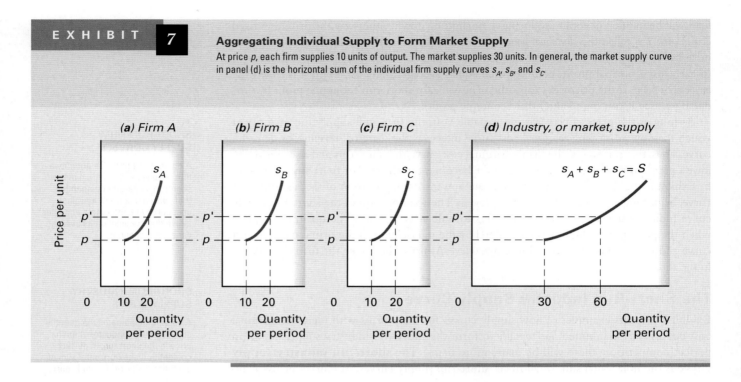

Aggregating Individual Supply to Form Market Supply
At price *p*, each firm supplies 10 units of output. The market supplies 30 units. In general, the market supply curve in panel (d) is the horizontal sum of the individual firm supply curves s_A, s_B, and s_C.

output is supplied. At price *p*, each of the three firms supplies 10 units, for the market supplies 30 units. At *p'*, which is above *p*, each firm supplies 20 units, so the market supplies 60 units.

Firm Supply and Market Equilibrium

Exhibit 8 shows the relationship between the short-run profit-maximizing output of the individual firm and market equilibrium price and quantity. Suppose there are 100,000 identical wheat farmers in this industry. Their individual supply curves (represented by the portions of the marginal cost curve at or rising above the average variable cost) are summed horizontally to yield the market, or industry, supply curve. The market supply curve appears in panel (b), where it intersects the market demand curve to determine the market price of $5 per bushel. At that price, each farmer supplies 12 bushels per day, as shown in panel (a), which sums to 1,200,000 bushels for the market, as shown in panel (b). Each farmer in the short run earns an economic profit of $12 per day, represented by the shaded rectangle in panel (a).

In summary: *A perfectly competitive firm supplies the short-run quantity that maximizes profit or minimizes loss. When confronting a loss, a firm either supplies an output that minimizes that loss or shuts down temporarily.* Given the conditions for perfect competition, the market will converge toward the equilibrium price and quantity. But how is that equilibrium actually reached? In the real world, markets operate based on customs and conventions, which vary across markets. For example, the rules acceptable on the New York Stock Exchange are not the same as those followed in the market for fresh fish. The following case study discusses one mechanism for reaching equilibrium—auctions.

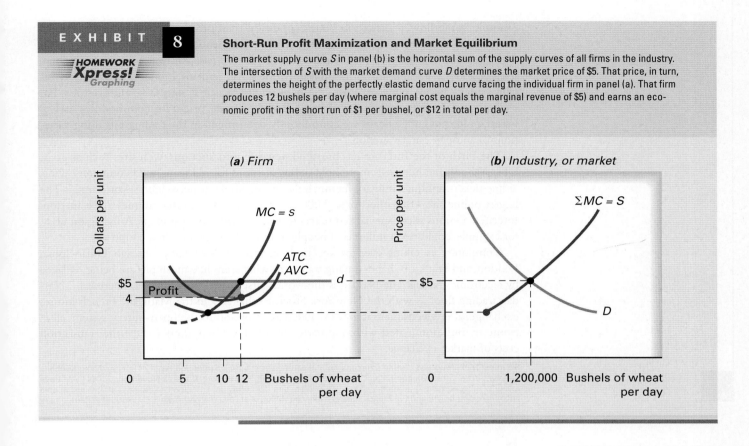

Short-Run Profit Maximization and Market Equilibrium

The market supply curve *S* in panel (b) is the horizontal sum of the supply curves of all firms in the industry. The intersection of *S* with the market demand curve *D* determines the market price of $5. That price, in turn, determines the height of the perfectly elastic demand curve facing the individual firm in panel (a). That firm produces 12 bushels per day (where marginal cost equals the marginal revenue of $5) and earns an economic profit in the short run of $1 per bushel, or $12 in total per day.

(a) Firm

(b) Industry, or market

Auction Markets

Five days a week, in a huge building 10 miles outside Amsterdam, some 2,500 buyers gather to participate in Flower Auction Holland, the largest auction of its kind in the world. Over 14 million flowers from 5,600 growers around the globe are auctioned off each day in the world's largest commercial building, spread across the equivalent of 100 football fields. Flowers are grouped and auctioned off by type—long-stemmed roses, tulips, and so on. Hundreds of buyers are seated in theater settings with their fingers on buttons. Once the flowers are presented, a clock-like instrument starts ticking off descending prices until a buyer pushes a button. The winning bidder gets to choose how many and which items to take. The clock starts again until another buyer stops it, and so on, until all flowers are sold. Buyers can also bid from remote locations over the Internet. Auctions occur rapidly—on average a transaction occurs every 4 seconds.

This is an example of a *Dutch auction,* which starts at a high price and works down. Dutch auctions are more common when selling multiple lots of similar, though not identical, items, such as flowers in Amsterdam, tobacco in Canada, and fish in seaports around the world. Because there is some difference among the products for sale in a given market—for

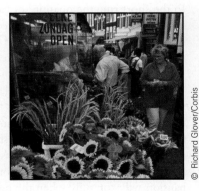

***Case* Study**

World of Business

*e*Activity
Are you fast enough to compete in the Dutch Flower Auction Simulation? Try your hand in a computer simulation at http://research.haifa.ac.il/~avinoy/auction/dutch/. How often did a winning bid appear before the price fell to the point where you could earn a profit? Did you lose out on any profitable opportunities? Were you tempted to bid faster and too high after losing out a few times? If so, you can return to the entry page to choose a slower clock speed. If you think you can go faster, try increasing the speed.

example, some flower lots are in better condition than others—this is not quite perfect competition because perfectly competitive markets sell identical products.

More common than the Dutch auction is the *English open outcry auction,* where bidding starts at a low price and moves up until only one buyer remains. Products sold this way include stocks, bonds, wine, art (think Sotheby's and Christie's), antiques, and livestock. For example, on markets, such as the Chicago Board of Trade, prices for commodities such as wheat, gold, and coffee beans are continuously determined in the trading pits using variations of an open outcry auction.

The birth of the Internet has breathed new life into auctions. Web sites such as eBay, Ubid, Yahoo!, and hundreds more hold online auctions for old maps, used computers, wine, airline tickets, antiques, military memorabilia, comic books, paperweights—you name it. The largest online site, eBay, offers over 2,000 categories in a forum that mimics a live auction. Internet auctions allow specialized sellers to reach a world of customers. A listing on eBay, for example, could reach millions of people in more than one hundred countries.

Computers are taking over markets in other ways. In New York, Chicago, Philadelphia, London, and Frankfurt, hand-waving traders in what seem like mosh pits are being replaced by electronic trading. The Nasdaq is the world's first virtual stock market. There is no Nasdaq trading floor as with the New York Stock Exchange. On the Matif, the French futures exchange, after electronic trading was added as an option to the open-outcry system, electronic trading dominated within a matter of months. Computers reduce the transaction costs of market exchange.

Sources: Nick Wingfield, "eBay's Results Keep a Strong Pace," *Wall Street Journal*, 17 October 2003; Michelle Slatalla, "At a Virtual Garage Sale, It Frequently Pays to Wait," *New York Times*, 2 November 2000; "We Have Lift-Off," *Economist*, 3 February 2001. The Web site for eBay is http://www.ebay.com/; Nasdaq's is http://nasdaq.com/; and the French trading exchange, Matif, is at http://www.matif.com/indexE4.htm.

N e t **Bookmark**

Quick links to numerous online auctions, such as eBay, can be found at the most popular search engines. Google offers a list of particular online auctions: http://www.google.com (search for online auctions), and Yahoo! presents http://auctions.yahoo.com/. What are the most frequently listed types of goods available through online auctions? Are these the types of goods you would expect to find offered in perfectly competitive market? Can you distinguish which goods are fads? Some of the search engines bring you directly to auctions for particular goods, but are they running the auction? Who is "powering" the auction processes? Does the auctioning business appear to be perfectly competitive?

Perfect Competition in the Long Run

In the short run, the quantity of variable resources can change, but other resources, which mostly determine firm size, are fixed. In the long run, however, firms have time to enter and leave and to adjust their size—that is, to adjust the *scale* of their operations. In the long run, there is no distinction between fixed and variable cost because all resources under the firm's control are variable.

Short-run economic profit will, in the long run, encourage new firms to enter the market and may prompt existing firms to get bigger. Economic profit will attract resources from industries where firms are losing money or earning only a normal profit. This expansion in the number and size of firms will shift the industry supply curve rightward in the long run, driving down the price. New firms will continue to enter a profitable industry and existing firms will continue to expand as long as economic profit is greater than zero. Entry and expansion will stop only when the resulting increase in supply drives down the price enough to erase economic profit. In the case of wheat farming, economic profit attracts new wheat farmers and may encourage existing wheat farmers to expand their scale of operation. *Short-run economic profit attracts new entrants in the long run and may cause existing firms to expand. Market supply thereby increases, driving down the market price until economic profit disappears.*

On the other hand, a short-run loss will, in the long run, force some firms to leave the industry or to reduce their scale of operation. In the long run, departures and reductions in scale shift the market supply curve to the left, thereby increasing the market price until remaining firms just break even—that is, earn a normal profit.

Zero Economic Profit in the Long Run

In the long run, firms in perfect competition earn just a normal profit, which means zero economic profit. Exhibit 9 shows a firm and the market in long-run equilibrium. In the long run, market supply adjusts as firms enter or leave or change their size. *This long-run adjustment continues until the market supply curve intersects the market demand curve at a price that corresponds to the lowest point on each firm's long-run average cost curve, or LRAC curve.* Because the long run is a period during which all resources under a firm's control can be varied, *a firm in the long run will be forced by competition to adjust its scale until its average cost of production is minimized.* A firm that fails to minimize cost will not survive in the long run. At point *e* in panel (a) of Exhibit 9, the firm is in equilibrium, producing *q* units and earning just a normal profit. At point *e*, price, marginal cost, short-run average total cost, and long-run average cost are all equal. No firm in the market has any reason to change its output rate, and no outside firm has any incentive to enter this industry, because firms in this market are earning normal, but not economic, profit.

The Long-Run Adjustment to a Change in Demand

To explore the long-run adjustment process, let's consider how a firm and an industry respond to an increase in market demand. Suppose that the costs facing each firm do not depend on the number of firms in the industry (this assumption will be explained soon).

Effects of an Increase in Demand

Exhibit 10 shows a perfectly competitive firm and industry in long-run equilibrium, with the market supply curve intersecting the market demand curve at point *a* in panel (b). The

HOMEWORK
Xpress!
Ask the Instructor
Video

E X H I B I T   9

Long-Run Equilibrium for a Firm and the Industry

In long-run equilibrium, the firm produces *q* units of output per period and earns a normal profit. At point *e*, price, marginal cost, short-run average total cost, and long-run average cost are all equal. There is no reason for new firms to enter the market or for existing firms to leave. As long as the market demand and supply curves remain unchanged, the industry will continue to produce a total of *Q* units of output at price *p*.

(a) Firm

(b) Industry, or market

Long-Run Adjustment to an Increase in Demand

An increase in market demand from *D* to *D′* in panel (b) moves the short-run market equilibrium from *a* to *b*. Output rises to Q_b, and price increases to *p′*. The price increase corresponds to the rise of the firm's demand curve from *d* to *d′* in panel (a). The firm responds to the higher price by increasing output to *q′* and earns economic profit, identified by the shaded rectangle. Economic profit attracts new firms to the industry in the long run. Market supply shifts right to *S′* in panel (b), pushing the market price back down to *p*. In panel (a), the firm's demand curve shifts back down to *d*, eliminating economic profit. The short-run adjustment is from point *a* to point *b* in panel (b), but the long-run adjustment is from point *a* to point *c*.

(a) Firm

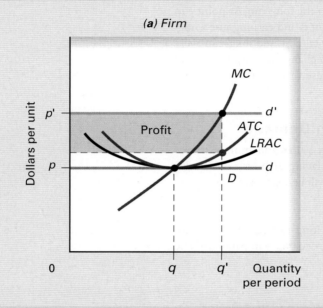

(b) Industry, or market

market-clearing price is *p*, and the market quantity is Q_a. The firm, shown in panel (a), supplies *q* units at that market price, earning a normal profit in long-run equilibrium. This representative firm produces at a level where price, or marginal revenue, equals marginal cost, short-run average total cost, and long-run average cost. (Remember, a normal profit is included in the firm's average total cost curve.)

Now suppose market demand increases, as reflected by a shift to the right in the market demand curve, from *D* to *D′*, causing the market price to increase in the short run to *p′*. Each firm responds to the higher price by expanding output along its short-run supply, or marginal cost, curve until the quantity supplied increases to *q′*, shown in panel (a) of Exhibit 10. At that output, the firm's marginal cost curve intersects the new marginal revenue curve, which is also the firm's new demand curve, *d′*. Because all firms expand, industry output increases to Q_b. Note that in the short run, each firm now earns an economic profit, shown by the shaded rectangle.

Economic profit attracts new firms in the long run. Their entry adds additional supply to the market, shifting the market supply curve to the right and pushing the price down. Firms continue to enter as long as they can earn economic profit. The market supply curve eventually shifts to *S′*, where it intersects *D′* at point *c*, returning the price to its initial equilibrium level, p. The firm's demand curve drops from d' back down to d. As a result, each firm reduces output from q' back to q, and once again, each earns just a normal profit. Notice that although industry output increases from Q_a to Q_c, each firm's output returns to q. In this example, the additional output comes entirely from new firms drawn to the industry rather than from more output by existing firms (existing firms don't expand in this example because an increase in scale would increase average cost).

New firms are attracted to the industry by short-run economic profits resulting from the increase in demand. But this new entry increases market supply, pushing the price down until economic profit disappears. In panel (b) of Exhibit 10, the short-run adjustment to increased demand is from point a to point b; the long-run adjustment moves to point c.

Effects of a Decrease in Demand

Next, let's consider the effect of a decrease in demand on the long-run market adjustment process. The initial long-run equilibrium situation in Exhibit 11 is the same as in Exhibit 10. Market demand and supply curves intersect at point a in panel (b), yielding the equilibrium price p and an equilibrium quantity Q_a. As shown in panel (a), the firm earns a normal profit in the long run by producing output rate q, where price, or marginal revenue, equals marginal cost, short-run average total cost, and long-run average cost.

EXHIBIT 11

Long-Run Adjustment to a Decrease in Demand

A decrease in demand to D'' in panel (b) disturbs the long-run equilibrium at point a. The price is driven down to p'' in the short run; output falls to Q_f. In panel (a), the firm's demand curve shifts down to d''. Each firm reduces its output to q'' and suffers a loss. As firms leave the industry in the long run, the market supply curve shifts left to S''. Market price rises to p as output falls further to Q_g. At price p, the firms once again earn a normal profit. Thus, the short-run adjustment is from point a to point f in panel (b); the long-run adjustment is from point a to point g.

(a) Firm

(b) Industry or market

Now suppose that the demand for this product declines, as reflected by a leftward shift of the market demand curve, from D back to D''. In the short run, this reduces the market price to p''. As a result, the demand curve facing each individual firm drops from d to d''. Each firm responds in the short run by cutting its output to q'', where marginal cost equals the now-lower marginal revenue, or price. Market output falls to Q_f. Because the lower market price is below short-run average total cost, each firm operates at a loss. This loss is shown by the shaded rectangle. Note, the price must still be above the average variable cost, because the firm's short-run supply curve, MC, is defined as that portion of the firm's marginal cost curve at or above its average variable cost curve.

A short-run loss, if it continues, will in the long run force some firms out of business. As firms exit, market supply decreases, so the price increases. Firms continue to leave until the market supply curve decreases to S'', where it intersects D'' at point g. Market output has fallen to Q_g, and price has returned to p. With the price back up to p, remaining firms once again earn a normal profit. When the dust settles, each firm produces q, the initial equilibrium quantity. But, because some firms have left the industry, market output has fallen from Q_a to Q_g. Again, note that the adjustment involves the departure of firms from the industry rather than a reduction in the scale of firms, as a reduction in scale would increase each firm's long-run average cost.

The Long-Run Industry Supply Curve

Thus far, we have looked at a firm's and industry's response to changes in demand, distinguishing between a short-run adjustment and a long-run adjustment. In the short run, a firm alters quantity supplied by moving up or down its marginal cost curves (that portion at or above average variable cost) until marginal cost equals marginal revenue, or price. If price is too low to cover minimum average variable cost, a firm shuts down in the short run. An economic profit (or loss) will, in the long run, prompt some firms to enter (or leave) the industry or to adjust firm size until remaining firms earn a normal profit.

In Exhibits 10 and 11, we began with an initial long-run equilibrium point; then, in response to a shift of the demand curve, we found two more long-run equilibrium points. In each case, the price changed in the short run but was unchanged in the long run. Industry output increased in Exhibit 10 and decreased in Exhibit 11. Connecting these long-run equilibrium points yields the *long-run industry supply curve,* labeled S^* in Exhibits 10 and 11. The **long-run industry supply curve** shows the relationship between price and quantity supplied once firms fully adjust to any short-term economic profit or loss resulting from a change in demand.

Constant-Cost Industries

The industry we have examined thus far is called **constant-cost industry** because each firm's long-run average cost curve does not shift up or down as industry output changes. In a constant-cost industry, each firm's per-unit costs are independent of the number of firms in the industry. *The long-run supply curve for a constant-cost industry is horizontal,* as is depicted in Exhibits 10 and 11. A constant-cost industry uses such a small portion of the resources available that increasing output does not bid up resource prices. For example, output in the pencil industry can expand without bidding up the prices of wood, graphite, and rubber, because the pencil industry uses such a small share of the market supply of these resources.

LONG-RUN INDUSTRY SUPPLY CURVE

A curve that shows the relationship between price and quantity supplied by the industry once firms adjust fully to any change in market demand

CONSTANT-COST INDUSTRY

An industry that can expand or contract without affecting the long-run per-unit cost of production; the long-run industry supply curve is horizontal

Increasing-Cost Industries

The firms in some industries encounter higher average costs as industry output expands in the long run. Firms in these **increasing-cost industries** find that expanding output bids up the prices of some resources or otherwise increases per-unit production costs, and these higher costs shift up each firm's cost curves. For example, a market expansion of oil production could bid up the price of drilling rigs and the wages of petroleum engineers and geologists, raising per-unit production costs for each oil firm. Likewise, more housing construction could bid up what developers must pay for land, carpenters, lumber, and other building materials.

To illustrate the equilibrium adjustment process for an increasing-cost industry, we begin again in long-run equilibrium in Exhibit 12, with the firm shown in panel (a) and the industry in panel (b). Market demand curve D in panel (b) intersects short-run market supply curve S at equilibrium point a to yield market price p_a and market quantity Q_a. When the price is p_a, the demand (and marginal revenue) curve facing each firm is d_a, as shown in panel (a). The firm produces the quantity q, where the price, or marginal revenue, equals marginal cost. At that output, average total cost equals the price, so the firm earns no economic profit in this long-run equilibrium.

Suppose an increase in the demand for this product shifts the market demand curve in panel (b) to the right from D to D'. The new demand curve intersects the short-run market supply curve S at point b, yielding the price p_b and market quantity Q_b. With an increase in the market price, each firm's demand curve shifts from d_a up to d_b. The new short-run equilibrium occurs at point b in panel (a), where the marginal cost curve intersects the new demand curve, which is also the marginal revenue curve. Each firm produces output q_b. In the short run, each firm earns an economic profit equal to q_b times the difference between price p_b and the average total cost at that rate of output. So far, the sequence of events is the same as for a constant-cost industry.

Economic profit attracts new firms. Because this is an increasing-cost industry, new entrants drive up the cost of production, raising each firm's marginal and average cost curves. In panel (a) of Exhibit 12, MC and ATC shift up to MC' and ATC'. (We assume for simplicity that new average cost curves are vertical shifts of the initial ones, so the minimum efficient plant size remains the same.)

The entry of new firms also shifts the short-run industry supply curve to the right in panel (b), thus reducing the market price. *New firms enter the industry until the combination of a higher production cost and a lower price squeezes economic profit to zero.* This long-run equilibrium occurs when the entry of new firms has shifted the short-run industry supply curve out to S', which lowers the price until it equals the minimum on each firm's new average total cost curve. The market price does not fall back to the initial equilibrium level because each firm's average total cost curve has increased, or shifted up, with the expansion of industry output. The intersection of the new short-run market supply curve, S', and the new market demand curve, D', determines the new long-run market equilibrium point, c. Points a and c in panel (b) are on the *upward-sloping* long-run supply curve, S^*, for this increasing-cost industry.

In constant-cost industries, each firm's costs depend simply on the scale of its plant and its rate of output. For increasing-cost industries, each firm's costs depend also on the number of firms in the market. By bidding up the price of resources, long-run expansion in an increasing-cost industry increases each firm's marginal and average costs. The long-run supply curve slopes upward, like S^* in Exhibit 12.

EXHIBIT **12**

An Increasing-Cost Industry

An increase in demand to D' in panel (b) disturbs the initial equilibrium at point *a*. Short-run equilibrium is established at point *b*, where D' intersects the short-run market supply curve S. At the higher price p_b, the firm's
demand curve shifts up to d_b, and its output increases to q_b in panel (a). At point *b*, the firm is now earning
economic profit, which attracts new firms. As new firms enter, input prices get bid up, so each firm's marginal and
average cost curves rise. New firms increase the short-run market supply curve from S to S'. The intersection of
the new market supply curve, S', with D' determines the market price, p_c. At p_c, individual firms are earning a
normal profit. Point *c* shows the long-run equilibrium combination of price and quantity. By connecting long-run
equilibrium points *a* and *c* in panel (b), we obtain the upward-sloping long-run market supply curve S^* for this
increasing-cost industry.

(a) Firm

(b) Industry, or market

To review: Firms in perfect competition can earn an economic profit, a normal profit, or
an economic loss in the short run. But in the long run, the entry or exit of firms and adjustments in firm scale force economic profit to zero, so firms earn only a normal profit.
This is true whether the industry in question exhibits constant costs or increasing costs in
the long run. Notice that, regardless of the nature of costs in the industry, the market supply
curve is more elastic in the long run than in the short run. In the long run, firms can adjust
all their resources, so they are better able to respond to changes in price. One final point:
Firms in an industry could theoretically experience a lower average cost as output expands
in the long run, resulting in a downward-sloping long-run industry supply curve. But such
an outcome is considered so rare that we have not examined it.

As mentioned at the outset, perfect competition provides a useful benchmark for evaluating the efficiency of markets. Let's examine the qualities of perfect competition that make
it so useful.

Perfect Competition and Efficiency

Economics in
the Movies

How does perfect competition stack up as an efficient user of resources? Two concepts of efficiency are used to judge market performance. The first, called *productive efficiency,* refers to producing output at the least possible cost. The second, called *allocative efficiency,* refers to producing the output that consumers value the most. Perfect competition guarantees both productive efficiency and allocative efficiency in the long run.

Productive Efficiency: Making Stuff Right

Productive efficiency occurs when the firm produces at the minimum point on its long-run average cost curve, so the market price equals the minimum average cost. The entry and exit of firms and any adjustment in the scale of each firm ensure that each firm produces at the minimum point on its long-run average cost curve. Firms that do not reach minimum long-run average cost must, to avoid continued losses, either adjust their scale or leave the industry. Thus, *perfect competition produces output at minimum average cost in the long run.*

PRODUCTIVE EFFICIENCY

The condition that exists when market output is produced using the least-cost combination of inputs; minimum average cost in the long run

Allocative Efficiency: Making the Right Stuff

Just because *production* occurs at the least possible cost does not mean that the *allocation* of resources is the most efficient one possible. The goods being produced may not be the ones consumers want. This situation is akin to that of the airline pilot who informs passengers that there's good news and bad news: "The good news is that we're making record time. The bad news is that we're lost!" Likewise, firms may be producing goods efficiently but producing the wrong goods—that is, making stuff right but making the wrong stuff.

Allocative efficiency occurs when firms produce the output that is most valued by consumers. How do we know that perfect competition guarantees allocative efficiency? The answer lies with the market demand and supply curves. Recall that the demand curve reflects the marginal value that consumers attach to each unit of the good, so the market price is the amount people are willing and able to pay for the final unit they consume. We also know that, in both the short run and the long run, the equilibrium price in perfect competition equals the marginal cost of supplying the last unit sold. Marginal cost measures the opportunity cost of all resources employed to produce that last unit sold. Thus, the demand and supply curves intersect at the combination of price and quantity at which *the marginal value, or the marginal benefit that consumers attach to the final unit purchased, just equals the opportunity cost of the resources employed to produce that unit.*

ALLOCATIVE EFFICIENCY

The condition that exists when firms produce the output most preferred by consumers; marginal benefit equals marginal cost

As long as marginal benefit equals marginal cost, the last unit produced is valued as much as, or more than, any other good those resources could have produced. There is no way to reallocate resources to increase the total value of output. Thus, there is no way to reallocate resources to increase the total utility or total benefit consumers reap from production. *When the marginal benefit that consumers derive from a good equals the marginal cost of producing that good, that market is said to be allocatively efficient.*

$$\text{Marginal benefit} = \text{Marginal cost}$$

Firms not only are making stuff right, they are making the right stuff.

What's So Perfect About Perfect Competition?

If the marginal cost of supplying a good just equals the marginal benefit to consumers, does this mean that market exchange confers no net benefits to participants? No. Market exchange usually benefits both consumers and producers. Recall that consumers enjoy a surplus from market exchange because the maximum amount they would be willing and able to pay for each unit of the good exceeds the amount they actually do pay. Exhibit 13 depicts a market in short–run equilibrium. The *consumer surplus* in this exhibit is represented by blue shading, which is the area below the demand curve but above the market-clearing price of $10.

Producers in the short run also usually derive a net benefit, or a surplus, from market exchange, because the amount they receive for their output exceeds the minimum amount they would require to supply that amount in the short run. Recall that the short-run market supply curve is the sum of that portion of each firm's marginal cost curve at or above the minimum point on its average variable cost curve. Point *m* in Exhibit 13 is the minimum point on the market supply curve; it indicates that at a price of $5, firms are willing to supply 100,000 units. At prices below $5, quantity supplied is zero because firms could not cover variable costs and would shut down. At point *m*, firms in this industry gain no net benefit from production over shutting down in the short run. At a price of $5, each firm's total revenue just covers the firm's variable cost.

If the price rises to $6, firms increase their quantity supplied until their marginal cost equals $6. Market output increases from 100,000 to 120,000 units, and total market revenue increases from $500,000 to $720,000. Part of the increased revenue covers the higher marginal cost of production. But the rest provides a bonus to producers, who would have been willing to supply the first 100,000 units for only $5 each. If the price is $6, they get to sell

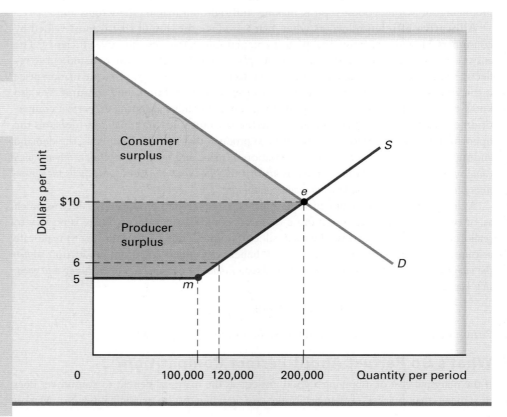

EXHIBIT 13

Consumer Surplus and Producer Surplus for a Competitive Market

Consumer surplus is represented by the area above the market-clearing price of $10 per unit and below the demand curve; it appears as the blue triangle. Producer surplus is represented by the area above the short-run market supply curve and below the market-clearing price of $10 per unit; it appears as the gold area. At a price of $5 per unit, there would be no producer surplus. At a price of $6 per unit, producer surplus would be the gold shaded area between $5 and $6.

these 100,000 units for $6 each rather than $5 each. Producer surplus at a price of $6 is the shaded area between $5 and $6.

In the short run, **producer surplus** is the total revenue producers are paid minus their variable cost of production. In Exhibit 13, the market-clearing price is $10 per unit, and producer surplus is depicted by the gold-shaded area under the price but above the market supply curve. That area represents the market price minus the marginal cost of each unit produced. The most the firm can lose in the short run is to shut down. Any price that exceeds average variable cost will reduce that short-run loss, and a high enough price could yield economic profit.

The combination of consumer surplus and producer surplus shows the gains from voluntary exchange. Productive and allocative efficiency in the short run occurs at equilibrium point *e*, which also is the combination of price and quantity that maximizes the sum of consumer surplus and producer surplus, thus maximizing social welfare. **Social welfare** is the overall well-being of people in the economy. Even though marginal cost equals marginal benefit for the final unit produced and consumed, both producers and consumers usually derive a surplus, or a bonus, from market exchange.

The gains from market exchange have been examined in an experimental setting, as discussed in the following case study.

Experimental Economics

Economists have limited opportunities to carry out the kind of controlled experiments available in the physical and biological sciences. But about four decades ago, Professor Vernon Smith, now at the George Mason University in Virginia, began some experiments to see how quickly and efficiently a group of test subjects could achieve market equilibrium. His original experiment involved 22 students, 11 of whom were designated as "buyers" and 11 as "sellers." Each buyer was given a card indicating the value of purchasing one unit of a hypothetical commodity; these values ranged from $3.25 down to $0.75, forming a downward-sloping demand curve. Each seller was given a card indicating the cost of supplying one unit of that commodity; these costs ranged from $0.75 up to $3.25, forming an upward-sloping supply curve. Each buyer and seller knew only what was on his or her own card.

© Stewart Cohen/Index Stock Imagery

To provide market incentives, participants were told they would receive a cash bonus at the end of the experiment based on the difference between the price they negotiated in the market and their value (for buyers) or their cost (for sellers). As a way of trading, Smith employed a system in which any buyer or seller could announce a bid or an offer to the entire group—a system called a *double-continuous auction*—based on rules similar to those governing stock markets and commodity exchanges. A transaction occurred whenever any buyer accepted an offer to sell or when any seller accepted an offer to buy. *Smith found that the price quickly moved to the market-clearing level,* which in his experiment was $2.00.

Economists have since performed thousands of experiments to test the properties of markets. These show that under most circumstances, markets are extremely efficient in moving goods from producers with the lowest costs to consumers who place the highest value on the goods. This movement maximizes the sum of consumer and producer surplus and thus maximizes social welfare. One surprising finding is how few participants are required

---

PRODUCER SURPLUS

A bonus for producers in the short run; the amount by which total revenue from production exceeds variable cost

SOCIAL WELFARE

The overall well-being of people in the economy; maximized when the marginal cost of production equals the marginal benefit to consumers

C a s e **S t u d y**

The Information Economy

*e*Activity

Market.Econ brings "experimental economics to the Internet" at http://market.econ.arizona.edu/. By supplying your email address, you can receive a password and play one of their games online. Be sure to read through any rules carefully. Rules and results of a variety of other games are available at http://eeps.caltech.edu/ from Caltech's Laboratory for Experimental Economics and Political Science. The director is Professor Charles Plott, an early innovator of experimental economics. Be sure to check out the *Jaws* animation, a QuickTime video presentation of changing equilibrium prices. Charles Holt of the University of Virginia, an innovator in using games in the classroom, maintains a Web site with instructions and game sheets for some experiments at http://www.people.virginia.edu/~cah2k/programs.html.

to establish a market price. Market experiments sometimes use only four buyers and four sellers, each capable of trading several units. Some experiments use only two sellers, yet the competitive equilibrium model performs quite well under double-continuous auction rules. Professor Smith won the Nobel Prize in 2002 for his work in experimental economics.

Incidentally, most U.S. retail markets, such as supermarkets and department stores, use *posted-offer pricing*—that is, the price is marked, not negotiated. Experiments show that posted pricing does not adjust to changing market conditions as quickly as does a double-continuous auction. Despite their slow response time, posted prices may be the choice for large, relatively stable markets, because posted prices involve low transaction costs—that is, buyer and seller don't have to haggle over each purchase. In contrast, double-continuous-auction pricing involves high transaction costs and, in the case of stock and commodity markets, requires thousands of people in full-time negotiations to maintain prices at their equilibrium levels (although, as discussed in the previous case study, the Internet is reducing these transaction costs).

Experiments have provided empirical support for economic theory and have yielded insights about how market rules affect market outcomes. They have also helped shape markets that did not exist before, such as the market for pollution rights or for broadcast spectrum rights—markets to be discussed in later chapters. Experiments also offer a safe and inexpensive way for people in emerging market economies to learn how markets work. The rapid development of online auctions has opened up a world of data for experimentalists.

Experimental economics is now a hot area for research and industry. For example, the number of papers published in the field jumped from fewer than 20 a year in the 1970s to more than ten times that. Most top U.S. business schools employ experimental economists. And some top corporations, such as Hewlett-Packard and IBM, have opened experimental-economics labs.

Sources: Vernon Smith, "Experimental Methods in Economics," *The New Palgrave Dictionary of Economics*, Vol. 2, edited by J. Eatwell et al. (Hampshire, England: Stockton Press, 1987), pp. 241–249; T. C. Bergstrom and J. H. Miller, *Experiments with Economic Principles*, Second Edition (New York: McGraw-Hill, 1999); Vernon Smith and Lynne Kiesling, "Socket to California," *Wall Street Journal*, 10 November 2003; and the University of Arizona's Economic Science Laboratory at http://www.econlab.arizona.edu/.

Conclusion

Let's review the assumptions of a perfectly competitive market and see how each relates to ideas developed in this chapter. *First,* there are many buyers and many sellers. This assumption ensures that no individual buyer or seller can influence the price (although recent experiments show that competition occurs even when there are few buyers and sellers). *Second,* firms produce a commodity, or a uniform product. If consumers could distinguish between the products of different suppliers, they might prefer one firm's product even at a higher price, so different producers could sell at different prices. In that case, not every firm would be a price taker—that is, each firm's demand curve would no longer be horizontal. *Third,* market participants have full information about all prices and all production processes. Otherwise, some producers could charge more than the market price, and some uninformed consumers would pay that higher price. Also, through ignorance, some firms might select outdated technology or fail to recognize opportunities for short-run economic profits. *Fourth,* all resources are mobile in the long run, with nothing preventing firms in the long run from entering profitable markets or leaving losing markets. If firms couldn't enter profitable markets, then some firms already in that market could earn economic profit in the long run.

Perfect competition is not the most common market structure observed in the real world. The markets for agricultural products, commodities such as gold and silver, widely traded stocks, and foreign exchange come close to being perfect. But even if not a single industry could be found, the model would still be useful for analyzing market behavior. As you will see in the next two chapters, perfect competition provides a valuable benchmark for evaluating the efficiency of other market structures.

SUMMARY

1. Market structures describe important features of the economic environment in which firms operate. These features include the number of buyers and sellers in the market, the ease or difficulty of entering the market, differences in the product across firms, and the forms of competition among firms.

2. Perfectly competitive markets are characterized by (a) a large number of buyers and sellers, each too small to influence market prices; (b) firms in the market produce a commodity, or undifferentiated product; (c) buyers and sellers possess full information about the availability and prices of all resources, goods, and technologies; and (d) firms and resources are freely mobile in the long run. Firms in perfect competition are said to be price takers because no firm can influence the market price. Each firm can vary only the amount it supplies at that price.

3. The market price in perfect competition is determined by the intersection of the market demand and market supply curves. Each firm then faces a demand curve that is a horizontal line at the market price. The firm's demand curve also shows the average revenue and marginal revenue received at each rate of output.

4. For a firm to produce in the short run, the market price must at least equal the firm's average variable cost. If price is below average variable cost, the firm will shut down. That portion of the marginal cost curve at or rising above the average variable cost curve becomes the perfectly competitive firm's short-run supply curve. The horizontal sum of all firms' supply curves forms the market supply curve. Each perfectly competitive firm maximizes profit or minimizes loss by producing where marginal revenue equals marginal cost.

5. Because firms are not free to enter or leave the market in the short run, economic profit or loss is possible. In the long run, however, some firms may adjust their scale of operation and other firms enter or leave the market until any economic profit or loss is eliminated.

6. Each firm in the long run will produce at the lowest point on its long-run average cost curve. At this rate of output, marginal revenue equals marginal cost and also equals the price and average cost. Firms that fail to produce at this least-cost combination will not survive in the long run.

7. In the short run, a firm alters the quantity supplied in response to a change in market demand by moving up or down its marginal cost, or supply, curve. The long-run adjustment to a change in market demand involves firms entering or leaving the market and perhaps existing firms changing their scale of operation until firms still in the industry earn just a normal profit. As the industry expands or contracts in the long run, the long-run industry supply curve has a shape that reflects either constant costs or increasing costs.

8. Perfectly competitive markets exhibit both productive efficiency (because output is produced using the most efficient combination of resources available) and allocative efficiency (because the goods produced are those most valued by consumers). In equilibrium, a perfectly competitive market allocates goods so that the marginal cost of the final unit produced equals the marginal value that consumers attach to that final unit. In the long run, market pressure minimizes the average cost of production. Voluntary exchange in competitive markets maximizes the sum of consumer surplus and producer surplus, thus maximizing social welfare.

QUESTIONS FOR REVIEW

1. *(Market Structure)* Define *market structure.* What factors are considered in determining the market structure of a particular industry?

2. *(Demand Under Perfect Competition)* What type of demand curve does a perfectly competitive firm face? Why?

3. *(Total Revenue)* Look back at Exhibit 3, panel (a) in this chapter. Explain why the total revenue curve is a straight line from the origin, whereas the slope of the total cost curve changes.

4. *(Profit in the Short Run)* Look back at Exhibit 3, panel (b), in this chapter. Why doesn't the firm choose the output that maximizes average profit (i.e., the output where average cost is the lowest)?

5. *(The Short-Run Firm Supply Curve)* An individual competitive firm's short-run supply curve is the portion of its marginal cost curve that equals or rises above the average variable cost. Explain why.

6. *(Case Study: Auction Markets)* Which of the characteristics of the perfectly competitive market structure are found in the Flower Auction Holland?

7. *(Long-Run Industry Supply)* Why does the long-run industry supply curve for an increasing-cost industry slope upward? What causes the increasing costs in an increasing-cost industry?

8. *(Perfect Competition and Efficiency)* Define productive efficiency and allocative efficiency. What conditions must be met to achieve them?

9. *(Case Study: Experimental Economics)* In Professor Vernon Smith's experiment, which "buyers" ended up with a surplus at the market-clearing price of $2? Which "sellers" had a surplus? Which "buyers" or "sellers" did not engage in transactions?

PROBLEMS AND EXERCISES

10. *(Short-Run Profit Maximization)* A perfectly competitive firm has the following fixed and variable costs in the short run. The market price for the firm's product is $150.

Output	FC	VC	TC	TR	Profit/ Loss
0	$100	$ 0	____	____	____
1	100	100	____	____	____
2	100	180	____	____	____
3	100	300	____	____	____
4	100	440	____	____	____
5	100	600	____	____	____
6	100	780	____	____	____

a. Complete the table.
b. At what output rate does the firm maximize profit or minimize loss?
c. What is the firm's marginal revenue at each positive level of output? Its average revenue?

d. What can you say about the relationship between marginal revenue and marginal cost for output rates below the profit-maximizing (or loss-minimizing) rate? For output rates above the profit-maximizing (or loss-minimizing) rate?

11. *(The Short-Run Firm Supply Curve)* Use the following data to answer the questions below:

Q	VC	MC	AVC
1	$10	____	____
2	16	____	____
3	20	____	____
4	25	____	____
5	31	____	____
6	38	____	____
7	46	____	____
8	55	____	____
9	65	____	____

a. Calculate the marginal cost and average variable cost for each level of production.

b. How much would the firm produce if it could sell its product for $5? For $7? For $10?

c. Explain your answers.

d. Assuming that its fixed cost is $3, calculate the firm's profit at each of the production levels determined in part (b).

12. *(The Short-Run Firm Supply Curve)* Each of the following situations could exist for a firm in the short run. In each case, indicate whether the firm should produce in the short run or shut down in the short run, or whether additional information is needed to determine what it should do in the short run.

a. Total cost exceeds total revenue at all output levels.

b. Total variable cost exceeds total revenue at all output levels.

c. Total revenue exceeds total fixed cost at all output levels.

d. Marginal revenue exceeds marginal cost at the current output level.

e. Price exceeds average total cost at all output levels.

f. Average variable cost exceeds price at all output levels.

g. Average total cost exceeds price at all output levels.

13. *(Perfect Competition in the Long Run)* Draw the short- and long-run cost curves of a competitive firm in long-run equilibrium. Indicate the long-run equilibrium price and quantity.

a. Discuss the firm's short-run response to a reduction in the price of a variable resource.

b. Assuming that this is a constant-cost industry, describe the process by which the industry returns to long-run equilibrium following a change in market demand.

14. *(The Long-Run Industry Supply Curve)* A normal good is being produced in a constant-cost, perfectly competitive industry. Initially, each firm is in long-run equilibrium.

a. Graphically illustrate and explain the short-run adjustments of the market and the firm to a decrease in consumer incomes. Be sure to discuss any changes in output levels, prices, profits, and the number of firms.

b. Next, show on your graph and explain the long-run adjustment to the income change. Be sure to discuss any changes in output levels, prices, profits, and the number of firms.

15. *(The Long-Run Industry Supply Curve)* The following graph shows possible long-run market supply curves for a perfectly competitive industry. Determine which supply curve indicates a constant-cost industry and which an increasing-cost industry.

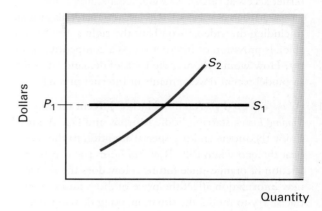

a. Explain the difference between a constant-cost industry and an increasing-cost industry.

b. Distinguish between the long-run impact of an increase in market demand in a constant-cost industry and the impact in an increasing-cost industry.

16. *(What's So Perfect About Perfect Competition)* Use the following data to answer the questions.

Quantity	Marginal Cost	Marginal Benefit
0	—	—
1	$ 2	$10
2	3	9
3	4	8
4	5	7
5	6	6
6	8	5
7	10	4
8	12	3

a. For the product shown, assume that the minimum point of each firm's average variable cost curve is at $2. Construct a demand and supply diagram for the product and indicate the equilibrium price and quantity.

b. On the graph, label the area of consumer surplus as *f*. Label the area of producer surplus as *g*.

c. If the equilibrium price were $2, what would be the amount of producer surplus?

EXPERIENTIAL EXERCISES

17. The National Council of Economic Education's EconEd-Link has an interesting module on the economics of Internet access at http://www.econedlink.org/lessons/index.cfm?lesson=NN10. Review the materials provided (including the video, if you have the right software available). Is provision of Internet access a competitive industry? How would you use the tools of demand and supply to model recent developments in Internet pricing?

18. (*C a s e* **S t u d y:** Auction Markets) Rent the movie *Trading Places,* starring Eddie Murphy and Dan Ackroyd. Enjoy the movie and pay special attention to the scene near the end when Billy Ray and Louis participate in an auction of orange-juice futures. How does the arrival of new information affect the price of those futures contracts? Try to model the situation, using demand and supply curves.

19. *(Wall Street Journal)* Financial markets are quintessential examples of perfectly competitive markets. And, of course, the *Wall Street Journal* features in-depth coverage of these markets. Turn to the Money and Investing section of today's *Wall Street Journal,* and choose one or two articles that seem interesting to you. Then, try to determine how financial markets contribute to productive and allocative efficiency in the U.S. economy.

20. *(Wall Street Journal)* Commodities often trade in markets that are examples of perfect competition. Look in the Money and Investing section of the *Wall Street Journal.* In the index, locate commodities and turn to the page where commodities are covered. Find a commodity that you believe trades in a perfectly competitive market. Describe why you believe this is so.

HOMEWORK XPRESS! EXERCISES

These exercises require access to McEachern Homework Xpress! If Homework Xpress! did not come with your book, visit **http://homeworkxpress.swlearning.com** *to purchase.*

Charles Cobbler, maker of fine shoes, sells in a competitive market and must decide how to respond to any particular market price.

1. At the current price P the firm is earning above normal profits. Draw typical marginal cost, average cost, and average cost curves that would illustrate the firm's situation. Identify the quantity the firm would choose to produce at this price.

2. Draw a marginal revenue curve for a price at which the firm would suffer losses but continue to operate in the short-run given the marginal cost, average total cost, and average variable costs in the diagram. Identify the price as P and the quantity the firm would choose to produce. Identify the average total cost per unit at this quantity as C.

3. Draw a marginal revenue curve for a price at which the firm would suffer such severe losses that it would choose to shut down in the short run given the marginal cost, average total cost, and average variable costs in the diagram.

4. Supply schedules for three firms, A, B, and C that sell identical products in a competitive market are given in the table below. Each firm has slightly different costs. Draw supply curves for each, labeling them S_A, S_B, and S_C, accordingly. Use the data in the table to derive and draw the industry supply curve. Label this curve as *S.*

Price	Firm A	Firm B	Firm C
$ 2	1	2	3
4	2	3	4
6	3	4	5

Monopoly

© Tim Wright/Corbis

How can a firm monopolize a market? Why aren't most markets monopolized? Why don't most monopolies last? Why don't monopolies charge the highest possible price? Why do some firms offer discounts to students, senior citizens, and other groups? Why are some airfares lower with a weekend stay? These and other questions are answered in this chapter, which looks at our second market structure—monopoly.

Monopoly is from the Greek, meaning "one seller." In some parts of the United States, monopolists sell electricity, cable TV service, and local phone service. Monopolists also sell postage stamps, hot dogs at sports arenas, some patented products, and other goods and services with no close substitutes. You have probably heard

BARRIER TO ENTRY

Any impediment that prevents new firms from entering an industry and competing on an equal basis with existing firms

PATENT

A legal barrier to entry that grants its holder the exclusive right to sell a product for 20 years from the date the patent application is filed

INNOVATION

The process of turning an invention into a marketable product

about the evils of monopoly. You may have even played the board game *Monopoly* on a rainy day. Now we will sort out fact from fiction.

Like perfect competition, pure monopoly is not as common as other market structures. But by understanding monopoly, you will grow more familiar with market structures that lie between the extremes of perfect competition and pure monopoly. This chapter examines the sources of monopoly power, how a monopolist maximizes profit, differences between monopoly and perfect competition, and why a monopolist sometimes charges different prices for the same product. Topics include:

- Barriers to entry
- Price elasticity and marginal revenue
- Profit maximization and loss minimization

- Monopoly and resource allocation
- Welfare cost of monopoly
- Price discrimination
- The monopolist's dream

Barriers to Entry

As noted in Chapter 3, a *monopoly* is the sole supplier of a product with no close substitutes. Why do some markets come to be dominated by a single supplier? A monopolized market is characterized by **barriers to entry**, which are restrictions on the entry of new firms into an industry. Because of barriers, new firms cannot profitably enter that market. Let's examine three types of entry barriers: legal restrictions, economies of scale, and the monopolist's control of an essential resource.

Legal Restrictions

One way to prevent new firms from entering a market is to make entry illegal. Patents, licenses, and other legal restrictions imposed by the government provide some producers with legal protection against competition.

Patents and Invention Incentives

In the United States, a **patent** awards an inventor the exclusive right to produce a good or service for 20 years from the date the patent is filed with the patent office. Originally enacted in 1790, patent laws encourage inventors to invest the time and money required to discover and develop new products and processes. If others could simply copy successful products, inventors would have less incentive to incur the up-front costs of invention. Patents also provide the stimulus to turn inventions into marketable products, a process called **innovation.**

Licenses and Other Entry Restrictions

Governments often confer monopoly status by awarding a single firm the exclusive right to supply a particular good or service. Federal licenses give certain firms the right to broadcast radio and TV signals. State licenses authorize suppliers of medical care, haircuts, and legal advice. A license may not grant a monopoly, but it does block entry and often confers the power to charge a price above the competitive level. Thus, a license can serve as an effective barrier against new competitors. Governments also grant monopoly rights to sell hot dogs at civic auditoriums, collect garbage, provide bus and taxi service, and supply services ranging from electricity to cable TV. The government itself may claim that right by outlawing competitors. For example, many states sell liquor and lottery tickets, and the U.S. Postal Service has the exclusive right to deliver first-class mail to your mailbox.

Economies of Scale

A monopoly sometimes occurs naturally when a firm experiences *economies of scale,* as reflected by the downward-sloping, long-run average cost curve shown in Exhibit 1. In such instances, a single firm can supply market demand at a lower average cost per unit than could two or more firms each producing less. Put another way, market demand is not great enough to allow more than one firm to achieve sufficient economies of scale. Thus, a single firm will emerge from the competitive process as the only supplier in the market. For example, even though the *production* of electricity has become more competitive, the *transmission* of electricity still exhibits economies of scale. Once wires are run throughout a community, the marginal cost of linking additional households to the power grid is relatively small. Consequently, the average cost of delivering electricity declines as more and more households are wired into the system.

A monopoly that emerges from the nature of costs is called a *natural monopoly,* to distinguish it from the artificial monopolies created by government patents, licenses, and other legal barriers to entry. A new entrant cannot sell enough to enjoy the economies of scale enjoyed by an established natural monopolist, so market entry is naturally blocked. A later chapter will discuss the regulation of natural monopolies.

Control of Essential Resources

Sometimes the source of monopoly power is a firm's control over some resource critical to production. Here are four examples: (1) Alcoa was the sole

EXHIBIT 1

Economies of Scale as a Barrier to Entry

A monopoly sometimes emerges naturally when a firm experiences economies of scale as reflected by a downward-sloping, long-run average cost curve. One firm can satisfy market demand at a lower average cost per unit than could two or more firms each operating at smaller rates of output.

U.S. maker of aluminum from the late 19th century until World War II. Its monopoly power initially stemmed from production patents that expired in 1909, but for the next three decades, it controlled the supply of bauxite, the key raw material. (2) Professional sports leagues try to block the formation of competing leagues by signing the best athletes to long-term contracts and by seeking the exclusive use of sports stadiums and arenas. (3) China is a monopoly supplier of pandas to the world's zoos. The National Zoo in Washington, D.C., for example, rents its pair of pandas from China for $1 million a year. As a way of controlling the panda supply, China stipulates that any offspring from the pair becomes China's property.[1] Finally, (4) since the 1930s, the world's diamond trade has been controlled primarily by De Beers Consolidated Mines, which mines diamonds and also buys most of the world's supply of rough diamonds, as discussed in the following case study.

Is a Diamond Forever?

In 1866, a child walking along the Orange River in South Africa picked up an odd pebble that turned out to be a 21-carat diamond. That discovery on a farm owned by Johannes De Beers sparked the largest diamond mine in history. Ever since the Great Depression caused a slump in diamond prices, De Beers Consolidated Mines has tried to control the world supply of uncut diamonds. The company has kept prices high by carefully limiting supply and by advertising. For example, De Beers spent $183 million in 2003 trying to convince people that diamonds are scarce, valuable, and perfect reflections of love. One promotional coup was to persuade *Baywatch,* a TV show now seen in reruns around the world, to devote an episode to a diamond engagement ring. The story played up the De Beers line that the ring should cost two months' salary. An episode of *The Drew Carey Show* had a similar theme. The latest attempt to boost the demand for diamonds is the "spirit ring," a diamond worn on a woman's right hand as a sign of independence.

De Beers limits the supply of rough diamonds reaching the market. The company, which is sometimes called "The Syndicate," invites about one hundred wholesalers to London, where each is offered a box of uncut diamonds for a set price—no negotiating. If De Beers needs to prop up the price of a certain size and quality of diamond, then few of those will show up in the boxes, thus restricting their supply. The company's actions violate U.S. antitrust laws (De Beers executives could be arrested if they traveled to America). But there are no laws prohibiting U.S. wholesalers from buying from De Beers.

It might surprise you that, as gems go, diamonds are not especially rare, either in nature or in jewelry stores. Diamonds may be the most common natural gemstone. Jewelry stores sell more diamonds than any other gem. Jewelers are willing to hold large inventories because they are confident that De Beers will keep prices up. De Beers' slogan, "A diamond is forever," sends several messages, including (1) a diamond lasts forever, and so should love; (2) diamonds should remain in the family and not be sold; and (3) diamonds retain their value. This slogan is aimed at keeping secondhand diamonds, which are good substitutes for new ones, off the market, where they could otherwise increase supply and drive down the price.

But De Beers has recently lost control of some rough diamond supplies. Russian miners have been selling half their diamonds to independent dealers. Australia's Argyle mine, now

1. Francis Clines, "Capital Exults Over Pandas," *New York Times,* 7 December 2000.

the world's largest, stopped selling to De Beers in 1996. And Yellowknife, a huge Canadian mine, began operations in 1998, but De Beers is guaranteed only about one-third of its output. As a result of all this erosion, DeBeers' share of the world's uncut diamond supply slipped from nearly 90 percent in the mid-1980s to about 62 percent in 2002. Worse still for De Beers, newly developed synthetic diamonds are starting to appear on the market. To counter that threat, De Beers is supplying precision equipment to jewelers so they can spot synthetic diamonds.

A monopoly that relies on the control of a key resource, as De Beers does, loses its power once that control slips away. In a reversal of policy, De Beers now says it will abandon efforts to control the world diamond supply and will instead become the "supplier of choice" by promoting the DeBeers brand of diamonds. But as of 2004 there are only a few DeBeers retail stores worldwide, in London and in Tokyo. De Beers is now trying to settle U.S. antitrust charges so it can open stores in the states. (Americans account for only 5 percent of the world's population but for half the world's diamond purchases.) In an effort to differentiate its diamonds, De Beers is etching the company name and an individual security number on some diamonds. Whether this branding effort will work remains to be seen.

Sources: Phyllis Berman and Lea Goldman, "The Billionaire Who Cracked De Beers," *Forbes*, 15 September 2003; Rob Walker, "The Right-Hand Diamond Ring," *New York Times*, 4 January 2004; Joshua Davis, "The New Diamond Age," *Wired Magazine*, September 2003; John Wilke, "De Beers Is in Talks to Settle Charges of Price Fixing," *Wall Street Journal*, 24 February 2004; and the De Beers home page at http://www.adiamondisforever.com/.

Local monopolies are more common than national or international monopolies. In rural areas, monopolies may include the only grocery store, movie theater, or restaurant for miles around. These are natural monopolies for products sold in local markets. But long-lasting monopolies are rare because, as we will see, a profitable monopoly attracts competitors. Also, over time, technological change tends to break down barriers to entry. For example, the development of wireless transmission of long-distance calls created competitors to AT&T. Wireless transmission will soon erase the monopoly held by local cable TV providers and even local phone service. Likewise, fax machines, email, the Internet, and firms such as FedEx now compete with the U.S. Postal Service's monopoly, as we will see in a later case study.

Revenue for the Monopolist

Because a monopoly, by definition, supplies the entire market, the demand for goods or services produced by a monopolist is also the market demand. The demand curve for the monopolist's output therefore slopes downward, reflecting the law of demand—price and quantity demanded are inversely related. Let's look at demand, average revenue, and marginal revenue.

Demand, Average Revenue, and Marginal Revenue

Suppose De Beers controls the entire diamond market. Exhibit 2 shows the demand curve for 1-carat diamonds. De Beers, for example, can sell three diamonds a day at $7,000 each. That price-quantity combination yields total revenue of $21,000 (=$7,000 × 3). Total revenue divided by quantity is the *average revenue per diamond,* which also is $7,000. Thus, the monopolist's price equals the average revenue per unit. To sell a fourth diamond, De Beers must drop the price to $6,750. Total revenue for four diamonds is $27,000 (=$6,750 × 4) and average revenue is $6,750. All along the demand curve, price equals average revenue. Therefore, *the demand curve is also the monopolist's average revenue curve,* just as the perfectly competitive firm's demand curve is that firm's average revenue curve.

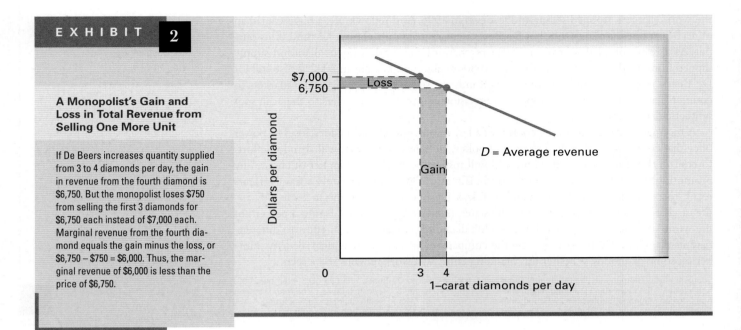

EXHIBIT 2

A Monopolist's Gain and Loss in Total Revenue from Selling One More Unit

If De Beers increases quantity supplied from 3 to 4 diamonds per day, the gain in revenue from the fourth diamond is $6,750. But the monopolist loses $750 from selling the first 3 diamonds for $6,750 each instead of $7,000 each. Marginal revenue from the fourth diamond equals the gain minus the loss, or $6,750 − $750 = $6,000. Thus, the marginal revenue of $6,000 is less than the price of $6,750.

What's the monopolist's marginal revenue from selling a fourth diamond? When De Beers drops the price from $7,000 to $6,750, total revenue goes from $21,000 to $27,000. Thus, *marginal revenue*—the change in total revenue from selling one more diamond—is $6,000, which is less than the price, or average revenue, of $6,750. *For a monopolist, marginal revenue is less than the price, or average revenue.* Recall that for a perfectly competitive firm, marginal revenue equals the price, or average revenue, because that firm can sell all it wants to at the market price.

The Gains and Loss from Selling One More Unit

A closer look at Exhibit 2 reveals why a monopolist's marginal revenue is less than the price. By selling another diamond, De Beers gains the revenue from that sale. For example, De Beers gets $6,750 from the fourth diamond, as shown by the blue-shaded vertical rectangle marked "Gain." But to sell that fourth unit, De Beers must sell all four diamonds for $6,750 each. Thus, to sell a fourth diamond, De Beers must sacrifice $250 on each of the first three diamonds, which could have been sold for $7,000 each. This loss in revenue from the first three units totals $750 (=$250 × 3) and is identified in Exhibit 2 by the pink-shaded horizontal rectangle marked "Loss." The net change in total revenue from selling the fourth diamond—that is, the marginal revenue from the fourth diamond—equals the *gain* minus the *loss,* which equals $6,750 minus $750, or $6,000. So marginal revenue equals the gain minus the loss, or the price minus the revenue forgone by selling all units for a lower price. Because a monopolist's marginal revenue equals the price minus the loss, you can see why the price exceeds marginal revenue.

Incidentally, this analysis assumes that all units of the good are sold at the market price; for example, the four diamonds are sold for $6,750 each. Although this is usually true, later in the chapter you will learn how some monopolists try to increase profit by charging different customers different prices.

(1) 1-Carat Diamonds per Day (Q)	(2) Price (average revenue) (p)	(3) Total Revenue ($TR = p \times Q$)	(4) Marginal Revenue ($MR = \Delta TR/\Delta Q$)
0	$7,750	0	___
1	7,500	$ 7,500	$7,500
2	7,250	14,500	7,000
3	7,000	21,000	6,500
4	6,750	27,000	6,000
5	6,500	32,500	5,500
6	6,250	37,500	5,000
7	6,000	42,000	4,500
8	5,750	46,000	4,000
9	5,500	49,500	3,500
10	5,250	52,500	3,000
11	5,000	55,000	2,500
12	4,750	57,000	2,000
13	4,500	58,500	1,500
14	4,250	59,500	1,000
15	4,000	60,000	500
16	3,750	60,000	0
17	3,500	59,500	-500

EXHIBIT 3

Revenue for De Beers, a Monopolist

To sell more, the monopolist must lower the price on all units sold. Because the revenue lost from selling all units at a lower price must be subtracted from the revenue gained by selling another unit, marginal revenue is less than the price. At some point, marginal revenue turns negative, as shown here when the price is reduced to $3,500.

Revenue Schedules

Let's flesh out more fully the revenue schedules behind the demand curve of Exhibit 2. Column (1) of Exhibit 3 lists the quantity of diamonds demanded per day, and column (2) lists the corresponding price, or average revenue. The two columns together are the demand schedule facing De Beers for 1-carat diamonds. The price in column (2) times the quantity in column (1) yields the monopolist's *total revenue*, shown in column (3). So $TR = p \times Q$. As De Beers expands output, total revenue increases until quantity reaches 15 diamonds.

Marginal revenue, the change in total revenue from selling one more diamond, appears in column (4). In shorthand, $MR = \Delta TR/\Delta Q$, or the change in total revenue divided by the change in quantity. Note in Exhibit 3 that after the first unit, marginal revenue is less than price. As the price declines, the gap between price and marginal revenue widens because the *loss* from selling all diamonds for less increases (because quantity increases) and the gain from selling another diamond decreases (because the price falls).

Revenue Curves

The data in Exhibit 3 are graphed in Exhibit 4, which shows the demand and marginal revenue curves in panel (a) and the total revenue curve in panel (b). Recall that total revenue equals price times quantity. Note that *the marginal revenue curve is below the demand curve and*

**Monopoly Demand and
Marginal Total Revenue**

Where demand is price elastic, marginal revenue is positive, so total revenue increases as the price falls. Where demand is price inelastic, marginal revenue is negative, so total revenue decreases as the price falls. Where demand is unit elastic, marginal revenue is zero, so total revenue is at a maximum, neither increasing nor decreasing.

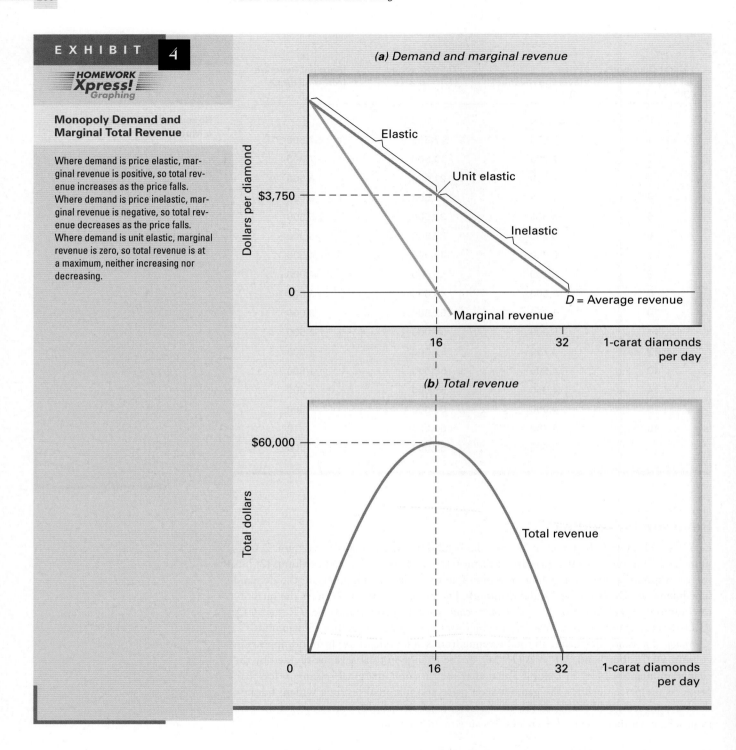

(a) Demand and marginal revenue

(b) Total revenue

that total revenue reaches a maximum when marginal revenue reaches zero. Take a minute now to study these relationships—they are important.

Again, at any level of sales, price equals average revenue, so the demand curve is also the monopolist's average revenue curve. In Chapter 5 you learned that the price elasticity for a straight-line demand curve decreases as you move down the curve. When demand is elastic—that is, when the percentage increase in quantity demanded more than offsets the percentage decrease in price—a decrease in price increases total revenue. Therefore, *where demand is elastic, marginal revenue is positive, and total revenue increases as the price falls.* On the other hand, where demand is inelastic—that is, where the percentage increase in quantity demanded is less than the percentage decrease in price—a decrease in price reduces total revenue. In other words, the loss in revenue from selling all diamonds for the lower price overwhelms the gain in revenue from selling more diamonds. Therefore, *where demand is inelastic, marginal revenue is negative, and total revenue decreases as the price falls.*

From Exhibit 4, you can see that marginal revenue turns negative if the price drops below $3,750, indicating inelastic demand below that price. *A profit-maximizing monopolist would never willingly expand output to where demand is inelastic because doing so would reduce total revenue.* It would make no sense to sell more just to see total revenue drop. Also note that demand is unit elastic at the price of $3,750. At that price, marginal revenue is zero and total revenue reaches a maximum.

The Firm's Costs and Profit Maximization

In the case of perfect competition, each firm's choice is confined to *quantity* because the market already determines the price. The perfect competitor is a *price taker.* The monopolist, however, can choose either the price or the quantity, but choosing one determines the other—they come in pairs. For example, if De Beers decides to sell 10 diamonds a day, consumers would buy that many only at a price of $5,250. Alternatively, if De Beers decides to sell diamonds for $6,000 each, consumers would buy 7 a day at that price. Because the monopolist can select the price that maximizes profit, we say the monopolist is a *price maker.* More generally, any firm that has some control over what price to charge is a **price maker.**

PRICE MAKER

A firm that must find the profit-maximizing price when the demand curve for its output slopes downward

Profit Maximization

Exhibit 5 repeats the revenue data from Exhibits 3 and 4 and also includes short-run cost data reflecting costs similar to those already introduced in the two previous chapters. Take a little time now to become familiar with this table. Then ask yourself, which price-quantity combination should De Beers select to maximize profit? As was the case with perfect competition, the monopolist can approach profit maximization in two ways—the total approach and the marginal approach.

Total Revenue Minus Total Cost

The profit-maximizing monopolist employs the same decision rule as the competitive firm. *The monopolist produces the quantity at which total revenue exceeds total cost by the greatest amount.* Economic profit appears in column (8) of Exhibit 5. As you can see, the maximum profit is $12,500 per day, which occurs when output is 10 diamonds per day and the price is $5,250 per diamond. At that quantity, total revenue is $52,500 and total cost is $40,000.

Marginal Revenue Equals Marginal Cost

De Beers, as a profit-maximizing monopolist, increases output as long as selling more diamonds adds more to total revenue than to total cost. So De Beers expands output as long as marginal revenue, shown in column (4) of Exhibit 5, exceeds marginal cost, shown in column (6). But De Beers will stop short of where marginal cost exceeds marginal revenue. Again, profit is maximized at $12,500 when output is 10 diamonds per day. For the 10th diamond, marginal revenue is $3,000 and marginal cost is $2,750. As you can see, if output

EXHIBIT	5	Short-Run Costs and Revenue for a Monopolist

(1) Diamonds per Day (Q)	(2) Price (p)	(3) Total Revenue (TR = p × Q)	(4) Marginal Revenue (MR = ΔTR/ΔQ)	(5) Total Cost (TC)	(6) Marginal Cost (MC = ΔTC /ΔQ)	(7) Average Total Cost (ATC = TC/Q)	(8) Total Profit or Loss (= TR − TC)
0	$7,750	0	—	$15,000	—	—	−$15,000
1	7,500	$7,500	$7,500	19,750	$4,750	$19,750	−12,250
2	7,250	14,500	7,000	23,500	3,750	11,750	−9,000
3	7,000	21,000	6,500	26,500	3,000	8,833	−5,500
4	6,750	27,000	6,000	29,000	2,500	7,750	−2,000
5	6,500	32,500	5,500	31,000	2,000	6,200	1,500
6	6,250	37,500	5,000	32,500	1,500	5,417	5,000
7	6,000	42,000	4,500	33,750	1,250	4,821	8,250
8	5,750	46,000	4,000	35,250	1,500	4,406	10,750
9	5,500	49,500	3,500	37,250	2,000	4,139	12,250
10	**5,250**	**52,500**	**3,000**	**40,000**	**2,750**	**4,000**	**12,500**
11	5,000	55,000	2,500	43,250	3,250	3,932	11,750
12	4,750	57,000	2,000	48,000	4,750	4,000	9,000
13	4,500	58,500	1,500	54,500	6,500	4,192	4,000
14	4,250	59,500	1,000	64,000	9,500	4,571	−4,500
15	4,000	60,000	500	77,500	13,500	5,167	−17,500
16	3,750	60,000	0	96,000	18,500	6,000	−36,000
17	3,500	59,500	−500	121,000	25,000	7,117	−61,500

exceeds 10 diamonds per day, marginal cost exceeds marginal revenue. An 11th diamond's marginal cost of $3,250 exceeds its marginal revenue of $2,500. For simplicity, we say that *the profit-maximizing output occurs where marginal revenue equals marginal cost,* which, you will recall, is the golden rule of profit maximization.

Graphical Solution

The cost and revenue data in Exhibit 5 are graphed in Exhibit 6, with per-unit cost and revenue curves in panel (a) and total cost and revenue curves in panel (b). The intersection of the two marginal curves at point *e* in panel (a) indicates that profit is maximized when 10 diamonds are sold. At that quantity, we move up to the demand curve to find the profit-maximizing price of $5,250. The average total cost of $4,000 is identified by point *b*. The average profit per diamond equals the price of $5,250 minus the average total cost of $4,000. Economic profit is the average profit per unit of $1,250 multiplied by the 10 diamonds sold, for a total profit of $12,500 per day, as identified by the shaded rectangle. *So the profit-maximizing rate of output is found where the rising marginal cost curve intersects the marginal revenue curve.*

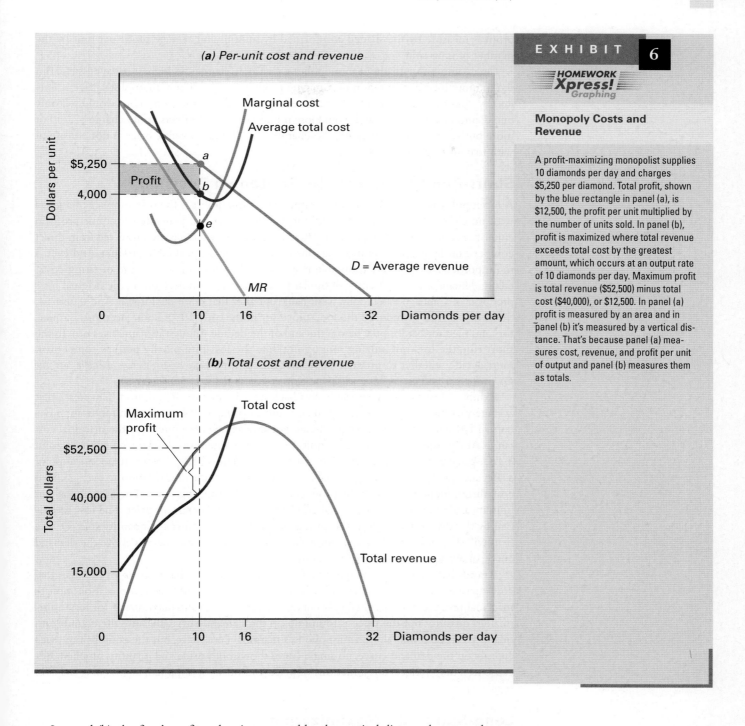

(a) Per-unit cost and revenue

Marginal cost

Average total cost

Dollars per unit

$5,250 — — — — — a

Profit   b

4,000 — — — — —

                     e

D = Average revenue

MR

0   10   16   32   Diamonds per day

(b) Total cost and revenue

Maximum
profit

Total cost

Total dollars

$52,500 — — — — —

40,000 — — — — —

Total revenue

15,000 —

0   10   16   32   Diamonds per day

EXHIBIT   6

HOMEWORK
Xpress!
Graphing

**Monopoly Costs and
Revenue**

A profit-maximizing monopolist supplies
10 diamonds per day and charges
$5,250 per diamond. Total profit, shown
by the blue rectangle in panel (a), is
$12,500, the profit per unit multiplied by
the number of units sold. In panel (b),
profit is maximized where total revenue
exceeds total cost by the greatest
amount, which occurs at an output rate
of 10 diamonds per day. Maximum profit
is total revenue ($52,500) minus total
cost ($40,000), or $12,500. In panel (a)
profit is measured by an area and in
panel (b) it's measured by a vertical distance. That's because panel (a) measures cost, revenue, and profit per unit
of output and panel (b) measures them
as totals.

In panel (b), the firm's profit or loss is measured by the vertical distance between the total revenue and total cost curves. De Beers will expand output as long as the increase in total revenue from selling one more diamond exceeds the increase in total cost. *The profit-maximizing firm will produce where total revenue exceeds total cost by the greatest amount.* Again, profit
is maximized where De Beers sells 10 diamonds per day. Note again that in panel (b), total
profit is measured by the *vertical distance* between the two total curves, and in panel (a), total

profit is measure by the shaded *area* formed by multiplying average profit per unit by the number of units sold.

One common myth about monopolies is that they charge the highest price possible. But the monopolist is interested in maximizing profit, not price. The monopolist's price is limited by consumer demand. De Beers, for example, could charge $7,500 but would sell only one diamond at that price and would lose money. Indeed, De Beers could charge $7,750 or more but would sell no diamonds. So charging the highest possible price is not consistent with maximizing profit.

Short-Run Losses and the Shutdown Decision

A monopolist is not assured a profit. Although a monopolist is the sole supplier of a good with no close substitutes, the demand for that good may not generate economic profit in either the short run or the long run. After all, many new products are protected from direct competition by patents, yet most patents never turn into a profitable product. And even a monopolist that is initially profitable may eventually suffer losses because of rising costs, falling demand, or market entry of similar products. For example, Coleco, the original mass producer of Cabbage Patch dolls, went bankrupt after that craze died down. And Cuisinart, the company that introduced the food processor in the early 1980s, soon faced many imitators and filed for bankruptcy before the end of the decade (though its name lives on). In the short run, the loss-minimizing monopolist, like the loss-minimizing perfect competitor, must decide whether to produce or to shut down. *If the price covers average variable cost, the firm will produce. If not, the firm will shut down, at least in the short run.*

Exhibit 7 brings average variable cost back into the picture. Recall from Chapter 7 that average variable cost and average fixed cost sum to average total cost. Loss minimization occurs in Exhibit 7 at point *e*, where the marginal revenue curve intersects the marginal cost curve. At the equilibrium rate of output, Q, price *p* is found on the demand curve at point *b*. That price exceeds average variable cost, at point *c*, but is below average total cost, at point *a*. Because price covers average variable cost and makes some contribution to average fixed cost, this monopolist loses less by producing Q than by shutting down. The average loss per unit, measured by *ab*, is average total cost minus average revenue, or price. The loss, identified by the shaded rectangle, is the average loss per unit, *ab*, times the quantity sold, Q. The firm will shut down in the short run if the average variable cost curve is above the demand curve, or average revenue curve, at all output rates.

Recall that a perfectly competitive firm's supply curve is that portion of the marginal cost curve at or above the average variable cost curve. The intersection of a monopolist's marginal revenue and marginal cost curves identifies the profit-maximizing (or loss-minimizing) quantity, but the price is found up on the demand curve. Because the equilibrium quantity can be found along a monopolist's marginal cost curve, but the equilibrium price appears on the demand curve, no single curve shows both price and quantity supplied. Because no curve reflects combinations of price and quantity supplied, *there is no monopolist supply curve.*

Long-Run Profit Maximization

For perfectly competitive firms, the distinction between the short run and the long run is important because entry and exit of firms can occur in the long run, erasing any economic profit or loss. For the monopolist, the distinction between the short run and long run is less important. *If a monopoly is insulated from competition by high barriers that block new entry, economic profit can persist in the long run.* Yet short-run profit is no guarantee of long-run profit.

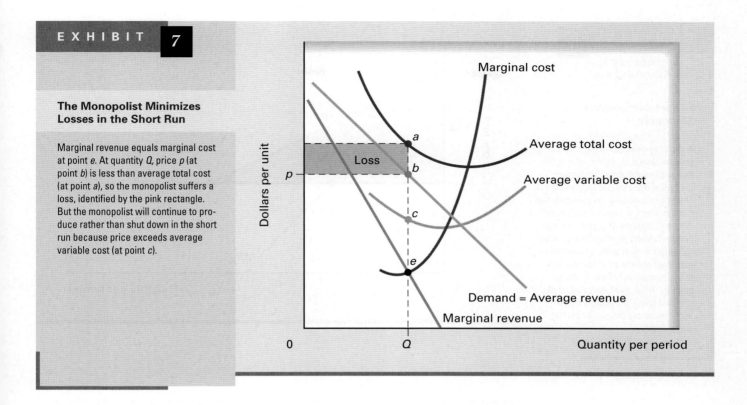

EXHIBIT 7

The Monopolist Minimizes Losses in the Short Run

Marginal revenue equals marginal cost at point *e*. At quantity *Q*, price *p* (at point *b*) is less than average total cost (at point *a*), so the monopolist suffers a loss, identified by the pink rectangle. But the monopolist will continue to produce rather than shut down in the short run because price exceeds average variable cost (at point *c*).

For example, suppose the monopoly relies on a patent. Patents last only so long and even while its product is under patent, the monopolist often must defend it in court (patent litigation has increased more than half in the last decade). On the other hand, a monopolist may be able to erase a loss (most start-up firms lose money initially) or increase profit in the long run by adjusting the scale of the firm or by advertising to increase demand. A monopolist unable to erase a loss will leave the market.

Monopoly and the Allocation of Resources

If monopolists are no greedier than perfect competitors (because both maximize profit), if monopolists do not charge the highest possible price, and if monopolists are not guaranteed a profit, then what's the problem with monopoly? To get a handle on the problem, let's compare monopoly with the benchmark established in the previous chapter—perfect competition.

Price and Output Under Perfect Competition

Let's begin with the long-run equilibrium price and output for a perfectly competitive market. Suppose the long-run market supply curve in perfect competition is horizontal, as shown by S_c in Exhibit 8. Because this is a constant-cost industry, the horizontal long-run supply curve also shows marginal cost and average total cost at each quantity. Equilibrium occurs at point *c*, where market demand and market supply curves intersect to yield price p_c and quantity Q_c. Remember, the demand curve reflects the marginal benefit of each unit purchased. In competitive equilibrium, the marginal benefit equals the marginal cost to

Perfect Competition and Monopoly

A perfectly competitive industry would produce output Q_c, determined by the intersection of the market demand curve D and the market supply curve S_c. The price would be p_c. A monopoly that could produce output at the same minimum average cost as a perfectly competitive industry would produce output Q_m, determined at point b, where marginal cost and marginal revenue intersect. The monopolist would charge price p_m. Thus, given the same costs, output is lower and price is higher under monopoly than under perfect competition.

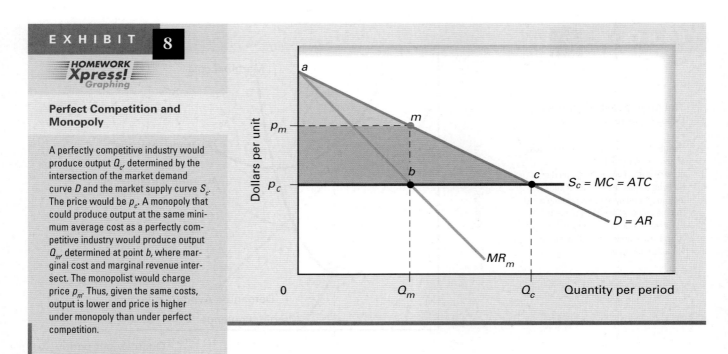

society of producing the final unit sold. As noted in the previous chapter, when the marginal benefit that consumers derive from a good equals the marginal cost of producing that good, that market is said to be allocatively efficient and to maximize social welfare. There is no way of reallocating resources to increase the total value of output or to increase social welfare. Because consumers are able to purchase Q_c units at price p_c, they enjoy a net benefit from consumption, or a consumer surplus, measured by the entire shaded triangle, acp_c.

Price and Output Under Monopoly

When there is only one firm in the industry, the industry demand curve becomes the monopolist's demand curve, so the price the monopolist charges determines how much gets sold. Because the monopolist's demand curve slopes downward, the marginal revenue curve also slopes downward and is beneath the demand curve, as is indicated by MR_m in Exhibit 8. Suppose the monopolist can produce at the same constant cost in the long run as can the competitive industry. The monopolist maximizes profit by equating marginal revenue with marginal cost, which occurs at point b, yielding equilibrium price p_m and output Q_m. Again, the price shows the consumers' marginal benefit for unit Q_m. This marginal benefit, identified at point m, exceeds the monopolist's marginal cost, identified at point b. Because marginal benefit exceeds marginal cost, society would be better off if output were expanded beyond Q_m. The monopolist restricts quantity below what would maximize social welfare. Even though the monopolist restricts output, consumers still derive some benefit; consumer surplus is shown by the smaller triangle, amp_m.

Allocative and Distributive Effects

Consider the allocative and distributive effects of monopoly versus perfect competition. In Exhibit 8, consumer surplus under perfect competition was the large triangle, acp_c. Under monopoly, consumer surplus shrinks to the smaller triangle amp_m, which in this example is only one-fourth as large. The monopolist earns economic profit equal to the shaded rectangle. By comparing the situation under monopoly with that under perfect competition, you can see that the monopolist's economic profit comes entirely from what was consumer surplus under perfect competition. Because the profit rectangle reflects a transfer from consumer surplus to monopoly profit, this amount is not lost to society and so is not considered a welfare loss.

Notice, however, that consumer surplus has been reduced by more than the profit rectangle. Consumers have also lost the triangle *mcb,* which was part of the consumer surplus under perfect competition. The *mcb* triangle is called the **deadweight loss of monopoly** because it is a loss to consumers but a gain to nobody. This loss results from the *allocative inefficiency arising from the higher price and reduced output of monopoly.* Again, society would be better off if output exceeded the monopolist's profit-maximizing quantity, because the marginal benefit of more output exceeds its marginal cost. Under monopoly, the price, or marginal benefit, always exceeds marginal cost. Empirical estimates of the annual deadweight loss of monopoly in the United States range from about 1 percent to about 5 percent of national income. Applied to national income data for 2004, these estimates imply a deadweight loss ranging from about $400 to $2,000 per capita, not a trivial amount.

DEADWEIGHT LOSS OF MONOPOLY

Net loss to society when a firm uses its market power to restrict output and increase price

Problems Estimating the Deadweight Loss of Monopoly

The actual cost of monopoly could differ from the deadweight loss described above. These costs could be lower or higher. Here's the reasoning.

Why the Deadweight Loss of Monopoly Might Be Lower

If economies of scale are substantial enough, a monopolist might be able to produce output at a lower cost per unit than could competitive firms. Therefore, the price, or at least the cost of production, could be lower under monopoly than under competition. The deadweight loss shown in Exhibit 8 may also overstate the true cost of monopoly because monopolists might, in response to public scrutiny and political pressure, keep prices below what the market could bear. Although monopolists would like to earn as much profit as possible, they realize that if the public outcry over high prices and high profit grows loud enough, some sort of government intervention could reduce or even erase that profit. For example, the prices and profit of drug companies, which individually are monopoly suppliers of patented medicines, come under scrutiny from time to time by federal legislators who want to regulate drug prices. Drug firms might try to avoid such treatment by keeping prices below the level that would maximize profit. Finally, a monopolist might keep the price below the profit-maximizing level to avoid attracting new competitors to the market. For example, some observers claim that Alcoa, when it was the only U.S. producer of aluminum, kept prices low enough to discourage new entry.

Why the Deadweight Loss Might Be Higher

Another line of reasoning suggests that the deadweight loss of monopoly might, in fact, be greater than shown in our simple diagram. *If resources must be devoted to securing and maintaining a monopoly position, monopolies may involve more of a welfare loss than simple models suggest.* For example, radio and TV broadcasting rights confer on the recipient the use a particular band of the scarce broadcast spectrum. In the past, these rights have been given away by government agencies to the applicants deemed most deserving. Because these rights are so valuable, numerous applicants spend millions on lawyers' fees, lobbying expenses, and other costs associated with making themselves appear the most deserving. The efforts devoted to securing and maintaining a monopoly position are largely a social waste because they use up scarce resources but add not one unit to output. Activities undertaken by individuals or firms to influence public policy in a way that will directly or indirectly redistribute income to them are referred to as **rent seeking.**

The monopolist, insulated from the rigors of competition in the marketplace, might also grow fat and lazy—and become inefficient. Because some monopolies could still earn an economic profit even if the firm is inefficient, corporate executives might waste resources creating a more comfortable life for themselves. Long lunches, afternoon golf, plush offices, corporate jets, and extensive employee benefits might make company life more pleasant, but they increase the cost of production and raise the price.

Monopolists have also been criticized for being slow to adopt the latest production techniques, being reluctant to develop new products, and generally lacking innovation. Because monopolists are largely insulated from the rigors of competition, they might take it easy. It's been said "The best of all monopoly profits is a quiet life."

The following case study discusses the performance of one of the nation's oldest monopolies, the U.S. Postal Service.

Case **Study**

Public Policy

eActivity

How has the U.S. Postal Service dealt with competition and change? A chapter in its online history, at http://www.usps.com/history/his3_5. htm, describes the reforms made in the 1990s to compete with for-profit firms and email. How does the Postal Service set rates now that it is no longer a monopoly? The process is described at http://www.usps.com/ratecase/ how_rates.htm. What role do forces of competition play in rate setting? Online cost calculators are provided by both USPS at http://postcalc.usps.gov/ and UPS (United Parcel Service) at http://wwwapps.ups.com/QCC WebApp/request. Try finding the cost of sending a letter to Uruguay. Which is cheaper—USPS or UPS? Why?

The Mail Monopoly

The U.S. Post Office was granted a monopoly in 1775 and has operated under federal protection ever since. In 1971, Congress converted the Post Office Department into a semi-independent agency called the U.S. Postal Service, or USPS, with total revenue of about $70 billion in 2003. About 800,000 USPS employees handle more than half a billion pieces of mail a day—over 40 percent of the world's total. USPS pays no taxes and is exempt from local zoning laws. It has a legal monopoly in delivering regular, first-class letters and has the exclusive right to use the space inside your mailbox. Outfits like FedEx or UPS cannot deliver to mail boxes or post office boxes.

© Frank Siteman Studio

The USPS monopoly has suffered in recent years because of rising costs and stiff competition from new technologies. The price of a first-class stamp climbed from 6 cents in 1970 to 37 cents by 2003—a growth rate double that of inflation. Long-distance phone service, one possible substitute for first-class mail, has become cheaper since 1970. New technologies such as fax machines and email also compete with USPS (email messages now greatly outnumber first-class letters). Because the monopoly applies only to regular first-class mail, USPS has lost chunks of other business to private firms offering lower rates and better service. The United Parcel Service (UPS) is more mechanized and more containerized than the USPS and thus has lower costs and less breakage. The USPS has tried to emulate UPS but with only limited success. Postal employees are paid more on average than those at UPS or other private-sector delivery services, such as FedEx.

When the Postal Service raised third-class ("junk" mail) rates, businesses substituted other forms of advertising, including cable TV and telemarketing. UPS and other rivals now account for 75 percent of the ground-shipped packages. Even USPS's first-class monopoly is being threatened, because FedEx and others have captured 90 percent of the overnight mail business. Thus, USPS is losing business because of competition from overnight mail and from new technologies.

USPS has been fighting back, trying to leverage its monopoly power while increasing efficiency. On the electronic front, USPS tried to offer online postage purchases, online bill-paying service, and secure online document transmission service. But by December 2003, these new products had been scrapped as failures. In more successful efforts, USPS has partnered with eBay to confirm delivery of auctioned items and expedite payments. USPS also provides some local delivery service—the so-called "last mile"—for several major shippers including DHL, Emery, and FedEx. Despite these efforts, changing technology and competition are eroding the government-granted monopoly power.

Sources: Rick Brooks, "New UPS Service Sends Packages Through the Post Office," *Wall Street Journal*, 6 November 2003; Angela Kean, "Modernizing USPS," *Traffic World*, 9 June 2003; Mark Fitzgerald, "USPS' Snail-Mail Spam," *Editor & Publisher*, 14 April 2003; Rick Brooks, "Postal Service to Discontinue Online Bill-Payment Service," *Wall Street Journal*, 14 November 2003; and the USPS home page at http://www.usps.com.

Not all economists believe that monopolies, especially private monopolies, manage their resources with any less vigilance than perfect competitors do. Some argue that because monopolists are protected from rivals, they are in a good position to capture the fruits of any innovation and therefore will be more innovative than competitive firms are. Others believe that if a private monopolist strays from the path of profit maximization, its share price will drop enough to attract someone who will buy controlling interest and shape up the company. This market for corporate control is said to keep monopolists on their toes.

Price Discrimination

In the model developed so far, a monopolist, to sell more output, must lower the price. In reality, a monopolist can sometimes increase profit by charging higher prices to those who value the product more. This practice of charging different prices to different groups of consumers is called **price discrimination.** For example, children, students, and senior citizens often pay lower admission prices to ball games, movies, plays, and other events. Firms offer certain groups reduced prices because doing so boosts profits. Let's see how and why.

Conditions for Price Discrimination

To practice price discrimination, a firm's product must meet certain conditions. First, the demand curve for the firm's product must slope downward, indicating that the firm is a price maker—the producer has some market power, some control over the price. Second, there must be at least two groups of consumers for the product, each with a different price elasticity of demand. Third, the firm must be able, at little cost, to charge each group a different price for essentially the same product. Finally, the firm must be able to prevent those who pay the lower price from reselling the product to those who pay the higher price.

A Model of Price Discrimination

Exhibit 9 shows the effects of price discrimination. Consumers are sorted into two groups with different demand elasticities. For simplicity, we assume that the firm produces at a constant long-run average and marginal cost of $1.00. *At a given price*, the price elasticity of demand in panel (b) is greater than that in panel (a). Think of panel (b) as reflecting the demand of college students, senior citizens, or some other group more sensitive to the price. *This firm maximizes profit by finding the price in each market that equates marginal revenue with marginal cost.* For example, consumers with a lower price elasticity pay $3.00, and those with a higher price elasticity pay $1.50. Profit maximization results in charging a lower price to the group with the more elastic demand. Despite the price difference, the firm gets the same marginal revenue from the last unit sold to each group. Note that charging both groups $3.00 would eliminate any profit from that right-hand group of consumers, who would be priced out of the market. Charging both groups $1.50 would lead to negative marginal revenue from the left-hand group, which would reduce profit. No single price could generate the profit achieved through price discrimination.

Examples of Price Discrimination

Let's look at some examples of price discrimination. Because businesspeople face unpredictable yet urgent demands for travel and communication, and because their employers pay such expenses, businesspeople are less sensitive to price than are householders. In other words, businesspeople have a less elastic demand for business travel and long-distance phone use than do householders, so airlines and telephone services try to maximize profits by charging business customers higher rates than residential customers.

But how do firms distinguish between customer groups? Telephone companies are able to sort out customers by charging different rates based on the time of day. Long-distance rates are often higher during normal *business* hours than during evenings and weekends, when householders, who have a higher price elasticity of demand, make social calls. Airlines distinguish between business and household customers based on the terms under which tickets are purchased. Householders usually plan their trips well in advance and often spend the weekend. But business travel is more unpredictable, more urgent, and seldom involves a

EXHIBIT 9

HOMEWORK
Xpress!
Graphing

Price Discrimination with Two Groups of Consumers

A monopolist facing two groups of consumers with different demand elasticities may be able to practice price discrimination to increase profit or reduce loss. With marginal cost the same in both markets, the firm charges a higher price to the group in panel (a), which has less elastic demand than the group in panel (b).

weekend stay. The airlines sort out the two groups by limiting discount fares to travelers who buy tickets well in advance and who stay over Saturday night. Airline tickets for business class costs much more than for coach class.

Here's another example of price discrimination: IBM wanted to charge business users of its laser printer more than home users. To distinguish between the two groups, IBM decided to slow down the home printer to 5 pages a minute (versus 10 for the business model). To do this, they added an extra chip that inserted pauses between pages.[2] Thus, IBM could sell the home model for less than the business model without cutting into sales of its business model.

Here's a final example. Major amusement parks, such as Disney World and Universal Studios, distinguish between local residents and out-of-towners when it comes to the price of admission. Out-of-towners typically spend a substantial amount on airlines and lodging just to be there, so they are less sensitive to the admission price than are local residents. The problem is how to charge a lower price to locals. The parks do this by making discount coupons available at local businesses, such as dry cleaners, which vacationers are less likely to visit.

Perfect Price Discrimination: The Monopolist's Dream

The demand curve shows the marginal value of each unit consumed, which is also the maximum amount consumers would pay for each unit. If the monopolist could charge a different price for each unit sold—a price reflected by the height of the demand curve—the firm's marginal revenue from selling one more unit would equal the price of that unit. Thus, the demand curve would become the firm's marginal revenue curve. A **perfectly discriminating monopolist** would charge a different price for each unit sold.

In Exhibit 10, again for simplicity, the monopolist is assumed to produce at a constant average and marginal cost in the long run. A perfectly discriminating monopolist, like any producer, would maximize profit by producing the quantity at which marginal revenue equals marginal cost. Because the demand curve is now the marginal revenue curve, the profit-maximizing quantity occurs where the demand, or marginal revenue, curve intersects the marginal cost curve, identified at point *e* in Exhibit 10. Price discrimination is a way of increasing profit. The area of the shaded triangle *aec* defines the perfectly discriminating monopolist's economic profit.

By charging a different price for each unit sold, the perfectly discriminating monopolist is able to convert every dollar of consumer surplus into economic profit. Although this practice may seem unfair to consumers, perfect price discrimination gets high marks based on allocative efficiency. Because such a monopolist does not have to lower the price to all customers to sell more, there is no reason to restrict output. In fact, because this is a constant-cost industry, *Q* is the same quantity produced in perfect competition (though in perfect competition, the triangle *aec* would be consumer surplus, not economic profit). As in the perfectly competitive outcome, the marginal benefit of the final unit produced and consumed just equals its marginal cost. And although perfect price discrimination yields no consumer surplus, the total benefits consumers derive just equal the total amount they pay for the good. Note also that because the monopolist does not restrict output, there is no deadweight loss. Thus, perfect price discrimination enhances social welfare when compared with monopoly output in the absence of price discrimination. But the monopolist reaps all net gains from production, while consumers just break even on the deal because their total benefit equals their total cost.

PERFECTLY DISCRIMINATING MONOPOLIST

A monopolist who charges a different price for each unit sold; also called the monopolist's dream

WALL STREET JOURNAL
Reading It **Right**

What's the relevance of the following statement from the Wall Street Journal: *"Any merchant would love to sell a product at the highest price each customer will pay."*

2. Carl Shapiro and Hal Varian, *Information Rules: A Strategic Guide to the Network Economy* (Boston: Harvard Business School Press, 1999), p. 59.

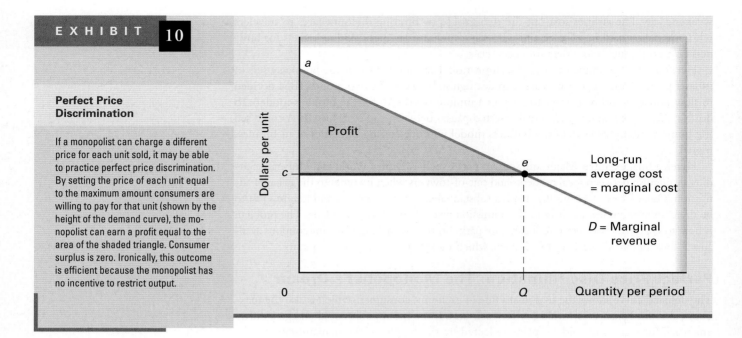

Perfect Price Discrimination

If a monopolist can charge a different price for each unit sold, it may be able to practice perfect price discrimination. By setting the price of each unit equal to the maximum amount consumers are willing to pay for that unit (shown by the height of the demand curve), the monopolist can earn a profit equal to the area of the shaded triangle. Consumer surplus is zero. Ironically, this outcome is efficient because the monopolist has no incentive to restrict output.

Examples of attempts to capture consumer surplus include pricing schemes for Internet service, cable television, and cellular phone service. For example, a cellular phone service offers several pricing alternatives, such as (1) price per minute with no basic fee, (2) a flat rate for the month plus a price per minute, and (3) a flat rate for unlimited calls. These alternatives allow the company to charge those who use fewer minutes more per minute than those who call more frequently. Such suppliers are trying to convert some consumer surplus into profit.

Conclusion

Pure monopoly, like perfect competition, is not that common. Perhaps the best examples are firms producing patented items with unique characteristics, such as certain prescription drugs. Some firms may have monopoly power in the short run, but the lure of economic profit encourages rivals to hurdle seemingly high entry barriers in the long run. Changing technology also works against monopoly in the long run. For example, the railroad monopoly was erased by the interstate highway system. AT&T's monopoly on long-distance phone service crumbled as microwave technology replaced copper wire. The U.S. Postal Service's monopoly on first-class mail is being eroded by overnight delivery, fax machines, and email. De Beers is losing its grip on the diamond market. And cable TV service is losing its local monopoly to technological breakthroughs in fiber-optics technology, wireless broadband, and the Internet.

Although perfect competition and pure monopoly are relatively rare, our examination of them yields a framework to help understand market structures that lie between the two extremes. As we will see, many firms have some degree of monopoly power—that is, they face downward-sloping demand curves. In the next chapter, we will consider the two market structures that lie in the gray region between perfect competition and monopoly.

SUMMARY

1. A monopolist sells a product with no close substitutes. Short-run economic profit earned by a monopolist can persist in the long run only if the entry of new firms is blocked. Three barriers to entry are (a) legal restrictions, such as patents and operating licenses; (b) economies of scale over a broad range of output; and (c) control over a key resource.

2. Because a monopolist is the sole supplier of a product with no close substitutes, its demand curve is also the market demand curve. Because a monopolist that does not price discriminate can sell more only by lowering the price for all units, marginal revenue is less than the price. Where demand is price elastic, marginal revenue is positive and total revenue increases as the price falls. Where demand is price inelastic, marginal revenue is negative and total revenue decreases as the price falls. A monopolist will never voluntarily produce where demand is inelastic because charging a higher price would increase total revenue.

3. If the monopolist can at least cover variable cost, profit is maximized or loss is minimized in the short run by finding the output rate that equates marginal revenue with marginal cost. At the profit-maximizing quantity, the price is found on the demand curve.

4. In the short run, a monopolist, like a perfect competitor, can earn economic profit but will shut down unless price at least covers average variable cost. In the long run, a monopolist, unlike a perfect competitor, can continue to earn economic profit as long as entry of other firms is blocked.

5. Resources are usually allocated less efficiently under monopoly than under perfect competition. If costs are similar, the monopolist will charge a higher price and supply less output than will a perfectly competitive industry. Monopoly usually results in a deadweight loss when compared with perfect competition because the loss of consumer surplus exceeds the gains in monopoly profit.

6. To increase profit through price discrimination, the monopolist must have at least two identifiable groups of customers, each with a different price elasticity of demand at a given price, and must be able to prevent customers charged the lower price from reselling to those charged the higher price.

7. A perfect price discriminator charges a different price for each unit of the good sold, thereby converting all consumer surplus into economic profit. Perfect price discrimination seems unfair because the monopolist "cleans up," but this approach is as efficient as perfect competition because the monopolist has no incentive to restrict output.

QUESTIONS FOR REVIEW

1. *(Barriers to Entry)* Complete each of the following sentences:

   a. A U.S. _____ awards inventors the exclusive right to production for 20 years.
   b. Patents and licenses are examples of government-imposed _____ that prevent entry into an industry.
   c. When economies of scale make it possible for a single firm to satisfy market demand at a lower cost per unit than could two or more firms, the single firm is considered a _____.
   d. A potential barrier to entry is a firm's control of a(n) _____ critical to production in the industry.

2. *(Barriers to Entry)* Explain how economies of scale can be a barrier to entry.

3. *(Case Study: Is a Diamond Forever?)* How did the De Beers cartel try to maintain control of the price in the diamond market? How has this control been threatened?

4. *(Revenue for the Monopolist)* How does the demand curve faced by a monopolist differ from the demand curve faced by a perfectly competitive firm?

5. *(Revenue for the Monopolist)* Why is it impossible for a profit-maximizing monopolist to choose any price *and* any quantity it wishes?

6. *(Revenue Schedules)* Explain why the marginal revenue curve for a monopolist lies below its demand curve, rather than coinciding with the demand curve, as is the case for a perfectly competitive firm. Is it ever possible for a monop-

olist's marginal revenue curve to coincide with its demand curve?

7. *(Revenue Curves)* Why would a monopoly firm never knowingly produce on the inelastic portion of its demand curve?

8. *(Profit Maximization)* Review the following graph showing the short-run situation of a monopolist. What output level will the firm choose in the short run? Why?

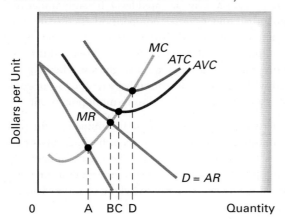

9. *(Allocative and Distributive Effects)* Why is society worse off under monopoly than under perfect competition, even if both market structures face the same constant long-run average cost curve?

10. *(Welfare Cost of Monopoly)* Explain why the welfare loss of a monopoly may be smaller or larger than the loss shown in Exhibit 8 in this chapter.

11. (*C a s e* **Study**: The Mail Monopoly) Can the U.S. Postal Service be considered a monopoly in first-class mail? Why or why not? What has happened to the price elasticity of demand for first-class mail in recent years?

12. *(Conditions for Price Discrimination)* What four conditions must be met for a monopolist to price discriminate successfully?

13. *(Price Discrimination)* Explain how it may be profitable for South Korean manufacturers to sell new autos at a lower price in the United States than in South Korea, even with transportation costs included.

14. *(Perfect Price Discrimination)* Why is the perfectly discriminating monopolist's marginal revenue curve identical to the demand curve it faces?

PROBLEMS AND EXERCISES

15. *(Short-Run Profit Maximization)* Answer the following questions on the basis of the monopolist's situation illustrated in the following graph.

a. At what output rate and price will the monopolist operate?

b. In equilibrium, approximately what will be the firm's total cost and total revenue?

c. What will be the firm's profit or loss in equilibrium?

16. *(Monopoly)* Suppose that a certain manufacturer has a monopoly on the sorority and fraternity ring business (a constant-cost industry) because it has persuaded the "Greeks" to give it exclusive rights to their insignia.

a. Using demand and cost curves, draw a diagram depicting the firm's profit-maximizing price and output level.

b. Why is marginal revenue less than price for this firm?

c. On your diagram, show the deadweight loss that occurs because the output level is determined by a monopoly rather than by a competitive market.

d. What would happen if the Greeks decided to charge the manufacturer a royalty fee of $3 per ring?

EXPERIENTIAL EXERCISES

17. *(The Welfare Cost of Monopoly)* In many larger U.S. cities, monopoly owners of sports franchises have been lobbying local governments for new publicly financed sports stadiums. Is this a form of rent seeking? Go to Heartland Institute's Web site at http://www.heartland.org/Index.cfm, conduct a search for sports stadiums, and look at one of the documents collected there. Is there convincing evidence of rent seeking? If so, how does that relate to the welfare cost of monopoly?

18. *(Price Discrimination)* The Robinson–Patman Act is a federal statute that outlaws certain forms of price discrimination. Review the main provisions of the Act as outlined by RPAMall at http://www.lawmall.com/rpa/. Then visit a local supermarket and look for evidence of price discrimination. Are the conditions for price discrimination, as outlined in this chapter, met there? Do you think the forms of price discrimination you found are legal under the Robinson–Patman Act?

19. *(Wall Street Journal)* The Legal Beat column, found in the Marketplace section of the Wall Street Journal, chronicles court decisions and legal trends that affect American businesses. In the legal arena, firms and the government often struggle over monopoly power. Find an article describing a firm seeking to restrict competition or a government action aimed at reducing monopoly power. See if you can use the monopoly model to understand the issues involved.

20. *(Wall Street Journal)* Look at the Travel page in the Weekend section of Friday's Wall Street Journal. Find the section displaying airfares. You will find that there are often a number of different fares between identical locations. Do these price differences necessarily represent the use of price discrimination? Why or Why not?

HOMEWORK XPRESS! EXERCISES

*These exercises require access to McEachern Homework Xpress! If Homework Xpress! did not come with your book, visit **http://homeworkxpress.swlearning.com** to purchase.*

Sal's Sandals has obtained a patent for its innovative footwear. Sal's estimate of demand for the firm's sandals is shown in the table.

1. Use Sal's values to plot the demand curve and to find and plot the marginal revenue curve for his sandals.

Quantity of sandals per period	Price
0	$ 50
10	45
20	40
30	35
40	30
50	25
60	20

2. Sal's estimates of demand and marginal revenue are as from Problem 1. Add a marginal cost curve so that the profit maximizing quantity is 30. Identify the price Sal would charge. Add an average total cost curve so that the average cost per unit is $30. Create a shaded box illustrating profits.

3. Sal's estimates of demand and marginal revenue are as from Problem 1. Draw typically shaped marginal cost, average total cost, and average variable cost curves to illustrate when Sal might choose to operate at a loss in the short run. Identify the quantity he would produce and the price he would charge. Create a shaded box illustrating his loss.

4. Red River Valley Electric Power has a monopoly in the supply of electric power in its region. Draw a diagram with a downward sloping demand curve and the corresponding marginal revenue curve. Add a constant average cost curve and identify the quantity produced and price charged when Red River exercises its monopoly power.

    However, the industry is soon to be opened to competition. Identify the price and quantity that would be expected in a competitive market for electric power. Shade in the area that represents the deadweight loss eliminated when the market is opened to competition.

Monopolistic Competition and Oligopoly

© Andrew Winning/Reuters/Corbis

W hy is Perrier water sold in green, tear-shaped bottles? Why are some shampoos sold only in salons? Why do some pizza makers deliver? Why do airlines engage in airfare warfare? Why was the oil cartel, OPEC, created, and why has it met with only spotty success? Why is there a witness protection program? To answer these and other questions, we turn in this chapter to the vast gray area that lies between perfect competition and monopoly.

Perfect competition and monopoly are extreme market structures. Under perfect competition, many suppliers offer an identical product and, in the long run, can enter or leave the industry with ease. A monopolist supplies a product with no close substitutes in a market where natural and artificial barriers keep out would-be competitors. These polar market structures are logically appealing and offer a useful description of some industries observed in the economy.

But most firms fit into neither market structure. Some markets have many sellers producing goods that vary slightly, such as the many convenience stores that abound. Other markets consist of just a few sellers that in some industries produce commodities (such as oil) and in other industries produce differentiated goods (such as automobiles). This chapter examines the two remaining market structures that together include most firms in the economy. Topics discussed include:

- Monopolistic competition
- Product differentiation
- Excess capacity
- Oligopoly
- Collusion
- Prisoner's dilemma

Monopolistic Competition

During the 1920s and 1930s, economists began formulating models that fit between perfect competition and monopoly. Two models of *monopolistic competition* were developed independently. In 1933 Edward Chamberlin of Harvard University published *The Theory of Monopolistic Competition*. Across the Atlantic that same year, Joan Robinson of Cambridge University published *The Economics of Imperfect Competition*. Although the theories differed, their underlying principles were similar. We will discuss Chamberlin's approach.

Characteristics of Monopolistic Competition

As the expression **monopolistic competition** suggests, this market structure contains elements of both monopoly and competition. Chamberlin used the term to describe a market in which many producers offer products that are substitutes but are not viewed as identical by consumers. Because the products of different suppliers differ slightly—for example, some convenience stores are closer to you than others—the demand curve for each is not horizontal but slopes downward. Each supplier has some power over the price it can charge. Thus, the firms that populate this market are not *price takers,* as they would be under perfect competition, but are *price makers.*

Because barriers to entry are low, firms in monopolistic competition can, in the long run, enter or leave the market with ease. Consequently, there are enough sellers that they behave competitively. There are also enough sellers that each tends to get lost in the crowd. For example, in a large metropolitan area, an individual restaurant, gas station, drugstore, video store, dry cleaner, or convenience store tends to act *independently.* In other market structures, there may be only two or three sellers in each market, so they keep an eye on one another; they act *interdependently.* You will understand the relevance of this distinction later in the chapter.

Product Differentiation

In perfect competition, the product is a commodity, meaning it's identical across producers, such as a bushel of wheat. In monopolistic competition, the product differs somewhat among sellers, as with the difference between one rock radio station and another. Sellers differentiate their products in four basic ways.

Physical Differences

The most obvious way products differ is in their physical appearance and their qualities. Packaging is also designed to make a product stand out in a crowded field, such as a distinctive bottle of water (Perrier) and instant soup in a cup (Cup O' Soup®). Physical differences

MONOPOLISTIC COMPETITION

A market structure with many firms selling products that are substitutes but different enough that each firm's demand curve slopes downward; firm entry is relatively easy

are seemingly endless: size, weight, color, taste, texture, and so on. Shampoos, for example, differ in color, scent, thickness, lathering ability, and bottle design. Particular brands aim at consumers with dandruff and those with normal, dry, or oily hair.

Location

The number and variety of locations where a product is available are other ways of differentiation—*spatial differentiation.* Some products seem to be available everywhere, including the Internet; finding other products requires some search and travel. If you live in a metropolitan area, you are no doubt accustomed to the many convenience stores that populate the region. Each wants to be closest to you when you need that gallon of milk or loaf of bread—thus, the proliferation of stores. As the name says, these mini grocery stores are selling *convenience.* Their prices are higher and selections more limited than those of regular grocery stores, but they are likely to be nearer customers, they don't have long lines, and some are open all night.

Services

Products also differ in terms of their accompanying services. For example, some pizza sellers, like Domino's, and some booksellers, like Amazon.com, deliver; others don't. Some retailers offer product demonstrations by a well-trained staff; others are mostly self-service. Some products include online support and toll-free numbers; others provide no help at all. Some offer money-back guarantees; others say "no returns." The quality and range of service often differentiate otherwise close substitutes.

Product Image

A final way products differ is in the image the producer tries to foster in the consumer's mind. For example, suppliers of sportswear, clothing, watches, and cosmetics often pay for endorsements from athletes, models, and other celebrities. Some producers try to demonstrate high quality based on where products are sold, such as shampoo sold only in hair salons. Some products tout their all-natural ingredients, such as Ben & Jerry's ice cream and Tom's of Maine toothpaste, or appeal to environmental concerns by focusing on recycled packaging, such as the Starbucks coffee cup insulating sleeve "made from 60% postconsumer recycled fiber." Producers try to create and maintain brand loyalty through product promotion and advertising.

Short-Run Profit Maximization or Loss Minimization

Because each monopolistic competitor offers a product that differs somewhat from what others supply, each has some control over the price charged. This *market power* means that each firm's demand curve slopes downward. Because many firms are selling substitutes, any firm that raises its price can expect to lose some customers, but not all, to rivals. By way of comparison, a price hike would cost a monopolist fewer customers but would cost a perfect competitor *all* customers. Therefore, a monopolistic competitor faces a demand curve that tends to be more elastic than a monopolist's but less elastic than a perfect competitor's.

Recall that the availability of substitutes for a given product affects its price elasticity of demand. The price elasticity of the monopolistic competitor's demand depends on (1) the number of rival firms that produce similar products and (2) the firm's ability to differentiate its product from those of its rivals. *A firm's demand curve will be more elastic the more substitutes there are and the less differentiated its product is.*

Marginal Revenue Equals Marginal Cost

From our study of monopoly, we know that the downward-sloping demand curve means the marginal revenue curve also slopes downward and lies beneath the demand curve. Exhibit 1 depicts demand and marginal revenue curves for a monopolistic competitor. The exhibit also presents average and marginal cost curves. Remember that the forces that determine the cost of production are largely independent of the forces that shape demand, so there is nothing special about a monopolistic competitor's cost curves. In the short run, a firm that can at least cover its variable cost will increase output as long as marginal revenue exceeds marginal cost. A monopolistic competitor maximizes profit just as a monopolist does: *the profit-maximizing quantity occurs where marginal revenue equals marginal cost; the profit-maximizing price for that quantity is found up on the demand curve.* Exhibit 1 shows the price and quantity combinations that maximize short-run profit in panel (a), and minimize short-run loss in panel (b). In each panel, the marginal cost and marginal revenue curves intersect at point *e*, yielding equilibrium output *q*, equilibrium price *p*, and average total cost *c*.

Maximizing Profit or Minimizing Loss in the Short Run

Recall that the short run is a period too brief to allow firms to enter or leave the market. The demand and cost conditions shown in panel (a) of Exhibit 1 indicate that this firm will earn economic profit in the short run. At the firm's profit-maximizing quantity, average total

EXHIBIT **1**

HOMEWORK
Xpress!
Graphing

Monopolistic Competitor in the Short Run

The monopolistically competitive firm produces the level of output at which marginal revenue equals marginal cost (point *e*) and charges the price indicated by point *b* on the downward-sloping demand curve. In panel (a), the firm produces *q* units, sells them at price *p*, and earns a short-run economic profit equal to (*p* – *c*) multiplied by *q*, shown by the blue rectangle. In panel (b), the average total cost exceeds the price at the output where marginal revenue equals marginal cost. Thus, the firm suffers a short-run loss equal to (*c* – *p*) multiplied by *q*, shown by the pink rectangle.

(a) Maximizing short-run profit

(b) Minimizing short-run loss

EXHIBIT 2

HOMEWORK
Xpress!
Graphing

Long-Run Equilibrium in Monopolistic Competition

If existing firms earn economic profits, new firms will enter the industry in the long run. This entry reduces the demand facing each firm. In the long run, the demand curve shifts leftward until marginal revenue equals marginal cost (point *a*) and the demand curve is tangent to the average total cost curve (point *b*). Economic profit is zero at output *q*. With zero economic profit, no more firms will enter, so the industry is in long-run equilibrium. The same long-run outcome will occur if firms suffer a short-run loss. Firms will leave until remaining firms earn just a normal profit.

cost, c , is below the price, p. Price minus average total cost is the firm's profit per unit, which, when multiplied by the quantity, yields economic profit, shown by the shaded rectangle. Again, the profit-maximizing quantity is found where marginal revenue equals marginal cost; price is found up on the demand curve at that quantity. Thus, a monopolistic competitor, like a monopolist, has no supply curve—that is, *there is no curve that uniquely relates alternative prices and corresponding quantities supplied.*

The monopolistic competitor, like other firms, has no guarantee of economic profit. The firm's demand and cost curves could be as shown in panel (b), where the average total cost curve lies entirely above the demand curve, so no quantity would allow the firm to break even. In such a situation, the firm must decide whether to produce or to shut down temporarily. The rule here is the same as with perfect competition and monopoly: as long as the price exceeds average variable cost, the firm in the short run will lose less by producing than by shutting down. If no price covers average variable cost, the firm will shut down. Recall that the halt in production may be only temporary; shutting down is not the same as going out of business. Firms that expect economic losses to persist may, in the long run, leave the industry.

Short-run profit maximization in monopolistic competition is quite similar to that under monopoly. But the stories differ in the long run, as we'll see next.

Zero Economic Profit in the Long Run

Low barriers to entry in monopolistic competition mean that short-run economic profit will attract new entrants in the long run. Because new entrants offer products that are similar to those offered by existing firms, they draw customers away from existing firms, thereby

reducing the demand facing each firm. Entry will continue in the long run until economic profit disappears. *Because of the ease of entry to the market, monopolistically competitive firms earn zero economic profit in the long run.*

If they continue to suffer short-run losses, some monopolistic competitors will leave the industry in the long run, redirecting their resources to products expected to earn at least a normal profit. As firms leave, their customers will switch to the remaining firms, increasing the demand for those products. Firms will continue to leave in the long run until the remaining firms have sufficient customers to earn normal profit, but not economic profit.

Exhibit 2 shows long-run equilibrium for a typical monopolistic competitor. In the long run, entry and exit will alter each firm's demand curve until economic profit disappears— that is, until price equals average total cost. In Exhibit 2, the marginal revenue curve intersects the marginal cost curve at point *a*. At the equilibrium quantity, *q,* the average total cost curve at point *b* is tangent to the demand curve. Because average total cost equals the price, the firm earns no economic profit but does earn a normal profit. At all other rates of output, the firm's average total cost is above the demand curve, so the firm would lose money if it reduced or expanded its output.

Thus, because entry is easy in monopolistic competition, short-run economic profit will draw new entrants into the industry in the long run. The demand curve facing each monopolistic competitor shifts left until economic profit disappears. A short-run economic loss will prompt some firms to leave the industry in the long run until remaining firms earn just a normal profit. In summary: *Monopolistic competition is like monopoly in the sense that firms in each industry face demand curves that slope downward. Monopolistic competition is like perfect competition in the sense that easy entry and exit eliminate economic profit or economic loss in the long run.*

One way to understand how firm entry erases short-run economic profit is to consider the evolution of an industry, as is discussed in the following case study.

Fast Forward

The introduction of videocassette recorders, or VCRs, fueled demand for videotaped movies. The initial surge in demand was magnified by rentals of older movies that consumers had missed at theaters. The first wave of outlets charged about $5 per day, required security deposits for tapes, and imposed membership fees of up to $100. In the late 1970s and early 1980s, most rental stores faced little competition and many earned short-run economic profits. But because entry was relatively easy, this profit attracted competitors. Convenience stores, grocery stores, bookstores, even drugstores began renting videos as a sideline. Between 1982 and 1987, the number of video outlets quadrupled, growing faster than the demand for VCRs. Once consumers caught up with the backlog of older movies, demand focused primarily on new releases.

Thus, the supply of rental outlets increased faster than the demand. The 1990s brought more bad news for the industry, when hundreds of cable channels and pay-per-view options offered substitutes for video rentals. The greater supply of rentals along with the increased availability of substitutes had the predictable effect on market prices. Rental rates crashed to as little as $0.99. Membership fees and tape deposits disappeared. Rental stores that could

C a s e **Study**

World of Business

*e*Activity
Movielink, LLC, at http://www.
movielink.com, is a joint venture
of Metro-Goldwyn-Mayer Studios, Paramount Pictures, Sony Pictures
Entertainment, Universal Studios, and
Warner Bros. Studios. Movielink
provides downloadable movies from a
wide selection of listings, including
independent films. Visit its site and
read about the company and its
management. What problems provided
the catalyst for this company's creation? Is the company practicing monopolistic competition? Or something
else?

not survive folded. So many failed that a market developed to buy and resell their tape inventories.

The video rental business grew little during the 1990s. The industry "shakeout" is still going on. Even after the addition of DVDs and video games, rental revenue per store declined in 2003. Blockbuster has grown to more than 6,000 U.S. stores, and now accounts for more than a third of the U.S. market, four times the share of second-ranked Hollywood Video. Blockbuster is transforming the rental industry from monopolistic competition to *oligopoly,* a market structure to be examined later in the chapter. But Blockbuster faces its own growing pains, including an "excess inventory" of tapes and a failed effort to sell books, magazines, and snacks at its rental stores.

The latest threat to the rental business is on-demand movies delivered by broadband cable. With a remote control and a digital cable box, customers can rent, rewind, pause, and replay movies, all without leaving the couch. Five of the largest Hollywood studios launched an Internet service called Movielink to supply downloaded movies. Blockbuster is trying to get into the broadband business, but success there could cannibalize its rental business. With an inventory of over 12,000 tapes and DVDs per store, Blockbuster would get stuck with more than 75 million tapes nationwide. Such is the dynamic nature of market evolution— out with the old and in with the new, in a competitive process that has been aptly called *creative destruction.*

Sources: "VHS and DVD Rental Spending," *Video Business,* 5 April 2004; Janet Whitman, "Blockbuster's Poor Sales Results Cast Shadow Over Rise in Net," *Wall Street Journal,* 22 October 2003; and "Movie Mayhem with Video-on-Demand," *Retail Merchandiser,* January 2003. Blockbuster's home page is http://www.blockbuster.com/.

Monopolistic Competition and Perfect Competition Compared

How does monopolistic competition compare with perfect competition in terms of efficiency? In the long run, neither can earn economic profit, so what's the difference? The difference arises because of the different demand curves facing individual firms in each of the two market structures. Exhibit 3 presents the long-run equilibrium price and quantity for a typical firm in each market structure, assuming each firm has identical cost curves. In each case, the marginal cost curve intersects the marginal revenue curve at the quantity where the average total cost curve is tangent to the firm's demand curve.

A perfect competitor's demand curve is a horizontal line drawn at the market price, as shown in panel (a). This demand curve is tangent to the lowest point of the long-run average total cost curve. Thus, a perfect competitor in the long run produces at the lowest possible average cost. In panel (b), a monopolistic competitor faces a downward-sloping demand curve because its product differs somewhat from those of other suppliers. In the long run, the monopolistic competitor produces less than required to achieve the lowest possible average cost. Thus, the price and average cost under monopolistic competition, identified as *p'* in panel (b), exceed the price and average cost under perfect competition, identified as *p* in panel (a). *If firms have the same cost curves, the monopolistic competitor produces less and charges more than the perfect competitor does in the long run, but neither earns economic profit.*

Firms in monopolistic competition are not producing at minimum average cost. They are said to have **excess capacity**, because production falls short of the quantity that would achieve the lowest average cost. Excess capacity means that each producer could easily serve more customers and in the process would lower average cost. *The marginal value of increased output would exceed its marginal cost, so greater output would increase social welfare.* Such excess

EXCESS CAPACITY

The difference between a firm's profit-maximizing quantity and the quantity that minimizes average cost

capacity exists with gas stations, drugstores, convenience stores, restaurants, motels, book-stores, flower shops, and firms in other monopolistic competitive industries. A specific ex-ample is the funeral business. Industry analysts argue that the nation's 22,000 funeral direc-tors could efficiently handle 4 million funerals a year, but only about 2.3 million people die. So the industry operates at less than 60 percent of capacity, resulting in a higher average cost per funeral because valuable resources remain idle much of the time.

One other difference between perfect competition and monopolistic competition does not show up in Exhibit 3. Although the cost curves drawn in each panel of the exhibit are identical, firms in monopolistic competition advertise more to differentiate their products than do firms in perfect competition. These higher advertising costs shift up their average cost curves.

Some economists have argued that monopolistic competition results in too many suppli-ers and artificial product differentiation. The counterargument is that consumers are willing to pay a higher price for a wider selection. According to this latter view, consumers benefit from more choice among gas stations, restaurants, convenience stores, clothing stores, video

EXHIBIT 3	**Perfect Competition Versus Monopolistic Competition in Long-Run Equilibrium**

Cost curves are assumed to be the same in each panel. The perfectly competitive firm of panel (a) faces a demand curve that is horizontal at market price *p*. Long-run equilibrium occurs at output *q*, where the demand curve is tan-gent to the average total cost curve at its lowest point. The monopolistically competitive firm of panel (b) is in long-run equilibrium at output *q′*, where demand is tangent to average total cost. Because the demand curve slopes downward in panel (b), however, the tangency does not occur at the minimum point of average total cost. Thus, the monopolistically competitive firm produces less output and charges a higher price than does a perfectly com-petitive firm with the same cost curves. Neither firm earns economic profit in the long run.

(a) Perfect competition

(b) Monopolistic competition

stores, drugstores, textbooks, hiking boots, and many other goods and services. For example, what if half of the restaurants in your area were to close just so the remaining ones could reduce their excess capacity? Some consumers, including you, might be disappointed if a favorite closed.

Perfect competitors and monopolistic competitors are so numerous in their respective markets that an action by any one of them has little or no effect on the behavior of others in the market. Another important market structure on the continuum between perfect competition and monopoly has just a few firms. We explore this market structure in the balance of the chapter.

An Introduction to Oligopoly

OLIGOPOLY

A market structure characterized by a few firms whose behavior is interdependent

The final market structure we examine is *oligopoly*, a Greek word meaning "few sellers." When you think of "big business," you are thinking of **oligopoly,** a market dominated by just a few firms. Perhaps three or four account for more than half the market supply. Many industries, including steel, automobiles, oil, breakfast cereals, cigarettes, personal computers, and operating systems software, are *oligopolistic*. Because an oligopoly has only a few firms, each must consider the effect of its own actions on competitors' behavior. Oligopolists are therefore said to be *interdependent*.

Varieties of Oligopoly

UNDIFFERENTIATED OLIGOPOLY

An oligopoly that sells a commodity, or a product that does not differ across suppliers, such as an ingot of steel or a barrel of oil

DIFFERENTIATED OLIGOPOLY

An oligopoly that sells products that differ across suppliers, such as automobiles or breakfast cereal

In some oligopolies, such as steel or oil, the product is identical, or undifferentiated, across producers. Thus, an **undifferentiated oligopoly** sells a commodity, such as an ingot of steel or a barrel of oil. But in other oligopolies, such as automobiles or breakfast cereals, the product is differentiated across producers. A **differentiated oligopoly** sells products that differ across producers, such as a Toyota Camry versus a Ford Taurus or General Mills's Wheaties versus Kellogg's Corn Flakes.

The more similar the products, the greater the interdependence among firms in the industry. For example, because steel ingots are essentially identical, steel producers are quite sensitive to each other's prices. A small rise in one producer's price will send customers to rivals. But with differentiated oligopoly, such as the auto industry, producers are not quite as sensitive about each other's prices. As with monopolistic competitors, oligopolists differentiate their products through (1) physical qualities, (2) sales locations, (3) services provided with the product, and (4) the image of the product established in the consumer's mind.

Because of interdependence, the behavior of any particular firm is difficult to predict. *Each firm knows that any changes in its product's quality, price, output, or advertising policy may prompt a reaction from its rivals. And each firm may react if another firm alters any of these features.* Monopolistic competition is like a professional golf tournament, where each player strives for a personal best. Oligopoly is more like a tennis match, where each player's actions depend on how and where the opponent hits the ball.

Why have some industries evolved into oligopolies, dominated by only a few firms? Although the reasons are not always clear, *an oligopoly can often be traced to some form of barrier to entry, such as economies of scale, legal restrictions, brand names built up by years of advertising, or control over an essential resource.* In the previous chapter, we examined barriers to entry as they applied to monopoly. The same principles apply to oligopoly. The following case study considers some barriers to entry in the airline industry.

The Unfriendly Skies

At one time, airline routes were straight lines from one city to another. Now they radiate like the spokes of a wagon wheel from a "hub" city. From about 30 hub airports across the country, the airlines send out planes along the spokes to about 400 commercial airports and then quickly bring them back to the hubs. Major airlines dominate hub airports. For example, half the passengers at Dallas–Fort Worth airport fly United Airlines. A new airline trying to enter the industry must secure a hub airport as well as landing slots at crowded airports around the country—not an easy task because hubs are crowded and landing slots are scarce. Hubs and landing slots create the first barrier to entry in the airline industry. Research shows that ticket prices at airports dominated by a single airline are higher than at more competitive airports.

© George Hall/Corbis

A second barrier to entry is frequent-flyer mileage programs. The biggest airlines fly more national and international routes, so they offer more opportunities both to accumulate frequent-flyer miles and to use them. Thus, the biggest airlines have the most attractive programs. A third barrier to entry is federal restrictions that prevent foreign ownership of U.S. airlines and block foreign airlines from offering connecting service between U.S. cities. Thus, scarce hubs and gates, frequent-flier programs, and restrictions against foreign competition create barriers to entry in the airline industry. Seven airlines account for over 80 percent of all passenger service.

But the entry of low-cost carriers is now challenging the top airlines. Upstart Jet Blue and Southwest Airlines were among the few to earn a profit in recent years. Both airlines fill a higher proportion of their seats than does the industry on average. So the entry barriers discussed above apparently have not blocked all entry.

Sources: "Low Cost Airlines: Crowded Skies," *The Economist;* 24 April 2004; "Southwest's Entry Shakes Up Airline Competition at Philadelphia Airport," *Philadelphia Inquirer,* 29 October 2003; Nick Pachetti, "Jet Blue Skies," *Money,* 1 April 2003; and Steven Morrison and Clifford Winston, *The Evolution of the Airline Industry* (Washington, D.C.: Brookings Institution, 1995). The travel site formed by the world's major airlines is http://www.orbitz.com/.

Economies of Scale

Perhaps the most important barrier to entry is economies of scale. Recall that the minimum efficient scale is the lowest output at which the firm takes full advantage of economies of scale. If a firm's minimum efficient scale is relatively large compared to industry output, then only a few firms are needed to satisfy industry demand. For example, an automobile plant of minimum efficient scale could make enough cars to supply nearly 10 percent of the U.S. market. If there were 100 auto plants, each would supply such a tiny portion of the market that the average cost per car would be higher than if only 10 plants manufacture autos. In the automobile industry, economies of scale create a barrier to entry. To compete with existing producers, a new entrant must sell enough automobiles to reach a competitive scale of operation.

Exhibit 4 presents the long-run average cost curve for a typical firm in the industry. If a new entrant sells only S cars, the average cost per unit, c_a, far exceeds the average cost, c_b, of a manufacturer that sells enough cars to reach the minimum efficient size, M. If autos sell for less than c_a, a potential entrant can expect to lose money, and this prospect will discour-

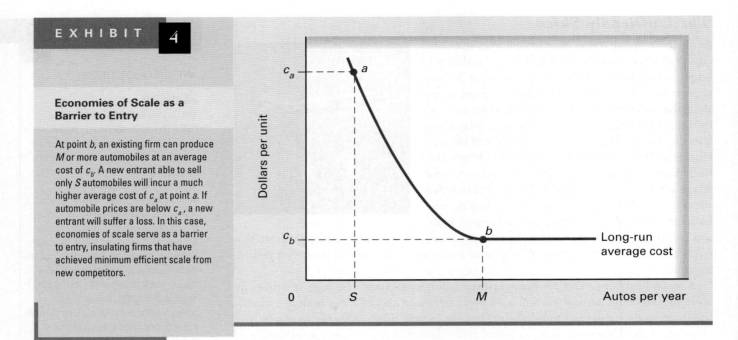

E X H I B I T　4

Economies of Scale as a Barrier to Entry

At point b, an existing firm can produce M or more automobiles at an average cost of c_b. A new entrant able to sell only S automobiles will incur a much higher average cost of c_a at point a. If automobile prices are below c_a, a new entrant will suffer a loss. In this case, economies of scale serve as a barrier to entry, insulating firms that have achieved minimum efficient scale from new competitors.

age entry. For example, John Delorean tried to break into the auto industry in the early 1980s with a modern design featured in the movie *Back to the Future*. But his company built only 8,583 Deloreans before going bankrupt.

The High Cost of Entry

Potential entrants into oligopolistic industries may face another problem. The total investment needed to reach the minimum efficient size is often gigantic. A new auto plant or new semiconductor plant can cost over $2 billion. The average cost of developing and testing a new drug exceeds $500 million. Advertising a new product enough to compete with established brands may also require enormous outlays.

High start-up costs and established brand names create substantial barriers to entry, especially because the market for new products is so uncertain (four out of every five new consumer products don't survive). An unsuccessful product could cripple an upstart firm. The prospect of such losses discourages many potential entrants. Most new products come from established firms, which can better withstand the possible losses. For example, Colgate-Palmolive spent $100 million introducing Total toothpaste, as did McDonald's in its failed attempt to sell the Arch Deluxe. Unilever lost $160 million when its new detergent, Power, washed out.

Firms often spend millions and sometimes billions trying to differentiate their products. Some of these outlays offer consumers valuable information and wider choice. But some spending seems to offer neither. For example, Pepsi and Coke spend billions on messages such "Joy of Pepsi" or "Life is Good." Regardless, *product differentiation expenditures create a barrier to entry*.

Crowding Out the Competition

Oligopolies compete with existing rivals and try to block new entry by offering a variety of products. Entrenched producers may flood the market with new products in part to crowd out any new entrants. For example, a few cereal makers offer more than a dozen products each. Many of these variations offer little that is new. One study of 25,500 new products introduced one year found only 7 percent offered new or added benefits.[1] *Multiple products from the same brand dominate shelf space and attempt to crowd out new entrants.*

Models of Oligopoly

Because oligopolists are interdependent, analyzing their behavior is complicated. No single model or single approach explains oligopoly behavior completely. At one extreme, oligopolists may try to coordinate their behavior so they act collectively as a single monopolist, forming a cartel, such as the Organization of Petroleum Exporting Countries (OPEC). At the other extreme, oligopolists may compete so fiercely that price wars erupt, such as those that break out among airlines, tobacco companies, computer chip makers, and wireless service providers.

Many theories have been developed to explain oligopoly behavior. We will study three of the better-known approaches: collusion, price leadership, and game theory. As you will see, each approach has some relevance in explaining observed behavior, although none is entirely satisfactory as a general theory of oligopoly. Thus, *there is no general theory of oligopoly but rather a set of theories, each based on the diversity of observed behavior in an interdependent market.*

Collusion and Cartels

In an oligopolistic market, there are just a few firms so, to decrease competition and increase profits, they may try to *collude,* or conspire to rig the market. **Collusion** is an agreement among firms in the industry to divide the market and fix the price. A **cartel** is a group of firms that agree to collude so they can act as a monopoly to increase economic profit. Cartels are more likely among sellers of a commodity, like oil or steel. Colluding firms, compared with competing firms, usually produce less, charge more, block new firms, and earn more profit. Consumers pay higher prices, and potential entrants are denied the opportunity to compete.

Collusion and cartels are illegal in the United States. Still, monopoly profit can be so tempting that some U.S. firms break the law. For example, top executives at Archer Daniels Midland were convicted in 1998 of conspiring with four Asian competitors to rig the $650 million world market for lysine, an amino acid used in animal feed. Some other countries are more tolerant of cartels and a few even promote cartels, as with the 11 member-nations of OPEC. But if OPEC ever met in the United States, its representatives could be arrested for price fixing. Cartels can operate worldwide because there are no international laws against them.

Suppose all firms in an industry formed a cartel. The market demand curve, *D,* appears in Exhibit 5. What price will maximize the cartel's profit, and how will output be allocated among participating firms? The first task of the cartel is to determine its marginal cost of production. Because a cartel acts like a monopoly that is operating many plants, the marginal cost curve in Exhibit 5 is the horizontal sum of each firm's marginal cost curve. The cartel's marginal cost curve intersects the market's marginal revenue curve to determine output that maximizes the cartel's profit. This intersection yields quantity *Q.* The cartel's price, *p,* is read off the demand curve at that quantity.

COLLUSION

An agreement among firms to increase economic profit by dividing the market or fixing the price

CARTEL

A group of firms that agree to coordinate their production and pricing decisions to act like a monopolist

---

1. The study was carried out by Market Intelligence Service and was reported in "Market Makers," *The Economist,* 14 March 1998.

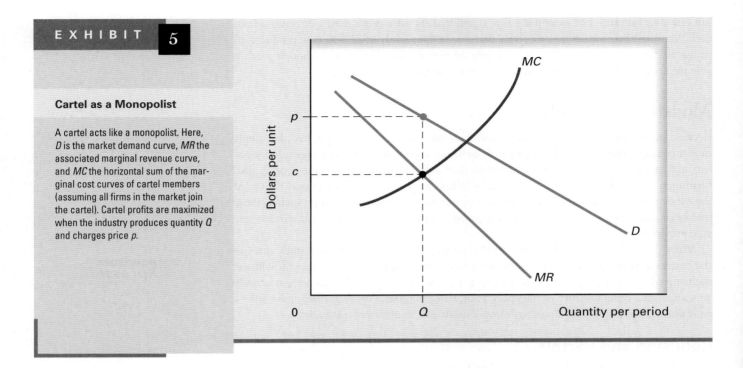

So far, so good. To maximize cartel profit, output Q must be allocated among cartel members so that each member's marginal cost equals c. Any other allocation would lower cartel profit. Thus, *for cartel profit to be maximized, output must be allocated so that the marginal cost for the final unit produced by each firm is identical.* Let's look at why this is easier said than done.

Differences in Average Cost

If all firms have identical average cost curves, output and profit would be easily allocated across firms (each firm would produce the same amount), but if costs differ, as they usually do, problems arise. The greater the difference in average costs across firms, the greater the differences in economic profits among firms. If cartel members try to equalize each firm's total profit, a high-cost firm would need to sell more than would a low-cost firm. But this allocation scheme would violate the cartel's profit-maximizing condition. Thus, *if average costs differ across firms, the output allocation that maximizes cartel profit will yield unequal profit across cartel members.* Firms that earn less profit could drop out of the cartel, thereby undermining it. Usually, the allocation of output is the result of haggling among cartel members. Firms that are more influential or more adept at bargaining get a larger share of output and profit. Allocation schemes are sometimes based on geography or on the historical division of output among firms. OPEC, for example, allocates output in proportion to each member country's share of estimated oil reserves.

Number of Firms in the Cartel

The more firms in an industry, the more difficult it is to negotiate an acceptable allocation of output among them. *Consensus becomes harder to achieve as the number of firms grows.* And the more firms in the industry, the more likely that some will become dissatisfied and bolt from the cartel.

New Entry into the Industry

If a cartel can't prevent new entry into the market, new firms will eventually force prices down, squeeze economic profit, and disrupt the cartel. The profit of the cartel attracts entry, entry increases market supply, and increased supply forces the price down. A cartel's success therefore depends on barriers that block the entry of new firms.

Cheating

Perhaps the biggest problem in keeping the cartel together is the powerful temptation to cheat on the agreement. Because oligopolists usually operate with excess capacity, some cheat on the established price. By offering a price slightly below the established price, any cartel member can usually increase sales and profit. Even if cartel members keep an eagle eye on each firm's price, one firm can increase sales by offering extra services, secret rebates, or other concessions. Cartels collapse if cheating becomes widespread.

OPEC's Spotty History

The problems of establishing and maintaining a cartel are reflected in the spotty history of OPEC. Many members are poor countries that rely on oil as their major source of revenue, so they argue over the price and their market share. OPEC members also cheat on the cartel. In 1980, the price of oil reached $80 a barrel (measured in 2004 dollars). For the last decade, the price has averaged around $32 a barrel, and it has been as low as $10 a barrel. Like other cartels, OPEC has also experienced difficulty with new entrants. The high prices resulting from OPEC's early success attracted new oil supplies from the North Sea, Mexico, and Siberia. Over 60 percent of the world's oil now comes from non-OPEC countries. Efforts to cartelize the world supply of a number of products, including bauxite, copper, and coffee, have failed so far.

In summary: Establishing and maintaining an effective cartel is more difficult if (1) the product is differentiated among firms, (2) average costs differ among firms, (3) there are many firms in the industry, (4) entry barriers are low, or (5) cheating on the cartel agreement becomes widespread.

Price Leadership

An informal, or *tacit,* form of collusion occurs if there is a **price leader** who sets the price for the rest of the industry. Typically, a dominant firm sets the market price, and other firms follow that lead, thereby avoiding price competition. The price leader also initiates any price changes, and, again, others follow. The steel industry was an example of the price-leadership form of oligopoly. Typically, U.S. Steel, the largest firm in the industry, would set the price for various products. Public pressure on U.S. Steel not to raise prices shifted the price-leadership role onto less prominent producers, resulting in a rotation of leadership among firms. Although the rotating price leadership reduced price conformity, price leadership kept prices high.

Like other forms of collusion, price leadership faces obstacles. Most importantly, the practice violates U.S. antitrust laws. Second, the greater the product differentiation among sellers, the less effective price leadership will be as a means of collusion. Third, there is no guarantee that other firms will follow the leader. Firms that fail to follow a price increase take business away from firms that do. Fourth, unless there are barriers to entry, a profitable price will attract new entrants, which could destabilize the price-leadership agreement. And finally, as with formal cartels, some firms are tempted to cheat on the agreement to boost sales and profits.

PRICE LEADER

A firm whose price is adopted by other firms in the industry

Game Theory

How will firms act when they recognize their interdependence but either cannot or do not collude? Because oligopoly involves interdependence among a few firms, we can think of interacting firms as players in a game. **Game theory** examines oligopolistic behavior as a series of strategic moves and countermoves among rival firms. It analyzes the behavior of decision makers, or players, whose choices affect one another. Game theory is not really a separate model of oligopoly but a general approach, an approach that can focus on each player's incentives to cooperate—say, through cartels or price leaders—or to compete, in ways to be discussed now.

To get some feel for game theory, let's work through the **prisoner's dilemma,** the most widely examined game. The game originally considered a situation in which two thieves, let's call them Ben and Jerry, are caught near the crime scene and brought to police headquarters, where they are interrogated in separate rooms. The police know the two guys did it but can't prove it, so they need a confession. Each faces a choice of confessing, thereby "squealing" on the other, or "clamming up," thereby denying any knowledge of the crime. If one confesses, turning state's evidence, he is granted immunity from prosecution and goes free, while the other guy is put away for 10 years. If both clam up, each gets only a 1-year sentence on a technicality. If both confess, each gets 5 years.

What will Ben and Jerry do? The answer depends on the assumptions about their behavior—that is, what *strategy* each pursues. A **strategy** reflects a player's game plan. In this game, suppose each player tries to save his own skin—each tries to minimize his time in jail, regardless of what happens to the other (after all, there is no honor among thieves). Exhibit 6 shows the *payoff matrix* for the prisoner's dilemma. A **payoff matrix** is a table listing the rewards (or, in this case, the penalties) that Ben and Jerry can expect based on the strategy each pursues.

Ben's choices are shown down the left margin and Jerry's across the top. Each prisoner can either confess or clam up. The numbers in the matrix indicate the prison time in years each can expect based on the corresponding strategies. Ben's numbers are in red and Jerry's in blue. Take a moment now to see how the matrix works. Notice that the sentence each player receives depends on the strategy he chooses *and* on the strategy the other player chooses.

What strategies are rational assuming that each player tries to minimize jail time? For example, put yourself in Ben's shoes. You know that Jerry, who is being questioned in another room, will either confess or clam up. If Jerry confesses, the left column of Exhibit 6 shows the penalties. If you confess too, you both get 5 years in jail, but if you clam up, you get 10 years and Jerry "walks." So, if you think Jerry will confess, you should too.

What if you believe Jerry will clam up? The right-hand column shows the two possible outcomes. If you confess, you do no time, but if you clam up too, you each get 1 year in jail. Thus, if you think Jerry will clam up, you're better off confessing. In short, whatever Jerry does, Ben is better off confessing. The same holds for Jerry. He is better off confessing, regardless of what Ben does. So each has an incentive to confess and both get 5 years in jail. This is called the **dominant-strategy equilibrium** of the game because each player's action does not depend on what he thinks the other player will do.

But notice that if each crook could just hang tough and clam up, both would be better off. After all, if both confess, each gets 5 years, but if both clam up, the police can't prove otherwise, so each gets only 1 year in jail. If each could trust the other to clam up, they both would be better off. But there is no way for the two to communicate or to coordinate their actions. That's why police investigators keep suspects apart, that's why organized crime

GAME THEORY

An approach that analyzes oligopolistic behavior as a series of strategic moves and counter-moves by rival firms

PRISONER'S DILEMMA

A game that shows why players have difficulty cooperating even though they would benefit from cooperation

STRATEGY

In game theory, the operational plan pursued by a player

PAYOFF MATRIX

In game theory, a table listing the payoffs that each player can expect based on the actions of the other player

DOMINANT-STRATEGY EQUILIBRIUM

In game theory, the outcome achieved when each player's choice does not depend on what the other player does

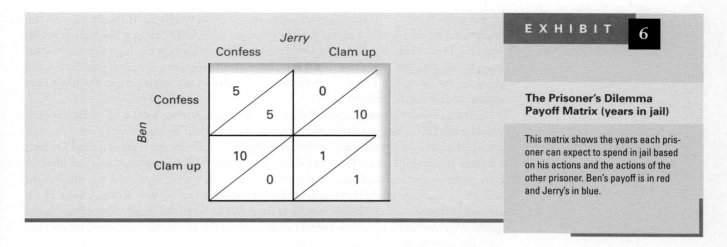

EXHIBIT 6

The Prisoner's Dilemma Payoff Matrix (years in jail)

This matrix shows the years each prisoner can expect to spend in jail based on his actions and the actions of the other prisoner. Ben's payoff is in red and Jerry's in blue.

threatens "squealers" with death, and that's why the witness protection program tries to shield "squealers."

Price-Setting Game

The prisoner's dilemma applies to a broad range of economic phenomena including pricing policy and advertising strategy. For example, consider the market for gasoline in a rural community with only two gas stations, Texaco and Exxon. Here the oligopoly consists of two sellers, or a **duopoly.** Suppose customers are indifferent between the brands and focus only on the price. Each station sets its daily price early in the morning before knowing the price set by the other. To keep it simple, suppose only two prices are possible—a low price or a high price. If both charge the low price, they split the market and each earns a profit of $500 per day. If both charge the high price, they also split the market, but profit jumps to $700 each. If one charges the high price but the other the low one, the low-price station gets most of the business, earning a profit of $1,000, leaving the high-price station with only $200.

Exhibit 7 shows the payoff matrix, with Texaco's strategy down the left margin and Exxon's across the top. Texaco's profit appears in red, and Exxon's in blue. Suppose you are

DUOPOLY

A market with only two producers; a type of oligopoly market structure

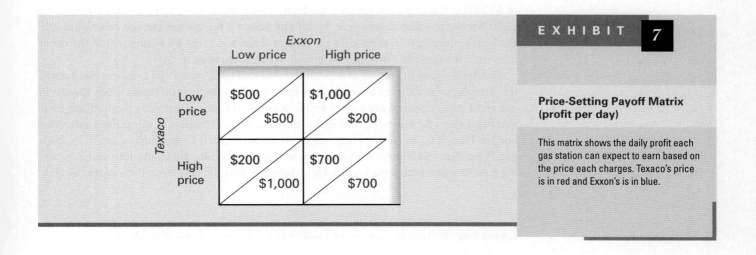

EXHIBIT 7

Price-Setting Payoff Matrix (profit per day)

This matrix shows the daily profit each gas station can expect to earn based on the price each charges. Texaco's price is in red and Exxon's is in blue.

running the Texaco station and are trying to decide what to charge. If Exxon charges the low price, you earn $500 charging the low price but only $200 charging the high price. So you earn more charging the low price. If, instead, Exxon charges the high price, you earn $1,000 charging the low price and $700 charging the high price. Again, you earn more charging the low price. Exxon faces the same incentives. Thus, each charges the low price, regardless of what the other does.

In this prisoner's dilemma, each charges the low price, earning $500 a day, although each would earn $700 charging the high price. Think of yourself as a member of the oil cartel discussed earlier, where the cartel determines the price and sets production quotas for each member. If you think other firms in the cartel will stick with their quotas, you can increase your profit by cutting your price and increasing quantity sold. If you think the other firms will cheat and overproduce, then you should too—otherwise, you will get your clock cleaned by those cheaters. Either way, your incentive as a cartel member is to cheat on the quota. All members have an incentive to cheat, although all would earn more by sticking with the agreement that maximizes joint profit.

This incentive to cut prices suggests why price wars sometimes break out among oligopolists. For example, in recent years automakers have aggressively matched and exceeded one another's price cuts and rebate programs, cutting auto prices sharply. In 2003, for example, the Cadillac DeVille with a sticker price of $48,000 sold for under $35,000. General Motors managed a profit in the third quarter of 2003 of just $15 on each car and truck sold, and Ford lost money on each vehicle.[2] A bitter price war with Dell in 2003 cut Hewlett-Packard's earnings on each $500 personal computer sold to a razor-thin $1.75.[3] And just before a recent Thanksgiving weekend, a price war erupted in airfares. American Airlines first announced holiday discounts. Delta responded with cuts of up to 50 percent. Within hours, American, United, and other major carriers said they would match Delta's reductions. All these airlines were losing money at the time. So go the price wars.

Cola War Game

As a final example of a prisoner's dilemma, consider the marketing strategies of Coke and Pepsi. Suppose each is putting together a promotional budget for the coming year, not knowing the other's plans. The choice boils down to adopting either a moderate budget or a big budget that involves multiple Super Bowl ads, showy in-store displays, and other efforts aimed mostly at attracting customers from each other. If each adopts a big budget, their costly efforts will, for the most part, cancel each other out and limit each company's profit to $2 billion a year. If each adopts a moderate promotional budget, the money saved boosts profit for each to $3 billion a year. And if one adopts a big budget but the other does not, the heavy promoter captures a bigger market share and earns $4 billion, while the other loses market share and earns only $1 billion. What to do, what to do?

Exhibit 8 shows the payoff matrix for the two strategies, with Pepsi's choices listed down the left margin and Coke's across the top. In each cell of the matrix, Pepsi's profit appears in red, and Coke's in blue. Let's look at Pepsi's decision. If Coke adopts a big promotional budget, Pepsi earns $2 billion by doing the same but only $1 billion by adopting a moderate budget. Thus, if Coke adopts a big budget, so should Pepsi. If Coke adopts a moderate budget, Pepsi earns $4 billion with a big budget and $3 billion with a moderate one. Again, Pepsi earns more with a big budget. Coke faces the same incentives, so both adopt big bud-

---

2. Micheline Maynard, "Car Sticker Prices Mask Some Big Bargains," *New York Times,* 29 October 2003.
3. David Bank, "H-P Posts 10% Increase in Revenue," *Wall Street Journal,* 20 November 2003.

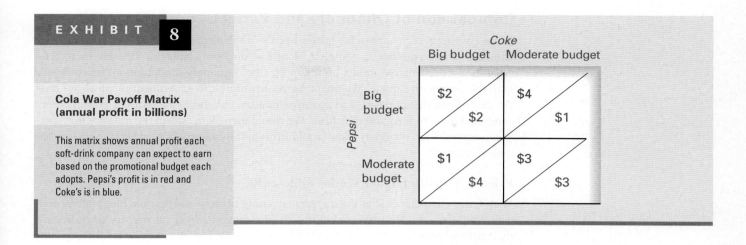

EXHIBIT 8

Cola War Payoff Matrix (annual profit in billions)

This matrix shows annual profit each soft-drink company can expect to earn based on the promotional budget each adopts. Pepsi's profit is in red and Coke's is in blue.

gets, earning $2 billion each in profit, even though each would have earned $3 billion with a moderate budget.

One-Shot Versus Repeated Games

The outcome of a game often depends on whether it is a *one-shot game* or a *repeated game*. The classic prisoner's dilemma is a one-shot game. If the game is to be played just once, the strategy of confessing makes you better off regardless of what the other player does. Your choice won't influence the other player's behavior. But if the same players repeat the prisoner's dilemma, as would likely occur with the price-setting game, the cola war game, and the OPEC cartel, other possibilities unfold. In a repeated-game setting, each player has a chance to establish a reputation for cooperation and thereby can encourage other players to do the same. After all, the cooperative solution—whether that involves clamming up, maintaining a high price, or adopting a moderate promotional budget—makes both players better off than if both fail to cooperate.

Experiments have shown that the strategy with the highest payoff in repeated games turns out to be the simplest—**tit-for-tat.** You begin by cooperating in the first round. On every round thereafter, you cooperate if the other player cooperated in the previous round, and you cheat if your opponent cheated in the previous round. In short, in any given round, you do whatever your opponent did in the previous round. The tit-for-tat strategy offers the other player an immediate punishment for cheating and an immediate reward for cooperation. Some cartels seem to employ tit-for-tat strategies.

Our discussion has given you some idea of game theory by focusing on the prisoner's dilemma. Other games can be more complicated and involve more strategic interaction. Because firms are interdependent, oligopoly gives rise to all kinds of behavior and many approaches. Each approach helps explain certain phenomena observed in oligopolistic markets. The *cartel,* or *collusion,* model shows why oligopolists might want to cooperate to set the market price; that model also explains why a cartel is hard to establish and maintain. The *price-leadership* model explains why and how firms may charge the same price without actually establishing a formal cartel. Finally, *game theory,* expressed here by the prisoner's dilemma, shows how difficult a cooperative solution might be even though players benefit from cooperation. Game theory is more of an approach than a distinct model.

TIT-FOR-TAT

In game theory, a strategy in repeated games when a player in one round of the game mimics the other player's behavior in the previous round; an optimal strategy for encouraging the other player to cooperate

Comparison of Oligopoly and Perfect Competition

As we have seen, each approach explains a piece of the oligopoly puzzle. But each has limitations, and none provides a complete picture of oligopoly behavior. Because there is no typical, or representative, model of oligopoly, "the" oligopoly model cannot be compared with the competitive model. We might, however, imagine an experiment in which we took the many firms that populate a competitive industry and, through a series of giant mergers, combined them to form, say, four firms. We would thereby transform the industry from perfect competition to oligopoly. How would firms in this industry behave before and after the massive merger?

Price Is Usually Higher Under Oligopoly

With fewer competitors after the merger, remaining firms would become more interdependent. Oligopoly models presented in this chapter suggest why firms may try to coordinate their pricing policies. *If oligopolists engaged in some sort of implicit or explicit collusion, industry output would be smaller and the price would be higher than under perfect competition.* Even if oligopolists did not collude but simply operated with excess capacity, the price would be higher and the quantity lower with oligopoly than with perfect competition. The price could become lower under oligopoly compared with perfect competition only if a price war broke out among oligopolists. Behavior will also depend on whether there are barriers to entry. The lower the barriers to entry into the oligopoly, the more oligopolists will act like perfect competitors.

Higher Profits Under Oligopoly

In the long run, easy entry prevents perfect competitors from earning more than a normal profit. With oligopoly, however, there may be barriers to entry, such as economies of scale or brand names, which allow firms in the industry to earn long-run economic profit. *If there are barriers to entry, we should expect profit in the long run to be higher under oligopoly than under perfect competition.* Profit rates do in fact appear to be higher in industries where a few firms account for a high proportion of industry sales. Some economists view these higher profit rates as troubling evidence of market power. But not all economists share this view. Some note that the largest firms in oligopolistic industries tend to earn the highest rate of profit. Thus, the higher profit rates observed in oligopolistic industries do not necessarily stem from market power per se. Rather, these higher profit rates stem from the greater efficiency arising from economies of scale in these large firms. Many of these issues will be revisited later, when we explore the government's role in promoting market competition.

Conclusion

This chapter has moved us from the extremes of perfect competition and monopoly to the gray area inhabited by most firms. Exhibit 9 compares features and examples of the four market structures. Please take a moment now to review these key distinctions.

Firms in monopolistic competition and in oligopoly face a downward-sloping demand curve for their products. With monopolistic competition, there are so many firms in the market that each tends to get lost in the crowd. Each behaves independently. But with oligopoly, there are so few firms in the market that each must consider the impact its pricing, output, and marketing decisions will have on other firms. Each oligopolist behaves interdependently, and this makes oligopoly difficult to analyze. As a result, there are different models and approaches to oligopoly, three of which were discussed in this chapter.

EXHIBIT 9   **Comparison of Market Structures**

	Perfect Competition	Monopoly	Monopolistic Competition	Oligopoly
Number of firms	Most	One	Many	Few
Control over price	None	Complete	Limited	Some
Product differences	None	None	Some	None or some
Barriers to entry	None	Insurmountable	Low	Substantial
Examples	Wheat	Local electricity	Convenience stores	Automobiles

The analytical results derived in this chapter are not as clear-cut as for the polar cases of perfect competition and monopoly. Still, we can draw some general conclusions, using perfect competition as a guide. In the long run, perfect competitors operate at minimum average cost, while other types of firms usually operate with excess capacity. Therefore, given identical cost curves, monopolists, monopolistic competitors, and oligopolists tend to charge higher prices than perfect competitors do, especially in the long run. In the long run, monopolistic competitors, like perfect competitors, earn only a normal profit because entry barriers are low. Monopolists and oligopolists can earn economic profit in the long run if new entry is restricted. In a later chapter, we will examine government policies aimed at increasing competition. *Regardless of the market structure, however, profit maximization prompts firms to produce where marginal revenue equals marginal cost.*

SUMMARY

1. Whereas the output of a monopolist has no substitutes, a monopolistic competitor must contend with many rivals. But because of differences among the products offered by different firms, each monopolistic competitor faces a downward-sloping demand curve.

2. Sellers in monopolistic competition and in oligopoly differentiate their products through (a) physical qualities, (b) sales locations, (c) services provided with the product, and (d) the product image.

3. In the short run, monopolistic competitors that can at least cover their average variable costs will maximize profits or minimize losses by producing where marginal revenue equals marginal cost. In the long run, easy entry and exit of firms ensures that monopolistic competitors earn

only a normal profit, which occurs where the average total cost curve is tangent to a firm's downward-sloping demand curve.

4. An oligopoly is an industry dominated by a few sellers, some of which are large enough relative to the market to influence the price. In undifferentiated oligopolies, such as steel or oil, the product is a commodity. In differentiated oligopolies, such as automobiles or breakfast cereals, the product differs across firms.

5. Because an oligopoly consists of just a few firms, each may react to another firm's changes in quality, price, output, services, or advertising. Because of this interdependence, the behavior of oligopolists is difficult to analyze. No single approach characterizes all oligopolistic markets.

6. In this chapter, we considered three approaches of oligopoly behavior: (a) collusion, in which firms form a cartel to act collectively like a monopolist; (b) price leadership, in which one firm, usually the biggest one, sets the price for the industry and other firms follow the leaders; and (c) game theory, which analyzes oligopolistic behavior as a series of strategic moves by rival firms.

QUESTIONS FOR REVIEW

1. *(Characteristics of Monopolistic Competition)* Why does the demand curve facing a monopolistically competitive firm slope downward in the long run, even after the entry of new firms?

2. *(Product Differentiation)* What are four ways in which a firm can differentiate its product? What role can advertising play in product differentiation? How can advertising become a barrier to entry?

3. *(Zero Economic Profit in the Long Run)* In the long run, a monopolistically competitive firm earns zero economic profit, which is exactly what would occur if the industry were perfectly competitive. Assuming that the cost curves for each firm are the same whether the industry is perfectly or monopolistically competitive, answer the following questions.

   a. Why don't perfectly and monopolistically competitive industries produce the same equilibrium quantity in the long run?
   b. Why is a monopolistically competitive industry said to be economically inefficient?
   c. What benefits might cause us to prefer the monopolistically competitive result to the perfectly competitive result?

4. *(Varieties of Oligopoly)* Do the firms in an oligopoly act independently or interdependently? Explain your answer.

5. *(**C a s e Study**:* The Unfriendly Skies) One complaint frequently heard about airfares is that flying from an airline's hub city airport is more expensive than flying from a nearby city that is not a hub. How might this reflect a different level of competition in hub city airports?

6. *(Collusion and Cartels)* Why would each of the following induce some members of OPEC to cheat on their cartel agreement?

   a. Newly joined cartel members are less-developed countries.
   b. The number of cartel members doubles from 10 to 20.
   c. International debts of some members grow.
   d. Expectations grow that some members will cheat.

7. *(Price Leadership)* Why might a price-leadership model of oligopoly not be an effective means of collusion in an oligopoly?

8. *(Market Structures)* Determine whether each of the following is a characteristic of perfect competition, monopolistic competition, oligopoly, and/or monopoly:

   a. A large number of sellers
   b. Product is a commodity
   c. Advertising by firms
   d. Barriers to entry
   e. Firms are price makers

PROBLEMS AND EXERCISES

9. *(Short-Run Profit Maximization)* A monopolistically competitive firm faces the following demand and cost structure in the short run:

Output	Price	FC	VC	TC	TR	Profit/Loss
0	$100	$100	$0	___	___	___
1	90	___	50	___	___	___
2	80	___	90	___	___	___
3	70	___	150	___	___	___
4	60	___	230	___	___	___
5	50	___	330	___	___	___
6	40	___	450	___	___	___
7	30	___	590	___	___	___

  a. Complete the table.
  b. What is the best profit or loss available to this firm?
  c. Should the firm operate or shut down in the short run? Why?
  d. What is the relationship between marginal revenue and marginal cost as the firm increases output?

10. *(Case Study: Fast Forward)* Use a cost-and-revenue graph to illustrate and explain the short-run profits in the video rental business. Then, use a second graph to illustrate the long-run situation. Explain fully.

11. *(Monopolistic Competition and Perfect Competition Compared)* Illustrated below are the marginal cost and average total cost curves for a small firm that is in long-run equilibrium.

  a. Locate the long-run equilibrium price and quantity if the firm is perfectly competitive.
  b. Label the price and quantity p_1 and q_1.
  c. Draw in a demand and marginal revenue curve to illustrate long-run equilibrium if the firm is monopolistically competitive. Label the price and quantity p_2 and q_2.

  d. How do the monopolistically competitive firm's price and output compare to those of the perfectly competitive firm?
  e. How do long-run profits compare for the two types of firms?

12. *(Collusion and Cartels)* Use revenue and cost curves to illustrate and explain the sense in which a cartel behaves like a monopolist.

13. *(Game Theory)* Suppose there are only two automobile companies, Ford and Chevrolet. Ford believes that Chevrolet will match any price it sets. Use the following price and profit data to answer the following questions.

Ford's Selling Price	Chevrolet's Selling Price	Ford's Profits (millions)	Chevrolet's Profits (millions)
$ 4,000	$4,000	$8	$8
4,000	8,000	12	6
4,000	12,000	14	2
8,000	4,000	6	12
8,000	8,000	10	10
8,000	12,000	12	6
12,000	4,000	2	14
12,000	8,000	6	12
12,000	12,000	7	7

  a. What price will Ford charge?
  b. What price will Chevrolet charge?
  c. What is Ford's profit after Chevrolet's response?
  d. If the two firms collaborated to maximize joint profits, what prices would they set?
  e. Given your answer to part (d), how could undetected cheating on price cause the cheating firm's profit to rise?

14. *(Game Theory)* While grading a final exam, an economics professor discovers that two students have virtually identical answers. She is convinced the two cheated but cannot prove it. The professor speaks with each student separately and offers the following deal: Sign a statement admitting to cheating. If both students sign the statement, each will receive an "F" for the course. If only one signs, he is allowed to withdraw from the course while the other student is expelled. If neither signs, both receive a "C" because the professor does not have sufficient evidence to prove cheating.

  a. Draw the payoff matrix.
  b. Which outcome do you expect? Why?

EXPERIENTIAL EXERCISES

15. *(Product Differentiation)* One important way monopolistic competitors differentiate their products is by location. Review John Campbell's article, "Time to Shop: The Geography of Retailing," from the Federal Reserve Bank of Boston's Regional Review at http://www.bos.frb.org/economic/nerr/rr1996/summer/rgrv96_3.htm. What locational strategies are retailers using? What does the theory of monopolistic competition predict about the success of such strategies in the short run and in the long run?

16. *(OPEC)* OPEC is the economist's favorite cartel to study. That is partly because it had such a spectacular short-run success and partly because oligopoly theory could be used to predict how OPEC pricing actually evolved. Take a look at the U.S. Department of Energy's OPEC Fact Sheet at http://www.eia.doe.gov/emeu/cabs/opec.html. What are some recent developments in petroleum pricing? How relevant are the factors listed in this chapter as affecting the difficulty of maintaining a cartel?

17. *(Wall Street Journal)* If you look carefully, you can often find evidence of price leadership. For example, the *Wall Street Journal* frequently runs stories about airfares. Typically, one airline will raise its fares—on certain routes or across the board—and other airlines will match those changes within a day or two. As you read through the *Wall Street Journal* this week, be on the lookout for such stories. They are typically reported on the front page—in the "What's News" column. When you find such a story, check back over the next few days. Did other airlines match the leader, or was the leader forced to back off its price changes?

18. *(Wall Street Journal)* Read the *Wall Street Journal* and look for articles that discuss firms that have successfully utilized product differentiation to create competitive advantage. Describe the actions of a firm that has been successful. Was advertising important?

HOMEWORK XPRESS! EXERCISES

*These exercises require access to McEachern Homework Xpress! If Homework Xpress! did not come with your book, visit **http://homeworkxpress.swlearning.com** to purchase.*

1. Giorgio's Brick Oven Pizza is the only pizzeria with a brick oven in town. It is not the only pizza seller so it faces a downward-sloping demand curve. The demand schedule is:

Quantity of Pizzas	Price
0	$20
10	16
20	12
30	8
40	4
50	0

   Draw the demand curve and the corresponding marginal revenue curve. Add a marginal cost curve so that the profit-maximizing price of a Giorgio's pizza will be $14. Add an average total cost curve so that the profit on each pizza is two dollars. Illustrate total profits.

2. Draw a downward-sloping demand curve and the corresponding marginal revenue curve for a monopolistically competitive firm. Add a marginal cost curve and an average total cost curve so that the firm is in long-run equilibrium. Identify the price it would set and the quantity it would choose to produce.

3. Draw a downward-sloping demand curve and the corresponding marginal revenue curve for a monopolistically competitive firm. Add a marginal cost curve and an average total cost curve so that the firm is in long-run equilibrium. Identify the price it would set and the quantity it would choose to produce. Add a demand curve the firm would face if it is in a perfectly competitive market and earning zero economic profits. Identify the price it faces and the quantity it would choose to produce.

4. Draw a world demand curve for bananas. A cartel, OBEC, the Organization of Banana Exporting Countries, is founded in an attempt to drive up the world price of bananas. Add a marginal revenue curve corresponding to the demand curve and a marginal cost curve representing the sum of the marginal cost curves of the cartel members. Identify the quantity that would maximize profits for the industry and the price the cartel would charge.

Resource Markets

© Eyewire/Fonts.com

Why do surgeons earn twice as much as general practitioners? Why do truck drivers in the United States earn at least 20 times more than rickshaw drivers in India? Why does prime Iowa corn acreage cost more than scrubland in the high plains of Montana? Why are buildings taller in downtown Chicago than those in the suburbs? To answer these and other questions, we turn to the demand and supply of resources.

You say you've been through this demand-and-supply drill already? True. But your earlier focus was on the product market—that is, on the market for final goods and services. Goods and services are produced by resources—labor, capital, natural resources, and entrepreneurial ability. Demand and supply in resource markets determine the price and quantity of resources. And the ownership of resources determines the distribution of income throughout the economy.

Because your earnings depend on the market value of your resources, you should find resource markets particularly relevant to your future. Certainly one consideration in your career decision will be the expected income associated with alternative careers. The next three chapters examine how demand and supply interact to establish market prices for various resources. Topics discussed include:

- Demand and supply of resources
- Opportunity cost and economic rent
- Marginal revenue product
- Marginal resource cost
- Changes in resource demand

The Once-Over

Just to prove you already know more about resource markets than you may think, try answering the questions that arise in the following examples of resource demand and supply.

Resource Demand

Let's begin with the demand for labor. The manager of Wal-Mart estimates that hiring another sales clerk would increase total revenue by $500 per week and increase total cost by $400 per week. Should another sales clerk be hired? Sure, because Wal-Mart's profit would increase by $100 per week. *As long as the additional revenue from employing another worker exceeds the additional cost, the firm should hire that worker.*

What about capital? Suppose that you operate a lawn service during the summer, earning an average of $40 per lawn. You mow about 15 lawns a week, for total revenue of $600. You are thinking of upgrading to a larger, faster mower called the Lawn Monster, but it would cost you an extra $400 per week. The bigger mower would cut your time per lawn in half, enabling you to mow 30 lawns per week, so your total revenue would double to $1,200. Should you make the switch? Because the additional revenue of $600 exceeds the additional cost of $400, you should move up to the Monster.

What about natural resources? A neighbor offers Farmer Jones the chance to lease 100 acres of farmland. Jones figures that farming the extra land would cost $70 per acre but would yield $60 per acre in additional revenue. Should Jones lease the extra land? What do you think? Because the additional cost of farming that land would exceed the additional revenue, the answer is no.

These examples show that a *producer demands another unit of a resource as long as its marginal revenue exceeds its marginal cost.*

Resource Supply

You likely also understand the economic logic behind resource supply. Suppose you are trying to decide between two jobs that are identical except that one pays more than the other. Is there any question which job you'll take? If the working conditions are equally attractive, you would choose the higher-paying job. Now let's say your choice is between two jobs that pay the same. One has normal 9-to-5 hours, but the other starts at 5 A.M., an hour when your body tends to reject conscious activity. Which would you choose? You would pick one that suits your tastes.

People will supply their resources to the highest-paying alternative, other things constant. Because other things are not always constant, people must be paid more for jobs less suited to their tastes. Your utility depends on both monetary and nonmonetary aspects of the job. Generally, people must be paid more for jobs that are dirty, dangerous, dull, exhausting, illegal, low status, have no future, have no benefits, and involve inconvenient hours than for jobs that are clean, safe, interesting, energizing, legal, high status, have bright prospects, have good benefits, and involve convenient hours.

The Demand and Supply of Resources

In the market for goods and services—that is, in the product market—households are the demanders and firms are suppliers. Households demand the goods and services that maximize utility, and firms supply the goods and services that maximize profit. In the resource market, roles are reversed: Firms are demanders and households are suppliers. Firms demand resources to maximize profit, and households supply resources to maximize utility. *Any differences between the profit-maximizing goals of firms and the utility-maximizing goals of households are reconciled through voluntary exchange in markets.*

Exhibit 1 presents the market for a particular resource—in this case, carpenters. As you can see, the demand curve slopes downward and the supply curve slopes upward. *Like the demand and supply for final goods and services, the demand and supply for resources depend on the willingness and ability of buyers and sellers to engage in market exchange.* This market will converge to the equilibrium wage, or the market price, for this type of labor.

The Market Demand for Resources

Why do firms employ resources? Resources produce goods and services, which firms try to sell for a profit. A firm values not the resource itself but the resource's ability to produce goods and services. Because the value of any resource depends on the value of what it produces, the demand for a resource is said to be a **derived demand**—arising from the

DERIVED DEMAND

Demand that arises from the demand for the product the resource produces

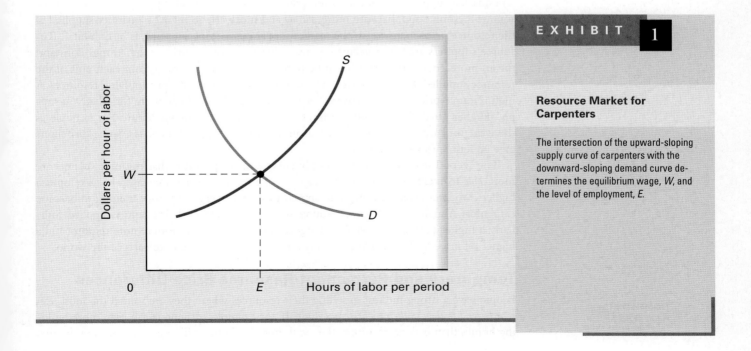

EXHIBIT 1

Resource Market for Carpenters

The intersection of the upward-sloping supply curve of carpenters with the downward-sloping demand curve determines the equilibrium wage, *W*, and the level of employment, *E*.

demand for the final product. For example, a carpenter's pay derives from the demand for the carpenter's output, such as a cabinet or a new deck. A professional baseball player's pay derives from the demand for ballgames. A truck driver's pay derives from the demand for transporting goods. The derived nature of resource demand helps explain why professional baseball players usually earn more than professional hockey players, why brain surgeons earn more than tree surgeons, and why drivers of big rigs earn more than drivers of delivery vans.

The market demand for a particular resource is the sum of demands for that resource in all its different uses. For example, the market demand for carpenters adds together the demands for carpenters in residential and commercial construction, remodeling, cabinetmaking, and so on. Similarly, the market demand for the resource, timber, sums the demand for timber as lumber, railway ties, firewood, furniture, pencils, toothpicks, paper products, and so on. The demand curve for a resource, like the demand curves for the goods produced by that resource, slopes downward, as depicted in Exhibit 1.

As the price of a resource falls, producers are more willing and able to employ that resource. Consider first the producer's greater *willingness* to hire resources as the resource price falls. In developing the demand curve for a particular resource, we assume the prices of other resources remain constant. So if the price of a particular resource falls, it becomes relatively cheaper compared with other resources the firm could use to produce the same output. Firms therefore are more willing to hire this resource rather than hire other, now relatively more costly, resources. Thus, we observe *substitution in production*—carpenters for masons, coal for oil, security alarms for security guards, and backhoes for grave diggers, as the relative prices of carpenters, coal, security alarms, and backhoes fall.

A lower price for a resource also increases a producer's *ability* to hire that resource. For example, if the wage of carpenters falls, home builders can hire more carpenters for the same total cost. The lower resource price means the firm is *more able* to buy the resource.

The Market Supply of Resources

The market supply curve for a resource sums all the individual supply curves for that resource. Resource suppliers are more *willing* and more *able* to increase quantity supplied as the resource price increases, so the market supply curve slopes upward, as in Exhibit 1. Resource suppliers are more *willing* because a higher resource price, other things constant, means more goods and services can be purchased with the earnings from each unit of the resource supplied. Resource prices are signals about the rewards for supplying resources. A high resource price tells the resource owner, "The market will pay more for what you supply." Higher prices draw resources from lower-valued uses, including leisure. For example, as the wage for carpenters increases, the quantity of labor supplied increases. Some carpenters give up leisure to work more hours.

The second reason a resource supply curve slopes upward is that resource owners are more *able* to increase the quantity supply as the resource price increases. For example, a higher carpenter's wage means more apprentices can undergo extensive training to become carpenters. A higher wage *enables* resource suppliers to increase their quantity supplied. Similarly, a higher timber price enables loggers to harvest trees in more remote regions, and a higher oil price enables producers to drill deeper and explore remote parts of the world.

Temporary and Permanent Resource Price Differences

People have a strong interest in selling their resources where they are valued the most. *Resources tend to flow to their highest-valued use.* If, for example, carpenters can earn more building homes than making furniture, they will shift into home building until wages in the two uses are equal. Because resource owners seek the highest pay, *other things constant,* the prices paid for identical resources should tend toward equality. For example, suppose carpenters who build homes earn $25 per hour, which is $5 more than carpenters who make furniture. This difference is shown in Exhibit 2 by an initial wage of $25 per hour in panel (a) and an initial wage of $20 per hour in panel (b). This gap will encourage some carpenters to move from furniture making to home building, pulling up the wage in furniture making and driving down the wage in home building. Carpenters will move into home building until wages equalize. In Exhibit 2, supply shifts leftward for furniture making and rightward for home building until the wage reaches $24 in both markets. Note that 2,000 hours of labor per day shift from furniture making to home building. *As long as the nonmonetary benefits of supplying resources to alternative uses are identical and as long as resources are freely mobile, resources will adjust across uses until they earn the same in different uses.*

Sometimes earnings appear to differ between seemingly similar resources. For example, corporate economists on average earn more than academic economists, and land in the city

EXHIBIT 2

Market for Carpenters in Alternative Uses

Suppose initially the wage of carpenters is $25 in the home-building market but only $20 in the furniture-making market. This differential will prompt carpenters to shift from furniture making to home building until the wage is identical in the two markets. In panel (b), the reduction of labor supplied to furniture making increases the market wage from $20 to $24. In panel (a), the increase of labor supplied to home building reduces the market wage from $25 to $24. Note that 2,000 carpenter hours per day shift from furniture making to home building.

costs more than land in the country. As you will now see, these differences also reflect the workings of demand and supply.

Temporary Differences in Resource Prices

Resource prices might differ temporarily across markets because adjustment takes time. For example, sometimes wage differences occur among workers who appear equally qualified. As you have seen, however, a difference between the prices of similar resources prompts resource owners and firms to make adjustments that drive resource prices toward equality, as with the carpenters in Exhibit 2. The process may take years, but when resource markets are free to adjust, price differences trigger the reallocation of resources, which equalizes earnings for similar resources.

Permanent Differences in Resource Prices

Not all resource price differences cause reallocation. For example, land along New York's Fifth Avenue sells for as much as $36,000 a *square yard!* For that amount, you could buy several acres in Upstate New York. Yet such a difference does not prompt upstate landowners to supply their land to New York City—obviously that's impossible. Likewise, the price of farmland itself varies widely, reflecting differences in the land's productivity and location. Such differences do not trigger shifts in resource supply. Similarly, certain wage differentials stem in part from the different costs of acquiring the education and training required to perform particular tasks. This difference explains why brain surgeons earn more than tree surgeons, why ophthalmologists earn more than optometrists, and why airline pilots earn more than truck drivers.

Differences in the nonmonetary aspects of similar jobs also lead to pay differences. For example, other things constant, most people require more pay to work in a grimy factory than in a pleasant office. Similarly, academic economists earn less than corporate economists, in part because academic economists typically have more freedom in their daily schedules, their attire, their choices of research topics, and even in their public statements.

Some price differences are temporary because they spark shifts of resource supply away from lower-paid uses and toward higher-paid uses. Other price differences cause no such shifts and are permanent. Permanent price differences are explained by *a lack of resource mobility* (urban land versus rural land), *differences in the inherent quality of the resource* (fertile land versus scrubland), *differences in the time and money involved in developing the necessary skills* (certified public accountant versus file clerk), or *differences in nonmonetary aspects of the job* (lifeguard at Malibu Beach versus prison guard at San Quentin).

Opportunity Cost and Economic Rent

Shaquille O'Neal earned about $30 million in 2004 playing basketball plus at least $10 million more from product endorsements. But he would probably have been willing to play basketball and endorse products for less. The question is, how much less? What is his best alternative? Suppose his best alternative is to become a full-time rap artist, something he now does in his spare time (as of 2004, he had released six rap albums). Suppose, as a full-time rapper, he could earn $1 million a year, including endorsements. And suppose, aside from the pay gap, he's indifferent between basketball and rap, so the nonmonetary aspects of the two jobs even out. Thus, he must be paid at least $1 million to remain in basketball, and this amount represents his opportunity cost. *Opportunity cost is what that resource could earn in its best alternative use.*

The amount O'Neal earns in excess of his opportunity cost is called *economic rent*. **Economic rent** is that portion of a resource's earnings that is not necessary to keep

ECONOMIC RENT

Portion of a resource's total earnings that exceeds its opportunity cost; earnings greater than the amount required to keep the resource in its present use the resource in its present use. Economic rent is, as the saying goes, "pure gravy." In O'Neal's case, economic rent is at least $39 million. Economic rent is producer surplus earned by resource suppliers. The *division* of earnings between opportunity cost and economic rent depends on the resource owner's elasticity of supply. *In general, the less elastic the resource supply, the greater the economic rent as a proportion of total earnings.* To develop a feel for the difference between opportunity cost and economic rent, let's go over three cases.

Case A: All Earnings Are Economic Rent

If the supply of a resource to a particular market is perfectly inelastic, that resource has no alternative use. Thus, there is no opportunity cost, and all earnings are economic rent. For example, scrubland in the high plains of Montana has no use other than for grazing cattle. The supply of this land is depicted by the red vertical line in panel (a) of Exhibit 3, which indicates that the 10 million acres have no alternative use. Because supply is fixed, the amount paid to rent this land for grazing has no effect on the quantity supplied. *The land's opportunity cost is zero, so all earnings are economic rent, shown by the blue-shaded area.* Here, fixed supply determines the equilibrium quantity of the resource, but demand determines the equilibrium price.

Case B: All Earnings Are Opportunity Costs

At the other extreme is the case in which a resource can earn as much in its best alternative use as in its present use. This situation is illustrated by the perfectly elastic supply curve in panel (b) of Exhibit 3, which shows the market for janitors in the local school system. Here, janitors earn $10 an hour to supply 1,000 hours of labor per day. If the school system paid less than $10 per hour, janitors would find jobs elsewhere, perhaps in nearby factories, where the wage is $10 per hour. *Janitors earn their opportunity costs.* In this case, the horizontal supply curve determines the equilibrium wage, but demand determines the equilibrium quantity.

Case C: Earnings Include Both Economic Rent and Opportunity Costs

If the supply curve slopes upward, most resource suppliers earn economic rent in addition to their opportunity cost. For example, if the market wage for unskilled work in your college community increases from $5 to $10 per hour, the quantity of labor supplied would increase, as would the economic rent earned by these workers. This situation occurs in panel (c) of Exhibit 3, where the pink shading identifies opportunity costs and the blue shading, economic rent. If the wage increases from $5 to $10 per hour, the quantity supplied will increase by 5,000 hours. For those who were willing to work for $5 per hour, the difference between $5 and $10 is economic rent. *When supply slopes upward, as it usually does, earnings consist of both opportunity cost and economic rent.* In the case of an upward-sloping supply curve and a downward-sloping demand curve, both demand and supply determine equilibrium price and quantity.

Note that specialized resources tend to earn a higher proportion of economic rent than do resources with many alternative uses. Thus, Shaquille O'Neal earns a greater *proportion* of his income as economic rent than does the janitor who cleans the Miami Heat's locker room. O'Neal would take a huge pay cut if he didn't play professional basketball, but the Heat's janitor could probably find another semiskilled job that would pay nearly as much.

To review: Given a resource demand curve that slopes downward, when the resource supply curve is vertical (perfectly inelastic), all earnings are economic rent; when that supply curve is horizontal (perfectly elastic), all earnings are opportunity cost; and when that supply curve slopes upward (an elasticity greater than zero but less than infinity), earnings divide between opportunity cost and economic rent. Remember, *the opportunity cost of a*

HOMEWORK
Xpress!
*Ask the Instructor
Video*

EXHIBIT 3

Opportunity Cost and Economic Rent

In panel (a), the resource supply curve is vertical, indicating that the resource has no alternative use. The price is demand determined, and all earnings are economic rent. In panel (b), the resource supply curve is horizontal at $10 per hour, indicating that the resource can also earn that much in its best alternative use. Employment is demand determined, and all earnings are opportunity costs. Panel (c) shows an upward-sloping resource supply curve. Earnings are partly opportunity costs and partly economic rent. Both demand and supply determine the equilibrium price and quantity.

(a) All resource earnings are economic rent   *(b) All resource earnings are opportunity costs*

(c) Resource earnings are divided between economic rent and opportunity cost

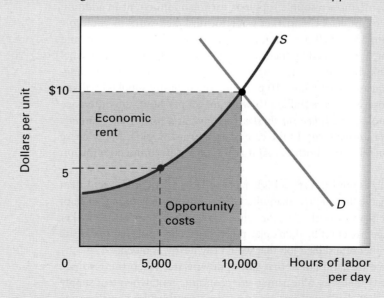

resource is what that resource could earn in its best alternative use. Economic rent is earnings in excess of opportunity cost.

This completes our introduction to resource supply. In the balance of this chapter, we take a closer look at resource demand. The determinants of the demand for a resource are largely the same whether we are talking about labor, capital, or natural resources. The supply of different resources, however, has certain peculiarities depending on the resource, so the supply of resources will be taken up in the next chapter.

A Closer Look at Resource Demand

Although production usually involves many resources, we will cut the analysis down to size by focusing on a single resource, assuming that the quantities of other resources employed remain constant. As usual, we will assume that firms try to maximize profit and households try to maximize utility.

The Firm's Demand for a Resource

You may recall that when the firm's costs were first introduced, we considered a moving company, where labor was the only variable resource in the short run. We examined the relationship between the quantity of labor employed and the amount of furniture moved per day. We use the same approach in Exhibit 4, where only one resource varies. Column (1) in the table lists possible employment levels of the variable resource, here measured as workers per day. Column (2) lists the amount produced, or total product, and column (3) lists the marginal product. The *marginal product* of labor is the change in total product from employing one more unit of labor.

When one worker is employed, total product is 10 units and so is the marginal product. The marginal product of adding the second worker is 9 units. As the firm hires more

(1) Workers per Day	(2) Total Product	(3) Marginal Product	(4) Product Price	(5) Total Revenue (5) = (2) × (4)	(6) Marginal Revenue Product (6) = (3) × (4)
0	0	—	$20	$ 0	—
1	10	10	20	200	$200
2	19	9	20	380	180
3	27	8	20	540	160
4	34	7	20	680	140
5	40	6	20	800	120
6	45	5	20	900	100
7	49	4	20	980	80
8	52	3	20	1040	60

EXHIBIT 4

Marginal Revenue Product When a Firm Sells in a Competitive Market

Because of diminishing marginal returns, the marginal product of labor declines as more labor is employed, as shown in column (3). Because this firm sells in a competitive market, it can sell all it wants at the market price of $20 per unit of output, as shown in column (4). The marginal product of labor in column (3) times the product price of $20 in column (4) yields the marginal revenue product of labor in column (6). Labor's marginal revenue product is the change in total revenue as a result of hiring another unit of labor.

workers, the marginal product of labor declines, reflecting the law of diminishing marginal returns. Notice in this example that diminishing marginal returns set in immediately—that is, right after the first worker.

Although labor is the variable resource here, we could examine the marginal product of any resource. For example, we could consider how many lawns could be cut per week by varying the quantity of capital employed. We might start off with very little capital—imagine cutting grass with a pair of scissors—and then move up to a push mower, a power mower, and the Lawn Monster. By holding labor constant and varying the quantity of capital employed, we could compute the marginal product of capital. Likewise, we could compute the marginal product of natural resources by examining crop production for varying amounts of farmland, holding other inputs constant.

Marginal Revenue Product

The important question is: what happens to the firm's *revenue* when additional workers are hired? The first three columns of Exhibit 4 show output as the firm hires more workers. The *marginal revenue product* of labor indicates how much total revenue changes as more labor is employed, other things constant. The **marginal revenue product** of any resource is the change in the firm's total revenue resulting from employing an additional unit of the resource, other things constant. You could think of the marginal revenue product as the firm's "marginal benefit" from hiring one more unit of the resource. *A resource's marginal revenue product depends on how much additional output the resource produces and the price at which output is sold.*

Selling Output in Competitive Markets

The calculation of marginal revenue product is simplest when the firm sells in a perfectly competitive market, which is the assumption underlying Exhibit 4. An individual firm in perfect competition can sell as much as it wants at the market price. The marginal revenue product, listed in column (6) of Exhibit 4, is the change in total revenue that results from changing input usage by one unit. For the perfectly competitive firm, the marginal revenue product is simply the marginal product of the resource multiplied by the product price of $20. Notice that because of diminishing returns, the marginal revenue product falls steadily as the firm uses more of the resource.

Selling Output with Some Market Power

If the firm has some market power in the product market—that is, some ability to set the price—the demand curve for that firm's output slopes downward. To sell more, the firm must lower its price. Exhibit 5 reproduces the first two columns of Exhibit 4. Column (3) now shows the price at which that output can be sold. Total output multiplied by the price yields the firm's total revenue, which appears in column (4).

The marginal revenue product of labor, which is the change in total revenue resulting from a 1-unit change in the quantity of labor employed, appears in column (5). For example, the first worker produced 10 units per day, which sell for $40 each, yielding total revenue of $400. Hiring the second worker adds 9 more units to total product, but to sell 9 more units, the firm must lower the price of each unit from $40 to $35.20. Total revenue increases to $668.80, which means the marginal revenue product from hiring a second worker is $268.80. For firms selling with some market power, the marginal revenue product curve slopes downward both because of diminishing marginal returns and because additional output can be sold only if the price falls.

(1) Workers per day	(2) Total Product	(3) Product Price	(4) Total Revenue (4) = (2) × (3)	(5) Marginal Revenue Product
0	0	—	—	—
1	10	$40.00	$400.00	$400.00
2	19	35.20	668.80	268.80
3	27	31.40	847.80	179.00
4	34	27.80	945.20	97.40
5	40	25.00	1000.00	54.80
6	45	22.50	1012.50	12.50
7	49	20.50	1004.50	−8.00
8	52	19.00	988.00	−16.50

EXHIBIT 5

The Marginal Revenue Product When a Firm Sells with Market Power

To sell more, this firm must lower the price, as indicated in column (3). Total revenue in column (4) equals total product in column (2) times the product price in column (3). Labor's marginal revenue product in column (5) equals the change in total revenue from hiring another worker. The marginal revenue product declines both because of diminishing marginal returns from labor and because the product price must fall to sell more.

Again, *the marginal revenue product is the additional revenue that results from employing each additional worker.* The profit-maximizing firm should be willing and able to pay as much as the marginal revenue product for an additional unit of the resource. Thus, *the marginal revenue product curve can be thought of as the firm's demand curve for that resource.* You could think of the marginal revenue product curve as the marginal benefit to the firm of hiring each additional unit of the resource.

To review: Whether a firm sells its product in a competitive market or sells with some market power, the marginal revenue product of a resource is the change in total revenue resulting from a 1-unit change in that resource, other things constant. The marginal revenue product curve of a resource is the demand curve for that resource—it shows the most a firm would be willing and able to pay for each additional unit of the resource. For firms selling in competitive markets, the marginal revenue product curve slopes downward only because of diminishing marginal returns to the resource. For firms selling with some market power, the marginal revenue product curve slopes downward both because of diminishing marginal returns and because additional output can be sold only if the price falls. *For all types of firms, the marginal revenue product is the change in total revenue resulting from hiring an additional unit of the resource.*

Marginal Resource Cost

If we know a firm's marginal revenue product, can we determine how much labor that firm should employ to maximize profit? Not yet, because we must also know how much labor costs the firm. Specifically, what is the **marginal resource cost**—what does another unit of labor cost the firm? The typical firm hires such a tiny fraction of the available resource that its hiring decision has no effect on the market price of the resource. Thus, each firm usually faces a given market price for the resource and decides only on how much to hire at that price.

For example, panel (a) of Exhibit 6 shows the market for factory workers, measured as workers per day. The intersection of market demand and market supply determines the

MARGINAL RESOURCE COST

The change in total cost when an additional unit of a resource is hired, other things constant

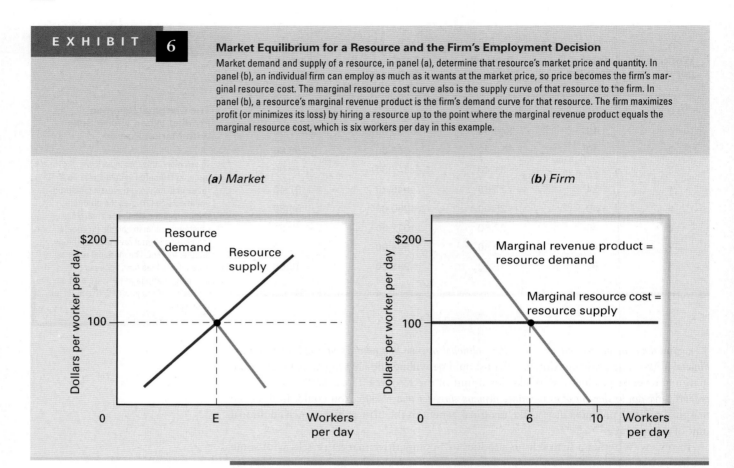

EXHIBIT 6

Market Equilibrium for a Resource and the Firm's Employment Decision
Market demand and supply of a resource, in panel (a), determine that resource's market price and quantity. In panel (b), an individual firm can employ as much as it wants at the market price, so price becomes the firm's marginal resource cost. The marginal resource cost curve also is the supply curve of that resource to the firm. In panel (b), a resource's marginal revenue product is the firm's demand curve for that resource. The firm maximizes profit (or minimizes its loss) by hiring a resource up to the point where the marginal revenue product equals the marginal resource cost, which is six workers per day in this example.

(a) Market

(b) Firm

market wage of $100 dollars per day. Panel (b) shows the situation for the firm. The market wage becomes the marginal resource cost of labor to the firm. The *marginal resource cost* curve is shown by the horizontal line drawn at the $100 level in panel (b); this is the labor supply curve to the firm. Panel (b) also shows the marginal revenue product curve, or resource demand curve, based on the schedule presented in Exhibit 4. The marginal revenue product curve indicates the additional revenue the firm receives as a result of employing another unit of labor.

Given a marginal resource cost of $100 per worker per day, how much labor will the firm employ to maximize profit? *The firm will hire more labor as long as doing so adds more to revenue than to cost—that is, as long as the marginal revenue product exceeds the marginal resource cost. The firm will stop hiring labor only when the two are equal.* If marginal resource cost is a constant $100 per worker, the firm will hire six workers per day because the marginal revenue product from hiring a sixth worker equals $100. Thus, the firm hires additional resources up to the level at which

Marginal revenue product = Marginal resource cost

This equality holds for all resources employed, whether the firm sells in competitive markets or has some market power. Profit maximization occurs where labor's marginal revenue product equals the market wage. Based on data presented so far, we can't yet determine the firm's actual profit because we don't yet know the firm's other costs. We do know, however, that in Exhibit 6, a seventh worker would add $100 to cost but would add less than that to revenue, so hiring a seventh worker would reduce the firm's profit (or increase its loss).

Whether a firm sells in competitive markets or with some market power, the profit-maximizing level of employment occurs where the marginal revenue product of labor equals its marginal resource cost. Similarly, profit-maximizing employment of other resources, such as natural resources and capital, occurs where their respective marginal revenue products equal their marginal resource costs. Each resource must "pull its own weight"—it must yield additional revenue that at least equals the additional cost.

In earlier chapters, you learned how to find the profit-maximizing level of output. Maximum profit (or minimum loss) occurs where the marginal revenue from *output* equals its marginal cost. Likewise, maximum profit (or minimum loss) occurs where the marginal revenue from an *input* equals its marginal resource cost. Although the first rule focuses on output and the second on input, the two are equivalent ways of deriving the same principle of profit maximization. For example, in Exhibit 6, the firm maximizes profit by hiring six workers when the market wage is $100 per day. Exhibit 4 indicates that a sixth worker adds five units to output, which sell for $20 each, yielding labor's marginal revenue product of $100. The *marginal revenue* of that output is the change in total revenue from selling another unit of output, which is $20. The *marginal cost* of that output is the change in total cost, $100, divided by the change in output, 5 units; so the marginal cost of output is $100/5, or $20. Thus, *in equilibrium, the marginal revenue of output equals its marginal cost*. Now that you have some idea of how to derive the demand for a resource, let's discuss what could shift resource demand.

Shifts of the Demand for Resources

As we have seen, a resource's marginal revenue product consists of two components: the resource's marginal product and the price at which that product is sold. Two factors can change a resource's marginal product: a change in the amount of other resources employed and a change in technology. One factor can change the price of the product: a change in demand for the product. Let's first consider changes that could affect marginal product, then changes that could affect demand for the product.

Change in the Price of Other Resources

Although our analysis so far has focused on a single input, in reality the marginal product of any resource depends on the quantity and quality of other resources used in production. Sometimes resources are *substitutes*. For example, coal substitutes for oil in generating electricity. And automatic teller machines, or ATMs, substitute for tellers in handling bank transactions. If two resources are **substitutes,** an increase in the price of one increases the demand for the other. An increase in the price of oil increases the demand for coal, and an increase in the wage of tellers increases the demand for ATMs.

Sometimes resources are *complements*—trucks and truck drivers, for example. If two resources are **complements,** a decrease in the price of one leads to an increase in the demand for the other. If the price of tractor-trailers decreases, the quantity demanded increases, which increases the demand for truck drivers. More generally, any increase in the quantity and quality of a complementary resource, such as trucks, hikes the marginal productivity of the resource in question, such as truck drivers, and so increases the demand for that resource. A bigger and better truck makes the driver more productive. One reason a truck driver in the United States earns much more than a rickshaw driver in India is the truck.

RESOURCE SUBSTITUTES

Resources that substitute in production; an increase in the price of one resource increases the demand for the other

RESOURCE COMPLEMENTS

Resources that enhance one another's productivity; an increase in the price of one resource decreases the demand for the other

Changes in Technology

Technological improvements can boost the productivity of some resources but can make others obsolete. The introduction of computer-controlled machines increased the demand for computer-trained machinists but decreased the demand for machinists without computer skills. The development of synthetic fibers, such as rayon and Orlon, increased the demand for acrylics and polyesters but reduced the demand for natural fibers, such as cotton and wool. Breakthroughs in fiber-optic and satellite telecommunication increased the demand for fiberglass and satellites and reduced the demand for copper wire.

Computer programs are changing job prospects in fields such as law, medicine, and accounting. For example, Quicken's WillMaker software has written more wills than any lawyer alive. In medicine, software such as Iliad helps doctors diagnose more than a thousand diseases. And in accounting, software such as TurboTax completes tax forms with ease. As software and hardware get cheaper, better, and more accessible, the demand for some professional services declines and the demand for others increases.

Changes in the Demand for the Final Product

Because the demand for a resource is *derived* from the demand for the final output, any change in the demand for output affects resource demand. For example, an increase in the demand for automobiles increases their market price and thereby increases the marginal revenue product of autoworkers. Let's look at the derived demand for architects in the following case study.

The Derived Demand for Architects

Architects design mostly buildings, particularly nonresidential structures such as offices, shopping centers, schools, and health-care facilities. After a boom in the 1980s, construction in the 1990s cooled significantly because of slower workforce growth and increased telecommuting. These changes reduced the demand for architects. In New York City, for example, the number of classified ads for architectural positions fell from 5,000 in 1987 to 500 in 1991. Similar drops occurred in other major U.S. cities. Employment at one national architectural firm shrank from 1,600 in 1988 to 700 in 1992.

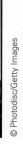

© Photodisc/Getty Images

Among new architects, job losses were compounded by better architectural software. Drafting jobs long represented the entry-level positions for architects, but computer-aided design and drafting (CADD) software coupled with cheaper and more powerful computers reduced the demand for young architects. Programs such as 3D Manager helped configure all aspects of a structure and create plans that could be manipulated in three-dimensional space, something impossible with traditional drawings. Design software such as 3D Home Architect came with online support for amateurs. Whereas construction-grade blueprints drafted by an architect cost about $550 a set, do-it-yourself CDs sold for $40 to $70. Thus, software substituted for entry-level architectural positions.

The recession of 2001 and job losses that continued over the next two years also cut into the demand for architects. Those who couldn't find jobs struggled on their own. About one in four architects are now self-employed, which is about three times the self-employment rate of similar professionals.

The declining demand for architects had a predictable effect on the demand for higher education, which itself is a derived demand. Enrollment in undergraduate architecture classes declined as entry-level positions disappeared. Enrollment in graduate courses, however, remained relatively stable. Apparently, many out-of-work architects decided to pursue graduate study, because the poor job market reduced their opportunity cost. The exception that proves the rule about derived demand is that those architectural firms that specialized in the health-care industry flourished because health care is the fastest-growing sector of the economy.

Sources: Reed Abelson, "Generous Medicare Payments Spur Specialty Hospital Boom," *New York Times*, 26 October 2003; D. W. Dunlap, "Recession Is Ravaging Architects' Firms," *New York Times*, 17 May 1992; Alex Frangos, "More Women Design Their Way to the Top," *Wall Street Journal*, 5 November 2003; and http://autodesk.com/siteselect.htm.

In summary: The demand for a resource depends on its marginal revenue product, which is the change in total revenue resulting from employing one more unit of the resource. Any change that increases a resource's marginal revenue product will increase resource demand.

The Optimal Use of More Than One Resource

As long as the marginal revenue product exceeds the marginal resource cost, a firm can increase profit or reduce a loss by employing more of that resource. Again, the firm will hire more of a resource until the marginal revenue product just equals the marginal resource cost. This principle holds for each resource employed. The opening paragraph asked why buildings in downtown Chicago are taller than those in the suburbs. Land and capital, to a large extent, substitute in the production of building space. Because land is more expensive downtown than in the suburbs, builders there substitute capital for land, building up instead of out. Hence, buildings are taller when they are closer to the center of the city and are tallest in cities where land is most expensive. Buildings in Chicago and New York City are taller than those in Salt Lake City and Tucson, for example.

The high price of land in metropolitan areas has other implications for the efficient employment of resources. For example, in New York City, as in many large cities, sidewalk vending carts sell everything from hot dogs to ice cream. Why are these carts so popular, with over 3,000 in New York City alone? Consider the resources used to supply hot dogs: land, labor, capital, entrepreneurial ability, plus intermediate goods such as hot dogs, buns, and other ingredients. Which of these do you suppose is most expensive in New York City? Retail space along Madison Avenue rents for an average of $550 a year per square foot. Because operating a hot dog cart requires about 4 square yards, it could cost as much as $20,000 a year to rent that much commercial space. Aside from the necessary public permits, however, space on the public sidewalk is free to vendors. Profit-maximizing street vendors substitute public sidewalks for costly commercial space. (Incidentally, does this free space mean sidewalk vendors earn long-run economic profit?)

Government policy can affect resource allocation in other ways, as discussed in this closing case study.

The McMinimum Wage

Case **Study**

Public Policy

In March 2000, Congress sent to President Clinton a measure to increase the minimum wage by $1.00 to $6.15 over two years; the legislation was vetoed because it was tied to a tax cut for businesses. Ever since a federal minimum wage of 25 cents was established in 1938, economists have been debating the benefits and costs of the law. The law initially covered only 43 percent of the workforce—primarily workers in large firms involved in

eActivity

The U.S. Department of Labor maintains a Minimum Wage page at http://www.dol.gov/esa/minwage/q-a.htm with questions and answers about the legal aspects and history of the minimum wage. A continually updated chart can be found at the Employment Policies Institute Web site at: http://www.epionline.org/mw_statistics_annual.cfm. The site also provides links to Questions and Answers about the economic impact of the minimum wage, living wage, and other labor issues. There are also links to several research reports on the impacts of minimum-wage laws. The liberal view can be found at the Economic Policy Institute's Web page on labor markets at http://epinet.org/subjectpages/labor.html.

WALL STREET JOURNAL
Reading It Right

What's the relevance of the following statement from the Wall Street Journal*: "'I'm afraid you are going to unemploy more people,' Sen. Don Nickles, R-Okla., said of what would happen if a minimum wage increase is included."*

interstate commerce. Over the years, the minimum wage has been raised and the coverage has been broadened. By 2003, coverage doubled to about 86 percent of the workforce (groups still not covered include those in small retail establishments and small restaurants). In 2003 only 3 percent of workers earned the minimum wage or less; this number is down from 15 percent in 1980.

When the 2000 legislation was vetoed, about 7 percent of the workforce earned between $5.15 and $6.15 an hour and thus could have been affected by an increase. This group included mostly young workers, the majority working part time, primarily in service and sales occupations. For example, 8 of 10 working teenagers earned less than a dollar above the minimum wage. Eleven states and the District of Columbia have a minimum wage exceeding the federal level. As of 2004, Washington had the highest state minimum at $7.16 per hour. In addition, at least 110 municipalities across the nation have so-called *living-wage laws* that exceed federal and state minimums. Among the highest is in Santa Monica, California's, where the minimum is $12.25 per hour for jobs without health-care benefits (this is three times the minimum wage *per day* in nearby Mexico).

Advocates of minimum-wage legislation argue that it can increase the income of the poorest workers. Critics claim that it can encourage employers either to cut nonwage compensation or to scale back employment. Dozens of studies have examined the effects of the minimum wage on employment. A few found a small positive effect on employment, but most found either no effect or a negative effect, particularly among teenage workers. One reason a higher minimum wage may not reduce total employment is that employers often respond by substituting part-time jobs for full-time jobs, by substituting more-qualified minimum-wage workers (such as college students) for less-qualified workers (such as high school dropouts), and by adjusting nonwage components of the job to reduce costs or increase worker productivity.

Here are some of nonwage adjustments an employer could impose on workers in response to a higher minimum wage: less convenient work hours, greater expected work effort, less on-the-job training, less time for meals and breaks, less extra pay for night shifts, less paid vacation, fewer paid holidays, less sick leave, fewer health-care benefits, stricter tardiness policy, and so on. For example, one researcher found that restaurants responded to a higher minimum wage by reducing vacation time and night-shift premiums.

Of most concern to economists is a possible reduction in on-the-job training of young workers, especially those with little education. A higher minimum wage also raises the opportunity cost of staying in school. According to one study, a higher minimum wage encouraged some 16- to 19-year-olds to quit school and look for work, though many failed to find jobs. Thus, an increase in the minimum wage may have the unintended consequence of cutting school enrollment. And those who had already dropped out were more likely to become unemployed.

A survey of 193 labor economists found that 87 percent believed "a minimum wage increases unemployment among young and unskilled workers." Minimum-wage increases, however, have broad public support. In one poll, the highest support, 81 percent, came from those aged 18 to 29, the group most likely to be affected by a hike in the minimum wage.

Sources: Robert Whaples, "Is There Consensus Among American Labor Economists?" *Journal of Labor Research* 27 (Fall 1996): 725–734; David Francis, "New Efforts Surface to Raise Minimum Wage," *Christian Science Monitor*, 15 September 2003; William Alpert, *The Minimum Wage in the Restaurant Industry* (New York: Praeger, 1986); and William Carrington and Bruce Fallick, "Do Some Workers Have Minimum Wage Careers?" *Monthly Labor Review* (May 2001): 7–26, which can also be found online at http://www.bls.gov/opub/mlr/mlrhome.htm.

Conclusion

A firm hires each resource until the marginal revenue product of that resource equals its marginal cost. The objective of profit maximization ensures that to produce any given level of output, firms will employ the least-cost combination of resources and thereby will use the economy's resources most efficiently. Although our focus has been on the marginal productivity of each resource, we should keep in mind that an orchestra of resources combine to produce output, so the marginal productivity of a particular resource depends in part on the amount and quality of other resources employed.

SUMMARY

1. Firms demand resources to maximize profits. Households supply resources to maximize utility. The profit-maximizing goals of firms and the utility-maximizing goals of households are reconciled through voluntary exchange in resource markets.

2. Because the value of any resource depends on what it produces, the demand for a resource is a derived demand—arising from the demand for the final product. Resource demand curves slope downward because firms are more willing and able to increase quantity demanded as the price of a resource declines. Resource supply curves slope upward because resource owners are more willing and able to increase quantity supplied as their reward for doing so increases.

3. Some differences in the market prices of similar resources trigger the reallocation of resources to equalize those prices. Other price differences do not cause a shift of resources among uses because of a lack of resource mobility, differences in the inherent quality of the resources, differences in the time and money involved in developing necessary skills, and differences in nonmonetary aspects of jobs.

4. Resource earnings divide between (a) earnings that reflect the resource's opportunity cost and (b) economic rent—that portion of earnings that exceeds opportunity cost. If a resource has no alternative use, earnings consist entirely of economic rent; if a resource has other uses that pay as well, earnings consist entirely of opportunity cost. Most resources earn both opportunity cost and rent.

5. A firm's demand curve for a resource is the resource's marginal revenue product curve, which shows the change in total revenue from employing one more unit of the resource, other things constant. If a firm sells output in a competitive market, the marginal revenue product curve slopes downward because of diminishing marginal returns. If a firm has some market power in the product market, the marginal revenue product curve slopes downward both because of diminishing marginal returns and because the product price must fall to sell more output.

6. The demand curve for a resource shifts to the right if there is an increase either in its marginal productivity or in the price of the output. The demand curve for a resource also shifts to the right with an increase in the price of a substitute resource or a decrease in the price of a complement resource.

7. Marginal resource cost is the change in total cost resulting from employing one more unit of a resource, other things constant. A firm maximizes profit by employing each resource up to the point where its marginal revenue product equals its marginal resource cost.

QUESTIONS FOR REVIEW

1. *(Resource Demand and Supply)* Answer each of the following questions about the labor market:

   a. Which economic decision makers determine the demand for labor? What is their goal, and what decision criteria do they use in trying to reach that goal?

   b. Which economic decision makers determine the supply of labor? What is their goal and what decision criteria do they use in trying to reach that goal?

   c. In what sense is the demand for labor a derived demand?

2. *(Market Supply for Resources)* Explain why the market supply curve of a resource slopes upward.

3. *(Resource Price Differences)* Distinguish between how the market reacts to a temporary difference in prices for the same resource and how the market reacts to a permanent difference. Why do the reactions differ?

4. *(Opportunity Cost and Economic Rent)* On-the-job experience typically enhances a person's productivity in that particular job. If the person's salary increases to reflect increased experience but the additional experience has no relevance for other jobs, does this higher salary reflect an increase in opportunity cost or in economic rent?

5. *(Firm's Demand for a Resource)* How does the law of diminishing marginal returns affect a firm's demand for labor?

6. *(Shifts of Resource Demand)* Many countries are predominantly agricultural. How would changes in the supply of fertilizer affect the marginal product, and thus the income, of farmers in such countries?

7. *(Optimal Use of More Than One Resource)* Explain the rule for determining optimal resource use when a firm employs more than one resource.

PROBLEMS AND EXERCISES

8. *(Opportunity Cost and Economic Rent)* Define economic rent. In the graph below, assume that the market demand curve for labor is initially D_1.

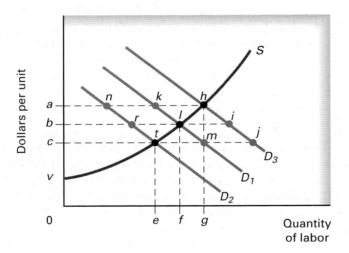

   a. What are the equilibrium wage rate and employment level? What is the economic rent?

   b. Next assume that the price of a substitute resource increases, other things constant. What happens to demand for labor? What are the new equilibrium wage rate and employment level? What happens to economic rent?

   c. Suppose instead that demand for the final product drops, other things constant. Using labor demand curve D_1 as your starting point, what happens to the demand for labor? What are the new equilibrium wage rate and employment level? Does the amount of economic rent change?

9. *(Firm's Demand for a Resource)* Use the following data to answer the questions below. Assume a perfectly competitive product market.

Units of Labor	Units of Output
0	0
1	7
2	13
3	18
4	22
5	25

   a. Calculate the marginal revenue product for each additional unit of labor if output sells for $3 per unit.

   b. Draw the demand curve for labor based on the above data and the $3-per-unit product price.

c. If the wage rate is $15 per hour, how much labor will be hired?

d. Using your answer to part (c), compare the firm's total revenue to the total amount paid for labor. Who gets the difference?

e. What would happen to your answers to parts (b) and (c) if the price of output increased to $5 per unit, other things constant?

10. *(Selling Output as a Price Taker)* If a competitive firm hires another full-time worker, total output will increase from 100 units to 110 units per week. Suppose the market price of output is $25 per unit. What is the maximum weekly wage at which the firm would hire that additional worker?

11. *(Shifts in Resource Demand)* A local pizzeria hires college students to make pizza, wait on tables, take phone orders,

and deliver pizzas. For each situation described, determine whether the demand for student employees by the restaurant would increase, decrease, or remain unchanged. Explain each answer.

a. The demand for pizza increases.

b. Another pizzeria opens up next door.

c. An increase in the minimum wage raises the cost of hiring student employees.

d. The restaurant buys a computer system for taking phone orders.

12. *(C a s e **S t u d y**: The Derived Demand for Architects)* Use a demand-and-supply diagram to illustrate the change in the market for entry-level architects as described in the case study. Explain your conclusions.

EXPERIENTIAL EXERCISES

13. *(Resource Demand)* The *Occupational Outlook Handbook* (OOH) is a U.S. Department of Labor publication that projects employment trends. Using the search feature available at the OOH Web site at http://www.bls.gov/oco/, search several occupations. What factors seem to be affecting employment prospects in those fields? What role does derived demand play? How about technological change?

14. A table from the Department of Labor with the real minimum wage in the United States can be found at: http://www.dol.gov/ILAB/media/reports/oiea/wagestudy/FS-UnitedStates.htm. A better alternative, however, is a continually updated chart with nominal and real mini-

mum wage that can be found at the Employment Policy Institute Web site at: http://www.epionline.org/mw_statistics_annual.cfm.

15. *(Wall Street Journal)* Review the "Work Week" column on the front page of Tuesday's *Wall Street Journal*. Choose an interesting article, read it, and then try to interpret it using the tools developed in this chapter. Did labor supply, labor demand, or both change? Was only a single labor market affected, or were the effects felt in several markets simultaneously? Be sure that your explanation accounts for what happened to both the wage rate and the level of employment.

HOMEWORK XPRESS! EXERCISES

*These exercises require access to McEachern Homework Xpress! If Homework Xpress! did not come with your book, visit **http://homeworkxpress.swlearning.com** to purchase.*

1. Every summer, pool managers and park directors hire lifeguards. Many of the workers are high school and college students looking for summer jobs. In the diagram, draw a demand curve for lifeguards that illustrates how those making the employment decisions will choose to be open

for fewer hours and hire fewer guards, the higher the wage that is paid. Draw a supply curve that illustrates how students would be willing to sacrifice more hours of summer leisure the higher the wage rate. Identify the market equilibrium wage and hours of labor.

2. Many of the skills required for life-guarding are also required for guiding whitewater rafting trips. Word gets around among students who usually work as lifeguards that outfitters hiring guides are paying $5 per hour more than the average for life-guarding at pools and beaches. Use the diagram from Problem 11-1 to illustrate the effects of this wage differential in the market for lifeguards.

3. Commercial fishing is often the lowest rated occupation on lists ranking the attractiveness of various jobs. For people living in and wanting to remain in small coastal communities, other job opportunities are few and the wage rate needed to attract them would be low. However, if there are few such workers, higher wage rates will have to be offered to attract more fishers. Use the demand-and-supply diagram for labor in commercial fishing to identify the equilibrium wage rate and quantity of labor. Use the diagram to illustrate the economic rent earned by workers who would fish at wage rates below the market equilibrium by shading in the appropriate area.

4. On a lobster boat, the more hands working, the more traps that can be checked per day, and the more lobsters landed. The relationship between workers per day and total product for a typical boat are as shown in the table. Find the marginal revenue product for workers per day and plot this as the demand curve for labor in the diagram, given a price of $10 per lobster landed. Add a marginal resource cost curve at $30 per day per worker and identify the number of workers employed per day on a typical boat.

Workers per day	Total Product
0	0
1	5
2	9
3	12
4	14
5	15

Labor Markets and Labor Unions

© Robert Galbraith/Reuters/Corbis

H ow do you divide your time between work and leisure? Why do many people work *less* if the wage increases enough? For example, why do unknown

rock bands play for hours for peanuts, while famous bands play much less for much

more? Why are butchers more likely than surgeons to mow their own lawns? What

determines the wage structure in the economy? What else besides the wage affects

your labor supply? This chapter digs deeper into wage determination.

You can be sure of one thing: demand and supply play a central role in the wage

structure. You have already examined the demand for resources. Demand depends

on a resource's marginal revenue product. The first half of this chapter focuses on the

supply of labor, and then brings demand and supply together to arrive at the market wage. The second half considers the role of labor unions. We examine the economic impact of unions and review recent trends in union membership. Topics discussed include:

- Theory of time allocation
- Backward-bending labor supply curve
- Nonwage factors in labor supply
- Why wages differ
- Unions and collective bargaining
- Union wages and employment
- Trends in union membership

Labor Supply

As a resource supplier, you have a labor supply curve for each of the many possible uses of your labor. To some markets, your quantity supplied is zero over the realistic range of wages. The qualifier "over the realistic range" is added because, for a high enough wage (say, $1 million per hour), you might supply labor to just about *any* activity. In most labor markets, your quantity supplied may be zero either because you are *willing* but *unable* to perform the job (professional golfer, airline pilot, novelist) or because you are *able* but *unwilling* to do so (soldier of fortune, prison guard, P.E. instructor).

So you have as many individual supply curves as there are labor markets, just as you have as many individual demand curves as there are markets for goods and services. Your labor supply to each market depends, among other things, on your abilities, your taste for the job, and the opportunity cost of your time. Your supply to a particular labor market assumes that wages in other markets are constant, just as your demand for a particular product assumes that other prices are constant.

Labor Supply and Utility Maximization

Recall the definition of economics: *the study of how people use their scarce resources in an attempt to satisfy their unlimited wants*—that is, how individuals attempt to use their scarce resources to maximize their utility. Two sources of utility are of special interest to us in this chapter: the consumption of goods and services and the enjoyment of leisure. The utility derived from consuming goods and services serves as the foundation for consumer demand. Another valuable source of utility is leisure—time spent relaxing with friends, sleeping, eating, watching TV, and other recreation. Leisure is a normal good that, like other goods, is subject to the law of diminishing marginal utility. Thus, the more leisure time you have, the less you value an additional hour of it. Sometimes you may have so much leisure that you "have time on your hands" and are "just killing time." As that sage of the comic page Garfield the cat once lamented, "Spare time would be more fun if I had less to spare." Or as Shakespeare wrote, "If all the year were playing holidays, to sport would be as tedious as to work." Leisure's diminishing marginal utility explains why some of the idle rich grow bored in their idleness.

Three Uses of Time

Some of you are at a point in your careers when you have few resources other than your time. Time is the raw material of life. You can use your time in three ways. First, you can undertake **market work**—selling your time in the labor market in return for income. When you supply labor, you usually surrender control of your time to the employer in return for a wage. Second, you can undertake **nonmarket work**—using time to produce your own goods and services. Nonmarket work includes the time you spend doing your laundry,

MARKET WORK

Time sold as labor

NONMARKET WORK

Time spent getting an education or producing goods and services for personal consumption making a sandwich, or cleaning up after yourself. Nonmarket work also includes the time spent acquiring skills and education to enhance your productivity. Although studying and attending class may provide little immediate payoff, you are betting that the knowledge and perspective so gained will enrich your future. Third, you can spend time as **leisure**—using your time in nonwork pursuits.

LEISURE
Time spent on nonwork activities

Work and Utility

Unless you are one of the fortunate few, work is not a pure source of utility, as it often generates some boredom, discomfort, and aggravation. In short, time spent working can be "a real pain," a source of *disutility*—the opposite of utility. And work is subject *to increasing marginal disutility*—the more you work, the greater the marginal disutility of working another hour. You may work nonetheless, because your earnings buy goods and services. You expect the utility from these products to more than offset the disutility of work. Thus, the *net utility of work*—the utility of the consumption made possible through earnings minus the disutility of the work itself—usually makes some amount of work an attractive use of your time. In the case of market work, your income buys goods and services. In the case of nonmarket work, either you produce goods and services directly, as in making yourself a sandwich, or you invest your time in education with an expectation of higher future earnings and higher future consumption. The additional utility you expect from the sandwich and higher future consumption possibilities resulting from education are the marginal benefits of nonmarket work.

Utility Maximization

Within the limits of a 24-hour day, seven days a week, you balance your time among market work, nonmarket work, and leisure to maximize utility. As a rational consumer, *you attempt to maximize utility by allocating your time so that the expected marginal utility of the last unit of time spent in each activity is identical.* Thus, in the course of a week or a month, the expected marginal utility of the last hour of leisure equals the expected net marginal utility of the last hour of market work, which equals the expected net marginal utility of the last hour of nonmarket work. In the case of time devoted to acquiring more human capital, you must consider the marginal utility expected from the future increase in earnings that will result from your enhanced productivity.

Maybe at this point you are saying, "Wait a minute. I don't know what you're talking about. I don't allocate my time like that. I just sort of bump along, doing what feels good." Economists do not claim that you are even aware of making these marginal calculations. But as a rational decision maker, you allocate your scarce time trying to satisfy your unlimited wants, or trying to maximize utility. And utility maximization, or "doing what feels good," implies that you act *as if* you allocated your time to derive the same expected net marginal utility from the last unit of time spent in each alternative use.

You probably have settled into a rough plan for meals, work, entertainment, study, sleep, and so on—a plan that fits your immediate objectives. This plan is probably in constant flux as you make expected and unexpected adjustments in your use of time. For example, last weekend you may have failed to crack a book, despite good intentions. This morning you may have slept later than you planned because you were up late. Over a week, a month, or a year, however, your use of time is roughly in line with an allocation that maximizes utility as you perceive it at the time. Put another way, if you could alter your use of time to increase your utility, you would do so. Nobody's stopping you! You may emphasize immediate gratification over long-term goals, but, hey, that's your choice and you bear the consequences. *This time-allocation process ensures that at the margin, the expected net utilities from the last unit of time spent in each activity are equal.*

Because information is costly and because the future is uncertain, you sometimes make mistakes. You don't always get what you expect. Some mistakes are minor, such as going to a movie that turns out to be a waste of time. But other mistakes can be costly. For example, some people are now studying for a field that will grow crowded by the time they graduate, or some people may be acquiring skills that new technology will make obsolete.

Implications

The theory of time allocation described thus far has several implications for individual choice. First, consider the choices of market work, nonmarket work, and leisure. The higher your market wage, other things constant, the higher your opportunity cost of leisure and nonmarket work. For example, those who earn a high wage will spend less time in nonmarket work, other things constant. Surgeons are less likely to mow their lawns than are butchers. And among those earning the same wage, those more productive in nonmarket work—handy around the house, good cooks—will do more for themselves. Conversely, those who are all thumbs around the house and have trouble boiling water will hire more household services and eat out more frequently.

By the same logic, the higher the expected earnings right out of high school, other things constant, the higher the opportunity cost of attending college. Most young, successful movie stars do not go to college, and some even drop out of high school, as noted earlier. Promising athletes often turn pro right after high school or before completing college. But the vast majority of people, including female basketball stars, do not face such a high opportunity cost of higher education. As one poor soul lamented, "Since my wife left me, my kids joined a cult, my job is history, and my dog died, I think now might be a good time to go back for an MBA."

Wages and Individual Labor Supply

To breathe life into the time-allocation problem, consider your choices for the summer. If you can afford to, you can take the summer off, spending it entirely on leisure, perhaps as a fitting reward for a rough academic year. Or you can supply your time to market work. Or you can undertake nonmarket work, such as cleaning the garage, painting the house, or attending summer school. As a rational decision maker, you will select the combination of leisure, market work, and nonmarket work that you expect will maximize your utility. And the optimal combination is likely to involve allocating time to each activity. For example, even if you work, you might still take one or two summer courses.

Suppose the only summer job available is some form of unskilled labor, such as working in a fast-food restaurant or for the municipal parks department. For simplicity, let's assume that you view all such jobs as equally attractive (or unattractive) in terms of their nonmonetary aspects, such as working conditions, working hours, and so on. (These nonmonetary aspects are discussed in the next section.) If there is no difference among these unskilled jobs, the most important question for you in deciding how much market labor to supply is: What's the market wage?

Suppose the wage is $6 per hour. Rather than working at a wage that low, you might decide to work around the house, attend summer school full time, take a really long nap, travel across the country to find yourself, or perhaps pursue some combination of these. In any case, you supply no market labor at such a low wage. The market wage must rise to $7 before you supply any market labor. Suppose at a wage of $7, you supply 20 hours per week, perhaps taking fewer summer courses and shorter naps.

As the wage increases, your opportunity cost of time spent in other activities rises, so you substitute market work for other uses of your time. You decide to work 30 hours per week at a wage of $8 per hour, 40 hours at $9, 48 hours at $10, and 55 hours at $11. At a wage of $12 you go to 60 hours per week; you are starting to earn serious money—$720 a week. If the wage hits $13 per hour, you decide to cut back to 58 hours per week. Despite the cutback, your pay rises to $754, which is more than when the wage was $12. Finally, if the wage hits $14, you cut back to 55 per week, earning $770. To explain why you may eventually reduce the quantity of labor supplied, let's consider the impact of wage increases on your time allocation.

Substitution and Income Effects

An increase in the wage has two effects on your use of time. First, because each hour of work now buys more goods and services, a higher wage makes you want to work more. A higher wage increases the opportunity cost of leisure and nonmarket work. Thus, as the wage increases, you substitute market work for other activities; this is the **substitution effect of a wage increase.** But a higher wage means a higher income for the same number of hours. A higher income increases your demand for all normal goods. Because leisure is a normal good, a higher income increases your demand for leisure, thereby reducing your allocation of time to market work. This **income effect of a wage increase** tends to reduce the quantity of labor supplied to market work.

As the wage increases, the substitution effect causes you to work more, but the income effect causes you to work less and demand more leisure. In our example, the substitution effect exceeds the income effect for wages up to $12 per hour, resulting in more labor supplied as the wage increases. When the wage reaches $13, however, the income effect exceeds the substitution effect, causing you to reduce the quantity of labor supplied.

Backward-Bending Labor Supply Curve

The labor supply curve just described appears in Exhibit 1. As you can see, this slopes upward until a wage of $12 per hour is reached; then it bends backward. The **backward-bending supply curve** gets its shape because the income effect of a higher wage eventually dominates the substitution effect, reducing the quantity of labor supplied as the wage increases. We see evidence of a backward-bending supply curve particularly among high-wage individuals, who reduce their work and consume more leisure as their wage increases. For example, entertainers typically perform less as they become more successful. Unknown musicians will play for hours for hardly any money; famous musicians play much less for much more. The income effect of rising real wages helps explain the decline in the U.S. workweek from an average of 60 hours in 1900 to less than 40 hours today.

Flexibility of Hours Worked

The model we have been discussing assumes that workers have some control over the number of hours they work. Opportunities for part-time work and overtime allow workers to put together their preferred quantity of hours. Workers also have some control over the timing and length of their vacations. More generally, individuals can control how long to stay in school, when to enter or leave the workforce, and when to retire. Thus, they actually have more control over the number of hours worked than you might think if you focused simply on the benchmark of, say, a 40-hour work week.

Nonwage Determinants of Labor Supply

The supply of labor to a particular market depends on a variety of factors other than the wage, just as the demand for a particular good depends on factors other than the price. As we have already seen, the supply of labor to a particular market depends on wages in other

SUBSTITUTION EFFECT OF A WAGE INCREASE

A higher wage encourages more work because other activities now have a higher opportunity cost

INCOME EFFECT OF A WAGE INCREASE

A higher wage increases a worker's income, increasing the demand for all normal goods, including leisure, so the quantity of labor supplied to market work decreases

BACKWARD-BENDING SUPPLY CURVE OF LABOR

As the wage rises, the quantity of labor supplied may eventually decline; the income effect of a higher wage increases the demand for leisure, which reduces the quantity of labor supplied enough to more than offset the substitution effect of a higher wage

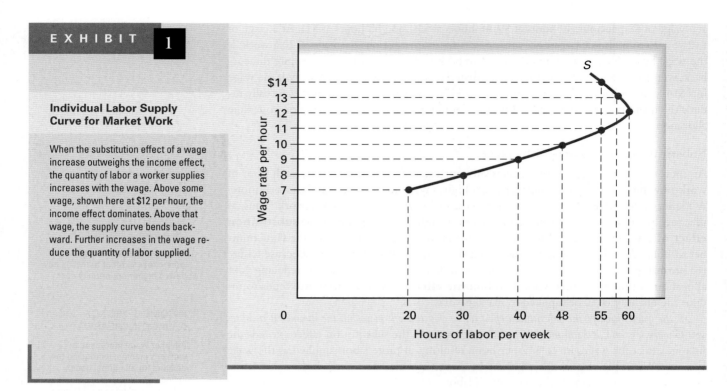

**Individual Labor Supply
Curve for Market Work**

When the substitution effect of a wage
increase outweighs the income effect,
the quantity of labor a worker supplies
increases with the wage. Above some
wage, shown here at $12 per hour, the
income effect dominates. Above that
wage, the supply curve bends backward. Further increases in the wage reduce the quantity of labor supplied.

labor markets. But what are the nonwage factors that shape a college student's labor supply
for the summer?

Other Sources of Income

Although some jobs are rewarding in a variety of nonmonetary ways, the main reason people work is to earn money. Thus, the willingness to supply time to a labor market depends
on income from other sources, including from prior savings, borrowing, family, and scholar-
ships. A student who receives a generous scholarship, for example, faces less pressure for
summer earnings. More generally, wealthy people have less incentive to work. For example,
multimillion-dollar lottery winners often quit their jobs.

Nonmonetary Factors

Labor is a special kind of resource. Unlike capital and natural resources, which can be supplied regardless of the whereabouts of the resource owner, the supplier of labor must be in
the same place the work is performed. Because individuals must usually be physically present to supply labor, such *nonmonetary factors* as the difficulty of the job, the quality of the
work environment, and the status of the position become important in labor supply. For example, deckhands on fishing boats in the Bering Sea off Alaska earn over $3,000 for five
days' work, but the winter temperature seldom exceeds zero and daily shifts allow only three
hours for sleep.

   Consider the different working conditions you might encounter. A campus job that lets
you study on the job is more attractive than one with no study time. Some jobs have flexible hours; others have rigid schedules. Is the workplace air-conditioned, or do you have to
sweat it out? The more attractive the working conditions, the more labor you supply to that
market, other things constant. Finally, some jobs convey more status than others. For

example, the president of the United States earns less than one-tenth the average pay of corporate heads, but there is no shortage of presidential candidates. Similarly, U.S. Supreme Court justices typically take a huge pay cut to accept the job.

The Value of Job Experience

All else equal, you are more inclined to take a job that provides valuable experience. Serving as the assistant treasurer for a local business during the summer provides better job experience and looks better on a résumé than serving mystery meat at the college cafeteria. Some people are willing to accept relatively low wages now for the promise of higher wages in the future. For example, new lawyers are eager to fill clerkships for judges, though the pay is low and the hours long, because these positions offer experience and contacts future employers value. Likewise, athletes who play in the minor leagues for little pay believe that experience will help them get to the major leagues. Thus, *the more a job enhances future earning possibilities, the greater the supply of labor to that occupation, other things constant.* Consequently, the pay is usually lower than for jobs that impart less valuable experience. Sometimes the pay is zero, as with some internships.

Taste for Work

Just as the tastes for goods and services differ among consumers, the tastes for work also differ among labor suppliers. Some people prefer physical labor and hate office work. Some become surgeons; others can't stand the sight of blood. Some become airline pilots; others are afraid to fly. Teenagers prefer jobs at Starbucks and Gap to those at McDonald's and Burger King.[1] Many struggling writers, artists, actors, and dancers could earn more elsewhere, but prefer the creative process and the chance, albeit slim, of becoming rich and famous in the arts (for example, members of the Screen Actors Guild average less than $20,000 a year). Some people have such strong preferences for certain jobs that they work for free, such as auxiliary police officers or volunteer firefighters.

As with the taste for goods and services, economists do not try to explain the origin of tastes for work. They simply argue that your tastes are relatively stable and you supply more labor to jobs you like. Based on tastes, workers seek jobs in a way that tends to minimize the disutility of work. This is not to say that everyone will end up in his or her most preferred position. The transaction costs of job information and of changing jobs may prevent some matchups that might otherwise seem desirable. But in the long run, people tend to find jobs that suit them. We are not likely to find tour guides who hate to travel, zookeepers who are allergic to animals, or garage mechanics who hate getting their hands dirty.

Market Supply of Labor

In the previous section, we considered those factors, both monetary and nonmonetary, that influence individual labor supply. *The supply of labor to a particular* market *is the horizontal sum of all the individual supply curves.* The horizontal sum is found by adding the quantities supplied by each worker at each particular wage. If an individual supply curve of labor bends backward, does this mean that the market supply curve for labor also bends backward? Not necessarily. Because different individuals have different opportunity costs and different tastes for work, the bend in the supply curve occurs at different wages for different individuals. And, for some individuals, the labor supply curve may not bend backward over the realistic range of wages. Exhibit 2 shows how just three individual labor supply curves sum to yield a market supply curve that slopes upward.

---

1. Dirk Johnson, "For Teenagers, Fast Food Is a Snack, Not a Job," *New York Times*, 8 January 2001.

EXHIBIT 2   **Deriving the Market Labor Supply Curve from Individual Labor Supply Curves**

The individual labor supply curve in panel (a) bends backward. The market supply curve, however, may still slope upward over the relevant range of wages.

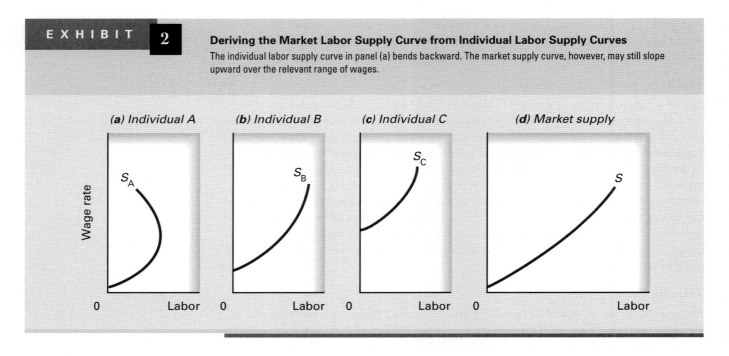

(a) *Individual A*   **(b)** *Individual B*   **(c)** *Individual C*   **(d)** *Market supply*

Why Wages Differ

Just as both blades of scissors contribute equally to cutting paper, both labor demand and labor supply determine the market wage. Exhibit 3 shows average hourly wages for the 128 million U.S. workers. Workers are sorted into 22 occupations from the highest to the lowest average wage. Management earns the highest wage, at $34 an hour. The lowest is the $8 an hour averaged by workers preparing and serving food. Wage differences across labor markets trace to differences in labor demand and in labor supply, as you will see. In the previous chapter, we discussed the elements that influence the demand for resources and examined labor in particular. In brief, *a profit-maximizing firm hires labor up to the point where labor's marginal revenue product equals its marginal resource cost*—that is, where the last unit employed increases total revenue enough to cover the added cost. Because we have already discussed what affects the demand for labor—namely, labor's marginal revenue product—let's focus more on labor supply.

Differences in Training, Education, Age, and Experience

Some jobs pay more because they require a long and expensive training period, which reduces market supply because few are willing to incur the time and expense required. But such training increases labor productivity, thereby increasing demand for the skills. Reduced supply and increased demand both raise the market wage. For example, certified public accountants (CPAs) earn more than file clerks because the extensive training of CPAs limits the supply to this field and because this training increases the productivity of CPAs compared to file clerks.

Exhibit 4 shows how education and experience affect earnings. Age groups are indicated on the horizontal axis and average annual earnings on the vertical axis. To standardize things, pay figures are for the highest level of education achieved. The relationship between income and education is clear. At every age, those with more education earn more. For example, among the three age groups between 35 and 64, those with professional degrees averaged *five times* more pay than those with less than a ninth-grade education.

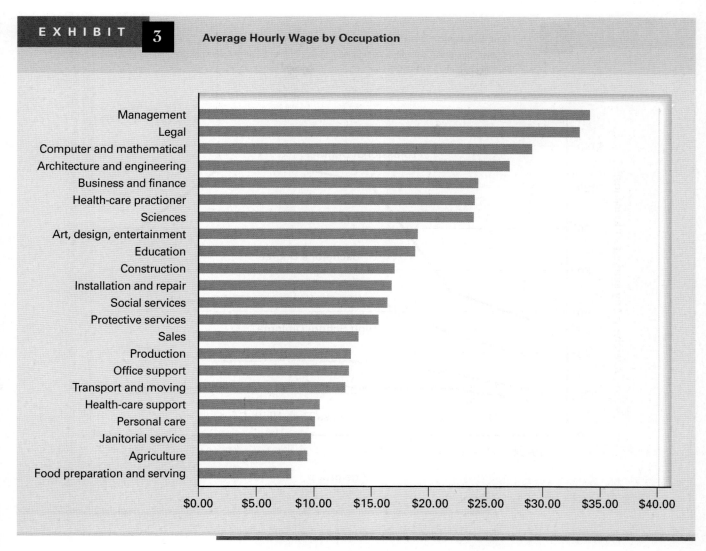

EXHIBIT 3 　 **Average Hourly Wage by Occupation**

Source: U.S. Bureau of Labor Statistics. Figures are for 2001. For the latest figures, go to http://www.bls.gov/bls/blswage.htm.

Age itself also has an important effect on income. Earnings tend to increase as workers acquire job experience and get promoted. Among educated workers, experience pays more. For example, among those with a professional degree, workers in the 45–54 age group earned on average 86 percent more than those in the 25–34 age group. But among those with less than a ninth-grade education, workers in the 45–54 age group earned on average only 8 percent more than those in the 25–34 age group. Differences in earnings reflect the normal workings of resource markets, whereby workers are rewarded according to their marginal productivity.

Differences in Ability

Because they are more able and talented, some individuals earn more than others with the same training and education. For example, two lawyers may have identical educations, but

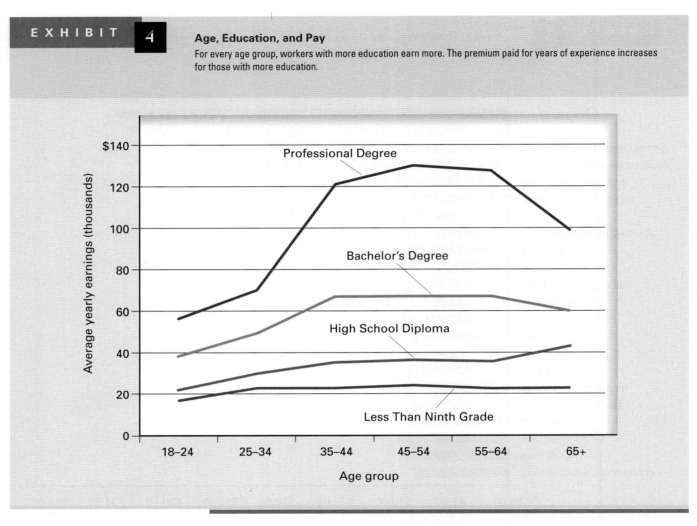

Source: U.S. Census Bureau. Figures are average earnings for all full-time, year-round workers in 2001.

WINNER-TAKE-ALL LABOR MARKETS

Markets in which a few key employees critical to the overall success of an enterprise are richly rewarded

Case **Study**

World of Business

eActivity

For current news stories about executive compensation, visit *Forbes* maga-

one earns more because of differences in underlying ability. Most executives have extensive training and business experience, but only a few get to head large corporations. In professional sports such as basketball and baseball, some players earn up to 50 times more than others. From lawyers to executives to professional athletes, pay differences reflect differing abilities and different marginal productivities. The following case study examines why the premium awarded greater marginal productivity has grown in recent decades.

Winner–Take–All Labor Markets

Each year *Forbes* magazine lists the multimillion-dollar earnings of top entertainers and professional athletes. Entertainment and pro sports have come to be called **winner-take-all labor markets** because a few key people critical to the overall success of an enterprise are richly rewarded. For example, the credits at the end of a movie list a hundred or more people directly involved in the production. Hundreds, sometimes thousands, more work behind the scenes. Despite a huge cast and crew, the difference between a movie's financial success and failure depends primarily on the performance of just a few critical people—the screenwriter, the director, and the lead actors. The same happens in sports. Although thousands compete each year in professional tennis, the value of television time, ticket sales, and endorsements is based on the drawing power of just the top few players. In professional golf tournaments, attendance and TV ratings have been significantly higher with Tiger Woods in the mix. Thus, top performers generate a high marginal revenue product.

zine's subsection about trends in this area at http://www.forbes.com/ compensation/. What is the latest explanation for the pay differential? Who are the highest-paid CEOs? For a union's view on the executive pay differential, read the United Auto Workers' (UAW) article on unionization and executive compensation at http://www.uaw.org/publications/jobs_ pay/00/0700/jpe04.html. Why does the UAW believe that stock compensation for executives may not improve executives' performance?

But high marginal productivity alone is not enough. To be paid anywhere near their marginal revenue product, there must be an open competition for top performers. This bids up pay, such as the $20 million per movie garnered by top stars—more than 1,000 times the average annual earnings of Screen Actors Guild members. In professional sports, before the free-agency rule was introduced (which allows players to seek the highest bidder), top players couldn't move on their own from team to team. They were stuck with the team that drafted them, earning only a fraction of their marginal revenue product.

Relatively high pay in entertainment and sports is not new. What is new is the spread of winner-take-all to other U.S. markets. The "star" treatment now extends to such fields as management, law, banking, finance, even academia. Consider, for example, corporate pay. In 1974, the chief executive officers (CEOs) of the 200 largest U.S. corporations earned about 35 times more than the average production worker. By 2000, this multiple topped 150. Comparable multiples were lower in Germany and Japan. Why the big U.S. jump?

First, the U.S. economy has grown sharply in recent decades and is by far the largest in the world—with output equaling that of the next three economies combined. So U.S. businesses serve a wider market, making the CEO potentially more productive and more valuable. Second, breakthroughs in communications, production, and transportation mean that a well-run U.S. company can now sell a valued product around the world. Third, wider competition for the top people has increased their pay. For example, in the 1970s, U.S. businesses usually hired CEOs from company ranks, promoting mainly from within (a practice still common today in Germany and Japan). Because other firms were not trying to bid away the most talented executives, companies were able to retain them for just a fraction of the pay that now prevails in a more competitive market. Today top executives are often drawn from outside the firm—even outside the industry and the country. One final reason why top CEO pay has increased in America is that high salaries are more socially acceptable here than they once were. High salaries are still frowned on in some countries, such as Japan and Germany.

Sources: Stefan Fatsis, "Thanks to Tiger's Roar, PGA Tour Signs Record TV Deal Through 2007," *Wall Street Journal*, 17 July 2001; "Making Companies Work," *Economist*, 25 October 2003; Barbara Whitaker, "Producers and Actors Reach Accord," *New York Times*, 5 July 2001; and *Economic Report of the President*, February 2004, at http://www.gpoaccess.gov/eop/index.html.

Differences in Risk

Research indicates that jobs with a higher probability of injury or death, such as coal mining, pay more, other things constant. Russians working at the partially disabled nuclear power plant, Chernobyl, earned 10 times the national average. Truck drivers for American contractors in Iraq earn over $100,000 a year, but the job is dangerous. Workers also earn more, other things constant, in seasonal jobs such as construction, where the risk of unemployment is greater.

Geographic Differences

People have a strong incentive to sell their resources in the market where they earn the most. For example, the National Basketball Association attracts talent from around the world. About 20 percent of NBA players in 2004 came from 36 other countries. Likewise, thousands of foreign-trained physicians migrate here each year for the high pay. The flow of labor is not all one way: Some Americans seek their fortune abroad, with American basketball players going to Europe and baseball players going to Japan. Workers often face migration hurdles. Any reduction in these hurdles would reduce wage differentials across countries.

Job Discrimination

Sometimes wage differences stem from racial or gender discrimination in the job market. Although such discrimination is illegal, history shows that certain groups—including African Americans, Hispanics, and women—have systematically earned less than others of equal ability.

Union Membership

Other things equal, members of organized labor earn more than nonmembers. The balance of this chapter discusses the effects of unions on the market for labor.

Unions and Collective Bargaining

Economics
in the Movies

Few aspects of the labor market make the news more often than the activities of labor unions. Labor negotiations, strikes, picket lines, confrontations between workers and employers—all fit TV's "action news" format. Despite media attention, only about one in seven U.S. workers is a union member and the overwhelming share of union agreements are reached without a strike. Let's examine the tools that unions use to seek higher pay and better benefits for their members.

Types of Unions

A **labor union** is a group of workers who join together to improve their terms of employment. Labor unions in the United States date back to the early days of national independence, when workers in various crafts—such as carpenters, shoemakers, and printers—formed local groups to seek higher wages and shorter work hours. A **craft union** was confined to people with a particular skill, or craft. Craft unions eventually formed their own national organization, the *American Federation of Labor (AFL)*. The AFL, founded in 1886 under the direction of Samuel Gompers, a cigar maker, was not a union itself but rather an organization of national unions, each retaining its autonomy.

By the beginning of World War I, the AFL, still under Gompers, was viewed as the voice of labor. The Clayton Act of 1914 exempted labor unions from antitrust laws, meaning that *unions at competing companies could legally join forces.* Unions were also tax exempt. Membership jumped during World War I but fell by half between 1920 and 1933, as the government retreated from its support of union efforts.

The *Congress of Industrial Organizations (CIO)* was formed in 1935 to serve as a national organization of unions in mass-production industries, such as autos and steel. Whereas the AFL organized workers in particular crafts, such as plumbers and carpenters, the CIO consisted of unions whose membership embraced all workers in a particular industry. These **industrial unions** included unskilled, semiskilled, and skilled workers in an industry, such as all autoworkers or all steelworkers.

LABOR UNION

A group of workers who organize to improve their terms of employment

CRAFT UNION

A union whose members have a particular skill or work at a particular craft, such as plumbers or carpenters

INDUSTRIAL UNION

A union of both skilled and unskilled workers from a particular industry, such as autoworkers or steelworkers

Collective Bargaining

Collective bargaining is the process by which representatives of union and management negotiate a mutually agreeable contract specifying wages, employee benefits, and working conditions. A tentative agreement, once reached, goes before the membership for a vote. If the agreement is rejected, the union can strike or can continue negotiations.

Mediation and Arbitration

If negotiations reach an impasse and the public interest is involved, government officials may ask an independent mediator to step in. A **mediator** is an impartial observer who listens to each side separately and then suggests a resolution. If each side still remains open to a settlement, the mediator brings them together to work out a contract, but the mediator has no power to impose a settlement. In certain critical sectors, such as police and fire protection, where a strike could harm the public interest, differences are sometimes settled through **binding arbitration.** A neutral third party evaluates each position and issues a ruling that both sides must accept. Some disputes skip the mediation and arbitration steps and go directly from impasse to strike.

The Strike

A major source of union power is a **strike,** which is a union's attempt to withhold labor to stop production, thereby hoping the firm will accept the union's position. But strikes are also risky for workers, who earn no pay or benefits during the strike and could lose their jobs. Union funds and, in some states, unemployment benefits, may aid strikers, but incomes still fall substantially. *Although neither party usually wants a strike, both sides, rather than concede on key points, usually act as if they could endure one.* Unions usually picket to prevent or discourage so-called strikebreakers, or "scabs," from crossing the picket lines to work. But the targeted firm, by hiring temporary workers and nonstriking union workers, can sometimes continue production.

Union Wages and Employment

Samuel Gompers, the AFL's long-time head, was once asked what unions want. "More," he roared. Union members, like everyone else, have unlimited wants. But because resources are scarce, choices must be made. A menu of union desires includes higher wages, more benefits, greater job security, better working conditions, and so on. To keep the analysis manageable, let's focus on a single objective, higher wages, and consider three ways unions might increase wages: (1) by forming an inclusive, or industrial, union; (2) by forming an exclusive, or craft, union; and (3) by increasing the demand for union labor.

Inclusive, or Industrial, Unions: Negotiating a Higher Industry Wage

With the *inclusive, or industrial,* approach, the union tries to negotiate an industry-wide wage for each class of labor. The market demand and supply curves for a particular type of labor are labeled D and S in panel (a) of Exhibit 5. In the absence of a union, the market wage is W and employment is E. At the market wage, each firm faces a horizontal, or perfectly elastic, supply of labor, as depicted by s in panel (b) of Exhibit 5. Thus, each firm can hire as much labor as it wants at the market wage of W. The firm hires up to the point where labor's marginal revenue product equals its marginal resource cost, resulting in e units of labor in panel (b). As we saw earlier, in equilibrium, labor is paid a wage just equal to its marginal revenue product.

COLLECTIVE BARGAINING

The process by which union and management negotiate a labor agreement

MEDIATOR

An impartial observer who helps resolve differences between union and management

BINDING ARBITRATION

Negotiation in which union and management must accept an impartial observer's resolution of a dispute

STRIKE

A union's attempt to withhold labor from a firm to stop production

N e t Bookmark

Does it make any difference to the quality of your job if your workplace is unionized? The AFL-CIO, an umbrella organization of most of the nation's unions, certainly believes it makes a difference. A Web page making the argument that better pay, benefits, and stability can come to union members can be found at http://www.aflcio.org/aboutunions/joinunions/whyjoin/uniondifference/. Also a history of the founding of Labor Day is available from the U.S. Department of Labor at http://www.dol.gov/opa/aboutdol/laborday.htm.

Effects of a Union's Wage Floor

Without a labor union, the market wage is *W* in panel (a). At that wage, each firm can hire as much labor as it wants. The individual firm in panel (b) hires more labor until the marginal revenue product equals the market wage, *W*. Each firm hires *e* units of labor, and total employment is *E*. If a union negotiates a wage *W'*, which is above the market wage *W*, the supply curve facing the firm shifts up from *s* to *s'*. Each firm hires less labor, *e'*, so total employment falls to *E'*. At the union wage there is now an excess quantity of labor supplied equal to *E"*– *E'*.

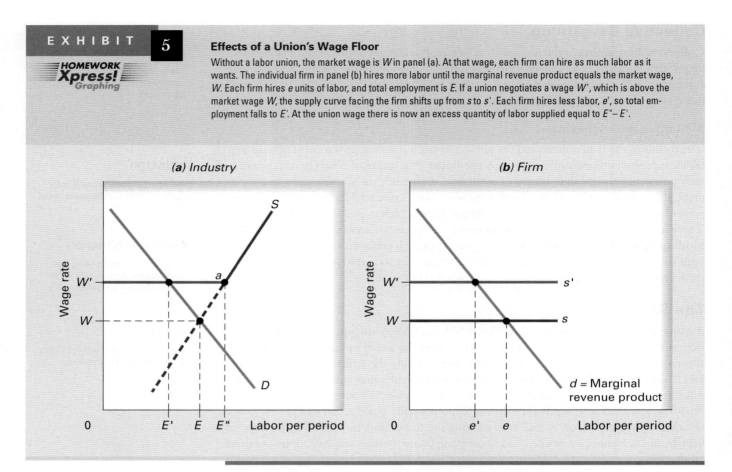

(a) Industry

(b) Firm

Now suppose the union negotiates a wage above the market-clearing level. Specifically, suppose the wage negotiated is *W'* in panel (a), meaning that no labor will be supplied at a lower wage. In effect, the market supply of labor is perfectly elastic at the union wage out to point *a*. Beyond point *a*, however, the wage floor no longer applies; *aS* becomes the relevant portion of the labor supply curve. For an industry facing a wage floor of *W'*, the entire labor supply curve becomes *W'aS*, which has a kink where the wage floor joins the upward-sloping portion of the original labor supply curve.

Once this wage floor is established, each firm faces a horizontal supply curve of labor at the collectively bargained wage, *W'*. Because the wage is now higher than the market-clearing wage, each firm hires less labor. Consequently, the higher wage leads to a reduction in total employment; the quantity demanded by the industry drops from *E* to *E'* in panel (a). At wage *W'* workers in the industry would like to supply, *E"*, which exceeds the labor demanded, *E'*. Ordinarily this excess quantity supplied would force the wage down. But because union members agree *collectively* to the union wage, individual workers can't work for less, nor can employers hire them for less. *With the inclusive, or industrial, union, which negotiates with the entire industry, the wage is higher and employment lower than they would be in the absence of a union.*

The union must somehow ration the limited jobs available, such as by awarding them based on worker seniority or personal connections within the union. Those who can't find

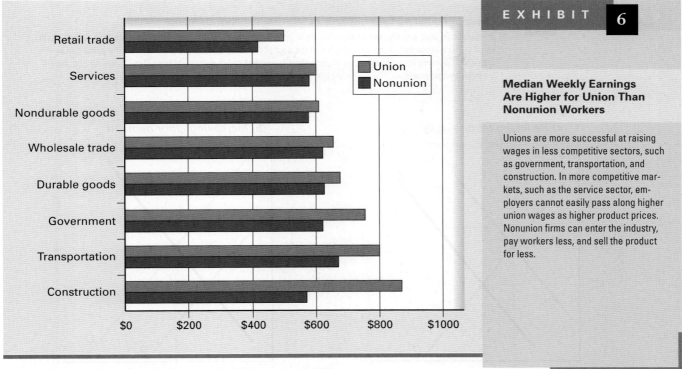

EXHIBIT 6

Median Weekly Earnings Are Higher for Union Than Nonunion Workers

Unions are more successful at raising wages in less competitive sectors, such as government, transportation, and construction. In more competitive markets, such as the service sector, employers cannot easily pass along higher union wages as higher product prices. Nonunion firms can enter the industry, pay workers less, and sell the product for less.

Source: U.S. Bureau of Labor Statistics. Figures are for full-time workers in 2001.

union jobs turn to the nonunion sector. *This increases the supply of labor in the nonunion sector, which drives down the nonunion wage.* So wages are relatively higher in the union sector first, because unions bargain for a wage that exceeds the market-clearing wage, and second, because those unable to find union jobs crowd into the nonunion sector. Studies show that union wages average about 15 percent above the wages of similarly qualified nonunion workers. Exhibit 6 compares median weekly earnings of union and nonunion workers. Note that unions are more successful at raising wages in less-competitive sectors. For example, unions have less impact on service industries, where product markets tend to be competitive. Unions have greater impact on wages in government, transportation, and construction, which tend to be less competitive. When there is more competition in the product market, employers cannot easily pass along higher union wages as higher product prices. New, nonunion, firms can enter the industry, pay lower wages, and sell the product for less.

Exclusive, or Craft, Unions: Reducing Labor Supply

One way to increase wages while avoiding an excess quantity of labor supplied is to somehow reduce the supply of labor, shown as a leftward shift of the labor supply curve in panel (a) of Exhibit 7. This supply reduction increases the wage and reduces employment. Successful supply restrictions of this type require that the union first limit its membership and second force all employers in the industry to hire only union members. The union can restrict membership with high initiation fees, long apprenticeship periods, tough qualification exams, restrictive licensing requirements, and other devices aimed at slowing down or

7

Effect of Reducing Labor Supply or Increasing Labor Demand

If a union can successfully restrict labor supply in an industry, the supply curve shifts to the left from *S* to *S'*, as in panel (a). The wage rises from *W* to *W'*, but at the cost of reducing employment from *E* to *E'.* If a union can increase the demand for union labor, as in panel (b), the demand curve shifts right from *D* to *D'*, raising both the wage and employment.

(a) *Reducing labor supply*

(b) *Increasing labor demand*

discouraging new membership. But even if unions restrict membership, they still have difficulty unionizing all firms in the industry.

Whereas wage setting is more typical of industrial unions, restricting supply is more typical of craft unions, such as unions of carpenters, plumbers, or bricklayers. Professional groups—doctors, lawyers, and accountants, for instance—also impose entry restrictions through education and examination standards. These restrictions, usually defended as protecting the public, are often little more than self-serving attempts to increase wages by restricting labor supply.

Increasing Demand for Union Labor

A third way to increase the wage is to increase the demand for union labor by somehow shifting the labor demand curve outward as from *D* to *D"* in panel (b) of Exhibit 7. This is an attractive alternative *because it increases both the wage and employment,* so there is no need to restrict labor supply or to ration jobs among union members. Here are some ways unions try to increase the demand for union labor.

Increase Demand for Union-Made Goods

The demand for union labor may be increased through a direct appeal to consumers to buy only union-made products. Because the demand for labor is a derived demand, increasing the demand for union-made products increases the demand for union labor.

Restrict Supply of Nonunion-Made Goods

Another way to increase the demand for union labor is to restrict the supply of products that compete with union-made products. Again, this approach relies on the derived nature of labor demand. The United Auto Workers (UAW), for example, supports restrictions on imported cars. Fewer imported cars means greater demand for cars produced by U.S. workers, who are mostly union members.

Increase Productivity of Union Labor

Some observers claim union representation improves labor-management relations. According to this theory, unions increase worker productivity by minimizing conflicts, resolving differences, and at times even straightening out workers who are goofing off. In the absence of a union, a dissatisfied worker may simply quit, causing job turnover. Turnover is costly to the firm because the departing worker leaves with company-specific, on-the-job training that increases workers' productivity. With a union, however, workers can resolve dissatisfactions through union channels. Quit rates are in fact significantly lower among union workers (although this could also be due to the higher pay). If unions increase the productivity of workers, the demand for union labor will increase.

Featherbedding

Yet another way unions try to increase the demand for union labor is by **featherbedding,** which makes employers hire more labor than they want or need. For example, union rules require that each Broadway theater have a permanent "house" carpenter, electrician, and property manager. Once the play run begins, these workers show up only on payday. The box office must be staffed by three people. The musicians' union requires that from 9 to 22 musicians be employed at each theater staging a musical, even if the show calls for just a piano player.

FEATHERBEDDING

Union efforts to force employers to hire more workers than wanted or needed

Featherbedding does not create a true increase in demand, in the sense of shifting the demand curve to the right. Instead, it forces the firm to a point to the right of its true labor demand curve. For example, changing one light bulb for the Broadway play *The Iceman Cometh* required a three-person crew, each earning $43.36 an hour.[2] The union tries to limit a firm to an all-or-none choice: Either hire so many workers for the job, or we'll strike. Thus, with featherbedding, *the union attempts to dictate not only the wage but also the quantity that must be hired at that wage, thereby moving employers to the right of their labor demand curve.*

To review: We have examined three ways in which unions try to raise members' wages: (1) by negotiating a wage floor above the equilibrium wage for the industry and somehow rationing the limited jobs among union members, (2) by restricting the supply of labor, and (3) by increasing the demand for union labor. Unions try to increase the demand for union labor in four ways: (1) through a direct public appeal to buy only union-made products, (2) by restricting the supply of products made by nonunion labor, (3) by reducing labor turnover and thereby increasing labor's marginal productivity, and (4) through featherbedding, which forces employers to hire more union labor than they want or need.

Recent Trends in Union Membership

In 1955, about one-third of U.S. workers belonged to unions. Union membership as a fraction of the workforce has since declined. Now, only one in seven U.S. workers belongs to a union. Government workers, who account for just one in six U.S. workers, now make up nearly half of all union members. A typical union member is a schoolteacher. Compared

2. Jesse McKinley, "$100 Tickets? Here's Why," *New York Times*, 8 April 1999.

WALL STREET JOURNAL

Reading It Right

What's the relevance of the following statement from the Wall Street Journal: *"The United Auto Workers lost its bid to represent 4,800 workers at Nissan Motor Co.'s auto factory in Smyrna, Tenn. . . . the latest in a string of failed efforts."*

RIGHT-TO-WORK STATES

States where workers in unionized companies do not have to join the union or pay union dues

with other industrialized countries, the United States ranks relatively low in the extent of unionization, though rates abroad are also declining.

The bar graph in Exhibit 8 indicates U.S. union membership rates by age and gender. The rates for men, shown by the green bars, are higher than the rates for women, in part because men are in manufacturing and women work more in the service sector, where union membership is lower. The highest membership rates are for middle-aged males. Although the exhibit does not show it, black employees have a higher union membership rate than their white counterparts (17 percent versus 13 percent), in part because black people are employed more by government and by heavy industries such as autos and steel, where union representation is higher. Union membership among those of Hispanic origin, who can be of any race, averaged only 11 percent.

Union membership rates also vary across states. New York had the highest unionization rate at 26.7 percent and North Carolina has the lowest at 3.7 percent. Unionization rates in right-to-work states average only half the rates in other states. In **right-to-work states**, workers in unionized companies do not have to join the union or pay union dues. Over the years, the number of right-to-work states has increased and this has hurt the union movement. The decline in membership rates is also due partly to structural changes in the U.S. economy. Unions have long been more important in the industrial sector than in the service sector. But employment in the industrial sector, which includes manufacturing, mining, and construction, has declined in recent decades as a share of all jobs. Another factor in the decline of the union movement is a growth in market competition, particularly from

EXHIBIT 8

Unionization Rates by Age and Gender

Unionization rates for men, shown by the green bars, are higher than the rates for women, in part because men are in manufacturing and women work more in the service sector, where union membership is lower. The highest membership rates are for middle-aged males.

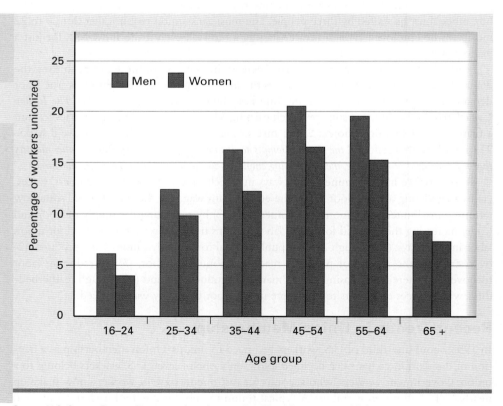

Source: U.S. Census Bureau. Figures are for union membership and percentage of U.S. wage and salary workers for 2002. For the latest figures go to http://www.bls.gov/.

imports. Increased competition from nonunion employers, both foreign and domestic, has reduced the ability of unionized firms to pass on higher labor costs as higher prices. And fewer union members mean fewer voters who belong to unions, so unions have lost political clout.

Finally, the near disappearance of the strike has cut union power. During the 1970s, there were about 300 strikes a year in the United States involving 1,000 or more workers. Such strikes now average only one-tenth that rate. Many recent strikes ended badly for union workers; companies such as Caterpillar, Phelps Dodge Copper, Continental Airlines, and Hormel Foods hired replacement workers. Union members are less inclined to strike because of the increased willingness of employers to hire strikebreakers and the increased willingness of workers—both union and nonunion—to cross picket lines. Strikes also cut company profits, which hurts workers who share in profits, thus dampening the incentive to strike. For example, a recent strike against General Motors cut each worker's average profit share to just $200 from more than $6,000 the year before. Because the strike and the threat of a strike have become less important, the power of unions has diminished.

The final case study examines why unions have achieved only limited success in organizing the fastest growing job sector—that for information technology workers.

Unionizing Information Technology Workers

Despite the demise of many online ventures and the outsourcing of software-related work overseas, information technology (IT) workers still make up a growing sector of the U.S. labor force. The U.S. Bureau of Labor Statistics predicts that job growth in computer and data processing will exceed that of most other fields during the next decade. Because labor unions want to grow, why don't they focus on IT jobs? Well, unions have tried to organize IT workers, but this group poses some special challenges for union organizers.

Compared to traditional union members, such as blue-collar and government workers, IT workers tend to be younger and comprise a motley crew of regular workers, telecommuters, part-timers, temporary workers, freelancers, and a growing number of foreigners on short-term work visas. Unions have a hard time even communicating with such a fragmented, independent bunch. IT firms are also more dynamic than traditional labor strongholds, such as autos, steel, and public schools. By the time a union has targeted an IT firm for organizing, that firm may have already moved, merged with another firm, or folded.

The only union with a significant presence among IT workers is the Communications Workers of America (CWA), which began decades ago with the then regulated phone monopoly, AT&T. The breakup of that monopoly in the early 1980s coupled with technological breakthroughs such as fiberglass and wireless transmission turned telecommunications into a hot, high-tech industry. Thus, CWA was in the right place at the right time. But the union has had difficulty moving into other IT industries. For example, since 1996 it has tried to organize Microsoft's 55,000 workers but has signed up few members. At Silicon Valley firms such as Intel and Hewlett-Packard, unions have successfully organized janitors but not IT workers. Worse yet for CWA, traditional telephone systems are losing ground to Internet-based technologies supplied by companies with no union members, such as Cisco. To keep from falling too far behind, CWA has even hired Cisco to help retrain some CWA members.

C a s e **S t u d y**

The Information Economy

*e*Activity
How successful has the Communications Workers of America (CWA) union been in organizing information technology workers? Check out the union's list of new CWA workplaces at http://www.cwa-union.org/news/articles.asp?category=New+CWA+Workplaces to find the latest on its successes. How many of the latest organizing victories are IT firms? For general news about the labor movement's progress in the IT industry go to *Industry Week*'s Web site at http://www.industryweek.com/ and conduct a search for news on union organizing.

The Internet has reduced the transaction costs of having software development and maintenance carried out overseas. As a result, firms also are outsourcing more IT work overseas to places like India and Ireland, putting that labor out of reach of union organizers. Thus, American IT workers now see their job security threatened by foreign workers on temporary visas and by outsourcing IT work overseas. This trend could motivate some U.S. workers to unionize.

In summary, IT workers are an independent bunch, not easily organized by unions. Trying to organize IT workers has been like trying to herd cats. But the loss of IT jobs to foreign workers could spur greater unionization as American workers seek greater job security.

Sources: Jeff Nachtigal, "Tech Workers, Unions Protest Offshore Outsourcing Conference," *WashTech News*, 17 September 2003; Aliza Earnshaw, "Portland Techies Look for Union Label," *Portland Business Journal*, 27 October 2003; Scott Thurm, "Cisco Systems Helps to Train Union Workers in Web's Ways," *Wall Street Journal*, 3 July 2001; and the CWA Web site at http://www.cwa-union.org/.

Finally, some observers argue that unions have been in decline because employers have discouraged organizing efforts. Although federal law bars employers from firing or penalizing workers for supporting a union, a federal study estimates that employers punished or fired over 125,000 workers between 1992 and 1997 for trying to establish a union.[3] This amount seems like a lot, but it works out to be only about one in a thousand workers during the six-year period. Others say that unions have failed to grow not so much because of what employers do but because of the larger forces in the economy already discussed—right-to-work laws at the state level, growing global competition, the economy's shift from manufacturing to services, the increased reluctance to strike, and the inability to unionize IT workers.

Conclusion

The first half of this chapter focused on labor supply and explained why wages differ across occupations and among individuals within an occupation. The interaction of labor demand and supply determines wages and employment. The second half of the chapter explored the effect of unions on the labor market. At one time unions dominated some key industries. But as global competition intensifies, employers have a harder time passing higher union labor costs along to consumers. Both in the United States and in other industrial economies, union members represent a dwindling segment of the labor force.

SUMMARY

1. The demand for labor curve shows the relationship between the wage and the quantity of labor producers are willing and able to hire, other things constant. The supply of labor curve shows the relationship between the wage and the quantity of labor workers are willing and able to supply, other things constant. The intersection of labor demand and labor supply curves determines the market wage and market employment.

2. People allocate their time to maximize utility. There are three uses of time: market work, nonmarket work, and leisure. A person attempts to maximize utility by allocating time so that the expected marginal utility of the last unit of time spent in each activity is identical.

3. The higher the wage, other things constant, the more goods and services can be purchased with that wage, so a higher wage encourages labor suppliers to substitute

3. The National Labor Relations Board study was discussed in Steven Greenhouse, "Report Faults Law for Slowing Growth of Unions," *New York Times*, 24 October 2000.

market work for other uses of their time. But a higher wage also increases income, increasing the demand for all normal goods, including leisure. The net effect of a higher wage on the quantity of labor supplied depends on both the substitution effect and the income effect.

4. The supply of labor depends on factors other than the wage, including (a) other sources of income, (b) job amenities, (c) the value of job experience, and (d) worker tastes.

5. Market wages differ because of (a) differences in training and education; (b) differences in the skill and ability of workers; (c) risk differences, both in terms of the workers' safety and the chances of getting laid off; (d) geographic differences; (e) racial and gender discrimination; and (f) union membership.

6. Unions and employers try to negotiate a labor contract through collective bargaining. A major source of union power has been the threat of a strike, which is an attempt to withhold labor from the firm.

7. Inclusive, or industrial, unions attempt to establish a wage floor that exceeds the competitive, or market-clearing, wage. But a wage above the market-clearing level creates an excess quantity of labor supplied, so the union must somehow ration the limited jobs among its members. Exclusive, or craft, unions try to raise the wage by restricting the supply of labor. Another way to raise union wages is to increase the demand for union labor.

8. Union membership as a percentage of the labor force has been falling for decades. Today, only one in seven workers is a union member, compared to one in three in 1955. Reasons for the decline include right-to-work laws, greater global competition, a shift in employment from goods to services, a greater willingness to hire replacements for striking workers, a greater willingness of union members and others to cross picket lines, less political support for the labor movement, and difficulty signing up IT workers.

QUESTIONS FOR REVIEW

1. *(Uses of Time)* Describe the three possible uses of an individual's time, and give an example of each.

2. *(Work and Utility)* Explain the concept of the "net utility of work." How is it useful in developing the labor supply curve?

3. *(Utility Maximization)* How does a rational consumer allocate time among competing uses?

4. *(Substitution and Income Effects)* Suppose that the substitution effect of an increase in the wage rate exactly offsets the income effect as the hourly wage increases from $12 to $13. What would the supply of labor curve look like over this range of wages? Why?

5. *(Substitution and Income Effects)* Suppose that the cost of living increases, thereby reducing the purchasing power of your income. If your money wage doesn't increase, you may work *more* hours because of this cost-of-living increase. Is this response predominantly an income effect or a substitution effect? Explain.

6. *(Nonwage Determinants of Labor Supply)* Suppose that two jobs are exactly the same except that one is performed in

an air-conditioned workplace. How could you measure the value workers attach to such a job amenity?

7. *(Why Wages Differ)* Why might permanent wage differences occur between different markets for labor or within the same labor market?

8. *(Mediation and Arbitration)* Distinguish between mediation and binding arbitration. Under what circumstances do firms and unions use these tools? What is the role of a strike in the bargaining process?

9. *(The Strike)* Why might firms in industries with high fixed costs be inclined to prevent strikes or end strikes quickly?

10. *(Industrial Unions)* Why are unions more effective at raising wages in oligopolistic industries than in competitive industries?

11. *(Craft Unions)* Both industrial unions and craft unions attempt to raise their members' wages, but each goes about it differently. Explain the difference in approaches and describe the impact these differences have on excess quantity of labor supplied.

12. (*C a s e* **S t u d y** : Unionizing Information Technology Workers) Why haven't unions been more successful in organizing IT workers? Graduate and research assistants at New York University in 2000 were granted the right to join unions, but a federal body reversed that decision in 2004. Do you think the unions would have been more successful in organizing this group than IT workers? Why or why not?

PROBLEMS AND EXERCISES

13. *(Market Supply of Labor)* The following table shows the hours per week supplied to a particular market by three individuals at various wage rates. Calculate the total hours per week (Q_T) supplied to the market.

Hourly Wage	Hours per Week			
	Q_1	Q_2	Q_3	Q_T
$ 5	20	0	0	____
6	25	0	0	____
7	35	10	0	____
8	45	25	10	____
9	42	40	30	____
10	38	37	45	____

Which individuals, if any, have backward-bending supply curves in the wage range shown? Does the market supply curve bend backward in the wage range shown in the table?

14. *(Industrial Unions)* Review the logic underlying Exhibit 5. Then determine the effect, on the industry and a typical firm, of an increase in the demand for industry output. Show your conclusions on a graph. Does the magnitude of the increase in demand make a difference?

EXPERIENTIAL EXERCISES

15. *(Wall Street Journal)* On Tuesday the *Wall Street Journal* includes articles and information on careers in the Marketplace section. Turn to the Career Opportunities section where employment opportunities are detailed. Read several position descriptions for jobs that are of interest to you. Identify the education and skill requirements of the positions.

16. *(Wages and Labor Supply)* Interview five of your classmates to determine the nature of their labor supply curves for a summer job. Ask each of them how many hours of work he or she would be willing to supply at wage rates of $10, $15, $20, $25, and $30 per hour. Plot the results on a labor supply diagram. Do any of these individuals exhibit a backward-bending labor supply curve? Is the market supply curve for these five individuals backward bending?

17. (*C a s e* **S t u d y** : Winner-Take-All Labor Markets) Robert Frank's "Talent and the Winner-Take-All-Society" appeared in *The American Prospect* (21 March, 1994) at http://www.prospect.org/print/V5/17/frank-r.html. Read this nontechnical article. What are some of the problems that Frank identifies?

18. *(Unions and Collective Bargaining)* Visit the AFL–CIO Executive Council Actions page at http://www.aflcio.org/aboutaflcio/ecouncil/ and look at some recent actions. Choose one and depict its intended effects, using the models developed in this chapter.

19. *(Wall Street Journal)* It shouldn't be too hard to find a *Wall Street Journal* story dealing with labor unions. Check the Economy page in the First Section, the Work Week report on the front page of the Tuesday *Journal,* or the "Legal Beat" column inside the Marketplace section. What's going on in the world of organized labor? Is the example you found consistent with the trends described in this chapter?

*These exercises require access to McEachern Homework Xpress! If Homework Xpress! did not come with your book, visit **http://homeworkxpress.swlearning.com** to purchase.*

1. Kelly is willing to work 20 hours per week if she's paid $10 per hour. She will work up to 45 hours per week if the wage rate is $20 per hour. However, for each additional dollar per hour, she would cut back on work by one hour per week. In the diagram, sketch both parts of Kelly's labor supply curve.

2. Labor supply schedules for three individuals A, B, and C who work in the same labor market are given in the table below. Each individual has different preferences with respect to how many hours to work for the given set of hourly wages. Draw labor supply curves for each, labeling them S_a, S_b, and S_c accordingly. Use the data in the table to derive and draw the market supply curve.

Wage Rate	Individual A	Individual B	Individual C
$ 0	0	0	0
10	0	20	0
15	0	30	0
20	40	40	0
25	35	50	30

3. New England shoe manufacturers hired workers in a competitive labor market. Use demand and supply curves for labor to illustrate how a wage rate was determined in the market for shoemakers. Shoemakers later formed a union and negotiated a higher wage with all shoe manufacturers. Show the effects of a union wage rate that is higher than the market wage rate. Be sure to identify the quantity of labor that would be demanded and the quantity of labor workers would like to supply.

4. Broadway theater producers must either hire at least nine musicians for each show they stage requiring even one musician or face picket lines of protesting musicians outside their theater doors that keep theatergoers away. Illustrate the effect in the market for musicians when the musicians are successful in having their demands met.

Capital, Interest, and Corporate Finance

W hy can first-run movie theaters charge more than other theaters? Why do you burn your mouth eating pizza? What's seed money and why can't Farmer Jones grow anything without it? What's the big deal with pirated software and music? Why are state lottery jackpots worth much less than the advertised millions? These and other questions are answered in this chapter, which examines capital and investment.

So far, our discussion of resources has focused primarily on labor markets. This emphasis is appropriate because labor generates most income—more than two-thirds of the total. The rewards to labor, however, depend in part on the amount and quality of the other resources employed, particularly capital. A farmer plowing a field with a tractor is more productive than one scraping the soil with a stick. This chapter looks at the role of capital in production—its cost and its expected return. You will learn about the optimal use of capital and how firms finance their investments. Topics include:

- Production, saving, and time
- Consumption, saving, and time
- Optimal investment
- Loanable funds market
- Present value and discounting
- Corporate finance
- Stocks, bonds, and retained earnings

The Role of Time in Production and Consumption

Time is important in both production and consumption. In this section, we first consider the role of time on the production decision, and then show why firms borrow household savings. Next, we consider the role of time in the consumption decision and show why households are rewarded to save, or to defer present consumption. By bringing together borrowers and savers, we find the market interest rate.

Production, Saving, and Time

Economics in the Movies

Suppose Jones is a primitive farmer in a simple economy. Isolated from any neighbors or markets, he literally scratches out a living on a plot of land, using only crude sticks. While his crop is growing, none of it is available for current consumption. Because production takes time, to survive, Jones must rely on food saved from prior harvests. The longer the growing season, the more Jones must save. Thus, even in this simple example, it is clear that *production cannot occur without prior saving.*

Suppose that with his current resources, consisting of land, labor, seed corn, fertilizer, and some crude sticks, Jones grows about 200 bushels of corn a year. He soon realizes that if he had a plow—a type of investment good, or capital—his productivity would increase. Making a plow in such a primitive setting, however, is time consuming and would keep him away from his fields for a year. Thus, the plow has an opportunity cost of 200 bushels of corn. He could not survive this drop in production without enough saving from previous harvests.

The question is: should he invest his time in the plow? The answer depends on the costs and benefits of the plow. We already know that the plow's opportunity cost is 200 bushels—the forgone output. The benefit depends on how much the plow will increase crop production and how long it will last. Jones figures that the plow would boost his annual yield by 100 bushels and would last his lifetime. In making the investment decision, he compares current costs to future benefits. Suppose he decides that adding 100 bushels a year outweighs the one-time cost of 200 bushels sacrificed to make the plow.

In making the plow, Jones engages in *roundabout production.* Rather than working the soil with his crude sticks, he produces capital to increase his productivity. More roundabout production in an economy means more capital, so more goods can be produced in the future. Advanced industrial economies are characterized by much roundabout production and thus abundant capital accumulation.

You can see why production cannot occur without prior saving. *Production requires saving because both direct and roundabout production require time—time during which goods and services are not available from current production.* Now let's modernize the example by introducing the ability to borrow. Many farmers visit the bank each spring to borrow enough "seed money" to get by until their crops come in. Likewise, other businesses often borrow at least a portion of the start-up funds needed to get going. Thus, in a modern economy, producers need not rely on their own prior saving. Banks and other financial institutions serve as *intermediaries* between savers and borrowers. As you will see toward the end of the chapter, financial markets for stocks and bonds also help channel savings to producers. Let's take a look at the incentive to save.

Consumption, Saving, and Time

Did you ever burn the roof of your mouth eating a slice of pizza that hadn't sufficiently cooled? Have you done this more than once? Why do you persist in such self-mutilation? You persist because that bite of pizza is worth more to you now than the same bite two minutes from now. In fact, you are willing to risk burning your mouth rather than wait until the pizza has lost its destructive properties. In a small way, this phenomenon reflects the fact that you and other consumers value *present* consumption more than *future* consumption. You and other consumers are said to have a **positive rate of time preference.**

Because you value present consumption more than future consumption, you are willing to pay more to consume now rather than wait. And prices often reflect this greater willingness to pay. Consider the movies. You pay more at a first-run theater than at other theaters. If you are patient, you can wait to rent the DVD. The same is true for books. By waiting for the paperback, you can save more than half the hardback price. Photo developers, dry cleaners, fast-food restaurants, convenience stores, cable news networks, and other suppliers tout the speed of their services, knowing that consumers prefer earlier availability. Thus, *impatience* is one explanation for a positive rate of time preference. Another is *uncertainty*. If you wait, something might prevent you from consuming the good. A T-shirt slogan captures this point best: "Life is uncertain. Eat dessert first."

Because people value present consumption more than future consumption, they must be rewarded to postpone consumption. Interest is the reward for postponing consumption. By saving a portion of their incomes in financial institutions such as banks, people forgo present consumption for a greater ability to consume in the future. The **interest rate** is the annual reward for saving as a percentage of the amount saved. For example, if the interest rate is 5 percent, the reward, or interest, is $5 per year for each $100 saved. The higher the interest rate, other things constant, the more consumers are rewarded for saving, so the more they save. You will learn more about this later in the chapter.

Optimal Investment

In a market economy characterized by specialization and exchange, Farmer Jones no longer needs to produce his own capital, nor must he rely on his own saving. He can purchase capital using borrowed funds. Suppose he wants to buy some farm equipment. He estimates how each piece of equipment will affect his productivity. Column (1) in panel (a) of Exhibit 1 identifies six pieces of farm machinery that Jones has ranked from most to least productive. The total product of the equipment is listed in column (2), and the marginal product of each piece is listed in column (3). Note that other resources are assumed to be constant.

With just his crude sticks, Jones can grow 200 bushels of corn per year. He figures that a tractor-tiller would boost the harvest to 1,200 bushels. Thus, the tractor-tiller would yield a marginal product of 1,000 bushels per year. The addition of a combine would increase total output to 2,000 bushels, yielding a marginal product of 800 bushels. Note that in this example, diminishing marginal returns from capital set in immediately. Marginal product continues to decrease as more capital is added, dropping to zero for a post-hole digger, which Jones has no use for.

Suppose Jones sells corn in a perfectly competitive market, so he can sell all he wants at the market price of $4 a bushel. The marginal product from column (3) multiplied by $4 yields capital's *marginal revenue product* listed in column (4). The marginal revenue product of

POSITIVE RATE OF TIME PREFERENCE

Consumers value present consumption more than future consumption

INTEREST RATE

Interest per year as a percentage of the amount saved or borrowed

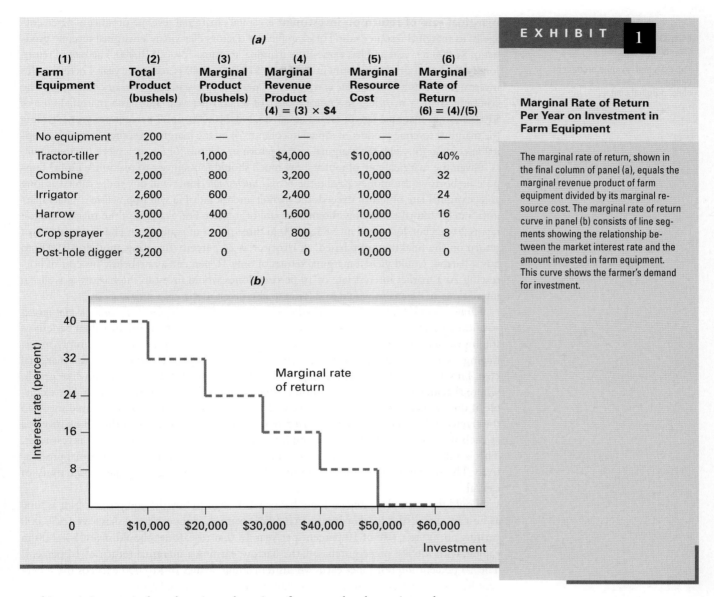

(a)

(1) Farm Equipment	(2) Total Product (bushels)	(3) Marginal Product (bushels)	(4) Marginal Revenue Product (4) = (3) × $4	(5) Marginal Resource Cost	(6) Marginal Rate of Return (6) = (4)/(5)
No equipment	200	—	—	—	—
Tractor-tiller	1,200	1,000	$4,000	$10,000	40%
Combine	2,000	800	3,200	10,000	32
Irrigator	2,600	600	2,400	10,000	24
Harrow	3,000	400	1,600	10,000	16
Crop sprayer	3,200	200	800	10,000	8
Post-hole digger	3,200	0	0	10,000	0

(b)

EXHIBIT 1

Marginal Rate of Return Per Year on Investment in Farm Equipment

The marginal rate of return, shown in the final column of panel (a), equals the marginal revenue product of farm equipment divided by its marginal resource cost. The marginal rate of return curve in panel (b) consists of line segments showing the relationship between the market interest rate and the amount invested in farm equipment. This curve shows the farmer's demand for investment.

machinery is its marginal product times the price of corn, or the change in total revenue resulting from adding another piece of farm equipment.

For simplicity, suppose each piece of farm equipment costs $10,000. Thus, the marginal resource cost is $10,000, as listed in column (5). Suppose also that the equipment is so durable that it is expected to last indefinitely, that operating expenses are negligible, and that the price of corn is expected to remain at $4 per bushel in the future. This farm equipment will increase revenue not only in the first year but every year into the future. The optimal investment decision requires Jones to take *time* into account. He can't simply equate marginal resource cost with marginal revenue product, because the marginal cost is an outlay this year, whereas the marginal product is an annual amount this year and each year in the future. As we will see, *markets bridge time with the interest rate.*

Jones must decide how much to invest in farm equipment. His first task is to compute the *marginal rate of return* he would earn each year by investing in farm machinery. The

marginal rate of return on investment is capital's marginal revenue product as a percentage of its marginal resource cost. For example, the tractor-tiller yields a marginal revenue product of $4,000 per year and has a one-time marginal resource cost of $10,000. The rate of return Jones could earn on this investment is $4,000/$10,000, or 40 percent per year. Therefore, this investment yields a *marginal rate of return* of 40 percent per year, as shown in column (6). The combine yields a marginal revenue product of $3,200 per year and has a marginal cost of $10,000, so its marginal rate of return equals $3,200/$10,000, or 32 percent per year. Dividing the marginal revenue product of capital in column (4) by the marginal resource cost of that capital in column (5) yields the marginal rate of return in column (6) for each piece of equipment.

Given the marginal rate of return, how much should Jones invest to maximize profit? Suppose he borrows the money, paying the *market interest rate*. Jones will buy more capital as long as its marginal rate of return exceeds the market interest rate. He will stop before capital's marginal rate of return falls below the market rate of interest. For example, if the market interest rate is 20 percent, Jones will invest $30,000 in three pieces of equipment. The marginal rate of return on the final item purchased, an irrigator, is 24 percent. Investing another $10,000 to buy a harrow would yield a marginal return of only 16 percent, a rate below his cost of borrowing. At a market interest rate of 10 percent, Jones would invest in the harrow as well. An interest rate of 6 percent would lead Jones to also invest in the crop sprayer.

Farmer Jones should increase his investment as long as the marginal rate of return on that investment exceeds the market rate of interest. The marginal rate of return is the marginal benefit of the investment, and the market interest rate is the marginal cost, so Jones is simply maximizing profit (or minimizing loss) by investing until marginal benefit equals the marginal cost. The data in column (6) are depicted in panel (b) of Exhibit 1 as a step-like graph, where the solid lines reflect the amount Jones will invest at each interest rate. For example, if the market interest rate is between 32 percent and 40 percent, Jones should invest in the tractor-tiller. Because the marginal rate of return shows how much should be invested at each interest rate, this step-like graph represents the farmer's demand for investment. This is a derived demand, based on each additional piece of equipment's marginal productivity. The demand curve steps down to reflect the diminishing marginal productivity of capital.

Would the example change if Jones has saved enough to buy the equipment? Not as long as he can save at the market interest rate. For example, suppose Jones has saved $50,000 earning an interest rate of 10 percent per year. In that case, Jones should invest $40,000 in capital, with the last piece purchased, the harrow, earning a marginal return of 16 percent. The 10 percent interest Jones earns on his remaining savings of $10,000 exceeds the 8 percent he could earn by investing that amount in the crop sprayer. Thus, as long as he can borrow and save at the same interest rate, Jones ends up with the same equipment whether he borrows funds or draws down his own savings. *Whether Jones borrows the money or uses savings on hand, the market interest rate represents his opportunity cost of investing.*

Let's review the steps to determine the optimal amount of investment. First, compute the marginal revenue product of capital. Next, divide the marginal revenue product by the marginal resource cost to determine the marginal rate of return. The marginal rate of return curve becomes a firm's demand curve for investment—that is, it shows the amount a firm is willing and able to invest at each interest rate. The market interest rate is the opportunity cost of investing either borrowed funds or savings, and can be thought of as the supply of investment funds to the firm. A firm should invest more as long as the marginal rate of return on capital exceeds the market rate of interest.

We have now discussed investing in physical capital. Let's shift gears and turn to a less tangible form of capital in the following case study, intellectual property.

The Value of a Good Idea—Intellectual Property

One potentially valuable capital asset is information, or so-called *intellectual property*. But the market for information is unusual. On the demand side, consumers are uncertain about the value of information until they acquire it. But they can't acquire it until they pay for it. So there is a circularity problem. There is also a problem on the supply side. Information is costly to produce, but, once produced, it can be supplied at low cost. For example, the first copy of a new software program may cost over a $100 million to produce, but each additional copy can be streamed over the Internet for virtually nothing.

© Royalty-Free/Corbis

Because of these demand and supply problems, producers of information may have difficulty getting paid for their product. As soon as the producer sells information, that first customer becomes a potential supplier of that information. (Do you have any pirated software?) The original producer has difficulty controlling distribution of the product. To address these problems, laws grant property rights to the creators of new ideas and new inventions. Originators are thereby better able to benefit from their creations. A *patent* establishes property rights to an invention or other technical advances. A *copyright* confers property rights to an original expression of an author, artist, composer, or programmer. And a *trademark* establishes property rights in unique commercial marks and symbols, such as McDonald's golden arches or Nike's swoosh.

Granting property rights is one thing; enforcing them is quite another. Much of the software, music CDs, and movie videos sold around the world, particularly in Vietnam, China, and Russia, are pirated editions of products developed in the United States. In fact, some movies are available on the black market as DVDs before they appear in U.S. theaters. Enforcement of property rights is costly, which diminishes the incentive to create new products and new ideas. Even within the United States, the music industry has been devastated by the ease with which music can shared over the Internet through services such as Napster. Sharing music files online is not a victimless crime: between 1999 and 2003, more than one-fifth of music industry workers lost their jobs as sales declined.

Pirated videos, music, computer games, and software bring no royalties to the artists, no wages to industry workers, no profits to the producers or programmers, and no taxes to the government. For example, Microsoft's XP Professional, which retails for about $400 in the United States, sells in pirated form for only $1.50 in Vietnam. In Russia alone, pirated software costs U.S. producers about $500 million a year in lost revenue. It was concern about piracy that prompted Warner Brothers to release *The Matrix Revolutions* in more than 100 countries simultaneously—an effort to show the movie before it became available on the black market.

The ability to exchange files online now extends beyond music to movies and other forms of intellectual property. Some digital gurus argue that the ease of duplicating data on the Internet dooms copyright protection. They say that anything that can be reduced to bits can be copied. The courts are currently sorting this out. Intellectual property is a capital asset that fuels the information economy. How society nurtures incentives to create new ideas, inventions, and artistic creations will affect economic development around the globe this century.

Sources: Mark McDonald, "Piracy, Counterfeiting on the Rise in Russia," *Knight Ridder Newspapers,* 15 October 2003; Bruce Orwall, "New 'Matrix' Posts Ticket Sales Below the Previous Release," *Wall Street Journal,* 10 November 2003; Ethan Smith, "Music Industry's Woes Deepen with New Job Cuts at Universal," *Wall Street Journal,* 16 October 2003; and the World Intellectual Property Organization at http://www.wipo.int/.

The Market for Loanable Funds

You earlier learned why producers are willing to pay interest to borrow money: *Money provides a command over resources, making both direct production and roundabout production possible.* The simple principles developed for Farmer Jones can be generalized to other producers. The major demanders of loans are firms that borrow to start firms and to invest in physical capital, such as machines, trucks, and buildings, and in intellectual capital, such as patents, copyrights, and trademarks. At any time, a firm has a variety of investment opportunities. The firm ranks its opportunities from highest to lowest, based on the expected marginal rates of return. The firm will increase its investment until the expected marginal rate of return just equals the market interest rate. With other inputs held constant, as they were on the farm, the demand curve for investment slopes downward.

But firms are not the only demanders of loans. As we have seen, households value present consumption more than future consumption; they are often willing to pay extra to consume now rather than later. One way to ensure that goods and services are available now is to borrow for present consumption. Some people also borrow to invest in their human capital. Home mortgages, car loans, credit-card purchases, and college loans are examples of household borrowing. The household's demand curve for loans, like the firm's demand for loans, slopes downward, reflecting consumers' greater willingness and ability to borrow at lower interest rates, other things constant. The government sector and the rest of the world are also demanders of loans.

Banks are willing to pay interest on savings because they can, in turn, lend these savings to those who need credit, such as farmers, home buyers, college students, and entrepreneurs looking to start a new business or buy new capital. Banks play the role of *financial intermediaries* in what is known as the market for loanable funds. The **loanable funds market** brings together savers, or suppliers of loanable funds, and borrowers, or demanders of loanable funds, to determine the market interest rate.

The higher the interest rate, other things constant, the greater the reward for saving. As people save more, the quantity of loanable funds increases. The **supply of loanable funds** curve shows the positive relationship between the market interest rate and the quantity of savings supplied, other things constant, as reflected by the usual upward-sloping supply curve shown as *S* in Exhibit 2.

For the economy as a whole, if the amount of other resources and the level of technology are fixed, diminishing marginal productivity causes the marginal rate of return curve, which is the demand curve for investment, to slope downward. The **demand for loanable funds** curve is based on the expected marginal rate of return these borrowed funds yield when invested in capital. Each firm has a downward-sloping demand curve for loanable funds, reflecting a declining marginal rate of return on investment. With some qualifications, the demand for loanable funds by each firm can be summed horizontally to yield the market demand for loanable funds, shown as *D* in Exhibit 2. Factors assumed constant along this demand curve include the prices of other resources, the level of technology, and the tax laws.

The demand and supply of loanable funds together, as in Exhibit 2, determine the market interest rate. In this case, the equilibrium interest rate of 8 percent is the only one that exactly matches the wishes of borrowers and savers. The equilibrium quantity of loanable funds is $100 billion per year. Any change in the demand or supply of loanable funds will change the market interest rate. For example, a major technological breakthrough that increases the productivity of capital will increase its marginal rate of return and shift the demand curve for loanable funds rightward, as shown in the movement from *D* to *D'*. Such an increase in the demand for loanable funds would raise the equilibrium interest rate to 9 percent and increase the market quantity of loanable funds to $115 billion per year.

LOANABLE FUNDS MARKET

The market in which savers (suppliers of loanable funds) and borrowers (demanders of loanable funds) come together to determine the market interest rate and the quantity of loanable funds exchanged

SUPPLY OF LOANABLE FUNDS

The relationship between the market interest rate and the quantity of loanable funds supplied, other things constant

DEMAND FOR LOANABLE FUNDS

The relationship between the market interest rate and the quantity of loanable funds demanded, other things constant

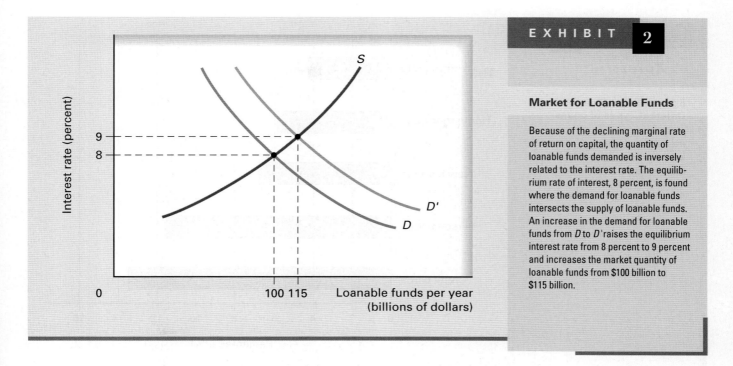

EXHIBIT 2

Market for Loanable Funds

Because of the declining marginal rate of return on capital, the quantity of loanable funds demanded is inversely related to the interest rate. The equilibrium rate of interest, 8 percent, is found where the demand for loanable funds intersects the supply of loanable funds. An increase in the demand for loanable funds from *D* to *D'* raises the equilibrium interest rate from 8 percent to 9 percent and increases the market quantity of loanable funds from $100 billion to $115 billion.

Why Interest Rates Differ

So far, we have been talking about *the* market interest rate, implying that only one rate prevails in the loanable funds market. At any particular time, however, a range of interest rates coexist in the economy. Exhibit 3 shows interest rates for loans in various markets. The lowest is the so-called **prime rate**, the interest rate lenders charge their most trustworthy business borrower. The highest is the rate charged on credit card balances, which is triple the prime rate. Let's see why interest rates differ.

Risk

Some borrowers are more likely than others to *default* on their loans—that is, not to pay them back. Before a bank lends money, it usually requires that a borrower put up **collateral**, which is an asset pledged by the borrower that can be sold to pay off the loan in the event of a default. With business loans, any valuable assets owned by the firm can serve as collateral. With a home mortgage, the home itself becomes collateral. And with car loans, the car becomes collateral. The more valuable the collateral backing up the loan, other things constant, the lower the interest rate changed on that loan. For example, the interest rate charged on car loans is usually higher than on home loans. A car loses its value more quickly than a home does, and a car can be driven away by a defaulting borrower, whereas a home usually increases in value and stays put. So a car offers worse collateral than a home. Interest rates are higher still for personal loans and credit cards, because such borrowers usually offer no collateral.

Duration of the Loan

The future is uncertain, and the further into the future a loan is to be repaid, the more uncertain that repayment becomes. Thus, as the duration of a loan increases, lenders become less willing to supply funds and require a higher interest rate to compensate for the greater

PRIME RATE

The interest rate lenders charge their most trustworthy business borrowers

COLLATERAL

An asset pledged by the borrower that can be sold to pay off the loan in the event the loan is not repaid

Interest Rates Charged for Different Types of Loans

Interest rates are higher for riskier loans. The most trustworthy business customers enjoy the prime rate, the lowest rate. Personal loans and credit card balances face the highest rates, because these loans are riskier—that is, the likelihood borrowers will not repay the loans is greater.

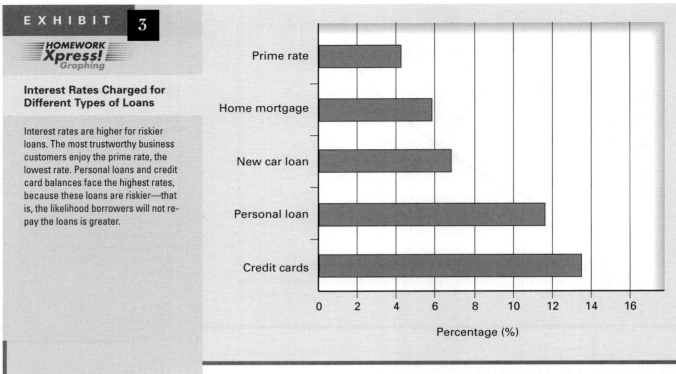

Source: Federal Reserve Board. Interest rates are annual averages during 2002, except for the prime rate, which is for December 2002.

TERM STRUCTURE OF INTEREST RATES

The relationship between the duration of a loan and the interest rate charged; typically interest rates increase with the duration of the loan

risk. The **term structure of interest rates** is the relationship between the duration of a loan and the interest rate charged. *The interest rate usually increases with the duration of the loan, other things constant.*

Cost of Administration

The costs of executing the loan agreement, monitoring the loan, and collecting payments are called the *administration costs* of the loan. These costs, as a proportion of the loan, decrease as the size of the loan increases. For example, the cost of administering a $100,000 loan will be less than 10 times the cost of administering a $10,000 loan. Consequently, that portion of the interest charge reflecting administration costs becomes smaller as the size of the loan increases, other things constant, thus reducing the interest rate for larger loans.

Tax Treatment

Differences in the tax treatment of different types of loans will also affect the interest rate charged. For example, the interest earned on loans to state and local governments is not subject to federal income taxes. Because lenders focus on their after-tax rate of interest, state and local governments can pay a lower interest rate than other borrowers pay.

Present Value and Discounting

Because present consumption is valued more than future consumption, present and future consumption cannot be directly compared. A way of standardizing the discussion is to measure all consumption in terms of its present value. **Present value** is the current value of a payment or payments that will be received in the future. For example, how much would you pay now to receive $100 one year from now? Put another way, what is the *present value* to you of receiving $100 one year from now?

Present Value of Payment One Year Hence

Suppose the market interest rate is 10 percent, so you can either lend or borrow at that rate. One way to determine how much you would pay for the opportunity to receive $100 one year from now is to ask how much you would have to save now, at the market interest rate, to end up with $100 one year from now. Here's the problem we are trying to solve: What amount of money, if saved at a rate of, say, 10 percent, would accumulate to $100 one year from now? We can calculate the answer with a simple formula:

$$\text{Present value} \times 1.10 = \$100$$

or:

$$\text{Present value} = \frac{\$100}{1.10} = \$90.91$$

Thus, if the interest rate is 10 percent, $90.91 is the present value of receiving $100 one year from now; it is the most you would be willing to pay today to receive $100 one year from now. Rather than pay more than $90.91, you could simply deposit your $90.91 at the market interest rate and end up with $100 a year from now (ignoring taxes). The procedure of dividing the future payment by 1 plus the prevailing interest rate to express it in today's dollars is called **discounting.**

The present value of $100 to be received one year from now depends on the interest rate. The more that present consumption is preferred to future consumption, the higher the interest rate that must be offered savers to defer consumption. *The higher the interest rate, the more the future payment is discounted and the lower its present value.* Put another way, the higher the interest rate, the less you need to save now to yield a given amount in the future. For example, if the interest rate is 15 percent, the present value of receiving $100 one year from now is $100/1.15, which equals $86.96.

Conversely, the less present consumption is preferred to future consumption, the less savers need to be paid to defer consumption so the lower the interest rate. The lower the interest rate, the less the future income is discounted and the greater its present value. A lower interest rate means that you must save more now to yield a given amount in the future. As a general rule, the present value of receiving an amount one year from now is:

$$\text{Present value} = \frac{\text{Amount received one year from now}}{1 + \text{interest rate}}$$

For example, when the interest rate is 5 percent, the present value of receiving $100 one year from now is:

$$\text{Present value} = \frac{\$100}{1 + 0.05} = \frac{\$100}{1.05} = \$95.24$$

Present Value for Payments in Later Years

Now consider the present value of receiving $100 two years from now. What amount of money, if deposited at the market interest rate of 5 percent, would yield $100 two years from now? At the end of the first year, the value would be the present value times 1.05, which would then earn the market interest rate during the second year. At the end of the second year, the deposit would have accumulated to the present value times 1.05 times 1.05. Thus, we have the equation:

$$\text{Present value} \times 1.05 \times 1.05 = \text{Present value} \times (1.05)^2 = \$100$$

Solving for the present value yields:

$$\text{Present value} = \frac{\$100}{(1.05)^2} = \frac{\$100}{1.1025} = \$90.70$$

If the $100 were to be received three years from now, we would discount the payment over three years:

$$\text{Present value} = \frac{\$100}{(1.05)^3} = \$86.38$$

If the interest rate is *i*, the present value of *M* dollars *t* years from now is:

$$\text{Present value} = \frac{M}{(1 + i)^t}$$

Because $(1 + i)$ is greater than 1, the more times it is multiplied by itself (as determined by *t*), the bigger the denominator and the smaller the present value. Thus, *the present value of a given payment will be smaller the further into the future that payment is to be received.*

Present Value of an Income Stream

The previous method is used to compute the present value of a single sum to be paid at some date in the future. Most investments, however, yield a stream of income over time. In cases where the income is received for a period of years, the present value of each receipt can be computed individually and the results summed to yield the present value of the entire income stream. For example, the present value of receiving $100 next year and $150 the year after is simply the present value of the first year's receipt plus the present value of the second year's receipt. If the interest rate is 5 percent:

$$\text{Present value} = \frac{\$100}{1.05} = \frac{\$150}{(1.05)^2} = \$231.29$$

Present Value of an Annuity

ANNUITY

A given sum of money received each year for a specified number of years

A given sum of money received each year for a specified number of years is called an **annuity.** Such an income stream is called a *perpetuity* if it continues indefinitely into the future, as it would with the indestructible farm machinery. The present value of receiving a certain amount forever seems like it should be a very large sum indeed. But because future income is valued less the more distant into the future it is to be received, the present value of receiving a particular amount forever is not much more than that of receiving it for, say, 20 years.

To determine the present value of receiving $100 a year forever, we need only ask how much money must be deposited in a savings account to yield $100 in interest each year. If the interest rate is 10 percent, a deposit of $1,000 will earn $100 per year. Thus, the present value of receiving $100 a year indefinitely when the interest rate is 10 percent is $1,000. More generally, the present value of receiving a sum forever equals the amount received each year divided by the interest rate.

The concept of present value is useful in making investment decisions. Farmer Jones, by investing $10,000 in the crop sprayer, expected to earn $800 more per year. So his marginal rate of return was 8 percent. At a market interest rate of 8 percent, the present value of a cash flow of $800 per year discounted at that rate would be $800/0.08, which equals $10,000. Thus, *Jones was willing to invest capital until, at the margin, his investment yields a cash stream with a present value just equal to the marginal cost of the investment.*

What about your decision to invest in human capital—to go to college? A chart in the previous chapter showed that those with at least a college degree earned twice as much as those with just a high school education. We could compute the present value of an education by discounting earnings based on that level of education, then summing total earnings over your working life. Even without carrying out those calculations, we can say with reasonable certainty that the present value of at least a college education will be more than twice that of just a high school education. You also learned way back in Chapter 1 that some college majors earn more than others. For example, among people 35 to 44 years old with a college degree as their highest degree, males who majored in economics had median earnings 55 percent higher than those who majored in philosophy. Among females, that advantage was 91 percent for the same majors. If such an advantage prevailed throughout all working years, the present value of a degree in economics would be 55 percent higher than the present value of a degree in philosophy for males and 91 percent higher for females.

To develop a hands-on appreciation for present value and discounting, let's put the payoff from state lotteries in perspective.

The Million–Dollar Lottery?

Since 1963, when New Hampshire introduced the first modern state-run lottery, 38 states and the District of Columbia have followed suit, generating profits of over $12 billion a year. Publicity photos usually show the winner receiving an oversized check for $1 million or more. But winners get paid in annual installments, so the present value of the prize is much less than the advertised millions. For example, a million-dollar prizewinner usually gets $50,000 a year for 20 years. To put this in perspective, keep in mind that at an interest rate of 10 percent, the $50,000 received in the 20th year has a present value of only $7,432. If today you deposited $7,432 in an account earning 10 percent interest, you would wind up with $50,000 in 20 years (if we ignore taxes).

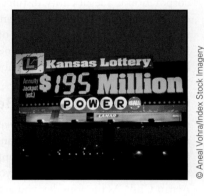

If the interest rate is 10 percent, the present value of a $50,000 annuity for the next 20 years is $425,700. Thus the present value of actual payments is less than half of the promised million, which is why lottery officials pay in installments. The Multistate-Powerball lottery pays out over 25 years, so it's worth even less. Incidentally, we might consider the present value of receiving $50,000 a year forever. Using the formula for an annuity discussed earlier, the present value with an interest rate of 10 percent is $50,000/0.10 = $500,000. Because the present value of receiving $50,000 for 20 years is $425,700, continuing the $50,000 annual payment *forever* adds only $74,300 to the present value. This example shows the dramatic effect of discounting.

In some states, lottery winners can sell their jackpots. Winners typically receive only 40 cents on the dollar for the 20-year annuity. So a million-dollar pot, if sold by the winner, would fetch only $400,000. At tax rates prevailing in 2004, federal income taxes on $400,000 for a single tax filer amount to about $125,000. State and local income taxes could whack another $40,000, depending on the state. Because of time and taxes, the much-touted million could shrink to about $235,000 in after-tax income—less than one-fourth the advertised million.

Among all the forms of legal gambling, state lotteries offer the smallest payout—only $0.55 of every dollar wagered on average goes to winners. Still, lotteries apparently seem like a good bet to some people, especially to the 5 percent of the population who buys half of all the lottery tickets sold.

Sources: "State Lottery Scandals Are Multiplying," *United Press International*, 9 February 2004; Tedra DeSue, "Tennessee Governor Giving Nod to New State Lottery, *The Bond Buyer*, 11 June 2003; Phil Kabler, "West Virginia Lawmakers Fear State Lottery Is Peaking," *Charleston Gazette*, 5 February 2004; and an index of lottery sites found at http://www.state.wv.us/lottery/links.htm.

This discussion of present value and discounting concludes our treatment of capital and interest. We now have the tools to consider how firms, especially corporations, are financed.

Corporate Finance

During the Industrial Revolution, labor-saving machinery made large-scale production more profitable, but building huge factories filled with heavy machinery required substantial investments. The corporate structure became the easiest way to finance such outlays, and by 1920, corporations accounted for most employment and output in the U.S. economy. Way back in Chapter 3, you learned about the pros and cons of the corporate form of business. Thus far, however, little has been said about corporate finance. As noted in Chapter 3, a corporation is a legal entity, distinct from its shareholders. The corporation may own property, earn a profit, sue or be sued, and incur debt. Stockholders, the owners of the corporation, are liable only to the extent of their investment in the firm. Use of the abbreviation Inc. or Corp. in the company name serves as a warning to potential creditors that stockholders will not accept personal liability for the debts the company incurs.

Corporate Stock and Retained Earnings

Corporations acquire funds for investment in three ways: by issuing stock, by retaining some of their profits, and by borrowing. Corporations issue and sell stock to raise money for operations and for new plants and equipment. Suppose you have developed a recipe for a hot, spicy chili that your friends have convinced you will be a best-seller. You start a company called Six-Alarm Chili. As the founder, you are that firm's entrepreneur. An **entrepreneur** is a profit-seeking decision maker who organizes an enterprise and assumes the risk of operation. An entrepreneur pays resource owners for the opportunity to use their resources in the firm. The entrepreneur need not actually manage the firm's resources as long as he or she has the power to hire and fire the manager—that is, as long as the entrepreneur controls the manager.

Your company meets with early success, but you find that to remain competitive, you need to grow faster. To fund that growth, you decide to incorporate. The newly incorporated company issues 1,000,000 shares of stock. You take 100,000 shares yourself as your *owner's equity* in the corporation. The rest are sold to the public for $10 per share, which raises $9 million for the company. You, in effect, pay for your shares with the "sweat equity" required to found the company and get it rolling. The initial sale of stock to the public is called an **initial public offering,** or **IPO.** A *share* of **corporate stock** represents a claim on the net income and assets of a corporation, as well as the right to vote on corporate directors and on other important matters. A person who buys 1 percent of the 1,000,000 shares issued thereby owns 1 percent of the corporation, is entitled to 1 percent of any profit, and gets to cast 1 percent of the votes.

ENTREPRENEUR

A profit-seeking decision maker who organizes an enterprise and assumes the risk of its operation

INITIAL PUBLIC OFFERING (IPO)

The initial sale of corporate stock to the public

CORPORATE STOCK

Certificate reflecting part ownership of a corporation

Corporations must pay corporate income taxes on any profit. After-tax profit is either paid as **dividends** to shareholders or reinvested in the corporation. Reinvested profit, or **retained earnings,** helps the firm finance expansion. Stockholders usually expect dividends, but the corporation is not required to pay dividends. Once shares are issued, their price tends to fluctuate directly with the firm's profit prospects. People buy stock because of the dividends and because they hope the share price will appreciate, or increase.

Corporate Bonds

Again, your corporation can acquire funds by issuing stock, by retaining earnings, or by borrowing. To borrow money, the corporation can go to a bank for a loan or it can issue and sell bonds. A **bond** is the corporation's promise to pay back the holder a fixed sum of money on the designated *maturity date* plus make interest payments until that date. For example, a corporation might sell for $1,000 a bond that promises to make an annual interest payment of, say, $100 and to repay the $1,000 at the end of 20 years.

The payment stream for bonds is more predictable than that for stocks. Unless this corporation goes bankrupt, it must pay bondholders the promised amounts. In contrast, stockholders are last in line when resource suppliers get paid, so bondholders get paid before stockholders. Investors usually consider bonds less risky than stocks, although bonds involve risks as well. Risks include corporate bankruptcy and higher market interest rates. For example, suppose you buy bonds that pay 6 percent interest. After that purchase, the market interest rate increases, so newly issued bonds pay 8 percent interest. Your 6 percent bonds are less attractive than the new bonds, so the market value of your bonds will decline.

Securities Exchanges

Once stocks and bonds have been issued and sold, owners of these securities are free to resell them on *securities exchanges.* In the United States, there are seven securities exchanges registered with the *Securities and Exchange Commission (SEC),* the federal body that regulates securities markets. The largest is the New York Stock Exchange, which trades the securities of about 2,800 major corporations, including about 500 non-U.S. companies. Altogether about 10,000 corporations trade on various U.S. exchanges.

Nearly all the securities traded each business day are *secondhand securities* in the sense that they have already been issued by the corporation. So the bulk of daily transactions do not finance firms in need of investment funds. Most money from daily trading goes from a securities buyer to a securities seller. *Institutional investors,* such as banks, insurance companies, and mutual funds, account for over half the trading volume on major exchanges. By providing a *secondary market* for securities, exchanges enhance the *liquidity* of these securities—that is, the exchanges make the securities more readily sold for cash and thus more attractive to own.

The secondary markets for stocks also determine the current market value of the corporation. The market value of a firm at any given time can be found by multiplying the share price by the number of shares issued. Because the share price changes throughout the trading day, so does the value of the corporation. In theory, the share price reflects the present value of the discounted stream of expected profit. Just to give you some idea, General Electric, the top-valued U.S. firm, had a market value of $346.2 billion at the end of the trading day on September 1, 2004. The 2,300 U.S. corporations traded on the New York Stock Exchange had a combined value of about $12 trillion.

Securities prices give the firm's management some indication of the wisdom of raising investment funds through retained earnings, new stock issues, or new bond issues. The greater a corporation's expected profit, other things constant, the higher the value of shares on the stock market and the lower the interest rate that would have to be paid on new bond issues. Securities markets usually promote the survival of the fittest by allocating investment funds to those firms that seem able to make the most profitable use of those funds. *Thus, securities markets allocate funds more readily to successful firms than to firms in financial difficulty.* Some firms may be in such poor shape that they can't issue new securities.

One final point: When economists talk about investing, they have in mind purchases of new capital, such as new machines and new buildings. When the media talk about investing, they usually mean buying stocks and bonds. To an economist, Farmer Jones is investing only when he buys new farm machinery, not when he buys stocks. As noted already, the overwhelming share of stock transactions are in secondary markets, so the money goes from buyers to sellers, and does not go toward new capital purchases.

Conclusion

This chapter introduced you to capital, interest, and corporate finance. Capital is a more complicated resource than this chapter has conveyed. For example, the demand curve for investment is a moving target, not the stable relationship drawn in Exhibit 1. An accurate depiction of the investment demand curve calls for knowledge of the marginal product of capital and the price of output in the future. But capital's marginal productivity changes with breakthroughs in technology and with changes in the employment of other resources. The future price of the product can also vary widely. Consider, for example, the dilemma of a firm contemplating an investment in oil-drilling rigs in recent years, when the price of crude oil fluctuated between $10 and more than $50 per barrel, as it has since 1998.

SUMMARY

1. Production cannot occur without savings, because both direct production and roundabout production require time—time during which the resources required for production must be paid. Because people value present consumption more than future consumption, they must be rewarded to defer consumption. Interest is the reward to savers for forgoing present consumption and the cost to borrowers for being able to spend now.

2. Choosing the profit-maximizing level of capital is complicated because capital purchased today yields a stream of benefit for years into the future. The marginal rate of return on capital equals the marginal revenue product of that capital as a percent of its marginal resource cost. The profit-maximizing firm invests up to the point where its marginal rate of return on capital equals the market rate

of interest. The market interest rate is the opportunity cost of investment.

3. The demand and supply of loanable funds determine the market interest rate. At any given time, interest rates may differ because of differences in risk, maturity, administrative costs, and tax treatment.

4. Corporations secure investment funding from three sources: new stock issues, retained earnings, and borrowing (either directly from a bank or by issuing bonds). Once new stocks and bonds are issued, they are then bought and sold on securities markets. The value of corporate stocks and bonds tends to vary directly with the firm's profit prospects. More profitable firms have more ready access to funds needed for expansion.

QUESTIONS FOR REVIEW

1. *(Role of Time)* Complete the following sentences with a word or a phrase:

   a. If Bryan values current consumption more than future consumption, he has a _____.

   b. The reward to households for forgoing current consumption is _____.

   c. Producing capital goods rather than producing final goods is known as _____.

2. *(Consumption, Saving, and Time)* Explain why the supply of loanable funds curve slopes upward to the right.

3. *(Why Interest Rates Differ)* At any given time, a range of interest rates prevails in the economy. What are some factors that contribute to differences among interest rates?

4. *(Present Value of an Annuity)* Why is $10,000 a close approximation of the price of an annuity that pays $1,000 each year for 30 years at 10 percent annual interest?

5. *(Present Value of an Annuity)* Suppose you are hired by your state government to determine the profitability of a lottery offering a grand prize of $10 million paid out in equal annual installments over 20 years. Show *how* to calculate the cost to the state of paying out such a prize. Assume payments are made at the end of each year.

6. (*C a s e* **S t u d y:** The Million-Dollar Lottery?) In many states with lotteries, people can take their winnings in a single, discounted, lump-sum payment or in a series of annual payments for 20 years. What factors should a winner consider in determining how to take the money?

7. *(Corporate Finance)* Describe the three ways in which corporations acquire funds for investment.

8. *(Securities Exchanges)* What role do securities exchanges play in financing corporations?

PROBLEMS AND EXERCISES

9. *(Optimal Investment)* Look back at Exhibit 1 in this chapter. If the marginal resource cost rose to $24,000 what would be the optimal investment at a market interest rate of 10 percent? If the interest rate then rose to 16.6 percent, what would be the optimal level of investment?

10. *(Market for Loanable Funds)* Using the demand-supply for loanable funds diagram, show the effect on the market interest rate of each of the following:

    a. An increase in the marginal resource cost of capital
    b. An increase in the marginal productivity of capital
    c. A shift in preferences toward present consumption and away from future consumption

11. *(Present Value)* Calculate the present value of each of the following future payments. (For some of these problems you may wish to use the online calculator available at http://www.moneychimp.com/articles/finworks/fmpresval.htm.)

    a. A $10,000 lump sum received 1 year from now if the market interest rate is 8 percent
    b. A $10,000 lump sum received 2 years from now if the market interest rate is 10 percent
    c. A $1,000 lump sum received 3 years from now if the market interest rate is 5 percent
    d. A $25,000 lump sum received 1 year from now if the market interest rate is 12 percent
    e. A $25,000 lump sum received 1 year from now if the market interest rate is 10 percent
    f. A perpetuity of $500 per year if the market interest rate is 6 percent

12. *(Present Value of an Income Stream)* Suppose the market interest rate is 10 percent. Would you be willing to lend $10,000 if you were guaranteed to receive $1,000 at the end of each of the next 12 years plus a $5,000 payment 15 years from now? Why or why not?

EXPERIENTIAL EXERCISES

13. (*C a s e* **S t u d y :** The Value of a Good Idea—Intellectual Property) MIT's Michael Kremer has suggested an interesting way to encourage innovation in drug development. The basic idea is explained in a nontechnical article in the 15 June 1996 issue of *The Economist* at http://rider. wharton.upenn.edu/~faulhabe/790/patent_cure-all.html. Take a look at the article and determine how Kremer places a value on an innovation.

14. (*Corporate Finance*) Read Jane Katz, "Who Should Be in Charge," in the Federal Reserve Bank of Boston's *Regional Review* at http://www.bos.frb.org/economic/nerr/ rr1997/fall/katz97_4.htm.. What are some of the current issues in corporate finance outlined by Katz?

15. (*Wall Street Journal*) Each day, the *Wall Street Journal* highlights a key interest rate in a graph in the left column of the first page of the Money and Investing section. Compare the graphs over several days and you will see the movements in rates for different securities. How have interest rates changed over the past year? Compare the graphs for several different securities. Have the rates on the various securities moved identically?

HOMEWORK XPRESS! EXERCISES

These exercises require access to McEachern Homework Xpress! If Homework Xpress! did not come with your book, visit **http://homeworkxpress.swlearning.com** *to purchase.*

1. Medical Receptionists, Inc. (MRI), handles the paperwork for filing of medical insurance claims. The work can be done entirely by hand, but by investing in computers the company can process more forms in the same amount of time. The relationship between the number of computers in which MRI invests and the total product—number of claims processed—is shown in the table below. MRI receives $20 per claim processed. Each computer would require an investment of $2,000. Given this information find the marginal rate of return on each computer and plot the data in the diagram.

Number of Computers	Total product
0	100
1	600
2	1,000
3	1,300
4	1,500
5	1,600
6	1,600

2. In the graph, draw a supply of loanable funds. Add a demand for loanable funds such that the equilibrium interest rate is 5 percent and the quantity of funds loaned is $100 billion per year. Show how an increase in demand for loanable funds arising from newfound optimism in the business community about future economic growth could increase the interest rate to 7 percent, while the amount of lending increases to $120 billion per year.

3. In the graph, draw a demand for loanable funds. Add a supply of loanable funds that are available for home mortgages and identify the market rate of interest for mortgages and the quantity of funds lent. Lenders are less willing to lend for new car loans than for homes, so draw a second supply curve representing the supply of loanable funds for new car loans. Identify the rate of interest and quantity of funds lent for purchasing new cars.

Transaction Costs, Imperfect Information, and Market Behavior

© Ken Osborn/Index Stock Imagery

G eneral Motors offers car loans and issues credit cards, so why don't some credit card companies make automobiles? Why do some firms, such as Domino's Pizza, specialize in a single product, while other firms, such as General Electric, make hundreds of different products? Why stop at hundreds? Why not thousands? In fact, why isn't there a giant firm that makes everything? Why is proper spelling important on your résumé? Why is buying a used car so dicey? Why do some winners of online auctions end up losers? Answers to these and other seemingly unrelated questions are addressed in this chapter, which digs deeper into assumptions about firms and the availability information in the market.

In the first half of this chapter, we will step inside the firm to reconsider some simplifying assumptions about how firms work. We ask: Why do firms exist? How do they decide what to make and what to buy from other firms? These steps toward realism move us beyond the simple depiction of the firm employed to this point. In the second half of this chapter, we challenge some simplifying assumptions about the information available to market participants. We ask: How does the lack of certain information affect the behavior and shape market outcomes? Overall, this chapter should help you develop a more realistic view of how markets work. Topics discussed include:

- Transaction costs
- Vertical integration
- Economies of scope
- Optimal search
- Winner's curse

- Asymmetric information
- Adverse selection
- Principal-agent problem
- Moral hazard
- Signaling and screening

Rationale for the Firm and Its Scope of Operation

The competitive model assumes that all participants in the market know everything they need to about the price and availability of all inputs, outputs, and production processes. The firm is assumed to be headed by a brilliant decision maker with a computer-like ability to calculate all the relevant marginal products. This individual knows everything necessary to solve complex production and pricing problems. The irony is that if the marginal products of all inputs could be measured easily and if prices for all inputs could be determined without cost, there would be little reason for production to take place in firms. In a world characterized by perfect competition, perfect information, constant returns to scale, and costless exchange, the consumer could bypass the firm to deal directly with resource suppliers, purchasing inputs in the appropriate amounts. Someone who wanted a table could buy timber, have it milled, contract with a carpenter, contract with a painter, and end up with a finished product. The consumer could carry out transactions directly with each resource supplier.

The Firm Reduces Transaction Costs

So why is production carried out within firms? Nearly 70 years ago, in a classic article entitled "The Nature of the Firm," Nobel Prize winner Ronald Coase asked the question, "Why do firms exist?"[1] Why do people organize in the hierarchical structure of the firm and coordinate their decisions through a manager rather than simply rely on market exchange? His answer would not surprise today's students of economics: *Organizing activities through the hierarchy of the firm is usually more efficient than market exchange because production requires the coordination of many transactions among many resource suppliers.* In short, firms are superior to markets when production is complicated.

Consider again the example of purchasing a table by contracting directly with all the different resource suppliers—from the timber logger to the painter who applied the finishing varnish. Using resource markets directly involves (1) the cost of determining what inputs are needed and how they should be combined and (2) the cost of reaching an agreement with each resource supplier *over and above* the direct costs of the timber, nails, machinery, paint, and labor required to make the table. Where inputs are easily identified, measured, priced, and hired, production can be carried out through a price-guided "do it yourself" approach using the market. For example, getting your house painted is a relatively simple

1. *Economica* 4 (November 1937): 386–405.

task: You can buy the paint and brushes and hire painters by the hour. You become your own painting contractor, hiring inputs in the market and combining them to do the job.

Where the costs of identifying the appropriate inputs and negotiating for each specific contribution are high, the consumer minimizes transaction costs by purchasing the finished product from a firm. For example, although some people serve as their own contractor when painting a house, fewer do so when building a house; most buy a home already built or hire a building contractor. *The more complicated the task, the greater the ability to economize on transaction costs through specialization and centralized control.* For example, attempting to buy a car by contracting with the thousands of suppliers required to assemble one would be time consuming, costly, and impossible for most anyone. What type of skilled labor should be hired and at what wages? How much steel, aluminum, plastic, glass, paint, and other materials should be purchased? How should resources be combined and in what proportions? Anyone without detailed knowledge of auto production couldn't do it. (General Motors and Ford, for example, deal with some 30,000 suppliers.) That's why consumers buy assembled cars rather than contract separately with each resource supplier.

At the margin, some activities could go either way, with some consumers using firms and some hiring resources directly in markets. The choice depends on each consumer's skill and opportunity cost of time. For example, some people may not want to be troubled with hiring all the inputs to get their house painted. Instead, they simply hire a firm for an agreed-on price—they hire a painting contractor. As you will see later in the chapter, however, hiring a contractor may give rise to other problems of quality control.

The Boundaries of the Firm

So far, the chapter has explained why firms exist: *Firms minimize the transaction costs and the production costs of economic activity.* The next question is: What are the efficient boundaries of the firm? The theory of the firm described in earlier chapters is largely silent on the boundaries of the firm—that is, on the appropriate degree of vertical integration. **Vertical integration** is the expansion of a firm into stages of production earlier or later than those in which it specializes. For example, a steel company may decide (1) to integrate backward to mine iron ore or even mine the coal used to smelt iron ore (U.S. Steel owns coal mines) or (2) to integrate forward to fashion raw steel into various components. A large manufacturer employs an amazing variety of production processes, but on average about half of the cost of production goes to purchase inputs from other firms. For example, General Motors and Ford each spend over $80 billion a year on parts, materials, and services. The combined total exceeds the annual output of most economies of the world.

VERTICAL INTEGRATION

The expansion of a firm into stages of production earlier or later than those in which it specializes, such as a steel maker that also mines iron ore

How does the firm determine which activities to undertake and which to purchase from other firms? Should IBM manufacture its own computer chips or buy them from another firm? The answer depends on the benefits and costs of internal production versus market purchases. The point bears repeating: *Internal production and market purchases are alternative ways of organizing transactions.* The choice will depend on which is a more efficient way of carrying out the transaction in question. Keep in mind that market prices coordinate transactions *between* firms, whereas managers coordinate activities *within* firms. The market coordinates resources by meshing the independent plans of separate decision makers, but a firm coordinates resources through the conscious direction of the manager.

The usual assumption is that transactions will be organized by market exchange unless markets pose problems. Market exchange allows each firm to benefit from specialization and comparative advantage. For example, IBM can specialize in making computers and buy chips from Intel, a specialist. Computer chips are a standard product, but sometimes the input is not standardized or the exact performance requirements are hard to specify. For example, suppose one firm wants to hire another firm to supply research and development services. The uncertainty involved in such a nonspecific service makes it difficult to write, execute, and enforce a purchase agreement covering all possible contingencies that could arise. What if the R&D supplier, in the course of fulfilling the agreement, makes a valuable discovery for a different application? Who has the right to that discovery—the firm that paid for the R&D service or the firm that came up with it? And who determines if the application is different? Because incomplete contracts create potentially troublesome situations, conducting research and development *within the firm* often involves a lower transaction cost than purchasing it in the market.

At this point, it might be useful to discuss specific criteria the firm considers when deciding whether to purchase a particular input from the market, thereby benefiting from another producer's comparative advantage, or to produce that input internally.

Bounded Rationality of the Manager

To direct and coordinate activity in a conscious way in the firm, a manager must understand how all the pieces of the puzzle fit together. As the firm takes on more and more activities, however, the manager may start losing track of details, so the quality of managerial decisions suffers. The more tasks the firm takes on, the longer the lines of communication between the manager and the production workers who must implement the decision. One constraint on vertical integration is the manager's **bounded rationality,** which limits the amount of information a manager can comprehend about the firm's operation. As the firm takes on more and more functions, coordination and communication become more difficult. The firm can experience diseconomies similar to those it experiences when it expands output beyond the efficient scale of production. The solution is for the firm to reduce its functions to those it does best. Such cutbacks occurred when automakers increased the proportion of parts they purchased from other firms.

Minimum Efficient Scale

As noted when firm costs were first discussed, the *minimum efficient scale* is the minimum level of output at which economies of scale are fully exploited. For example, suppose that minimum efficient scale in the production of personal computers is 1 million per year, as shown by the long-run average cost curve in panel (a) of Exhibit 1. Suppose this turns out to be the amount the firm needs to produce to maximize profit. Because the computer chip is an important component in a personal computer, should the PC maker integrate backward into chip production? What if the minimum efficient scale in chip production is 5 million per year? As you can see in panel (b) of Exhibit 1, the average cost of producing 1 million chips is much higher than the average cost at the minimum efficient scale of chip production. The PC manufacturer therefore minimizes costs by buying chips from a chip maker of optimal size. More generally, *other things constant, a firm should buy an input if the market price is below what it would cost the firm to make.*

Easily Observable Quality

If an input is well defined and its quality is easily determined at the time of purchase, that input is more likely to be purchased in the market than produced internally, other things constant. For example, a flourmill will typically buy wheat in the market rather than grow its own, as the quality of the wheat can be easily assessed on inspection. In contrast, the quality of certain inputs can be determined only as they are produced. Firms whose reputations depend on the operation of a key component are likely to produce the component, especially if the quality varies widely across producers over time and can't be easily observed by

BOUNDED RATIONALITY

The notion that there is a limit to the information that a firm's manager can comprehend and act on

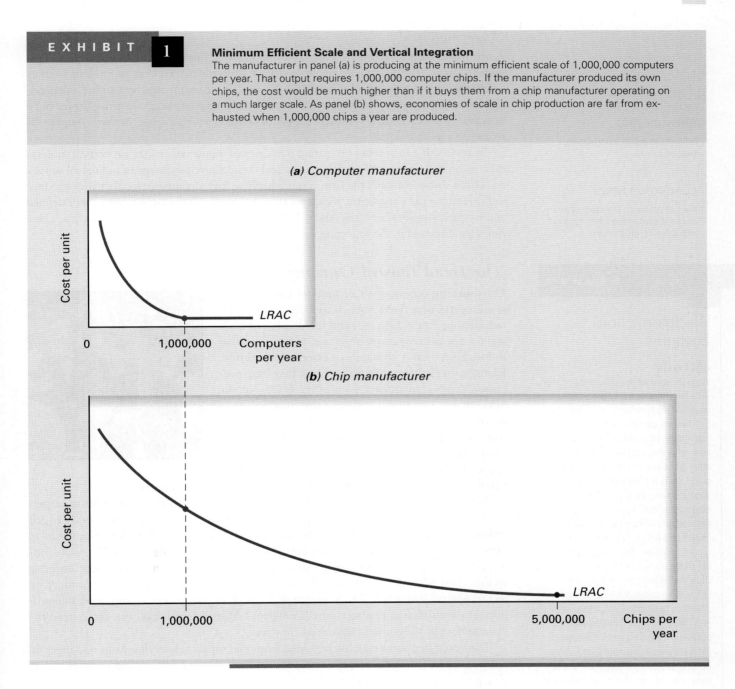

EXHIBIT 1

Minimum Efficient Scale and Vertical Integration
The manufacturer in panel (a) is producing at the minimum efficient scale of 1,000,000 computers per year. That output requires 1,000,000 computer chips. If the manufacturer produced its own chips, the cost would be much higher than if it buys them from a chip manufacturer operating on a much larger scale. As panel (b) shows, economies of scale in chip production are far from exhausted when 1,000,000 chips a year are produced.

(a) Computer manufacturer

(b) Chip manufacturer

inspection. For example, suppose that the manufacturer of a sensitive measuring instrument requires a crucial gauge, the quality of which can be observed only as the gauge is assembled. If the firm produces the gauge itself, it can closely monitor quality.

Producers sometimes integrate backward so they can offer consumers a guarantee about the quality of the components or ingredients in a product. For example, some chicken suppliers such as Tyson and Purdue can advertise the upbringing of their chickens because they raise their own. KFC, however, omits this family background because the company makes no claim about raising them.

Many Suppliers

A firm wants an uninterrupted source of components. If there are many suppliers of a component, a firm is more likely to purchase that input in the market than to produce it internally, other things constant. Not only does the existence of many suppliers ensure a dependable source of components, competition among these suppliers keeps the price down. But a firm that cannot rely on a consistent supply of components may make its own components to ensure a reliable supply.

To review: If a firm relies on market purchases of inputs rather than on vertical integration, it can benefit from the specialization and comparative advantage of individual suppliers. Other things constant, the firm is more likely to buy a component rather than produce it if (1) buying the component is cheaper than making it, (2) the component is well defined and its quality easily observable, and (3) there are many suppliers of the component. These issues are discussed in the following case study.

The Trend Toward Outsourcing

© Brian Lee/Corbis

Outsourcing occurs when a firm buys products, such as auto parts, or services, such as data processing, from outside suppliers. A firm relies on the division of labor and the law of comparative advantage to focus on what it does best, what it considers its **core competency**. Firms, particularly manufacturing firms, have long purchased some components from other firms, but the outsourcing movement extends this practice to a broader range of products and activities that typically had been produced internally. Japanese firms pioneered outsourcing to reduce production costs and enhance quality. In the United States, outsourcing blossomed in manufacturing during the 1980s and spread to virtually every industry.

For example, DuPont, which produces hundreds of products from chemicals to carpeting, outsources the shipping of all imports and exports. Dell Computer, the world's largest online, phone, and mail-order seller of personal computers, also turns over shipping to an outside firm. Many computer firms outsource computer assembly. Even Microsoft outsources some software development. About a dozen wine makers outsource grape crushing to the Napa Wine Company. And in what may be the largest outsourcing contract on record, Merrill Lynch is paying $1 billion for IT support provided by a team of outside vendors. The outsourcing contract runs 1,500 pages. Merrill Lynch has even outsourced the management of all its other outsourced contracts.

The boom in outsourcing has benefited firms that supply what other firms no longer do for themselves. IBM's major business has shifted from selling hardware and software to servicing firms that have outsourced their information technology needs. As noted in a previous chapter, firms in India have sprung up to offer IT services to major U.S. corporations, usually supplying these services over the Internet. Many U.S. corporations have outsourced customer-service call centers to India and the Philippines. For example, Microsoft customers now get their email and phone call queries answered from India.

Perhaps the poster child of outsourcing is Stone Mountain Accessories. Not long ago the company had 500 employees scattered across three manufacturing and distribution plants in Georgia. But Stone Mountain was losing money and would have failed had it not outsourced most functions and trimmed down to a 12-person marketing and design firm. Out-

---

OUTSOURCING

A firm buys inputs from outside suppliers

CORE COMPETENCY

Area of specialty; the product or phase of production a firm supplies with greatest efficiency

Case **Study**

The Information Economy

*e*Activity

Want to learn more about outsourcing? Visit the Outsourcing FAQ at http://www.outsourcing-faq.com/. Should a firm hire an outside consultant to help manage its outsourcing? There are now firms that specialize in helping other firms with outsourcing. For example, Everest provides outsourcing management services at http://www.everestgrp.com/. Look under Our Knowledge and browse through White Papers and Articles to read some of its reports, such as "The Changing Face of the Outsourcing Marketplace." The Outsourcing Institute (http://www.outsourcing.com/content.asp?page=01i/index.html) provides an Internet B2B ("B2B" is short for "business to business.") meeting place for outsourcing managers, consultants, and others. Go to Outsourcing Intelligence and review some of the articles available free to the public to learn more about how outsourcing is evolving.

sourcing allowed the company to lower its price enough to quadruple handbags sales and become profitable.

One problem with outsourcing is the loss of control. For example, when Compaq outsourced some laptop production to a Japanese manufacturer, problems mushroomed in design, cost, and quality. Compaq now has a management team that oversees outsourced activities. Some companies fear that outsourcing can weaken customer ties. For example, several automakers had to recall 8 million vehicles because of faulty seat belts from a Japanese supplier. Customers blamed the auto companies for the recall, not the subcontractor. But in general, outsourcing allows a firm to focus on what it does best and turn over everything else to other firms that focus on what they do best. The law of comparative advantage reduces the cost of production and benefits consumers.

Sources: Todd Datz, "IT Outsourcing: Merrill Lynch's $1 Billion Bet," *CIO Magazine*, 15 September 2003; Lisa Fickenscher, "Handbag Maker Plays China Card," *Crain's New York Business*, 19 January 2004, http://www. crainsny.com; James Hookway, "At 2 A.M. in Manila, It's Time to Break for a Midday Snack," *Wall Street Journal*, 20 October 2003; "Microsoft's India Outsourcing Raises Protests," *CNET Asia*, 3 July 2003, http://asia.cnet. com; *Outsourcing Journal*, http://www.outsourcing-journal.com/; and the Outsourcing Institute at http://www. outsourcing.com/.

Economies of Scope

So far we have considered issues affecting the optimal degree of vertical integration in producing a particular product. Even with outsourcing, the focus is on how best to produce a particular product, such as an automobile or a computer. But some firms branch into product lines that do not have a vertical relationship. **Economies of scope** exist when it's cheaper to produce two or more different items in one firm than to produce them in separate firms. For example, General Electric produces hundreds of different products ranging from light bulbs to jet engines to NBC Universal. By spreading outlays for research and development and marketing ("Imagination at work") over different products, GE can reduce those costs. Or consider economies of scope on the farm. A farmer often grows a variety of crops and raises different farm animals—animals that recycle damaged crops and food scraps into useful fertilizer. With economies of *scale*, the average cost per unit of output falls as the *scale* of the firm increases; *with economies of scope, average costs per unit fall as the firm supplies more types of products—that is, as the scope of the firm increases.* The cost of some fixed resources, such as specialized knowledge, can be spread across product lines.

Some combinations don't work out. For example, in 1994, Quaker Oats paid $1.7 billion for the Snapple drink business. After Snapple sales dropped, Quaker Oats sold that business in 1997 for $300 million, less than one-fifth the purchase price. In 1991 AT&T bought NCR, which provides hardware and software for customer transactions. AT&T paid $7.5 billion and after spending another $2 billion trying to make the marriage work, it sold NCR in 1997 for $3.4 billion—taking a $6.1 billion haircut on the deal. Some mergers don't yield the expected economies of scope.

Our focus has been on why firms exist, why they often integrate vertically, why they outsource, and why they sometimes produce a range of products. These steps toward realism move us beyond the simple picture of the firm created earlier. The rest of the chapter challenges some simplifying assumptions about the amount of information available to market participants.

Market Behavior with Imperfect Information

For the most part, our analysis of market behavior has assumed that market participants have full information about products and resources. For consumers, full information involves

ECONOMIES OF SCOPE
Average costs decline as a firm makes different products rather than just one

knowledge about a product's price, quality, and availability. For firms, full information includes knowledge about the marginal productivity of various resources, about the appropriate technology for combining them, and about the demand for the firm's product. In reality, *reliable information is often costly for both consumers and producers.* This section examines the impact of less-than-perfect information on market behavior.

Optimal Search with Imperfect Information

Suppose you want to buy a new computer. You need information about the quality and features of each model and the prices at various retail outlets, mail-order firms, and online sites. To learn more about your choices, you may talk with friends and experts, read promotional brochures and computer publications, and visit online sites. Once you narrow your choice to one or two models, you may visit the mall, or let your fingers do the walking through the *Yellow Pages,* computer catalogs, Internet search engines, newspaper ads, and the like. Searching for the lowest price for a particular model involves a cost, primarily the opportunity cost of your time. This cost will obviously vary from individual to individual and from item to item. Some people actually enjoy shopping, but this "shop 'til you drop" approach does not necessarily carry over to all items. *For most of us, the process of gathering consumer information can be considered nonmarket work.*

Marginal Cost of Search

In your quest for product information, you gather the easy and obvious information first. You may check on the price and availability at the few computer stores at the mall. But as your search widens, the *marginal cost* of information increases, both because you may have to travel greater distances to check prices and services and because the opportunity cost of your time increases as you spend more time acquiring information. Consequently, the marginal cost curve for information slopes upward, as is shown in Exhibit 2. Note that a certain amount of information, I_f, is common knowledge and is freely available, so its marginal cost is zero.

Marginal Benefit of Search

The *marginal benefit* from acquiring additional information is a better quality for a given price or a lower price for a given quality. The marginal benefit is relatively large at first, but as you gather more information and grow more acquainted with the market, additional information yields less and less marginal benefit. For example, the likelihood of uncovering valuable information, such as an attractive feature or a lower price, at the second store or Web site visited is greater than the likelihood of finding this information at the twentieth store or Web site visited. Thus, the marginal benefit curve for additional information slopes downward, as is shown in Exhibit 2.

Optimal Search

Market participants will continue to gather information as long as the marginal benefit of additional information exceeds its marginal cost. *Optimal search occurs where the marginal benefit just equals the marginal cost,* which in Exhibit 2 occurs where the two marginal curves intersect. Notice that at search levels exceeding the equilibrium amount, the marginal benefit of additional information is still positive, but it's below the marginal cost. Notice also that at some point the value of additional information reaches zero, as identified by I_p on the horizontal axis. This level of information could be identified as *full information.* The high marginal cost of acquiring I_p, however, makes it impractical to become fully informed. Thus, firms and consumers, by gathering the optimal amount of information, I^*, have less-than-perfect information about the price, availability, and quality of products and resources.

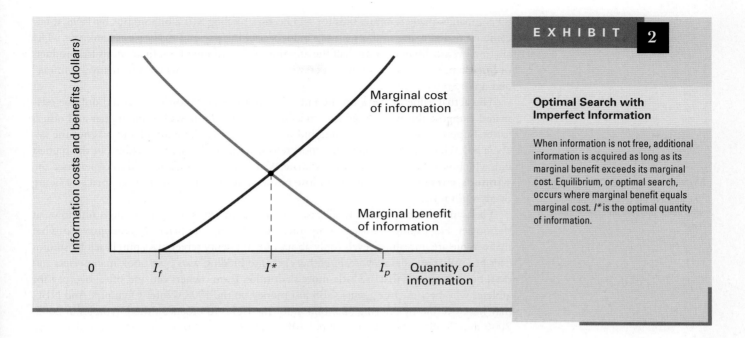

EXHIBIT 2

Optimal Search with Imperfect Information

When information is not free, additional information is acquired as long as its marginal benefit exceeds its marginal cost. Equilibrium, or optimal search, occurs where marginal benefit equals marginal cost. I^* is the optimal quantity of information.

Implications

The search model we have described was developed by Nobel laureate George Stigler, who showed that the price of a product can differ among sellers because some consumers are unaware of lower prices offered by some sellers.[2] Thus, *search costs result in price dispersion, or different prices, for the same product.* Some sellers call attention to price dispersions by claiming to have the lowest prices around and by promising to match any competitor's price (Gateway Computers does this). *Search costs also lead to quality differences across sellers, even for identically priced products, because consumers find it too costly to shop for the highest quality product.* There are other implications of Stigler's search model. The more expensive the item, the greater the price dispersion in dollar terms, so the greater the incentive to shop around. You are more likely to shop around for a new car than for a new comb. Also, as earnings increase, so does the opportunity cost of time, resulting in less searching and more price dispersion. On the other hand, any technological change that reduces the marginal cost of information will lower the marginal cost curve in Exhibit 1, increasing the optimal amount of information and reducing price dispersion. For example, some Internet sites, like mySimon.com, identify the lowest prices for books, airfares, automobiles, computers, and dozens of other products. And some Internet sellers, like Buy.com, maintain the lowest prices on the Web as a way of attracting customers who undertake such searches. Thus, by reducing search costs, the Internet reduces price dispersion.

The Winner's Curse

In 1996, the federal government auctioned off leases to valuable space on the scarce radio spectrum. The space was to be used for cell phones, wireless networks, and portable fax machines. The bidding was carried out in the face of much uncertainty about these new markets. Thus, bidders had little experience with the potential value of such leases. At the time,

---

2. George Stigler, "The Economics of Information," *Journal of Political Economy* (June 1961): 213–225.

89 companies made winning bids for 493 licenses totaling $10.2 billion. But by 1998, it became clear that many of the winning bidders couldn't pay, and many went bankrupt.[3] The auction eventually raised only half the amount of the winning bids. In auctions for products of uncertain value, such as wireless communications licenses, why do so many "winners" end up losers?

The actual value of space on the radio spectrum was unknown and could only be estimated. Suppose the average bid for a license was $10 million, with some higher and others lower. Suppose also that the winning bid was $20 million. The winning bid was not the average bid, which may have been the most reliable estimate of the true value, but the highest bid, which was the most optimistic estimate. Winners of such bids are said to experience the **winner's curse** because they often lose money after winning the bid, the price of being overly optimistic.

The winner's curse applies to all cases of bidding in which the true value is unknown at the outset. For example, movie companies often bid up the price of screenplays to what many argue are unrealistic levels (only about one in twenty screenplays purchased by studios ever become movies). Likewise, publishers get into bidding wars over book manuscripts and even book proposals that are little more than titles. Team owners bid and often overpay for athletes who become free agents. CBS lost money on the 1998 Winter Olympics. And NBC may have overbid by offering $2.3 billion for the rights to broadcast the Olympics in 2002, 2006, and 2008; at the time of the bid, Olympic cities had not even been selected. Online auctions, like eBay, often sell items of unknown value. With perfect information about market value, potential buyers would never bid more than that market value. But *when competitive bidding is coupled with imperfect information, the winning bidder often ends up an overly optimistic loser.*

Asymmetric Information in Product Markets

Economics
in the Movies

We have considered the effects of costly information and limited information on market behavior. But the issue becomes more complicated when one side of the market knows more than the other side does, a situation in which there is **asymmetric information.** There are two types of information that a market participant may want but lack: information about a product's *characteristics* and information about *actions* taken by the other party to the transaction. This section examines several examples of asymmetric information in the product market and the effect on market efficiency.

Hidden Characteristics: Adverse Selection

When one side of the market knows more than the other side about important product characteristics, the asymmetric information problem involves **hidden characteristics.** For example, the seller of a used car normally has abundant personal experience with important *characteristics* of that car: accidents, breakdowns, gas mileage, maintenance record, performance in bad weather, and so on. A prospective buyer can only guess at these characteristics based on the car's appearance and perhaps a test drive. The buyer cannot really know how good the car is without driving it for several months under varying traffic and weather conditions.

To simplify the problem, suppose there are only two types of used cars for sale: good ones and bad ones, or "lemons." A buyer who is certain about a car's type would be willing to pay $10,000 for a good used car but only $4,000 for a lemon. Again, only the seller knows

WINNER'S CURSE

The plight of the winning bidder who overestimates an asset's true value

ASYMMETRIC INFORMATION

One side of the market has more reliable information about the product than does the other side

HIDDEN CHARACTERISTICS

One side of the market knows more than the other side about product characteristics that are important to the other side

---

3. Scott Ritter, "FCC Says Several Bidders to Return Wireless Licenses," *Wall Street Journal,* 18 June 1998.

which type is for sale. A buyer who believes that half the used cars on the market are good ones and half are lemons would be willing to pay, say, $7,000 for a car of unknown quality (the average perceived value of cars on the market). Would $7,000 be the equilibrium price of used cars?

So far, the analysis has ignored the actions of potential sellers, who know which type of car they have. Because sellers of good cars can get only $7,000 for cars they know to be worth $10,000 on average, many will keep their cars or will sell them only to friends or relatives. But sellers of lemons will find $7,000 an attractive price because they know their cars are worth only $4,000. As a result, the proportion of good cars on the market will fall and the proportion of lemons will rise, reducing the average value of used cars on the market. As buyers come to realize that the mix has shifted toward lemons, they will reduce what they are willing to pay for cars of unknown quality. As the market price of used cars falls, potential sellers of good cars become even more reluctant to sell at such a low price, so the proportion of lemons increases, leading to still lower prices. The process could continue until very few good cars are sold on the open market. More generally, *when sellers have better information about a product's quality than buyers do, lower-quality products dominate the market.*

When those on the informed side of the market self-select in a way that harms the uninformed side of the market, the problem is one of **adverse selection.** In our example, car sellers, the informed side, self-select—that is, they decide whether or not to offer their cars for sale—in a way that increases the proportion of lemons for sale. Because of adverse selection, those still willing to buy on the open market often get stuck with lemons.

Hidden Actions: The Principal-Agent Problem

A second type of problem occurs when one side of a transaction can pursue an unobservable *action* that affects the other side. Whenever one side of an economic relationship can take a relevant action that the other side cannot observe, the situation is described as one of **hidden actions.** In this age of specialization, there are many tasks we do not perform for ourselves because others do them better and because others have a lower opportunity cost of time. Suppose your car needs a repair that you can't do yourself. The mechanic you hire may have other objectives, such as maximizing on-the-job leisure or maximizing the garage's profit. But the mechanic's actions are hidden from you. Although your car's problem may be only a loose electrical wire, the mechanic could inflate the bill by charging you for work not needed or not performed. This asymmetric information problem occurs because one side of a transaction can pursue *hidden actions* that affect the other side. When buyers have difficulty monitoring and evaluating the quality of goods or services purchased, some suppliers may substitute poor-quality resources or exercise less diligence in providing the service.

The problem that arises from hidden actions is called the **principal-agent problem,** which describes a relationship in which one party, known as the **principal,** contracts with another party, known as the **agent,** in the expectation that the agent will act on behalf of the principal. *The problem arises when the goals of the agent are incompatible with those of the principal and when the agent can pursue hidden actions.* You could confront a principal-agent problem when you deal with a doctor, lawyer, auto mechanic, or stockbroker, to name a few. Any employer-employee relationship could become a principal-agent problem. Again, the problem arises because the agent's objectives are not the same as the principal's *and* because the agent's actions are hidden. Not all principal-agent relationships pose a problem. For example, when you hire someone to mow your lawn or cut your hair, there are no hidden actions and you can judge the results for yourself.

HOMEWORK Xpress!
Ask the Instructor Video

ADVERSE SELECTION

Those on the informed side of the market self-select in a way that harms those on the uninformed side of the market

HIDDEN ACTIONS

One side of an economic relationship can do something that the other side cannot observe

PRINCIPAL-AGENT PROBLEM

The agent's objectives differ from those of the principal's, and one side can pursue hidden actions

PRINCIPAL

A person or firm who hires an agent to act on behalf of that person or firm

AGENT

A person or firm who is supposed to act on behalf of the principal

Asymmetric Information in Insurance Markets

Asymmetric information also creates problems in insurance markets. For example, from an insurer's point of view, ideal candidates for health insurance are those who lead long, healthy lives and then die peacefully in their sleep. But many people are poor risks for health insurers because of hidden characteristics (bad genes) or hidden actions (smoking and drinking excessively, getting exercise only on trips to the refrigerator, and thinking of a seven-course meal as beef jerky and a six-pack of beer). In the insurance market, it is the buyers, not the sellers, who have more information about the characteristics and actions that predict their likely need for insurance in the future.

If the insurance company has no way of distinguishing among applicants, it must charge those who are good health risks the same price as those who are poor ones. This price is attractive to poor health risks but not to good health risks, some of whom will not buy insurance. Because some healthy people opt out, the insured group becomes less healthy on average, so rates must rise, making insurance even less attractive to healthy people. *Because of adverse selection, insurance buyers tend to be less healthy than the population as a whole.* Adverse selection has been used as an argument for national health insurance.

The insurance problem is compounded by the fact that once people buy insurance, their behavior may change in a way that increases the probability that a claim will be made. For example, those with health insurance may take less care of their health, those with theft insurance may take less care of insured valuables, and those with fire insurance may take less care in fire prevention. This incentive problem is referred to as *moral hazard*. **Moral hazard** occurs when an individual's behavior changes in a way that increases the likelihood of an unfavorable outcome. More generally, *moral hazard is a principal-agent problem because it occurs when those on one side of a transaction have an incentive to shirk their responsibilities because the other side is unable to observe them.* The responsibility could be to repair a car, maintain one's health, or safeguard one's valuables. Both the mechanic and the policy buyer may take advantage of the ignorant party. In the car-repair example, the mechanic is the agent; in the insurance example, the policy buyer is the principal. Thus, moral hazard arises when someone can undertake hidden action; this could be either the agent or the principal, depending on the situation.

MORAL HAZARD

A situation in which one party, as a result of a contract, has an incentive to alter their behavior in a way that harms the other party to the contract

Coping with Asymmetric Information

There are ways of reducing the consequences of asymmetric information. An incentive structure or an information-revealing system can be developed to reduce the problems associated with the lopsided availability of information. For example, some states have "lemon laws" that offer compensation to buyers of new or used cars that turn out to be lemons. Used-car dealers may offer warranties to reduce the buyer's risk of getting stuck with a lemon. Most auto-repair garages provide written estimates before a job is done, and some return the defective parts to the customer as evidence that the repair was necessary and was carried out. Consumers often get multiple estimates for major repairs.

Health insurance companies deal with adverse selection and moral hazard in a variety of ways. Most require applicants to take a physical exam and to answer questions about their medical histories and lifestyles. To avoid adverse selection, an insurer often covers all those in a group, such as all company employees, not just those who would otherwise self-select. Insurers reduce moral hazard by making the policyholder pay, say, the first $250 of a claim as a "deductible" or by requiring the policyholder to co-pay a percentage of a claim. Also, if more claims are filed on a policy, the premiums go up and the policy may be canceled. Property insurers reduce rates to those who install security systems, smoke alarms, sprinkler systems, and who undertake other safety precautions.

HOMEWORK
Xpress!
Ask the Instructor
Video

Asymmetric Information in Labor Markets

Our market analysis for particular kinds of labor typically assumes that workers are more or less interchangeable. In equilibrium, each worker in a particular labor market is assumed to be paid the same wage, a wage equal to the marginal revenue product of the last unit of labor hired. But what if ability differs across workers? Differences in ability present no particular problem as long as these differences can be readily observed by the employer. If the productivity of each worker is easily quantified through a measure such as the quantity of oranges picked, the number of garments sewn, or the number of cars sold, that measure itself can and does serve as the basis for pay. And such per-unit incentives seem to affect output. For example, when the British National Health Service changed the way dentists were paid from "contact hours" with patients to the number of cavities filled, dentists found more cavities and filled them in only a third of the time they took under the contact-hour pay scheme.[4]

But because production often occurs through the coordinated efforts of several workers, the employer may not be able to attribute specific outputs to particular workers. Because information about each worker's marginal productivity may be hard to come by, employers usually pay workers by the hour rather than try to keep track of each worker's contribution to total output. Sometimes the pay combines an hourly rate and incentive pay linked to a measure of productivity. For example, a sales representative typically receives a base salary plus a commission tied to sales. At times, the task of evaluating performance is left to the consumer. Workers who provide personal services, such as waiters, barbers, beauticians, pizza deliverers, and bellhops, are paid partly in tips. These services are "personal" and visible, so customers are usually in the best position to judge the quality and timeliness of service and to tip accordingly.

Adverse Selection in Labor Markets

Suppose an employer wants to hire a program coordinator for a new project, a job that calls for imagination, organizational skills, and the ability to work independently. The employer would like to attract the most qualified person in the market, but the qualities demanded are not directly observable. The employer offers the going wage for such a position. Individual workers are able to evaluate this market wage in light of their own abilities and opportunities. Talented people will find the wage too low and will be less inclined to apply for the job. Less-talented people, however, will find this wage attractive and will be more inclined to seek the position. Because of this adverse selection, the employer ends up with a pool of applicants of below-average ability.

Before being hired, a worker's true abilities—motivation, work habits, skills, ability to get along with others, and the like—are, to a large extent, *hidden characteristics*. In a labor market with hidden characteristics, employers might be better off offering a higher wage. The higher the wage, the more attractive the job is to more-qualified workers. Paying a higher wage also encourages workers not to goof off or otherwise do anything that would risk losing an attractive job. Paying a higher wage to attract and retain more-productive workers is called paying **efficiency wages.**

EFFICIENCY WAGE THEORY

The idea that offering high wages attracts a more talented labor pool, making it easier for firms to hire and retain more-productive workers

Signaling and Screening

The person on the side of the market with hidden characteristics and hidden actions has an incentive to say the right thing. For example, a job applicant might say, "Hire me because I am hardworking, reliable, prompt, highly motivated, and just an all-around great employee." Or a

4. John Pencavel, "Piecework and On-the-Job Screening," *Working Paper,* Stanford University, June 1975.

SIGNALING

Using a proxy measure to communicate information about unobservable characteristics; the signal is more effective if more-productive workers find it easier to send than do less-productive workers

SCREENING

The process used by employers to select the most qualified workers based on readily observable characteristics, such as a job applicant's level of education and course grades

producer might say, "At Ford, quality is job one." But such claims appear self-serving and thus are not necessarily believable. To cut through this fog, both sides of the market have an incentive to develop credible ways of communicating reliable information about qualifications.

Signaling is the attempt by the informed side of the market to communicate information that the other side would find valuable. Consider signaling in the job market. Because some jobs require abilities that are unobservable on a résumé or in an interview, job applicants offer proxy measures, such as years of education, college grades, and letters of recommendation. A proxy measure is called a *signal,* which is an observable indicator of some hidden characteristic. A signal is sent by the informed side of the market to the uninformed side and will be useful as long as less-qualified applicants face more difficulty sending the same signal.

To identify the best workers, employers try to *screen* applicants. **Screening** is the attempt by the uninformed side of the market to uncover the relevant but hidden characteristics of the informed party. An initial screen might check each résumé for spelling and typographical errors. Although not important in themselves, such errors suggest a lack of attention to detail—which would reduce labor productivity. The uninformed party must detect signals that less-productive individuals will have more difficulty sending. A signal that can be sent with equal ease by all workers, regardless of their productivity, does not provide a useful way of screening applicants. But if, for example, more-productive workers find it easier to graduate from college than do less-productive workers, a college degree is a measure worth using to screen workers. In this case, education may be valuable, not so much because of its direct effect on a worker's productivity, but simply because it enables employers to distinguish among types of workers. Indeed, the actual pay increase resulting from a fourth year of college that results in graduation is several times the pay increase from just a third year of college. This finding is consistent with the screening theory of education.

To summarize: Because the potential productivity of job applicants cannot be measured directly, an employer must rely on proxy measures to screen applicants. *The most valuable proxy is a signal that can be sent more easily by more-productive workers and also is a good predictor of future productivity.* The problems of adverse selection, signaling, and screening are discussed in the following case study of how McDonald's chooses franchisees.

The Reputation of a Big Mac

McDonald's has 29,000 restaurants and nearly 500,000 employees in more than 121 countries. The secret to their success is that more than 40 million customers served around the world each day can count on product consistency whether they buy a Big Mac in Anchorage, Moscow, or Hong Kong. McDonald's has grown because it has attracted competent and reliable franchise owners and has provided these owners with appropriate incentives and constraints to offer a product of consistent quality.

To avoid adverse selection, McDonald's seldom advertises for franchisees but still has plenty of applicants for each new restaurant. Even to be granted an interview, applicants must show substantial financial resources and good business experience. Those who pass the initial screening must come up with a security deposit and complete the nine-month training program. A franchise costs anywhere from $460,000 to $800,000, depending on the size and location, plus an opening fee of $45,000. Of that amount, the new franchisee must come up with a minimum of $175,000 in cash; this money can't come from friends or relatives. Having so much saved is used by McDonald's as a signal of the individual's business sense and ability to manage money. The balance can be borrowed from a bank, so McDonald's, in effect, uses the bank's loan officers to screen the applicant's creditworthiness. Those selected as franchisees must also divest themselves of any other business interests.

McDonald's Hamburger University trains thousands each year (offering simultaneous translations in more than 27 different languages). During this training period, the applicant is paid nothing, not even expenses. Some who complete the training are rejected for a franchise. Once the restaurant opens, a franchisee must work full time.

Thus, the franchisee has a clear financial stake in the success of the operation. As a further incentive, successful owners may get additional restaurants. If all goes well, the franchise is valid for 20 years and renewable after that, but it can be canceled *at any time* if the restaurant fails the company's standards of quality, pricing, cleanliness, hours of operation, and so on. The franchisee is bound to the company by highly specific investments of money and time, such as time learning McDonald's operating system. The loss of a franchise would represent a huge financial blow. In selecting and monitoring franchisees, McDonald's has successfully addressed problems stemming from hidden characteristics and hidden actions.

Through its franchise policies, McDonald's is trying to protect its most valuable asset—the reputation of its brand name. McDonald's is the second most recognized symbol of any kind in the world (the Olympic rings rank first). To leverage that brand recognition, the company is experimenting with other products such as McDonald's ketchup in Germany, Golden Arch Hotels in Switzerland, and McCafé coffee bars around the world. The company also will put its McKids brand on a range of products, including toys, bicycles, jungle gyms, apparel, and interactive DVDs. Extending the brand involves some risk. For example, the company could get a black eye if one of these branded products turns out to be defective.

Source: Richard Gibson, "McDonald's Plans to Make 'McKids' a Multifaceted Brand," *Wall Street Journal*, 13 November 2003; "McD's 'I'm Lovin' It' Breaks in U.S.," *Adweek*, 28 September 2003; D. L. Noren, "The Economics of the Golden Arches," *American Economist* (Fall 1990); and "McDonald's Corporate Franchising" at http://www.mcdonalds.com/corp/franchise/faqs.html.

Conclusion

The firm has evolved through a natural selection process as the form of organization that minimizes both transaction and production costs. Ways of organizing production that are efficient will be selected by the economic system for survival. Attributes that yield an economic profit will thrive, and those that do not will fall away. The form of organization selected may not be optimal in the sense that it cannot be improved, but it will be the most efficient of those that have been tried. If there is a way to organize production that is more efficient, some entrepreneur will stumble on it one day and will be rewarded with greater profit. The improvement may not always be the result of any conscious design. Once a more efficient way of organizing production is uncovered, others will imitate it.

In conventional demand-and-supply analysis, trades occur in impersonal markets, and the buyer has no special concern about who is on the sell side. But with asymmetric information, the mix and characteristics of the other side of the market become important. When the problem of adverse selection is severe enough, some markets may cease to function. Market participants try to overcome the limitations of asymmetric information by signaling, screening, and trying to be quite explicit and transparent about the terms of the transaction.

SUMMARY

1. According to Ronald Coase, firms arise when production is more efficient using the hierarchy of the firm than using market transactions. Because production requires elaborate coordination of many resources, all this activity can usually be carried out more efficiently under the direction of a firm's manager than by having a consumer negotiate detailed performance contracts with many resource suppliers.

2. The extent to which a firm integrates vertically will depend on both the transaction and the production costs of economic activity. Other things constant, the firm is more likely to buy a component rather than produce it if (a) it's cheaper to buy it than make it, (b) the item is well defined and its quality easily observable, and (c) there are many suppliers of the item. Economies of scope exist when it is cheaper to produce two or more different products in one firm than to produce them in separate firms.

3. A buyer searches for product information as long as the marginal benefit of search exceeds its marginal cost. Because information is costly, product prices may differ across suppliers.

4. Asymmetric information occurs when one side of the market is better informed about a product than the other side is. The uninformed side may not know about hidden characteristics or about hidden actions. Because of adverse selection, those on the uninformed side of the market may find they are dealing with exactly the wrong people.

5. When the productivity of job applicants is not directly observable, an employer may try to screen them based on some signal that more-productive workers can send more easily than can less-productive workers.

QUESTIONS FOR REVIEW

1. *(Rationale for the Firm)* Explain Ronald Coase's theory of why firms exist. Why isn't all production consolidated in one large firm?

2. *(Bounds of the Firm)* Define vertical integration. What factors should a firm consider when determining what degree of vertical integration to undertake?

3. *(Bounds of the Firm)* Ashland Oil buys its crude oil in the market. Larger oil refiners, such as Texaco, drill for their own crude oil. Why do some oil companies drill for their own crude oil and others buy crude oil in the market?

4. (*C a s e* **Study:** The Trend Toward Outsourcing) In the movement to downsize government, advocates often recommend turning over some government services to private firms hired by the government. What are the potential benefits and costs of such outsourcing? Prepare your answer by reviewing The Outsourcing Institute's "Top 10 Reasons Companies Outsource" at http://www.horizontech.net/toptenreasons.htm.

5. *(Economies of Scope)* Distinguish between economies of scale and economies of scope. Why do some firms produce multiple product lines, while others produce only one?

6. *(Search with Imperfect Information)* Fifty years ago, people shopped by mail using catalogs from large mail-order houses. In the last few years, catalog shopping has again become a widely used method of buying. Online shopping is also growing. What reasons can you suggest for the growth in these forms of shopping?

7. *(Asymmetric Information)* Define asymmetric information. Distinguish between hidden characteristics and hidden actions. Which type of asymmetric information contributes to the principal-agent problem?

8. *(The Principal-Agent Problem)* Discuss the nature of the principal-agent problem. Determine which is the principal and which is the agent in each of the following relationships:

   a. A firm that produces export goods and the export management company that helps market its goods
   b. The management of a firm and its stockholders
   c. A homeowner and the plumber hired to make repairs
   d. A dentist and a patient
   e. An employee-pension management firm and the company using its services

9. *(Adverse Selection and Moral Hazard)* Describe the problems faced by health insurance companies as a result of adverse selection and moral hazard. How do insurance companies try to reduce these problems?

10. *(Signaling)* Give an example of signaling in each of the following situations:

  a. Choosing a doctor
  b. Applying to graduate school
  c. Filling out a form for a dating service

11. *(Signaling and Screening)* What roles do signaling and screening play in a labor market with asymmetric information?

12. (*C a s e* **S t u d y :** The Reputation of a Big Mac) Explain how the time and financial requirements involved in obtaining a McDonald's franchise relate to the hidden-characteristics problem. Why would existing franchise owners have an interest in the maintenance of high application standards for new franchise owners?

PROBLEMS AND EXERCISES

13. *(Search with Imperfect Information)* The following questions concern the accompanying graph.

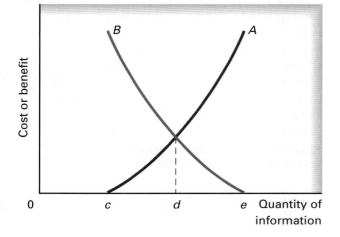

  a. Identify the two curves shown on the graph, and explain their upward or downward slopes.
  b. Why does curve *A* intersect the horizontal axis?
  c. What is the significance of quantity *d*?
  d. What does *e* represent?
  e. How would the optimal quantity of information change if the marginal benefit of information increased—that is, if the marginal benefit curve shifted upward?

14. *(Search with Imperfect Information)* Determine the effect of each of the following on the optimal level of search.

  a. The consumer's wage increases.
  b. One seller guarantees to offer the lowest price on the market.
  c. The technology of gathering and transmitting market information improves.

EXPERIENTIAL EXERCISES

15. *(Market Behavior with Imperfect Information)* Kenneth Arrow, a Nobel laureate, has contributed many important ideas in the economics of information. Read the interview with Arrow in *The Region* at http://woodrow.mpls.frb.fed.us/pubs/region/95-12/int9512.cfm. What does he think are the policy implications that arise because of imperfect information?

16. *(Adverse Selection)* Adverse selection is a serious problem for health insurers. As an example, read the brief analysis

in "Medical Savings Accounts for Medicare" at http://www.ncpa.org/ba/ba183.html. What is the mechanism by which adverse selection can make health insurance unprofitable for private insurers to provide?

17. (*Wall Street Journal*) Once you learn about the economics of asymmetric information, you begin to see examples all around you. To demonstrate this point, check today's *Wall Street Journal*. It should not be too hard to find a story that describes some new development that is a response to an

asymmetric information problem. Look on the Economy page in the First Section or in the Marketplace section. When you've found an article, try to analyze it using the ideas developed in this chapter.

18. (*Wall Street Journal*) Many firms utilize both the concepts of outsourcing and economies of scope. Find an example

of a firm using one of these concepts in the *Wall Street Journal* (try the lead stories, or Industry/Corporate Focus, which appear daily, or the Monday Outlook sections). Analyze the firm's decision in the context of the theories developed in this chapter.

HOMEWORK XPRESS! EXERCISES

These exercises require access to McEachern Homework Xpress! If Homework Xpress! did not come with your book, visit **http://homeworkxpress.swlearning.com** *to purchase.*

1. Charles Cobbler, Inc., maker of fine shoes, could tan the 1,000 units of leather needed for use in its shoes or it could purchase leather from a tannery that produces 10,000 units of leather and supplies numerous shoe producers. Draw a long-run average cost curve and illustrate how economies of scale would enable Charles Cobbler to purchase the leather at a lower cost, C', than if it produces its own at cost C.

2. Ashley is considering purchasing a new car. To obtain quotes on prices from dealers, she plans to visit the dealers' showrooms. One dealer is within walking distance of her home, but others are farther away. The cost of each additional quote therefore rises, as she has to travel farther to get to the showroom. The marginal cost of each is shown in the table. Plot this information in the diagram. Add a downward-sloping marginal benefit of information curve such that the optimal number of quotes is 4.

Quantity of Information	Marginal Cost of Information
1	$ 0
2	1
3	3
4	6
5	10
6	15

3. Anthony and Linda are considering buying their own home. They intend to begin the process by conducting an online search of real estate listings. The value of their time in reviewing each listing is $5. The first five listings that appear as a result of their search most closely match their stated preferences and therefore are the most valuable. Each additional five are less likely to match what they are looking for and therefore are less valuable. The marginal benefits of additional sets of listings are as shown in the table. In the diagram, draw a marginal cost curve illustrating the cost of their time for searching and reviewing each listing. Add the marginal benefit data. Identify the optimal number of listings to review.

Quantity of Information	Marginal Benefit of Information
5	$ 25
10	17
15	11
20	5
25	0

CHAPTER

15

Economic Regulation and Antitrust Policy

© Richard T. Nowitz/Corbis

I f the "invisible hand" of competition yields such desirable results for the economy, why does the government need to regulate business? Is a monopoly ever better than competition? Who benefits the most when government regulates monopoly? Why did the government haul Microsoft into court? Is the U.S. economy getting more competitive or less competitive? Answers to these and other questions are addressed in this chapter, which discusses government regulation of business.

Businesspeople praise competition but they love monopoly. They praise competition because it harnesses the diverse and often conflicting objectives of various market participants and channels them into the efficient production of goods and services. Competition does this as if by "an invisible hand." Businesspeople love monopoly because it provides the surest path to economic profit in the long run—

and, after all, profit is the name of the game. The fruits of monopoly are so tempting that a firm might try to eliminate competitors or conspire with them. As Adam Smith remarked more than two centuries ago, "People of the same trade seldom meet together, even for merriment or diversion, but the conversation ends in a conspiracy against the public, or in some contrivance to raise prices."

The tendency of firms to seek monopolistic advantage is understandable, but monopoly usually harms consumers. Public policy can play a role by promoting competition in those markets where competition seems desirable and by reducing the harmful effects of monopoly in those markets where the output can be most efficiently produced by one or a few firms. Topics discussed include:

- Regulating natural monopolies
- Theories of economic regulation
- Deregulation
- Antitrust policy

- Per se illegality
- Rule of reason
- Merger waves
- Competitive trends

Business Behavior, Public Policy, and Government Regulation

You'll recall that a monopolist supplies a product with no close substitutes, so a monopolist can charge a higher price than would prevail with more competition. When a few firms account for most of the sales in a market, those firms are sometimes able to coordinate their actions, either explicitly or implicitly, to act like a monopolist. The ability of a firm to raise its price without losing all its sales to rivals is called **market power.** Any firm facing a downward-sloping demand curve has some control over the price and thus some market power. The presumption is that a monopoly, or a group of firms acting as a monopoly, restricts output to charge a higher price than competing firms would charge. With output restricted, the marginal benefit of the final unit produced exceeds its marginal cost, so expanding output would increase social welfare. By failing to expand output to the point where marginal benefit equals marginal cost, firms with market power produce too little of the good than would be socially optimal.

Other distortions have also been associated with monopolies. For example, some critics argue that because a monopoly is insulated from competition, it is not as innovative as aggressive competitors would be. Worse still, because of their size and economic importance, monopolies may influence political outcomes, which they use to protect and enhance their monopoly power.

Three kinds of government policies are designed to alter or control firm behavior: social regulation, economic regulation, and antitrust policy. **Social regulation** tries to improve health and safety, such as control over unsafe working conditions and dangerous products. Social regulation has economic consequences, but we will not discuss social regulation in this chapter. **Economic regulation** controls the price, output, the entry of new firms, and the quality of service *in industries in which monopoly appears inevitable or even desirable.* Government controls over *natural monopolies,* such as local electricity transmission, local phone service, and a subway system, are examples of economic regulation. Several other industries, such as land and air transportation, have also been regulated in the past. Federal, state, and local governments carry out economic regulation. **Antitrust policy** outlaws attempts to monopolize, or cartelize, markets in which competition is desirable. Antitrust policy is pursued in the courts by government attorneys and by individual firms that charge other firms with violating antitrust laws. Economic regulation and antitrust policy will be examined in this chapter.

MARKET POWER

The ability of a firm to raise its price without losing all its customers to rival firms

SOCIAL REGULATION

Government regulations aimed at improving health and safety

ECONOMIC REGULATION

Government regulation of natural monopoly, where, because of economies of scale, average production cost is lowest when a single firm supplies the market

ANTITRUST POLICY

Government regulation aimed at preventing monopoly and fostering competition in markets where competition is desirable

Let's turn first to economic regulation—specifically, the regulation of natural monopolies.

Regulating Natural Monopolies

Because of economies of scale, natural monopolies have a long-run average cost curve that slopes downward over the range of market demand. This means that the lowest average cost is achieved when one firm serves the entire market. For example, a subway system is a natural monopoly. If two competing subway systems tunnel parallel routes throughout a city, the average cost per trip would be higher than if a single system provided this service.

Unregulated Profit Maximization

Exhibit 1 shows the demand and cost conditions for a natural monopoly, in this case a metropolitan subway system. A natural monopoly usually faces huge initial capital costs, such as those associated with digging a subway system, building a natural gas pipeline, or wiring a city for electricity. Because of the heavy capital outlays, once capital is in place, average cost falls as output increases, so the average cost curve slopes downward over a broad range of output. In this situation, average cost is lowest when a single firm supplies the market.

An unregulated monopolist will choose the price-quantity combination that maximizes profit. In Exhibit 1, the monopolist—in this case, the operator of a subway system—maximizes profit by producing where marginal revenue equals marginal cost, which occurs at 50 million riders per month paying $4 per trip. The monopolist will reap the profit identified by the blue-shaded rectangle. The *abc* triangle, which is below the demand curve and above the $4 price, measures the consumer surplus, a measure of consumers' net gain from riding the subway. The problem with letting the monopolist maximize profit is that the resulting price-output combination is inefficient in terms of social welfare. Consumers pay a price that far exceeds the marginal cost of providing the service. The marginal value of additional output exceeds its marginal cost, so social welfare would increase if output expanded.

One option for government is to allow the monopolist to maximize profit. But government can increase social welfare by forcing the monopolist to expand output and lower price. To accomplish this, government can either operate the monopoly itself, as with most urban transit systems, or can *regulate* a privately owned monopoly, as it does with some urban transit systems, local phone services, and electricity transmission. Government-owned or government-regulated monopolies are called **public utilities.** Here we focus on government regulation, though the issues discussed are similar if the government chose to own and operate the monopoly.

PUBLIC UTILITIES

Government-owned or government-regulated monopolies

Setting Price Equal to Marginal Cost

Many facets of a natural monopoly have been regulated, but the price-output combination gets the most attention. Suppose government regulators require the monopolist to produce the level of output that is efficient—that is, where the price, which also measures the marginal benefit to consumers, equals the marginal cost of the good. This price-output combination is depicted in Exhibit 1 as point *e,* where the demand curve, or the marginal benefit curve, intersects the marginal cost curve, yielding a price of $0.50 per trip and quantity of 105 million trips per month. Consumers will clearly prefer this price to the $4 charged by the unregulated monopolist. The consumer surplus from riding the subway increases from triangle *abc* without regulation to triangle *aef* with regulation.

Notice, however, that the monopolist now has a problem. The average cost of supplying 105 million trips per month is $1.25, identified by point *g* on the average cost curve. This amount is more than double the regulated price of $0.50. Rather than earning a profit, the monopolist suffers a loss—in this case, $0.75 per trip, for a total loss of about $80 million a month, identified by the pink-shaded rectangle. *Forcing a natural monopolist to produce where price, or marginal benefit, equals marginal cost results in an economic loss to the monopolist.* In the long run, the monopolist would go out of business rather than endure such a loss.

Subsidizing the Natural Monopolist

How can regulators encourage the monopolist to stay in business yet still produce where price equals marginal cost? The government can cover the loss—*subsidize* the firm so it earns a normal profit. Bus and subway fares are typically set below the average cost of providing the service, with the difference made up by a government subsidy. For example, the Washington, D.C., Metro subway system gets over $200 million per year in federal subsidies. Amtrak requires a federal subsidy of at least $1.5 billion per year. One drawback with

---

| EXHIBIT | 1 | **Regulating a Natural Monopoly** |

With a natural monopoly, the long-run average cost curve slopes downward where it intersects with the demand curve. The unregulated firm maximizes profit by producing where marginal revenue equals marginal cost, in this case, 50 million trips per month at a price of $4.00 per trip. This outcome is inefficient because price, or marginal benefit, exceeds marginal cost. To achieve the efficient level of output, regulators could set the price at $0.50 per trip. The subway would sell 105 million trips per month, which would be an efficient outcome. But at that price, the subway would lose money and would require a subsidy to keep going. As an alternative, regulators could set the price at $1.50 per trip. The subway would sell 90 million trips per month and would break even (because price equals average cost). Although the subway would earn a normal profit, social welfare could still be increased by expanding output as long as the price, or marginal benefit, exceeds marginal cost, but that would result in an economic loss, requiring a subsidy.

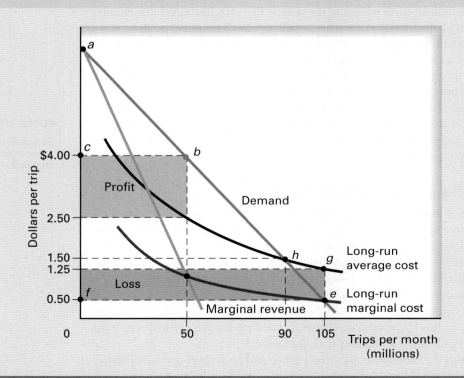

the subsidy solution is that, to provide the subsidy, the government must raise taxes or forgo public spending in some other area. Thus, the subsidy has an opportunity cost and could easily result in inefficiencies elsewhere in the economy.

Setting Price Equal to Average Cost

Although some public utilities are subsidized, most are not. Instead, regulators try to establish a price that will provide the monopolist with a "fair return." Recall that the average cost curve includes a normal profit. Thus, *setting price equal to average cost* provides a normal, or "fair," profit for the monopolist. In Exhibit 1, the demand curve intersects the average cost curve at point *h,* yielding a price of $1.50 and a quantity of 90 million trips a month. This price-output combination will allow the monopolist to stay in business without a subsidy.

Setting price equal to average total cost enhances social welfare compared to the unregulated situation. The monopolist would prefer an economic profit but will accept a normal profit to stay in business. After all, a normal profit is the best this firm could expect if resources were redirected to their best alternative uses. But note that the marginal benefit of the 90 millionth trip exceeds its marginal cost. Therefore, expanding output beyond 90 million trips per month would increase social welfare.

The Regulatory Dilemma

Setting price equal to marginal cost yields the *socially optimal* allocation of resources because *the consumers' marginal benefit from the last unit sold equals the marginal cost of producing that last unit.* In our example, setting the price at $0.50 equates marginal benefit and marginal cost, but the monopolist will face losses unless government provides a subsidy. These losses disappear if price equals average cost, which in our example is $1.50. The higher price ensures a normal profit, but the output is 15 million trips below the socially optimal level.

Thus, the dilemma facing the regulator is whether to set price equal to marginal cost, which is socially optimal but requires a government subsidy, or to set a break-even price even though output falls short of the socially optimal level. There is no right answer. Compared with the unregulated profit-maximizing price of $4, both reduce the price, increase output, erase economic profit, increase consumer surplus, and increase social welfare. Although Exhibit 1 lays out the options neatly, regulators usually face a cloudier picture. Demand and cost curves can only be estimated, and the regulated firm may withhold or distort information. For example, a utility may overstate its costs so it can charge more.

Alternative Theories of Economic Regulation

Why do governments regulate certain industries? Why not let market forces allocate resources? There are two views of government regulation. The first has been implicit in the discussion so far—namely, economic regulation is in the *public interest.* Economic regulation promotes social welfare by keeping prices down when one or just a few firms serve a market. A second, darker, view is that economic regulation is not in the public interest but is in the *special interest* of producers. According to this view, *well-organized producer groups expect to profit from economic regulation and persuade public officials to impose restrictions that existing producers find attractive, such as limiting entry into the industry or preventing competition among existing firms.* Individual producers have more to gain or to lose from regulation than do individual consumers. Producers typically are also better organized and more focused than consumers and are therefore better able to bring about regulations that favor producers.

Producers' Special Interest in Economic Regulation

To understand how and why producer interests could influence public regulation, think back to the last time you had your hair cut. Most states regulate the training and licensing of barbers and beauticians. If any new regulation affecting the profession is proposed, such as longer training requirements, who do you suppose has more interest in that legislation, you or those who cut hair for a living? *Producers have a strong interest in matters that affect their livelihood, so they play a disproportionately large role in trying to influence such legislation.* If there are public hearings on haircut regulations, the industry will provide self-serving testimony, while consumers will largely ignore the whole thing.

As a consumer, you do not specialize in getting haircuts. You purchase haircuts, cold cuts, hardware, software, underwear, and thousands of other goods and services. You have no *special interest* in haircuts. Some critics argue that because consumers fail to focus on such matters, business regulations often favor producer interests. Well-organized producer groups, as squeaky wheels in the legislative machinery, get the most grease in the form of favorable regulations. Such regulations are usually introduced under the guise of advancing consumer interests. Producer groups may argue that unbridled competition in their industry would hurt consumers. For example, the alleged problem of "cutthroat" competition among cab drivers has led to regulations that eliminate price competition and restrict the number of cabs in most large metropolitan areas. New York City has 10,000 fewer cabs now than it did 70 years ago. As a result, cabs there are harder to find and fares are more expensive. To operate a cab in New York City, someone must purchase a "medallion." The purchase price reflects the market value to cab owners of regulations that restrict entry and fix cab fares above the competitive level. The average price of a cab medallion increased from $27,000 in 1968 to $225,000 in 2003.[1] Regulation gives medallion owners an abiding interest in blocking new entry. If market entry and cab fares were deregulated, cabs would become more plentiful, fares would fall, and medallions would become worthless.

Regulation may be introduced under the guise of quality control, such as keeping unlicensed "quacks" from certain professions. But these supply restrictions usually reduce competition and increase the price. The special-interest theory may be valid even when the initial intent of the legislation was in the consumer interest. Over time, the regulatory machinery may shift toward the special interests of producers, who, in effect, "capture" the regulating agency. This **capture theory of regulation** was discussed by George Stigler, the Nobel laureate mentioned in the previous chapter. He argued that "as a general rule, regulation is acquired by the industry and is designed and operated for its benefit."[2]

Perhaps it would be useful at this point to discuss the regulation and, more recently, deregulation of a particular industry—airlines.

Airline Regulation and Deregulation

The Civil Aeronautics Board (CAB), established in 1938, once tightly regulated interstate airlines. Anyone trying to enter a particular airline market had to first persuade the CAB that the route needed another airline. During the 40 years prior to deregulation, potential entrants submitted more than 150 applications for long-distance routes, *but not a single new interstate airline was authorized.* The CAB also enforced strict compliance with regulated prices. In effect, the CAB had created a cartel that fixed prices among the 10 major airlines

---

1. These numbers were noted by Michael Luo, "46 Years in Cab, Recalling That Tip from Marylyn," *New York Times*, 7 December 2003.
2. George Stigler, "The Theory of Economic Regulation," *Bell Journal of Economics and Management Science* (Spring 1971): 3.

CAPTURE THEORY OF REGULATION

Producers' political power and strong stake in the regulatory outcome lead them, in effect, to "capture" the regulating agency and prevail on it to serve producer interests

C a s e **S t u d y**

Public Policy

eActivity

A review of airline deregulation from a conservative viewpoint is available online from the Heritage Foundation's magazine at http://www.heritage.org/Research/Regulation/BG1173es.cfm. What actions was the Department of and blocked new entry. This was a perfect example of the capture theory of regulation.

Regulation had insulated the industry from price competition, allowing labor unions to secure higher wages than they could in a more competitive setting. For working less than two weeks a month, airline pilots in 1978 earned more than $300,000 a year on average (in 2004 dollars). Some had so much free time they pursued second careers. Just how attractive a pilot's job was became apparent after deregulation. America West, a nonunion airline that sprouted from deregulation, paid its pilots $64,000 a year (in 2004 dollars) and required them to work 40 hours a week, performing other duties when they were not flying. Yet the company received more than 4,000 applications for its 29 pilot openings.

© Peter Schulz/Index Stock Imagery

Transportation considering at the time this review was written? What nonregulatory alternatives does the author suggest? The concerns of airline pilots about employment security and getting what they see as their fair share of industry revenues are presented through the Air Line Pilots' Association Web site at http://www.alpa.org/. What particular issues related to industry structure are of current concern to the pilots?

Although the CAB prohibited price competition, *nonprice competition flourished*. Airlines competed based on the frequency of flights, the quality of meals, the width of the seats, even the friendliness of the staff. For example, American Airlines put pianos in their jumbo jets. United Airlines countered with guitars and wine tastings. Such competition increased operating costs until firms earned only a normal rate of return. Thus, *airfares set above competitive levels coupled with entry restrictions were no guarantee of economic profit as long as airlines were free to compete in other ways, such as in the frequency of flights.*

The CAB had no regulatory power over airlines that flew only *intrastate* routes—flights between Los Angeles and San Francisco, for instance. The record shows that fares on intrastate airlines were only half those on identical routes flown by regulated airlines.

Airline Deregulation. Despite opposition from the existing airlines and labor unions, Congress passed the Airline Deregulation Act in 1978, which allowed price competition and new entry. By 2000, airfares in inflation-adjusted dollars averaged 27 percent below regulated prices. The airlines could afford to lower fares because they became more productive by filling a greater percentage of seats. The hub-and-spoke system developed under deregulation also allowed airlines to route planes more efficiently. Airline routes used to be straight lines from one city to another. Now they radiate like the spokes of a wagon wheel from a "hub" airport. From 30 hubs across the country, airlines send out planes along the spokes to over 400 commercial airports and then quickly bring them back to the hubs. Passenger miles flown nearly tripled since deregulation, and the net benefits to passengers now exceed $20 billion a year, or about $75 per U.S. resident.

Critics of deregulation worried that quality and safety would deteriorate. But the Federal Aviation Administration still regulates quality and safety. Since deregulation, accident rates have declined by anywhere from 10 to 45 percent, depending on the specific measure used. Also, because of lower fares, more people fly now rather than drive, thereby saving thousands of lives that would have been lost driving (per passenger mile, flying is about 20 times safer than driving).

Another concern with deregulation was that small communities would lose service. Because of the hub-and-spoke system, however, the number of scheduled departures from small cities and rural communities has increased more than one-third. The latest development in air travel is regional jets that bypass the hub-and-spoke system to fly 40 to 70 passengers from, say, Hartford, Connecticut, to Rochester, New York. The demand for air travel has increased enough to make such point-to-point service profitable.

Airport Capacity Limits Competition. Although airline traffic has more than doubled since deregulation, the air traffic control system has not expanded, and only one major new airport, Denver's, has opened. Airports and the air traffic control system are owned and operated by government agencies. *The government did not follow up deregulation with an expansion of airport capacity.* Revenue from taxes on airline tickets goes elsewhere. Departure gates, landing rights, and hub airports became the scarce resources in the industry. The major airlines may not have pushed for airport expansions because additional capacity could encourage more entry, which would increase competition.

Some passengers complain that the quality of food has declined in recent years, but that's because many consumers apparently prefer the lower fares of no-frills airlines. Most consumers view air travel as a commodity, and consider airlines as interchangeable. Thus, consumers seek the lowest fare. Low-cost, no-frills carriers such as Southwest Airlines and Jet Blue are grabbing market share and forcing down fares wherever they fly. Competition has been fierce and several airlines have disappeared or filed for bankruptcy. But, on the whole, deregulation has benefited consumers.

Sources: Steven Morrison and Clifford Winston, "The Remaining Role for Government Policy in the Deregulated Airline Industry," in *Deregulation of Network Industries: What's Next;* Sam Peltzman and Clifford Winston, eds. Brookings Institution, 2000, pp. 1–40; Scott McCartney, "AMR Is Challenging Jet Blue with Free Ticket Promotion," *Wall Street Journal,* 7 January 2004; and http://flyaow.com/, with links to nearly 500 airlines worldwide.

The course of regulation and deregulation raises some interesting questions about the true objectives of regulation. Recall the alternative views of regulation: one holds that regulation is in the public, or consumer, interest; the other holds that regulation is in the special, or producer, interest. In the airline industry, regulation appeared more in accord with producer interests, and producer groups fought deregulation, which benefited consumers.

This concludes our discussion of economic regulation, which tries to reduce the harmful consequences of monopolistic behavior in those markets where the output can be most efficiently supplied by one or a few firms. We now turn to antitrust policy, which tries to promote competition in those markets where competition seems desirable.

Antitrust Law and Enforcement

Although competition typically ensures the most efficient use of the nation's resources, an individual competitor would prefer to operate as a monopolist. If left alone, a firm might try to create a monopoly by driving competitors out of business, by merging with competitors, or by colluding with competitors. *Antitrust policy* is the government's attempt to reduce anticompetitive behavior and promote a market structure that will lead to greater competition. *Antitrust policy attempts to promote socially desirable market performance.*

Origins of Antitrust Policy

Economic developments in the last half of the 19th century created bigger firms serving wider markets. Perhaps the two most important developments were (1) technological breakthroughs that led to a larger optimal plant size in manufacturing and (2) the rise of the railroad from 9,000 miles of track in 1850 to 167,000 miles by 1890, which reduced transport costs. *Economies of scale and cheaper transport costs extended the geographical size of markets,* so firms grew larger and served a wider geographical market.

Sharp declines in the national economy in 1873 and in 1883, however, panicked large manufacturers. Because their heavy fixed costs required large-scale production, they cut prices in an attempt to stimulate sales. Price wars erupted, creating economic turmoil. Firms desperately sought ways to stabilize their markets. One solution was for each firm to form a *trust* by transferring their voting stock to a single board of trustees, which would vote in the interest of the industry. Early trusts were formed in the sugar, tobacco, and oil industries. Although the impact of these early trusts is still debated today, they allegedly pursued anticompetitive practices to develop and maintain a monopoly advantage. Gradually the word **trust** came to represent any firm or group of firms that tried to monopolize a market.

Trusts provoked widespread criticism and their creators were called "robber barons." Most farmers, especially, were hurt by these early trusts, for while farm prices were pushed down by technological change in agriculture, the prices farmers had to pay for supplies were higher because of trusts. At the time, farmers accounted for 40 percent of the U.S. workforce and thus had political clout. Some states, primarily agricultural, enacted *antitrust* laws in the 1880s, prohibiting trusts. But these laws were largely ineffective because a trust could simply move to a state without such restrictions.

Sherman Antitrust Act of 1890

In the presidential election of 1888, the major political parties put antitrust planks in their platforms. This consensus culminated in the **Sherman Antitrust Act of 1890,** the first national legislation in the world against monopoly. The law prohibited trusts, restraint of trade, and monopolization, but the law's vague language allowed much anticompetitive activity to slip by.

Clayton Act of 1914

The **Clayton Act of 1914** was passed to outlaw certain practices not prohibited by the Sherman Act and to help government stop a monopoly before it develops. For example, the Clayton Act outlaws price discrimination when this practice creates a monopoly. You'll recall that *price discrimination* is charging different customers different prices for the same good. The act also prohibits *tying contracts* and *exclusive dealing* if they substantially lessen competition. **Tying contracts** require the buyer of one good to purchase another good as part of the deal. For example, a seller of a patented machine might require customers to buy other supplies. **Exclusive dealing** occurs when a producer will sell a product only if the buyer agrees not to buy from other suppliers of the product. For example, a manufacturer might sell computer chips to a computer maker only if the computer maker agrees not to buy any chips elsewhere. Another prohibition of the act is **interlocking directorates,** whereby the same individual serves on the boards of directors of competing firms. Finally, acquiring of the corporate stock of a competing firm is outlawed if this would substantially lessen competition.

Federal Trade Commission Act of 1914

The **Federal Trade Commission (FTC) Act of 1914** established a federal body to help enforce antitrust laws. The president appoints the five commissioners, who are assisted by a staff of economists and lawyers. The Sherman, Clayton, and FTC acts provide the framework for antitrust laws. Subsequent amendments and court decisions have clarified and embellished these laws. A loophole in the Clayton Act was closed in 1950 with the passage of the *Celler-Kefauver Anti-Merger Act,* which prevents one firm from buying the *physical assets* of another firm if the effect is to reduce competition. This law can block both **horizontal mergers,** or the merging of firms that produce the same product, such as Coke and Pepsi, and **vertical mergers,** or the merging of firms where one supplies inputs to the other or demands output from the other, such as Microsoft and Dell.

TRUST

Any firm or group of firms that tries to monopolize a market

SHERMAN ANTITRUST ACT OF 1890

First national legislation in the world against monopoly; prohibited trusts, restraint of trade, and monopolization, but the law was vague and, by itself, ineffective

CLAYTON ACT OF 1914

Beefed up the Sherman Act; outlawed certain anticompetitive practices not prohibited by the Sherman Act, including price discrimination, tying contracts, exclusive dealing, interlocking directorates, and buying the corporate stock of a competitor

TYING CONTRACT

A seller of one good requires a buyer to purchase other goods as part of the deal

EXCLUSIVE DEALING

A supplier prohibits customers from buying from other suppliers of the product

INTERLOCKING DIRECTORATE

A person serves on the boards of directors of two or more competing firms

FEDERAL TRADE COMMISSION (FTC) ACT OF 1914

Established a federal body to help enforce antitrust laws; run by commissioners assisted by economists and lawyers

HORIZONTAL MERGER

A merger in which one firm combines with another that produces the same product

VERTICAL MERGER

A merger in which one firm combines with another from which it had purchased inputs or to which it had sold output

Antitrust Law Enforcement

Any law's effectiveness depends on the vigor and vigilance of enforcement. The pattern of antitrust enforcement goes something like this. Either the Antitrust Division of the U.S. Justice Department or the FTC charges a firm or group of firms with breaking the law. Federal agencies are often acting on a complaint by a customer or a competitor. At that point, those charged with the wrongdoing may be able, without admitting guilt, to sign a **consent decree,** whereby they agree not to continue doing what they had been charged with. If the accused contests the charges, evidence from both sides is presented in a court trial, and a judge renders a decision. Some decisions may be appealed all the way to the Supreme Court, and in such cases the courts may render new interpretations of existing laws.

CONSENT DECREE

The accused party, without admitting guilt, agrees to stop the alleged activity if the government drops the charges

Per Se Illegality and the Rule of Reason

The courts have interpreted antitrust laws in essentially two different ways. One set of practices has been declared **per se illegal**—that is, illegal regardless of the economic rationale or consequences. For example, under the Sherman Act, all formal agreements among competing firms to fix prices, restrict output, or otherwise restrain competition are viewed as per se illegal. To prove guilt under a per se rule, the government need only show that the offending practice took place. Thus, the government need only examine the firm's *behavior*.

Another set of practices falls under the **rule of reason.** Here the courts engage in a broader inquiry into the facts surrounding the particular offense—namely, the reasons why the offending practice was adopted and its effect on competition. The rule of reason was first set forth in 1911, when the Supreme Court held that Standard Oil had illegally monopolized the petroleum refining industry. Standard Oil allegedly had come to dominate 90 percent of the market by acquiring more than 120 former rivals and by practicing **predatory pricing** to drive remaining rivals out of business—for example, by temporarily selling below marginal cost or dropping the price only in certain markets. In finding Standard Oil guilty, the Court focused on both the company's *behavior* and the *market structure* that resulted from that behavior. Based on this approach, the Court found that the company had behaved *unreasonably* and ruled that the monopoly should be broken up.

But in 1920, the rule of reason led the Supreme Court to find U.S. Steel not guilty of monopolization. In that case, the Court ruled that not every contract or combination in restraint of trade is illegal—only those that "unreasonably" restrained trade violated antitrust laws. The Court said that *mere size is not an offense.* Although U.S. Steel clearly possessed market power, the company, in the Court's view, had not violated antitrust laws because it had not unreasonably used that power. The Court switched positions in 1945, ruling that although Alcoa's conduct might be reasonable and legal, its mere possession of market power—Alcoa controlled 90 percent of the aluminum ingot market—violated antitrust laws. Here the Court was using *market structure* rather than firm *behavior* as the test of legality.

PER SE ILLEGAL

In antitrust law, business practices that are deemed illegal regardless of their economic rationale or their consequences

RULE OF REASON

Before ruling on the legality of certain business practices, a court examines why they were undertaken and what effect they have on market competition

PREDATORY PRICING

Pricing tactics employed by a dominant firm to drive competitors out of business, such as temporarily selling below marginal cost or dropping the price only in certain markets

Mergers and Public Policy

Some firms have pursued rapid growth by merging with other firms or by acquiring other firms. Much of what the Antitrust Division in the U.S. Justice Department and the FTC's Bureau of Competition do is approve or deny proposed mergers and acquisitions. In determining possible harmful effects that a merger might have on competition, one important consideration is its impact on the share of sales accounted for by the largest firms in the industry. If a few firms account for a relatively large share of sales, the industry is said to be *concentrated.* As a measure of sales concentration, the Justice Department uses the **Herfindahl-Hirschman Index,** or **HHI,** which is found by squaring the percentage of market share

HERFINDAHL-HIRSCHMAN INDEX, OR HHI

A measure of market concentration that squares each firm's percentage share of the market then sums these squares

Firm	Industry I		Industry II		Industry III	
	Market Share (percent)	Market Share Squared	Market Share (percent)	Market Share Squared	Market Share (percent)	Market Share Squared
A	23	529	15	225	57	3,249
B	18	324	15	225	1	1
C	13	169	15	225	1	1
D	6	36	15	225	1	1
Remaining 40 firms	1 each	40	1 each	40	1 each	40
HHI		1,098		940		3,292

EXHIBIT 2

Herfindahl-Hirschman Index (HHI) Based on Market Share in Three Industries

Each of the three industries shown has 44 firms. The HHI is found by squaring each firm's market share then summing the squares. Under each industry, each firm's market share is shown in the left column and the square of the market share is shown in the right column. For ease of exposition, only the market share of the top four firms differs across industries. The remaining 40 firms have 1 percent market share each. The HHI for Industry III is nearly triple that for each of the other two industries.

of each firm in the market and then summing those squares. For example, if the industry consists of 100 firms of equal size, the HHI is 100 [$= 100 \times (1)^2$]. If the industry is a monopoly, its index is 10,000 [$= (100)^2$], the largest possible value. The more firms there are in the industry and the more equal their size, the smaller the HHI. This index gives greater weight to firms with larger market shares, as can be seen for the three examples presented in Exhibit 2. Each industry has 44 firms, but, for ease of exposition, only the market share of the top 4 firms differs across industries. Note that the index for Industry III is nearly triple that for each of the two other industries. Take a minute now to work through the logic of the exhibit.

The Justice Department's guidelines sort all mergers into one of two categories: *horizontal mergers,* which involve firms in the same market, and *nonhorizontal mergers,* which include all other types of mergers. Of greatest interest for antitrust purposes are horizontal mergers, such as a merger between competing oil companies like Mobil and Exxon. The Justice Department generally challenges any merger in an industry that meets two conditions: (1) the post-merger HHI exceeds 1,800 and (2) the merger increases the index by more than 100 points. Mergers in an industry that would have a post-merger index of less than 1,000 are seldom challenged.[3] Other factors, such as the ease of entry into the market and gains in efficiency, are considered for indexes between 1,000 and 1,800.

Merger Waves

There have been four merger waves in this country over the last century, as outlined in Exhibit 3. Between 1887 and 1904 some of today's largest firms, including U.S. Steel and Standard Oil, were formed. Mergers during this first wave tended to be horizontal. For example, the firm that is today U.S. Steel was created in 1901 through a billion-dollar merger that involved dozens of individual steel producers and two-thirds of the industry's production

3. Merger guidelines are laid out by the U.S. Department of Justice at http://www.usdoj.gov/atr/public/guidelines/horiz_book/hmg1.html.

E X H I B I T **3**

U.S. Merger Waves in the Past Century

Wave	Years	Dominant Type of Merger	Examples	Stimulus
First	1887–1904	Horizontal	U.S. Steel, Standard Oil	Span national markets
Second	1916–1929	Vertical	Copper refiner with fabricator	Stock market boom
Third	1948–1969	Conglomerate	Litton Industries	Diversification
Fourth	1982– present	Horizontal and vertical	Banking, tele- communications, health services, insurance	Span national and global markets, stock market boom

HOMEWORK
Xpress!
Ask the Instructor Video

CONGLOMERATE MERGER

A merger of firms in different industries

capacity. This merger wave was a reaction to technological progress in transportation, communication, and manufacturing. Simply put, it became easier and cheaper to run a corporation that stretched across the nation, so firms merged to achieve national size. During this first wave, similar merger waves occurred in Canada, Great Britain, and elsewhere, creating dominant firms, some of which still exist today. The U.S. merger wave cooled with the severe national recession of 1904 and with the first stirrings of antitrust laws with real bite.

Because antitrust laws began to restrain *horizontal* mergers, *vertical* mergers became more common during the second merger wave, which occurred between 1916 and 1929. A vertical merger is one between a firm that either supplies the other firm inputs or demands the other firm's outputs—the merger of firms at different stages of the production process. For example, a copper refiner merges with a copper fabricator. The stock market boom of the 1920s fueled this second wave, and the stock market crash stopped it cold in 1929.

The Great Depression and World War II cooled mergers for two decades, but the third merger wave got under way after the war. More than 200 of the 1,000 largest firms in 1950 disappeared by the early 1960s as a result of the third merger wave, which occurred between 1948 and 1969. In that span, many large firms were absorbed by other, usually larger, firms. The third merger wave peaked during 1964 to 1969, when **conglomerate mergers,** which join firms in different industries, accounted for four-fifths of all mergers. For example, Litton Industries combined firms that made calculators, appliances, electrical equipment, and machine tools. Merging firms were looking to diversify their product mix and perhaps achieve some *economies of scope*—meaning, to reduce average costs by producing a variety of goods.

The fourth merger wave began in 1982 and involved both horizontal and vertical mergers. Some large conglomerate mergers from the third wave were dissolved during the fourth wave, as the core firm sold off unrelated operations. About one-third of mergers in the 1980s resulted from *hostile takeovers,* where one firm would buy control of another against the wishes of the target firm's management. Hostile takeovers dwindled to less than one-tenth of mergers during the 1990s.

Merger activity gained momentum during the latter half of the 1990s, with the dollar value of each new merger topping the previous record. Most mergers during this period were financed by the exchange of corporate stock and were spurred on by a booming stock market (like the mergers of the 1920s). The dissolution of the Soviet Union ended the Cold War and boosted capitalism around the world. Companies merged to achieve a stronger competitive position in global markets. The largest mergers in history were proposed during the late 1990s, with the biggest action in banking, radio and television, insurance, telecommunications, and health services.

In recent years, there have been fewer objections to mergers on antitrust grounds either from academics or regulatory officials. The government shifted from rules that restrict big mergers to a more flexible approach that allows big companies to merge. For example, the government approved Boeing's $15 billion acquisition of McDonnell Douglas, the commercial aircraft manufacturer, because the airlines said it made no difference to them whether or not the two combined. Boeing still competes fiercely with Airbus, its European rival, in the world market for aircraft. Antitrust officials ask "will the merger hurt competition?"[4] Most apparently do not. Regulators ultimately challenged only about 2 percent of all mergers proposed in recent years, though just the threat of a legal challenge has deterred countless potentially anticompetitive mergers and acquisitions.

Competitive Trends in the U.S. Economy

For years, there has been concern about the sheer size of some firms because of the real or potential power they might exercise in economic and political arenas. One way to measure the power of the largest corporations is to calculate the share of the nation's corporate assets controlled by the 100 largest firms. The 100 largest manufacturers now control about half of all manufacturing assets in the United States, up from a 40 percent share after World War II. We should recognize, however, that size alone is not synonymous with market power. A very big firm, such as a large automaker, may face stiff competition from other large automakers both foreign and domestic. On the other hand, the only movie theater in an isolated community may be able to raise its price with less concern about competition.

Market Competition over Time

More important than the size of the largest firms in the nation is the market structure of each industry. Various studies have examined the level of competition by industry and changes in competition over the years. All have begun with some measure of market share, such as the HHI. Among the most comprehensive is the research of William G. Shepherd, who relied on many sources to determine the competitiveness of each industry in the U.S. economy.[5] He sorted industries into four groups: (1) pure monopoly, in which a single firm controlled the entire market and was able to block entry; (2) dominant firm, in which a single firm had more than half the market share and had no close rival; (3) tight oligopoly, in which the top four firms supplied more than 60 percent of market output, with stable market shares and evidence of cooperation; and (4) effective competition, in which firms in the industry exhibited low concentration, low entry barriers, and little or no collusion.

Exhibit 4 presents Shepherd's breakdown of U.S. industries into the four categories for 1939, 1958, and 1988. Between 1939 and 1958, the table shows a modest trend toward increased competition, with the share of those industries rated as "effectively competitive"

---

4. "Prepared Remarks of Timothy J. Muris, Chairman, Federal Trade Commission," 17 February 2004 at http://www.ftc.gov/speeches/muris/040217hmgwksp.htm#N_4_.

5. William G. Shepherd, "Causes of Increased Competition in the U.S. Economy, 1939–1980," *Review of Economics and Statistics* 64 (November 1982); and William G. Shepherd, *The Economics of Industrial Organization*, 3rd ed. (Englewood Cliffs, N.J.: Prentice Hall, 1990), 15.

EXHIBIT 4   **Competitive Trends in the U.S. Economy**

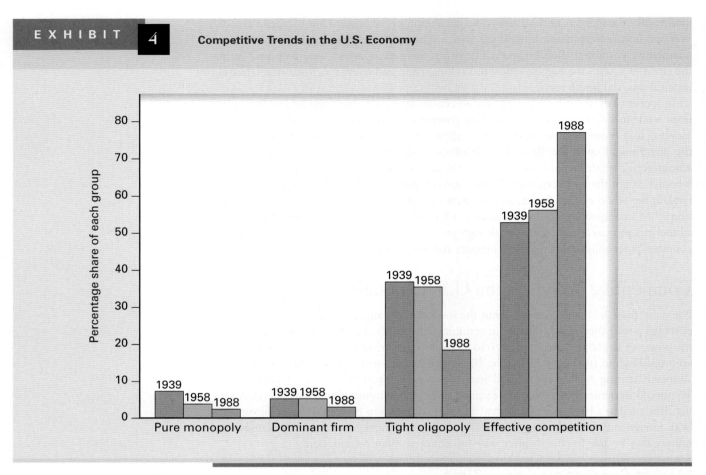

Sources: William G. Shepherd, "Causes of Increased Competition in the U.S. Economy, 1939–1980," *Review of Economics and Statistics* 64 (November 1982); and William G. Shepherd, *The Economics of Industrial Organization*, 3rd ed. (Englewood Cliffs, N.J.: Prentice Hall, 1997), 15.

growing from 52 percent to 56 percent of all industries. Between 1958 and 1988, however, there was a sharp rise in competitiveness in the economy, with the share of effectively competitive industries jumping from 56 percent to 77 percent.

According to Shepherd, the growth in competition from 1958 to 1988 can be traced to three sources: (1)*competition from imports,* (2) *deregulation, and* (3) *antitrust policy.* Foreign imports between 1958 and 1988 increased competition in 13 major industries, including autos, tires, and steel. The growth in imports accounted for one-sixth of the overall increase in competition. Imports were attractive to consumers because of their superior quality and lower price. Finding themselves at a cost and technological disadvantage, U.S. producers initially sought protection from foreign competitors through trade barriers, such as quotas and tariffs.

Shepherd argues that deregulation accounted for one-fifth of the increase in competition. Trucking, airlines, securities trading, banking, and telecommunications were among the industries deregulated between 1958 and 1988. We have already discussed some of the effects of deregulation in airlines, particularly in reducing barriers to entry and in eliminating

HOMEWORK
Xpress!
*Ask the Instructor
Video*

uniform pricing schedules. With regard to telecommunications, in 1982, AT&T was forced to sell its 22 subsidiaries, which provided most of the country's local phone service. Since 1984, AT&T's share of the long-distance market declined from 88 percent to less than 40 percent today. This enhanced competition reduced long-distance rates.

Although it is difficult to attribute an increase in competition to specific antitrust cases, Shepherd credits antitrust policy with two-fifths of the growth in competition between 1958 and 1988. To summarize: According to Shepherd, the three primary reasons for increased competition were international trade, deregulation, and antitrust policy. One-sixth of the growth in competition between 1958 and 1988 came from imports, one-fifth from deregulation, and two-fifths, the largest share, from antitrust policy. In light of the important role that Shepherd accords antitrust policy, let's look at the most significant antitrust case in the last decade.

Microsoft on Trial

Microsoft released its long-awaited Windows 98 operating system in June 1998 under a cloud. The U.S. Justice Department and 20 state attorneys general had filed lawsuits a month earlier alleging that Microsoft tried to protect its operating-system monopoly and to extend that monopoly into Internet software. At the time, Windows software was used on 90 percent of the nation's desktop computers. The government charged that Microsoft's integration of its browser, Internet Explorer, into Windows 98 was not, as the company claimed, solely to make life easier for customers, but was aimed at boosting Explorer's market share. Con-

© Jeff Christensen/AFP/Getty Images

trolling the gateway to the Internet would be a first step toward controlling Internet traffic and commerce. Government officials wanted Windows customers to have a choice of browsers. Microsoft disputed the charges and said the government was interfering with its right to create new products that benefit consumers.

Prior to any judicial ruling, Microsoft's choices were: (1) to separate its Internet browser from Windows 98, a task the company claimed would take "months if not years"; (2) to ship its major rival's browser, Netscape Navigator, as well as its own browser with Windows 98— a task Microsoft head Bill Gates likened to "requiring Coke to include three cans of Pepsi in every six-pack it sells"; or (3) to ship Windows 98 with Microsoft's browser bundled in the software. Microsoft chose the third alternative, which involved some risk because the practice could ultimately be deemed illegal.

The trial began in October 1998. The government argued that Microsoft engaged in predatory practices aimed at winning the browser war and harming competitors (the company's behavior would be considered illegal only if Microsoft was found to possess monopoly power). The government, by focusing on Microsoft's anticompetitive *behavior*, was using a rule-of-reason approach. Microsoft, for its part, characterized itself as an aggressive but legal player in a fiercely competitive industry. Microsoft's lawyers said that the company would not hold such a huge market share if it failed to improve quality and value with each new version. They argued that the high market share "does not begin to reflect the intense competitive dynamic in the software industry." Even such a market share, they said, was "susceptible to rapid deterioration should the market leader fail to innovate at a rapid and competitive pace."

WALL STREET JOURNAL

Reading It **Right**

What's the relevance of the following statement from the Wall Street Journal: *"Microsoft hasn't been shy about flexing its political muscle in Washington to influence lawmakers and regulators."*

After 78 days of testimony and months of deliberation, Judge Thomas Penfield Jackson ruled that Microsoft maintained a monopoly in operating-system software by anticompetitive means and attempted to monopolize the Web browser market by unlawfully "tying" Internet Explorer with Windows. He called Microsoft "an untrustworthy monopoly that refuses to abandon illegal business practices that crush competitors and harm consumers." As a remedy, he proposed restricting Microsoft's business practices and dividing the firm into a Windows-based operating-system company and an applications-software company.

Microsoft appealed the decision, arguing that it did not hold a monopoly and had not engaged in anticompetitive practices. Microsoft also charged that Judge Jackson showed bias in his ruling. In June 2001, the U.S. Court of Appeals upheld unanimously the finding that Microsoft violated antitrust laws and acted illegally in maintaining a monopoly in its operating system. But the appeals court also found that Judge Jackson had engaged in "serious judicial misconduct" in making derogatory comments about Microsoft to the media, so a new judge was chosen to decide on the punishment.

In November 2001, Microsoft reached a settlement with the Justice Department and with most of the state attorneys general. The settlement gives personal-computer makers greater freedom to install non-Microsoft software on new machines and to remove access to competing Microsoft features, such as Internet browsers. It also bans retaliation against companies that take advantage of these freedoms, prohibits exclusive contracts, and requires Microsoft to disclose design information to hardware and software makers so they can build competing products that will run smoothly with Windows. The court approved this settlement but that decision was appealed. By early 2004, Massachusetts remained the only state that had failed to settle with Microsoft. In July 2004, the U.S. Court of Appeals rejected that state's appeal, likely ending the court case in the United States. But Microsoft still faced charges brought by the European Union's antitrust authorities, who allege the company tried to extend monopoly power to its Windows Media Player. Fines, legal expenses, and dispute settlements cost Microsoft at least $2.5 billion in 2004. Still, Microsoft remains a huge company, with projected revenue in 2005 of $38 billion and a projected profit of $16 billion.

Sources: Brandon Mitchener and Matthew Newman, "Microsoft, EU Regulators Face More Pressure to Settle," *Wall Street Journal*, 24 November 2003; John Wilke and Ted Bridis, "Justice Department Says It Won't Seek Court-Ordered Breakup of Microsoft," *Wall Street Journal*, 7 September 2001; "Windows of Opportunity," *Economist*, 15 November 2003; and Brier Dudley, "Microsoft's Antitrust Settlement Upheld," *Seattle Times*, 1 July 2004.

Recent Competitive Trends

Shepherd's analysis of competition extended only to 1988. What has been the trend since then? Growing world trade has increased competition in the U.S. economy. For example, the share of the U.S. market controlled by the three major automakers fell from 80 percent in 1970 to 60 percent by 2000. And federal action to deregulate international phone service forced down the average price of international phone calls from $0.88 a minute in 1997 to well under $0.20 a minute by 2004. In an effort to reduce international phone rates, federal officials subpoenaed Filipino phone executives who were attending a conference in Hawaii, alleging they colluded on phone rates to the United States.[6]

Technological change is boosting competition in many markets. For example, the prime-time audience share of the three major television networks (NBC, CBS, and ABC) dropped from 90 percent in 1980 to under 40 percent in 2004 as satellite and cable tech-

6. Raissa Robles, "FBI Swoop Sparks Manila-U.S. Row," *South China Morning Post*, 15 January 2004.

nology delivered many more networks and channels. Despite Microsoft's dominance in operating systems, the software market barely existed in 1980 but now flourishes in a technology-rich environment populated by nearly 10,000 producers. And the Internet has opened far-ranging possibilities for greater competition in a number of industries, from online stock trading to all manner of electronic commerce.

Problems with Antitrust Policy

Despite the publicity and hoopla surrounding the Microsoft antitrust case (there was even a thinly disguised movie about Microsoft called *Antitrust*), there is growing doubt about the economic value of the lengthy antitrust cases pursued in the past. A case against Exxon, for example, was in the courts for 17 years before the company was cleared of charges in 1992. Another case began in 1969 when IBM, with nearly 70 percent of domestic sales of electronic data-processing equipment, was accused of monopolizing that market. IBM responded that its large market share was based on its innovative products and on its economies of scale. The trial began in 1975, the government took nearly three years to present its case; litigation dragged on for four more years. In the meantime, many other computer makers emerged both in this country and abroad to challenge IBM's dominance. In 1982, the government dropped the case, noting that the threat of monopoly had diminished enough that the case was "without merit." As noted already, the U.S. case against Microsoft took nearly six years to resolve.

Too Much Emphasis on the Competitive Model

Joseph Schumpeter argued half a century ago that competition should be viewed as a dynamic process, one of "creative destruction." Firms are continually in flux—introducing new products, phasing out old ones, trying to compete for the consumer's dollar in a variety of ways. In light of this, antitrust policy should not necessarily aim at increasing the *number* of firms in each industry. In some cases, firms will grow large because they are more efficient than rivals at offering what consumers want. Accordingly, firm size should not be the primary concern. Moreover, as noted in the chapter on perfect competition, economists have shown through market experiments that most of the desirable properties of perfect competition can be achieved with relatively few firms.[7] For example, the two leading chip makers, Intel and Advanced Micro Devices, have been locked in a price war for years, as each fights for market share. Likewise, Boeing is the only U.S. maker of commercial jets but it competes fiercely with Europe's Airbus for every new contract.

Abuse of Antitrust

Parties that can show injury from firms that violate antitrust laws can sue the offending company and recover three times the amount of the damages sustained. These so-called *treble damage* suits increased after World War II. More than 1,000 are filed each year. Courts have been relatively generous to those claiming to have been wronged. Even foreign firms have started suing in U.S. courts. But studies show that such suits can be used to intimidate an aggressive competitor or to convert a contract dispute between, say, a firm and its supplier into treble damage payoffs. The result can have a chilling effect on competition. Many economists now believe that the anticompetitive costs from this abuse of treble damage suits may exceed any competitive benefits of these laws.

---

7. See, for example, Vernon Smith, "Markets as Economizers of Information: Experimental Examinations of the 'Hayek Hypothesis,'" *Economic Inquiry* 20 (1982); and Douglas Davis and Charles Holt, *Experimental Economics* (Princeton, N.J.: Princeton University Press, 1993).

Growing Importance of International Markets

Finally, a standard approach to measuring the market power of a firm is its share of the market. With greater international trade, however, the local or even national market share becomes less relevant. General Motors may dominate U.S. auto manufacturing, accounting for half of national sales by U.S. firms. But when Japanese and European producers are included, GM's share of the U.S. auto market falls to only 28 percent. GM's share of world production has declined steadily since the mid-1950s. *Where markets are open to foreign competition, antitrust enforcement that focuses on domestic producers makes less economic sense.* In response to the global nature of markets, antitrust policy is starting to take an international approach. The U.S. government has signed cooperative agreements with some other governments, including Japan and the European Union, to promote antitrust enforcement and reduce conflicting decisions. For example, on February 12, 2003, antitrust investigators from the United States, the European Union, Japan, and Canada simultaneously raided 14 companies in 5 countries in a price fixing probe of the polyvinyl chloride market.

Conclusion

Competition has been growing in recent decades because of changing technology, greater international trade, industry deregulation, and antitrust policy. Federal Reserve Chairman Alan Greenspan, testifying before Congress, expressed skepticism about some antitrust intervention, arguing that changes in market conditions and in technologies tend to undermine monopolies over time. He called for "a higher degree of humility when enforcers make . . . projections" about the lasting effects of monopoly power. But, Joel Klein, then the antitrust chief for the Justice Department, said "we reject categorically the notion that markets will self-correct and we should sit back and watch."[8] So goes the debate about antitrust policy.

SUMMARY

1. In this chapter, we examined two forms of government regulation of business: (a) economic regulation, such as the regulation of natural monopolies, and (b) antitrust policy, which promotes competition and prohibits efforts to monopolize, or to cartelize, an industry.

2. Governments regulate natural monopolies so that output is greater and prices lower than if the monopolist was allowed to maximize profits. One problem with regulation is that the price that maximizes social welfare results in an economic loss, whereas the price that allows the firm to earn a normal profit does not maximize social welfare.

3. There are two views of economic regulation. The first is that economic regulation is in the public, or consumer,

interest because it controls natural monopolies where production by one or just a few firms is most efficient. A second view is that regulation is not in the public, or consumer, interest, but is more in the special interest of producers that use regulations to fix the price and block entry.

4. Regulations in effect for 50 years in the airline industry restricted entry and fixed prices. Deregulation in 1978 stimulated new entry, unleashed price competition, and reduced prices overall. Price wars in the industry are now common, and consumers have benefited.

5. Antitrust laws are aimed at promoting competition and prohibiting efforts to cartelize, or monopolize, an industry.

8. As quoted in John R. Wilke, "Greenspan Questions Government's Antitrust-Enforcement Campaigns," *Wall Street Journal,* 17 June 1998.

The Sherman, Clayton, and FTC acts provide the legal and institutional framework for antitrust enforcement, a framework that subsequent amendments and court cases have clarified and embellished.

6. Competition in U.S. industries has been increasing since World War II. Four sources of growing competition are greater international trade, deregulation, antitrust policy, and technological change.

QUESTIONS FOR REVIEW

1. *(Business Behavior and Public Policy)* Define market power, and then discuss the rationale for government regulation of firms with market power.

2. *(Government Regulation)* What three types of government policies are used to alter or control firm behavior? Determine which type of regulation is used for each of the following:

   a. Preventing a merger that the government believes would lessen competition
   b. The activities of the Food and Drug Administration
   c. Regulation of fares charged by a municipal bus company
   d. Occupational safety and health regulations that affect working conditions

3. *(Regulating Natural Monopolies)* What is the "regulatory dilemma?" That is, what trade-offs do regulators have to consider when deciding how to control a natural monopoly?

4. *(Theories of Regulation)* Why do producers have more interest in government regulations than consumers do?

   a. Compare and contrast the public-interest and special-interest theories of economic regulation. What is the capture theory of regulation?

   b. Which of these theories best describes the case of airline deregulation? Which best explains the government's case against Microsoft?

5. *(Case Study: Airline Regulation and Deregulation)* Consumers now treat air travel like a commodity and meals on some airlines are nonexistent. Does this mean that consumers have suffered because of airline deregulation?

6. *(Antitrust Law and Enforcement)* Discuss the difference between per se illegality and the rule of reason.

7. *(Antitrust Activity)* "The existence of only two or three big U.S. auto manufacturers is evidence that the market structure is anticompetitive and that antitrust laws are being broken." Evaluate this assertion.

8. *(Mergers and Public Policy)* Under what circumstances, and why, would the government be opposed to a merger of two firms? How does the Justice Department decide which mergers to challenge?

9. *(Competitive Trends in the U.S. Economy)* William Shepherd's study of U.S. industries showed a clear increase in competition in the U.S. economy between 1958 and 1988. How did Shepherd explain this trend?

PROBLEMS AND EXERCISES

10. *(Regulating Natural Monopolies)* The following graph represents a natural monopoly.

a. Why is this firm considered a natural monopoly?

b. If the firm is unregulated, what price and output would maximize its profit? What would be its profit or loss?

c. If a regulatory commission establishes a price with the goal of achieving allocative efficiency, what would be the price and output? What would be the firm's profit or loss?

d. If a regulatory commission establishes a price with the goal of allowing the firm a "fair return," what would be the price and output? What would be the firm's profit or loss?

e. Which one of the prices in parts b, c, and d maximizes consumer surplus? What problem, if any, occurs at this price?

11. *(Origins of Antitrust Policy)* Identify the type of anticompetitive behavior illustrated by each of the following:

a. A university requires buyers of season tickets for its basketball games to buy season tickets for its football games as well.

b. Dairies that bid on contracts to supply milk to school districts collude to increase what they charge.

c. The same individual serves on the boards of directors of General Motors and Ford.

d. A large retailer sells merchandise below cost in certain regions to drive competitors out of business.

e. A producer of carbonated soft drinks sells to a retailer only if the retailer agrees not to buy from the producer's major competitor.

12. *(Mergers and Public Policy)* Calculate the Herfindahl-Hirschman Index (HHI) for each of the following industries. Which industry is the most concentrated?

a. An industry with five firms that have the following market shares: 50 percent, 30 percent, 10 percent, 5 percent, and 5 percent

b. An industry with five firms that have the following market shares: 60 percent, 20 percent, 10 percent, 5 percent, and 5 percent

c. An industry with five firms, each of which has a 20 percent market share

EXPERIENTIAL EXERCISES

13. *(Mergers and Public Policy)* Find the Department of Justice and Federal Trade Commission merger guidelines at http://www.usdoj.gov/atr/public/guidelines/horiz_book/toc.html. How does the government use the Herfindahl-Hirschman Index to determine which proposed mergers to allow and which to challenge? Do these guidelines indicate that the Justice Department is using the per-se-illegality or rule-of-reason approach to antitrust enforcement?

14. *(C a s e* **Study:** Microsoft on Trial) The latest information on the Justice Department's case against Microsoft is available at http://www.usdoj.gov/atr/cases/ms_index.htm. To get the other side of the story, check Microsoft's PressPass page at http://microsoft.com/presspass/legalnews.asp. What has happened with the case in Europe since this textbook went to press?

15. (*Wall Street Journal*) The best place for finding late-breaking information about antitrust activity is in the "Legal Beat" column of the *Wall Street Journal.* You can find it inside the Marketplace section. Try to find at least one relevant article and determine the basis for the antitrust action. Were the Justice Department guidelines and the Herfindahl–Hirschman index mentioned in the article?

16. (*Regulatory Policy*) Research a recent antitrust case at the Department of Justice Web site (http://www.usdoj. gov/atr). Summarize the case including: the parties involved, the legal basis for the case, and the current status.

HOMEWORK XPRESS! EXERCISES

These exercises require access to McEachern Homework Xpress! If Homework Xpress! did not come with your book, visit **http://homeworkxpress.swlearning.com** *to purchase.*

York Local Phone Company, Inc. (YLPC) has a natural monopoly in the supply of land lines in Yorktown. Information about the demand, marginal revenue, long-run average cost, and long-run marginal cost are given in the table below. Plot all four in a diagram.

Quantity (10,000)	Price	Marginal Revenue	Long-Run Average Cost	Long-Run Marginal Cost
0	$60	$60	—	—
10	50	40	$37	$30
20	40	20	30	20
30	30	0	24	15
40	20		20	11
50	10		15	10
60	0		12	9

1. Identify the price YLPC would charge and the quantity of land lines that would be demanded at this price if left unregulated. Create a shaded box to illustrate its profit or loss.

2. Identify the price YLPC would charge and the quantity of land lines that would be demanded if a regulatory commission sets the price it can charge with the goal of achieving allocative efficiency. Create a shaded box to illustrate its profit or loss.

3. Identify the price YLPC would charge and the quantity of land lines that would be demanded at this price if a regulatory commission sets the price it can charge with the goal of allowing the firm a fair rate of return.

Public Goods
and Public Choice

How do public goods differ from private goods? Why do most people remain largely ignorant about what's happening in the public sector? Why is voter turnout so low? Why do politicians talk about their concern for the middle class, while they are acting on the concerns of special interests? Why are elected officials more likely than challengers to support campaign spending limits? Answers to these and related questions are discussed in this chapter, which focuses on the public sector—both the rationale for public goods and public choices about those goods.

The effects of government are all around us. Stitched into the clothes you donned this morning are government-required labels providing washing instructions. Prices of the milk and sugar you put on your Cheerios are propped up by government price supports as are the oats in the Cheerios. Governments regulate the motor vehicle that provided your transportation as well the speed and the sobriety of the driver. Your education is subsidized by taxpayers in a variety of ways. Yes, government plays a major role in the economy. The federal government alone spends each year more than $2,400,000,000,000.00—more than $2.4 *trillion*—including $1 million on paper clips. State and local governments tax and spend more than $1 trillion on their own.

The role of government has been discussed throughout this book. For the most part, we assumed that government makes optimal adjustments to the shortcomings of the private sector; that is, when confronted with market failure, government adopts and implements the appropriate program to address the problem. But, just as there are limits to the market's effectiveness, there are limits to government's effectiveness. In this chapter, we look at the pros and cons of government activity. We begin with public goods, discuss the decision-making process, and then examine the limitations of that process. Topics discussed include:

- Private versus public goods
- Representative democracy
- Rational ignorance
- Special-interest legislation
- Rent seeking
- The underground economy
- Bureaucratic behavior
- Private versus public production

Public Goods

Throughout most of this book, we have been talking about *private goods*, such as pizzas and haircuts. As noted in Chapter 3, private goods have two important features. First, they are *rival* in consumption, meaning that the amount consumed by one person is unavailable for others to consume. For example, when you and friends share a pizza, each slice others eat is one less available for you (which is why you usually eat a little faster when sharing). A second key feature of private goods is that suppliers can easily *exclude* those who don't pay. Only paying customers get pizzas. Thus, private goods are said to be *rival* and *exclusive*.

Private Goods, Public Goods, and In Between

In contrast to private goods, *public goods*, such as national defense, the national weather service, the Centers for Disease Control, or a local mosquito-control program, are *nonrival* in consumption. One person's consumption does not diminish the amount available to others. Once produced, such goods are available to all in equal amount; the marginal cost of supplying the good to an additional consumer is zero. But once a public good is produced, suppliers cannot easily deny it to those who fail to pay. There are no vending machines for public goods. For example, if a firm sprays a neighborhood for mosquitoes, all households in the neighborhood benefit. The firm can't easily exclude those who fail to pay. Thus, the mosquito spraying is *nonexclusive*—it benefits all those in the neighborhood. Some people figure, "Since I can enjoy the benefits without paying, why bother paying?" As a consequence, for-profit firms can't profitably sell public goods. In this case of market failure, the government comes to the rescue by providing public goods and paying for them through enforced taxation. Sometimes nonprofit agencies also provide public goods, funding them through contributions and other revenue sources.

But the economy consists of more than just private and public goods. Some goods are *nonrival* but *exclusive*. For example, additional households can tune in a TV show without affecting the reception of other viewers. It's not as if there is only so much TV signal to go around. Television signals are nonrival in consumption. Yet the program's producers, should they choose to, could charge each household for reception, as with cable TV, so the TV

QUASI-PUBLIC GOOD

A good that is nonrival in consumption but exclusive, such as cable TV

OPEN-ACCESS GOOD

A good that is rival in consumption but nonexclusive, such as ocean fish

signal is nonrival but exclusive. A good that is nonrival but exclusive is called a **quasi-public good.** Along the same lines, short of the point of congestion, additional people can benefit from a golf course, swimming pool, rock concert, or highway without diminishing the benefit to other users. These goods, when not congested, are nonrival. Yet producers can, with relative ease, exclude those who don't pay the greens fee, pool admission, ticket price, or road toll. These uncongested goods are both nonrival and exclusive and are therefore quasi-public goods. Once congestion sets in, however, these goods become rival—space is scarce on a backed-up golf course, in a crowded swimming pool, at a jam-packed concert, or on a traffic-clogged highway. Once congestion sets in, these quasi-public goods become private goods—both rival and exclusive.

Some other goods are *rival* but *nonexclusive.* The fish in the ocean are rival in the sense that every fish caught is not available for others to catch; the same goes for migratory game, like geese. But ocean fish and migratory game are nonexclusive in that it would be costly or impossible for a private firm to prevent access to these goods. A good that is rival but nonexclusive is called an **open-access good** because it would be difficult and costly to prevent individuals from consuming the good. Problems that arise with open-access goods will be examined in the next chapter.

Exhibit 1 sorts out the four categories of goods. Across the top, goods are either *rival* or *nonrival,* and along the left margin, goods are either *exclusive* or *nonexclusive.* Private goods are usually provided by the private sector. Quasi-public goods are sometimes provided by the private sector, as with a private golf course, and sometimes provided by government, as with a municipal golf course. Open-access goods are usually regulated by government, as you will see in the next chapter. And public goods are usually provided by the government.

Optimal Provision of Public Goods

Because private goods are rival in consumption, the market demand for a private good is the sum of the quantities demanded by each consumer. For example, the market quantity of

EXHIBIT 1

Categories of Goods

	Rival	Nonrival
Exclusive	1. Private Goods —Pizza —Crowded swimming pool	2. Quasi-Public Goods —Cable TV —Uncrowded swimming pool
Nonexclusive	3. Open-Access Goods —Ocean fish —Migratory birds	4. Public Goods —National defense —Mosquito control

pizza demanded when the price is $10 is the quantity demanded by Alan plus the quantity demanded by Maria plus the quantity demanded by all other consumers in the market. The market demand curve for a private good is the *horizontal* sum of individual demand curves, an idea developed in Exhibit 7 of Chapter 6. The efficient quantity of a private good occurs where the market demand curve intersects the market supply curve.

But a public good is nonrival in consumption, so that good, once produced, is available to all consumers. For example, the market demand for a given level of mosquito control reflects the marginal benefit that Alan gets from that amount of the good plus the marginal benefit that Maria gets from that amount plus the marginal benefit that all others in the community get from that amount of the good. Therefore, the market demand curve for a public good is the *vertical* sum of each consumer's demand for the public good. To arrive at the efficient level of the public good, we find where the market demand curve intersects the marginal cost curve—that is, where the sum of the marginal valuations equals the marginal cost.

Suppose the public good in question is mosquito control in a neighborhood, which, for simplicity, has only two households, one headed by Alan and the other by Maria. Alan spends more time in the yard than does Maria and thus values a mosquito-free environment more than she does. Their individual demand curves are shown in Exhibit 2 as D_a and D_m, reflecting the marginal benefits that Alan and Maria enjoy at each rate of output. Quantity is measured here as hours of mosquito spraying per week. By vertically summing marginal valuations at each rate of output, we derive the neighborhood demand curve, D, for mosquito spraying. For example, when the town sprays two hours a week, Maria values the second hour at $5 and Alan values it at $10. To get the market demand for two hours of spraying, we simply add each resident's marginal benefit to get $15, as identified by point e.

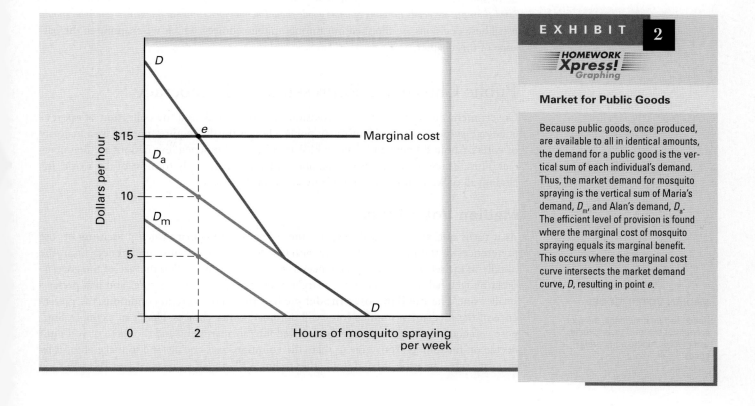

EXHIBIT **2**

≡HOMEWORK≡
Xpress!
≡ ≡ *Graphing*

Market for Public Goods

Because public goods, once produced, are available to all in identical amounts, the demand for a public good is the vertical sum of each individual's demand. Thus, the market demand for mosquito spraying is the vertical sum of Maria's demand, D_m, and Alan's demand, D_a. The efficient level of provision is found where the marginal cost of mosquito spraying equals its marginal benefit. This occurs where the marginal cost curve intersects the market demand curve, D, resulting in point e.

How much mosquito spraying should the government provide? Suppose the marginal cost of spraying is a constant $15 an hour, as shown in Exhibit 2. The efficient level of output is found where the marginal benefit to the neighborhood equals the marginal cost, which occurs where the neighborhood demand curve intersects the marginal cost curve. In our example, these curves intersect where quantity is two hours per week.

Paying for Public Goods

The government pays for the mosquito spray through taxes, user fees, or some combination of the two. The efficient approach would be to impose a tax on each resident equal to his or her marginal valuation. Simple enough, but there are at least two problems with this. First, once people realize their taxes are based on how much the government thinks they value the good, people tend to understate their true valuation. Why admit you really value the good if, as a result, you get socked with a higher tax bill? So taxpayers are reluctant to offer information about their true valuation of public goods. This creates the **free-rider problem,** which occurs because people try to benefit from the public good without paying for it. For example, they can enjoy mosquito abatement whether or not they pay. But even if the government has accurate information about marginal valuations, some households have a greater ability to pay taxes than others. In our example, Alan values mosquito control more because he spends more time in the yard than does Maria. What if Alan is around more because he can't find a job? Should his taxes be double those of Maria, who, say, has a high-paying job? *Taxing people according to their marginal valuations of the public good may be efficient, but it may not be fair if incomes differ.*

Once the public good is produced, only that quantity is available, such as two hours of mosquito spraying per week. With private goods, each consumer can purchase any quantity he or she prefers and each can purchase a different amount. Thus, *public goods are more complicated than private goods in terms of what goods should be provided, in what quantities, and who should pay.* These decisions are thrashed out through public choices, which we examine in the balance of this chapter.

Public Choice in a Representative Democracy

Government decisions about the provision of public goods and the collection of tax revenues are *public choices.* In a democracy, public choices usually require approval by a majority of voters. About 60 percent of the world's two hundred independent nations are democracies. Thus, issues raised in this section about majority rule apply to most of the world, including all of Western Europe and nearly all of the Americas.

Median Voter Model

As it turns out, we can usually explain the outcome of majority rule by focusing on the preferences of the median voter. The *median voter* is the one whose preferences lie in the middle of the set of all voters' preferences. For example, if the issue is the size of the government budget, half the voters prefer a larger budget than the median voter and half prefer a smaller one. The **median voter model** predicts that under certain conditions, the preference of the median, or middle, voter will dominate other choices. Here's an example. Suppose you and two roommates have just moved into an apartment, and the three of you must decide on furnishings. You agree to share the common costs equally and to make choices by majority rule. The issue at hand is whether to buy a TV and, if so, of what size. But you each

FREE-RIDER PROBLEM

Because a public good is nonexclusive, people may try to reap the benefits of the good without paying for it

MEDIAN VOTER MODEL

Under certain conditions, the preferences of the median, or middle, voter will dominate other preferences have a different preference. Your studious roommate considers a TV an annoying distraction and would rather go without; otherwise, the smaller, the better. Your other roommate, a real TV fan, prefers a 48-inch screen but would settle for a smaller one rather than go without. A 27-inch screen is your first choice, but you would accept the 48-inch screen rather than go without. What to do, what to do?

You all agree to make the decision by voting on two alternatives at a time, then pairing the winner against the remaining alternative until one dominates the others. When the 27-inch set is paired with the no-TV option, the 27-inch gets both your vote and the TV fan's vote. When the 27-inch screen is then paired with the 48-inch screen, the 27-inch screen wins again, this time because your studious roommate sides with you rather than voting for the super screen.

Majority voting in effect delegates the public choice to the person whose preference is the median for the group. As the median voter in this example, you get your way. You have the votes for any choice between no TV and a 48 incher. Similarly, *the median voter in an electorate often determines public choices. Political candidates try to get elected by appealing to the median voter.* This is why candidates focus their rhetoric on "hard-working Americans," "middle America," or "American families." They are targeting the median voter. This is one reason why candidates often seem so much alike. Note that under majority rule, only the median voter gets his or her way. Other voters must go along with the median choice. Thus, other voters usually end up paying for what they consider to be either too much or too little of the public good. In private markets people get whatever they are willing and able to buy.

People vote directly on issues at New England town meetings and on the occasional referendum, but *direct democracy* is not the most common means of public choice. When you consider the thousands of choices made in the public sector—from the number of teachers to hire to what software to use for municipal records—it becomes clear that direct democracy for all public choices through referenda would be unwieldy and impractical. Rather than make decisions by direct referenda, voters elect *representatives,* who, at least in theory, make public choices that reflect their constituents' views. Under certain conditions, the resulting public choices reflect the preferences of the median voter. Some complications of making public choices through representative democracy are explored next.

Special Interest and Rational Ignorance

We assume that consumers maximize utility and firms maximize profit, but what about governments? As noted in Chapter 3, there is no common agreement about what, if anything, governments try to maximize or, more precisely, what elected officials try to maximize. One theory that parallels the rational self-interest assumption employed in private choices is that elected officials attempt to *maximize their political support.*

Elected officials may cater to special interests rather than serve the interest of the public. The possibility arises because of the asymmetry between special interest and public interest, an idea introduced in the previous chapter. Consider only one of the thousands of decisions that are made each year by elected representatives: funding an obscure federal program that subsidizes U.S. wool production. Under the wool-subsidy program, the federal government guarantees that a floor price is paid to sheep farmers for each pound of wool they produce, a subsidy that costs taxpayers over $75 million per year. During deliberations to renew the program, the only person to testify before Congress was a representative of the National Wool Growers Association, who claimed that the subsidy was vital to the nation's economic welfare. Why didn't a single taxpayer challenge the subsidy? Why were sheep farmers able to pull the wool over taxpayers' eyes?

Households consume so many different public and private goods and services that they have neither the time nor the incentive to understand the effects of public choices on every product. What's more, voters realize that each of them has only a tiny possibility of influencing public choices. And even if an individual voter is somehow able to affect the outcome, the impact on that voter is likely to be small. For example, if a taxpayer could successfully stage a grassroots campaign to eliminate the wool subsidy, the taxpayer would save, on average, less than $0.55 per year in federal income taxes (based on about 135 million tax filers in 2004). Therefore, unless voters have a *special* interest in the legislation, they adopt a stance of **rational ignorance,** which means that they remain largely oblivious to most public choices. The cost to the typical voter of acquiring information about each public choice and acting on it usually exceeds any expected benefit. It's not easy to interest the public in the public interest.

In contrast, consumers have much more incentive to gather and act on information about decisions they make in private markets because they benefit directly from such information. *Because information and the time required to acquire and digest it are scarce, consumers concentrate on private choices rather than public choices. The payoff in making better private choices is usually more immediate, more direct, and more substantial.* For example, a consumer in the market for a new car has an incentive to examine the performance records of different models, test-drive a few, and check prices at dealerships and on the Internet. That same individual has less incentive to examine the performance records of candidates for public office because that single voter has virtually no chance of deciding the election. What's more, because candidates aim to please the median voter anyway, they often take positions that are similar.

Distribution of Benefits and Costs

Let's turn now to a different topic—how the costs and benefits of public choices are spread across the population. Depending on the issue, the benefits of particular legislation may affect only a small group or much of the population. Likewise, the costs of that legislation may be imposed either narrowly or widely over the population. The possible combinations of benefits and costs yield four categories of distributions: (1) widespread benefits and widespread costs, (2) concentrated benefits and widespread costs, (3) widespread benefits and concentrated costs, and (4) concentrated costs and concentrated benefits.

Traditional public-goods legislation, such as for national defense or a system of justice, have widespread benefits and widespread costs—nearly everyone benefits and nearly everyone pays. Traditional public-goods legislation usually has a positive impact on the economy because total benefits exceed total costs.

With **special-interest legislation,** benefits are concentrated but costs widespread. For example, as you'll see shortly, price supports for dairy products benefit dairy farmers with higher prices. The program's costs are spread across nearly all consumers and taxpayers. Legislation that caters to special interests usually harms the economy, on net, because total costs often exceed total benefits. Special-interest legislation of narrow geographical interest is called **pork-barrel spending.** For example, a recent federal budget appropriated $50,000 for a tattoo removal program in San Luis Obispo, California; $150,000 to restore the Augusta Historic Theater in Georgia; and $2 million for a statue of a Roman god in Birmingham, Alabama.[1] To boost their reelection prospects, members of Congress "bring home the bacon" by delivering pork-barrel programs for their constituents.

RATIONAL IGNORANCE

A stance adopted by voters when they find that the cost of understanding and voting on a particular issue exceeds the benefit expected from doing so

TRADITIONAL PUBLIC-GOODS LEGISLATION

Legislation that involves widespread costs and widespread benefits—nearly everyone pays and nearly everyone benefits

SPECIAL-INTEREST LEGISLATION

Legislation with concentrated benefits but widespread costs

PORK-BARREL SPENDING

Special-interest legislation with narrow geographical benefits but funded by all taxpayers

---

1. Dan Morgan and Helen Dewar, "GOP Dishes Out Pork in Growing Portions," *Washington Post,* 24 November 2003.

Populist legislation involves widespread benefits but concentrated costs. Populist legislation usually has a tough time getting approved because the widespread group that benefits typically remains rationally ignorant of the proposed legislation, so these voters provide little political support. But the concentrated group getting whacked will object strenuously. Most economists agree that tort-reform legislation, for example, would benefit the economy as a whole by limiting product liability lawsuits, reducing insurance costs, and bringing some goods to the market that, because of liability suits, have all but disappeared, such as personal aircraft. But trial lawyers, the group that would be most harmed by such limits, have successfully blocked reforms for years. Because the small group that bears the cost is savvy about the impact of the proposed legislation but those who would reap the benefits remain rationally ignorant, populist legislation has little chance of approval, unless elected officials can somehow get the issue on the voter's radar screen.

Finally, **competing-interest legislation** involves both concentrated benefits and concentrated costs, such as legislation affecting the power of labor unions in their dealings with employers, or legislation affecting steel makers versus steel-using industries. These are the fiercest political issues because both sides have a heavy stake in the outcome.

Exhibit 3 arrays the four categories of distributions. Across the top, benefits of legislation are either *widespread* or *concentrated,* and along the left margin, costs are either *widespread* or *concentrated.* Box 1 shows *traditional public-goods legislation,* such as national defense, with both widespread benefits and widespread costs. Box 2 shows *special-interest legislation,* such as farm subsidies, with concentrated benefits but widespread costs. Box 3 shows *populist legislation,* such as tort reform, with widespread benefits but concentrated costs. And Box 4 shows *competing-interest legislation,* such as labor union issues, with both concentrated benefits and concentrated costs.

The following case study considers a special-interest program—milk price supports.

POPULIST LEGISLATION

Legislation with widespread benefits but concentrated costs

COMPETING-INTEREST LEGISLATION

Legislation that confers concentrated benefits on one group by imposing concentrated costs on another group

Distribution of Benefits

	Widespread	Concentrated
Widespread	1. Traditional Public Goods —National defense	2. Special Interest —Farm subsidies
Concentrated	3. Populist —Tort reform	4. Competing Interest —Labor union issues

Distribution of Costs

EXHIBIT 3

Categories of Legislation Based on the Distribution of Costs and Benefits

© Photodisc/Getty Images

C a s e **S t u d y**

Public Policy

*e*Activity

"Provisions of the Federal Agriculture Improvement and Reform Act of 1996," available at http://www.ers.usda.gov/ publications/aib729/, describes legislation aimed at reducing farmers' reliance on price support programs. You can learn about its impact on the dairy sector by reading the summary of "Structure of Dairy Markets: Past, Present, Future" at http://www.ers.usda. gov/publications/aer757. Which type of firm buys most of the fluid milk produced by dairy farmers? What does the future hold for dairy markets?

Farm Subsidies

The Agricultural Marketing Agreement Act became law in 1937 to prevent what was viewed as "ruinous competition" among farmers. In the years since, the government introduced a variety of policies that set floor prices for a wide range of farm products. Farm subsidies will cost U.S. taxpayers at least $20 billion a year for the next decade. In much of the country, milk prices are the most regulated of farm products. Explaining the intricacies of the price support program for milk takes up three volumes of the *Code of Federal Regulations,* and administering the regulations employs hundreds of people at the U.S. Department of Agriculture—more than oversee the entire federal budget in the Office of Management and Budget.

Let's see how price supports work in the dairy industry, using a hypothetical example. Exhibit 4 simplifies the market for milk. Without government intervention, suppose the market price of milk would average $1.50 per gallon for 100 million gallons per month. In long-run equilibrium, dairy farmers would earn a normal profit in this competitive industry. Consumer surplus is shown by the blue-shaded area. Recall that consumer surplus is the difference between the most that consumers would be willing to pay for that quantity and the amount they actually pay.

But suppose the dairy lobby persuades Congress that the market price is too low, so legislation establishes a price floor for milk of, say, $2.50 per gallon. The higher price encourages farmers to increase the quantity supplied to 150 million gallons per month. Consumers, however, reduce their quantity demanded to 75 million gallons per month. To make

EXHIBIT 4

Effects of Milk Price Supports

In the absence of government intervention, the market price of milk is $1.50 per gallon, and 100 million gallons are sold per month. If government establishes a floor price of $2.50 per gallon, then the quantity supplied will increase and the quantity demanded will decrease. To maintain the higher price, the government must buy the excess quantity at $2.50 per gallon.

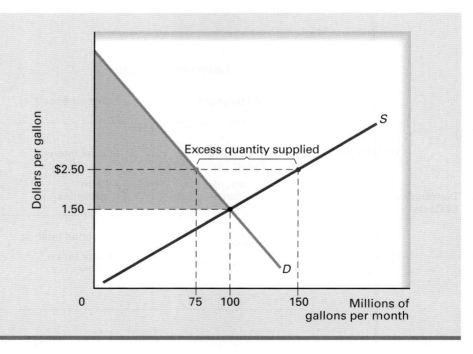

the higher price stick, the government must buy the 75 million gallons of surplus milk generated by the floor price or somehow get dairy farmers to restrict their output to 75 million gallons per month. For example, to reduce production, the government could buy cows from farmers (as occurred in the 1980s).

Consumers end up paying dearly to subsidize farmers. First, the price consumers pay increases by $1 per gallon. Second, as taxpayers, consumers must also buy the surplus milk or otherwise pay farmers not to supply that milk. And third, if the government buys the surplus, taxpayers must then pay for storage. So consumers pay $2.50 for each gallon they buy on the market, another $2.50 for each surplus gallon the government buys, plus, say, an extra $0.50 per gallon to convert surplus milk into powder and to store it. Instead of paying a free-market price of just $1.50 per gallon, the typical consumer-taxpayer in effect pays $5.50 (=$2.50 + $2.50 + $0.50), or nearly four times that, for each gallon actually consumed.

How do farmers make out? Each receives an extra $1 per gallon in revenue compared to the free-market price. As farmers increase their output, however, their marginal cost of production increases. At the margin, the higher price just offsets the higher marginal cost of production. The subsidy also increases the value of specialized resources, such as cows and especially grazing land. Farmers who own these resources when the subsidy is introduced will benefit. Farmers who purchase them after that (and, hence, after resource prices have increased) earn only a normal rate of return on their investment. Because farm subsidies were originally introduced more than half a century ago, most farmers today earn just a normal return on their investment, despite the billions spent annually on subsidies.

If the extra $1 per gallon that farmers receive for milk were pure profit, farm profits would increase by $150 million per month. But consumer-taxpayer costs increase by $300 million per month ($75 million for milk consumed, plus $187.5 million in higher taxes to pay for the 75 million surplus gallons purchased by the government, plus $37.5 million to store the 75 million surplus gallons). Thus, costs to consumer-taxpayers are double the farmers' maximum possible gain of $150 million. Like other special-interest legislation, farm subsidies have a negative impact on the economy, as the losses outweigh the gains. The only winners are those who owned specialized resources when the subsidy was first introduced. New farmers must pay more to get in a position to reap the subsidies. About half the nation's agricultural land is rented out by landlords who likely purchased the land after the subsidy program went into effect, and thus already paid to get in on the subsidy. Farmers who lease that land pay higher land rent because of the subsidy. Ironically, subsidies aimed at preserving the family farm raise the costs of becoming a farmer.

The dairy industry is supported in other ways. Some states ensure even higher price floors. Foreign imports of liquid milk are tightly restricted. Other laws promote the consumption of dairy products more generally. For example, some states prohibit restaurants from serving margarine instead of butter unless the customer specifically requests margarine.

The profound long-run problem for dairy farmers is that technological breakthroughs, such as genetically engineered hormones that stimulate milk production, have increased the milk yield per cow, making each farmer far more productive. Yet, despite the widely advertised "Got milk?" and milk-mustache campaigns, milk consumption remains flat. The combination of increased supply and stagnant demand creates excess quantity supplied.

Sources: "The Farmland Bubble," *New York Times*, 26 December 2003; "U.S. Dairy Farmers Seek Government Help to Slow Milk Product Imports," *Dow Jones Newswire*, 13 December 2003; Scott Kilman, "Dairy Aisle's Secret: Milk Is a Cash Cow," *Wall Street Journal*, 28 July 2003; "Ditching the Peace," *Economist*, 1 January 2004; and the U.S. Department of Agriculture's dairy products site at http://www.ams.usda.gov/dairy/index.htm.

Rent Seeking

An important feature of representative democracy is the incentive and political power it offers participants to employ legislation to increase their wealth, either through direct transfers or through favorable public expenditures and regulations. Special-interest groups, such
as dairy farmers and trial lawyers, try to persuade elected officials to provide the special interest with some market advantage or some outright transfer or subsidy. Such benefits are
often called *rents*. The term in this context means that the government transfer or subsidy
constitutes a payment to the resource owner that exceeds the earnings necessary to call forth
that resource—*a payment exceeding opportunity cost.* The activity that interest groups undertake to secure these special favors from government is called *rent seeking,* a term already
introduced.

The government frequently bestows some special advantage on a producer or group of
producers, and abundant resources are expended to acquire these rights. For example, *political action committees,* known more popularly as *PACs,* contribute millions to congressional
campaigns. About 4,000 PACs try to shape federal legislation. The top contributors recently
included the tobacco lobby and the American Trial Lawyers Association. Tobacco interests
would like to influence cigarette legislation, and lawyers fear reforms that would limit liability lawsuits.

To the extent that special-interest groups engage in rent seeking, they shift resources
from productive endeavors that create output and income to activities that focus more on
transferring income to their special interests. *Resources employed to persuade government to redistribute income and wealth are unproductive because they do nothing to increase total output and
usually end up reducing it.* Often many firms compete for the same government advantage,
thereby wasting still more resources. If the advantage conferred by government on some
special-interest group requires higher income taxes, the net return individuals expect from
working and investing will fall, so they may work less and invest less. If this happens, productive activity declines.

As a firm's profitability becomes more and more dependent on decisions made in Washington, resources are diverted from productive activity to rent seeking, or lobbying efforts,
to gain special advantage. One firm may thrive because it secured some special government
advantage at a critical time; another firm may fail because its managers were more concerned with productive efficiency than with rent seeking.

Think of the economy's output in a particular period as depicted by a pie. The pie represents the total value of goods and services produced. In answering the what, how, and for
whom questions introduced in Chapter 2, policy makers have three alternatives: (1) they
can introduce changes that increase the size of the pie (that is, positive-sum changes);
(2) they can decide simply to carve up the existing pie differently (redistribute income); or
(3) they can start fighting over how the pie is carved up, causing some of it to end up on
the floor (negative-sum changes).

Special-interest groups have little incentive to make the economy more efficient. In fact,
they will usually support legislation that transfers wealth to them even if the economy's
overall efficiency declines. For example, suppose that the American Trial Lawyers Association is able to revise product liability laws in a way that boosts lawyers' annual incomes by a
total of $1 billion, or about $1,900 for each lawyer in private practice. Suppose, too, that this
measure drives up insurance premiums, raising the total cost of production by, say, $2 billion
per year. Lawyers themselves will have to bear part of this higher cost, but because they account for only about 1 percent of the spending in the economy, they will bear only about

1 percent of the $2 billion in higher costs, or about $20 million. This amounts to about $40 per lawyer per year. Thus, the legislation is a good deal for lawyers because their annual incomes grow about $1,900 each but their annual costs increase only about $40 each, resulting in the net average gain of $1,860 per lawyer. Much special-interest legislation leads to a net reduction in social welfare. For example, some of the nation's best minds are occupied with devising schemes to avoid taxes or divert income to favored groups at the expense of market efficiency.

There are hundreds of special-interest groups representing farmers, physicians, lawyers, teachers, manufacturers, barbers, and so on. One way special interests try to gain access to the political process is through campaign contributions. The tricky issue of campaign finance reform is discussed in the following case study.

Campaign Finance Reform

Critics have long argued that American politics is awash in special-interest money. Most Americans seem to agree. Two-thirds of those surveyed in a recent poll support public financing of campaigns if it eliminates funding from large private donations and organized interest groups. Since the 1970s, presidential campaigns have been in part publicly funded, but not congressional races. Candidates who accept public funds must abide by campaign spending limits. But, by rejecting public funds in the primary, as John Kerry and George W. Bush did in the 2004 presidential primaries, candidates can ignore spending limits.

© Photodisc/Getty Images

Senators John McCain and Russ Feingold proposed a ban on so-called soft-money contributions to national parties. *Soft money* allows political parties to raise unlimited amounts from individuals, corporations, and labor unions and to spend it freely on party-building activities, such as get-out-the-vote efforts, but not on direct support for candidates. *Hard money* is the cash parties raise under rules that limit individual contributions and require public disclosure of donors. Before recent increases, individual contributions to candidates had been limited to $1,000 per person. The McCain-Feingold measure was approved as the Bipartisan Campaign Reform Act of 2002. The act bans the solicitation of soft money by federal candidates and prohibits political advertising by special interest groups in the weeks just before an election. The contribution limit was raised from $1,000 to $2,000.

Limits on special-interest contributions may reduce their influence in the political process, but such limits heighten the current advantage of incumbents. About 95 percent of congressional incumbents are reelected. Incumbents benefit from a taxpayer-funded staff and free mailing privileges; these mailings often amount to campaign literature masquerading as official communications. Limits on campaign spending also magnify the advantages of incumbency by reducing a challenger's ability to appeal directly to voters. Some liberal *and* conservative thinkers agree that the supply of political money should be increased, not decreased. As Curtis Gans, director of the Committee for the Study of the American Electorate argued, "The overwhelming body of scholarly research . . . indicates that low spending limits will undermine political competition by enhancing the existing advantages of incumbency." *Money matters more to challengers than to incumbents* because the public knows less about challengers than about incumbents. Challengers must be able to spend enough to get their message out. One study found a positive relationship between spending by challengers and their election success but found no relationship between spending by incumbents and their reelection success. So campaign spending limits favor incumbents.

According to Common Cause, national party groups took in a total of $441 million in soft money for the 2000 election, with $225 million raised by Republicans and $216 million by Democrats. That money was used to fund presidential and congressional races across the country. Nearly half a billion dollars sounds like a lot of money, but Coke spent over four times that on advertising in 2000. The point is that legislation often has unintended consequences. Efforts to limit campaign spending may or may not reduce the influence of special-interest groups, but *a limit reduces a challenger's ability to reach the voters and thereby increase the advantage of incumbency, thus reducing political competition.*

Sources: David Stout, "Divided Court Says Government Can Ban 'Soft Money,'" *New York Times*; 10 December 2003; Jeanne Cummings et al., "Supreme Court Upholds Key Parts of New Campaign-Finance Law," *Wall Street Journal*, 11 December 2003; the Federal Election Commission at http://www.fec.gov/; and Common Cause at http://www.commoncause.org.

The Underground Economy

A per-unit government subsidy promotes production, as we saw in the case study on milk price supports. Conversely, a per-unit tax discourages production. Perhaps it would be more accurate to say that when government taxes productive activity, less production gets *reported*. If you ever worked as a waitress or waiter, did you faithfully report all your tip income to the Internal Revenue Service? If you didn't, your unreported income became part of the underground economy. The **underground economy** is a term used for all market activity that goes unreported either to avoid taxes or because the activity itself is illegal. Income arising in the underground economy ranges from unreported tips to the earnings of drug dealers.

The introduction of a tax on productive activity has two effects. First, resource owners may supply less of the taxed resource because the after-tax wage declines. Second, to evade taxes, some people will shift from the formal, reported economy to an underground, "off the books" economy. Thus, when the government taxes market exchange or the income it generates, less market activity gets reported.

We should take care to distinguish between tax *avoidance* and tax *evasion*. Tax avoidance is a *legal* attempt to arrange one's economic affairs to pay the least tax possible, such as buying municipal bonds because they yield interest free of federal income taxes. Tax evasion, on the other hand, is *illegal;* it takes the form of either failing to file a tax return or filing a fraudulent return by understating income or overstating deductions. Research around the world indicates that the underground economy grows more when (1) government regulations increase, (2) tax rates increase, and (3) government corruption is more widespread.[2]

The U.S. Commerce Department estimates that official figures capture only about 90 percent of U.S. income. An Internal Revenue Service survey estimates that only about 90 percent of taxable income gets reported on tax returns. These studies suggest an underground economy of about $1 trillion in 2004.

Those who pursue rent-seeking activity and those involved in the underground economy view government from opposite sides. Rent seekers want government to become actively involved in transferring wealth to them, but those in the underground economy want to avoid government contact. *Subsidies and other advantages bestowed by government draw some groups closer to government; taxes drive others underground.*

---

2. For a summary of these studies, see Simon Johnson et al., "Regulatory Discretion and the Unofficial Economy," *American Economic Review* 88 (May 1998): 387–392.

UNDERGROUND ECONOMY

An expression used to describe market activity that goes unreported either because it is illegal or because those involved want to evade taxes

HOMEWORK Xpress!
Ask the Instructor Video

Bureaucracy and Representative Democracy

Elected representatives approve legislation, but the task of implementing that legislation is typically left to **bureaus,** which are government departments and agencies whose activities are financed by appropriations from legislative bodies.

BUREAUS

Government agencies charged with implementing legislation and financed by appropriations from legislative bodies

Ownership and Funding of Bureaus

We can get a better feel for government bureaus by comparing them to corporations. Ownership of a corporation is based on the shares owned by stockholders. Stockholders share any profit or loss arising from the firm's operations. Stockholders also get to vote on important corporate matters based on the number of shares owned. Ownership in a corporation is *transferable:* the shares can be bought and sold in the stock market. Taxpayers are in a sense the "owners" of government bureaus. If the bureau earns a "profit," taxes may decline; if the bureau operates at a "loss," as most do, this loss must be made up by taxes. Each taxpayer has just one vote, regardless of the taxes he or she pays. Ownership in the bureau is surrendered only if the taxpayer dies or moves out of the jurisdiction; ownership is not transferable—it cannot be bought or sold directly.

Whereas firms receive their revenue when customers voluntarily purchase their products, bureaus are typically financed by a budget appropriation from the legislature. Most of this budget comes from taxpayers. Some bureaus earn revenue through user charges, such as admission fees to state parks or tuition at state colleges, but supplementary funds for these activities often come from taxpayers. Because of these differences in the forms of ownership and in the sources of revenue, bureaus have different incentives than do for-profit firms, so they are likely to behave differently.

Ownership and Organizational Behavior

A central assumption of economics is that people behave rationally and respond to economic incentives. The more tightly compensation is linked to individual incentives, the more people will behave in accordance with those incentives. For example, if a letter carrier's pay is based on customer satisfaction, the carrier will make a greater effort to deliver mail promptly and intact.

A private firm receives a steady stream of consumer feedback. If the price is too high or too low to clear the market, surpluses or shortages become obvious. Not only is consumer feedback abundant, but the firm's owners have a profit incentive to act on that information to satisfy consumer wants. The promise of profits also creates incentives to produce output at minimum cost. Thus, the firm's owners stand to gain from any improvement in customer satisfaction or any reduction in cost.

Because public goods and services are not sold in markets, government bureaus receive less consumer feedback and have less incentive to act on any feedback they do receive. There are usually no prices and no obvious shortages or surpluses. For example, how would you know whether there was a shortage or a surplus of police protection in your community? (Would gangs of police officers hanging around Dunkin' Donuts indicate a surplus?) Not only do bureaus receive less consumer feedback than firms do, they also have less incentive to act on the information available. Because any "profit" or "loss" arising in the bureau is spread among all taxpayers, and because there is no transferability of ownership, bureaus have less incentive to satisfy customers or to produce their output using the least-cost combination of resources. (Laws prevent bureaucrats from taking home any "profit.")

Some pressure for customer satisfaction and cost minimization may be communicated by voters to their elected representatives and thereby to the bureaus. But this discipline is not very precise, particularly because any gains or losses in efficiency are spread across taxpayers. For example, suppose that you are one of a million taxpayers in a city and you learn that by having FedEx Kinko's do all public copying, the city could save $1 million a year. If, through letters to the editor and calls to local officials, you somehow convince the city to adopt this cost-saving measure, you, as a typical taxpayer, would save yourself about a dollar a year in taxes.

Voters can leave a jurisdiction if they believe government is inefficient. This mechanism, whereby people "vote with their feet," does promote some efficiency and consumer satisfaction at the state and local levels, but it's rather crude. What if you like some public programs but not others? Moreover, voters dissatisfied with the biggest spender, the federal government, cannot easily vote with their feet. Even if you move abroad, you, as a U.S. citizen, must still pay U.S. federal taxes on your worldwide income (some other countries, such as Canada, tax only domestic income).

Because of differences between public and private organizations—in the owners' ability both to transfer ownership and to appropriate profits—we expect bureaus to be less concerned with satisfying consumer demand and with minimizing costs than private firms are. A variety of empirical studies compares costs for products that are provided by both public bureaus and private firms, such as garbage collection. Of those studies that show a difference, most find private firms to be more efficient.

Bureaucratic Objectives

Assuming that bureaus are not simply at the beck and call of the legislature—that is, assuming that bureaucrats have some autonomy—what sort of objectives will *they* pursue? The traditional view is that bureaucrats are "public servants," who try to serve the public as best they can. No doubt many public employees do just that, but is this a realistic assumption for bureaucrats more generally? Why should we assume self-sacrificing behavior by public-sector employees when we make no such assumption about private-sector employees?

One widely discussed theory of bureaucratic behavior claims that bureaus try to *maximize their budget,* for along with a bigger budget come size, prestige, amenities, staff, and pay—all features that are valued by bureaucrats.[3] According to this view, bureaus are monopoly suppliers of their output to the legislature. Rather than charge a price per unit, bureaus offer the legislature the entire amount as a package deal in return for the requested appropriation. This theory assumes that the legislature has only limited ability to dig into the budget and cut particular items. If the legislature does try to cut the bureau's budget, the bureau will threaten to make those cuts as painful to the legislature and constituents as possible. For example, if city officials attempt to reduce the school budget, school bureaucrats, rather than increase teaching loads, may threaten to eliminate kindergarten, abolish the high school football team, disband the school band, or cut textbook purchases. If such threats force the legislature to back off, the government budget turns out to be larger than most taxpayers would prefer. *Budget maximization results in a larger budget than that desired by the median voter.* The key to this argument is that bureaus are monopoly suppliers of the product and elected officials have only limited ability to cut that budget. If taxpayers have alternatives in the private sector, the monopoly power of the bureau is diminished.

3. William A. Niskanen Jr., in *Bureaucracy and Representative Government* (New York: Aldine-Atherton, 1971).

Private Versus Public Production

Simply because some goods and services are financed by the government does not mean that they must be produced by the government. Elected officials may contract directly with private firms to produce public output. For example, city officials may contract with a private firm to handle garbage collection for the city. Profit-making firms now provide everything from fire protection to prisons in some jurisdictions. Elected officials may also use some combination of bureaus and firms to produce the desired output. For example, the Pentagon, a giant bureau, hires and trains military personnel, yet contracts with private firms to develop and produce various weapon systems. State governments typically hire private contractors to build roads but employ state workers to maintain them. The mix of firms and bureaus varies over time and across jurisdictions, but the trend is toward increased *privatization,* or production by the private sector, of public goods and services.

When governments produce public goods and services, they are using *the internal organization of the government*—the bureaucracy—to supply the product. When governments contract with private firms to produce public goods and services, they are using *the market* to supply the product. While private firms have more incentives to be efficient than bureaus do, legislators sometimes prefer dealing with bureaus. In situations where it would be difficult to specify a contract for the public good in question, a bureau may be more responsive to the legislature's concerns than a for-profit firm would be. For example, suppose the service provided by social workers is put out for bid. The firm that wins the bid may be tempted to skimp on quality, particularly if quality can be determined only by direct observation at the time the service is provided. The governments would have difficulty monitoring the service quality provided by a private contractor. The services of social workers might be better provided by a government bureau. Because profit is not its goal, a bureau may be less inclined to minimize cost by reducing quality.

Conclusion

Governments attempt to address market failures in the private economy. But simply turning problems of perceived market failure over to government may not always be the best solution, because government has limitations and failings of its own. Participation in markets is based on voluntary exchange. Governments, however, have the legal power to enforce public choices. We should employ at least as high a standard in judging the performance of government, where allocations have the force of law, as we do in judging the private market, where allocations are decided by voluntary exchange between consenting parties. In other words, we should scrutinize a system that is compulsory at least as much as we scrutinize a system that is voluntary. After all, nobody is forcing you to buy tofu, but you can be forced to pay taxes for programs you may not like.

SUMMARY

1. Private goods are rival and exclusive, such as a pizza. Public goods are nonrival and nonexclusive, such as national defense. Goods that are in between public and private goods include quasi-public goods, which are nonrival but exclusive, such as cable TV, and open-access goods, which are rival but nonexclusive, such as ocean fish. Because private-sector producers cannot easily exclude nonpayers from consuming a public good, public goods are typically provided by government, which has the power to collect taxes.

2. Public choice based on majority rule usually reflects the preferences of the median voter. Other voters often must "buy" either more or less of the public good than they would prefer.

3. Producers have an abiding interest in any legislation that affects their livelihood. Consumers, however, purchase thousands of different goods and services and thus have no special interest in legislation affecting any particular product. Most consumers adopt a posture of rational ignorance, because the expected costs of keeping up with special-interest issues usually outweigh the expected benefits.

4. The intense interest that producer groups express in relevant legislation, coupled with the rational ignorance of voters on most issues, leaves government vulnerable to rent seeking by special interests. Elected officials trying to maximize their political support may serve special interests at the expense of the public interest.

5. Bureaus differ from firms in the amount of consumer feedback they receive, in their incentives to minimize costs, and in the transferability of their ownership. Because of these differences, bureaus may not be as efficient or as sensitive to consumer preferences as for-profit firms are.

QUESTIONS FOR REVIEW

1. *(Private and Public Goods)* Distinguish among private goods, quasi-public goods, open-access goods, and public goods. Provide examples of each.

2. *(Free Rider)* Does the free-rider problem arise from the characteristics of consumption rivalry, excludability, or both?

3. *(Median Voter Model)* In a single-issue majority vote, such as the TV example in this chapter, will the median voter always get his or her most preferred outcome?

4. *(Representative Democracy)* Major political parties typically offer "middle of the road" platforms rather than take extreme positions. Is this consistent with the concepts of the median voter and rational ignorance discussed in this chapter?

5. *(Distribution of Costs and Benefits)* Why are consumer interest groups usually less effective than producer lobbies in influencing legislation?

6. *(Distribution of Costs and Benefits)* Which groups typically bear the costs and which groups enjoy the benefits of (a) traditional public goods, (b) special-interest legislation, and (c) competing-interest legislation?

7. *(Case Study: Farm Subsidies)* "Subsidizing the price of milk or other agricultural products is not very expensive considering how many consumers there are in the United States. Therefore, there is little harmful effect from such subsidies." Evaluate this statement.

8. *(Case Study: Farm Subsidies)* Subsidy programs are likely to have a number of secondary effects in addition to the direct effect on dairy prices. What impact do you suppose farm subsidies are likely to have on the following?
   a. Housing prices
   b. Technological change in the dairy industry
   c. The price of dairy product substitutes

9. *(Rent Seeking)* Explain how rent seeking can lead to a drop in production of goods and services. What role might the underground economy play in lessening the drop in productive activities?

10. *(The Underground Economy)* What is the underground economy? What is the impact on the underground economy of instituting a tax on a certain productive activity?

11. *(Bureaucracy and Representative Democracy)* How do the incentives and feedback for government bureaus differ from those for profit-making firms?

12. *(Bureaucracy and Representative Democracy)* A firm is described as combining managerial coordination with market exchange in order to produce its good or service. Does similar behavior occur in government bureaus? Explain.

PROBLEMS AND EXERCISES

13. *(Optimal Provision of Public Goods)* Using at least two individual consumers, show how the market demand curve is derived from individual demand curves (a) for a private good and (b) for a public good. Once you have derived the market demand curve in each case, introduce a market supply curve and then show the optimal level of production.

14. *(Distribution of Costs and Benefits)* Suppose that the government decides to guarantee an above-market price for a good by buying up any surplus at that above-market price.

Using a conventional supply-demand diagram, illustrate the following gains and losses from such a price support:

a. The loss of consumer surplus
b. The gain of producer surplus in the short run
c. The cost of running the government program (assuming no storage costs)
d. What is the total cost of the program to consumers?
e. Are the costs and benefits of the support program widespread or concentrated?

EXPERIENTIAL EXERCISES

15. *(Rational Ignorance)* Loren Lomasky, in "The Booth and Consequences" at http://www.magnolia.net/~leonf/sd/tbac.html wrestles with the question of why people bother to vote. Read the article and decide for yourself: Is voting rational?

16. *(Wall Street Journal)* "The Politics & Policy" column in the First Section of the *Wall Street Journal* is a good source for articles on politics at every level. Choose one such article and decide which it describes: special-interest or tradi-

tional public-goods legislation. Classify the benefits and the costs as either concentrated or widespread.

17. The federal budget revenues and expenditures are detailed at http://www.whitehouse.gov/omb/budget. Browse the site and locate the section detailing spending. Find several expenditures that you find interesting. Identify the groups bearing the costs and those reaping the benefits of the expenditures.

HOMEWORK XPRESS! EXERCISES

These exercises require access to McEachern Homework Xpress! If Homework Xpress! did not come with your book, visit **http://homeworkxpress.swlearning.com** *to purchase.*

1. When the Red River floods, the Prescotts—who live on the east side of the river—and the Walkers—who live on the west side of the river—suffer flood damages. A project to deepen the river by dredging would reduce the damages for both families. The deeper the dredging, the less the damages. The marginal benefits to each family are given in the table. Plot each family's demand curve for the project. Calculate and plot the market demand curve for the project.

Depth in feet	Prescotts	Walkers
0	—	—
10	$10	$6
20	8	3
30	6	0
40	4	0
50	2	0

2. Rice farmers find that they face the market conditions illustrated in the table on the next page. Plot the demand

and supply curves given these data. Identify the market equilibrium price and quantity. Rice farmers are well organized, and have promoted rice consumption with their ad campaign "Rice is nice." Despite this effort, they are not satisfied with the market price and they successfully lobby the government for a price support of $0.80 per bushel. Show the quantity that would be supplied and the quantity that would be demanded at this government-mandated price.

Quantity (millions of bushels)	Price per Bushel	Marginal Cost per Bushel
0	—	$0.00
1	$1.00	0.20
2	0.90	0.40
3	0.80	0.60
4	0.70	0.80
5	0.60	1.00
6	0.50	1.20

3. Rice farmers find that for each $.05 increase in the government mandated price, each farmer's revenues increase by $50,000. The lobbying cost per farmer for each $.05 increment in price support is increasing, as illustrated in the table below, because convincing additional politicians with less interest in the rice industry becomes increasingly expensive. Plot the marginal revenue per increase in the subsidy and the marginal cost per farmer in a diagram, and identify the level of subsidy worth lobbying for.

Subsidy per Bushel	Marginal Cost of Lobbying per Farmer
$0.00	$ 0
0.05	5,000
0.10	15,000
0.15	30,000
0.20	50,000
0.25	75,000
0.30	105,000

Externalities and the Environment

© Tim Brown/Index Stock Imagery

The rivers in Jakarta, Indonesia, are dead—killed by acid, alcohol, and oil. Coral reefs in the South Pacific have been ripped apart by dynamite fishing. The tropical rainforest is shrinking because of slash-and-burn claims on the land's resources. In Mexico City, some people buy oxygen tanks for home use because the air is so bad. And some streams in Colorado are still considered toxic from gold mining that ended more than a century ago. What does all this have to do with economics? These environmental problems are all negative externalities, which result from the actions of producers or consumers that affect bystanders. Markets can allocate resources efficiently only as long as property rights are well defined and can be easily enforced. But property rights to clean water, air, and soil, to fish in the ocean, to peace and quiet, and to scenic vistas are hard to establish and enforce. This lack of property rights to some resources results in externalities.

Externalities may be either negative, such as air and water pollution, or positive, such as the general improvement in the civic climate that results from better education. This chapter discusses externalities and explores how well-designed public policies can increase efficiency by reducing negative externalities and increasing positive externalities. Topics discussed include:

- Exhaustible resources
- Renewable resources
- Common-pool problem
- Private property rights
- Optimal pollution

- Marginal social cost
- Marginal social benefit
- Coase theorem
- Markets for pollution rights
- Environmental protection

Externalities and the Common-Pool Problem

Let's begin by distinguishing between exhaustible resources and renewable resources. An **exhaustible resource** such as oil or coal does not renew itself and so is available in a finite amount. Technology may improve the ability to extract these resources from the ground, but each gallon of oil burned is gone forever. Sooner or later, all oil wells will run dry. The world's oil reserves are *exhaustible*.

Renewable Resources

A resource is **renewable** if, when used conservatively, it can be drawn on indefinitely. Thus, timber is a renewable resource if seedlings replace felled trees. The atmosphere and rivers are renewable resources to the extent that they can absorb and neutralize a certain level of pollutants. More generally, biological resources like fish, game, forests, rivers, grasslands, and agricultural soil are renewable if managed appropriately.

Some renewable resources are also open-access goods, an idea introduced in the previous chapter. An open-access resource is rival in consumption, but exclusion is costly. Fish caught in the ocean, for example, are not available for others to catch, so fish are rival in consumption. Yet it would be difficult for a person or a firm to "own" fish still swimming in the ocean and to prevent others from catching them, so ocean fish are nonexclusive. An open-access good is often subject to the **common-pool problem,** which results because people consume such a good until the marginal value of additional use drops to zero. People will fish the ocean until it becomes "fished out." Open-access goods are overfished, overhunted, overused, and overharvested. Because the atmosphere is an open-access resource, the air gets used as a dump for unwanted gases. Air pollution is a negative externality imposed on society by polluters.

In a market system, specific individuals usually own the rights to resources and therefore have a strong interest in using those resources efficiently. *Private property rights*, a term introduced in Chapter 2, allow individuals to use resources or to charge others for their use. Private property rights are defined and enforced by government, by informal social actions, and by ethical norms. But because specifying and enforcing property rights to open-access resources, such as the air, are quite costly or even impossible, these resources usually are not owned as private property.

Pollution and other negative externalities arise because there are no practical, enforceable, private property rights to open-access resources, such as the air. Market prices usually fail to include the costs that negative externalities impose on society. For example, the price you pay for a gal-

---

EXHAUSTIBLE RESOURCE

A resource in fixed supply, such as crude oil or coal

RENEWABLE RESOURCE

A resource that regenerates itself and so can be used indefinitely if used conservatively, such as a properly managed forest

COMMON-POOL PROBLEM

Unrestricted access to a resource results in overuse until its marginal value drops to zero lon of gasoline does not reflect the costs imposed by the dirtier air and the greater traffic congestion your driving creates. Electric rates in the Midwest do not reflect the negative externalities, or external costs, that sulfur dioxide emissions impose on people living downwind from fossil-fueled power plants. Note that externalities are unintended side effects of actions that are themselves useful and purposeful. Electricity producers, for example, did not go into business to pollute.

Resolving the Common-Pool Problem

Users of the atmosphere, waterways, wildlife, or other open-access resources tend to ignore the impact of their use on the resource's renewal ability. As quality and quantity diminish from overuse, the resource grows scarcer and could disappear. For example, Georges Bank, located off the New England coast, long one of the world's most productive fishing grounds, became so depleted by overfishing that by the 1990s the catch was down 85 percent from peak years.[1] The United Nations reports that 11 of the world's 15 primary fishing grounds are seriously depleted.

By imposing restrictions on resource use, government regulations may be able to reduce the common-pool problem. Output restrictions or taxes could force firms to use the resource at a rate that is socially optimal. For example, in the face of the tendency to overfish and to catch fish before they are sufficiently mature, the U.S. government has imposed a variety of restrictions on the fishing industry. The laws limit the total catch, the size of fish, the length of the fishing season, the equipment used, and other aspects of the business.

More generally, when imposing and enforcing private property rights would be too costly, government regulations may improve allocative efficiency. For example, stop signs and traffic lights allocate the scarce road space at an intersection, minimum size restrictions control lobster fishing, hunting seasons control the stock of game, and official study hours may calm the din in the dormitory.

But not all regulations are equally efficient. For example, fishing authorities sometimes limit the total industry catch and allow all firms to fish until that total is reached. Consequently, when the fishing season opens, there is a mad scramble to catch as much as possible before the industry limit is reached. Because time is of the essence, fishing boats make no effort to fish selectively. And the catch reaches processors all at once, creating congestion throughout the supply chain. Also, each firm has an incentive to expand its fishing fleet to catch more in those precious few weeks. Thus, large fleets of technologically efficient fishing vessels operate for a few weeks until the limit is reached then sit in port for the rest of the year. Each firm is acting rationally, but the collective effect of the regulation is grossly inefficient in terms of social welfare. Consider the complicated and sometimes confounding fishing regulations in Iceland:

> *The Icelandic government realized that it would have to curb the capacity of its own fleet. But the fishermen compensated by buying more trawlers. Then the government restricted the size of the fleet and the number of days at sea; the fishermen responded by buying larger, more efficient gear. The cod stocks continued to decline. In 1984, the government introduced quotas on species per vessel per season. This was a controversial and often wasteful system. A groundfish hauled up from 50 fathoms [300 feet] is killed by the change in pressure. But if it is a cod and the cod quota has been used up, it is thrown overboard. Or if the price of cod is low that week and cod happens to come in the haddock*

1. Deborah Cramer, "Troubled Waters," *Atlantic Monthly* (June 1995): 22–26.

net, the fishermen will throw them overboard because they do not want to use up their cod quota when they are not getting a good price.[2]

Ocean fish remain a common-pool resource because firms have not yet been able to establish and enforce rights to particular schools of fish. But advances in technology may some day allow the creation of private property rights to ocean fish, migrating birds, and other open-access resources. Establishing property rights to cattle on the Great Plains once seemed impossible, but the invention of barbed wire allowed ranchers to fence the range. In a sense, barbed wire tamed the Wild West.

Optimal Level of Pollution

Economics
in the Movies

Though the science is far from resolved, research suggests that the sulfur dioxide emitted by coal-fired electricity generators mixes with moisture in the air to form sulfuric acid, which is carried by the prevailing winds and falls as acid rain. Many argue that acid rain has killed lakes and forests and has corroded buildings, bridges, and other structures. Electricity production, therefore, involves the external cost of using the atmosphere as a gas dump. For example, Ohio is the largest U.S. polluter based on coal-fired plants located there.[3] In this section, we analyze this externality problem.

External Costs with Fixed Technology

Suppose *D* in Exhibit 1 depicts the demand for electricity in the Midwest. Recall that a demand curve reflects consumers' marginal benefit of each quantity. The lower horizontal line

---

EXHIBIT **1**

Negative Externalities: The Market for Electricity in the Midwest

If producers base their output on marginal private cost, 50 million kilowatt-hours of electricity are produced per month. The marginal external cost of electricity reflects the cost of pollution imposed on society. The marginal social cost curve includes both the marginal private cost and the marginal external cost. If producers base their output decisions on marginal social cost, only 35 million kilowatt-hours are produced, which is the optimal output. The total social gain from basing production on marginal social cost is reflected by the blue-shaded triangle.

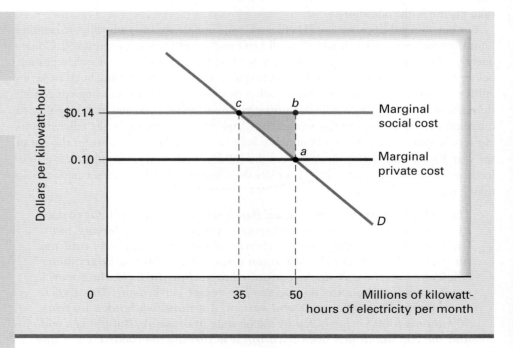

2. Mark Kurlansky, *Cod: A Biography of the Fish That Changed the World* (New York: Walker & Co., 1997), p. 172.
3. Robert Melnbardis, "Report: Coal, Oil-Fired Power Plants Top Polluters," *Reuters,* 20 July 2001.

reflects the marginal private cost of electricity. If producers base their pricing and output decisions on their private marginal costs, the equilibrium quantity per month is 50 million kilowatt-hours and the equilibrium price is $0.10 per kilowatt-hour. At that price and quantity, the marginal private cost of production just equals the marginal benefit enjoyed by consumers of electricity.

Electricity production involves not only the private cost of the resources employed but also the external cost of using the atmosphere as a gas dump. Suppose that the marginal external cost imposed on the environment by the generation of electricity is $0.04 per kilowatt-hour. When the only way of reducing emissions is by reducing the generation of electricity, then the relationship between the production of electricity and the production of pollution is fixed; the pollution in this case occurs with **fixed-production technology.**

The vertical distance between the marginal private cost curve and the marginal social cost curve in Exhibit 1 shows the marginal external cost of $0.04 per kilowatt-hour. The **marginal social cost** includes both the marginal private cost and the marginal external cost that production imposes on society. Because the marginal external cost is assumed to be a constant $0.04 per kilowatt-hour, the two cost curves are parallel. Notice that at the private-sector equilibrium output level of 50 million kilowatt-hours, the marginal social cost, identified at point *b*, exceeds society's marginal benefit of electricity, identified on the demand curve at point *a*. The 50-millionth kilowatt-hour of electricity costs society $0.14 but yields only $0.10 of marginal benefit. Because the marginal social cost exceeds the marginal benefit, too much electricity is produced.

The efficient quantity of 35 million kilowatt-hours is found where the demand, or marginal benefit, curve intersects the marginal social cost curve. This intersection is identified at point *c*. How could output be restricted to the socially efficient amount? If regulators knew the demand and marginal cost curves, they could simply limit production to 35 million kilowatt-hours, the efficient quantity. Or, on each kilowatt hour, they could impose a tax equal to the marginal external cost of $0.04. Such a pollution tax would lift the marginal private cost curve up to the marginal social cost curve. Thus, the tax would bring private costs in line with social costs.

With a tax of $0.04 per kilowatt-hour, the equilibrium combination of price and output moves from point *a* to point *c*. The price rises from $0.10 to $0.14 per kilowatt-hour, and output falls to 35 million kilowatt-hours. Setting the tax equal to the marginal external cost results in the efficient level of output. At point *c*, the marginal social cost of production equals the marginal benefit. Notice that pollution is not eliminated at point *c*, but the utilities no longer generate electricity for which marginal social cost exceeds marginal benefit. The total social gain from reducing production to the socially optimal level is shown by the blue-shaded triangle in Exhibit 1. This triangle also measures the total social cost of allowing firms to ignore the external cost of pollution. Although Exhibit 1 offers a tidy solution, the external costs of pollution often cannot be easily calculated or taxed. At times, government intervention may result in more or less production than the optimal solution requires.

External Costs with Variable Technology

The previous example assumes that the only way to reduce pollution is to reduce output. But power companies, particularly in the long run, can usually change their resource mix to reduce emissions for any given level of electricity. If pollution can be reduced by altering the production process rather than by simply adjusting the quantity, these externalities are said to be produced under conditions of **variable technology.** With variable technology, the objective is to find the optimal level of pollution for a given quantity of electricity.

FIXED-PRODUCTION TECHNOLOGY

Occurs when the relationship between the output rate and the generation of an externality is fixed; the only way to reduce the externality is to reduce the output

MARGINAL SOCIAL COST

The sum of the marginal private cost and the marginal external cost of production or consumption

VARIABLE TECHNOLOGY

Occurs when the amount of externality generated at a given rate of output can be reduced by altering the production process

Let's look at Exhibit 2. The horizontal axis measures air quality for a given level of electricity. Air quality can be improved by adopting cleaner production technology. For example, coal-burning plants can be fitted with smoke "scrubbers" to reduce toxic emissions. Yet the production of cleaner air, like the production of other goods, is subject to diminishing marginal returns. Cutting emissions of the largest particles may involve simply putting a screen over the smokestack, but eliminating successively finer particles calls for more sophisticated and more expensive processes. Thus, the marginal social cost of cleaning the air increases, as shown by the upward-sloping marginal social cost curve in Exhibit 2.

The **marginal social benefit** curve reflects the additional benefit society derives from better air quality. When air quality is poor, an improvement can save lives and thus will be valued by society more than when air quality is already excellent. Cleaner air, like other goods, has a declining marginal benefit to society (though the total benefit still increases). The marginal social benefit curve from cleaner air therefore slopes downward, as shown in Exhibit 2.

The optimal level of air quality for a given quantity of electricity is found at point *a*, where the marginal social benefit of cleaner air equals the marginal social cost. In this example, the optimal level of air quality is *A*. If firms made their production decisions based simply on their private cost—that is, if the cost of pollution is external to the firm—then firms would have no incentive to search for production methods that reduce pollution, so too much pollution would result.

What if the government regulators decree that air quality should exceed *A*? For example, suppose a law sets *A'* as the minimum acceptable level. The marginal social cost, identified as *c*, of achieving that level of air quality exceeds the marginal social benefit, identified

MARGINAL SOCIAL BENEFIT

The sum of the marginal private benefit and the marginal external benefit of production or consumption

---

E X H I B I T   2

The Optimal Level of Air Quality

The optimal level of air quality is found at point *a*, where the marginal social benefit of cleaner air equals its marginal social cost. If some higher level of air quality were dictated by the government, the marginal social cost would exceed the marginal social benefit, and social waste would result. The total social waste resulting from a higher-than-optimal air quality is shown by the pink-shaded triangle.

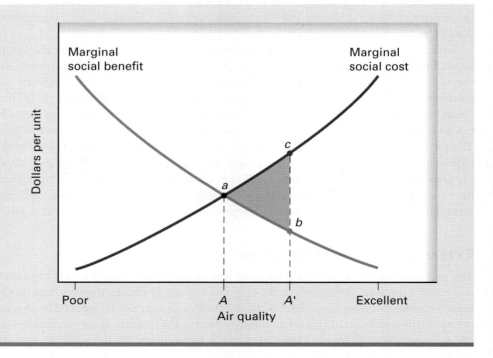

as *b*. The total social waste associated with imposing a greater-than-optimal level of air quality is shown by the pink-shaded triangle, *abc*. This area is the total amount by which the additional social costs of cleaner air (associated with a move from *A* to *A'*) exceed the additional social benefits. The idea that all pollution should be eliminated is a popular misconception. Improving air quality benefits society only if the marginal benefit of cleaner air exceeds its marginal cost.

What would happen to the optimal level of air quality if either the marginal costs or the marginal benefits of air quality changed? For example, suppose some technological breakthrough reduces the marginal cost of cleaning the air. As shown in panel (a) of Exhibit 3, the marginal social cost curve of air quality would shift downward to *MSC'*, thereby increasing the optimal level of air quality from *A* to *A'*. *The simple logic is that the lower the marginal cost of reducing pollution, other things constant, the greater the optimal level of air quality.*

An increase in the marginal benefit of air quality would have a similar effect. For example, recent research indicates that deaths from heart and lung disease would decrease 0.7 percent in large U.S. cities if suspended particulates decrease by just 1/100,000th of a gram per cubic meter of air.[4] This finding increases the perceived benefits of cleaner air. Thus, the marginal benefit of cleaner air would increase, as reflected in panel (b) of Exhibit 3 by a shift upward of the marginal social benefit curve to *MSB'*. As a result, the optimal level of air quality would increase. *The greater the marginal benefit of cleaner air, other things constant, the greater the optimal level of air quality.*

The atmosphere has the ability to cleanse itself of some emissions, but the destruction of the tropical rainforest has reduced this ability, as discussed in the following case study.

EXHIBIT   3   **Effect of Changes in Costs and Benefits on the Optimal Level of Air Quality**

Either a reduction in the marginal social cost of cleaner air, as shown in panel (a), or an increase in the marginal social benefit of cleaner air, as shown in panel (b), will increase the optimal level of air quality.

4. Jonathan M. Samet et al., "Fine Particulate Air Pollution and Mortality in 20 U.S. Cities, 1987–1994," *New England Journal of Medicine*, 14 December 2000.

C a s e **S t u d y**

Public Policy

eActivity

The Rainforest Alliance at http://www.rainforest-alliance.org/ is an international nonprofit organization dedicated to the conservation of tropical forests. Its goal is to promote economically viable alternatives to the destruction of this endangered natural resource. Look through this site to find examples of the role economics plays in the projects and research the group supports. The Rainforest Action Network is another group devoted to rainforest conservation but focuses more on citizen activism. Go to its site at http://www.ran.org/, and compare the approaches of these two groups.

Destruction of the Tropical Rainforests

The tropical rainforests have been called the lungs of the world because they naturally recycle carbon dioxide into oxygen and wood, thus eliminating heat-trapping gases and helping to maintain the world's atmospheric balance. These rainforests cover only 6 to 7 percent of the Earth's land surface but contain over half of the world's plant and animal species. The Amazon rainforest, for example, contains the largest collection of plant and animal life on Earth, along with 20 percent of the world's supply of fresh water. Of the tens of millions of species on Earth, scientists have named only about 1.5 million and have studied even fewer in depth.

The world's rainforests are located in countries that are relatively poor, such as Bolivia, Brazil, Colombia, Indonesia, Sudan, Venezuela, and the Philippines. Landless peasants and settlers burn down these forests to create farmland and pastures. Worse yet, to meet the worldwide demand for timber, loggers strip rainforests. Because the rainforest amounts to an open-access resource where property rights are not easily established, poor settlers and timber companies usually pursue a slash-and-burn approach. The world's tropical forests cover only half the area of 50 years ago, and another 30 million acres are lost each year—an area the size of Pennsylvania.

Burning the world's rainforests spells trouble for the environment. The fires add harmful gases to the atmosphere. The loss of trees reduces the atmosphere's ability to cleanse itself and increases flash flooding and mud slides. Stripped of trees, the land contains huge amounts of carbon subject to oxidization. Soil gets eroded by rains and baked by the sun and runs out of nutrients after just two growing seasons. With nutrients lost, the system is not very resilient—*it takes a century for a clear-cut forest to return to its original state.* The loss of the tropical forests involves other costs. A canopy of trees protects a rich, genetically diverse, ecosystem.

The tropical rainforests, by serving as the lungs of the world, confer benefits around the globe. But these benefits are usually ignored in the decision to clear the land. It's not the greed of peasants and timber companies that leads to inefficient, or wasteful, uses of resources. The problem is that the rainforests and the atmosphere are open-access resources that can be degraded with little immediate personal cost to those who clear the land. The costs of deforestation are imposed on people around the globe.

Poverty in the rainforest countries combined with the lack of legal title to the land encourage people to exploit that timber and soil rather than maximize the long-term value of these resources. For example, a secure property right to the land would reduce the need to clear a lot to claim some value. A farmer with title to the land could even leave a forest bequest to heirs. Research shows that people granted rights to the Amazon rainforest manage their land more conservatively. Property rights promote efficient harvesting of hardwoods and reforestation, allowing the forest to serve as an air filter. For example, the frequency of reforestation among those settlers granted land title was about 15 times greater than among those without title. Without title, the only way to gain some of the land's value is through a slash-and-burn approach. Thus, granting peasants and settlers property rights can help conserve the rainforests.

Other efforts are under way to protect the rainforests. With help from the World Bank and the World Wildlife Fund, Brazil plans to protect an area of rainforest the size of Colorado. And a timber company has given up harvesting rights to what is considered the most pristine rainforest in Africa. The United States now cancels some developing countries' government debts in exchange for their efforts to preserve their rainforests. To help crops that are environmentally friendly, the Rainforest Alliance now certifies farms using such methods. Other ideas are on the drawing board, but a systematic solution is still a long way off.

Sources: R. Godoy, et al., "The Role of Tenure Security and Private Time Preference in Neotropical Deforestation," *Land Economics*, 74 (May 1998): 162–170; Charles Wood and Robert Walker, "Saving the Trees by Helping the Poor," *Resources for the Future* (Summer 1999): 14–17; Jeffrey Ball, "If an Oak Eats CO_2 in a Forest, Who Gets the Emissions Credits?' *Wall Street Journal*, 10 December 2003; Juan Forero, "Seeking Balance: Growth vs. Culture in Amazon," *New York Times*, 10 December 2003; and the Rainforest Alliance at http://www.rainforest-alliance.org/.

The Coase Theorem

The traditional analysis of externalities assumes that market failures arise because people ignore the external effects of their actions. For example, suppose a research laboratory that tests delicate equipment is next door to a manufacturer of heavy machinery. The vibrations caused by the manufacturing process throw off the delicate equipment next door. Professor Ronald Coase, who won the Nobel Prize in 1991, would argue that the negative externality in this case is not necessarily imposed by the heavy machinery—rather, it arises from the incompatible activities of the two firms. The externality is the result of both vibrations created by the factory *and* the location of the testing lab next door. One possible solution might be to modify the machines in the factory; another might be to make the equipment in the testing lab more shock resistant or to move the lab elsewhere.

According to Coase, the efficient solution depends on which party can avoid the externality problem at the lower cost. Suppose it would cost $2 million for the factory to reduce vibrations enough for the lab to function normally. On the other hand, if the factory makes no changes, the lab can't insulate equipment enough to operate accurately, so the lab would have to relocate at a cost of $1 million. Based on this information, the least-cost solution would be for the testing lab to relocate at a cost of $1 million. Coase argues that, as long as transaction costs are low, the parties will reach the efficient solution if one party is assigned the property right. *This efficient solution will be achieved regardless of which party gets the property right.*

Suppose the testing lab is granted the right to operate free of vibrations from next door, so the testing lab can force the factory to reduce its vibration. Rather than cut vibrations at a cost of $2 million, the factory can pay the lab to relocate. Any payment greater than $1 million but less than $2 million will make both sides better off, because the lab would receive more than its moving cost and the factory would pay less than its cost of reducing vibrations. Thus, the lab will move, which is the efficient outcome.

Alternatively, suppose the factory is granted the right to generate vibrations in its production process, regardless of the impact on the testing lab. For the factory, this means business as usual. Because the minimum payment the factory would accept to reduce vibrations is $2 million, the lab would rather relocate at a cost of $1 million. Thus, whether property rights are granted to the lab or to the factory, the lab will move, which is the efficient, or least-cost, solution. The **Coase theorem** says that as long as bargaining costs are small, the assignment of property rights will generate an efficient solution to an externality problem regardless of which party is assigned property rights. A particular assignment of property rights determines only who incurs the externality costs, not the efficient outcome.

Inefficient outcomes do occur, however, when the transaction costs of arriving at a solution are high. For example, an airport located in a populated area would have difficulty negotiating noise levels with all the surrounding residents. Or a power plant emitting sulfur

COASE THEOREM

As long as bargaining costs are low, an efficient solution to the problem of externalities will be achieved by assigning property rights to one party or the other dioxide would have trouble negotiating with the millions of people scattered across the downwind states. Or peasants contemplating clearing a portion of the tropical rainforest cannot negotiate with the millions, and perhaps, billions, of people ultimately affected by that decision. When the number of parties involved in the transaction is large, Coase's solution of assigning property rights isn't enough.

Markets for Pollution Rights

According to the Coase theorem, the assignment of property rights is often sufficient to resolve the market failure typically associated with externalities. Additional government intervention is not necessary. If pollution can be easily monitored and polluters easily identified, the government may be able to achieve an efficient solution to the problem of pollution simply by assigning the right to pollute. To see how this could work, let's look at an example. Firms that dump into a river evidently value the ability to discharge waste in this way. For them, the river provides a low-cost outlet for by-products that otherwise would have to be disposed of at greater cost. The river provides a disposal service, and the demand curve for that service slopes downward, just like the demand for other resources.

The demand for the river as a discharge system is presented as *D* in Exhibit 4. The horizontal axis measures the tons of discharge dumped into the river per day, and the vertical axis measures firms' marginal benefits of disposing of their waste in this way. The demand curve thus measures the marginal value to firms of using the river as a disposal service. With no restrictions on river pollution—that is, if all firms were free to dump waste into the river—dumping would continue as long as doing so continues to yield some private marginal benefit to producers. This marginal benefit falls to zero in Exhibit 4 when 250 tons per day are discharged.

The river, like the atmosphere and the soil, can absorb and neutralize a certain amount of discharge per day without deteriorating in quality. What if voters make the public choice

EXHIBIT 4

Optimal Allocation of Pollution Rights

Suppose the demand for a river as a discharge service is *D*. In the absence of any environmental controls, polluters would dump 250 tons per day, where the marginal benefit of discharge is zero. If regulatory authorities establish 100 tons as the maximum daily level of discharge and then sell the rights, the market for these pollution rights will clear at $25 per ton. If the demand for pollution rights increases to *D'*, the market-clearing price of pollution rights will rise to $35 per ton.

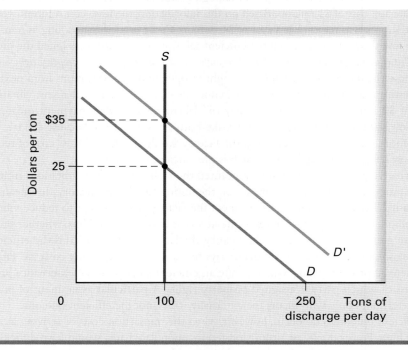

that the river should remain clean enough for swimming and fishing? Suppose engineers determine this level of water quality can be maintained as long as no more than 100 tons are discharged per day. Thus, the "supply" of the discharge service provided by the river is fixed at 100 tons per day, shown by the vertical supply curve, *S*, in Exhibit 4.

If government regulators can easily identify polluters and monitor their behavior, authorities can allocate permits to discharge 100 tons per day. If polluters are simply given these permits (that is, if the price of permits is zero), there will be an excess demand for them, because the quantity supplied is 100 tons but the quantity demanded at a price of zero would be 250 tons. An alternative is to sell permits for 100 tons of pollution at the market-clearing price. The intersection of supply curve *S* and demand curve *D* yields a permit price of $25 per ton, which is the marginal value of discharging the 100th ton into the river each day. To most permit buyers, the marginal value of a permit will exceed $25 per ton.

The beauty of this system is that producers who value the discharge rights the most will ultimately end up with them. Producers who attach a lower marginal value apparently have cheaper ways of resolving their waste problems, including changing production techniques. And if conservation groups, such as the Sierra Club, want a higher river quality than the government's standard, such as water clean enough to drink, they can purchase pollution permits but not exercise them.

What if additional firms spring up along the river and are willing to pay more than $25 per ton for pollution rights? This added demand is reflected in Exhibit 4 by *D'*. This increase of demand would bid up the market price of pollution permits to, say, $35 per ton. Some existing permit holders will sell their rights to those who value them more. Regardless of the comings and goings of would-be polluters, the total quantity of discharge rights is restricted to 100 tons per day, so the river's quality will be maintained. Thus, the value of pollution permits, but not the total amount of pollution, may fluctuate over time.

If the right to pollute could be granted, monitored, and enforced, then what had been a negative externality problem could be solved through market allocation. Historically, the U.S. government had relied on setting discharge standards and fining offenders. But in 1989, a pollution rights market for fluorocarbon emissions was established and was followed in 1990 by a market for sulfur dioxide. During the 1990s, sulfur dioxide emissions in the nation fell by more than half, exceeding the goals of the authorizing legislation. So the market for pollution rights is alive and growing.[5] Even China is now experimenting with this approach.

Pollution Rights and Public Choice

Unfortunately, legislation dealing with pollution is affected by the same problems of representative democracy that trouble other public policy questions. Polluters have a special interest in government proposals relating to pollution, and they fight measures to reduce pollution. But members of the public remain rationally ignorant about pollution legislation. So pollution regulations may be less in accord with the public interest than with the special interests of polluters. This is why a portion of pollution permits are often given to existing firms. For example, under the sulfur dioxide program, the nation's 101 dirtiest power plants receive credits equal to between 30 and 50 percent of the pollution they emitted before the program began. Because they received something of value, polluters were less inclined to oppose the legislation. Once permits were granted, some recipients found it profitable to sell their permits to

5. For a discussion of the market for sulfur dioxide emissions, see Paul Joskow, Richard Schmalensee, and Elizabeth Bailey, "The Market for Sulfur-Dioxide Emissions," *American Economic Review* 88 (September 1998): 669–685.

COMMAND-AND-CONTROL ENVIRONMENTAL REGULATIONS

An approach that required polluters to adopt particular technologies to reduce emissions by specific amounts; inflexible regulations based on engineering standards that ignore each firm's unique cost of reducing pollution

ECONOMIC EFFICIENCY APPROACH

An approach that offers each polluter the flexibility to reduce emissions as cost-effectively as possible, given its unique cost conditions; the market for pollution rights is an example

other firms that valued them more. Thus, a market emerged that led to an efficient allocation of pollution permits. According to some analysts, the sulfur dioxide program saves up to $3 billion annually compared with the old system. More generally, a system of marketable pollution rights can reduce the cost of pollution abatement by as much as 75 percent.

Before 1990, **command-and-control environmental regulations** were the norm—an approach that required polluters, such as electric utilities, to introduce particular technologies to reduce emissions by specific amounts. These regulations were based on engineering standards and did not recognize unique circumstances across generating plants, such as plant design, ability to introduce scrubbers, and the ease of switching to low-sulfur fuels. But the market for pollution rights reflects an **economic efficiency approach** that offers each electrical utility the flexibility to reduce emissions in the most cost-effective manner, given its unique operation. Firms with the lowest costs of emission control have an incentive to implement the largest reduction in emissions and then sell unused pollution permits to those with greater control costs.

Now that you know something about the theory of externalities, let's turn to an important application of the theory—environmental protection.

Environmental Protection

Federal efforts to address the common-pool problems of air, water, and soil pollution are coordinated by the Environmental Protection Agency (EPA). Four federal laws and subsequent amendments underpin U.S. efforts to protect the environment: the Clean Air Act of 1970, the Clean Water Act of 1972, the Resource Conservation and Recovery Act of 1976 (which governs solid waste disposal), and the Superfund law of 1980 (legislation focusing on toxic waste dumps). When the EPA was created in 1970, it began with about 4,000 employees and a budget of $1 billion (in 2004 dollars). By 2004, it had about 18,000 employees and a budget exceeding $8 billion.

According to EPA estimates, compliance with pollution-control regulations cost U.S. producers and consumers about $220 billion in 2004, an amount equivalent to 2 percent of gross domestic product, the market value of all final goods and services produced in the economy. We can divide pollution control spending into three categories: spending for air pollution abatement, spending for water pollution abatement, and spending for solid waste disposal. About 40 percent of the pollution control expenditures in the United States goes toward cleaner air, another 40 percent goes toward cleaner water, and 20 percent goes toward disposing of solid waste. In this section, we will consider, in turn, air pollution, water pollution, Superfund activities, and disposing of solid waste.

Air Pollution

In the Clean Air Act of 1970 and in subsequent amendments, Congress set national standards for the amount of pollution that could be emitted into the atmosphere. Congress thereby recognized the atmosphere as an economic resource, which, like other resources, has alternative uses. The air can be used as a source of life-giving oxygen, as a prism for viewing breathtaking vistas, or as a dump for carrying away unwanted soot and gases. The 1970 act gave Americans the right to breathe air of a certain quality and at the same time gave producers the right to emit particular amounts of specified pollutants.

Smog is the most visible form of air pollution. Automobile emissions account for 40 percent of smog. Another 40 percent comes from consumer products, such as paint thinner, fluorocarbon sprays, dry-cleaning solvents, and baker's yeast by-products. Surprisingly, only 15 percent of smog comes from manufacturing. The 1970 Clean Air Act mandated a reduction of 90 percent in auto emissions, leaving it to the auto industry to achieve this target. At the time, automakers said the target was impossible. Between 1970 and 1990, however, average emissions of lead fell 97 percent, carbon monoxide emissions fell 41 percent, and sulfur oxide emissions fell 25 percent. In fact, a recent EPA study concluded that because auto emissions and industrial smoke have been reduced, *air pollution on average is now greater indoors than outdoors.* For example, in the Los Angeles area, a smog alert, meaning the air reached dangerous levels, occurred on a weekly basis during the 1980s, but by 2000 there were no smog alerts. U.S. air quality is now considered good compared to the air quality in much of the world. Only one U.S. city, New York, ranks among the world's 10 worst when it comes to nitrogen oxide, and no U.S. city ranks among the world's 20 worst in sulfur dioxide.

Despite recent improvements in air quality, the United States is still a major source of carbon dioxide emissions. As you can see from Exhibit 5, which shows the world's 20 worst nations in carbon dioxide emissions per capita in 2000, the United States ranks third worst with 5.4 tons per capita. The following case study examines the problem of cleaning up the polluted air in the capital city of one developing country.

City in the Clouds

Mexico City was once known for its spectacular views of snow-capped volcanoes. Now the distant hills seldom appear. The problem? Population surged from 3 million in 1950 to 20 million today. More people mean more industry and more vehicles. Nearly half of Mexico's industrial output is produced in or near Mexico City. Over 3.5 million vehicles (30 percent are more than 20 years old) plus tens of thousands of small, poorly regulated businesses spew a soup of pollution.

The city's geography and altitude compound the pollution problem. Mountains border on three sides, so the wind that blows in from the north (the open side) traps pollution over the city. Worse yet, at 7,400 feet above sea level, the city's altitude reduces the air's oxygen content by about one-quarter. The low oxygen content causes incomplete fuel combustion in engines, and results in yet more pollution. The combination of high pollution, low oxygen, and a tropical sun makes for unhealthy air—which is why some people call the place "Makesicko City."

Traffic is a snarl. The average commuting time is three hours per day, with one-fifth of commuters spending four hours or more. City officials have taken steps to address the common-pool problem, but the task is daunting. Emission limits for new cars were recently imposed but the growing popularity of sports utility vehicles, or SUVs, adds to the problem. They are less fuel efficient, spew more emissions, and take up more space on already crowded roads. In September 2003, some 10 percent of motor vehicles were temporarily ordered off the roads when ozone levels reached 2.5 times acceptable limits.

Part of the problem is that low incomes in Mexico make environmental protection a costly luxury. For example, the minimum wage is the equivalent of about $4 per day. Despite all this, there are some hopeful signs. Catalytic converters, a switch to unleaded fuel, and higher gasoline prices are starting to brighten the picture. The North American Free-Trade Agreement (NAFTA) has encouraged some producers to move closer to the U.S. border. With industry moving out of Mexico City, levels of lead, carbon dioxide, and sulfur dioxide are beginning to show some improvement. Make no mistake, the air in Mexico City

© Allen Russell/Index Stock Imagry

C a s e **S t u d y**

Public Policy

*e*Activity
GAIA, a collaborative effort of European research centers and universities, builds multimedia tools for environmental education and management. It presents an interesting case study, "Urban Air Pollution in Mexico City," at http://www.ess.co.at/GAIA/CASES/MEX/index.html. What are the major sources of air pollutants in Mexico City, and what are their primary effects? What plans are there to control emissions? A photographic essay illustrating the problem is archived by the National Geographic Society at http://www.nationalgeographic.com/features/96/mexico/a011.html.

Part 5 *Market Failure and Public Policy*

is still bad, but it's better than it was five years ago. For the first time in a long while, a patch of blue sky sometimes shows through.

Sources: Andrew Churg et al., "Chronic Exposure to High Levels of Chronic Air Pollution: A Case Study of Mexico City," *Environmental Health Perspectives*, Vol. 111 (May 2003); Tim Weiner, "Terrific News in Mexico City: Air Is Sometimes Breathable," *New York Times*, 5 January 2001; "Mexico City Declares Air Pollution Emergency, Orders 350,000 Cars Off the Streets," *Associated Press*, 20 September 2002; and Planet Ark at http://www. planetark.org.

EXHIBIT 5   **Fossil-Fuel Carbon Dioxide Emissions per Capita: The 20 Worst Nations**

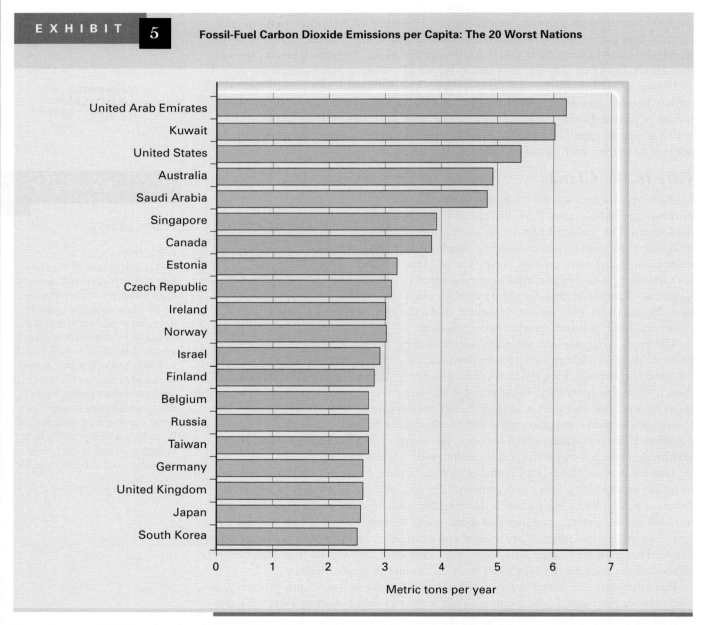

Source: Figures are for 2000 and are from "A Compendium of Data on Global Change" by the Carbon Dioxide Information Analysis Center at http://cdiac. esd.ornl.gov/home.html.

There have been efforts to address air quality on an international scale. A tentative accord reached in Kyoto, Japan, in 1997, would require the 38 industrial countries to reduce emissions of carbon dioxide and other so-called greenhouse gases by one-third over 10 years. The measure would impose a carbon tax on coal, natural gas, and oil. The cost to the U.S. economy could reach $300 billion a year, according to one study. Only industrial countries would be required to reduce emissions; developing countries need not participate. Thus, even if industrial nations met their Kyoto targets, carbon dioxide emissions would continue to rise because most of the projected global increase would come from exempted countries. Critics of the treaty argue that cleaner air should require a greater commitment from the developing world, such as China and India, which are major polluters. Argentina was the first developing nation offering to cut back greenhouse emissions. But the United States and Russia have rejected the treaty, thus dooming it.

Water Pollution

Two major sources of water pollution are sewage and chemicals. For decades, U.S. cities had an economic incentive to dump their sewage directly into waterways rather than clean it up first. The current or tides would carry off the waste to become someone else's problem. Although each community found it rational, based on a narrow view of the situation, to dump into waterways, the combined effect of these individual choices was water pollution, a negative externality imposed by one community on other communities.

Federal money over the years has funded sewage treatment plants, and subsidizing treatment plants has cut water pollution substantially. Hundreds of once-polluted waterways have been cleaned up enough for swimming and fishing. Nearly all U.S. cities now have modern sewage control systems. A notable exception is New York City, which teams up with New Jersey to dump some raw sewage into the Atlantic Ocean, using a discharge point about 100 miles out to sea.

Chemicals are another source of water pollution. Chemical pollution may conjure up an image of a pipe spewing chemicals into a river, but only about 10 percent of chemical pollution in the water comes from point pollution—pollution from factories and other industrial sites. About two-thirds come from nonpoint pollution—mostly runoff from agricultural pesticides and fertilizer. Congress has been reluctant to limit the use of pesticides, although pesticides pollute water and contaminate food. Industrial America seems an easier target than Old MacDonald's farm.

In 1970, Congress shifted control of pesticides from the U.S. Department of Agriculture to the newly created Environmental Protection Agency (EPA). But the EPA already had its hands full administering the Clean Water Act, so it turned pesticide regulation over to the states. Most states gave the job to their departments of agriculture. But these departments usually promote the interests of farmers, not restrict what farmers can do. The EPA now reports that in most states pesticides have fouled some groundwater. The EPA also argues that pesticide residues on food pose more health problems than do toxic waste dumps or even air pollution. The EPA's inspector general said that federal and state officials failed to enforce the nation's clean air and water laws. For example, most streams in Missouri are not clean enough for swimming. So that state failed to achieve the Clean Water Act's central goal.[6]

Hazardous Waste and the Superfund

The U.S. synthetic chemical industry has flourished in the last 50 years, and over 50,000 chemicals are now in common use. Some have harmful effects on humans and other living

6. John Cushman, "E.P.A. and States Found to Be Lax on Pollution Law," *New York Times*, 7 June 1998.

creatures. These chemicals can pose risks at every stage of their production, use, and disposal. New Jersey manufactures more toxic chemicals than any other state and, not surprisingly, has the worst toxic waste burden. Prior to 1980, the disposal of toxic waste created get-rich-quick opportunities for anyone who could rent or buy a few acres of land to open a toxic waste dump. As an extreme example, one site in New Jersey took in 71 million gallons of hazardous chemicals during a three-year period.[7]

Before 1980, once a company paid someone to haul away its hazardous waste, the company was no longer responsible. The Comprehensive Environmental Response, Compensation, and Liability Act of 1980, known more popularly as the Superfund law, now requires any company that generates, stores, or transports hazardous wastes to pay to clean up any wastes that are improperly disposed. A producer or hauler who is the source of even one barrel of pollution dumped at a site can be held liable for cleaning up the entire site.

The Superfund law gives the federal government authority over sites contaminated with toxins. But to get an offending company to comply, the EPA frequently must sue. The process is slow, and nearly half the budget goes to lawyers, consultants, and administrators rather than to site cleanups. The law did not require that benefits exceed costs or even that such comparisons be attempted. Although billions have been spent so far, a recent EPA study concluded that the health hazards of Superfund sites have been vastly exaggerated. Chemicals in the ground often move slowly, sometimes taking years to travel a few feet, so any possible health threat is confined to the site itself. People know when they live near toxic waste sites, and they can exert political pressure to get something done, whereas people exposed to polluted air, water, and pesticide residue may develop health problems but not make the connection to their environment. Thus, people see less reason to press public officials for cleaner air and water. Toxic waste sites, because of their greater political urgency and media appeal, tend to receive more attention than air or water pollution. And with the federal government picking up the tab, localities demand all the cleanup they can get.

Solid Waste: "Paper or Plastic?"

Throughout most of history, households tossed their trash outside as fodder for pigs and goats. New York City, like other cities, had no trash collections, so domestic waste was thrown into the street, where it mixed with mud and manure. Decades of such behavior explains why the oldest Manhattan streets are anywhere from 3 to 15 feet above their original levels. About 200 years ago, people buried their trash near their homes or took it to the town dump. Now U.S. households generate about 4 pounds of garbage per resident per day—more than twice the 1960 level and the most per capita in the world. Much of the solid waste consists of packaging material. The question is, how do we dispose of the more than 200 million tons of household garbage generated in this country each year?

Advanced economies produce and buy more than less developed economies, so there is more to throw away. And because of higher incomes in advanced economies, the opportunity cost of time is higher, so we tend to discard items rather than repair or recycle them. For example, it's cheaper to buy a new toaster for $25 than to pay someone $40 an hour to fix a broken one, assuming you can even find a repair service. (Look up "Appliance Repair, Small" in the *Yellow Pages* of the Internet's Super Pages and see if you can find even one such shop in your area.)

About 70 percent of the nation's garbage is bulldozed and covered with soil in landfills. Although a well-managed landfill poses few environmental concerns, at one time, communities dumped all kinds of toxic materials in them—stuff that could leach into the soil, con-

7. Jason Zweig, "Real-Life Horror Story," *Forbes,* 12 December 1988.

taminating wells and aquifers. So landfills got a bad reputation. The prevailing attitude with landfills is Nimby! (Not in my backyard!). We all want our garbage picked up but nobody wants it put down anywhere nearby.

As the cost of solid waste disposal increases, some state and local governments are economizing, charging households by the pound for trash pickups, and requiring more recycling and returnable bottles. **Recycling** is the process of converting waste products into reusable materials. Nearly half of U.S. households participate in curbside recycling programs. Still, according to the EPA, only about 15 percent of U.S. garbage gets recycled; about 15 percent is incinerated and, as noted already, the remaining 70 percent goes into landfills. Of the recycled material, three-quarters consists of corrugated boxes, newspapers, office paper, newspapers, and other paper products. Some of the paper is shipped to Korea, Taiwan, and China, where it becomes packaging material for U.S. imports such as DVD players and computer components. Exhibit 6 ranks the world's top 20 paper recyclers among advance economies in 2000. Germany heads the list, recycling 70 percent of its paper. The United States ranks 16th, recycling 42 percent, double that of 1985.

Most of the 15 percent of garbage that is incinerated gets burned in trash-to-energy plants, which generate electricity using the heat from incineration. Until recently, such plants looked like the wave of the future, but less favorable tax treatment and environmental concerns over incinerator locations (Nimby strikes again!) have taken the steam out of the trash-to-energy movement.

To repeat, about 70 percent of U.S. garbage goes to landfills, and only 30 percent is incinerated or recycled. In contrast, the Japanese recycle 40 percent of their waste and incinerate 33 percent, leaving only 27 percent to be deposited in landfills. Japanese households sort their trash into as many as 21 categories. Because land is scarcer in Japan—we know this because it costs relatively more—it is not surprising that the Japanese deposit a smaller share of their garbage in landfills.

Some recycling is clearly economical—such as aluminum cans, which are a cheap source of aluminum compared to producing raw aluminum. About two out of three aluminum cans now get recycled, though only 10 states require returnable deposits. The average American uses 12 pounds of aluminum each year in aluminum cans; so about 8 pounds of that is recycled. Recycling paper and cardboard is also economical and occurred long before the environmental movement. Still, such old standbys as paper drives, drop-off bins, and redemption centers still collect more tonnage than curbside programs. Most recycling results from salvaging scrap material from business and industry, a practice that goes back decades.

Governments have tried to stimulate demand for recycled material—for example, by requiring newspapers to use a certain amount of recycled newsprint. Other recycled products are not in such demand. In fact, some recycled products have become worthless and must be hauled to landfills. Recycling imposes its own cost on the environment. Curbside recycling requires fleets of trucks that pollute the air. Newsprint must first be de-inked, creating a sludge that must be disposed. But greater environmental awareness has made consumers more receptive to more efficient packaging material. For example, liquid laundry detergent is now available in a concentrated "ultra" form, which cuts volume in half. And labels for all kinds of products proudly identify the recycled content of the packaging.

Positive Externalities

To this point, we have considered only negative externalities. But externalities are sometimes positive, or beneficial. Positive externalities occur when consumption or production benefits other consumers or other firms. For example, people who get inoculated against a

RECYCLING
The process of converting waste products into reusable material

EXHIBIT   **6**   **Paper and Cardboard Recycling: Top 20 Among Advanced Economies**

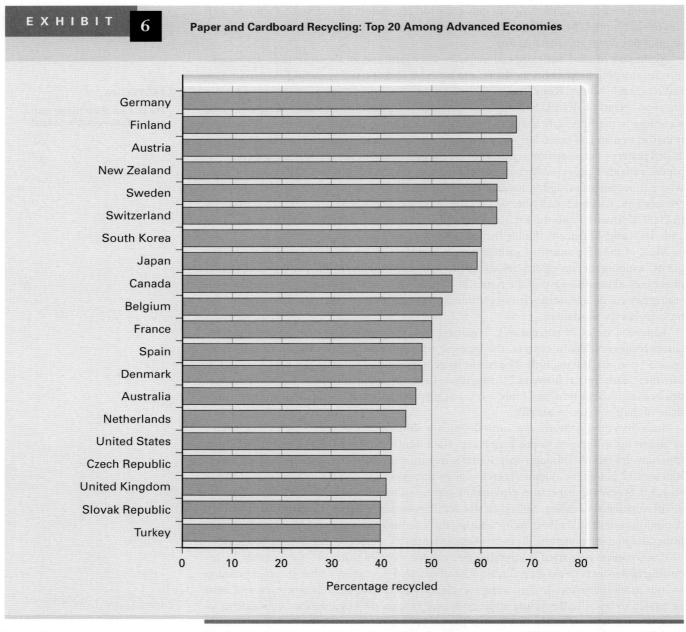

Source: Figures are rankings among members of the Organization of Economic Cooperation and Development as reported in *OECD Environmental Data 2002*, Table 5.4A, p. 21. This can be found at http://www.oecd.org/document/21/0,2340,en_2825_495628_2516565_1_1_1_1,00.html. Figures are for 2000, except for Canada, which is for 1996, and the United States, which is for 1999.

disease reduce their own likelihood of contracting the disease, but in the process they also reduce the risk of transmitting the disease to others. Inoculations thus provide external benefits to others. Society as a whole receives external benefits from education because those who acquire more education become better citizens, can read road signs, are better able to support themselves and their families, and are less likely to require public assistance or to re-

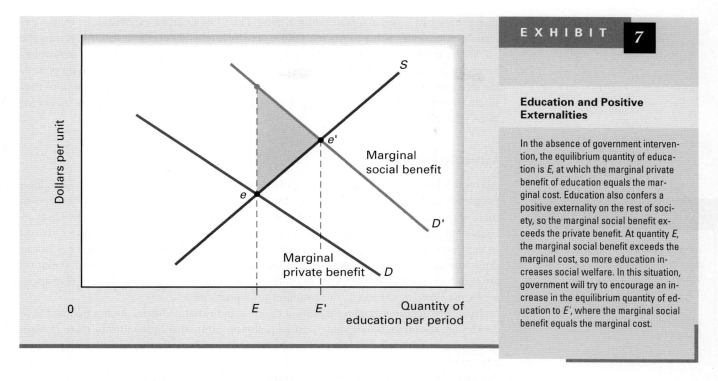

EXHIBIT 7

Education and Positive Externalities

In the absence of government intervention, the equilibrium quantity of education is *E*, at which the marginal private benefit of education equals the marginal cost. Education also confers a positive externality on the rest of society, so the marginal social benefit exceeds the private benefit. At quantity *E*, the marginal social benefit exceeds the marginal cost, so more education increases social welfare. In this situation, government will try to encourage an increase in the equilibrium quantity of education to *E'*, where the marginal social benefit equals the marginal cost.

sort to crime for income. Thus, education provides private benefits but it also confers additional social benefits on others.

The effect of external benefits on the optimal level of consumption is illustrated in Exhibit 7, which presents the demand and supply of education. The demand curve, *D*, represents the private demand for education, which reflects the marginal private benefit for those who acquire the education. More education is demanded at a lower price than at a higher price.

The benefit of education, however, spills over to others in society. If we add this positive externality, or marginal external benefit, to the marginal private benefit of education, we get the marginal social benefit of education. The marginal social benefit includes all the benefit society derives from education, both private and external. The marginal social benefit curve is above the private demand curve in Exhibit 7. At each level of education, the marginal social benefit exceeds the marginal private benefit by the amount of marginal external benefit generated by that particular level of education.

If education were a strictly private decision, the amount purchased would be determined by the intersection of the private demand curve *D* with supply curve *S*. The supply curve reflects the marginal cost of producing each unit of the good. This intersection at point *e* yields education level *E*, where the marginal private benefit of education equals its marginal cost. But at level *E*, the marginal social benefit of education exceeds its marginal cost. Social welfare will increase if education expands beyond *E*. As long as the marginal social benefit of education exceeds its marginal cost, social welfare increases if education expands. Social welfare is maximized at point *e'* in Exhibit 7, where *E'* units of education are provided—that is, where the marginal social benefit equals the marginal cost, as reflected by the supply curve. The blue-shaded triangle identifies the increase in social welfare that results from increasing education from *E* to *E'*.

Thus, society is better off if the level of education exceeds the private equilibrium. When positive externalities are present, decisions based on private marginal benefits result in less than the socially optimal quantity of the good. Thus, like negative externalities, positive externalities typically point to market failure, which is why government often gets into the act. When there are external benefits, public policy aims to increase the level of output beyond the private optimum. For example, governments try to increase education by providing free primary and secondary education, by requiring students to stay in school until they reach 16 years of age, by subsidizing public higher education, and by offering tax breaks for some education costs.

Conclusion

About 6.5 billion people inhabit the globe, doubling in the last 40 years. Over 72 million people are added each year. World population is projected to reach 9 billion by 2050, with most of this growth occurring in countries where most people barely eke out a living. Population pressure coupled with a lack of incentives to conserve open-access resources results in deforestation, dwindling fish stocks, and polluted air, land, and water. Market prices can direct the allocation of resources only as long as property rights are well defined. Pollution arises not so much from the greed of producers and consumers as from the fact that open-access resources are subject to the common-pool problem.

Ironically, because of tighter pollution controls, industrial countries are less polluted than developing countries, where there is more pollution from what little industry there is. Most developing countries have such profound economic problems that environmental quality is not a high priority. For example, when India's Supreme Court recently tried to close some polluting factories in New Delhi, thousands of workers torched buses, threw stones, and blocked major roads, demanding the factories stay open. Although New Delhi's air is so filthy that it often masks any trace of a blue sky, workers believe their jobs are more important. Here's one account of New Delhi's air quality:

In the heat of the afternoons, a yellow-white mixture hung above the city, raining acidic soot into the dust and exhaust fumes. At night the mixture condenses into a dry, choking fog that envelops the headlights of passing cars, and creeps its stink into even the tightest houses. The residents could do little to keep the poison out of their lungs or the lungs of their children, and if they were poor, they could not even try.[8]

SUMMARY

1. An exhaustible resource is available in fixed supply, such as crude oil or coal. A renewable resource regenerates itself and so can be used periodically if used conservatively, such as a properly managed forest. Some resources suffer from a common-pool problem because unrestricted access leads to overuse.

2. Production that generates negative externalities results in too much output. Production that generates positive externalities results in too little output. Public policy should tax or otherwise limit production that generates negative externalities and should subsidize or otherwise promote production that generates positive externalities.

3. The optimal amount of environmental quality occurs where the marginal social benefit of an improvement equals its marginal social cost. An upward shift of the marginal benefit curve of environmental quality or a downward shift of its marginal cost curve will increase the optimal level of environmental quality.

8. William Langewiesche, "The Shipbreakers," *Atlantic Monthly* (August 2000): 42.

4. The world's tropical rainforests recycle noxious gases into oxygen and wood. Because rainforests are open-access resources, settlers and loggers cut them down to make a living. This destruction reduces the environment's ability to cleanse itself.

5. The Coase theorem argues that as long as bargaining costs are low, assigning property rights to one party leads to an efficient solution to an externality problem. The market for pollution permits reflects the Coase theorem in action.

6. The nation's
is cleaner b
vehicles, ar
spent on s
pose as g
such as
the me

378

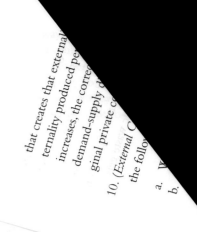

that creates that externa
ternality produced pe
increases, the corre
demand-supply
ginal private c

10. (External C
the follo
a.
b.

QUESTIONS FOR REVIEW

1. (*Externalities*) Complete each of the following sentences:

    a. Resources that are available only in a fixed amount are _____ resources.
    b. The possibility that a nonexcludable resource will be used until the net marginal value of additional use equals zero is known as the _____.
    c. Resources for which periodic use can be continued indefinitely are known as _____ resources.

2. (*Resolving the Common-Pool Problem*) Why have authorities found it so difficult to regulate the fishing catch to allow for a sustainable yield?

3. (*Optimal Level of Pollution*) Explain the difference between fixed-production technology and variable technology. Should the government set a goal of reducing the marginal social cost of pollution to zero in industries with fixed-production technology? Should they do so in industries with variable technology?

4. (*Case Study: Destruction of the Tropical Rainforests*) Why does a solution to the overharvesting of timber in the tropical rainforests require some form of international cooperation? Would this be a sufficient solution to the deforestation problem?

5. (*The Coase Theorem*) Suppose a firm pollutes a stream that has a recreational value only when pollution is below a certain level. If transaction costs are low, why does the assignment of property rights to the stream lead to the same (efficient) level of pollution whether the firm or recreational users own the stream?

6. (*The Coase Theorem*) Ronald Coase points out that a market failure does not arise simply because people ignore the external cost of their actions. What other condition is necessary? What did Coase consider to be an efficient solution to a negative externality?

7. (*Positive Externalities*) The value of a home depends in part on how attractive other homes and yards in the neighborhood are. How do local zoning ordinances try to promote land uses that generate external benefits for neighbors?

PROBLEMS AND EXERCISES

8. (*External Costs with Fixed-Production Technology*) Review the situation illustrated in Exhibit 1 in this chapter. If the government sets the price of electricity at the socially optimal level, why is the net gain equal to triangle *abc*, even though consumers now pay a higher price for electricity?

What would the net gain be if the government set the price above the optimal level?

9. (*Negative Externalities*) Suppose you wish to reduce a negative externality by imposing a tax on the activity

ity. When the amount of the ex-
unit of output increases as output
t tax can be determined by using a
agram; show this. Assume that the mar-
st curve slopes upward.

osts) Use the data in the table below to answer
ving questions.

What is the external cost per unit of production?
What level will be produced if there is no regulation
of the externality?
c.   What level should be produced to achieve economic
efficiency?
d.   Calculate the dollar value of the net gain to society
from correcting the externality.

Quantity	Marginal Private Benefit (demand)	Marginal Private Cost (supply)	Marginal Social Cost
0	—	$ 0	$ 0
1	$10	2	4
2	9	3	5
3	8	4	6
4	7	5	7
5	6	6	8
6	5	7	9
7	4	8	10
8	3	9	11
9	2	10	12
10	1	11	13

11. (*External Costs with Variable Technology*) Think of an industry that pollutes the water and has access to variable technology for reducing that water pollution. Graphically illustrate and explain the impact of each of the following, other
things constant, on the optimal level of water quality:

a.   New evidence is discovered of a greater risk of cancer
from water pollution.
b.   The cost of pollution control equipment increases.
c.   A technological improvement reduces the cost of pollution control.

12. (*Market for Pollution Rights*) The following graph shows the
market for pollution rights.

a.   If there are no restrictions on pollution, what amount
will be discharged?
b.   What will be the quantity supplied and the quantity
demanded if the government restricts the amount of
discharge to Q* but gives the permits away?
c.   Where is market equilibrium if the government sells
the permits? Illustrate this on the graph.
d.   What happens to market equilibrium if the government reduces the amount of discharge permitted to
Q**? Illustrate this on the graph.

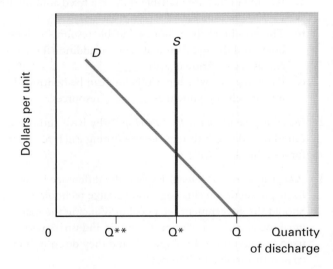

EXPERIENTIAL EXERCISES

13. (***C a s e S t u d y:*** City in the Clouds) Suppose you are
the mayor of Mexico City. How can you use some of the
techniques outlined in this chapter to control pollution
there? (For background information, check
http://www.ess.co.at/GAIA/CASES/MEX/index.html.)

14. (*The Common-Pool Problem*) Garrett Hardin's 1968 article,
"The Tragedy of the Commons," is available online at
http://www.garretthardinsociety.org/articles/art_tragedy_
of_the_commons.html. Read this clearly written article,
and then describe some examples of the common-pool
problem or, as he calls it, the tragedy of the commons.

15. *(External Costs with Fixed Technology)* Read Betty Joyce Nash's "Pollution Allowances Help Clear the Air" at http://www.rich.frb.org/pubs/cross/cross134/2.html. Based on what you've learned in this chapter, evaluate Nash's case for pollution allowances as a way of controlling negative externalities.

16. *(Wall Street Journal)* The Marketplace section of the *Wall Street Journal* is a good place to look for information related to externalities. On a given day, see how many stories you can find that deal with externalities—positive or negative. Are businesses taking steps to "internalize" externalities? What role does technology play in controlling negative externalities?

17. Visit the Environmental Protection Agency's Web site and examine information on general interest programs (at http://www.epa.gov/epahome/general.htm). The EPA has implemented a number of programs aimed at improving air and water quality. Describe one program and the problem it addresses. Graphically illustrate and explain the EPA's approach.

HOMEWORK XPRESS! EXERCISES

*These exercises require access to McEachern Homework Xpress! If Homework Xpress! did not come with your book, visit **http://homeworkxpress.swlearning.com** to purchase.*

1. The production of clean, white paper is really a dirty job. Paper mills generate air and water pollutants. In the diagram, draw a downward sloping demand for paper and a horizontal marginal private cost curve at $20. Identify the private-sector equilibrium level of output of paper. Then add a marginal social cost curve showing that each ton of paper produced generates an additional $2 per ton of external costs. Identify the socially efficient level of output.

2. The runoff of water from streets, lawns, and construction sites is a major source of pollutants for our lakes and streams. Various methods are available for controlling runoff and improving water quality—some cheap, others more costly. In the diagram draw the marginal social cost line that illustrates this. Add a marginal social benefit line that shows how the additional benefits of control decrease. Identify the optimal level of water quality. Suppose the government mandates control efforts that result in a higher level of quality. Illustrate the social waste associated with making the water too clean.

3. Improving the quality of drinking water in developing economies is one of the most beneficial investments that can be made. However, controlling discharges that reduce water quality is costly. Use marginal social cost and marginal social benefits lines to illustrate the optimal level of water quality in any particular area. Then illustrate the effect on the optimal level of water quality of a technological improvement that reduces control costs.

Income Distribution and Poverty

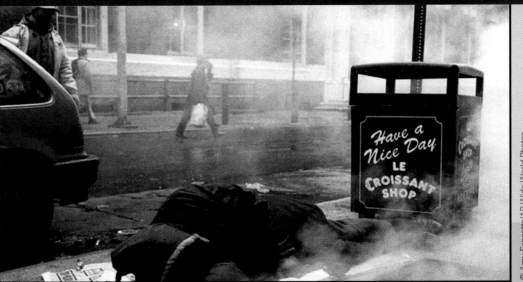

© Amy Sancetta/AP Wide World Photos

Why are some people poor even in the most productive economy on Earth? Who are the poor, how did they get that way, and how long do they remain poor? What's been the trend in poverty over time? How has the changing family structure affected poverty? What public programs aim to reduce poverty, and how well have they worked? Answers to these and related questions are addressed in this chapter, which discusses income distribution and poverty in America.

To establish a reference point, we first examine the distribution of income in the United States, paying special attention to trends in recent decades. We then evaluate the "social safety net"—government programs aimed at helping poor people. We also consider the impact of the changing family structure on poverty, focusing in particular on the increase in households headed by women. We close by examining recent welfare reforms. Topics discussed include:

HOMEWORK Xpress!

Use Homework Xpress! for economic application, graphing, videos, and more.

- Distribution of income
- Official poverty level
- Public policy and poverty
- The feminization of poverty
- Poverty and discrimination
- Welfare reforms

The Distribution of Household Income

In a market economy, income depends primarily on earnings, which depend on the productivity of one's resources. The problem with allocating income according to productivity is that some people have few productive resources to sell. People with mental or physical disabilities and poor education, those facing discrimination, bad luck, or the demands of caring for small children, and the elderly may be less productive or unable to earn a living.

Income Distribution by Quintiles

As a starting point, let's consider the distribution of income in the economy and see how it has changed over time, focusing on the household as the economic unit. After dividing the total number of U.S. households into five groups of equal size, or *quintiles,* ranked according to income, we can examine the percentage of income received by each quintile. Such a division is presented in Exhibit 1 since 1970. Take a moment to look over this exhibit. Notice that households in the lowest, or poorest, fifth of the population received only 4.1 percent of the income in 1970, whereas households in the highest, or richest, fifth received 43.3 percent of the income. The U.S. Census Bureau measures income after cash transfer payments are received but before taxes are paid.

In recent decades, the share of income going to the top fifth has increased, and the share going to the bottom fifth has declined. The richest group's share of income increased from 43.3 percent in 1970 to 49.7 percent in 2002. A primary contributor to the larger share of income going to the highest group has been the growth of two-earner households in that top group. A primary contributor to the smaller share going to the lowest group has been the growth of single-parent households in the bottom group.

Also shown in Exhibit 1 is the share of income going to the top 5 percent of households; that share has grown since 1980, accounting for all the growth of the top 20 percent of households. Because of substantial reductions in the top marginal tax rates in 1981 and 1986, high-income people had less incentive to engage in tax avoidance and tax evasion, so their reported income increased, boosting the share of reported income going to the richest 5 percent of households.

The Lorenz Curve

We have just examined the distribution of income using a bar chart. Another way to picture that distribution is with a Lorenz curve. A **Lorenz curve** shows the percentage of total income received by any given percentage of households when incomes are arrayed from smallest to largest. As shown in Exhibit 2, the cumulative percentage of households is measured along the horizontal axis, and the cumulative percentage of income is measured along the vertical axis. Any given distribution of income can be compared to an equal distribution of income among households. If income were evenly distributed, each 20 percent of households would also receive 20 percent of the total income, and the Lorenz curve would be a straight line with a slope equal to 1.0, as shown in Exhibit 2.

As the distribution becomes more uneven, the Lorenz curve is pulled down to the right, away from the line of equal distribution. The Lorenz curves in Exhibit 2 were calculated for

LORENZ CURVE

A curve showing the percentage of total income received by a given percentage of recipients whose incomes are arrayed from smallest to largest

EXHIBIT 1   **Share of Aggregate Household Income by Quintile: 1970, 1980, 1990, and 2002**

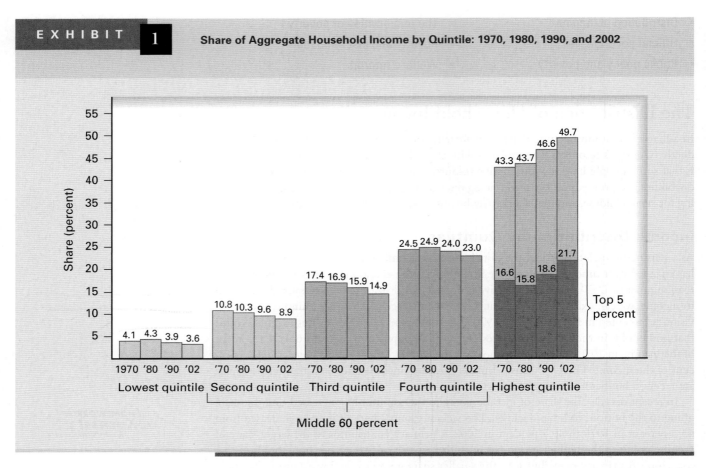

Source: U.S. Census Bureau, *Income in the United States: 2002*, Current Population Reports, September 2003, Table A-3, http://www.census.gov/prod/2003pubs/p60-221.pdf.

1970 and 2002 based on the data in Exhibit 1. As a reference, point *a* on the 1970 Lorenz curve indicates that in that year, the bottom 80 percent of families received 56.7 percent of the income, and the top 20 percent received 43.3 percent of the income. The Lorenz curve for 2002 is farther from the line of equal distribution than is the Lorenz curve for 1970, showing that income among households has become more unevenly distributed. Point *b* on the 2002 curve shows that the bottom 80 percent received 50.3 percent of the income and the top 20 percent received 49.7 percent of the income.

A College Education Pays More

Also contributing to the dominance of the top group is a growing premium paid those with college educations. In the last two decades, the median wage (adjusted for inflation) for people with only high school diplomas declined 6 percent, while the median wage for college graduates rose 12 percent. The **median wage** is the middle wage when wages are ranked from lowest to highest. Why have more-educated workers done better? First, trends such as industry deregulation, declining unionization, and freer international trade have reduced the demand for workers with less education. Labor unions, for example, raised the wages of many workers who would have otherwise ended up in the bottom half of the income dis-

MEDIAN WAGE

The middle wage when wages of all workers are ranked from lowest to highest

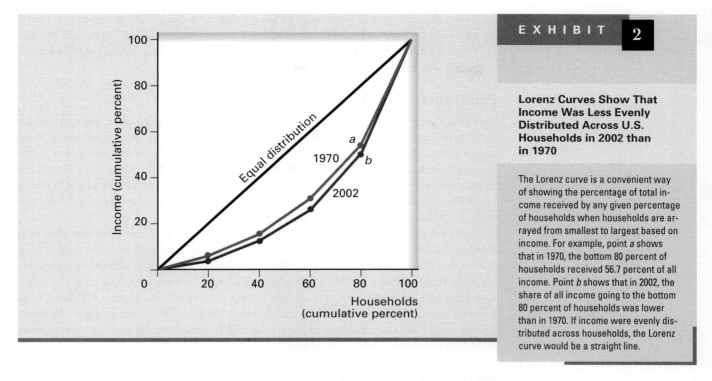

EXHIBIT 2

Lorenz Curves Show That Income Was Less Evenly Distributed Across U.S. Households in 2002 than in 1970

The Lorenz curve is a convenient way of showing the percentage of total income received by any given percentage of households when households are arrayed from smallest to largest based on income. For example, point *a* shows that in 1970, the bottom 80 percent of households received 56.7 percent of all income. Point *b* shows that in 2002, the share of all income going to the bottom 80 percent of households was lower than in 1970. If income were evenly distributed across households, the Lorenz curve would be a straight line.

tribution. But the share of the workforce that is unionized declined from 26 percent in 1973 to only 14 percent in 2002.

Second, new computer-based information technologies have reduced the demand for low-skilled clerical workers, because their jobs became computerized. Computers also offered more timely and accurate information to management, allowing for organizational innovations that made managers and other professionals more productive.[1] So computers reduced the demand for workers with low skills, such as clerical staff and bank tellers, and increased the demand for those who use computers to boost labor productivity, such as managers and accountants.

Third, the supply of less-educated workers increased more than the supply of more-educated workers, thus increasing the rewards of education. For example, compared to average residents, recent U.S. immigrants tend to be less educated, including an estimated 8 million illegal aliens, half of whom are from Mexico. The Hispanic population more than doubled between 1980 and 2000, and the percentage of foreign-born Hispanics increased. Among males age 25 and older, only 57 percent of Hispanics had at least a high school education in 2000, compared with 85 percent of whites and 79 percent of blacks. More generally, the foreign-born share of the U.S. population doubled from 5 percent in 1970 to 11 percent in 2000, the largest share since the 1930s. Thus, immigration has increased the supply of relatively poorly educated workers, which has depressed wages of the less educated generally.

So economic and migration trends in recent years have benefited the better educated, and this helps explain the growing disparity in household income. Income in the United States is less evenly distributed than in other developed countries throughout the world, such as Canada, France, Great Britain, Italy, and Australia, but is more evenly distributed than in most developing countries, such as Brazil, Chile, Mexico, Nigeria, and the Philippines. Some countries also

1. Timothy Bresnahan, "Computerization and Wage Dispersion: An Analytical Reinterpretation," *Economic Journal* (June 1999).

have far more extensive redistribution programs than does the United States, basing a variety of public policies on income. For example, Finland's traffic fines increase with the driver's income. One young tycoon speeding 43 miles per hour in a 25-mile-an-hour zone paid a $71,400 fine.[2]

Problems with Distribution Benchmarks

One problem with assessing income distributions is that there is no objective standard for evaluating them. The usual assumption is that a more equal distribution of income is more desirable, but is equal distribution most preferred? If not, then how uneven should it be? For example, among major league baseball players, well over half the pay goes to 20 percent of the players. Professional basketball pay skews even more, with top NBA players earning up to 50 times more than the bottom players. Does this mean the economy, as a whole, is in some sense "fairer" than these professional sports?

A second problem is that because Exhibits 1 and 2 measure money income after cash transfers but before taxes they neglect the effects of taxes and in-kind transfers, such as food stamps and free medical care for poor families. The tax system as a whole is progressive, meaning that families with higher incomes pay a larger fraction of their incomes in taxes. In-kind transfers benefit the lowest income groups the most. Consequently, if Exhibit 1 incorporated the effects of taxes and in-kind transfers, the share of income going to the lower groups would increase, the share going to the higher groups would decrease, and income would become more evenly distributed.

Third, focusing on the share of income going to each income quintile overlooks the fact that household size differs across quintiles. Most households in the bottom quintile consist of one person living alone. Only one in 16 households in the top quintile consists of one person living alone. Households in the top quintile average two-thirds larger than those in the bottom quintile, which helps to explain some of the difference in income share going to each quintile.

Fourth, Exhibits 1 and 2 include only *reported* income. If people receive payment "under the table" to evade taxes, or if they earn money through illegal activities, their actual income will exceed their reported income. The omission of unreported income will distort the data if unreported income as a percentage of total family income differs across income levels.

Finally, Exhibits 1 and 2 focus on the distribution of *income*, but a better measure of household welfare would be the distribution of *spending*. Available evidence indicates that *spending by quintiles is much more evenly distributed than income by quintiles.*

Why Incomes Differ

Income differences across households stem in part from differences in the *number* of workers in each household. Thus, *one reason household incomes differ is that the number of household members who are working differs.* For example, among households in the bottom 20 percent based on income, only one in five includes a full-time, year-round worker. Consider the link between median income and the number of workers. The **median income** of all households is the middle income when incomes are ranked from lowest to highest. In any given year, half the households are above the median income and half are below it. The median income for households with two earners is 87 percent higher than for households with only one earner and is about four times higher than for households with no earners.

HOMEWORK Xpress!
Ask the Instructor Video

MEDIAN INCOME

The middle income when all incomes are ranked from smallest to largest

---

2. Seven Stecklow, "Finnish Drivers Don't Mind Sliding Scale, But Instant Calculation Gets Low Marks," *Wall Street Journal,* 2 January 2001.

Incomes also differ for all the reasons labor incomes differ, such as differences in education, ability, job experience, and so on. At every age, people with more education earn more, on average. As noted a few chapters back, those with a professional degree earn about four times more than those with only a high school education. Age itself also has an important effect on income. As workers mature, they acquire valuable job experience, get promoted, and earn more.

Differences in earnings based on age and education reflect a normal *life cycle* pattern of income. In fact, most income differences across households reflect the normal workings of resource markets, whereby workers are rewarded according to their productivity. Because of these lifetime patterns, it is not necessarily the same households that remain rich or poor over time. Indeed, one study of income mobility found that more than three-quarters of people in the bottom 20 percent in 1975 had moved into the top 40 percent for at least one year by 1991.[3] Despite this mobility over time, we can still characterize rich and poor households at a point in time. A high-income household usually consists of a well-educated couple with both spouses employed. A low-income household is usually headed by a single parent who is young, female, poorly educated, and not working. Low incomes are a matter of public concern, especially when children are involved, as we will see in the next section.

Poverty and the Poor

Because poverty is such a relative concept, how do we measure it objectively, and how do we ensure that the measure can be applied with equal relevance over time? The federal government has developed a method for calculating an official poverty level, which serves as a benchmark for poverty analysis in the United States.

Official Poverty Level

To derive the **U.S. official poverty level,** the U.S. Department of Agriculture in 1959 first estimated the cost of a nutritionally adequate diet. Then, based on the assumption that the poor spend about one-third of their income on food, the official poverty level was calculated by multiplying this food cost by three. The U.S. Census Bureau tracks the official poverty level, making adjustments for family size and for inflation. For example, the official poverty level of money income for a family of four was $18,392 in 2002; a family of four at or below that income threshold was regarded as living in poverty. Poverty levels in 2002 ranged from $9,183 for a person living alone to $37,062 for a family of nine. The poverty definition is based on pretax money income, including cash transfers, but it excludes the value of noncash transfers such as food stamps, Medicaid, subsidized housing, or employer-provided health insurance.

Each year since 1959, the Census Bureau has conducted a survey comparing each family's cash income to the annual poverty level applicable to that family. Results of this survey are presented in Exhibit 3, which indicates both the millions of people living below the official poverty level and the percentage of the U.S. population below that level. Periods of U.S. recession are also shown (a recession is defined as two or more successive quarters of declining gross domestic product). Note that poverty increased during recessions.

The biggest decline in poverty occurred before 1970; *the poverty rate dropped from 22.4 percent in 1959 to 12.1 percent in 1969.* During that period, the number of poor people decreased from about 40 million to 24 million. The poverty rate has not shown huge fluctua-

U.S. OFFICIAL POVERTY LEVEL

Benchmark level of income computed by the federal government to track poverty over time; initially based on three times the cost of a nutritionally adequate diet

3. W. Michael Cox and Richard Arm, "By Our Own Bootstraps," *Federal Reserve Bank of Dallas: 1995 Annual Report.*

EXHIBIT **3**   **Number and Percentage of U.S. Population in Poverty: 1959–2002**

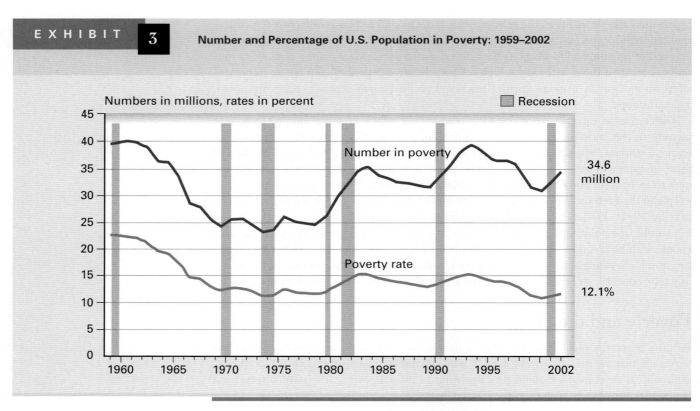

Source: U.S. Census Bureau, *Poverty in the United States: 2002*, Current Population Reports, September 2003, Figure 1, p.3, http://www.census.gov/prod/2003pubs/p60-222.pdf.

tions since that initial drop. After declining from 1994 to 2000, the poverty rate and the number of poor people increased during the next two years because of the national recession in 2001.

Poverty is a relative term. If we examined the distribution of income across countries, we would find huge gaps between rich and poor nations. The U.S. official poverty level of income is many times greater than the average income for three-fourths of the world's population. The U.S. poverty level for a family of four in 2002 works out to be a $12.60 per person per day. Most nations employ a much lower poverty level. For example, the World Bank uses an *international poverty line* of $1 per person per day. Based on that benchmark, about 16 percent of those in China, 35 percent of those in the India, and 47 percent of sub-Saharan Africans lived in poverty.[4]

Programs to Help the Poor

What should society's response to poverty be? The best predictor of family poverty is whether someone in that family has a job. Overall, the poverty rate is about four times greater in families with no workers than in families with at least one worker. One way to reduce poverty, therefore, is to ensure a healthy economy. The stronger the economy, the greater the job opportunities, and the more likely people will find work. Perhaps the best

4. Poverty rates can be found at the World Bank Group's site at http://www.worldbank.org/research/povmonitor/.

indicator of whether or not jobs are readily available is the *unemployment rate*, which shows the percentage or the labor force out of work. The *lower* the unemployment rate, the *higher* the likelihood that someone who wants a job has found one. Thus, the lower the unemployment rate, the lower the poverty rate. Exhibit 4 shows poverty rates and unemployment rates in the United States each year since 1969. As you can see, the poverty rate, shown by the top line, tends to rise when the unemployment rate increases and fall when the unemployment rate declines. For example, between 1979 and 1982 the unemployment rate spiked from 5.8 percent to 9.7 percent. During that period, the nation's poverty rate climbed from 11.7 percent to 15.0 percent. The unemployment rate fell from 7.5 percent in 1992 to 4.0 percent in 2000. During that period, poverty declined from 14.8 percent to 11.3 percent. After 2000, both unemployment and poverty increased with the national recession of 2001.

Thus, the government's first line of defense in fighting poverty is to promote a healthy economy. Yet even when the unemployment rate is low, some people are still poor. Although some antipoverty programs involve direct market intervention, such as minimum-wage laws, the most visible antipoverty programs redistribute income after the market has made an initial distribution. Since the mid-1960s, social welfare expenditures at all levels of government have increased significantly. We can divide these programs into two broad categories: social insurance and income assistance.

Social Insurance

Social insurance programs are designed to help make up for the lost income of people who worked but are now retired, temporarily unemployed, or unable to work because of disability or work-related injury. The major social insurance program is **Social Security,** established during the Great Depression to supplement retirement income of those with a

SOCIAL INSURANCE

Government programs designed to help make up for lost income of people who worked but are now retired, unemployed, or unable to work because of disability or work-related injury

SOCIAL SECURITY

Supplements retirement income to those with a record of contributing to the program during their working years; by far the largest government redistribution program

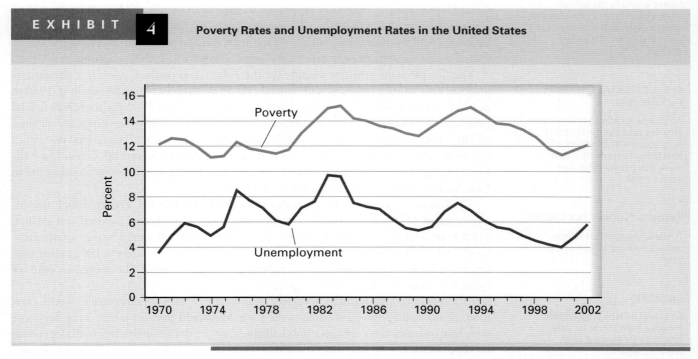

| EXHIBIT | 4 | **Poverty Rates and Unemployment Rates in the United States** |

Sources: U.S. Census Bureau and U.S. Bureau of Labor Statistics.

work history and a record of contributing to the program. **Medicare,** another social insurance program, provides health insurance for short-term medical care, mostly to those age 65 and older, regardless of income. There are over 40 million Social Security and Medicare beneficiaries. Other social insurance programs include *unemployment insurance* and *workers' compensation,* which supports workers injured on the job; both programs require that beneficiaries have a prior record of employment.

The social insurance system deducts "insurance premiums" from workers' pay to provide benefits to other retired, disabled, and unemployed individuals. These programs protect some families from poverty, particularly the elderly receiving Social Security, but they are aimed more at those with a work history. Still, the social insurance system tends to redistribute income from rich to poor and from young to old. Most current Social Security beneficiaries receive far more in benefits than they paid into the program, especially those with a brief work history or a record of low wages.

Income Assistance

Income assistance programs—what we usually call welfare programs—provide money and in-kind assistance to the poor. Unlike social insurance programs, income assistance programs do not require recipients to have a history of work or to have contributed to the program. Income assistance programs are means tested. In a **means-tested program,** a household's income and assets must fall below a certain level to qualify for benefits. The federal government funds two-thirds of welfare spending, and state and local governments fund one-third.

The two primary *cash transfer* programs are **Temporary Assistance for Needy Families (TANF),** which provides cash to poor families with dependent children, and **Supplemental Security Income (SSI),** which provides cash to the elderly poor and the disabled. Cash transfers vary inversely with family income from other sources. In 1997, TANF replaced Aid for Families with Dependent Children (AFDC), which began during the Great Depression and originally supported widows with young children. Whereas AFDC was a federal *entitlement* program, meaning that anyone who met the criteria was *entitled* to benefits, TANF is under the control of each state and carries no federal entitlement. The federal government gives each state a fixed grant to help fund TANF programs.

The SSI program provides support for the elderly and disabled poor. It is the fastest-growing cash transfer program, with federal outlays quadrupling from $8 billion in 1980 to nearly $31 billion by 2002, when 6.5 million people averaged $380 per month in federal benefits. SSI coverage has been broadened to include people addicted to drugs and alcohol, children with learning disabilities, and, in some cases, the homeless. The federal portion of this program is uniform across states, but states can supplement federal aid. Benefits in California average twice those in Alabama. Most states also offer modest *General Assistance* aid to those who are poor but do not qualify for TANF or SSI.

The federal government also provides an **earned-income tax credit,** which supplements wages of the working poor. For example, a family with two children and earning $14,500 in 2002 would not only pay no federal income tax but would receive a cash transfer of $4,140. More than 19.2 million recipients received such transfers in 2002, when outlays topped $30 billion, nearly double federal spending on TANF. The earned income tax credit lifts millions of families out of poverty.

In addition to cash transfers, a variety of *in-kind transfer* programs provide health care, food stamps, and housing assistance to the poor. **Medicaid** pays for medical care for those with low incomes who are aged, blind, disabled, or are living in families with dependent children. *Medicaid is by far the largest welfare program, costing nearly twice as much as all cash transfer programs combined.* It has grown more than any other poverty program, quadrupling in the last decade and accounting for nearly a quarter of the typical state's budget (though states receive federal grants covering half or more of their Medicaid budget). The qualifying level of income is set by each state, and some states are strict. Therefore, the proportion of poor covered by Medicaid varies across states. In 2002, about 40 million people received Medicaid benefits at a total cost of over $240 billion; outlays averaged about $6,000 per recipient. For many elderly, Medicaid covers long-term nursing care, which can exceed $100,000 per year. Although half the nation's welfare budget goes for health care, nearly 44 million U.S. residents, or one in seven people, still had no health insurance in 2002.

Food stamps are vouchers that the poor can redeem for food. In 2003, nearly 21.5 million people received food stamps in the average month, down from an all-time high of 27.5 million recipients in 1994. Monthly benefits averaged $82 per person in 2003. Four of 10 people eligible for food stamps do not apply for them.

Housing assistance programs include direct assistance for rental payments and subsidized low-income housing. Spending for housing assistance has more than doubled since 1990. About 10 million people receive some form of housing assistance. Other in-kind transfer programs include the *school lunch program* for poor children; supplemental food vouchers for pregnant women, infants, and children; *energy assistance* to help pay the energy bills of poor families; and *education and training assistance* for poor families, such as Head Start. *In all, there are about 75 means-tested federal welfare programs.*

FOOD STAMPS

An in-kind transfer program that offers low-income households vouchers redeemable for food; benefit levels vary inversely with household income

Who Are the Poor?

Economics
in the Movies

Who are the poor, and how has the composition of this group changed over time? We will slice poverty statistics in several ways to examine the makeup of the group. Keep in mind that we are relying on official poverty estimates, which ignore the value of in-kind transfers, so, to that extent, official estimates overstate poverty.

Poverty and Age

Earlier we looked at poverty among the U.S. population. Here we focus on poverty and age. Exhibit 5 presents the poverty rates for three age groups since 1959: people less than 18 years old, those between 18 and 64, and those 65 and older. As you can see, poverty rates for each group declined between 1959 and 1968. Between the mid-1970s and the early 1980s, the rate among those under 18 trended upward, but then declined from 22.7 percent in 1993 to 16.7 percent in 2002.

In 1959, the elderly were the poorest group, with a poverty rate of 35 percent. Poverty among the elderly has declined to 10.4 percent by 2002, slightly below the rate of 10.6 percent for people 18 to 64 years of age. The decline in poverty among the elderly stems from the tremendous growth in spending for Social Security and Medicare. In real terms—that is, after adjusting for the effects of inflation—those two programs have grown more than twelvefold since 1959 (Medicare didn't even exist until 1965). *Although not welfare programs in a strict sense, Social Security and Medicare have been hugely successful in reducing poverty among the elderly.*

Poverty and Public Choice

In a democracy, public policies depend very much on the political power of the interest groups involved. In recent years, the elderly have become a powerful political force. The voter participation rate of those 65 and over is higher than that of any other age group. For example, people 65 years of age and older vote at triple the rate of those between 18 and 24

Poverty Rates by Age: 1959–2002

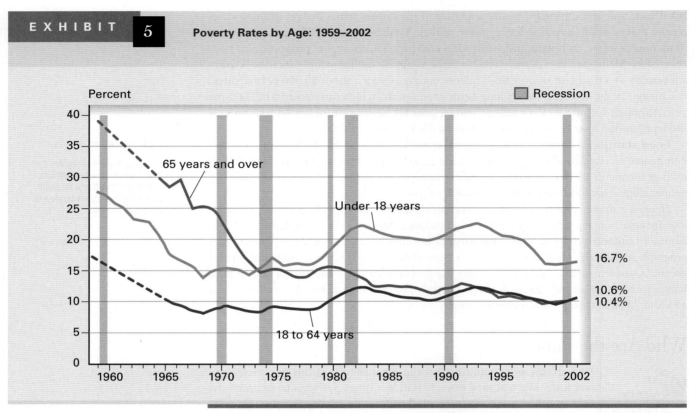

Source: U.S. Census Bureau, *Poverty in the United States: 2002*, Current Population Reports, September 2003, Figure 2, http://www.census.gov/prod/2003pubs/p60-222.pdf.

and four times that of welfare recipients. The political muscle of the elderly has been flexed whenever a question of Social Security benefits are considered.

Unlike most interest groups, the elderly make up a group we all expect to join one day. The elderly are actually represented by five constituencies: (1) the elderly themselves; (2) people under 65 who are concerned about the current benefits to their parents or other elderly relatives; (3) people under 65 who are concerned about their own benefits in the future; (4) people who earn their living by caring for the elderly, such as doctors, nurses, and nursing-home operators; and (5) candidates for office who want to harvest the votes that seniors deliver. So the elderly have a broad constituency, and this pays off in terms of redistribution of wealth to the elderly and in the reduction of poverty among this group.

The Feminization of Poverty

Another way to look at poverty is based on the status of the household head. Exhibit 6 compares poverty rates among families headed by females with no husband present with poverty rates for other families. Two trends are unmistakable. First, poverty rates among families headed by females are much higher than rates among other families—about five times higher on average. Second, poverty rates among female-headed families have declined in the last decade, falling from 39.7 percent in 1991 to 28.8 percent in 2002.

The exhibit compares poverty among female householders to other families. What it doesn't show is the growth in the number of female-headed households. The number of families

EXHIBIT   6   **Poverty Rates Are Much Higher for Families Headed by Females But Have Declined in the Last Decade**

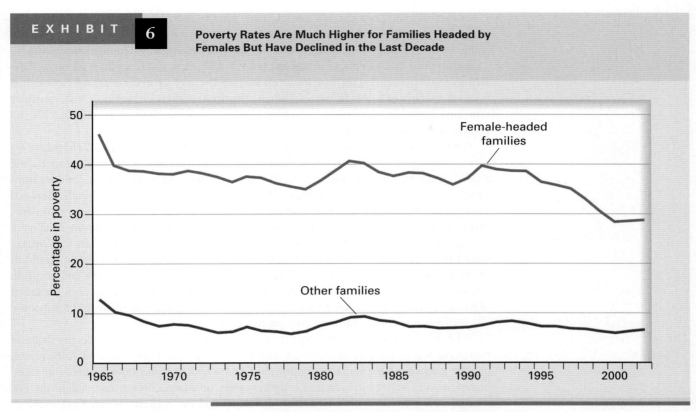

Source: Developed from data in U.S. Census Bureau, *Poverty in the United States: 2002*, Current Population Reports, September 2003, Appendix Table A-1, http://www.census.gov/prod/2003pubs/p60-222.pdf.

headed by women increased 148 percent between 1965 and 2002, while all other families grew just 21 percent. The percentage of births to unmarried mothers is five times greater today than in the 1960s. In 1960, only 1 in 200 children lived with a single parent who had never married. Today, 1 in 10 children lives with a single parent who has never married.

The United States has the highest teenage pregnancy rate in the developed world—twice the rate of Great Britain and 15 times that of Japan. Because the fathers in such cases typically provide little child care or support, children born outside marriage are likely to be poorer than other children. The divorce rate has also increased since 1960. Because of the higher divorce rate, even children born to married couples now face a greater likelihood of living in a one-parent household before they grow up. Divorce usually reduces the resources available to the children.

The growth in the number of poor families since 1965 resulted overwhelmingly from a growth in the number of female householders. The U.S. economy has generated 70 million new jobs in the last four decades. Families with a female householder were in the worst position to take advantage of this job growth. *Children of female householders are five times more likely to live in poverty than are other children. Young, single motherhood is a recipe for poverty.* Often the young mother drops out of school, which reduces her future earning possibilities when and if she seeks work outside the home. Even a strong economy is little aid to households with nobody in the labor force. Worse yet, young, single mothers-to-be are less likely to seek adequate medical care; the result is a higher proportion of premature, underweight babies. This is one reason why the

U.S. infant mortality rate exceeds that of many other industrialized countries. Compared to two-parent families, children in one-parent families are twice as likely to drop out of school, and girls from one-parent families are twice as likely to become single mothers themselves.

Because of a lack of education and limited job skills, most single mothers go on welfare. Before recently imposed lifetime limits on welfare, the average never-married mother had been on welfare for a decade, twice as long as divorced mothers on welfare. Of all teenagers who gave birth, the proportion unmarried was 13 percent in 1950, 30 percent in 1970, 67 percent in 1990, and 80 percent in 2002.[5]

Poverty has therefore become increasingly feminized, mostly because female householders have become more common. Children from mothers who finished high school, married before having a child, and gave birth after age 20 are 10 times less likely to be poor than children from mothers who fail to do these things.[6] Because the number of female householders has grown more rapidly among black women, the feminization of poverty has been more dramatic in those households. Sixty-eight percent of all births to black mothers in 2002 were to unmarried women compared with 43 percent of all births among women of Hispanic origin and 23 percent of births among non-Hispanic whites.[7] But we should be careful in drawing conclusions about the role of race or ethnicity per se, because black and Hispanic households are poorer than white households. Low income alone could account for much of the difference in birth rates. In other words, a better comparison would adjust for income differences across groups, but such data are not available.

Exhibit 7 shows the poverty rates for each of the 50 states. States with a deeper shade of pink have higher poverty rates. States with no shading have lower rates. As you can see, poverty rates are higher across the bottom half of the United States. Poverty rates tend to be higher in states where births to single mothers make up a larger percentage of all births. For example, New Mexico, Louisiana, and Mississippi had the highest poverty rates in 2002. They also had the highest rates of births to unmarried mothers. Nearly half of all births in these three states were to unmarried mothers.

Poverty and Discrimination

To what extent has racial discrimination limited job opportunities and increased poverty among minorities? Discrimination can occur in many ways: in school funding, in housing, in employment, in career advancement. Also, discrimination in one area can affect opportunities in another. For example, housing discrimination can reduce job opportunities if a black family cannot move within commuting distance of the best employers. Job-market discrimination can take many forms. An employer may fail to hire a black job applicant because the applicant lacks training. But this lack of training can arise from discrimination in the schools, in union apprenticeship programs, or in training programs run by other employers. For example, evidence suggests that black workers receive less on-the-job training than otherwise similar white workers.

After adjusting for a variety of factors that could affect the wage, such as education and work experience, research shows that white people earn more than black people. The gap between the two narrowed between 1940 and 1976 to the point where black workers earned only 7 percent less than white workers; then it widened somewhat.[8] Since 1993, the gap has again narrowed. Could explanations besides job discrimination account for the wage gap? Though the data adjust for *years* of schooling, some research suggests that black workers

HOMEWORK
Xpress!
Ask the Instructor
Video

5. *National Vital Statistics Report,* Vol. 51, No.11 (25 June 2003), Table C.
6. James Q. Wilson, "Human Remedies for Social Disorder," *Public Interest* (Spring 1998): 27.
7. *National Vital Statistics Report,* Vol. 51, No. 11 (25 June 2003), Table A.
8. M. Boozer, A. Krueger, and S. Wolken, "Race and School Quality Since Brown v. Board of Education," *Brookings Papers on Economic Activity: Microeconomics* (1992): 269–326.

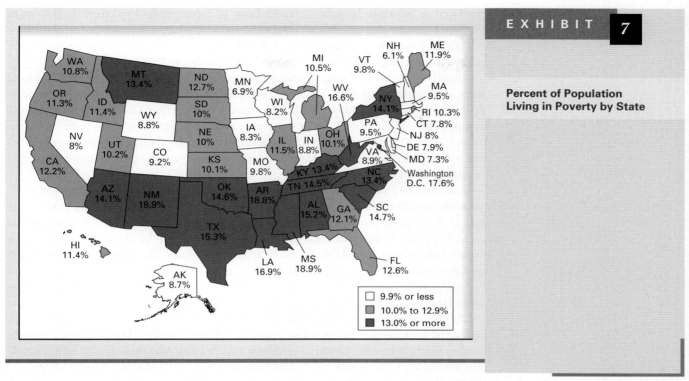

EXHIBIT   7

Percent of Population Living in Poverty by State

Map labels:
WA 10.8%, MT 13.4%, ND 12.7%, MN 6.9%, MI 10.5%, NH 6.1%, ME 11.9%, VT 9.8%, WV 16.6%, MA 9.5%, NY 14.1%, RI 10.3%, PA 9.5%, CT 7.8%, NJ 8%, DE 7.9%, MD 7.3%, OR 11.3%, ID 11.4%, WY 8.8%, SD 10%, WI 8.2%, OH 10.1%, VA 8.9%, Washington D.C. 17.6%, NV 8%, UT 10.2%, NE 10%, IA 8.3%, IL 11.5%, IN 8.8%, KY 13.4%, NC 13.4%, CA 12.2%, CO 9.2%, KS 10.1%, MO 9.8%, TN 14.5%, SC 14.7%, AZ 14.1%, NM 18.9%, OK 14.6%, AR 18.8%, AL 15.2%, GA 12.1%, HI 11.4%, TX 15.3%, LA 16.9%, MS 18.9%, FL 12.6%, AK 8.7%

Legend:
☐ 9.9% or less
▨ 10.0% to 12.9%
■ 13.0% or more

Source: *Poverty in the United States: 2002,* U.S. Census Bureau, September 2003, Table 4, http://www.census.gov/prod/2003pubs/p60-222.pdf. Rates are averaged for 2001 and 2002 to provide more reliable figures.

received a lower *quality* of schooling than white workers. For example, black students are less likely to use computers in school. Inner-city schools often have more problems with classroom discipline, which takes time and attention away from instruction. Such quality differences could account for at least a portion of the remaining gap in standardized wages.

Evidence of discrimination comes from studies where otherwise similar white and black candidates are sent to the same source to seek jobs, rent apartments, or apply for mortgage loans. For example, white and black job applicants with similar qualifications and résumés applied for the same job. These studies find that employers are less likely to interview or offer a job to minority applicants. Minority applicants also tend to be treated less favorably by real estate agents and lenders. The President's Council of Economic Advisers concluded that discrimination against members of racial and ethnic minorities, while "far less pervasive and overt" than in the past, still persists.[9]

Affirmative Action

The Equal Employment Opportunity Commission, established by the Civil Rights Act of 1964, monitors cases involving unequal pay for equal work and unequal access to promotion. All companies doing business with the federal government had to set numerical hiring, promotion, and training goals to ensure that these firms did not discriminate in hiring on the basis of race, sex, religion, or national origin. Black employment increased in those firms required to file affirmative action plans.[10] The fraction of the black labor force

9. *Economic Report of the President,* February 1998, 152.

10. James Smith and Finis Welch, "Black Economic Progress After Myrdal," *Journal of Economic Literature* 27 (June 1989): 519–563.

employed in white-collar jobs increased from 16.5 percent in 1960 to 40.5 percent in 1981—an increase that greatly exceeded the growth of white-collar jobs in the labor force as a whole. Research also suggests that civil rights legislation played a role in narrowing the black-white earnings gap between 1960 and the mid-1970s.[11]

Attention focused on hiring practices and equality of opportunity at the state and local levels as well, as governments introduced so-called *set-aside* programs to guarantee minorities a share of contracts. But a 1995 U.S. Supreme Court decision challenged affirmative action programs, ruling that Congress must meet a rigorous legal standard to justify any contracting or hiring practice based on race, especially programs that reserve jobs for minorities and women. Programs must be shown to be in response to injustices created by past discrimination, said the Court.

In summary, evidence suggests that black workers earn less than white workers after adjustment for other factors that could affect wages, such as education and job experience. Part of this wage gap may reflect differences in the quality of education, differences that could themselves be the result of discrimination. Keep in mind that unemployment rates are higher among black people than among white people and are higher still among black teenagers, the group most in need of job skills and job experience. *But we should also note that black families are not a homogeneous group. In fact, the distribution of income is more uneven among black families than it is among the population as a whole.*

On the upside, according to the *Economic Report of the President:* Since 1993, the median income of black families has risen faster than that of white families. The proportion of black families living below the poverty line fell to a record low. And there is a growing middle class among black households. Since 1970, the number of black doctors, nurses, college professors, and newspaper reporters has more than doubled; the number of black engineers, computer programmers, accountants, managers, and administrators has more than tripled; the number of black elected officials has quadrupled; and the number of black lawyers has increased sixfold. Three of the most admired Americans are black—talk show host Oprah Winfrey, basketball legend Michael Jordan, and Secretary of State Colin Powell, who arguably could get elected U.S. president if he chose to run.

Unintended Consequences of Income Assistance

On the plus side, antipoverty programs increase the consumption possibilities of poor families, and this is important, especially because children are the largest poverty group. But programs to assist the poor have secondary effects that limit their ability to reduce poverty. Here we consider some unintended consequences.

Disincentives

Society, through government, tries to provide families with an adequate standard of living, but society also wants to ensure that only those in need receive benefits. As we have seen, income assistance consists of a combination of cash and in-kind transfer programs. Because these programs are designed to help the poor and only the poor, the level of benefits varies inversely with income from other sources. This inverse relationship has resulted in a system where transfers decline sharply as earned income increases, in effect imposing a high marginal tax rate on that earned income. An increase in earnings may reduce benefits from TANF, Medicaid, food stamps, housing assistance, energy assistance, and other programs.

11. David Card and Alan Krueger, "Trends in Relative Black-White Earnings Revisited," *American Economic Review* 83 (May 1993): 85–91.

With a loss in support from each program as earned income increases, working may lead to little or no increase in total income. Over certain income ranges, the welfare recipient may lose more than $1 in welfare benefits for each additional $1 in earnings. Thus, the *marginal tax rate* on earned income could exceed 100 percent.

Holding even a part-time job involves additional expenses—for clothing, transportation, and child care, for instance—not to mention the loss of free time. Such a system of perverse incentives can frustrate people trying to work their way off welfare. *The high marginal tax rate discourages employment and self-sufficiency.* In many cases, the value of welfare benefits exceeds the disposable income resulting from full-time employment.

The longer people are out of the labor force, the more their job skills deteriorate, so when they do look for work, their productivity and their pay are lower than when they were last employed. This lowers their expected wage, making work even less attractive. Some economists argue that in this way, welfare benefits can lead to long-term dependency. While welfare seems to be a rational choice in the short run, it has unfavorable long-term consequences for the family, for society, and for the economy.

Welfare programs can cause other disincentives. For example, children may be eligible for Supplemental Security Income if they have a learning disability. According to one first-hand account, some low-income parents encouraged poor performance in school so their children would qualify for this program.[12]

Does Welfare Cause Dependency?

A relatively brief stay on welfare would be evidence of little dependency. But the same family staying on welfare year after year is a matter of concern. To explore the question of whether welfare causes dependency, a University of Michigan study tracked 5,000 families over a number of years, paying particular attention to economic mobility both from year to year and from one generation to the next.[13] The study first examined poverty from year to year, or dependency within a generation. It found that most received welfare for less than a year, but about 30 percent remained on welfare for at least eight years. Thus, there was a core of long-term recipients.

A serious concern is whether the children on welfare end up on welfare as adults. Is there a cycle of dependency? Why might we expect one? Children in welfare households may learn the ropes about the welfare system and may come to view welfare as a normal way of life rather than as a temporary bridge over a rough patch. Research indicates that daughters from welfare families are more likely than daughters in other families to participate in the welfare system themselves and are more likely to have premarital births.[14] It is difficult to say whether welfare "causes" the link between mother and daughter, because the same factors that contribute to a mother's welfare status can also contribute to her daughter's welfare status. Evidence of a link is weaker when it comes to sons from welfare families.

Welfare Reform

There has been much dissatisfaction with the welfare system, among both those who pay for the programs and direct beneficiaries. Welfare reforms introduced in recent years have been aimed at reducing long-term dependency.

---

12. Jacqueline Goldwyn Kingon, "Education Life: A View from the Trenches," *New York Times,* 8 April 2001.
13. Greg J. Duncan et al., *Years of Poverty, Years of Plenty* (Ann Arbor: University of Michigan Press, 1984).
14. Robert Moffit, "Incentive Effects of the U.S. Welfare System: A Review," *Journal of Economic Literature* 30 (March 1992): 37.

Recent Reforms

Some analysts believe that one way to reduce poverty is to provide welfare recipients with job skills and make them find jobs. Even before the 1996 federal reform of welfare, to be discussed shortly, some sort of "workfare" component for welfare recipients operated in most states. In these states, as a condition of receiving welfare, the head of the household had to participate in education and training programs, search for work, or take some paid or unpaid position. The idea was to expose people on welfare to the job market. Evidence from various states indicates that programs involving mandatory job searches, short-term unpaid work, and training could operate at low cost and could increase employment. The government saved money because those in welfare-to-work programs left welfare rolls sooner.

Reforms at the state level set the stage for federal reforms. By far the biggest reform in the welfare system in the last 70 years came with the 1996 legislation that replaced Aid to Families with Dependent Children (AFDC) with Temporary Assistance for Needy Families (TANF). Whereas the AFDC program set eligibility rules and left federal costs open-ended through matching grants to the states, TANF offers a fixed grant to the states to run their welfare programs. States ended AFDC and began TANF by July 1, 1997. Under the new system, states have much control over their own welfare programs. But concerns about welfare dependency fostered some special provisions. The act imposes a five-year lifetime limit on cash transfers and requires states to move a certain percentage of people from welfare to work.

Aside from the time limits and work participation rates imposed by the federal government, states are free to set benefit levels and experiment however they choose. For example, about half the states impose time limits shorter than five years. Some observers fear that states now have an incentive to keep welfare costs down by cutting benefits. To avoid becoming destinations for poor people—that is, to avoid becoming "welfare magnets"—states may be tempted to offer relatively low benefits. The fear is that states will undercut benefits in what has been called a "race to the bottom."

The following case study surveys some results of welfare reform so far.

HOMEWORK
Xpress!
econ-apps debate

Is Welfare-to-Work Working?

Here are some preliminary conclusions about the course of welfare reform. Work requirements and time limits have resulted in substantial declines in the welfare caseload. The number of welfare recipients peaked in January 1994 at 14.2 million, mostly single women with children. By 2003 the rolls had fallen to 4.9 million—65 percent below the peak. Exhibit 8 shows the percentage of the U.S. population on welfare since 1960. Note the sharp decline in recent years. As a share of the U.S. population, welfare recipients fell from 5.5 percent in 1994 to 1.7 percent in 2003, the lowest rate since 1960. Fortunately, the reforms were introduced during

© Gilles Mingasson/Liaison/Getty Images

an expanding economy, with the unemployment rate the lowest in three decades. But welfare rolls continued to decline, albeit at a slower rate, during the recession year of 2001, and in 2002 and 2003, years when the U.S. economy continued to lose jobs. One study found that those in welfare-to-work programs experienced longer job tenure than other employees.

Because most people on welfare are poorly educated and have few job skills, wages for those who find jobs remain low. Part-time work is common. On the plus side, the earned-income tax credit provides additional income to low-income workers—up to $4,140 in

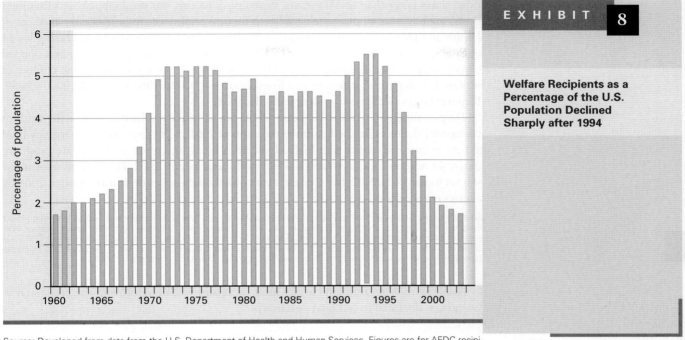

EXHIBIT 8

Welfare Recipients as a Percentage of the U.S. Population Declined Sharply after 1994

Source: Developed from data from the U.S. Department of Health and Human Services. Figures are for AFDC recipients before 1997 and TANF recipients for 1997 and later.

2002. Most of those going to work can continue to receive food stamps, child care, and Medicaid. Because the welfare rolls have declined but federal grants have not, welfare spending per recipient has increased significantly. Most states are combining tough new rules with an expanded menu of welfare services. States have made large investments in work-related services such as job placement, transportation, and especially child care.

Other positive developments include falling rates of crime and drug abuse; the greatest decline in child poverty, especially black child poverty, since the 1960s; and a substantial increase in employment among mothers who head families, especially those who have never married. The proportion of black children living with married parents increased from 35 percent in 1995 to 39 percent in 2000. And a Michigan study found that former welfare mothers with jobs are significantly less likely than mothers still on welfare to report domestic violence or homelessness.

One effect of the work requirements of welfare reform has been to raise the "price" of going on welfare. As one welfare director noted, a lot of people who are leaving welfare are saying, "It's not worth the hassle." We might say that the demand curve for welfare is downward sloping, with "hassle" measuring the price on the vertical axis. The greater the "hassle," the less the amount of welfare demanded. Many on welfare had other ways to support themselves. One expert who counted everything from food stamps to unreported income found cash transfers accounted for only about 34 percent of the average welfare recipient's income. Food stamps provided about 25 percent, and 36 percent came from unreported sources such as secret jobs, boyfriends, relatives, and charities.

Welfare rolls declined more in states where efforts to get people to work are greater. For example, Wisconsin and Minnesota had similar economies, as reflected by identical unemployment rates, but Wisconsin's more aggressive work requirements cut welfare rolls there

WALL STREET JOURNAL

Reading It **Right**

What's the relevance of the following statement from the Wall Street Journal*: "Family households maintained by women without a husband present saw incomes rise 4.0 percent to $28,116 from 1999 to 2000, the Census Department said. Other types of households had no significant change in their median household income."*

three times faster than in Minnesota. Wisconsin's success was no doubt behind President Bush's appointment of that state's governor, Tommy Thompson, to head the Department of Health and Human Services, the agency that runs federal welfare programs. During his 14 years as governor, Thompson reduced welfare payments to parents whose children skipped school and paid teenage parents more if they got married. During his tenure, the number of welfare families in the state dropped from about 100,000 in 1986 to only 16,000 in 2000. Reported cases of domestic violence also declined.

Despite the good news, some poor people are still having a hard time. The demand for emergency shelters increased with the recession of 2001, as did requests for emergency food aid. As mentioned earlier, although Medicaid is by far the most costly welfare program, nearly 44 million Americans still lacked health insurance in 2002. The welfare reform law was set to expire in 2002, but Congress has continued the measure at least through 2004 by a series of extensions.

Sources: Susan Goodin and Margo Bailey, "Welfare and Work: Job-Retention Outcomes of Federal Welfare-to-Work Employees," *Public Administration Review*, January 2001; Tyrone Cheng, "Welfare Recidivism Among Former Welfare Recipients," *Families and Society: The Journal of Contemporary Human Services*; Jan.–Mar., 2003; "HHS Announces Declines in TANF Caseloads," U.S. Department of Health and Human Services, 2 December 2003; and the federal site on welfare reform at http://www.acf.hhs.gov/programs/ofa/welfare/index.htm.

Along with Wisconsin, one of the most successful welfare reforms in the country is in Oregon, as discussed in our final case study.

Oregon's Program of "Tough Love"

Welfare reform in Oregon began in 1994, when the state received a federal waiver to operate under its own rules. The number receiving welfare fell from 116,390 in January 1994 to 42,341 by March 2002, for a drop of 64 percent, also the average U.S. decline. The Oregon decline came not as a result of strict time limits or tougher eligibility standards but by providing strong work incentives and working more closely with welfare beneficiaries. The state combines training and education with help for drug abuse, mental health, domestic violence, and other barriers to employment, even encouraging some people to hold out for better jobs.

© Jim McGuire/Index Stock Imagery.

After leaving TANF for work, people in Oregon continue to qualify for several programs including (1) health benefits for at least a year, (2) child care until income reaches 200 percent of the federal poverty level, (3) food stamps for those who are eligible, and (4) the federal earned-income tax credit, which in effect can raise the wage more than $1 an hour. By working full time at the state's minimum wage of $7 an hour in 2003, a family's living standard would exceed 130 percent of the poverty level. In comparison, the typical family on welfare and food stamps was living at only 75 percent of the poverty level. Thus, work becomes more attractive than welfare. What's more, the average starting wage in the first job after welfare exceeded the minimum wage.

One federal study tracked 5,500 welfare recipients in Oregon over a two-year period, where half the group participated in the welfare-to-work program and half did not. Taking part in the welfare-to-work program increased employment by 18 percent, raised average earnings over the two years by 35 percent, and boosted the proportion of individuals with employer-provided health insurance by 71 percent.

Oregon became the first state to require drug addicts to attend treatment to qualify for welfare. An evaluation of that program found that clients who completed drug treatment earned 65 percent more than similar clients in a comparison group. Those completing treatment for addiction were 45 percent less likely to be arrested and only half as likely to be investigated for child abuse or neglect. The study also found that every dollar Oregon spent on drug treatment saved $5.60 on other social services. The approach in most other states is simply to ban recent drug felons from receiving aid.

The Oregon program offers abundant services, but welfare applicants must first spend a month looking for work before getting help. The federal government requires states to enroll 50 percent of their recipients in job-related activity. Oregon had 89 percent of its recipients in job-related activity. Perhaps the most persuasive evidence that Oregon's approach of tough love is working is that after 18 months, only 8 percent of those who left welfare returned to the rolls. Statewide, the number of child abuse victims fell from 11,241 in 1999 to 8,424 in 2002.

Still, the road to welfare reform has not been smooth, even in Oregon. People coming off welfare often start near the poverty line. A University of Oregon study followed 1,000 Oregon families who left welfare during the first quarter of 1998. After two years, about 70 percent were employed and about 70 percent had health-care coverage, though wages for many still hovered around the federal poverty level.

Sources: Tom Detzel, "Oregon Officials Bracing for Cuts in Welfare Services," *The Oregonian*, 21 September 2003; *National Evaluation of Welfare Strategies*, Manpower Demonstration Research Corporation, June 2000; and Elizabeth Davis and Roberta Walker, "The Dynamics of Child Care Subsidy Use by Rural Families in Oregon," *American Journal of Agricultural Economics*, 15 November 2001. An overview of Oregon's welfare programs is available at http://www.dhs.state.or.us/assistance/. State-by-state caseload information appears at http://www.acf.dhhs.gov/news/tables.htm.

Conclusion

Government redistribution programs have been most successful at reducing poverty among the elderly. But until recently, poverty rates among children increased because of the growth in the number of female householders. We might ask why transfer programs have reduced poverty rates more among the elderly than among female householders. Transfer programs do not encourage people to get old; that process occurs naturally and is independent of the level of transfers. But the level and availability of transfer programs at the margin could influence some young unmarried women as they are deciding whether or not to have a child and may, at the margin, influence a married mother's decision to get divorced.

Most transfers in the economy are not from the government but are in-kind transfers within the family, from parents to children. Thus, any change in a family's capacity to earn income has serious consequences for dependent children. Family structure is a primary determinant of family income. One in six children in the United States lives in poverty. Children are the innocent victims of the changing family structure. Recent welfare reforms are aimed at breaking the cycle of poverty and dependency.

SUMMARY

1. Money income in the United States became less evenly distributed between 1970 and 2002. Since 1959, the poverty rate has dropped most among the elderly, thanks to Social Security and Medicare.

2. Young, single motherhood is a recipe for poverty. Often the young mother drops out of school, which reduces her future earning possibilities when and if she seeks work outside the home. Growth in the number of female

householders in the last three decades increased poverty among children, though that poverty rate has declined since peaking in 1993.

3. The wage gap between black and white workers narrowed between 1940 and 1976, widened until the early 1990s, and has been narrowing again since 1993. Affirmative action programs and gains in education seem to have increased employment opportunities among black workers.

4. Among the undesirable effects of income assistance is a high marginal tax rate on earned income, which discour-

ages employment and encourages welfare dependency. Before recent welfare reforms, about 30 percent of families on welfare remained there for eight years or more.

5. Welfare reforms introduced by the states set the stage for federal welfare reforms aimed at promoting the transition from welfare to work. The states began experimenting with different systems to encourage greater personal responsibility. As a result of state reforms, federal welfare reform, and a strengthening economy, welfare rolls dropped by about 65 percent between 1994 and 2003.

QUESTIONS FOR REVIEW

1. *(Distribution of Household Income)* Look back at Exhibit 1 in this chapter. How would you explain the shift of the U.S. income distribution in the last two decades?

2. *(Lorenz Curve)* What is a Lorenz curve? What does the Lorenz curve in Exhibit 2 illustrate?

3. *(Official Poverty Level)* Although the poverty rate among single mothers has decreased since 1960, the number of poor children from such families has more than doubled. Explain.

4. *(Income Differences)* List some reasons why household incomes differ. Which factors are the most important?

5. *(Official Poverty Level)* How does the U.S. Department of Agriculture calculate the official poverty level? What government assistance programs does the Census Bureau consider when calculating household income? What programs are ignored?

6. *(Programs to Help the Poor)* Distinguish between social insurance programs and income assistance programs. Identify key examples of each.

7. *(Poverty and Age)* Poverty among the elderly fell dramatically between 1959 and 1974 and has continued to decline. However, poverty among that portion of the U.S.

population that is less than 18 years old is no lower today than in the 1970s. Why have the experiences of these two age groups differed?

8. *(Poverty and Public Choice)* Why is it difficult to pass legislation to reduce Social Security or Medicare benefits?

9. *(Poverty and Discrimination)* Which types of discrimination may cause an earnings gap between white and black workers? Consider discrimination in schooling, for example. How would researchers detect such discrimination?

10. *(Disincentives)* How does the implicit tax on earned income (in the form of lost benefits from government assistance programs as earned income increases) affect work incentives? How do some people avoid the implicit tax?

11. *(Welfare Reform)* What has happened to the welfare caseload in recent years? Discuss some differences in results across states.

12. (*C a s e* **S t u d y**: Is Welfare-to-Work Working?) Discuss the key features of welfare reforms introduced by the federal government in 1996. Why were policy makers worried that turning welfare over to the states would result in a "race to the bottom"?

EXPERIENTIAL EXERCISES

13. *(Poverty and the Poor)* Visit the Census Bureau's page on poverty statistics at http://www.census.gov/hhes/www/poverty.html. Look at the Small Area Income and Poverty Estimates, and find the latest poverty estimate for your county. How does the poverty rate there compare with the overall rate in your state and in the United States as a whole?

14. *(Wall Street Journal)* The front page of the Marketplace section of the *Wall Street Journal* often carries articles on income distribution and the personal impact of poverty. Pay particular attention to the "Work & Family" and "Business and Race" columns in the Wednesday paper. How are the actions of U.S. businesses affecting income distribution and poverty?

HOMEWORKXPRESS! EXERCISES

These exercises require access to McEachern Homework Xpress! If Homework Xpress! did not come with your book, visit ***http://homeworkxpress.swlearning.com*** *to purchase.*

The distribution of income among quintiles can be illustrated using a Lorenz curve.

1. In the diagram draw a line representing an equal distribution of income. Then add Lorenz curves for 1980 and 2005 based on the hypothetical data in the table.

Households (cumulative percent)	Income (cumulative percent)	
	1980	2005
0	0	0
20	10	5
40	20	15
60	35	30
80	60	50
100	100	100

2. In the diagram for this exercise is a line representing an equal distribution of income. Sketch a Lorenz curve representing a typical distribution of income in the United States. Brazil is noted for having one of the most unequal distributions of income among major economies. Add a Lorenz curve for Brazil illustrating how the distribution there is significantly more unequal than in the United States.

International Trade

T his morning you pulled on your Levi's jeans from Mexico, pulled over your Benetton sweater from Italy, and laced up your Timberland boots from Thailand. After a breakfast that included bananas from Honduras and coffee from Brazil, you climbed into your Volvo from Sweden fueled by Venezuelan oil and headed for a lecture by a visiting professor from Hungary. If the United States is such a rich and productive country, why do we import so many goods and services? Why don't we produce everything ourselves? And why do some groups try to restrict foreign trade? Answers to these and other questions are addressed in this chapter.

The world is a giant shopping mall, and Americans are big spenders. Americans buy Japanese cars, French wine, Chinese kitchen gadgets, European vacations, and thousands of other goods and services from around the globe. But foreigners buy American products too—grain, personal computers, aircraft, movies, trips to New

© Gary Conner/Index Stock Imagery

York City, and thousands of other goods and services. In this chapter, we examine the gains from international trade and the effects of trade restrictions on the allocation of resources. The analysis is based on the familiar tools of demand and supply. Topics discussed include:

- Gains from trade
- Absolute and comparative advantage revisited
- Tariffs

- Import quotas
- Welfare loss from trade restrictions
- Arguments for trade restrictions

The Gains from Trade

A family from Virginia that sits down for a meal of Kansas prime rib, Idaho potatoes, and California string beans, with Georgia peach cobbler for dessert, is benefiting from interstate trade. You already understand why the residents of one state trade with those of another. Back in Chapter 2, you learned about the gains arising from specialization and exchange. You may recall how you and your roommate could maximize output when you each specialized. The law of comparative advantage says that the individual with the lowest opportunity cost of producing a particular good should specialize in producing that good. Just as individuals benefit from specialization and exchange, so do states and, indeed, nations. To reap the gains that arise from specialization, countries engage in international trade. *With trade, each country specializes in the goods that it produces at the lowest opportunity cost.*

A Profile of Exports and Imports

Just as some states are more involved in interstate trade than others, some nations are more involved in international trade than others. For example, exports account for about one-quarter of the gross domestic product (GDP) in Canada and the United Kingdom; about one-third of GDP in Germany, Sweden, and Switzerland; and about half of GDP in the Netherlands. Despite the perception that Japan has a huge export sector, exports make up only about one-seventh of its GDP.

U.S. Exports

In the United States, exports of goods and services amounted to about 10 percent of GDP in 2003. Although small relative to GDP, exports play a growing role in the U.S. economy. The left panel of Exhibit 1 shows the composition of U.S. merchandise exports by major category. Capital goods account for 41 percent of all exports. Capital goods include high-tech products, such as computers and jet aircraft. Next most important are industrial supplies and materials, at 24 percent of the total. Together, capital goods and industrial supplies and materials make up 65 percent, or nearly two-thirds, of U.S. exports. Thus, most U.S. exports help foreign manufacturers make stuff. Consumer goods (except food, which is included in another category) account for only 13 percent of exports. This category includes entertainment products, such as movies and recorded music.

U.S. Imports

U.S. imports of goods and services were 14 percent relative to GDP in 2003. The right panel of Exhibit 1 shows the composition of U.S. merchandise imports. Whereas consumer goods accounted for only 13 percent of U.S. exports, they are the largest category of imports at 27 percent of the total. Imported consumer goods include electronics from Taiwan, shoes from Brazil, and kitchen gadgets from China. The next most important category of imports, at

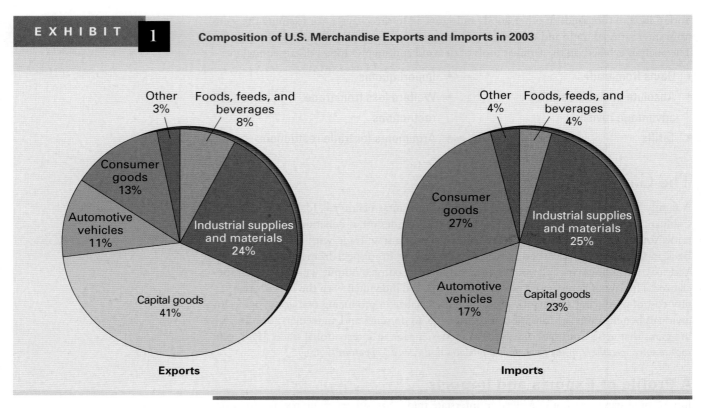

EXHIBIT 1   Composition of U.S. Merchandise Exports and Imports in 2003

Source: Based on government figures reported by Christopher Bach, "U.S. International Transactions, 2003," *Survey of Current Business* (April 2004), Table D, p. 63.

25 percent, is industrial supplies and materials, such as crude oil from Venezuela and the Middle East and raw metals, including lead, zinc, and copper, from around the world. Ranked third is capital goods, at 23 percent, such as printing presses from Germany. Note that automotive vehicles are only 11 percent of exports but 17 percent of imports.

Raw Materials

Let's focus just on raw materials. Exhibit 2 shows, for 12 key commodities, U.S. production as a percentage of U.S. consumption. If production falls short of consumption, the United States imports the difference. For example, because America grows coffee only in Hawaii, U.S. production is only 1 percent of U.S. consumption, so nearly all coffee is imported. The exhibit also shows that U.S. production falls short of consumption for oil and metals such as lead, zinc, copper, and aluminum. If production exceeds consumption, the United States exports the difference. For example, U.S.-grown wheat amounts to 184 percent of U.S. wheat consumption, so nearly half of U.S.-grown wheat is exported. U.S. production also exceeds consumption for other crops, including cotton, oil seeds (soybeans, sunflower seeds, canola), and coarse grains (corn, barley, oats). In short, when it comes to basic commodities, the United States is a net importer of oil and metals and a net exporter of crops.

Trading Partners

To give you some feel for America's trading partners in 2003, here are the top 10 destinations for U.S. goods in order of importance: Canada, Mexico, Japan, Great Britain, Germany,

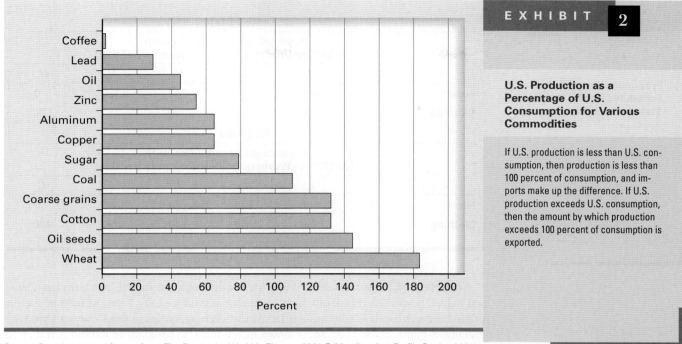

Source: Based on annual figures from *The Economist World in Figures: 2001 Edition* (London: Profile Books, 2001).

China, South Korea, France, the Netherlands, and Taiwan. The top 10 sources of U.S. imports consist of Canada, China, Mexico, Japan, Germany, Great Britain, South Korea, Taiwan, France, and Italy. China makes the biggest jump in the ranks, going from sixth as a destination for U.S. exports to second as a source of U.S. imports.

Production Possibilities Without Trade

The rationale behind most international trade is obvious. The United States grows little coffee because our climate is not suited to coffee. More revealing, however, are the gains from trade where the comparative advantage is not so obvious. Suppose that just two goods—food and clothing—are produced and consumed and that there are only two countries in the world—the United States, with a labor force of 100 million workers, and the mythical country of Izodia, with 200 million workers. The conclusions derived from this simple model have general relevance for international trade.

Exhibit 3 presents production possibilities tables for each country, based on the size of the labor force and the productivity of workers in each country. The exhibit assumes that each country has a given technology and labor is fully and efficiently employed. If no trade occurs between countries, Exhibit 3 presents each country's *consumption possibilities* table as well. The production numbers imply that each worker in the United States can produce either 6 units of food or 3 units of clothing per day. If all 100 million U.S. workers are in the food industry, they produce 600 million units per day, as shown in column U_1 in panel (a). If all U.S. workers make clothing, they turn out 300 million units per day, as shown in column U_6. The columns in between show some workers making food and some making clothing. Because a U.S. worker can produce either 6 units of food or 3 units of clothing, *the opportunity cost of 1 more unit of food is ½ unit of clothing.*

EXHIBIT 3							

(a) United States

Production Possibilities with 100 Million Workers (millions of units per day)

	U_1	U_2	U_3	U_4	U_5	U_6
Food	600	480	360	240	120	0
Clothing	0	60	120	180	240	300

(b) Izodia

Production Possibilities with 200 Million Workers (millions of units per day)

	I_1	I_2	I_3	I_4	I_5	I_6
Food	200	160	120	80	40	0
Clothing	0	80	160	240	320	400

Production Possibilities Schedules for the United States and Izodia

Suppose Izodian workers are less educated, work with less capital, and farm less-fertile soil than U.S. workers (think of China), so each can produce only 1 unit of food or 2 units of clothing per day. If all 200 million Izodian workers specialize in food, they can produce 200 million units of food per day, as shown in column I_1 in panel (b) of Exhibit 3. If they all make clothing, total output is 400 million units of clothing per day, as shown in column I_6. Some intermediate production possibilities are also listed in the exhibit. Because an Izodian worker can produce either 1 unit of food or 2 units of clothing, *the opportunity cost of 1 more unit of food is 2 units of clothing.*

We can convert the data in Exhibit 3 to a production possibilities frontier for each country, as shown in Exhibit 4. In each diagram, the amount of food produced is measured on the vertical axis and the amount of clothing on the horizontal axis. U.S. combinations are shown in the left panel by U_1, U_2, and so on; Izodian combinations are shown in the right panel by I_1, I_2, and so on. Because we assume that resources are perfectly adaptable to the production of each commodity, each production possibilities curve is a straight line reflecting a constant opportunity cost.

Exhibit 4 illustrates the possible combinations of food and clothing that residents of each country can produce and consume if all resources are fully and efficiently employed and there is no trade between the two countries. **Autarky** is the situation of national self-sufficiency, in which there is no economic interaction with foreign producers or consumers. Suppose that U.S. producers maximize profit and U.S. consumers maximize utility with the combination of 240 million units of food and 180 million units of clothing—combination U_4. This will be called the *autarky equilibrium*. Suppose also that Izodians are in autarky equilibrium, identified as combination I_3, of 120 million units of food and 160 million units of clothing.

AUTARKY

A situation of national self-sufficiency; there is no economic interaction with foreigners

Consumption Possibilities Based on Comparative Advantage

Economics in the Movies

In our example, each U.S. worker can produce more clothing and more food per day than can each Izodian worker, so Americans have an *absolute advantage* in the production of both goods. Recall from Chapter 2 that having an absolute advantage means being able to produce something using fewer re-

Production Possibilities Frontiers for the United States and Izodia Without Trade (millions of units per day)

Panel (a) shows the U.S. production possibilities curve; its slope indicates that the opportunity cost of an additional unit of food is ½ unit of clothing. Panel (b) shows production possibilities in Izodia; an additional unit of food costs 2 units of clothing. Food is produced at a lower opportunity cost in the United States.

sources than other producers require. Should the U.S. economy remain in autarky—that is, self-sufficient in both food and clothing productions—or could there be gains from trade?

As long as the opportunity cost of production differs between the two countries, there are gains from specialization and trade. The opportunity cost of producing 1 more unit of food is ½ unit of clothing in the United States compared with 2 units of clothing in Izodia. *According to the law of comparative advantage, each country should specialize in producing the good with the lower opportunity cost.* Because the opportunity cost of producing food is lower in the United States than in Izodia, both countries will gain if the United States specializes in food and exports some to Izodia, and Izodia specializes in clothing and exports some to the United States.

Before countries can trade, they must somehow agree on how much of one good exchanges for another—that is, they must establish the **terms of trade.** As long as Americans can get more than ½ unit of clothing for each unit of food, and as long as Izodians can get more than ½ unit of food for each unit of clothing, both countries will be better off by specialization and exchange rather than autarky. Suppose that market forces shape the terms of trade so that 1 unit of clothing exchanges for 1 unit of food. Americans thus trade 1 unit of food to Izodians for 1 unit of clothing. To produce 1 unit of clothing themselves, Americans would have to sacrifice 2 units of food. Likewise, Izodians trade 1 unit of clothing to Americans for 1 unit of food, which is only half what Izodians would sacrifice to produce 1 unit of food themselves.

Exhibit 5 shows that with 1 unit of food trading for 1 unit of clothing, Americans and Izodians can consume anywhere along their blue consumption possibilities frontiers. *The consumption possibilities frontier* shows a nation's possible combinations of goods available as a result of production and foreign trade. (Note that the U.S. consumption possibilities curve does not extend to the right of 400 million units of clothing, because that's the most Izodians can produce.) The amount each country actually consumes will depend on the relative preferences for food and clothing. Suppose Americans select combination *U* in panel (a) and Izodians select point *I* in panel (b).

Without trade, the United States produces and consumes 240 million units of food and 180 million units of clothing. With trade, the United States specializes in food by producing

TERMS OF TRADE

How much of one good exchanges for a unit of another good

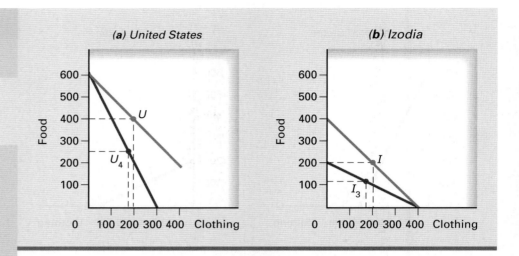

Production (and Consumption) Possibility Frontiers with Trade (millions of units per day)

If Izodia and the United States can trade at the rate of 1 unit of clothing for 1 unit of food, both can benefit. Consumption possibilities at these terms of trade are shown by the blue lines. The United States was previously producing and consuming U_4. By trading with Izodia, it can produce only food and still consume combination U, which has more food and more clothing than U_4. Likewise, Izodia can attain preferred combination I by trading its clothing for U.S. food. Both countries are better off as a result of international trade.

600 million units; Americans eat 400 million units and exchange the rest for 200 million units of Izodian clothing. This consumption combination is reflected by point U. Through exchange, Americans increase their consumption of both food and clothing.

Without trade, Izodians produce and consume 120 million units of food and 160 million units of clothing. With trade, Izodians specialize to produce 400 million units of clothing; they wear 200 million units and exchange the rest for 200 million units of U.S. food. This consumption combination is shown by point I. Through trade, Izodians, like Americans, are able to increase their consumption of both goods. How is this possible?

Because Americans are more efficient in the production of food and Izodians more efficient in the production of clothing, total output increases when each specializes. Without specialization, total world production was 360 million units of food and 340 million units of clothing. With specialization, food increases to 600 million units and clothing to 400 million units. Thus, both countries increase consumption with trade. *Although the United States has an absolute advantage in both goods, differences in the opportunity cost of production between the two nations ensure that specialization and exchange result in mutual gains.* Remember that comparative advantage, not absolute advantage, creates gains from specialization and trade. The only constraint on trade is that, for each good, *total world production must equal total world consumption.*

We simplified trade relations in our example to highlight the gains from specialization and exchange. We assumed that each country would completely specialize in producing a particular good, that resources were equally adaptable to the production of either good, that the costs of transporting goods from one country to another were inconsequential, and that there were no problems in arriving at the terms of trade. The world is not that simple. For example, we don't expect a country to produce just one good. Regardless, the law of comparative advantage still leads to gains from trade.

Reasons for International Specialization

Countries trade with one another—or, more precisely, people and firms in one country trade with those in another—because each side expects to gain from exchange. How do we know what each country should produce and what each should trade?

Differences in Resource Endowments

Trade is often prompted by differences in resource endowment that results in differences in the opportunity cost of production across countries. Some countries are blessed with an abundance of fertile land and favorable growing seasons. The United States, for example, has been called the "breadbasket of the world" because of its rich farmland ideal for growing corn. Coffee grows best in the climate and elevation of Colombia, Brazil, and Jamaica. Honduras has the ideal climate for growing bananas. Thus, the United States exports corn and imports coffee and bananas. Differences in the seasons across countries also serve as a basis for trade. For example, during the winter, Americans import fruit from Chile, and Canadians travel to Florida for sun and fun. During the summer, Americans export fruit to Chile, and Americans travel to Canada for camping and hiking.

Mineral resources are often concentrated in particular countries: oil in Saudi Arabia, bauxite in Jamaica, diamonds in South Africa. The United States has abundant coal supplies, but not enough oil to satisfy domestic demand. Thus, the United States exports coal and imports oil. More generally, *countries export products they can produce more cheaply in return for those that are unavailable domestically or are more costly to produce than to buy from other countries.* Remember, trade is based on comparative advantage, which is the ability to produce something at a lower opportunity cost than other producers face.

Economies of Scale

If production is subject to *economies of scale*—that is, if long-run average cost falls as a firm expands its scale of operation—countries can gain from trade if each nation specializes. Such specialization allows firms in each nation to produce more, which reduces average costs. The primary reason for establishing the single integrated market of the European Union was to offer producers there a large, open market of over 450 million consumers so that producers could achieve economies of scale, and thereby produce at a lower opportunity cost than faced by foreign producers. Firms and countries producing at the lowest opportunity costs are most competitive in international markets.

Differences in Tastes

Even if all countries had identical resource endowments and combined those resources with equal efficiency, each country would still gain from trade as long as tastes differed among countries. Consumption patterns differ across countries and some of this likely results from differences in tastes. For example, the Czechs and Irish drink three times as much beer per capita as do the Swiss and Swedes. The French drink three times as much wine as do Australians. The Danes eat twice as much pork as do Americans. Americans eat twice as much chicken as do Hungarians. Soft drinks are four times more popular in the United States than in Europe. The English like tea; Americans, coffee. Algeria has an ideal climate for growing grapes, but its large Muslim population abstains from alcohol; thus, Algeria exports wine.

Trade Restrictions and Welfare Loss

Despite the benefits of international trade, nearly all countries at one time or another erect trade barriers. Trade restrictions usually benefit some domestic producers but harm some other domestic producers and all domestic consumers. In this section, we will consider the effects of restrictions and the reasons they are imposed.

Tariffs

A *tariff*, a term first introduced in Chapter 3, is a tax on imports. (Tariffs can apply to exports, too, but we will focus on import tariffs.) A tariff can be either *specific*, such as a tariff of $5 per barrel of oil, or *ad valorem*, such as 10 percent on the import price of jeans. Consider the effects of a specific tariff on a particular good. In Exhibit 6, *D* is the U.S. demand for sugar and *S* is the supply of sugar from U.S. growers (there were about 10,000 U.S. sugarcane growers in 2004). Suppose that the world price of sugar is $0.10 per pound, as it was recently. The **world price** is determined by the world supply and demand for a product. It is the price at which any supplier can sell output on the world market and at which any demander can purchase output on the world market.

With free trade, U.S. consumers can buy any amount desired at the world price of $0.10 per pound, so the quantity demanded is 70 million pounds per month, of which U.S. producers supply 20 million pounds and 50 million pounds are imported. Because U.S. buyers can purchase sugar at the world price, U.S. producers can't charge more than that. Now

WORLD PRICE

The price at which a good is traded on the world market; determined by the world supply and world demand for the good

---

EXHIBIT **6**

HOMEWORK
Xpress!
Graphing

Effect of a Tariff

At a world price of $0.10 per pound, U.S. consumers demand 70 million pounds of sugar per month, and U.S. producers supply 20 million pounds per month; the difference is imported. After the imposition of a $0.05 per pound tariff, the U.S. price rises to $0.15 per pound. U.S. producers increase production to 30 million pounds, and U.S. consumers cut back to 60 million pounds. Imports fall to 30 million pounds. At the higher U.S. price, consumers are worse off; their loss of consumer surplus is the sum of areas *a*, *b*, *c*, and *d*. Area *a* represents an increase in producer surplus; this area is transferred from consumers to producers. Area *b* reflects the higher marginal cost of domestically producing sugar that could have been produced more cheaply abroad; thus *b* is a net U.S. welfare loss. Area *c* shows government revenue from the tariff. Area *d* reflects the loss of consumer surplus resulting from the drop in consumption. The net welfare loss to the U.S. economy consists of areas *b* and *d*.

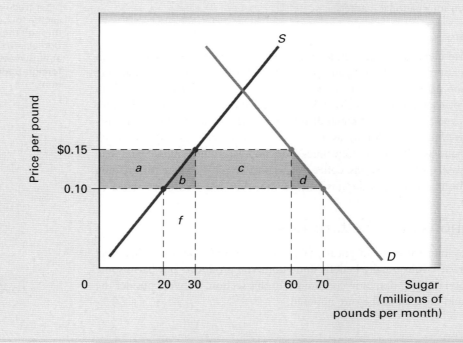

suppose that a specific tariff of $0.05 is imposed on each pound of imported sugar, raising its price from $0.10 to $0.15 per pound. U.S. producers can therefore raise their own price to $0.15 per pound as well without losing customers to imports. At the higher price, the quantity supplied by U.S. producers increases to 30 million pounds, but the quantity demanded by U.S. consumers declines to 60 million pounds. Because quantity demanded has declined and quantity supplied by U.S. producers has increased, U.S. imports fall from 50 million to 30 million pounds.

Because the price is higher after the tariff, consumers are worse off. Their loss in consumer surplus is identified in Exhibit 6 by the combination of the blue- and pink-shaded areas. Because both the U.S. price and the quantity supplied by U.S. producers have increased, U.S. producers' total revenue increases by the areas *a* plus *b* plus *f.* But only area *a* represents an increase in producer surplus. The increased revenue represented by the areas *f* plus *b* merely offsets the higher marginal cost of expanding U.S. sugar production from 20 million to 30 million pounds per month. Area *b* represents part of the net welfare loss to the domestic economy because those 10 million pounds could have been imported for $0.10 per pound rather than produced domestically at a higher marginal cost.

Government revenue from the tariff is identified by area *c,* which equals the tariff of $0.05 per pound multiplied by the 30 million pounds that are imported, or $1.5 million per month. Tariff revenue represents a loss to consumers, but because the tariff goes to the government, it can be used to lower taxes or to increase public services, so it's not a loss to society. Area *d* shows a loss in consumer surplus because less sugar is consumed at the higher price. This loss is not redistributed to anyone else, so area *d* reflects part of the net welfare loss of the tariff. Therefore, areas *b* and *d* show the domestic economy's net welfare loss of the tariff; *the two triangles measure a loss in consumer surplus that is not offset by a gain to anyone in the domestic economy.*

In summary: Of the total loss in U.S. consumer surplus (areas *a, b, c,* and *d*) resulting from the tariff, area *a* is redistributed to U.S producers, area *c* becomes government revenue, and areas *b* and *d* are net losses in domestic social welfare because of the tariff.

Import Quotas

An *import quota* is a legal limit on the amount of a particular commodity that can be imported. Quotas usually target imports from certain countries. For example, a quota may limit automobiles from Japan or shoes from Brazil. To have an impact on the domestic market, a quota must be less than would be imported under free trade. Consider a quota on the U.S. market for sugar. In panel (a) of Exhibit 7, *D* is the U.S. demand curve and *S* is the supply curve of U.S. sugar producers. Suppose again that the world price of sugar is $0.10 per pound. With free trade, that price would prevail in the U.S. market as well, and a total of 70 million pounds would be demanded. U.S. producers would supply 20 million pounds and importers, 50 million pounds. With a quota of 50 million pounds or more per month, the U.S. price would remain the same as the world price of $0.10 per pound, and quantity would be 70 million pounds per month. In short, a quota of at least 50 million pounds would not raise the U.S. price above the world price. A more stringent quota, however, would reduce imports, which, as we'll see, would raise the U.S. price.

Suppose U.S. trade officials impose an import quota of 30 million pounds per month. As long as the U.S. price is at or above the world price of $0.10 per pound, foreign producers supply 30 million pounds. So at prices at or above $0.10 per pound, the total supply of sugar to the U.S. market is found by adding 30 million pounds of imported sugar to the amount supplied by U.S. producers. U.S. and foreign producers would never sell for less than $0.10 per

Effect of a Quota

In panel (a), *D* is the U.S. demand curve and *S* is the supply curve of U.S. producers. When the government estab-lishes a sugar quota of 30 million pounds per year, the supply curve from both U.S. production and imports be-comes horizontal at the world price of $0.10 per pound and remains horizontal until the quantity supplied reaches 50 million pounds. For higher prices, the supply curve equals the horizontal sum of the U.S. supply curve, *S*, and the quota. The new U.S. price, $0.15 per pound, is determined by the intersection of the new supply curve, *S'*, with the U.S. demand curve, *D*. Panel (b) shows the welfare effect of the quota. As a result of the higher U.S. price, con-sumer surplus is cut by the shaded area. Area *a* represents a transfer from U.S. consumers to U.S. producers. Triangular area *b* reflects a net loss; it represents the amount by which the cost of producing an extra 10 million pounds of sugar in the United States exceeds the cost of buying it from abroad. Rectangular area *c* shows the gain to those who can sell foreign-grown sugar at the higher U.S. price instead of the world price. Area *d* also reflects a net loss—a reduction in consumer surplus as consumption falls because of the price increase. Thus, the blue-shaded areas illustrate the loss in consumer surplus that is captured by domestic producers and those who are permitted to fulfill the quota, and the pink-shaded triangles illustrate the net welfare cost of the quota on the U.S. economy.

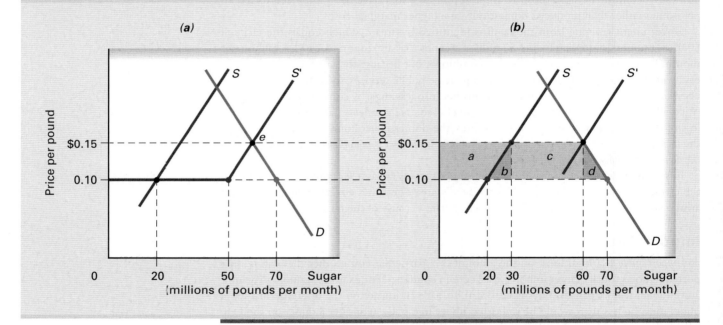

pound in the U.S. market because they can always get that price on the world market. Thus, the supply curve that sums domestic production and imports is horizontal at the world price of $0.10 per pound and remains so until the quantity supplied reaches 50 million pounds.

Again, for prices above $0.10 per pound, the new supply curve, *S'*, adds horizontally the 30-million-pound quota to *S*, the supply curve of U.S. producers. The U.S. price is found where this new supply curve, *S'*, intersects the domestic demand curve, which in the left panel of Exhibit 7 occurs at point *e*. *By limiting imports, the quota raises the domestic price of sugar above the world price and reduces quantity below the free-trade level.* (Note that to compare more easily the effects of tariffs and quotas, this quota is designed to yield the same equilibrium price and quantity as the tariff examined earlier.)

Panel (b) of Exhibit 7 shows the distribution and efficiency effects of the quota. As a re-sult of the quota, U.S. consumer surplus declines by the combined blue and pink areas. Area *a* becomes producer surplus and thus involves no loss of U.S. welfare. Area *c* shows the increased economic profit to those permitted by the quota to sell Americans 30 million pounds at $0.15 per pound, or $0.05 above the world price. If foreign exporters rather than U.S. importers reap this profit, area *c* reflects a net loss in U.S. welfare.

Area *b* shows a welfare loss to the U.S. economy, because sugar could have been purchased abroad for $0.10 per pound, and the U.S. resources employed to increase sugar production could have been used more efficiently producing other goods. Area *d* is also a welfare loss because it reflects a reduction in consumer surplus with no offsetting gain to anyone. Thus, areas *b* and *d* in panel (b) of Exhibit 7 measure the minimum U.S. welfare loss from the quota. If the profit from quota rights (area *c*) accrues to foreign producers, this increases the U.S. welfare loss.

Quotas in Practice

The United States has granted quotas to specific countries. These countries, in turn, distribute these quota rights to their exporters through a variety of means. *By rewarding domestic and foreign producers with higher prices, the quota system creates two groups intent on securing and perpetuating these quotas.* Lobbyists for foreign producers work the halls of Congress, seeking the right to export to the United States. This strong support from producers, coupled with a lack of opposition from consumers (who remain rationally ignorant for the most part), has resulted in quotas that have lasted for decades. For example, sugar quotas have been around more than 50 years. In 2003 the world price of sugar averaged about $0.07 a pound, but U.S. businesses that need sugar to make products, such as candy, paid about $0.21 a pound, costing consumers an extra $2 billion a year.[1]

Some economists have argued that if quotas are to be used, the United States should auction them off to foreign producers, thereby capturing the difference between the world price and the U.S. price. Auctioning off quotas would not only increase federal revenue but would reduce the profitability of quotas, which would reduce pressure on Washington to perpetuate quotas.

Tariffs and Quotas Compared

Consider the similarities and differences between a tariff and a quota. Because both have identical effects on the price in our example, they both lead to the same change in quantity demanded. In both cases, U.S. consumers suffer the same loss of consumer surplus, and U.S. producers reap the same gain of producer surplus. The primary difference is that the revenue from the tariff goes to the government, whereas the revenue from the quota goes to whoever secures the right to sell foreign goods in the U.S. market. *If quota rights accrue to foreigners, then the domestic economy is worse off with a quota than with a tariff.* But even if quota rights go to domestic importers, quotas, like tariffs, still increase the domestic price, restrict quantity, and thereby reduce consumer surplus. Quotas and tariffs can also raise production costs. For example, U.S. candy manufacturers face higher production costs because of sugar quotas, as do U.S. automakers because of steel quotas. Finally, and most importantly, quotas and tariffs encourage foreign governments to retaliate with quotas and tariffs of their own, thus shrinking U.S. export markets, so the loss in welfare is greater than shown in Exhibits 6 and 7.

Other Trade Restrictions

Besides tariffs and quotas, a variety of other measures limit free trade. A country may provide *export subsidies* to encourage exports and *low-interest loans* to foreign buyers to promote

1. "America's Sugar Daddies," *New York Times*, 29 November 2003.

exports of large capital goods. Some countries impose *domestic content requirements* specifying that a certain portion of a final good must be produced domestically. Other requirements concerning health, safety, or technical standards often discriminate against foreign goods. For example, European countries prohibit beef from hormone-fed cattle, a measure aimed at U.S. beef. Purity laws in Germany bar many non-German beers. The European Union bans Brazil nuts, claiming the shells contain a cancer causing agent. Until the European Community adopted uniform standards, differing technical requirements forced manufacturers to offer as many as seven different versions of the same TV for that market. Sometimes exporters will voluntarily limit exports, as when Japanese automakers agreed to cut exports to the United States. The point is that *tariffs and quotas are only two of many devices that restrict foreign trade.*

Recent research on the cost of protectionism indicates that international trade barriers slow the introduction of new goods and improved technologies. So, rather than simply raising domestic prices, trade restrictions slow economic progress.

Freer Trade by Multilateral Agreement

Mindful of how high tariffs cut world trade during the Great Depression, the United States, after World War II, invited its trading partners to negotiate lower tariffs and other trade barriers. The result was the **General Agreement on Tariffs and Trade (GATT),** an international trade treaty adopted in 1947 by 23 countries, including the United States. Each GATT member agreed to (1) reduce tariffs through multinational negotiations, (2) reduce import quotas, and (3) treat all members equally with respect to trade.

Trade barriers have been reduced through trade negotiations among many countries, or "trade rounds," under the auspices of GATT. Trade rounds offer a package approach rather than an issue-by-issue approach to trade negotiations. Concessions that are necessary but otherwise difficult to defend in domestic political terms can be made more acceptable in the context of a package that also contains politically and economically attractive benefits. Most early GATT trade rounds were aimed at reducing tariffs. The Kennedy Round in the mid-1960s included new provisions against **dumping,** which is selling a commodity abroad for less than is charged in the home market. The Tokyo Round of the 1970s was a more sweeping attempt to extend and improve the system.

The most recently completed round was launched in Uruguay in September 1986 and ratified by 123 participating countries in 1994. The number of signing countries grew to 142 more recently. This so-called **Uruguay Round,** the most comprehensive of the eight postwar multilateral trade negotiations, included 550 pages of tariff reductions on 85 percent of world trade. The Uruguay Round also created the World Trade Organization (WTO) to succeed GATT.

The World Trade Organization

The **World Trade Organization (WTO)** now provides the legal and institutional foundation for world trade. Whereas GATT was a multilateral agreement with no institutional foundation, the WTO is a permanent institution in Geneva, Switzerland. A staff of about 500 economists and lawyers helps shape policy and resolves trade disputes between member countries. Whereas GATT involved only merchandise trade, the WTO also covers services and trade-related aspects of intellectual property, such as books, movies, and computer programs. Quotas will eventually be phased out by the WTO, but tariffs will remain legal. Average tariffs will fall from 6 percent to 4 percent of the value of imports (when GATT began in 1947, tariffs averaged 40 percent).

GENERAL AGREEMENT ON TARIFFS AND TRADE (GATT)

An international tariff-reduction treaty adopted in 1947 that resulted in a series of negotiated "rounds" aimed at freer trade; the Uruguay Round created GATT's successor, the World Trade Organization (WTO)

DUMPING

Selling a product abroad for less than charged in the home market

URUGUAY ROUND

The most recently concluded multilateral trade negotiation under GATT; this 1994 agreement cut tariffs, formed the World Trade Organization (WTO), and will eventually eliminate quotas

WORLD TRADE ORGANIZATION (WTO)

The legal and institutional foundation of the multilateral trading system that succeeded GATT in 1995

Whereas GATT relied on voluntary cooperation, the WTO settles disputes in a way that is faster, more automatic, and less susceptible to blockage than the GATT system was. The WTO resolved more trade disputes in its first decade than GATT did in nearly 50 years. Since 2000, developing countries have filed 60 percent of the disputes. But the WTO has also become a lightning rod for globalization issues, as discussed in the following case study.

The WTO and the "Battle in Seattle"

When WTO members met in Seattle in November 1999 to set an agenda and timetable for the next round of trade talks, all hell broke loose, as 50,000 protesters disrupted the city. Most were peaceful, but police made more than 500 arrests over three days, and property damage reached $3 million. T-shirts sold the week before the meeting dubbed the event the "Battle in Seattle," and so it was. The less-peaceful protestors targeted multinational companies, smashing windows at Starbucks, McDonald's, Nike Town, and Old Navy, and burning khakis in front of the Gap. Across the Atlantic, about 2,000 protested in London, where 40 were arrested for overturning vehicles and starting fires.

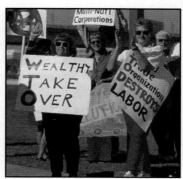
© Todd Bigelow/Aurora Photos

The "Battle in Seattle" was by far the largest demonstration against free trade in the United States. Organizers used free trade as a recruiting and fund-raising focus for a variety of groups, including labor unions and environmental groups. Protestors could pick their favorite cause—union members' fear of losing jobs overseas, environmentalists' fear that producers would seek out countries with lax regulations, and other groups' fear of developments such as hormone-fed beef and genetically modified food. (If you want to sample their concerns, plug "stop the WTO" into any Internet search engine.)

Protestors would probably have been surprised to learn that WTO members are not of one mind about trade issues. For example, the United States and Europe usually push to protect worker rights around the world, but developing countries, including Mexico, Egypt, India, and Pakistan, object strenuously to discussing worker rights. These poorer nations are concerned that the clothing, shoes, and textiles they make have not gained access to rich nations quickly enough. Many developing countries view attempts to impose labor and environmental standards as just the latest effort to keep poor countries poor.

Without international groups such as the WTO to provide a forum for discussing labor and environmental issues around the world, conditions in poor countries would probably be worse. Working conditions, especially in poor countries, have been slowly improving, thanks in part to trade opportunities along with pressure for labor rights from WTO and other international groups. For example, Cambodia is one of the poorest countries in the world, but the highest wages in the country are earned by the 1 percent of the population working in the export sector. For example, Deth worked in the June Textile factory in Cambodia sewing T-shirts and shorts, mostly for Nike and the Gap. She worked from 6:15 A.M. to 2:15 P.M. with a half hour for lunch, extra pay for overtime, and double pay for working holidays. Though her pay was low by U.S. standards, it supported her family and was more than twice what judges and doctors averaged in Cambodia. Her pay and working conditions were also far more attractive than in her previous line of work—prostitution. Factories tend to hire young women, a group that otherwise has few job opportunities. Factory jobs have provided this group with status and social equality they never had.

Child labor still occurs in poor countries, but it's more likely to be on the family farm than in a factory. One in six 10- to 14-year-olds in Cambodia works, the highest rate in Southeast Asia. But the manufacturing and trade sectors account for only about 10 percent of Cambodia's estimated 600,000 child workers, according to the United Nations Development Program. The rest work on family farms or fisheries, with some hired out to neighboring families for work. Some children try to use fake IDs to get hired in factories, where the minimum age is 15. The trade-barrier reductions from the Uruguay Round are projected to boost world income by $510 billion in 2005 (the target date for full implementation), or about $100 per person on Earth. In Cambodia and in other poor countries around the world this extra income could be a lifesaver.

The Seattle WTO meeting adjourned without a date or an agenda for the next round of trade talks, so demonstrators succeeded in disrupting deliberations. In part because of media pressure, Nike ended its contract with the June Textile factory in Cambodia. Deth was worried. "I don't know what the fate of my children will be if I lose my job," she told *Asiaweek*.

After failing to get off the ground in Seattle, the current round of WTO talks was finally launched two years later in Doha, Qatar. In setting the groundwork for the **Doha Round,** members agreed to improve market access around the world, phase out export subsidies, and substantially reduce distorting government subsidies in agriculture. But that round has not gone smoothly so far. Talks in Cancun ended bitterly in September 2003. Headed by Brazil, a group of developing countries demanded stronger commitments from the richer countries to curb agricultural subsidies in the United States, Europe, and Japan. These subsidies harm farmers in poor countries.

Sources: Brian Lindsey, "The Miami Fizzle—What Else But Cancun Redux," *Wall Street Journal*, 28 November 2003; Gina Chon, "Dropped Stitches," *Asiaweek*, 22 December 2000; Nicholas Kristoff, "Inviting All Democrats," 14 January 2004; David Postman and Linda Mapes, "Why WTO Unified So Many Foes," *Seattle Times*, 6 December 1999; and the Web site for the World Trade Organization at http://www.wto.org.

DOHA ROUND

The current multilateral trade negotiations, which aims at lowering tariffs on a wide range of industrial and agricultural products; the first trade round under WTO

Common Markets

Some countries have looked to the success of the U.S. economy, which is essentially a free trade zone across 50 states, and have tried to develop free trade zones of their own. The largest and best known is the European Union, which began in 1958 with a half dozen countries and has expanded to 25. The idea was to create a barrier-free European market like the United States in which goods, services, people, and capital are free to flow to their highest-valued use. Twelve members of the European Union have adopted a common currency, the *euro,* which replaced national currencies in 2002.

The United States, Canada, and Mexico have developed a free trade pact called the North American Free Trade Agreement (NAFTA). Through NAFTA, Mexico hopes to attract more U.S. investment by guaranteeing companies that locate there duty-free access to U.S. markets, which is where over two-thirds of Mexico's exports go. Mexico's 110 million people represent an attractive export market for U.S. producers, and Mexico's oil reserves could ease U.S. energy problems. The United States would also like to support Mexico's efforts to become more market oriented, as is reflected, for example, by Mexico's privatization of its phone system and banks. After a decade of NAFTA, agricultural exports to Mexico doubled, as did overall trade among the three nations, but Americans bought much more from Mexicans and Canadians than the other way around.

Free trade areas are proliferating. The United States and other countries are negotiating the Central American Free Trade Agreement, or CAFTA. A half dozen Latin American countries form Mercosur, the association of Southeast Asian nations make up ASEAN, and South Africa and its four neighboring countries make up the Southern African Customs

Union. Regional trade agreements require an exception to WTO rules because bloc members can make special deals among themselves and thus discriminate against outsiders. Under WTO's requirements, any trade concession granted one country must usually be granted to *all other* WTO members.

Arguments for Trade Restrictions

Trade restrictions often appear to be little more than handouts for the domestic industries they protect. Given the loss in social welfare that results from these restrictions, it would be more efficient simply to transfer money from domestic consumers to domestic producers. But such a bald transfer would be politically unpopular. Arguments for trade restrictions avoid mention of transfers to domestic producers and instead cite loftier goals. As we shall now see, some of these arguments are more valid than others.

HOMEWORK
Xpress!
econ-apps news

National Defense Argument

Some industries claim they need protection from import competition because their output is vital for national defense. Products such as strategic metals and military hardware are often insulated from foreign competition by trade restrictions. Thus, national defense considerations outweigh concerns about efficiency and equity. How valid is this argument? Trade restrictions may shelter the defense industry, but other means, such as government subsidies, might be more efficient. Or the government could stockpile basic military hardware so that maintaining an ongoing productive capacity would become less essential, though technological change soon makes certain weapons obsolete. Because most industries can play some role in national defense, instituting trade restrictions on this basis can get out of hand. For example, U.S. wool producers gained protection at a time when some military uniforms were made of wool.

Infant Industry Argument

The infant industry argument was formulated as a rationale for protecting emerging domestic industries from foreign competition. In industries where a firm's average cost of production falls as output expands, new firms may need protection from imports until these firms grow big enough to be competitive. Trade restrictions let new firms achieve the economies of scale needed to compete with mature foreign producers.

But how do we identify industries that merit protection, and when do they become old enough to look after themselves? Protection often fosters inefficiencies. The immediate cost of such restrictions is the net welfare loss from higher domestic prices. These costs may become permanent if the industry never realizes the expected economies of scale and thus never becomes competitive. As with the national defense argument, policy makers should be careful in adopting trade restrictions based on the infant industry argument. Here again, temporary production subsidies may be more efficient than import restrictions.

Antidumping Argument

As we have noted already, *dumping* is selling a product abroad for less than in the home market. Exporters may be able to sell the good for less overseas because of export subsidies, or firms may simply find it profitable to sell for less in foreign markets where demand is more price elastic—that is, firms price discriminate. Critics of dumping call for a tariff to raise the price of dumped goods. But why shouldn't U.S. consumers pay as little as possible, even if these low prices result from a foreign subsidy or price discrimination? If dumping is *persistent,* the increase in consumer surplus would more than offset losses to domestic producers. *There is no good reason why consumers should not be allowed to buy imports for a persistently lower price.*

An alternative form of dumping, termed *predatory dumping,* is the *temporary* sale abroad at prices below the home market or even below cost to eliminate competitors in that foreign market. Once the competition is gone, so the story goes, the exporting firm can raise the price in the foreign market. The trouble with this argument is that if dumpers try to take advantage of their monopoly position by sharply increasing the price, then other firms, either domestic or foreign, could enter the market and sell for less. There are few documented cases of predatory dumping.

Sometimes dumping may be *sporadic,* as firms occasionally try to unload excess inventories. Retailers hold periodic "sales" for the same reason. Sporadic dumping can be unsettling for domestic producers, but the economic impact is not a matter of great public concern. Regardless, all dumping is prohibited in the United States by the Trade Agreements Act of 1979, which calls for the imposition of tariffs when a good is sold for less in the United States than in its home market. In addition, WTO rules allow for offsetting tariffs when products are sold for "less than fair value" and when there is "material injury" to domestic producers. For example, U.S. producers of lumber and beer have accused their Canadian counterparts of dumping.

Jobs and Income Argument

One rationale for trade restrictions that is commonly heard in the United States, and was voiced by WTO protestors, is that they protect U.S. jobs and wage levels. Using trade restrictions to protect domestic jobs is a strategy that dates back centuries. One problem with such a policy is that other countries will likely retaliate by restricting *their* imports to save *their* jobs, so international trade is reduced, jobs are lost in export industries, and potential gains from trade fail to materialize. That happened during the Great Depression.

Wages in other countries, especially developing countries, are often a small fraction of wages in the United States. Looking simply at differences in wages, however, narrows the focus too much. Wages represent just one component of the total production cost and may not necessarily be the most important. Employers are interested in the labor cost per unit of output, which depends on both the wage and labor productivity. Wages are high in the United States partly because U.S. labor productivity remains the highest in the world. High productivity can be traced to education and training and to the abundant computers, machines, and other physical capital that make workers more productive. U.S. workers also benefit from a stable business climate.

But what about the lower wages in many developing countries? These low wages are often linked to workers' lack of education and training, to the meager physical capital available to each worker, and to a business climate that is less stable and less attractive for producers. But once multinational firms build plants and provide technological know-how in developing countries, U.S. workers lose some of their competitive edge, and their relatively high wages could price some U.S. products out of the world market. This has already happened in the stereo and consumer electronics industries. China now makes 80 percent of the toys sold in the United States. Some U.S. toy sellers, such as the makers of Etch A Sketch, would no longer survive if they had not outsourced manufacturing to China.

Domestic producers do not like to compete with foreign producers whose costs are lower, so they often push for trade restrictions. But if restrictions negate any cost advantage a foreign producer might have, the law of comparative advantage becomes inoperative and domestic consumers are denied access to the lower-priced goods.

Over time, as labor productivity in developing countries increases, wage differentials among countries will narrow, much as wage differentials narrowed between northern and southern U.S. states. As technology and capital spread, U.S. workers, particularly unskilled workers, cannot expect to maintain wage levels that are far above those in other countries. So far, research and development has kept U.S. producers on the cutting edge of technological developments, but staying ahead in the technological race is a constant battle.

Declining Industries Argument

Where an established domestic industry is in jeopardy of closing because of lower-priced imports, could there be a rationale for *temporary* import restrictions? After all, domestic producers employ many industry-specific resources—both specialized machines and specialized labor. This physical and human capital is worth less in its best alternative use. If the extinction of the domestic industry is forestalled through trade restrictions, specialized machines can be allowed to wear out naturally, and specialized workers can retire voluntarily or can gradually pursue more promising careers.

Thus, in the case of declining domestic industries, trade protection can help lessen shocks to the economy and can allow for an orderly transition to a new industrial mix. But the protection offered should not be so generous as to encourage continued investment in the industry. Protection should be of specific duration and should be phased out over that period.

The clothing industry is an example of a declining U.S. industry. The 22,000 U.S. jobs saved as a result of one recent trade restriction paid an average of about $23,000 per year. But a Congressional Budget Office study estimated that, because of higher domestic clothing prices, U.S. consumers paid between $39,000 and $74,000 per year for each textile and apparel job saved. Trade restrictions in the U.S. clothing and textile industry are being phased out beginning in 2005 under the Uruguay Round of trade agreements.

Free trade may displace some U.S. jobs through imports, but it also creates U.S. jobs through exports. When people celebrate a ribbon-cutting ceremony for a new software company, nobody credits free trade for those jobs, but when a steel plant closes, everyone talks about how those jobs went overseas. What's more, many foreign companies have built plants in the United States and employ U.S. workers. For example, a dozen foreign television manufacturers and all major Japanese automobile manufacturers now have U.S. plants.

The number of jobs in the United States has more than doubled since 1960. To recognize this job growth is not to deny the problems facing workers who are displaced by imports. Some displaced workers, particularly those in blue-collar jobs in steel and other unionized industries, are not likely to find jobs that will pay as well as the ones they lost. As with infant industries, however, the problems posed by declining industries need not require trade restrictions. To support the affected industry, the government could offer wage subsidies or special tax breaks that decline over time. The government has also funded programs to retrain affected workers for jobs that are in greater demand.

Problems with Protection

Trade restrictions raise a number of problems in addition to those already mentioned. First, protecting one stage of production usually requires protecting downstream stages of production. Protecting the U.S. textile industry from foreign competition, for example, raises the cost of cloth to U.S. apparel manufacturers, reducing their competitiveness. Thus, if the government protects domestic textile manufacturers, the domestic garment industry also needs protection. Second, the cost of protection includes not only the welfare loss arising from the higher domestic price but also the cost of the resources used by domestic producers and groups to secure the favored protection. The cost of *rent seeking*—lobbying fees, propaganda, and legal actions—can equal or exceed the direct welfare loss from restrictions. A third problem with trade restrictions is the transaction costs of enforcing the myriad quotas, tariffs, and other trade restrictions. A fourth problem is that economies insulated from foreign competition become less innovative and less efficient. And a final problem with imposing trade restrictions is that other countries usually retaliate, thus shrinking the gains from trade. Retaliation can set off still greater trade restrictions, leading to an outright trade war. Consider the recent steel tariffs discussed in the following case study.

Bush's Steel Tariffs

Case Study

Public Policy

eActivity

For more on the union perspective about the repeal of the steel tariffs visit the AFL-CIO's Web page on the issue at http://www.aflcio.org/issuespolitics/manufacturing/ns12042003.cfm, which includes links to additional union statements. For the European view visit the BBC World News to read about the proposed retaliatory tariffs at http://news.bbc.co.uk/1/hi/business/3243423.stm and look at a Q&A about the trade dispute at http://news.bbc.co.uk/1/hi/business/3291675.stm. On what basis did the Europeans select the goods on which to impose the countervailing duties? Why do you think President Bush changed his mind about the tariffs?

The U.S. steel industry has been suffering a long, painful decline for decades—a death from a thousand cuts. From 1997 to 2001, about 30 percent of U.S. steel producers filed for bankruptcy, including Bethlehem Steel and National Steel. During that same stretch, 45,000 steel jobs disappeared, leaving about 180,000 jobs remaining. Imports accounted for 30 percent of the U.S. market, with most of that steel coming from Europe.

© Photodisc/Getty Images

Industry leaders turned to the White House for help. Many of the jobs lost were in "rust-belt" states, such as Ohio, West Virginia, and Pennsylvania, states that President George W. Bush hoped to win in his 2004 reelection bid. We can only speculate what role politics played in the decision, but in March 2002, the Bush administration imposed tariffs on imported steel, claiming imports caused "material injury" to the U.S. steel industry. The tariffs, which ranged from 8 to 30 percent on 10 steel categories, were scheduled to last three years.

As expected, the tariffs cut imports and boosted the domestic price of steel. By 2003, steel imports reached their lowest level in a decade. The higher price of steel helped U.S. steel makers but made steel-using industries less competitive on world markets. For example, the tariffs added about $300 to the average cost of a U.S. automobile. According to one conservative estimate, the tariffs lost 15,000 to 20,000 jobs in the steel user industries.

The European Union and other affected nations complained to the WTO. In November 2003, the WTO ruled that the tariffs violated trade agreements. The European Union, with about 300,000 steel jobs at stake, announced that if the tariffs were not lifted by mid-December 2003, EU countries would retaliate with tariffs on U.S. exports. Japan and South Korea also threatened retaliatory tariffs.

In early December 2003, the Bush administration repealed the tariffs, arguing that they had served their purpose. Approximately $650 million in higher tariffs had been collected during the 20 months they were imposed. The steelworkers union called the repeal "an affront to all workers." But union members should not have been surprised in light of the WTO ruling, the threatened retaliation from abroad, and the fact that several months earlier, the steelworkers union endorsed a Democrat for president.

Sources: Neil King et al., "U.S. Steel Tariffs Ruled Illegal, Sparking Potential Trade War," *Wall Street Journal*, 11 November 2003; Carlos Tejeda, "After Removal of Steel Tariffs, Many Are Without Scrap Heap," *Wall Street Journal*, 15 December 2003; Carlos Tejeda, "Tariffs Retreat May Affect Talks," *Wall Street Journal*, 8 December 2003; and "Rolled Over," *Economist*, 6 December 2003.

Import Substitution Versus Export Promotion

An economy's progress usually involves moving from agriculture and raw material to manufacturing then to services. If a country is fortunate, this transformation occurs gradually through natural market forces. Sometimes governments push along the evolution. Many developing countries, including Argentina and India, pursued a strategy called **import substitution,** whereby the country manufactured products that until then had been imported. To insulate domestic producers from foreign competition, the government imposed tariffs and quotas. This development strategy became popular for several reasons. First, demand already existed for these products, so the "what to produce" question was easily answered. Second, import substitution provided infant industries a protected market. Finally, import substitution was popular with those who supplied capital, labor, and other resources to the favored domestic industries.

Like all protection measures, however, import substitution erased the gains from specialization and comparative advantage among countries. Often the developing country replaced low-cost foreign goods with high-cost domestic goods. And domestic producers, shielded from foreign competition, usually failed to become efficient. Worse still, other countries often retaliated with their own trade restrictions.

Critics of import substitution claim that export promotion is a surer path to economic development. **Export promotion** concentrates on producing for the export market. This development strategy begins with relatively simple products, such as textiles. As a developing country builds its technological and educational base—that is, as the developing economy learns by doing—producers can then export more complex products. Economists favor export promotion over import substitution because the emphasis is on comparative advantage and trade expansion rather than on trade restriction. Export promotion also forces producers to grow more efficient in order to compete on world markets. Research shows that global competition boosts domestic efficiency.[2] What's more, export promotion requires less government intervention in the market than does import substitution.

Of the two approaches, export promotion has been more successful around the world. For example, the newly industrialized countries of East Asia (Taiwan, South Korea, Hong Kong, and Singapore) have successfully pursued export promotion, while Argentina, India, and Peru have failed with their import-substitution approach. Since 1965, the four newly industrialized economies of East Asia raised their average real incomes from only 20 percent of industrial economies to over 70 percent. Most Latin American nations, which for decades had favored import substitution, are now pursuing free trade agreements with the United States. Even India is dismantling its trade barriers.

IMPORT SUBSTITUTION

A development strategy that emphasizes domestic manufacturing of products that were imported

EXPORT PROMOTION

A development strategy that concentrates on producing for the export market

Conclusion

International trade arises from voluntary exchange among buyers and sellers pursuing their self-interest. Since 1950 world output has risen sevenfold, while world trade has increased seventeenfold. World trade offers many advantages to the trading countries: access to markets around the world, lower costs through economies of scale, the opportunity to utilize abundant resources, better access to information about markets and technology, improved quality honed by competitive pressure, and lower prices for consumers. Comparative advantage, specialization, and trade allow people to use their scarce resources most efficiently to satisfy their unlimited wants.

---

2. See Martin Baily and Hans Gersbach, "Efficiency in Manufacturing and the Need for Global Competition," in *Brookings Papers on Economic Activity: Microeconomics,* M. Baily, P. Reiss, and C. Winston, eds. (Washington, D.C.: Brookings Institution, 1995), 307–347.

Despite the clear gains from free trade, restrictions on international trade date back centuries, and pressure to impose trade restrictions continues today. Domestic producers (and their resource suppliers) benefit from trade restrictions because they can sell their products for more. Protection insulates domestic producers from the rigors of global competition, in the process stifling innovation and leaving the industry vulnerable to technological change elsewhere. Under a system of quotas, the winners also include those who have secured the right to import goods at the world prices and sell them at the domestic prices. Consumers, who must pay higher prices for protected goods, suffer from trade restrictions, as do the domestic producers who use imported resources. Other losers are U.S. exporters, who face higher trade barriers as foreigners retaliate with their own trade restrictions.

Producer groups have a laser-like focus on trade legislation, but consumers remain largely oblivious. Consumers purchase thousands of different goods and thus have no special interest in the effects of trade policy on any particular good. Congress tends to support the group that makes the most noise, so trade restrictions often persist, despite the widespread gains from free trade.

SUMMARY

1. Even if a country has an absolute advantage in all goods, that country should specialize in producing the goods in which it has a comparative advantage. If each country specializes and trades according to the law of comparative advantage, all countries will have greater consumption possibilities.

2. Tariff revenues could be used to lower taxes or fund government programs. Quotas benefit those with the right to buy goods at the world price and sell them at the higher domestic price. Both tariffs and quotas harm domestic consumers more than they help domestic producers, although tariffs at least yield government revenue, which can be used to fund valued public programs or to cut taxes.

3. Despite the gains from free trade, trade restrictions have been imposed for centuries. The General Agreement on Tariffs and Trade (GATT) was an international treaty ratified in 1947 to reduce trade barriers. Subsequent negotiations lowered tariffs and reduced trade restrictions. The Uruguay Round, ratified in 1994, lowered tariffs, phased out quotas, and created the World Trade Organization (WTO) as the successor to GATT.

4. Arguments used by producer groups to support trade restrictions include promoting national defense, nurturing infant industries, preventing foreign producers from dumping goods in domestic markets, protecting domestic jobs, and allowing declining industries time to wind down.

5. Import substitution is a development strategy that emphasizes domestic production of goods that are currently imported. Export promotion concentrates on producing for the export market. Over the years, export promotion has been more successful than import substitution because it relies on specialization and comparative advantage.

QUESTIONS FOR REVIEW

1. *(Profile of Imports and Exports)* What are the major U.S. exports and imports? How does international trade affect consumption possibilities?

2. *(Reasons for Trade)* What are the primary reasons for international trade?

3. *(Gains from Trade)* Complete each of the following sentences:

   a. When a nation has no economic interaction with foreigners and produces everything it consumes, the nation is in a state of _____.

   b. According to the law of comparative advantage, each nation should specialize in producing the goods in which it has the lowest _____.

   c. The amount of one good that a nation can exchange for one unit of another good is known as the _____.

   d. Specializing according to comparative advantage and trading with other nations results in _____.

4. *(Reasons for International Specialization)* What determines which goods a country should produce and export?

5. *(Tariffs)* High tariffs usually lead to black markets and smuggling. How is government revenue reduced by such activity? Relate your answer to the graph in Exhibit 5 in this chapter. Does smuggling have any social benefits?

6. *(Trade Restrictions)* Exhibits 6 and 7 show net losses to the economy of a country that imposes tariffs or quotas on imported sugar. What kinds of gains and losses would occur in the economies of countries that export sugar?

7. *(The World Trade Organization)* What is the World Trade Organization (WTO) and how does it help foster multilateral trade? (Check the WTO Web site at http://www.wto.org/.)

8. (*Case Study*: The WTO and the "Battle in Seattle") Why did protesters demonstrate during the WTO meetings in Seattle in November 1999?

9. *(Arguments for Trade Restrictions)* Explain the national defense, declining industries, and infant industry arguments for protecting a domestic industry from international competition.

10. *(Arguments for Trade Restrictions)* Firms hurt by cheap imports typically argue that restricting trade will save U.S. jobs. What's wrong with this argument? Are there ever any reasons to support such trade restrictions?

11. (*Case Study*: Bush's Steel Tariffs) How did Bush's steel tariff affect the domestic steel industry, the workers in the steel industry, and consumers?

PROBLEMS AND EXERCISES

12. *(Comparative Advantage)* Suppose that each U.S. worker can produce 8 units of food or 2 units of clothing daily. In Fredonia, which has the same number of workers, each worker can produce 7 units of food or 1 unit of clothing daily. Why does the United States have an absolute advantage in both goods? Which country enjoys a comparative advantage in food? Why?

13. *(Comparative Advantage)* The consumption possibilities frontiers shown in Exhibit 4 assume terms of trade of 1 unit of clothing for 1 unit of food. What would the consumption possibilities frontiers look like if the terms of trade were 1 unit of clothing for 2 units of food?

14. *(Import Quotas)* How low must a quota be to have an impact? Using a demand-and-supply diagram, illustrate and explain the net welfare loss from imposing such a quota. Under what circumstances would the net welfare loss from an import quota exceed the net welfare loss from an equivalent tariff (one that results in the same price and import level as the quota)?

15. *(Trade Restrictions)* Suppose that the world price for steel is below the U.S. domestic price, but the government requires that all steel used in the United States be domestically produced.

   a. Use a diagram like the one in Exhibit 5 to show the gains and loses from such a policy.

   b. How could you estimate the net welfare loss (deadweight loss) from such a diagram?

   c. What response to such a policy would you expect from industries (like automobile producers) that use U.S. steel?

   d. What government revenues are generated by this policy?

16. *(Import Substitution Versus Export Promotion)* Two strategies frequently used to stimulate economic development are export promotion and import substitution. Describe the advantages and disadvantages of each strategy.

EXPERIENTIAL EXERCISES

17. *(Arguments for Trade Restrictions)* Visit the Office of the U.S. Trade Representative at http://www.ustr.gov/. The U.S. Trade Representative is a cabinet member who acts as the principal trade advisor, negotiator, and spokesperson for the president on trade and related investment matters. Look at some of the most recent press releases. What are some of the trade-related issues the United States is currently facing?

18. *(Wall Street Journal)* The *Wall Street Journal* is one of the world's best sources of information regarding international trade. A good place to look is the International page inside the First Section of each day's edition. Look at today's issue and find an article dealing with trade barriers—tariffs, quotas, and so on. Model the trade barrier using a graph, and try to determine who benefits and who bears the costs. If you are lucky, the article will provide sufficient information to allow you to actually estimate costs and benefits in dollar terms. If you can't find a relevant article in today's paper, go to previous issues until you come up with one.

HOMEWORK XPRESS! EXERCISES

*These exercises require access to McEachern Homework Xpress! If Homework Xpress! did not come with your book, visit **http://homeworkxpress.swlearning.com** to purchase.*

1. Canada and Bolivia both can produce two goods—chairs and sweaters. The production possibilities for each are shown in the diagram. Identify how many sweaters Canada can produce if it produces 30 chairs. Add a consumption possibilities curve if each country specializes and trades 1 chair for 10 sweaters. Identify how many sweaters Canadians can have if they keep 30 chairs and trade the rest for sweaters.

2. Demand and domestic supply curves for crude oil in the nation of Yacimiento are shown in the diagram. The world price for crude oil is $20 per barrel. Identify the quantity demanded and domestic quantity supplied at this price. The government decides to lessen dependence on im- ported oil by imposing a $10 per barrel tariff on imported crude. Identify the quantity demanded and domestic quantity supplied with the tariff. Shade the area representing government revenue generated by the tariff.

3. Demand and domestic supply curves for crude oil in the nation of Yacimiento are shown in the diagram. The world price for crude oil is $20 per barrel. Identify the quantity demanded at the world price. The government decides to lessen dependence on imported oil by imposing a quota on imports of .25 billion barrels. Draw the part of the new supply curve that will intersect the demand curve. Identify the new price of oil in Yacimiento and the quantity demanded at this price.

Introduction to Macroeconomics

© M. SAT Editions SARL/Corbis Sygma

What's the big idea with macroeconomics? Why is its focus the national economy? How do we measure the economy's performance over time? Which has more impact on your standard of living, the economy's ups and downs or its long-term growth? Answers to these and related questions are provided in this chapter, which introduces macroeconomics. Macroeconomics looks at the big picture—not the demand for Dunkin' Donuts but the demand for everything produced in the economy; not the price of gasoline but the average price of all goods and services produced in the economy; not consumption by the Martinez household but consumption by all households; not investment by the Disney Corporation but investment by all firms in the economy.

Macroeconomists develop and test theories about how the economy as a whole works—theories that can help predict the consequences of economic policies and events. Macroeconomists are concerned not only with what determines such big-picture indicators as production, employment, and the price level but also with understanding how and why these measures change over time. Macroeconomists are especially interested in what makes an economy grow, because a growing economy creates more jobs and more goods and services—in short, faster growth means a higher standard of living. What determines the economy's ability to use resources productively, to adapt, to grow? This chapter begins exploring such questions. Topics discussed include:

- The national economy
- Economic fluctuations
- Aggregate demand
- Aggregate supply

- Equilibrium level of price and aggregate output
- Short history of the U.S. economy
- Demand-side economics
- Supply-side economics

The National Economy

ECONOMY

The structure of economic activity in a community, a region, a country, a group of countries, or the world

Macroeconomics concerns the overall performance of the *economy*. The term **economy** describes the structure of economic life, or economic activity, in a community, a region, a country, a group of countries, or the world. We could talk about the Chicago economy, the Illinois economy, the Midwest economy, the U.S. economy, the North American economy, or the world economy. We measure an economy's size in different ways, such as the amount produced, the number of people working, or their total income. The most common yardstick is *gross product,* which measures the market value of final goods and services produced in a particular geographical region during a given period, usually one year.

If the focus is the Illinois economy, we consider the *gross state product*. If the focus is the U.S. economy, we consider the **gross domestic product,** or **GDP,** which measures the market value of all final goods and services produced in the United States during a given period, usually a year. GDP adds up production of the economy's incredible variety of goods and services, from trail bikes to pedicures. We can use the gross domestic product to compare different economies at the same time or to track the same economy over time.

GROSS DOMESTIC PRODUCT (GDP)

The market value of all final goods and services produced in the nation during a particular period, usually a year

What's Special About the National Economy?

The national economy deserves special attention. Here's why. If you were to drive west on Interstate 10 in Texas, you would hardly notice crossing the state line into New Mexico. But if you took the Juarez exit south into Mexico, you would be stopped at the border, asked for identification, and possibly searched. You would become quite aware of crossing an international border. Like most countries, the United States and Mexico usually allow people and goods to move more freely *within* their borders than *across* their borders.

The differences between the United States and Mexico are far greater than the differences between Texas and New Mexico. For example, each country has its own standard of living and currency, its own culture and language, its own communication and transportation system, its own system of government, and its own "rules of the game"—that is, its own laws, regulations, customs, and conventions for conducting economic activity both within and across its borders.

Macroeconomics typically focuses on the performance of the national economy, including how the national economy interacts with other economies around the world. The U.S. economy is the largest and most complex in the world, with about 110 million households, 24 million businesses, and 87,400 separate government jurisdictions. The world economy includes about 200 sovereign nations, ranging from tiny Liechtenstein, with only 33,000 residents, to China, with 1.3 billion people. These numbers offer snapshots, but the economy is a moving picture, a work in progress—too complex to capture in snapshots. This is why we use theoretical models to focus on key relationships. To help you get your mind around the economy, let's begin with a simple analogy.

The Human Body and the U.S. Economy

Consider the similarities and differences between the human body and the economy. The body consists of millions of cells, each performing particular functions yet each linked to the entire body. Similarly, the U.S. economy is composed of millions of decision makers, each acting with some independence yet each connected with the economy as a whole. The economy, like the body, is continually renewing itself, with new households, new businesses, a changing group of public officials, and new foreign competitors and customers. Blood circulates throughout the body, facilitating the exchange of oxygen and vital nutrients among cells. Similarly, *money* circulates throughout the economy, facilitating the exchange of resources and products among individual economic units. In fact, blood and money are each called a *medium of exchange*. In Chapter 1 we saw that the movement of money, products, and resources throughout the economy follows a *circular flow*, as does the movement of blood, oxygen, and nutrients, throughout the body.

Flow and Stock Variables

Just as the same blood recirculates as a medium of exchange in the body, the same dollars recirculate as a medium of exchange in the economy to finance transactions. The dollars you spend on croissants are spent by the baker on butter and then spent by the dairy farmer on work boots. Dollars *flow* through the economy. To measure a flow, we use a **flow variable,** which is an amount per unit of time, such as your average spending per week or your heartbeats per minute. In contrast, a **stock variable** is an amount measured at a particular point in time, such as the amount of money you have with you right now or your weight this morning.

Testing New Theories

Physicians and other natural scientists test their theories using controlled experiments. Macroeconomists, however, have no laboratories and little ability to run economy-wide experiments. Granted, they can study different economies around the world, but each economy is unique, so comparisons are tricky. Controlled experiments also provide natural scientists with something seldom available to macroeconomists—the chance, or serendipitous, discovery (such as penicillin). Macroeconomists studying the U.S. economy have only one patient, so they can't introduce particular policies in a variety of alternative settings. Cries of "Eureka!" are seldom heard from macroeconomists.

Knowledge and Performance

Throughout history, little was known about the human body, yet many people still enjoyed good health. For example, the fact that blood circulates in our bodies was not discovered until 1638; it took scientists another 150 years to figure out why. Similarly, over the millennia, various complex economies developed and flourished, although there was little known about how these economies worked.

The economy is much like the body: As long as it functions smoothly, policy makers need not understand how it works. But if a problem develops—severe unemployment, high inflation, or sluggish growth, for example—we must know how a healthy economy works before we can consider if and how the problem can be corrected. We need not know every

FLOW VARIABLE

A variable that measures something over an interval of time, such as your income per week

STOCK VARIABLE

A variable that measures something at a particular point in time, such as the amount of money you have with you right now detail of the economy, just as we need not know every detail of the body. But we must understand essential relationships among key variables. For example, does the economy work well on its own, or does it often perform poorly? If it performs poorly, what remedies are available? Can we be sure that the proposed remedy would not do more harm than good? When doctors didn't understand how the human body worked, their attempted "cures" were often worse than the diseases. Much of the history of medicine describes misguided efforts to deal with maladies. Even today, medical care is based on less scientific evidence than you might think. According to one study, only one in seven medical interventions is supported by reliable scientific evidence.[1]

Likewise, policy makers may adopt the wrong prescription because of a flawed theory about how the economy works. At one time, for example, a nation's economic vitality was thought to spring from the stock of precious metals accumulated in the public treasury. This theory spawned a policy called **mercantilism,** which held that, as a way of accumulating gold and silver, a nation should try to export more than it imports. To achieve this, nations restricted imports by such barriers as tariffs and quotas. But these restrictions led to retaliations by other countries, reducing international trade and the gains from specialization. Another flawed economic theory prompted President Herbert Hoover to introduce a major tax *increase* during the Great Depression. Economists have since learned that such a policy does more harm than good.

We turn now to the performance of the U.S. economy.

Economic Fluctuations and Growth

The U.S. economy and other industrial market economies historically have experienced alternating periods of expansion and contraction in economic activity. **Economic fluctuations** are the rise and fall of economic activity relative to the long-term growth trend of the economy. These fluctuations, or *business cycles,* vary in length and intensity, yet some features appear common to all. The ups and downs usually involve the entire nation and often the world and they affect nearly all dimensions of economic activity, not just production and employment.

U.S. Economic Fluctuations

Perhaps the easiest way to understand economic fluctuations is to examine their components. During the 1920s and 1930s, Wesley C. Mitchell, director of the National Bureau of Economic Research (NBER), analyzed economic fluctuations, noting that the economy has two phases: periods of *expansion* and periods of *contraction.* Prior to World War II, a contraction might be so severe as to be called a **depression,** which is a sharp reduction in the nation's total production lasting more than a year and accompanied by high unemployment. A milder contraction is called a **recession,** which is a decline in total output lasting at least two consecutive quarters, or at least six months. The U.S. economy experienced both recessions and depressions before World War II. Since then, there have been recessions but no depressions, so things have improved.

Despite these ups and downs, the U.S. economy has grown dramatically over the long run. The economy produced about 12 times more output in 2004 than it did in 1929. Output is measured by real GDP, the value of final goods and services after stripping away changes due to **inflation,** which is an increase in the economy's price level. Production increased because

MERCANTILISM

The incorrect theory that a nation's economic goal should be to accumulate precious metals in the public treasury; this theory prompted trade barriers to reduce imports, but other countries retaliated, reducing trade and the gains from specialization

ECONOMIC FLUCTUATIONS

The rise and fall of economic activity relative to the long-term growth trend of the economy; also called business cycles

DEPRESSION

A sharp reduction in an economy's total output accompanied by high unemployment lasting more than a year; a severe economic contraction

RECESSION

A decline in the economy's total output lasting at least two consecutive quarters, or six months; an economic contraction

INFLATION

An increase in the economy's average price level

1. As reported by Sherwin Nuland, "Medical Fads: Bran, Midwives and Leeches," *New York Times,* 25 January 1995.

of (1) increases in the amount and quality of resources, especially labor and capital; (2) better technology; and (3) improvements in the *rules of the game* that facilitate production and exchange, such as property rights, patent laws, the legal system, and market practices.

Exhibit 1 shows such a long-term growth trend in real GDP as an upward-sloping straight line. Economic fluctuations reflect movements around this growth trend. A contraction begins after the previous expansion has reached its *peak,* or high point, and continues until the economy reaches a *trough,* or low point. The period between a peak and trough is a *contraction,* and the period between a trough and subsequent peak is an **expansion.** Note that expansions last longer than contractions, but the length of the full cycle varies.

Analysts at NBER have tracked the U.S. economy back to 1854. Since then, the nation has experienced 32 peak-to-trough-to-peak cycles. No two have been exactly alike. The longest contraction lasted five and a half years from 1873 to 1879. The longest expansion lasted nearly 10 years, beginning in the spring of 1991. Year-to-year changes in output since 1929 appear in Exhibit 2, which shows the annual percentage change in real GDP. Years of declining real GDP are shown as red bars and years of increasing real GDP as blue bars. The big decline during the Great Depression of the early 1930s and the sharp jump during World War II stand in stark contrast. Growth averaged 3.4 percent a year for the entire period. Since 1948, the economy has experienced 10 full cycles, with expansions averaging just under five years and recessions just under one year. Notice that since 1948 the annual declines have been less frequent and less negative.

The intensity of U.S. economic fluctuations varies across regions. A recession hits hardest those regions that produce capital goods, such as heavy machinery, and durable goods, such as appliances, furniture, and automobiles. The demand for these goods falls more during hard times than does the demand for other goods and services. Because of seasonal fluctuations

EXPANSION

A phase of economic activity during which the economy's output increases

N e t B o o k m a r k

Read the Economic Review articles for the third quarter of 2003 at http://www.kc.frb.org/publicat/econrev/er03q3.htm. Some of the articles focus on urban growth, travel and tourism, and entrepreneurship, all of which are aspects of expansion. How long do economic expansions last? Why do they end? Read some of the Chicago Fed National Activity Index reports, from most recent to those in 2001 or 2002, at http://www.chicagofed.org. How do the numbers and tone of the reports compare? What do they say about economic expansion?

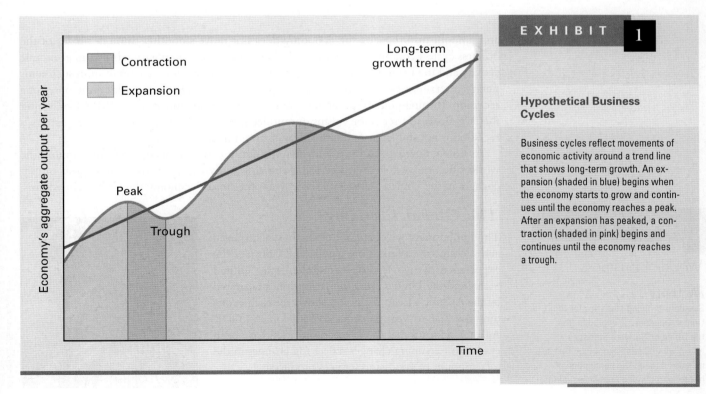

EXHIBIT 1

Hypothetical Business Cycles

Business cycles reflect movements of economic activity around a trend line that shows long-term growth. An expansion (shaded in blue) begins when the economy starts to grow and continues until the economy reaches a peak. After an expansion has peaked, a contraction (shaded in pink) begins and continues until the economy reaches a trough.

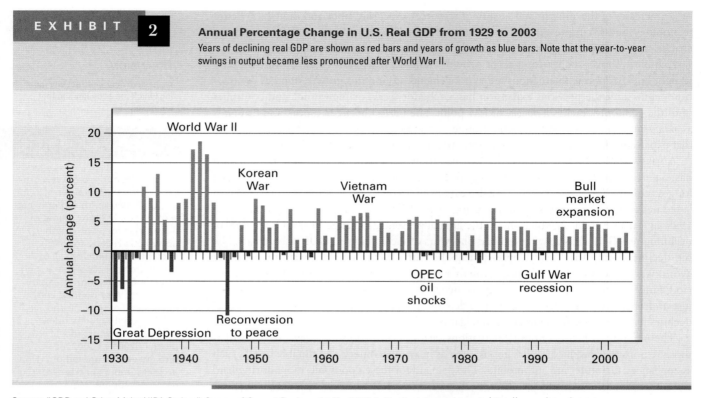

EXHIBIT	2	**Annual Percentage Change in U.S. Real GDP from 1929 to 2003**

Years of declining real GDP are shown as red bars and years of growth as blue bars. Note that the year-to-year swings in output became less pronounced after World War II.

Source: "GDP and Other Major NIPA Series," *Survey of Current Business* 84 (April 2004). For the latest data, go to http://www.bea.doc.gov.

and random disturbances, the economy does not move smoothly through phases of the business cycle. Economists can't always distinguish between temporary setbacks in economic activity and the beginning of a downturn. A drop in production may result from such temporary interruptions as a snowstorm or a poor harvest rather than marking the onset of a recession. Turning points—peaks and troughs—are thus identified by the NBER only after the fact. Because a recession means output declines for at least two consecutive quarters, a recession is not so designated until at least six months after it begins.

As noted, fluctuations usually involve the entire nation. Indeed, economies around the world often move together. The following case study compares the year-to-year output changes in the United States with those in another major economy, the United Kingdom.

Case **Study**

World of Business

eActivity
Standard-of-living statistics for the United Kingdom are available from the Office of National Statistics at http://www.statistics.gov.uk/. This site includes data on the percentage of households owning appliances, autos,

The Global Economy

Though business cycles are not perfectly synchronized across countries, a link is often apparent. Consider the experience of two leading economies—the United States and the United Kingdom, economies separated by the Atlantic Ocean. Exhibit 3 shows for each economy the year-to-year percentage change in real GDP. Again, *real* means that the effects of inflation have been erased, so remaining changes reflect *real* changes in the total amount of goods and services produced.

If you spend a little time following the annual changes in each economy, you will see the similarities. For example, both economies went into recession in the early 1980s, grew well for the rest of the decade, entered another recession in 1991, recovered for the rest of the decade, then slowed down in 2001. And both economies picked up steam in 2004.

One problem with the linkage across economies is that a slump in other major economies could worsen a recession in the United States, and vice versa. For example, the terrorist attacks on the United States in September 2001 affected economies around the world, reducing airline travel and lowering stock market prices. At the time people feared difficulties in the top two economies in the world, the United States and Japan, would feed into each other, dragging other economies down with them.

Sources: Edmund Andrews, "America's Economic Cloud Extends to Europe," *New York Times*, 28 September 2001; Michael Williams et al., "Japan Must Finish Its Stalled Reform," *Wall Street Journal*, 16 March 2001; *Economic Report of the President*, February 2004; *OECD Economic Outlook* 75 (June 2004); and the Bureau of Economic Analysis Web site at http://www.bea.gov/.

etc. Compare the availability of cars and telephones in the United Kingdom to the United States by viewing the U.S. Census reports at http://www.census.gov/apsd/www/cqc.html

EXHIBIT 3

U.S. and U.K. Annual Growth Rates in Output Are Similar

Though economic fluctuations are not perfectly synchronized across major economies, a link is usually apparent. For example, although the United States and the United Kingdom are separated by the Atlantic Ocean, their real GDPs changed from year to year by roughly similar percentages during the last quarter century.

Source: U.S. growth estimates from Bureau of Economic Analysis, U.S. Department of Commerce. For the latest, go to http://www.bea.gov/ then click on Gross Domestic Product. U.K. growth estimates from *OECD Economic Outlook* 75 (June 2004).

Leading Economic Indicators

Certain events foreshadow a turning point in economic activity. Months before a recession is fully under way, changes in leading economic indicators point to the coming storm. In the early stages of a recession, business slows down, orders for machinery and computers slip, and the stock market, anticipating lower profits, turns down. Consumer confidence in the economy also begins to sag, so households spend less, especially on big-ticket items like automobiles and homes. Unsold goods start piling up. All these signs are called **leading economic indicators** because they usually predict, or *lead to,* a downturn. Upturns in leading indicators point to an economic recovery. But leading indicators cannot predict precisely *when* a turning point will occur, or even whether one will occur. Sometimes leading indicators sound a false alarm, and sometimes the economy slows down but does not contract.

Some economic indicators measure what's going on in the economy right now. **Coincident economic indicators** are those measures that reflect peaks and troughs as they occur. Coincident indicators include total employment, personal income, and industrial production. And some economic indicators measure what has already happened. **Lagging economic indicators** follow, or trail, changes in overall economic activity. Lagging indicators include the interest rate and how long on average people have been out of work.

Our introduction to economic fluctuations has been largely mechanical, focusing on the history and measurement of these fluctuations. We have not discussed why economies fluctuate, in part because such a discussion requires firmer footing in macroeconomic theory and in part because the causes remain in dispute. In the next section, we begin to build a macroeconomic framework by introducing a key model of analysis.

Aggregate Demand and Aggregate Supply

The economy is so complex that we need to simplify matters, or to abstract from the millions of relationships to isolate the important ones. We must step back from all the individual economic transactions to survey the resulting mosaic.

Aggregate Output and the Price Level

Let's begin with something you already know. Picture a pizza. Got that? Now picture food more generally. Food, of course, includes not just pizza but thousands of other items. Although food is more general than pizza, you probably have no difficulty picturing food. Now make the leap from food to all goods and services produced in the economy—food, housing, clothing, entertainment, transportation, medical care, and so on. Economists call this **aggregate output.** Because *aggregate* means total, aggregate output is the total amount of goods and services produced in the economy during a given period. The best measure of aggregate output is *real GDP.*

Just as we can talk about the demand for pizza, or the demand for food, we can talk about the demand for aggregate output. **Aggregate demand** is the relationship between the average price of aggregate output and the quantity of aggregate output demanded. The average price of aggregate output is called the economy's **price level.** You are more familiar than you may think with these aggregate measures. Headlines refer to the growth of aggregate output—as in "Growth Slows in Second Quarter." News accounts also report on changes in the "cost of living," reflecting movements in the economy's price level—as in "Prices Jump in June."

In a later chapter, you will learn how the economy's price level is computed. All you need to know now is that the price level in any year is an *index number,* or a reference number, comparing average prices that year to average prices in some base, or reference, year. If we say that the price level is higher, we mean compared with where it was. In Chapter 4, we talked about the price of a particular product, such as pizza, *relative to the prices of other products*. Now we talk about the *average price* of all goods and services produced in the economy *relative to the price level in some base year*.

The price level in the *base year* is standardized to a benchmark value of 100, and price levels in other years are expressed relative to the base-year price level. For example, in 2003, the U.S. price level, or price index, was 106, indicating that the price level that year was 6 percent higher than its value of 100 in the base year of 2000. The price level, or price index, is used not only to make comparisons in prices across time but also to make accurate comparisons of real aggregate output over time. Economists use the *price index* to eliminate any year-to-year change in GDP due solely to a change in the price level. What's left is the change in real output—the change in the amount of goods and services produced. After adjusting GDP for price level changes, we end up with what is called the **real gross domestic product,** or **real GDP.** So the price index (1) shows how the economy's price level changes over time and (2) can be used to figure out real GDP each year. You will get a better idea of these two roles as we discuss the U.S. economy.

REAL GROSS DOMESTIC PRODUCT (REAL GDP)

The economy's aggregate output measured in dollars of constant purchasing power

The Aggregate Demand Curve

In Chapter 4, you learned about the demand for a particular product. Now let's talk about the demand for our composite measure of output—aggregate output, or real GDP. The **aggregate demand curve** shows the relationship between the price level in the economy and real GDP demanded, other things constant. Exhibit 4 shows a hypothetical aggregate demand curve, *AD*. The vertical axis measures an index of the economy's price level relative to a 2000 base-year price level of 100. The horizontal axis shows real GDP, which measures output in dollars of constant purchasing power (here we use 2000 prices).

AGGREGATE DEMAND CURVE

A curve representing the relationship between the economy's price level and real GDP demanded per period, with other things constant

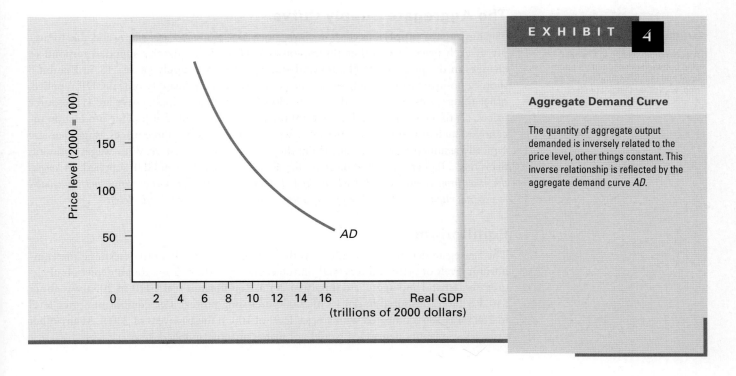

EXHIBIT 4

Aggregate Demand Curve

The quantity of aggregate output demanded is inversely related to the price level, other things constant. This inverse relationship is reflected by the aggregate demand curve *AD*.

The aggregate demand curve in Exhibit 4 reflects an inverse relationship between the price level in the economy and real GDP demanded. Aggregate demand sums demands of the four economic decision makers: households, firms, governments, and the rest of the world. As the price level increases, other things constant, households demand less housing and furniture, firms demand fewer trucks and tools, governments demand less computer software and military hardware, and the rest of the world demands less U.S. grain and U.S. aircraft.

The reasons behind this inverse relationship will be examined more closely in later chapters, but here's a quick summary. Real GDP demanded depends in part on household *wealth*. Some wealth is typically held in bank accounts and currency. An increase in the price level, other things constant, decreases the purchasing power of bank accounts and currency. Households are therefore poorer when the price level increases, so the quantity of real GDP they demand decreases. Conversely, a reduction in the price level increases the purchasing power of bank accounts and currency. Because households are richer as the price level decreases, the quantity of real GDP demanded increases.

Among the factors held constant along a given aggregate demand curve are the price levels in other countries as well as the exchange rates between the U.S. dollar and foreign currencies. When the U.S. price level increases, U.S. products become more expensive relative to foreign products. Consequently, households, firms, and governments both here and abroad decrease the quantity of U.S. real GDP demanded. On the other hand, a lower U.S. price level makes U.S. products cheaper relative to foreign products, so the quantity of U.S. real GDP demanded increases.

Consider the demand for a particular product versus aggregate demand. If the price of a particular product, such as pizza, increases, quantity demanded declines in part because pizza becomes more costly compared to substitutes. If the economy's price level increases, the quantity of U.S. real GDP demanded declines in part because U.S. products become more costly compared to foreign products.

The Aggregate Supply Curve

AGGREGATE SUPPLY CURVE

A curve representing the relationship between the economy's price level and real GDP supplied per period, with other things constant

The **aggregate supply curve** shows how much U.S. producers are willing and able to supply at each price level, other things constant. How does quantity supplied respond to changes in the price level? The upward-sloping aggregate supply curve, *AS*, in Exhibit 5 shows a positive relationship between the price level and the quantity of real GDP supplied, other things constant. Assumed constant along an aggregate supply curve are (1) resource prices, (2) the state of technology, and (3) the rules of the game that provide production incentives, such as patent and copyright laws. With regard to resource prices, wage rates are typically assumed to be constant along the aggregate supply curve. With wages constant, firms find a higher price level more profitable, so they increase real GDP supplied. *As long as the prices firms receive for their products rise faster than their cost of production, firms find it profitable to expand output, so real GDP supplied varies directly with the economy's price level.*

Equilibrium

The aggregate demand curve intersects the aggregate supply curve to determine the equilibrium levels of price and real GDP in the economy. Exhibit 5 is a rough depiction of aggregate demand and aggregate supply in 2003. Equilibrium real GDP in 2003 was about $10.4 trillion (measured in dollars of 2000 purchasing power). The equilibrium price level in 2003 was 106 (compared with a price level of 100 in the base year of 2000). At any other price level, quantity demanded would not match quantity supplied.

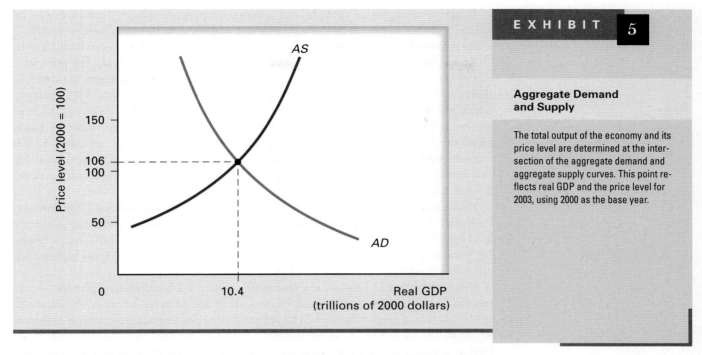

Aggregate Demand and Supply

The total output of the economy and its price level are determined at the intersection of the aggregate demand and aggregate supply curves. This point reflects real GDP and the price level for 2003, using 2000 as the base year.

Incidentally, although employment is not measured directly along the horizontal axis, firms usually must hire more workers to produce more output. So higher levels of real GDP can be beneficial because (1) more goods and services become available in the economy, and (2) more people are usually employed. Perhaps the best way to understand aggregate demand and aggregate supply is to apply these tools to the U.S. economy. The following section simplifies U.S. economic history to review changes in the price and output levels over time.

A Short History of the U.S. Economy

The history of the U.S. economy can be divided roughly into four economic eras: (1) before and during the Great Depression, (2) after the Great Depression to the early 1970s, (3) from the early 1970s to the early 1980s, and (4) since the early 1980s. The first era was marked by recessions and depressions, culminating in the Great Depression of the 1930s. These depressions were often accompanied by a falling price level. The second era was one of generally strong economic growth, with only moderate increases in the price level. The third era saw both high unemployment and high inflation at the same time. And the fourth era was more like the second, with good economic growth on average and only moderate increases in the price level.

The Great Depression and Before

Before World War II, the U.S. economy alternated between hard times and prosperity. As noted earlier, the longest contraction on record occurred between 1873 and 1879, when 80 railroads went bankrupt and most of the steel industry was shut down. During the depression of the 1890s the unemployment rate topped 18 percent. In October 1929, the stock market crash began what was to become the deepest, though not the longest, economic contraction in our nation's history, the Great Depression of the 1930s.

In terms of aggregate demand and aggregate supply, the Great Depression can be viewed as a shift to the left of the aggregate demand curve, as shown in Exhibit 6. AD_{1929} is the aggregate demand curve in 1929, before the onset of the depression. Real GDP in 1929 was $865 billion (measured in dollars of 2000 purchasing power), and the price level was 11.9 (relative to a 2000 base-year price level of 100). By 1933, aggregate demand had shifted leftward, decreasing to AD_{1933}. Why did aggregate demand decline? Though economists still debate the causes, most agree that the stock market crash of 1929 was the trigger. From there, grim business expectations cut investment, consumer spending fell, banks failed, the nation's money supply dropped, and world trade was severely restricted. All this contributed to a big decline in aggregate demand. The aggregate supply curve probably also shifted somewhat during this period, but the drop in aggregate demand was the dominant factor.

Because of the decline in aggregate demand, both the price level and real GDP dropped. Real GDP fell 27 percent, from $865 billion in 1929 to $636 billion in 1933, and the price level fell 25 percent, from 11.9 to 8.9. As real GDP declined, unemployment soared, climbing from only 3 percent of the labor force in 1929 to 25 percent in 1933, the highest U.S. rate ever recorded.

Before the Great Depression, macroeconomic policy was based primarily on the *laissez-faire* philosophy of Adam Smith. Smith, you may recall, argued in his famous book, *The Wealth of Nations*, that if people are allowed to pursue their self-interest in free markets, resources would be guided as if by an "invisible hand" to produce the most efficient and most valued level of aggregate output. Although the U.S. economy had suffered many sharp contractions since the beginning of the 19th century, most economists of the day viewed these as a natural phase of the economy—unfortunate but ultimately therapeutic and essentially *self-correcting*.

The Age of Keynes: After the Great Depression to the Early 1970s

The Great Depression was so severe that it stimulated new thinking about how the economy worked (or didn't work). In 1936, John Maynard Keynes (1883–1946) published *The*

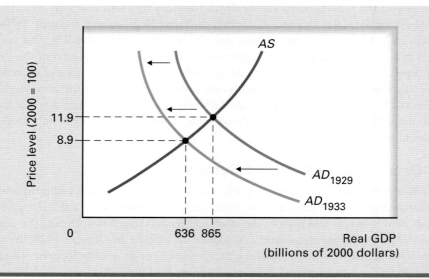

EXHIBIT 6

The Decrease in Aggregate Demand from 1929 to 1933

The Great Depression of the 1930s can be represented by a shift to the left of the aggregate demand curve, from AD_{1929} to AD_{1933}. In the resulting depression, real GDP fell from $865 billion to $636 billion, and the price level dropped from 11.9 to 8.9, measured relative to a price level of 100 in the base year 2000.

General Theory of Employment, Interest, and Money, the most famous economics book of the 20th century. In it, Keynes argued that aggregate demand was inherently unstable, in part because investment decisions were often guided by the unpredictable "animal spirits" of business expectations. If businesses grew pessimistic about the economy, they would invest less, which would reduce aggregate demand, output, and employment. For example, investment dropped more than 80 percent between 1929 and 1933. Keynes saw no natural market forces operating to ensure that the economy, even if allowed a reasonable time to adjust, would get output and employment back on the right track.

Keynes proposed that the government jolt the economy out of its depression by increasing aggregate demand. He recommended an expansionary fiscal policy to offset contractions. The government could achieve this stimulus either directly by increasing its own spending, or indirectly by cutting taxes to stimulate consumption and investment. But either action could create a federal budget deficit. A **federal budget deficit** is a flow variable that measures, for a particular period, the amount by which federal outlays exceed federal revenues.

To understand what Keynes had in mind, imagine federal budget policies that would increase aggregate demand in Exhibit 6, shifting the aggregate demand curve to the right, back to its original position. Such a shift would raise real GDP, which would increase employment. According to the Keynesian prescription, the miracle drug of fiscal policy—changes in government spending and taxes—could compensate for what he viewed as the instability of private spending, especially investment. If demand in the private sector declined, Keynes said the government should pick up the slack. We can think of the Keynesian approach as **demand-side economics** because it focused on how changes in aggregate demand could promote full employment. Keynes argued that government stimulus could shock the economy out of its depression. Once investment returned to normal levels, the government's shock treatment would no longer be necessary.

The U.S. economy bounced back some during the second half of the 1930s (see Exhibit 2). Then World War II broke out, boosting war-related demand for tanks, ships, aircraft, and the like. Government spending increased more than sixfold between 1940 and 1944. The explosion of output and sharp drop in the unemployment seemed to confirm the powerful role government spending could play in the economy. The increase in government spending, with no significant increase in tax rates, created federal deficits during the war.

Immediately after the war, memories of the Great Depression were still vivid. Trying to avoid another depression, Congress approved the *Employment Act of 1946,* which imposed a clear responsibility on the federal government to promote "maximum employment, production, and purchasing power." The act also required the president to appoint a *Council of Economic Advisers,* a three-member team of economists to provide economic advice and report annually on the economy.

The economy seemed to prosper during the 1950s largely without the added stimulus of fiscal policy. The 1960s, however, proved to be the *golden age of Keynesian economics,* a period when fiscal policy makers thought they could "fine-tune" the economy for top performance—just as a mechanic fine-tunes a racecar. During the early 1960s, nearly all advanced economies around the world enjoyed low unemployment and healthy growth with only modest inflation. In short, the world economy was booming, and the U.S. economy was on top of the world.

The economy was on such a roll that toward the end of the 1960s some economists believed the business cycle was history. As a sign of the times, the name of a federal publication, *Business Cycle Developments,* was changed to *Business Conditions Digest.* In the early 1970s, however, fluctuations returned with a fury. Worse yet, the problems of recession were compounded by inflation, which increased during the recessions of 1974–1975 and of

FEDERAL BUDGET

A plan for federal government outlays and revenues for a specific period, usually a year

FEDERAL BUDGET DEFICIT

A flow variable that measures the amount by which federal government outlays exceed federal government revenues in a particular period, usually a year

DEMAND-SIDE ECONOMICS

Macroeconomic policy that focuses on shifting the aggregate demand curve as a way of promoting full employment and price stability

1979–1980. Until then, inflation was limited primarily to periods of expansion. Confidence in demand-side policies was shaken, and the expression "fine-tuning" dropped from the economic vocabulary. What ended the golden age of Keynesian economics?

The Great Stagflation: 1973 to 1980

During the late 1960s, federal spending increased on both the war in Vietnam and social programs at home. This combined stimulus increased aggregate demand enough that in 1968 the *inflation rate,* the annual percentage increase in the price level, rose to 4.4 percent, after averaging only 2.0 percent during the previous decade. Inflation climbed to 4.7 percent in 1969 and to 5.3 percent in 1970. These rates were so alarming that in 1971, President Richard Nixon imposed ceilings on prices and wages. Those ceilings were eliminated in 1973, about the time that crop failures around the world caused grain prices to soar. To compound these problems, the Organization of Petroleum Exporting Countries (OPEC) cut its supply of oil, so oil prices jumped. Crop failures around the world plus the OPEC action reduced aggregate supply, shown in Exhibit 7 by the leftward shift of the aggregate supply curve from AS_{1973} to AS_{1975}. This resulted in **stagflation,** meaning a *stag*nation, or a contraction, in the economy's aggregate output and in*flation,* or increase, in the economy's price level. Real GDP declined by about $30 billion between 1973 and 1975, and unemployment climbed from 4.9 percent to 8.5 percent. During the same period, the price level jumped 19 percent.

Stagflation hit again five years later, fueled again by OPEC cutbacks. Between 1979 and 1980, real GDP declined but the price level increased by 9.1 percent. Macroeconomics has not been the same since. Because stagflation was on the supply side, not on the demand side, the demand-management prescriptions of Keynes seemed ineffective. Increasing aggregate demand might reduce unemployment but would worsen inflation.

HOMEWORK
Xpress!
Ask the Instructor
Video

STAGFLATION

A contraction, or *stagnation*, of a nation's output accompanied by in*flation* in the price level

---

E X H I B I T   7

Stagflation from 1973 to 1975

The stagflation of the mid-1970s can be represented as a leftward shift of the aggregate supply curve from AS_{1973} to AS_{1975}. Aggregate output fell from $4.34 trillion in 1973 to $4.31 trillion in 1975, for a decline of about $30 billion (*stag*nation). The price level rose from 31.9 to 38.0, for a growth of 19 percent (in*flation*).

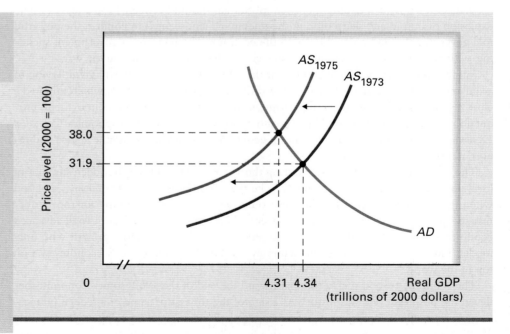

Experience Since 1980

Increasing aggregate supply seemed an appropriate way to combat stagflation, for such a move would both lower the price level and increase output and employment. Attention therefore turned from aggregate demand to aggregate supply. A key idea behind **supply-side economics** was that the federal government, by lowering tax rates, would increase after-tax wages, which would provide incentives to increase the supply of labor and other resources. According to advocates of the supply-side approach, the resulting increase in aggregate supply would achieve the happy result of expanding real GDP and reducing the price level. But this was easier said than done.

In 1981, to provide economic incentives to increase aggregate supply, President Ronald Reagan and Congress cut personal income tax rates by an average of 23 percent to be phased in over three years. Their hope was that aggregate supply would increase output and employment enough to increase tax revenue. Put another way, they believed the tax cuts would stimulate economic growth enough that the government's smaller share of a bigger pie would exceed what had been its larger share of a smaller pie.

But before the tax cut took effect, recession hit in 1981, contracting output and pushing the unemployment rate to 10 percent by 1982. Once the recession ended, the economy began what at the time was to be the longest peacetime expansion on record. For the rest of the decade, output grew, unemployment fell, and inflation settled down. But the growth in federal spending exceeded the growth in federal tax revenues during this period, so federal budget deficits swelled.

Deficits worsened with the onset of a recession in 1990. Even though that recession officially ended in March 1991, the deficit climbed, topping $290 billion in 1992. Annual deficits accumulated as a huge federal debt. **Government debt** is a stock variable that measures the net accumulation of prior deficits. To reduce federal deficits, President George H. W. Bush increased taxes in 1990, President William Clinton in 1993 increased tax rates for those in the highest tax bracket, and in 1995 a newly elected Republican Congress put the brakes on federal spending. Higher tax rates and a slower growth in federal spending combined with an improving economy to cut federal deficits. By 1998, the federal budget had turned into a surplus. By late 2000, the U.S. economic expansion became the longest on record, a stretch during which 22 million jobs were added, the unemployment rate dropped from 7.5 percent to 4.2 percent, and inflation remained tame. But after achieving this record, the economy slipped into recession by early 2001 and stretched into November of that year, aggravated by the terrorist attacks of September 2001. The recovery was slow and uneven and the unemployment continued to rise, peaking at 6.3 percent in June 2003. President Bush pushed through tax cuts "to get the economy moving again." Output was growing even though employment was not because those working had become more productive. But the tax cuts and spending programs increased the federal budget deficit, which exceeded $400 billion in 2004. Despite uncertainty created by the war in Iraq and higher oil prices, the U.S. economy started adding jobs in 2004.

Focusing on the ups and downs of the economy can miss the point that the U.S. economy over the long run has been an incredible creator of jobs and output—the most productive economy in the world. To underscore that point, we close with a case study that shows U.S. economic growth since 1929.

SUPPLY-SIDE ECONOMICS

Macroeconomic policy that focuses on a rightward shift of the aggregate supply curve through tax cuts or other changes that increase production incentives

GOVERNMENT DEBT

A stock variable that measures the net accumulation of annual budget deficits

WALL STREET JOURNAL

Reading It **Right**

What's the relevance of the following statement from the Wall Street Journal: *"Federal Reserve Chairman Alan Greenspan painted a grim picture of short-run economic weakness in the aftermath of last week's terrorist attacks, echoing widespread concerns about weak corporate earnings and rising layoffs that sent markets tumbling again."*

Case **Study**

Public Policy

eActivity

Are you interested in learning more about the economic history of the past century? J. Bradford De Long's brief article, "Slouching Toward Utopia," provides one economist's evaluation of key developments. You can read it at http://www.bos.frb.org/economic/nerr/rr1998/q3/delo98_3.htm

Over Seven Decades of Real GDP and Price Levels

Exhibit 8 traces the U.S. real GDP and price level for each year since 1929. Aggregate demand and aggregate supply curves are shown for 2003, but all points in the series reflect such intersections. Years of growing GDP are indicated as blue points and years of declining GDP as red ones. Despite the Great Depression of the 1930s and the 10 recessions since World War II, the long-term growth in output is unmistakable. Real GDP, measured along the horizontal axis in 2000 constant dollars, grew from $0.9 trillion in 1929 to $10.4 trillion in 2003—a twelvefold increase and an average annual growth rate of 3.4 percent. The price level also rose, but not quite as much, rising from 11.9 in 1929 to 105.7 in 2003—nearly a ninefold increase and an average inflation rate of 3.0 percent per year.

Because the U.S. population is growing, the economy must create new jobs just to employ the additional people looking for work. For example, the U.S. population grew from 122 million in 1929 to 291 million in 2003, a rise of 139 percent. Fortunately, employment grew even faster, from 47 million in 1929 to 138 million in 2003, for a growth of 194 percent. So, since 1929, employment grew more than enough to keep up with a growing population. The United States has been an impressive job machine.

EXHIBIT   8

Tracking U.S. Real GDP and Price Level Since 1929

As you can see, both real GDP and the price level trended higher since 1929. Blue points indicate years of growing real GDP, and red points are years of declining real GDP. Real GDP in 2003 was 12 times greater than in 1929, and the price level was nearly nine times greater.

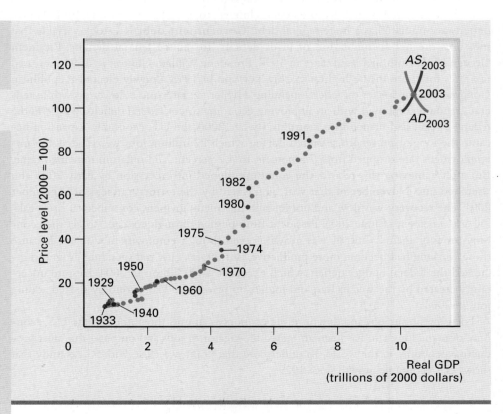

Not only did the number of workers more than double, their average education increased as well. Other resources, especially capital, also rose sharply. What's more, the level of technology improved steadily, thanks to breakthroughs like the computer chip and the Internet. The availability of more and higher-quality human capital and physical capital increased the productivity of each worker, contributing to the twelvefold jump in real GDP since 1929.

Real GDP is important, but the best measure of the average standard of living is an economy's **real GDP per capita,** which tells us how much an economy produces on average per resident. Because real GDP grew much faster than the population, real GDP *per capita* jumped fivefold from $6,740 in 1929 to about $35,700 in 2003. The United States is the largest economy in the world and a leader in output per capita. We will examine U.S. productivity and growth more closely in the next chapter.

REAL GDP PER CAPITA

Real GDP divided by the population; the best measure of an economy's standard of living

Sources: "National Income and Product Account Tables," *Survey of Current Business* 84 (February 2004); *Economic Report of the President*, February 2004; *Economic Report of the President*, January 1980; and *OECD Economic Outlook* 75 (June 2004). For the latest real GDP and price level data, go to http://www.bea.doc.gov.

Conclusion

Because macroeconomists have no test subjects and cannot rely on luck, they hone their craft by developing models of the economy and then searching for evidence to support or reject these models. In this sense, macroeconomics is retrospective, always looking at recent developments for hints about which model works best. The macroeconomist is like a traveler who can see only the road behind and must find the way using a collection of poorly drawn maps. The traveler must continually check each map (or model) against the landmarks to see whether one map is more consistent with the terrain than the others. Each new batch of information about the economy causes macroeconomists to shuffle through their "maps" to check their models. Macroeconomics often emphasizes what can go wrong with the economy. Sagging output, high unemployment, and rising inflation capture much of the attention. But perhaps the most important performance measure is economic growth, which is examined in the next chapter. In a later chapter, we discuss two potential problems confronting the economy: unemployment and inflation.

SUMMARY

1. Macroeconomics focuses on the national economy. A standard measure of performance is the growth of real gross domestic product, or real GDP, the value of final goods and services produced in the nation during the year.

2. The economy has two phases: periods of expansion and periods of contraction. No two business cycles are the same; since 1948 peacetime expansions averaged just under five years and contractions averaged just less than one year. Before World War II, expansions were shorter and contractions longer. Despite these ups and downs, the economy has grown twelvefold since 1929 and jobs have grown faster than the population.

3. The aggregate demand curve slopes downward, reflecting a negative, or inverse, relationship between the price level and real GDP demanded. The aggregate supply curve slopes upward, reflecting a positive, or direct, relationship between the price level and real GDP supplied. The intersection of the two curves determines the economy's real GDP and price level.

4. The Great Depression and earlier depressions prompted John Maynard Keynes to argue that the economy is inherently unstable, largely because the components of private spending, particularly business investment, are erratic. Keynes did not believe that depressions were self-correcting, as

most economists before him believed. He argued that whenever aggregate demand sagged, the federal government should spend more or tax less to stimulate aggregate demand. His demand-side policies dominated macroeconomic thinking between World War II and the late 1960s.

5. During the 1970s, higher oil prices and global crop failures reduced aggregate supply. The result was stagflation, the troublesome combination of declining real GDP and rising inflation. Demand-side policies appeared less effective in an economy suffering from a reduction in aggregate supply, because stimulating aggregate demand would worsen inflation.

6. Supply-side tax cuts in the early 1980s were supposed to increase aggregate supply, thereby increasing output while dampening inflation. But federal spending increased faster than federal revenue, resulting in big budget deficits, which grew into the early 1990s. Tax increases, a slower growth in government spending, and an expanding economy all helped erase budget deficits by 1998, creating a federal budget surplus. But after the longest expansion on record, the economy suffered a recession. The recession ended in November 2001, but unemployment continued to rise into 2003. Tax cuts and a sluggish recovery boosted the federal deficit. Jobs began growing once again in 2004.

QUESTIONS FOR REVIEW

1. *(The National Economy)* Why do economists pay more attention to national economies (for example, the U.S. or Canadian economies) than to state or provincial economies (such as California or Ontario)?

2. *(The Human Body and the U.S. Economy)* Based on your own experiences, extend the list of analogies between the human body and the economy as outlined in this chapter. Then, determine which variables in your list are stocks and which are flows.

3. *(Stocks and Flows)* Differentiate between stock and flow variables. Give an example of each.

4. *(Economic Fluctuations)* Describe the various components of fluctuations in economy activity over time. Because the economic activity fluctuates, how is long-term growth possible?

5. *(Economic Fluctuations)* Why doesn't the National Bureau of Economic Research identify the turning points in economic activity until months after they occur?

6. *(C a s e **Study**: The Global Economy)* How are economic fluctuations linked among national economies? Could a recession in the United States trigger a recession abroad?

7. *(Leading Economic Indicators)* Define *leading economic indicators* and give some examples. You may wish to take a look

at The Conference Board's index of leading economic indictors at http://www.conference-board.org/economics/indicators.cfm.

8. *(Aggregate Demand and Aggregate Supply)* Why does a decrease in aggregate demand result in a lower level of employment, given an aggregate supply curve?

9. *(Aggregate Demand and Aggregate Supply)* Is it possible for the price level to fall while production and employment both rise? If it is possible, how could this happen? If it is not possible, explain why not.

10. *(Aggregate Demand Curve)* Describe the relationship illustrated by the aggregate demand curve. Why does this relationship exist?

11. *(Demand-Side Economics)* What is the relationship between demand-side economics and the federal budget deficit?

12. *(Stagflation)* What were some of the causes of the stagflations of 1973 and 1979? In what ways were these episodes of stagflation different from the Great Depression of the 1930s?

13. *(C a s e **Study**: Over Seven Decades of Real GDP and Price Levels)* The price level grew faster than real GDP between 1947 and 2003. Does this mean that the rising price level masked an actual decline in output? Why or why not?

PROBLEMS AND EXERCISES

14. *(Aggregate Demand and Supply)* Review the information on demand and supply curves in Chapter 4. How do the aggregate demand and aggregate supply curves presented in this chapter differ from the market curves of Chapter 4?

15. *(Aggregate Demand and Supply)* Determine whether each of the following would cause a shift of the aggregate demand curve, the aggregate supply curve, neither, or both. Which curve shifts, and in which direction? What happens to aggregate output and the price level in each case?

a. The price level changes
b. Consumer confidence declines
c. The supply of resources increases
d. The wage rate increases

16. *(Supply-Side Economics)* One supply-side measure introduced by the Reagan administration was a cut in income tax rates. Use an aggregate demand-supply diagram to show what effect was intended. What might happen if such a tax cut also generated a change in aggregate demand?

EXPERIENTIAL EXERCISES

17. *(Economic Fluctuation)* The National Bureau of Economic Research maintains a Web page devoted to business cycle expansions and contractions at http://www.nber.org/cycles.html. Take a look at this page and see if you can determine how the business cycle has been changing in recent decades. Has the overall length of cycles been changing? Have recessions been getting longer or shorter?

18. *(Experience Since 1980)* Review the Summary of Commentary on Current Economic Conditions by Federal Reserve District (Beige Book), available through the Federal Reserve System at http://www.federalreserve.gov/FOMC/BeigeBook/2004/default.htm.

a. Summarize the national economic conditions for the most recent period covered in the report. Overall, is the economy healthy? If not, what problems is it experiencing?

b. Go to the summary applicable to your district. Summarize the economic conditions for the last reporting period. Is the economy in your district healthy? If not, what problems is it experiencing?

19. *(Wall Street Journal)* This chapter introduced the tools of aggregate demand and supply. Can you use them? Test your understanding by finding an article in today's *Wall Street Journal* describing an event that may affect the U.S. price level and real GDP. Look under "Economy" or "International" in the First Section of the newspaper. Draw an initial set of *AD* and *AS* curves and then determine which curve will be affected and in which direction it will shift. What do you predict will happen to the price level and real GDP?

HOMEWORK XPRESS! EXERCISES

These exercises require access to McEachern Homework Xpress! If Homework Xpress! did not come with your book, visit **http://homeworkxpress.swlearning.com** *to purchase.*

1. In the diagram, sketch an aggregate demand curve for the year 2000 when real GDP was $9.8 trillion.

2. In the diagram, the aggregate demand curve is for the year 2002. Sketch an aggregate supply curve that shows the economy at an equilibrium real GDP of $10.1 trillion. Identify the price level.

3. In the diagram, the aggregate supply curve is for the year 2000. Sketch an aggregate demand curve that shows the economy at an equilibrium real GDP of $9.8 trillion. Illustrate how a shift of aggregate demand could decrease the equilibrium level of real GDP to $9.5 trillion. Identify the price level for this new equilibrium.

4. In the diagram, the aggregate demand curve is for the year 1995. Sketch in an aggregate supply curve that shows the economy at an equilibrium real GDP of $8 trillion. Identify the price level. Illustrate how a shift of aggregate supply could decrease the equilibrium level of GDP to $7.5 trillion. Identify the price level for this new equilibrium.

Productivity and Growth

© Ralf-Finn Hestoft/Index Stock Imagery

W hy is the standard of living so much higher in some countries than in oth-

ers? How does an economy increase its living standard? Why is the long-

term growth rate more important than short-term fluctuations in economic activ-

ity? What's labor productivity and why has it picked up in recent years? What's the

impact of the recent surge in labor productivity on your living standard? Answers to

these and other questions are addressed in this chapter, which focuses on arguably

the most important criteria for judging an economy's performance—productivity

and growth.

The single most important determinant of a nation's standard of living in the long

run is the productivity of its resources. Even seemingly low growth in productivity,

if sustained for years, can have a substantial effect on the average living standard—

that is, on the average availability of goods and services per capita. Growing productivity is therefore critical to a rising standard of living and has kept the U.S. economy a world leader.

Economic growth is a complicated process, one that even experts do not yet fully understand. Since before Adam Smith inquired into the *Wealth of Nations,* economists have puzzled over what makes some economies prosper while others founder. Because a market economy is not the product of conscious design, it does not reveal its secrets readily, nor can it be easily manipulated in pursuit of growth. We can't simply push here and pull there to achieve the desired result. Changing the economy is not like remodeling a home by knocking out a wall to expand the kitchen. Because we have no clear blueprint of the economy, we cannot make changes to specifications.

Still, there is much economists do know. In this chapter, we first develop a few simple models to examine productivity and growth. Then, we use these models to help explain why some nations are rich and some poor. U.S. performance gets special attention, particularly compared with other major economies around the world. We close with some current issues of technology and growth. Topics include:

- Labor productivity
- The production function
- U.S. productivity and growth
- Technological change and unemployment
- Research and development
- Convergence

Theory of Productivity and Growth

Two centuries ago, 90 percent of the American workforce was in agriculture, where the hours were long and rewards unpredictable. Other workers had it no better, toiling from sunrise to sunset for a wage that bought just the bare necessities. People had little intellectual stimulation and little contact with the outside world. A skilled worker's home in 1800 was described as follows: "Sand sprinkled on the floor did duty as a carpet. . . . What a stove was he did not know. Coal he had never seen. Matches he had never heard of. . . . He rarely tasted fresh meat. . . . If the food of a [skilled worker] would now be thought coarse, his clothes would be thought abominable."[1]

Over the last two centuries, there has been an incredible increase in the U.S. *standard of living* as measured by the amount of goods and services available on average per person. An economy's standard of living grows over the long run because of (1) increases in the amount and quality of resources, especially labor and capital, (2) better technology, and (3) improvements in the *rules of the game* that facilitate production and exchange, such as tax laws, property rights, patent laws, the legal system, and customs of the market. Perhaps the easiest way to introduce economic growth is by beginning with something you have already read about, the production possibilities frontier.

Growth and the Production Possibilities Frontier

The *production possibilities frontier,* or *PPF,* first introduced in Chapter 2, shows what the economy can produce if available resources are used efficiently. Let's briefly review the assumptions made in developing the frontier shown in Exhibit 1. During the period under consideration, usually a year, the quantity of resources in the economy and the level of technology are assumed to be fixed. Although not mentioned in Chapter 2, also assumed fixed during the period are the rules of the game that facilitate production and exchange. We clas-

1. E. L. Bogart, *The Economic History of the United States* (New York: Longmans, Green, and Co., 1912), pp. 157–158.

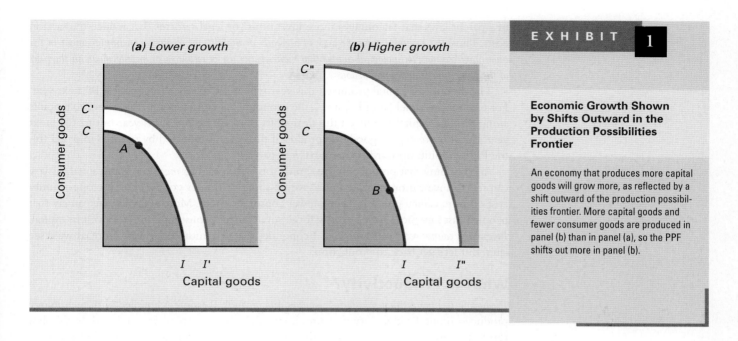

(a) Lower growth

(b) Higher growth

E X H I B I T   1

Economic Growth Shown by Shifts Outward in the Production Possibilities Frontier

An economy that produces more capital goods will grow more, as reflected by a shift outward of the production possibilities frontier. More capital goods and fewer consumer goods are produced in panel (b) than in panel (a), so the PPF shifts out more in panel (b).

sify all production into two broad categories—in this case, consumer goods and capital goods. Capital goods are used to produce other goods. For example, the economy can make pizzas and pizza ovens. Pizzas are consumer goods and ovens are capital goods.

When resources are employed efficiently, the production possibilities frontier *CI* in each panel of Exhibit 1 shows the possible combinations of consumer goods and capital goods that can be produced in a given year. Point *C* depicts the quantity of consumer goods produced if all the economy's resources are employed efficiently to produce them. Point *I* depicts the same for capital goods. Points inside the frontier show inefficient combinations, and points outside the frontier show unattainable combinations, given the resources, technology, and rules of the game. The production possibilities frontier is bowed out because resources are not perfectly adaptable to the production of both goods; some resources are specialized.

Economic growth is an outward shift of the production possibilities frontier, as shown in each panel of Exhibit 1. What can cause growth? An increase in resources, such as a growth in the labor supply or in the capital stock, shifts the frontier outward. Labor supply can increase either because of population growth or because the existing population is willing to work more. The capital stock expands if the economy produces more capital this year. The more capital produced this year, the more the economy grows, as reflected by an outward shift of the production frontier.

Breakthroughs in technology also expand the frontier by making more efficient use of existing resources. Technological change often improves the quality of capital, but it can enhance the productivity of any resource. Technological change often can free up resources for other uses. For example, the development of synthetic dyes in the 19th century freed up millions of acres of agricultural land that had been devoted to dye crops such as madder (red) and indigo (blue). The development of fiber-optic cable and cellular technology freed up the world's largest stock of copper in the form of existing telephone wires strung on poles across the nation.

Finally, any improvement in the rules of the game that nurtures production and exchange promotes growth and expands the frontier. For example, the economy can grow as a result of a patent laws that encourages more inventions[2] or legal reforms that reduce transaction costs. Thus, *the economy grows because of a greater availability of resources, an improvement in the quality of resources, technological change that makes better use of resources, or improvements in the rules of the game that enhance production.*

The amount of capital produced this year will affect the location of the PPF next year. For example, in panel (a) of Exhibit 1, the economy has chosen point *A* from possible points along *CI*. The capital produced this year shifts the PPF from *CI* this year out to *C'I'* next year. But if more capital goods are produced this year, as reflected by point *B* in panel (b), the PPF will shift outward farther next year, to *C"I"*.

An economy that produces more capital this year is said to *invest* more in capital. As you can see, to invest more, people must give up some consumer goods. Thus, the opportunity cost of more capital goods is having fewer consumer goods. More generally, we can say that people must *save* more now—that is, forgo some current consumption—to invest in capital. *Investment cannot occur without saving.* Economies that save more can invest more, as we'll see later. But let's get back to production.

What Is Productivity?

Production is a process that transforms resources into products. Resources coupled with technology produce output. Productivity measures how efficiently resources are employed. In simplest terms, the greater the productivity, the more goods and services can be produced from a given amount of resources, and the farther out will be the production possibilities frontier. Economies that use resources more efficiently create a higher standard of living, meaning that more goods and services are produced per capita.

PRODUCTIVITY

The ratio of a specific measure of output, such as real GDP, to a specific measure of input, such as labor; in this case productivity measures real GDP per hour of labor

LABOR PRODUCTIVITY

Output per unit of labor; measured as real GDP divided by the hours of labor employed to produce that output

Productivity is defined as the ratio of total output to a specific measure of input. It usually reflects an average, expressing total output divided by the amount of a particular kind of resource employed. For example, **labor productivity** is the output per unit of labor and measures total output divided by the hours of labor employed to produce that output.

We can talk about the productivity of any resource, such as labor, capital, or natural resources. When agriculture accounted for most output in the economy, land productivity, or bushels of grain per acre, was a key measure of economic welfare. Where soil was rocky and barren, people were poorer than where soil was fertile and fruitful. Even today, soil productivity determines the standard of living in some economies. Industrialization and trade, however, have liberated many from dependence on soil fertility. Today, some of the world's most productive economies have little land or have land of poor fertility. For example, Japan has a high living standard even though its population, which is nearly half that of the United States, lives on a land area only one twenty-fifth the U.S. land area.

Labor Productivity

Labor is the resource most commonly used to measure productivity. Why labor? First, labor accounts for most production cost—about 70 percent on average. Second, labor is more easily measured than other inputs, whether we speak of hours per week or full-time workers per year. Statistics about employment and hours worked are more readily available and more reliable than those about other resources used.

But the resource most responsible for increasing labor productivity is capital. As introduced in Chapter 1, the two broad categories are human capital and physical capital. *Human*

2. For evidence how the greater protection of intellectual property stimulates technological change, see Sunil Kanwar and Robert Evenson, "Does Intellectual Property Protection Spur Technological Change?" *Oxford Economic Papers* 55 (April 2003): 235–264.

capital is the accumulated knowledge, skill, and experience of the labor force. As workers acquire more human capital, their productivity and their incomes grow. That's why surgeons earn more than butchers and accountants earn more than file clerks. You are reading this book right now to enhance your human capital. *Physical capital* includes the machines, buildings, roads, airports, communication networks, and other manufactured creations used to produce goods and services. Think about digging a ditch with bare hands versus using a shovel. Now switch the shovel for a backhoe. More physical capital obviously makes diggers more productive. Or consider picking oranges with bare hands versus using a picking machine that combs the trees with steel bristles. In less than 15 minutes the machine can pick 18 tons of oranges from 100 trees, catch the fruit, and drop it into storage carts. Without the machine, that would take four workers all day.[3]

In poorer countries labor is cheap and capital dear, so producers substitute labor for capital. For example, in India a beverage truck will make its rounds festooned with workers, as many as 10, so as to minimize the time the truck, the valuable resource, spends at each stop. In the United States, where labor is more costly (compared to capital), the truck will make its rounds with just the driver. As another example, in Haiti, the poorest country in the Western Hemisphere, a ferry service could not afford to build a dock, so it hired workers to carry passengers through the water to and from the ferry on their shoulders.[4]

As an economy accumulates more capital per worker, labor productivity increases and the standard of living grows. The most productive combination of all is human capital combined with physical capital. For example, one certified public accountant with a computer and specialized software can sort out a company's finances more quickly and more accurately than can a thousand high-school-educated file clerks with pencils and paper.

The Per-Worker Production Function

We can express the relationship between the amount of capital per worker and the output per worker as an economy's **per-worker production function.** Exhibit 2 shows the relationship between the amount of capital per worker, measured along the horizontal axis, and average output per worker, or labor productivity, measured along the vertical axis, other things constant—including the level of technology and rules of the game. Any point on the production function, *PF,* shows how much output can be produced per worker for each amount of capital per worker. For example, when there are *k* units of capital per worker, average output per worker in the economy is *y.* The curve slopes upward from left to right because an increase in capital per worker helps each worker produce more output. For example, a bigger truck makes the driver more productive.

As the quantity of capital per worker increases, output per worker increases but at a diminishing rate, as reflected by the shape of the per-worker production function. The diminishing slope of this curve reflects the *law of diminishing marginal returns from capital,* which says that beyond some level of capital per worker, increases in capital add less and less to output per worker. For example, adding to the size and number of trucks at a shipping company initially increases the productivity of drivers. Once all drivers have big trucks, however, more trucks add little to total output. Thus, given the supply of other resources, the level of technology, and the rules of the game, additional gains from more capital per worker eventually diminish. An increase in the amount of capital per worker is called **capital deepening** and is one source of rising productivity. *Capital deepening contributes to labor productivity and economic growth.*

PER-WORKER PRODUCTION FUNCTION

The relationship between the amount of capital per worker in the economy and average output per worker

CAPITAL DEEPENING

An increase in the amount of capital per worker; one source of rising labor productivity

---

3. Eduardo Porter, "In Florida Groves, Cheap Labor Means Machines," *New York Times,* 22 March 2004.
4. This example was noted by Tyler Cowen, "The Ricardo Effect in Haiti," 23 February 2004, http://www.marginalrevolution.com.

Per-Worker Production Function

The per-worker production function, *PF*, shows a direct relationship between the amount of capital per worker, *k*, and the output per worker, *y*. The bowed shape of *PF* reflects the law of diminishing marginal returns from capital, which holds that as more capital is added to a given number of workers, gains in output diminish.

Technological Change

Held constant along a per-worker production function is the level of technology in the economy. Technological change usually improves the *quality* of capital and represents another source of increased productivity. For example, a tractor is more productive than a horse-drawn plow, a word processor more productive than a typewriter, and an Excel spreadsheet more productive than pencil and paper. Better technology is reflected in Exhibit 3 by an upward rotation in the per-worker production function from *PF* to *PF'*. As a result of a technological breakthrough, more is produced at each level of capital per worker. For example, if there are *k* units of capital per worker, a major breakthrough in technology increases the output per worker in the economy from *y* to *y'*.

Simon Kuznets, who won a Nobel Prize in part for his analysis of economic growth, claimed that technological change and the ability to apply such breakthroughs to all aspects of production were the driving forces behind economic growth in market economies.

Impact of a Technological Breakthrough on the Per-Worker Production Function

A technological breakthrough increases output per worker at each level of capital per worker. Better technology makes workers more productive. This is shown by a rotation upward in the per-worker production function from *PF* to *PF'*. An improvement in the rules of the game would have a similar effect.

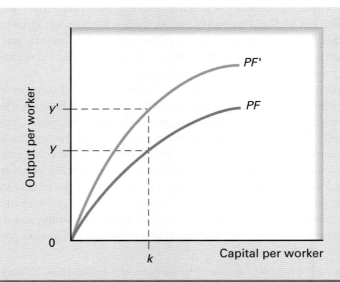

Kuznets argued that changes in the *quantities* of labor and capital account for only one-tenth of the increase in economic growth. Nine-tenths came from improvements in the *quality* of inputs. As technological breakthroughs become *embodied* in new capital, resources are combined more efficiently, increasing total output. *From the wheel to the assembly-line robot, capital embodies the fruits of discovery and drives economic growth.*

Thus, two kinds of changes in capital improve worker productivity: (1) an increase in the *quantity* of capital per worker, as reflected by a movement along the per-worker production function, and (2) an improvement in the *quality* of capital per worker, as reflected by technological change that rotates the curve upward. More capital per worker and better capital per worker result in more output per worker, which, over time, translates into more output per capita, meaning a higher standard of living.

Rules of the Game

Perhaps the most elusive ingredients for productivity and growth are the **rules of the game,** the formal and informal institutions that promote economic activity: the laws, customs, conventions, and other institutional elements that encourage people to undertake productive activity. A stable political environment and system of well-defined property rights are important. Less investment will occur if potential investors believe their capital could be appropriated by government, stolen by thieves, destroyed by civil unrest, or blown up by terrorists. Improvements in the rules of the game could result in more output for each level of capital per worker, thus reflected in a rotation up in the per-worker production function. Simply put, a more stable political climate could have a similar beneficial effect on productivity as a technological improvement. Conversely, events that foster instability can harm an economy's productivity and rotate the per-worker production function downward. The terrorist attack of the World Trade Center and Pentagon was such a destabilizing event. According to Albert Abadie, a Harvard economist, the attack affected "the spinal cord of any favorable business environment"—the ability of business and workers "to meet and communicate effectively without incurring risks."[5] For example, airport security has clearly added to the cost of flying. Shops in countries plagued by suicide bombers must hire guards to deter such horror, and this adds to the cost of doing business.

Now that you have some idea about the theory of productivity and growth, let's look at them in practice, beginning with the vast difference in performance among economies around the world. Then we turn to the United States.

Productivity and Growth in Practice

Economics in the Movies

Differences in the standard of living among countries are profound. To give you some idea, per capita output in the United States, the world leader, is about 50 times that of the world's poorest countries. With only one-twentieth of the world's population, the United States produces more than all the nations comprising the bottom half of the world's population put together. At the risk of appearing simplistic, we might say that poor countries are poor because they experience low labor productivity. We can sort the world's economies into two broad groups. **Industrial market countries,** or *developed countries,* make up about 20 percent of the world's population. They consist of the economically advanced capitalist countries of Western Europe, North America, Australia, New Zealand, and Japan, plus the newly

5. As quoted in Greg Ip and John McKinnon, "Economy Likely Won't See Gain from War Against Terrorism," *Wall Street Journal,* 25 September 2001.

RULES OF THE GAME

The formal and informal institutions that promote economic activity; the laws, customs, conventions, and other institutional elements that determine transaction costs and thereby affect people's incentive to undertake production and exchange

WALL STREET JOURNAL
Reading It **Right**

What's the relevance of the following statement from the Wall Street Journal: *"Some economists say productivity growth will take an additional and longer-lasting hit in the terrorist attack's aftermath."*

INDUSTRIAL MARKET COUNTRIES

Economically advanced capitalist countries of Western Europe, North America, Australia, New Zealand, and Japan, plus the newly industrized Asian economies of Taiwan, South Korea, Hong Kong, and Singapore

DEVELOPING COUNTRIES

Countries with a low living standard because of little human and physical capital per worker

industrialized Asian countries of Taiwan, South Korea, Hong Kong, and Singapore. Industrial market countries were usually the first to experience long-term economic growth during the 19th century, and today have the world's highest standard of living based on abundant human and physical capital. The rest of the world, the remaining 80 percent of the world's population, consists of **developing countries,** which have a lower standard of living because they have less human and physical capital. Most workers in developing countries are farmers. Because farming methods there are primitive, labor productivity is low and most people barely subsist, much like Americans two centuries ago.

Education and Economic Development

Another important source of productivity is human capital—the skill, experience, and education of workers. If knowledge is lacking, other resources may not be used efficiently. For example, a country may be endowed with fertile land, but farmers may lack knowledge of irrigation and fertilization techniques. What exactly is the role of education in economic development? *Education makes workers aware of the latest production techniques and more receptive to new ideas and methods.* Countries today with the most advanced educational systems were also the first to develop. For example, America led the world in education during the last century and is today the world's premier economy.

Exhibit 4 shows the average years of schooling of the working-age population in the United States and six other industrial market economies (together called the *Group of Seven,* or *G-7*). In 1970, the U.S. working population averaged 11.6 years of schooling, the highest in the world. Among other advanced economies, education ranged from a low of 6.6 years in Italy to 11.3 years in Canada. The U.S. average grew to 12.7 years by 1998, but other countries became even more educated, so Americans ranked third behind Germany, at 13.6 years, and Canada, at 12.9 years.

EXHIBIT 4

Average Years of Education of Working-Age Populations in 1970 and 1998

In 1970 the United States led major economies in average education of the working-age population. By 1998 education increased more in Germany and Canada than in the United States, ranking America third.

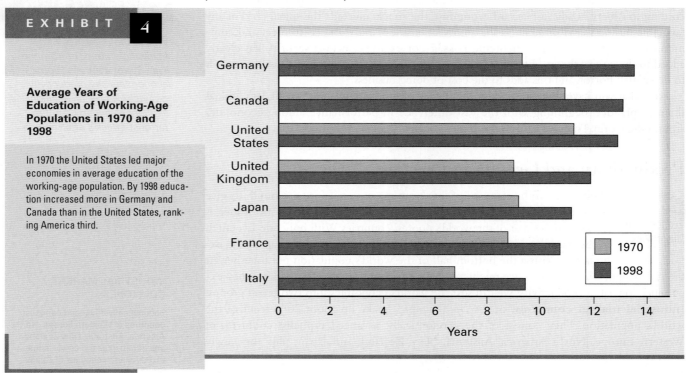

Source: Based on estimates developed in *OECD Economic Outlook* 68 (December 2000), Figure IV.1.

Not shown in Exhibit 4 are developing countries, which have far lower levels of education. For example, while the literacy rate exceeds 95 percent in industrial market economies, more than half the adults in the world's poorest countries can't read or write.

U.S. Labor Productivity

What has been the record of labor productivity in the United States? Exhibit 5 offers a long-run perspective, showing growth in real output per work hour. Annual productivity growth is averaged by decade. The huge dip during the Great Depression and the strong rebound during World War II are unmistakable. Growth slowed during the 1970s and 1980s but recovered since 1990. Labor productivity has grown an average of 2.1 percent per year since 1870. This may not impress you, but because of the power of compounding, output per hour has jumped over 1,500 percent during the period. To put this in perspective, if a roofer in 1870 could shingle one roof in a day, today's roofer could shingle 16 roofs in a day.

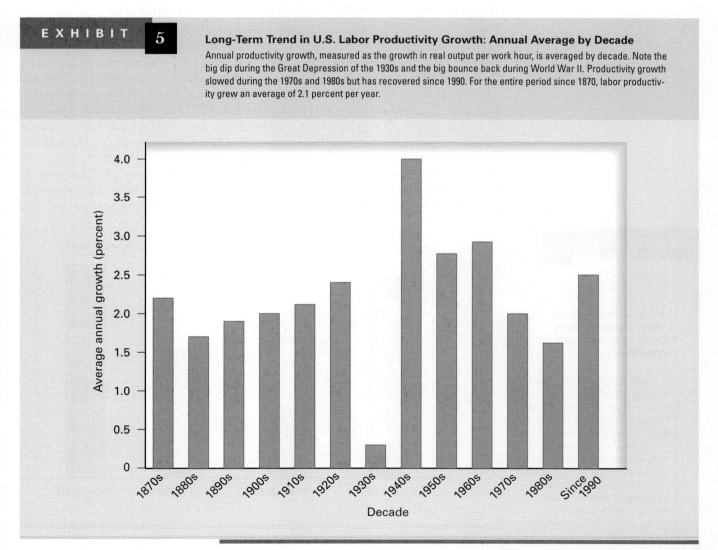

EXHIBIT 5

Long-Term Trend in U.S. Labor Productivity Growth: Annual Average by Decade

Annual productivity growth, measured as the growth in real output per work hour, is averaged by decade. Note the big dip during the Great Depression of the 1930s and the big bounce back during World War II. Productivity growth slowed during the 1970s and 1980s but has recovered since 1990. For the entire period since 1870, labor productivity grew an average of 2.1 percent per year.

Sources: Angus Maddison, *Phases of Capitalist Development* (New York: Oxford University Press, 1982) and U.S. Bureau of Labor Statistics. "Since 1990" goes through 2003. For the latest data, go to http://www.bls.gov/lpc/.

Over long periods, small differences in productivity can make huge differences on the economy's ability to produce and therefore on the standard of living. For example, if productivity grew only 1.1 percent per year instead of 2.1 percent, output per work hour since 1870 would have increased by only 333 percent, not 1,520 percent. On the other hand, if productivity grew 3.1 percent per year, output per work hour since 1870 would have jumped 5,880 percent! The wheels of progress seem to grind slowly but they grind very fine, and the cumulative effect is powerful.

So far, we have averaged productivity growth for all workers. Productivity has grown more in some industries than in others. In ocean shipping, for example, cargo carried per worker hour is now about 80 times greater than it was in 1900, for an average annual growth of 4.3 percent. On the other hand, those making wooden office furniture are only three times more productive today than in 1900, for an average annual growth in productivity of only 1.1 percent.

Slowdown and Rebound in Productivity Growth

You can see in Exhibit 5 that productivity growth slowed during the 1970s and 1980s and has recovered since 1990. By breaking the data down into intervals other than decades, we can get a better feel for years since World War II. Exhibit 6 offers average annual growth for four periods. Labor productivity growth averaged 2.9 percent per year between 1948 and 1973, but, between 1974 and 1982, fell to only about a third of that, averaging only 1.0 percent. Why the slowdown? First, oil prices jumped from 1973 to 1974 and again from 1979 to 1980 as a result of OPEC actions, boosting inflation and contributing to three recessions during the period. Second, legislation in the early 1970s necessary to protect the environment and improve workplace safety increased production costs.

Fortunately, productivity rebounded off the 1974–1982 low, growing 1.8 percent from 1983 to 1995 and 3.1 percent from 1996 to 2003. Why the rebound? The information revolution powered by the computer chip started paying off, as discussed in the following case study.

EXHIBIT 6

U.S. Labor Productivity Growth Slowed During 1974 to 1982 and Then Rebounded

The growth in labor productivity declined from an average of 2.9 percent per year between 1948 and 1973 to only 1.0 percent between 1974 and 1982. A jump in the price of oil helped contribute to three recessions during that stretch, and new environmental and workplace regulations, though necessary and beneficial, slowed down productivity growth temporarily. The information revolution powered by the computer chip has boosted productivity in recent years.

Source: Averages based on annual estimates from the U.S. Bureau of Labor Statistics. For the latest data go to http://www.bls.gov/lpc/home.htm.

Computers and Productivity Growth

The first microprocessor, the Intel 4004, could execute about 400 computations per second when it hit the market in 1971. IBM's first personal computer, introduced a decade later, could execute 330,000 computations per second. Today a $500 PC can handle over 2 billion computations per second, or *5 million* times what the 1971 Intel 4004 could handle. Such advances in computing power have fueled a boom in computer use. There are over 65 PCs per 100 persons in the United States, the world leader. There are now more computers in the United States than automobiles. U.S. companies and universities are well ahead of other countries in high-technology applications, ranging from software to biotechnology.

© Photodisc/Getty Images

The Information Economy

eActivity

The application of computing technologies by U.S. firms has grown drastically, but until recently the connection between computer use and business productivity growth has been unclear. Read "Computer Use and Productivity Growth" in *National Economic Trends* from the Federal Reserve Bank of St. Louis, at http://research.stlouisfed.org/publications/net/20031201/cover.pdf.

PCs are moving beyond word processing and spreadsheet analysis to help people work together. For example, design engineers in California can use the Internet to test new ideas with marketers in New York, cutting development time in half. Sales representatives on the road can use laptops or other wireless devices to log orders and serve customers. U.S. insurance companies can coordinate data entry done as far away as India to handle claims more efficiently. An operator of multiple restaurants can use the Internet to track sales up to the minute, check the temperatures of freezers, refrigerators, and fryers, and observe each restaurant through a live video feed. A new generation of machines monitors itself and sends messages to a service center, detailing any problems as they arise. For example, General Electric uses the Internet to keep tabs on factory equipment thousands of miles away. Some home appliances, such as refrigerators, are also Internet compatible. Computers not only improve the quality and safety in many industries, including automobiles and airlines, but they increase the versatility of machines, which can be reprogrammed for different tasks.

A study by economists from the Federal Reserve System notes that computers boost productivity through two channels: (1) efficiency gains in the production of computers and semiconductors and (2) greater computer use by industry. These two channels accounted for much of the gain in productivity growth since 1996. Although computer hardware manufacturers make up only a small fraction of the U.S. economy, their pace of innovation quickened enough since 1996 to boost overall U.S. productivity growth. For example, Intel's 1.7-gigahertz Pentium 4 processor sold for $342 when introduced, much less than the $990 for the 1.1-gigahertz Pentium 3 it replaced. What's more, the efficiency in semiconductor production and the price declines since 1996 advanced IT use by business more generally, which also enhanced labor productivity. America invested more and earlier in IT than did other big economies, so economic benefits should show up here first. In fact, labor productivity grew an impressive 4.9 percent in 2002, 4.5 percent in 2003, and 3.1 percent in the first half of 2004. This growth was the fastest pace of consecutive years in more than 50 years. What's also impressive is that since 1996 productivity growth in services has exceeded that in manufacturing.

Sources: Kevin Kliesen, "Was Y2K Behind the Business Investment Boom and Bust?" *Federal Reserve Bank of St. Louis Review,* (January–February 2003): 31–42; Hal Varian, "Information Technology May Cure Low Productivity," *New York Times,* 12 February 2004; and Stephen Oliner and Daniel Sichel, "Information Technology and Productivity," *Economic Review,* Federal Reserve Bank of Atlanta (Third Quarter 2002): 15–44. The federal government's labor productivity home page is http://www.bls.gov/lpc/home.htm.

Higher labor productivity growth can easily make up for output lost during recessions. For example, if over the next 10 years the U.S. labor productivity grew an average of 3.1 percent per year (the average from 1996 to 2003) instead of 1.8 percent (the average from 1982 to 1995), that higher growth would add nearly $2 trillion to GDP in the 10th year—more than enough to make up for the output lost during three typical recessions. *This cumulative power of productivity growth is why economists now pay less attention to short-term fluctuations in output and more to long-term growth.*

Output per Capita

So far, we have focused on rising labor productivity as an engine of economic growth—that is, growth achieved by getting more output from each hour worked. But even if labor productivity did not increase, total output would grow if the quantity of labor increased. After all, because labor productivity equals real GDP divided by the quantity of labor, then real GDP equals labor productivity times the quantity of labor. Therefore, total output can grow as a result of higher labor productivity, more labor, or both.

As noted earlier, the best measure of an economy's standard of living is output per capita. *Output per capita,* or real GDP divided by the population, indicates how much an economy produces on average per resident. Let's relate output per capita to labor productivity by using an example. Suppose labor productivity in the economy averages $70,000 per worker per year. If there is one worker for every two people in the economy, then *output per capita* equals output per worker divided by two, which is $70,000/2, or $35,000.

Even if labor productivity does not change over time, output per capita would grow if the number of workers grows faster than the population—that is, if the worker–population ratio increases. More generally, output per capita increases if (1) labor productivity increases for a given worker–population ratio, (2) the worker–population ratio increases for given labor productivity, or (3) labor productivity and the worker–population ratio both increase. In fact, output per capita would increase as long an increase in one of the variables more than offsets any decrease in the other one. For example, if labor productivity increases 2.3 percent but the worker–population ratio declines 2.0 percent, output per capita would increase. Before you move on, please take a minute now to reread this paragraph and give it some thought.

Exhibit 7 presents real GDP per capita for the United States since 1959. Notice the general upward trend, interrupted by seven recessions, indicated by the pink-shaded bars. Real GDP per capita nearly tripled (in 2000 dollars) from about $13,700 in 1959 to $35,700 in 2003, for an average annual growth rate of 2.2 percent. Incidentally, since 1959, labor productivity grew an average of 2.1 percent. Output per capita grew faster than did labor productivity because the number of workers grew faster than did the population, so the worker–population ratio increased.

International Comparisons

How does U.S. output per capita compare with that of other industrial countries? Exhibit 8 compares GDP per capita in 2002 for the United States and the six other leading industrial nations. The United States stands alone at the top, with a per capita income 18 percent above second-ranked Canada and about 40 percent above the rest. Thus, the United States produced more per capita than any other major economy.

Exhibit 8 looks at the level of output per capita. What about the growth in output per capita? Exhibit 9 shows growth in real GDP per capita from 1982 to 2002. With an average growth of 2.2 percent per year, the United States ranked second among the seven major economies. The United Kingdom ranked first, thanks in part to Prime Minister Margaret

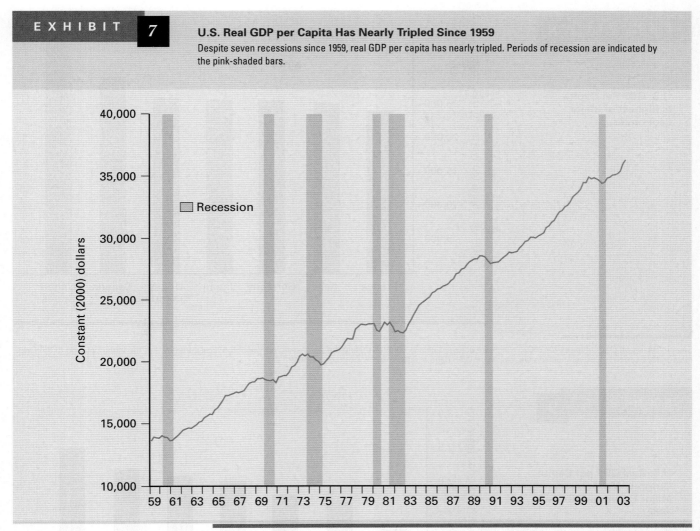

EXHIBIT 7

U.S. Real GDP per Capita Has Nearly Tripled Since 1959

Despite seven recessions since 1959, real GDP per capita has nearly tripled. Periods of recession are indicated by the pink-shaded bars.

Source: *Survey of Current Business* 84 (April 2004). For the latest data, go to http://www.bea.doc.gov/bea/pubs.htm. Select the most recent month, go to the "National Data" section toward the end of the page, and then select "Charts."

Thatcher, who converted crusty government enterprises into dynamic for-profit firms. Industries she *privatized* during the 1980s include coal, iron and steel, gas, electricity, railways, trucking, airlines, telecommunications, and the water supply. She also reduced income tax rates.

To review, over the last 130 years, U.S. labor productivity has grown an average of 2.1 percent per year. Output per hour of work is now 16 times its 1870 level. Growth slowed between 1974 and 1982, because of spikes in energy prices and implementation of necessary but costly new environmental and workplace regulations. Since 1982 labor productivity growth has picked up, especially since 1996, due primarily to breakthroughs in information technology. Among the seven major economies, the United States experienced the second fastest growth in per capita income from 1982 to 2002, and in 2002 boasted the highest GDP per capita among major economies.

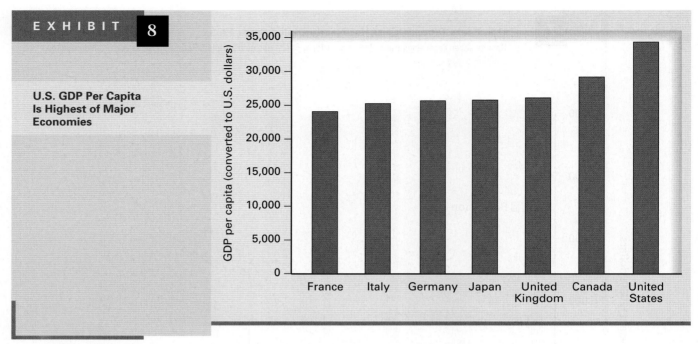

EXHIBIT 8

U.S. GDP Per Capita Is Highest of Major Economies

Source: Based on OECD figures for 2002, which are adjusted across countries using the purchasing power of the local currency. For the latest data, go to the Organization for Economic Cooperation and Development Web page at http://www.oecd.org/home/.

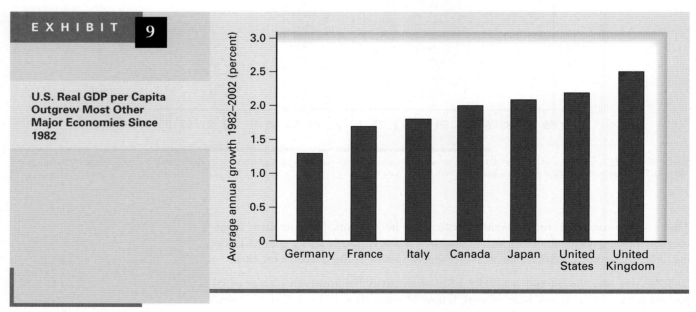

EXHIBIT 9

U.S. Real GDP per Capita Outgrew Most Other Major Economies Since 1982

Source: Based on annual figures from 1982 through 2002 from the U.S. Bureau of Labor Statistics at http://www.stats.bls.gov/fls/flsgdp.pdf. Figures were converted into U.S. dollars based on the purchasing power of local currency. For the latest data, go to http://www.stats.bls.gov/fls/.

Other Issues of Technology and Growth

In this section we consider some other issues of technology and growth, beginning with the question of whether technological change creates unemployment.

Does Technological Change Lead to Unemployment?

Because technological change can reduce the labor needed to produce a given amount of output, some observers fear technological change will increase unemployment. True, technological change can create dislocations as displaced workers try to find jobs elsewhere. But technological change can also make products more affordable. For example, the introduction of the assembly line cut the cost of automobiles, making them more affordable for the average household. This change increased the quantity demanded, boosting production and employment in the auto industry. The same happened with personal computers. Even in industries where machines displace some workers, those who keep their jobs are more productive, so they earn more. And *because human wants are unlimited, displaced workers will usually find jobs producing other goods and services demanded in a growing economy.*

Although data from the 19th century are sketchy, there is no evidence that the unemployment rate is any higher today than it was in 1870. Since then, worker productivity has increased over 1,500 percent, and the length of the average workweek has been cut nearly in half. Although technological change may displace some workers in the short run, long-run benefits include higher real incomes and more leisure—in short, a higher standard of living.

If technological change caused unemployment, then the recent spurt in productivity growth should have increased unemployment compared to the slow-growth years from 1974 to 1982. But the unemployment rate, the percentage of the workforce looking for jobs, averaged 7.2 percent during 1974 to 1982, compared to only 4.9 percent since 1996. And if technological change causes unemployment, then unemployment rates should be lower in economies where the latest technology has not yet been adopted, such as in developing countries. But unemployment rates are much higher there, and those who do find work earn little because they are not very productive.

Again, there is no question that technological change sometimes creates job dislocations and hardships in the short run, as workers scramble to adjust to a changing world. Some workers with specialized skills made obsolete by technology may be unable to find jobs that pay as well as the ones they lost. These temporary dislocations are one price of progress. Over time, however, most displaced workers find other jobs, often in new industries created by technological change. In a typical year, the U.S. economy eliminates about 10 million jobs but creates nearly 12 million new ones. Out with the old, in with the new.

Research and Development

As noted several times already, a major contributor to productivity growth has been an improvement in the quality of human and physical capital. In terms of human capital, this improvement results from more education and more job training. In terms of physical capital, this improvement springs from better technology embodied in this capital. For example, because of extensive investments in cellular transmission, new satellites, and fiber-optic technology, labor productivity in the telecommunications industry has increased by an average of 5.5 percent per year during the past three decades.

Improvements in technology arise from scientific discovery, which is the fruit of research. We can distinguish between basic research and applied research. **Basic research,** the search for knowledge without regard to how that knowledge will be used, is a first step toward technological advancement. In terms of economic growth, however, scientific discoveries are meaningless until they are implemented, which requires applied research. **Applied research** seeks to answer particular questions or to apply scientific discoveries to the development of specific products. Because technological breakthroughs may or may not have commercial possibilities, the payoff is less immediate with basic research than with applied research. *Yet basic research yields a higher return to society as a whole than does applied research.*

BASIC RESEARCH

The search for knowledge without regard to how that knowledge will be used

APPLIED RESEARCH

Research that seeks answers to particular questions or to apply scientific discoveries to develop specific products

Part 7 *Fundamentals of Macroeconomics*

Because technological change is the fruit of research and development (R&D), investment in R&D aims to improve productivity through technological discovery. One way to track R&D spending is to measure it relative to gross domestic product, or GDP. Exhibit 10 shows R&D spending as a share of GDP for the United States and the six other major economies for the 1980s and 1990s. Overall R&D spending in the United States averaged 2.7 percent of GDP in both the 1980s and the 1990s. During the 1990s, R&D as a share of GDP ranked the United States second among the major economies, slightly behind Japan, at 2.9 percent, but well ahead of last placed Italy, at only 1.1 percent.

Bar segments in the chart distinguish between R&D by businesses and R&D by governments and nonprofit institutions. Business R&D is more likely to target applied research and

E X H I B I T 10 **R&D Spending as a Percentage of GDP for Major Economies During the 1980s and 1990s**

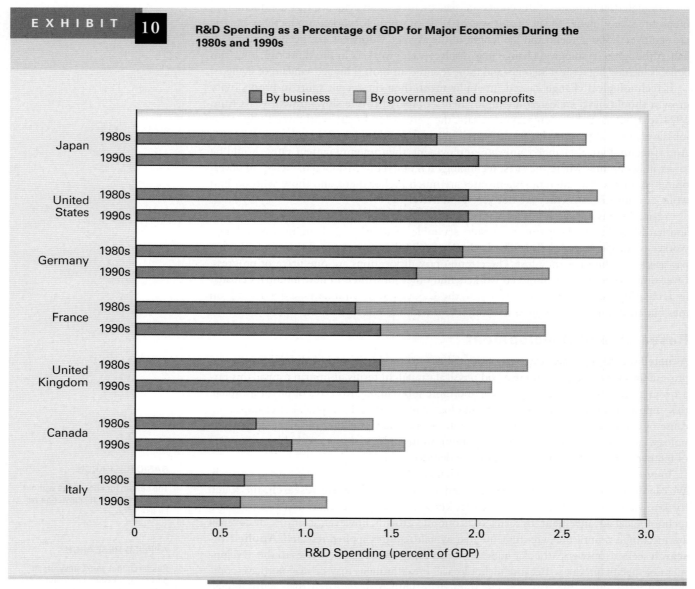

Source: Based on estimates developed in *OECD Economic Outlook 68* (December 2000). Figure IV.2.

innovations. R&D spending by governments and nonprofits, such as universities, may generate basic knowledge that has applications in the long run (for example, the Internet sprang from R&D spending on national defense). R&D by U.S. businesses averaged 1.9 percent of GDP in the 1990s, the same as in the 1980s. Three of the six other major countries experienced an increase in business R&D between the 1980s and 1990s, and three saw a decrease. Again, only Japan had higher business R&D than the United States in the 1990s, at 2.0 percent of GDP. Italy had the lowest at 0.6 percent.

In short, the United States devotes more resources to R&D than most other advanced economies, and this should help America maintain a higher standard of living.

Do Economies Converge?

If given enough time, will poor countries eventually catch up with rich ones? The **convergence** theory argues that developing countries can grow faster than advanced ones and should eventually close the gap. Here's why: It is easier to copy new technology once it is developed than to develop that technology in the first place. Countries that are technologically backward can grow faster by copying existing technology. But economies that already use the latest technology can boost productivity only with a steady stream of new breakthroughs.

Advanced countries, such as the United States, will find their growth limited by the rate of creation of new knowledge and improved technology. But follower countries can grow more quickly by, for example, adding computers where they previously had none. Until 1995, the United States, which makes up just 5 percent of the world's population, accounted for most of the world's computer purchases by households. But by 2000, most computers were bought by non-U.S. households.

What's the evidence on convergence? Some poor countries have begun to catch up with richer ones. For example, the newly industrialized Asian economies of Hong Kong, Singapore, South Korea, and Taiwan have invested heavily in technology acquisition and human resources and are closing the gap with the world leaders, moving from the ranks of developing nations to the ranks of industrial market economies. For example, real output per capita in South Korea has grown three times faster than the average for the seven major economies. But these so-called *Asian Tigers* are the exceptions. Among the nations that comprise the poorest third of the world's population, consumption per capita has grown only about 1.0 percent per year over the last two decades compared with a 2.5 percent growth in the rest of the world,[6] so the standard of living in the poorest third of the world has grown somewhat in absolute terms but has fallen further behind in relative terms.

One reason per capita consumption has grown so slowly in the poorest economies is that birthrates there are double those in richer countries, so poor economies must produce still more just to keep up with a growing population. Another reason why convergence has not begun, particularly for the poorest third of the world, is the vast difference in the quality of human capital across countries. Whereas technology is indeed portable, the knowledge, skill, and training needed to take advantage of that technology are not. Countries with a high level of human capital can make up for other shortcomings. For example, much of the capital stock in Japan and Germany was destroyed during World War II. But the two countries retained enough of their well-educated and highly skilled labor force to rejoin elite industrial market economies in little more than a generation. But some countries, such as those in Africa, simply lack the human capital needed to identify and absorb new technology. As noted already, such poor economies tend to have low education levels and low literacy rates.

CONVERGENCE

A theory predicting that the standard of living in economies around the world will grow more similar over time, with poorer countries eventually catching up with richer ones

---

6. Based on figures developed by the World Bank in *World Development Report 2002/2003* (New York: Oxford University Press, 2003), Tables 1 and 2.

What's more, some countries lack the stable macroeconomic environment and the established institutions needed to nurture economic growth. Many developing countries have serious deficiencies in their infrastructures, lacking, for example, the reliable source of electricity to power new technologies. For example, in Northern Nigeria, near the Sahara, 90 percent of the villages have no electricity. Some of the poorest nations have been ravaged by civil war for years. And simply communicating can be challenging in some developing countries. In Nigeria, for example, more than 400 languages are spoken by 250 distinct ethnic groups.

Industrial Policy

Policy makers have debated whether government should become more involved in shaping an economy's technological future. One concern is that technologies of the future will require huge sums to develop, sums that an individual firm cannot easily raise and put at risk. Another concern is that some technological breakthroughs spill over to other firms and other industries, but the firm that develops the breakthrough may not be in a position to reap benefits from these spillover effects, so individual firms may underinvest in such research. One possible solution is more government involvement.

Industrial policy is the idea that government, using taxes, subsidies, regulations, and coordination of the private sector, could help nurture the industries and technologies of the future to give domestic industries an advantage over foreign competition. The idea is to secure a leading global role for domestic industry. One example of European industrial policy is Airbus Industrie, a four-nation aircraft consortium. With an estimated $20 billion in government aid, the aircraft maker has become Boeing's main rival. When Airbus seeks aircraft orders around the world, it can draw on government backing to promise favorable terms, such as landing rights at key European airports and an easing of regulatory constraints. U.S. producers get less government backing. Industrial policy is discussed in the following case study.

Picking Technological Winners

U.S. industrial policy over the years was aimed at creating the world's most advanced military production capacity. With the demise of the Soviet Union, however, defense technologies became less important. Some argue that U.S. industrial policy should shift from a military to a civilian focus. Former President Clinton once talked about establishing a powerful agency to help finance and coordinate R&D for what he called "cutting-edge products and technologies." He also proposed bringing together businesses, universities, and laboratories to carry out R&D in civilian technologies.

Many state governments are also trying to identify what industries to support. Economists have long recognized that firms in some industries gain a performance advantage by *clustering*—that is, by locating in a region already thick with firms in the same industry or in related industries. Clusters such as Hollywood entertainers, Wall Street brokers, Broadway theaters, Las Vegas casinos, and Silicon Valley software makers facilitate communication and promote healthy competition among cluster members. The flow of information and cooperation between firms, as well as the competition among firms in close proximity, stimulates regional innovation and propels growth. By locating in a region already settled with similar firms, a firm can also tap into established local markets for specialized labor and for other inputs.

### Sidebar

INDUSTRIAL POLICY

The view that government—using taxes, subsidies, and regulations—should nurture the industries and technologies of the future, thereby giving these domestic industries an advantage over foreign competition

---

***Case*Study**

Public Policy

eActivity

State and local governments sometimes engage in industrial policies of their own. For examples and arguments against such policies, read Melvin L. Burstein and Arthur J. Rolnick's "Congress Should End the Economic War Among the States" at http://minneapolisfed.org/pubs/ar/ar1994.cfm. Also read a prize-winning essay on this subject by a high school student, "The Economic War Among the States Subsidizes Inefficiency" found also at the Minneapolis Fed Web site, http://minneapolisfed.org/econed/essay/results/1-97.cfm. What guarantees come with government subsidies for industrial development? For more examples of how a state tries to attract business, visit Virginia is for Business

But skeptics wonder whether the government should be trusted to identify emerging technologies and to pick the industry clusters that will lead the way. Critics of industrial policy believe that markets allocate scarce resources better than governments do. For example, European governments' costly attempt to develop the supersonic transport Concorde did not work. As another example, in the early 1980s, the U.S. government spent $1 billion to help military contractors develop a high-speed computer circuit. But Intel, a company getting no federal aid, was the first to develop the circuit. Japan has had the most aggressive support for favored industries, an approach that includes discouraging competition and encouraging joint research. But those Japanese industries getting the most government help, like chemicals and aircraft manufacturing, simply became uncompetitive in the world market. Meanwhile, industries with little government backing, like automobiles, cameras, and video games, turned out to be innovative world leaders.

There is also concern that an industrial policy would evolve into a government giveaway program. Rather than going to the most promising technologies, the money and the competitive advantages would go to the politically connected. Critics also wonder how wise it is to sponsor corporate research when beneficiaries may share their expertise with foreign companies and may build factories abroad. Most economists would prefer to let Microsoft, General Electric, or some start-up bet on the important technologies of the future.

Sources: "The Complications of Clustering," *Economist*, 2 January 1999; Michael Porter, "Japan: What Went Wrong," *Wall Street Journal*, 21 March 2001; and Ron Martin, "The New 'Geographical' Turn in Economics," *Cambridge Journal of Economics*, January 1999. The Web site for a firm advising governments about clustering can be found at http://www.sri.com/policy/csted/economics/clustering.html.

at http://www.yesvirginia.org/ or use a search engine such as Google to find a similar Web site for your state.

Conclusion

Productivity and growth depend on the supply and quality of resources, the level of technology, and the rules of the game that nurture production and exchange. These elements tend to be correlated with one another. An economy with an unskilled and poorly educated workforce will usually be deficient in physical capital, in technology, and in the institutional support that promotes production and exchange. Similarly, an economy with a high-quality workforce will likely excel in the other sources of productivity and growth.

We should distinguish between an economy's standard of living, as measured by output per capita, and improvements in that standard of living, as measured by the growth in output per capita. Growth in output per capita can occur when labor productivity increases or when the number of workers in the economy grows faster than the population. *In the long run, productivity growth and the growth in workers relative to the growth in population will determine whether or not the United States continues to enjoy the world's highest standard of living.*

In the next chapter, you will learn how to measure output in the economy and how to adjust for changes in the price level. In later chapters, you will develop aggregate demand and aggregate supply curves to build a model of the economy. Once you have an idea how a healthy economy works, you can consider the policy options in the face of high unemployment, high inflation, or both.

SUMMARY

1. If the population is continually increasing, an economy must produce more goods and services simply to maintain its standard of living, as measured by output per capita. If output grows faster than the population, the standard of living will rise.

2. An economy's standard of living grows over the long run because of (a) increases in the amount and quality of resources, especially labor and capital, (b) better technology, and (c) improvements in the rules of the game that facilitate production and exchange, such as tax laws, property

rights, patent laws, the legal system, and customs of the market.

3. The per-worker production function shows the relationship between the amount of capital per worker in the economy and the output per worker. As capital per worker increases, so does output per worker but at a decreasing rate. Technological change and improvements in the rules of the game shift the per-worker production function upward, so more is produced for each ratio of capital per worker.

4. Since 1870, U.S. labor productivity growth has averaged 2.1 percent per year. Output per work hour has grown sixteen-fold. The *quality* of labor and capital is much more important than the *quantity* of these resources. Labor productivity growth slowed between 1974 and 1982, in part because of spikes in energy prices and implementation of costly but necessary environmental and workplace regulations. Since 1983 productivity growth has picked up, especially since 1996, due primarily to information technology.

5. Among the seven major industrial market economies, the United States has the highest standard of living as measured by real GDP per capita.

6. Technological change sometimes creates job dislocations and hardships in the short run, as workers scramble to adjust to a changing world. Over time, however, most displaced workers find other jobs, sometimes in new industries created by technological change. There is no evidence that, in the long run, technological change increases unemployment in the economy.

7. Convergence is a theory predicting that economies around the world will grow more alike, as poorer countries catch up with richer ones. Some Asian countries that had been poor are catching up with the leaders, but most poor countries around the world have failed to close the gap.

8. Some governments use industrial policy in an effort to nurture the industries and technologies of the future, giving domestic industries an advantage over foreign competitors. But critics are wary of the government's ability to pick the winning technologies of the future.

QUESTIONS FOR REVIEW

1. *(Productivity)* As discussed in the text, per capita GDP in many developing countries depends on the productivity of land there. However, many richer economies have little land or land of poor quality. How can a country with little land or unproductive land become rich?

2. *(Labor Productivity)* What two kinds of changes in the capital stock can improve labor productivity? How can each type be illustrated with a per-worker production function? What determines the slope of the per-worker production function?

3. *(Slowdown in Labor Productivity Growth)* What contributed to the slower rate of growth in labor productivity during the 1974–1982 period?

4. *(Output per Capita)* Explain how output per capita can grow faster than labor productivity. Is it possible for labor productivity to grow faster than output per capita?

5. *(Technology and Productivity)* What measures can government take to promote the development of practical technologies?

6. *(Basic and Applied Research)* What is the difference between basic research and applied research? Relate this to the human genome project—research aimed at developing a complete map of human chromosomes, showing the location of every gene.

7. *(Rules of the Game)* How do "rules of the game" affect productivity and growth? What types of "rules" should a government set to encourage growth?

8. (*Case* **Study**: Computers and Productivity Growth) How has the increased use of computers affected U.S. productivity in the last few years? Is the contribution of computers expected to increase or decrease in the near future? Explain.

9. *(International Productivity Comparisons)* How does output per capita in the United States compare with output per capita in other industrial economies? How has this comparison changed over time?

10. *(Industrial Policy)* Define industrial policy. What are some arguments in favor of industrial policy?

11. (*C a s e* **Study**: Picking Technological Winners) What was the central focus of U.S. industrial policy in the past? Is the same focus appropriate today? What are the arguments against an active U.S. industrial policy?

12. *(Technological Change and Unemployment)* Explain how technological change can lead to unemployment in certain industries. How can it lead to increased employment?

13. *(Convergence)* Explain the convergence theory. Under what circumstances is convergence unlikely to occur?

14. *(Productivity)* What factors might contribute to a low *level* of productivity in an economy? Regardless of the level of labor productivity, what impact does slow *growth* in labor productivity have on the economy's standard of living?

PROBLEMS AND EXERCISES

15. *(Growth and the PPF)* Use the production possibilities frontier (PPF) to demonstrate economic growth.

    a. With consumption goods on one axis and capital goods on the other, show how the combination of goods selected this period affects the PPF in the next period.

    b. Extend this comparison by choosing a different point on this period's PPF and determining whether that combination leads to more or less growth over the next period.

16. *(Long-Term Productivity Growth)* Suppose that two nations start out in 2004 with identical levels of output per work hour—say, $100 per hour. In the first nation, labor productivity grows by 1 percent per year. In the second, it grows by 2 percent per year. Use a calculator or a spreadsheet to determine how much output per hour each nation will be producing 20 years later, assuming that labor

productivity growth rates do not change. Then, determine how much each will be producing per hour 100 years later. What do your results tell you about the effects of small differences in growth rates?

17. *(Technological Change and Unemployment)* What are some examples, other than those given in the chapter, of technological change that has caused unemployment? And what are some examples of new technologies that have created jobs? How do you think you might measure the net impact of technological change on overall employment and GDP in the United States?

18. *(Shifts in the PPF)* Terrorist attacks foster instability and may affect productivity over the short and long term. Do you think the September 11, 2001, terrorist attacks on the World Trade Center and the Pentagon affected short and/or long-term productivity in the United States? Explain your response and show any movements in the PPF.

EXPERIENTIAL EXERCISES

19. *(Labor Productivity)* Go to the Bureau of Labor Statistics (BLS) page on Quarterly Labor Productivity at http://www.bls.gov/lpc/ and get the latest news release on productivity and costs. Rank the various sectors of the U.S. economy from highest to lowest according to their most recent productivity growth rates. Does what you found make sense to you? Why or why not?

20. *(International Productivity Comparisons)* The BLS also compiles international data on manufacturing productivity at http://stats.bls.gov/news.release/prod4.toc.htm. For the most recent period, which nations have enjoyed the most rapid growth in manufacturing productivity? Which nations have experienced the slowest growth? Has productivity actually declined anywhere? How could this be related to the convergence theory explained in this chapter?

21. *(Wall Street Journal)* Technological change is an important driver of economic growth. Refer to the "Technology" column in the Marketplace section of a recent *Wall Street Journal*. Find a story about a technological innovation that seems interesting to you. How will this innovation affect the U.S. production possibilities frontier? Does it seem likely to affect employment as well? If so, which types of workers will be harmed, and which types will benefit?

HOMEWORK XPRESS! EXERCISES

These exercises require access to McEachern Homework Xpress! If Homework Xpress! did not come with your book, visit **http://homeworkxpress.swlearning.com** *to purchase.*

1. Two economies, the United States and country G, currently have identical production possibilities frontiers, *CI,* but have chosen differing combinations of capital and consumer goods as indicated. Illustrate how these choices will affect economic growth by adding a PPF for the United States ten years into the future, and then one for country G ten years from now.

2. Sketch a per-worker production function in the diagram that illustrates the law of diminishing marginal returns. Identify the level of output per worker produced given *k* capital per worker.

3. Sketch a per-worker production function in the diagram that illustrates the law of diminishing marginal returns. Identify the level of output per worker produced given *k* capital per worker. Illustrate the impact of technological changes that increase productivity. Identify the new level of output per worker that can be produced given *k* capital per worker.

4. A per-worker production function is shown in the diagram for an economy currently producing with *k* units of capital per worker. Illustrate how the economy can increase output per worker to y_1 by increasing capital per worker. Then illustrate how y_1 could be achieved by improving technology instead of increasing capital.

Measuring the Economy and the Circular Flow

© Leslie Harris/Index Stock Imagery

H ow do we keep track of the most complex economy in world history? What's gross about the gross domestic product? What's domestic about it? If you make yourself a tuna sandwich, how much does your effort add to the gross domestic product? Because prices change over time, how can we compare the economy's production in one year with that in other years? Answers to these and other questions are addressed in this chapter, which introduces an economic scorecard for a $12 trillion economy. That scorecard is the national income accounting system, which reduces a huge network of economic activity to a few aggregate measures.

As you will see, aggregate output can be measured either by the spending on that output or by the income derived from producing it. We examine each approach and see why they are equivalent. The major components and important equalities built into the national income accounts are offered here as another way of understanding how the economy works—not as a foreign language to be mastered before the next exam. The emphasis is more on economic intuition than on accounting precision. The body of the chapter provides the background you will need for later chapters. More details about the national income accounts are offered in the appendix. Topics discussed in this chapter include:

- National income accounts
- Expenditure approach to GDP
- Income approach to GDP
- Circular flow of income and expenditure

- Leakages and injections
- Limitations of national income accounting
- Consumer price index
- GDP price index

The Product of a Nation

How do we measure the economy's performance? During much of the 17th and 18th centuries, when the dominant economic policy was mercantilism, many thought that economic prosperity was best measured by the *stock* of precious metals a nation accumulated in the public treasury. Mercantilism led to restrictions on international trade, but this restriction had the unintended consequence of limiting the gains from comparative advantage. In the latter half of the 18th century, François Quesnay became the first to measure economic activity as a *flow.* In 1758 he published his *Tableau Économique,* which described the *circular flow* of output and income through different sectors of the economy. His insight was likely inspired by his knowledge of blood's circular flow in the body—Quesnay was court physician to King Louis XV of France.

Rough measures of national income were developed in England two centuries ago, but detailed calculations built up from microeconomic data were refined in the United States during the Great Depression. The resulting *national income accounting system* organizes huge quantities of data collected from a variety of sources across America. These data were summarized, assembled into a coherent framework, and reported by the federal government. The conception and implementation of these accounts has been hailed as one of the greatest achievements of the 20th century. The U.S. national income accounts are the most widely copied and most highly regarded in the world and earned their developer, Simon Kuznets, the Nobel Prize in 1971 for "giving quantitative precision to economic entities."

National Income Accounts

How do the national income accounts keep track of the economy's incredible variety of goods and services, from hiking boots to guitar lessons? The *gross domestic product,* or GDP, measures the market value of all final goods and services produced during a year by resources located in the United States, regardless of who owns the resources. For example, GDP includes production in the United States by foreign firms, such as a Japanese auto plant in Kentucky, but excludes foreign production by U.S. firms, such as a General Motors plant in Mexico. Incidentally, until 1992, the federal government's yardstick was gross *national* product, or GNP, which measures the market value of all goods and services produced by resources supplied by U.S. residents and firms, regardless of the location of the resources.

The national income accounts are based on the simple fact that *one person's spending is another person's income.* GDP can be measured either by total spending on U.S. production or by total income received from that production. The **expenditure approach** adds the spending on all final goods and services produced during the year. The **income approach** adds the earnings during the year by those who produce that output. In the *double-entry bookkeeping sys-*

EXPENDITURE APPROACH TO GDP

A method of calculating GDP by adding spending on all final goods and services produced in the nation during the year

INCOME APPROACH TO GDP

A method of calculating GDP by adding all payments for resources used to produce output in the nation during the year *tem* used to track the economy, spending on aggregate output is recorded on one side of the ledger and income from producing that aggregate output is recorded on the other side.

Gross domestic product includes only **final goods and services,** which are goods and services sold to the final, or end, user. A toothbrush, a pair of contact lenses, and a bus ride are examples of final goods and services. Whether a sale is to the final user depends on who buys the product. Your purchase of chicken from a grocer is reflected in GDP. When KFC buys chicken, however, this is not counted in GDP because KFC is not the final consumer. Only after the chicken is cooked and sold by KFC is the transaction counted in GDP.

Intermediate goods and services are those purchased for additional processing and resale, like KFC's chicken. This change may be imperceptible, as when a grocer buys canned goods to stock the shelves. Or the intermediate goods can be dramatically altered, as when a painter transforms a $100 canvas and $30 in oils into a work of art that sells for $5,000. Sales of intermediate goods and services are excluded from GDP to avoid the problem of **double counting,** which is counting an item's value more than once. For example, suppose the grocer buys a can of tuna for $0.60 and sells it for $1.00. If GDP counted both the intermediate transaction of $0.60 and the final transaction of $1.00, the recorded value of $1.60 would exceed its final value by $0.60. Hence, GDP counts only the final value. GDP also ignores most of the secondhand value of used goods, such as existing homes, used cars, and used textbooks. These goods were counted in GDP when they were produced. But just as the services provided by the grocer are included in GDP, so are the services provided by real estate agents, used-car dealers, and used-book sellers.

GDP Based on the Expenditure Approach

As noted already, one way to measure GDP is to add spending on all final goods and services produced in the economy during the year. The easiest way to understand the spending approach is to divide aggregate expenditure into its components: consumption, investment, government purchases, and net exports. **Consumption,** or more specifically, *personal consumption expenditures,* consists of purchases of final goods and services by households during the year. Consumption is the largest spending category, averaging about two-thirds of U.S. GDP during the last decade. Along with *services* like dry cleaning, haircuts, and air travel, consumption includes *nondurable goods,* like soap and soup, and *durable goods,* like furniture and major appliances. Durable goods are expected to last at least three years.

Investment, or more specifically, *gross private domestic investment,* consists of spending on new capital goods and on net additions to inventories. The most important investment is **physical capital,** such as new buildings and new machinery. Investment also includes new **residential construction.** Although it fluctuates from year to year, investment averaged about one-sixth of U.S. GDP during the last decade. More generally, investment consists of spending on current production that is not used for current consumption. A net increase to inventories also counts as investment because it represents current production not used for current consumption. **Inventories** are stocks of goods in process, such as computer parts, and stocks of finished goods, such as new computers awaiting sale. Inventories help manufacturers cope with unexpected changes in the supply of their resources or in the demand for their products.

Although investment includes purchasing a new residence, it excludes purchases of *existing* buildings and machines and purchases of financial assets, such as stocks and bonds. Existing buildings and machines were counted in GDP when they were produced. Stocks and bonds are not investments themselves but simply indications of ownership.

Government purchases, or more specifically, *government consumption and gross investment,* include government spending for goods and services—from clearing snowy roads to clearing court dockets, from library books to the librarian's pay. Government purchases

FINAL GOODS AND SERVICES

Goods and services sold to final, or end, users

INTERMEDIATE GOODS AND SERVICES

Goods and services purchased by firms for further reprocessing and resale

DOUBLE COUNTING

The mistake of including the value of intermediate goods plus the value of final goods in gross domestic product; counting the same good more than once

CONSUMPTION

Household purchases of final goods and services, except for new residences, which count as investments

INVESTMENT

The purchase of new plants, new equipment, new buildings, and new residences, plus net additions to inventories

PHYSICAL CAPITAL

Manufactured items used to produce goods and services; includes new plants and new equipment

RESIDENTIAL CONSTRUCTION

Building new homes or dwelling places

INVENTORIES

Producers' stocks of finished and in-process goods

GOVERNMENT PURCHASES

Spending for goods and services by all levels of government; government outlays minus transfer payments averaged a bit less than one-fifth of U.S. GDP during the last decade. Government purchases, and therefore GDP, exclude transfer payments, such as Social Security, welfare benefits, and unemployment insurance. Such payments are not true purchases by the government or true earnings by the recipients.

The final spending component, net exports, reflects international trade in goods and services. Goods, or *merchandise* traded, include physical items such as bananas and DVD players (stuff you can drop on your toes). Services, or so-called *invisibles,* include intangible items, such as European tours and online customer service from India. Foreign purchases of U.S. goods and services are counted as part of U.S. GDP. But U.S. purchases of foreign goods and services are subtracted from U.S. GDP. **Net exports** equal the value of U.S. exports of goods and services minus the value of U.S. imports of goods and services. U.S. imports have exceeded U.S. exports nearly every year since the 1960s, meaning U.S. net exports have been negative. During the last decade, net exports averaged a negative 2 percent of GDP, but this has increased to a negative 4 or 5 percent of GDP in recent years.

With the expenditure approach, the nation's **aggregate expenditure** equals the sum of consumption, C, investment, I, government purchases, G, and net exports, which is the value of exports, X, minus the value of imports, M, or $(X - M)$. Summing these yields aggregate expenditure, or GDP:

$$C + I + G + (X - M) = \text{Aggregate expenditure} = \text{GDP}$$

GDP Based on the Income Approach

The expenditure approach sums, or aggregates, spending on production. The income approach sums, or aggregates, income arising from that production. Again, double-entry bookkeeping ensures that the value of aggregate output equals the aggregate income paid for resources used to produce that output: the wages, interest, rent, and profit arising from production. The price of a Hershey Bar reflects the income of resource suppliers along the way. **Aggregate income** equals the sum of all the income earned by resource suppliers in the economy. Thus, we can say that

$$\text{Aggregate expenditure} = \text{GDP} = \text{Aggregate income}$$

A product usually goes through stages involving several firms on its way to the consumer. A wooden desk, for example, starts as raw timber, which is typically cut by one firm, milled by another, made into a desk by a third, and retailed by a fourth. We avoid double counting either by including only the market value of the desk when it is sold to the final user or by *calculating the value added at each stage of production.* The **value added** by each firm equals that firm's selling price minus payments for inputs from other firms. The value added at each stage is the income earned by resource suppliers at that stage. *The value added at all stages sums to the market value of the final good, and the value added for all final goods sums to GDP based on the income approach.* For example, suppose you buy a wooden desk for $200. This final market value gets added directly into GDP. Consider the history of that desk. Suppose the tree that gave its life for your studies was cut into a log and sold to a miller for $20. That log was milled into lumber and sold for $50 to a manufacturer, who built your desk and sold it for $120 to a retailer, who sold it to you for $200.

Column (1) of Exhibit 1 lists the selling price at each stage of production. If all these transactions were added up, the total of $390 would exceed the $200 market value of the desk. To avoid double counting, we include only the value added at each stage, listed in column (3) as the difference between the purchase price and the selling price at that stage. Again, *the value added at each stage equals the income earned by those who supplied their resources at*

NET EXPORTS

The value of a country's exports minus the value of its imports

AGGREGATE EXPENDITURE

Total spending on final goods and services during a given period, usually a year

AGGREGATE INCOME

The sum of all income earned by resource suppliers in an economy during a given period

VALUE ADDED

The difference at each stage of production between the selling price of a product and the cost of intermediate goods purchased from other firms

Stage of Production	(1) Sale Value	(2) Cost of Intermediate Goods	(3) Value Added
Logger	$ 20	——	$ 20
Miller	50	$ 20	30
Manufacturer	120	50	70
Retailer	200	120	80
		Market value of final good	**$200**

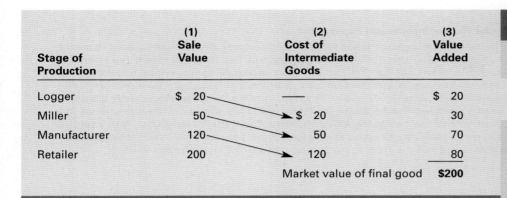

EXHIBIT 1

Computation of Value Added for a New Desk

The value added at each stage of production is the sale price at that stage minus the cost of intermediate goods, or column (1) minus column (2). The values added at each stage sum to the market value of the final good, shown at the bottom of column (3).

that stage. For example, the $80 in value added by the retailer consists of income to resource suppliers at that stage, from the salesperson to the janitor who cleans the showroom to the trucker who provides "free delivery" of your desk. The value added at all stages totals $200, which is both the final market value of the desk and the total income earned by all resource suppliers along the way.

To reinforce your understanding of the equality of income and spending, let's return to something introduced in the first chapter, the circular-flow model.

The Circular Flow of Income and Expenditure

The model in Exhibit 2 outlines the circular flow of income and spending in the economy for not only households and firms, as was the case in Chapter 1, but governments and the rest of the world too. The main stream flows clockwise around the circle, first as income from firms to households (in the lower half of the circle), and then as spending from households back to firms (in the upper half of the circle). For each flow of money, there is an equal and opposite flow of products or resources. Here we follow the money.

The Income Half of the Circular Flow

In the process of developing a circular flow of income and spending, we must make some simplifying assumptions. Specifically, by assuming that physical capital does not wear out (i.e., no capital depreciation) and that firms pay out all profits to firm owners (i.e., firms retain no earnings), we can say that *GDP equals aggregate income.* The circular flow is a continuous process, but the logic of the model is clearest if we begin at juncture (1) in Exhibit 2, where U.S. firms make production decisions. After all, production must occur before output can be sold and income earned. As Henry Ford explained, "It is not the employer who pays the wages—the employer only handles the money. It is the product that pays wages." Households supply their labor, capital, natural resources, and entrepreneurial ability to make products that sell to pay wages, interest, rent, and profit. Production of aggregate output, or GDP, gives rise to an equal amount of aggregate income.

Thus, at juncture (1), aggregate output equals aggregate income. But not all that income is available to spend. At juncture (2), governments collect taxes. Some of these tax dollars return as transfer payments to the income stream at juncture (3). By subtracting taxes and adding transfers, we transform aggregate income into **disposable income, *DI,*** which flows to households at juncture (4). Disposable income is take-home pay, which households can spend or save.

DISPOSABLE INCOME (DI)

The income households have available to spend or to save after paying taxes and receiving transfer payments

Circular Flow of Income and Expenditure

The circular-flow model captures important relationships in the economy. The bottom half depicts the income arising from production. At juncture (1), GDP equals aggregate income. Taxes leak from the flow at (2), but transfer payments enter the flow at (3). Taxes minus transfers equals net taxes, *NT*. Aggregate income minus net taxes equals disposable income, *DI*, which flows to households at juncture (4). The top half of the model shows the flow of expenditure. At (5), households either spend disposable income or save it. Consumption enters the spending flow directly. Saving leaks from the spending flow into financial markets, where it is channeled to borrowers. At (6), investment enters the spending flow. At (7), government purchases enter the spending flow. At (8), imports leak from the spending flow, and at (9), exports enter the spending flow. Consumption plus investment plus government purchases plus net exports add up to the aggregate expenditure on GDP received by firms at (10).

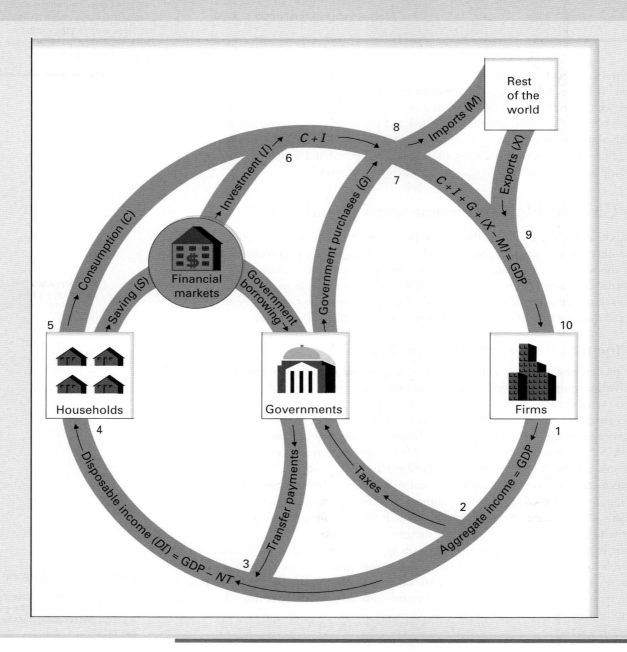

The bottom half of this circular flow is the *income half* because it focuses on the income arising from production. Aggregate income is the total income from producing GDP, and disposable income is the income remaining after taxes are subtracted and transfers added. To simplify the discussion, we define **net taxes, *NT*,** as taxes minus transfer payments. So *disposable income equals GDP minus net taxes.* Put another way, we can say that aggregate income equals disposable income plus net taxes:

$$GDP = \text{Aggregate income} = DI + NT$$

NET TAXES (NT)

Taxes minus transfer payments

At juncture (4), firms have produced output and have paid resource suppliers; governments have collected taxes and made transfer payments. With the resulting disposable income in hand, households must now decide how much to spend and how much to save. Because firms have already produced the output and have paid resource suppliers, firms wait to see how much consumers want to spend. Any unsold production gets added to firm inventories.

The Expenditure Half of the Circular Flow

Disposable income splits at juncture (5). Part goes for consumption, *C,* and the rest is saved, *S.* Thus,

$$DI = C + S$$

Spending on consumption remains in the circular flow and is the biggest aggregate expenditure, about two-thirds of the total. Household saving flows to **financial markets,** which consist of banks and other financial institutions that link savers to borrowers. For simplicity, Exhibit 2 shows households as the only savers, though governments, firms, and the rest of the world could save as well. The primary borrowers are firms and governments, but households borrow too, particularly for new homes, and the rest of the world also borrows. In reality, financial markets should be connected to all four economic decision makers, but we have simplified the flows to keep the model from looking like a plate of spaghetti.

FINANCIAL MARKETS

Banks and other financial institutions that facilitate the flow of funds from savers to borrowers

In our simplified model, firms pay resource suppliers an amount equal to the entire value of output. With nothing left for investment, firms must borrow to finance purchases of physical capital plus any increases in their inventories. Households also borrow to purchase new homes. Therefore, investment, *I,* consists of spending on new capital by firms, including inventory changes, plus spending on residential construction. Investment enters the circular flow at juncture (6), so aggregate spending at that point totals *C + I.*

Governments must also borrow whenever they incur deficits, that is, whenever their total *outlays*—transfer payments plus purchases of goods and services—exceed their revenues. Government purchases of goods and services, represented by *G,* enter the spending stream in the upper half of the circular flow at juncture (7). Remember that *G excludes* transfer payments, which already entered the stream as income at juncture (3).

Some spending by households, firms, and governments goes for imports. Because spending on imports flows to foreign producers, spending on imports, *M,* leaks from the circular flow at juncture (8). But the rest of the world buys U.S. products, so foreign spending on U.S. exports, *X,* enters the spending flow at juncture (9). Net exports, the impact of the *rest of the world* on aggregate expenditure, equal exports minus imports, *X − M,* which can be positive, negative, or zero.

The upper half of the circular flow, the *expenditure half,* tracks components of aggregate expenditure: consumption, *C,* investment, *I,* government purchases, *G,* and net exports, *X − M.* Aggregate expenditure flows into firms at juncture (10). Aggregate expenditure equals the market value of aggregate output, or GDP. In other words,

$$C + I + G + (X - M) = \text{Aggregate expenditure} = GDP$$

Leakages Equal Injections

Let's step back now to see the big picture. In the lower half of the circular flow, aggregate income equals disposable income plus net taxes. In the upper half, aggregate expenditure equals the total spending on U.S. output. *The aggregate income arising from production equals the aggregate expenditure on that production.* This is the first accounting identity. Thus, aggregate income (disposable income plus net taxes) equals aggregate expenditure (spending by each sector), or

$$DI + NT = C + I + G + (X - M)$$

Because disposable income equals consumption plus saving, we can substitute $C + S$ for DI in the above equation to yield

$$C + S + NT = C + I + G + (X - M)$$

After subtracting C from both sides and adding M to both sides, the equation reduces to

$$S + NT + M = I + G + X$$

Note that at various points around the circular flow, some of the flow leaks from the main stream. Saving, S, net taxes, NT, and imports, M, are **leakages** from the circular flow. **Injections** into the main stream also occur at various points around the circular flow. Investment, I, government purchases, G, and exports, X, are *injections* of spending into the circular flow. As you can see from the preceding equation, *leakages from the circular flow equal injections into that flow.* This leakages-injections equation demonstrates a second accounting identity based on double-entry bookkeeping.

Limitations of National Income Accounting

Imagine the difficulty of developing an accounting system that must capture the subtleties of such a complex and dynamic economy. In the interest of clarity and simplicity, certain features get neglected. In this section, we examine some limitations of the national income accounting system, beginning with productive activity not captured by GDP.

Some Production Is Not Included in GDP

With some minor exceptions, GDP includes only those products that are sold in markets, thereby neglecting all do-it-yourself household production—child care, meal preparation, house cleaning, home maintenance and repair. Thus, an economy in which householders are largely self-sufficient will have a lower GDP than will an otherwise similar economy in which households specialize and sell products to one another. During the 1950s, more than 80 percent of American mothers with small children remained at home caring for the family, but all this care added not one cent to GDP. Today most mothers with small children are in the workforce, where their labor gets counted in GDP. Meals, child care, and the like are now often purchased in markets and thus get reflected in GDP. In less developed economies, more economic activity is do-it-yourself.

GDP also ignores off-the-books production. The term **underground economy** describes market activity that goes unreported because either it's illegal or people want to evade taxes on otherwise legal activity. Although there is no official measure of the underground economy, most economists agree that it is substantial. A federal study suggests the equivalent of 7.5 percent of GDP is underground production; this would have amounted to about $800 billion in 2004.

LEAKAGE

Any diversion of income from the domestic spending stream; includes saving, taxes, and imports

INJECTION

Any spending other than by households or any income other than from resource earnings; includes investment, government purchases, exports, and transfer payments

WALL STREET JOURNAL

Reading It **Right**

What's the relevance of the following statement from the Wall Street Journal: *"The economic package approved by the Italian Parliament includes measures to encourage firms operating in the underground economy to come out in the open."*

UNDERGROUND ECONOMY

Market exchange that goes unreported either because it is illegal or because those involved want to evade taxes

For some economic activity, income must be *imputed,* or assigned, because market exchange does not occur. For example, included in GDP is an *imputed rental income* that homeowners receive from home ownership, even though no rent is actually paid or received. Also included in GDP is an imputed dollar amount for (1) wages paid *in kind,* such as employers' payments for employees' medical insurance, and (2) food produced by farm families for their own consumption. *GDP therefore includes some economic production that does not involve market exchange.*

Leisure, Quality, and Variety

The average U.S. workweek is much shorter now than it was a century ago, so people work less to produce today's output. People also retire earlier and live longer after retirement. Over the years, there has been an increase in the amount of leisure available. But leisure is not reflected in GDP because it is not directly bought and sold in a market. The quality and variety of products sold have also improved on average over the years because of technological advances and greater competition. Yet most of these improvements are not reflected in GDP. Recording systems, computers, tires, running shoes, and hundreds of other products have gotten better over the years. Also, new products are being introduced all the time, such as high-definition television and MP3 players. *The gross domestic product fails to capture changes in the availability of leisure time and often fails to reflect changes in the quality of products and the availability of new products.* The special problem of measuring production in an economy shaped by changing technology is discussed in the following case study.

Tracking a $12 Trillion Economy

© Photodisc/Getty Images

C a s e **S t u d y**

The Information Economy

*e*Activity
How does the Bureau of Economic Analysis go about incorporating changes to industry into national income statistics? Visit the site of National Income and Product Accounts for 2003 at http://www.bea.gov/bea/dn/2003benchmarck/CR2003content.htm, and click on "Highlights" to see the kinds of changes and the issues involved, and then select FAQs to learn more about this process. If you select "Interactive NIPA Tables," you can view some of the statistics.

Ever since Article I of the U.S. Constitution required a decennial population census, the federal government has been gathering data. The three data-gathering agencies are the Census Bureau, the Commerce Department's Bureau of Economic Analysis, and the Bureau of Labor Statistics. Since 1980, real GDP has more than doubled, employment has increased more than 40 million, and real foreign trade has more than tripled. Yet the federal budget for these agencies has declined in real terms. Only 0.2 percent of the federal budget goes toward keeping track of the nation and its economy.

Budget cuts have eliminated some data collection and have slowed down others. For example, computations of monthly international trade statistics have become so overwhelming that as many as half the imports counted for a particular month reflect a "carryover" from previous months. Some agencies must do more with the same staff. For example, in 1980, the Bureau of Labor Statistics had 18 analysts to monitor productivity in 95 different industries. The number of industries now tracked has quadrupled, but the number of analysts has changed little. The Census Bureau proposed collecting data on the Internet economy, but Congress said no.

Ways of monitoring economic activity were developed in the 1930s and 1940s, when manufacturing dominated. Because manufacturing is tangible, such as automobiles and toasters, output is easy to measure. But services are intangible, such as medical care and on-line services, and are harder to measure. Yet services now make up most of the GDP. Even where services would appear to be easily measured, government does not yet collect such data. For example, although there are thousands of nail salons in the country, nobody knows exactly how many and nobody keeps track of manicures and pedicures.

Because services are intangible, measures for the service sector tend to be less reliable than those for the manufacturing sector. Measures of service output often fail to reflect improvements in the speed or quality of services. For example, some trucking firms use on-board computers to map the most efficient route and remap the route should priorities change. The increased efficiency has reduced the number of ton-miles (tonnage times miles) carried per month. Yet, according to federal statisticians, these more efficient drivers appear to be producing less because output in this industry is measured by ton-miles.

Because of technological advances in health care, diagnosis is now more accurate, treatments are less invasive and less painful, and people recover faster, so hospital stays are shorter. These improvements suggest big cost savings and greater convenience for patients. But because output in health care is usually measured by inputs, such as the doctor's time and hospital-bed days, these measures miss the improved quality. Federal statisticians are working on getting better measures of services, but they still have difficulty measuring output in a wide range of industries, including medicine, banking, education, software, legal services, wholesale trade, and communications. Researchers have found that, after 1995, labor productivity in the service sector grew faster than in the goods sector.

Sources: "The U.S. Statistical System and a Rapidly Changing Economy," *Brookings Policy Brief*, No. 63 (July 2000): 2–8; Barry Bosworth and Jack Triplett, "Productivity in Services Industries: Trends and Measurement Issues," 17 November 2003, Brookings Institution, http://www.brookings.edu; and *Economic Report of the President*, February 2004. For the latest labor productivity data, go to http://www.bls.gov/lpc/home.htm.

What's Gross about Gross Domestic Product?

In the course of producing GDP, some capital wears out, such as the delivery truck that finally dies, and some capital becomes obsolete, such as an aging computer that can't run the latest software. A new truck that logs 100,000 miles its first year has been subject to wear and tear, and therefore has a diminished value as a resource. A truer picture of the *net* production that actually occurs during a year is found by subtracting this capital *depreciation* from GDP. **Depreciation** measures the value of the capital stock that is used up or becomes obsolete in the production process. Gross domestic product is called "gross" because it fails to take into account this depreciation. **Net domestic product** equals gross domestic product minus depreciation, the capital stock used up in the production process.

We can now have two measures of investment. *Gross investment* is the value of all investment during a year, and is used in computing GDP. *Net investment* equals gross investment less depreciation. The economy's production possibilities depend on what happens to net investment. If net investment is negative—that is, if depreciation exceeds gross investment—the economy's capital stock declines, so its contribution to output will decline as well. If net investment is zero, the capital stock remains constant, as does its contribution to output. And if net investment is positive, the capital stock grows, as does its contribution to output.

As the names imply, *gross* domestic product reflects gross investment and *net* domestic product reflects net investment. But estimating depreciation involves much guesswork. For example, what is the appropriate measure of depreciation for the roller coasters at Busch Gardens, the metal display shelves at Wal-Mart, or the parking lots at Disney World?

GDP Does Not Reflect All Costs

Some production and consumption degrades the quality of our environment. Trucks and automobiles pump pollution into the atmosphere. Housing displaces forests. Paper mills foul

DEPRECIATION

The value of capital stock used up to produce GDP or that becomes obsolete during a year

NET DOMESTIC PRODUCT

Gross domestic product minus depreciation

the lungs and burn the eyes. These negative externalities—costs that fall on those not directly involved in the transactions—are mostly ignored in GDP accounting, even though they diminish the quality of life and may limit future production. To the extent that growth in GDP also involves growth in negative externalities, a rising GDP may not be as attractive as it would first appear.

Although the national income accounts reflect the depreciation of buildings, machinery, vehicles, and other manufactured capital, this accounting ignores the depletion of natural resources, such as standing timber, fish stocks, and soil fertility. So national income accounts reflect depreciation of the manufactured capital stock but not the natural capital stock. For example, intensive farming may raise productivity temporarily and boost GDP, but this depletes soil fertility. Worse still, some economic development may cause the extinction of certain plants and animals. The U.S. Commerce Department is now in the process of developing so-called *green accounting*, or *green GDP*, to reflect the impact of production on air pollution, water pollution, soil depletion, and the loss of other natural resources.

GDP and Economic Welfare

In computing GDP, the market price of output is the measure of its value. Therefore, each dollar spent on handguns or cigarettes is counted in GDP the same as each dollar spent on baby formula or fitness programs. Positive economic analysis tries to avoid making value judgments about how people spend their money. Because the level of GDP provides no information about its composition, some economists question whether GDP is a good measure of the nation's economic welfare.

Despite the limitations of official GDP estimates, the trend of GDP offers a good snapshot of the U.S. economy. Inflation, however, clouds comparability over time. In the next section, we discuss how to adjust GDP for changes in the economy's price level.

Accounting for Price Changes

As noted earlier, the national income accounts are based on the market values of final goods and services produced in a particular year. Initially, gross domestic product measures the value of output in *current dollars*—that is, in the dollar values at the time production occurs. When GDP is based on current dollars, the national income accounts measure the *nominal value* of national output. Thus, the current-dollar GDP, or **nominal GDP,** is based on the prices prevailing when production takes place.

NOMINAL GDP

GDP based on prices prevailing at the time of the transaction; current-dollar GDP

National income accounts based on current, or nominal, dollars allow for comparisons among income or expenditure components in a particular year. Because the economy's average price level changes over time, however, current-dollar comparisons across years can be misleading. For example, between 1979 and 1980, nominal GDP increased by about 9 percent. That sounds impressive, but the economy's average price level rose more than 9 percent. So the growth in nominal GDP resulted entirely from inflation. Real GDP, or GDP measured in terms of the goods and services produced, in fact declined. If nominal GDP increases in a given year, part of this increase may simply reflect inflation—pure hot air. To make meaningful comparisons of GDP across years, we must take out the hot air, or *deflate* nominal GDP. We focus on *real* changes in production by eliminating changes due solely to inflation.

Price Indexes

To compare the price level over time, let's first establish a point of reference, a base year to which prices in other years can be compared. An *index number* compares the value of some variable in a particular year to its value in a base year, or reference year. Think about the simplest of index numbers. Suppose bread is the only good produced in an economy. As a reference point, let's look at its price in some specific year. The year selected is called the **base year;** prices in other years are expressed relative to the base-year price.

Suppose the base year is 2003, when a loaf of bread in our simple economy sold for $1.25. Let's say the price of bread increased to $1.30 in 2004 and to $1.40 in 2005. We construct a **price index** by dividing each year's price by the price in the base year and then multiplying by 100, as shown in Exhibit 3. For 2003, the base year, we divide the base price of bread by itself, $1.25/$1.25, which equals 1, so the price index in 2003 equals 1 × 100 = 100. *The price index in the base year is always 100.* The price index in 2004 is $1.30/$1.25, which equals 1.04, which when multiplied by 100 equals 104. In 2005, the index is $1.40/$1.25, or 1.12, which when multiplied by 100 equals 112. Thus, the index is 4 percent higher in 2004 than in the base year and 12 percent higher in 2005. The price index permits comparisons across years. For example, what if you were provided the indexes for 2004 and 2005 and asked what happened to the price level between the two years? By dividing the 2005 price index by the 2004 price index, 112/104, you find that the price level rose 7.7 percent.

This section has shown how to develop a price index assuming we already know the price level each year. Determining the price level is a bit more involved, as we'll now see.

Consumer Price Index

The price index most familiar to you is the **consumer price index,** or **CPI,** which measures changes over time in the cost of buying a "market basket" of goods and services purchased by a typical family. For simplicity, suppose a typical family's market basket for the year includes 365 packages of Twinkies, 500 gallons of heating oil, and 12 months of cable TV. Prices in the base year are listed in column (2) of Exhibit 4. The total cost of each product in the base year is found by multiplying price by quantity, as shown in column (3). The cost of the market basket in the base year is shown at the bottom of column (3) to be $1,184.85.

Prices in the current year are listed in column (4). Notice that not all prices changed by the same percentage since the base year. The price of fuel oil increased by 50 percent, but the price of Twinkies declined. The cost of purchasing that same basket in the current year increased to $1,398.35, shown as the sum of column (5). To compute the consumer price index for the current year, we simply divide the cost in the current year by the cost of that same basket in the base year, $1,398.35/$1,184.85, and then multiply by 100. This yields a price index of 118. We could say that between the base period and the current year, the "cost of living" increased by 18 percent, although not all prices increased by the same percentage.

BASE YEAR

The year with which other years are compared when constructing an index; the index equals 100 in the base year

PRICE INDEX

A number that shows the average price of goods; changes in a price index over time show changes in the economy's average price level

CONSUMER PRICE INDEX, OR CPI

A measure of inflation based on the cost of a fixed market basket of goods and services

EXHIBIT 3	Year	(1) Price of Bread in Current Year	(2) Price of Bread in Base Year	(3) Price Index (3) = (1)/(2) x 100
	2003	$1.25	$1.25	100
Hypothetical Example of a Price Index (base year = 2003)	2004	1.30	1.25	104
	2005	1.40	1.25	112

The price index equals the price in the current year divided by the price in the base year, all multiplied by 100.

EXHIBIT 4

Hypothetical Market Basket Used to Develop the Consumer Price Index

The cost of a market basket in the current year, shown at the bottom of column (5), sums the quantities of each item in the basket, shown in column (1), times the price of each item in the current year, shown in column (4).

Product	(1) Quantity in Market Basket	(2) Prices in Base Year	(3) Cost of Basket in Base Year (3) = (1) x (2)	(4) Prices in Current Year	(5) Cost of Basket in Current Year (5) = (1) x (4)
Twinkies	365 packages	$ 0.89/package	$ 324.85	$ 0.79	$ 288.35
Fuel Oil	500 gallons	1.00/gallon	500.00	1.50	750.00
Cable TV	12 months	30.00/month	360.00	30.00	360.00
			$1,184.85		$1,398.35

The federal government uses the 36 months of 1982, 1983, and 1984 as the base period for calculating the CPI for a market basket consisting of hundreds of goods and services. The CPI is reported monthly based on prices collected from about 23,000 sellers across the country in 87 metropolitan areas. In reality, each household consumes a unique market basket, so we could theoretically develop about 110 million CPIs—one for each household.

Problems with the CPI

Economics in the Movies

There is no perfect way to measure changes in the price level. As we have already seen, the quality and variety of some products are improving all the time, so some price increases may be as much a reflection of improved quality as of inflation. Thus, there is a *quality bias* in the CPI, because it assumes that the quality of the market basket remains relatively constant over time. *As a result of ignoring quality improvements, the CPI overstates the true extent of inflation.*

The CPI tends to overstate inflation for another reason. Recall that the CPI holds constant over time the kind and amount of goods and services in the typical market basket. Because not all items in the market basket experience the same rate of price change, relative prices change over time. A household would respond to changes in relative prices by purchasing less of the more expensive products and more of the cheaper products. But, because the CPI holds the market basket constant for long periods, the CPI is slow to incorporate consumer responses to changes in relative prices. *The CPI calculations, by not allowing households to shift away from goods that have become more costly, overestimates the true extent of inflation experienced by the typical household.*

The CPI has also failed to keep up with the consumer shift toward discount stores such as Wal-Mart, Target, and Home Depot. Government statisticians consider goods sold by discounters as different from goods sold by regular retailers. Hence, the discounter's lower price does not translate into a reduction in the cost of living.

Experts conclude the CPI has overestimated inflation by about 1 percent per year. This problem is of more than academic concern because changes in the CPI determines changes in tax brackets and in an array of payments, including wage agreements that include a cost-of-living adjustment, Social Security benefits, and welfare benefits. In fact, about 30 percent of federal outlays are tied to changes in the CPI. A 1 percent correction in the upward bias of the CPI would save the federal budget nearly $200 billion annually by 2010.

Overstating the CPI also distorts other measures, such as wages, that use the CPI to adjust for inflation. For example, based on the official CPI, the average real wage in the U.S. economy fell by a total of about 2 percent in the last two decades. But if the CPI overstated inflation by 1 percent per year, as researchers believe, then the average real wage, instead of dropping by 2 percent, actually increased by about 20 percent. The Bureau of Labor Statistics, the group that estimates the CPI, is now working on these problems and has introduced an experimental version of the CPI that would reduce measured inflation. One experiment uses scanner data at supermarkets to find out how consumers respond, for example, to a rise in the price of romaine lettuce relative to iceberg lettuce, two products assumed to be reasonable substitutes.

The GDP Price Index

GDP PRICE INDEX

A comprehensive price index of all goods and services included in the gross domestic product

Price indexes are weighted sums of various prices. Whereas the CPI focuses on just a sample of consumer purchases, a more complex and more comprehensive price index, the **GDP price index,** measures the average price of all goods and services produced in the economy. To calculate the GDP price index, we use the formula

$$\text{GDP price index} = \frac{\text{Nominal GDP} \times 100}{\text{Real GDP}}$$

where nominal GDP is the dollar value of GDP measured in current-year prices, and real GDP is the dollar value of GDP measured in base-year prices. If we know both nominal GDP and real GDP, then finding the GDP price index is easy. Nominal GDP is simply current-dollar GDP. The challenge is finding real GDP. Any measure of real GDP is constructed as the weighted sum of thousands of different goods and services produced in the economy. The question is what weights, or prices, to use. Between World War II and 1995, the Bureau of Economic Analysis (BEA) used prices for a particular base year (most recently 1987) to estimate real GDP. In this case, the quantity of each output in a particular year was valued by using the 1987 price of each output. So real GDP in, say, 1994 was the sum of 1994 output valued at 1987 prices.

Moving from Fixed Weights to Chain Weights

CHAIN-WEIGHTED SYSTEM

An index that adjusts the weights from year to year in calculating a price index, thereby getting rid of much of the bias caused by a fixed-price weighting system

Estimating real GDP by using prices from a base year yields an accurate measure of real GDP as long as the year in question is close to the base year. But BEA used prices that prevailed in 1987 to value production from 1929 to 1995. In early 1996, BEA switched from a fixed-price weighting system to a **chain-weighted system,** using a complicated process that changes price weights from year to year. All you need to know is that the chain-weighted real GDP adjusts the weights more or less continuously from year to year, reducing the bias caused by a fixed-price weighting system.

Even though the chain-type index adjusts the weights from year to year, any index, by definition, must still use some year as an anchor, or reference point—that is, any index must answer the question, "Compared to what?" To provide such a reference point, BEA measures U.S. real GDP and its components in *chained (2000) dollars.* Exhibit 5 presents current-dollar estimates of GDP as well as chained (2000) dollar estimates of real GDP. The blue line indicates current-dollar GDP, or nominal GDP, since 1959. The red line indicates real GDP since 1959, or GDP measured in chained (2000) dollars. The two lines intersect in 2000, because that's when real GDP equaled nominal GDP. Nominal, or current-dollar, GDP is be-

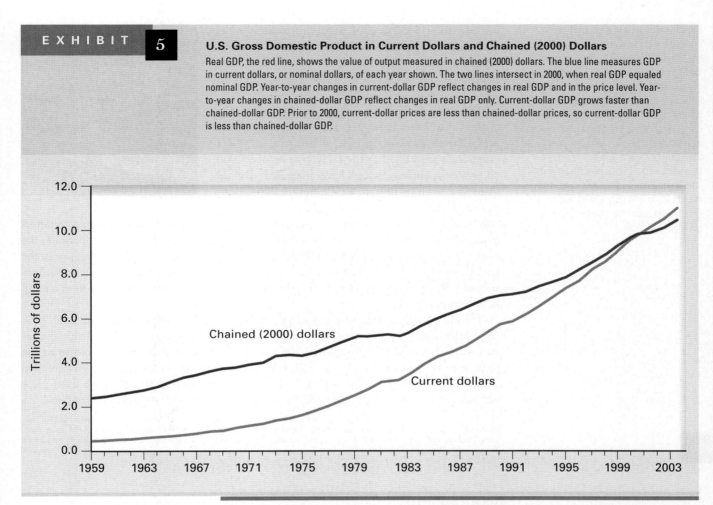

EXHIBIT 5

U.S. Gross Domestic Product in Current Dollars and Chained (2000) Dollars

Real GDP, the red line, shows the value of output measured in chained (2000) dollars. The blue line measures GDP in current dollars, or nominal dollars, of each year shown. The two lines intersect in 2000, when real GDP equaled nominal GDP. Year-to-year changes in current-dollar GDP reflect changes in real GDP and in the price level. Year-to-year changes in chained-dollar GDP reflect changes in real GDP only. Current-dollar GDP grows faster than chained-dollar GDP. Prior to 2000, current-dollar prices are less than chained-dollar prices, so current-dollar GDP is less than chained-dollar GDP.

Source: Based on annual estimates from the Bureau of Economic Analysis, U.S. Department of Commerce. For the latest data, go to http://www.bea.doc.gov/bea/pubs.htm.

low real GDP in years prior to 2000 because real GDP is based on chained (2000) prices, which on average are higher than prices prior to 2000. Current-dollar GDP reflects growth in real GDP and in the price level. Chained-dollar GDP reflects growth only in real GDP. So current-dollar GDP grows faster than chained-dollar GDP. An example of the bias resulting from a fixed-price weighting system involves computers, as discussed in this closing case study.

Computer Prices and GDP Estimation

As noted already, until 1996, federal statisticians based their real GDP estimates on 1987 prices. Relying on such estimates, economists believed that the recovery that began in the spring of 1991 was spurred by investment spending, especially spending on new computers. In this case study, we reconsider the role of computer production as an economic stimulus to that recovery.

Computer prices have fallen by an average of about 13 percent per year since 1982. Based on this rate of decline, a computer that cost, say, $10,000 in 1982 cost about $5,000 in 1987

*Case***Study**

Public Policy

eActivity
The Bureau of Economic Analysis is charged with estimating GDP and its components. You can find selected

National Income and Product Account tables at http://www.bea.doc.gov/bea/dn/nipaweb/index.asp. Summary Table S1 tells you by how much each component has grown. Summary Table S2 shows the contribution of each component to GDP growth. Can you explain the difference between these two types of statistics? The BEA also produces the monthly report, *Survey of Current Business,* with articles describing and interpreting national income data. The current issue and back issues are accessible through http://www.bea.doc.gov/bea/pubs.htm.

but only about $450 in 2004. According to these prices, that computer cost about the same in 1982 as a Chrysler minivan; in 2004, you could buy about 50 computers for the cost of a minivan. So the price of computers fell sharply between 1982 and 2004.

The sharp decline in computer prices spurred purchases for offices and homes. Suppose computer sales jumped from 1 million in 1982 to 5 million in 2004. If computers are valued at their 1987 price of $5,000, computer spending would have increased fivefold, from $5 billion in 1982 to $25 billion in 2004. But if priced in current, or nominal, dollars, of $10,000 in 1982 and $450 in 2004, computer spending would have declined more than three quarters from $10 billion in 1982 to only $2.2 billion in 2004. Using the 1987 price understates the value of computer production in 1982, overstates it in 2004, and thus exaggerates the growth between 1982 and 2004. It was this exaggeration in the value of computer production in 1991 that led to the incorrect belief that the recovery resulted primarily from a jump in investment spending.

The chain-weighted measure adjusts for some of the distortion that comes from using 1987 fixed prices. According to the chain-weighted measure, investment grew less during the recovery that began in 1991 than during the four previous recoveries, so investment turned out to be less of a factor in stimulating economic expansion than it had been in the previous two decades. The chain-weighted system, although it is more complicated than the fixed-price weighting system, provides a more reliable picture of year-to-year changes in real output.

Sources: "Dell Says That Revenues Are Ahead of Plan, But Profits Trail," *Wall Street Journal,* 9 April 2004; "Improved Estimates of the National Income and Product Accounts for 1959–95: Results of the Comprehensive Revision," *Survey of Current Business* 76 (January/February 1996); *Survey of Current Business* 84 (April 2004); and Dell's Web site at http://www.dell.com/. The home page for the Bureau of Economic Analysis is at http://www.bea.doc.gov/.

Conclusion

This chapter examined how GDP is measured and how it's adjusted for changes in the price level over time. The national income accounts have limitations, but they offer a reasonably accurate picture of year-to-year movements in the economy. The national income accounts are published in much greater detail than this chapter suggests. The appendix provides some flavor of the additional detail available. Subsequent chapters will refer to the distinction between real and nominal values.

SUMMARY

1. The gross domestic product, or GDP, measures the market value of all final goods and services produced during the year by resources located in the United States, regardless of who owns those resources.

2. The expenditure approach to GDP adds the market value of all final goods and services produced in the economy

during the year. The income approach to GDP adds all the income generated as a result of that production.

3. The circular-flow model summarizes the flow of income and spending through the economy. Saving, net taxes, and imports are leakages from the circular flow. These leakages equal the injections into the circular flow from investment, government purchases, and exports.

4. GDP reflects market production. Most household production and the underground economy are not captured by GDP. Improvements in the quality and variety of goods also are often missed in GDP. In other ways GDP may overstate production. GDP fails to subtract for the depreciation of the capital stock or for the depletion of natural resources and fails to account for negative externalities arising from production.

5. Nominal GDP in a particular year values output based on market prices prevailing at the time production occurs. To determine real GDP, nominal GDP must be adjusted for price changes. The consumer price index, or CPI, tracks prices for a basket of goods and services over time. The GDP price index tracks price changes for all output. No adjustment for price changes is perfect, but current approaches offer a reasonable estimate of real GDP over time.

QUESTIONS FOR REVIEW

1. *(National Income Accounting)* Identify the component of aggregate expenditure to which each of the following belongs:

   a. A U.S. resident's purchase of a new automobile manufactured in Japan
   b. A household's purchase of one hour of legal advice
   c. Construction of a new house
   d. An increase in semiconductor inventories over last year's level
   e. A city government's acquisition of 10 new police cars

2. *(National Income Accounting)* Define *gross domestic product*. Determine whether each of the following would be included in the 2004 U.S. gross domestic product:

   a. Profits earned by Ford Motor Company in 2004 on automobile production in Ireland
   b. Automobile parts manufactured in the United States in 2004 but not used until 2005
   c. Social Security benefits paid by the U.S. government in 2004
   d. Ground beef purchased and used by McDonald's in 2004
   e. Ground beef purchased and consumed by a private U.S. household in 2004
   f. Goods and services purchased in the United States in 2004 by a Canadian tourist

3. *(National Income Accounting)* Explain why intermediate goods and services generally are not included directly in GDP. Are there any circumstances under which they would be included directly?

4. *(Leakages and Injections)* What are the leakages from and injections into the circular flow? How are leakages and injections related to the circular flow?

5. *(Investment)* In national income accounting, one component of investment is net changes in inventories. Last year's inventories are subtracted from this year's inventories to obtain a net change. Explain why net inventory increases are counted as part of GDP. Also, discuss why it is not sufficient to measure the level of inventories only for the current year. (Remember the difference between stocks and flows.)

6. *(Limitations of National Income Accounting)* Explain why each of the following should be taken into account when GDP data are used to compare the "level of well-being" in different countries:

   a. Population levels
   b. The distribution of income
   c. The amount of production that takes place outside of markets
   d. The length of the average work week
   e. The level of environmental pollution

7. (*C a s e* **S t u d y**: Tracking a $12 Trillion Economy) Why has it become increasingly difficult for the federal government to monitor economic activity in the United States?

8. *(Nominal GDP)* Which of the following is a necessary condition—something that must occur—for nominal GDP to rise? Explain your answers.

   a. Actual production must increase.
   b. The price level must increase.
   c. Real GDP must increase.
   d. Both the price level and actual production must increase.
   e. Either the price level or real GDP must increase.

9. *(Price Indexes)* Home computers and DVD players have not been part of the U.S. economy for very long. Both goods have been decreasing in price and improving in quality. What problems does this pose for people responsible for calculating a price index?

10. *(GDP and Depreciation)* What is gross about gross domestic product? Could an economy enjoy a constant—or growing—GDP while not replacing worn-out capital?

11. *(Consumer Price Index)* One form of the CPI that has been advocated by lobbying groups is a "CPI for the elderly." The Bureau of Labor Statistics currently produces only indexes for "all urban households" and "urban wage earners and clerical workers." Should the BLS produce such an index for the elderly?

12. *(GDP Price Index)* The health expenditure component of the GDP price index has been rising steadily. How might this index be biased by quality and substitution effects? Are there any substitutes for health care?

13. (*C a s e* **S t u d y :** Computer Prices and GDP Estimation) Compared to the fixed-price weighting system, how does the chain-weighted system better account for the economic incentives provided by price changes?

PROBLEMS AND EXERCISES

14. *(Income Approach to GDP)* How does the income approach to measuring GDP differ from the expenditure approach? Explain the meaning of *value added* and its importance in the income approach. Consider the following data for the selling price at each stage in the production of a 5-pound bag of flour sold by your local grocer. Calculate the final market value of the flour.

Stage of Production	Sale Price
Farmer	$0.30
Miller	0.50
Wholesaler	1.00
Grocer	1.50

15. *(Expenditure Approach to GDP)* Given the following annual information about a hypothetical country, answer questions a through d.

	Billions of Dollars
Personal consumption expenditures	$200
Personal taxes	50
Exports	30
Depreciation	10
Government purchases	50
Gross private domestic investment	40
Imports	40
Government transfer payments	20

a. What is the value of GDP?
b. What is the value of net domestic product?
c. What is the value of net investment?
d. What is the value of net exports?

16. *(Investment)* Given the following data, answer questions a through c.

	Billions of Dollars
New residential construction	$500
Purchases of existing homes	250
Sales value of newly issued stocks and bonds	600
New physical capital	800
Depreciation	200
Household purchases of new furniture	50
Net change in firms' inventories	100
Production of new intermediate goods	700

a. What is the value of gross private domestic investment?
b. What is the value of net investment?
c. Are any intermediate goods counted in gross investment?

17. *(Consumer Price Index)* Calculate a new consumer price index for the data in Exhibit 4 in this chapter. Assume that current-year prices of Twinkies, fuel oil, and cable TV are $0.95/package, $1.25/gallon, and $15.00/month, respec-

tively. Calculate the current year's cost of the market basket and the value of the current year's price index. What is this year's percentage change in the price level compared to the base year?

18. *(Consumer Price Index)* Given the following data, what was the value of the consumer price index in the base year?

Calculate the annual rate of consumer price inflation in 2004 in each of the following situations:

a. The CPI equals 200 in 2003 and 240 in 2004.
b. The CPI equals 150 in 2003 and 175 in 2004.
c. The CPI equals 325 in 2003 and 340 in 2004.
d. The CPI equals 325 in 2003 and 315 in 2004.

EXPERIENTIAL EXERCISES

19. *(Limitations of National Income Accounting)* One often-heard criticism of the U.S. national income accounts is that they ignore the effect of environmental pollution. The World Bank's group on Environmental Economics and Indicators has been investigating ways of assessing environmental degradation. Take a look at their work on "green accounting" at http://lnweb18.worldbank.org/ESSD/envext.nsf/44ByDocName/GreenAccounting. What kinds of problems have they identified, and what proposals have they made to deal with those problems?

20. *(Problems with the CPI)* The importance of the bias in the U.S. consumer price index is reviewed in an article in the June 1997 issue of *Finance and Development* from the International Monetary Fund at http://www.imf.org/external/pubs/ft/fandd/1997/06/pdf/armknech.pdf. Tao Wu of the Federal Reserve Bank of San Francisco discusses current issues with the calculation of the consumer price index at

http://www.frbsf.org/publications/economics/letter/2003/el2003-24.html. What are the criticisms of the CPI as it is now calculated?

21. *(Wall Street Journal)* Data on the consumer price index are released near the middle of each month. Data on GDP are released on the last Friday of each month (in preliminary, revised, and then final form). Analysis of these data releases appears in the first section of the following weekday's *Wall Street Journal*. Look in the Economy section to find the story. What do the latest available data tell you about the current rate of inflation and the current rate of GDP growth? Is the economy in a recession or an expansion?

22. *(Wall Street Journal)* New economic data are regularly reported in the *Wall Street Journal*. Look in section C of the paper (the Money and Investing section) the day after a major piece of economic information was released to see how the stock market reacted to the news.

National Income Accounts

This chapter has focused on the gross domestic product, or GDP, the measure of output that will be of most interest in subsequent chapters. Other economic aggregates also convey useful information and receive media attention. One of these, *net domestic product,* has already been introduced. Exhibit 6 shows that net domestic product equals gross domestic product minus depreciation. In this appendix we examine other aggregate measures.

National Income

So far, we have been talking about the value of production from resources located in the United States, regardless of who owns them. Sometimes we want to know how much American resource suppliers earn for their labor, capital, natural resources, and entrepreneurial ability. **National income** captures all income earned by American-owned resources, whether located in the United States or abroad. To get the net value of production from American-owned resources, we add income earned by American resources abroad and subtract income earned by resources in the United States owned by those outside the country.

National income therefore equals net domestic product plus net earnings from American resources abroad. Exhibit 6

EXHIBIT 6	Deriving Net Domestic Product and National Income (in trillions of dollars)
Gross domestic product (GDP)	$11.00
Minus depreciation	−1.35
Net domestic product	9.65
Plus net earnings of American resources abroad	0.03
National income	$9.68

Source: Figures are current, or nominal, estimates for 2003 from the Bureau of Economic Analysis, U.S. Department of Commerce. For the latest figures, go to http://www.bea.doc.gov/bea/dn/nipaweb/populartables.asp.

shows how to go from net domestic product to national income. We have now moved from gross domestic product to net domestic product to national income. Next we peel back another layer from the onion to arrive at personal income, the income people actually receive.

Personal and Disposable Income

Some of the income received this year was not earned this year, and some of the income earned this year was not received this year by those who earned it. By adding to national income the income received but not earned and subtracting the income earned but not received, we move from national income to the income *received* by individuals, which is called **personal income,** a widely reported measure of economic welfare. The federal government computes and reports personal income monthly.

The adjustment from national income to personal income is shown in Exhibit 7. Income *earned but not received* in the current period includes the employer's share of Social Security taxes, taxes on production (e.g., sales and property taxes) net of to subsidies, corporate income taxes, and undistributed corporate profits, which are profits the firm retains rather than pays out as dividends. Income *received but not earned* in the current period includes government transfer payments, receipts from private pension plans, and interest paid by government and by consumers.

Although business taxes have been considered so far, we have not yet discussed personal taxes, which consist mainly of federal, state, and local personal income taxes and the employee's share of the Social Security tax. Subtracting personal taxes and other government charges from personal income yields *disposable income,* which is the amount available for spending or saving—the amount that can be "disposed of" by the household. Think of disposable income as take-home pay. Exhibit 7 shows that personal income minus personal taxes and other government charges yields disposable income.

Summary of National Income Accounts

Let's summarize the income side of national income accounts. We begin with *gross domestic product,* or *GDP,* the

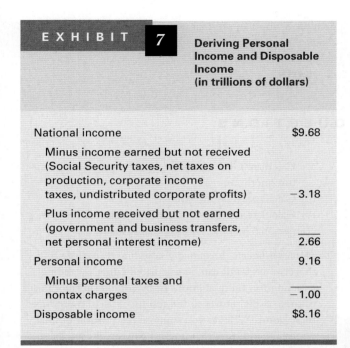

EXHIBIT 7	Deriving Personal Income and Disposable Income (in trillions of dollars)
National income	$9.68
Minus income earned but not received (Social Security taxes, net taxes on production, corporate income taxes, undistributed corporate profits)	−3.18
Plus income received but not earned (government and business transfers, net personal interest income)	2.66
Personal income	9.16
Minus personal taxes and nontax charges	−1.00
Disposable income	$8.16

Source: Figures are current, or nominal, estimates for 2003 from the Bureau of Economic Analysis, U.S. Department of Commerce. For the latest figures, go to http://www.bea.doc.gov/bea/dn/nipaweb/populartables.asp.

market value of all final goods and services produced during the year by resources located in the United States. We subtract depreciation from GDP to yield the *net domestic product.* To net domestic product we add net earnings from American resources abroad to yield *national income.* We obtain *personal income* by subtracting from national income all income earned this year but not received this year (for example, undistributed corporate profits) and by adding all income received this year but not earned this year (for example, transfer payments). By subtracting personal taxes and other government charges from personal income, we arrive at the bottom line: *disposable income,* the amount people are actually free either to spend or to save.

Summary Income Statement of the Economy

Exhibit 8 presents an annual income statement for the entire economy. The upper portion lists aggregate expenditure, which consists of consumption, gross investment, government purchases, and net exports. Because imports exceeded exports, net exports are negative. The aggregate income from this expenditure is allocated as shown in the lower portion of Exhibit 8. Some spending goes to cover depreciation

and net taxes on production, and so is not received as income by anyone. What remains are five income sources: employee compensation, proprietors' income, corporate profits, net interest, and rental income of persons. *Employee compensation,* by far the largest income source, includes both money wages and employer contributions to cover Social Security taxes, medical insurance, and other fringe benefits. *Proprietors' income* includes the earnings of unincorporated businesses. *Corporate profits* are the net revenues received by incorporated businesses but before subtracting corporate income taxes. *Net interest* is the interest received by individuals, excluding interest paid by consumers to businesses and interest paid by government.

Each family that owns a home is viewed as a tiny firm that rents that home to itself. Because homeowners do not, in fact, rent homes to themselves, an imputed rental value is estimated based on what the market rent would be. *Rental*

EXHIBIT 8	Expenditure and Income Statement for the U.S. Economy (in trillions of dollars)
Aggregate Expenditure	
Consumption (C)	$7.76
Gross investment (I)	1.67
Government purchases (G)	2.07
Net exports (X − M)	−0.50
GDP	$11.00
Aggregate Income	
Depreciation	$1.35
Net taxes on production	0.75
Compensation of employees	6.29
Proprietors' income	0.83
Corporate profits	1.02
Net interest	0.60
Rental income of persons	0.16
GDP	$11.00

Source: Figures are current, or nominal, estimates for 2003 from the Bureau of Economic Analysis, U.S. Department of Commerce. For the latest figures, go to http://www.bea.doc.gov/bea/dn/nipaweb/populartables.asp.

income of persons consists primarily of the imputed rental value of owner-occupied housing minus the cost of owning that property (such as property taxes, insurance, depreciation, and interest paid on the mortgage). From the totals in

Exhibit 8, you can see that *aggregate spending in the economy equals the income generated by that spending*, thus satisfying the accounting identity.

APPENDIX QUESTIONS

1. *(National Income Accounting)* Use the following data to answer the questions below:

	Billions of Dollars
Net investment	$110
Depreciation	30
Exports	50
Imports	30
Government purchases	150
Consumption	400
Indirect business taxes (net of subsidies)	35
Income earned but not received	60
Income received but not earned	70
Personal income taxes	50
Employee compensation	455
Corporate profits	60
Rental income	20
Net interest	30
Proprietor's income	40
Net earnings of U.S. resources abroad	40

a. Calculate GDP using the income and the expenditure methods.
b. Calculate gross investment.
c. Calculate net domestic product, national income, personal income, and disposable income.

2. *(National Income Accounting)* According to Exhibit 8 in this chapter, GDP can be calculated either by adding expenditures on final goods or by adding the allocations of these expenditures to the resources used to produce these goods. Why do you suppose the portion of final goods expenditures that goes to pay for intermediate goods or raw materials is excluded from the income method of calculation?

Unemployment and Inflation

W ho among the following would be counted as unemployed: a college student who is not working, a bank teller displaced by an automatic teller machine, Kirsten Dunst between movies, or baseball slugger Barry Bonds in the off-season? What type of unemployment might be healthy for the economy? What's so bad about inflation? Why is unanticipated inflation worse than anticipated inflation? These and other questions are answered in this chapter, where we explore two macroeconomic problems: unemployment and inflation.

To be sure, unemployment and inflation are not the only problems an economy could face. Sluggish growth and widespread poverty are other possibilities. But low unemployment and low inflation go a long way toward reducing other economic problems. Although unemployment and inflation are often related, each initially will

HOMEWORK
Xpress!

Use Homework Xpress! for
economic application,
graphing, videos, and more.

be described separately. The causes of each and the relationship between the two will become clearer as you learn more about how the economy works.

This chapter shows that not all unemployment or all inflation harms the economy. Even in a healthy economy, a certain amount of unemployment reflects the voluntary choices of workers and employers seeking their best options. And inflation that is fully anticipated creates fewer distortions than does unanticipated inflation. Topics discussed include:

- Measuring unemployment
- Frictional, structural, seasonal, and cyclical unemployment
- Full employment

- Sources and consequences of inflation
- Relative price changes
- Nominal and real interest rates

Unemployment

Economics
in the Movies

"They scampered about looking for work. . . . They swarmed on the highways. The movement changed them; the highways, the camps along the road, the fear of hunger and the hunger itself, changed them. The children without dinner changed them, the endless moving changed them."[1] There is no question, as John Steinbeck writes in *The Grapes of Wrath,* that a long stretch of unemployment profoundly affects the individual and the family. The most obvious loss is a steady paycheck, but the unemployed often lose self-esteem and part of their identity as well. According to psychologists, in terms of stressful events, the loss of a good job ranks only slightly below the death of a loved one or a divorce. Moreover, unemployment appears to be linked to a greater incidence of crime and to a variety of afflictions, including heart disease, suicide, and mental illness.[2] No matter how much people complain about their jobs, they rely on those same jobs not only for income but also for their personal identity. When strangers meet, one of the first questions asked is "what do you do?"

In addition to these personal costs, unemployment imposes a cost on the economy as a whole because fewer goods and services are produced. When those who are willing and able to work can't find jobs, that unemployed labor is lost forever. *This lost output coupled with the economic and psychological cost of unemployment on the individual and the family are the true costs of unemployment.* As we begin our analysis, keep in mind that the national unemployment rate reflects millions of individuals with their own stories. As President Harry Truman remarked, "It's a recession when your neighbor loses his job; it's a depression when you lose your own." For some lucky people, unemployment is a brief vacation between jobs. For others, a long stretch can have a lasting effect on family stability, economic welfare, self-esteem, and personal identity.

Measuring Unemployment

The unemployment rate is the most widely reported measure of the nation's economic health. What does the unemployment rate measure? What are the sources of unemployment? How has unemployment changed over time? These are some of the questions explored in this section. Let's first see how to measure unemployment.

---

1. John Steinbeck, *The Grapes of Wrath* (New York: Viking Press, 1939), p. 392.
2. For a study linking a higher incidence of suicides to recessions, see Christopher Ruhm, "Are Recessions Good for Your Health," *Quarterly Journal of Economics* 115 (May 2000): 617–650.

We begin with the U.S. *civilian noninstitutional adult population,* which consists of all civilians 16 years of age and older, except those in prison or in mental hospitals. The adjective *civilian* means the definition excludes those in the military. In this chapter, when we refer to the *adult population,* we mean the civilian noninstitutional adult population. The **labor force** consists of the people in the adult population who are either working or looking for work. *Those who want a job but can't find one are unemployed.* The Bureau of Labor Statistics interviews 55,000 households monthly and counts people as unemployed if they have no job but want one and have looked for work at least once during the preceding four weeks. Thus, the college student, the displaced bank teller, Kirsten Dunst, and Barry Bonds would all be counted as unemployed if they want a job and looked for work in the previous month. The unemployment rate measures the percentage of those in the labor force who are unemployed. Hence, the **unemployment rate,** which is reported monthly, equals the number unemployed—that is, people without jobs who are looking for work—divided by the number in the labor force.

Only a fraction of adults who are not working are considered unemployed. The others may have retired, are students, are caring for children at home, or simply don't want to work. Others may be unable to work because of long-term illness or disability. Some may have become so discouraged by a long, unfruitful job search that they have given up in frustration. These **discouraged workers** have, in effect, dropped out of the labor force, so they are not counted as unemployed. Finally, about one-third of those working part time would prefer to work full time, yet all part-timers are counted as employed. Because the official unemployment rate does not include discouraged workers and counts all part-time workers as employed, it may underestimate the true extent of unemployment in the economy. Later we will consider some factors that work in the opposite direction.

These definitions are illustrated in Exhibit 1, where circles represent the various groups, and the number (in millions) of individuals in each category and subcategory is shown in

LABOR FORCE

Those 16 years of age and older who are either working or looking for work

UNEMPLOYMENT RATE

The number unemployed as a percentage of the labor force

DISCOURAGED WORKERS

Those who drop out of the labor force in frustration because they can't find work

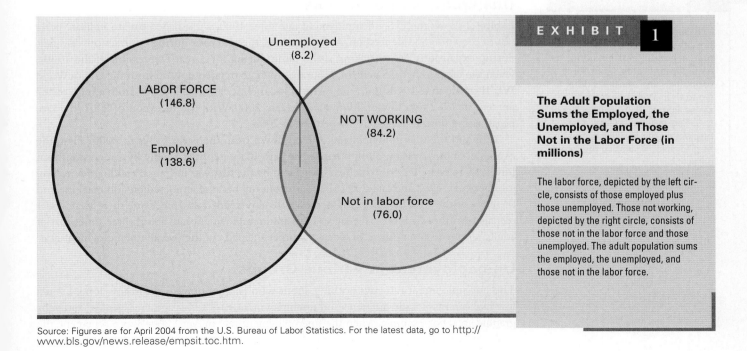

EXHIBIT 1

The Adult Population Sums the Employed, the Unemployed, and Those Not in the Labor Force (in millions)

The labor force, depicted by the left circle, consists of those employed plus those unemployed. Those not working, depicted by the right circle, consists of those not in the labor force and those unemployed. The adult population sums the employed, the unemployed, and those not in the labor force.

Source: Figures are for April 2004 from the U.S. Bureau of Labor Statistics. For the latest data, go to http://www.bls.gov/news.release/empsit.toc.htm.

parentheses. The circle on the left depicts the entire U.S. labor force, including both employed and unemployed people. The circle on the right represents members of the adult population who, for whatever reason, are not working. These two circles combined show the entire adult population. The overlapping area identifies the number of *unemployed* workers—that is, people in the labor force who are not working. The unemployment rate is found by dividing the number unemployed by the number in the labor force. In April 2004, 8.2 million people were unemployed in a labor force of 146.8 million, yielding an unemployment rate of 5.6 percent.

Labor Force Participation Rate

The productive capability of any economy depends in part on the proportion of adults in the labor force, measured as the *labor force participation rate*. In Exhibit 1, the U.S. adult population equals those in the labor force (146.8 million) plus those not in the labor force (76.0 million)—a total of 222.8 million. The **labor force participation rate** therefore equals the number in the labor force divided by the adult population, or 65.9 percent ($=146.8/222.8$). So, on average, two out of three adults are in the labor force. The labor force participation rate increased from about 60 percent in 1970 to about 67 percent in 1990, and has remained relatively steady since then.

One striking development since World War II has been the convergence in the labor force participation rates of men and women. In 1950, only 34 percent of adult women were in the labor force. Today 60 percent are, with the greatest increase among younger women. The labor force participation rate among men has declined from 86 percent in 1950 to about 75 percent today, primarily because of earlier retirement. The participation rate is slightly higher among white males than black males but higher among black females than white females. Finally, the participation rate increases with education—from 44.2 percent for those without a high school diploma to 77.6 percent among those with a college degree.

Unemployment over Time

Exhibit 2 shows the U.S. unemployment rate since 1900, with shaded bars to indicate periods of recession and depression. As you can see, the rate rises during contractions and falls during expansions. Most striking is the jump during the Great Depression of the 1930s, when the rate reached 25 percent. Note that the rate trended upward from the end of World War II in the mid-1940s until the early 1980s; then it came back down, from a high of 9.7 percent in 1982 to a low of 3.9 percent in late 2000. With the recession of 2001, the rate began rising until it peaked at 6.0 percent in 2003.

Why did the unemployment rate trend down from the early 1980s to 2000? First, the overall economy was on a roll during that period, interrupted briefly by a recession from July 1990 to March 1991, which was triggered by the first war in Iraq. By adding 35 million jobs between 1982 and late 2000, the U.S. economy became an incredible job machine and the envy of the world. The unemployment rate also trended down because there were fewer teenagers in the workforce. Teenagers have an unemployment rate about three times that of adults, so the declining share of teenage workers helped cut the overall unemployment rate.

Unemployment in Various Groups

The unemployment rate says nothing about who is unemployed or for how long. Even a low rate can mask wide differences in unemployment rates across age, race, gender, and geographic area. For example, when the unemployment rate in April 2004 was 5.6 percent, the

---

LABOR FORCE PARTICIPATION RATE

The labor force as a percentage of the adult population

HOMEWORK
Xpress!
Ask the Instructor Video

EXHIBIT 2

The U.S. Unemployment Rate Since 1900

Since 1900, the unemployment rate has fluctuated widely, rising during contractions and falling during expansions. During the Great Depression of the 1930s, the rate spiked to 25 percent.

Sources: U.S. Census Bureau, *Historical Statistics of the United States: Colonial Times to 1970* (Washington, D.C. U.S. Government Printing Office, 1975); *Economic Report of the President*, February 2004; and U.S. Bureau of Labor Statistics. For the latest unemployment rate, go to http://www.bls.gov/news.release/empsit.toc.htm.

rate was 16.9 percent among teenagers, 9.7 percent among black workers, and 7.2 percent among people of Hispanic ethnicity. Why are unemployment rates among teenagers so much higher than among older workers? Because young workers enter the job market with little training, they take unskilled jobs, and they are the first to be fired if demand softens. Young workers also move in and out of the job market more frequently during the year as they juggle school demands. Even those who have left school often shop around more than older workers, quitting one job in search of a better one.

Unemployment rates for different groups appear in Exhibit 3. Each panel shows the rate by race and by gender since 1972 (historical data are not available for those of Hispanic ethnicity). Panel (a) shows the rates for people 20 and older, and panel (b) the rates for 16 to 19 year olds. Years of recession are shaded pink. As you can see, rates are higher among black workers than among white, and rates are higher among teenagers than among those 20 and older. During recessions, the rates climbed for all groups. Rates peaked during the recession of 1982 and then trended down. After the recession of the early 1990s, unemployment rates continued downward, with the rate among black people falling in 2000 to the lowest on record. Rates rose again beginning with the recession of 2001.

Unemployment also varies by occupation. Professional and technical workers experience lower unemployment rates than blue-collar workers. Construction workers face high unemployment because that business is both seasonal and subject to wide swings over the business cycle.

Unemployment Varies Across Regions

The unemployment rate varies across the country. For example, in 2004, unemployment rates in Alaska, Michigan, and South Carolina were double those in North Dakota, South

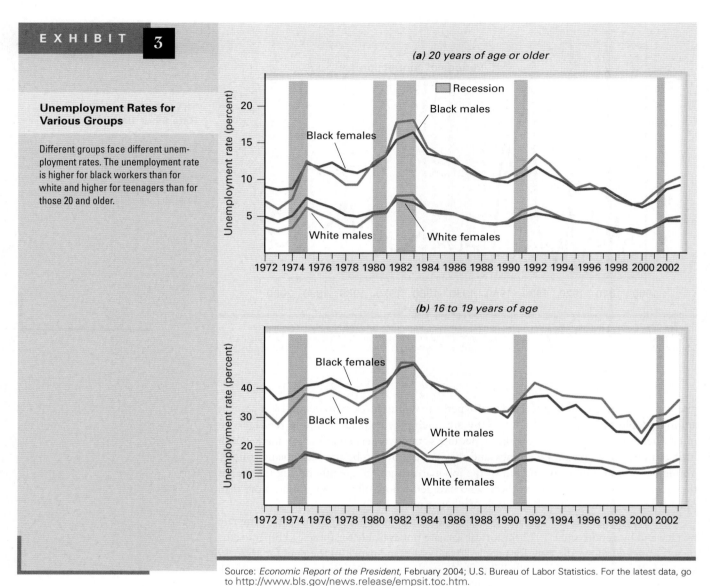

EXHIBIT **3**

Unemployment Rates for Various Groups

Different groups face different unemployment rates. The unemployment rate is higher for black workers than for white and higher for teenagers than for those 20 and older.

(a) *20 years of age or older*

(b) *16 to 19 years of age*

Source: *Economic Report of the President,* February 2004; U.S. Bureau of Labor Statistics. For the latest data, go to http://www.bls.gov/news.release/empsit.toc.htm.

Dakota, and Virginia. Even within states, unemployment varies widely. For example, in Virginia, the unemployment rate in Danville was triple that of Charlottesville. Exhibit 4 shows unemployment rates in 2004 for 26 U.S. metropolitan areas. As you can see, the unemployment in New York City, which was slow to recover from the 2001 recession and the terrorist attacks that year, was more than double the rate in Honolulu. The point is that the national unemployment rate masks wide differences across the country and even across an individual state. The following case study examines the plight of one troubled county in West Virginia.

EXHIBIT 4   **Unemployment Rates Differ Across U.S. Metropolitan Areas**

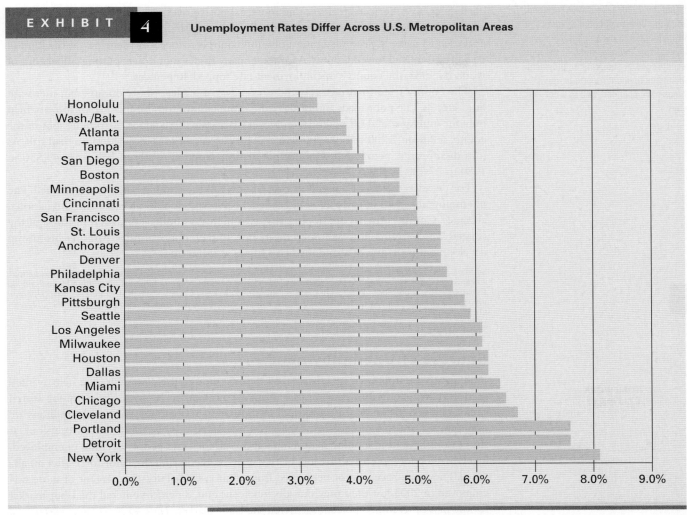

Source: Based on figures for March 2004 from the U.S. Bureau of Labor Statistics. For the latest figures, go to http://www.bls.gov/lau/home.htm.

Poor King Coal

For decades McDowell County, West Virginia, prospered by supplying the coal that fired the nation's steel mills. In 1980 mining jobs were abundant, accounting for half of all jobs in the county. And mining wages were attractive, with average pay exceeding $80,000 in today's dollars. Many young people quit school to become miners (more than half of those over age 25 in 1980 were high school dropouts). Mining companies dominated the county, owning most of the property and paying a chunk of local taxes.

But two developments in the early 1980s hurt McDowell County's coal industry. First, the value of the dollar rose relative to foreign

© Omni Photo Communications/ Index Stock Imagery

Case **Study**

World of Business

eActivity

Carolyn Sherwood-Call of the Federal Reserve Bank of San Francisco has written "The 1980s Divergence in State per Capita Incomes: What Does It Tell Us?" Access her article at http://www. frbsf.org/econrsrch/econrev/96-1/ 14-25.pdf to learn more about the shifting fortunes of various U.S. regions during the 1980s—your own included. Go to the Bureau of Labor Statistics at http://www.bls.gov/schedule/archives/laus_nr.htm and read some of the more recent regional and state employment and unemployment reports to see if things have changed, and in what ways.

currencies, so American steel became more expensive overseas and foreign steel became cheaper here. Steel imports rose substantially, reducing the demand for U.S. steel and the coal used to make it. Second, tighter pollution controls reduced the demand for the kind of coal mined in McDowell County. As a result, many mines shut down, putting miners out of work. By 1983, the county's unemployment rate topped 40 percent.

The county tried to attract new industry—even a nuclear-waste dump—but met with little success. The poor roads and bridges, the mountainous terrain, and a labor force trained only for mining scared off potential employers. Between 1980 and 2000, mining jobs in the county fell from 7,200 to only 700 while all private-sector jobs dropped more than half. As jobs disappeared, people left. County population dropped nearly in half from 49,550 in 1980 to 27,329 in 2000.

For decades, the county put all its eggs in one basket—mining—but that basket fell. The unemployment rate in early 2004 exceeded 11 percent; double the state and the national averages. County officials are hoping that two highways under construction through the rugged West Virginia hills will open the region to new opportunities. Another promising development is the use of abandoned coal mines as fish farms.

Sources: Walter Adams, "Steel," in *The Structure of American Industry*, edited by Walter Adams and James Brock (Englewood Cliffs, N.J.: Prentice Hall, 1995), pp. 93–118; and Beth Gorczyca, "Past Woes, Future Hope," *Herald Dispatch*, 18 September 2000. Information about McDowell County can be found at http://www.wv.gov/county.aspx?regID=3&cID=16. For the latest unemployment rate in the county, go to http://www.state.wv.us/bep/lmi/datarel/drcntyem.htm.

Sources of Unemployment

Pick up any metropolitan newspaper and thumb through the classifieds. The help-wanted section may include thousands of jobs, from accountants to X-ray technicians. Job search sites such as Monster.com list hundreds of thousands of openings. Why, when millions are unemployed, are so many jobs available? To understand this, we must take a closer look at the reasons behind unemployment. Think about all the ways people become unemployed. They may be looking for a first job, or they may be reentering the labor force after an absence. They may have quit or been fired from their last job. Fifty-five percent of those unemployed in 2003 lost their previous job, 9 percent quit, 8 percent entered the labor market for the first time, and 28 percent reentered the labor market. *Thus, 45 percent were unemployed either because they quit jobs or because they were just joining or rejoining the labor force.*

There are four sources of unemployment: frictional, seasonal, structural, and cyclical.

Frictional Unemployment

Just as employers do not always hire the first applicant who comes through the door, job seekers do not always accept the first offer. Both employers and job seekers need time to explore the job market. Employers need time to learn about the talent available, and job seekers need time to learn about employment opportunities. The time required to bring together employers and job seekers causes **frictional unemployment.** Although unemployment often creates economic and psychological hardships, not all unemployment is necessarily bad. Frictional unemployment does not usually last long and it results in a better match between workers and jobs, so the entire economy becomes more efficient. Policy makers are not that concerned with frictional unemployment.

Seasonal Unemployment

Unemployment caused by seasonal changes in labor demand during the year is called **seasonal unemployment**. During cold winter months, demand for farm hands, lifeguards,

Ask the Instructor
Video

FRICTIONAL UNEMPLOYMENT

Unemployment that occurs because job seekers and employers need time to find each other

SEASONAL UNEMPLOYMENT

Unemployment caused by seasonal changes in the demand for certain kinds of labor landscapers, and construction workers shrinks, as it does for dozens of other seasonal occupations. Likewise, tourism in places such as Miami and Phoenix melts in the summer heat. The Christmas season increases the demand for sales clerks, postal workers, and Santa Clauses. Those holding seasonal jobs know those jobs will disappear in the off-season. Some even choose such jobs to complement their lifestyles or academic schedules. To eliminate seasonal unemployment, we would have to outlaw winter and abolish Christmas. Monthly employment statistics are "seasonally adjusted" to smooth out the bulges that result from seasonal factors. Policy makers are not that concerned with seasonal unemployment.

Structural Unemployment

A third reason why job vacancies and unemployment coexist is that unemployed workers often do not have the skills demanded by employers or do not live where their skills are demanded. For example, the Lincoln Electric Company in Euclid, Ohio, could not fill 200 openings because few among the thousands who applied could operate computer-controlled machines. Unemployment arising from a mismatch of skills or geographic location is called **structural unemployment.** *Structural unemployment occurs because changes in tastes, technology, taxes, and competition reduce the demand for certain skills and increase the demand for other skills.* In our dynamic economy, some workers, such as the coal miners in West Virginia, are stuck with skills no longer demanded. Likewise, golf carts replaced caddies, ATMs replaced bank tellers, and office technology is replacing clerical staff. For example, because of email, voice mail, PCs, PDAs, and other wireless devices, the number of secretaries, typists, and administrative assistants in the United States has fallen by half since 1987.

> **STRUCTURAL UNEMPLOYMENT**
>
> Unemployment because (1) the skills in demand do not match those of the unemployed, or (2) the unemployed do not live where the jobs are

Whereas most frictional unemployment is short-term and voluntary, structural unemployment poses more of a problem because workers must develop the skills demanded in the local job market or look elsewhere. For example, unemployed coal miners and bank tellers must seek work in other industries or in other regions. But moving where the jobs are is easier said than done. Most prefer to remain near friends and relatives. Those laid off from good jobs hang around in hopes of getting rehired. Married couples with one spouse still employed may not want to give up one job to seek two jobs elsewhere. Finally, available jobs may be in regions where the living cost is much higher. So those structurally unemployed often stay put. Federal retraining programs aim to reduce structural unemployment.

Cyclical Unemployment

As output declines during recessions, firms reduce their demand for inputs, including labor. **Cyclical unemployment** increases during recessions and decreases during expansions. Between 1932 and 1934, when unemployment averaged about 24 percent, there was clearly much cyclical unemployment. Between 1942 and 1945, when unemployment averaged less than 2 percent, there was no cyclical unemployment. Cyclical unemployment means the economy is operating inside its production possibilities frontier. Government policies that stimulate aggregate demand during recessions aim to reduce cyclical unemployment.

> **CYCLICAL UNEMPLOYMENT**
>
> Unemployment that fluctuates with the business cycle, increasing during contractions and decreasing during expansions

The Meaning of Full Employment

In a dynamic economy such as ours, changes in product demand and in technology continually alter the supply and demand for particular types of labor. Thus, even in a healthy economy, there will be some frictional, structural, and seasonal unemployment. The economy is viewed as operating at *full employment* if there is no cyclical unemployment. When economists talk about "full employment," they do not mean zero unemployment but low unemployment, with estimates ranging from 4 to 6 percent. Even when the economy is at **full employment,** there will be some frictional, structural, and seasonal unemployment. After

> **FULL EMPLOYMENT**
>
> Employment level when there is no cyclical unemployment

all, nearly half of those unemployed have quit their last job or are new entrants or reentrants into the labor force. We can't expect people to find jobs overnight. Many in this group would be considered frictionally unemployed.

Unemployment Compensation

As noted at the outset, unemployment often imposes an economic and psychological hardship. For a variety of reasons, however, the burden of unemployment on the individual and the family may not be as severe today as it was during the Great Depression. Today, many households have two workers in the labor force, so if one loses a job, another is likely to still have one—a job that may provide health insurance and other benefits. Having more than one family member in the labor force cushions the shock of unemployment.

Moreover, unlike the experience during the Great Depression, most who lose their jobs now collect unemployment benefits. In response to the Great Depression, Congress passed the Social Security Act of 1935, which provided unemployment insurance financed by a tax on employers. Unemployed workers who meet certain qualifications can receive **unemployment benefits** for up to six months, provided they actively seek work. During recessions, benefits often extend beyond six months in states with especially high unemployment. Benefits go mainly to people who have lost jobs. Those just entering or reentering the labor force are not covered, nor are those who quit their last job or those fired for just cause, such as excessive absenteeism or theft. Because of these restrictions, about half those unemployed receive benefits.

Unemployment benefits replace on average about 40 percent of a person's take-home pay, with a higher share for those whose jobs paid less. Benefits averaged about $260 per week in 2003. Because these benefits reduce the opportunity cost of remaining unemployed, they may reduce the incentives to find work. For example, if faced with a choice of washing dishes for $240 per week or collecting $200 per week in unemployment benefits, which would you choose? Evidence suggests that those collecting unemployment benefits remain out of work weeks longer than those without benefits. So although unemployment insurance provides a safety net, it may reduce the urgency of finding work, thereby increasing unemployment. On the plus side, because beneficiaries need not take the first job that comes along, unemployment insurance allows for a higher quality search. As a result of a higher quality job search, there is a better match between job skills and job requirements, and this promotes economic efficiency.

International Comparisons of Unemployment

How do U.S. unemployment rates compare with those around the world? Exhibit 5 shows rates since 1982 for the United States, Japan, and the average of four major Western European economies. Over the last two decades, unemployment trended down in the United States, trended up in Japan, and remained high in Western Europe. At the beginning of the period, the United States had the highest rates among the three economies. More recently, the U.S. rate was well below Western Europe's and only slightly above Japan's.

Why are rates so high in Western Europe? The ratio of unemployment benefits to average pay is higher in Western Europe than in the United States, and unemployment benefits last longer there, sometimes years. So those collecting unemployment benefits have less incentive to find work. What's more, government regulations make European employers more reluctant to hire new workers because firing them is difficult. For example, Germany imposes penalties on firms for "socially unjustified" layoffs.

Historically, unemployment has been low in Japan because many firms there offered job security for life. Thus, some employees there who do little or no work are still carried on

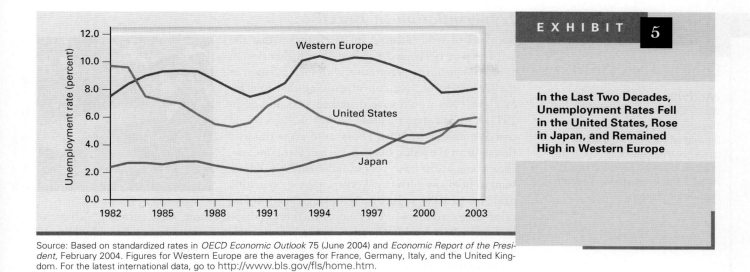

Source: Based on standardized rates in *OECD Economic Outlook* 75 (June 2004) and *Economic Report of the President*, February 2004. Figures for Western Europe are the averages for France, Germany, Italy, and the United Kingdom. For the latest international data, go to http://www.bls.gov/fls/home.htm.

company payrolls. Both labor laws and social norms limit layoffs in Japan. Unemployment has increased there in the last decade because firms went bankrupt.

Problems with Official Unemployment Figures

Official unemployment statistics are not without their problems. As we saw earlier, not counting discouraged workers as unemployed understates unemployment. Official employment data also ignore the problem of **underemployment,** which arises because people are counted as employed even if they can find only part-time work or are vastly overqualified for their job, as when someone with a Ph.D. in literature can find only a clerk's position. Counting overqualified and part-time workers as employed tends to understate the actual amount of unemployment.

On the other hand, because unemployment benefits and most welfare programs require recipients to seek employment, some people may go through the motions of looking for work just to qualify for benefits. If they do not in fact want a job, counting them as unemployed overstates actual unemployment. Likewise, some people who would prefer to work part time can find only full-time jobs, and some forced to work overtime and weekends would prefer to work less. To the extent that people must work more than they want to, the official unemployment rate overstates the actual rate. Finally, people in the underground economy may not admit they have jobs because they are breaking the law. *On net, however, because discouraged workers aren't counted as unemployed and because underemployed workers are counted as employed, most experts believe that official U.S. unemployment figures tend to underestimate unemployment.* Still, the size of this underestimation may not be large. For example, counting discouraged workers as unemployed would have raised the unemployment rate in April 2004 from 5.6 percent to 5.9 percent.

Despite these qualifications and limitations, the unemployment rate is a useful measure of trends over time. We turn next to another major problem: inflation.

Inflation

As noted already, *inflation* is a sustained increase in the economy's average price level. Let's begin with a case study that underscores the cost of high inflation.

UNDEREMPLOYMENT

Workers are overqualified for their jobs or work fewer hours than they would prefer

Bringing Theory to Life

*e*Activity

What's happening in Brazil? Look at the Economic Bulletin from the Brazilian Development Bank at http://www. bndes.gov.br/english/bndes/synop.pdf to access the latest news and reports on the economic situation and current stabilization policies.

Hyperinflation in Brazil

Six years of wild inflation in Brazil meant that the price level in 1994 was *3.6 million* times higher than in 1988! To put this in perspective, with such inflation in the United States, a gallon of gasoline that sold for $1.25 in 1988 would have soared to $4.5 million in 1994. A pair of jeans that sold for $25 in 1988 would cost $90 million in 1994. Those were crazy times in Brazil. With the value of their currency, the *cruzeiro*, cheapening by the hour, people understandably did not want to hold any currency. Workers insisted on getting paid at least daily, immediately buying things before prices increased more or exchanging their cruzeiros for a more stable currency, such as the U.S. dollar. With such wild inflation, everyone, including merchants, had difficulty keeping up with prices. Different price increases among sellers of the same product encouraged buyers to shop around more.

The exploding price level meant even the simplest transactions required mountains of cash. Think again in terms of dollars. As a consequence of such inflation, dinner for two would cost more than $120 million. Such a stack of $100 bills would weigh more than a ton, literally. Because carrying enough money for even modest purchases became physically impossible, currency was issued in ever larger denominations. Between the mid-1980s and 1994, new denominations were issued five times, each a huge multiple of the previous one. For example, the new *cruzeiro real* issued in 1994 exchanged for 2,750 of the cruzeiro it replaced. Larger denominations facilitated purchases. Still, lugging money around, searching for the lowest price, and generally obsessing about money sucked up time and energy and, in the process, reduced productivity. This focus on money was rational for each individual but wasteful for the economy as a whole.

Since 1994 inflation in Brazil has dropped to single digits (the rate in 2004 was down to 6 percent). Fernando Henrique Cardoso, the finance minister in 1994, became a national hero for taming inflation. He was elected president in1994 and reelected in 1998. Although Brazil ended its inflation nightmare, hyperinflation is usually a problem somewhere in the world. The latest casualty was Zimbabwe, where the price level quadrupled in 2003.

Sources: "Battle Begins for Cardoso's Successor," *Economist*, 6 January 2001; "Emerging Market Indicators," *Economist*, 14 May 2004; and "Brazil," *Britannica Book of the Year* (Chicago: Encyclopedia Britannica, 1995). For more on the Brazilian economy, go to http://www.latin-focus.com/latinfocus/countries/brazil/brazil.htm.

HYPERINFLATION

A very high rate of inflation

DEFLATION

A sustained decrease in the price level

DISINFLATION

A reduction in the rate of inflation

We have already discussed inflation in different contexts. If the price level bounces around—moving up one month, falling back the next month—any particular increase in the price level would not necessarily be called inflation in a meaningful sense. We typically measure inflation on an annual basis. The annual *inflation rate* is the percentage increase in the average price level from one year to the next. For example, between January 2003 and January 2004, the U.S. *consumer price index* increased 1.8 percent. Extremely high inflation, as in Brazil, is called **hyperinflation.** A sustained *decrease* in the average price level is called **deflation,** as occurred in the United States during the Great Depression and most recently in Japan, Hong Kong, and Israel. And a reduction in the rate of inflation is called **disinflation**, as occurred in the United States during the first half of the 1980s and first half of the 1990s.

In this section, we first consider two sources of inflation. Then, we examine the extent and consequences of inflation in the United States and around the world.

Two Sources of Inflation

Inflation is a sustained increase in the economy's price level; it results from an increase in aggregate demand, a decrease in aggregate supply, or both. Panel (a) of Exhibit 6 shows that an increase in aggregate demand raises the economy's price level from P to P'. In such cases, a shift to the right of the aggregate demand curve *pulls up* the price level. Inflation resulting from increases in aggregate demand is called **demand-pull inflation.** To generate continuous demand-pull inflation, the aggregate demand curve would have to keep shifting out along a given aggregate supply curve. Rising U.S. inflation during the late 1960s resulted from demand-pull inflation, when federal spending for the Vietnam War and expanded social programs boosted aggregate demand.

Alternatively, inflation can arise from reductions in aggregate supply, as shown in panel (b) of Exhibit 6, where a leftward shift of the aggregate supply curve raises the price level. For example, crop failures and OPEC price hikes reduced aggregate supply during 1974 and 1975, thereby raising the price level. Inflation stemming from decreases in aggregate supply is called **cost-push inflation,** suggesting that increases in the cost of production *push up* the price level. Prices increase and real GDP decreases, a combination identified earlier as *stagflation*. Again, to generate sustained and continuous cost-push inflation, the aggregate supply curve would have to keep shifting left along a given aggregate demand curve.

DEMAND-PULL INFLATION

A sustained rise in the price level caused by a rightward shift of the aggregate demand curve

COST-PUSH INFLATION

A sustained rise in the price level caused by a leftward shift of the aggregate supply curve

---

E X H I B I T 6   **Inflation Caused by Shifts of Aggregate Demand and Aggregate Supply Curves**

Panel (a) illustrates demand-pull inflation. An outward shift of the aggregate demand to AD' "pulls" the price level up from P to P'. Panel (b) shows cost-push inflation. A decrease of aggregate supply to AS' "pushes" the price level up from P to P'.

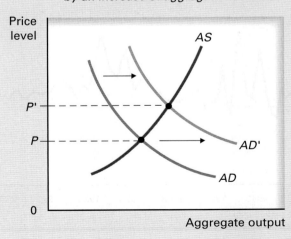

(a) *Demand-pull inflation: inflation induced by an increase of aggregate demand*

(b) *Cost-push inflation: inflation induced by a decrease of aggregate supply*

A Historical Look at Inflation and the Price Level

Economics in the Movies

The consumer price index is the price measure you most often encounter, so it gets attention here. As you learned in the previous chapter, the *consumer price index,* or *CPI,* measures the cost of a market basket of consumer goods and services over time. Exhibit 7 shows prices in the United States since 1913, using the consumer price index. Panel (a) shows the price *level,* measured by an

EXHIBIT 7

Consumer Price Index Since 1913

Panel (a) shows that, despite fluctuations, the price level, as measured by the consumer price index, was lower in 1940 than in 1920. Since 1940, the price level has risen nearly every year. Panel (b) shows the annual rate of change in the price level. Since 1948, the inflation rate has averaged 3.9 percent annually.

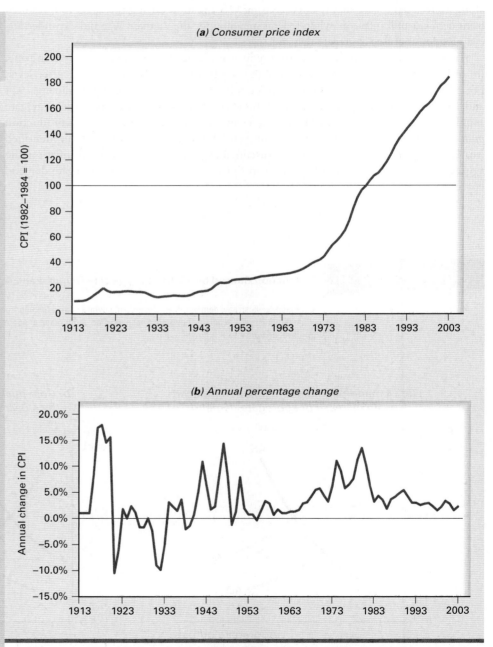

Source: The CPI home page of the U.S. Bureau of Labor Statistics is at http://www.bls.gov/cpi/home.htm. Go there for the latest figures.

index relative to the base period of 1982 to 1984. As you can see, the price level was lower in 1940 than in 1920. Since 1940, however, it has risen steadily, especially during the 1970s.

People are concerned less about the price level and more about year-to-year changes in that level. The lower panel shows the annual *rate of change* in the CPI, or the annual rate of *inflation* or *deflation*. The decade of the 1970s was not the only period of high inflation. Inflation exceeded 10 percent from 1916 to 1919 and in 1947—periods associated with world wars. Prior to the 1950s, high inflation was war related and was usually followed by deflation. Such an inflation-deflation cycle stretches back over the last two centuries. In fact, between the Revolutionary War and World War II, the price level fell in about as many years as it rose. At the end of World War II, the price level was about where it stood at the end of the Civil War.

So fluctuations in the price level are nothing new. But prior to World War II, years of inflation and deflation balanced out over the long run. Therefore, people had good reason to believe the dollar would retain its purchasing power over the long term. Since the end of World War II, however, the CPI has increased by an average of 3.9 percent per year. That may not sound like much, but it translates into an *eightfold* increase in the consumer price index since 1947. *Inflation erodes confidence in the value of the dollar over the long term.*

Anticipated Versus Unanticipated Inflation

What is the effect of inflation on the economy? *Unanticipated inflation* creates more problems than *anticipated inflation*. To the extent that inflation is higher or lower than anticipated, it arbitrarily creates winners and losers. If inflation is higher than expected, the winners are buyers who agreed to a price that anticipated lower inflation. The losers are those who agreed to sell at that price. If inflation is lower than expected, the situation is reversed: The winners are sellers who agreed to a price that anticipated higher inflation, and the losers are buyers who agreed to that price.

Suppose inflation is expected to be 3 percent next year, and you agree to a 4 percent increase in your nominal, or money, wage. You expect your *real* wage—that is, your wage measured in dollars of constant purchasing power—to increase by 1 percent. If inflation turns out to be 3 percent, you and your employer will both be satisfied with your nominal wage increase of 4 percent. If inflation turns out to be 5 percent, your real wage will fall by 1 percent, so you will be a loser and your employer a winner. If inflation turns out to be only 1 percent, your real wage will increase by 3 percent, so you will be a winner and your employer a loser. *The arbitrary gains and losses arising from unanticipated inflation is one reason inflation is so unpopular.* Inflation just doesn't seem fair.

The Transaction Costs of Variable Inflation

During long periods of price stability, people correctly believe that they can predict future prices and can therefore plan accordingly. If inflation changes unexpectedly, however, the future is cloudier, so planning gets harder. Uncertainty about inflation undermines money's ability to link the present with the future. Firms dealing with the rest of the world face an added burden. They must not only plan for U.S. inflation, they must also anticipate how the value of the dollar might change relative to foreign currencies. Inflation uncertainty and the resulting exchange-rate uncertainty complicate international transactions. In this more uncertain environment, managers must shift their attention from production decisions to anticipating the effects of inflation and exchange-rate changes on the firm's finances. Market transactions, particularly long-term contracts, become more complicated as inflation becomes more unpredictable. Some economists believe that the high and variable U.S. inflation during the 1970s and early 1980s cut economic growth during those periods.

Inflation Obscures Relative Price Changes

Even with no inflation, some prices would increase and some would decrease, reflecting normal market activity. For example, since 1980 the U.S. price level doubled, yet the prices of color televisions, computers, phone service and many other products fell sharply. Because the prices of various goods change by different amounts, *relative prices* change. Consider price changes over a longer period. In the last hundred years, consumer prices overall increased about 2,000 percent, but the price of a hotel room in New York City jumped 7,500 percent, while the price of a three-minute phone call from New York to Chicago dropped 99 percent. Whereas the economy's price level describes the exchange rate between a market basket and *money*, relative prices describe the exchange rate between goods—that is, how much one good costs compared to another.

Inflation does not necessarily cause a change in relative prices, but it can obscure that change. During periods of volatile inflation, there is greater uncertainty about the price of one good relative to another—that is, about relative prices. But relative price changes are important for allocating the economy's resources efficiently. If all prices moved together, suppliers could link the selling prices of their goods to the overall inflation rate. Because prices usually do not move in unison, however, tying a particular product's price to the overall inflation rate may result in a price that is too high or too low based on market conditions. The same is true of agreements to link wages with inflation. If the price of an employer's product grows more slowly than the rate of inflation in the economy, the employer may be hard-pressed to increase wages by the rate of inflation. Consider the problem confronting oil refiners who signed labor contracts agreeing to pay their workers cost-of-living wage increases. In some years, those employers had to provide pay increases at a time when the price of oil was falling like a rock.

Inflation Across Metropolitan Areas

Inflation rates differ across regions mostly because of differences in housing prices, which grow faster in some places than in others. But most prices, such as for automobiles, refrigerators, or jeans, do not differ that much across regions. The federal government tracks separate CPIs for each of 26 metropolitan areas. Based on these CPIs from 1994 to 2004, the average annual inflation rate is presented in Exhibit 8. Average annual inflation during the decade ranged from a low of 1.4 percent in Honolulu to a high of 3.2 percent in Denver. Most cities averaged between 2.0 percent and 3.0 percent per year. The median city averaged 2.4 percent per year, which was also the U.S. average annual inflation rate during the 10-year period.

Inflation Across Countries

Exhibit 9 shows annual inflation based on the CPI for the past two decades in the United States, Japan, and the Western European economy, represented here as the average of four major nations. All three economies show a similar trend, with declining inflation, or disinflation, during the first half of the 1980s, rising inflation during the second half of the 1980s to a peak in the early 1990s, and then another trend lower. The overall trend during the two decades was toward lower inflation. Inflation rates in Western Europe were similar to those in the United States. Rates in Japan were consistently lower, even dipping into deflation in recent years. Inflation since 1980 averaged 4.2 percent in Western Europe, 3.6 percent in the United States, and 1.2 percent in Japan.

The quantity and quality of data going into the price index varies across countries. Governments in less-developed countries sample fewer products and measure prices only in the

EXHIBIT	8	Average Annual Inflation from 1994 to 2004 Differed across U.S. Metropolitan Areas

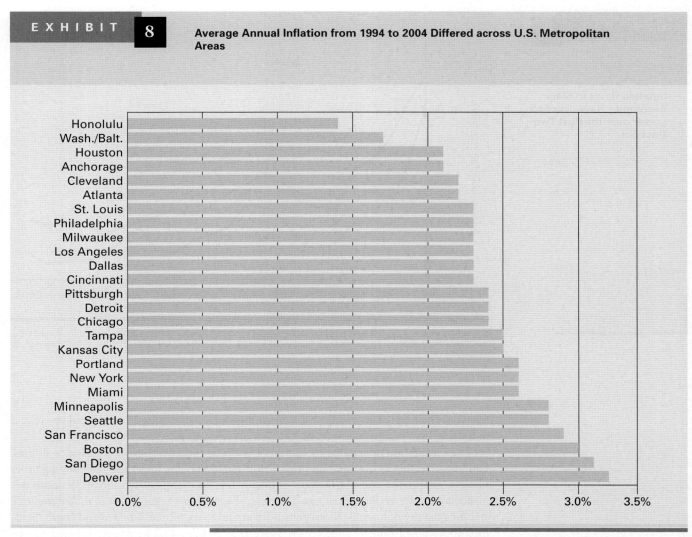

Source: Annual averages for 1994 to 2004 based on CPI estimates from the U.S. Bureau of Labor Statistics. For the latest figures go to http://www.bls.gov/cpi/home.htm and find "Regional Resources."

capital city. Whereas hundreds of items are sampled to determine the U.S. consumer price index, as few as 30 might be sampled in some developing countries.

Inflation and Interest Rates

No discussion of inflation would be complete without some mention of the interest rate. **Interest** is the dollar amount paid by borrowers to lenders. Lenders must be rewarded for forgoing present consumption, and borrowers are willing to pay a premium to spend now. The **interest rate** is the amount paid per year as a percentage of the amount borrowed. For example, an interest rate of 5 percent means $5 per year on a $100 loan. The greater the interest rate, other things constant, the greater the reward for lending money. The amount of money people are willing to lend, called *loanable funds,* increases as the interest rate rises, other things

INTEREST

The dollar amount paid by borrowers to lenders

INTEREST RATE

Interest per year as a percentage of the amount loaned

Inflation Rates in Major Economies Have Trended Lower over the Past Two Decades

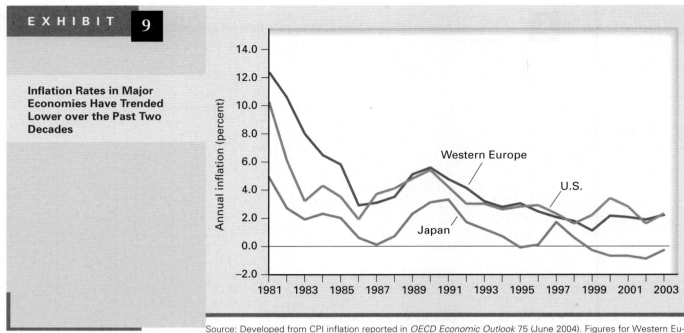

Source: Developed from CPI inflation reported in *OECD Economic Outlook* 75 (June 2004). Figures for Western Europe are the averages for France, Germany, Italy, and the United Kingdom. For the latest data, go to http://www.bls.gov/fls/home.htm.

constant. The supply curve for loanable funds therefore slopes upward, as indicated by curve *S* in Exhibit 10.

These funds are demanded by households, firms, and governments to finance homes, buildings, machinery, college, and other major purchases. The lower the interest rate, other things constant, the cheaper the cost of borrowing. So the quantity of loanable funds demanded increases as the interest rate decreases, other things constant. That is, the interest rate and the quantity of loanable funds demanded are inversely related. The demand curve therefore slopes downward, as indicated by curve *D* in Exhibit 10. The downward-sloping demand curve and the upward-sloping supply curve intersect to yield the equilibrium nominal rate of interest, *i*.

NOMINAL INTEREST RATE

The interest rate expressed in current dollars as a percentage of the amount loaned; the interest rate on the loan agreement

REAL INTEREST RATE

The interest rate expressed in dollars of constant purchasing power as a percentage of the amount loaned; the nominal interest rate minus the inflation rate

The **nominal interest rate** measures interest in terms of the current dollars paid. The nominal rate is the one that appears on the loan agreement; it is the rate discussed in the news media and is often of political significance. The **real interest rate** equals the nominal rate minus the inflation rate:

$$\text{Real interest rate} = \text{Nominal interest rate} - \text{Inflation rate}$$

For example, if the nominal interest rate is 5 percent and the inflation rate is 3 percent, the real interest rate is 2 percent. With no inflation, the nominal rate and the real rate would be identical. But with inflation, the nominal rate exceeds the real rate. If inflation is unexpectedly high—higher, for example, than the nominal rate—then the real interest rate would be negative. In this case, the nominal interest earned for lending money would not even cover the loss in spending power caused by inflation. Lenders would lose purchasing power. This is why lenders and borrowers are concerned more about the real rate than the nominal rate. The real interest rate, however, is known only after the fact—that is, only after inflation actually occurs.

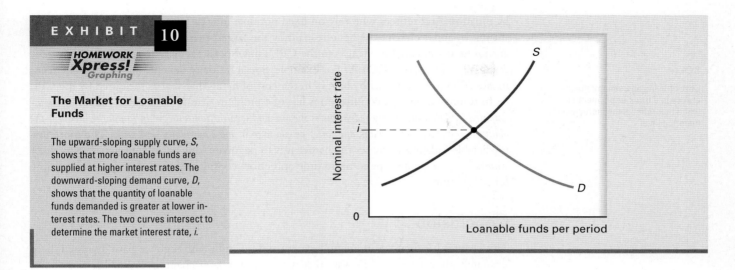

The Market for Loanable Funds

The upward-sloping supply curve, *S*, shows that more loanable funds are supplied at higher interest rates. The downward-sloping demand curve, *D*, shows that the quantity of loanable funds demanded is greater at lower interest rates. The two curves intersect to determine the market interest rate, *i*.

Because the future is uncertain, lenders and borrowers must form expectations about inflation, and they base their willingness to lend and borrow on these expectations. The higher the *expected* inflation, the higher the nominal rate of interest that lenders require and that borrowers are willing to pay. Lenders and borrowers base their decisions on the *expected* real interest rate, which equals the nominal rate minus the expected inflation rate.

Although the discussion has implied that there is only one market rate of interest, there are many rates. Rates differ depending on such factors as the duration of the loan, and tax treatment of interest, and the risk the loan will not be repaid.

Why Is Inflation Unpopular?

Whenever the price level increases, spending increases just to buy the same amount of goods and services. If you think of inflation only in terms of spending, you consider only the problem of paying those higher prices. But if you think of inflation in terms of the higher money income that result, you see that higher prices mean higher receipts for resource suppliers, including higher wages for workers. When viewed from the income side, inflation is not so bad.

If every higher price is received by some resource supplier, why are people so troubled by inflation? People view their higher incomes as well-deserved rewards for their labor, but they see inflation as a penalty that unjustly robs them of purchasing power. Most people do not stop to realize that unless their labor productivity increases, higher wages *must* result in higher prices. Prices and wages are simply two sides of the same coin. To the extent that nominal wages on average keep up with inflation, workers retain their purchasing power.

Presidents Ford and Carter could not control inflation and were turned out of office. Inflation slowed significantly during President Reagan's first term, and he won reelection easily, even though the unemployment rate was higher during his first term than during President Carter's tenure. During the 1988 election, George H. W. Bush won in part by reminding voters what inflation was in 1980, the last time a Democrat was president. But he lost his bid at reelection in part because inflation spiked to 6.0 percent in 1990, the highest in a decade. Inflation remained under 3.0 percent during President Clinton's first term, and he was reelected easily. In the elections of 2000 and 2004, inflation was low enough as not to be an issue in either presidential election.

Although inflation affects everyone to some extent, it hits hardest those whose incomes are fixed in nominal terms. For example, pensions are often fixed amounts and are eroded by inflation. And retirees who rely on fixed nominal interest income also see their incomes shrunk by inflation. But the benefits paid by the largest pension program, Social Security, are adjusted annually for changes in the CPI. Thus, Social Security recipients get a cost-of-living adjustment, or a **COLA.** For example, Social Security benefits increased 2.1 percent in late 2003 to keep up with changes in the cost of living that year as measured by the CPI.

COLA

Cost-of-living adjustment; the increase in a transfer payment or wage that reflects the increase in the price level

In summary, anticipated inflation is less of a problem than unanticipated inflation. *Unanticipated inflation arbitrarily redistributes income and wealth from one group to another, reduces the ability to make long-term plans, and forces people to focus more on money and prices.* The more unpredictable inflation becomes the harder it is to negotiate long-term contracts. Productivity suffers because people spend more time and effort coping with inflation, leaving less time for production.

Conclusion

This chapter has focused on unemployment and inflation. Although we have discussed them separately, they are related in ways that will unfold in later chapters. Politicians sometimes add the unemployment rate to the inflation rate to come up with what they refer to as the "misery index." In 1980, for example, an unemployment rate of 7.1 percent combined with a CPI increase of 13.6 percent to yield a misery index of 20.7—a number that helps explain why President Carter was not reelected. By 1984 the misery index had dropped to 11.8, and by 1988 to 9.6; Republicans retained the White House in both elections. In 1992, the index climbed slightly to 10.4 percent, spelling trouble for President George H. W. Bush. And in 1996, the index fell back to 8.4 percent, assuring President Clinton's reelection. During the election of 2000, the misery index was down to 7.7, which should have helped Al Gore, the candidate of the incumbent party. But during the campaign, Gore distanced himself from President Clinton and thus was not able to capitalize on the strong economy. And in the 2004 election the misery index remained about the same as in 2000, which helps explains why challenger John Kerry had difficulty making an issue of the economy.

SUMMARY

1. The unemployment rate is the number of people looking for work divided by the number in the labor force. The unemployment rate masks differences among particular groups and across regions. The rate is lowest among white adults and highest among black teenagers.

2. There are four sources of unemployment. Frictional unemployment arises because employers and qualified job seekers need time to find one another. Seasonal unemployment stems from the effects of weather and the seasons on certain industries, such as construction and agriculture. Structural unemployment arises because changes in tastes, technology, taxes, and competition reduce the demand for certain skills and increase the demand for other skills. And cyclical unemployment results from fluctuations in employment caused by the business cycle. Pol-

icy makers are less concerned with frictional and seasonal unemployment. Full employment occurs when cyclical unemployment is zero.

3. Unemployment often creates both an economic and a psychological hardship. For some, this burden is reduced by an employed spouse and by unemployment insurance. Unemployment insurance provides a safety net for some, but it may also reduce incentives to find work.

4. Inflation is a sustained rise in the average price level. An increase in aggregate demand can cause demand–pull inflation. A decrease in aggregate supply can cause cost-push inflation. Until World War II, both inflation and deflation were common, but since then the price level has increased virtually every year.

5. Anticipated inflation causes fewer distortions in the economy than unanticipated inflation. Unanticipated inflation arbitrarily creates winners and losers, and forces people to spend more time and energy coping with the effects of inflation. The negative effects of high and variable inflation on productivity can be observed in countries that have experienced hyperinflation, such as Brazil.

6. Because not all prices change by the same amount during inflationary periods, people have trouble keeping track of changes in relative prices. Unexpected inflation makes long-term planning more difficult and more risky.

7. The intersection of the demand and supply curves for loanable funds yields the market interest rate. The real interest rate is the nominal interest rate minus the inflation rate. Borrowers and lenders base decisions on the expected real interest rate.

QUESTIONS FOR REVIEW

1. *(Labor Force)* Refer to Exhibit 1 in the chapter to determine whether each of the following statements is true or false.
   a. Some people who are officially unemployed are not in the labor force.
   b. Some people in the labor force are not working.
   c. Everyone who is not unemployed is in the labor force.
   d. Some people who are not working are not unemployed.

2. *(Unemployment in Various Groups)* Does the overall unemployment rate provide an accurate picture of the impact of unemployment on all U.S. population groups?

3. *(Case Study: Poor King Coal)* Was the high unemployment in McDowell County primarily frictional, seasonal, structural, or cyclical? Explain your answer, using the text definitions for these categories of unemployment.

4. *(The Meaning of Full Employment)* When the economy is at full employment, is the unemployment rate at 0 percent? Why or why not? How would a more generous unemployment insurance system affect the full employment figure?

5. *(International Comparisons of Unemployment)* In recent years how has the U.S. unemployment rate compared with rates in other major economies? Why should we be careful in comparing unemployment across countries?

6. *(Official Unemployment Figures)* Explain why most experts believe that official U.S. data underestimate the actual rate of unemployment. What factors could make the official rate overstate the actual unemployment rate?

7. *(Case Study: Hyperinflation in Brazil)* In countries such as Brazil and Russia, which had problems with high inflation, the increased use of another country's currency (such as the U.S. dollar) became common. Why do you suppose this occurred?

8. *(Sources of Inflation)* What are the two sources of inflation? How would you illustrate them graphically?

9. *(Anticipated Versus Unanticipated Inflation)* If actual inflation exceeds anticipated inflation, who will lose purchasing power and who will gain?

10. *(Inflation and Relative Price Changes)* What does the consumer price index measure? Does the index measure changes in relative prices? Why, or why not?

11. *(Inflation and Interest Rates)* Explain as carefully as you can why borrowers would be willing to pay a higher interest rate if they expected the inflation rate to increase in the future.

12. *(Inflation)* Why is a relatively constant and predictable inflation rate less harmful to an economy than a rate that fluctuates unpredictably?

13. *(Inflation)* Why do people dislike inflation?

PROBLEMS AND EXERCISES

14. *(Measuring Unemployment)* Determine the impact on each of the following if 2 million formerly unemployed workers decide to return to school full time and stop looking for work:

    a. The labor force participation rate
    b. The size of the labor force
    c. The unemployment rate

15. *(Measuring Unemployment)* Suppose that the U.S. noninstitutional adult population is 230 million and the labor force participation rate is 67 percent.

    a. What is the size of the U.S. labor force?
    b. If 85 million adults are not working, what is the unemployment rate?

16. *(Types of Unemployment)* Determine whether each of the following would be considered frictional, structural, seasonal, or cyclical unemployment:

    a. A UPS employee who was hired for the Christmas season is laid off after Christmas.
    b. A worker is laid off due to reduced aggregate demand in the economy.
    c. A worker in a video rental stores becomes unemployed as video-on-demand cable service becomes more popular.
    d. A new college graduate is looking for employment.

17. *(Inflation)* Here are some recent data on the U.S. consumer price index:

Year	CPI	Year	CPI	Year	CPI
1988	118.3	1994	148.2	1999	166.6
1989	124.0	1995	152.4	2000	172.2
1990	130.7	1996	156.9	2001	177.1
1991	136.2	1997	160.5	2002	179.9
1992	140.3	1998	163.0	2003	184.0
1993	144.5				

Compute the inflation rate for each year 1989–2003 and determine which were years of inflation. In which years did deflation occur? In which years did disinflation occur? Was there hyperinflation in any year?

18. *(Sources of Inflation)* Using the concepts of aggregate supply and aggregate demand, explain why inflation usually increases during wartime.

19. *(Inflation and Interest Rates)* Using a demand-supply diagram for loanable funds (like Exhibit 10), show what happens to the nominal interest rate and the equilibrium quantity of loans when both borrowers and lenders increase their estimates of the expected inflation rate from 5 percent to 10 percent.

EXPERIENTIAL EXERCISES

20. *(Measuring Unemployment)* The chapter explains the definitions the government employs in measuring unemployment. Interview 10 members of your class to determine their labor market status—employed, unemployed, or not in the labor force. Include yourself, and then compute the unemployment rate and the labor force participation rate for these 11 people.

21. *(International Comparisons of Inflation)* In recent years, how has the U.S. inflation rate compared with rates in other industrial economies? Why should we be careful in comparing inflation rates across countries? The Federal Reserve Bank of St. Louis maintains a Web page devoted to

international economic trends: http://www.stls.frb.org/publications/iet/. Choose two countries and compare their recent inflation experiences. (If you have Adobe Acrobat Reader, you can look at bar charts of the data.)

22. *(Wall Street Journal)* Scan the Economy page in the First Section of today's *Wall Street Journal*. You are almost sure to find a discussion of a policy proposal that will affect unemployment, inflation, or both. Use the aggregate demand and supply model to describe the effect of the proposal—if enacted—on the U.S. unemployment and inflation rates.

23. In January 1997, the U.S. Treasury began issuing inflation-indexed bonds. The bonds pay a fixed rate of interest and

the par value of the bond is increased each year by the rate of inflation, as measured by the CPI. Look in the Money & Investing section of the *Wall Street Journal* on the page where U.S. Treasury bond information is provided and compare the rates on these inflation indexed bonds with nonindexed U.S. Treasury bonds.

HOMEWORK XPRESS! EXERCISES

These exercises require access to McEachern Homework Xpress! If Homework Xpress! did not come with your book, visit **http://homeworkxpress.swlearning.com** *to purchase.*

In the diagram for this exercise, use aggregate demand and aggregate supply curves to show an economy initially at equilibrium and identify the price level as P.

1. Illustrate how demand–pull inflation arises.

2. Illustrate how cost–push inflation arises.

3. Illustrate how a change in aggregate demand would cause deflation.

4. Illustrate how a change in aggregate supply would cause deflation.

Aggregate Expenditure Components

© Wendell Metzen/Index Stock Imagery

When driving through a neighborhood new to you, how can you figure out the income of the residents? How would your spending change if you won the lottery? What's the most predictable and useful relationship in macroeconomics? Why are consumer confidence and business confidence in the economy so important? Answers to these and other questions are addressed in this chapter, which focuses on the makeup of aggregate expenditure. Consumption is the most important, accounting for about two-thirds of all spending. But in this short chapter, we also examine investment, government purchases, and net exports. We will discuss how each relates to income in the economy.

Let's see where this leads. In the next chapter, we combine these spending components to derive the aggregate demand curve. After that, we derive the aggregate supply curve and see how it interacts with the aggregate demand curve to determine the economy's equilibrium levels of price and output. Topics in the current chapter include:

- Consumption and income
- Marginal propensities to consume and to save
- Changes in consumption and in saving

- Investment
- Government purchases
- Net exports
- Composition of spending

Consumption

What if a new college friend invites you home for the weekend? On your first visit, you would get some idea of the family's standard of living. Is their house a mansion, a dump, or in between? Do they drive a new BMW or take the bus? The simple fact is that consumption tends to reflect income. Although some households can temporarily live beyond their means and others still have the first nickel they ever earned, in general consumption depends on income. *The positive and stable relationship between consumption and income, both for the household and for the economy as a whole, is the main point of this chapter.* Got it?

A key decision in the circular-flow model developed two chapters back was how much households spent and how much they saved. Consumption depends primarily on income. Although this relationship seems obvious, the link between consumption and income is fundamental to understanding how the economy works. Let's look at this link in the U.S. economy over time.

A First Look at Consumption and Income

Exhibit 1 shows consumer spending, or consumption, in the United States since 1959 as the red line and *disposable income* as the blue line. Disposable income, remember, is the income actually available for consumption and saving. Data have been adjusted for inflation so that dollars are of constant purchasing power—in this case, 2000 dollars. Notice that consumer spending and disposable income move together over time. Both increased nearly every year, and the relationship between the two appears stable. Specifically, consumer spending has averaged about 90 percent of disposable income. Disposable income minus consumption equals saving. In Exhibit 1, saving is measured by the vertical distance between the two lines. Saving has averaged about 10 percent of disposable income.

Another way to graph the relationship between consumption and income over time is shown in Exhibit 2, where consumption is measured along the vertical axis and disposable income along the horizontal axis. Notice that each axis measures the same units: trillions of 2000 dollars. Each year is depicted by a point that reflects two values: disposable income and consumption. For example, the combination for 1985, identified by the red point, shows that when disposable income (measured along the horizontal axis) was $4.6 trillion, consumption (measured along the vertical axis) was $4.1 trillion.

As you can see, there is a clear and direct relationship between consumption and disposable income, a relationship that should come as no surprise after Exhibit 1. You need little imagination to see that by connecting the dots in Exhibit 2, you could trace a line relating consumption to income. That relationship has special significance in macroeconomics.

EXHIBIT 1

Disposable Income, Consumption, and Saving in the United States

There is a clear and direct relationship between consumption, shown by the red line, and disposable income, shown by the blue line. Disposable income minus consumption equals saving, shown by the vertical distance between disposable income and consumption.

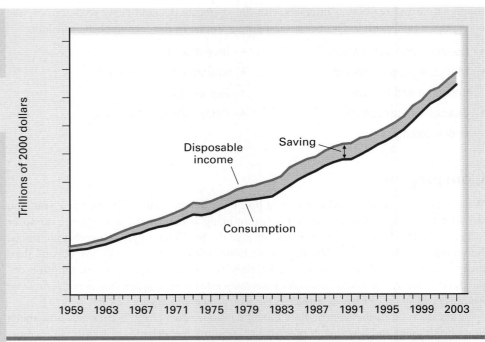

Source: Based on annual estimates from the Bureau of Economic Analysis, U.S. Department of Commerce. For the latest data, go to http://www.bea.doc.gov/bea/pubs.htm.

EXHIBIT 2

U.S. Consumption Depends on Disposable Income

Consumption is on the vertical axis and disposable income on the horizontal axis. Notice that each axis measures trillions of 2000 dollars. For example, in 1985, identified by the red point, consumption was $4.1 trillion and disposable income $4.6 trillion. There is a clear and direct relationship over time between disposable income and consumption. As disposable income increases, so does consumption.

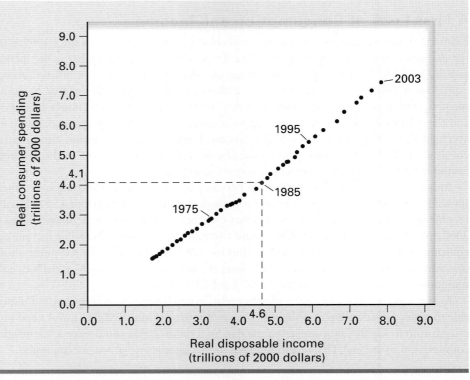

Source: Based on estimates from the Bureau of Economic Analysis, U.S. Department of Commerce. For the latest data, go to http://www.bea.doc.gov/bea/pubs.htm.

The Consumption Function

After examining the link between consumption and income, we found it to be quite stable. Based on their disposable income, households decide how much to consume and how much to save. So consumption depends on disposable income. *Consumption is the dependent variable and disposable income, the independent variable.* Because consumption depends on income, we say that consumption is a *function* of income. Exhibit 3 presents for the economy a hypothetical **consumption function,** which shows that consumption increases with disposable income, assuming other determinants of consumption remain constant. Again, both consumption and disposable income are in real terms, or in inflation-adjusted dollars. Notice that this hypothetical consumption function reflects the historical relationship between consumption and income shown in Exhibit 2.

Marginal Propensities to Consume and to Save

In Chapter 1, you learned that economic analysis focuses on activity at the margin. For example, what happens to consumption if income changes by a certain amount? Suppose U.S. households receive another billion dollars in disposable income. Some of it will be spent on consumption, and the rest will be saved. The fraction of the additional income that is spent is called the marginal propensity to consume. More precisely, the **marginal propensity to consume,** or **MPC,** equals the change in consumption divided by the change in income. Likewise, the fraction of that additional income that is saved is called the marginal propensity to save. More precisely, the **marginal propensity to save,** or **MPS,** equals the change in saving divided by the change in income.

For example, if U.S. income increases from $12.0 trillion to $12.5 trillion, consumption increases by $0.4 trillion and saving by $0.1 trillion. The marginal propensity to consume

CONSUMPTION FUNCTION

The relationship between consumption and income, other things constant

MARGINAL PROPENSITY TO CONSUME (MPC)

The fraction of a change in income that is spent on consumption; the change in consumption divided by the change in income that caused it

MARGINAL PROPENSITY TO SAVE (MPS)

The fraction of a change in income that is saved; the change in saving divided by the change in income that caused it

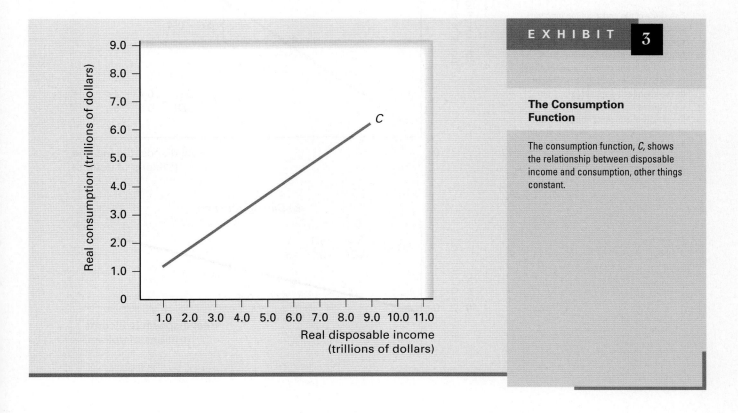

EXHIBIT 3

The Consumption Function

The consumption function, *C*, shows the relationship between disposable income and consumption, other things constant.

equals the change in consumption divided by the change in income. In this case, the change in consumption is $0.4 trillion and the change in income is $0.5 trillion, so the marginal propensity to consume is 0.4/0.5, or 4/5. Income not spent is saved. Saving increases by $0.1 trillion as a result of the $0.5 trillion increase in income, so the marginal propensity to save equals 0.1/0.5, or 1/5. Because disposable income is either spent or saved, the marginal propensity to consume plus the marginal propensity to save must sum to 1. In our example, 4/5 + 1/5 = 1. We can say more generally that $MPC + MPS = 1$.

MPC, MPS, and the Slope of the Consumption and Saving Functions

You may recall from the appendix to Chapter 1 that the slope of a straight line is the vertical distance between any two points divided by the horizontal distance between those same two points. Consider, for example, the slope between points a and b on the consumption function in panel (a) of Exhibit 4, where Δ means "change in." The horizontal distance between these points shows the change in disposable income, denoted as ΔDI—in this case, $0.5 trillion. The vertical distance shows the change in consumption, denoted as ΔC—in

(a) Consumption function

$$MPC = \frac{\Delta C}{\Delta DI} = \frac{0.4}{0.5} = \frac{4}{5}$$

$\Delta C = 0.4$

$\Delta DI = 0.5$

Real disposable income (trillions of dollars)

Consumption (trillions of dollars)

(b) Saving function

$$MPS = \frac{\Delta S}{\Delta DI} = \frac{0.1}{0.5} = \frac{1}{5}$$

$\Delta S = 0.1$

$\Delta DI = 0.5$

Real disposable income (trillions of dollars)

Saving (trillions of dollars)

this case, $0.4 trillion. The slope equals the vertical distance divided by the horizontal distance, or 0.4/0.5, which equals the marginal propensity to consume of 4/5.

Thus, *the marginal propensity to consume is measured graphically by the slope of the consumption function.* After all, the slope is nothing more than the increase in consumption divided by the increase in income. *Because the slope of any straight line is constant everywhere along the line, the MPC for any linear, or straight-line, consumption function is constant at all incomes.* We assume for convenience that the consumption function is a straight line, though it need not be.

Panel (b) of Exhibit 4 presents the **saving function,** *S,* which relates saving to income. The slope between any two points on the saving function measures the change in saving divided by the change in income. For example, between points *c* and *d* in panel (b) of Exhibit 4, the change in income is $0.5 trillion and the resulting change in saving is $0.1 trillion. The slope between these two points therefore equals 0.1/0.5, or 1/5, which by definition equals the marginal propensity to save. Because the marginal propensity to consume and the marginal propensity to save are simply different sides of the same coin, from here on we focus more on the marginal propensity to consume.

SAVING FUNCTION

The relationship between saving and income, other things constant

Nonincome Determinants of Consumption

Along a given consumption function, consumer spending depends on disposable income in the economy, other things constant. Now let's see what factors are held constant and how changes in them could cause the entire consumption function to shift.

Net Wealth and Consumption

Given the economy's income, an important influence on consumption is each household's **net wealth**—that is, the value of all assets that each household owns minus any liabilities, or debts. Your family's assets may include a home, furnishings, automobiles, bank accounts, cash, and the value of stocks, bonds, and pensions. Your family's liabilities, or debts, may include a mortgage, car loans, student loans, credit card balances, and the like. According to the Federal Reserve, the net wealth of U.S. households totaled $44.3 trillion at the end of 2003, the highest on record.[1] Net wealth increased in 2003 because of rising house prices and a recovery in stock market prices. Net wealth is a stock variable. Consumption and income are flow variables. Net wealth is assumed to be constant along a given consumption function.

NET WEALTH

The value of a assets minus liabilities

A decrease in net wealth would make consumers less inclined to spend and more inclined to save at each income level. To see why, suppose prices fall sharply on the stock market. Stockholders are poorer than they were, so they spend less. For example, following the stock market crash of October 1987, consumption declined and saving increased. Household saving as a percentage of disposable income increased from 3.9 percent in the quarter before the crash to 5.7 percent in the quarter following the crash. Spending on new homes and cars fell. As another example, stock market declines in 2000, 2001, and 2002 cut into the purchases of luxury goods. Our original consumption function is depicted as line *C* in Exhibit 5. If net wealth declines, the consumption function shifts from *C* down to *C'*, because households now spend less and save more at every income level.

Conversely, suppose stock prices increase sharply. This increase in net wealth increases the desire to spend. For example, stock prices surged in 1999, increasing stockholders' net wealth. Consumers spent 94 percent of disposable income that year compared with an average of about 90 percent during the first half of the 1990s. Purchases of homes and cars

1. James Hagerty and Deborah Lagomarsino, "U.S. Household Wealth Hits Record," *Wall Street Journal*, 5 March 2004.

Shifts of the Consumption Function

A downward shift of the consumption function, such as from *C* to *C'*, can be caused by a decrease in wealth, an increase in the price level, an unfavorable change in consumer expectations, or an increase in the interest rate. An upward shift, such as from *C* to *C"*, can be caused by an increase in wealth, a decrease in the price level, a favorable change in expectations, or a decrease in the interest rate.

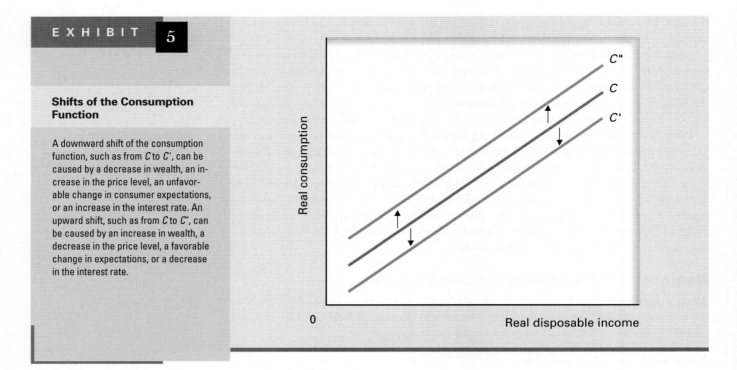

soared. Because of an increase in net wealth, the consumption function shifts from *C* up to *C"*, reflecting households' desire to spend more at each income level. Research by the Federal Reserve indicates that consumer spending eventually rises or falls between three to five cents for every dollar rise or fall in the value of stock market holdings.

Again, *it is a change in net wealth, not a change in disposable income, that shifts the consumption function. A change in disposable income, other things constant, means a movement along a given consumption function, not a shift of that function.* Be mindful of the difference between a movement along the consumption function, which results from a change in income, and a shift of the consumption function, which results from a change in one of the nonincome determinants of consumption, such as net wealth.

The Price Level

Another variable that can affect the consumption function is the price level prevailing in the economy. As we have seen, net wealth is an important determinant of consumption. The greater the net wealth, other things constant, the greater consumption will be at each income level. Some household wealth is held as money, such as cash and bank accounts. When the price level changes, so does the real value of cash and bank accounts.

For example, suppose your wealth consists of a $20,000 bank account. If the economy's price level increases by 5 percent, your bank account will buy about 5 percent less in real terms. You feel poorer because you are poorer. To rebuild the real value of your money holdings to some desired comfort level, you decide to spend less and save more. *An increase in the price level reduces the purchasing power of money holdings, causing households to consume less and save more at each income level.* So the consumption function would shift downward from *C* to *C'*, as shown in Exhibit 5.

Conversely, should the price level ever fall, as it did frequently before World War II and recently in Japan and Hong Kong, the real value money holdings increases. Households would be wealthier, so they decide to consume more and save less at each income level. For example, if the price level declined by 5 percent, your $20,000 bank account would then buy about 5 percent more in real terms. A drop in the price level would shift the consumption function from C up to C''. *At each income, a change in the price level influences consumption by affecting the real value of money holdings.*

The Interest Rate

Interest is the reward savers earn for deferring consumption and the cost borrowers pay for current spending power. When graphing the consumption function, we assume a given interest rate in the economy. If the interest rate increases, other things constant, savers or lenders are rewarded more, and borrowers are charged more. The higher the interest rate, the less is spent on those items typically purchased on credit, such as cars. Thus, at a higher interest rate, households save more, borrow less, and spend less. Greater saving at each income level means less consumption. Simply put, *a higher interest rate, other things constant, shifts the consumption function downward.* Conversely, *a lower interest rate, other things constant, shifts the consumption function upward.*

Expectations

Expectations influence economic behavior in a variety of ways. For example, suppose as a college senior, you land a good job that starts after graduation. Your consumption will probably jump long before the job actually begins because you expect an increase in your income; you might buy a car, for example. Conversely, a worker who gets a layoff notice to take effect at the end of the year will likely reduce consumption immediately, well before the actual date of the layoff. More generally, if people grow concerned about their job security, they will reduce the amount they consume at each income level.

Changing expectations about price levels and interest rates also affect consumption. For example, a change that leads householders to expect higher car prices or higher interest rates in the future will prompt some to buy new cars now. On the other hand, a change leading householders to expect lower prices or lower interest rates in the future will cause some to defer car purchases. Thus, expectations affect spending at each income, and a change in expectations can shift the consumption function. This is why economic forecasters monitor consumer confidence so closely.

Keep in mind the distinction between *movements along a given consumption function,* which result from a change in income, and *shifts in the consumption function,* which result from a change in one of the factors assumed to remain constant along a given consumption function. We conclude our introduction to consumption with the following case study, which discusses consumption and saving patterns over a lifetime.

The Life-Cycle Hypothesis

Do people with high incomes save a larger fraction of their incomes than those with low income? Both theory and evidence suggest they do. The easier it is to make ends meet, the more income is left over for saving. Does it follow from this that richer economies save more than poorer ones—that economies save a larger fraction of total disposable income as they grow? In his famous book, *The General Theory of Employment, Interest, and Money,* published in 1936, John Maynard Keynes drew that conclusion. But as later economists studied the

© EPA/AKIO SUG/AP Photo

Case **Study**

Bringing
Theory to Life

eActivity
Until quite recently, the Japanese government had been trying various changes in government spending and tax policies to encourage more consumer spending. However, the

Japanese public often would just put any extra income into savings. How could they be persuaded to spend more? An innovative policy was to issue purchase vouchers. The Japanese Information Network reports on these at http://web-japan.org/trends98/hon-bun/ntj981201.html. To whom did the government intend to distribute these coupons? Why? Would receiving 20,000 yen in vouchers ensure that spending would increase by that amount?

LIFE-CYCLE MODEL OF CONSUMPTION AND SAVING

Young people borrow, middle agers pay off debts and save, and older people draw down their savings; on average net savings over a lifetime is small

data—such as that presented in Exhibit 2—it became clear that Keynes was wrong. *The fraction of disposable income saved in an economy seems to stay constant as the economy grows.*

So how can it be that richer people save more than poorer people, yet richer countries do not necessarily save more than poorer ones? Several answers have been proposed. One of the most important is the **life-cycle model of consumption and saving.** According to this model, young people tend to borrow to finance education and home purchases. In middle age, people pay off debts and save more. In old age, they draw down their savings, or dissave. Some still have substantial wealth at death, because they are not sure when death will occur and because some parents want to bequeath wealth to their children. And some people die in debt. But on average net savings over a person's lifetime tend to be small. The life-cycle hypothesis suggests that the saving rate for an economy as a whole depends on, among other things, the relative number of savers and dissavers in the population.

Other factors that influence the saving rate across countries include the tax treatment of interest, the convenience and reliability of saving institutions, national customs, and the relative cost of a household's major purchase—housing. In Japan, for example, about 24,000 post offices nationwide offer convenient savings accounts. Japan's postal savings system holds over $2 trillion in savings deposits, more than one-third of Japan's total. Also, a home buyer in Japan must come up with a substantial down payment, one that represents a large fraction of the home's purchase price, and housing there is more expensive than in the United States. Finally, borrowing is considered by some Japanese to be shameful, so households save to avoid having to borrow. Because saving in Japan is necessary, convenient, and consistent with an aversion to borrowing, the country has one of the highest saving rates in the world. In a recent year, for example, Japanese households saved 13 percent of their disposable income compared with a saving rate of only about 4 percent in the United States.

Sources: "Leviathan Unbound," *The Economist*, 27 May 2003; Martin Browning and Thomas Crossley, "The Life-Cycle Model of Consumption and Saving," *Journal of Economic Perspective* 15 (Summer 2001): 3–22; *OECD Economic Outlook* 75 (June 2004); and "Overview of the Postal Savings Operation" at http://www.yu-cho.japanpost.jp/e_index.htm.

We turn next to the second component of aggregate expenditure—investment. Keep in mind that our initial goal is to understand the relationship between total spending and income.

Investment

The second component of aggregate expenditure is investment, or, more precisely, *gross private domestic investment*. Again, by *investment* we do not mean buying stocks, bonds, or other financial assets. Investment consists of spending on (1) new factories, office buildings, malls, and new equipment, such as computers; (2) new housing; and (3) net increases to inventories. Firms invest now in the expectation of a future return. Because the return is in the future, a would-be investor must estimate how much a particular investment will yield this year, next year, the year after, and in all years during the productive life of the investment. *Firms buy new capital goods only if they expect this investment to yield a higher return than other possible uses of their funds.*

The Demand for Investment

To understand the investment decision, let's consider a simple example. The operators of the Hacker Haven Golf Course are thinking about buying some solar-powered golf carts. The model under consideration, called the Weekend Warrior, sells for $2,000, requires no maintenance or operating expenses, and is expected to last indefinitely. *The expected rate of return of each cart equals the expected annual earnings divided by the cart's purchase price.* The first cart is expected to generate rental income of $400 per year. This income, divided by the cost of the cart, yields an expected rate of return on the investment of $400/$2,000, or 20 percent per year. Additional carts will be used less. A second is expected to generate $300 per year in rental income, yielding a rate of return of $300/$2,000, or 15 percent; a third cart, $200 per year, or 10 percent; and a fourth cart, $100 per year, or 5 percent. They don't expect a fifth cart will get rented at all, so it has a zero expected rate of return.

Should the operators of Hacker Haven invest in golf carts, and if so, how many? Suppose they plan to borrow the money to buy the carts. The number of carts they purchase will depend on the interest rate they must pay for borrowing. If the market interest rate exceeds 20 percent, the cost of borrowing would exceed the expected rate of return for even the first cart, so the club would buy no carts. What if the operators have enough cash on hand to buy the carts? The market interest rate also reflects what club owners could earn on savings. If the interest rate paid on savings exceeded 20 percent, course owners would earn more saving their money than buying golf carts. *The market interest rate is the opportunity cost of investing in capital.*

Suppose the market rate is 8 percent per year. At that rate, the first three carts, all with expected returns exceeding 8 percent, would each yield more than the market rate. A fourth cart would lose money, because its expected rate of return is only 5 percent. Exhibit 6 measures the nominal interest rate along the vertical axis and the amount invested in golf carts along the horizontal axis. The step-like relationship shows the expected rate of return earned on additional dollars invested in golf carts. This relationship also indicates the amount invested in golf carts at each interest rate, so you can view this step-like relationship as Hacker Haven's demand curve for this type of investment. For example, the first cart costs $2,000 and earns a rate of return of 20 percent. A firm should reject any investment with an expected rate of return that falls below the market rate of interest.

The horizontal line at 8 percent indicates the market interest rate, which is Hacker Haven's opportunity cost of investing. The course operators' objective is to choose an investment strategy that maximizes profit. Profit is maximized when $6,000 is invested in the

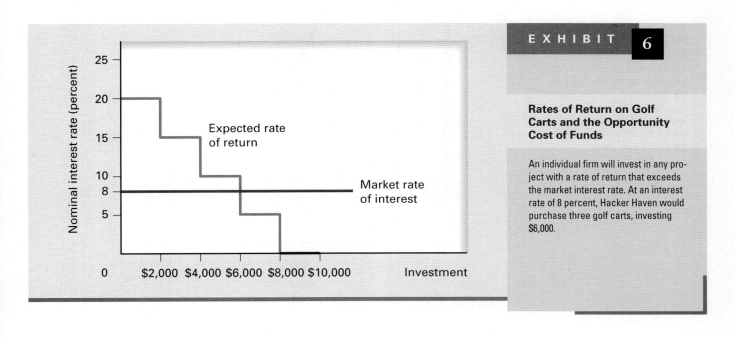

EXHIBIT 6

Rates of Return on Golf Carts and the Opportunity Cost of Funds

An individual firm will invest in any project with a rate of return that exceeds the market interest rate. At an interest rate of 8 percent, Hacker Haven would purchase three golf carts, investing $6,000.

carts—that is, when three carts are purchased. The expected return from a fourth cart is 5 percent, which is below the opportunity cost of funds. Therefore, investing in four or more carts would lower total profit.

From Micro to Macro

So far, we have looked at the investment decision for a single golf course, but there are over 13,000 golf courses in the United States. The industry demand for golf carts shows the relationship between the amount all courses invest and the expected rate of return. Like the step-like relationship in Exhibit 6, the investment demand curve for the golf industry slopes downward.

Let's move beyond golf carts and consider the invest decisions of all industries: publishing, hog farming, fast food, software, and thousands more. Individual industries have downward-sloping demand curves for investment. More is invested when the opportunity cost of borrowing is lower, other things constant. A downward-sloping investment demand curve for the entire economy can be derived, with some qualifications, from a horizontal summation of all industries' downward-sloping investment demand curves. The economy's *investment demand curve* is represented as *D* in Exhibit 7, which shows the inverse relationship between the quantity of investment demanded and the market interest rate, other things—including business expectations—held constant. For example, in Exhibit 7, when the market rate is 8 percent, the quantity of investment demanded is $1.0 trillion. If the interest rate rises to 10 percent, investment declines to $0.9 trillion, and if the rate falls to 6 percent, investment increases to $1.1 trillion. Assumed constant along the investment demand curve are business expectations about the economy. If firms grow more optimistic

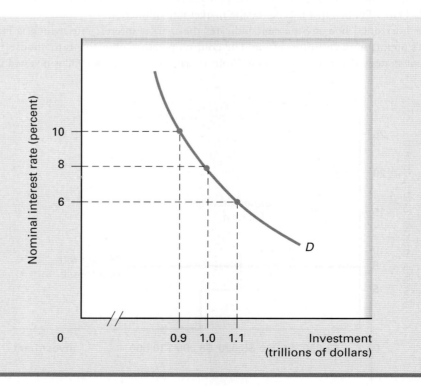

EXHIBIT 7

Investment Demand Curve for the Economy

The investment demand curve for the economy sums the investment demanded by each firm at each interest rate. At lower interest rates, more investment projects become profitable for individual firms, so total investment in the economy increases.

about profit prospects, the demand for investment increases, so the investment demand curve shifts to the right.

Planned Investment and the Economy's Income

To integrate the discussion of investment with our earlier analysis of consumption, we need to know if and how investment varies with income in the economy. Whereas we were able to present evidence relating consumption to income over time, the link between investment and income is weaker. Investment in a particular year shows little relation to income that year. *Investment depends more on interest rates and on business expectations than on the prevailing income.* One reason investment is less related to income is that some investments, such as a new power plant, take years to build. And investment, once in place, is expected to last for years, sometimes decades. The investment decision is thus said to be *forward looking*, based more on expected profit than on current income.

So how does the amount firms plan to invest relate to income? The simplest **investment function** assumes that *planned investment* is unrelated to disposable income. Planned investment is assumed to be **autonomous** with respect to disposable income. For example, suppose that, given current business expectations and an interest rate of 8 percent, firms plan to invest $1.0 trillion per year, regardless of the economy's income level. Exhibit 8 measures disposable income on the horizontal axis and planned investment on the vertical axis. Planned investment of $1.0 trillion is shown by the flat investment function, *I*. As you can see, along *I*, planned investment does not vary even though real disposable income does.

Nonincome Determinants of Planned Investment

The investment function isolates the relationship between income in the economy and *planned investment*—the amount firms would like to invest, other things constant. We have already mentioned two determinants that are assumed constant: the interest rate and business expectations. Now let's look at how changes in these factors affect investment.

N e t **B o o k m a r k**

For a personal view on Keynes and his work, read "Cairncross on Keynes," an obituary written by one of his students, Sir Alec Cairncross. It originally appeared in the *Economist* and is now available online at a site maintained by Professor Brad DeLong at http://econ161. berkeley.edu/Economists/ cairncrossonkeynes.html.

INVESTMENT FUNCTION

The relationship between the amount businesses plan to invest and the economy's income, other things constant

AUTONOMOUS

A term that means "independent"; for example, autonomous investment is independent of income

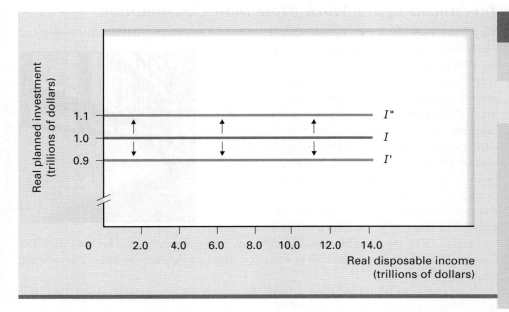

E X H I B I T   8

Planned Investment Function

Planned investment is assumed to be independent of income, as shown by the horizontal lines. Thus, planned investment is assumed to be autonomous. An increase in the interest rate or less favorable business expectations would decrease investment at every level of income, as shown by the downward shift from *I* to *I'*. A decrease in the interest rate or more upbeat business expectations would increase investment at every level of income, as shown by the upward shift from *I* to *I"*.

Market Interest Rate

Exhibit 7 shows that if the interest rate is 8 percent, planned investment is $1.0 trillion. This investment is also shown as *I* in Exhibit 8. If the interest rate increases because of, say, a change in the nation's monetary policy (as happened in 2004), the cost of borrowing increases, which increases the opportunity cost of investment. For example, if the interest rate increases from 8 percent to 10 percent, planned investment drops from $1.0 trillion to $0.9 trillion. This decrease is reflected in Exhibit 8 by a shift of the investment function from *I* down to *I'*. Conversely, if the interest rate decreases because of, say, a change in the nation's monetary policy (as happened in 2001 and 2002), the cost of borrowing decreases, which reduces the opportunity cost of investment. For example, a drop in the rate of interest from 8 percent to 6 percent, other things remaining constant, will reduce the cost of borrowing and increase planned investment from $1.0 trillion to $1.1 trillion, as reflected by the upward shift of the investment function from *I* to *I"*. Notice that the shifts in Exhibit 8 match interest rate movements along the investment demand curve in Exhibit 7.

Business Expectations

Investment depends primarily on business expectations, or on what Keynes called the "animal spirits" of business. Suppose planned investment initially is $1.0 trillion, as depicted by *I* in Exhibit 8. If firms now become more pessimistic about their profit prospects, perhaps expecting the worst, as in 2001 when terrorists leveled the World Trade Center, planned investment will decrease at every income, as reflected in Exhibit 8 by a shift of the investment function from *I* down to *I'*. On the other hand, if profit expectations become rosier, as they did in 2003, firms become more willing to invest, thereby increasing the investment function from *I* up to *I"*. *Examples of factors that could affect business expectations, and thus investment plans, include wars, technological change, tax changes, and destabilizing events such as terrorist attacks.* Changes in business expectations also shift the investment demand curve in Exhibit 7.

Now that we have examined consumption and investment individually, let's take a look at their year-to-year variability in the following case study.

Investment Varies Much More than Consumption

We already know that consumption makes up about two-thirds of GDP and that investment varies from year to year, averaging about one-sixth of GDP over the last decade. Now let's compare their year-to-year variability. Exhibit 9 shows the annual percentage changes in GDP, consumption, and investment, all measured in real terms. Two points are obvious. First, investment fluctuates much more than either consumption or GDP. For example, in the recession year of 1982, GDP declined 1.9 percent but investment crashed 14.0 percent; consumption actually increased 1.4 percent. In 1984, GDP increased 7.2 percent, consumption rose 5.3 percent, but investment soared 29.5 percent. Second, fluctuations in consumption and in GDP appear to be entwined, although consumption varies a bit less than GDP. Consumption varies less than GDP because consumption depends on disposable income, which varies less than GDP.

During years of falling GDP since 1959, the average decline in GDP was 0.6 percent, but investment dropped an average of 11.7 percent. Consumption actually increased 0.6

WALL STREET JOURNAL
Reading It Right

What's the relevance of the following statement from the Wall Street Journal: *"Indeed, a major contributor to economic cycles is that businesses spend enthusiastically on buildings and equipment when times are good and cut back sharply when times are bad."*

Case Study

Public Policy

*e*Activity
Visit the Web site for the Research Seminar in Quantitative Economics at the University of Michigan at http://rsqe.econ.lsa.umich.edu/index. html. RSQE is "an economic modeling and forecasting unit which has been in operation at the University of Michigan since 1952. RSQE provides forecasts of the economic outlook for the U.S. and Michigan economies, based on quarterly econometric models." Read the executive summary for their latest U.S. forecast. What are the "seeds" or sources of the predicted trend? How, specifically, do the forecasters believe

EXHIBIT	9	**Annual Percentage Change in U.S. Real GDP, Consumption, and Investment**

Investment varies much more year-to-year than consumption does and accounts for nearly all the variability in real GDP. This is why economic forecasters pay special attention to the business outlook and investment plans.

Source: Bureau of Economic Analysis, U.S. Department of Commerce. For the latest data, go to http://www.bea.doc.gov/bea/pubs.htm.

percent. So *while consumption is the largest spending component, investment varies much more than consumption and accounts for nearly all the year-to-year variability in real GDP.* Note that GDP does not always fall during years in which a recession occurs. For example, in the 2001 recession, GDP managed a tiny gain for the year of 0.5 percent and consumption increased 2.5 percent. It was the 8.3 percent fall in investment that caused the recession. This is why economic forecasters pay special attention to business expectations and investment plans.

that the types of consumption and investment spending cited in the text will change and affect real GDP?

Sources: *Economic Report of the President*, February 2004; U.S. Department of Commerce, *Survey of Current Business* 84, various months for 2004; and *OECD Economic Outlook* 75 (June 2004). For data and articles about economic aggregates, go to the Bureau of Economic Analysis site at http://www.bea.doc.gov/.

Government

The third component of aggregate expenditure is government purchases of goods and services. Federal, state, and local governments purchase thousands of goods and services, ranging from weapon systems to road signs. During the last decade, government purchases in the United States accounted for a little less than one-fifth of GDP, most of that by state and local governments.

Government Purchase Function

The **government purchase function** relates government purchases to income in the economy, other things constant. Decisions about government purchases are largely under the control of public officials, such as the decision to build an interstate highway or to boost military spending. These purchases do not depend directly on income in the economy. We therefore assume that *government purchases* are autonomous, or independent of income. Such a function would relate to income as a flat line similar to the investment function shown in Exhibit 8. An increase in government purchases would result in an upward shift of the government purchase function. And a decrease in government purchases would result in a downward shift of the government purchase function.

Net Taxes

As noted earlier, government purchases represent only one of the two components of government outlays; the other is *transfer payments,* such as Social Security, welfare benefits, and unemployment benefits. Transfer payments, which make up about a third of government outlays, are outright grants from governments to households and are thus not considered part of aggregate expenditure. Transfer payments vary inversely with income—as income increases, transfer payments decline.

To fund government outlays, governments impose taxes. Taxes vary directly with income; as income increases, so do taxes. *Net taxes* equal taxes minus transfers. Because taxes tend to increase with income but transfers tend to decrease with income, for simplicity, let's assume that net taxes do not vary with income. Thus, we assume for now that *net taxes* are *autonomous,* or independent of income.

Net taxes affect aggregate spending indirectly by changing disposable income, which in turn changes consumption. We saw from the discussion of circular flow that by subtracting net taxes, we transform real GDP into *disposable income.* Disposable income is take-home pay—the income households can spend or save. We will examine the impact of net taxes in the next few chapters.

Net Exports

The rest of the world affects aggregate expenditure through imports and exports and has a growing influence on the U.S. economy. The United States, with only one-twentieth of the world's population, accounts for about one-sixth of the world's imports and one-ninth of the world's exports.

Net Exports and Income

How do imports and exports relate to the economy's income? When incomes rise, Americans spend more on all normal goods, including imports. Higher incomes lead to more spending on Persian rugs, French wine, Korean DVD players, German cars, Chinese toys, European vacations, African safaris, and thousands of other foreign goods and services.

How do U.S. exports relate to the economy's income? U.S. exports depend on the income of foreigners, not on U.S. income. U.S. disposable income does not affect French purchases of U.S. computers or Saudi Arabian purchases of U.S. military hardware. The **net export function** shows the relationship between net exports and U.S. income, other things constant. Because our exports are insensitive to U.S. income but our imports tend to increase with income, *net exports,* which equal the value of exports minus the value of imports, tend to decline as U.S. incomes increase. Such an inverse relationship is developed

Net Export Function

Net exports here are assumed to be independent of disposable income, as shown by the horizontal lines. $X - M$ is the net export function when autonomous net exports equal $-\$200$ billion. An increase in the value of the dollar relative to other currencies would decrease net exports at each level of income, as shown by the shift down to $X' - M'$. A decrease in the value of the dollar would increase net exports at each level of income, as shown by the shift up to $X'' - M''$.

graphically in the appendix to this chapter. For now, we assume that net exports are *autonomous,* or independent of income.

If exports exceed imports, net exports are positive; if imports exceed exports, net exports are negative; and if exports equal imports, net exports are zero. U.S. net exports have been negative nearly every year during the past three decades, so let's suppose net exports are autonomous and equal to $-\$0.2$ trillion, or $-\$200$ billion, as shown by the net export function $X - M$ in Exhibit 10.

Nonincome Determinants of Net Exports

Factors assumed constant along the net export function include the U.S. price level, price levels in other countries, interest rates here and abroad, foreign income levels, and the exchange rate between the dollar and foreign currencies. Consider the effects of a change in one of these factors. Suppose the value of the dollar increases relative to foreign currencies such as those of Asia, as happened in 1998. With the dollar worth more on world markets, foreign products become cheaper for Americans, and U.S. products become more costly for foreigners. A rise in the dollar's exchange value will increase imports and decrease exports, thus reducing net exports, shown in Exhibit 10 by a parallel drop in the net export line from $X - M$ down to $X' - M'$, a decline from $-\$200$ billion to $-\$220$ billion.

A decline in the value of the dollar, as occurred in 2003, will have the opposite effect, increasing exports and decreasing imports. An increase in autonomous net exports is shown in our example by a parallel increase in the net export function, from $X - M$ up to $X'' - M''$, reflecting an increase in autonomous net exports from $-\$200$ billion to $-\$180$ billion. A country sometimes tries to devalue its currency in an attempt to increase its net exports and thereby increase employment. The effect of changes in net exports on aggregate spending will be taken up in the next chapter.

Composition of Aggregate Expenditure

Now that we have examined each component of aggregate spending, let's get a better idea of spending over time. Exhibit 11 shows the composition of spending in the United States

EXHIBIT 11

U.S. Spending Components as Percentages of GDP Since 1959

The composition of U.S. GDP has not changed much since 1959. Consumption's share edged up from an average of 62 percent during the 1960s to 68 percent during the last decade. Investment has fluctuated from year to year but with no clear long-term trend up or down. Government purchases declined slightly from an average of 22 percent of GDP during the 1960s to an average of 18 percent in the last decade. And net exports have become more negative, expressed by that portion exceeding 100 percent of GDP.

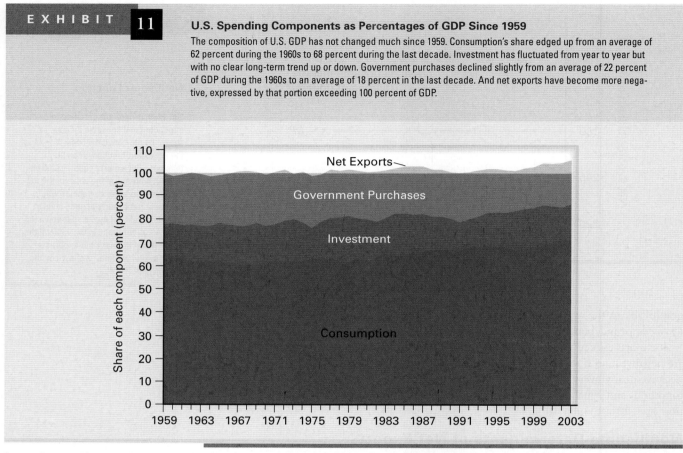

Source: Computed from annual estimates in *Survey of Current Business* 84 (February 2004). For the latest data, go to http://www.bea.doc.gov/bea/pubs.htm.

since 1959. As you can see, consumption's share of GDP appears stable from year to year, but the long-term trend shows an increase from an average of 62 percent during the 1960s to 68 percent during the last decade. Investment fluctuates more from year to year but with no long-term trend up or down.

Government purchases declined from an average of 22 percent of GDP during the 1960s to an average of 18 percent during the last decade, due primarily to decreases in defense spending. (But defense spending has picked up lately with the war on terrorism.) Net exports averaged 0.3 percent of GDP in the 1960s but were negative nearly every year since then, averaging a minus 2.5 percent of GDP during the last decade. Negative net exports mean that the sum of spending on consumption, investment, and government purchases exceeds GDP, the amount produced in the U.S. economy. Americans are spending more than they make, and they are covering the difference by borrowing from abroad. U.S. spending exceeds U.S. GDP by the amount shown as negative net exports. Because the spending components must sum to GDP, *negative* net exports are expressed in Exhibit 11 by that portion of spending that exceeds 100 percent of GDP.

In summary: During the last four decades, consumption's share of total spending increased and government purchases decreased. Investment's share bounced around and net exports' share turned negative, meaning that imports exceeded exports.

Conclusion

This chapter has focused on the relationship between spending and income. We considered the four components of aggregate expenditure: consumption, investment, government purchases, and net exports. Consumption increases with income. Investment relates more to interest rates and business expectations than it does to income. Government purchases also tend to be autonomous, or independent of income. And net exports are assumed, for now, to be affected more by such factors as the exchange rate than by U.S. income. The appendix to this chapter develops a more realistic but also more complicated picture by showing how net exports decline as income increases. In the next chapter, we will see how aggregate spending depends on income and how this link helps shape the aggregate demand curve.

SUMMARY

1. The most predictable and most useful relationship in macroeconomics is between consumption and income. The more people have to spend, the more they spend on consumption, other things constant.

2. The consumption function shows the link between consumption and income in the economy. The slope of the consumption function reflects the marginal propensity to consume, which equals the change in consumption divided by the change in income. The slope of the saving function reflects the marginal propensity to save, which equals the change in saving divided by the change in income.

3. Certain factors can cause consumers to change the amount they want to spend at each income level. An increase in net wealth reduces the need to save, thus increasing consumption at every income. A higher price level reduces the value of money holdings, thereby reducing net wealth, which in turn reduces consumption. An increase in the interest rate makes saving more rewarding and borrowing more costly, thus increasing saving and decreasing consumption at each income. Expectations about future incomes, prices, and interest rates also influence consumption.

4. Planned investment depends on the market interest rate and on business expectations. Investment fluctuates from year to year but averaged about one-sixth of GDP during the last decade. We assume for now that investment in the economy is unrelated to income.

5. Government purchases of goods and services averaged a little less than one-fifth of GDP during the last decade. Government purchases are based on the public choices of elected officials and are assumed to be autonomous, or independent of the economy's income level. Net taxes, or taxes minus transfer payments, are also assumed for now to be unrelated to income.

6. Net exports equal the value of exports minus the value of imports. U.S. exports depend on foreign income, not on U.S. income. Imports increase with U.S. income. So net exports decline as income increases. For simplicity, however, we initially assume that net exports are autonomous, or unrelated to domestic income.

QUESTIONS FOR REVIEW

1. *(Consumption Function)* How would an increase in each of the following affect the consumption function? How would it affect the saving function?

   a. Autonomous net taxes
   b. The interest rate
   c. Consumer optimism, or confidence
   d. The price level
   e. Consumers' net wealth
   f. Disposable income

2. *(Consumption Function)* A number of factors can cause the consumption function to shift. What, if anything, happens to the saving function when the consumption function shifts? Explain.

3. *(C a s e* **S t u d y :** The Life-Cycle Hypothesis) According to the life-cycle hypothesis, what is the typical pattern of saving for an individual over his or her lifetime? What impact does this behavior have on an individual's lifetime consumption pattern? What impact does the behavior have on the saving rate in the overall economy?

4. *(Investment)* What are the components of gross private domestic investment? What is the difference between the investment curve shown in Exhibit 6 and the one shown in Exhibit 7?

5. *(Investment)* Why would the following investment expenditures increase as the interest rate declines?

   a. Purchases of a new plant and equipment
   b. Construction of new housing
   c. Accumulation of planned inventories

6. *(Nonincome Determinants of Investment)* What are some factors assumed to be constant along the autonomous planned investment function? What kinds of changes in each factor could cause investment spending to increase at each level of real disposable income?

7. *(C a s e* **S t u d y :** Investment Varies Much More Than Consumption) Why do economic forecasters pay special attention to investment plans? Take a look at the Conference Board's index of leading economic indictors at http://www.conferenceboard.org. Which of those indicators might affect investment?

8. *(Government Spending)* How do changes in disposable income affect government purchases and the government purchase function? How do changes in net taxes affect the consumption function?

9. *(Net Exports)* What factors are assumed constant along the net export function? What would be the impact on net exports of a change in real disposable income?

PROBLEMS AND EXERCISES

10. *(Consumption)* Use the following data to answer the questions below:

Real Disposable Income (billions)	Consumption Expenditures (billions)	Saving (billions)
$100	$150	$_____
200	200	_____
300	250	_____
400	300	_____

   a. Graph the consumption function, with consumption spending on the vertical axis and disposable income on the horizontal axis.
   b. If the consumption function is a straight line, what is its slope?
   c. Fill in the saving column at each level of income. If the saving function is a straight line, what is its slope?

11. *(MPC and MPS)* If consumption increases by $12 billion when disposable income increases by $15 billion, what is the value of the MPC? What is the relationship between the MPC and the MPS? If the MPC increases, what must happen to the MPS? How is the MPC related to the consumption function? How is the MPS related to the saving function?

12. *(Consumption and Saving)* Suppose that consumption equals $500 billion when disposable income is $0 and that each increase of $100 billion in disposable income causes consumption to increase by $70 billion. Draw a graph of the saving function using this information.

13. *(Investment Spending)* Review Exhibit 6 in this chapter. If the operators of the golf course revised their revenue estimates so that each cart is expected to earn $100 less, how many carts would they buy at an interest rate of 8 percent? How many would they buy if the interest rate is 3 percent?

EXPERIENTIAL EXERCISES

14. *(Marginal Propensity to Consume)* Find some recent data on U.S. real disposable income and real consumption spending. (One possible source is the *Economic Report of the President* at http://w3.access.gpo.gov/eop/, but there are many others.) Use the data to compute the marginal propensity to consume for each year, 1991 to 2004. Has the MPC been relatively constant?

15. *(Variability of Consumption and Investment)* Expectations and consumer confidence are important in determining fluctuations in aggregate spending. What is the present status of consumer confidence as measured by the Conference Board's index? You can find the data, with interpretation, at The Conference Board at http://www.conference-board.org/economics/consumerConfidence.cfm.

16. *(Wall Street Journal)* Business investment spending is an important component of aggregate expenditure. Review the "Business Bulletin" column on the front page of Thursday's *Wall Street Journal*. What are some recent trends in investment spending? Are they likely to increase or decrease aggregate expenditure? (Remember that purchases of stocks and bonds are not investment, in the sense described in this chapter!)

HOMEWORK XPRESS! EXERCISES

These exercises require access to McEachern Homework Xpress! If Homework Xpress! did not come with your book, visit **http://homeworkxpress.swlearning.com** *to purchase.*

1. In the diagram for this exercise, plot the consumption function line for the data in the table below. Calculate savings at each level of real disposable income and plot the savings function.

Real Disposable Income (trillions)	Consumption (trillions)
$2.00	$2.50
3.00	3.25
4.00	4.00
5.00	4.75
6.00	5.50
7.00	6.25
8.00	7.00

2. In the diagram draw a linear consumption function. Illustrate the effect on the consumption function of an increase in net wealth. Then illustrate the effect on the consumption function of an increase in the price level.

3. In the diagram sketch an investment demand curve illustrating the relationship between the quantity of investment undertaken and the interest rate.

4. In the diagram sketch an autonomous investment function showing the level of investment as $1 trillion at the current market interest rate. Illustrate the effect on the function of an inprovement in business expectations. Then illustrate the effect of an increase in the interest rate.

5. In the diagram, sketch an autonomous net export function showing the U.S. economy with a trade balance of $−50 billion. Illustrate how a decrease in the value of the U.S. dollar could lead to a positive trade balance. Then illustrate the effect of a decrease in the value of the currency of a major trading partner.

Variable Net Exports

In this appendix, we examine the relationship between net exports and U.S. income. We first look at exports and imports separately and then consider exports minus imports, or net exports.

Net Exports and Income

As noted earlier in the chapter, the amount of U.S. output purchased by foreigners depends not on U.S. income but on income in foreign countries. We therefore assume that U.S. exports do not vary with U.S. income. Specifically, suppose the rest of the world spends $0.9 trillion, of $900 billion, per year on U.S. exports of goods and services. The export function, X, is as shown in panel (a) of Exhibit 12. But when income increases, Americans spend more on all goods and services, including imports. Thus, the relationship between imports and income is positive, as expressed by the upward-sloping import function, M, in panel (b) of Exhibit 12. If Americans spend 10 percent of their disposable income on imports, when disposable income is $9.0 trillion, imports are $0.9 trillion.

So far, we have considered imports and exports as separate functions of income. What matters in terms of total spending on U.S. products are exports, X, minus imports, M, or net exports, $X - M$. Because money spent on imports goes to foreign producers, not U.S. producers, imports get subtracted from the circular flow of spending. By subtracting the import function depicted in panel (b) from the export function in panel (a), we derive the *net export function*, depicted as $X - M$ in panel (c) of Exhibit 12.

Because exports in panel (a) equal $0.9 trillion at all levels of income, net exports equal zero when U.S. disposable income is $9.0 trillion. At incomes less than $9.0 trillion, net exports are positive because exports exceed imports. At incomes greater than $9.0 trillion, net exports are negative because imports exceed exports. As a case in point, recessions in 1991 and 2001 reduced the trade deficits those years as imports declined. As the economy recovered, the trade deficit increased, reaching a record to that point in 2004.

Shifts of Net Exports

The net export function, $X - M$, shows the relationship between net exports and disposable income, other things constant. Suppose the value of the dollar increases relative to for-

EXHIBIT 12

Imports, Exports, and Net Exports (in trillions of dollars)

Exports are independent of income, as shown in panel (a). Imports are positively related to income, as shown in panel (b). Net exports equal exports minus imports. Net exports are negatively related to income, as shown in panel (c). Net exports are zero when disposable income is $9.0 trillion.

eign currencies, as happened in 1999. With the dollar worth more, foreign products become cheaper for Americans, and U.S. products become more expensive for foreigners. The impact of a rising dollar is to decrease exports but increase imports at each income level, thus decreasing net exports. This relationship is shown in Exhibit 13 by the shift from $X - M$ down to $X' - M'$. A decline in the dollar's value, as occurred in 2003, has the opposite effect, increasing exports and de-

creasing imports, as reflected in Exhibit 13 by an upward shift of the net export function from $X - M$ to $X'' - M''$.

In summary, in this appendix we assumed that imports relate positively to income, whereas exports are independent of domestic income. Therefore, net exports, which equal exports minus imports, vary inversely with income. The net export function shifts downward if the value of the dollar rises and shifts upward if the value of the dollar falls.

EXHIBIT 13

Shifts of Net Exports (in trillions of dollars)

A rise in the value of the dollar, other things constant, will decrease exports and increase imports, thereby decreasing net exports, as shown by the shift from $X - M$ down to $X' - M'$. A decrease in the value of the dollar will increase exports and decrease imports, causing net exports to rise, as shown by the shift from $X - M$ up to $X'' - M''$.

APPENDIX QUESTION

1. *(Rest of the World)* Using a graph of net exports $(X - M)$ against disposable income, show the effects of the following. Explain each of your answers.

   a. An increase in foreign disposable income
   b. An increase in U.S. disposable income

   c. An increase in the U.S. interest rate
   d. An increase in the value of the dollar against foreign currencies

Aggregate Expenditure and Aggregate Demand

Now that we have considered consumption, investment, government purchases, and net exports, how do we combine them to get aggregate expenditure for the economy? How is aggregate expenditure linked to income? How does a change in spending ripple through the economy, magnifying the impact? For example, how did the fear of flying after the terrorist attacks of September 11 affect the economy as a whole? What happens to spending if the economy's price level changes? Answers to these and other questions are covered in this chapter, which develops the aggregate demand curve.

Your economic success depends in part on the overall performance of the economy. When the economy grows, job opportunities expand, so your chances of finding a good job increase. When the economy contracts, job opportunities shrink, and so do your job prospects. Thus, you have a personal stake in the economy's success.

Use Homework Xpress! for
economic application,
graphing, videos, and more.

The previous chapter showed how each spending component relates to income in the economy. In this chapter, these components are added to learn how total spending, or aggregate expenditure, relates to income. We then see how a change in the economy's price level affects aggregate expenditure. All this is aimed at getting to the economy's aggregate demand curve. Aggregate supply will be developed in the next chapter. The effects of government spending and taxing will be explored in the chapter after that. Topics discussed include:

- Aggregate expenditure line
- Real GDP demanded
- Changes in aggregate expenditure

- Simple spending multiplier
- Changes in the price level
- Aggregate demand curve

Aggregate Expenditure and Income

In the previous chapter, the big idea was the link between consumption and income, a link that is the most stable in all of macroeconomics. In this section, we build on that connection to uncover the link between total spending in the economy and income. If we try to confront the economy head-on, it soon becomes a bewildering maze, which is why we make progress by beginning with simple models. We continue to assume, as we did in developing the circular-flow model, that there is no capital depreciation and no business saving. Thus, we can say that *each dollar of spending translates directly into a dollar of aggregate income.* Therefore, gross domestic product, or GDP, equals aggregate income. We also continue to assume that investment, government purchases, and net exports are *autonomous,* or independent of the income. Appendix A shows what happens when imports increase with income, and Appendix B develops the algebra behind all this.

The Components of Aggregate Expenditure

Let's begin developing the aggregate demand curve by asking how much aggregate output would be demanded at a given price level. By finding the quantity demanded at a given price level, we'll identify a single point on the aggregate demand curve. We begin by considering the relationship between aggregate spending in the economy and aggregate income. To get us started, suppose the price level in the economy is 130, or 30 percent higher than in the base year. We want to find out how much will be spent at various levels of real income, or real GDP. By *real* GDP, we mean GDP measured in terms of real goods and services produced. Exhibit 1 puts into tabular form relationships introduced in the previous chapter—consumption, saving, planned investment, government purchases, net taxes, and net exports. Although the entries are hypothetical, they bear some relation to levels observed in the U.S. economy. For example, real GDP in the U.S. economy is nearly $12 trillion a year.

Column (1) lists possible real GDP levels in the economy, symbolized by Y. Remember, real GDP also means real income in the economy. Column (2) shows *net taxes,* or *NT,* assumed here to be $1.0 trillion at each real GDP level. Subtracting net taxes from real GDP yields *disposable income,* listed in column (3) as $Y - NT$. Note that at each real GDP level, disposable income equals real GDP minus net taxes of $1.0 trillion. Because net taxes do not vary with income, each time real GDP increases by $0.5 trillion, disposable income also increases by $0.5 trillion.

Households have only two possible uses for disposable income: consumption and saving. Columns (4) and (5) show that the levels of *consumption, C,* and *saving, S,* increase with disposable income. Each time real GDP and disposable income increase by $0.5 trillion, con-

| | EXHIBIT 1 | Real GDP with Net Taxes and Government Purchases (trillions of dollars) |

(1) Real GDP (Y)	(2) Net Taxes (NT)	(3) Disposable Income (Y − NT) (3) =(1) − (2)	(4) Consumption (C)	(5) Saving (S)	(6) Planned Investment (I)	(7) Government Purchases (G)	(8) Net Exports (X − M)	(9) Planned Aggregate Expenditure (AE)	(10) Unplanned Inventory Adjustment (Y − AE) (10) = (1) − (9)
11.0	1.0	10.0	9.4	0.6	1.0	1.0	−0.2	11.2	−0.2
11.5	1.0	10.5	9.8	0.7	1.0	1.0	−0.2	11.6	−0.1
12.0	**1.0**	**11.0**	**10.2**	**0.8**	**1.0**	**1.0**	**−0.2**	**12.0**	**0.0**
12.5	1.0	11.5	10.6	0.9	1.0	1.0	−0.2	12.4	+0.1
13.0	1.0	12.0	11.0	1.0	1.0	1.0	−0.2	12.8	+0.2

sumption increases by $0.4 trillion and saving increases by $0.1 trillion. Thus, as in the previous chapter, the marginal propensity to consume is 4/5, or 0.8, and the marginal propensity to save is 1/5, or 0.2.

Columns (6), (7), and (8) list three now-familiar injections of spending into the circular flow: *planned investment* of $1.0 trillion, *government purchases* of $1.0 trillion, and *net exports* of −$0.2 trillion. In the table, government purchases equal net taxes, so the government budget is balanced. We first want to see how a balanced budget works before we consider the effects of budget deficits or surpluses, which will be discussed in the chapter after next. *The sum of consumption, C, planned investment, I, government purchases, G, and net exports, X − M, is listed in column (9) as planned aggregate expenditure, AE, which shows how much households, firms, governments, and the rest of the world plan to spend on U.S. output at each level of real GDP, or real income.* Note that the only spending component that varies with real GDP is consumption. As real GDP increases, so does disposable income, which increases consumption.

The final column in Exhibit 1 lists any unplanned adjustment to inventories, which equal real GDP minus planned aggregate expenditure, or Y − AE. For example, when real GDP is $11.0 trillion, planned aggregate expenditure is $11.2 trillion. Because planned spending exceeds the amount produced by $0.2 trillion, firms must rely on inventories to make up the shortfall in output. So when real GDP is $11.0 trillion, the unplanned inventory adjustment in the final column is −$0.2 trillion. Because firms cannot reduce inventories indefinitely, they respond to shortfalls in output by increasing production, and they continue to do so until they produce the amount people want to buy—that is, until real GDP equals planned aggregate expenditure.

If the amount produced exceeds planned spending, firms get stuck with unsold goods, which become unplanned increases in inventories. For example, if real GDP is $13.0 trillion, planned aggregate expenditure is only $12.8 trillion, so $0.2 trillion in output remains unsold. Thus, inventories increase by $0.2 trillion. Firms respond by reducing output and do so until they produce the amount people want to buy.

Note the distinction here between **planned investment,** the amount firms plan to invest, and **actual investment,** which includes both planned investment and any unplanned

PLANNED INVESTMENT

The amount of investment that firms plan to undertake during a year

ACTUAL INVESTMENT

The amount of investment actually undertaken; equals planned investment plus unplanned changes in inventories changes in inventories. Unplanned increases in inventories cause firms to smarten up and decrease their production next time around so as not to get stuck with more unsold goods. When the amount people plan to spend equals the amount produced, there are no unplanned inventory adjustments. And when there are no unplanned adjustments in inventories, planned investment equals actual investment. More precisely, *at a given price level, the quantity of real GDP demanded occurs where spending plans match the amount produced*. In Exhibit 1, this occurs where both planned aggregate expenditure and real GDP equal $12.0 trillion.

Real GDP Demanded

Using a table, we have seen how firms adjust output until production just equals desired spending. You may find graphs easier. Graphs are more general than tables and can show relationships between variables without focusing on specific numbers. The tabular relationship between real GDP and planned aggregate expenditure in Exhibit 1 can be expressed as an **aggregate expenditure line** in Exhibit 2. Like the planned aggregate expenditure amounts shown in column (9) of Exhibit 1, the aggregate expenditure line in Exhibit 2 reflects the sum of consumption, planned investment, government purchases, and net exports, or $C + I + G + (X - M)$. Aggregate expenditure is measured on the vertical axis.

Real GDP, measured along the horizontal axis in Exhibit 2, can be viewed in two ways—as the value of *aggregate output* and as the *aggregate income* generated by that output. Because real GDP, or aggregate income, is measured on the horizontal axis and aggregate expenditure is measured on the vertical axis, this graph is often called the **income-expenditure model.** To gain perspective on the relationship between income and expenditure, we use a handy analytical tool: the 45-degree ray from the origin. The special feature of this line is that any point along it is the same distance from each axis. Thus, the 45-degree line

AGGREGATE EXPENDITURE LINE

A relationship showing, for a given price level, planned spending at each income, or real GDP; the total of $C + I + G + (X - M)$ at each income, or real GDP

INCOME-EXPENDITURE MODEL

A relationship between aggregate income and aggregate spending that determines, for a given price level, where the amount people plan to spend equals the amount produced

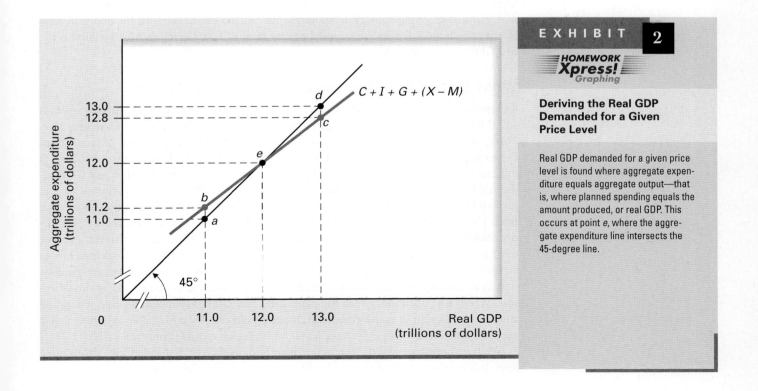

EXHIBIT 2

HOMEWORK
Xpress!
Graphing

Deriving the Real GDP Demanded for a Given Price Level

Real GDP demanded for a given price level is found where aggregate expenditure equals aggregate output—that is, where planned spending equals the amount produced, or real GDP. This occurs at point *e*, where the aggregate expenditure line intersects the 45-degree line.

identifies all points where planned expenditure equals real GDP. *Aggregate output demanded at a given price level occurs where planned aggregate expenditure, measured along the vertical axis, equals real GDP, measured along the horizontal axis.* In Exhibit 2, this occurs at point *e,* where the aggregate expenditure line intersects the 45-degree line. At point *e,* the amount people plan to spend equals the amount produced. We conclude that, at the given price level of 130, the quantity of real GDP demanded equals $12.0 trillion.

What If Planned Spending Exceeds Real GDP?

To find the real GDP demanded at the given price level, consider what happens when real GDP is initially less than $12.0 trillion. As you can see from Exhibit 2, when real GDP is less than $12.0 trillion, the aggregate expenditure line is above the 45-degree line, indicating that planned spending exceeds the amount produced (give this a little thought). For example, if real GDP is $11.0 trillion, planned spending is $11.2 trillion, as indicated by point *b* on the aggregate expenditure line, so planned spending exceeds output by $0.2 trillion. When the amount people plan to spend exceeds the amount produced, something has to give. Ordinarily what gives is the price, but remember that we are seeking the real GDP demanded for a given price level, so the price level is assumed to remain constant, at least for now. What gives in this model are *inventories.* Unplanned reductions in inventories make up the $0.2 trillion shortfall in output. Because firms can't draw down inventories indefinitely, *unplanned inventory reductions* prompt firms to produce more. That increases employment and consumer income, leading to more spending. As long as planned spending exceeds output, firms increase production to make up the difference. This process of more output, more income, and more spending will continue until planned spending equals real GDP, an equality achieved at point *e* in Exhibit 2.

When output reaches $12.0 trillion, planned spending exactly matches output, so no unintended inventory adjustments occur. More importantly, when output reaches $12.0 trillion, planned spending equals the amount produced and equals the total income generated by that production. Earlier we assumed a price level of 130. Therefore, $12.0 trillion is the real GDP demanded at that price level.

What If Real GDP Exceeds Planned Spending?

To reinforce the logic of the model, consider what happens when real GDP initially exceeds $12.0 trillion—that is, when the aggregate expenditure line is below the 45-degree line. Notice in Exhibit 2 that, to the right of point *e,* planned spending falls short of production. For example, if the amount produced in the economy is $13.0 trillion, planned spending, as indicated by point *c* on the aggregate expenditure line, is $0.2 trillion less than real GDP, indicated by point *d* on the 45-degree line. Because real GDP exceeds the amount people plan to buy, unsold goods accumulate. This swells inventories by $0.2 trillion more than firms planned. Rather than allow inventories to pile up indefinitely, firms reduce production, which reduces employment and income. As an example of such behavior, a recent news account read, "General Motors will idle two assembly plants in a move to trim inventories in the wake of slowing sales." *Unplanned inventory buildups* cause firms to cut production until the amount they produce equals aggregate spending, which occurs, again, where real GDP is $12.0 trillion. Given the price level, real GDP demanded is found where the amount people plan to spend equals the amount produced. *For a given price level, there is only one point along the aggregate expenditure line at which planned spending equals real GDP.*

We have now discussed the forces that determine real GDP demanded for a given price level. In the next section, we examine changes that can shift planned spending.

The Simple Spending Multiplier

In the previous section, we used the aggregate expenditure line to find real GDP demanded for a particular price level. In this section, we continue to assume that the price level remains unchanged as we trace the effects of changes in planned spending. Like a stone thrown into a still pond, the effect of any shift of planned spending ripples through the economy, generating changes in aggregate output that exceed the initial change in spending.

An Increase in Planned Spending

We begin at point *e* in Exhibit 3, where planned spending equals real GDP at $12.0 trillion. Now let's consider the effect of an increase in one of the components of spending. Suppose that firms become more optimistic about future profits and decide to increase their investment from $1.0 trillion to $1.1 trillion per year. Exhibit 3 reflects this change by a shift upward of the aggregate expenditure line by $0.1 trillion, from $C + I + G + (X - M)$ to $C + I' + G + (X - M)$.

What happens to real GDP demanded? An instinctive response is to say that real GDP demanded increases by $0.1 trillion. In this case, however, instinct is a poor guide. As you can see, the new spending line intersects the 45-degree line at point *e'*, where real GDP demanded is $12.5 trillion. How can a $0.1 trillion increase in planned spending increase real GDP demanded by $0.5 trillion? What's going on?

The idea of the circular flow is central to an understanding of the adjustment process. As noted earlier, real GDP can be thought of as both the value of production and the income arising from that production. Recall that production yields income, which generates spending. We can think of each trip around the circular flow as a "round" of income and spending.

EXHIBIT 3

Effect of an Increase in Investment on Real GDP Demanded

The economy is initially at point *e*, where spending and real GDP equal $12.0 trillion. A $0.1 trillion increase in autonomous investment shifts the aggregate expenditure line up vertically by $0.1 trillion from $C + I + G + (X - M)$ to $C + I' + G + (X - M)$. Real GDP increases until it equals planned spending at point *e'*. As a result of the $0.1 trillion increase in autonomous investment, real GDP demanded increases by $0.5 trillion, to $12.5 trillion.

Round One

An upward shift of the aggregate expenditure line means that, at the initial real GDP of $12.0 trillion, planned spending now exceeds output by $0.1 trillion, or $100 billion. This is shown in Exhibit 3 by the distance between point *e* and point *f*. Initially, firms match this increased spending by an unplanned reduction in inventories. But reduced inventories prompt firms to expand production by $100 billion, as shown by the movement from point *f* to point *g*. This generates $100 billion more income. The movement from *e* to *g* shows the first round in the multiplier process. The income-generating process does not stop there, however, because those who earn this additional income spend some of it and save the rest, leading to round two of spending and income.

Round Two

Given a marginal propensity to consume of 0.8, those who earn the additional $100 billion will spend $80 billion on toasters, backpacks, gasoline, restaurant meals, and thousands of other goods and services. They save the other $20 billion. The move from point *g* to point *h* in Exhibit 3 shows this $80 billion spending increase. Firms respond by increasing their output by $80 billion, shown by the movement from point *h* to point *i*. Thus, the initial $100 billion in new income increases real GDP by $80 billion during round two.

Round Three and Beyond

We know that four-fifths of the $80 billion earned during round two will get spent during round three and one-fifth will get saved. Thus, $64 billion is spent during round three on still more goods and services, as reflected by the movement from point *i* to point *j*. The remaining $16 billion gets saved. The added spending causes firms to increase output by $64 billion, as shown by the movement from point *j* to point *k*. Round three's additional production generated $64 billion more income, which sets up subsequent rounds of spending, output, and income. *As long as planned spending exceeds output, production will increase, thereby creating more income, which will generate still more spending.*

Exhibit 4 summarizes the multiplier process, showing the first three rounds, round 10, and the cumulative effect of all rounds. The new spending each round is shown in the second column and the accumulation of new spending appears in the third column. For example, the new spending accumulated as of the third round is $244 billion—the sum of the first three rounds of spending ($100 billion + $80 billion + $64 billion). The new saving

EXHIBIT 4	Round	New Spending This Round	Cumulative New Spending	New Saving This Round	Cumulative New Saving
	1	100	100	—	—
	2	80	180	20	20
Tracking the Rounds of Spending Following a $100 Billion Increase in Investment (billions of dollars)	3	64	244	16	36
	⋮	⋮	⋮	⋮	⋮
	10	13.4	446.3	3.35	86.6
	⋮	⋮	⋮	⋮	⋮
	∞	0	500	0	100

from each round appears in the fourth column, and the accumulation of new saving appears in the final column.

Using the Simple Spending Multiplier

In our model, consumers spend four-fifths of their income each round, with each new round equal to spending from the previous round times the marginal propensity to consume, or the MPC. This goes on round after round, leaving less and less to fuel more spending and income. At some point, the new rounds of income and spending become so small that they disappear and the process stops. The question is, by how much does total spending increase? We can get some idea of the total by working through a limited number of rounds. For example, as shown in Exhibit 4, total new spending after 10 rounds sums to $446.3 billion. But calculating the exact total for all rounds would require us to work through an infinite number of rounds—an impossible task.

Fortunately, we can borrow a shortcut from mathematicians, who have found that the sum of an infinite number of rounds, each of which is MPC times the previous round, equals $1/(1 - MPC)$ times the initial change. Translated, the cumulative spending equals $1/(1 - MPC)$, which, in our example, was 1/0.2, or 5, times the initial increase in spending, which was $100 billion. In short, the increase in planned investment eventually boosts real GDP demanded by 5 times $100 billion, or $500 billion.

The **simple spending multiplier** is the factor by which real GDP demanded changes for a given initial change in spending.

$$\text{Simple spending multiplier} = \frac{1}{1 - MPC}$$

The simple spending multiplier provides a shortcut to the total change in real GDP demanded. This multiplier depends on the MPC. The larger the MPC, the larger the simple spending multiplier. That makes sense—the more people spend from each dollar of fresh income, the more total spending will increase. For example, if the MPC was 0.9 instead of 0.8, the denominator of multiplier formula would equal 1.0 minus 0.9, or 0.1, so the multiplier would be 1/0.1, or 10. With an MPC of 0.9, a $0.1 trillion investment increase would boost real GDP demanded by $1.0 trillion. On the other hand, an MPC of 0.75 would yield a denominator of 0.25 and a multiplier of 4. So a $0.1 trillion investment increase would raise real GDP demanded by $0.4 trillion.

Let's return to Exhibit 3. The $0.1 trillion rise in autonomous investment raised real GDP demanded from $12.0 trillion to $12.5 trillion. Note that real GDP demanded would have increased by the same amount if consumers had decided to spend $0.1 trillion more at each income level—that is, if the consumption function, rather than the investment function, had shifted up by $0.1 trillion. Real GDP demanded likewise would have increased if government purchases or net exports increased $0.1 trillion. *The change in aggregate output demanded depends on how much the aggregate expenditure line shifts, not on which spending component causes the shift.*

In our example, planned investment increased by $0.1 trillion in the year in question. *If this greater investment is not sustained the following year, real GDP demanded will fall back.* For example, if planned investment returns to its initial level, other things constant, real GDP demanded would return to $12.0 trillion. Finally, recall from the previous chapter that the MPC and the MPS sum to 1, so 1 minus the MPC equals the MPS. With this information, we can define the simple spending multiplier in terms of the MPS as follows:

SIMPLE SPENDING MULTIPLIER

The ratio of a change in real GDP demanded to the initial change in spending that brought it about; the numerical value of the simple spending multiplier is $1/(1 - MPC)$, called "simple" because only consumption varies with income

$$\text{Simple spending multiplier} = \frac{1}{1 - MPC} = \frac{1}{MPS}$$

We can see that the smaller the MPS, the less leaks from the spending stream as saving. Because less is saved, more gets spent each round, so the spending multiplier is greater. Incidentally, this spending multiplier is called "simple" because consumption is the only spending component that varies with income.

As an example of how a decline in aggregate expenditure can ripple through the economy, consider what happened to air travel in the wake of the September 11 terrorist attacks.

Fear of Flying

When hijacked planes hit the World Trade Center and the Pentagon, America's sense of domestic security changed. The thousands of lives lost and the billions of dollars of property destroyed were chronicled at length in the media. Let's look at the impact of the tragedy on just one industry—air travel—to see how slumping demand there had a multiplier effect on aggregate expenditure.

Once aviation regulators became aware of the hijackings, they grounded all nonmilitary aircraft immediately. This cost the airlines hundreds of millions of dollars a day during the week of the shutdown. During the days following the attack, video of the second plane crashing into the twin towers was shown again and again, freezing this image in people's minds and heightening concerns about airline safety. These worries, coupled with the airport delays from added security (passengers were told to arrive up to three hours before flights), reduced the demand for air travel. Two weeks after the attacks, airlines were operating only 75 percent of their flights, and these flights were only 30 percent full instead of the usual 75 percent full. Airlines requested federal support, saying they would go bankrupt otherwise. Congress quickly approved a $15 billion package of loans and grants.

Despite the promise of federal aid, airlines laid off 85,000 workers, or about 20 percent of their workforce. Flight reductions meant that as many as 900 aircraft would be parked indefinitely, so investment in new planes collapsed. Boeing, the major supplier of new planes, announced layoffs of 30,000 workers. This triggered layoffs among suppliers of airline parts, such as jet engine and electronic components. For example, Rockwell Collins, an electronics supplier, said 15 percent of its workforce would lose jobs. Other suppliers in the airline food chain also cut jobs. Sky Chef, a major airline caterer, laid off 4,800 of its 16,000 employees.

Airports began rethinking their investment plans. Half the major U.S. airports said they were reevaluating their capital improvement plans to see if these investments made sense in this new environment. Honolulu airport, for example, suspended plans to add extra gates and renovate its overseas terminals.

Just within the first three weeks after the attacks, job cuts announced in the industry exceeded 150,000. These were part of only the first round of reduced consumption and investment. In an expanding economy, job losses in one sector can be made up by job expansions in other sectors. But the U.S. economy was already in a recession at the time of the attack. People who lost jobs or who feared for their jobs reduced their demand for housing, clothing, entertainment, restaurant meals, and other goods and services. For example, unemployed flight attendants would be less likely to buy a new car, reducing the income of autoworkers and suppliers. People who lost jobs in this declining auto industry would reduce *their* demand for goods and services. So the reductions in airline jobs had a multiplier effect.

Airlines are only one part of the travel industry. With fewer people traveling, fewer needed hotels, rental cars, taxi rides, and restaurant meals. Each of those sectors generated a cascade of job losses. The terrorist attacks also shook consumer confidence, which in September 2001 suffered its largest monthly drop since October 1990, on the eve of the first Persian Gulf War. Within 10 days following the attacks, the number of people filing for unemployment benefits jumped to a nine-year high. Again, these early job losses could be viewed as just part of the first round of reduced aggregate expenditure. The second round would occur when people who lost jobs or who feared they would lose their jobs started spending less. The U.S. economy continued to lose jobs for nearly two more years.

Sources: Scott McCartney, "Coast-to-Coast Fares Drop to New Lows," *Wall Street Journal,* 12 May 2004; Susan Carey, "UAL Reports a Narrower Loss, But Profits Remain Elusive," *Wall Street Journal,* 29 April 2004; Will Pinkston, "Airports Reconsider Expansion Plans as Future of Air Travel Gets Murkier," *Wall Street Journal,* 27 September 2001; Luke Timmerman, "Boeing Warns Bad May Get Worse," *Seattle Times,* 21 September 2001; and the Federal Aviation Administration at http://www.faa.gov/.

The Aggregate Demand Curve

In this chapter, we have used the aggregate expenditure line to find real GDP demanded *for a given price level.* But what happens to planned spending if the price level changes? As you will see, for each price level, there is a specific aggregate expenditure line, which yields a unique real GDP demanded. By altering the price level, we can derive the aggregate demand curve.

A Higher Price Level

What is the effect of a higher price level on planned spending and, in turn, on real GDP demanded? Recall that consumers hold many assets that are fixed in dollar terms, such as currency and bank accounts. A higher price level decreases the real value of these money holdings. This cuts consumer wealth, making people less willing to spend at each income level. For reasons that will be explained in a later chapter, a higher price level also tends to increase the market interest rate, and a higher interest rate reduces investment. Finally, a higher U.S. price level means that foreign goods become cheaper for U.S. consumers, and U.S. goods become more expensive abroad. So imports rise and exports fall, decreasing net exports. Therefore, *a higher price level reduces consumption, planned investment, and net exports, which all reduce aggregate spending.* This decrease in planned spending reduces real GDP demanded.

Exhibit 5 represents two different ways of expressing the effects of a change in the price level on real GDP demanded. Panel (a) offers the income-expenditure model, and panel (b) offers the aggregate demand curve, showing the inverse relationship between the price level and real GDP demanded. The idea is to find the real GDP demanded for a given price level in panel (a) and show that price-quantity combination as a point on the aggregate demand curve in panel (b). The two panels measure real GDP on the horizontal axes. At the initial price level of 130 in panel (a), the aggregate expenditure line, now denoted simply as *AE,* intersects the 45-degree line at point *e* to yield real GDP demanded of $12.0 trillion. Panel (b) shows more directly the link between real GDP demanded and the price level. As you can see, when the price level is 130, real GDP demanded is $12.0 trillion. This combination is identified by point *e* on the aggregate demand curve.

What if the price level increases from 130 to, say, 140? As you've just learned, an increase in the price level reduces consumption, planned investment, and net exports. This reduction

EXHIBIT   5

HOMEWORK
Xpress!
Graphing

The Income-Expenditure Approach and the Aggregate Demand Curve

At the initial price level of 130, the aggregate expenditure line is *AE*, which identifies real GDP demanded of $12.0 trillion. This combination of a price level of 130 and a real GDP demanded of $12.0 trillion determines one combination (point *e*) on the aggregate demand curve in panel (b).

At the higher price level of 140, the aggregate expenditure line shifts down to *AE'*, and real GDP demanded falls to $11.5 trillion. This price-quantity combination is plotted as point *e'* in panel (b).

At the lower price level of 120, the aggregate expenditure line shifts up to *AE"*, which increases real GDP demanded. This combination is plotted as point *e"* in panel (b).

Connecting points *e, e',* and *e"* in panel (b) yields the downward-sloping aggregate demand curve, which shows the inverse relation between price and real GDP demanded.

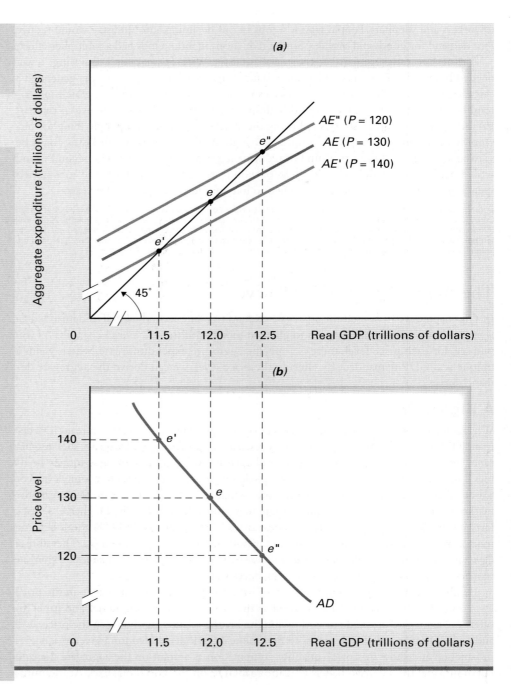

in planned spending is reflected in panel (a) by a downward shift of the aggregate expenditure line from *AE* to *AE'*. As a result, real GDP demanded declines from $12.0 trillion to $11.5 trillion. Panel (b) shows that an increase in the price level from 130 to 140 decreases real GDP demanded from $12.0 trillion to $11.5 trillion, as reflected by the movement from point *e* to point *e'*.

A Lower Price Level

The opposite occurs if the price level falls. At a lower price level, the value of bank accounts, currency, and other money holdings increases. Consumers on average are richer and thus consume more at each real GDP. A lower price level also tends to decrease the market interest rate, which increases investment. Finally, a lower U.S. price level, other things constant, makes U.S. products cheaper abroad and foreign products more expensive here, so exports increase and imports decrease. *Because of a decline in the price level, consumption, investment, and net exports increase at each real GDP.*

Refer again to Exhibit 5 and suppose the price level declines from 130 to, say, 120. This increases planned spending at each income level, as reflected by an upward shift of the spending line from *AE* to *AE"* in panel (a). An increase in planned spending increases real GDP demanded from $12.0 trillion to $12.5 trillion, as indicated by the intersection of the top aggregate expenditure line with the 45-degree line at point *e"*. This same price decrease can be viewed more directly in panel (b). As you can see, when the price level decreases to 120, real GDP demanded increases to $12.5 trillion.

The aggregate expenditure line and the aggregate demand curve present real output from different perspectives. The aggregate expenditure line shows, for a given price level, how planned spending relates to real GDP in the economy. Real GDP demanded is found where planned spending equals real GDP. The aggregate demand curve shows, for various price levels, the quantities of real GDP demanded.

The Multiplier and Shifts in Aggregate Demand

Now that you have some idea how changes in the price level shift the aggregate expenditure line to generate the aggregate demand curve, let's reverse course and return to the situation where the price level is assumed to remain constant. What we want to do now is trace through the effects of a shift of a spending component on aggregate demand, assuming the price level does not change. For example, suppose that a bounce in business confidence spurs a $0.1 trillion increase in planned investment at each real GDP level. Each panel of Exhibit 6 shows a different way of expressing the effects of an increase in planned spending on real GDP demanded, assuming the price level remains unchanged. Panel (a) presents the income-expenditure model and panel (b), the aggregate demand model. Again, the two panels measure real GDP on the horizontal axes. At a price level of 130 in panel (a), the aggregate expenditure line, $C + I + G + (X - M)$, intersects the 45-degree line at point *e* to yield $12.0 trillion in real GDP demanded. Panel (b) shows more directly the link between real GDP demanded and the price level. As you can see, when the price level is 130, real GDP demanded is $12.0 trillion, identified as point *e* on the aggregate demand curve.

Exhibit 6 shows how a shift of the aggregate expenditure line relates to a shift of the aggregate demand curve, given a constant price level. In panel (a), a $0.1 trillion increase in investment shifts the aggregate expenditure line up by $0.1 trillion. Because of the multiplier effect, real GDP demanded climbs from $12.0 trillion to $12.5 trillion. Panel (b) shows the effect of the increase in spending on the aggregate demand curve, which shifts to the right, from *AD* to *AD'*. At the prevailing price level of 130, real GDP demanded increases from $12.0 trillion to $12.5 trillion as a result of the $0.1 trillion increase in planned investment.

Our discussion of the simple spending multiplier exaggerates the actual effect we might expect. For one thing, we have assumed that the price level remains constant. As we shall see in the next chapter, incorporating aggregate supply into the analysis reduces the multiplier because of the resulting price change. Moreover, as income increases there are leakages from the circular flow in addition to saving, such as higher income taxes and greater imports; these

546

Part 7 *Fundamentals of Macroeconomics*

EXHIBIT **6**

HOMEWORK
Xpress!
Graphing

A Shift of the Aggregate Expenditure Line That Shifts the Aggregate Demand Curve

A shift of the aggregate expenditure line at a given price level shifts the aggregate demand curve. In panel (a), an increase in investment of $0.1 trillion, with the price level constant at 130, causes the aggregate expenditure line to increase from $C + I + G + (X - M)$ to $C + I' + G + (X - M)$. As a result, real GDP demanded increases from $12.0 trillion to $12.5 trillion. In panel (b), the aggregate demand curve has shifted from AD out to AD'. At the prevailing price level of 130, real GDP demanded has increased by $0.5 trillion.

(a)

(b)

leakages reduce the multiplier. Finally, although we have presented the process in a timeless framework, the spending multiplier takes time to work through rounds—perhaps a year or more.

In summary: For a given price level, the aggregate expenditure line relates spending plans to income, or real GDP. A change in the price level will shift the aggregate expenditure line, changing real GDP demanded. Changes in the price level and consequent changes in real GDP demanded generate points along an aggregate demand curve. But at a given price level, changes in spending plans, such as changes in planned investment, consumption, or government purchases, will shift the aggregate demand curve.

We close with a case study that considers the problem created when Japanese consumers decided to spend less and save more.

Falling Consumption Triggers Japan's Recession

As noted already, consumer spending is the largest component of aggregate expenditure, accounting for about two-thirds of the total. Consumption depends primarily on disposable income. But at any given income level, consumption depends on several other factors, including household wealth, the interest rate, and consumer expectations. Look what happened in Japan, where by 2003 the stock market stood two-thirds below its 1990 level, taking a big bite from household wealth. A collapse in the once-booming real estate market cut household wealth even more.

C a s e **S t u d y**

**Bringing
Theory to Life**

eActivity
Keep track of what is happening in the Japanese economy through a Web page from NikkeiNet at http://www. nni.nikkei.co.jp sponsored by Nikkei, "the primary source of business information for top executives and decision makers in Japan." What current policies for stimulating consumption can you find among the most current headlines? What are the latest economic indicators reported?

This sharp reduction in household wealth, combined with an erosion of consumer confidence in the economy, prompted Japanese consumers to spend less and save more. Japan's consumption function shifted downward, and their saving function shifted upward. The drop in consumption reduced aggregate expenditure and shifted the aggregate demand curve to the left. The decline in aggregate demand resulted in Japan's longest economic downturn in 50 years, with the unemployment rate doubling between 1990 and 2003. Retail sales declined in 2003 for the seventh consecutive year. Japan, the second largest economy in the world (after the United States), is by far the largest economy in Asia. A weak economy in Japan hurts the already troubled economies across Asia because Japan is a customer for their exports. Thus, the decline in consumption in Japan had global implications. But by 2004 Japan was starting to show signs of life, with a growing real GDP.

Sources: "Japanese Retail Sales Fell Last Year, *Taipei Times*, 29 January 2004; and "Japan Is Flying Again," *The Economist*, 14 February 2004. For a survey of the Japanese economy, go to http://www.oecd.org/home/.

Conclusion

Three ideas central to this chapter are (1) certain forces determine the quantity of real GDP demanded at a given price level, (2) changes in the price level generate the aggregate demand curve, and (3) at a given price level, changes in planned spending shift the aggregate demand curve. The simple multiplier provides a crude but exaggerated idea of how a change in spending plans affects real GDP demanded.

This chapter focused on aggregate spending. A simplifying assumption used throughout was that net exports do not vary with income. Appendix A adds more realism by considering what happens when imports increase with income. Because spending on imports leak from the circular flow, this more realistic approach reduces the spending multiplier.

So far, we have derived real GDP demanded using several approaches, including intuition, tables, and graphs. With the various approaches, we find that for each price level there is a specific quantity of real GDP demanded, other things constant. Appendix B uses algebra to show the same results.

SUMMARY

1. The aggregate expenditure line indicates, for a given price level, planned spending at each income level. At a given price level, real GDP demanded is found where the amount that people plan to spend equals the amount produced.

2. The simple spending multiplier indicates the multiple by which a shift of planned spending changes real GDP demanded. The simple spending multiplier developed in this chapter is $1/(1 - MPC)$. The larger the MPC, the more will be spent and the less will be saved, so the larger the simple multiplier.

3. A higher price level causes a downward shift of the aggregate expenditure line, leading to a lower real GDP de-

manded. A lower price level causes an upward shift of the aggregate expenditure line, increasing real GDP demanded. By tracing the impact of price changes on real GDP demanded, we can derive an aggregate demand curve.

4. The aggregate expenditure line and the aggregate demand curve portray real output from different perspectives. The aggregate expenditure line shows, for a given price level, how much people plan to spend at each income level. Real GDP demanded is found where planned spending equals the amount produced. The aggregate demand curve shows, for various price levels, the quantities of real GDP demanded. At a given price level, a change in spending plans shifts the aggregate demand curve.

QUESTIONS FOR REVIEW

1. *(Aggregate Expenditure)* What are the components of aggregate expenditure? In the model developed in this chapter, which components vary with changes in the level of real GDP? What determines the slope of the aggregate expenditure line?

2. *(Real GDP Demanded)* In your own words, explain the logic of the income-expenditure model. What determines the amount of real GDP demanded?

3. *(Real GDP Demanded)* What equalities hold at the level of real GDP demanded? When determining real GDP demanded, what do we assume about the price level? What do we assume about inventories?

4. *(When Output and Spending Differ)* What role do inventories play in determining real GDP demanded? In answering this question, suppose initially that firms are either producing more than people plan to spend, or producing less than people plan to spend.

5. *(Simple Spending Multiplier)* "A rise in planned investment in an economy will lead to a rise in the amount of planned spending." Use the spending multiplier to verify this statement.

6. (*Case* **Study**: Fear of Flying) How do events, such as the World Trade Center and Pentagon attacks described in the case study "Fear of Flying," affect the aggregate expenditure line and the aggregate demand curve? Explain fully.

7. *(The Aggregate Demand Curve)* What is the effect of a lower price level, other things constant, on the aggregate expenditure line and real GDP demanded? How does the multiplier interact with the price change to determine the new real GDP demanded?

8. (*Case* **Study**: Falling Consumption Triggers Japan's Recession) What happened to consumption in Japan? Why did this happen? What was the impact on aggregate demand there?

PROBLEMS AND EXERCISES

9. *(Simple Spending Multiplier)* For each of the following values for the MPC, determine the size of the simple spending multiplier and the total change in real GDP demanded following a $10 billion decrease in autonomous spending:

   a. $MPC = 0.9$
   b. $MPC = 0.75$
   c. $MPC = 0.6$

10. *(Simple Spending Multiplier)* Suppose that the MPC is 0.8 and that $12 trillion of real GDP is currently being demanded. The government wants to increase real GDP demanded to $13 trillion at the given price level. By how much would it have to increase government purchases to achieve this goal?

11. *(Simple Spending Multiplier)* Suppose that the MPC is 0.8, while planned investment, government purchases, and net exports sum to $500 billion. Suppose also that the government budget is in balance.

   a. What is the sum of saving and net taxes when desired spending equals real GDP? Explain.
   b. What is the value of the multiplier?
   c. Explain why the multiplier is related to the slope of the consumption function.

12. *(Investment and the Multiplier)* This chapter assumes that investment is autonomous. What would happen to the size of the multiplier if investment increases as real GDP increases? Explain.

13. *(Shifts of Aggregate Demand)* Assume the simple spending multiplier equals 10. Determine the size and direction of any changes of the aggregate expenditure line, real GDP demanded, and the aggregate demand curve for each of the following changes in autonomous spending:

   a. Autonomous spending rises by $8 billion.
   b. Autonomous spending falls by $5 billion.
   c. Autonomous spending rises by $20 billion.

EXPERIENTIAL EXERCISES

14. (*C a s e* **Study**: Falling Consumption Triggers Japan's Recession) Professor Nouriel Roubini of New York University maintains an extensive Web page at http://www. stern.nyu.edu/globalmacro/ devoted to global financial crises. Visit the page and determine what are the latest developments in Japan and around the world.

15. *(Wall Street Journal)* This chapter pointed out that net exports are an important influence on aggregate demand.

Find a story in today's *Wall Street Journal* that describes an event that will affect U.S. imports or exports. A good place to look is the "International" page in the first section of the *Journal*. Analyze the story you have chosen, and illustrate the event using both the aggregate expenditure line and the aggregate demand curve.

HOMEWORK XPRESS! EXERCISES

*These exercises require access to McEachern Homework Xpress! If Homework Xpress! did not come with your book, visit **http://homeworkxpress.swlearning.com** to purchase.*

1. Use the diagram for this exercise to draw a level of aggregate expenditures that would lead to an economy at an equilibrium, *E,* with a real GDP of $8 trillion.

2. Use the diagram for this exercise to draw a level of aggregate expenditures that would lead to an economy at an equilibrium, *E,* with a real GDP of $8 trillion. Illustrate how a change in aggregate expenditures would lead to an increase in the equilibrium level of GDP to $10 trillion.

3. Use the diagram to draw in a level of aggregate expenditures that would lead to an economy at an equilibrium, *E,* with a real GDP of $8 trillion for a price level of *P* = 100. Illustrate the effect of an increase in the price level to *P* = 120. Identify the new equilibrium.

4. In the diagram, draw a level of aggregate expenditures that would lead to an economy at an equilibrium, *E,* with a real GDP of $8 trillion for a price level of *P* = 100. Illustrate the effect of a decrease in the price level to *P* = 80. Identify the new equilibrium.

5. Draw an aggregate demand curve that shows the economy at an equilibrium level of real GDP of $8 trillion when the price level is *P* = 120.

Variable Net Exports Revisited

This chapter has assumed that net exports do not vary with income. A more realistic approach has net exports varying inversely with income. Such a model was developed in the appendix to the previous chapter. The resulting net export function, $X - M$, is presented in panel (a) of Exhibit 7. Recall that the higher the income level in the economy, the more is spent on imports, so the lower the net exports. (If this is not clear, review the appendix to the previous chapter.) Panel (b) of Exhibit 7 shows what happens when vari-

able net exports are added to consumption, government purchases, and investment. We add the variable net export function to $C + I + G$ to get $C + I + G + (X - M)$. Perhaps the easiest way to see how introducing net exports affects planned spending is to begin where real GDP equals $10.0 trillion. Because net exports equal zero when real GDP equals $10.0 trillion, the addition of net exports has no effect on planned spending. So the $C + I + G$ and $C + I + G + (X - M)$ lines intersect where real GDP equals $10.0

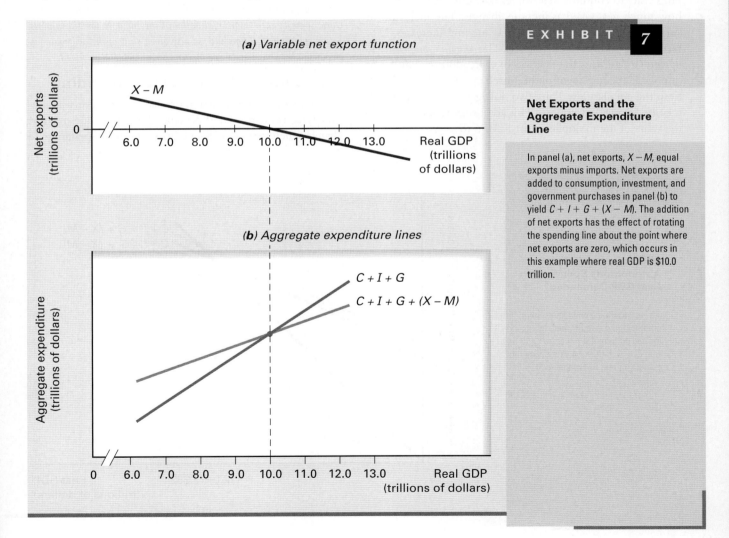

EXHIBIT 7

Net Exports and the Aggregate Expenditure Line

In panel (a), net exports, $X - M$, equal exports minus imports. Net exports are added to consumption, investment, and government purchases in panel (b) to yield $C + I + G + (X - M)$. The addition of net exports has the effect of rotating the spending line about the point where net exports are zero, which occurs in this example where real GDP is $10.0 trillion.

trillion. At real GDP levels less than $10.0 trillion, net exports are positive, so the $C + I + G + (X - M)$ line is above the $C + I + G$ line. At real GDP levels greater than $10.0 trillion, net exports are negative, so the $C + I + G + (X - M)$ line is below the $C + I + G$ line. *Because variable net exports and real GDP are inversely related, the addition of variable net exports has the effect of flattening out, or reducing the slope of, the aggregate expenditure line.*

Net Exports and the Spending Multiplier

The inclusion of variable net exports makes the model more realistic but more complicated, and it requires a reformulation of the spending multiplier. If net exports are autonomous, or independent of income, only the marginal propensity to consume determines how much gets spent and how much gets saved as income changes. The inclusion of variable net exports means that, as income increases, U.S. residents spend more on imports. The *marginal propensity to import*, or *MPM*, is the fraction of each additional dollar of disposable income spent on imported products. Imports leak from the circular flow. Thus, two leakages now increase with income: saving and imports. This additional leakage changes the value of the multiplier from $1/MPS$ to:

$$\text{spending multiplier with variable net exports} = \frac{1}{MPS + MPM}$$

The larger the marginal propensity to import, the greater the leakage during each round of spending and the smaller the resulting spending multiplier. Suppose the MPM equals 1/10, or 0.1. If the marginal propensity to save is 0.2 and the marginal propensity to import is 0.1, then only $0.70 of each additional dollar of disposable income gets spent on output produced in the United States. We can compute the new multiplier as follows:

$$\text{Spending multiplier with variable net exports}$$
$$= \frac{1}{MPS + MPM} = \frac{1}{0.2 + 0.1} = \frac{1}{0.3} = 3.33$$

Thus, the inclusion of net exports reduces the spending multiplier in our hypothetical example from 5 to 3.33. *Because some of each additional dollar of income goes toward imports, less is spent on U.S. products, so any given shift of the aggregate expenditure line has less of an impact on real GDP demanded.*

A Change in Autonomous Spending

Given the net export function described in the previous section, what is the real GDP demanded, and how does income change when there is a change in autonomous spending? To

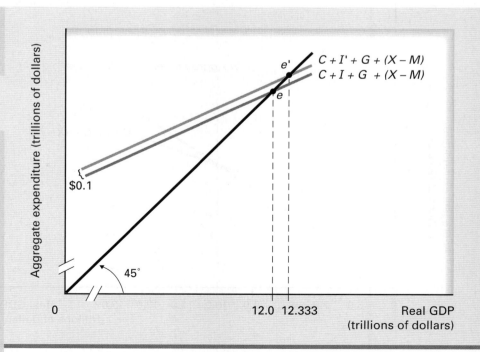

EXHIBIT 8

Effect of a Shift of Autonomous Spending on Real GDP Demanded

An increase in planned investment, other things constant, shifts the spending line up from $C + I + G + (X - M)$ to $C + I' + G + (X - M)$, increasing the quantity of real GDP demanded.

answer these questions, let's begin in Exhibit 8 with an aggregate expenditure line of $C + I + G + (X - M)$, where net exports vary inversely with income. This aggregate expenditure line intersects the 45-degree line at point e, determining real GDP demanded of $12.0 trillion. Suppose now that planned investment increases by $0.1 trillion at every income, with the price level unchanged. This will shift the entire aggregate expenditure line up by $0.1 trillion, from C $+ I + G + (X - M)$ to $C + I' + G + (X - M)$, as shown in Exhibit 8. Output demanded increases from $12.0 trillion to $12.333 trillion, representing an increase of $0.333 trillion, or $333 billion, which is $0.1 trillion times the spending multiplier with variable exports of 3.33. The derivation of the output level and the size of the multiplier are explained in Appendix B.

APPENDIX A QUESTION

1. (*Net Exports and the Spending Multiplier*) Suppose that the marginal propensity to consume (MPC) is 0.8 and the marginal propensity to import (MPM) is 0.05.

   a. What is the value of the spending multiplier?
   b. By how much would the real GDP demanded change if planned investment increased by $100 billion?

   c. Using your answer to part (b), calculate the change in net exports caused by the change in aggregate output.

The Algebra of Income and Expenditure

This appendix explains the algebra behind real GDP demanded. You should see some similarity between this and the circular-flow explanation of national income accounts.

The Aggregate Expenditure Line

We first determine where planned spending equals output and then derive the relevant spending multipliers, assuming a given price level. Initially, let's assume net exports are autonomous. Then we'll incorporate variable net exports into the framework.

Real GDP demanded for a given price level occurs where planned spending equals income, or real GDP. Planned spending is equal to the sum of consumption, C, planned investment, I, government purchases, G, and net exports, X − M. Algebraically, we can write the equality as

$$Y = C + I + G + (X - M)$$

where Y equals income, or real GDP. To find where real GDP equals planned spending, we begin with the heart of the income-expenditure model: the consumption function. The consumption function used throughout this chapter is a straight line; the equation for that line can be written as

$$C = 1.4 + 0.8\ (Y - 1.0)$$

The marginal propensity to consume is 0.8, Y is income, or real GDP, and 1.0 is autonomous net taxes in trillions of dollars. Thus (Y − 1.0) is real GDP minus net taxes, which equals disposable income. The consumption function can be simplified to

$$C = 0.6 + 0.8Y$$

Consumption at each real GDP, therefore, equals $0.6 trillion (which could be called autonomous consumption—that is, consumption that does not vary with income), plus 0.8 times income, which is the marginal propensity to consume times income.

The second component of spending is investment, I, which we have assumed is autonomous and equal to $1.0 trillion. The third component of spending is autonomous government purchases, G, which we assumed to be $1.0 trillion. Net exports, X − M, the final spending component, we assumed to be −$0.2 trillion at all levels of income. Sub-

stituting the numerical values for each spending component in planned spending, we get

$$Y = 0.6 + 0.8Y + 1.0 + 1.0 - 0.2$$

Notice there is only one variable in this expression: Y. If we rewrite the expression as

$$Y - 0.8Y = 0.6 + 1.0 + 1.0 - 0.2$$

$$0.2Y = 2.4$$

we can solve for real GDP demanded:

$$Y = \$12.0 \text{ trillion}$$

A More General Form of Income and Expenditure

The advantage of algebra is that it allows us to derive the equilibrium quantity of real GDP demanded in a more general way. Let's begin with a consumption function of the general form

$$C = a + b\ (Y - NT)$$

where b is the marginal propensity to consume and NT is net taxes. Consumption can be rearranged as

$$C = a - bNT + bY$$

where a − bNT is *autonomous* consumption (the portion of consumption that is independent of income) and bY is *induced* consumption (the portion of consumption generated by higher income in the economy). Real GDP demanded equals the sum of consumption, C, planned investment, I, government purchases, G, and net exports, X − M, or

$$\text{Income} = \text{Expenditure}$$

$$Y = a - bNT + bY + I + G + (X - M)$$

Again, by rearranging terms and isolating Y on the left side of the equation, we get

$$Y = \frac{1}{1 - b}(a - bNT + I + G + X - M)$$

The (a − bNT + I + G + X − M) term represents autonomous spending—that is, the amount of spending that is independent of income. And $(1 - b)$ equals 1 minus the MPC. In the chapter, we showed that $1/(1 - MPC)$ equals the simple spending multiplier. One way of viewing what's going on is to keep in mind that autonomous spending is *multiplied* through the economy to arrive at real GDP demanded.

The formula that yields real GDP demanded can be used to derive the spending multiplier. We can increase autonomous spending by, say, $1, to see what happens to real GDP demanded.

$$Y' = \frac{1}{1 - b}(a - bNT + I + G + X - M + \$1)$$

The difference between this expression and the initial one (that is, between Y' and Y) is $\$1/(1 - b)$. Because b equals the MPC, the simple multiplier equals $1/(1 - b)$. Thus, the change in equilibrium income equals the change in autonomous spending times the multiplier.

Varying Net Exports

Here we explore the algebra behind variable net exports, first introduced in the appendix to the previous chapter. We begin with the equality

$$Y = C + I + G + (X - M)$$

Exports are assumed to equal $0.9 trillion at each income level. Imports increase as disposable income increases, with a marginal propensity to import of 0.1. Therefore, net exports equal

$$X - M = 0.9 - 0.1 (Y - 1.0)$$

After incorporating the values for *C, I,* and *G* presented earlier, we can express the equality as

$$Y = 0.6 + 0.8Y + 1.0 + 1.0 + 0.9 - 0.1 (Y - 1.0)$$

which reduces to $0.3Y = \$3.6$ trillion, or $Y = \$12.0$ trillion.

Algebra can be used to generalize these results. If m represents the marginal propensity to import, net exports become $X - m(Y - NT)$. Real GDP demanded can be found by solving for Y in the expression

$$Y = a + b(Y - NT) + I + G + X - m(Y - NT)$$

which yields

$$Y = \frac{1}{1 - b + m}(a - bNT + I + G + X + mNT)$$

The expression in parentheses represents autonomous spending. In the denominator, $1 - b$ is the marginal propensity to save and m is the marginal propensity to import. Appendix A demonstrated that $1/(MPS - MPM)$ equals the spending multiplier when variable net exports are included. Thus, real GDP demanded equals the spending multiplier times autonomous spending. And an increase in autonomous spending times the multiplier gives us the resulting increase in real GDP demanded.

APPENDIX B QUESTION

---

1. Suppose that $C = 100 + 0.75(Y - 100)$, $I = 50$, $G = 30$, and $X - M = -100$, all in billions of dollars. What is the simple spending multiplier? What is real GDP demanded? What would happen to real GDP demanded if government purchases increased to $40 billion?

Aggregate Supply

W hat is your normal capacity for academic work, and when do you exceed that effort? If the economy is already operating at full employment, how can it produce more? What valuable piece of information do employers and workers lack when they negotiate wages? Why do employers and workers fail to agree on pay cuts that might save jobs? How might a long stretch of high unemployment reduce the economy's ability to produce in the future? These and other questions are answered in this chapter, which develops the aggregate supply curve in the short run and in the long run.

Up to this point, we have focused on aggregate demand. We have not yet brought in aggregate supply, a much debated topic. The debate involves the shape of the aggregate supply curve and the reasons for that shape. This chapter develops a single, coherent framework for aggregate supply. Although the focus continues to be on economic aggregates, you should keep in mind that aggregate supply reflects billions of individual production decisions made by millions of individual resource suppliers and firms in the economy. Each firm operates in its own little world, dealing with its own suppliers and customers, and keeping a watchful eye on existing and potential competitors. Yet each firm recognizes that success also depends on the performance of the economy as a whole. The theory of aggregate supply described here must be consistent with both the microeconomic behavior of individual suppliers and the macroeconomic behavior of the economy. Topics discussed include:

- Expected price level and long-term contracts
- Potential output
- Short-run aggregate supply
- Long-run aggregate supply
- Expansionary gap
- Contractionary gap
- Changes in aggregate supply

Aggregate Supply in the Short Run

Aggregate supply is the relationship between the price level in the economy and the aggregate output firms are willing and able to supply, with other things constant. Assumed constant along a given aggregate supply curve are resource prices, the state of technology, and the set of formal and informal institutions that structure production incentives, such as the system of property rights, patent laws, tax systems, respect for the laws, and the customs and conventions of the marketplace. The greater the supply of resources, the better the technology, and the more effective the production incentives provided by the economic institutions, the greater the aggregate supply. Let's begin by looking at the key resource—labor.

Labor and Aggregate Supply

Labor is the most important resource, accounting for about 70 percent of production cost. The supply of labor in an economy depends on the size and abilities of the adult population and their preferences for work versus leisure. Along a given labor supply curve—that is, for a given adult population with given preferences for work and leisure—the quantity of labor supplied depends on the wage. The higher the wage, other things constant, the more labor supplied.

So far, so good. But things start getting complicated once we recognize that the purchasing power of any given nominal wage depends on the economy's price level. *The higher the price level, the less any given money wage will purchase, so the less attractive that wage is to workers.* Consider wages and the price level over time. Suppose a worker in 1970 was offered a job paying $20,000 per year. That salary may not impress you today, but its real purchasing power back then would exceed $75,000 in today's dollars. Because the price level matters, we must distinguish between the **nominal wage,** or money wage, which measures the wage in current dollars, and the **real wage,** which measures the wage in constant dollars—that is, dollars measured by the goods and services they will buy. A higher real wage means workers can buy more goods and services.

Both workers and employers care more about the real wage than about the nominal wage. The problem is that nobody knows for sure how the price level will change during the life of the wage agreement, so labor contracts must be negotiated in terms of nominal wages, not real wages. Some resource prices, such as wages set by long-term contracts, remain in force for extended periods, often for two or three years. Workers as well as other resource suppliers must therefore reach agreements based on the *expected* price level.

NOMINAL WAGE

The wage measured in current dollars; the dollar amount on a paycheck

REAL WAGE

The wage measured in dollars of constant purchasing power; the wage measured in terms of the quantity of goods and services it will buy

Even where there are no explicit labor contracts, there is often an implicit agreement that the wage, once negotiated, will not change for a while. For example, in many firms the standard practice is to revise wages annually. So wage agreements may be either *explicit* (based on a labor contract) or *implicit* (based on labor market practices). These explicit and implicit agreements are difficult to renegotiate while still in effect, even if the price level in the economy turns out to be higher or lower than expected.

Potential Output and the Natural Rate of Unemployment

Here's how resource owners and firms negotiate resource price agreements for a particular period, say, a year. Firms and resource suppliers expect a certain price level to prevail in the economy during the year. You could think of this as the *consensus* view for the upcoming year. Based on consensus expectations, firms and resource suppliers reach agreements on resource prices, such as wages. For example, firms and workers may expect the price level to increase 3 percent next year, so they agree on a nominal wage increase of 4 percent, which would increase the real wage by 1 percent. If these price-level expectations are realized, the agreed-on nominal wage translates into the expected real wage, so everyone is satisfied with the way things work out—after all, that's what they willingly negotiated. When the actual price level turns out as expected, we call the resulting output the economy's potential output. *The potential output is the amount produced when there are no surprises about the price level.* So, at the agreed-on real wage, workers are supplying the quantity of labor they want and firms are hiring the quantity of labor they want. Both sides are content with the outcome.

We can think of **potential output** as the economy's maximum sustainable output, given the supply of resources, the state of technology, and the formal and informal production incentives offered by the rules of the game. Potential output is also referred to by other terms, including the *natural rate of output* and the *full-employment rate of output.*

The unemployment rate that occurs when the economy is producing its potential GDP is called the **natural rate of unemployment.** That rate prevails when cyclical unemployment is zero. When the economy is producing its potential output, the number of job openings equals the number of people unemployed for frictional, structural, and seasonal reasons. Widely accepted estimates of the natural rate of unemployment range from about 4 percent to about 6 percent of the labor force.

Potential output provides a reference point, an anchor, for the analysis in this chapter. *When the price-level expectations of both workers and firms are fulfilled, the economy produces its potential output.* Complications arise, however, when the actual price level differs from expectations, as we'll see next.

Actual Price Level Higher than Expected

As you already know, each firm's goal is to maximize profit. Profit equals total revenue minus total cost. Suppose workers and firms reach a wage agreement. What if the economy's price level then turns out to be higher than they expected? What happens *in the short run* to real GDP supplied? The **short run** in macroeconomics is a period during which some resource prices remain fixed by contract. Does output in the short run exceed the economy's potential, fall short of that potential, or equal that potential?

The prices of many resources have been fixed for the duration of contracts, so firms welcome a higher than expected price level. After all, the selling prices of their products, on average, are higher than expected, while the costs of at least some of the resources they employ remain constant. *Because a price level that is higher than expected results in a higher profit per unit, firms have an incentive in the short run to increase production beyond the economy's potential level.*

At first it might appear contradictory to talk about producing beyond the economy's potential, but remember that potential output means not zero unemployment but the natural rate of unemployment. Even in an economy producing its potential output, there is some unemployed labor and some unused production capacity. If you think of potential GDP as the economy's *normal capacity,* you get a better idea of how production can temporarily exceed that capacity. For example, during World War II, the United States pulled out all the stops to win the war. Factories operated around the clock. The unemployment rate dropped below 2 percent—well under the natural rate. Overtime was common. People worked longer and harder for the war effort than they normally would have.

Think about your own study habits. During most of the term, you display your normal capacity for academic work. As the end of the term draws near, however, you may shift into high gear, finishing term papers, studying late into the night for final exams, and generally running yourself ragged trying to pull things together. During those final frenzied days of the term, you study beyond your normal capacity, beyond the schedule you would prefer to follow on a regular or sustained basis. We often observe workers exceeding their normal capacity for short bursts: fireworks technicians around the Fourth of July, accountants during tax time, farmers during harvest time, and elected officials toward the end of a campaign or legislative session. Similarly, firms and their workers are able, *in the short run,* to push output beyond the economy's potential.

Why Costs Rise When Output Exceeds Potential

The economy is flexible enough to expand output beyond potential GDP, but as output expands, the cost of additional output increases. Although many workers are bound by contracts, wage agreements may require overtime pay for extra hours or weekends. As the economy expands and the unemployment rate declines, additional workers are harder to find. Retirees, homemakers, and students may require extra pay to draw them into the labor force. Some firms may resort to hiring workers who are not prepared for the available jobs—those who had been structurally unemployed. If few additional workers are available, if workers require additional pay for overtime, or if available workers are less qualified, the nominal cost of labor will increase as output expands in the short run, even though most wages remain fixed by long-term agreements.

As production increases, the demand for nonlabor resources increases as well, so the prices of those resources in markets where prices are flexible—such as the market for oil—will increase, reflecting their greater scarcity. Also, as production increases, firms use their machines and trucks more intensively, so equipment wears out faster and is more subject to breakdown. Thus, the nominal cost per unit of output rises when production is pushed beyond the economy's potential output. But *because the prices of some resources are fixed by contracts, the price level rises faster than the per-unit production cost, so firms find it profitable to increase the quantity supplied.*

When the economy's actual price level exceeds the expected price level, the real value of an agreed-on nominal wage declines. We might ask why workers would be willing to increase the quantity of labor they supply when the price level is higher than expected. One answer is that because labor agreements require workers to offer their labor at the agreed-on nominal wage, workers are simply complying with their contracts, at least until they have a chance to renegotiate.

In summary: If the price level is higher than expected, firms have a profit incentive to increase the quantity of goods and services supplied. At higher rates of output, however, the per-unit cost of additional output increases. Firms will expand output as long as the revenue from additional production exceeds the cost of that production.

An Actual Price Level Lower than Expected

We have discovered that if the price level is greater than expected, firms expand output in the short run, but as they do, the per-unit cost of additional production increases. Now let's look at the effects of a price level that turns out to be lower than expected. Again, suppose that resource suppliers and firms expect a certain price level. If it turns out to be lower than expected, production is less attractive to firms. The prices they receive for their output are on average lower than they expected, yet many of their production costs, such as the nominal wage, do not fall.

Because production is less profitable when prices are lower than expected, firms reduce their quantity supplied, so the economy's output falls below its potential. As a result, some workers are laid off, those who keep their jobs may work fewer hours, and unemployment exceeds the natural rate. Not only is less labor employed, but machines go unused, delivery trucks sit idle, and entire plants may shut down—for example, automakers sometimes halt production for weeks.

Just as some costs increase in the short run when output is pushed beyond the economy's potential, some costs decline when output falls below that potential. Some resources become unemployed, so the prices of resources decline in markets where the price is flexible. Moreover, with an abundance of unemployed resources, firms can become more selective about which resources to retain, laying off the least productive first (recent hires, who typically have the least experience, are usually the first to go).

To review: If the economy's price level turns out to be higher than expected, firms maximize profit by increasing the quantity supplied beyond the economy's potential output. As output expands, the per-unit cost of additional production increases, but firms expand production as long as prices rise more than costs. If the price level turns out to be lower than expected, firms reduce output below the economy's potential output because prices fall more than costs. All of this is a long way of saying that *there is a direct relationship in the short run between the actual price level and real GDP supplied.*

The Short-Run Aggregate Supply Curve

What we have been describing so far traces out the **short-run aggregate supply (SRAS) curve,** which shows the relationship between the actual price level and real GDP supplied, other things remaining constant. Again, the *short run* in this context is the period during which some resource prices, especially those for labor, are fixed by implicit or explicit agreement. For simplicity, we can think of the short run as the duration of labor contracts, which are based on the expected price level.

Suppose the expected price level is 130. The short-run aggregate supply curve in Exhibit 1, $SRAS_{130}$, is based on that expected price level (hence the subscript 130). If the price level turns out to be 130, as expected, producers supply the economy's *potential output,* which in Exhibit 1 is $12.0 trillion. Although not shown in the exhibit, for the price level to turn out as expected, the aggregate demand curve would have to intersect the aggregate supply curve at point *a.* So, given the economy's potential output, the short-run aggregate supply curve depends on the expected price level, which depends on expectations about aggregate demand. If the economy produces its potential output, unemployment is at the *natural rate.* Nobody is surprised, and all are content with the outcome. There is no tendency to move away from point *a* even if workers and firms have a chance to renegotiate wages.

In Exhibit 1, output levels that fall short of the economy's potential are shaded red, and output levels that exceed the economy's potential are shaded blue. The slope of the short-run aggregate supply curve depends on how sharply the cost of additional production rises

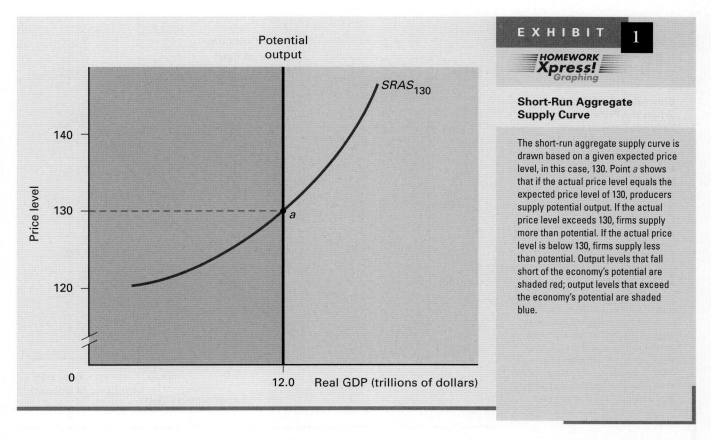

EXHIBIT **1**

HOMEWORK
Xpress!
Graphing

**Short-Run Aggregate
Supply Curve**

The short-run aggregate supply curve is drawn based on a given expected price level, in this case, 130. Point *a* shows that if the actual price level equals the expected price level of 130, producers supply potential output. If the actual price level exceeds 130, firms supply more than potential. If the actual price level is below 130, firms supply less than potential. Output levels that fall short of the economy's potential are shaded red; output levels that exceed the economy's potential are shaded blue.

as real GDP expands. If per-unit costs increase modestly as output expands, the supply curve will be relatively flat. If these costs increase sharply as output expands, the supply curve will be relatively steep. Much of the controversy about the short-run aggregate supply curve involves its shape. Shapes range from flat to steep. Notice that the short-run aggregate supply curve becomes steeper as output increases, because resources become scarcer and thus more costly as output increases.

From the Short Run to the Long Run

This section begins with the price level exceeding expectations in the short run to see what happens in the long run. The long run is long enough that firms and resource suppliers can renegotiate all agreements based on knowledge of the actual price level. *So in the long run, there are no surprises about the price level.*

Closing an Expansionary Gap

Let's begin our look at the long-run adjustment in Exhibit 2 with an expected price level of 130. The short-run aggregate supply curve for that expected price level is $SRAS_{130}$. Given this short-run aggregate supply curve, the equilibrium price level and real GDP depend on the aggregate demand curve. The actual price level will equal the expected price level only if the aggregate demand curve intersects the aggregate supply curve at point *a*— that is, where the short-run quantity equals potential output. Point *a* reflects potential output of $12.0 trillion and a price level of 130, which is the expected price level.

**Short-Run Equilibrium
When the Price Level
Exceeds Expectations**

If the expected price level is 130, the short-run aggregate supply curve is $SRAS_{130}$. If the actual price level turns out as expected, the quantity supplied is the potential output of $12.0 trillion. Given the aggregate demand curve shown here, the price level ends up higher than expected, and output exceeds potential, as shown by the short-run equilibrium at point *b*. The amount by which actual output exceeds the economy's potential output is called the expansionary gap. In the long run, price-level expectations and nominal wages will be revised upward. Costs will rise and the short-run aggregate supply curve will shift leftward to $SRAS_{140}$. Eventually, the economy will move to long-run equilibrium at point *c*, thus closing the expansionary gap.

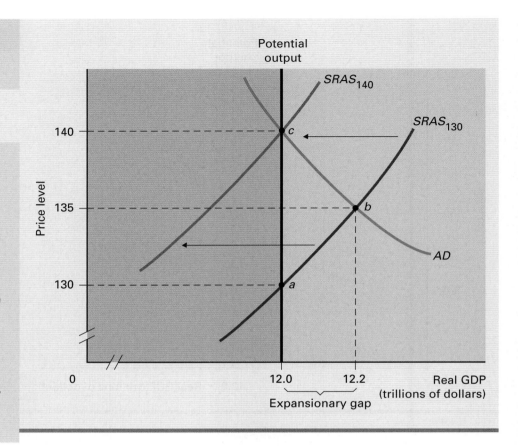

SHORT-RUN EQUILIBRIUM

The price level and real GDP that occur when the aggregate demand curve intersects the short-run aggregate supply curve

EXPANSIONARY GAP

The amount by which output in the short run exceeds the economy's potential output

LONG RUN

In macroeconomics, a period during which wage contracts and resource price agreements can be renegotiated; there are no surprises about the economy's actual price level

But what if aggregate demand turns out to be greater than expected, as shown by curve *AD,* which intersects the short-run aggregate supply curve $SRAS_{130}$ at point *b*. Point *b* is the **short-run equilibrium,** reflecting a price level of 135 and a real GDP of $12.2 trillion. The actual price level in the short run is higher than expected, and output exceeds the economy's potential of $12.0 trillion.

The amount by which short-run output exceeds the economy's potential is called an **expansionary gap.** In Exhibit 2, that gap is the short-run output of $12.2 trillion minus potential output of $12.0 trillion, or $0.2 trillion. When real GDP exceeds its potential, the unemployment rate is below its natural rate. Employees are working overtime, machines are being pushed to their limits, and farmers are sandwiching extra crops between usual plantings. Remember that the nominal wage was negotiated based on an expected price level of 130; because the actual price level is higher, that nominal wage translates into a lower-than-expected real wage. As we will see, output exceeding the economy's potential creates inflationary pressure. *The more that short-run output exceeds the economy's potential, the larger the expansionary gap and the greater the upward pressure on the price level.*

What happens in the long run? The **long run** is a period during which firms and resource suppliers know about market conditions, particularly aggregate demand and the actual price level, and have the time to renegotiate resource payments based on that knowledge. Because the higher-than-expected price level cuts the real value of the nominal wage originally agreed to, workers will try to negotiate a higher nominal wage at their earliest opportunity. Workers and other resource suppliers negotiate higher nominal payments, raising production costs for firms, so the short-run aggregate supply curve shifts leftward, resulting in cost-push inflation. In Exhibit 2, the expansionary gap causes the short-run aggregate supply curve to shift leftward to $SRAS_{140}$, which results in an expected price level of 140. Notice that the short-run aggregate supply curve shifts until the equilibrium quantity equals the economy's potential output. *Actual output can exceed the economy's potential in the short run but not in the long run.*

As shown in Exhibit 2, the expansionary gap is closed by long-run market forces that shift the short-run aggregate supply curve from $SRAS_{130}$ left to $SRAS_{140}$. Whereas $SRAS_{130}$ was based on resource contracts reflecting an expected price level of 130, $SRAS_{140}$ is based on resource contracts reflecting an expected price level of 140. At point *c* the expected price level and the actual price level are identical, so the economy is not only in short-run equilibrium but also is in **long-run equilibrium.** Consider all the equalities that hold at point *c*: (1) the expected price level equals the actual price level; (2) the quantity supplied in the short run equals potential output, which also equals the quantity supplied in the long run; and (3) the quantity supplied equals the quantity demanded. Looked at another way, *long-run equilibrium occurs where the aggregate demand curve intersects the vertical line drawn at potential output.* Point *c* will continue to be the equilibrium point unless there is some change in aggregate demand or in aggregate supply.

LONG-RUN EQUILIBRIUM

The price level and real GDP that occurs when (1) the actual price level equals the expected price level, (2) real GDP supplied equals potential output, and (3) real GDP supplied equals real GDP demanded

Note that the situation at point *c* is no different *in real terms* from what had been expected at point *a*. At both points, firms supply the economy's potential of $12.0 trillion real GDP. The same amounts of labor and other resources are employed, and although the price level, the nominal wage, and other nominal resource payments are higher at point *c*, the real wage and the real return to other resources are the same as they would have been at point *a*. For example, suppose the nominal wage averaged $13 per hour when the expected price was 130. If the expected price level increased from 130 to 140, an increase of 7.7 percent, the nominal wage would also increase by that same percentage to an average of $14 per hour, leaving the real wage unchanged. With no change in the real wage between points *a* and *c*, firms demand enough labor and workers supply enough labor to produce $12.0 trillion in real GDP.

Thus, if the price level turns out to be higher than expected, the short-run response is to increase quantity supplied. But production exceeding the economy's potential creates inflationary pressure. In the long run this causes the short-run aggregate supply curve to shift to the left, reducing output, increasing the price level, and closing the expansionary gap.

If an increase in the price level was predicted accurately year after year, firms and resource suppliers would build these expectations into their long-term agreements. The price level would move up each year by the expected amount, but the economy's output would remain at potential GDP, thereby skipping the round-trip beyond the economy's potential and back.

Closing a Contractionary Gap

Let's begin again with an expected price level of 130 as presented in Exhibit 3, where blue shading indicates output exceeding potential and red shading indicates output below potential. If the price level turned out as expected, the resulting equilibrium combination would occur at *a*, which would be both a short-run and a long-run equilibrium. Suppose this time that the aggregate demand curve intersects the short-run aggregate supply curve to the left of potential output, yielding a price level below that expected. The intersection of the aggregate demand curve, AD'', with $SRAS_{130}$ establishes the short-run equilibrium point, *d*, where the price level is below expectations and production is less than the economy's potential. The amount by which actual output falls short of potential GDP is called a

E X H I B I T   **3**

≡HOMEWORK≡
Xpress!≡
            Graphing

Short-Run Equilibrium When the Price Level Is Below Expectations

When the actual price level is below expectations, as indicated by the intersection of the aggregate demand curve *AD″* with the short-run aggregate supply curve $SRAS_{130}$, short-run equilibrium occurs at point *d*. Production below the economy's potential opens a contractionary gap. If prices and wages are flexible enough in the long run, nominal wages will be renegotiated lower. As resource costs fall, the short-run aggregate supply curve eventually shifts rightward to $SRAS_{120}$ and the economy moves to long-run equilibrium at point *e*, with output increasing to the potential level of $12.0 trillion.

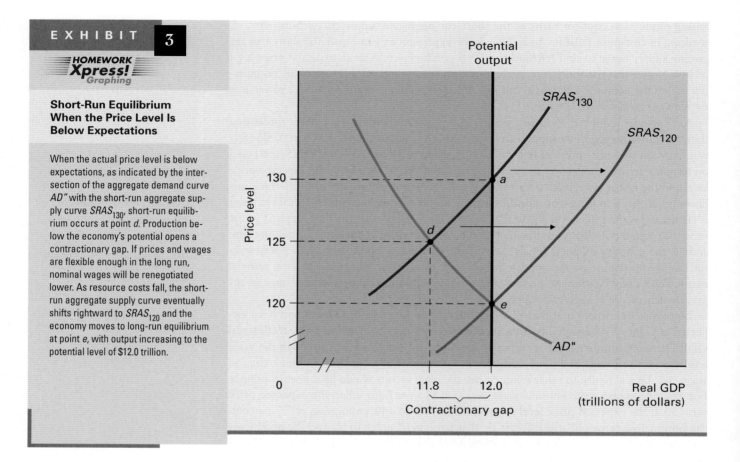

CONTRACTIONARY GAP

The amount by which actual output in the short run falls short of the economy's potential output

contractionary gap. In this case, the contractionary gap is $0.2 trillion, and unemployment exceeds its natural rate.

Because the price level turns out to be lower than expected, the nominal wage, which is based on the expected price level, translates into a higher real wage in the short run. What happens in the long run? With the price level lower than expected, employers are no longer willing to pay as high a nominal wage. And with the unemployment rate higher than the natural rate, more workers are competing for jobs, putting downward pressure on the nominal wage. If the price level and the nominal wage are flexible enough, the combination of a lower price level and a pool of unemployed workers competing for jobs should make workers more willing to accept lower nominal wages when wage agreements are negotiated.

If firms and workers negotiate lower nominal wages, the cost of production decreases, shifting the short-run aggregate supply curve rightward, leading to deflation and greater output. The short-run supply curve will continue to shift rightward until it intersects the aggregate demand curve where the economy produces its potential output. This increase in supply is reflected in Exhibit 3 by a rightward shift of the short-run aggregate supply curve from $SRAS_{130}$ to $SRAS_{120}$. *If the price level and nominal wage are flexible enough, the short-run aggregate supply curve will move rightward until the economy produces its potential output.* The new short-run aggregate supply curve is based on an expected price level of 120. Because the expected price level and the actual price level are now identical, the economy is in long-run equilibrium at point *e*.

Although the nominal wage is lower at point *e* than that originally agreed to when the expected price level was 130, the real wage is the same at point *e* as it was at point *a*. Because the real wage is the same, the amount of labor that workers supply is the same and real output is the same. All that has changed between points *a* and *e* are nominal measures—the price level, the nominal wage, and other nominal resource prices.

We conclude that when incorrect expectations cause firms and resource suppliers to overestimate the actual price level, output in the short run falls short of the economy's potential. As long as wages and prices are flexible enough, however, firms and workers should be able to renegotiate wage agreements based on a lower expected price level. The negotiated drop in the nominal wage will shift the short-run aggregate supply curve to the right until the economy once again produces its potential output. If wages and prices are not flexible, they will not adjust quickly to a contractionary gap, so shifts of the short-run aggregate supply curve may be slow to move the economy to its potential output. The economy can therefore get stuck at an output and employment level below its potential.

We are now in a position to provide an additional interpretation of the red- and blue-shaded areas of our exhibits. *If a short-run equilibrium occurs in the blue-shaded area, that is, to the right of potential output, then market forces in the long run will increase nominal resource costs, shifting the short-run aggregate supply to the left. If a short-run equilibrium occurs in the red-shaded area, then market forces in the long run will reduce nominal resource costs, shifting the short-run aggregate supply curve to the right.* Closing an expansionary gap involves inflation and closing a contractionary gap involves deflation.

Tracing Potential Output

If wages and prices are flexible enough, the economy will produce its potential output in the long run, as indicated in Exhibit 4 by the vertical line drawn at the economy's potential GDP of $12.0 trillion. This vertical line is called the economy's **long-run aggregate supply (LRAS) curve.** *The long-run aggregate supply curve depends on the supply of resources in the economy, the level of technology, and the production incentives provided by the formal and informal institutions of the economic system.*

In Exhibit 4, the initial price level of 130 is determined by the intersection of *AD* with the long-run aggregate supply curve. If the aggregate demand curve shifts out to *AD'*, then in the long run, the equilibrium price level will increase to 140 and equilibrium output will remain at $12.0 trillion, the economy's potential GDP. Conversely, a decline in aggregate demand from *AD* to *AD''* will, in the long run, lead only to a fall in the price level from 130 to 120, with no change in output. Note that these long-run movements are more like tendencies than smooth and timely adjustments. It may take a long time for resource prices to adjust, particularly when the economy faces a contractionary gap. As long as wages and prices are flexible, the economy's potential GDP is consistent with any price level. *In the long run, equilibrium output equals long-run aggregate supply, which is also potential output. The equilibrium price level depends on the aggregate demand curve.*

Wage Flexibility and Employment

What evidence is there that a vertical line drawn at the economy's potential GDP depicts the long-run aggregate supply curve? Except during the Great Depression, unemployment over the last century has varied from year to year but typically has returned to what would be viewed as a natural rate of unemployment—again, estimates range from 4 percent to 6 percent.

An *expansionary* gap creates a labor shortage that eventually results in a higher nominal wage and a higher price level. But a *contractionary* gap does not necessarily generate enough downward pressure to lower the nominal wage. Studies indicate that nominal wages are slow

LONG-RUN AGGREGATE SUPPLY (LRAS) CURVE

A vertical line at the economy's potential output; aggregate supply when there are no surprises about the price level and all resource contracts can be renegotiated

Long-Run Aggregate Supply Curve

In the long run, when the actual price level equals the expected price level, the economy produces its potential. In the long run, $12.0 trillion in real GDP will be supplied regardless of the actual price level. As long as wages and prices are flexible, the economy's potential GDP is consistent with any price level. Thus, shifts of the aggregate demand curve will, in the long run, not affect potential output. The long-run aggregate supply curve, *LRAS*, is a vertical line at potential GDP.

to adjust to high unemployment. Nominal wages have declined in particular industries; during the 1980s, for example, nominal wages fell in airlines, steel, and trucking. But seldom have we observed actual declines in nominal wages across the economy, especially since World War II. Nominal wages do not adjust downward as quickly or as substantially as they adjust upward, and the downward response that does occur tends to be slow and modest. Consequently, we say that nominal wages tend to be "sticky" in the downward direction. *Because nominal wages fall slowly, if at all, the supply-side adjustments needed to close a contractionary gap may take so long as to seem ineffective.* What, in fact, usually closes a contractionary gap is an increase in aggregate demand as the economy pulls out of its funk.

Although the nominal wage seldom falls, an actual decline in the nominal wage is not necessary to close a contractionary gap. All that's needed is a fall in the real wage. And *the real wage will fall as long as the price level increases more than the nominal wage.* For example, if the price level increases by 4 percent and the nominal wage increases by 2 percent, the real wage falls by 2 percent. If the real wage falls enough, firms will be willing to demand enough additional labor to produce the economy's potential output.

In the following case study, we look more at output gaps and discuss why wages are not more flexible.

U.S. Output Gaps and Wage Flexibility

Let's look at estimates of actual and potential GDP. Exhibit 5 measures actual GDP minus potential GDP as a percentage of potential GDP for the United States. When actual output exceeds potential output, the output gap is positive and the economy has an expansionary gap. For example, actual output in 2000 was 2.2 percent above potential output, amounting to an expansionary gap of about $200 billion (in 2000 dollars). When actual output falls short of potential output, the output gap is negative and the economy suffers a contractionary gap. For example, actual output in 2003 was 1.4 percent below potential output, amounting to

a contractionary gap of about $150 billion (in 2000 dollars). Note that the economy need not be in recession for actual output to fall short of potential output. For example, from 1992 to 1995, and from 2002 to 2004, the economy expanded, yet actual output fell short of potential output. As long as unemployment exceeds its natural rate, the economy will suffer a contractionary gap.

Employers and employees clearly would have been better off if these contractionary gaps had been reduced or eliminated. After all, more workers would have been employed, and more goods and services would have increased the standard of living. If workers and employers fail to reach an outcome that seems possible and that all would prefer, then they have failed to coordinate in some way. Contractionary gaps can thus be viewed as resulting from a **coordination failure.**

If employers and workers can increase output and employment by agreeing to lower nominal wages, why doesn't such an agreement occur quickly? As we have already seen,

Case **Study**

Public Policy

*e*Activity

For the latest on output gaps among the world's leading economies, go to the OECD's Web site at http://www.oecd.org/home/. From there you can access Publications & Documents, which will lead you to the latest OECD Outlook and the Annex tables. What is the current output gap in the United States? How does the U.S. gap compare to that in the other leading economies?

COORDINATION FAILURE

A situation in which workers and employers fail to achieve an outcome that all would prefer

Source: Developed from estimates by the *OECD*. Figures for 2004 and 2005 are projections. OECD data can be found at http://www.oecd.org/home/.

EXHIBIT 5

U.S. Output Gap Measures Actual Output Minus Potential Output as Percentage of Potential Output

The output gap each year equals actual GDP minus potential GDP as a percentage of potential GDP. When actual output exceeds potential output, the output gap is positive and the economy has an expansionary gap, as shown by the blue bars. When actual output falls short of potential output, the output gap is negative and the economy suffers a contractionary gap, as shown by the red bars. Note that the economy need not be in recession for actual output to fall below potential output.

some workers are operating under long-term contracts, so wages are not very flexible, particularly in the downward direction. But if long-term contracts are a problem, why not negotiate shorter ones? First, negotiating contracts is costly and time-consuming (for example, airline worker contracts take an average of 1.3 years to negotiate). Longer contracts reduce the frequency, and thus the average annual cost, of negotiations. Second, long-term contracts reduce the frequency of strikes, lockouts, and other settlement disputes. Thus, both workers and employers gain from longer contracts, even though such contracts make wages more sticky and contractionary gaps more likely to linger.

When demand is slack, why do employers choose to lay off workers rather than cut nominal wages? Yale economist Truman Bewley interviewed over 300 managers, union officials, and employment recruiters and concluded that resistance to pay cuts comes, not from workers or unions, but from employers. Employers think pay cuts damage worker morale more than layoffs do. By lowering morale, pay cuts increase labor turnover and reduce productivity. In contrast, the damage from layoffs is brief and limited because laid off workers are soon gone and cannot disrupt the workplace. What's more, even during the sharpest of recessions, more than nine in ten workers still keep their jobs (or soon find other jobs), so most workers have little incentive to support a wage cut to increase employment.

Another reason workers may be reluctant to accept lower nominal wages is unemployment benefits. When a worker is laid off, the incentive to accept a lower wage is reduced by the prospect of unemployment benefits. The greater these benefits and the longer their duration, the less the pressure to accept a lower wage. For example, in the latter part of the 1920s, unemployment benefits nearly tripled in Great Britain and eligibility requirements were loosened. Despite record high unemployment, money wages remained unchanged during the period. For some people, unemployment benefits had become a viable alternative to accepting a lower wage.

Sources: Truman Bewley, *Why Wages Don't Fall During a Recession* (Cambridge, Mass.: Harvard University Press, 2000); Andrew von Nordenflycht, "Labor Contract Negotiations in the Airline Industry," *Monthly Labor Review* (July 2003): 18–28; Laurence Ball and David Romer, "Sticky Prices and Coordination Failures," *American Economic Review* 81 (June 1991): 539–552; Daniel Benjamin and Levis Kochin, "Searching for an Explanation of Unemployment in Interwar Britain," *Journal of Political Economy* 87 (June 1979): 441–470; and *Survey of Current Business* 84 (April 2004).

To review: When the actual price level differs from the expected price level, output in the short run will depart from the economy's potential. In the long run, however, market forces will shift the short-run aggregate supply curve until the economy once again produces its potential output. Thus, surprises about the price level will change real GDP in the short run but not in the long run. Shifts of the aggregate demand curve change the price level but do not affect potential output, or long-run aggregate supply.

Changes in Aggregate Supply

In this section, we consider factors other than changes in the expected price level that may affect aggregate supply. We begin by distinguishing between long-term trends in aggregate supply and **supply shocks,** which are unexpected events that affect aggregate supply, sometimes only temporarily.

Increases in Aggregate Supply

The economy's potential output is based on the willingness and ability of households to supply resources to firms, the level of technology, and the institutional underpinnings of the economic system. Any change in these factors could affect the economy's potential output. Changes in the economy's potential output over time were introduced in the earlier chapter

SUPPLY SHOCKS

Unexpected events that affect aggregate supply, sometimes only temporarily that focused on U.S. productivity and growth. The supply of labor may change over time because of a change in the size, composition, or quality of the labor force or a change in preferences for labor versus leisure. For example, the U.S. labor force has doubled since 1948 as a result of population growth and a growing labor force participation rate, especially among women with children. At the same time, job training, education, and on-the-job experience increased the quality of labor. Increases in both the quantity and the quality of the labor force have increased the economy's potential GDP, or long-run aggregate supply.

The quantity and quality of other resources also change over time. The capital stock—machines, buildings, and trucks—increases whenever the economy's gross investment exceeds the depreciation of capital. Even the quantity and quality of land can be increased—for example, by claiming land from the sea, as is done in the Netherlands and Hong Kong, or by revitalizing soil that has lost its fertility. These increases in the quantity and quality of resources increase the economy's potential output.

Finally, institutional changes that define property rights more clearly or make contracts more enforceable, such as the introduction of clearer patent and copyright laws, will increase the incentives to undertake productive activity, thereby increasing potential output. *Changes in the labor force, in the supply of other resources, and in the institutional arrangements of the economic system tend to occur gradually.* Exhibit 6 depicts a gradual shift of the economy's potential output from $12.0 trillion to $12.5 trillion. The long-run aggregate supply curve shifts from *LRAS* out to *LRAS'*.

In contrast to the gradual, or long-term, changes that often occur in the supply of resources, *supply shocks* are unexpected events that change aggregate supply, sometimes only temporarily. **Beneficial supply shocks** increase aggregate supply; examples include (1) abundant harvests that increase the food supply, (2) discoveries of natural resources, such as oil in Alaska or the North Sea, (3) technological breakthroughs that allow firms to combine resources more efficiently, such as faster computers or the Internet, and (4) sudden changes in the economic system that promote more production, such as tax cuts that stimulate production incentives or new limits on frivolous product liability suits.

Exhibit 7 shows the effect of a beneficial supply shock from a technological breakthrough. The beneficial supply shock shown here shifts the short-run and long-run aggregate supply curves rightward. Along the aggregate demand curve, *AD,* the equilibrium

BENEFICIAL SUPPLY SHOCKS

Unexpected events that increase aggregate supply, sometimes only temporarily

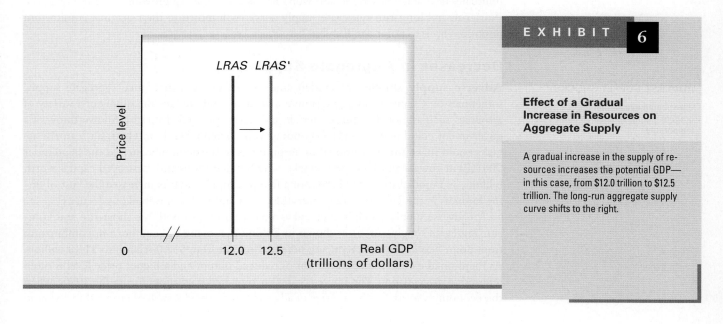

E X H I B I T   6

Effect of a Gradual Increase in Resources on Aggregate Supply

A gradual increase in the supply of resources increases the potential GDP—in this case, from $12.0 trillion to $12.5 trillion. The long-run aggregate supply curve shifts to the right.

EXHIBIT 7

Effects of a Beneficial Supply Shock on Aggregate Supply

Given the aggregate demand curve, a beneficial supply shock that has a lasting effect, such as a breakthrough in technology, will permanently shift both the short-run aggregate supply curve and the long-run aggregate supply curve, or potential output. A beneficial supply shock lowers the price level and increases output, as reflected by the change in equilibrium from point *a* to point *b*. A temporary beneficial supply shock, such as would result from an unusually favorable growing season, will shift the aggregate supply curves only temporarily. If the next growing season returns to normal, the aggregate supply curves will return to their original equilibrium position at point *a*.

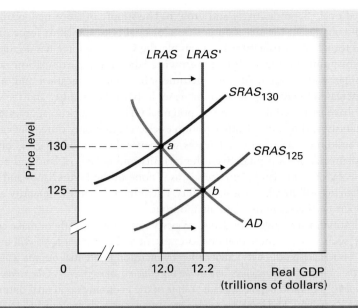

ADVERSE SUPPLY SHOCKS

Unexpected events that reduce aggregate supply, sometimes only temporarily

combination of price and output moves from point *a* to point *b*. *For a given aggregate demand curve, the happy outcome of a beneficial supply shock is an increase in output and a decrease in the price level.* The new equilibrium at point *b* is a short-run and a long-run equilibrium in the sense that there is no tendency to move from that point as long as whatever caused the beneficial effect continues, and a technological discovery usually has a lasting effect. Likewise, substantial new oil discoveries benefit the economy for a long time. On the other hand, an unusually favorable growing season won't last. When a normal growing season returns, the short-run and long-run aggregate supply curves will return to their original equilibrium position—back to point *a* in Exhibit 7.

Decreases in Aggregate Supply

Adverse supply shocks are sudden, unexpected events that reduce aggregate supply, sometimes only temporarily. For example, a drought could reduce the supply of a variety of resources, such as food, building materials, and water-powered electricity. An overthrow of a government could destabilize the economy, as occurred recently in Haiti. Or terrorist attacks could shake the institutional underpinnings of the economy, such as the September 2001 Twin Towers and Pentagon attacks, which killed thousands, destroyed capital worth billions, and eroded the civil liberties of a free nation. The attacks increased the cost of doing business in the United States—everything from airline travel to building security.

An adverse supply shock is depicted as a leftward shift of both the short-run and long-run aggregate supply curves, as shown in Exhibit 8, moving the equilibrium combination from point *a* to point *c* and reducing potential output from $12.0 trillion to $11.8 trillion. As mentioned earlier, the combination of reduced output and a higher price level is often referred to as stagflation. The United States encountered stagflation during the 1970s, when the economy was rocked by a series of adverse supply shocks, such as crop failures around

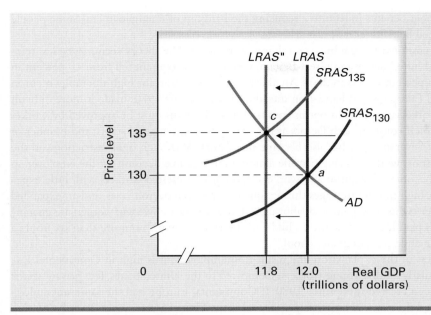

E X H I B I T **8**

≡HOMEWORK≡
Xpress!
Graphing

Effects of an Adverse Supply Shock on Aggregate Supply

Given the aggregate demand curve, an adverse supply shock, such as an increased threat of terrorism, shifts the short-run and long-run aggregate supply curves to the left, increasing the price level and reducing real GDP, a movement called stagflation. This change is shown by the move in equilibrium from point *a* to point *c*. If the shock is just temporary, the shift of the aggregate supply curves will be temporary.

the globe and the oil price hikes by OPEC in 1974 and 1979. If the effect of the adverse supply shock is temporary, such as a poor growing season, the aggregate supply curve returns to its original position once things return to normal. But some economists question an economy's ability to bounce back, as discussed in the following case study.

Why Is Unemployment So High in Europe?

Between World War II and the mid-1970s, unemployment in Western Europe was low. From 1960 to 1974, for example, the unemployment rate in France never got as high as even 4 percent. The worldwide recession of the mid-1970s, however, jacked up unemployment rates. But unemployment continued to climb in Continental Europe long after the recession ended. Unemployment in France and Italy remained above 10 percent during most of the 1980s. After a modest decline in the late 1980s, rates again topped 10 percent during the 1990s. In 2004, the rates were 8 percent in Italy, 10 percent in Germany and France, 11 percent in Spain,

© Sean Gallup/Getty Images

and 12 percent in Belgium. Some observers claim that the natural rate of unemployment has increased in these countries.

Economists have borrowed a term from physics, **hysteresis** (pronounced *his-ter-eé-sis*), to argue that the natural rate of unemployment depends in part on the recent history of unemployment. *The longer the actual unemployment rate remains above what had been the natural rate, the more the natural rate itself will increase.* For example, those unemployed can lose valuable job skills, such as the computer programmer who loses touch with the latest developments. As weeks of unemployment turn into months and years, the shock and stigma may diminish, so the work ethic weakens. What's more, some European countries offer generous

HYSTERESIS

The theory that the natural rate of unemployment depends in part on the recent history of unemployment; high unemployment rates increase the natural rate of unemployment

C a s e **S t u d y**

Public Policy

*e*Activity
Learn about unemployment rates in Europe by finding the most current press release from Eurostat at http://europa.eu.int/comm/eurostat/. The OECD follows trends in market reforms in Europe designed to reduce the structural impediments to lowering the unemployment rate. You can access the latest reports and analyses at http://www.oecd.org/home/. Go to By Topic, then to Employment, and follow the link to Labour Markets. What changes have been made in employment protection and other labor laws in the European countries to deal with high rates of unemployment? What types of liberalization and other changes can you find that have been made in labor and product markets to promote employment?

unemployment benefits indefinitely, reducing the hardship of unemployment. Some people have collected benefits *for more than a decade.*

No consensus exists regarding the validity of hysteresis. The theory seems to be less relevant in the United States and Great Britain, where unemployment fell from 10 percent in 1982 to 5.6 percent or less in 2004. An alternative explanation for high unemployment in Continental Europe is that legislation introduced there in the 1970s made it more difficult to lay off workers. In most European countries, job dismissals must be approved by worker councils, which consider such factors as the worker's health, marital status, and number of dependents. Severance pay has also become mandatory. With such tight restrictions on the ability to dismiss workers, hiring became almost an irreversible decision for the employer, so firms have become reluctant to add workers, particularly untested workers with little experience. Also, high minimum wages throughout Europe, high payroll taxes, and an expanded list of worker rights have increased labor costs. For example, in Sweden, women are guaranteed a year's paid leave on having a child and the right to work no more than six hours a day until the child reaches grade school.

Regardless of the explanation, the result is unemployment is high in Continental Europe, particularly among young workers. Compared to the United States, few private sector jobs have been created there since 1980. If Continental Europe had the same unemployment rate and the same labor participation rate as the United States, about 30 million more people there would be working.

Sources: Russell Smyth, "Unemployment Hysteresis in Australian States and Territories," *Australian Economic Review*, 36 (June 2003): 181–192; Horst Siebert, "Labor Market Rigidities: At the Root of Unemployment in Europe," *Journal of Economic Perspectives* 11 (Summer 1997): 37–54; "Economic and Financial Indicators," *Economist*, 15 May 2004; and *OECD Economic Outlook* 75 (June 2004).

Conclusion

This chapter explains why the aggregate supply curve slopes upward in the short run and is vertical at the economy's potential output in the long run. Firms and resource suppliers negotiate contracts based on the economy's expected price level, which depend on expectations about aggregate demand. Unexpected changes in the price level can move output in the short run away from its potential level. But as firms and resource suppliers fully adjust to price surprises, the economy in the long run moves toward its potential output. Potential output is the anchor for analyzing aggregate supply in the short run and long run.

SUMMARY

1. Short-run aggregate supply is based on resource demand and supply decisions that reflect the expected price level. If the price level turns out as expected, the economy produces its potential output. If the price level exceeds expectations, short-run output exceeds the economy's potential, creating an expansionary gap. If the price level is below expectations, short-run output falls short of the economy's potential, creating a contractionary gap.

2. Output can exceed the economy's potential in the short run, but in the long run, higher nominal wages will be negotiated at the earliest opportunity. This increases the cost of production, shifting the short-run aggregate supply curve leftward along the aggregate demand curve until the economy produces its potential output.

3. If output in the short run is less than the economy's potential, and if wages and prices are flexible enough, lower

nominal wage will reduce production costs in the long run. These lower costs shift the short-run aggregate supply curve rightward along the aggregate demand curve until the economy produces its potential output.

4. Evidence suggests that when output exceeds the economy's potential, nominal wages and the price level increase. But there is less evidence that nominal wages and the price level fall when output is below the economy's potential. Wages appear to be "sticky" in the downward direction. What usually closes a contractionary gap is an increase in aggregate demand.

5. The long-run aggregate supply curve, or the economy's potential output, depends on the amount and quality of resources available, the state of technology, and formal and informal institutions, such as patent laws and business practices, that structure production incentives. Increases in resource availability, improvements in technology, or institutional changes that provide more attractive production incentives increase aggregate supply and potential output.

6. Supply shocks are unexpected, often temporary changes in aggregate supply. Beneficial supply shocks increase output, sometimes only temporarily. Adverse supply shocks result in stagflation—reduced output and a higher price level, sometimes only temporarily.

QUESTIONS FOR REVIEW

1. *(Short-Run Aggregate Supply)* In the short run, prices may rise faster than costs do. This chapter discusses why this might happen. Suppose that labor and management agree to adjust wages continuously for any changes in the price level. How would such adjustments affect the slope of the aggregate supply curve?

2. *(Potential Output)* Define the economy's potential output. What factors help determine potential output?

3. *(Actual Price Level Higher than Expected)* Discuss some instances in your life when your actual production for short periods exceeded what you considered your potential production. Why does this occur only for brief periods?

4. *(Nominal and Real Wages)* Complete each of the following sentences:

   a. The _____ wage measures the wage rate in current dollars, while the _____ wage measures it in constant dollars.

   b. Wage agreements are based on the _____ price level and negotiated in _____ terms. Real wages are then determined by the _____ price level.

   c. The higher the actual price level, the _____ is the real wage for a given nominal wage.

   d. If nominal wages are growing at 2 percent per year while the annual inflation rate is 3 percent, then real wages change by _____.

5. *(Contractionary Gaps)* After reviewing Exhibit 3 in this chapter, explain why contractionary gaps occur only in the short run and only when the actual price level is below what was expected.

6. *(Short-Run Aggregate Supply)* In interpreting the short-run aggregate supply curve, what does the adjective *short-run* mean? Explain the role of labor contracts along the *SRAS* curve.

7. *(Contractionary Gap)* What does a contractionary gap imply about the actual rate of unemployment relative to the natural rate? What does it imply about the actual price level relative to the expected price level? What must happen to real and nominal wages in order to close a contractionary gap?

8. *(Expansionary Gap)* How does an economy that is experiencing an expansionary gap adjust in the long run?

9. *(Output Gaps and Wage Flexibility)* What are some reasons why nominal wages may not fall during a contractionary gap?

10. *(C a s e **S t u d y**: U.S. Output Gaps and Wage Flexibility)* Unemployment is costly to employers, employees, and the economy as a whole. What are some explanations for the *coordination failures* that prevent workers and employers from reaching agreements?

11. *(Long-Run Adjustment)* In the long run, why does an actual price level that exceeds the expected price level lead to changes in the nominal wage? Why do these changes cause shifts of the short-run aggregate supply curve?

12. *(Long-Run Aggregate Supply)* The long-run aggregate supply curve is vertical at the economy's potential output level. Why is the long-run aggregate supply curve located at this output rather than below or above potential output?

13. *(Long-Run Aggregate Supply)* Determine whether each of the following, other things held constant, would lead to an increase, a decrease, or no change in long-run aggregate supply:

    a.   An improvement in technology
    b.   A permanent decrease in the size of the capital stock

    c.   An increase in the actual price level
    d.   An increase in the expected price level
    e.   A permanent increase in the size of the labor force

14. *(Changes in Aggregate Supply)* What are supply shocks? Distinguish between beneficial and adverse supply shocks. Do such shocks affect the short-run aggregate supply curve, the long-run aggregate supply curve, or both? What is the resulting impact on potential GDP?

PROBLEMS AND EXERCISES

15. *(Real Wages)* In Exhibit 2 in this chapter, how does the real wage rate at point *c* compare with the real wage rate at point *a*? How do nominal wage rates compare at those two points? Explain your answers.

16. *(Natural Rate of Unemployment)* What is the relationship between potential output and the natural rate of unemployment?

    a.   If the economy currently has a frictional unemployment rate of 2 percent, structural unemployment of 2 percent, seasonal unemployment of 0.5 percent, and cyclical unemployment of 2 percent, what is the natural rate of unemployment? Where is the economy operating relative to its potential GDP?
    b.   What happens to the natural rate of unemployment and potential GDP if cyclical unemployment rises to 3 percent with other types of unemployment unchanged from part (a)?
    c.   What happens to the natural rate of unemployment and potential GDP if structural unemployment falls to 1.5 percent with other types of unemployment unchanged from part (a)?

17. *(Expansionary and Contractionary Gaps)* Answer the following questions on the basis of the following graph:

    a.   If the actual price level exceeds the expected price level reflected in long-term contracts, real GDP equals _____ and the actual price level equals _____ in the short run.

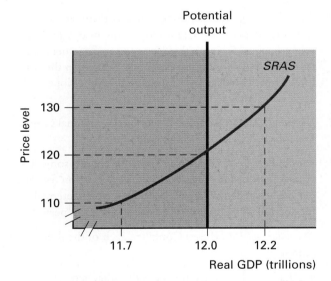

    b.   The situation described in part (a) results in a(n) _____ gap equal to _____.
    c.   If the actual price level is lower than the expected price level reflected in long-term contracts, real GDP equals _____ and the actual price level equals _____ in the short run.
    d.   The situation described in part (c) results in a(n) _____ gap equal to _____.
    e.   If the actual price level equals the expected price level reflected in long-term contracts, real GDP equals _____ and the actual price level equals _____ in the short run.

f. The situation described in part (e) results in _____ gap equal to _____.

18. *(Long-Run Adjustment)* The ability of the economy to eliminate any imbalances between actual and potential output is sometimes called self-correction. Using an aggregate supply and aggregate demand diagram, show why this self-correction process involves only temporary periods of inflation or deflation.

19. *(Changes in Aggregate Supply)* List three factors that can change the economy's potential output. What is the impact of shifts of the aggregate demand curve on potential output? Illustrate your answers with a diagram.

20. *(Supply Shocks)* Give an example of an adverse supply shock and illustrate graphically. Now do the same for a beneficial supply shock.

EXPERIENTIAL EXERCISES

21. (*C a s e* **S t u d y :** Why Is Unemployment So High in Europe?) European unemployment is a hot topic. Use any Web browser to search for the words "European unemployment." Just by scanning the headlines, see how many possible explanations you can list. How do they compare to the explanations reviewed in the chapter case study?

22. *(Wall Street Journal)* In the short run, some workers' wages are determined by contracts, and some are not. The split between costs that change as production changes and those that do not is a key determinant of the shape of the short-run aggregate supply curve. To get a better feel for wage determination, look at the "Work Week" column in the first section of Tuesday's *Wall Street Journal.* Determine how some of the developments described there are likely to affect aggregate supply. Make sure that you distinguish between the short-run and the long-run effects. Draw a diagram to illustrate your conclusions.

HOMEWORK XPRESS! EXERCISES

These exercises require access to McEachern Homework Xpress! If Homework Xpress! did not come with your book, visit **http://homeworkxpress.swlearning.com** *to purchase.*

1. In the diagram sketch a line representing a potential output of $10 trillion. Sketch a short-run aggregate supply curve when the expected price level is 120.

2. In the diagram for this exercise, use aggregate demand and short-run aggregate supply curves to show an economy at a short-run equilibrium with an expansionary gap, when potential output is $10 trillion. Then illustrate how the gap would close in the long run.

3. In the diagram, use aggregate demand and short-run aggregate supply curves to show an economy at a short-run equilibrium with a contractionary gap, when potential output is $10 trillion. Then illustrate how the gap would close in the long run.

4. In the diagram for this exercise, sketch a line representing a long-run aggregate supply at $10 trillion. Illustrate the effect of an increase in long-run aggregate supply. Then illustrate the effect of a decrease in long-run aggregate supply.

5. In the diagram use aggregate demand and short-run and long-run aggregate supply curves to show an economy at a long-run equilibrium of $10 trillion. Then illustrate the effects of an adverse supply shock.

CHAPTER

27

Fiscal Policy

© Vince Streano/Corbis

P resident George W. Bush pushed through tax cuts to "get the country moving again." The Japanese government cut taxes and increased spending to stimulate its troubled economy. These are examples of *fiscal policy,* which focuses on the effect of taxing and public spending on aggregate economic activity. What is the proper role of fiscal policy in the economy? Can fiscal policy reduce swings in the business cycle? Why did fiscal policy fall on hard times for nearly two decades, and what has brought it to life? Does fiscal policy affect aggregate supply? Answers to these and other questions are addressed in this chapter, which examines the theory and practice of fiscal policy.

In this chapter, we first explore the effects of fiscal policy on aggregate demand. Next, we bring aggregate supply into the picture to consider the impact of taxes and government purchases on the level of income and employment in the economy.

Then, we examine the role of fiscal policy in moving the economy to its potential output. Finally, we review fiscal policy as it has been practiced since World War II. Throughout the chapter, we use simple tax and spending programs to explain fiscal policy. A more complex treatment, along with the algebra behind it, appears in the appendix to this chapter. Topics discussed include:

- Theory of fiscal policy
- Discretionary fiscal policy
- Automatic stabilizers

- Lags in fiscal policy
- Limits of fiscal policy
- The supply-side experiment

Theory of Fiscal Policy

Our macroeconomic model so far has viewed government as passive. But government purchases and transfer payments at all levels in the United States now exceed $3 trillion a year, making government an important player in the economy. From tax cuts to highways to national defense, fiscal policy affects the economy in myriad ways. We now move fiscal policy to center stage. As introduced in Chapter 3, *fiscal policy* refers to government purchases, transfer payments, taxes, and borrowing as they affect macroeconomic variables such as real GDP, employment, the price level, and economic growth. When economists study fiscal policy, they usually focus on the federal government, although governments at all levels affect the economy.

Fiscal Policy Tools

The tools of fiscal policy sort into two broad categories: automatic stabilizers and discretionary fiscal policy. **Automatic stabilizers** are revenue and spending programs in the federal budget that automatically adjust with the ups and downs of the economy to stabilize disposable income and, consequently, consumption and real GDP. For example, the federal income tax is an automatic stabilizer because (1) once adopted, it requires no congressional action to operate year after year, so it's *automatic*, and (2) it reduces the drop in disposable income during recessions and reduces the jump in disposable income during expansions, so it's a *stabilizer*. **Discretionary fiscal policy,** on the other hand, requires the deliberate manipulation of government purchases, taxation, and transfers to promote macroeconomic goals like full employment, price stability, and economic growth. President Bush's tax cuts are examples of discretionary fiscal policy. Some discretionary policies are temporary, such as a boost in government spending to fight a recession. The Bush tax cuts were originally scheduled to expire, and thus would remain discretionary fiscal policy measures unless they are made permanent.

Using the income–expenditure framework developed earlier, we will initially focus on the demand side to consider the effect of changes in government purchases, transfer payments, and taxes on real GDP demanded. The short story is that *at any given price level, an increase in government purchases or in transfer payments increases real GDP demanded, and an increase in net taxes decreases real GDP demanded, other things constant.* Next, we see how and why.

Changes in Government Purchases

Let's begin by looking at Exhibit 1, with real GDP demanded of $12.0 trillion, as reflected at point *a,* where the aggregate expenditure line crosses the 45-degree line. This equilibrium was determined two chapters back, where government purchases and net taxes each equaled $1.0 trillion and did not vary with income. Because government purchases equal net taxes, the government budget is balanced.

AUTOMATIC STABILIZERS

Structural features of government spending and taxation that reduce fluctuations in disposable income, and thus consumption, over the business cycle

DISCRETIONARY FISCAL POLICY

The deliberate manipulation of government purchases, taxation, and transfer payments to promote macroeconomic goals, such as full employment, price stability, and economic growth

Effect of a $0.1 Trillion Increase in Government Purchases on Aggregate Expenditure and Real GDP Demanded

As a result of a $0.1 trillion increase in government purchases, the aggregate expenditure line shifts up by $0.1 trillion, increasing the level of real GDP demanded by $0.5 trillion. This model assumes the price level remains unchanged.

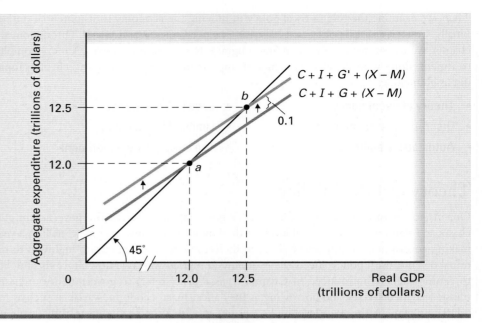

N *e t* **B o o k m a r k**

The Office of Management and Budget prepares *A Citizen's Guide to the Federal Budget* each year, with numerous, easy-to-read charts and graphs indicating sources of revenue and the types of spending. Access to these guides and other budget documents for the current year and previous years is available at http://www.whitehouse.gov/omb/budget/fy2002/guide.html.

Now suppose the federal policy makers, troubled by rising unemployment, decide to stimulate aggregate demand by increasing government purchases $0.1 trillion, or by $100 billion. To consider the effect on aggregate demand, let's initially assume that nothing else changes, including the price level and net taxes. This additional spending shifts the aggregate expenditure line up by $0.1 trillion to $C + I + G' + (X - M)$. At real GDP of $12.0 trillion, planned spending now exceeds output, so production will increase. This increase in production increases income, which in turn increases planned spending, and so it goes through the series of spending rounds.

The initial increase of $0.1 trillion in government purchases eventually increases real GDP demanded at the given price level from $12.0 trillion to $12.5 trillion, shown as point *b* in Exhibit 1. Because output demanded increases by $0.5 trillion as a result of an increase of $0.1 trillion in government purchases, the government purchases multiplier in our example is equal to 5. *As long as consumption is the only spending component that varies with income, the multiplier for a change in government purchases, other things constant, equals* $1/(1 - MPC)$, *or* $1/(1 - 0.8)$ in our example. Thus, we can say that for a given price level, and assuming that only consumption varies with income,

$$\Delta \text{ Real GDP demanded} = \Delta G \times \frac{1}{1 - MPC}$$

where, again, Δ means "change in." This same multiplier appeared two chapters back, when we discussed shifts in consumption, investment, and net exports.

Changes in Net Taxes

A change in net taxes also affects real GDP demanded, but the effect is less direct. A *decrease* in net taxes, other things constant, *increases* disposable income at each level of real GDP, so consumption increases. In Exhibit 2, we begin again at equilibrium point *a,* with real GDP demanded equal to $12.0 trillion. To stimulate aggregate demand, suppose federal policy makers cut net taxes by $0.1 trillion, or by $100 billion, other things constant. We continue to assume that net taxes are autonomous—that is, that they do not vary with income. A $100 billion reduction in net taxes could result from a tax cut, an increase in transfer payments, or some combination of the two. The $100 billion decrease in net taxes increases disposable income by $100 billion at each level of real GDP. Because households now have more disposable income, they spend more and save more at each level of real GDP.

Because households save some of the tax cut, consumption increases in the first round of spending by less than the full tax cut. Specifically, *consumption spending at each level of real GDP rises by the decrease in net taxes multiplied by the marginal propensity to consume.* In our example, consumption at each level of real GDP increases by $100 billion times 0.8, or $80 billion. Decreasing net taxes by $100 billion causes the aggregate expenditure line to shift up by $80 billion, or $0.08 trillion, at all levels of income, as shown in Exhibit 2. This initial increase in spending triggers subsequent rounds of spending, following a now-familiar pattern in the income-expenditure cycle based on the marginal propensities to consume and to save. For example, the $80 billion increase in consumption increases output and income by $80 billion, which in the second round leads to $64 billion in consumption and $16 billion in saving, and so on through successive rounds. As a result, real GDP demanded eventually increases from $12.0 trillion to $12.4 trillion per year, or by $400 billion.

The effect of a change in net taxes on real GDP demanded equals the resulting shift of the aggregate expenditure line times the simple spending multiplier. Thus, we can say that the effect of a change in net taxes is

$$\Delta \text{Real GDP demanded} = (-MPC \times \Delta NT) \times \frac{1}{1 - MPC}$$

The simple spending multiplier is applied to the shift of the aggregate expenditure line that results from the change in net taxes. This equation can be rearranged as

EXHIBIT 2

Effect of a $0.1 Trillion Decrease in Autonomous Net Taxes on Aggregate Expenditure and Real GDP Demanded

As a result of a decrease in autonomous net taxes of $0.1 trillion, or $100 billion, consumers, who are assumed to have a marginal propensity to consume of 0.8, spend $80 billion and save $20 billion. The consumption function shifts up by $80 billion, or $0.08 trillion, as does the aggregate expenditure line. An $80 billion increase in the aggregate expenditure line eventually increases real GDP demanded by $0.4 trillion. Keep in mind that the price level is assumed to remain constant.

$$\Delta \text{ Real GDP demanded} = \Delta \text{NT} \times \frac{-MPC}{1 - MPC}$$

where $-MPC/(1 - MPC)$ is the **simple tax multiplier,** which can be applied directly to the change in net taxes to yield the change in real GDP demanded at a given price level. This tax multiplier is called *simple* because, by assumption, only consumption varies with income. For example, with an MPC of 0.8, the simple tax multiplier equals -4. In our example, a *decrease* of $0.1 trillion in net taxes results in an *increase* in real GDP demanded of $0.4 trillion, assuming a given price level. As another example, an *increase* in net taxes of $0.2 trillion would, other things constant, *decrease* real GDP demanded by $0.8 trillion.

Note two differences between the government purchase multiplier and the simple tax multiplier. First, the government purchase multiplier is positive, so an increase in government purchases leads to an increase in real GDP demanded. The tax multiplier is negative, so an increase in net taxes leads to a decrease in real GDP demanded. Second, the multiplier for a given change in government purchases is larger by 1 than the absolute value of the multiplier for an identical change in net taxes. In our example, the government purchase multiplier is 5, while the absolute value of the tax multiplier is 4. This holds because changes in government purchases affect aggregate spending directly—a $100 billion increase in government purchases increases spending in the first round by $100 billion. In contrast, a $100 billion decrease in net taxes increases consumption indirectly by way of a change in disposable income. Thus, each $100 billion decrease in net taxes increases disposable income by $100 billion, which, given an MPC of 0.8, increases consumption in the first round by $80 billion; people save the other $20 billion. In short, an increase in government purchases has a greater impact than does an identical tax cut because some of the tax cut gets saved, so it leaks from the spending flow.

To summarize: An increase in government purchases or a decrease in net taxes, other things constant, increases real GDP demanded. Although not shown, the combined effect of changes in government purchases and in net taxes is found by adding their individual effects.

Including Aggregate Supply

To this point in the chapter, we have focused on the amount of real GDP demanded at a given price level. We are now in a position to bring aggregate supply into the picture. The previous chapter introduced the idea that natural market forces may take a long time to close a contractionary gap. Let's consider the possible effects of discretionary fiscal policy in such a situation.

Discretionary Fiscal Policy to Close a Contractionary Gap

What if the economy produces less than its potential? Suppose aggregate demand curve *AD* in Exhibit 3 intersects the aggregate supply curve at point *e,* yielding the short-run output of $11.5 trillion and price level of 125. Output falls short of the economy's potential, opening up a contractionary gap of $0.5 trillion. Unemployment exceeds the natural rate. If markets adjusted naturally to high unemployment, the short-run aggregate supply curve would shift rightward in the long run to achieve equilibrium at the economy's potential output, point *e″*. History suggests, however, that wages and other resource prices could be slow to respond to a contractionary gap.

Suppose policy makers believe that natural market forces will take too long to return the economy to potential output. They also believe that the appropriate increase in government purchases, decrease in net taxes, or some combination of the two could increase aggregate

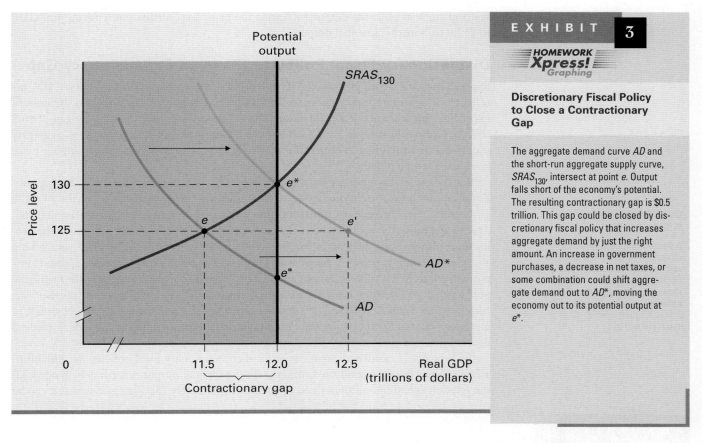

EXHIBIT 3

HOMEWORK
Xpress!
Graphing

**Discretionary Fiscal Policy
to Close a Contractionary
Gap**

The aggregate demand curve *AD* and
the short-run aggregate supply curve,
$SRAS_{130}$, intersect at point *e*. Output
falls short of the economy's potential.
The resulting contractionary gap is $0.5
trillion. This gap could be closed by discretionary fiscal policy that increases
aggregate demand by just the right
amount. An increase in government
purchases, a decrease in net taxes, or
some combination could shift aggregate demand out to AD^*, moving the
economy out to its potential output at
e^*.

demand enough to return the economy to its potential output. A $0.2 trillion increase in
government purchases reflects an **expansionary fiscal policy** that increases aggregate demand, as shown in Exhibit 3 by the rightward shift from *AD* to AD^*. If the price level remains at 125, the additional spending would increase the quantity demanded from $11.5 to
$12.5 trillion. This increase of $1.0 trillion reflects the simple multiplier effect, given a constant price level.

At the original price level of 125, however, excess quantity demanded causes the price
level to rise. As the price level rises, real GDP supplied increases, but real GDP demanded
decreases along the new aggregate demand curve. The price level will rise until quantity demanded equals quantity supplied. In Exhibit 3, the new aggregate demand curve intersects
the aggregate supply curve at e^*, where the price level is 130, the one originally expected,
and output equals potential GDP of $12.0 trillion. Note that *an expansionary fiscal policy aims
to close a contractionary gap.*

The intersection at point e^* is not only a short-run equilibrium but a long-run equilibrium. If fiscal policy makers are accurate enough (or lucky enough), the appropriate fiscal stimulus can close the contractionary gap and foster a long-run equilibrium at potential GDP. But
the increase in output results in a higher price level. What's more, if the federal budget was in
balance before the fiscal stimulus, the increase in government spending creates a budget deficit.
In fact, the federal government has run deficits nearly every year since the early 1970s.

What if policy makers overshoot the mark and stimulate aggregate demand more than
needed to achieve potential GDP? In the short run, real GDP will exceed potential output.
In the long run, the short-run supply curve will shift back until it intersects the aggregate

**EXPANSIONARY
FISCAL POLICY**

An increase in government purchases, decrease in net taxes, or
some combination of the two aimed
at increasing aggregate demand
enough to return the economy to its
potential output thereby reducing
unemployment; policy used to
close a contractionary gap

demand curve at potential output, increasing the price level further but reducing real GDP to $12.0 trillion, the potential output.

Discretionary Fiscal Policy to Close an Expansionary Gap

Suppose output exceeds potential GDP. In Exhibit 4, the aggregate demand curve, *AD'*, intersects the aggregate supply curve to yield short-run output of $12.5 trillion, an amount exceeding the potential of $12.0 trillion. The economy faces an expansionary gap of $0.5 trillion. Ordinarily, this gap would be closed by a leftward shift of the short-run aggregate supply curve, which would return the economy to potential output but at a higher price level, as shown by point *e''*.

But the use of discretionary fiscal policy introduces another possibility. By reducing government purchases, increasing net taxes, or employing some combination of the two, the government can implement a **contractionary fiscal policy** to reduce aggregate demand. This would move the economy to potential output without the resulting inflation. If the policy succeeds, aggregate demand in Exhibit 4 will shift leftward from *AD'* to *AD★*, establishing a new equilibrium at point *e★*. Again, with just the right reduction in aggregate demand, output will fall to $12.0 trillion, the potential GDP. Closing an expansionary gap through fiscal policy rather than through natural market forces results in a lower price level, not a higher one. Increasing net taxes or reducing government purchases also reduces a government deficit or increases a surplus. So a contractionary fiscal policy could reduce inflation and reduce a federal deficit. Note that *a contractionary fiscal policy aims to close an expansionary gap.*

Such precisely calculated expansionary and contractionary fiscal policies are difficult to achieve. Their proper execution assumes that (1) potential output is accurately gauged, (2) the relevant spending multiplier can be predicted accurately, (3) aggregate demand can be

CONTRACTIONARY FISCAL POLICY

A decrease in government purchases, increase in net taxes, or some combination of the two aimed at reducing aggregate demand enough to return the economy to potential output without worsening inflation; policy used to close an expansionary gap

EXHIBIT 4

Discretionary Fiscal Policy to Close an Expansionary Gap

The aggregate demand curve *AD'* and the short-run aggregate supply curve, *SRAS*₁₃₀, intersect at point *e'*, resulting in an expansionary gap of $0.5 trillion. Discretionary fiscal policy aimed at reducing aggregate demand by just the right amount could close this gap without inflation. An increase in net taxes, a decrease in government purchases, or some combination could shift the aggregate demand curve back to *AD** and move the economy back to potential output at point *e**.

shifted by just the right amount, (4) various government entities can somehow coordinate their fiscal efforts, and (5) the shape of the short-run aggregate supply curve is known and will remain unaffected by the fiscal policy.

The Multiplier and the Time Horizon

In the short run, the aggregate supply curve slopes upward, so a shift of aggregate demand changes both the price level and the level of output. When aggregate supply gets in the act, we find that the simple multiplier overstates the amount by which output changes. The exact change of equilibrium output in the short run depends on the steepness of the aggregate supply curve, which in turn depends on how sharply production costs increase as output expands. *The steeper the short-run aggregate supply curve, the less impact a given shift of the aggregate demand curve has on real GDP and the more impact it has on the price level, so the smaller the spending multiplier.*

If the economy is already producing its potential, then in the long run, any change in fiscal policy aimed at stimulating demand will increase the price level but will not affect output. Thus, *if the economy is already producing its potential, the spending multiplier in the long run is zero.*

You now have some idea of how fiscal policy can work in theory. Let's take a look at fiscal policy in practice.

The Evolution of Fiscal Policy

Before the 1930s, discretionary fiscal policy was seldom used to influence the macroeconomy. Prior to the Great Depression, public policy was shaped by the views of **classical economists,** who advocated *laissez-faire,* the belief that free markets were the best way to achieve economic prosperity. Classical economists did not deny that depressions and high unemployment occurred from time to time, but they argued that the sources of such crises lay outside the market system, in the effects of wars, tax increases, poor growing seasons, changing tastes, and the like. Such external shocks could reduce output and employment, but classical economists believed that natural market forces, such as changes in prices, wages, and interest rates, could correct these problems.

Simply put, classical economists argued that if the economy's price level was too high to sell all that was produced, prices would fall until the quantity supplied equaled the quantity demanded. If wages were too high to employ all who wanted to work, wages would fall until the labor supplied equaled the labor demanded. And if the interest rate was too high to invest all that had been saved, interest rates would fall until the amount invested equaled the amount saved.

So the classical approach implied that natural market forces, through flexible prices, wages, and interest rates, would move the economy toward potential GDP. There appeared to be no need for government intervention. What's more, the government, like households, was expected to live within its means. The idea of government running a deficit was considered immoral. Thus, before the onset of the Great Depression, most economists believed that discretionary fiscal policy could do more harm than good. Besides, the federal government itself was a bit player in the economy. At the onset of the Great Depression, for example, federal outlays were less than 3 percent of GDP (compared to about 20 percent today).

The Great Depression and World War II

Economics in the Movies

Although classical economists acknowledged that capitalistic, market-oriented economies could experience high unemployment from time to time, the prolonged depression of the 1930s strained belief in the economy's ability to mend itself. The Great Depression was marked by unemployment reaching 25 percent

CLASSICAL ECONOMISTS

A group of 18th- and 19th-century economists who believed that economic downturns were short-run phenomena that corrected themselves through natural market forces; thus, they believed the economy was self-correcting and needed no government intervention

HOMEWORK Xpress!
Ask the Instructor Video

with many factories sitting idle. With vast unemployed resources, output and income fell well short of the economy's potential.

The stark contrast between the natural market adjustments predicted by classical economists and the years of high unemployment during the Great Depression represented a collision of theory and fact. In 1936, John Maynard Keynes of Cambridge University, England, published *The General Theory of Employment, Interest, and Money,* a book that challenged the classical view and touched off what would later be called the Keynesian revolution. *Keynesian theory and policy were developed to address the problem of unemployment arising from the Great Depression.* Keynes's main quarrel with the classical economists was that prices and wages did not seem to be flexible enough to ensure the full employment of resources. According to Keynes, prices and wages were relatively inflexible in the downward direction—they were "sticky"—so natural market forces would not return the economy to full employment in a timely fashion. Keynes also believed business expectations might at times become so grim that even very low interest rates would not spur firms to invest all that consumers might save.

It is said that geologists learn more about the nature of the Earth's crust from one major upheaval, such as a huge earthquake or major volcanic eruption, than from a dozen more-common events. Likewise, economists learned more about the economy from the Great Depression than from many more-modest business cycles. Even though this depression began nearly eight decades ago, economists continue to sift through the rubble, looking for hints about how the economy really works.

Three developments in the years following the Great Depression bolstered the use of discretionary fiscal policy in the United States. The first was the influence of Keynes's *General Theory,* in which he argued that natural forces would not necessarily close a contractionary gap. Keynes thought the economy could get stuck well below its potential, requiring the government to increase aggregate demand so as to boost output and employment. The second development was the impact of World War II on output and employment. The demands of war greatly increased production and erased cyclical unemployment during the war years, pulling the U.S. economy out of its depression. The third development, largely a consequence of the first two, was the passage of the **Employment Act of 1946**, which gave the federal government responsibility for promoting full employment and price stability.

Prior to the Great Depression, the dominant fiscal policy was a balanced budget. Indeed, to head off a modest deficit in 1932, federal tax rates were raised, which only deepened the depression. In the wake of Keynes's *General Theory* and World War II, however, policy makers grew more receptive to the idea that fiscal policy could improve economic stability. The objective of fiscal policy was no longer to balance the budget but to promote full employment with price stability even if budget deficits resulted.

Automatic Stabilizers

This chapter has focused mostly on discretionary fiscal policy—conscious decisions to change taxes and government spending. Now let's get a clearer picture of automatic stabilizers. *Automatic stabilizers smooth out fluctuations in disposable income over the business cycle, thereby stimulating aggregate demand during recessions and dampening aggregate demand during expansions.* Consider the federal income tax. For simplicity, we assumed net taxes to be independent of income. In reality, the federal income tax system is progressive, meaning that the fraction of income paid in taxes increases as income increases. During an economic expansion, taxes claim a growing fraction of income, slowing the growth in disposable income and, hence, slowing the growth in consumption. Therefore, the progressive income tax relieves some of the inflationary pressure that might otherwise arise as output exceeds its potential during an economic expansion. Conversely, when the economy is in recession, output declines, but taxes decline

EMPLOYMENT ACT OF 1946

Law that assigned to the federal government the responsibility for promoting full employment and price stability faster, so disposable income does not fall as much as GDP. Thus, the progressive income tax cushions declines in disposable income, in consumption, and in aggregate demand.

Another automatic stabilizer is unemployment insurance. During economic expansions, the system automatically increases the flow of unemployment insurance taxes from the income stream into the unemployment insurance fund, thereby moderating aggregate demand. During recessions, unemployment increases and the system reverses itself. Unemployment payments automatically flow from the insurance fund to the unemployed, increasing disposable income and propping up consumption and aggregate demand. Likewise, welfare transfer payments automatically increase during hard times as more people become eligible. *Because of these automatic stabilizers, GDP fluctuates less than it otherwise would, and disposable income varies proportionately less than does GDP.* Because disposable income varies less than GDP does, consumption also fluctuates less than GDP does (as we saw in an earlier case study).

The progressive income tax, unemployment insurance, and welfare benefits were initially designed not so much as automatic stabilizers but as income redistribution programs. Their roles as automatic stabilizers were secondary effects of the legislation. Automatic stabilizers do not eliminate economic fluctuations, but they do reduce their magnitude. The stronger and more effective the automatic stabilizers are, the less need for discretionary fiscal policy. Because of the greater influence of automatic stabilizers, *the economy is more stable today than it was during the Great Depression and before.* As a measure of just how successful these automatic stabilizers have become in cushioning the impact of recessions, real consumption increased on average during the last six recession years. Without much fanfare, automatic stabilizers have been quietly doing their work, keeping the economy on a more even keel.

From the Golden Age to Stagflation

The 1960s was the Golden Age of fiscal policy. John F. Kennedy was the first president to propose a federal budget deficit to stimulate an economy experiencing a contractionary gap. Fiscal policy was also used on occasion to provide an extra kick to an expansion already under way, as in 1964, when Kennedy's successor, Lyndon B. Johnson, cut income tax rates to keep an expansion alive. *This tax cut, introduced to stimulate business investment, consumption, and employment, was perhaps the shining example of fiscal policy during the 1960s.* The tax cut seemed to work wonders, increasing disposable income and consumption. The unemployment rate dropped under 5 percent for the first time in seven years, the inflation rate dipped under 2 percent, and the federal budget deficit in 1964 equaled only about 1 percent of GDP (compared with about 4 percent in recent years).

Discretionary fiscal policy is a demand-management policy; the objective is to increase or decrease aggregate demand to smooth economic fluctuations. Demand-management policies were applied during much of the 1960s. But during the 1970s came a different problem—stagflation, the double trouble of higher inflation and higher unemployment resulting from a decrease in aggregate supply. The aggregate supply curve shifted left because of crop failures around the world, sharply higher OPEC-driven oil prices, and other adverse supply shocks. Demand-management policies were ill suited to cure stagflation because an increase of aggregate demand would worsen inflation, whereas a decrease of aggregate demand would worsen unemployment.

Other concerns also caused economists and policy makers to question the effectiveness of discretionary fiscal policy. These concerns included the difficulty of estimating the natural rate of unemployment, the time lags involved in implementing fiscal policy, the distinction between current and permanent income, and the possible feedback effects of fiscal policy on aggregate demand. We will consider each in turn.

Fiscal Policy and the Natural Rate of Unemployment

As we have seen, the unemployment that occurs when the economy is producing its potential GDP is called the *natural rate of unemployment*. Before adopting discretionary policies, public officials must correctly estimate this natural rate. Suppose the economy is producing its potential output of $12.0 trillion, as in Exhibit 5, where the natural rate of unemployment is 5.0 percent. Also suppose that public officials mistakenly believe the natural rate to be 4.0 percent, and they attempt to reduce unemployment and increase real GDP through discretionary fiscal policy. As a result of their policy, the aggregate demand curve shifts to the right, from *AD* to *AD'*. In the short run, this stimulation of aggregate demand expands output to $12.2 trillion and reduces unemployment to 4.0 percent, so the policy appears successful. But stimulating aggregate demand opens up an expansionary gap, which in the long run results in a leftward shift of the short-run aggregate supply curve. This reduction in aggregate supply pushes up prices and reduces real GDP to $12.0 trillion, the economy's potential. Thus, policy makers believe temporarily their plan worked, but pushing production beyond the economy's potential leads only to inflation in the long run.

Lags in Fiscal Policy

The time required to approve and implement fiscal legislation may hamper its effectiveness and weaken discretionary fiscal policy as a tool of macroeconomic stabilization. Even if a fiscal prescription is appropriate for the economy at the time it is proposed, the months and sometimes years required to approve and implement legislation means the medicine could do more harm than good. The policy might kick in only after the economy has already

EXHIBIT 5

When Discretionary Fiscal Policy Overshoots Potential Output

If public officials underestimate the natural rate of unemployment, they may attempt to stimulate aggregate demand even if the economy is already producing its potential output, as at point *a*. In the short run, this expansionary policy yields a short-run equilibrium at point *b*, where the price level and output are higher and unemployment is lower, so the policy appears to succeed. But the resulting expansionary gap will, in the long run, reduce the short-run aggregate supply curve from $SRAS_{130}$ to $SRAS_{140}$, eventually reducing output to its potential level of $12.0 trillion while increasing the price level to 140. Thus, attempts to increase production beyond potential GDP lead only to inflation in the long run.

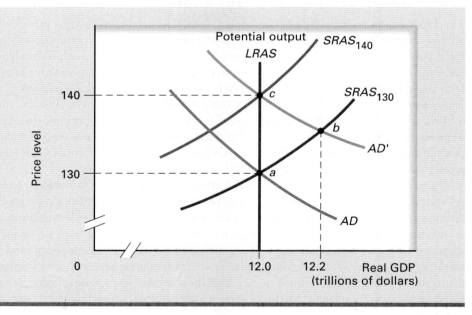

turned itself around. Because a recession is not usually identified until at least six months after it begins, and because the 10 recessions since 1945 lasted only 11 months on average, discretionary fiscal policy allows little room for error (more in a later chapter about timing problems).

Discretionary Fiscal Policy and Permanent Income

It was once believed that discretionary fiscal policy could be turned on and off like a water faucet, stimulating the economy at the right time by just the right amount. Given the marginal propensity to consume, tax changes could increase or decrease disposable income to bring about desired change in consumption. A more recent view suggests that people base their consumption decisions not merely on changes in their current income but on changes in their permanent income.

Permanent income is the income a person expects to receive on average over the long term. Changing tax rates for a year or two will not affect consumption much as long as people view the changes as only temporary. In 1967, for example, the escalating war in Vietnam increased military spending, pushing real GDP beyond its potential. The combination of a booming domestic economy and higher defense spending opened up an expansionary gap by 1968. That year, Congress approved a *temporary* tax hike, raising rates for 18 months. Higher taxes were supposed to soak up some disposable income, thereby reducing consumption to relieve inflationary pressure in the economy. But the reduction in aggregate demand turned out to be disappointingly small, and inflation was hardly affected. The *temporary* nature of the tax increase meant that consumers faced only a small cut in their permanent income. Because permanent income changed little, consumption changed little. Consumers simply saved less. As another example, in late 1997, Japanese officials introduced an income tax cut intended to stimulate Japan's flat economy. People expected the cut would be repealed after a year, so economists were skeptical that the plan would work, and it didn't. In short, *to the extent that consumers base spending decisions on their permanent income, attempts to fine-tune the economy with temporary tax changes will be less effective.*

The Feedback Effects of Fiscal Policy on Aggregate Supply

So far we have limited the discussion of fiscal policy to its effect on aggregate demand. Fiscal policy may also affect aggregate supply, although the effect is usually unintentional. For example, suppose the government increases unemployment benefits, paid with higher taxes on workers. If the marginal propensity to consume is the same for both groups, the reduced spending by workers should just offset the increased spending by beneficiaries. There should be no change in aggregate demand and thus no change in equilibrium real GDP, simply a redistribution of disposable income from the employed to the unemployed.

But could the program affect labor supply? Unemployed beneficiaries have less incentive to find work, so they may search at a more leisurely pace. A higher tax on workers reduces their opportunity cost of leisure, so they may work less. In short, the supply of labor could decrease as a result of offsetting changes in transfers and taxes. A decrease in the supply of labor would decrease aggregate supply, reducing the economy's potential GDP.

Both automatic stabilizers, such as unemployment insurance and the progressive income tax, and discretionary fiscal policies, such as changes in tax rates, may affect individual incentives to work, spend, save, and invest, although these effects are usually unintended consequences. We should keep these secondary effects in mind when we evaluate fiscal policies. It was concern about the effects of taxes on the supply of labor that motivated the tax cuts approved in 1981, as we will see next.

WALL STREET JOURNAL

Reading It **Right**

What's the relevance of the following statement from the Wall Street Journal: *"Inevitably, there is a big, long lag between the time spending is ordered by Congress and the time spending actually shows up in the economy."*

PERMANENT INCOME

Income that individuals expect to receive on average over the long term

U.S. Budget Deficits of the 1980s and 1990s

In 1981, President Reagan and Congress agreed on a 23 percent reduction in average income tax rates and a major buildup in defense programs, with no substantial offsetting reductions in domestic programs. Reagan argued that a reduction in tax rates would make people more willing to work and to invest because they could keep more of what they earned. Lower taxes would increase the supply of labor and the supply of other resources in the economy, thereby increasing the economy's potential output. In its strongest form, this supply-side theory held that output would increase enough to increase tax revenues despite the cut in tax rates. In other words, a smaller tax share of a bigger pie would exceed a larger tax share of a smaller pie. What happened as a result of the tax cut? Let's review events during the 1980s in the following case study.

Case Study

Public Policy

eActivity

Visit SciForums.com and read the varied opinions about supply-side economics at http://www.sciforums.com/showthread.php?t=32680. Are a majority of the opinions for or against supply-side economics? Does supply-side economics work? Based on what you've learned in this chapter, do you agree with any of the opinions?

The Supply-Side Experiment

Taking 1981 to 1988 as the time frame for examining the supply-side experiment, we can make some observations about the effects of the 1981 federal income tax cut, which was phased in over three years. After the tax cut was approved but before it took effect, a recession hit the economy and the unemployment rate climbed to nearly 10 percent in 1982.

© Stephen Chernin/Getty Images

Although it is difficult to untangle the growth generated by the tax cuts from the cyclical upswing following the recession of 1981–1982, we can say that between 1981 and 1988, the number employed climbed by 15 million and number unemployed fell by 2 million. Real GDP per capita, a good measure of the standard of living, increased by about 2.5 percent per year between 1981 and 1988. This rate was higher than the 1.4 percent average annual increase between 1973 and 1981 but lower than the 3.1 percent annual growth rate between 1960 and 1973.

Does the growth in employment and in real GDP mean the supply-side experiment was a success? Part of the growth in employment and output could be explained by the huge federal stimulus resulting from deficits during the period. The tax cuts, in effect, resulted in an expansionary fiscal policy. *The stimulus from the tax cut helped sustain a continued expansion during the 1980s—the longest peacetime expansion to that point in the nation's history.*

Despite the job growth, government revenues did not increase enough to offset the combination of tax cuts and increased government spending. Between 1981 and 1988, federal outlays grew an average of 7.1 percent per year, and federal revenues averaged 6.3 percent. So the tax cut failed to generate the revenue required to fund growing government spending. Before 1981, deficits had been relatively small—typically less than 1 percent compared with GDP. But deficits grew to about 4 percent compared with GDP by the middle of the decade. These were the largest peacetime deficits to that point on record. The recession of the early 1990s pushed the federal deficit up to 5 percent of GDP by 1992. These deficits accumulated into a huge national debt. *The national debt, which is the accumulation of annual deficits, nearly doubled relative to GDP from 33 percent in 1981 to 64 percent in 1992.*

Sources: *Economic Report of the President*, February 2004; *Survey of Current Business*, April 2004; and Herbert Stein, *The Fiscal Revolution in America*, 2nd ed. (Washington, D.C.: The AEI Press, 1996).

Given the effects of fiscal policy, particularly in the short run, we should not be surprised that elected officials might use it to get reelected. Let's look at how political considerations may shape fiscal policies.

Discretionary Fiscal Policy and Presidential Elections

After the recession of 1990–1991, the economy was slow to recover. At the time of the 1992 presidential election, the unemployment rate still languished at 7.5 percent, up two percentage points from when President George H. W. Bush took office in 1989. The higher unemployment rate was too much of a hurdle to overcome, and Bush lost his reelection bid to challenger Bill Clinton. Clinton's guide to the campaign was: "It's the economy, stupid."

© Michael Kleinfld/UPI/Landov

The link between economic performance and re-election success has a long history. Ray Fair of Yale University examined presidential elections dating back to 1916 and found, not surprisingly, that the state of the economy during the election year affected the outcome. Specifically, Fair found that a declining unemployment rate and strong growth rate in GDP per capita increased election prospects for the incumbent party. Another Yale economist, William Nordhaus, developed a theory of **political business cycles,** arguing that incumbent presidents use expansionary policies to stimulate the economy, often only temporarily, during an election year. For example, observers claim that President Nixon used expansionary policies to increase his chances for reelection in 1972. The evidence to support the theory of political business cycles is not entirely convincing. One problem is that the theory limits presidential motives to reelection, when in fact presidents may have other objectives. For example, President Bush passed up an opportunity in 1992 to sign a tax cut for the middle class because that measure would also have increased taxes on a much smaller group—upper-income taxpayers.

An alternative to the theory of political business cycles is that Democrats care more about unemployment and less about inflation than do Republicans. This view is supported by evidence indicating that during Democratic administrations, unemployment is more likely to fall and inflation is more likely to rise than during Republican administrations. Republican presidents tend to pursue contractionary policies soon after taking office and are more willing to endure a recession to reduce inflation. The country suffered a recession in the first term of the last six Republican presidents, including President George W. Bush. Democratic presidents tend to pursue expansionary policies to reduce unemployment and are willing to put up with higher inflation to do so. But George W. Bush pushed tax cuts early in his administration to fight a recession. Bush, like Reagan before him, seemed less concerned about the impact of tax cuts on federal deficits.

A final problem with the political business cycle is that other issues sometimes compete with the economy for voter attention. For example, in the 2004 election, President Bush's handling of the war on terrorism, especially in Iraq, became at least as much of a campaign issue as his handling of the economy.

Sources: *Economic Report of the President*, February 2004; Ray Fair, "The Effects of Economic Events on Votes for President," *Review of Economics and Statistics* (May 1978): 159–172; Ray Fair, *Predicting Presidential Elections and Other Things* (Stanford, Calif.: Stanford University Press, 2002); and William Nordhaus, "Alternative Approaches to the Political Business Cycle," *Brookings Papers on Economic Activity*, No. 2 (1989): 1–49.

The large federal budget deficits of the 1980s and first half of the 1990s reduced the use of discretionary fiscal policy as a tool for economic stabilization. Because deficits were already large during economic expansions, it was hard to justify increasing deficits to stimulate the economy. For example, President Clinton proposed a modest stimulus package in early 1993 to help the recovery that was under way. His opponents blocked the measure, arguing that it would increase the deficit.

Balancing the Federal Budget—Temporarily

Clinton did not get his way with the stimulus package, but in 1993, he did manage to substantially increase taxes on high-income households, a group that now pays the lion's share of federal income taxes (the top 10 percent of earners pay about two-thirds of federal income taxes collected). The Republican Congress elected in 1994 imposed more discipline on federal spending as part of a plan to balance the budget. Meanwhile, the economy experienced a vigorous recovery fueled by growing consumer spending and rising business optimism based on technological innovation, market globalization, and the strongest stock market in history. The confluence of these events—tax increases on the rich, spending restraints, and a strengthening economy—changed the dynamic of the federal budget. Tax revenues gushed into Washington, growing an average of 8.3 percent per year between 1993 and 1998; meanwhile, federal outlays remained in check, growing only 3.2 percent per year. By 1998, that one-two punch knocked out the federal deficit, a deficit that only six years earlier reached a record at the time of $290 billion. The federal surplus grew from $70 billion in 1998 to $236 billion in 2000.

But by early 2001, the economy was in recession, so newly elected President George W. Bush pushed through an across-the-board $1.35 trillion, 10-year tax cut to "get the economy moving again." Then on September 11, 2001, nineteen men in four hijacked airplanes ended thousands of lives and ended chances of a strong economic recovery. Given the softening economy and uncertainty created by the terrorist attacks, consumers took a wait-and-see approach. Unemployment rose.

The president and Congress approved measures to help rebuild New York City, support the troubled airlines, beef up domestic security, and wage a worldwide war on terrorism. These programs coupled with tax cuts provided fiscal stimulus to an ailing economy. According to the President's Council of Economic Advisors, these measures "provided substantial short-term stimulus to economic activity and helped put the economy on the road to recovery."[1] Although the recession officially ended in November 2001, the recovery was slow and uneven and the unemployment rate rose until peaking in June 2003 at 6.3 percent. But the tax cuts and spending programs, including the war in Iraq, increased the federal deficit, which was projected to exceed $400 billion in 2004.

Conclusion

This chapter reviewed several factors that reduce the size of the spending and taxing multipliers. In the short run, the aggregate supply curve slopes upward, so the impact on equilibrium output of any change in aggregate demand is blunted by a change in the price level. In the long run, aggregate supply is a vertical line, so if the economy is already producing at its potential, the spending multiplier is zero. To the extent that consumers respond primarily to changes in their permanent incomes, temporary changes in taxes affect consumption less, so the tax multiplier will be smaller.

1. *Economic Report of the President,* February 2004, p. 43.

Throughout this chapter, we assumed net taxes and net exports would remain unchanged with changes in income. In reality, income taxes increase with income and net exports decrease with income. The appendix introduces these more realistic assumptions. The resulting spending multipliers and tax multipliers are smaller than those developed to this point.

Because of huge federal deficits between 1982 and 1996, discretionary fiscal policy fell out of favor in the 1980s and most of the 1990s. But fiscal policy came back into the picture during the recession of 2001. During the time when discretionary fiscal policy was dormant, monetary policy took center stage as *the* tool of economic stabilization. Monetary policy is the regulation of the money supply by the Federal Reserve. The next three chapters introduce money and financial institutions, review monetary policy, and discuss the impact of monetary and fiscal policy on economic stability and growth. Once we bring money into the picture, we will consider yet another reason why the simple spending multiplier is overstated.

SUMMARY

1. The tools of fiscal policy are automatic stabilizers and discretionary fiscal measures. Automatic stabilizers, such as the federal income tax, once implemented, operate year after year without congressional action. Discretionary fiscal policy results from specific legislation about government spending, taxation, and transfers.

2. The effect of an increase in government purchases on aggregate demand is the same as that of an increase in any other type of spending. Thus, the simple multiplier for a change in government purchases is $1/(1 - MPC)$.

3. A decrease in net taxes (taxes minus transfer payments) affects consumption by increasing disposable income. A decrease in net taxes does not increase spending as much as would an identical increase in government purchases because some of the tax cut is saved. The multiplier for a change in autonomous net taxes is $-MPC/(1 - MPC)$.

4. An expansionary fiscal policy can close a contractionary gap by increasing government purchases, reducing net taxes, or both. Because the short-run aggregate supply curve slopes upward, an increase in aggregate demand raises both output and the price level in the short run. A contractionary fiscal policy can close an expansionary gap by reducing government purchases, increasing net taxes, or both. Fiscal policy that reduces aggregate demand to close an expansionary gap reduces both output and the price level.

5. Fiscal policy focuses primarily on the demand side, not the supply side. The problems of the 1970s, however, resulted more from a decline of aggregate supply than from a decline of aggregate demand, so demand-side remedies seemed less effective.

6. The tax cuts of the early 1980s were introduced as a way of increasing aggregate supply. But government spending grew faster than tax revenue, creating budget deficits that stimulated aggregate demand, leading to the longest peacetime expansion to that point in the nation's history. These huge deficits discouraged additional discretionary fiscal policy as a way of stimulating aggregate demand further, but success in reducing the deficit in the late 1990s spawned renewed interest in discretionary fiscal policy, as reflected by President Bush's tax cuts and spending programs beginning in 2001.

7. Tax cuts and new spending helped fight the recession of 2001 and strengthened a weak recovery. But these federal programs, combined with the recession and its aftermath, resulted in huge budget deficits in 2003 and 2004. The 2004 election became a referendum on President Bush's handling of the economy and the war on terror.

QUESTIONS FOR REVIEW

1. *(Fiscal Policy)* Define *fiscal policy*. Determine whether each of the following, other factors held constant, would lead to an increase, a decrease, or no change in the level of real GDP demanded:

   a. A decrease in government purchases
   b. An increase in net taxes
   c. A reduction in transfer payments
   d. A decrease in the marginal propensity to consume

2. *(The Multiplier and the Time Horizon)* Explain how the steepness of the short-run aggregate supply curve affects the government's ability to use fiscal policy to change real GDP.

3. *(Evolution of Fiscal Policy)* What did classical economists assume about the flexibility of prices, wages, and interest rates? What did this assumption imply about the self-correcting tendencies in an economy in recession? What disagreements did Keynes have with classical economists?

4. *(Automatic Stabilizers)* Often during recessions, the number of young people who volunteer for military service increases. Could this rise be considered a type of automatic stabilizer? Why or why not?

5. *(Permanent Income)* "If the federal government wants to stimulate consumption by means of a tax cut, it should employ a permanent tax cut. If the government wants to stimulate saving in the short run, it should employ a temporary tax cut." Evaluate this statement.

6. *(Fiscal Policy)* Explain why effective discretionary fiscal policy requires information about each of the following:

   a. The slope of the short-run aggregate supply curve
   b. The natural rate of unemployment
   c. The size of the multiplier
   d. The speed with which self-correcting forces operate

7. *(Automatic Stabilizers)* Distinguish between discretionary fiscal policy and automatic stabilizers. Provide some examples of automatic stabilizers. What is the impact of automatic stabilizers on disposable income as the economy moves through the business cycle?

8. *(Fiscal Policy Effectiveness)* Determine whether each of the following would make fiscal policy more effective or less effective:

   a. A decrease in the marginal propensity to consume
   b. Shorter lags in the effect of fiscal policy
   c. Consumers suddenly becoming more concerned about permanent income than about current income
   d. More accurate measurement of the natural rate of unemployment

9. *(C a s e* **S t u d y:** The Supply-Side Experiment) Explain why it is difficult to determine whether or not the supply-side experiment was a success.

10. *(C a s e* **S t u d y:** Discretionary Fiscal Policy and Presidential Elections) Suppose that fiscal policy changes output faster than it changes the price level. How might such timing play a role in the theory of political business cycles?

11. *(Balancing the Federal Budget)* Once the huge federal budget deficits of the 1980s and the first half of the 1990s turned into budget surpluses, why were policy makers more willing to consider discretionary fiscal policy?

PROBLEMS AND EXERCISES

12. *(Changes in Government Purchases)* Assume that government purchases decrease by $10 billion, with other factors held constant. Calculate the change in the level of real GDP demanded for each of the following values of the MPC. Then, calculate the change if the government, instead of reducing its purchases, increased autonomous net taxes by $10 billion.

    a. 0.9
    b. 0.8

    c. 0.75
    d. 0.6

13. *(Fiscal Multipliers)* Explain the difference between the government purchases multiplier and the net tax multiplier. If the MPC falls, what happens to the tax multiplier?

14. *(Changes in Net Taxes)* Using the income-expenditure model, graphically illustrate the impact of a $15 billion drop in government transfer payments on aggregate ex-

penditure if the MPC equals 0.75. Explain why it has this impact. What is the impact on the level of real GDP demanded, assuming the price level remains unchanged?

15. *(Fiscal Policy with an Expansionary Gap)* Using the aggregate demand–aggregate supply model, illustrate an economy with an expansionary gap. If the government is to close the gap by changing government purchases, should it increase or decrease those purchases? In the long run, what happens to the level of real GDP as a result of government intervention? What happens to the price level? Illustrate this on an AD–AS diagram, assuming that the government changes its purchases by exactly the amount necessary to close the gap.

16. *(Fiscal Policy)* This chapter shows that increased government purchases, with taxes held constant, can eliminate a contractionary gap. How could a tax cut achieve the same result? Would the tax cut have to be larger than the increase in government purchases? Why or why not?

17. *(Multipliers)* Suppose investment, in addition to having an autonomous component, also has a component that varies directly with the level of real GDP. How would this affect the size of the government purchase and net tax multipliers?

EXPERIENTIAL EXERCISES

18. *(Fiscal Policy)* The University of Washington's Fiscal Policy Center at http://depts.washington.edu/fpcweb/center/links.htm provides an extensive list of links about U.S. fiscal policy. Visit that site and use the links to determine what tax and spending proposals have been made in Congress during the past six months. Choose one of those proposals and use the *AD–AS* framework to explain its likely impact.

19. *(The Evolution of Fiscal Policy)* In the United States, fiscal policy is determined jointly by the president and Congress. The Congressional Budget Office at http://www.cbo.gov/ provides analysis to Congress, and the Office of

Management and Budget at http://www.whitehouse.gov/omb/index.html does the same for the executive branch. Visit these Web sites to get a sense of the kinds of analysis these groups do and how they might be used in determining fiscal policy.

20. *(Wall Street Journal)* "Washington Wire" is a column that appears on the front page of the *Wall Street Journal* each Friday. Review the latest column to determine what fiscal policy proposals are under consideration. Do the proposals deal more with discretionary fiscal policy or with automatic stabilizers? Are they designed to affect aggregate demand or aggregate supply?

HOMEWORK XPRESS! EXERCISES

*These exercises require access to McEachern Homework Xpress! If Homework Xpress! did not come with your book, visit **http://homeworkxpress.swlearning.com** to purchase.*

1. Use the diagram for this exercise with the helping line to draw a level of aggregate expenditure that would lead to an economy at an equilibrium with a real GDP of $9 trillion. Illustrate the effect of an increase in government purchases of $200 billion when the marginal propensity to consume is 0.75

2. Use the diagram with the helping line to draw a level of aggregate expenditure that would lead to an economy at an equilibrium with a real GDP of $9 trillion. Illustrate the effect of a decrease in autonomous net taxes of $200 billion when the marginal propensity to consume is 0.75

3. In the diagram use aggregate demand and short-run aggregate supply curves to show an economy at a short-run equilibrium, with a $0.5 trillion contractionary gap when

potential output is $9.5 trillion. Identify the equilibrium point and price level. Illustrate how fiscal policy can close the contractionary gap.

4. In the diagram use aggregate demand and short-run aggregate supply curves to show an economy at a short-run with a $0.5 trillion expansionary gap when potential output is $9.5 trillion. Identify the equilibrium point and price level. Illustrate how fiscal policy can close the expansionary gap.

5. In the diagram use aggregate demand and short-run aggregate supply curves to show an economy at equilibrium at its potential output of $9.5 trillion. Identify the equilibrium point and price level. Illustrate how fiscal policy can create an expansionary gap of $0.5 trillion.

The Algebra of Demand-Side Equilibrium

In this appendix, we continue to focus on aggregate demand, using algebra. In Appendix B two chapters back, we solved for real GDP demanded at a particular price level, then derived the simple multiplier for changes in spending, including government purchases. The change in real GDP demanded, here denoted as ΔY, resulting from a change in government purchases, ΔG, is

$$\Delta Y = \Delta G \times \frac{1}{1 - MPC}$$

The government spending multiplier is $1/(1 - MPC)$. In this appendix, we first derive the multiplier for net taxes that do not vary with income. Then, we incorporate proportional income taxes and variable net exports into the framework. *Note the simple multiplier assumes a shift of the aggregate demand curve at a given price level. By ignoring the effects of aggregate supply, we exaggerate the size of the multiplier.*

Net Tax Multiplier

How does a $1 increase in net taxes that do not vary with income affect real GDP demanded? We begin with Y, real GDP demanded, originally derived in Appendix B two chapters back:

$$Y = \frac{1}{1 - b}(a - bNT + I + G + X - M)$$

where b is the marginal propensity to consume and $a - bNT$ is that portion of consumption that is independent of the level of income (review Appendix B two chapters back if you need a refresher).

Now let's increase net taxes by $1 to see what happens to the level of real GDP demanded. Increasing net taxes by $1 yields

$$Y' = \frac{a - b(NT + \$1) + I + G + X - M}{1 - b}$$

The difference between Y' and Y is

$$Y - Y' = \frac{\$1(-b)}{1 - b}$$

Because b is the marginal propensity to consume, this difference can be expressed as $\$1 \times -MPC/(1 - MPC)$, which is the net tax multiplier discussed in this chapter. With the MPC equal to 0.8, the net tax multiplier equals $-0.8/0.2$, or -4, so the effect of decreasing net taxes by $1 is to increase GDP demanded by $4, with the price level assumed

constant. For any change larger than $1, we simply scale up the results. For example, the effect of decreasing net taxes by $10 billion is to increase GDP demanded by $40 billion. A different marginal propensity to consume will yield a different multiplier. For example, if the MPC equals 0.75, the net tax multiplier equals $-0.75/0.25$, or -3.

The Multiplier When Both *G* and *NT* Change

Although we did not discuss in the chapter the combined effects of changing both government purchases and net taxes, we can easily summarize these effects here. Suppose both increase by $1. We can bring together the two changes in the following equation:

$$Y'' = \frac{a - b(NT + \$1) + I + G + \$1 + X - M}{1 - b}$$

The difference between this equilibrium and Y (the income level before introducing any changes in G or NT) is

$$Y'' - Y = \frac{\$1(-b) + \$1}{1 - b}$$

which simplifies to

$$Y'' - Y = \frac{\$1(1 - b)}{1 - b} = \$1$$

Equilibrium real GDP demanded increases by $1 as a result of $1 increases in both government purchases and net taxes. This result is referred to as the *balanced budget multiplier*, which is equal to 1.

More generally, we can say that if ΔG represents the change in government purchases and ΔNT represents the change in net taxes, the resulting change in aggregate output demanded, ΔY, can be expressed as

$$\Delta Y = \frac{\Delta G - b\Delta NT}{1 - b}$$

The Multiplier with a Proportional Income Tax

A net tax of a fixed amount is easy to manipulate, but it is not realistic. Instead, suppose we introduce a *proportional income tax* rate equal to t, where t lies between 0 and 1. Incidentally, the proportional income tax is also the so-called *flat tax* discussed as an alternative to the existing progressive income tax. Tax collections under a proportional income tax equal the tax rate, t, times real GDP, Y. With tax collections of tY, disposable income equals

$$Y - tY = (1 - t)Y$$

We plug this value for disposable income into the equation for the consumption function to yield

$$C = a + b(1 - t)Y$$

To consumption, we add the other components of aggregate expenditure, I, G, and $X - M$, to get

$$Y = a + b(1 - t)Y + I + G + (X - M)$$

Moving the Y terms to the left side of the equation yields

$$Y - b(1 - t)Y = a + I + G + (X - M)$$

or

$$Y[1 - b(1 - t)] = a + I + G + (X - M)$$

By isolating Y on the left side of the equation, we get

$$Y = \frac{a + I + G + (X - M)}{1 - b(1 - t)}$$

The numerator on the right side consists of the autonomous spending components. A \$1 change in any of these components would change real GDP demanded by

$$\Delta Y = \frac{\$1}{1 - b(1 - t)}$$

Thus, the spending multiplier with a proportional income tax equals

$$\frac{1}{1 - b(1 - t)}$$

As the tax rate increases, the denominator increases, so the multiplier gets smaller. *The higher the proportional tax rate, other things constant, the smaller the multiplier.* A higher tax rate reduces consumption during each round of spending.

Including Variable Net Exports

The previous section assumed that net exports remained independent of disposable income. If you have been reading the appendixes along with the chapters, you already know how variable net exports fit into the picture. *The addition of variable net exports causes the aggregate expenditure line to flatten out because net exports decrease as real income increases.* Real GDP demanded with a proportional income tax and variable net exports is

$$Y = a + b(1 - t)Y + I + G + X - m(1 - t)Y$$

where $m(1 - t)Y$ shows that imports are an increasing function of disposable income. The above equation reduces to

$$Y = \frac{a + I + G + X}{1 - b + m + t(b - m)}$$

The higher the proportional tax rate, t, or the higher the marginal propensity to import, m, the larger the denominator, so the smaller the spending multiplier. If the marginal propensity to consume is 0.8, the marginal propensity to import is 0.1, and the proportional income tax rate is 0.2, the spending multiplier would be about 2.3, or less than half the simple spending multiplier of 5. And this still assumes the price level remains unchanged.

Since we first introduced the simple spending multiplier, we have examined several factors that reduce that multiplier: (1) a marginal propensity to consume that responds primarily to permanent changes in income, not transitory changes; (2) a marginal propensity to import; (3) a proportional income tax; and (4) the upward-sloping aggregate supply curve in the short run and a vertical aggregate supply curve in the long run. After we introduce money in the next two chapters, we will consider still other factors that reduce the size of the spending multiplier.

APPENDIX QUESTIONS

1. (*The Algebra of Demand-Side Equilibrium*) Suppose that the autonomous levels of consumption, investment, government purchases, and net exports are \$500 billion, \$300 billion, \$100 billion, and \$100 billion, respectively. Suppose further that the MPC is 0.85, that the marginal propensity to import is 0.05, and that income is taxed at a proportional rate of 0.25.

   a. What is the level of real GDP demanded?

   b. What is the size of the government deficit (or surplus) at this output level?
   c. What is the size of net exports at the level of real GDP demanded?
   d. What is the level of saving at this output?
   e. What change in autonomous spending is required to change equilibrium real GDP demanded by \$500 billion?

2. *(Spending Multiplier)* If the MPC is 0.8, the MPM is 0.1, and the proportional income tax rate is 0.2, what is the value of the spending multiplier? Determine whether each of the following would increase the value of the spending multiplier, decrease it, or leave it unchanged:

   a. An increase in the MPM
   b. An increase in the MPC
   c. An increase in the proportional tax rate
   d. An increase in autonomous net taxes

3. *(The Multiplier with a Proportional Income Tax)* Answer the following questions using the following data, all in billions. Assume an MPC of 0.8.

Disposable Income	Consumption
$ 0	$ 500
500	900
1,000	1,300
1,500	1,700

   a. Assuming that net taxes are equal to $200 billion regardless of the level of income, graph consumption against income (as opposed to disposable income).
   b. How would an increase in net taxes to $300 billion affect the consumption function?
   c. If the level of taxes were related to the level of income (i.e., income taxes were proportional to income), how would this affect the consumption function?

Money and the Financial System

Why are you willing to exchange a piece of paper bearing Alexander Hamilton's portrait and the number 10 in each corner for a pepperoni pizza with extra cheese? If Russia can't pay its bills, why don't they simply print more rubles? Why are only a few of the world's largest banks American? Why was someone able to cash a check written on underpants? And why is there so much fascination with money? These and other questions are answered in this chapter, which introduces money and banking.

The word *money* comes from the name of the goddess (*Juno Moneta*) in whose temple Rome's money was coined. Money has come to symbolize all personal and business finance. You can read *Money* magazine and the "Money" section of *USA Today*, watch TV shows such as *Moneyline*, *Moneyweek*, and *Your Money*, and go to Web sites such as money.cnn.com, moneycentral.msn.com/home.asp, and smartmoney.com. With money, you can articulate your preferences—after all, money talks. And when it talks, it says a lot, as in, "Put your money where your mouth is" and "Show me the money." Money is the grease that lubricates the wheels of commerce (in fact, the old expression "grease the palm" means to pay someone). Just as grease makes for an easier fit among gears, money reduces the friction—the transaction costs—of market exchange. Too little can leave some parts creaking; too much can gum up the works.

This chapter is obviously about money. We begin with the evolution of money, tracing its use from primitive economies to our own. Then we turn to developments in the United States.

Topics discussed in this chapter include:

- Barter
- Functions of money
- Commodity and fiat money

- The Federal Reserve System
- Depository institutions
- Banking developments

The Evolution of Money

In the beginning, there was no money. The earliest families were largely self-sufficient. Each produced all it consumed and consumed all it produced, so there was little need for exchange. Without exchange, there was no need for money. When specialization first emerged, as some people went hunting and others took up farming, hunters and farmers had to trade. Thus, the specialization of labor resulted in exchange, but the assortment of goods traded was limited enough that people could easily exchange their products directly for other products—a system called *barter*.

Barter and the Double Coincidence of Wants

DOUBLE COINCIDENCE OF WANTS

Two traders are willing to exchange their products directly

Barter depends on a **double coincidence of wants,** which occurs when one trader is willing to exchange his or her product for something another trader offers. If a hunter was willing to exchange hides for a farmer's corn, that was a coincidence. But if the farmer was also willing to exchange corn for the hunter's hides, that was a double coincidence—a *double coincidence of wants*. As long as specialization was limited, to, say, two or three goods, mutually beneficial trades were relatively easy to realize—that is, trade wasn't much of a coincidence. As specialization increased, however, finding the particular goods that each trader wanted became more difficult.

In a barter system, traders must not only discover a double coincidence of wants, they must also agree on an exchange rate. How many hides should the farmer get for a bushel of corn? If only two goods are produced, only one exchange rate needs to be worked out. As the types of goods traded increased, however, exchange rates increased too. Specialization raised the transaction costs of barter. A huge difference in the values of the units to be exchanged can also made barter difficult. For example, a hunter who wanted a home that exchanged for 1,000 hides would be hard-pressed to find a home seller needing so many hides. High transaction costs of barter gave birth to money.

The Earliest Money and Its Functions

Nobody actually recorded the emergence of money. We can only speculate now about how it first came into use. Through experience with barter, traders may have found they could always find ready buyers for certain goods. If a trader could not find a good that he or she desired personally, some good with a ready market could be accepted instead. So traders began to accept a certain good not for immediate consumption but because that good was readily accepted by others and therefore could be retraded later. For example, corn might become accepted because traders knew that it was always in demand. As one good became generally accepted in return for all other goods, that good began to function as **money.** *Any commodity that acquires a high degree of acceptability throughout an economy becomes money.*

Money fulfills three important functions: a *medium of exchange,* a *unit of account,* and a *store of value.* Let's consider each.

Medium of Exchange

Separating the sale of one good from the purchase of another requires an item acceptable to all involved in the transactions. If a society, by luck or by design, can find a commodity that everyone will accept in exchange for whatever is sold, traders can save time, disappointment, and sheer aggravation. Suppose corn plays this role, a role that clearly goes beyond its role as food. We then call corn a medium of exchange because it is accepted in exchange by all buyers and sellers, whether or not they want corn for food. A **medium of exchange** is anything that is generally accepted in payment for goods and services. The person who accepts corn in exchange for some product believes corn can be traded later for whatever is desired.

In this example, corn is both a *commodity* and *money,* so we call it **commodity money.** The earliest money was commodity money. Gold and silver have been used as money for at least 4,000 years. Cattle served as money, first for the Greeks, then for the Romans. In fact, the word *pecuniary* (meaning "of or relating to money") comes from the Latin word for cattle, *pecus.* Salt also served as money. Roman soldiers received part of their pay in salt; the salt portion was called the *salarium,* the origin of the word *salary.* Also used as money were wampum (polished strings of shells) and tobacco in colonial America, tea pressed into small cakes in Russia, rice in Japan, and palm dates in North Africa. Note that commodity money was a good, not a service; a service is intangible and cannot be held for later exchange.

Unit of Account

A commodity such as corn that grows to be widely accepted becomes a **unit of account,** a standard on which prices are based. The price of shoes or pots or hides is measured in bushels of corn. Thus, corn serves not only as a medium of exchange; it also becomes a common denominator, a yardstick, for *measuring the value* of each product. Rather than having to determine exchange rates among all products, as with a barter economy, people can price everything using a single measure, such as corn. For example, if a pair of shoes sells for 2 bushels of corn and a 5-gallon pot sells for 1 bushel of corn, then a pair of shoes has the same value in exchange as two 5-gallon pots.

Store of Value

Because people do not want to make purchases every time they sell something, the purchasing power acquired through a sale must somehow be preserved. Money serves as a **store of value** when it retains purchasing power over time. The better it preserves purchasing power, the better money serves as a store of value, and the more willing people are to hold it. Consider again the distinction between a stock and a flow. Recall that a *stock* is an amount measured at a particular point in time, such as the amount of food in your refrigerator, or the amount of money you have with you right now. In contrast, a *flow* is an amount per unit of time, such as the calories you consume per day, or the income you earn per week. *Money* is a stock and *income* is a flow. Don't confuse money with income. The role of money as a stock is best reflected by money's role as a store of value.

MONEY

Anything that is generally accepted in exchange for goods and services

MEDIUM OF EXCHANGE

Anything that facilitates trade by being generally accepted by all parties in payment for goods or services

COMMODITY MONEY

Anything that serves both as money and as a commodity; money that has intrinsic value

UNIT OF ACCOUNT

A common unit for measuring the value of each good or service

STORE OF VALUE

Anything that retains its purchasing power over time

Desirable Qualities of Money

The introduction of commodity money reduced the transaction costs of exchange compared with barter, but commodity money also involves some transaction costs. First, if the commodity money is perishable, as is corn, it must be properly stored or its quality deteriorates; even then, it won't maintain its quality for long. Coins have a projected life of 30 years, a dollar note, only 18 months. So money should be *durable*. Second, if the commodity money is bulky, major purchases can become unwieldy. For example, many cartloads of corn would be needed to purchase a home selling for 5,000 bushels of corn. So money should be *portable*, or easily carried. Dollar notes are easier to carry than dollar coins, which may explain why dollar coins have never become popular. Third, some commodity money was not easily divisible into smaller units to offer a range of prices. For example, when cattle served as money, any price involving a fraction of a cow posed an exchange problem. So money should be *divisible*.

Fourth, if commodity money like corn is valued equally in exchange, regardless of its quality, people will keep the best corn and trade away the rest. As a result, the quality remaining in circulation will decline, reducing its acceptability. Sir Thomas Gresham wrote back in the 16th century that "bad money drives out good money"; this has come to be known as **Gresham's law.** People tend to trade away inferior money and hoard the best. Over time, the quality of money in circulation becomes less acceptable. To avoid this problem, money should be of *uniform quality*.

Fifth, commodity money usually ties up otherwise valuable resources, so it has a higher opportunity cost than, say, paper money. For example, corn that is used for money cannot at the same time be used for corn on the cob, corn flour, popcorn, or other food. So money should have *a low opportunity cost*.

If the supply or demand for money fluctuates unpredictably, so will the economy's price level, and this is the final problem with commodity money. For example, if a bumper crop increases the supply of corn, more corn is required to purchase other goods. This we call *inflation*. Likewise, any change in the demand for corn *as food* from, say, the invention of corn chips, would affect the exchange value of corn. Erratic fluctuations in the market for corn limit its usefulness as money, particularly as a unit of account and a store of value. So money *should maintain a relatively stable value*. Money supplied by a responsible issuing authority is likely to retain its value better than money whose supply depends on uncontrollable forces of nature such as good or bad growing seasons.

What all this boils down to is that *the best money is durable, portable, divisible, of uniform quality; has a low opportunity cost; and is relatively stable in value*. These qualities are offered in Exhibit 1, which also lists the rationale, good examples, and bad examples. Please spend a minute reviewing the table.

GRESHAM'S LAW

People tend to trade away inferior money and hoard the best

Coins

The division of commodity money into units was often natural, as in bushels of corn or heads of cattle. When rock salt was used as money, it was cut into uniform bricks. Because salt was usually of consistent quality, a trader had only to count the bricks to determine the total amount of money. When silver and gold were used as money, both their quantity and quality were open to question. Because precious metals could be *debased* with cheaper metals, the quantity and the quality of the metal had to be determined with each exchange.

This quality control problem was addressed by coining the metal. *Coinage determined both the amount and quality of the metal.* Coins allowed payment by count rather than by weight. A table on which this money was counted came to be called the *counter*, a term still used to-

EXHIBIT 1 Six Desirable Qualities of Money

Quality	Rationale	Good Examples	Bad Examples
1. Durable	Money should not wear out quickly	Coins; sea shells	Strawberries; seafood
2. Portable	Money should be easy to carry, even relatively large sums	Diamonds; paper money	Lead bars; potatoes
3. Divisible	Market exchange is easier if denominations support a range of possible prices	Honey; paper money and coins	Cattle; diamonds
4. Uniform Quality	If money is not of uniform quality, people will hoard the best and spend the rest, reducing its quality	Salt bricks; paper money; coins	Diamonds; DVDs
5. Low Opportunity Cost	The fewer resources tied up in creating money, the more available for other uses	Iron coins; paper money	Gold, silver; diamonds
6. Stable Value	People are more willing to accept and hold money if they believe it will keep its value over time	Anything whose supply can be controlled by issuing authority, such as paper money	Farm crops; gold

day. Initially, coins were stamped with an image on only one side, but before spending the coin someone could shave of the precious metal from the smooth side. To prevent this, coins came to be stamped with an image on both sides. But another problem arose because bits of metal could still be clipped from the edge. To prevent clipping, coins were bordered with a well-defined rim. If you have a dime or a quarter, notice the tiny serrations on the edge. These serrations, throwbacks from the time when coins were silver or gold rather than cheaper metals, reduced the chances of "getting clipped."

The power to issue coins, which was vested in the *seignior,* or feudal lord, was considered an act of sovereignty. Counterfeiting was considered an act of treason. If the face value of the coin exceeded the cost of coinage, minting coins was profitable. **Seigniorage** (pronounced "seen´-your-edge") refers to the profit earned by the seignior from coinage. **Token money** is money whose face value exceeds its production cost. Coins and paper money now in circulation in the United States are token money. For example, the 25-cent coin costs the U.S. Mint only about 3 cents to make. Coin production nets the federal government about $500 million a year in seigniorage. Paper money is a far greater source of seigniorage, as we'll see later.

Money and Banking

The word *bank* comes from the Italian word *banca,* meaning "bench." Italian money changers originally conducted their business on benches. Banking spread from Italy to England, where London goldsmiths offered "safekeeping" for money and other valuables. The goldsmith gave depositors their money back on request, but because deposits by some people tended to offset withdrawals by others, the amount of idle cash, or gold, in the vault changed

SEIGNIORAGE

The difference between the face value of money and the cost of supplying it; the "profit" from issuing money

TOKEN MONEY

Money whose face value exceeds its cost of production

N e t B o o k m a r k

Tour the American Currency Exhibit, an online money museum created by the Federal Reserve Bank of San Francisco at http://www.frbsf.org/currency/index.html. You can view pictures of the types of currency used throughout U.S. history. For an informative history of money in America, follow the "Tour Historical Context" link. Who produced money before the Federal Reserve was created? What determined the value(s) of a dollar?

little over time. Goldsmiths found that they could earn interest by making loans from this pool of idle cash.

Goldsmiths offered depositors safekeeping, but visiting the goldsmith to get money to pay for each purchase became a nuisance. For example, a farmer might visit the goldsmith to withdraw enough money to buy a horse. The farmer would then pay the horse trader, who would promptly deposit the receipts with the goldsmith. Thus, money took a round trip from goldsmith to farmer to horse trader and back to goldsmith. Because depositors soon grew tired of visiting the goldsmith every time they needed money, they began instructing the goldsmith to pay someone from their account. The payment amounted to moving gold from one stack (the farmer's) to another (the horse trader's). *These written instructions to the goldsmith were the first checks.* **Checks** have since become official-looking, but they need not be, as evidenced by the actions of a Montana man who paid a speeding fine with a check written on clean but frayed underpants. The Western Federal Savings and Loan of Missoula honored the check.

By combining the ideas of cash loans and checks, the goldsmith soon discovered how to make loans by check. Rather than lend idle cash, the goldsmith could simply create a checking balance for the borrower. *The goldsmith could extend a loan by creating an account against which the borrower could write checks. In this way goldsmiths, or banks, were able to create a medium of exchange, or to "create money."* This money, based only on an entry in the goldsmith's ledger, was accepted because of the public's confidence that these claims would be honored.

The total claims against the goldsmith consisted of claims by people who had deposited their money plus claims by borrowers for whom the goldsmith had created deposits. Because these claims exceeded the value of gold on reserve, this was the beginning of a **fractional reserve banking system,** a system in which reserves amounted to just a fraction of total deposits. The *reserve ratio* measured reserves as a percentage of total claims against the goldsmith, or total deposits. For example, if the goldsmith had reserves of $5,000 but deposits of $10,000, the reserve ratio would be 50 percent.

Paper Money

Another way a bank could create money was by issuing bank notes. **Bank notes** were pieces of paper promising the bearer specific amounts of gold or silver when the notes were presented to the issuing bank for redemption. In London, goldsmith bankers introduced bank notes about the same time they introduced checks. *Whereas checks could be redeemed only if endorsed by the payee, notes could be redeemed by anyone who presented them.* Paper money was often "as good as gold," because the bearer could redeem it for gold. In fact, paper money was more convenient than gold because it was less bulky and more portable. Bank notes that exchange for a specific commodity, such as gold, were called **representative money**. The paper money *represented* gold in the bank's vault.

The amount of paper money issued by a bank depended on that bank's estimate of the proportion of notes that would be redeemed. The greater the redemption rate, the fewer notes could be issued based on a given amount of reserves. Initially, these promises to pay were issued by private individuals or banks, but over time, governments took a larger role in printing and circulating notes. Once paper money became widely accepted, it was perhaps inevitable that governments would begin issuing **fiat money,** which derives its status as money from the power of the state, or by *fiat*. Fiat (pronounced "fee´at") money is money because the government says so. The word *fiat* is from the Latin and means "so be it." Fiat money is not redeemable for anything other than more fiat money; it is not backed by something of intrinsic value. You can think of fiat money as mere paper money. It is acceptable not because it is intrinsically useful or valuable—as is corn or gold—but because the

---

CHECK

A written order instructing the bank to pay someone from an amount deposited

FRACTIONAL RESERVE BANKING SYSTEM

Only a portion of bank deposits is backed by reserves

BANK NOTES

Originally, papers promising a specific amount of gold or silver to anyone who presented them to issuing banks for redemption; today, Federal Reserve notes are mere paper money

REPRESENTATIVE MONEY

Bank notes that exchange for a specific commodity, such as gold

FIAT MONEY

Money not redeemable for any commodity; its status as money is conferred initially by the government but eventually by common experience government says it's money. Fiat money is declared **legal tender** by the government, meaning that you have made a valid and legal offer of payment of your debt when you pay with such money. *Gradually, people came to accept fiat money because they believed that others would accept it as well.* The currency issued in the United States today, and indeed paper money throughout most of the world, is fiat money.

A well-regulated system of fiat money is more efficient for an economy than commodity money. Fiat money uses only paper (a dollar note costs about 5 cents to make), but commodity money ties up something intrinsically valuable. Paper money makes up only part of the money supply. Modern money also includes checking accounts, which are electronic entries in bank computers.

LEGAL TENDER

U.S. currency that constitutes a valid and legal offer of payment of debt

The Value of Money

Economics in the Movies

Money has grown increasingly more abstract—from a physical commodity, to a piece of paper representing a claim on a physical commodity, to a piece of paper of no intrinsic value, to an electronic entry representing a claim on a piece of paper of no intrinsic value. So why does money have value? The commodity feature of early money bolstered confidence in its acceptability. Commodities such as corn, tobacco, and gold had value in use even if for some reason they became less acceptable in exchange. When paper money came into use, its acceptability was initially fostered by the promise to redeem it for gold or silver. But because most paper money throughout the world is now fiat money, there is no promise of redemption. So why can a piece of paper bearing the portrait of Alexander Hamilton and the number 10 in each corner be exchanged for a pizza or anything else selling for $10? *People accept these pieces of paper because, through experience, they have reason to believe that others will do so as well.* The acceptability of money, which we now take for granted, is based on years of experience with the stability of its value and with the willingness of others to accept it as payment. As we will soon see, when money's value becomes questionable, so does its acceptability.

The *purchasing power* of money is the rate at which it exchanges for goods and services. The higher the price level in the economy, the less can be purchased with each dollar, so the less each dollar is worth. The purchasing power of each dollar over time varies inversely with the economy's price level. As the price level increases, the purchasing power of money falls. To measure the purchasing power of the dollar in a particular year, you first compute the price index for that year and then divide 100 by that price index. For example, relative to the base period of 1982 through 1984, the consumer price index for April 2004 was 188. The purchasing power of a dollar in April 2004 was therefore 100/188, or $0.53, measured in 1982–1984 dollars. Exhibit 2 shows the steady decline in the value of the dollar since 1960, when it was worth $3.38 in 1982–1984 dollars.

When Money Performs Poorly

One way to understand the functions of money is to look at instances when money did not perform well. In an earlier chapter, we examined hyperinflation in Brazil. With prices growing by the hour, money no longer served as a reliable store of value, so people couldn't wait to exchange their money for goods or for some "hard" currency—that is, a more stable currency. If inflation gets high enough, people no longer accept the nation's money and instead resort to some other means of exchange. On the other hand, if the supply of money dries up or if the price system is not allowed to function properly, barter may be the only alternative. The following case study discusses instances when money performed poorly because of too much money, too little money, or a hobbled price system.

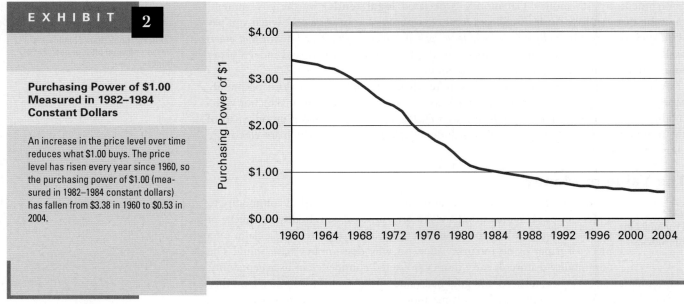

Source: Developed with CPI figures from the U.S. Bureau of Labor Statistics. For the latest CPI, go to http://bls.gov/cpi/home.htm.

Case **Study**

Public Policy

eActivity

Are U.S. dollars still flowing into Russia? Find out from the Bank of Russia's statistics page at http://www.cbr.ru/eng/statistics/credit_statistics/ See how the flow of dollars has changed over time. For an Internet guide to Russian banks and finance, visit Russia on the Net at http://www.ru/.

When Monetary Systems Break Down

What happens when there is too much money in circulation? We already discussed the transaction costs and distortions created by hyperinflation in Brazil. As a different example, hyperinflation in Russia following the breakup of the Soviet Union increased demand for so-called hard currencies, especially the dollar. Advertisers even quoted prices in "bucks." In keeping with Gresham's law, Russians traded rubles and hoarded dollars.

Consider the opposite problems: What if there isn't enough money to go around? Money became extremely scarce in 19th-century Brazil because a copper shortage halted minting of copper coins. People hoarded rather than traded the limited supply of coins available. In response, some merchants and tavern keepers printed vouchers redeemable for products sold by those merchants and taverns. These vouchers circulated as money until enough copper coins reappeared. Similarly, people coped with the shortage of money in the early American colonies by maintaining careful records, showing who owed what to whom.

For a more recent example of a money shortage, consider Panama, a Central American country that uses U.S. dollars as its currency. In 1988, the United States, responding to charges that Panama's leader was dealing drugs, froze Panamanian assets in the United States. This touched off a panic in Panama as bank customers tried to withdraw their dollars. Banks were forced to close for nine weeks. Dollars were hoarded, so people resorted to barter. Because barter is less efficient than a smoothly functioning monetary system, the currency shortage contributed to Panama's 30 percent GDP decline in 1988.

Finally, what happens when the price system is not allowed to operate? After Germany lost World War II, money in that country became close to useless. Despite tremendous inflationary pressure in the German economy, those who won the war imposed strict price controls. Because most price ceilings were set well below the market clearing level, sellers stopped accepting money, and this forced people to barter. Experts estimate that the lack of a viable currency cut German output in half. Germany's "economic miracle" of 1948 was due largely to the adoption of a reliable monetary system.

Thus, when the official money fails to serve as a medium of exchange because of price controls or hyperinflation or when hoarding dries up money in circulation, some other means of exchange emerges. But this diverts more resources from production to exchange. A poorly functioning monetary system increases the transaction costs of exchange. *No machine increases the economy's productivity as much as properly functioning money.* Indeed, it seems hard to overstate the value of a reliable monetary system. This is why we pay so much attention to money and banking.

Sources: Michael Casey, "Argentina Gets First Whiff of Inflation—Is It Back?" *Dow Jones Newswire*, 10 May 2004; and Michael Bryan et al., "Who Is That Guy on the $10 Bill?" *Economic Commentary: Federal Reserve Bank of Cleveland*, July 2000. Recent inflation rates around the world are available in the *World Development Report*; for the latest, go to http://econ.worldbank.org/wdr/.

Let's turn now to the development of money and banking in the United States.

Financial Institutions in the United States

You have already learned about the origin of modern banks: Goldsmiths lent money from deposits held for safekeeping. So you already have some idea of how banks work. Recall from the circular-flow model that household saving flows into financial markets where it is lent to investors. Financial institutions accumulate funds from savers and lend them to borrowers. Financial institutions, or **financial intermediaries,** earn a profit by "buying low and selling high"—that is, by paying a lower interest rate to savers than they charge borrowers.

Commercial Banks and Thrifts

A wide variety of financial intermediaries respond to the economy's demand for financial services. **Depository institutions**—such as commercial banks, savings banks, and credit unions—obtain funds primarily by accepting customer *deposits*. Depository institutions play a key role in providing the nation's money supply. Depository institutions can be classified broadly into commercial banks and thrift institutions.

Commercial banks are the oldest, largest, and most diversified of depository institutions. They are called **commercial banks** because historically they made loans primarily to *commercial* ventures, or businesses, rather than to households. Commercial banks hold about two-thirds of all deposits held by depository institutions. **Thrift institutions,** or **thrifts,** include savings banks and credit unions. Historically, savings banks specialized in making home mortgage loans. Credit unions, which are more numerous but smaller than savings banks, extend loans only to their "members" to finance homes or other major consumer purchases, such as new cars.

The Birth of the Fed

Before 1863, banks were chartered by the states in which they operated, so they were called *state banks.* These banks, like the English goldsmiths, issued bank notes. Thousands of different notes circulated and nearly all were redeemable for gold. The National Banking Act of

FINANCIAL INTERMEDIARIES

Institutions that serve as go-betweens, accepting funds from savers and lending them to borrowers

DEPOSITORY INSTITUTIONS

Commercial banks and thrift institutions; financial institutions that accept deposits from the public

COMMERCIAL BANKS

Depository institutions that historically made short-term loans primarily to businesses

THRIFT INSTITUTIONS, OR THRIFTS

Savings banks and credit unions; depository institutions that historically lent money to households

What's the relevance of the following statement from the Wall Street Journal: *One of Russia's biggest private banks, Alfa Bank, moved to reassure the market that it has enough money to meet obligations after lines of depositors formed outside its branches."*

FEDERAL RESERVE SYSTEM, OR THE FED

The central bank and monetary authority of the United States

RESERVES

Funds that banks use to satisfy the cash demands of their customers and the reserve requirements of the Fed; reserves consist of cash held by banks plus deposits at the Fed

1863 and later amendments created a new system of federally chartered banks called *national banks.* National banks were authorized to issue notes and were regulated by the Office of the Comptroller of the Currency, part of the U.S. Treasury. State bank notes were taxed out of existence, but state banks survived by creating checking accounts for borrowers. To this day, the United States has a *dual banking system* consisting of state banks and national banks.

During the 19th century, the economy experienced a number of panic "runs" on banks by depositors seeking to withdraw their funds. A panic was usually set off by the failure of some prominent financial institution. Following such a failure, fearful customers besieged their banks. Borrowers wanted additional loans and extensions of credit, and depositors wanted their money back. *As many depositors tried to withdraw their money, they couldn't because each bank held only a fraction of its deposits as reserves.* The failure of the Knickerbocker Trust Company in New York triggered the Panic of 1907. This banking calamity so aroused the public that Congress authorized a study that led to the creation of the **Federal Reserve System** in 1913 as the central bank and monetary authority of the United States.

Nearly all industrialized countries had formed central banks by 1900—the Bundesbank in Germany, the Bank of Japan, the Bank of England. But the American public's suspicion of such monopoly power led to the establishment of not one central bank but separate banks in 12 Federal Reserve districts around the country. The new banks were named after the cities in which they were located—the Federal Reserve Banks of Boston, New York, Chicago, San Francisco, and so on, as shown in Exhibit 3 (which district are you in?). *Throughout most of its history, the United States had what is called a decentralized banking system. The Federal Reserve Act moved the country toward a system that was partly centralized and partly decentralized.* All national banks joined the Federal Reserve System and were thus subject to new regulations issued by *the Fed,* as it came to be called (don't confuse *the Fed* with *the Feds,* shorthand for the FBI or other federal crime fighters). For state banks, membership was voluntary, and, to avoid the new regulations, most did not join.

Powers of the Federal Reserve System

The founding legislation established the Federal Reserve Board "to exercise general supervision" over the Federal Reserve System and to ensure sufficient money and credit in the banking system needed to support a growing economy. The power to issue bank notes was taken away from national banks and turned over to Federal Reserve Banks. (Take out a $1 note and notice what it says across the top: "Federal Reserve Note." On the $1 note, the seal to the left of George Washington's portrait identifies which Federal Reserve Bank issued the note.) The Federal Reserve was also given other powers: *to buy and sell government securities, to extend loans to member banks, to clear checks, and to require that member banks hold reserves equal to at least some specified fraction of their deposits.*

Federal Reserve Banks do not deal with the public directly. Each may be thought of as a bankers' bank. Reserve banks hold deposits of member banks, just as depository institutions hold deposits of the public, and they extend loans to member banks, just as depository institutions extend loans to the public. The name *reserve bank* comes from the responsibility to hold member bank *reserves* on deposit. **Reserves** are cash that banks have on hand or on deposit with the Fed to promote banking safety, to facilitate interbank transfers of funds, to satisfy the cash demands of their customers, and to comply with Federal Reserve regulations. By holding bank reserves, a reserve bank can clear a check written by a depositor at one bank and deposited at another bank, much like the goldsmith's moving of gold reserves from the farmer's account to the horse trader's account. Reserve banks were also authorized to lend to banks in need of reserves; the interest rate charged is called the *discount rate.*

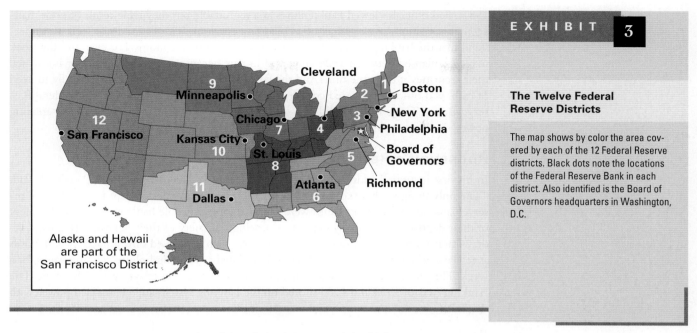

Source: Federal Reserve Board Web page at http://www.federalreserve.gov/otherfrb.htm.

A member bank is required to own stock in its district Federal Reserve Bank, and this entitles the bank to a specified dividend. Any additional profit earned by the reserve banks is turned over to the U.S. Treasury. So, technically, the reserve banks are owned by the member banks in the district.

Banking During the Great Depression

Economics in the Movies

From 1913 to 1929, both the Federal Reserve System and the national economy performed relatively well. But the stock market crash of 1929 was followed by the Great Depression, creating a new set of problems for the Fed, such as bank runs caused by panicked depositors. The Fed, however, dropped the ball by failing to act as a lender of last resort—that is, the Fed did not lend banks the money they needed to satisfy deposit withdrawals in cases of runs on otherwise sound banks.

The Federal Reserve System was established precisely to prevent such panics and to add stability to the banking system. What went wrong? In a word, everything. Between 1930 and 1933, the support offered banks by the Federal Reserve System seemed to crumble in stages. As businesses failed, they were unable to repay their loans. These loan defaults led to the initial bank failures. As the crisis deepened, the public worried about the safety of their deposits, so cash withdrawals increased. To satisfy the greater demand for currency, banks were forced to sell their holdings of stocks and bonds. But with many banks trying to sell and with few buyers, securities prices collapsed, sharply reducing the market value of bank assets. Many banks did not survive. Between 1930 and 1933, about one-third of all U.S. banks failed.

Because the Fed failed to understand its role as the lender of last resort, it failed to extend loans on a large scale to banks experiencing short-run shortages of cash (in contrast, the Fed was a ready source of loans a half century later during the stock market crash of

1987). Fed officials viewed bank failures as a regrettable but inevitable result of poor management or simply as the effect of a collapsing economy. The Fed did not seem to understand that the banking system's instability was hurting the economy. For example, the stock market collapsed between 1929 and 1933 in part because many banks were trying to sell their securities at the same time. And the collapse came just when banks were badly in need of cash. Fed officials appeared concerned primarily with the solvency of the Federal Reserve Banks. These officials did not seem to realize they had unlimited money-creating power, so they could not fail.

Roosevelt's Reforms

In his first inaugural address in 1933, newly elected President Franklin D. Roosevelt said, "The only thing we have to fear is fear itself," a statement especially apt for a fractional reserve banking system. Most banks were sound as long as people had confidence in the safety of their deposits. But if many depositors, fearing the safety of their deposits, tried to withdraw their money, they could not do so because each bank held only a fraction of deposits as reserves. When he took office, Roosevelt declared a "banking holiday," closing banks for a week. This drastic measure was welcomed as a sign that something would be done. The Banking Acts of 1933 and 1935 shored up the banking system and centralized power with the Fed. Consider some important features of these acts.

Board of Governors

The Federal Reserve Board was renamed the *Board of Governors* and became responsible for setting and implementing the nation's monetary policy. *Monetary policy,* a term introduced in Chapter 3, is the regulation of the economy's money supply and interest rates to promote macroeconomic objectives. All 12 reserve banks moved under the Board of Governors, which consists of seven members appointed by the president and confirmed by the Senate. Each member serves a 14-year nonrenewable term, with one appointed every two years. *The long tenure of office was designed to insulate board members from political pressure.* A new U.S. president can be sure of appointing or reappointing only two members during a presidential term, so a new president could not change much. One governor is also appointed to chair the Board of Governors for a four-year renewable term.

Federal Open Market Committee

Originally, the power of the Federal Reserve System was vested in each of the 12 reserve banks. The Banking Acts established the **Federal Open Market Committee** (**FOMC**) to consolidate decisions about the key tool of monetary policy, **open-market operations**— the Fed's buying and selling government securities (tools of monetary policy will be examined in the next chapter). The FOMC consists of the 7 board governors plus 5 of the 12 presidents of the reserve banks; the chair of the Board of Governors heads the group. Because the New York Federal Reserve Bank carries out open-market operations, that bank's president always sits on the FOMC. The structure of the Federal Reserve System as it now stands is presented in Exhibit 4. The FOMC and, less significantly, the Federal Advisory Committee (which consists of a commercial banker from each of the 12 reserve bank districts) advise the board.

Regulating the Money Supply

Because reserves amount to just a fraction of deposits, the United States has a *fractional reserve* banking system, as already noted. The Banking Acts gave the Board of Governors more authority in setting reserve requirements, thereby giving the Fed an additional tool of

FEDERAL OPEN MARKET COMMITTEE (FOMC)

The 12-member group that makes decisions about open-market operations—purchases and sales of U.S. government securities by the Fed that affect the money supply and interest rates; consists of the 7 Board governors plus 5 of the 12 presidents of the reserve banks

OPEN-MARKET OPERATIONS

Purchases and sales of government securities by the Federal Reserve in an effort to influence the money supply

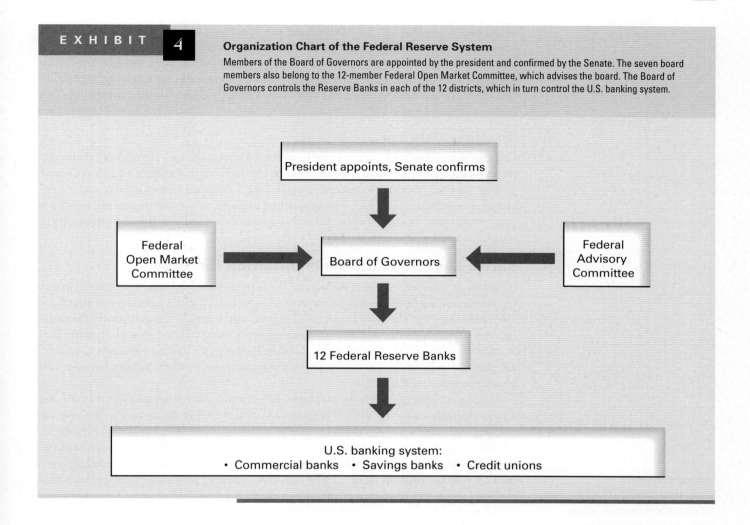

EXHIBIT 4

Organization Chart of the Federal Reserve System

Members of the Board of Governors are appointed by the president and confirmed by the Senate. The seven board members also belong to the 12-member Federal Open Market Committee, which advises the board. The Board of Governors controls the Reserve Banks in each of the 12 districts, which in turn control the U.S. banking system.

monetary policy. Thus, as of 1935, the Federal Reserve System has a variety of tools to regulate the money supply, including *(1) conducting open-market operations—buying and selling U.S. government securities; (2) setting the discount rate—the interest rate charged by reserve banks for loans to member banks; and (3) setting legal reserve requirements for member banks.* We will explore these tools in greater detail in the next chapter.

Deposit Insurance

Panic runs on banks stemmed from fears about the safety of bank deposits. The *Federal Deposit Insurance Corporation (FDIC)* was established in 1933 to insure the first $2,500 of each deposit account. Today the insurance ceiling is $100,000 per account. Banks purchase FDIC insurance. Over 90 percent of all banks now buy FDIC insurance. Other insurance programs take care of the rest. *Deposit insurance, by calming fears about the safety of bank deposits, worked wonders to reduce bank runs.*

Restricting Bank Investment Practices

As part of the Banking Act of 1933, commercial banks could no longer own corporate stocks and bonds, financial assets that fluctuate widely in value and contributed to instability of the banking system. The act limited bank assets primarily to loans and government securities—bonds issued by federal, state, and local governments. A *bond* is an IOU, so a government bond is an IOU from the government. Also, bank failures were thought to have resulted in part from fierce interest-rate competition among banks for customer deposits. To curb such competition, the Fed was empowered to set a ceiling on the interest rate that banks could pay depositors.

Objectives of the Fed

Over the years, the Fed has accumulated additional responsibilities. Here are six frequently mentioned goals of the Fed: (1) a high level of employment in the economy, (2) economic growth, (3) price stability, (4) interest rate stability, (5) financial market stability, and (6) exchange rate stability. *These goals boil down to high employment; economic growth; and stability in prices, interest rates, financial markets, and exchange rates.* As we will see, not all of these objectives can be achieved simultaneously.

Banks Lost Deposits When Inflation Increased

Restrictions imposed on banks during the 1930s made banking a heavily regulated industry. Banks lost much of their freedom to wheel and deal, and the federal government insured most deposits. The assets banks could acquire were carefully limited, as were the interest rates they could offer depositors (checking deposits earned no interest). Banking thus became a highly regulated, even stuffy, industry. Bankers operated on what was facetiously called the "3-6-3 rule"—pay 3 percent interest for deposits, charge 6 percent for loans, and get on the golf course by 3 P.M.

Ceilings on interest rates reduced interest-rate competition for deposits *among* banks. But a surge of inflation during the 1970s increased interest rates in the economy. Banking has not been the same since. When market interest rates rose above what banks could legally offer, many customers withdrew their deposits and put them into higher-yielding alternatives. In 1972, Merrill Lynch, a major brokerage house, introduced an account combining a **money market mutual fund** with limited check-writing privileges. Money market mutual fund shares are claims on a portfolio, or collection, of short-term interest-earning assets. These mutual funds became stiff competition for bank deposits, especially checkable deposits, which at the time paid no interest at banks.

Banks, like the London goldsmiths, used deposits to make loans. When people withdrew their deposits, banks had to support their loans by borrowing at prevailing interest rates, which were typically higher than the rates banks earned on their existing loans. Commercial banks, because their loans were usually for short periods, got in less trouble than savings banks did when interest rates rose. Savings banks had made loans for long-term mortgages, loans that would not be fully repaid for 30 years. Because they had to pay more interest to borrow funds than they were earning on these mortgages, savings banks were in big trouble, and many failed.

Bank Deregulation

In response to the loss of deposits and other problems, Congress tried to ease regulations, giving banks greater discretion in their operations. For example, interest-rate ceilings for deposits were eliminated, and all depository institutions were allowed to offer money market deposit accounts. Such accounts jumped from only $8 billion in 1978 to $200 billion in 1982. Some states, like California and Texas, also deregulated state-chartered savings banks. The combination of deposit insurance, unregulated interest rates, and wider latitude in the kinds of assets that savings banks could purchase gave them a green light to compete for large deposits in national markets. Once-staid financial institutions moved into the fast lane.

MONEY MARKET MUTUAL FUND

A collection of short-term interest-earning assets purchased with funds collected from many shareholders

Savings banks could wheel and deal but with the benefit of deposit insurance. The combination of deregulation and deposit insurance encouraged some on the verge of failing to take bigger risks—to "bet the bank"—because their depositors would be protected by deposit insurance. This created a *moral hazard,* which in this case was the tendency of bankers to take unwarranted risks in making loans because deposits were insured. Banks that were virtually bankrupt—so-called "zombie" banks—were able to attract additional deposits because of deposit insurance. Zombie banks, by offering higher interest rates, also drew deposits away from healthier banks. Meanwhile, because depositors were insured, most paid little attention to their banks' health. Thus, *deposit insurance, originally introduced during the Great Depression to prevent bank panics, caused depositors to become complacent about the safety of their deposits. Worse still, it caused those who ran the banks to take wild gambles to survive.*

Savings Banks on the Ropes

Many of these gambles didn't pay off, particularly loans to real estate developers, and banks lost a ton of money. The insolvency and collapse of a growing number of savings banks prompted Congress in 1989 to approve the largest financial bailout of any U.S. industry in history—a measure that would eventually cost about $250 billion. Taxpayers paid nearly two-thirds of the total, and savings banks paid the remaining third through higher deposit insurance premiums. The money was spent to shut down failing banks and to pay off insured depositors. Exhibit 5 shows the number of savings bank failures in the United States

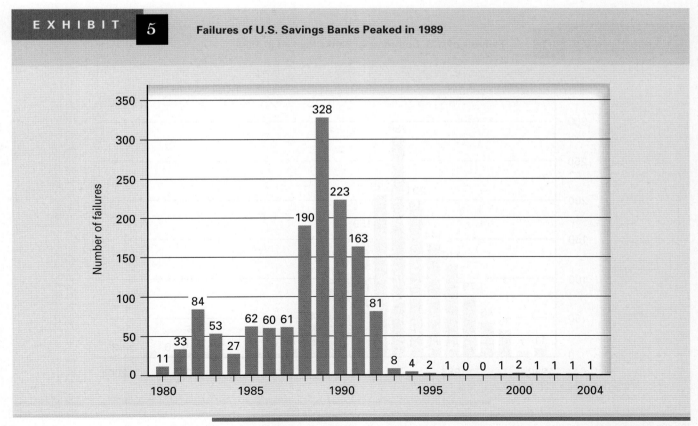

EXHIBIT   5   Failures of U.S. Savings Banks Peaked in 1989

Source: Based on annual reports from the Federal Deposit Insurance Corporation. For the latest figures, go to http://www2.fdic.gov/hsob/SelectRpt.asp? EntryTyp=30.

by year since 1980. From their 1989 peak of 328, annual failures dropped to 2 or fewer since 1995. Because of failures and mergers the number of FDIC-insured savings banks fell from 3,418 in 1984 to 1,404 by 2004, a drop of 59 percent.

Credit unions, which make up the bulk of thrift institutions, got into less trouble than savings banks because credit unions typically lend for shorter periods. Still, because of failures and mergers, the number of federally insured credit unions declined about 25 percent from 12,596 in 1992 to 9,490 in 2004.

Commercial Banks Were Also Failing

The U.S. banking system experienced more change and upheaval during the 1980s and early 1990s than at any other time since the Great Depression. As was the case of savings banks, risky decisions based on deposit insurance coupled with a slump in real estate values hastened the demise of many commercial banks. Banks in Texas and Oklahoma failed when loans to oil drillers and farmers proved unsound. Banks in the Northeast failed because of falling real estate values, which caused borrowers to default. Hundreds of troubled banks, like Continental Illinois Bank, First Republic Bank of Dallas, and the Bank of New England, were taken over by the FDIC or forced to merge with healthier competitors. Exhibit 6 shows commercial bank failures since 1980. The rising tide during the 1980s is clear, with failures peaking at 280 in 1988. But by the mid-1990s, failures fell sharply, and have been in

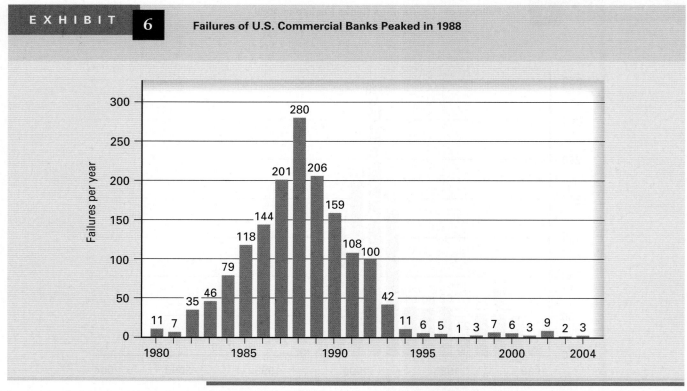

EXHIBIT 6   Failures of U.S. Commercial Banks Peaked in 1988

Source: Based on annual reports from the Federal Deposit Insurance Corporation. For the latest figures, go to http://www2.fdic.gov/hsob/SelectRpt.asp?EntryTyp=30.

single digits since 1995. Because of failures, mergers, and acquisitions, the number of FDIC-insured commercial banks fell from 14,496 in 1984 to 7,712 by 2004, a drop of 47 percent.

U.S. Banking Structure

As failed banks disappeared or merged with stronger banks, the industry got healthier. Bank profits grew fourfold during the 1990s. Although the number of commercial banks fell nearly by half over the last two decades, the United States still has more than any other country. Other major economies have fewer than 1,000 commercial banks. The large number of U.S. banks reflects past restrictions on **bank branches**, which are additional offices that carry out banking operations. Again, Americans, fearing monopoly power, did not want any one bank to become too large and too powerful. The combination of intrastate and interstate restrictions on branching spawned the many commercial banks that exist today, most of which are relatively small. For example, the largest 5 percent of commercial banks hold 86 percent of all commercial bank assets in 2004, meaning that 95 percent of commercial banks hold only 14 percent of the assets. Branching restrictions create inefficiencies, because banks cannot achieve optimal size and could not easily diversify their portfolios of loans across different regions.

In recent years, federal legislation has lifted restrictions on interstate branching and on the kinds of assets that banks can own. Two developments have allowed banks to get around branching restrictions: bank holding companies and mergers. A **bank holding company** is a corporation that may own several different banks. The *Graham-Leach-Bliley Act* of 1999 repealed some Depression-era restrictions on the kinds of assets a bank could own. A holding company can provide other services that banks are not authorized to offer, such as financial advising, leasing, insurance, credit cards, and securities trading. Thus, holding companies have blossomed in recent years. More than three-quarters of the nation's checking deposits are in banks owned by holding companies.

Another important development that allowed banks to expand their geographical reach is *bank mergers,* which have spread the presence of some banks across the country. Banks are merging because they want more customers and expect the higher volume of transactions to reduce operating costs per customer. Nationwide banking is also seen as a way of avoiding the concentration of bad loans that sometimes occur in one geographical area. The merger movement was fueled by a rising stock market during the 1990s and by federal legislation that facilitates consolidation of merged banks.

Bank holding companies and bank mergers have reduced the number of banks, but increased the number of branches. Exhibit 7 shows the number of commercial banks and bank branches in the United States since 1934. The number of banks remained relatively constant between 1934 and the mid-1980s but then declined, falling nearly in half since 1984 as a result of failures, mergers, and holding companies. The number of bank branches increased steadily, however, nearly doubling since 1984. So the number of branches per bank increased. In 1984, the average U.S. bank had about three branches; by 2003, the average bank had more than eight branches.

Exhibit 8 (a) shows the top 10 U.S. banks based on assets. The top three clearly dominate, with triple the assets of the next three. The top three banks grew mostly through mergers and acquisitions. For example, BankAmerica and NationsBank merged to form Bank of America, which then acquired FleetBoston, a major bank in the Northeast, which itself was a product of several mergers. Bank of America now stretches from coast to coast with over 6,000 branches. As another example of growth through merger, J.P Morgan

BANK BRANCHES
A bank's additional offices that carry out banking operations

BANK HOLDING COMPANY
A corporation that owns banks

| EXHIBIT | 7 | The Number of Commercial Banks Declined over the Last Two Decades, but the Number of Branches Continues to Grow |

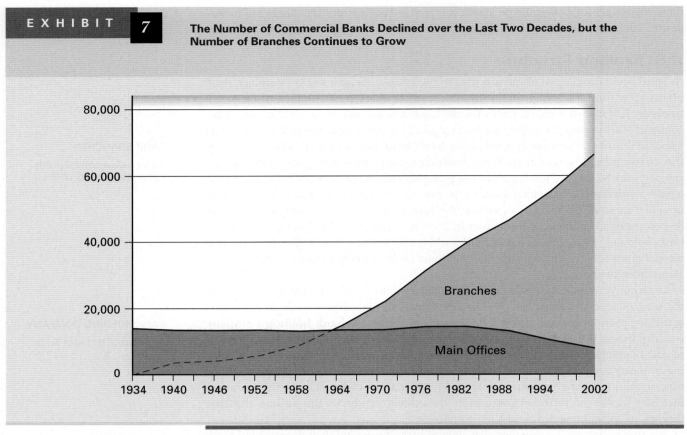

Source: Figures are for FDIC-insured commercial banks in the United States based on Federal Deposit Insurance Corporation data.

Chase in 2004 acquired Bank One, which had been the nation's sixth largest. National banks are the wave of the future.

How big are U.S. banks on the world stage? As indicated by Exhibit 8 (b), three of the largest four banks in the world are now American. Citigroup, the world's largest, had 275,000 employees as of 2004 in 100 countries on six continents. Citibank continues to expand, in 2004 acquiring over 400 branches from Washington Mutual and buying KorAm Bank of Korea. In the first quarter of 2004, Citibank earned $5.3 billion, a near record for any U.S. corporation. Although the top three U.S. banks are among the largest in the world, the next ranking U.S. bank was well down the 2004 list, ranking 35th. So there are only three world–class U.S. banks.

While U.S. banks were getting stronger and more global, Japanese banks were getting weaker. American banks have displaced Japanese banks at the top. Japan still placed three banks among the top 10, and a giant merger could soon create the largest bank in the world, but banking in Japan has suffered since 1990, as discussed in the following case study.

EXHIBIT 8

Top 10 Banks in America and the World

Among America's top 10 banks in panel (a), the top three are each more than twice the size of any other U.S. banks. Among the world's top 10 banks in panel (b), three of the top four are American.

(a) America's 10 largest banks based on assets

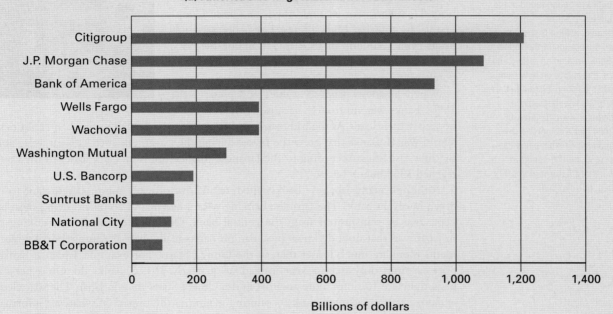

Billions of dollars

(b) World's 10 largest banks based on assets

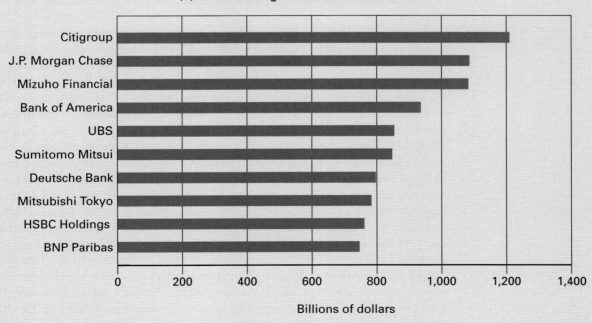

Billions of dollars

(a) Source: SNL Financial. Figures are for 2003 but have been updated by the author to reflect mergers announced as of early 2004.
(b) Source: *The Banker*. Figures are for 2003 but have been updated by the author to reflect mergers announced as of early 2004.

Public Policy

eActivity

Numerous banks in Japan failed in the early 2000s, leaving Mizuho Financial Group the largest, after a restructuring that included absorption of the formerly stable Fuji Bank. To read an article and view statistical graphics on how things were in Japan's banking system in early 2004 visit http://www.die-bank.de/index.asp?channel=121010&art=305&issue=022004. For a comprehensive report of Japanese banking since the Asian crisis, read the IMF report at http://www.imf.org/External/Pubs/FT/GFSR/2003/01/pdf/chp2.pdf.

Banking Troubles in Japan

© Tom Wagner/Corbis Saba

Prior to the 1980s, financial markets in Japan were heavily regulated, with restrictions on the interest rates that banks could offer. After deregulation, banks became more aggressive in attracting deposits and more willing to make riskier loans, particularly in real estate (sound familiar?). For example, the Kizu Credit Cooperative, by offering high interest rates, increased deposits from $2 billion in 1988 to $12 billion by 1995. Kizu lent these deposits to finance risky real estate purchases.

When Japanese property values collapsed in the 1990s, banks were in trouble because borrowers could not repay their loans. As the bad loans piled up, Japan experienced its first bank failures since World War II. Banks that grew the fastest during the go-go era, such as Kizu, were among the first casualties. According to the Japanese finance minister, bank losses in the country reached $350 billion by 1997.

Although many Japanese banks failed, regulatory officials appeared reluctant to close down insolvent banks. The Japanese banking system had many "zombies," living-dead banks kept alive by transfusions from the central bank. One problem with the banking crisis in Japan was that nobody knew how bad off banks really were because reporting requirements there are much looser than in the United States. For example, Japanese banks report earnings only once a year instead of quarterly, as U.S. banks do. On a per-capita basis, there are 12 times more auditors in the United States than in Japan. The so-called *lack of transparency* in Japanese bank accounting magnifies the impact of whatever information does become public. For example, when Fuji Bank reported that its problem loans were higher than it had previously disclosed, Fuji's share price plunged, along with shares of other banks.

To help resolve its banking crisis, the Japanese government in 1998 began using public funds to bail out troubled banks. By early 1999, about $75 billion had been earmarked to shore up 15 major banks. But by April 2001, Japanese banks and credit unions had as much as $1.2 trillion in problem loans, equivalent to about 30 percent of Japan's GDP. This made Japan's banking problem about five times bigger, in relative terms, than the U.S. savings bank problem.

Two major banks required bailouts by the central bank in 2003, but in 2004 Japan's economy began to brighten. Retail sales edged up, real GDP grew 3 percent, and unemployment fell. A decline in corporate bankruptcies cut the amount of *nonperforming loans*, or loans not being repaid. A rise in the stock market also dressed up bank balance sheets, because banks in Japan own much stock. The three Japanese banks ranked among the world's top 10 all showed a profit in 2004 for the first time in more than a decade. But Japan's fourth largest bank, UFJ Holdings, lost $4 billion in 2004 because of bad loans. Still Japanese banks were on course to cut their bad loans in half between 2002 and 2005. The Bank of Japan has encouraged banks to strengthen their liquidity management and become more transparent. Healthier banks are now helping the economy in Japan because they are in a better position to lend money to firms making capital investments. Japanese banks' troubles over the years were compounded by the "blanket deposit insurance" in place during the troubled times. This gave banks an incentive to gamble because depositors could not lose. The Bank of Japan plans to remove that blanket coverage in 2005. When UFJ Holdings merges with Mitsubishi Tokyo Financial Group in September 2005, the resulting bank will displace Citibank as the world's largest.

Sources: Ginny Parker, "Japan's Banks Post Profits," *Wall Street Journal*, 25 May 2004; "Economic and Financial Indicators," *Economist*, 5 June 2004; Hussain Kahn, "Ripples from a Japanese Bank Collapse," *Asia Times Online*, 15 December 2003, http://www.atimes.com; "Top 1000 World Banks," *The Banker*, 2 July 2003; Leika Kihara, "Japan Takenaka: No Comment On UFJ-MTFG Merger Talks," Dow Jones Newswires, 13 July 2004; an English-language Web site for Japan's central bank can be found at http://www.boj.or.jp/en/index.htm.

Conclusion

Money has grown increasingly more abstract over time, moving from commodity money to paper money that represented a claim on some commodity such as gold, to paper money with no intrinsic value. As you will see, paper money constitutes only a fraction of the money supply. Modern money also consists of electronic entries in the banking system's computers. So money has changed from a physical commodity to an electronic entry. Money today does not so much change hands as change computer accounts.

Money and banking have been intertwined ever since the early goldsmiths offered to hold customers' valuables for safekeeping. Banking has evolved from one of the most staid and regulated industries to one of the most competitive. Deregulation, branching innovations, and mergers have increased competition and have expanded the types of bank deposits. Reforms have given the Federal Reserve System more uniform control over depository institutions and have given the institutions greater access to the services provided by the Fed. Thus, all depository institutions can compete on more equal footing.

Deregulation provided greater freedom not only to prosper but also to fail. Failures of depository institutions create a special problem, however, because these institutions provide the financial underpinning of the nation's money supply, as you will see in the next chapter. There we will examine more closely how banks operate and supply the nation's money.

SUMMARY

1. Barter was the first means of exchange. As specialization grew, it became more difficult to discover the double coincidence of wants that barter required. The time and inconvenience of barter led even simple economies to develop money.

2. Anything that acquires a high degree of acceptability throughout an economy thereby becomes money. The first moneys were commodities, such as gold. Eventually, what changed hands were pieces of paper that could be redeemed for something of value, such as gold. As paper money became widely accepted, governments introduced fiat money—pieces of paper not redeemable for anything. Fiat money is money by law, or by fiat. Most currencies throughout the world today are fiat money. People accept

fiat money because, through experience, they believe that other people will do so as well.

3. The value of money depends on what it buys. If money fails to serve as a medium of exchange, traders find other means of exchange, such as barter, careful record keeping, some informal commodity money, or some other nation's currency. If a monetary system breaks down, more time must be devoted to exchange, leaving less time for production, so efficiency suffers.

4. The Federal Reserve System, or the Fed, was established in 1913 to regulate the banking system and issue the nation's currency. After a third of the nation's banks failed during the Great Depression, the Fed's powers were increased and centralized. After the Great Depression, the

primary powers of the Fed were to (a) conduct open-market operations (buying and selling U.S. government securities), (b) set the discount rate (the interest rate the Fed charges borrowing banks), and (c) establish reserve requirements (the share of deposits banks must hold in reserve).

5. Regulations introduced during the Great Depression turned banking into a closely regulated industry. Reforms in the 1980s gave banks more flexibility to compete for deposits with other kinds of financial intermediaries.

Some banks used this flexibility to make risky loans, but these gambles often failed, causing bank failures. In 1989, Congress approved a measure to close failing banks, pay off insured depositors, and impose tighter regulations. By the mid-1990s, U.S. banks were thriving once again, but Japanese banks remained troubled. Mergers and holding companies are creating banks that span the nation and are becoming the largest in the world.

QUESTIONS FOR REVIEW

1. *(Barter)* Define a double coincidence of wants and explain its role in a barter system.

2. *(Money Versus Barter)* "Without money, everything would be more expensive." Explain this statement. Then take a look at a Web page devoted to barter at http://www.ex.ac.uk/~RDavies/arian/barter.html. What are some current developments in barter exchange?

3. *(Functions of Money)* What are the three important functions of money? Define each of them.

4. *(Functions of Money)* "If an economy had only two goods (both *nondurable*), there would be no need for money because exchange would always be between those two goods." What important function of money does this statement disregard?

5. *(Characteristics of Money)* Why is universal acceptability such an important characteristic of money? What other characteristics can you think of that might be important to market participants?

6. *(Commodity Money)* Why do you think rice was chosen to serve as money in medieval Japan? What would happen to the price level if there was a particularly good rice harvest one year?

7. *(Commodity Money)* Early in U.S. history, tobacco was used as money. If you were a tobacco farmer and had two loads of tobacco that were of different qualities, which would you supply as money and which would you supply for smoking? Under what conditions would you use both types of tobacco for money?

PROBLEMS AND EXERCISES

8. *(Origins of Banking)* Discuss the various ways in which London goldsmiths functioned as early banks.

9. *(Types of Money)* Complete each of the following sentences:

   a. If the face value of a coin exceeds the cost of coinage, the resulting revenue to the issuer of the coin is known as _____.

   b. A product that serves both as money and as a commodity is _____.

   c. Coins and paper money circulating in the United States have face values that exceed the value of the

   materials from which they are made. Therefore, they are forms of _____.

   d. If the government declares that creditors must accept a form of money as payment for debts, the money becomes _____.

   e. A common unit for measuring the value of every good or service in the economy is known as a(n) _____.

10. *(Fiat Money)* Most economists believe that the better fiat money serves as a store of value, the more acceptable it is. What does this statement mean? How could people lose faith in money?

11. *(The Value of Money)* When the value of money was based on its gold content, new discoveries of gold were frequently followed by periods of inflation. Explain.

12. (*C a s e* **S t u d y :** When Monetary Systems Break Down) In countries where the monetary system has broken down, what are some alternatives to which people have resorted to carry out exchange?

13. *(Depository Institutions)* What is a depository institution, and what types of depository institutions are found in the United States? How do they act as intermediaries between savers and borrowers? Why do they play this role?

14. *(Federal Reserve System)* What are the main powers and responsibilities of the Federal Reserve System?

15. *(Bank Deregulation)* Some economists argue that deregulated deposit rates combined with deposit insurance led to the insolvency of many depository institutions. On what basis do they make such an argument?

16. *(The Structure of U.S. Banking)* Discuss the impact of bank mergers on the structure of American banking. Why do banks merge?

17. (*C a s e* **S t u d y :** Banking Troubles in Japan) Discuss problems with the banking system in Japan. In what ways are they similar to U.S. banking problems in the late 1980s and early 1990s? What is the current status of bank restructuring in Japan?

EXPERIENTIAL EXERCISES

18. *(When Money Performs Poorly)* Visit Glyn Davies's History of Money site at http://www.ex.ac.uk/~RDavies/ arian/llyfr.html. Click on "A Comparative Chronology of Money" and check the years since 1939. How many hyperinflations are mentioned for those years? What does that tell you about the relationship between monetary systems and economic well-being?

19. *(U.S. Banking Structure)* The Federal Reserve Bank of Philadelphia often runs informative articles that are accessible to introductory economics students. At http://www.phil.frb.org/econ/wps/wp02.html, read the Working Paper titled "Do Bankers Sacrifice Value to Build Empires? Managerial Incentives, Industry Consolidation, and Financial Performance" by Joseph P. Hughes, William

W. Lang, Loretta J. Mester, Choon-Geol Moon, and Michael S. Pagano. Consider the numerous bank mergers of the early 2000s. Are bank mergers a good thing? What are the authors' conclusions about this?

20. *(Wall Street Journal)* The *Wall Street Journal* prints several features that track key interest rates. The daily Money Rates box lists the current prime lending rate, along with a variety of short-term rates. The weekly Key Interest Rates table reports on Treasury securities. And a weekly Consumer Savings Rates List shows the rates paid by 100 large banks. Take a look at these sources—you can find them on the Money and Credit Markets pages—and determine the extent to which all these interest rates move together.

Banking and the Money Supply

© Michael S. Yamashita/Corbis

How do banks create money? Why are banks called First Trust or Security National rather than Benny's Bank or Easy Money Bank and Trust? Why are we so interested in banks, anyway? After all, isn't banking a business like any other, such as dry cleaning, auto washing, or home remodeling? Why not devote a chapter to the home-remodeling business? Answers to these and related questions are provided in this chapter, which examines banking and the money supply.

In this chapter, we take a closer look at the unique role banks play in the economy. Banks are special in macroeconomics because, like the London goldsmith, they can convert a borrower's IOU into money, one key to a healthy economy. Because regulatory reforms have eliminated many of the distinctions between commercial banks and thrift institutions, and because thrifts represent a dwindling share of depository institutions, all depository institutions will usually be referred to more simply as *banks*.

We begin by going over the definitions of money, from the narrowest to the broadest. Then, we look at how banks work and how they create money. We also consider the Fed in more detail. As you will see, the Fed attempts to control the money supply directly by issuing currency and indirectly by regulating bank reserves. Topics discussed in this chapter include:

- Money aggregates
- Checkable deposits
- Balance sheets
- Money creation
- Money multiplier
- Tools of the Fed

Money Aggregates

When you think of money, what comes to mind is probably currency—dollar notes and coins. But as you learned in the last chapter, dollar notes and coins account for only part of the money supply. In this section, we consider three definitions of money.

The Narrow Definition of Money: M1

Suppose you have some cash with you right now—dollar notes and coins. Dollar notes and coins are part of the money supply as it's narrowly defined. If you were to deposit this cash in your checking account, you could then write checks directing your bank to pay someone from your account. **Checkable deposits,** or deposits against which checks can be written, are another part of the narrow definition of money. Checkable deposits can also be tapped with an ATM card or a debit card, usable at a growing number of retailers. Banks hold a variety of checkable deposits. In recent years, financial institutions have developed other kinds of accounts that carry check-writing privileges but also earn interest.

Money aggregates are various measures of the money supply defined by the Federal Reserve. The narrowest definition, called **M1,** consists of currency (including coins) held by the nonbanking public, checkable deposits, and traveler's checks. Note that currency sitting in bank vaults is not counted as part of the money supply because it is not being used as a medium of exchange. But checkable deposits are money because their owners can write checks or use debit cards to tap them. Checkable deposits are the liabilities of the issuing banks, which stand ready to convert them into cash. But unlike cash, checks are *not* legal tender, as signs that say "No Checks!" attest.

The primary currency circulating in the United States consists of Federal Reserve notes, which are produced by the U.S. Bureau of Engraving and Printing and are issued by and are liabilities of the 12 Federal Reserve Banks. Over 90 percent of the Fed's liabilities consist of Federal Reserve notes. The Fed spends about $750 million a year printing, storing, and distributing notes—the Fed's largest single expense. Because Federal Reserve notes are redeemable for nothing other than more Federal Reserve notes, U.S. currency is *fiat money.* The other component of currency is coins, manufactured and distributed by the U.S. Mint. Like paper money, U.S. coins are token money because their metal value is usually less than their face value (as noted in the previous chapter, a quarter costs about 3 cents to make).

About 60 percent of Federal Reserve notes now in circulation are in foreign hands. Some countries, such as Panama, Ecuador, and El Salvador, use U.S. dollars as their currency. This is actually a good deal for Americans because a $100 note that costs only about 5 cents to print can be "sold" to foreigners for $100 worth of goods and services. It's as if these countries were granting us an interest-free loan during the period the $100 note circulates abroad, usually several years. But having our currency used around the world poses special problems when it comes to counterfeiting, as discussed in the following case study.

CHECKABLE DEPOSITS

Deposits in financial institutions against which checks can be written and ATM or debit cards can be applied

MONEY AGGREGATES

Measures of the economy's money supply

M1

The narrowest measure of the money supply, consisting of currency and coins held by the nonbanking public, checkable deposits, and traveler's checks

Public Policy

eActivity

Visit the information page about the new $50 notes from the U.S. Treasury Department at http://www. moneyfactory.com/newmoney/ main.cfm/currency/new50 for a detailed explanation of the new design and security features of the $50 Grant note. What has happened to the Federal Reserve seal that traditionally identifies the issuing bank? Will all the new currency designs get the same level of protection as the $50 bill? Who is paying for these design changes?

WALL STREET JOURNAL

Reading It **Right**

What's the relevance of the following statement from the Wall Street Journal: *"The Bank of Mexico will begin issuing new high-denomination bills next week that include improved security features to dissuade counterfeiters. New counterfeit techniques allow for the mass production of false bills."*

Faking It

One threat to the integrity of U.S. currency is the so-called supernote—a counterfeit $100 note of extremely high quality that began circulating around 1990. It's a remarkable forgery, including sequential serial numbers and a polymer security thread that took Crane & Company, the supplier of paper for U.S. currency since 1879, years to develop. By perfectly emulating the ferrous oxide inked in Benjamin Franklin's portrait, the supernote sometimes fools currency-scanning machines at the nation's 12 Federal Reserve Banks. Supernotes are ubiquitous abroad, especially in Europe. Up to one-fifth of the $100 notes circulating in Russia in a recent year were believed to be fake. Because of the supernote, merchants and bank tellers in Europe and the Far East grew reluctant to accept $100 notes.

© 2003, Mark Wilson/Getty Images

Expert engravers produced the supernote, but technological improvements in copy machines, computers, and printers now allow even amateurs to make passable counterfeits. About half the fake notes found in a recent year were produced with computers, copiers, and printers, up from just 1 percent in 1995. On U.S. soil, the Secret Service seizes most counterfeit money before it circulates. But foreign counterfeiting poses a problem for the U.S. Secret Service, which is primarily a domestic police force (few of the 2,000 agents work abroad). Most counterfeit money seized here is printed abroad, and seizures abroad have been growing.

To combat technological improvements in counterfeiting, U.S. currency was recently redesigned for the first time since 1929. In fact, U.S. currency had changed so little that on the back of a $10 note the car driving by the U.S. Treasury building was from the 1920s. The U.S. Treasury will redesign U.S. currency every 7 to 10 years to keep ahead of counterfeiters. In the first round of changes, the new notes remained the same size as the old ones and were printed on the same Crane paper in the same green and black ink. Changes to the $100 note included a new off-center portrait of Franklin, microprinting around the portrait that repeats the phrase "The United States of America," a watermark image of Franklin, and a "100" that shifts from green to black when viewed from different angles. A new security thread buried in the paper repeats "USA 100" in print 42-thousandths of an inch tall. This lettering is visible when the note is held up to light but is not reproducible on a photocopier, and the thread glows red under ultraviolet light. New $50, $20, $10, and $5 notes were also issued during that first round, each with its own security features, such as a security strip with a distinct color under ultraviolet light. The $1 note is not scheduled for a makeover because it is not popular with counterfeiters. Apparently, the cost of counterfeiting a $1 note and the risk of trying to pass it exceed the expected benefits.

Counterfeiters are fighting back. The watermark is faked by light printing. The security strip is faked by laboriously threading material between the two thin sheets of paper that make up the note. The hardest features to fake are microprinting, fine-line printing patterns, and details in the U.S. Treasury seal. The $20 note is most popular among domestic counterfeiters, and the $100 note most popular among foreign counterfeiters. Colombia is now the world's largest source of bogus American currency, accounting for 40 percent of the world total. Colombia borders on Ecuador, which converted to the U.S. dollar in 2000 and thus offers a ready outlet for counterfeits. In some countries, such as El Salvador, the U.S. dollar circulates alongside the native currency, which offers outlets for counterfeiters.

U.S. currency is now going through its second redesign in a decade, with a new $20 note introduced in 2003 and the $50 note in 2004. The most noticeable difference in the newly designed $20 note is the subtle background colors of peach and blue on both sides of the note. This marks the first coloring of U.S. currency other than black or green in modern American history. The $50 note adds a blue and red background to both sides of the note.

The United States has a policy of never recalling currency for fear that the world's hoarders of dollars might switch to other currencies, like euros or yen (remember, we want foreigners to hold onto their U.S. dollars). Over time, preference for the new currency and the replacement of old notes as they pass through the Fed will eventually eliminate old notes. But different designs of the same denomination will circulate side by side for some time, especially $100 notes. To give you some idea how long this could take, U.S. notes of $500 and up were last printed in 1946, and the Fed began taking them out of circulation in 1969. Yet hundreds of thousands of these big denominations are still hoarded by the public, about 60 years after they were last printed. Some big notes still show up at Federal Reserve Banks, where they are destroyed. But they remain legal tender. In fact, every U.S. note issued since 1861 remains legal tender today. That's one reason U.S. dollars are prized around the world.

Sources: Timothy O'Brien, "Lockboxes, Iraqi Loot and a Trail to the Fed," *New York Times*, 6 June 2004; "Spotting Counterfeit Currency," Federal Reserve Bank of Atlanta, http://www.frbatlanta.org; "The Use and Counterfeiting of U.S. Currency Abroad," *A Report to the Congress by the Secretary of the Treasury*, January 2000, at http://www.federalreserve.gov/boarddocs/rptcongress/counterfeit.pdf. The U.S. Treasury has a Web site providing information about new notes at http://www.moneyfactory.com/section.cfm/4.

Broader Money Aggregates

Economists regard currency and checkable deposits as money because each serves as a medium of exchange, a unit of account, and a store of value. Some other financial assets perform the store-of-value function and can be converted into currency or to checkable deposits. Because these are so close to money, they are called money under a broader definition.

Savings deposits earn interest but have no specific maturity date. Banks often allow depositors to shift funds from savings accounts to checking accounts by phone, an ATM card, or online, so distinctions between narrow and broad definitions of money have become blurred. **Time deposits** (also called *certificates of deposit,* or *CDs*) earn a fixed rate of interest if held for a specified period, ranging from several months to several years. Premature withdrawals are penalized by forfeiture of several months' interest. Neither savings deposits nor time deposits serve directly as media of exchange, so they are not included in M1, the narrowest definition of money.

Money market mutual fund accounts, mentioned in the previous chapter, are another component of money when defined more broadly. But, because of restrictions on the minimum balance, on the number of checks that can be written per month, and on the minimum amount of each check, these popular accounts are not viewed as money when narrowly defined.

Recall that M1 consists of currency (including coins) held by the nonbanking public, checkable deposits, and traveler's checks. **M2** includes M1 as well as savings deposits, small-denomination time deposits, and money market mutual fund accounts. **M3** includes M2 plus large-denomination time deposits ($100,000 or more). M3 is less liquid than M2, which is less liquid than M1. Exhibit 1 shows the size and relative importance of each aggregate. As you can see, compared to M1, M2 is nearly five times larger and M3 is nearly seven times larger. Thus, the narrowest definition of money includes only a fraction of broader aggregates. But distinctions between M1 and M2 become less meaningful as banks allow depositors to transfer funds from one account to another.

SAVINGS DEPOSITS
Deposits that earn interest but have no specific maturity date

TIME DEPOSITS
Deposits that earn a fixed rate of interest if held for the specified period, which can range from several months to several years; also called certificates of deposit

M2
A money aggregate consisting of M1 plus savings deposits, small-denomination time deposits, and money market mutual funds

M3
A money aggregate consisting of M2 plus large-denomination time deposits

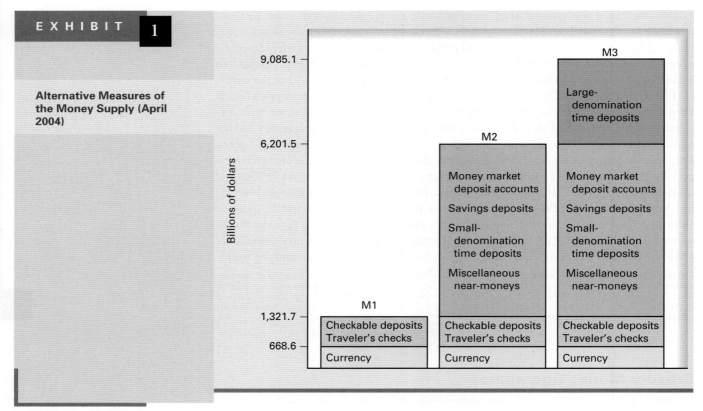

EXHIBIT **1**

Alternative Measures of the Money Supply (April 2004)

Billions of dollars

M3

Large-denomination time deposits

M2

Money market deposit accounts

Savings deposits

Small-denomination time deposits

Miscellaneous near-moneys

Money market deposit accounts

Savings deposits

Small-denomination time deposits

Miscellaneous near-moneys

M1

Checkable deposits
Traveler's checks
Currency

Checkable deposits
Traveler's checks
Currency

Checkable deposits
Traveler's checks
Currency

9,085.1

6,201.5

1,321.7

668.6

Source: Based on seasonally adjusted monthly figures from the Federal Reserve Board. For the latest data, go to http://www.federalreserve.gov/releases/h6/Current/.

Credit Cards and Debit Cards: What's the Difference?

You may be curious why the definitions of money include debit cards but not credit cards. After all, most sellers accept credit cards as readily as they accept cash or checks (some, such as Internet sites, even prefer credit cards to checks), and credit cards finance more than 20 percent of all consumer purchases. Credit cards offer an easy way to get a loan from the card issuer. If you buy an airline ticket with a credit card, the card issuer lends you the money to pay for the ticket. You don't need money until you repay the credit card issuer. The credit card has not eliminated your use of money, merely delayed it. Three in four households have credit cards. About half of those with credit cards carry a balance from month to month, and that group's median balance was about $2,000 in 2003.

On the other hand, when you use your debit card at a grocery store or drugstore, you tap directly into your checking account, paying with electronic money—part of M1. Debit cards get their name because they *debit*, or reduce, your bank balance immediately. A **debit card**, also called a check card, combines the functions of an ATM card and a check. Debit cards are issued by banks, sometimes jointly with Visa, MasterCard, or other major card issuers. Even though debit cards look like credit cards, and even may bear a name such as Visa, they are not credit cards.

Many people prefer debit cards to checks because no checkbook is required and payments are made directly and immediately. Like ATM cards, debit cards usually require a personal identification number, or PIN, to use. In that regard, debit cards are safer than credit

DEBIT CARD

Cards that tap directly into the depositor's bank account to fund purchases; also called a check card, and usually doubles as an ATM card cards, which could be more easily used by a thief. But debit cards have some disadvantages. Whereas a debit cards draws down your checking account immediately, credit cards provide a 20- to 30-day grace period between a purchase and required payment. And some people prefer to borrow beyond the grace period—that is, they carry a balance from month to month. Also, because debit cards immediately reduce your bank account, you can't dispute a bill or withhold payment as you can with a credit card and you can't stop payment as you can with a check. Still, debit cards came from nowhere a few years ago to be used by half the households surveyed in 2003.[1]

How Banks Work

Banks attract deposits from savers to lend to borrowers, earning a profit on the difference between the interest paid depositors and the interest charged borrowers. Savers need a safe place for their money, and borrowers need credit; banks try to earn a profit by serving both groups. To inspire depositor confidence, banks usually present an image of trust and assurance. For example, banks are more apt to be called Fidelity Trust, Security National, Surety Bank, or Federal Savings than Benny's Bank, Easy Money Bank and Trust, Loans 'R' Us, or Loadsamoney. In contrast, *finance companies* are financial intermediaries that do not get their funds from depositors, so they can choose names aimed at borrowers—names such as Household Finance, The Money Store, or Home Improvement Loan Online.

Banks Are Financial Intermediaries

By bringing together both sides of the money market, banks serve as financial intermediaries, or as go-betweens. They gather various amounts from savers and repackage these funds into the amounts demanded by borrowers. Some savers need their money next week, some next year, some only after retirement. Likewise, borrowers need credit for different lengths of time. Banks, as intermediaries, offer desirable durations to both groups. In short, *banks reduce the transaction costs of channeling savings to creditworthy borrowers.* Here's how.

Coping with Asymmetric Information

Banks, as lenders, try to identify borrowers who are willing to pay interest and are able to repay the loans. But borrowers have more reliable information about their own credit history and financial plans than do lenders. Thus, in the market for loans, there is **asymmetric information**—an inequality in what's known by each party to the transaction. Asymmetric information is unequal information. This wouldn't be a problem if borrowers could be trusted to report relevant details to lenders. Some borrowers, however, have an incentive to suppress important information, such as other debts outstanding, a troubled financial history, or plans to use the borrowed funds in a risky venture. Because of their experience and expertise in evaluating loan applicants, banks can better cope with asymmetric information than could an individual saver. Banks also know more about lending agreements than do individual savers. Thus, savers, rather than lending their money directly, are better off depositing their money in banks, and let banks do the lending. *The economy is more efficient because banks develop expertise in evaluating creditworthiness, structuring loans, and enforcing loan contracts.*

ASYMMETRIC INFORMATION

A situation in which one side of the market has more reliable information than the other side

Reducing Risk Through Diversification

By developing a diversified portfolio of assets rather than lending funds to a single borrower, banks reduce the risk to each individual saver. A bank, in effect, lends a tiny fraction of each

---

1. Survey results reported by C. E. Anguelov et al. "U.S. Consumers and Electronic Banking, 1995–2003," *Federal Reserve Bulletin* (Winter 2004): 1–18, also available at http://www.federalreserve.gov/pubs/bulletin/2004/winter04_ca.pdf.

saver's deposits to each of its many borrowers. If one borrower fails to repay a loan, it hardly affects a large, diversified bank. Certainly such a default does not represent the personal disaster it would if one saver's entire nest egg was loaned directly to that defaulting borrower.

Starting a Bank

We could consider the operation of any type of depository institution (commercial bank, savings bank, or credit union), but let's focus on starting a commercial bank because they are the most important in terms of total assets. What's more, the operating principles apply to other depository institutions as well. Suppose some business leaders in your hometown want to establish a commercial bank called Home Bank. To obtain a *charter,* or the right to operate, they must apply to the state banking authority in the case of a state bank or to the U.S. Comptroller of the Currency in the case of a national bank. The chartering agency reviewing the application judges the quality of management, the need for another bank in the region, and the likely success of the bank.

Suppose the founders plan to invest $500,000 in the bank, and they so indicate on their application for a national charter. If their application is approved, they incorporate, issuing themselves shares of stock—certificates of ownership. Thus, they exchange $500,000 for shares of stock in the bank. These shares are called the *owners' equity,* or the **net worth,** of the bank. Part of the $500,000, say $50,000, is used to buy shares in their district Federal Reserve Bank. So Home Bank is now a member of the Federal Reserve System. With the remaining $450,000, the owners acquire and furnish the bank building.

To focus our discussion, we will examine the bank's **balance sheet,** presented in Exhibit 2. As the name implies, a balance sheet shows a balance between the two sides of the bank's accounts. The left side lists the bank's assets. An **asset** is any physical property or financial claim owned by the bank. At this early stage, assets include the building and equipment owned by Home Bank plus its stock in the district Federal Reserve Bank. The right side lists the bank's liabilities and net worth. A **liability** is an amount the bank owes. So far the bank owes nothing, so the right side includes only the net worth of $500,000. The two sides of the ledger must always be equal, or in *balance,* which is why we call it a *balance sheet.* So assets must equal liabilities plus net worth:

$$\text{Assets} = \text{Liabilities} + \text{Net worth}$$

The bank is now ready for business. Opening day is the bank's lucky day, because the first customer carries in a briefcase full of $100 notes and deposits $1,000,000 into a new checking account. In accepting this, the bank promises to repay the depositor that amount. The

NET WORTH

Assets minus liabilities

BALANCE SHEET

A financial statement that shows assets, liabilities, and net worth at a given point in time; all these are stock measures; because assets must equal liabilities plus net worth, the statement is in balance

ASSET

Anything of value that is owned

LIABILITY

Anything that is owed to another individual or institution

EXHIBIT 2	Assets		Liabilities and Net Worth	
	Building and furniture	$450,000	Net worth	$500,000
	Stock in district Fed	50,000		
Home Bank's Balance Sheet	Total	$500,000	Total	$500,000

Assets		Liabilities and Net Worth	
Cash	$1,000,000	Checkable deposits	$1,000,000
Building and furniture	450,000	Net worth	500,000
Stock in district Fed	50,000		
Total	$1,500,000	Total	$1,500,000

EXHIBIT 3

Home Bank's Balance Sheet After $1,000,000 Deposit into Checking Account

deposit therefore is an amount the bank owes—it's a liability of the bank. As a result of this deposit, the bank's assets increase by $1,000,000 in cash and its liabilities increase by $1,000,000 in checkable deposits. Exhibit 3 shows the effects of this transaction on Home Bank's balance sheet. The right side now shows two claims on the bank's assets: claims by the owners, called net worth, and claims by nonowners, called liabilities, which at this point consist of checkable deposits.

Reserve Accounts

Where do we go from here? As mentioned in the previous chapter, banks are required by the Fed to set aside, or to hold in reserve, a percentage of their checkable deposits. The dollar amount that must be held in reserve is called **required reserves**—checkable deposits multiplied by the required reserve ratio. The **required reserve ratio** dictates the minimum proportion of deposits the bank must hold in reserve. The current reserve requirement is 10 percent on checkable deposits (other types of deposits have no reserve requirement). All depository institutions are subject to the Fed's reserve requirements. Reserves are held either as cash in the bank's vault or as deposits at the Fed, but neither earns the bank any interest. Home Bank must therefore hold $100,000 as reserves, or 10 percent times $1,000,000.

Suppose Home Bank deposits $100,000 in a reserve account with its district Federal Reserve Bank. Home Bank's reserves now consist of $100,000 in required reserves on deposit with the Fed and $900,000 in **excess reserves** held as cash in the vault. So far Home Bank has not earned a dime. Excess reserves, however, can be used to make loans or to purchase interest-bearing assets, such as government bonds. By law, the bank's interest-bearing assets are limited primarily to loans and to government securities (if a bank is owned by a holding company, the holding company has broader latitude in the kinds of assets it can hold).

Liquidity Versus Profitability

Like the early goldsmiths, modern banks must be prepared to satisfy depositors' requests for funds. A bank loses reserves whenever a depositor withdraws cash or writes a check that gets deposited in another bank. The bank must be in a position to satisfy all depositor demands, even if many depositors ask for their money at the same time. Required reserves are not meant to be used to meet depositor requests for funds; therefore, banks often hold excess reserves or other assets, such as government bonds, that can be easily converted to cash to satisfy any unexpected demand for funds. Banks may also want to hold excess reserves in case a valued customer needs immediate credit.

REQUIRED RESERVES

The dollar amount of reserves a bank is obligated by regulation to hold

REQUIRED RESERVE RATIO

The ratio of reserves to deposits that banks are obligated by regulation to hold

EXCESS RESERVES

Bank reserves exceeding required reserves

LIQUIDITY

A measure of the ease with which an asset can be converted into money without a significant loss of value

FEDERAL FUNDS MARKET

A market for overnight lending and borrowing of reserves among banks; the market for reserves on account at the Fed

FEDERAL FUNDS RATE

The interest rate charged in the federal funds market; the interest rate banks charge one another for overnight borrowing; the Fed's target interest rate

The bank manager must therefore structure the portfolio of assets with an eye toward liquidity but must not forget that survival also depends on profitability. **Liquidity** is the ease with which an asset can be converted into cash without a significant loss of value. *The objectives of liquidity and profitability are at odds.* For example, more liquid assets yield lower interest than less liquid assets do. The most liquid asset is bank reserves, either in the bank's vault as cash or on account with the Fed, but reserves earn no interest.

At one extreme, suppose a bank is completely liquid, holding all its assets as cash reserves. Such a bank would have no difficulty meeting depositors' demands for funds. This bank is playing it safe—too safe. The bank earns no interest and will fail. At the other extreme, suppose a bank uses all its excess reserves to acquire high-yielding but illiquid assets, such as long-term loans. Such a bank will run into problems whenever withdrawals exceed new deposits. There is a trade-off between liquidity and profitability. The portfolio manager's task is to strike the right balance between liquidity, or safety, and profitability.

Because reserves earn no interest, banks try to keep excess reserves to a minimum. Banks continuously "sweep" their accounts to find excess reserves that can be put to some interest-bearing use. They do not let excess reserves remain idle even overnight. The **federal funds market** provides for day-to-day lending and borrowing among banks of excess reserves on account at the Fed. These funds usually do not leave the Fed—instead, they shift among accounts. For example, suppose that at the end of the business day, Home Bank has excess reserves of $100,000 on account with the Fed and wants to lend that amount to another bank that finished the day short $100,000 in required reserves. These two banks are brought together by a broker who specializes in the market for federal funds—that is, the market for reserves at the Fed. The interest rate paid on this loan is called the **federal funds rate;** this is the rate the Fed targets as a tool of monetary policy, but more on that later.

How Banks Create Money

Let's now discuss how the Fed, Home Bank, and the banking system as a whole can create fiat money. Excess reserves are the raw material the banking system uses to create money. Again, our discussion focuses on commercial banks because they are the largest and most important depository institutions, although thrifts operate the same way.

Creating Money Through Excess Reserves

Suppose Home Bank has already used its $900,000 in excess reserves to make loans and buy government bonds and has no excess reserves left. In fact, let's assume there are no excess reserves in the banking system. With that as a point of departure, let's walk through the money creation process.

Round One

To start, suppose the Fed buys a $1,000 U.S. government bond from a securities dealer, with the transaction handled by the dealer's bank—Home Bank. The Fed pays the dealer by crediting Home Bank's reserve account with $1,000, so Home Bank can increase the dealer's checking account by $1,000. Where does the Fed get these reserves? It makes them up—creates them out of thin air, out of electronic ether! The securities dealer has exchanged one asset, a U.S. bond, for another asset, checkable deposits. A U.S. bond is not money, but checkable deposits are, so the money supply increases by $1,000 in this first round. Exhibit 4 shows changes in Home Bank's balance sheet as a result of the Fed's bond purchase. On the assets side, Home Bank's reserves at the Fed increase by $1,000. On the liabilities side, checkable deposits increase by $1,000. Of the dealer's $1,000 checkable deposit, Home Bank must set aside $100 in

Assets		Liabilities and Net Worth	
Reserves at Fed	+ $1,000	Checkable deposits	+ $1,000

EXHIBIT 4

Changes in Home Bank's Balance Sheet After Fed Buys a $1,000 Bond from Securities Dealer

Assets		Liabilities and Net Worth	
Loans	+$900	Checkable deposits	+$900

EXHIBIT 5

Changes in Home Bank's Balance Sheet After Lending $900 to You

required reserves (based on a 10 percent required reserve ratio). The remaining $900 becomes excess reserves, which can fuel a further increase in the money supply.

Round Two

Suppose Home Bank is your regular bank, and you apply for a $900 student loan to help pay student fees. Home Bank approves your loan and increases your checking account by $900. *Home Bank has converted your promise to repay, your IOU, into a $900 checkable deposit. Because checkable deposits are money, this action increases the money supply by $900.* The money supply has increased by a total of $1,900 to this point—the $1,000 increase in the securities dealer's checkable deposits and now the $900 increase in your checkable deposits. In the process, what had been $900 in Home Bank's excess reserves now back up its loan to you (remember, a bank can lend no more than its excess reserves). As shown in Exhibit 5, Home Bank's loans increase by $900 on the assets side because your IOU becomes the bank's asset. On the bank's liabilities side, checkable deposits increase by $900 because the bank has increased your account by that amount. In short, Home Bank has created $900 in checkable deposits based on your promise to repay the loan.

When you write a $900 check for student fees, your college promptly deposits the check into its checking account at Merchants Trust, which increases the college's account by $900, and sends your check to the Fed. The Fed transfers $900 in reserves from Home Bank's account to Merchants Trust's account. The Fed then sends the check to Home Bank, which reduces your checkable deposits by $900. The Fed has thereby "cleared" your check by settling the claim that Merchants Trust had on Home Bank. The $900 in checkable deposits has simply shifted banks, so the total increase in the money supply to this point is still $1,900.

Round Three

But Merchants Trust now has $900 more in reserves on deposit with the Fed. After setting aside $90 as required reserves, or 10 percent of your college's checkable deposit increase, the bank has $810 in excess reserves. Suppose Merchants Trust lends this $810 to an English major starting a new business called "Note This," an online note-taking service for students in large classes. Exhibit 6 shows assets at Merchants Trust are up by $810 in loans, and liabilities are up by $810 in checkable deposits. At this point, checkable deposits in the banking system, and the money supply in the economy, are up by a total of $2,710 (= $1,000 + $900 + $810), all springing from the Fed's original $1,000 bond purchase.

The $810 loan is spent at the college bookstore, which deposits the check in its account at Fidelity Bank. Fidelity credits the bookstore's checkable deposits with $810 and sends the check to the Fed for clearance. The Fed reduces Merchants Bank's reserves by $810 and increases Fidelity's by the same. The Fed then sends the check to Merchants, which reduces the English major's checkable deposits by $810. So checkable deposits are down by $810 at Merchants and up by the same amount at Fidelity. Checkable deposits are still up by $2,710, as the $810 in checkable deposits has simply shifted from Merchants Trust to Fidelity Bank.

Round Four and Beyond

We could continue the process with Fidelity Bank setting aside $81 in required reserves and lending $729 in excess reserves, but you get some idea of money creation by now. Notice the pattern of deposits and loans. Each time a bank gets a fresh deposit, 10 percent goes to required reserves. The rest becomes excess reserves, which fuel new loans or other asset acquisitions. Excess reserves are a prerequisite to support a loan that increases the borrower's checkable deposits. The borrower writes a check, which the recipient deposits in a checking account, thereby generating excess reserves to support still more loans. Because this example began with the Fed, the Fed can rightfully claim, "The buck starts here"—a slogan that appears on a large plaque in the Federal Reserve chairman's office.

An individual bank can lend no more than its excess reserves. When the borrower spends those funds, reserves at one bank usually fall, but total reserves in the banking system do not. The recipient bank uses most of the new deposit to extend more loans, creating more checkable deposits. The potential expansion of checkable deposits in the banking system therefore equals some multiple of the initial increase in reserves. Note that our example assumes that banks do not allow excess reserves to sit idle, that borrowed funds do not idle in checking accounts, and that the public does not choose to hold some of the newly created money as cash. If excess reserves remained just that or if borrowed funds idled in checking

---

EXHIBIT 6

Changes in Merchants Trust's Balance Sheet After Lending $810 to English Major

Assets		Liabilities and Net Worth	
Loans	+ $810	Checkable deposits	+ $810

accounts, they could not fuel an expansion of the money supply. And if people chose to hold borrowed funds in cash rather than in checking accounts, that idle cash could not add to reserves in the banking system.

A Summary of the Rounds

Let's review the money creation process: *The initial and most important step is the Fed's injection of $1,000 in fresh reserves into the banking system.* By buying the bond from the securities dealer, the Fed immediately increased the money supply by $1,000. Home Bank set aside $100 as required reserves and lent you its $900 in excess reserves. You paid your college fees, and the $900 ended up in your college's checkable account. This fueled more money creation, as shown in a series of rounds of Exhibit 7. As you can see, during each round, the increase in checkable deposits (column 1) minus the increase in required reserves (column 2) equals the potential increase in loans (column 3). Checkable deposits in this example can potentially increase by as much as $10,000.

In our example, money creation results from the Fed's $1,000 bond purchase from the securities dealer, but excess reserves would also have increased if the Fed purchased a $1,000 bond from Home Bank, lent Home Bank $1,000, or freed up $1,000 in excess reserves by lowering the reserve requirement.

What if the Fed paid the securities dealer in cash? By exchanging Federal Reserve notes, which become part of the money supply in the hands of the public, for a U.S. bond, which is not part of the money supply, the Fed would have increased the money supply by $1,000. Once the securities dealer put this cash into a checking account—or spent the cash, so the money ended up in someone else's checking account—the banking system's money creation process would have been off and running.

Reserve Requirements and Money Expansion

The banking system as a whole eliminates excess reserves by expanding the money supply. With a 10 percent reserve requirement, the Fed's initial injection of $1,000 in fresh reserves could support up to $10,000 in new checkable deposits in the banking system as a whole, *assuming no bank holds excess reserves, borrowers do not let their funds sit idle, and borrowers do not want to hold cash.*

The multiple by which the money supply increases as a result of an increase in the banking system's reserves is called the **money multiplier.** The **simple money multiplier** equals the reciprocal of the required reserve ratio, or $1/r$, where r is the reserve ratio. In our

MONEY MULTIPLIER

The multiple by which the money supply increases as a result of an increase in fresh reserves in the banking system

SIMPLE MONEY MULTIPLIER

The reciprocal of the required reserve ratio, or $1/r$; the maximum multiple of fresh reserves by which the money supply can increase

Bank	(1) Increase in Checkable Deposits	(2) Increase in Required Reserves	(3) Increase in Loans (3) = (1) − (2)
1. Home Bank	$ 1,000	$ 100	$ 900
2. Merchants Trust	900	90	810
3. Fidelity Bank	810	81	729
All remaining rounds	7,290	729	6,561
Totals	$10,000	$1,000	$9,000

EXHIBIT 7

Summary of the Money Creation Resulting from Fed's Purchase of $1,000 U.S. Government Bond

example, the reserve ratio was 10 percent, or 0.1, so the reciprocal is 1/0.1, which equals 10. The formula for the multiple expansion of money supply can be written as:

$$\text{Change in the money supply} = \text{Change in fresh reserves} \times 1/r$$

Again, the simple money multiplier assumes that banks hold no excess reserves, that borrowers do not let the funds sit idle, and that people do not want to hold cash. The higher the reserve requirement, the greater the fraction of deposits that must be held as reserves, so the smaller the money multiplier. A reserve requirement of 20 percent instead of 10 percent would require each bank to set aside twice as much in required reserves. The simple money multiplier in this case would be 1/0.2, which equals 5, and the maximum possible increase in checkable deposits resulting from an initial $1,000 increase in fresh reserves would therefore be $1,000 × 5, or $5,000. *Excess reserves fuel the deposit expansion process, and a higher reserve requirement drains this fuel from the banking system, thereby reducing the amount of new money that can be created.*

On the other hand, with a reserve requirement of only 5 percent, banks would set aside less for required reserves, leaving more excess reserves available for loans. The simple money multiplier in that case would be 1/0.05, or 20. With $1,000 in fresh reserves and a 5 percent reserve requirement, the banking system could increase the money supply by a maximum of $1,000 × 20, which equals $20,000. Thus, the change in the required reserve ratio affects the banking system's ability to create money.

In summary, money creation usually begins with the Fed injecting new reserves into the banking system. An individual bank lends an amount no greater than its excess reserves. The borrower's spending ends up in someone else's checking account, fueling additional loans. *The fractional reserve requirement is the key to the multiple expansion of checkable deposits.* If each $1 deposit had to be backed by $1 in required reserves, the money multiplier would be reduced to 1, which is no multiplier at all.

Limitations on Money Expansion

Various leakages from the multiple expansion process reduce the size of the money multiplier, which is why 1/r is called the *simple* money multiplier. You could think of "simple" as meaning maximum. To repeat, our example assumed (1) that banks do not let excess reserves sit idle, (2) that borrowers do something with the money, and (3) that people do not choose to increase their cash holdings. How realistic are these assumptions? With regard to the first, banks have a profit incentive to make loans or buy some other interest-bearing asset with excess reserves. The second assumption is also easy to defend. Why would people borrow money if they didn't plan to spend it? The third assumption is trickier. Cash may sometimes be preferable to checking accounts because cash is more versatile, so people may choose to hold some of the newly created money as cash. To the extent that people prefer to hold cash, this drains reserves from the banking system. With reduced reserves, banks are less able to make loans, reducing the money multiplier. Incidentally, for the money multiplier to operate, a particular bank need not use excess reserves in a specific way; it could use them to pay all its employees a Christmas bonus, for that matter. As long as that spending ends up as checkable deposits in the banking system, away we go with the money expansion process.

Multiple Contraction of the Money Supply

We have already outlined the money creation process, so the story of how the Federal Reserve System can reduce bank reserves, thereby reducing the money supply, can be a brief one. Again, we begin by assuming there are no excess reserves in the system and the reserve requirement is 10 percent. Suppose the Fed *sells* a $1,000 U.S. bond to a securities dealer and gets paid with a check drawn on the security dealer's account at Home Bank. So the Fed gets paid by drawing down Home Bank's reserves at the Fed by $1,000. The Fed has thereby reduced the money supply by $1,000 in this first round.

Because the dealer's checking account was reduced by $1,000, Home Bank no longer needs to hold $100 in required reserves. But Home Bank is still short $900 in required reserves (remember, when we started, there were no excess reserves in the banking system). To replenish reserves, Home Bank must recall loans (ask for repayment before the due date), sell some other asset, or borrow additional reserves. Suppose the bank calls in $900 loaned to a local business, and the loan is repaid with a check written against Merchants Bank. When the check clears, Home Bank's reserves are up by $900, just enough to satisfy its reserve requirement, but Merchants Bank's reserves and checkable deposits are down by $900. Checkable deposits are now down $1,900 as a result of the Fed's purchase of a $1,000 bond. Because there were no excess reserves at the outset, the loss of $900 in reserves leaves Merchants $810 short of its required level of reserves, forcing that bank to get more reserves.

And so it goes down the line. The Fed's sale of government bonds reduces bank reserves, forcing banks to recall loans or to somehow replenish reserves. This reduces checkable deposits each additional round. *The maximum possible effect is to reduce the money supply by the original reduction in bank reserves times the simple money multiplier, which again equals 1 divided by the reserve requirement, or 1/r.* In our example, the Fed's sale of $1,000 in U.S. bonds could reduce the money supply by as much as $10,000.

For a change of pace, let's end this section with a case study that looks at new developments in banking sparked by the revolution in personal computers and the Internet.

Banking on the Net

The Bank of Internet USA never closes. It's open 24 hours a day, 365 days a year. From anywhere in the world with Internet access, bank customers can pay bills, check balances, or apply for a loan. Virtual banks have little physical presence beyond ATMs. For example, the Bank of Internet USA has a single, 6,000-square-foot office with only 20 employees. But the bank's customers can withdraw funds and make deposits at more than 300,000 ATMs around the country and the world. They can even print out deposit slips online.

© EPA/QILAI SHEN/AP Photo

With the money saved on buildings and bank tellers, Internet banks can offer depositors higher interest rates. At a time when money market rates averaged less than 1.0 percent, most Internet banks offered interest at least twice that. The three banks offering the highest interest rates in 2004 were Internet banks: Bank of Internet USA, VirtualBank, and National InterBank.

But virtual banks remain the exception. The overwhelming share of banks now accessible via the Internet consist of physical banks that offer Internet banking for customer convenience. For example, Wells Fargo, a bank with about 3,000 branches in 23 states and 16 million customers, has invested $1 billion in online banking and claims to be the market leader. Like some other banks, Wells Fargo also offers customers the ability to verify online all account balances, *including accounts at other banks*. Many banks even offer wireless banking for customers with Web-enabled cell phones or personal digital assistants.

With such easy access, customers are increasingly shopping nationwide for the best rates for deposits, credit cards, and loans. So a customer in St. Louis can get a mortgage in Atlanta,

ELECTRONIC BANKING, OR E-BANKING

Conducting banking transactions over the Internet

a car loan in Phoenix, a credit card in Boston, a checking account in New York, and a savings account in Los Angeles. For example, ING Direct offers 2.1 percent interest on FDIC-insured savings accounts with no minimum balance and no fees. Customers can transfer funds online between this account and online checking accounts at other banks.

For the banks, **electronic banking,** or **e-banking,** speeds processing, lowers costs, and helps attract and keep customers. For depositors, e-banking saves time, money, and is often more convenient. Households can manage their money, pay bills, and can keep track of their credit. There has been an increase in the share of bank customers using a variety of e-banking technologies. According to a broad survey, the share of households banking by computer tripled from 10 percent in 1999 to 32 percent in 2003. These newer technologies tend to be used by higher income, higher asset, younger, and more educated households.

The Internet could become the biggest market in history, and banks want to be part of it. Over the long run, the Internet offers convenience for customers and potential cost savings for banks. The Internet reduces the need for branches and branch personnel. Citibank, for example, encourages online use by eliminating fees for those who bank online. Because e-banking reduces the search costs of shopping around for the best deal, banking will become more competitive, squeezing down interest rate differences across banks for similar products.

Sources: John Kimelman, "How Internet Banks Have Inched Ahead on Rates," *New York Times*; 28 December 2003; Bambi Francisco, "Internet Banking Surges," CBS.MarketWatch.com, 17 June 2004; and C. E. Anguelov et al. "U.S. Consumers and Electronic Banking, 1995–2003," *Federal Reserve Bulletin* (Winter 2004): 1–18, also available at http://www.federalreserve.gov/pubs/bulletin/2004/winter04_ca.pdf. The Bank of Internet USA is at http://www.bankofinternet.com/. VirtualBank is at http://www.virtualbank.com/. National InterBank is at http://www.nationalinterbank.com/nib/. Wells Fargo's is http://www.wellsfargo.com/. And ING Direct is http://home.ingdirect.com/.

N e t **B o o k m a r k**

For an online introduction to the Federal Reserve System and a monetary policy link to the Federal Reserve Bank of New York, go to the introduction page at http://www.ny.frb.org/introduce/. This site provides a very readable overview of the Fed's structure and operations. It includes links giving more details about particular terms. Be sure to take a peek inside the gold vault.

Now that you have some idea how fractional reserve banking works, we are in a position to summarize the Federal Reserve's role in the economy.

The Fed's Tools of Monetary Control

As mentioned in the previous chapter, in its capacity as a bankers' bank, the Fed clears checks for, extends loans to, and holds deposits of banks. The Fed, through its regulation of financial markets, also tries to prevent major disruptions and financial panics. For example, during the dark days following the terrorist attacks on America of September 11, 2001, people used their ATM cards to load up on cash. Some were hoarding cash. To provide the banking system with sufficient liquidity, the Fed bought all the government securities offered for sale, purchasing a record $150 billion worth in two days.[2] The Fed also eased some regulations to facilitate bank clearances, especially for banks hit by the attacks. Fed Chairman Alan Greenspan also worked behind the scenes to ensure that banks had sufficient liquidity to calm panics in 1987, 1989, and 1998, when financial crises threatened. The Fed also stockpiles cash in bank vaults around the country and around the world in case of emergencies.

As noted already, about half of the narrow definition of money (M1) consists of checkable deposits. The Fed's control over checkable deposits works indirectly through its control over reserves in the banking system. You are already familiar with the Fed's three tools for

2. Anita Rachavan, Susan Pulliam, and Jeff Opdyke, "Banks and Regulators Drew Together to Calm Rattled Markets After Attack," *Wall Street Journal,* 18 October 2001.

controlling reserves: (1) open-market operations, or the buying and selling of U.S. government bonds; (2) the discount rate, which is the interest rate the Fed charges for loans it makes to banks; and (3) the required reserve ratio, which is the minimum fraction of reserves that banks must hold against deposits. Let's examine each of these in more detail.

Open-Market Operations and the Federal Funds Rate

The Fed carries out open-market operations whenever it buys or sells U.S. government bonds in the open market. To increase the money supply, the Fed directs the New York Fed to buy U.S. bonds. This is called an **open-market purchase**. To reduce the money supply, the Fed can carry out an **open-market sale**. Policy decisions about open-market operations are made by the Federal Open Market Committee, or FOMC, which meets every six weeks and during emergencies. Open-market operations are relatively easy to carry out. They require no change in laws or regulations and can be executed in any amount—large or small—chosen by the Fed. Their simplicity and ease of use make them the tool of choice for the Fed.

Through open-market operations, the Fed influences bank reserves and the *federal funds rate,* which is the interest rate banks charge one another for borrowing excess reserves at the Fed, typically just for a day or two. Banks that need reserves can borrow excess reserves from other banks, paying the federal funds rate. The federal funds rate serves as a good indicator of the "tightness" of monetary policy. For example, suppose the Fed buys bonds in the open market and thereby increases reserves in the banking system. As a result, more banks have excess reserves. Demand for excess reserves in the federal funds market will fall and supply will increase, so the federal funds rate—the interest rate for reserves in this market—will decline. We can expect that this lower federal funds rate will spread quickly to the economy at large: The excess reserves that have created the lower federal funds rate will prompt banks to lower short-term interest rates in general and this will increase the quantity of loans demanded by the public.

OPEN-MARKET PURCHASE
The purchase of U.S. government bonds by the Fed to increase the money supply

OPEN-MARKET SALE
The sale of U.S. government bonds by the Fed to reduce the money supply

The Discount Rate

The second monetary policy tool available to the Fed is the **discount rate**, which is the interest rate the Fed charges for loans it makes to banks. Banks borrow from the Fed to satisfy their reserve requirements. A lower discount rate reduces the cost of borrowing, encouraging banks to borrow reserves from the Fed. But the Fed considers itself as the "lender of last resort," and a lender during a financial crisis. The Fed does not encourage banks to borrow through the discount window. There are actually two discount rates. The *primary discount rate* is usually one percentage point above the federal funds rate. Thus, discount borrowing is less attractive than borrowing through the federal funds market. But during a financial crisis, the Fed could lower the primary discount rate to supply liquidity to the banking system. The Fed charges more interest on loans to banks considered less sound than other banks. This *secondary discount rate* is usually about one-half a percentage point higher than the primary discount rate.

The Fed uses the discount rate more as a signal to financial markets about its monetary policy than as a tool for increasing or decreasing the money supply. The discount rate might also be thought of as an emergency tool for injecting liquidity into the banking system in the event of some financial crisis, such as a stock market crash. Banks would prefer to borrow reserves from other banks in the federal funds market rather than borrow reserves directly from the Fed. The discount rate has become largely symbolic, and discount lending has declined sharply in the last two decades.

DISCOUNT RATE
The interest rate the Fed charges banks that borrow reserves

Reserve Requirements

The Fed also influences the money supply through reserve requirements, which are regulations regarding the minimum amount of reserves that banks must hold to back up deposits. Reserve requirements determine how much money the banking system can create with each dollar of fresh reserves. If the Fed increases the reserve requirement, then banks have less excess reserves to lend out. This reduces the banking system's ability to create money. On the other hand, a lower reserve requirement increases the banking system's ability to create money. Reserve requirements can be changed by a simple majority vote of the Board of Governors. But changes in the reserve requirement disrupt the banking system, so the Fed seldom makes such changes. As noted already, the current reserve requirement is 10 percent on checkable deposits and zero on other deposits. Some countries such as Australia, Canada, and the United Kingdom have no reserve requirement. Banks there still hold reserves to deal with everyday cash requirements and can borrow from their central banks (at high rates) if necessary.

The Fed Is a Money Machine

One way to get a better idea of the Fed is to review its balance sheet, shown as Exhibit 8, with assets on the left and liabilities and net worth on the right. Note that U.S. government bonds account for over 90 percent of Fed assets. These IOUs from the federal government result from open-market operations, and they earn the Fed interest. On the other side of the ledger, Federal Reserve notes outstanding account for over 90 percent of Fed liabilities. These notes—U.S. currency—are IOUs from the Fed and are therefore liabilities of the Fed, but the Fed pays no interest on these notes. Thus, the Fed's primary asset—U.S. government bonds—earns interest, whereas the Fed's primary liability—Federal Reserve notes—requires no interest payments by the Fed. *The Fed is therefore both literally and figuratively a money machine. It is literally a money machine because it supplies the economy with Federal Reserve notes; it is figuratively a money machine because its main asset earns interest, but its main liability requires no interest payments.* The Fed also earns revenue from various services it provides banks. After covering its operating costs, the Fed turns over any remaining income, some years in excess of $20 billion, to the U.S. Treasury.

The asset side of Exhibit 8 also indicates how tiny the Fed's discount loans are relative to total assets. As of the end of 2003, the Fed's discount lending stood at only $62 million. On the right side of the ledger, you can see that depository institutions' reserves at the Fed totaled $23,058 million, or about $23 billion. You can also see that the Fed held deposits of the U.S. Treasury, a reminder that the Fed is the federal government's banker.

Conclusion

Banks play a unique role in the economy because they can transform someone's IOU into a checkable deposit, and a checkable deposit is money. The banking system's ability to expand the money supply depends on the amount of excess reserves in that system. In our example, it was the purchase of a $1,000 U.S. bond that started the ball rolling. The Fed can also increase reserves by lowering the discount rate enough to stimulate bank borrowing from the Fed (although the Fed uses changes in the discount rate more to signal its policy than to alter the money supply). And, by reducing the required reserve ratio, the Fed not only instantly creates excess reserves in the banking system but also increases the money multiplier. In practice, the Fed rarely changes the reserve requirement because of the disruptive effect of such a change on the banking system. *To control the money supply, the Fed relies primarily on open-market operations.*

Assets		Liabilities and Net Worth	
U.S. Treasury securities	$ 710,415	Federal Reserve notes outstanding	$ 689,754
Foreign currencies	19,868	Depository institution reserves	23,058
Bank buildings	1,630	U.S. Treasury balance	5,723
Discount loans to depository institutions	62	Other liabilities	37,665
Other assets	41,919	Net worth	17,694
Total	$ 773,894	Total	$ 773,894

E X H I B I T 8

≡HOMEWORK≡
Xpress!
Graphing

Federal Reserve Bank Balance Sheet as of December 31, 2003 (Millions of dollars)

Source: Developed from data in *90th Annual Report: 2003*, Federal Reserve Board, Table 1, p. 260. This report is available at http://www.federalreserve.gov/boarddocs/rptcongress/annual03/default.htm. For the latest, go to http://www.federalreserve.gov/publications.htm, click on "Annual Report," then find "Statistical Tables."

Open-market operations can have a direct effect on the money supply, as when the Fed buys bonds from the public. But the Fed also affects the money supply indirectly, as when the Fed's bond purchase increases bank reserves, which then serve as fuel for the money multiplier. In the next chapter, we will consider the effects of changes in the money supply on the economy.

SUMMARY

1. The money supply is narrowly defined as M1, which consists of currency held by the nonbanking public plus checkable deposits and traveler's checks. Broader money aggregates include other kinds of bank deposits. M2 includes M1 plus savings deposits, small-denomination time deposits, and money market mutual funds. M3 includes M2 plus time deposits of $100,000 and up.

2. Banks are unlike other businesses because they can turn a borrower's IOU into money—they can create money. Banks match the different desires of savers and borrowers. Banks also evaluate loan applications and diversify portfolios of assets to reduce the risk to any one saver.

3. In acquiring portfolios of assets, banks try to maximize profit while maintaining enough liquidity to satisfy depositors' requests for money. Assets that earn the bank more interest are usually less liquid.

4. Any single bank can expand the money supply by the amount of its excess reserves. For the banking system as a whole, however, the maximum expansion of the money supply equals a multiple of fresh bank reserves. The simple money multiplier is the reciprocal of the reserve ratio. This multiplier is reduced to the extent that (a) banks allow excess reserves to remain idle, (b) borrowers sit on their proceeds, and (c) the public withdraws cash from the banking system and holds it.

5. The key to changes in the money supply is the Fed's impact on excess reserves in the banking system. To increase excess reserves and thus increase the money supply, the Fed can buy U.S. government bonds, reduce the discount rate, or lower the reserve requirement. To reduce excess reserves and thus reduce the money supply, the Fed can sell U.S. government bonds, increase the discount rate, or increase the reserve requirement. By far the most important monetary tool for the Fed is open-market operations—buying or selling U.S. bonds.

QUESTIONS FOR REVIEW

1. *(Money Aggregates)* What are the three measures of the money supply and how is each measure determined?

2. *(Money Aggregates)* What portion of U.S. Federal Reserve notes circulate outside the United States? How does this affect the United States?

3. (*C a s e* **S t u d y**: Faking It) Why did the U.S. government consider it important to redesign the $100 note in order to combat the effects of the "supernote"?

4. *(Money Aggregates)* Determine whether each of the following is included in any of the M1, M2, or M3 measures of the money supply:

   a. Currency held by the nonbanking public
   b. Available credit on credit cards held by the nonbanking public
   c. Savings deposits
   d. Large-denomination time deposits
   e. Money market mutual fund accounts

5. *(Banks Are Financial Intermediaries)* In acting as financial intermediaries, what needs and desires of savers and borrowers must banks consider?

6. *(Money Aggregates)* Suppose that $1,000 is moved from a savings account at a commercial bank to a checking account at the same bank. Which of the following statements are true and which are false?

   a. The amount of currency in circulation will fall.
   b. M1 will increase.
   c. M2 will increase.

7. *(Bank Deposits)* Explain the differences among checkable deposits, savings deposits, and time deposits. Explain whether each of these deposits represents a bank asset or a bank liability.

8. *(Reserve Accounts)* Explain why a reduction in the required reserve ratio cannot, at least initially, increase total reserves in the banking system. Is the same true of lowering the discount rate? What would happen if the Fed bought U.S. bonds from, or sold them to, the banking system?

9. *(Liquidity Versus Profitability)* Why must a bank manager strike a balance between liquidity and profitability on the bank's balance sheet?

10. *(Creating Money)* Often it is claimed that banks create money by making loans. How can commercial banks create money? Is the government the only institution that can legally create money?

11. *(Fed Tools of Monetary Control)* What three tools can the Fed use to change the money supply? Which tool is used most frequently? What are three limitations on the money expansion process?

12. *(Discount Rate)* What is the difference between the federal funds rate and the discount rate? What is the ultimate impact on the money supply of an increase in the discount rate?

13. *(Federal Funds Market)* What is the federal funds market? How does it help banks strike a balance between liquidity and profitability?

14. *(The Fed Is a Money Machine)* Why is the Fed both literally and figuratively a money machine?

15. (*C a s e* **S t u d y**: Banking on the Net) What impact is increased Internet banking likely to have on money's function as a medium of exchange?

PROBLEMS AND EXERCISES

16. *(Monetary Aggregates)* Calculate M1, M2, and M3 using the following information:

Large-denomination time deposits	$304 billion
Currency and coin held by the non-banking public	$438 billion
Checkable deposits	$509 billion
Small-denomination time deposits	$198 billion
Traveler's checks	$18 billion
Savings deposits	$326 billion
Money market mutual fund accounts	$637 billion

17. *(Money Creation)* Show how each of the following *initially* affects bank assets, liabilities, and reserves. Do *not* include the results of bank behavior resulting from the Fed's action. Assume a required reserve ratio of 0.05.

    a. The Fed purchases $10 million worth of U.S. government bonds from a bank.
    b. The Fed loans $5 million to a bank.
    c. The Fed raises the required reserve ratio to 0.10.

18. *(Money Creation)* Show how each of the following would initially affect a bank's assets and liabilities.

    a. Someone makes a $10,000 deposit into a checking account.
    b. A bank makes a loan of $1,000 by establishing a checking account for $1,000.
    c. The loan described in part (b) is spent.
    d. A bank must write off a loan because the borrower defaults.

19. *(Reserve Accounts)* Suppose that a bank's customer deposits $4,000 in her checking account. The required reserve ratio is 0.25. What are the required reserves on this new deposit? What is the largest loan that the bank can make on the basis of the new deposit? If the bank chooses to hold reserves of $3,000 on the new deposit, what are the excess reserves on the deposit?

20. *(Money Multiplier)* Suppose that the Federal Reserve lowers the required reserve ratio from 0.10 to 0.05. How does this affect the simple money multiplier, assuming that excess reserves are held to zero and there are no currency leakages? What are the money multipliers for required reserve ratios of 0.15 and 0.20?

21. *(Money Creation)* Suppose Bank A, which faces a reserve requirement of 10 percent, receives a $1,000 deposit from a customer.

    a. Assuming that it wishes to hold no excess reserves, determine how much the bank should lend. Show your answer on Bank A's balance sheet.
    b. Assuming that the loan shown in Bank A's balance sheet is redeposited in Bank B, show the changes in Bank B's balance sheet if it lends out the maximum possible.
    c. Repeat this process for three additional banks: C, D, and E.
    d. Using the simple money multiplier, calculate the total change in the money supply resulting from the $1,000 initial deposit.
    e. Assume Banks A, B, C, D, and E each wish to hold 5 percent excess reserves. How would holding this level of excess reserves affect the total change in the money supply?

22. *(Monetary Control)* Suppose the money supply is currently $500 billion and the Fed wishes to increase it by $100 billion.

    a. Given a required reserve ratio of 0.25, what should it do?
    b. If it decided to change the money supply by changing the required reserve ratio, what change should it make?

EXPERIENTIAL EXERCISES

23. *(Fed Tools of Monetary Control)* Review the Fed's online brochure on the Federal Open Market Committee (FOMC) at http://www.federalreserve.gov/pubs/frseries/frseri2.htm, especially the sections titled "The Decisionmaking Process" and "Reports." What information does the FOMC consider as it plans open-market operations? Look at the minutes of the most recent meeting to determine what kinds of open-market operations are going on now.

24. (*C a s e* **S t u d y :** Banking on the Net) The *Journal of Internet Banking and Commerce* at http://www.arraydev.com/commerce/JIBC/current.asp is a Web-based magazine devoted to Internet banking and related issues. Take a look at the current edition and see whether you can determine what effect electronic banking is having on the Fed's ability to control the U.S. money supply. Also, see what you can learn about the status of Internet banking outside the United States.

25. *(Wall Street Journal)* If you have access to the Interactive Edition of the *Wall Street Journal*, you can use the Briefing Books feature to obtain data on over 10,000 public companies. Use this feature to locate the briefing book on a large commercial bank in your area. Look at some of its press releases to determine how this bank has been influenced by Federal Reserve regulations and monetary policy operations.

26. *(Wall Street Journal)* Open-market operations, in which the Federal Reserve buys and sells U.S. government bonds, are an important tool of monetary control. Look in the *Wall Street Journal* in the Money and Investing section. Find the page where bond activity is reported. Is the market for U.S. government bills and bonds an active market? What impact does the liquidity of this market have on the ability of the Federal Reserve to exert monetary control?

Monetary Theory and Policy

© James Leynse/Corbis

W hy do people maintain checking accounts and have cash in their pockets, purses, wallets, desk drawers, coffee cans—wherever? In other words, why do people hold money? How does the stock of money in the economy affect your chances of finding a job, your ability to finance a new car, the interest rate you pay on credit cards, the ease of getting a student loan, and the interest rate on that loan? What have economic theory and the historical record taught us about the relationship between the quantity of money in the economy and other macroeconomic variables? Answers to these and related questions are addressed in this chapter, which examines monetary theory and policy.

The amount of money in the economy affects you in a variety of ways, but to understand these effects, we must dig a little deeper. So far, we have focused on how banks create money. But a more fundamental question is how money affects the economy, a topic called *monetary theory*. Monetary theory explores the effect of the money supply on the economy's price level, employment, and real GDP. The Fed's control over the money supply is called *monetary policy*. In the short run, changes in the money supply affect the economy by working through changes in the interest rate. In the long run, changes in the money supply affect the price level. In this chapter, we consider the theory behind each time frame. Topics discussed include:

- Demand and supply of money
- Money in the short run
- Federal funds rate
- Money in the long run
- Velocity of money
- Monetary policy targets

The Demand and Supply of Money

Let's begin by reviewing the important distinction between the *stock of money* and the *flow of income*. How much money do you have with you right now? That amount is a *stock*. Income, in contrast, is a *flow,* indicating how much money you earn per period. Income has no meaning unless the period is specified. You would not know whether to be impressed that a friend earned $400 unless you knew whether this was earnings per month, per week, per day, or per hour.

DEMAND FOR MONEY

The relationship between how much money people want to hold and the interest rate

The **demand for money** is a relationship between how much money people want to hold and the interest rate. Keep in mind that the quantity of money held is a stock measure. It may seem odd at first to be talking about the demand for money. You might think people would demand all the money they could get their hands on. But remember that money, the stock, is not the same as income, the flow. People express their demand for income by selling their labor and other resources. People express their demand for money by holding some of their wealth as money rather than holding other assets that earn more interest.

But we are getting ahead of ourselves. The question is: why do people demand money? Why do people have money on them, stash money around the house, and have money in checking accounts? The most obvious reason people demand money is that money is a convenient medium of exchange. *People demand money to carry out market transactions.*

The Demand for Money

Because barter represents an insignificant portion of exchange in the modern industrialized economy, households, firms, governments, and foreigners need money to conduct their daily transactions. Consumers need money to buy products, and firms need money to buy resources. *Money allows people to carry out economic transactions more easily and more efficiently.* With credit cards, the short-term loan delays the payment of money, but all accounts must eventually be settled with money.

The greater the value of transactions to be financed in a given period, the greater the demand for money. *So the more active the economy is—that is, the more goods and services exchanged, reflected by real output—the more money demanded.* Obviously an economy with a real GDP of $12 trillion will need more money than one-half that size. *Also, the higher the economy's price level, the greater the demand for money.* The more things cost on average, the more money is needed to buy them.

You demand the money needed to fund your normal spending in the course of the day or week, and you may need money for unexpected expenditures. If you plan to buy lunch tomorrow, you will carry enough money to pay for it. But you may also want to be able to pay for other possible contingencies. For example, you could have car trouble or you could come across an unexpected sale on a favorite item. You can use credit cards for some of these unexpected purchases, but you still feel safer with some extra cash. You may have a little extra money with you right now for who knows what. Even *you* don't know.

The demand for money is rooted in money's role as a medium of exchange. But as we have seen, money is more than a medium of exchange; it is also a store of value. People save for a new home, for college, for retirement. People can store their purchasing power as money or as other financial assets, such as corporate and government bonds. When people purchase bonds and other financial assets, they are lending their money and are paid interest for doing so.

The demand for any asset is based on the services it provides. The big advantage of money as a store of value is its liquidity: Money can be immediately exchanged for whatever is for sale. In contrast, other financial assets, such as corporate or government bonds, must first be *liquidated,* or exchanged for money, which can then be used to buy goods and services. Money, however, has one major disadvantage when compared to other financial assets. Money in the form of currency and traveler's checks earns no interest, and the rate earned on checkable deposits is well below that earned on other financial assets. So holding wealth as money means giving up some interest. For example, suppose a corporation could earn 3 percent more interest by holding financial assets other than money. The opportunity cost of holding $10 million as money rather than as some other financial asset would amount to $300,000 per year. *The interest forgone is the opportunity cost of holding money.*

Money Demand and Interest Rates

When the market interest rate is low, other things constant, the cost of holding money—the cost of maintaining liquidity—is low, so people hold more of their wealth in the form of money. When the interest rate is high, the cost of holding money is high, so people hold less of their wealth in money and more in other financial assets that pay higher interest. Thus, *other things constant, the quantity of money demanded varies inversely with the market interest rate.*

The money demand curve, D_m, in Exhibit 1 shows the quantity of money people demand at alternative interest rates, other things constant. Both the quantity of money and the

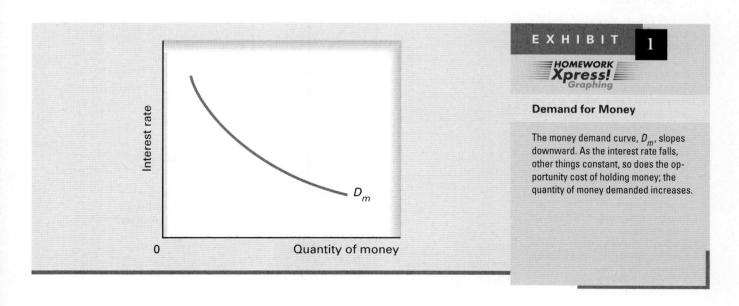

EXHIBIT 1

Demand for Money

The money demand curve, D_m, slopes downward. As the interest rate falls, other things constant, so does the opportunity cost of holding money; the quantity of money demanded increases.

interest rate are in nominal terms. *The money demand curve slopes downward because the lower the interest rate, the lower the opportunity cost of holding money.* Movements along the curve reflect the effects of changes in the interest rate on the quantity of money demanded, other things assumed constant. The quantity of money demanded is inversely related to the price of holding money, which is the interest rate. *Assumed constant along the curve are the price level and real GDP. If either increases, the demand for money increases, as reflected by a rightward shift of the money demand curve.*

The Supply of Money and the Equilibrium Interest Rate

The supply of money—the stock of money available in the economy at a particular time—is determined primarily by the Fed through its control over currency and over excess reserves in the banking system. The supply of money, S_m, is depicted as a vertical line in Exhibit 2. *A vertical supply curve implies that the quantity of money supplied is independent of the interest rate.*

The intersection of the demand for money, D_m, with the supply of money, S_m, determines the equilibrium interest rate, i—the interest rate that equates the quantity of money demanded in the economy with the quantity supplied. At interest rates above the equilibrium level, the opportunity cost of holding money is higher, so the quantity of money people want to hold is less than the quantity supplied. At interest rates below the equilibrium level, the opportunity cost of holding money is lower, so the quantity of money people want to hold exceeds the quantity supplied.

If the Fed increases the money supply, the money supply curve shifts to the right, as shown by the movement from S_m to S'_m in Exhibit 2. The quantity supplied now exceeds the quantity demanded at interest rate i. Because of the increased supply of money, people are *able* to hold more money. But at interest rate i they are *unwilling* to hold that much. Because people are now holding more of their wealth as money than they would like, they

EXHIBIT **2**

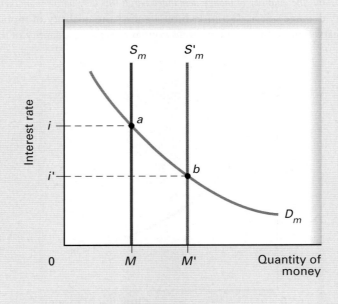

Effect of an Increase in the Money Supply

Because the supply of money is determined by the Federal Reserve, it can be represented by a vertical line. At point *a*, the intersection of supply of money, S_m, and the demand for money, D_m, determines the market interest rate, *i*. Following an increase in the money supply to S'_m, the quantity of money supplied exceeds the quantity demanded at the original interest rate, *i*. People attempt to exchange money for bonds or other financial assets. In doing so, they push down the interest rate to *i'*, where quantity demanded equals the new quantity supplied. This new equilibrium occurs at point *b*.

exchange some money for other financial assets, such as bonds. As the demand for bonds increases, bond sellers can pay less interest yet still attract enough buyers. The interest rate falls until the quantity of money demanded just equals the quantity supplied. With the decline in the interest rate to *i'* in Exhibit 2, the opportunity cost of holding money falls enough that the public is willing to hold the now-larger stock of money. Equilibrium moves from point *a* to point *b*. *For a given money demand curve, an increase in the supply of money drives down the market interest rate, and a decrease in the supply of money drives up the market interest rate.*

Now that you have some idea how money demand and supply determine the market interest rate, you are ready to see how money fits into our model of the economy. Specifically, let's see how changes in money supply affect aggregate demand and equilibrium output.

Money and Aggregate Demand in the Short Run

In the short run, money affects the economy through changes in the interest rate. Monetary policy influences the market interest rate, which in turn affects the level of planned investment, a component of aggregate demand. Let's work through the chain of causation.

Interest Rates and Planned Investment

Suppose the Fed believes that the economy is producing less than its potential and decides to stimulate output and employment by increasing the money supply. Recall from the previous chapter that the Fed's primary tool for increasing the money supply is open-market purchases of U.S. government securities. The three panels of Exhibit 3 trace the links between changes in the money supply and changes in aggregate demand. We begin with

---

E X H I B I T **3**	**Effects of an Increase in the Money Supply on Interest Rates, Investment, and Aggregate Demand**

In panel (a), an increase in the money supply drives the interest rate down to *i'*. With the cost of borrowing lower, the amount invested increases from *I* to *I'*, as shown in panel (b). This sets off the spending multiplier process, so the aggregate output demanded at price level *P* increases from *Y* to *Y'*. The increase is shown by the shift of the aggregate demand curve to the right in panel (c).

equilibrium interest rate *i,* which is determined in panel (a) by the intersection of the money demand curve D_m with the money supply curve S_m. Suppose the Fed purchases U.S. government bonds and thereby increases the money supply, as shown by a rightward shift of the money supply curve from S_m to S'_m. After the increase in the supply of money, people are holding more money than they would prefer at interest rate *i,* so they try to exchange one form of wealth, money, for other financial assets. Exchanging dollars for financial assets has no direct effect on aggregate demand, but it does reduce the market interest rate.

A decline in the interest rate to *i',* other things constant, reduces the opportunity cost of financing new plants and equipment, thereby making new investment more profitable. Likewise, a lower interest rate reduces the cost of financing a new house. So the decline in the interest rate increases the amount of investment demanded. Panel (b) shows the demand for investment, D_I, first introduced several chapters back. When the interest rate falls from *i* to *i',* planned investment increases from *I* to *I'.*

The spending multiplier magnifies this increase in investment, leading to a greater increase in aggregate demand, reflected in panel (c) by a rightward shift of the aggregate demand curve from *AD* to *AD'.* At the given price level *P,* real GDP increases from *Y* to *Y'.* The sequence of events can be summarized as follows:

$$M \uparrow \rightarrow i \downarrow \rightarrow I \uparrow \rightarrow AD \uparrow \rightarrow Y \uparrow$$

An increase in the money supply, *M,* reduces the interest rate, *i.* The lower interest rate stimulates investment, *I,* which increase in aggregate demand from *AD* to *AD'.* At a given price level, real GDP demanded increased from *Y* to *Y'.* The entire sequence is also traced out in each panel by the movement from point *a* to point *b.*

Note that the graphs presented here ignore any feedback effects of changes in real GDP on the demand for money. Because the demand for money depends on the level of real GDP, an increase in real GDP would shift the money demand curve to the right in panel (a). If we had shifted the money demand curve, the equilibrium interest rate would still have fallen, but not by as much, so investment and aggregate demand would not have increased by as much. Thus, Exhibit 2 is a simplified view, but it still offers the essential story of how changes in the money supply affect the economy.

Now let's consider the effect of a Fed-orchestrated *increase* in interest rates. In Exhibit 3 such a policy could be traced by moving from point *b* to point *a* in each panel, but we will dispense with a blow-by-blow discussion of the graphs. Suppose the Federal Reserve decides to reduce the money supply to cool down an overheated economy. A decrease in the money supply would increase the interest rate. At the higher interest rate, businesses find it more costly to finance plants and equipment, and households find it more costly to finance new homes. Hence, a higher interest rate reduces investment. The resulting decline in investment is magnified by the spending multiplier, leading to a greater decline in aggregate demand.

As long as the interest rate is sensitive to changes in the money supply, and as long as investment is sensitive to changes in the interest rate, changes in the money supply affect planned investment. The extent to which a given change in planned investment affects aggregate demand depends on the size of the spending multiplier.

Adding Short-Run Aggregate Supply

Even after tracing the effect of a change in the money supply on aggregate demand, we still have only half the story. To determine the effects of monetary policy on the equilibrium real GDP in the economy, we need the supply side. An aggregate supply curve will help show how a given shift of the aggregate demand curve affects real GDP and the price level. In the short run, the aggregate supply curve slopes upward, so the quantity supplied will expand only if the price level increases. *For a given shift of the aggregate demand curve, the steeper the short-run aggregate supply curve, the smaller the increase in real GDP and the larger the increase in the price level.*

Suppose the economy is producing at point *a* in Exhibit 4, where the aggregate demand curve *AD* intersects the short-run aggregate supply curve $SRAS_{130}$, yielding a short-run equilibrium output of $11.8 trillion and a price level of 125. As you can see, the actual price level of 125 is below the expected price level of 130, and the short-run equilibrium output of $11.8 trillion is below the economy's potential of $12.0 trillion, yielding a contractionary gap of $0.2 trillion.

At point *a*, real wages are higher than had been negotiated and many people are looking for jobs. The Fed can wait to see whether the economy recovers on its own. Market forces could cause employers and workers to renegotiate lower nominal wages. This would lower production costs, pushing the short-run aggregate supply curve rightward, thus closing the contractionary gap. But if the Fed has little confidence in natural market forces or thinks this would take too long, the Fed could intervene and attempt to close the gap using an expansionary monetary policy. For example, during 2001 and 2002, the Fed aggressively cut the federal funds rate to stimulate aggregate demand. If the Fed lowers the rate by just the right amount, this stimulates investment, thus increasing the aggregate demand curve enough to achieve a new equilibrium at point *b*, where the economy produces its potential output. Given all the connections in the chain of causality between changes in the money

EXHIBIT 4

HOMEWORK
Xpress!
Graphing

Expansionary Monetary Policy to Correct a Contractionary Gap

At point *a*, the economy is producing less than its potential in the short run, resulting in a contractionary gap of $0.2 trillion. If the Federal Reserve increases the money supply by just the right amount, the aggregate demand curve shifts rightward from *AD* to *AD'*. A short-run and long-run equilibrium is established at point *b*, with the price level at 130 and output at the potential level of $12.0 trillion.

supply and changes in equilibrium output, however, it would actually be quite remarkable for the Fed to execute monetary policy so precisely. If the Fed overshoots the mark and stimulates aggregate demand too much, this would create an expansionary gap, thus creating inflationary pressure in the economy.

To review: As long as the demand for money slopes downward and investment demand is sensitive to changes in the interest rate, an increase in the money supply will reduce the market interest rate, increasing planned investment and consequently increasing aggregate demand. And as long as the short-run aggregate supply curve slopes upward, the short-run effect of an increase in the money supply is an increase in both real output and the price level. But one final caution: Lowering the interest rate may not always stimulate investment. Economic prospects may be so grim that lower interest rates may fail to achieve the desired increase in aggregate demand. In Japan, for example, the central bank has lowered the interest rate to nearly zero, yet that economy remained stagnant for a decade.

That's the theory of monetary policy in the short run. The following case study looks at how the Fed executes that policy.

C a s e **S t u d y**

Public Policy

eActivity
The Federal Reserve Banks provide reports, surveys, speeches, and other information for Fed Watchers. At the Federal Reserve Bank of Philadelphia at http://www.phil.frb.org, click on Economic Research. Select a recent survey or report, such as the Survey of Professional Forecasters, and read the latest offering. What indications can you find about the future direction of interest rates?

Targeting the Federal Funds Rate

At 2:15 P.M. on June 25, 2003, immediately following a regular meeting, the Federal Open Market Committee (FOMC) announced that it would lower its target for the federal funds rate by one-quarter of a percentage point to 1 percent, the lowest rate since the Eisenhower administration of the 1950s. As you know by now, the federal funds rate is the one that banks charge one another for reserves on account at the Fed. Because lowering the rate reduces the cost of covering any reserve shortfall, banks are more willing to lend to the public. In cutting the target rate, the FOMC noted that the economy "has yet to exhibit sustainable growth," so "a slightly more expansive monetary policy would further support for an economy which it expects to improve over time." Between the beginning of 2001 and that June 2003 meeting, the Fed cut the rate 5.5 percentage points in 13 steps, its most concentrated effort to stimulate the economy ever. To lower the federal funds rate, the FOMC authorized the New York Fed to make open-market purchases to increase bank reserves until the rate fell to the target level.

For nearly four decades, the Fed has reflected its monetary policy in this interest rate. (For a few years, the Fed targeted money aggregates, but more on that later.) There are many interest rates in the economy—for credit cards, new cars, mortgages, home equity loans, personal loans, and more. Why focus on such an obscure rate? First, by changing bank reserves through open-market operations, the Fed has a direct lever on the federal funds rate, so the Fed's grip on this rate is tighter than on any other market rate. Second, the federal funds rate serves as a benchmark in the economy for determining other short-term interest rates. For example, after the Fed announced the rate cut, major banks around the country lowered by the same amount the prime interest rate—the interest rate they charge their best corporate customers.

Exhibit 5 shows the federal funds rate since early 1996. Let's walk through developments of the period. Between early 1996 and late 1998, the economy grew nicely with low inflation, so the FOMC kept the rate relatively stable in a range of 5.25 percent to 5.5 percent.

But in late 1998, a Russian default on its bonds and the near collapse of a U.S. financial institution prompted the FOMC to drop its target rate to 4.75 percent. By the summer of 1999, those fears abated, and instead the FOMC became concerned that robust economic growth would trigger higher inflation. In a series of steps, the federal funds target rate was raised from 4.75 percent to 6.5 percent. The FOMC announced at the time that the moves "should markedly diminish the risk of rising inflation going forward." Some observers suggest that the Fed's aggressive rate hikes contributed to the subsequent recession. In early 2001, concerns about waning consumer confidence, weaker capital spending, falling manufacturing output, and a sinking stock market prompted the FOMC to reverse course, beginning the series of rate cuts discussed already. As it turned out, the economy was already in recession at the time.

In 1994, the Fed began announcing after each FOMC meeting whether the target interest rate would increase, decrease, or remain unchanged. Later, the Fed began indicating the probable "bias" of policy in the near term—that is, whether or not its current level or direction of interest rate changes would continue. For example, with its June 2003 announcement, the FOMC was worried more about "substantial fall in inflation" than in "a pickup in inflation." This signaled financial markets that the Fed would not likely raise interest rates soon. With such concrete news coming after each meeting, these FOMC meetings became media events. Some of the cuts during the recent drop in rates came between regular meetings. Such intermeeting actions have a more dramatic impact on markets, particularly the stock market, because of the surprise element. Still, in announcing target rate cuts, the FOMC must be careful not to appear too alarmed about the economy, because those doubts could harm business and consumer confidence further. Also, the Fed has to avoid overdoing rate cuts. As one member of the Board of Governors warned, the Fed must not cut the rate so much that it "ends up adding to price pressure as the growth strengthens."

Before making a decision about changes in the target interest rate, the Fed tracks a variety of indicators, including real GDP and the unemployment rate. One of Chairman

WALL STREET JOURNAL

Reading It **Right**

What's the relevance of the following statement from the Wall Street Journal: *"[The Philadelphia Fed President] has warned about the danger of cutting interest rates too much this year because, given the 6- to 12-month lags with which monetary policy affects the economy, it could lead to the economy growing unsustainably quickly next year, fueling inflation pressure."*

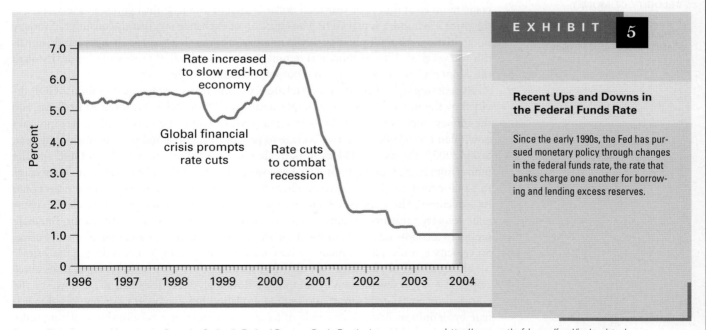

E X H I B I T 5

Recent Ups and Downs in the Federal Funds Rate

Since the early 1990s, the Fed has pursued monetary policy through changes in the federal funds rate, the rate that banks charge one another for borrowing and lending excess reserves.

Source: Based on monthly averages from the St. Louis Federal Reserve Bank. For the latest rates, go to http://www.stls.frb.org/fred/index.html.

Greenspan's favorites is the employment cost index, which measures changes in the cost of labor. If labor costs increase more than labor productivity, this signals to Greenspan that inflationary pressure is building in the economy, suggesting that an interest rate hike might be the appropriate remedy.

Sources: Aaron Luchetti, "Fed Sharpens Rate-Cut Shears," *Wall Street Journal*, 25 June 2003; Gregory Ip, "Fed to Keep Rates at Historic Low Despite Growth," *Wall Street Journal*, 14 November 2003; "Minutes of the Federal Open Market Committee" and "FOMC Statement on Interest Rates," various meetings. Find the latest FOMC minutes and statements at http://www.federalreserve.gov/fomc/#calendars.

Money and Aggregate Demand in the Long Run

When we looked at the impact of money on the economy in the short run, we found that money influences aggregate demand and equilibrium output through its effect on the interest rate. Here we look at the long-run effects of changes in the money supply on the economy. The long-run view of money is more direct: if the central bank supplies more money to the economy, sooner or later people spend more. But because the long-run aggregate supply curve is fixed at the economy's potential output, this greater spending simply increases the price level. Here are the details.

The Equation of Exchange

Every transaction in the economy involves a two-way swap: The buyer exchanges money for goods and the seller exchanges goods for money. One way of expressing this relationship among key variables in the economy is the **equation of exchange,** first developed by classical economists. Although this equation can be arranged in different ways, depending on the emphasis, the basic version is

$$M \times V = P \times Y$$

EQUATION OF EXCHANGE

The quantity of money, M, multiplied by its velocity, V, equals nominal GDP, which is the product of the price level, P, and real GDP, Y

VELOCITY OF MONEY

The average number of times per year each dollar is used to purchase final goods and services

where M is the quantity of money in the economy; V is the **velocity of money,** or the average number of times per year each dollar is used to purchase final goods and services; P is the price level; and Y is real GDP. The equation of exchange says that the quantity of money in circulation, M, multiplied by V, the number of times that money changes hands, equals the average price level, P, times real output, Y. The price level, P, times real output, Y, equals the economy's nominal income and output, or nominal GDP.

By rearranging the equation of exchange, we find that velocity equals nominal GDP divided by the money stock. For example, nominal GDP in 2003 was about $11 trillion, and the money stock as measured by M1 averaged $1.3 trillion. The velocity of money indicates how often each dollar is used on average to pay for final goods and services during the year. So in 2003, velocity was $11 trillion divided by $1.3 trillion, or 8.5. Given GDP and the money supply, each dollar must have been spent about eight and one-half times on average to pay for final goods and services. There is no other way these market transactions could have occurred. The value of velocity is implied by the values of the other variables. Incidentally, velocity measures spending only on final goods and services—not on intermediate products, secondhand goods, or financial assets, even though such spending also takes place. So velocity is really a low estimate of how hard the money supply works during the year.

The equation of exchange says that total spending $(M \times V)$ is always equal to total receipts $(P \times Y)$, as was the case in our circular-flow analysis. As described so far, however, the equation of exchange is simply an *identity*—a relationship expressed in such a way that it is true by definition. Another example of an identity would be a relationship equating miles per gallon to the distance driven divided by the gasoline required.

The Quantity Theory of Money

If velocity is relatively stable over time, or at least predictable, the equation of exchange turns from an identity into a theory—the quantity theory of money. The **quantity theory of money** states that if the velocity of money is stable, or at least predictable, then the equation of exchange can be used to predict the effects of changes in the money supply on *nominal* GDP, $P \times Y$. For example, if M is increased by 5 percent and V remains constant, then $P \times Y$, or nominal GDP, must also increase by 5 percent. For a while, some economists believed they could use the equation of exchange to predict nominal output in the short run. Now it's used primarily as a guide in the long run.

So an increase in the money supply results in more spending in the long run, which leads to a higher nominal GDP. How is this increase in $P \times Y$ divided between changes in the price level and changes in real GDP? The answer does not lie in the quantity theory, for that theory is stated only in terms of nominal GDP. The answer lies in the shape of the aggregate supply curve.

The long-run aggregate supply curve is vertical at the economy's potential level of output. With output, Y, fixed and the velocity of money, V, relatively stable, a change in the stock of money translates directly into a change in the price level. Exhibit 6 shows the effect of an increase in the supply of money in the long run. An increase in the money supply causes a rightward shift of the aggregate demand curve, which increases the price level but leaves output unchanged at potential GDP. So the economy's potential output level is not affected by changes in the money supply. *In the long run, increases in the money supply, with velocity stable or at least not decreasing, result only in higher prices.* For example, three years of an easy money policy began to catch up on the economy in early 2004, when the inflation rate doubled to four percent.[1] And an examination of 73 inflation periods across major economies since 1960 concludes that important triggers to inflation were expansionary policies.[2]

QUANTITY THEORY OF MONEY

If the velocity of money is stable, or at least predictable, changes in the money supply have predictable effects on nominal GDP

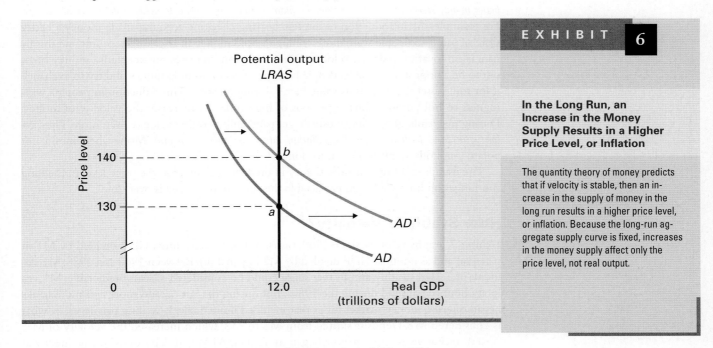

E X H I B I T   6

In the Long Run, an Increase in the Money Supply Results in a Higher Price Level, or Inflation

The quantity theory of money predicts that if velocity is stable, then an increase in the supply of money in the long run results in a higher price level, or inflation. Because the long-run aggregate supply curve is fixed, increases in the money supply affect only the price level, not real output.

1. E. S. Browning, "Investors Cross Fingers As Inflation Looms," *Wall Street Journal*, 7 June 2004.
2. John Boschen and Charles Weise, "What Starts Inflation: Evidence from OECD Countries," *Journal of Money, Credit and Banking* 35 (June 2003): 323–349.

To review: *If velocity is stable, or at least predictable, the quantity theory of money says that changes in the money supply will, in the long run, result in predictable effects on the economy's price level.* Velocity's stability and predictability are key to the quantity theory of money. Let's consider some factors that might influence velocity.

What Determines the Velocity of Money?

Velocity depends on the customs and conventions of commerce. In colonial times, money might be tied up in transit for days as a courier on horseback carried a payment from a merchant in Boston to one in Baltimore. Today, the electronic transmission of funds takes only an instant, so the same stock of money can move around much more quickly to finance many more transactions. *The velocity of money has also increased because of a variety of commercial innovations that facilitate exchange.* For example, a wider use of charge accounts and credit cards has reduced the need for shoppers to carry cash. Likewise, automatic teller machines have made cash more accessible at more times and in more places. What's more, debit cards are used at a growing number of retail outlets, such as grocery stores and drug stores, so people have reduced their "walking around" money.

Another institutional factor that determines velocity is the frequency with which workers get paid. Suppose a worker earns $26,000 per year and is paid $1,000 every two weeks. Earnings are spent evenly during the two-week period and are gone by the end of the period. In that case, a worker's average money balance during the pay period is $500. If a worker earns the same $26,000 per year but, instead, gets paid $500 weekly, the average money balance during the week falls to $250. *Thus, the more often workers get paid, other things constant, the lower their average money balances, so the more active the money supply and the greater its velocity.* Payment practices change slowly over time, and the effects of these changes on velocity are predictable.

Another factor affecting velocity depends on how stable money is as a store of value. *The better money serves as a store of value, the more money people want to hold, so the lower its velocity.* For example, the introduction of interest-bearing checking accounts made money a better store of value, so people were more willing to hold money in checking accounts and this financial innovation reduced velocity. When inflation increases unexpectedly, money turns out to be a poor store of value. People become reluctant to hold money and try to exchange it for some asset that retains its value better during inflation. This reduction in people's willingness to hold money during periods of high inflation increases the velocity of money. During hyperinflation, workers usually get paid daily, boosting velocity even more. Thus, *velocity increases with a rise in the inflation rate, other things constant.* Money becomes a hot potato—nobody wants to hold it for long.

The usefulness of the quantity theory in predicting changes in the price level in the long run hinges on how stable and predictable the velocity of money is over time.

How Stable Is Velocity?

Exhibit 7 graphs velocity since 1960, measured both as nominal GDP divided by M1 in panel (a) and as nominal GDP divided by M2 in panel (b). Between 1960 and 1980, M1 velocity increased steadily and in that sense could be considered at least predictable. M1 velocity bounced around during the 1980s. But during the last decade, more and more banks began offering money market funds that included limited check-writing privileges, or what is considered M2. Deposits shifted from M1 to M2, which increased the velocity of M1. Also in recent years, more people began using their ATM and debit cards to pay directly at grocery stores, drugstores, and a growing number of outlets, and this too increased the velocity of M1 because people had less need for walking-around money.

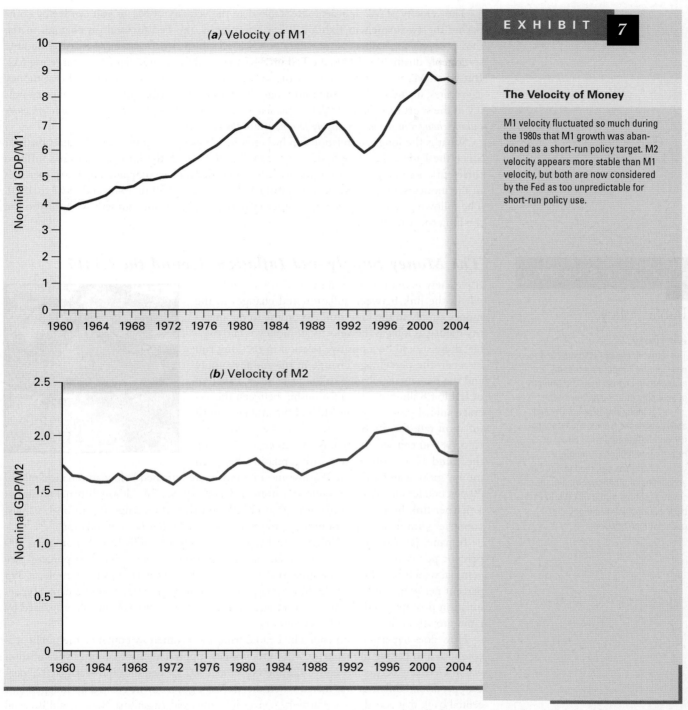

(a) Velocity of M1

(b) Velocity of M2

E X H I B I T 7

The Velocity of Money

M1 velocity fluctuated so much during the 1980s that M1 growth was abandoned as a short-run policy target. M2 velocity appears more stable than M1 velocity, but both are now considered by the Fed as too unpredictable for short-run policy use.

Source: *Economic Report of the President*, February 2004. To compute the latest velocity, go to http://w3.access.gpo.gov/eop/, find the statistical tables in the appendix then divide nominal GDP by M1 and by M2.

The velocity of M2 appears more stable than the velocity of M1, as you can see by comparing the two panels in Exhibit 7. For a few years, the Fed focused on changes in the money supply as a target for monetary policy in the short run. Because M1 velocity became so unstable during the 1980s, the Fed in 1987 switched from targeting M1 to targeting M2. But when M2 velocity became volatile in the early 1990s, the Fed announced that money aggregates, including M2, would no longer be considered reliable guides for monetary policy in the short run. *Since 1993, the equation of exchange has been considered more of a rough guide linking changes in the money supply to inflation in the long run.*

What is the long-run relationship between increases in the money supply and inflation? Since the Federal Reserve System was established in 1913, the United States has suffered three episodes of high inflation, and each was preceded and accompanied by sharp increases in the money supply. These occurred from 1913 to 1920, 1939 to 1948, and 1967 to 1980. The following case study examines other evidence linking money growth with inflation in the long run worldwide.

The Money Supply and Inflation Around the World

If we view economies around the world as evidence, what's the link between inflation and changes in the money supply in the long run? According to the quantity theory, as long as the velocity of money is fairly stable, there should be a positive relation in the long run between the percentage change in the money supply and the percentage change in the price level. Panel (a) of Exhibit 8 illustrates the relationship between the average annual growth rate in M2 and the average annual inflation rate for the 85 countries over a 10-year period. As you can see, the points fall rather neatly along the trend line, showing a positive relation between money growth and inflation. Because most countries are bunched below an inflation rate of 20 percent, let's break these points out in finer detail in panel (b). Although panel (a) shows a sharper link between money growth and inflation than does panel (b), in both panels, countries with higher rates of money growth experience higher rates of inflation.

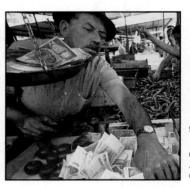
© Art Zamur/Gamma

In panel (a), Argentina, Bolivia, and Israel—countries with inflation of more than 100 percent per year—also experienced annual money growth exceeding 100 percent. Argentina, which had the highest inflation rate over the 10-year period in the sample, at 395 percent per year, also had the highest average annual money growth, at 369 percent. Hyperinflation first appeared about a century ago, and in every case it has been accompanied by rapid growth in the supply of paper money.

How does hyperinflation end? The central bank must somehow convince the public it is committed to halting the rapid growth in the money supply. The most famous hyperinflation was in Germany between August 1922 and November 1923, when inflation averaged 322 percent *per month*. Inflation was halted when the German government created an independent central bank that issued a new currency convertible into gold. Argentina, Bolivia, and Israel all managed to tame inflation, with inflation under 3 percent by 2000. Incidentally, households in all three countries, perhaps mindful of their hyperinflation, still hold a lot of U.S. currency.

Sources: *World Development Report 1997* (Oxford: Oxford University Press, 1997); Gerald Dwyer and R. W. Hafer, "Are Money Growth and Inflation Still Related?" *Federal Reserve Bank of Atlanta Economic Review* (Second Quarter 1999): 32–43; and "Emerging Market Indicators," *Economist*, 2 April 2004. Recent inflation rates around the world are available in the *World Development Report*; for the latest, go to http://econ.worldbank.org/wdr/.

Case Study

Public Policy

*e*Activity

The latest economic statistics and reports on the Argentine economy are available in English from the Ministry of Economy at http://www.mecon.gov.ar/default_english.htm. Or read about economic trends, monetary policy, and inflation rates in Israel at http://www.mof.gov.il/beinle/ie/israe_1.htm. You can read about the economies of other countries in the country profiles at the CIA World Factbook at http://www.cia.gov/cia/publications/factbook.

EXHIBIT 8

A Decade of Annual Inflation and Money Growth in 85 Countries (average annual percent)

Panel (a) shows that money growth is clearly linked with inflation based on a sample of 85 countries between 1980 and 1990. In each country that experienced hyperinflation, the inflation rate matched the growth in the money supply. Panel (b) offers finer detail for the subset of countries with inflation and money growth below 30 percent. Again, money growth and inflation are positively related in the long run.

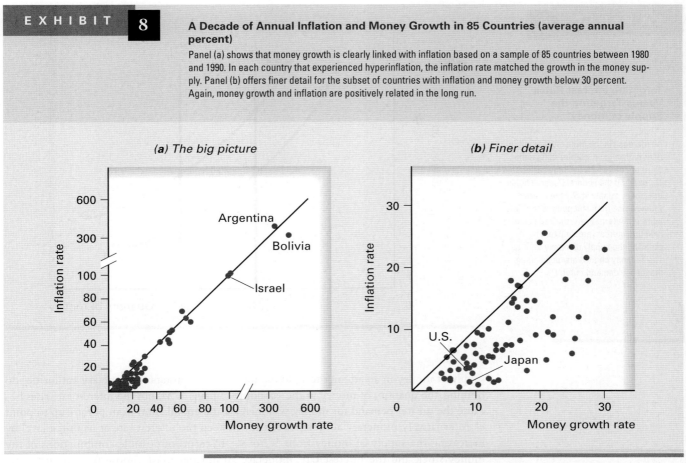

Source: The World Bank, *World Development Report 1992* (New York: Oxford University Press, 1992), Table 13. Figures are annual averages for 1980 to 1990.

Targets for Monetary Policy

In the short run, monetary policy affects the economy largely by influencing the interest rate. In the long run, changes in the money supply affect the price level, though with an uncertain lag. Should monetary authorities focus on the interest rates in the short run or the supply of money in the long run? As we will see, the Fed lacks the tools to focus on both at the same time.

Contrasting Policies

To demonstrate the effects of different policies, we begin with the money market in equilibrium at point *e* in Exhibit 9. The interest rate is *i* and the money stock is *M*, values the monetary authorities find appropriate. Suppose there is an increase in the demand for money in the economy, perhaps because of an increase in nominal GDP. The money demand curve shifts to the right, from D_m to D'_m.

When confronted with an increase in the demand for money, monetary authorities can choose to do nothing, thereby allowing the interest rate to rise, or they can increase the

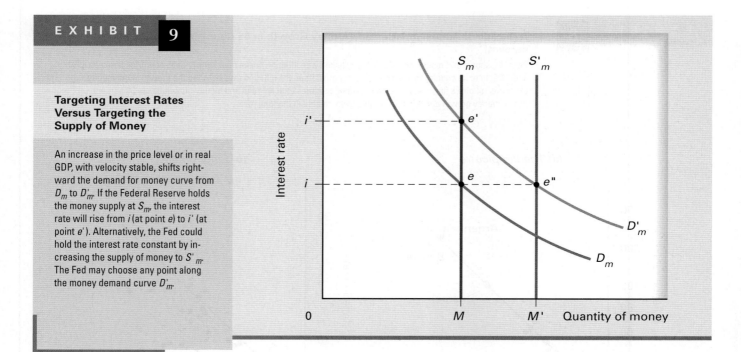

EXHIBIT 9

Targeting Interest Rates Versus Targeting the Supply of Money

An increase in the price level or in real GDP, with velocity stable, shifts rightward the demand for money curve from D_m to D'_m. If the Federal Reserve holds the money supply at S_m, the interest rate will rise from i (at point e) to i' (at point e'). Alternatively, the Fed could hold the interest rate constant by increasing the supply of money to S'_m. The Fed may choose any point along the money demand curve D'_m.

supply of money in an attempt to hold the interest rate constant. If monetary authorities do nothing, the quantity of money in the economy remains at M, but the interest rate rises because the greater demand for money will increase the equilibrium from point e up to point e'. Alternatively, monetary authorities can try to keep the interest rate at its initial level by increasing the supply of money from S_m to S'_m. In terms of possible combinations of the money stock and the interest rate, monetary authorities must choose from points lying along the new money demand curve, D'_m.

A growing economy usually needs a growing money supply to pay for the increase in aggregate output. If monetary authorities maintain a constant growth in the money supply, and if velocity remains stable, the interest rate will fluctuate unless the growth in the supply of money each period just happens to match the growth in the demand for money (as in the movement from e to e'' in Exhibit 9). Alternatively, monetary authorities could try to adjust the money supply each period by the amount needed to keep the interest rate stable. In this approach, changes in the money supply would have to offset any changes in the demand for money. This essentially is what the Fed does when it holds the federal funds target constant.

Interest rate fluctuations could be harmful if they created undesirable fluctuations in investment. For interest rates to remain stable during economic expansions, the money supply would have to grow at the same rate as the demand for money. Likewise, for interest rates to remain stable during economic contractions, the money supply would have to shrink at the same rate as the demand for money. Hence, for monetary authorities to maintain the interest rate at some specified level, the money supply must increase during economic expansions and decrease during contractions. But an increase in the money supply during an expansion would increase aggregate demand even more, and a decrease in the money supply during a contraction would reduce aggregate demand even more. *Such changes in the money supply would thus tend to worsen fluctuations in economic activity, thereby adding more instability to the economy.* With this in mind, let's examine monetary policy over the years.

Targets Before 1982

Between World War II and October 1979, the Fed attempted to stabilize interest rates. Stable interest rates were viewed as a prerequisite for an attractive investment environment and, thus, for a stable economy. Milton Friedman, the Nobel Prize winner, argued that this exclusive attention to interest rates made monetary policy a source of instability in the economy because changes in the money supply reinforced fluctuations in the economy. He said that the Fed should pay less attention to interest rates and instead should focus on a steady and predictable growth in the money supply. The debate raged during the 1970s, and Friedman won some important converts. Amid growing concern about the rising inflation rate, the Fed, under a new chairman, Paul Volcker, announced in October 1979 that it would deemphasize interest rates and would instead target specific money aggregates. Not surprisingly, interest rates became much more volatile.

But many observers believe that a sharp reduction in money growth in the latter half of 1981 caused the recession of 1982. Inflation declined rapidly, but unemployment jumped to 10 percent. People were worried. As you might expect, the Fed was widely criticized. Farmers, politicians, and businesspeople denounced Volcker. Emotions ran high. Volcker was reportedly even given Secret Service protection. In October 1982, three years after the focus on interest rates was dropped, Volcker announced that the Fed would again pay more attention to interest rates.

Targets After 1982

The Fed is always feeling its way, looking for signs about the direction of the economy. The rapid pace of financial innovations and deregulation during the 1980s made the definition and measurement of the money supply more difficult. Alan Greenspan, who became the Fed chairman in 1987, said that, in the short run, changes in the money supply "are not linked closely enough with those of nominal income to justify a single-minded focus on the money supply."[3] In 1993, he testified in Congress that the Fed would no longer target money aggregates, such as M1 and M2, as a guide to monetary policy. As we've seen, the Fed in recent years has targeted the federal funds rate. No central bank in a major economy now makes significant use of money aggregates to guide policy in the short run. Still, most policy makers also agree that in the long run, changes in the money supply influenced the price level and inflation.

Conclusion

This chapter has described two ways of viewing the effects of money on the economy's performance, but we should not overstate the differences. In the model that focuses on the short run, an increase in the money supply means that people are holding more money than they would like at the prevailing interest rate, so they exchange one form of wealth, money, for other financial assets, such as corporate or government bonds. This greater demand for other financial assets has no direct effect on aggregate demand, but it does reduce the interest rate, and this lower interest rate stimulates investment. The higher investment gets magnified by the spending multiplier, increasing aggregate demand. The effect of this increase in demand on real output and the price level depends on the shape of the short-run aggregate supply curve.

In the model that focuses on the long run, changes in the money supply act more directly on the price level. If velocity is relatively stable or at least fairly predictable, then

3. Quoted in "Greenspan Asks That Fed Be Allowed to Pay Interest," *Wall Street Journal,* 11 March 1992.

changes in the money supply will have a predictable effect on the price level in the long run. As long as velocity is not declining, an increase in the money supply means that people eventually spend more, increasing aggregate demand. But because long-run aggregate supply is fixed at the economy's potential output, increased aggregate demand leads simply to a higher price level, or to inflation.

SUMMARY

1. The opportunity cost of holding money is the higher interest forgone by not holding other financial assets instead. Along a given money demand curve, the quantity of money demanded relates inversely to the interest rate. The demand for money curve shifts rightward as a result of an increase in the price level, an increase in real GDP, or an increase in both.

2. The Fed determines the supply of money, assumed to be independent of the interest rate. The intersection of the supply and demand for money determines the equilibrium interest rate. In the short run, an increase in the supply of money reduces the interest rate, which increases investment. This boosts aggregate demand, which increases real output and the price level.

3. The long-run approach focuses on the role of money through the equation of exchange, which states that the quantity of money, M, multiplied by velocity, V, the average number of times each dollar gets spent, equals the price level, P, multiplied by real GDP, Y. So $M \times V = P \times Y$. Because the aggregate supply curve in the long run is a vertical line at the economy's potential output, a change in the money supply affects the price level but not real output.

4. Between World War II and October 1979, the Fed targeted stable interest rates as a way of promoting a stable investment environment. During the 1980s and early 1990s, the Fed paid more attention to growth in money aggregates, first M1 and then M2. But the velocity of M1 and M2 became so unstable that the Fed decided to shift focus back to interest rates, particularly the federal funds rate.

QUESTIONS FOR REVIEW

1. *(Demand for Money)* Determine whether each of the following would lead to an increase, a decrease, or no change in the quantity of money people wish to hold. Also determine whether there is a shift of the money demand curve or a movement along a given money demand curve.

   a. A decrease in the price level
   b. An increase in real output
   c. An improvement in money's ability to act as a store of value
   d. An increase in the market interest rate

2. *(Demand for Money)* If money is so versatile and can buy anything, why don't people demand all the money they can get their hands on?

3. *(Monetary Policy)* What is the impact of a decrease in the required reserve ratio on aggregate demand?

4. *(**Case Study**: Targeting the Federal Funds Rate)* Why has the Federal Reserve chosen to focus on the federal funds rate rather than some other interest rate as a tool of monetary policy?

5. *(Equation of Exchange)* Using the equation of exchange, show why fiscal policy alone cannot increase nominal GDP if the velocity of money is constant.

6. *(Velocity)* Why do some economists believe that higher expected inflation will lead to a rise in velocity?

7. *(Velocity of Money)* Determine whether each of the following would lead to an increase or a decrease in the velocity of money:

   a. Increasing the speed of funds transfers
   b. Decreased use of credit cards

c. Decreasing the frequency with which workers are paid

d. Increased customer use of ATM, or debit, cards at retailers

8. *(Quantity Theory of Money)* The quantity theory states that the impact of money on nominal GDP can be determined without details about the *AD* curve, so long as the velocity of money is predictable. Discuss the reasoning behind this claim.

9. *(Case Study: The Money Supply and Inflation Around the World)* According to Exhibit 8 in this chapter, what is the relationship between the rate of money supply growth and the inflation rate? How does this explain the hyperinflation experienced in some economies?

10. *(How Stable Is Velocity?)* What factors have led to changes in the velocity of M1 and M2 over the past 25 years?

11. *(Money Supply Versus Interest Rate Targets)* In recent years the Fed's monetary target has been the federal funds rate. How does the Fed raise or lower that rate, and how is that rate related to other interest rates in the economy such as the prime rate?

PROBLEMS AND EXERCISES

12. *(Money Demand)* Suppose that you never carry cash. Your paycheck of $1,000 per month is deposited directly into your checking account, and you spend your money at a constant rate so that at the end of each month your checking account balance is zero.

a. What is your average money balance during the pay period?

b. How would each of the following changes affect your average monthly balance?
   i. You are paid $500 twice monthly rather than $1,000 each month.
   ii. You are uncertain about your total spending each month.
   iii. You spend a lot at the beginning of the month (e.g., for rent) and little at the end of the month.
   iv. Your monthly income increases.

13. *(Money and Aggregate Demand)* Would each of the following increase, decrease, or have no impact on the ability of open-market operations to affect aggregate demand? Explain your answer.

a. Investment demand becomes less sensitive to changes in the interest rate.
b. The marginal propensity to consume rises.
c. The money multiplier rises.
d. Banks decide to hold additional excess reserves.
e. The demand for money becomes more sensitive to changes in the interest rate.

14. *(Monetary Policy and Aggregate Supply)* Assume that the economy is initially in long-run equilibrium. Using an *AD–AS* diagram, illustrate and explain the short-run and long-run impacts of an increase in the money supply.

15. *(Monetary Policy and an Expansionary Gap)* Suppose the Fed wishes to use monetary policy to close an expansionary gap.

a. Should the Fed increase or decrease the money supply?
b. If the Fed uses open-market operations, should it buy or sell government securities?
c. Determine whether each of the following increases, decreases, or remains unchanged in the short run: the market interest rate, the quantity of money demanded, investment spending, aggregate demand, potential output, the price level, and equilibrium real GDP.

16. *(Equation of Exchange)* Calculate the velocity of money if real GDP is 3,000 units, the average price level is $4 per unit, and the quantity of money in the economy is $1,500. What happens to velocity if the average price level drops to $3 per unit? What happens to velocity if the average price level remains at $4 per unit but the money supply rises to $2,000? What happens to velocity if the average price level falls to $2 per unit, the money supply is $2,000, and real GDP is 4,000 units?

17. *(Quantity Theory of Money)* What basic assumption about the velocity of money transforms the equation of exchange into the quantity theory of money? Also:

a. According to the quantity theory, what will happen to nominal GDP if the money supply increases by 5 percent and velocity does not change?

b. What will happen to nominal GDP if, instead, the money supply decreases by 8 percent and velocity does not change?

c. What will happen to nominal GDP if, instead, the money supply increases by 5 percent and velocity decreases by 5 percent?

d. What happens to the price level in the short run in each of these three situations?

18. *(Money Supply Versus Interest Rate Targets)* Assume that the economy's real GDP is growing.

a. What will happen to money demand over time?

b. If the Fed leaves the money supply unchanged, what will happen to the interest rate over time?

c. If the Fed changes the money supply to match the change in money demand, what will happen to the interest rate over time?

d. What would be the effect of the policy described in part (c) on the economy's stability over the business cycle?

EXPERIENTIAL EXERCISES

19. *(Money Supply Versus Interest Rate Targets)* A favorite activity of many macroeconomists is Fed watching. Go to the Federal Reserve Board's Web site and look for the most recent Congressional testimony of the Board Chairperson at http://www.federalreserve.gov/boarddocs/testimony/2004/. Is the Fed targeting interest rates, the money supply, or something else?

20. *(Targets After 1982)* The Federal Reserve Bank of Cleveland's monthly publication *Economic Trends* at http://www.clevelandfed.org/Research/index.htm is available online. Choose the current issue and find "Monetary Policy." What are some current developments in monetary policy? See if you can illustrate them using the *AD–AS* model.

21. *(Wall Street Journal)* The Federal Reserve Report appears in each Friday's *Wall Street Journal.* You can find it in the Money and Investing section. In addition to the weekly report, a monthly chart shows the recent performance of money supply indicators, compared with Fed targets. Does it look as if the Fed has been hitting its targets over the last year?

22. *(Wall Street Journal)* Look in the Money and Investing section of the *Wall Street Journal* for interest rate information. Find the current federal funds rate. How has it changed over the past year?

HOMEWORK XPRESS! EXERCISES

*These exercises require access to McEachern Homework Xpress! If Homework Xpress! did not come with your book, visit **http://homeworkxpress.swlearning.com** to purchase.*

1. In the Homework Xpress! graph for this problem, sketch a curve illustrating the relationship between the interest rate and the demand for money.

2. Draw a demand for money curve and a supply of money at $2 trillion. Identify the rate of interest at which people would hold this quantity of money. Illustrate the effect of an increase in the supply of money by the Fed.

3. In the diagram, sketch a line showing long-run aggregate supply at a potential output of $10 trillion. Sketch in an aggregate demand curve and identify the price level. Illustrate the long-run effect of an increase in the money supply.

4. Sketch a demand for money curve and a supply of money at $2 trillion. Identify the rate of interest at which people would hold this quantity of money. Illustrate the effect of an increase in the demand for money. Show how the Fed could act to keep the interest rate constant.

The Policy Debate: Active or Passive?

© William Philpott/AFP/Getty Images

D oes the private sector work fairly well on its own, or does it require active government intervention? Does government intervention do more harm than good? If people expect government to intervene if the economy falters, does this expectation affect people's behavior? What is the relationship between unemployment and inflation in the short run and in the long run? Answers to these and other questions are provided in this chapter, which examines the appropriate role for government in economic stabilization.

You have studied both fiscal and monetary policy and are now in a position to consider the overall impact of public policy on the U.S. economy. This chapter distinguishes between two general approaches: the *active approach* and the *passive approach*. The active approach views the private sector as relatively unstable and unable to recover from shocks when they occur. According to the active approach, economic fluctuations arise primarily from the private sector, particularly investment, and natural market forces may not help much or may be too slow when the economy gets off track. To move the economy to its potential output, the active approach calls for government intervention and discretionary policy. The passive approach, on the other hand, considers the private sector to be relatively stable and able to recover from shocks when they do occur. When the economy derails, natural market forces nudge it back on track in a timely manner. Not only is government intervention unnecessary, but according to the passive approach, such activism may do more harm than good.

In this chapter, we consider the pros and cons of *active* intervention in the economy versus *passive* reliance on natural market forces. We also examine the role that expectations play in determining the effectiveness of stabilization policy. You will learn why unanticipated stabilization policies have more impact on employment and output than do anticipated ones. Finally, the chapter explores the trade-off between unemployment and inflation. Topics discussed include:

- Active versus passive approaches
- Self-correcting mechanisms
- Rational expectations
- Policy rules and policy credibility
- The time-inconsistency problem
- Short-run and long-run Phillips curves
- Natural rate hypothesis

Active Policy Versus Passive Policy

According to the *active approach,* discretionary fiscal or monetary policy can reduce the costs of an unstable private sector, such as higher unemployment. According to the *passive approach,* discretionary policy may contribute to the instability of the economy and is therefore part of the problem, not part of the solution. The two approaches differ in their assumptions about how well natural market forces operate and the effectiveness of government intervention.

Closing a Contractionary Gap

Perhaps the best way to describe each approach is by examining a particular macroeconomic problem. Suppose the economy is in short-run equilibrium at point *a* in panel (a) of Exhibit 1, with real GDP at $11.8 trillion, which is below the economy's potential of $12.0 trillion. The contractionary gap of $0.2 trillion drives unemployment above its natural rate (the rate when the economy produces potential GDP). This gap could have resulted from lower-than-expected aggregate demand. What should public officials do?

Those who follow the passive approach, as did their classical predecessors, have more faith in the *self-correcting forces* of the economy than do those who favor the active approach. In what sense is the economy self-correcting? According to the passive approach, wages and prices are flexible enough to adjust within a reasonable period to labor shortages or surpluses. High unemployment will cause wages to fall, which will reduce production costs, which will shift the short-run aggregate supply curve rightward in panel (a) of Exhibit 1. (Money wages need not actually fall; money wage increases need only lag behind price increases, so that real wages fall.) The short-run aggregate supply curve will, within a reasonable period, shift from $SRAS_{130}$ to $SRAS_{120}$, moving the economy to its potential output at point *b. According to the passive approach, the economy is stable enough, gravitating in a reasonable time toward potential GDP. Consequently, advocates of passive policy see little reason for discretionary policy.* The passive approach is to let natural market forces close the contractionary gap. So

EXHIBIT 1

Closing a Contractionary Gap

At point *a* in both panels, the economy is in short-run equilibrium, with unemployment exceeding its natural rate. According to the passive approach, shown in panel (a), high unemployment eventually causes wages to fall, reducing the cost of doing business. The decline in costs shifts the short-run aggregate supply curve rightward from $SRAS_{130}$ to $SRAS_{120}$, moving the economy to its potential output at point *b*. In panel (b), the government employs an active approach to shift the aggregate demand curve from *AD* to *AD'*. If the active policy works, the economy moves to its potential output at point *c*.

(a) The passive approach

Potential output

$SRAS_{130}$
$SRAS_{120}$

Price level

130
125
120

a
b

AD

0   11.8 12.0   Real GDP
(trillions of dollars)

(b) The active approach

Potential output

$SRAS_{130}$

Price level

130
125

c
a

AD'
AD

0   11.8 12.0   Real GDP
(trillions of dollars)

the prescription of passive policy is to do nothing beyond the automatic stabilizers already built into taxes, transfers, and government purchases.

Advocates of an active approach, on the other hand, believe that prices and wages are not very flexible, particularly in the downward direction. They think that when adverse supply shocks or sagging demand push unemployment above its natural rate, market forces are slow to respond. The longer market forces take to reduce unemployment to the natural rate, the greater the output lost and the greater the economic and psychological cost to those unemployed. *Because advocates of an active policy associate a high cost with the passive approach, they advocate an active stabilization policy to stimulate aggregate demand.*

A decision by public officials to intervene in the economy to achieve potential output—that is, a decision to use discretionary policy—reflects an active approach. In panel (b) of Exhibit 1, we begin at the same point *a* as in panel (a). At point *a*, short-run equilibrium output is below potential output, so the economy is experiencing a contractionary gap. Through discretionary monetary policy, discretionary fiscal policy, or some of both, as occurred in 2001, active policy attempts to increase aggregate demand from *AD* to *AD'*, moving equilibrium from point *a* to point *c*, thus closing the contractionary gap.

What's the relevance of the following statement from the Wall Street Journal*: "The U.S. could rebound quickly from its downturn because of the monetary and fiscal stimulus already in the 'pipeline' in response to early signs of a slowdown and particularly in response to the terrorist attacks."*

In 2001, policy makers tried to revive a slowing economy using both fiscal and monetary policy. George W. Bush's first tax cut, the largest in a decade, was approved by Congress in May and was aimed, in Bush's words, at "getting the country moving again." Later that year, Congress and the president also approved a multibillion dollar package of federal outlays to support greater national security in the wake of the terrorist attacks. Meanwhile, throughout 2001, as noted in the previous chapter, the Fed cut its target interest rate a record amount. This combination of fiscal and monetary policy was the most concentrated attempt to boost aggregate demand since World War II. One possible cost of using discretionary policy to stimulate aggregate demand is an increase in the price level, or inflation. Another cost of fiscal stimulus is to increase the budget deficit, a cost addressed in the next chapter.

Closing an Expansionary Gap

Let's consider the situation in which the short-run equilibrium output exceeds the economy's potential. Suppose the actual price level of 135 exceeds the expected price level of 130, causing an expansionary gap of $0.2 trillion, as shown in Exhibit 2. The passive approach argues that natural market forces will prompt workers and firms to negotiate higher wages. These higher nominal wages will increase production costs, shifting the short-run supply curve leftward, from $SRAS_{130}$ to $SRAS_{140}$, as shown in panel (a). Consequently, the price level will increase and output will decrease to the economy's potential. So the natural adjustment process will result in a higher price level, or inflation.

An active approach sees discretionary policy as a way to reach potential output without increasing the price level. Advocates of active policy believe that if aggregate demand can be reduced from AD'' to AD', as shown in panel (b) of Exhibit 2, then the equilibrium point will move down along the initial aggregate supply curve from *d* to *c*. *Whereas the passive approach relies on natural market forces to close an expansionary gap through a decrease in short-run aggregate supply, the active approach relies on just the right discretionary policy to close the gap through a decrease of aggregate demand.* In the long run, the passive approach results in a higher price level and the active approach results in a lower price level. Thus, the correct discretionary policy can relieve the inflationary pressure associated with an expansionary gap. Whenever the Fed attempts to cool down an overheated economy by increasing its target interest rate, as it did in 2000, it employs an active monetary policy to close an expansionary gap. In 2000, when the economy was flying high, with output exceeding potential, the Fed tried to orchestrate a so-called *soft landing* to gently slow the rate of growth before that growth triggered inflation. Critics say the Fed overdid it and contributed to the recession of 2001.

Problems with Active Policy

The timely adoption and implementation of an active policy is not easy. One problem is identifying the economy's potential output and the natural rate of unemployment. Suppose the natural rate of unemployment is 5 percent, but policy makers believe it's 4 percent. As they pursue their elusive goal of 4 percent, they push output beyond its potential, fueling higher prices in the long run but with no permanent reduction in unemployment. Recall that when output exceeds the economy's potential, this opens up an expansionary gap, causing a leftward shift of the short-run aggregate supply curve until the economy returns to its potential output at a higher price level.

Even if policy makers can accurately estimate the economy's potential output and the natural rate of unemployment, formulating an effective policy requires detailed knowledge of current and future economic conditions. To craft an effective strategy, policy makers must first be able to forecast aggregate demand and supply without active intervention. In other

EXHIBIT 2

Closing an Expansionary Gap

At point *d* in both panels, the economy is in short-run equilibrium, producing $12.2 trillion, which exceeds the economy's potential output. Unemployment is below its natural rate. In the passive approach reflected in panel (a), the government makes no change in policy, so natural market forces eventually bring about a higher negotiated wage, increasing firm costs and shifting the short-run supply curve leftward to $SRAS_{140}$. The new equilibrium at point *e* results in a higher price level and lower output and employment. An active policy reduces aggregate demand, shifting the equilibrium in panel (b) from point *d* to point *c*, thus closing the expansionary gap without increasing the price level.

(a) The passive approach *(b)* The active approach

words, they must be able to predict what would happen with a passive approach. Second, they must have the tools needed to achieve the desired result relatively quickly. Third, they must be able to predict the effects of an active policy on the economy's key performance measures. Fourth, policy makers must work together, or at least not work at cross-purposes. Congress and the president pursue fiscal policy while the Fed pursues monetary policy; these groups often fail to coordinate their efforts. If an active policy requires coordination, the policy may not work as desired. In early 1995, for example, Congress was considering an expansionary tax cut while the Fed was pursuing a contractionary monetary policy. Fifth, policy makers must be able to implement the appropriate policy, even when this involves short-term political costs. For example, during inflationary times, the optimal policy may call for a tax increase or a tighter monetary policy—policies that are unpopular because they increase unemployment. Finally, policy makers must be able to deal with a variety of timing lags. As we will see next, these lags compound the problems of pursuing an active policy.

The Problem of Lags

So far, we have ignored the time required to implement policy. That is, we have assumed that the desired policy is selected and implemented instantaneously. We have also assumed that, once implemented, the policy works as advertised—again, in no time. Actually, there may be long, sometimes unpredictable, lags at several stages in the process. These lags reduce the effectiveness and increase the uncertainty of active policies.

First, is a **recognition lag**—the time it takes to identify a problem and determine how serious it is. For example, time is required to accumulate evidence that the economy is indeed performing below its potential. Even if initial data look troubling, data are usually revised later. For example, the government releases three estimates of quarterly GDP growth coming weeks apart—an *advanced* estimate, a *preliminary* estimate, and a *final* estimate. What's more these estimates are often revised years later or even a decade later. Therefore, policy makers sometimes wait for more proof before responding to what may turn out to be a false alarm. Because a recession is not identified until more than 6 months after it begins and because the average recession lasts only about 11 months, a typical recession will be more than half over before officially recognized as such.

RECOGNITION LAG

The time needed to identify a macroeconomic problem and assess its seriousness

Even after enough evidence accumulates, policy makers often take time deciding what to do, so there is a **decision-making lag.** In the case of discretionary fiscal policy, Congress and the president must agree on an appropriate course of action. Fiscal policy usually takes months to develop and approve; it could take more than a year. On the other hand, the Fed can implement monetary policy more quickly and does not even have to wait for regular meetings. For example, as the economy weakened in 2001, the Fed announced interest rate cuts three times between regular meetings. So the decision-making lag is shorter for monetary policy than for fiscal policy.

DECISION-MAKING LAG

The time needed to decide what to do once a macroeconomic problem has been identified

Once a decision has been made, the new policy must be introduced, which usually involves an **implementation lag.** Again, monetary policy has the advantage: After a policy has been adopted, the Fed can immediately buy or sell bonds to influence bank reserves and thereby change the federal funds rate. The implementation lag is longer for fiscal policy. If tax rates change, new tax forms must be printed and distributed advising employers of changes in tax withholding. If government spending changes, the appropriate government agencies must get involved. The implementation of fiscal policy can take more than a year. For example, in February 1983, the nation's unemployment rate reached 10.3 percent, with 11.5 million people unemployed. The following month, Congress passed the Emergency Jobs Appropriation Act, providing $9 billion to create what supporters claimed would be hundreds of thousands of new jobs. Fifteen months later, only $3.1 billion had been spent and only 35,000 new jobs had been created, according to a U.S. General Accounting Office study. By that time, the economy was already recovering on its own, lowering the unemployment rate from 10.3 percent to 7.1 percent and adding 6.2 million new jobs. So this public spending program was implemented only after the recession had bottomed out and recovered. Likewise, in spring 1993, President Clinton proposed a $16 billion stimulus package to boost what appeared to be a sluggish recovery. The measure was defeated because it would have increased what already was a large federal deficit, yet the economy still added 5.6 million jobs over the next two years. As a final example, in early 2001, President Bush proposed a tax cut to stimulate the economy. Although Congress passed the measure relatively quickly, tax rebate checks were not mailed until six months after Bush introduced the legislation.

IMPLEMENTATION LAG

The time needed to introduce a change in monetary or fiscal policy

Once a policy has been implemented, there is an **effectiveness lag** before the full impact of the policy registers on the economy. One problem with monetary policy is that the lag between a change in the federal funds rate and the change in aggregate demand and output can take from months to a year or more. Fiscal policy, once enacted, usually requires 3 to 6 months to take effect and between 9 and 18 months to register its full effect.

EFFECTIVENESS LAG

The time needed for changes in monetary or fiscal policy to affect the economy

These various lags make active policy difficult to execute. The more variable the lags, the harder it is to predict when a particular policy will take hold and what the state of the economy will be at that time. To advocates of passive policy, these lags are reason enough to avoid active discretionary policy. *Advocates of a passive approach argue that an active stabilization policy imposes troubling fluctuations in the price level and real GDP because it often takes hold only after market forces have already returned the economy to its potential output level.*

Talk in the media about "jump-starting" the economy reflects the active approach, which views the economy as a sputtering machine that can be fixed by an expert mechanic. The passive approach views the economy as more like a supertanker on automatic pilot. The policy question then becomes whether to trust that automatic pilot (the self-correcting tendencies of the economy) or to try to override the mechanism with active discretionary policies.

A Review of Policy Perspectives

The active and passive approaches embody different views about the stability and resiliency of the economy and the ability of Congress or the Fed to implement appropriate discretionary policies. So the two approaches disagree about the inherent stability of the private sector and the role of public policy in the economy. As we have seen, advocates of an active approach think that the natural adjustments of wages and prices can be excruciatingly slow, particularly when unemployment is high, as it was during the Great Depression. Prolonged high unemployment means that much output must be sacrificed, and the unemployed must suffer personal hardship during the slow adjustment period. If high unemployment lasts a long time, labor skills may grow rusty, and some may drop out of the labor force. Therefore, prolonged unemployment may cause the economy's potential GDP to fall, as suggested in the case study of hysteresis several chapters back.

Thus, active policy associates a high cost with the failure to pursue a discretionary policy. And, despite the lags involved, advocates of the active approach prefer action—through discretionary fiscal policy, discretionary monetary policy, or some combination of the two—to inaction. Passive policy advocates, on the other hand, believe that uncertain lags and ignorance about how the economy works prevent policy makers from accurately determining and effectively implementing the appropriate active policy. Therefore, the passive approach, rather than pursuing a misguided activist policy, relies more on the economy's natural ability to correct itself just using automatic stabilizers.

Differences between active and passive approaches emerged during the presidential campaign of 1992, when the economy was slow to recover from a recession, as discussed in the following case study.

Active Versus Passive Presidential Candidates

During the third quarter of 1990, after what at the time had become the longest peacetime economic expansion of the century, the U.S. economy slipped into a recession, triggered by Iraq's invasion of oil-rich Kuwait. Because of large federal deficits at the time, policy makers were reluctant to adopt discretionary fiscal policy to revive the economy. That task was left to monetary policy. The recession lasted only nine months, but the recovery was sluggish—so sluggish that unemployment continued to edge up in what was derisively called a "jobless recovery."

That sluggish recovery was the economic backdrop for the presidential election of 1992 between Republican President George H. W. Bush and

© Jeff Haynes/AFP/Getty Images

Read it to determine whether he was in favor of an active or passive approach to dealing with the sluggish recovery. Next compare President Clinton's last address to that of President George W. H. Bush. How activist did Clinton appear given economic conditions during his last year? What additional government programs and/or tax cuts was he proposing? Were these to stimulate the economy or for some other purpose? Also read President George W. Bush's State of the Union address for January of 2004. How does his approach compare to that of the first President Bush's approach?

Democratic challenger Bill Clinton. Because monetary policy did not seem to be providing enough kick, was additional fiscal stimulus needed? With the federal budget deficit in 1992 already approaching $300 billion, a record level to that point, would a higher deficit do more harm than good?

Bush's biggest political liabilities during the campaign were the sluggish recovery and ballooning federal deficits; these were Clinton's biggest political assets. Clinton argued that (1) Bush had not done enough to revive the economy; (2) Bush and his predecessor, Ronald Reagan, were responsible for the huge federal deficits; and (3) Bush could not be trusted because he broke his 1988 campaign pledge of "no new taxes" by signing a tax increase in 1990 to help cut federal deficits. Clinton promised to raise tax rates on the rich and cut them for the middle class. He also promised to create jobs through government spending that would "invest in America."

Bush tried to remind voters that, technically, the recession was over and the economy was on the mend. But that was a hard sell with unemployment averaging 7.6 percent during the six months leading up to the election. Bush blamed a Democratic Congress for blocking his recovery proposals, and he renewed his pledge of no new taxes. In fact, he promised to cut taxes by 1 percent, arguing that this would reallocate spending from government back to households.

Clinton saw a stronger role for government, and Bush saw a stronger role for the private sector. Clinton's approach was more *active* and Bush's more *passive*. In the end, the high unemployment rates during the campaign made people more willing to gamble on Clinton. Apparently, during troubled times, an active policy has more voter appeal than a passive one. Ironically, the economy at the time was stronger than conveyed by the media and by challenger Clinton ("It's the economy, stupid" became Clinton's rallying cry). Real GDP in 1992 grew 3.3 percent, which would turn out to be more than the 2.7 percent growth experienced during Clinton's first year in office. The unemployment rate began falling in October 1992, the month before the election (but the unemployment report came in early November—too late to help Bush). The unemployment rate then proceeded to fall *for the next eight years.* Bush's timing was awful; Clinton's, incredible.

George W. Bush was not about to make the same mistake as his father. Shortly after taking office in 2001, he proposed the first of three tax cuts to boost a lifeless economy. These cuts, along with a growth in government spending, offered the most fiscal stimulus in more than a decade. This expansionary fiscal policy combined with the Fed's interest rate cuts for the greatest stimulus of aggregate demand since World War II. Although the recession was over by the end of 2001, the unemployment rate continued to rise until its peak of 6.3 percent in June 2003. Jobs started coming back in earnest just before the 2004 presidential election.

Sources: David Wessel, "Wanted: Fiscal Stimulus Without Higher Taxes," *Wall Street Journal*, 5 October 1992; *Economic Report of the President*, February 2004; Bob Woodward, *The Agenda* (New York: Simon and Schuster, 1994); and the St. Louis Federal Reserve Bank's database at http://www.stls.frb.org/fred/index.html.

The Role of Expectations

The effectiveness of a particular government policy depends in part on what people expect. As we saw in an earlier chapter, the short-run aggregate supply curve is drawn for a given expected price level reflected in long-term wage contracts. If workers and firms expect continuing inflation, their wage agreements will reflect these inflationary expectations. One approach in macroeconomics, called **rational expectations,** argues that people form expectations on the basis of all available information, including information about the probable future actions of policy makers. Thus, aggregate supply depends on what sort of

RATIONAL EXPECTATIONS

A school of thought that argues people form expectations based on all available information, including the likely future actions of government policy makers macroeconomic course policy makers are expected to pursue. For example, if people were to observe policy makers using discretionary policy to stimulate aggregate demand every time output falls below potential, people would come to anticipate the effects of this policy on the price level and output. Robert Lucas, of the University of Chicago, won the 1995 Nobel Prize for his studies of rational expectations.

Monetary authorities are required to testify before Congress regularly, indicating the policy they plan to pursue. The Fed also announces, after each meeting of the FOMC, any changes in its interest rate targets and the likely direction of future changes. We will consider the role of expectations in the context of monetary policy by examining the relationship between policy pronouncements and equilibrium output. We could focus on fiscal policy, but monetary policy has been calling the shots for most of the last quarter century. Only with George W. Bush's tax cuts did fiscal policy make something of a comeback.

Monetary Policy and Expectations

Suppose the economy is producing potential output so unemployment is at its natural rate. At the beginning of the year, firms and employees must negotiate wage agreements. While negotiations are under way, the Fed announces that throughout the year, its monetary policy will aim at maintaining potential output while keeping the price level stable. This seems the appropriate policy because unemployment is already at the natural rate. Workers and firms understand that the Fed's stable price policy appears optimal under the circumstances because an expansionary monetary policy would lead only to higher inflation in the long run. Until the year is under way and monetary policy is actually implemented, however, the public cannot be sure what the Fed will do.

As long as wage increases do not exceed the growth in labor productivity, the Fed's plan of a stable price level should work. Alternatively, workers could try for higher wage growth, but that option would ultimately lead to inflation. Suppose workers and firms believe the Fed's pronouncements and agree on wage settlements based on a constant price level. If the Fed follows through as promised, the price level should turn out as expected. Output will remain at the economy's potential, and unemployment will remain at the natural rate. The situation is depicted in Exhibit 3. The short-run aggregate supply curve, $SRAS_{130}$, is based on wage contracts reflecting an expected price level of 130. If the Fed follows the announced course, aggregate demand will be AD and equilibrium will be at point *a*, where the price level is as expected and the economy is producing $12.0 trillion, the potential output.

Suppose, however, that after workers and firms have agreed on nominal wages—that is, after the short-run aggregate supply curve has been determined—public officials become dissatisfied with the unemployment rate. Perhaps election-year concerns with unemployment, a false alarm about a recession, or overestimating potential output convince the Fed to act. An expansionary monetary policy increases aggregate demand from $AD,$ the level anticipated by firms and employees, to AD'. This unexpected policy stimulates output and employment in the short run to equilibrium point *b*. Output increases to $12.2 trillion, and the price level increases to 135. This temporary boost in output and reduction in unemployment may last long enough to help public officials get reelected.

So the price level is now higher than workers expected, and their agreed-on wage buys less in real terms than workers bargained for. At their earliest opportunity, workers will negotiate higher wages. These higher wage agreements will eventually cause the short-run aggregate supply curve in Exhibit 3 to shift leftward, intersecting AD' at point *c,* the economy's potential output (to reduce clutter, the shifted short-run aggregate supply curve is not shown). So output once again returns to the economy's potential GDP, but in the process the price level rises to 142.

Short-Run Effects of an Unexpected Expansionary Monetary Policy

At point *a*, workers and firms expect a price level of 130; supply curve *SRAS*$_{130}$ reflect that expectation. If the Fed unexpectedly pursues an expansionary monetary policy, the aggregate demand curve becomes *AD'* rather than *AD*. Output in the short run (at point *b*) exceeds its potential, but in the long run costs increase, shifting *SRAS* leftward until the economy produces its potential output at point *c* (the resulting supply curve is not shown). The short-run effect of an unexpected monetary expansion is greater output, but the long-run effect is just a higher price level.

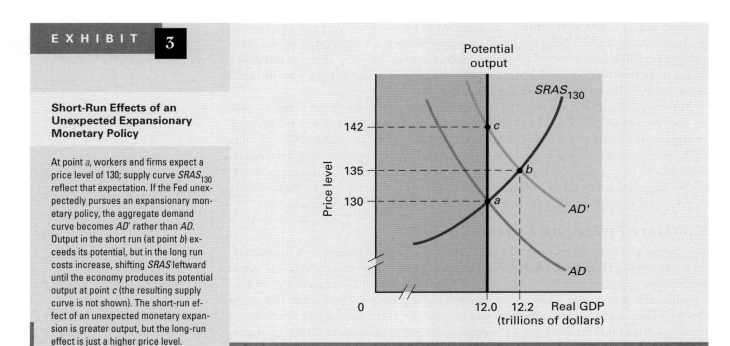

TIME-INCONSISTENCY PROBLEM

When policy makers have an incentive to announce one policy to influence expectations but then pursue a different policy once those expectations have been formed and acted on

Thus, the unexpected expansionary policy causes a short-run pop in output and employment. But in the long run, the increase in the aggregate demand curve yields only inflation. The **time-inconsistency problem** arises when policy makers have an incentive to announce one policy to shape expectations but then to pursue a different policy once those expectations have been formed and acted on.

Anticipating Monetary Policy

Workers may be fooled once by the Fed's actions, but they won't be fooled again. Suppose Fed policy makers become alarmed by the high inflation. The next time around, the Fed once again announces a monetary policy aimed at producing potential output while keeping the price level stable at 142. Based on their previous experience, however, workers and firms have learned that the Fed is willing to accept higher inflation in exchange for a temporary boost in output. Consequently, people take the Fed's announcement with a grain of salt. Workers, in particular, do not want to get caught again with their real wages down should the Fed implement a stimulative monetary policy. The bottom line is that workers and firms negotiate a high wage increase.

In effect, workers and firms are betting the Fed will pursue an expansionary policy regardless of pronouncement to the contrary. The short-run aggregate supply curve reflecting these higher wage agreements is depicted by *SRAS*$_{152}$ in Exhibit 4, where 152 is the expected price level. Note that *AD'* would result if the Fed followed its announced policy; that demand curve intersects the potential output line at point *c*, where the price level is 142. But *AD"* is the aggregate demand that workers and firms expect based on an expansionary monetary policy. They have agreed to wage settlements that will produce the economy's potential output if the Fed behaves as *expected*, not as *announced*. Thus, a price level of 152 is based on rational expectations. In effect, workers and firms expect the expansionary monetary policy to shift aggregate demand from *AD'* to *AD"*.

EXHIBIT 4

Short-Run Effects of the Fed Pursuing a More Expansionary Policy Than Announced

The Fed announces it plans to keep prices stable at 142. Workers and firms, however, do not believe this. Based on their experience, they expect monetary policy to be expansionary. The short-run aggregate supply curve, $SRAS_{152}$, reflects their expectations. If the Fed follows the announced stable-price policy, aggregate demand will be AD', and short-run output at point d will be less than the economy's potential output of $12.0 trillion. To keep the economy performing at its potential, the Fed must stimulate aggregate demand as much as workers and firms expect, but this is inflationary.

Monetary authorities must now decide whether to stick with their announced plan of holding the price level constant or to follow a more expansionary monetary policy. If they pursue the constant-price-level policy, aggregate demand will turn out to be AD' and short-run equilibrium will occur at point d. Short-run output will fall below the economy's potential, resulting in unemployment exceeding the natural rate. If monetary authorities want to keep output at its potential, they have only one alternative—to match public expectations. Monetary authorities must pursue an expansionary monetary policy, an action that reinforces public skepticism of policy announcements and increases inflation. This expansionary policy will result in an aggregate demand of AD'', leading to equilibrium at point e, where the price level is 152 and output equals the economy's potential.

Thus, workers and firms enter negotiations realizing that the Fed has an incentive to pursue an expansionary monetary policy. So workers and firms agree to higher wage increases, and the Fed follows with an expansionary policy, one that results in more inflation. Once workers and firms come to expect an expansionary monetary policy and the resulting inflation, such a policy does not spur even a temporary jump in output beyond the economy's potential. *Economists of the rational expectations school believe that if the economy is already producing its potential, an expansionary policy, if fully anticipated, has no effect on output or employment. Only unanticipated or incorrectly anticipated changes in policy can temporarily push output beyond its potential.*

Policy Credibility

If the economy was already producing its potential, an unexpected expansionary monetary policy would increase output and employment temporarily. The costs, however, include not only inflation in the long term but also a loss of credibility the next time around. Is there any way out of this? For the Fed to pursue a policy consistent with a constant price level, its announcements must somehow be *credible*, or believable. Worker and firms must believe that when the time comes to make a hard decision, the Fed will follow through as promised. Perhaps the Fed could offer some sort of guarantee to convince people it will stay the course—for example, the chairman of the Fed could promise to resign if the Fed does not pursue the announced policy. Ironically, policy makers are often more credible and therefore more effective if they have their discretion taken away. In this case, a hard-and-fast rule could be substituted for a policy maker's discretion. We will examine policy rules in the next section.

Consider the problems facing central banks in countries that have experienced hyperinflation. For an anti-inflation policy to succeed at the least possible cost in forgone output, the public must believe central bankers. How can central bankers in an economy ripped by hyperinflation establish credibility? Some economists believe that the most efficient anti-inflation policy is **cold turkey,** which is to announce and execute tough measures to stop inflation, such as halting the growth in the money supply. For example, in 1985, the annual rate of inflation in Bolivia was running at 20,000 percent when the new government announced a stern policy. The restrictive measures worked, and inflation was stopped within a month, with little loss in output. Around the world, credible anti-inflation policies have been successful.[1] Drastic measures sometimes involve costs. For example, some economists argue that the Fed's dramatic efforts to curb high U.S. inflation in the early 1980s triggered the worst recession since the Great Depression. Some say that the Fed's pronouncements were not credible and therefore resulted in a recession.

Much depends on the Fed's time horizon. If policy makers take the long view, they will not risk their long-run policy effectiveness for a temporary reduction in unemployment. If Fed officials realize that their credibility is hard to develop but easy to undermine, they will be reluctant to pursue policies that will ultimately just increase inflation.

Often Congress tries to pressure the Fed to stimulate the economy. By law, the Fed must "promote effectively the goals of maximum employment, stable prices, and moderate long-term interest rates." The law lets the Fed decide how best to do this. The Fed does not rely on congressional appropriations, so Congress cannot threaten to withhold funds. Thus, although the U.S. president appoints the Board of Governors, and the Senate must approve these appointments, the Fed operates somewhat independently. Consider the link around the world between central bank independence and price stability in the following case study.

COLD TURKEY

The announcement and execution of tough measures to reduce high inflation

Central Bank Independence and Price Stability

Some economists argue that the Fed would do better in the long run if it committed to the single goal of price stability. But to focus on price stability, a central bank should be insulated from political influence, because price stability may involve some painful remedies. When the Fed was established, several features insulated it from politics, such as the 14-year terms with staggered appointments of Board members. Also, the Fed has its own income source (interest on government securities and fees from bank services), so it does not rely on Congress for a budget.

Does central bank independence affect performance? When central banks for 17 advanced industrial countries were ranked from least

*Case*Study*

Public Policy

*e*Activity

With a currency board, a country fixes its exchange rate and backs its money supply entirely with foreign exchange, as Argentina did in the 1990s. Read articles, readings, and debates, and find more links at http://www.stern.nyu.edu/globalmacro/exchange_rates/currency_boards.html. What are the benefits of imposing the strict rules of currency boards? How does a currency board derive its own credibility?

---

1. For a discussion about how four hyperinflations in the 1920s ended, see Thomas Sargent, "The Ends of Four Big Inflations," in *Inflation: Causes and Consequences,* edited by Robert Hall (Chicago: University of Chicago Press, 1982), pp. 41–98.

independent to most independent, inflation turned out to be the lowest in countries with the most independent central banks and highest in countries with the least independent central banks. For example, the most independent central banks in the study were in Germany and Switzerland, and their inflation rates averaged about 3 percent per year during the 15-year span examined. The least independent banks were in Spain, New Zealand, Australia, and Italy, where inflation averaged 11.5 percent. The U.S. central bank is considered relatively independent, and U.S. inflation averaged 6.5 percent—between the most independent and least independent groups.

The trend around the world is toward greater central bank independence. For example, in 1990 the Central Bank of New Zealand adopted a monetary policy of inflation rate targeting, with price stability as the primary goal. Altogether, more than a dozen central banks adopted targets of low inflation and none has abandoned the goal. Chile, Colombia, and Argentina—developing countries that suffered hyperinflation—have legislated more central bank independence. The Maastricht agreement, which defined the framework for a single European currency, the euro, identified price stability as the main objective of the new European Central Bank. That bank announced a policy rule that it would not reduce its interest rate target as long as inflation exceeded 2.0 percent. In fact, the European Central Bank came under criticism recently for not cutting interest rate targets even though a recession loomed and unemployment topped 8 percent. And in March 2004 the Coalition Provisional Authority directed the Central Bank of Iraq to "maintain domestic price stability" as its primary objective.

Sources: Alberto Alesina and Lawrence Summers, "Central Bank Independence and Macroeconomic Performance: Some Comparative Evidence," *Journal of Money, Credit and Banking* 25 (May 1993): 151–162; Ben Bernanke, "A Perspective on Inflation Targeting: Why It Seems to Work," *Business Economics* 38 (July 2003): 7–15; "New Law Governing the Central Bank of Iraq," Coalition Provisional Authority, 7 March 2004; for links to more than 80 central bank Web sites, including all those discussed in this case study, go to http://www.bis.org/cbanks.htm.

Policy Rules Versus Discretion

Again, the active approach views the economy as unstable and in need of discretionary policy to eliminate excessive unemployment when it arises. The passive approach views the economy as stable enough that discretionary policy is not only unnecessary but may actually worsen economic fluctuations. In place of discretionary policy, the passive approach often calls for predetermined rules to guide the actions of policy makers. In the context of fiscal policy, these rules take the form of automatic stabilizers, such as unemployment insurance, a progressive income tax, and transfer payments, all of which are aimed at reducing economic fluctuations. In the case of monetary policy, passive rules might be the decisions to allow the money supply to grow at a predetermined rate, to maintain interest rates at some predetermined level, and to keep inflation below a certain rate. For example, as noted in the previous case study, the European Central Bank announced a rule that it would not lower its target interest rate as long as inflation exceeded 2.0 percent a year. Most central banks have committed to achieving low **inflation targets**, usually specifying a particular rate for the next year or two. Advocates of inflation targets say this would encourage workers, firms, and investors to plan on a low and stable inflation rate. Opponents of inflation targets worry that the Fed would pay less attention to economic growth.[2] In this section, we examine the arguments for policy rules versus discretion mostly in the context of monetary policy, because that's where the action has been in recent decades.

INFLATION TARGET

Central bankers commit not to exceed a certain inflation rate for the next year or two

---

2. Gregory Ip, "Fed Considers Targets for Inflation," *Wall Street Journal,* 20 October 2003.

Limitations on Discretion

The rationale for the passive approach rather than the use of active discretion arises from different views of how the economy works. One view holds that *the economy is so complex and economic aggregates interact in such obscure ways and with such varied lags that policy makers cannot comprehend what is going on well enough to pursue an active monetary or fiscal policy.* For example, if the Fed adopts a discretionary policy that is based on a misreading of the current economy or a poor understanding of the lag structure, the Fed may be lowering the target interest rate when a more appropriate course would be to leave the rate unchanged or even to raise it. As a case in point, during a meeting of the FOMC, one member lamented the difficulty of figuring out what was going on with the economy, noting, "As a lesson for the future, I'd like to remind us all that as recently as two meetings ago [in September] we couldn't see the strength that was unfolding in the second half [of the year]. . . . It wasn't in our forecast; it wasn't in the other forecasts; and it wasn't in the anecdotal reports. We were standing right on top of it and we couldn't see it. That's just an important lesson to remember going forward."[3]

A comparison of economic forecasters and weather forecasters may shed light on the position of those who advocate the passive approach. Suppose you are in charge of the heating and cooling system at a major shopping mall. You realize that weather forecasts are unreliable, particularly in the early spring, when days can be either warm or cold. Each day you must guess what the temperature will be and, based on that guess, decide whether to fire up the heater, turn on the air conditioner, or leave them both off. Because the mall is so large, you must start the system long before you know for sure what the weather will be. Once it's turned on, it can't be turned off until much later in the day.

Suppose you guess the day will be cold, so you turn on the heat. If the day turns out to be cold, your policy is correct and the mall temperature will be just right. But if the day turns out to be warm, the heater will make the mall unbearable. You would have been better off with nothing. In contrast, if you turn on the air conditioner expecting a warm day but the day turns out to be cold, the mall will be freezing. The lesson is that if you are unable to predict the weather, you should use neither heat nor air conditioning. Similarly, if policy makers cannot predict the course of the economy, they should not try to fine-tune monetary or fiscal policy. Complicating the prediction problem is the fact that policy officials are not sure about the lags involved with discretionary policy. The situation is comparable to your not knowing how long the system actually takes to come on once you flip the switch.

This analogy applies only if the cost of doing nothing—using neither heat nor air conditioning—is relatively low. In the early spring, you can assume that there is little risk of weather so cold that water pipes freeze or so hot that walls sweat. A similar assumption in the passive view is that the economy is fairly stable and periods of prolonged unemployment unlikely. In such an economy, the costs of *not* intervening are relatively low. In contrast, advocates of active policy believe that wide and prolonged swings in the economy (analogous to wide and prolonged swings in temperature) make doing nothing risky.

Rules and Rational Expectations

Another group of economists also advocates the passive approach, but not because they think the economy is too complex. Proponents of the rational expectations approach, discussed earlier, claim that people have a pretty good idea about how the economy works and

3. FOMC board member Thomas Melzer, in a transcript of the 22 December 1992 meeting of the Federal Open Market Committee, p. 14. Meeting transcripts are published after a five-year lag and are available at http://www.federalreserve.gov/fomc/transcripts/.

what to expect from government policy makers. For example, people know enough about the monetary policy pursued in the past to forecast, with reasonable accuracy, future policies and their effects on the economy. Some individual forecasts will be too high and some too low, but on average, forecasts will turn out to be about right. *To the extent that monetary policy is fully anticipated by workers and firms, it has no effect on the level of output; it affects only the price level.* Thus, only unexpected changes in policy can bring about short-run changes in output.

In the long run, changes in the money supply affect only inflation, not potential output, so followers of the rational expectations theory believe that the Fed should avoid discretionary monetary policy. Instead, the Fed should follow a predictable monetary rule. A monetary rule would reduce monetary surprises and keep output near the natural rate. *Whereas some economists favor rules over discretion because of ignorance about the lag structure of the economy, rational expectations theorists advocate a predictable rule to avoid surprises, which result in unnecessary departures from the potential output.*

Despite support by some economists for explicit rules rather than discretion, central bankers appear reluctant to follow hard-and-fast rules about the course of future policy. Discretion has been used more than explicit rules since the early 1980s, though policy has become more predictable because the Fed now announces the probable trend of future target rate changes. As former Fed Chairman Paul Volcker argued two decades ago:

> The appeal of a simple rule is obvious. It would simplify our job at the Federal Reserve, make monetary policy easy to understand, and facilitate monitoring of our performance. And if the rule worked, it would reduce uncertainty. . . . But unfortunately, I know of no rule that can be relied on with sufficient consistency in our complex and constantly evolving economy.[4]

This sentiment was echoed more recently by Fed Chairman Alan Greenspan:

> The Federal Reserve, should, some conclude, attempt to be more formal in its operations by tying its actions solely to the prescriptions of a formal policy rule. That any approach along these lines would lead to an improvement in economic performance, however, is highly doubtful.[5]

So far, we have looked at active stabilization policy, which focuses on shifts of the aggregate demand curve, and passive stabilization policy, which relies more on natural shifts of the short-run aggregate supply curve. In the final section, we focus on an additional model, the Phillips curve, to shed more light on the relationship between aggregate demand and aggregate supply in the short and long runs.

The Phillips Curve

At one time, policy makers thought they faced a long-run trade-off between inflation and unemployment. This view was suggested by the research of New Zealand economist A. W. Phillips, who in 1958 published an article that examined the historical relation between inflation and unemployment in the United Kingdom.[6] Based on about 100 years of evidence, his data traced an inverse relationship between the unemployment rate and the rate of

---

4. Former Federal Reserve Chairman Paul Volcker, before the Committee on Banking, Finance, and Urban Affairs, U.S. House of Representatives, August 1983.
5. Chairman Alan Greenspan, "Monetary Policy Under Uncertainty," Remarks at a symposium sponsored by the Federal Reserve Bank of Kansas City, Jackson Hole, Wyoming, 29 August 2003, which can be found at http://www.federalreserve.gov/boarddocs/speeches/2003/20030829/default.htm.
6. A. W. Phillips, "Relation Between Unemployment and the Rate of Change in Money Wage Rates in the United Kingdom, 1861–1957," *Economica* 25 (November 1958): 283–299.

PHILLIPS CURVE

A curve showing possible combinations of the inflation rate and the unemployment rate

change in nominal wages (serving as a measure of inflation). This relationship implied that the opportunity cost of reducing unemployment was higher inflation, and the opportunity cost of reducing inflation was higher unemployment.

The possible options with respect to unemployment and inflation are illustrated by the hypothetical **Phillips curve** in Exhibit 5. The unemployment rate is measured along the horizontal axis and the inflation rate along the vertical axis. Let's begin at point *a*, which depicts one possible combination of unemployment and inflation. Fiscal or monetary policy could be used to stimulate output and thereby reduce unemployment, moving the economy from point *a* to point *b*. Notice, however, that the reduction in unemployment comes at the cost of higher inflation. A reduction in unemployment with no change in inflation would be represented by point *c*. But as you can see, this alternative is not available.

Most policy makers of the 1960s came to believe that they faced a stable, long-run trade-off between unemployment and inflation. The Phillips curve was based on an era when inflation was low and the primary disturbances in the economy were shocks to aggregate demand. The effect of changes in aggregate demand can be traced as movements along a given short-run aggregate supply curve. If aggregate demand increases, the price level increases but unemployment falls. If aggregate demand decreases, the price level decreases but unemployment increases. With appropriate demand-management policies, policy makers believed they could choose any point along the Phillips curve.

The 1970s proved this view wrong in two ways. First, some of the biggest disturbances were adverse *supply* shocks, such as those created by oil embargoes and worldwide crop failures. These shocks shifted the aggregate supply curve leftward. A reduction in aggregate supply led to both higher inflation *and* higher unemployment. Stagflation was at odds with the Phillips curve. Second, economists learned that when short-run output exceeds potential, an expansionary gap opens. As this gap closes by a leftward shift of the short-run aggregate supply curve, greater inflation *and* higher unemployment result—again, an outcome inconsistent with a Phillips curve.

EXHIBIT 5

Hypothetical Phillips Curve

The Phillips curve shows an inverse relation between unemployment and inflation. Points *a* and *b* lie on the Phillips curve and represent alternative combinations of inflation and unemployment that are attainable as long as the curve itself does not shift. Points *c* and *d* are off the curve.

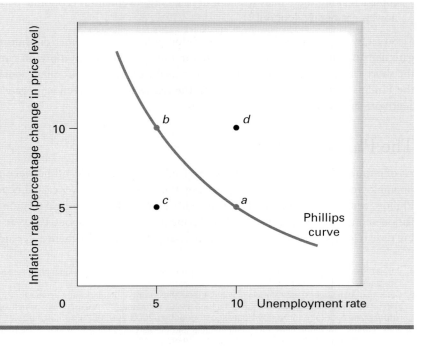

The combination of high inflation and high unemployment resulting from stagflation and the closing of expansionary gaps can be represented by an outcome such as point *d* in Exhibit 5. By the end of the 1970s, simultaneous increases in inflation and unemployment suggested either that the Phillips curve had shifted outward or that it no longer described economic reality. The situation called for a reexamination of the Phillips curve, which led to a distinction between the short-run Phillips curve and the long-run Phillips curve.

The Short-Run Phillips Curve

To discuss the underpinnings of the Phillips curve, we must return to the short-run aggregate supply curve. Suppose the price level this year is reflected by a price index of, say, 100, and that people expect prices to be about 3 percent higher next year. So the price level expected for next year is 103. Workers and firms therefore negotiate wage contracts based on an expected price level of 103. As the short-run aggregate supply curve in Exhibit 6(a) indicates, if *AD* is the aggregate demand curve and the price level is 103, as expected, output equals the economy's potential, shown here to be $12.0 trillion. Recall that when the economy produces its potential, unemployment is at the natural rate.

The short-run relationship between inflation and unemployment is presented in Exhibit 6(b) under the assumption that people expect inflation to be 3 percent. Unemployment is measured along the horizontal axis and inflation along the vertical axis. Panel (a) shows that when inflation is 3 percent, the economy produces its potential. Unemployment is at the natural rate, assumed in panel (b) to be 5 percent. The combination of 3 percent inflation and 5 percent unemployment is reflected by point *a* in panel (b), which corresponds to point *a* in panel (a).

What if aggregate demand turns out to be greater than expected, as indicated by *AD'*? In the short run, the greater demand results in point *b*, with a price level of 105 and output of $12.1 trillion. Because the price level exceeds the level reflected in wage contracts, inflation also exceeds expectations. Specifically, inflation turns out to be 5 percent, not 3 percent. Because output exceeds potential, unemployment falls below the natural rate to 4 percent. The new combination of unemployment and inflation is depicted by point *b* in panel (b), which corresponds to point *b* in panel (a).

What if aggregate demand turns out to be lower than expected, as indicated by *AD''*? In the short run, the lower demand results in point *c*, where the price level of 101 is less than expected and output of $11.9 trillion is below potential. Inflation of 1 percent is less than the expected 3 percent, and unemployment of 6 percent exceeds the natural rate. This combination is reflected by point *c* in panel (b), which corresponds to point *c* in panel (a).

Note that the short-run aggregate supply curve in panel (a) can be used to develop the inverse relationship between inflation and unemployment shown in panel (b), called a **short-run Phillips curve.** This curve is created by the intersection of alternative aggregate demand curves along a given short-run aggregate supply curve. *The short-run Phillips curve is based on labor contracts that reflect a given expected price level, which implies a given expected rate of inflation.* The short-run Phillips curve in panel (b) is based on an expected inflation of 3 percent. If inflation turns out as expected, unemployment equals the natural rate. If inflation exceeds expectations, unemployment in the short run falls below the natural rate. If inflation is less than expected, unemployment exceeds the natural rate.

The Long-Run Phillips Curve

If inflation exceeds expectations, output will exceed the economy's potential in the short run but not in the long run. Labor shortages and shrinking real wages will prompt higher

SHORT-RUN PHILLIPS CURVE

Based on an expected inflation rate, a curve that reflects an inverse relationship between the inflation rate and the unemployment rate

EXHIBIT 6

Aggregate Supply Curves and Phillips Curves in the Short Run and Long Run

If people expect a price level of 103, which is 3 percent higher than the current level, and if *AD* turns out to be the aggregate demand curve, then the price level will actually be 103 and output will be at its potential. Point *a* in both panels represents this situation. Unemployment will be the natural rate, assumed to be 5 percent in panel (b).

If aggregate demand turns out to be greater than expected (*AD'* instead of *AD*), the economy in the short run will be at point *b* in panel (a), where the price level of 105 will exceed expectations and output will exceed its potential. Higher inflation and lower unemployment are shown as point *b* in panel (b). If aggregate demand turns out to be less than expected (*AD"* instead of *AD*), short-run equilibrium will be at point *c* in panel (a), where the price level of 101 will be lower than expected and output will be short of potential. Lower inflation and higher unemployment are shown as point *c* in panel (b). In panel (b), points *a*, *b*, and *c* trace a short-run Phillips curve.

In the long run, the actual price level equals the expected price level. Output is at the potential level, $12.0 trillion, in panel (a). Unemployment is at the natural rate, 5 percent, in panel (b). Points *a*, *d*, and *e* depict long-run points in each panel. In panel (a) these points trace potential output, or long-run aggregate supply. In panel (b), these points trace a long-run Phillips curve.

(a) Short-run aggregate supply curve

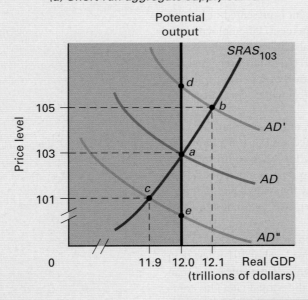

(b) Short-run and long-run Phillips curves

wage agreements. The short-run aggregate supply curve will shift leftward until it passes through point *d* in panel (a) of Exhibit 6, returning the economy to its potential output. The unexpectedly higher aggregate demand curve has no lasting effect on output or unemployment. Point *d* corresponds to a higher price level, and thus higher inflation. Closing the expansionary gap generates both higher unemployment and higher inflation, a combination depicted by point *d* in panel (b). Note that whereas points *a*, *b*, and *c* are on the same short-run Phillips curve, point *d* is not.

To trace the long-run effects of a lower-than-expected price level, let's return to point *c* in panel (a), where the actual price level is below the expected level, so output is below its potential. If workers and firms negotiate lower money wages (or if the growth in nominal wages trails inflation), the short-run aggregate supply curve will shift rightward until it passes through point *e*, where the economy returns once again to its potential output. Both inflation and unemployment will fall, as reflected by point *e* in panel (b).

Note that points *a, d,* and *e* in panel (a) depict long-run equilibrium points; the expected price level equals the actual price level. At those same points in panel (b), expected inflation equals actual inflation, so unemployment equals the natural rate. We can connect points *a, d,* and *e* in the right panel to form the **long-run Phillips curve.** *When workers and employers adjust fully to any unexpected change in aggregate demand, the long-run Phillips curve is a vertical line drawn at the economy's natural rate of unemployment.* As long as prices and wages are flexible, the rate of unemployment, in the long run, is independent of the rate of inflation. *Thus, according to proponents of this type of analysis, policy makers cannot, in the long run, choose between unemployment and inflation. They can choose only among alternative rates of inflation.*

The Natural Rate Hypothesis

The natural rate of unemployment occurs at the economy's potential output, discussed extensively already. An important idea that emerged from this reexamination of the Phillips curve is the **natural rate hypothesis,** which states that in the long run, the economy tends toward the natural rate of unemployment. This natural rate is largely independent of any *aggregate demand* stimulus provided by monetary or fiscal policy. Policy makers may be able to push output beyond its potential temporarily, but only if the policy surprises the public. The natural rate hypothesis implies that *the policy that results in low inflation is generally the optimal policy in the long run.*

Evidence of the Phillips Curve

What has been the actual relationship between unemployment and inflation in the United States? In Exhibit 7, each year since 1960 is represented by a point, with the unemployment

LONG-RUN PHILLIPS CURVE

A vertical line drawn at the economy's natural rate of unemployment that traces equilibrium points that can occur when workers and employers have the time to adjust fully to any unexpected change in aggregate demand

NATURAL RATE HYPOTHESIS

The natural rate of unemployment is largely independent of the stimulus provided by monetary or fiscal policy

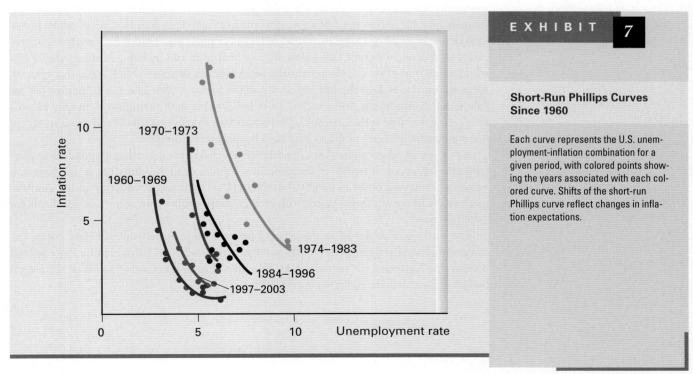

EXHIBIT 7

Short-Run Phillips Curves Since 1960

Each curve represents the U.S. unemployment-inflation combination for a given period, with colored points showing the years associated with each colored curve. Shifts of the short-run Phillips curve reflect changes in inflation expectations.

Source: Based on inflation and unemployment figures from the *Economic Report of the President*, February 2004, at http://www.gpoaccess.gov/eop/index.html.

rate measured along the horizontal axis and the inflation rate measured along the vertical axis. Superimposed on these points is a series of short-run Phillips curves showing patterns of unemployment and inflation during what turns out to be five distinct periods since 1960. Remember, each short-run Phillips curve is drawn for a given *expected inflation*. A change in inflationary expectations shifts the short-run Phillips curve.

The clearest trade-off between unemployment and inflation occurred between 1960 and 1969; the points for those years fit neatly along the curve. In the early part of the decade, inflation was low but unemployment relatively high; as the 1960s progressed, unemployment declined but actual inflation increased. Inflation during the decade averaged only 2.5 percent, and unemployment averaged 4.8 percent.

The short-run Phillips curve shifted to the right for the period from 1970 to 1973, when inflation and unemployment each climbed to an average of 5.2 percent. In 1974, sharp increases in oil prices and crop failures around the world reduced aggregate supply, which sparked another shift of the Phillips curve. During the 1974–1983 period, inflation averaged 8.2 percent and unemployment 7.5 percent. After two recessions in the early 1980s, the short-run Phillips curve shifted leftward, or inward. Average inflation for 1984–1996 fell to 3.7 percent and average unemployment fell to 6.1 percent. Finally, data for 1997 to 2003 suggest a new, lower short-run Phillips curve, with average inflation of only 2.3 percent and average unemployment of 4.9 percent. Thus, the Phillips curve shifted rightward between the 1960s and the early 1980s. Since then, the Fed has learned more about how to control inflation, thereby shifting the Phillips curve back to about where it started in the 1960s.

Conclusion

This chapter examined the implications of active and passive policy. The important question is whether the economy is essentially stable and self-correcting when it gets off track or essentially unstable and in need of active government intervention. Advocates of active policy believe that the Fed or Congress should reduce economic fluctuations by stimulating aggregate demand when output falls below its potential level and by dampening aggregate demand when output exceeds its potential level. Advocates of active policy argue that government attempts to reduce the ups and downs of the business cycle may not be perfect but are still better than nothing. Some activists also believe that high unemployment may be self-reinforcing, because some unemployed workers lose valuable job skills and grow to accept unemployment as a way of life, as may have happened in Europe.

Advocates of passive policy, on the other hand, believe that discretionary policy may contribute to the cyclical swings in the economy, leading to higher inflation in the long run with no permanent boost in potential output and no permanent reduction in the employment rate. This group favors passive rules for monetary policy and automatic stabilizers for fiscal policy.

The active-passive debate in this chapter has focused primarily on monetary policy because discretionary fiscal policy, until quite recently, had been hampered by large federal deficits that ballooned the national debt. The next chapter takes a closer look at the federal budget, federal deficits, and government debt.

SUMMARY

1. Advocates of active policy view the private sector—particularly fluctuations in investment—as the primary source of economic instability in the economy. Activists argue that achieving potential output through natural market forces can be slow and painful, so the Fed or Congress should stimulate aggregate demand when actual output falls below potential.

2. Advocates of passive policy argue that the economy has enough natural resiliency to return to potential output within a reasonable period if upset by some shock. They point to the variable and uncertain lags associated with discretionary policy as reason enough to steer clear of active intervention.

3. The effect of particular government policies on the economy depends on what people expect. The theory of rational expectations holds that people form expectations based on all available information including past behavior by public officials. According to the rational expectations school, government policies are mostly anticipated by the public, and therefore have less effect than unexpected policies.

4. The passive policy approach suggests that the government should follow clear and predictable policies and avoid discretionary intervention to stimulate or dampen aggregate demand over the business cycle. Passive policies are reflected in automatic fiscal stabilizers and in explicit monetary rules, such as maintaining a constant target interest rate or a steady growth in the money supply.

5. At one time, public officials thought they faced a stable trade-off between higher unemployment and higher inflation. More recent research suggests that if there is a trade-off, it exists only in the short run, not in the long run. Expansionary fiscal or monetary policies may stimulate output and employment in the short run. But if the economy is already at or near its potential output, these expansionary policies will, in the long run, result only in more inflation.

QUESTIONS FOR REVIEW

1. *(Active Versus Passive Policy)* Contrast the active policy view of the behavior of wages and prices during a contractionary gap to the passive policy view.

2. *(Active Policy)* Why do proponents of active policy recommend government intervention to close an expansionary gap?

3. *(Active Versus Passive Policy)* According to advocates of passive policy, what variable naturally adjusts in the labor market, shifting the short-run aggregate supply curve to restore unemployment to the natural rate? Why does the active policy approach assume that the short-run aggregate supply curve shifts leftward more easily and quickly than it shifts rightward?

4. *(Review of Policy Perspectives)* Why might an active policy approach be more politically popular than a passive approach, especially during a recession?

5. *(The Role of Expectations)* Some economists argue that only unanticipated increases in the money supply can affect real GDP. Explain why this may be the case.

6. *(Anticipating Monetary Policy)* In 1994, the Fed began announcing its interest rate targets immediately following each meeting of the FOMC. Prior to that, observers were left to draw inferences about Fed policy based on the results of that policy. What is the value of this greater openness?

7. *(Policy Credibility)* What is policy credibility and how is it relevant to the problem of reducing high inflation? How is credibility related to the time-inconsistency problem?

8. *(Case Study: Central Bank Independence and Price Stability)* One source of independence for the Fed is the length of term for members of the Board of Governors. In the chapter before last, we learned that the Fed is a "money machine." Does this suggest another source of Fed independence from Congress?

9. *(Rationale for Rules)* Some economists call for predetermined rules to guide the actions of government policy makers. What are two rationales that have been given for such rules?

10. *(Rational Expectations)* Suppose that people in an election year believe that public officials are going to pursue expansionary policies to enhance their reelection prospects. How could such expectations put pressure on officials to pursue expansionary policies even if they hadn't planned to?

11. *(Potential GNP)* Why is it hard for policy makers to decide if the economy is operating at its potential output level? Why is this uncertainty a problem?

12. *(Phillips Curves)* Describe the different policy trade-offs implied by the short-run Phillips curve and the long-run Phillips curve. What forces shift the long-run Phillips curve?

PROBLEMS AND EXERCISES

13. *(Active Versus Passive Policy)* Discuss the role each of the following plays in the debate between the active and passive approaches:

    a. The speed of adjustment of the nominal wage
    b. The speed of adjustment of expectations about inflation
    c. The existence of lags in policy creation and implementation
    d. Variability in the natural rate of unemployment over time

14. *(**C a s e Study**:* Active Versus Passive Presidential Candidates) What were the main differences between candidates Bush and Clinton in the 1992 presidential campaign? Illustrate their ideas using the aggregate supply and demand model.

15. *(Problems with Active Policy)* Use an *AD–AS* diagram to illustrate and explain the short-run and long-run effects on the economy of the following situation: Both the natural rate of unemployment and the actual rate of unemployment are 5 percent. However, the government believes that the natural rate of unemployment is 6 percent and that the economy is overheating. Therefore, it introduces a policy to reduce aggregate demand.

16. *(Policy Lags)* What lag in discretionary policy is described in each of the following statements? Why do long lags make discretionary policy less effective?

    a. The time from when the government determines that the economy is in recession until a tax cut is approved to reduce unemployment
    b. The time from when the money supply is increased until the resulting effect on the economy is felt
    c. The time from the start of a recession until the government identifies the existence and severity of the recession
    d. The time from when the Fed decides to reduce the money supply until the money supply actually declines

17. *(Rational Expectations)* Using an *AD–AS* diagram, illustrate the short-run effects on prices, output, and employment of an increase in the money supply that is correctly anticipated by the public. Assume that the economy is initially at potential output.

18. *(Long-Run Phillips Curve)* Suppose the economy is at point *d* on the long-run Phillips curve shown in Exhibit 6. If that inflation rate is unacceptably high, how can policy makers get the inflation rate down? Would rational expectations help or hinder their efforts?

E X P E R I E N T I A L   E X E R C I S E S

19. *(Active Versus Passive Policy)* The Federal Reserve Bank of Minneapolis's *The Region* at http://woodrow.mpls.frb. fed.us/pubs/region/int.cfm features an ongoing series of interviews with prominent U.S. policy makers. Choose a Fed governor or a regional Reserve Bank president and try to determine whether that person leans more toward an active or a passive policy view. What specific policy views does that person advocate?

20. (*C a s e* **S t u d y**: Central Bank Independence and Price Stability) The Bank for International Settlements maintains a list of links to central banks around the world at http://www.bis.org/cbanks.htm. Many of those banks maintain English-language Web pages. Choose one or two nations and explore their central bank Web pages. How much independence do those banks have? To what extent are their functions and goals similar to those of the U.S. Federal Reserve System?

21. *(Wall Street Journal)* A good source for the latest information regarding macroeconomic policy is the "Economy" column that appears in the daily *Wall Street Journal*. Take a look at today's issue and review the latest hot topics. Then, turn to the editorial pages, where the *Journal's* editorial board, contributors, and letter writers have their say.

H O M E W O R K   X P R E S S !   E X E R C I S E S

These exercises require access to McEachern Homework Xpress! If Homework Xpress! did not come with your book, visit **http://homeworkxpress.swlearning.com** *to purchase.*

1. In the diagram for this exercise, use aggregate demand and short–run and long–run aggregate supply curves to show an economy at a short–run equilibrium with a contractionary gap of $0.5 trillion when potential output is $10 trillion. Then illustrate how the gap would close in the long run if the economy is self-correcting.

2. In the diagram, use aggregate demand and short-run and long-run aggregate supply curves to show an economy at a short-run equilibrium with an expansionary gap of $0.5 trillion when potential output is $10 trillion. Then illustrate how the gap would close in the long run using an activist approach.

3. In the diagram, use aggregate demand and short-run and long-run aggregate supply curves to show an economy at a short-run equilibrium at its potential output of $10 trillion. Illustrate the short-run effects if the Fed unexpect-edly pursues an expansionary monetary policy. Then show the long-run effect.

4. In the diagram, use aggregate demand and long-run aggregate supply curves to show an economy at a long-run equilibrium at its potential output of $10 trillion and a price level of $P = 120$. Illustrate the effects if firms and workers do not believe that the Fed will maintain a price level of 120 but the Fed does not increase the money supply as expected.

5. In the diagram use aggregate demand and long-run aggregate supply curves to show an economy at a long-run equilibrium at its potential output of $10 trillion and a price level of $P = 120$. Illustrate the effects if firms and workers do not believe that the Fed will maintain a price level of 120 and the Fed increases the money supply as expected.

Federal Budgets and Public Policy

© AP Photo/APTN

How big is the federal budget, and where does the money go besides national defense? Why is the federal budget process such a tangled web? In what sense is the federal budgeting at odds with discretionary fiscal policy? How is a sluggish economy like an empty restaurant? Why has the federal budget been in deficit most years, and why did a surplus briefly materialize at the end of the 1990s? What is the federal debt, and who owes it to whom? Answers to these and other questions are examined in this chapter, which considers federal budgeting in theory and practice.

The word *budget* derives from the Old French word *bougette,* which means "little bag." The federal budget is now over $2,400,000,000,000—$2.4 trillion a year. That's big money! If this "little bag" held $100 notes, it would weigh more than 26,000 *tons!* These $100 notes could paper over a 14-lane highway stretching from northern Maine to southern California. This total could cover every U.S. family's mortgage and car payments for the year.

Government budgets have a tremendous impact on the economy. Government outlays at all levels amount to about 36 percent relative to GDP. Our focus in this chapter will be the federal budget, beginning with the budget process. We then look at the source of federal deficits and how they briefly became surpluses. We also examine the national debt and its impact on the economy. Topics discussed include:

- The budget process
- Rationale for deficit spending
- Impact of deficits

- Crowding out and crowding in
- The short-lived budget surplus
- The burden of the federal debt

The Federal Budget Process

The **federal budget** is a plan of outlays and revenues for a specified period, usually a year. Federal *outlays* include both government purchases and transfer payments. Exhibit 1 shows federal outlays by major category since 1960. As you can see, the share of outlays going to national defense dropped from over half in 1960 to only 20 percent in 2004. Social Security's share has grown every decade. Medicare, medical care for the elderly, was introduced in the 1965 and has also grown every year. In fact, Social Security and Medicare, programs aimed primarily at the elderly, now combine for 33 percent of federal outlays. For the last two decades, welfare spending, which consists of cash and in-kind transfer payments, has remained at about 15 percent of federal outlays. And, thanks to record low interest rates, 7 percent of the budget in 2004 paid interest on the national debt, down from 15 percent as recently as 1996. So 48 percent, or nearly half the federal budget in 2004, redistributed income (Social Security, Medicare, and welfare); 20 percent went toward defense; 7 percent serviced the national debt; and the remaining 25 percent paid for everything else in the federal budget—from environmental protection to federal prisons and aid to education.

FEDERAL BUDGET

A plan for federal government outlays and revenues for a specified period, usually a year

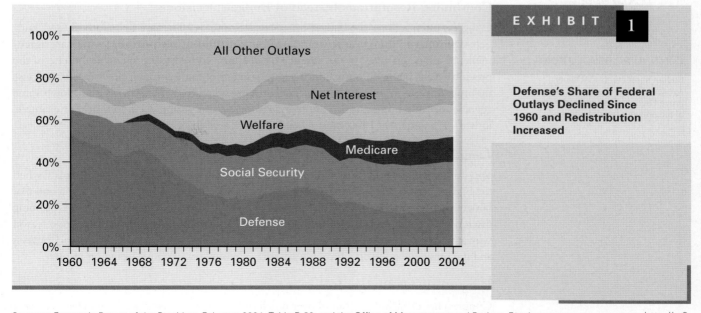

EXHIBIT 1

Defense's Share of Federal Outlays Declined Since 1960 and Redistribution Increased

Sources: *Economic Report of the President*, February 2004, Table B-80; and the Office of Management and Budget. For the most recent year, go to http://w3.access.gpo.gov/eop/.

BUDGET RESOLUTION

A congressional agreement about
total outlays, spending by major
category, and expected revenues;
it guides spending and revenue decisions by the many congressional
committees and subcommittees

CONTINUING RESOLUTIONS

Budget agreements that allow
agencies, in the absence of an approved budget, to spend at the rate
of the previous year's budget

The Presidential and Congressional Roles

The president's budget proposal begins to take shape a year before it is submitted to Congress, with each agency preparing a budget request. In late January or early February, the presidents submits to Congress *The Budget of the United States Government,* a big pile of books detailing spending and revenue proposals for the upcoming fiscal year, which begins October 1. At this stage, the president's budget is little more than detailed suggestions for congressional consideration. About the same time, the president's Council of Economic Advisors sends Congress the *Economic Report of the President,* which offers the president's take on the economy.

Budget committees in both the House and the Senate rework the president's budget until they agree on total outlays, spending by major category, and expected revenues. This agreement, called a **budget resolution,** establishes a framework to guide spending and revenue decisions and to guide the many congressional committees and subcommittees that authorize spending. The budget cycle is supposed to end before October 1, the start of the new fiscal year. Before that date, Congress should have approved detailed plans for outlays along with revenue projections. Thus, the federal budget has a congressional gestation period of about nine months—though, as noted, the president's budget usually begins taking shape a year before it's submitted to Congress.

The size and composition of the budget and the difference between outlays and revenues measure the budget's fiscal impact on the economy. *When outlays exceed revenues, the budget is in deficit. A deficit stimulates aggregate demand in the short run but reduces national saving, which in the long run could impede economic growth. Alternatively, when revenues exceed outlays, the federal budget is in surplus. A surplus dampens aggregate demand in the short run but enhances domestic saving, which in the long run could promote economic growth.*

Problems with the Federal Budget Process

The federal budget process sounds good on paper, but it does not work that well in practice. There are several problems.

Continuing Resolutions Instead of Budget Decisions

Congress often ignores the budget timetable. Because deadlines are frequently missed, budgets typically run from year to year based on **continuing resolutions,** which are agreements to allow agencies, in the absence of an approved budget, to spend at the rate of the previous year's budget. Poorly conceived programs continue through sheer inertia; successful programs cannot expand. On occasion, the president must temporarily shut down some agencies because not even the continuing resolution can be approved on time. For example, in late 1995 and early 1996, most federal offices closed for 27 days.

Lengthy Budget Process

You can imagine the difficulty of using the budget as a tool of discretionary fiscal policy when the budget process takes so long. Given that the average recession lasts less than a year and that budget preparations begin more than a year and a half before the budget takes effect, planning discretionary fiscal measures to smooth economic fluctuations is difficult. That's one reason why attempts to stimulate an ailing economy often seem so halfhearted; by the time Congress and the president agree on a fiscal remedy, the economy has often recovered on its own.

Uncontrollable Budget Items

Congress has only limited control over much of the budget. *About three-fourths of federal budget outlays are determined by existing laws.* For example, once Congress establishes eligibility criteria,

entitlement programs, such as Social Security and Medicare, take on lives of their own, with each annual appropriation simply reflecting the amount required to support the expected number of entitled beneficiaries. Congress has no say in such appropriations unless it chooses to change benefits or eligibility criteria. Most entitlement programs have such politically powerful constituencies that Congress is reluctant to mess with the structure.

No Separate Capital Budget

Congress approves a single budget that mixes together *capital* expenditures, like new federal buildings or aircraft carriers, with *operating* expenditures, like employee payrolls or military meals. Budgets for businesses and for state and local governments usually distinguish between a *capital budget* and an *operating budget.* The federal government, by mixing the two, offers a fuzzier picture of what's going on.

Overly Detailed Budget

The federal budget is divided into thousands of accounts and subaccounts, which is why it fills volumes. To the extent that the budget is a way of making political payoffs, such micromanagement allows elected officials to reward friends and punish enemies with great precision. For example, a recent budget included $176,000 for the Reindeer Herders Association in Alaska, $400,000 for the Southside Sportsman Club in New York, and $5 million for an insect-rearing facility in Mississippi. By budgeting in such detail, Congress may lose sight of the big picture. When economic conditions change or when the demand for certain public goods shifts, the federal government cannot easily reallocate funds. Detailed budgeting is not only time consuming, it reduces the flexibility of discretionary fiscal policy and is subject to political abuse.

Possible Budget Reforms

Some reforms might improve the budget process. First, the annual budget could become a two-year budget, or *biennial budget.* As it is, Congress spends nearly all of the year working on the budget. The executive branch is always dealing with three budgets: administering an approved budget, defending a proposed budget before congressional committees, and preparing the next budget for submission to Congress. With a two-year budget, Congress would not be continually involved with budget deliberations, and cabinet members could focus more on running their agencies (many states have adopted two-year budgets). A two-year budget, however, would require longer-term economic forecasts and would be less useful than a one-year budget as a tool of discretionary fiscal policy.

Another possible reform would be to simplify the budget document by concentrating only on major groupings and eliminating line items. Each agency head would receive a total budget, along with the discretion to allocate that budget in a manner consistent with the perceived demands for agency services. The drawback is that agency heads may have different priorities than those of elected representatives.

A final reform is to sort federal spending into a capital budget and an operating budget. A *capital budget* would include spending on physical capital such as buildings, highways, computers, military equipment, and other public infrastructure. An *operating budget* would include spending on the payroll, building maintenance, computer paper, and other ongoing expenses.

The Fiscal Impact of the Federal Budget

When government outlays—that is, government purchases plus transfer payments—exceed government revenue, the result is a *budget deficit,* a flow measure already introduced.

Although the federal budget was in surplus from 1998 to 2001, before that it had been in deficit every year but one since 1960 and in all but eight years since 1930. Since 2001 the budget has slipped back in the red. To place deficits in perspective, let's first examine the economic rationale for deficit financing.

The Rationale for Deficits

Deficit financing has been justified for outlays that increase the economy's productivity—capital outlays for investments such as highways, waterways, and dams. The cost of these capital projects should be borne in part by future taxpayers, who will also benefit from these investments. Thus, there is some justification for government borrowing to finance capital projects and for future taxpayers helping to pay for them. State and local governments issue debt to fund capital projects, such as schools. But, as noted already, the federal government does not budget capital projects separately, so there is no explicit link between capital budgets and federal deficits.

Before the Great Depression, federal deficits occurred only during wartime. Because wars involved much personal hardship, public officials were understandably reluctant to tax citizens much more to finance war-related spending. Deficits incurred during wars were largely self-correcting, however, because government spending dropped after a war, but the tax revenue did not.

The Depression led John Maynard Keynes to argue that public spending should offset any drop in private spending. As you know by now, Keynes said a federal budget deficit would stimulate aggregate demand. As a result of the Depression, automatic stabilizers were also introduced, which increased public outlays during recessions and decreased them during expansions. Deficits increase during recessions because tax revenues decline while spending programs such as unemployment benefits and welfare increase. For example, during the 1990–1991 recession, corporate tax revenue fell 10 percent but welfare spending jumped 25 percent. An economic expansion is the other side of the coin. As the economy picks up, so do personal income and corporate profits, boosting federal revenue. Unemployment compensation and welfare spending decline. Thus, federal deficits usually fall during the recovery stage of the business cycle.

Budget Philosophies and Deficits

ANNUALLY BALANCED BUDGET

Budget philosophy prior to the Great Depression; aimed at matching annual revenues with outlays, except during times of war

CYCLICALLY BALANCED BUDGET

A budget philosophy calling for budget deficits during recessions to be financed by budget surpluses during expansions

FUNCTIONAL FINANCE

A budget philosophy using fiscal policy to achieve the economy's potential GDP, rather than balancing budgets either annually or over the business cycle

Several budget philosophies have emerged over the years. Prior to the Great Depression, fiscal policy focused on maintaining an **annually balanced budget,** except during wartime. Because tax revenues rise during expansions and fall during recessions, an annually balanced budget means that spending increases during expansions and declines during recessions. But such a pattern magnifies fluctuations in the business cycle, overheating the economy during expansions and increasing unemployment during recessions.

A second budget philosophy calls for a **cyclically balanced budget,** meaning that budget deficits during recessions are covered by budget surpluses during expansions. Fiscal policy dampens swings in the business cycle without increasing the national debt. Nearly all states have established "rainy day" funds to build up budget surpluses during the good times for use during bad times.

A third budget philosophy is **functional finance,** which says that policy makers should be concerned less with balancing the budget annually, or even over the business cycle, and more with ensuring that the economy produces its potential output. If the budgets needed to keep the economy producing its potential involve chronic deficits, so be it. Since the Great Depression, budgets in this country have seldom balanced. *Although budget deficits have been larger during recessions than during expansions, the federal budget has been in deficit in all but a dozen years since 1930.*

Federal Deficits Since the Birth of the Nation

Between 1789, when the U.S. Constitution was adopted, and 1930, the first full year of the Great Depression, the federal budget was in deficit 33 percent of the years, primarily during wartime. After a war, government spending dropped more than government revenue. Thus, deficits arising during wars were largely self-correcting once the wars ended.

Since the onset of the Great Depression, however, federal budgets have been in deficit 85 percent of the time. Exhibit 2 shows federal deficits and surpluses as a percentage of GDP since 1934. Unmistakable are the huge deficits during World War II, which dwarf deficits in other years. Turning now to the last quarter century, we see that large tax cuts during the 1980s along with higher defense spending contributed to modern deficits. Supply-side economists argued that tax cuts would stimulate enough economic activity to keep tax revenues from falling. Unspecified spending cuts were supposed to erase a projected deficit, but Congress never made the promised cuts. Moreover, overly optimistic revenue projections—so-called rosy scenarios—were built into the budget. For example, the budget projected that real GDP would grow by 5.2 percent in 1982, but instead the economy fell into a recession, which cut output 2.0 percent that year. The recession triggered automatic stabilizers, reducing revenues and increasing spending still more. The deficit in 1982 amounted to 4 percent of GDP—at the time one of the largest peacetime deficits ever.

President Reagan's budget strategy during the 1980s called for defense increases but no new taxes and no cuts in Social Security. In short, the president and Congress cut tax rates but not expenditures. *Relative to GDP, federal revenues declined but federal spending increased.* The deficit climbed to 6 percent of GDP in 1983. As the economy improved during the 1990s,

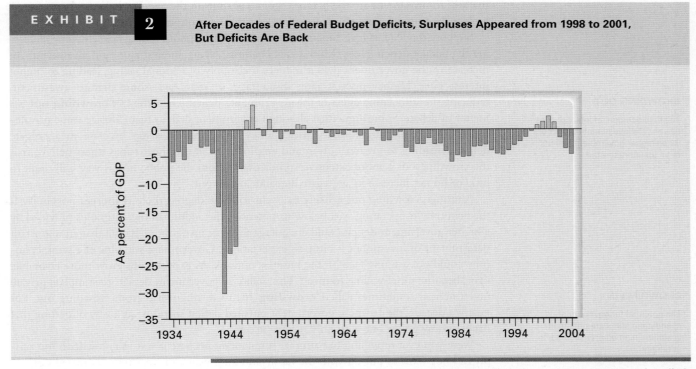

EXHIBIT 2 **After Decades of Federal Budget Deficits, Surpluses Appeared from 1998 to 2001, But Deficits Are Back**

Sources: *Economic Report of the President*, February 2004. Deficit for 2004 is a projection from the president and Congress. For the latest data, go to http://w3. access.gpo.gov/eop/.

the deficit decreased and then disappeared, turning into a surplus by 1998. But a recession in 2001, tax cuts, and higher federal spending turned surpluses into deficits. A weak recovery and the war against terrorism worsened the deficits in 2002, 2003, and 2004. By 2004 the deficit exceeded 4 percent of GDP, a level not seen since 1992.

That's a short history of federal deficits. Now let's consider why the federal budget has been in deficit so long.

Why Have Deficits Persisted?

As we have seen, huge deficits in the 1980s and more recently came from a combination of tax cuts and spending increases. But why has the budget been in deficit for all but 12 years since 1934? The most obvious answer is that, unlike budgeters in 49 states, federal officials are not required to balance the budget. But why deficits? One widely accepted model of the public sector assumes that elected officials try to maximize their political support, including votes and campaign contributions. Voters like public spending programs but hate paying taxes, so spending programs win support and taxes lose it. Because of this asymmetry, candidates try to maximize their chances of getting elected and reelected by offering budgets long on benefits but short on taxes. Moreover, members of Congress push their favorite programs with little concern about the overall budget. For example, a senator from Mississippi was able to include $1.5 billion in a recent budget for an amphibious assault ship to be built in his hometown of Pascagoula. The Navy never even asked for the ship.

Deficits, Surpluses, Crowding Out, and Crowding In

What effect do federal deficits and surpluses have on interest rates? Recall that interest rates affect investment, a critical component of economic growth. What's more, year-to-year fluctuations in investment are the primary source of shifts in the aggregate demand curve. Let's look at the impact of government deficits and surpluses on investment.

Suppose the federal government increases spending without raising taxes, thereby increasing the budget deficit. How will this affect national saving, interest rates, and investment? An increase in the government deficit reduces the supply of national saving, leading to higher interest rates. Higher interest rates discourage, or *crowd out,* some private investment, reducing the stimulating effect of the government's deficit. The extent of **crowding out** is a matter of debate. Some argue that although government deficits may displace some private-sector borrowing, discretionary fiscal policy will result in a net increase in aggregate demand, leading to greater output and employment in the short run. Others believe that the crowding out is more extensive, so borrowing from the public in this way will result in little or no net increase in aggregate demand and output.

Although crowding out is likely to occur to some degree, there is another possibility. If the economy is operating well below its potential, the additional fiscal stimulus provided by a higher government deficit could encourage firms to invest more. Recall that an important determinant of investment is business expectations. Government stimulus of a weak economy could put a sunny face on the business outlook. As expectations grow more favorable, firms become more willing to invest. This ability of government deficits to stimulate private investment is sometimes called **crowding in,** to distinguish it from crowding out. For nearly a decade, the Japanese government pursued deficit spending as a way of getting that flat economy going, but with only recent success.

Were you ever unwilling to patronize a restaurant because it was too crowded? You simply did not want to put up with the hassle and long wait and were thus "crowded out." As that baseball-player-turned-philosopher Yogi Berra said, "No one goes there nowadays. It's

CROWDING OUT

The displacement of interest-sensitive private investment that occurs when higher government deficits drive up interest rates

CROWDING IN

The potential for government spending to stimulate private investment in an otherwise dead economy too crowded." Similarly, large government deficits may "crowd out" some investors by driving up interest rates. On the other hand, did you ever pass up an unfamiliar restaurant because the place seemed dead—it had no customers? Perhaps you wondered why? If you had seen just a few customers, you might have stopped in—you might have been willing to "crowd in." Similarly, businesses may be reluctant to invest in a seemingly lifeless economy. The economic stimulus resulting from deficit spending could encourage some investors to "crowd in."

The Twin Deficits

To finance the huge deficits of the 1980s, the U.S. Treasury had to sell a lot of bonds, pushing up market interest rates. With U.S. interest rates relatively high, foreigners were more willing to buy dollar-denominated bonds. To buy them, foreigners had to exchange their currencies for dollars. This greater demand for dollars caused the dollar to appreciate relative to foreign currencies during the first half of the 1980s. The rising value of the dollar made foreign goods cheaper in the United States and U.S. goods more expensive abroad. Thus, U.S. imports increased and U.S. exports decreased, so the foreign trade deficit increased.

Higher trade deficits meant that foreigners were accumulating dollars. With these dollars, they purchased U.S. assets, including U.S. government bonds, and thereby helped fund federal deficits. The increase in funds from abroad is both good news and bad news for the U.S. economy. The supply of foreign saving increased investment spending in the United States over what would have occurred in the absence of these funds. Ask people what they think of foreign investment in their town; they will likely say it's great. But foreign funds to some extent simply offsets a decline in U.S. saving rates. Such a pattern could pose problems in the long run. The United States has surrendered a certain amount of control over its economy to foreign investors. And the return on foreign investments in the United States flows abroad. For example, a growing share of the federal government's debt is now owed to foreigners, as will be discussed later in this chapter.

The Short-Lived Budget Surplus

Exhibit 3 summarizes the federal budget since 1970, with outlays relative to GDP shown as the red line and revenues relative to GDP as the blue line. When outlays exceeded revenues, the federal budget was in deficit, measured each year by the vertical distance between the blue and red lines. The pink shading shows the annual deficit as a percent of GDP. In the early 1990s, outlays started to decline relative to GDP, while revenues increased. This shrank the deficit and, by 1998, created a surplus, as indicated by the blue shading. Specifically, the deficit in 1990, which amounted to 3.8 percent relative to GDP, became a surplus by 1998, which lasted until 2001. What turned a hefty deficit into a surplus, and why has the surplus turned back into a deficit?

Tax Increases

With concern about the deficit growing, Congress and President George H. W. Bush agreed in 1990 to a package of spending cuts and tax increases aimed at trimming budget deficits. Ironically, those tax increases not only may have cost President Bush reelection in 1992 (because it violated his 1988 election promise of "no new taxes"), but they also began the groundwork for erasing the budget deficit, for which President Clinton was able to take credit. For his part, President Clinton increased taxes on high-income households in 1993, boosting the top marginal tax rate from 31 percent to 40 percent. The economy also enjoyed a vigorous recovery during the 1990s, fueled by rising worker productivity, growing consumer spending, globalization of markets, and the strongest stock market in history. The combined effects of higher taxes on the rich and a strengthening economy raised federal revenue from 17.8 percent of GDP in 1990 to 20.3 percent in 2000.

Slower Growth in Federal Outlays

Because of spending discipline imposed by the 1990 legislation, growth in federal outlays slowed compared with those in the 1980s. What's more, the collapse of the Soviet Union reduced U.S. military commitments abroad. Between 1990 and 2000, military personnel dropped one-third and defense spending dropped 30 percent in real terms. An additional impetus for slower spending growth came from Republicans, who attained congressional majority in 1994. Between 1994 and 2000, domestic spending grew little in real terms. Another beneficial development was the drop in interest rates, which fell to their lowest level in 30 years, saving billions in interest charges on the national debt. In short, federal outlays dropped from 21.6 percent relative to GDP in 1990 to 17.9 percent in 2000.

A Reversal of Fortune in 2001

Thanks to the tax-rate increases and the strong economy, revenues gushed into Washington, growing an average of 8.4 percent per year between 1993 and 2000. Meanwhile, federal outlays remained in check, growing only 3.5 percent per year. By 2000, that combination created a federal budget surplus of $236 billion, quite a turnaround from a deficit that had topped $290 billion only eight years earlier. But in 2001 unemployment increased, the stock market sank, and terrorists crashed jets and spread anthrax. All this slowed federal revenues and accelerated federal spending. To counter the recession and cope with terrorism, Congress and the president cut taxes and increased federal spending. As a result, the federal bud-

EXHIBIT 3   **During the 1990s, Federal Outlays Declined Relative to GDP and Revenues Increased, Turning Deficits into Surpluses, But Not for Long**

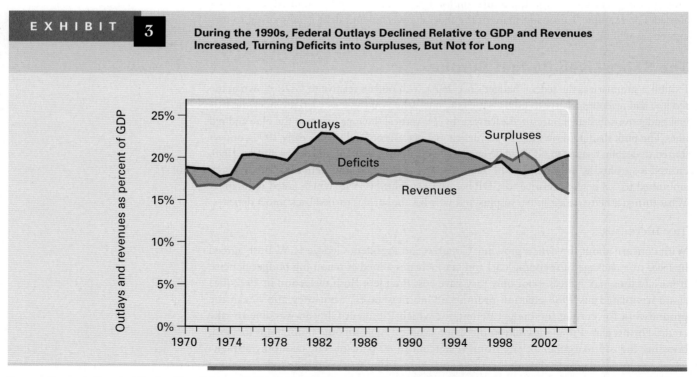

Sources: *Economic Report of the President*, February, Tables B-1 and B-78; and the Office of Management and Budget. For the latest data, go to http://w3.access.gpo.gov/eop/.

get surplus of 2001 turned into a deficit exceeding $400 billion by 2004. The era of federal budget surpluses was short-lived. Worse yet, two major federal programs spelled trouble for the budget in the long run, as discussed in the following case study.

Reforming Social Security and Medicare

Social Security is a federal redistribution program established during the Great Depression that collects payroll taxes from current workers and their employers to pay pensions to current retirees. About 40 million retirees averaged $880 per month from the program in 2004. For the first 50 years of the program, whenever tax revenues exceeded the cost of the program, Congress raised benefits, expanded eligibility, or spent the surplus. Medicare, a program established in 1965 to provide short-term medical care for the elderly, is also funded by a payroll tax. Social Security and Medicare are credited with helping reduce poverty among the elderly from more than 30 percent in 1960 to only 10 percent by 2002—a rate as low or lower than that of any other age group.

© Frank Siteman/Index Stock Imagery

C a s e S t u d y

Public Policy

*e*Activity
The National Academy of Social Insurance is a nonpartisan research organization formed to study Social Security and Medicare. Go to its Web site, at http://www.nasi.org, to access its publications. There you will find Briefs and Fact Sheets about the current status of and issues related to both Medicare and Social Security. How much progress has been made in implementing President George W. Bush's proposals to partially privatize Social Security? Do you think the prescription-drug coverage for those on Medicare will be viable?

In the early 1980s, policy makers recognized the tremendous impact that baby boomers would have on such a pay-as-you-go program. When 77 million baby boomers begin retiring in 2011, Social Security costs and, especially, Medicare costs are set to explode. Reforms adopted in 1983 raised the payroll tax rate, expanded the tax base by the rate of inflation, gradually increased the retirement age from 65 to 67, increased the penalty for early retirement, and offered incentives to delay retirement. These reforms ensured that revenues would exceed costs at least while baby boomers remain in the workforce. To help pay for baby boomer retirements, the 1983 reform began accumulating the resulting surplus in trust funds.

But here's the problem: Both programs are projected to go broke. Growth in beneficiaries and higher medical costs per beneficiary will bankrupt the Medicare Trust Fund by 2019. The problem is that the American population is aging and technological developments are boosting healthcare costs even as they extend lives. The Social Security Trust Fund is projected to go broke later—estimates range from 2042 to 2052. Things only get worse after that as retirees live longer and fewer new workers enter the labor force. In 1940, there were 42 workers per retiree. Today, there are 3.2 workers per retiree. By 2033 only two workers will support each retiree. Based on current benefits and payroll taxes, spending on the Social Security and Medicare, now about 7 percent of GDP, will claim 12 percent by 2030, and exceed 20 percent in 2078. The huge sucking sound will be Social Security and Medicare deficits.

What to do, what to do? These programs have been called the "third rail" of American politics: electrically charged and untouchable. Interest groups are so well organized and senior voter participation is so high that any legislator who proposes limiting benefits risks instant electrocution. Possible reforms include tax increases, delaying retirement, using a more accurate index to calculate the annual cost-of-living increase in benefits (meaning smaller annual increases), and raising the eligibility age. Federal Reserve Chairman Alan Greenspan urged Congress in 2004 to cut the growth of these programs. Lawmakers predictably distanced themselves from Greenspan's suggestions.

Recent changes in these programs will cost more money. President George W. Bush pushed through a new prescription-drug benefit expected to cost some $500 billion over the next 10 years. He also proposed offering young workers the chance to invest a small portion of their Social Security taxes in the stock market or some other asset, which could yield a better return than Social Security. Diverting payroll taxes to private investment could ultimately contribute to a long-term solution, but the near-term cost would be to reduce revenue supporting this pay-as-you-go plan.

In summary, Social Security and Medicare helped reduce poverty among the elderly, but the program will grow more costly as the elderly population increases and as the flow of young people into the workforce slows. Something has to give if these programs are to be available when you retire.

Sources: Laurence Kotlikoff and Scott Burns, *The Coming Generational Storm* (MIT Press, 2004); John McKinnon, "Medicare's Health to Fail, Rapidly," *Wall Street Journal*, 24 March 2004; "Status of the Social Security and Medicare Programs: A Summary of the 2004 Annual Report," Social Security and Medicare Boards of Trustees, at http://www.ssa.gov/OACT/TRSUM/trsummary.html.

The Relative Size of the Public Sector in the United States

So far, we have focused on the federal budget, but a fuller picture includes state and local governments as well. For added context, we can look at government budgets over time compared to the experience in other major economies. Exhibit 4 shows government outlays at all levels relative to GDP in 10 industrial economies in 1994 and in 2004. Government outlays in the United States in 2004 were 35.7 percent relative to GDP, the smallest share in the group. This amount is down slightly from 36.5 percent in 1994, a year when only Japan among the 10 industrial economies had a smaller government. Between 1994 and 2004, government outlays relative to GDP shrank in 9 of the 10 industrial economies; the average dropped from 46.5 percent to 43.1 percent. Why the drop? The demise of the Soviet Union in the early 1990s reduced defense spending in major economies, and the failure of the socialist experiment shifted sentiment more toward private markets, thus diminishing the role of government. The exception to the trend toward less government spending was Japan, where real estate and stock market prices crashed in 1990, crushing consumer confidence and hobbling the economy for more than a decade.

Let's now turn our attention to an unintended consequence of federal deficits—a sizable federal debt.

The National Debt

Federal deficits add up. It took 39 presidents, six wars, the Great Depression, and more than 200 years for the federal debt to reach $1 trillion, as it did in 1981. It took only 3 presidents and another 15 years for that debt to triple in real terms, as it did by 1996. Ironically, the biggest growth in debt occurred under President Reagan, who ran on a promise to balance the budget.

NATIONAL DEBT

The net accumulation of federal budget deficits

The federal deficit is a flow variable measuring the amount by which outlays exceed revenues in a particular year. The federal debt, or the **national debt,** is a stock variable measuring the net accumulation of past deficits, the amount owed by the federal government. This section puts the national debt in perspective by looking at (1) changes over time, (2) U.S. debt levels compared with those in other countries, (3) interest on the debt, and (4) the prospect of paying off the debt. Note that the national debt ignores the projected liabilities of Social Security, Medicare, or other federal retirement programs. If these liabilities were included, the national debt would triple.

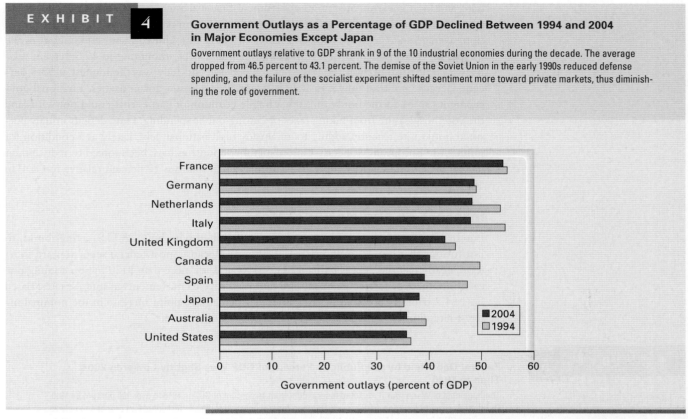

EXHIBIT 4

Government Outlays as a Percentage of GDP Declined Between 1994 and 2004 in Major Economies Except Japan

Government outlays relative to GDP shrank in 9 of the 10 industrial economies during the decade. The average dropped from 46.5 percent to 43.1 percent. The demise of the Soviet Union in the early 1990s reduced defense spending, and the failure of the socialist experiment shifted sentiment more toward private markets, thus diminishing the role of government.

Sources: *OECD Economic Outlook*, Vol. 75 (June 2004), Annex Table 28. For the latest data, go to http://www.oecd.org/home/, click on "Statistics," then find *OECD Economic Outlook*.

In talking about the national debt, we should distinguish between the gross debt and debt held by the public. The *gross debt* includes U.S. Treasury securities purchased by various federal agencies. Because the federal government owes this debt to itself, analysts often focus instead on *debt held by the public,* which includes debt held by households, firms, banks (including Federal Reserve Banks), and foreign entities. As of 2004, the gross federal debt stood at about $7.2 trillion, and the debt held by the public stood at $4.2 trillion.

One way to measure debt over time is relative to the economy's production and income, or GDP (just as a bank might compare the size of a mortgage to a borrower's income). Exhibit 5 shows federal debt held by the public relative to GDP. The cost of World War II ballooned the debt to over 100 percent relative to GDP by 1946. By 1980, it had dropped to 26 percent. But high deficits in the 1980s and early 1990s nearly doubled debt to 49 percent by 1993. Favorable developments already discussed cut debt to 33 percent relative to GDP by 2001. A recession, a stock market crash, tax cuts, and higher government spending created deficits that boosted debt to 38 percent relative to GDP by 2004, about where it was in 1940, after the Great Depression but before World War II.

International Perspective on Public Debt

Exhibit 6 compares the net government debt in the United States relative to GDP with those of nine other industrial countries. *Net debt* includes outstanding liabilities of federal, state, and local governments minus government financial assets, such as loans to students and farmers, securities, cash on hand, and foreign exchange on reserve. Net debt for the ten nations averaged 47.6 percent in 2004 relative to GDP. The United States ranks about in the middle for industrial countries, with net government debt amounting to 49.5 percent relative to GDP. Australia was the lowest at 2.4 percent, and Italy was the highest at 93.5 percent. Because political power in Italy is fragmented across a dozen parties, a national government can be formed only through a fragile coalition of parties that could not withstand the voter displeasure from hiking taxes or cutting public spending. Thus, deficits in Italy persisted until quite recently, adding to an already high national debt. Lately, as a condition for joining the European Monetary Union, member countries have been forced to reduce their federal deficits. Italy, for example, went from a deficit that was 12 percent relative to GDP in 1990 to only 3 percent by 2004.

Interest on the National Debt

Purchasers of federal securities range from individuals who buy $25 U.S. savings bonds to institutions that buy $1 million Treasury bonds. Because most federal securities are short term, nearly half the debt is refinanced every year. With more than $150 billion coming due each month, debt service payments are quite sensitive to movements in interest rates. Based on a $4.2 trillion debt held by the public, a 1 percentage point increase in the nominal interest rate ultimately increases costs by about $42 billion a year.

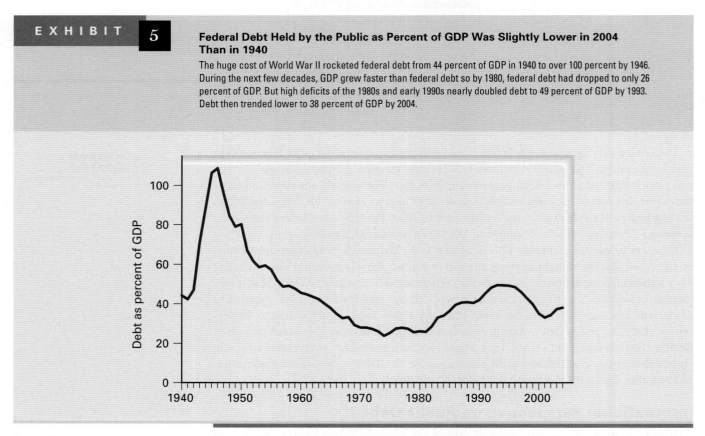

| EXHIBIT | 5 | **Federal Debt Held by the Public as Percent of GDP Was Slightly Lower in 2004 Than in 1940** |

The huge cost of World War II rocketed federal debt from 44 percent of GDP in 1940 to over 100 percent by 1946. During the next few decades, GDP grew faster than federal debt so by 1980, federal debt had dropped to only 26 percent of GDP. But high deficits of the 1980s and early 1990s nearly doubled debt to 49 percent of GDP by 1993. Debt then trended lower to 38 percent of GDP by 2004.

Source: Fiscal year figures from the *Economic Report of the President*, February 2004. Figures for 2004 are projections. For the latest data go to http://w3.access.gpo.gov/eop/.

Exhibit 7 shows interest on the federal debt held by the public as a percentage of federal outlays since 1960. After remaining relatively constant for two decades, interest climbed in the 1980s because growing deficits added to the debt and because of higher interest rates. Interest payments peaked at 15.4 percent of outlays in 1996, then began falling first because of budget surpluses and later because of falling interest rates. Thanks to the lowest interest rates in more than four decades, interest payments slipped to only 6.7 percent of the federal budget by 2004, the lowest since 1972. Interest's share of federal outlays is likely to climb as interest rates rise from their historic lows.

Who Bears the Burden of the Debt?

Deficit spending is a way of billing future taxpayers for current spending. The national debt raises moral questions about the right of one generation of taxpayers to bequeath to the next generation the burden of its borrowing. To what extent do deficits and debt shift the burden to future generations? Let's examine two arguments about the burden of the federal debt.

We Owe It to Ourselves

It is often argued that the debt is not a burden to future generations because, although future generations must service the debt, those same generations receive the payments. It's true that if U.S. citizens forgo present consumption to buy bonds, they or their heirs will be repaid, so debt service payments will stay in the country. Thus, future generations will both service the debt and receive the payments. In that sense, the debt is not a burden on future generations. It's all in the family, so to speak.

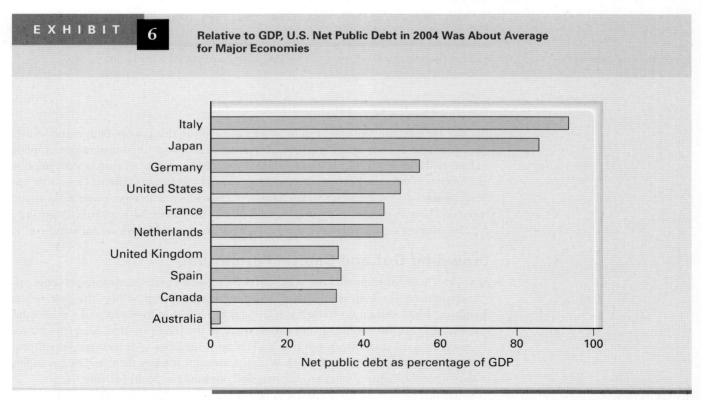

EXHIBIT 6 Relative to GDP, U.S. Net Public Debt in 2004 Was About Average for Major Economies

Source: *OECD Economic Outlook*, 75 (June 2004), Annex Table 35. Figures are projections for net debt at all levels of government in 2004. For the latest data, go to http://www.oecd.org/home/, click on "Statistics," then find *OECD Economic Outlook*.

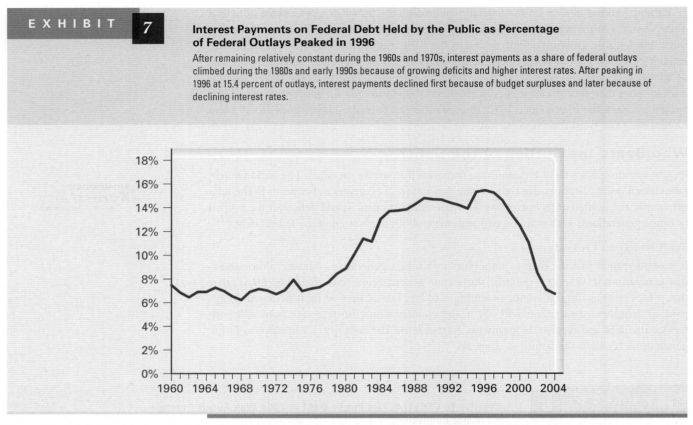

EXHIBIT	7

Interest Payments on Federal Debt Held by the Public as Percentage of Federal Outlays Peaked in 1996

After remaining relatively constant during the 1960s and 1970s, interest payments as a share of federal outlays climbed during the 1980s and early 1990s because of growing deficits and higher interest rates. After peaking in 1996 at 15.4 percent of outlays, interest payments declined first because of budget surpluses and later because of declining interest rates.

Source: *Economic Report of the President*, February 2004. Figure for 2004 is a projection. For the latest figures, go to http://w3.access.gpo.gov/eop.

Foreign Ownership of Debt

But the "we owe it to ourselves" argument does not apply to that portion of the national debt owed to foreigners. Foreigners who buy U.S. government bonds forgo present consumption and are paid back in the future. Foreign buyers reduce the amount of current consumption that Americans must sacrifice to finance a deficit. *A reliance on foreigners, however, increases the burden of the debt on future generations because future debt service payments no longer remain in the country.* Foreigners held 45 percent of all privately held debt by the end of 2003, up from 21 percent a decade earlier. So the burden of the debt on future generations of Americans has increased.

Crowding Out and Capital Formation

As we have seen, government borrowing can drive up interest rates, crowding out some private investment. The long-run effect of deficit spending depends on how the government spends the borrowed funds. If the funds are invested in better highways and a more educated workforce, this could enhance productivity in the long run. If, however, borrowed dollars go toward current expenditures such as farm subsidies or federal retirement programs, less capital formation will result. With less investment today, there will be less capital in the future, thus hurting labor productivity and our future standard of living.

Ironically, despite the large federal deficits during the last few decades, public investments in roads, bridges, and airports—so-called *public capital*—declined, perhaps because a growing share of the federal budget goes toward income redistribution, especially for the elderly. In 1970, the value of the nation's public infrastructure was about 50 percent relative to GDP; this figure has since declined to about 40 percent. Some argue that declining investment in the public infrastructure serves as a drag on productivity growth. For example, the failure to invest sufficiently in airport safety and efficiency and in the air traffic control system has led to congested airports and flight delays, a problem compounded by the terrorist attacks.

Therefore, government deficits of one generation can affect the standard of living of the next. Note again that our current measure of the national debt does not capture all burdens passed on to future generations. As mentioned earlier, if the unfunded liabilities of government retirement programs, especially Medicare, were included, this would triple the national debt. A model that considers some intergenerational issues of public budgeting is discussed in the following case study.

An Intergenerational View of Deficits and Debt

Harvard economist Robert Barro has developed a model that assumes parents are concerned about the welfare of their children who, in turn, are concerned about the welfare of *their* children, and so on for generations. Thus, the welfare of all generations is tied together. According to Barro, parents can reduce the burden of federal debt on future generations. Here's his argument. When the government runs deficits, it keeps current taxes lower than they would otherwise be, but taxes in the future must increase to service the higher debt. If there is no regard for the welfare of future generations, then the older people become, the more attractive debt becomes relative to current taxes. Older people can enjoy the benefits of public spending now but will not live long enough to help finance the debt through higher taxes or lower public benefits.

© Photodisc/Getty Images

Public Policy

*e*Activity
Visit the Third Millennium at http://www.thirdmil.org/, an organization of nonpartisan Generation Xers proposing solutions to long-term problems facing the United States. The site also provides links to other organizations concerned with like topics.

But parents can undo the harm that deficit financing imposes on their children by consuming less now and saving more. As governments substitute deficits for taxes, parents will consume less and save more to increase gifts and bequests to their children. If greater saving offsets federal deficits, deficit spending will not increase aggregate demand because the decline in consumption will negate the fiscal stimulus provided by deficits. According to Barro, this intergenerational transfer offsets the future burden of higher debt and neutralizes the effect of deficit spending on aggregate demand, output, and employment.

The large budget deficits caused in part by tax cuts and spending increases of the 1980s would seem to provide a natural experiment for testing Barro's theory. The evidence fails to support his theory because the large federal deficits coincided with lower, not higher, saving rates. Yet defenders of Barro's view say that maybe the saving rate was low because people were optimistic about future economic growth, an optimism reflected by the strong performance of stock markets. Or maybe the saving rate was low because people believed tax cuts would result not in higher future taxes but in lower government spending, as President Reagan promised.

But there are other reasons to question Barro's theory. First, those with no children may be less concerned about the welfare of future generations. Second, his theory assumes that people are well informed about federal spending and tax policies and about the future consequences of current policies. Most people, however, seem to know little about such matters. One survey found that few adults polled had any idea about the size of the federal deficit. In the poll, respondents were offered a range of choices, but only 1 in 10 said correctly that the deficit that year was between $100 billion and $400 billion.

Sources: Robert J. Barro, "The Ricardian Approach to Budget Deficits," *Journal of Economic Perspectives* 3 (Spring 1989); Jay Mathews, "How High Is the Deficit, the Dow? Most in Survey Didn't Know," *Hartford Courant*, 19 October 1995; and John McKinnon, "House Narrowly Passes Budget Plan," *Wall Street Journal*, 26 March 2004.

WALL STREET JOURNAL
Reading It Right

What's the relevance of the following statement from the Wall Street Journal*: "In a recent Oval Office meeting with his top aides, President Bush sought to sum up the administration's new economic philosophy by saying, 'We are both supply-siders and Keynesian.'"*

Conclusion

John Maynard Keynes introduced the idea that federal deficit spending is an appropriate fiscal policy when private aggregate demand is insufficient to achieve potential output. The federal budget has not been the same since. Beginning in 1960, the federal budget was in deficit every year but one until 1998. And beginning in the early 1980s, huge federal deficits dominated the fiscal policy debate, tripling the national debt in real terms and putting discretionary fiscal policy on hold. But after peaking at $290 billion in 1992, the deficit disappeared briefly because of higher tax rates on high-income households, lower growth in federal outlays, and a rip-roaring economy fueled by faster labor productivity growth and a dazzling stock market. The softening economy of 2001 and the terrorist attacks put discretionary fiscal policy back in the picture. A recession and weak recovery, tax cuts, and spending increases swelled the federal deficit by 2004 to rival those of the 1980s and early 1990s.

SUMMARY

1. The federal budget process suffers from a variety of problems, including overlapping committee jurisdictions, lengthy budget deliberations, continuing resolutions, budgeting in too much detail, failure to distinguish between capital costs and operating costs, and a lack of control over most of the budget. Suggested improvements include instituting a biennial budget, budgeting in less detail, and distinguishing between a capital budget and an operating budget.

2. Deficits usually increase during wars and severe recessions, but deficits remained high during the economic expansion of the 1980s. Those deficits arose from a combination of tax cuts during the early 1980s and growth in federal spending. As a percentage of GDP, the federal debt held by the public nearly doubled between 1980 and 1992.

3. To the extent that deficits crowd out private capital formation, this decline in private investment reduces the economy's ability to grow. This is one cost of deficit spending. Foreign holdings of debt also impose a burden on future generations because debt service payments go to foreigners. Thus, the deficits of one generation can reduce the standard of living of the next.

4. After peaking at $290 billion in 1992, the federal deficit turned into a surplus by 1998 because of higher tax rates, reduced outlays especially for defense, declining interest rates, and a strengthening economy fueled by growing labor productivity.

5. The recession of 2001 and terrorist attacks prompted tax cuts to "get the economy moving again." The weak recovery plus the tax cuts and federal spending increases all contributed to a growing federal deficit, which topped $400 billion in 2004. Interest payments on the national debt will likely increase as interest rates rise from their 40-year low.

QUESTIONS FOR REVIEW

1. *(The Federal Budget Process)* The federal budget passed by Congress and signed by the president shows the relationship between *budgeted* expenditures and *projected* revenues. Why does the budget require a forecast of the economy? Under what circumstances would actual government spending and tax revenue fail to match the budget as approved?

2. *(The Federal Budget Process)* In what sense is the executive branch of the U.S. government always dealing with three budgets?

3. *(The Budget Process)* In terms of the policy lags described in the previous chapter, discuss the following issues associated with the budget process:
   a. Continuing resolutions
   b. Uncontrollable budget items
   c. Overly detailed budget

4. *(Budget Philosophies)* Explain the differences among an annually balanced budget, a cyclically balanced budget, and functional finance. How does each affect economic fluctuations?

5. *(Budget Philosophies)* One alternative to balancing the budget annually or cyclically is to produce a government budget that would be balanced if the economy were at potential output. Given the cyclical nature of government tax revenues and spending, how would the resulting budget deficit or surplus vary over the business cycle?

6. *(Budget Philosophies)* The functional finance approach to budget deficits would set the federal budget to promote an economy operating at potential output. What problems would you expect if the country were to employ this kind of budgetary philosophy?

7. *(Crowding Out)* Is it possible for U.S. federal budget deficits to crowd out investment spending in other countries? How could German or British investment be hurt by large U.S. budget deficits?

8. *(Crowding Out)* How might federal deficits crowd out private domestic investment? How could this crowding out affect future living standards?

9. *(Interest on the Debt)* Why did interest payments on the national debt fall from 15.4 percent of the federal budget in 1996 to 6.7 percent in 2004. Why is this percentage expected to increase in the future?

10. *(Burden of the Debt)* Suppose that budget deficits are financed to a considerable extent by foreigners. How does this create a potential burden on future generations of Americans?

11. *(The Twin Deficits)* How is the U.S. budget deficit related to the trade deficit?

12. *(The Miraculous Budget Surplus)* Why did the federal budget go from a huge deficit in 1992 to a surplus in 1998? Explain the factors that contributed to the turnaround.

13. *(Case Study:* Reforming Social Security and Medicare) Why are the Social Security and Medicare programs headed for trouble? When will the trouble begin? What possible solutions have been proposed?

14. *(Crowding Out and Capital Formation)* In earlier chapters, we've seen that the government can increase GDP in the short run by running a budget deficit. What are some long-term effects of deficit spending?

15. *(Case Study: An Intergenerational View of Deficits and Debt)* Explain why Robert Barro argues that if parents are concerned about the future welfare of their children, the effects of deficit spending on the economy will be neutralized.

16. *(The Private Sector)* Look at Exhibit 4. How have government outlays as a percent of GDP changed in the industrial countries depicted between 1994 and 2004? Why has Japan been an exception to the trend?

PROBLEMS AND EXERCISES

17. *(The National Debt)* Try the following exercises to better understand how the national debt is related to the government's budget deficit.

    a. Assume that the gross national debt initially is equal to $3 trillion and the federal government then runs a deficit of $300 billion:
       i. What is the new level of gross national debt?
       ii. If 100 percent of the deficit is financed by the sale of securities to federal agencies, what happens to the amount of debt held by the public? What happens to the level of gross debt?
       iii. If GDP increased by 5 percent in the same year that the deficit is run, what happens to gross debt as a percentage of GDP? What happens to the level of debt held by the public as a percentage of GDP?

    b. Now suppose that the gross national debt initially is equal to $2.5 trillion and the federal government then runs a deficit of $100 billion:
       i. What is the new level of gross national debt?
       ii. If 100 percent of this deficit is financed by the sale of securities to the public, what happens to the level of debt held by the public? What happens to the level of gross debt?
       iii. If GDP increases by 6 percent in the same year as the deficit is run, what happens to gross debt as a percentage of GDP? What happens to the level of debt held by the public as a percentage of GDP?

EXPERIENTIAL EXERCISES

18. *(Federal Budget Deficits)* Try your hand at balancing the federal budget by trying the National Budget Simulation at UC Berkeley's Center for Community Economic Research at http://www.budgetsim.org/nbs/.

    a. Develop a budget and see what happens. Were you successful in balancing the budget? If not, how much of a deficit or surplus did you end up with? What does this exercise tell you about the process of creating a balanced budget?
    b. Reexamine the budget cuts or increases you made. What problems would such changes pose for a politician facing reelection?
    c. This budget simulator allows you only to change spending and tax expenditures over a one-year period. What problems does this pose to finding a realistic economic solution for balancing the budget?

19. (*Case*Study: Reforming Social Security and Medicare) Visit Econ-Debates Online at http://www.swlearning.com/economics/policy_debates/econ_debates_productivity.html. Review the materials on "Will Social Security survive into the 21st century?" What are some of the macroeconomic implications of Social Security reform?

20. *(Wall Street Journal)* You learned that the government pays billions of dollars in interest each year to finance the national debt. Those debt payments are sensitive to changes in the nominal interest rate. Check the "Treasury Issues" table in the Money and Investing section of today's *Wall Street Journal*. Have interest rates on Treasury bonds and bills been increasing or decreasing lately? What are the implications of interest rate changes for bond prices and for debt finance?

21. *(National Debt)* Go to the Web site for the Bureau of the Public Debt at http://www.publicdebt.treas.gov/. The site contains information on the current public debt of the United States, holders of the debt, and historical information. What is the current value of the national debt? How has this changed over the past year?

International Finance

© Brand X Pictures/Getty Images

H ow can the United States export more than any other country yet still have the world's highest trade deficit? Are high trade deficits a worry? What's a "strong dollar"? Why do U.S. consumers favor a strong dollar while U.S. producers have mixed feelings? How is the foreign exchange market like an all-night diner? Why do some nations try to influence the value of their currency? And what's the big idea with the European currency, the euro? Answers to these and other questions are explored in this chapter, which focuses on international finance.

A U.S. firm shopping for a German printing press will be quoted a price in euros. Suppose that machine costs 1 million euros. How many dollars is that? The cost in dollars will depend on the exchange rate. When trade takes place across international borders, two currencies are usually involved. Supporting the flows of goods and services are flows of currencies that connect all international transactions.

The *exchange rate* between two currencies—the price of one in terms of the other—is the means by which the price of a good produced in one country translates into the price paid by a buyer in another country. The willingness of buyers and sellers to strike deals therefore depends on the exchange rate. In this chapter we examine the international transactions that determine the relative value of one currency in terms of another. Topics discussed include:

- Balance of payments
- Trade deficits and surpluses
- Foreign exchange markets
- Purchasing power parity
- Flexible exchange rates
- Fixed exchange rates
- International monetary system
- Bretton Woods agreement
- Managed float

Balance of Payments

A country's gross domestic product measures the economy's output and income during a given period. To account for dealings abroad, countries also keep track of international transactions. A country's *balance of payments*, as introduced in Chapter 3, summarizes all economic transactions during a given period between residents of that country and residents of other countries. *Residents* include people, firms, and governments.

International Economic Transactions

The balance of payments measures economic transactions between countries, whether they involve goods and services, real and financial assets, or transfer payments. As a measure reflecting the volume of transactions during a particular period, usually a year, the balance of payments measures a *flow*. Some transactions reflected in the balance of payments do not involve actual payments. For example, if *Time* magazine ships a new printing press to its Australian subsidiary, no payment is involved, yet an economic transaction involving another country occurs. Similarly, if CARE sends food to Africa or the Pentagon provides military assistance to the Middle East, these transactions must be captured in the balance of payments. So remember, although we speak of the *balance of payments*, a more descriptive phrase would be the *balance of economic transactions*.

Balance-of-payments accounts are maintained according to the principles of *double-entry bookkeeping*, in which entries on one side of the ledger are called *credits*, and entries on the other side are called *debits*. As you will see, the balance of payments consists of several individual accounts. A deficit in one or more accounts must be offset by a surplus in the other accounts. Because total credits must equal total debits, there is a *balance* of payments. During a given period, such as a year, the inflow of receipts from the rest of the world, which are entered as credits, equals the outflow of payments to the rest of the world, which are entered as debits. The next few sections describe major accounts in the balance of payments.

The Merchandise Trade Balance

The *merchandise trade balance*, a term introduced in Chapter 3, equals the value of merchandise exports minus the value of merchandise imports. The merchandise account reflects trade in goods, or tangible products (stuff you can drop on your toe), like French wine and U.S. computers, and is often referred to simply as the *trade balance*. The value of U.S. merchandise exports is a credit in the U.S. balance-of-payments account because U.S. residents get *paid* for the exported goods. The value of U.S. merchandise imports is a debit in the balance-of-payments account because U.S. residents *pay* foreigners for imported goods.

If merchandise exports exceed merchandise imports, the trade balance is in *surplus*. If merchandise imports exceed merchandise exports, the trade balance is in *deficit*. The merchandise trade balance, which is reported monthly, influences foreign exchange markets, the stock market, and other financial markets. The trade balance depends on a variety of factors, including the relative strength and competitiveness of the domestic economy compared with other economies and the relative value of the domestic currency compared with other currencies.

U.S. merchandise trade since 1960 is depicted in Exhibit 1, where exports, the blue line, and imports, the red line, are expressed as a percentage of GDP. During the 1960s, exports exceeded imports, and the resulting trade surpluses are shaded blue. Since 1976, imports have exceeded exports, and the resulting trade deficits are shaded pink. Trade deficits as a percentage of GDP increased from 1.3 percent in 1991 to 5.0 percent in 2003, when the deficit reached a record $549 billion. Notice in Exhibit 1 that exports as a percentage of GDP dipped during the 1980s, when the value of the dollar rose sharply relative to other currencies (more on this later). Despite that dip, merchandise exports since 1980 have remained in the range of about 5 percent to 8 percent of GDP with no upward trend. But merchandise imports have trended up from about 9 percent in 1980 to about 12 percent in 2003.

The United States imports more goods from each of the world's major economies than it exports to them. Exhibit 2 shows the U.S. merchandise trade deficit with major economies or regions of the world in 2003. The $124 billion trade deficit with China was by far the largest, nearly double that with Japan or Latin America. The Chinese bought $28 billion in U.S. goods in 2003, but Americans bought $152 billion in Chinese goods, including $93 billion in nonfood consumer goods. So China sells America five times more than it buys from America. Chances are, most of the utensils in your kitchen were made in China; most toys are also Chinese made. The United States does not have a trade surplus with any major economy in the world and is the world's biggest importer.

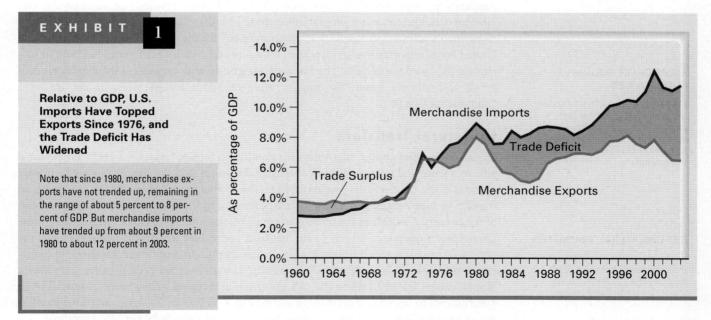

EXHIBIT 1

Relative to GDP, U.S. Imports Have Topped Exports Since 1976, and the Trade Deficit Has Widened

Note that since 1980, merchandise exports have not trended up, remaining in the range of about 5 percent to 8 percent of GDP. But merchandise imports have trended up from about 9 percent in 1980 to about 12 percent in 2003.

Source: Developed from merchandise trade data from the *Economic Report of the President*, February 2004, and *Survey of Current Business*, May 2004, U.S. Department of Commerce. For the latest data, go to http://www.bea.doc.gov/.

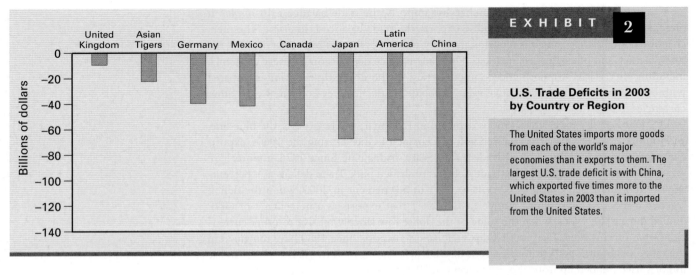

Source: Developed from data in "U.S. International Transactions, 2003," *Survey of Current Business*, April 2004, Table J. The so-called Asian Tigers are Hong Kong, Singapore, South Korea, and Taiwan.

The Balance on Goods and Services

The merchandise trade balance focuses on the flow of goods, but services are also traded internationally. *Services* are intangibles, such as transportation, insurance, banking, education, consulting, and tourism. Services also include the income earned from foreign investments less the income earned by foreigners from their investments in the U.S. economy. Services are often called "invisibles" because they are not tangible. The value of U.S. service exports, like when an Irish tourist visits New York City, is listed as a credit in the U.S. balance-of-payments account because U.S. residents get paid for these services. The value of U.S. service imports, like computer programming done in India, is listed as a debit in the balance-of-payments account because U.S. residents must pay for the imported services. Because the United States exports more services than it imports, the balance on services has been in surplus for the last three decades. The **balance on goods and services** is the export value of goods and services minus the import value of goods and services, or *net exports*, a component of GDP.

BALANCE ON GOODS AND SERVICES

The portion of a country's balance-of-payments account that measures the value of a country's exports of goods and services minus the value of its imports of goods and services

Unilateral Transfers

Unilateral transfers consist of government transfers to foreign residents, foreign aid, personal gifts to friends and relatives abroad, charitable donations, and the like. For example, private charities in the United States sent about $5 billion to foreign countries in 2003. U.S. unilateral transfers include money sent abroad by a U.S. resident to friends or relatives. Money sent out of the country is a debit in the balance-of-payments account. For example, immigrants to the United States often send money to families back home. **Net unilateral transfers** equal the unilateral transfers received from abroad by U.S. residents minus unilateral transfers sent to foreign residents by U.S. residents. U.S. net unilateral transfers have been negative since World War II, except for 1991, when the U.S. government received sizable transfers from foreign governments to help pay their share of the Persian Gulf War. In 2003, net unilateral transfers were a negative $68 billion, for an average net outflow of about $600 per U.S. household.

NET UNILATERAL TRANSFERS

The unilateral transfers (gifts and grants) received from abroad by residents of a country minus the unilateral transfers sent abroad

The United States places few restrictions on money sent out of the country. Other countries, particularly developing countries, strictly limit the amount that may be sent abroad. More generally, many developing countries, such as China, restrict the convertibility of their currency into other currencies.

When we add net unilateral transfers to the exports of goods and services minus the imports of goods and services, we get the **balance on current account,** which is reported quarterly. Thus, *the current account includes all transactions in currently produced goods and services plus net unilateral transfers.* It can be negative, reflecting a current account deficit; positive, reflecting a current account surplus; or zero.

The Capital Account

The current account records international transactions involving the flows of goods (including capital goods), services, and unilateral transfers. When economists talk about capital, they typically mean the physical goods employed to produce goods and services. But sometimes *capital* is just another word for *money*—money to acquire financial assets, such as stocks, bonds, and bank balances, and money to buy foreign land, housing, factories, and other physical assets. The **capital account** records international transactions involving foreign assets and liabilities. For example, U.S. residents purchase foreign securities to earn a higher rate of return and to diversify their portfolios. U.S. capital flows out when Americans buy foreign assets. Foreign capital flows in when foreigners buy U.S. assets.

Between 1917 and 1982, the United States ran a capital account deficit, meaning that U.S. residents purchased more foreign assets than foreigners purchased assets from the United States. The net income from these foreign assets improved our current account balance. But in 1983, for the first time in 65 years, high real interest rates in the United States (relative to those in the rest of the world) resulted in foreigners purchasing more assets in the United States than U.S. residents purchased abroad. Since 1983, foreigners have continued to buy more U.S. assets most years than the other way around, meaning there has usually been a surplus in our capital account.

Americans owe foreigners more and more each year. *The United States is now the world's largest net debtor nation.* This is not as bad as it sounds, because foreign purchases of assets in the United States add to America's productive capacity and promote employment and labor productivity. But the return on these assets flows to foreigners, not to Americans.

Deficits and Surpluses

Nations, like households, operate under a budget constraint. Spending cannot exceed income plus cash on hand and borrowed funds. We have distinguished between *current* transactions, which are the income and expenditures from exports, imports, and unilateral transfers, and *capital* transactions, which reflect international investments and borrowing. Any surplus or deficit in one account must be offset by deficits or surpluses in other balance-of-payments accounts. The current account has been in deficit since 1982, meaning that the sum of U.S. imports of goods and services plus unilateral transfers to foreigners has exceeded the sum spent by foreigners on our exports and sent as unilateral transfers to us.

Exhibit 3 presents the U.S. balance-of-payments statement for 2003. All transactions requiring payments from foreigners to U.S. residents are entered as credits, indicated by a plus sign (+), because they result in an inflow of funds from foreign residents to U.S. residents. All transactions requiring payments to foreigners from U.S. residents are entered as debits, indicated by a minus sign (−), because they result in an outflow of funds from

BALANCE ON CURRENT ACCOUNT

The portion of a country's balance-of-payments account that measures that country's balance on goods and services plus its net unilateral transfers

CAPITAL ACCOUNT

The record of a country's international transactions involving purchases or sales of financial and real assets

U.S. residents to foreign residents. As you can see, a surplus in the capital account of $579.0 billion more than offsets a current account deficit of $541.8 billion. The statistical discrepancy that *balances* payments is a negative $37.2 billion. Think of the statistical discrepancy as the official "fudge factor" that (1) measures the error in the balance-of-payments and (2) satisfies the double-entry bookkeeping requirement that total debits equal total credits.

Foreign exchange is the currency of another country needed to carry out international transactions. A country runs a deficit in its current account when the amount of foreign exchange that country gets from exporting goods and services and from receipts of unilateral transfers falls short of the amount needed to pay for its imports and to make unilateral transfers. The additional foreign exchange required must come from a net capital inflow (borrowing from abroad, foreign purchases of domestic stocks and bonds, foreigners buying a steel plant in Pittsburgh or a ski lodge in Aspen, and so forth). If a country runs a current account surplus, the foreign exchange received from selling exports and from unilateral transfers exceeds the amount required to pay for imports and to make unilateral transfers. This excess foreign exchange could be held in a bank account, converted to the domestic currency, or used to purchase foreign stocks, bonds, or other foreign assets, such as a shoe plant in Italy or a villa on the French Riviera.

When all transactions are considered, accounts must always balance, though specific accounts usually don't. A deficit in a particular account should not necessarily be viewed as a source of concern, nor should a surplus be a source of satisfaction. The deficit in the U.S. current account in recent years has been offset by a capital account surplus. As a result, foreigners are acquiring more claims on U.S. assets.

Current Account	
1. Merchandise exports	+713.8
2. Merchandise imports	−1,263.2
3. Trade balance (1 + 2)	−549.4
4. Service exports	+580.5
5. Service imports	−504.6
6. Goods and services balance (3 + 4 + 5)	−473.5
7. Net unilateral transfers	−68.3
8. Current account balance (6 + 7)	−541.8
Capital Account	
9. Outflow of U.S. capital	−277.7
10. Inflow of foreign capital	+856.7
11. Capital account balance (9 + 10)	+579.0
12. Statistical discrepancy	−37.2
TOTAL (8 + 11 + 12)	**0.0**

EXHIBIT 3

U.S. Balance of Payments for 2003 (billions of dollars)

Source: *Survey of Current Business*, May 2004, Table F-2, U.S. Department of Commerce. For the latest data, go to http://www.bea.doc.gov/.

Foreign Exchange Rates and Markets

Now that you have some idea about international flows, we can take a closer look at the forces that determine the underlying value of the currencies involved. Let's begin by looking at exchange rates and the market for foreign exchange.

Foreign Exchange

Foreign exchange, recall, is foreign money needed to carry out international transactions. The **exchange rate** is the price measured in one country's currency of buying one unit of another country's currency. Exchange rates are determined by the interaction of the households, firms, private financial institutions, governments, and central banks that buy and sell foreign exchange. The exchange rate fluctuates to equate the quantity of foreign exchange demanded with the quantity supplied. Typically, foreign exchange is made up of bank deposits denominated in the foreign currency. When foreign travel is involved, foreign exchange often consists of foreign paper money.

The foreign exchange market incorporates all the arrangements used to buy and sell foreign exchange. This market is not so much a physical place as a network of telephones and computers connecting financial centers all over the world. Perhaps you have seen pictures of foreign exchange traders in New York, Frankfurt, London, or Tokyo in front of computer screens amid a tangle of phone lines. The foreign exchange market is like an all-night diner—it never closes. A trading center is always open somewhere in the world.

We will consider the market for the euro in terms of the dollar. But first, a little background about the euro. For decades the nations of Western Europe have tried to increase their economic cooperation and trade. These countries believed they would be more productive and more competitive with the United States if they acted less like many separate economies and more like the 50 United States, with a single set of trade regulations and one currency. Imagine the hassle involved if each of the 50 states had its own currency.

In January 2002, euro notes and coins entered circulation in the 12 European countries adopting the common currency. The big advantage of a common currency is that Europeans no longer have to change money every time they cross a border or trade with another country in the group. Again, the inspiration for this is the United States, arguably the most successful economy in world history.

So the euro is now the common currency of the *euro area,* as the region is usually called. The price, or exchange rate, of the euro in terms of the dollar is the number of dollars required to purchase one euro. An increase in the number of dollars needed to purchase a euro indicates weakening, or **depreciation,** of the dollar. A decrease in the number of dollars needed to purchase a euro indicates strengthening, or **appreciation,** of the dollar. Put another way, a decrease in the number of euros needed to purchase a dollar is a depreciation of the dollar, and an increase in the number of euros needed to purchase a dollar is an appreciation of the dollar.

Because the exchange rate is a price, it is determined by demand and supply: The equilibrium price is the one that equates quantity demanded with quantity supplied. To simplify the analysis, suppose that the United States and the euro area make up the entire world, so the demand and supply for euros in international finance is the demand and supply for foreign exchange from the U.S. perspective.

EXCHANGE RATE

The price measured in one country's currency of purchasing 1 unit of another country's currency

HOMEWORK
Xpress!
Ask the Instructor
Video

CURRENCY DEPRECIATION

With respect to the dollar, an increase in the number of dollars needed to purchase 1 unit of foreign exchange in a flexible rate system

CURRENCY APPRECIATION

With respect to the dollar, a decrease in the number of dollars needed to purchase 1 unit of foreign exchange in a flexible rate system

The Demand for Foreign Exchange

Whenever U.S. residents need euros, they must buy them in the foreign exchange market, which could include their local bank, paying for them with dollars. Exhibit 4 depicts a market for foreign exchange—in this case, euros. The horizontal axis shows the quantity of foreign exchange, measured here in millions of euros. The vertical axis shows the price per unit of foreign exchange, measured here as the number of dollars required to purchase one euro. The demand curve D for foreign exchange shows the inverse relationship between the dollar price of the euro and the quantity of euros demanded, other things assumed constant. Assumed constant along the demand curve are the incomes and preferences of U.S. consumers, the expected inflation rates in the United States and the euro area, the euro price of goods in the euro area, and interest rates in the United States and the euro area. People have many reasons for demanding foreign exchange, but in the aggregate, the lower the dollar price of foreign exchange, other things constant, the greater the quantity demanded.

A drop in the dollar price of foreign exchange, in this case the euro, means that fewer dollars are needed to purchase each euro, so the dollar prices of euro area products (like German cars, Italian shoes, tickets to Euro Disney, and euro area securities), which list prices in euros, become cheaper. The cheaper it is to buy euros, the lower the dollar price of euro area products to U.S. residents, so the greater the quantity of euros demanded by U.S. residents, other things constant. For example, a cheap enough euro might persuade you to tour Rome, climb the Austrian Alps, wander the museums of Paris, or crawl the pubs of Dublin.

The Supply of Foreign Exchange

The supply of foreign exchange is generated by the desire of foreign residents to acquire dollars—that is, to exchange euros for dollars. Euro area residents want dollars to buy U.S.

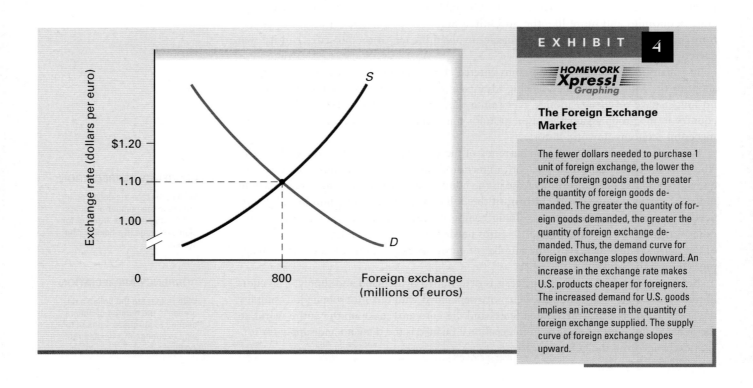

EXHIBIT 4

HOMEWORK
Xpress!
Graphing

The Foreign Exchange Market

The fewer dollars needed to purchase 1 unit of foreign exchange, the lower the price of foreign goods and the greater the quantity of foreign goods demanded. The greater the quantity of foreign goods demanded, the greater the quantity of foreign exchange demanded. Thus, the demand curve for foreign exchange slopes downward. An increase in the exchange rate makes U.S. products cheaper for foreigners. The increased demand for U.S. goods implies an increase in the quantity of foreign exchange supplied. The supply curve of foreign exchange slopes upward.

goods and services, acquire U.S. assets, make loans in dollars, or give cash gifts in dollars to their U.S. friends and relatives. Euros are supplied in the foreign exchange market to acquire the dollars people want. An increase in the dollar-per-euro exchange rate, other things constant, makes U.S. products cheaper for foreigners because foreign residents need fewer euros to get the same number of dollars. For example, suppose a Dell computer sells for $500. If the exchange rate is $1.00 per euro, that computer costs 500 euros; if the exchange rate is $1.25 per euro, it costs only 400 euros. The number of Dell computers demanded in the euro area increases as the dollar-per-euro exchange rate increases, other things constant, so more euros will be supplied on the foreign exchange market to buy dollars.

The positive relationship between the dollar-per-euro exchange rate and the quantity of euros supplied on the foreign exchange market is expressed in Exhibit 4 by the upward-sloping supply curve for foreign exchange (again, euros in our example). The supply curve assumes that other things remain constant, including euro area incomes and tastes, expectations about the rates of inflation in the euro area and the United States, and interest rates in the euro area and the United States.

Determining the Exchange Rate

Exhibit 4 brings together the demand and supply for foreign exchange to determine the exchange rate. At a rate of $1.10 per euro, the quantity of euros demanded equals the quantity supplied—in our example, 800 million euros. Once achieved, this equilibrium rate will remain constant until a change occurs in one of the factors that affect supply or demand. If the exchange rate is allowed to adjust freely, or to *float,* in response to market forces, the market will clear continually, as the quantities of foreign exchange demanded and supplied are equated.

What if the initial equilibrium is upset by a change in one of the underlying forces that affect supply or demand? For example, suppose higher U.S. incomes increase American demand for all normal goods, including those from the euro area. This shifts the U.S. demand curve for foreign exchange to the right, as Americans buy more Italian marble, Dutch chocolate, German machines, Parisian vacations, and euro securities.

This increased demand for euros is shown in Exhibit 5 by a rightward shift of the demand curve for foreign exchange. The demand increase from D to D' leads to an increase in the exchange rate per euro from $1.10 to $1.12. Thus, the euro increases in value, or appreciates, while the dollar falls in value, or depreciates. An increase in U.S. income should not affect the euro supply curve, though it does increase the *quantity of euros supplied.* The higher exchange value of the euro prompts those in the euro area to buy more American products and assets, which are now cheaper in terms of the euro.

To review: Any increase in the demand for foreign exchange or any decrease in its supply, other things constant, causes an increase in the number of dollars required to purchase one unit of foreign exchange, which is a depreciation of the dollar. On the other hand, any decrease in the demand for foreign exchange or any increase in its supply, other things constant, causes a reduction in the number of dollars required to purchase one unit of foreign exchange, which is an appreciation of the dollar.

Arbitrageurs and Speculators

Exchange rates between two currencies are nearly identical at any given time in markets around the world. For example, the dollar price of a euro is the same in New York, Frankfurt, Tokyo, London, Zurich, Hong Kong, Istanbul, and other financial centers. **Arbitrageurs**—dealers who take advantage of any difference in exchange rates between

ARBITRAGEUR

Someone who takes advantage of temporary geographic differences in the exchange rate by simultaneously purchasing a currency in one market and selling it in another market

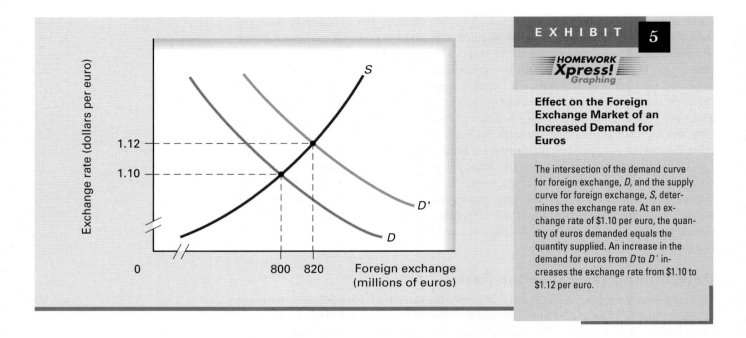

EXHIBIT 5

HOMEWORK Xpress!
Graphing

Effect on the Foreign Exchange Market of an Increased Demand for Euros

The intersection of the demand curve for foreign exchange, *D*, and the supply curve for foreign exchange, *S*, determines the exchange rate. At an exchange rate of $1.10 per euro, the quantity of euros demanded equals the quantity supplied. An increase in the demand for euros from *D* to *D'* increases the exchange rate from $1.10 to $1.12 per euro.

markets by buying low and selling high—ensure this equality. Their actions help to equalize exchange rates across markets. For example, if one euro costs $1.09 in New York but $1.10 in Frankfurt, an arbitrageur could buy, say, $10,000,000 worth of euros in New York and at the same time sell them in Frankfurt for $10,091,743, thereby earning $91,743 minus the transaction costs of the trades.

Because an arbitrageur buys and sells simultaneously, relatively little risk is involved. In our example, the arbitrageur increased the demand for euros in New York and increased the supply of euros in Frankfurt. These actions increased the dollar price of euros in New York and decreased it in Frankfurt, thereby squeezing down the difference in exchange rates. Exchange rates may still change because of market forces, but they tend to change in all markets simultaneously.

The demand and supply of foreign exchange arises from many sources—from importers and exporters, investors in foreign assets, central banks, tourists, arbitrageurs, and speculators. **Speculators** buy or sell foreign exchange in hopes of profiting by trading the currency at a more favorable exchange rate later. By taking risks, speculators aim to profit from market fluctuations—they try to buy low and sell high. In contrast, arbitrageurs take less risk, because they *simultaneously* buy currency in one market and sell it in another.

Finally, people in countries suffering from economic and political turmoil, such as recently occurred in Russia, Indonesia, and the Philippines, may buy *hard* currency as a hedge against the depreciation and instability of their own currencies. The dollar has long been accepted as an international medium of exchange. It is also the currency of choice in the world markets for oil and illegal drugs. But the euro eventually may challenge that dominance, in part because the largest euro denomination, the 500 euro note, is worth over five times the largest U.S. note, the $100 note. So it would be five times easier to smuggle euro notes than U.S. notes of equal value.

SPECULATOR

Someone who buys or sells foreign exchange in hopes of profiting from fluctuations in the exchange rate over time

Purchasing Power Parity

As long as trade across borders is unrestricted and as long as exchange rates are allowed to adjust freely, the **purchasing power parity (PPP) theory** predicts that the exchange rate between two currencies will adjust in the long run to reflect price-level differences between the two currency regions. *A given basket of internationally traded goods should therefore sell for about the same around the world (except for differences reflecting transportation costs and the like).* Suppose a basket of internationally traded goods that sells for $10,000 in the United States sells for 9,000 euros in the euro area. According to the purchasing power parity theory, the equilibrium exchange rate should be $1.11 per euro. If this were not the case—if the exchange rate were, say, $1.00 per euro—then you could exchange $9,000 for 9,000 euros, with which you buy the basket of commodities in the euro area. You could then sell the basket of goods in the States for $10,000, yielding you a profit of $1,000 minus any transaction costs. Selling dollars and buying euros will drive up the dollar price of euros.

The purchasing power parity theory is more of a long-run predictor than a day-to-day indicator of the relationship between changes in the price level and the exchange rate. For example, a country's currency generally appreciates when inflation is low compared with other countries and depreciates when inflation is high. Likewise, a country's currency generally appreciates when its real interest rates are higher than those in the rest of the world, because foreigners are more willing to buy and hold investments denominated in that high-interest currency. As a case in point, the dollar appreciated during the first half of the 1980s, when real U.S. interest rates were relatively high, and depreciated in the 2002 and 2003, when real U.S. interest rates were relatively low.

Because of trade barriers, central bank intervention in exchange markets, and the fact that many products are not traded or are not comparable across countries, the purchasing power parity theory usually does not explain exchange rates at a particular point in time. For example, if you went shopping in London tomorrow, you would soon notice a dollar does not buy as much there as it does in the United States. The following case study considers the purchasing power parity theory based on the price of Big Macs around the globe.

The Big Mac Price Index

As you have already learned, the PPP theory says that in the long run the exchange rate between two currencies should move toward the one that equalizes the prices in each country of an identical basket of internationally traded goods. A lighthearted test of the theory has been developed by *The Economist* magazine, which compares prices around the world for a "market basket" consisting simply of one McDonald's Big Mac—a product that, though not internationally traded, is essentially the same in more than 100 countries. *The Economist* begins with the price of a Big Mac in the local currency and then converts that price into dollars based on the exchange rate prevailing at the time. A comparison of the dollar price of Big Macs across countries offers a crude test of the PPP theory, which predicts that these prices should move toward equality in the long run.

Exhibit 6 lists the dollar price of a Big Mac in May 2004, in each of 30 surveyed countries plus the euro area average. By comparing the price of a Big Mac in the United States (shown as a green bar) with prices in other countries, we can derive a crude measure of

PURCHASING POWER PARITY (PPP) THEORY

The idea that the exchange rate between two countries will adjust in the long run to reflect price-level differences between the countries

C a s e **S t u d y**

Bringing Theory to Life

eActivity

The Economist has published several articles about the Big Mac Index. Go to http://www.economist.com/markets/Bigmac/Index.cfm to access the latest edition of the index. Which currencies have had the largest changes in value? Which currencies went from being overvalued to undervalued between 1989 and 2004?

whether particular currencies, relative to the dollar, are overvalued (red bars) or undervalued (blue bars). For example, because the price of a Big Mac in Switzerland, at $4.90, was 69 percent higher than the U.S. price of $2.90, the Swiss franc appears overvalued compared to the dollar. The euro was 13 percent overvalued. But Big Macs were cheaper in most of the countries surveyed. The cheapest was in Saudi Arabia, where a Big Mac price of 64 cents was 78 percent below the U.S. price.

Thus, Big Mac prices in May 2004 ranged from 69 percent above to 78 percent below the U.S. price. These prices lend little support to the PPP theory, but that theory relates only to traded goods. The Big Mac is not traded internationally. A large share of the total cost of a Big Mac is rent, which can vary substantially across countries. Taxes and trade barriers, such as tariffs and quotas on beef, may also distort local prices. And wages differ across countries, with a McDonald's worker averaging $7 an hour in the United States versus less than $1 an hour in China. So there are understandable reasons why Big Mac prices differ across countries.

Sources: "The Big Mac Index: Food for Thought," *Economist*, 27 May 2004; Michael Pakko and Patricia Pollard, "Burgernomics: A Big Mac Guide to Purchasing Power Parity," *Federal Reserve Bank of St. Louis Review*, (November/December 2003): 9–28; and the McDonald's Corporation Web site at http://www.mcdonalds.com.

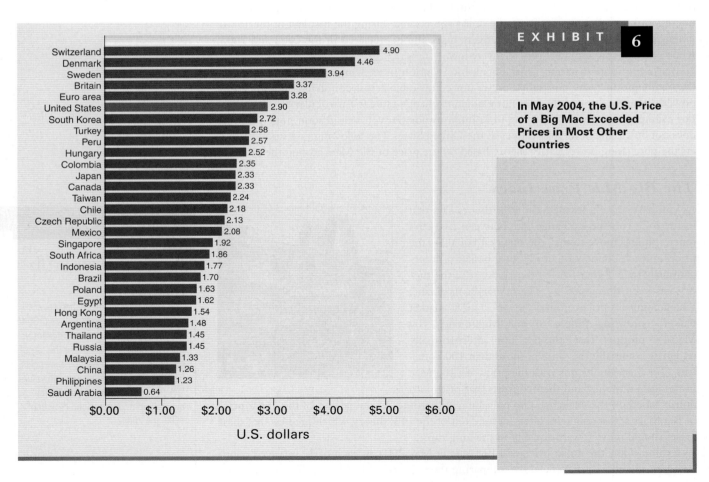

EXHIBIT 6

In May 2004, the U.S. Price of a Big Mac Exceeded Prices in Most Other Countries

Source: Developed from the price survey appearing in "The Big Mac Index: Food for Thought," *Economist*, 27 May 2004.

Flexible Exchange Rates

For the most part, we have been discussing a system of **flexible exchange rates,** with rates determined by demand and supply. Flexible, or *floating,* exchange rates adjust continually to the myriad forces that buffet the foreign exchange market. Consider how the exchange rate is linked to the balance-of-payments accounts. Debit entries in the current and capital accounts increase the demand for foreign exchange, resulting in a depreciation of the dollar. Credit entries in these accounts increase the supply of foreign exchange, resulting in an appreciation of the dollar.

Fixed Exchange Rates

When exchange rates are flexible, governments usually have little direct role in foreign exchange markets. But if governments try to set exchange rates, active and ongoing central bank intervention is necessary to establish and maintain these **fixed exchange rates.** Suppose the European Central Bank selects what it thinks is an appropriate rate of exchange between the dollar and the euro. It attempts to *fix,* or to *peg,* the exchange rate within a narrow band around the particular value selected. If the euro threatens to climb above the maximum acceptable exchange rate, monetary authorities must sell euros and buy dollars, thereby keeping the dollar price of the euro down. Conversely, if the euro threatens to drop below the minimum acceptable exchange rate, monetary authorities must sell dollars and buy euros. This increased demand for the euro will keep its value up relative to the dollar. Through such intervention in the foreign exchange market, monetary authorities try to stabilize the exchange rate, keeping it within the specified band.

If monetary officials must keep selling foreign exchange to maintain the pegged rate, they risk running out of foreign exchange reserves. Faced with this threat, the government has several options for eliminating the exchange rate disequilibrium. First, the pegged exchange rate can be increased, which is a **devaluation** of the domestic currency. (A decrease in the pegged exchange rate is called a **revaluation.**) Second, the government can reduce the domestic demand for foreign exchange directly by imposing restrictions on imports or on capital outflows. China and many other developing countries do this. Third, the government can adopt contractionary fiscal or monetary policies to reduce the country's income level, increase interest rates, or reduce inflation relative to that of the country's trading partners, thereby indirectly decreasing the demand for foreign exchange and increasing the supply of foreign exchange. Several Asian economies, such as South Korea and Indonesia, pursued such policies to stabilize their currencies in 1998. Finally, the government can allow the disequilibrium to persist and ration the available foreign reserves through some form of foreign exchange control.

This concludes our introduction to the theories of international finance. Let's examine international finance in practice.

Development of the International Monetary System

From 1879 to 1914, the international financial system operated under a **gold standard,** whereby the major currencies were convertible into gold at a fixed rate. For example, the U.S. dollar could be redeemed at the U.S. Treasury for one-twentieth of an ounce of gold. The British pound could be redeemed at the British Exchequer, or treasury, for one-fourth of an ounce of gold. Because each British pound could buy five times as much gold as each dollar, one British pound exchanged for $5.

The gold standard provided a predictable exchange rate, one that did not vary as long as currencies could be redeemed for gold at the announced rate. But the money supply in each country was determined in part by the flow of gold between countries, so each

FLEXIBLE EXCHANGE RATE

Rate determined by the forces of demand and supply without government intervention

FIXED EXCHANGE RATE

Rate of exchange between currencies pegged within a narrow range and maintained by the central bank's ongoing purchases and sales of currencies

CURRENCY DEVALUATION

An increase in the official pegged price of foreign exchange in terms of the domestic currency

CURRENCY REVALUATION

A reduction in the official pegged price of foreign exchange in terms of the domestic currency

GOLD STANDARD

An arrangement whereby the currencies of most countries are convertible into gold at a fixed rate country's monetary policy was influenced by the supply of gold. A balance-of-payments deficit resulted in a loss of gold, which theoretically caused a country's money supply to decline. A balance-of-payments surplus resulted in an increase in gold, which theoretically caused a country's money supply to rise. The supply of money throughout the world also depended on the vagaries of gold discoveries. When gold production did not keep pace with the growth in economic activity, the price level dropped. When gold production exceeded the growth in economic activity, the price level rose. For example, gold discoveries in Alaska and South Africa in the late 1890s expanded the U.S. money supply, leading to inflation.

The Bretton Woods Agreement

During World War I, many countries could no longer convert their currencies into gold, and the gold standard eventually collapsed, disrupting international trade during the 1920s and 1930s. Once an Allied victory in World War II appeared certain, the Allies met in Bretton Woods, New Hampshire, in July 1944 to formulate a new international monetary system. Because the United States had a strong economy and was not ravaged by the war, the dollar was selected as the key reserve currency in the new international monetary system. All exchange rates were fixed in terms of the dollar, and the United States, which held most of the world's gold reserves, stood ready to convert foreign holdings of dollars into gold at a rate of $35 per ounce. Even though exchange rates were fixed by the Bretton Woods agreement, *other* countries could adjust *their* exchange rates relative to the U.S. dollar if they found a chronic disequilibrium in their balance of payments—that is, if a country faced a large and persistent deficit or surplus.

The Bretton Woods agreement also created the **International Monetary Fund (IMF)** to set rules for maintaining the international monetary system, to standardize financial reporting for international trade, and to make loans to countries with temporary balance-of-payments problems. The IMF lends a revolving fund of $300 billion to economies in need of reserves. Headquartered in Washington, D.C., the IMF has more than 180 member countries and a staff of 2,500 drawn from around the world.

The Demise of the Bretton Woods System

During the latter part of the 1960s, inflation began heating up in the United States. Higher U.S. prices meant that those exchanging foreign currencies for dollars at the official exchange rates found these dollars bought fewer U.S. goods and services. Because of U.S. inflation, the dollar had become *overvalued* at the official exchange rate, meaning that the gold value of the dollar exceeded the exchange value of the dollar. With the dollar overvalued, foreigners redeemed more dollars for gold. To halt this outflow of gold, the United States in August 1971 stopped exchanging gold for dollars. In December 1971, the world's 10 richest countries met in Washington and devalued the dollar by 8 percent. The hope at the time was that this devaluation would put the dollar on firmer footing and would save the "dollar standard." With prices rising at different rates around the world, however, an international monetary system based on fixed exchange rates was doomed.

In 1971, U.S. merchandise imports exceeded merchandise exports for the first time since World War II. When the trade deficit tripled in 1972, it became clear that the dollar was still overvalued. In early 1973, the dollar was devalued another 10 percent, but this did not quiet foreign exchange markets. The dollar, for three decades the anchor of the international monetary system, suddenly looked vulnerable, and speculators began betting the dollar would fall

INTERNATIONAL MONETARY FUND (IMF)

An international organization that establishes rules for maintaining the international monetary system and makes loans to countries with temporary balance-of-payments problems even more. Dollars were exchanged for German marks because the mark appeared to be the most stable currency. Bundesbank, Germany's central bank, exchanged marks for dollars in an attempt to defend the official exchange rate and prevent an appreciation of the mark. Why didn't Germany want the mark to appreciate? Appreciation would make German goods more expensive abroad and foreign goods cheaper in Germany, thereby reducing German exports and increasing German imports. So the mark's appreciation would reduce German output and employment. But after selling $10 billion worth of marks, the Bundesbank gave up defending the dollar. As soon as the value of the dollar was allowed to float against the mark, the Bretton Woods system, already on shaky ground, collapsed.

The Current System: Managed Float

The Bretton Woods system has been replaced by a **managed float system,** which combines features of a freely floating exchange rate with sporadic intervention by central banks as a way of moderating exchange rate fluctuations among the world's major currencies. Most small countries, particularly developing countries, still peg their currencies to one of the major currencies (such as the U.S. dollar) or to a "basket" of major currencies. What's more, in developing countries, private international borrowing and lending are severely restricted; some governments allow residents to purchase foreign exchange only for certain purposes. In some countries, different exchange rates apply to different categories of transactions.

Critics of flexible exchange rates argue that they are inflationary, because they free monetary authorities to pursue expansionary policies; and they have often been volatile. This volatility creates uncertainty and risk for importers and exporters, increasing the transaction costs of international trade. Furthermore, exchange rate volatility can lead to wrenching changes in the competitiveness of a country's export sector. These changes cause swings in employment, resulting in louder calls for import restrictions. For example, the exchange rate between the Japanese yen and the U.S. dollar has been relatively unstable, particularly because of international speculation.

Policy makers are always on the lookout for a system that will perform better than the current managed float system, with its fluctuating currency values. *Their ideal is a system that will foster international trade, lower inflation, and promote a more stable world economy.* International finance ministers have acknowledged that the world must find an international standard and establish greater exchange rate stability.

The wild swings in exchange rates that sometimes occur with flexible exchange rates have triggered interventions to reduce undesirable fluctuations, as discussed in the following case study about recent financial troubles in Asia.

The Asian Contagion

The trouble started in Thailand in early 1997. Speculators began betting that the Thai currency, the baht, was in for a fall. The Thai central bank tried to defend the baht's value by buying baht and selling foreign reserves. At the time, the baht's value was pegged to the U.S. dollar. As the central bank's foreign reserves dwindled, the government decided in July 1997 to let the baht float. It lost 40 percent of its value against the dollar in a matter of weeks. With the baht worth so much less, Thai businesses and government had difficulty repaying foreign loans, most of which had to be paid back in dollars.

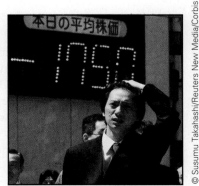

© Susumu Takahashi/Reuters New Media/Corbis

MANAGED FLOAT SYSTEM

An exchange rate system that combines features of freely floating rates with sporadic intervention by central banks

Case **Study**

World of Business

*e*Activity

The Institute for International Economics Policy Briefs, at http://www.iie.com/publications/pb/pb04.htm, presents an article, "Islam, Globalization, and Economic Performance in the Middle East" by Marcus Noland and

Howard Pack, which discusses the impact of globalization on countries in the Middle East. What explains the relative underperformance of the Middle East in the past few decades? Other economists' views and analyses are available at the Brookings Institution at http://www.brook.edu /index/papersarticles.htm.

WALL STREET JOURNAL
Reading It **Right**

What's the relevance of the following statement from the Wall Street Journal: *"While Japan's direct investment around the world has fallen 36 percent in the last 10 years as it has grappled with its own economic downturn, its investment in Southeast Asia has been cut in half."*

The crisis prompted a $17 billion bailout of Thailand, supervised by the International Monetary Fund (IMF) and aimed at helping Thailand pay back some foreign debt. But problems in Thailand deepened, as outside credit agencies continued to downgrade Thai debt. Falling currency values soon spread to neighboring Indonesia, Malaysia, and South Korea, as the so-called Asian Contagion ripped through the region, cutting real GDP in each of these countries more than 5 percent in 1998. Note that a plunging currency value was not so much the source of economic instability as a reflection of other problems in the economy, such as falling exports and an unstable banking sector due to bad loans. Indonesia and South Korea were forced to seek IMF assistance.

In Japan, where the economy had been on the ropes since 1990, matters worsened. In November 1997, four large financial institutions went bankrupt, the yen suffered its biggest drop against the dollar in years, and the stock market continued its eight-year slide. Japan, the second-largest economy in the world (after the United States), is by far the largest in Asia. A weakened Japan threatened the fragile economies of Asia as they tried to recover from financial chaos. A weakened Japan meant the country would buy less from its Asian neighbors, and a weakened yen meant Japanese exports would be cheaper on world markets, thus undercutting exports from elsewhere in Asia. Faced with growing problems in Asia, the U.S. government joined forces with the Japanese government to intervene in currency markets and spent $2 billion buying yen. By increasing the demand for yen, the U.S. intervention reversed the slide in the yen's value. In one day, the yen-per-dollar exchange rate appreciated 5 percent. By 2001, output in the other economies affected by the Asian Contagion was growing.

Asian economies have now recovered in large part because they used their cheap currencies to boost their exports to the United States. This strategy has generated growing trade surpluses with the United States and infused Asian central banks with billions of dollars. These banks have used these surplus dollars to buy dollar-denominated securities, primarily U.S. Treasury bonds. By 2004, Asians held about $1 trillion in U.S. bonds, or about 55 percent of the U.S. bonds held by foreigners. This is up from 40 percent in 1996, the year before the Asian Contagion started. Chinese holdings of U.S. bonds more than doubled between 2000 and 2004. This is an example of the twin deficits: the U.S. trade deficits put dollars in the hands of foreigners; they use those dollars to buy U.S. Treasury bonds, thus funding our federal deficit.

Sources: John Andrews, *Pocket Asia*, 7 ed. (The Economist Books, 2002); "Banking in South-East Asia?" 1 May 2004; "Emerging Market Indicators," *Economist*, 27 May 2004; "Stocks Stumble Across Asia as Yen Hits Lowest Since '90," *Wall Street Journal*, 11 June 1998; Craig Karmin et al., "Despite U.S. Bond Selloff, Asia Continues Buying," *Wall Street Journal*, 4 August 2003.

Conclusion

The United States is very much a part of the world economy, not only as the largest exporter but also as the largest importer. Although the dollar remains the unit of transaction in many international settlements—OPEC, for example, still states oil prices in dollars—gyrations of exchange rates have made those involved in international finance wary of putting all their eggs in one basket. The international monetary system is now going through a difficult period as it gropes for a new source of stability more than three decades after the collapse of the Bretton Woods agreement.

SUMMARY

1. The balance of payments reflects all economic transactions between one country and the rest of the world. The current account measures flows of (a) merchandise; (b) services, including investment income, military transactions, and tourism; and (c) unilateral transfers, or public and private transfer payments to and from foreign residents. The capital account measures international transactions in real and financial assets.

2. Foreign exchange funds the flow of goods and services across international borders. The interaction of the supply and demand for foreign exchange determines the equilibrium exchange rate.

3. Under a system of flexible exchange rates, the value of the dollar relative to foreign exchange varies over time. An increase in the demand for foreign exchange or a decrease in its supply, other things constant, will increase the value of foreign exchange relative to the dollar, which is a depreciation of the dollar. Conversely, a decrease in the demand for foreign exchange or an increase in its supply will decrease the value of foreign exchange relative to the dollar, which is an appreciation of the dollar.

4. Under a system of fixed exchange rates, monetary authorities try to stabilize the exchange rate, keeping it between a specified ceiling and floor value.

5. For much of this century, the international monetary system was based on fixed exchange rates. A managed float system has been in effect for the major currencies since the demise of the Bretton Woods system in the early 1970s. Although central banks often try to stabilize exchange rates, fluctuations in rates persist. These fluctuations usually reflect market forces but they still raise the transaction costs of international trade and finance.

QUESTIONS FOR REVIEW

1. *(Balance of Payments)* Suppose the United States ran a balance-on-goods-and-services surplus by exporting goods and services while importing nothing.

   a. How would such a surplus be offset elsewhere in the balance-of-payments accounts?
   b. If the level of U.S. production does not depend on the balance on goods and services, how would running this surplus affect our *current* standard of living?
   c. What is the relationship between total debits and total credits in the balance on goods and services?
   d. When all international economic transactions are considered, what must be true about the sum of debits and credits?
   e. What is the role of the statistical discrepancy?

2. *(Foreign Exchange)* What is the difference between a depreciation of the dollar and a devaluation of the dollar?

3. *(Purchasing Power Parity)* According to the theory of purchasing power parity, what will happen to the value of the dollar (against foreign currencies) if the U.S. price level doubles and price levels in other countries remain constant? Why is the theory more suitable to analyzing events in the long run?

4. *(Case Study: The Big Mac Price Index)* The Big Mac Price Index computed by *The Economist* has consistently found the U.S. dollar to be undervalued against some currencies and overvalued against others, which seems to call for a rejection of the purchasing power parity theory. Explain why this index may not be a valid test of the theory.

5. *(The Current System: Managed Float)* What is a managed float? What are the disadvantages of freely floating exchange rates that led countries to the managed float system?

6. *(Merchandise Trade Balance)* Explain why a U.S. recession that does not occur at the same time as recessions in the rest of the world will tend to reduce the U.S. trade deficit.

PROBLEMS AND EXERCISES

7. *(Balance of Payments)* The following are hypothetical data for the U.S. balance of payments. Use the data to calculate each of the following:
   a. Merchandise trade balance
   b. Balance on goods and services
   c. Balance on current account
   d. Capital account balance
   e. Statistical discrepancy

	Billions of Dollars
Merchandise exports	350.0
Merchandise imports	2,425.0
Service exports	170.0
Service imports	2,145.0
Net unilateral transfers	221.5
Outflow of U.S. capital	245.0
Inflow of foreign capital	70.0

8. *(Balance of Payments)* Explain where in the U.S. balance of payments an entry would be made for each of the following:
   a. A Hong Kong financier buys some U.S. corporate stock.
   b. A U.S. tourist in Paris buys some perfume to take home.
   c. A Japanese company sells machinery to a pineapple company in Hawaii.

   d. U.S. farmers make a gift of food to starving children in Ethiopia.
   e. The U.S. Treasury sells a bond to a Saudi Arabian prince.
   f. A U.S. tourist flies to France on Air France.
   g. A U.S. company sells insurance to a foreign firm.

9. *(Determining the Exchange Rate)* Use these data to answer the following questions about the market for British pounds:

Price of Pound (in $)	Quantity Demanded (of pounds)	Quantity Supplied (of pounds)
$4.00	50	100
3.00	75	75
2.00	100	50

   a. Draw the demand and supply curves for pounds, and determine the equilibrium exchange rate (dollars per pound).
   b. Suppose that the supply of pounds doubles. Draw the new supply curve.
   c. What is the new equilibrium exchange rate?
   d. Has the dollar appreciated or depreciated?
   e. What happens to U.S. imports of British goods?

EXPERIENTIAL EXERCISES

10. *(Foreign Exchange Rates and Markets)* Trade among European nations has been bolstered by the introduction of the euro. Visit http://www.euro.gov.uk/home.asp?f=1 to review the latest developments.

11. (***Case* Study:** The Asian Contagion) Visit the Business section of *Time* magazine's Asia edition at http://www.time.com/time/asia/biz/ and determine if the Asian economic situation seems to be easing or getting worse. You can also try Yahoo!, which maintains a page devoted

to the Asian economy at http://dailynews.yahoo.com/fc/Business/Asian_Economy.

12. *(Wall Street Journal)* The latest data on exchange rates appear in the "Currency Trading" column in the daily *Wall Street Journal.* You can find it in the Money and Investing section. Try tracking a particular foreign currency over the course of several weeks. Has the dollar been appreciating or depreciating relative to that currency? Try to explain why it has been appreciating or depreciating.

HOMEWORK XPRESS! EXERCISES

*These exercises require access to McEachern Homework Xpress! If Homework Xpress! did not come with your book, visit **http://homeworkxpress.swlearning.com** to purchase.*

1. In the diagram for this exercise, sketch demand and supply curves to represent the market for exchanging British pounds for U.S. dollars to illustrate an equilibrium exchange rate of $1.50 per pound for a volume of exchange of 500 million pounds.

2. In the diagram, sketch demand and supply curves to represent the market for exchanging British pounds for U.S. dollars to

illustrate an equilibrium exchange rate of $1.50 per pound for a volume of exchange of 500 million pounds. Then show how the exchange rate could increase to $1.80 with an increase in volume to 600 million pounds.

A

ability-to-pay tax principle Those with a greater ability to pay, such as those with a higher income or those who own more property, should pay more taxes

absolute advantage The ability to produce something using fewer resources than other producers use

accounting profit A firm's total revenue minus its explicit costs

actual investment The amount of investment actually undertaken; equals planned investment plus unplanned changes in inventories

adverse selection Those on the informed side of the market self-select in a way that harms those on the uninformed side of the market

adverse supply shocks Unexpected events that reduce aggregate supply, sometimes only temporarily

agent A person or firm who is supposed to act on behalf of the principal

aggregate demand The relationship between the economy's price level and the quantity of aggregate output demanded, with other things constant

aggregate demand curve A curve representing the relationship between the economy's price level and real GDP demanded per period, with other things constant

aggregate expenditure Total spending on final goods and services during a given period, usually a year

aggregate expenditure line A relationship showing, for a given price level, planned spending at each income, or real GDP; the total of $C + I + G + (X - M)$ at each income, or real GDP

aggregate income The sum of all income earned by resource suppliers in an economy during a given period

aggregate output A composite measure of all final goods and services produced in an economy during a given period; real GDP

aggregate supply curve A curve representing the relationship between the economy's price level and real GDP supplied per period, with other things constant

allocative efficiency The condition that exists when firms produce the output most preferred by consumers; marginal benefit equals marginal cost

alternative goods Other goods that use some or all of the same resources as the good in question

annually balanced budget Budget philosophy prior to the Great Depression; aimed at matching annual revenues with outlays, except during times of war

annuity A given sum of money received each year for a specified number of years

antitrust policy Government regulation aimed at preventing monopoly and fostering competition in markets where competition is desirable

applied research Research that seeks answers to particular questions or to apply scientific discoveries to develop specific products

arbitrageur Someone who takes advantage of temporary geographic differences in the exchange rate by simultaneously purchasing a currency in one market and selling it in another market

asset Anything of value that is owned

association-is-causation fallacy The incorrect idea that if two variables are associated in time, one must necessarily cause the other

asymmetric information A situation in which one side of the market has more reliable information than the other side

autarky A situation of national self-sufficiency; there is no economic interaction with foreigners

automatic stabilizers Structural features of government spending and taxation that reduce fluctuations in disposable income, and thus consumption, over the business cycle

autonomous A term that means "independent"; for example, autonomous investment is independent of income

average revenue Total revenue divided by output, or $AR = TR/q$; in all market structures, average revenue equals the market price

average total cost Total cost divided by output, or $ATC = TC/q$; the sum of average fixed cost and average variable cost, or $ATC = AFC + AVC$

average variable cost Variable cost divided by output, or $AVC = VC/q$

B

backward-bending supply curve of labor As the wage rises, the quantity of labor supplied may eventually decline; the income effect of a higher wage increases the demand for leisure, which reduces the quantity of labor supplied enough to more than offset the substitution effect of a higher wage

balance of payments A record of all economic transactions between residents of one country and residents of the rest of the world during a given period

balance on current account The portion of a country's balance-of-payments account that measures that country's balance on goods and services plus its net unilateral transfers

balance on goods and services The portion of a country's balance-of-payments account that measures the value of a country's exports of goods and services minus the value of its imports of goods and services

balance sheet A financial statement that shows assets, liabilities, and net worth at a given point in time; all these are stock measures; because assets must equal liabilities plus net worth, the statement is in balance

bank branches A bank's additional offices that carry out banking operations

bank holding company A corporation that owns banks

bank notes Originally, papers promising a specific amount of gold or silver to anyone who presented them to issuing banks for redemption; today, Federal Reserve notes are mere paper money

barrier to entry Any impediment that prevents new firms from entering an industry and competing on an equal basis with existing firms

barter The direct exchange of one good for another without using money

base year The year with which other years are compared when constructing an index; the index equals 100 in the base year

basic research The search for knowledge without regard to how that knowledge will be used

behavioral assumption An assumption that describes the expected behavior of economic decision makers, what motivates them

beneficial supply shocks Unexpected events that increase aggregate supply, sometimes only temporarily

benefits-received tax principle Those who receive more benefits from the government program funded by a tax should pay more taxes

binding arbitration Negotiation in which union and management must accept an impartial observer's resolution of a dispute

bond Certificate reflecting a firm's promise to pay the lender periodic interest and to pay a fixed sum of money on the designated maturity date

bounded rationality The notion that there is a limit to the information that a firm's manager can comprehend and act on

budget line A line showing all combinations of two goods that can be purchased at given prices with a given amount of income

budget resolution A congressional agreement about total outlays, spending by major category, and expected revenues; it guides spending and revenue decisions by the many congressional committees and subcommittees

bureaus Government agencies charged with implementing legislation and financed by appropriations from legislative bodies

C

capital The buildings, equipment, and human skill used to produce goods and services

capital account The record of a country's international transactions involving purchases or sales of financial and real assets

capital deepening An increase in the amount of capital per worker; one source of rising labor productivity

capture theory of regulation Producers' political power and strong stake in the regulatory outcome lead them, in effect, to "capture" the regulating agency and prevail on it to serve producer interests

cartel A group of firms that agree to coordinate their production and pricing decisions to act like a monopolist

chain-weighted system An index that adjusts the weights from year to year in calculating a price index, thereby getting rid of much of the bias caused by a fixed-price weighting system

check A written order instructing the bank to pay someone from an amount deposited

checkable deposits Deposits in financial institutions against which checks can be written and ATM or debit cards can be applied

circular-flow model A diagram that outlines the flow of resources, products, income, and revenue among economic decision makers

classical economists A group of 18th- and 19th-century economists who believed that economic downturns were short-run phenomena that corrected themselves through natural market forces; thus, they believed the economy was self-correcting and needed no government intervention

Clayton Act of 1914 Beefed up the Sherman Act; outlawed certain anti-competitive practices not prohibited by the Sherman Act, including price discrimination, tying contracts, exclusive dealing, interlocking directorates, and buying the corporate stock of a competitor

Coase theorem As long as bargaining costs are low, an efficient solution to the problem of externalities will be achieved by assigning property rights to one party or the other

coincident economic indicators Variables that reflect peaks and troughs as they occur; examples include employment, personal income, and industrial production

COLA Cost-of-living adjustment; the increase in a transfer payment or wage that reflects the increase in the price level

cold turkey The announcement and execution of tough measures to reduce high inflation

collateral An asset pledged by the borrower that can be sold to pay off the loan in the event the loan is not repaid

collective bargaining The process by which union and management negotiate a labor agreement

collusion An agreement among firms to increase economic profit by dividing the market or fixing the price

command-and-control environmental regulations An approach that required polluters to adopt particular technologies to reduce emissions by specific amounts; inflexible regulations based on engineering standards that ignore each firm's unique cost of reducing pollution

commercial banks Depository institutions that historically made short-term loans primarily to businesses

commodity A standardized product, a product that does not differ across producers, such as bushels of wheat or an ounce of gold

commodity money Anything that serves both as money and as a commodity; money that has intrinsic value

common-pool problem Unrestricted access to a resource results in overuse until its marginal value drops to zero

comparative advantage The ability to produce something at a lower opportunity cost than other producers face

competing-interest legislation Legislation that confers concentrated benefits on one group by imposing concentrated costs on another group

complements Goods, such as milk and cookies, that are related in such a way that an increase in the price of one shifts the demand for the other leftward

conglomerate merger A merger of firms in different industries

consent decree The accused party, without admitting guilt, agrees to stop the alleged activity if the government drops the charges

constant long-run average cost A cost that occurs when, over some range of output, long-run average cost neither increases nor decreases with changes in firm size

constant-cost industry An industry that can expand or contract without affecting the long-run per-unit cost of production; the long-run industry supply curve is horizontal

constant-elasticity demand curve The type of demand that exists when price elasticity is the same everywhere along the curve; the elasticity value is constant

consumer equilibrium The condition in which an individual consumer's budget is spent and the last dollar spent on each good yields the same marginal utility; therefore, utility is maximized

consumer price index, or CPI A measure of inflation based on the cost of a fixed market basket of goods and services

consumer surplus The difference between the maximum amount that a consumer is willing to pay for a given quantity of a good and what the consumer actually pays

consumption Household purchases of final goods and services, except for new residences, which count as investments

consumption function The relationship between consumption and income, other things constant

continuing resolutions Budget agreements that allow agencies, in the absence of an approved budget, to spend at the rate of the previous year's budget

contractionary fiscal policy A decrease in government purchases, increase in net taxes, or some combination of the two aimed at reducing aggregate demand enough to return the economy to potential output without worsening inflation; policy used to close an expansionary gap

contractionary gap The amount by which actual output in the short run falls short of the economy's potential output

convergence A theory predicting that the standard of living in economies around the world will grow more similar over time, with poorer countries eventually catching up with richer ones

coordination failure A situation in which workers and employers fail to achieve an outcome that all would prefer

core competency Area of specialty; the product or phase of production a firm supplies with greatest efficiency

corporate stock Certificate reflecting part ownership of a corporation

corporation A legal entity owned by stockholders whose liability is limited to the value of their stock

cost-push inflation A sustained rise in the price level caused by a leftward shift of the aggregate supply curve

craft union A union whose members have a particular skill or work at a particular craft, such as plumbers or carpenters

cross-price elasticity of demand The percentage change in the demand of one good divided by the percentage change in the price of another good

crowding in The potential for government spending to stimulate private investment in an otherwise dead economy

crowding out The displacement of interest-sensitive private investment that occurs when higher government deficits drive up interest rates

currency appreciation With respect to the dollar, a decrease in the number of dollars needed to purchase 1 unit of foreign exchange in a flexible rate system

currency depreciation With respect to the dollar, an increase in the number of dollars needed to purchase 1 unit of foreign exchange in a flexible rate system

currency devaluation An increase in the official pegged price of foreign exchange in terms of the domestic currency

currency revaluation A reduction in the official pegged price of foreign exchange in terms of the domestic currency

cyclical unemployment Unemployment that fluctuates with the business cycle, increasing during contractions and decreasing during expansions

cyclically balanced budget A budget philosophy calling for budget deficits during recessions to be financed by budget surpluses during expansions

D

deadweight loss of monopoly Net loss to society when a firm uses its market power to restrict output and increase price

debit card Cards that tap directly into the depositor's bank account to fund purchases; also called a check card, and usually doubles as an ATM card

decision-making lag The time needed to decide what to do once a macroeconomic problem has been identified

deflation A sustained decrease in the price level

demand A relation between the price of a good and the quantity that consumers are willing and able to buy during a given period, other things constant

demand curve A curve showing the relation between the price of a good and the quantity demanded during a given period, other things constant

demand for loanable funds The relationship between the market interest rate and the quantity of loanable funds demanded, other things constant

demand for money The relationship between how much money people want to hold and the interest rate

demand-pull inflation A sustained rise in the price level caused by a rightward shift of the aggregate demand curve

demand-side economics Macroeconomic policy that focuses on shifting the aggregate demand curve as a way of promoting full employment and price stability

dependent variable A variable whose value depends on that of the independent variable

depository institutions Commercial banks and thrift institutions; financial institutions that accept deposits from the public

depreciation The value of capital stock used up to produce GDP or that becomes obsolete during a year

depression A sharp reduction in an economy's total output accompanied by high unemployment lasting more than a year; a severe economic contraction

derived demand Demand that arises from the demand for the product the resource produces

developing countries Countries with a low living standard because of little human and physical capital per worker

differentiated oligopoly An oligopoly that sells products that differ across suppliers, such as automobiles or breakfast cereal

discount rate The interest rate the Fed charges banks that borrow reserves

discounting Converting future dollar amounts into present value

discouraged workers Those who drop out of the labor force in frustration because they can't find work

discretionary fiscal policy The deliberate manipulation of government purchases, taxation, and transfer payments to promote macroeconomic goals, such as full employment, price stability, and economic growth

diseconomies of scale Forces that may eventually increase a firm's average cost as the scale of operation increases in the long run

disequilibrium The condition that exists in a market when the plans of buyers do not match those of sellers; a temporary mismatch between quantity supplied and quantity demanded as the market seeks equilibrium

disinflation A reduction in the rate of inflation

disposable income (DI) The income households have available to spend or to save after paying taxes and receiving transfer payments

dividends After-tax corporate profit paid to stockholders rather than retained by the firm and reinvested

division of labor Organizing production of a good into its separate tasks

Doha Round The current multilateral trade negotiations, which aims at lowering tariffs on a wide range of industrial and agricultural products; the first trade round under WTO

dominant-strategy equilibrium In game theory, the outcome achieved when each player's choice does not depend on what the other player does

double coincidence of wants Two traders are willing to exchange their products directly

double counting The mistake of including the value of intermediate goods plus the value of final goods in gross domestic product; counting the same good more than once

dumping Selling a product abroad for less than charged in the home market

duopoly A market with only two producers; a type of oligopoly market structure

E

earned-income tax credit A federal program that supplements the wages of the working poor

economic efficiency approach An approach that offers each polluter the flexibility to reduce emissions as cost-effectively as possible, given its unique cost conditions; the market for pollution rights is an example

economic fluctuations The rise and fall of economic activity relative to the long-term growth trend of the economy; also called business cycles

economic growth An increase in the economy's ability to produce goods and services; an outward shift of the production possibilities frontier

economic profit A firm's total revenue minus its explicit and implicit costs

economic regulation Government regulation of natural monopoly, where, because of economies of scale, average production cost is lowest when a single firm supplies the market

economic rent Portion of a resource's total earnings that exceeds its opportunity cost; earnings greater than the amount required to keep the resource in its present use

economic system The set of mechanisms and institutions that resolve the what, how, and for whom questions

economic theory, or economic model A simplification of reality used to make predictions about cause and effect in the real world

economics The study of how people use their scarce resources to satisfy their unlimited wants

economies of scale Forces that reduce a firm's average cost as the scale of operation increases in the long run

economies of scope Average costs decline as a firm makes different products rather than just one

economy The structure of economic activity in a community, a region, a country, a group of countries, or the world

effectiveness lag The time needed for changes in monetary or fiscal policy to affect the economy

efficiency The condition that exists when there is no way resources can be reallocated to increase the production of one good without decreasing the production of another

efficiency wage theory The idea that offering high wages attracts a more talented labor pool, making it easier for firms to hire and retain more-productive workers

elastic demand A change in price has a relatively large effect on quantity demanded; the percentage change in quantity demanded exceeds the percentage change in price; the resulting price elasticity has an absolute value exceeding 1.0

elastic supply A change in price has a relatively large effect on quantity supplied; the percentage change in quantity supplied exceeds the percentage change in price; the resulting price elasticity of supply exceeds 1.0

electronic banking, or e-banking Conducting banking transactions over the Internet

Employment Act of 1946 Law that assigned to the federal government the responsibility for promoting full employment and price stability

entitlement programs Guaranteed benefits for those who qualify for government transfer programs such as Social Security and Medicare

entrepreneur A profit-seeking decision maker who organizes an enterprise and assumes the risk of its operation

entrepreneurial ability Managerial and organizational skills needed to start a firm, combined with the willingness to take risks

equation of exchange The quantity of money, M, multiplied by its velocity, V, equals nominal GDP, which is the product of the price level, P, and real GDP, Y

equilibrium The condition that exists in a market when the plans of buyers match those of sellers, so quantity demanded equals quantity supplied and the market clears

excess capacity The difference between a firm's profit-maximizing quantity and the quantity that minimizes average cost

excess reserves Bank reserves exceeding required reserves

exchange rate The price measured in one country's currency of purchasing 1 unit of another country's currency

exclusive dealing A supplier prohibits customers from buying from other suppliers of the product

exhaustible resource A resource in fixed supply, such as crude oil or coal

expansion A phase of economic activity during which the economy's output increases

expansion path A line connecting points of tangency that identify the least-cost input combinations for producing alternative output rates; the expansion path need not be a straight line, though it generally slopes upward

expansionary fiscal policy An increase in government purchases, decrease in net taxes, or some combination of the two aimed at increasing aggregate demand enough to return the economy to its potential output thereby reducing unemployment; policy used to close a contractionary gap

expansionary gap The amount by which output in the short run exceeds the economy's potential output

expenditure approach to GDP A method of calculating GDP by adding spending on all final goods and services produced in the nation during the year

explicit cost Opportunity cost of resources employed by a firm that takes the form of cash payments

export promotion A development strategy that concentrates on producing for the export market

externality A cost or a benefit that falls on a third party and is therefore ignored by the two parties to the market transaction

F

fallacy of composition The incorrect belief that what is true for the individual, or part, must necessarily be true for the group, or whole

featherbedding Union efforts to force employers to hire more workers than wanted or needed

federal budget A plan for federal government outlays and revenues for a specified period, usually a year

federal budget deficit A flow variable that measures the amount by which federal government outlays exceed federal government revenues in a particular period, usually a year

federal funds market A market for overnight lending and borrowing of reserves among banks; the market for reserves on account at the Fed

federal funds rate The interest rate charged in the federal funds market; the interest rate banks charge one another for overnight borrowing; the Fed's target interest rate

Federal Open Market Committee (FOMC) The 12-member group that makes decisions about open-market operations—purchases and sales of U.S. government securities by the Fed that affect the money supply and interest rates; consists of the 7 Board governors plus 5 of the 12 presidents of the reserve banks

Federal Reserve System, or the Fed The central bank and monetary authority of the United States

Federal Trade Commission (FTC) Act of 1914 Established a federal body to help enforce antitrust laws; run by commissioners assisted by economists and lawyers

fiat money Money not redeemable for any commodity; its status as money is conferred initially by the government but eventually by common experience

final goods and services Goods and services sold to final, or end, users

financial intermediaries Institutions that serve as go-betweens, accepting funds from savers and lending them to borrowers

financial markets Banks and other financial institutions that facilitate the flow of funds from savers to borrowers

firms Economic units formed by profit-seeking entrepreneurs who use resources to produce goods and services for sale

fiscal policy The use of government purchases, transfer payments, taxes, and borrowing to influence economy-wide activity such as inflation, employment, and economic growth

fixed cost Any production cost that is independent of the firm's rate of output

fixed exchange rate Rate of exchange between currencies pegged within a narrow range and maintained by the central bank's ongoing purchases and sales of currencies

fixed resource Any resource that cannot be varied in the short run

fixed-production technology Occurs when the relationship between the output rate and the generation of an externality is fixed; the only way to reduce the externality is to reduce the output

flexible exchange rate Rate determined by the forces of demand and supply without government intervention

flow variable A variable that measures something over an interval of time, such as your income per week

food stamps An in-kind transfer program that offers low-income households vouchers redeemable for food; benefit levels vary inversely with household income

foreign exchange Foreign money needed to carry out international transactions

fractional reserve banking system Only a portion of bank deposits is backed by reserves

free-rider problem Because a public good is nonexclusive, people may try to reap the benefits of the good without paying for it

frictional unemployment Unemployment that occurs because job seekers and employers need time to find each other

full employment Employment level when there is no cyclical unemployment

functional finance A budget philosophy using fiscal policy to achieve the economy's potential GDP, rather than balancing budgets either annually or over the business cycle

G

game theory An approach that analyzes oligopolistic behavior as a series of strategic moves and countermoves by rival firms

GDP price index A comprehensive price index of all goods and services included in the gross domestic product

General Agreement on Tariffs and Trade (GATT) An international tariff-reduction treaty adopted in 1947 that resulted in a series of negotiated "rounds" aimed at freer trade; the Uruguay Round created GATT's successor, the World Trade Organization (WTO)

gold standard An arrangement whereby the currencies of most countries are convertible into gold at a fixed rate

golden rule of profit maximization To maximize profit or minimize loss, a firm should produce the quantity at which marginal revenue equals marginal cost; this rule holds for all market structures

good A tangible item used to satisfy human wants

government debt A stock variable that measures the net accumulation of annual budget deficits

government purchase function The relationship between government purchases and the economy's income, other things constant

government purchases Spending for goods and services by all levels of government; government outlays minus transfer payments

graph A picture showing how variables relate in two-dimensional space; one variable is measured along the horizontal axis and the other along the vertical axis

Gresham's Law People tend to trade away inferior money and hoard the best

gross domestic product (GDP) The market value of all final goods and services produced in the nation during a particular period, usually a year

H

Herfindahl-Hirschman Index, or HHI A measure of market concentration that squares each firm's percentage share of the market then sums these squares

hidden actions One side of an economic relationship can do something that the other side cannot observe

hidden characteristics One side of the market knows more than the other side about product characteristics that are important to the other side

horizontal axis Line on a graph that begins at the origin and goes to the right and left; sometimes called the x axis

horizontal merger A merger in which one firm combines with another that produces the same product

hyperinflation A very high rate of inflation

hypothesis A theory about relationships among key variables

hysteresis The theory that the natural rate of unemployment depends in part on the recent history of unemployment; high unemployment rates increase the natural rate of unemployment

I

implementation lag The time needed to introduce a change in monetary or fiscal policy

implicit cost A firm's opportunity cost of using its own resources or those provided by its owners without a corresponding cash payment

import substitution A development strategy that emphasizes domestic manufacturing of products that were imported

income approach to GDP A method of calculating GDP by adding all payments for resources used to produce output in the nation during the year

income assistance programs Welfare programs that provide money and in-kind assistance to the poor; benefits do not depend on prior contributions

income effect of a price change A fall in the price of a good increases consumers' real income, making consumers more able to purchase goods; for a normal good, the quantity demanded increases

income effect of a wage increase A higher wage increases a worker's income, increasing the demand for all normal goods, including leisure, so the quantity of labor supplied to market work decreases

income elasticity of demand The percentage change in demand divided by the percentage change in consumer income; the value is positive for normal goods and negative for inferior goods

income-expenditure model A relationship between aggregate income and aggregate spending that determines, for a given price level, where the amount people plan to spend equals the amount produced

increasing-cost industry An industry that faces higher per-unit production costs as industry output expands in the long run; the long-run industry supply curve slopes upward

increasing marginal returns The marginal product of a variable resource increases as each additional unit of that resource is employed

independent variable A variable whose value determines that of the dependent variable

indifference curve A curve showing all combinations of goods that provide the consumer with the same satisfaction, or the same utility

indifference map A set of indifference curves representing each possible level of total utility that can be derived by a particular consumer from consumption of two goods; a map of the consumer's tastes for the two goods

individual demand The demand of an individual consumer

individual supply The supply of an individual producer

industrial market countries Economically advanced capitalist countries of Western Europe, North America, Australia, New Zealand, and Japan, plus the newly industrized Asian economies of Taiwan, South Korea, Hong Kong, and Singapore

industrial policy The view that government—using taxes, subsidies, and regulations—should nurture the industries and technologies of the future, thereby giving these domestic industries an advantage over foreign competition

Industrial Revolution Development of large-scale factory production that began in Great Britain around 1750 and spread to the rest of Europe, North America, and Australia

industrial union A union of both skilled and unskilled workers from a particular industry, such as autoworkers or steelworkers

inelastic demand A change in price has relatively little effect on quantity demanded; the percentage change in quantity demanded is less than the percentage change in price; the resulting price elasticity has an absolute value less than 1.0

inelastic supply A change in price has relatively little effect on quantity supplied; the percentage change in quantity supplied is less than the percentage change in price; the price elasticity of supply has a value less than 1.0

inferior good A good, such as used clothes, for which demand decreases, or shifts leftward, as consumer incomes rise

inflation An increase in the economy's average price level

inflation target Central bankers commit not to exceed a certain inflation rate for the next year or two

Information Revolution Technological change spawned by the invention of the microchip and the Internet that enhanced the acquisition, analysis, and transmission of information

initial public offering (IPO) The initial sale of corporate stock to the public

injection Any spending other than by households or any income other than from resource earnings; includes investment, government purchases, exports, and transfer payments

innovation The process of turning an invention into a marketable product

interest Payment to resource owners for the use of their capital; the dollar amount paid by borrowers to lenders

interest rate Interest per year as a percentage of the amount saved, borrowed, or loaned

interlocking directorate A person serves on the boards of directors of two or more competing firms

intermediate goods and services Goods and services purchased by firms for further reprocessing and resale

International Monetary Fund (IMF) An international organization that establishes rules for maintaining the international monetary system and makes loans to countries with temporary balance-of-payments problems

inventories Producers' stocks of finished and in-process goods

investment The purchase of new plants, new equipment, new buildings, and new residences, plus net additions to inventories

investment function The relationship between the amount businesses plan to invest and the economy's income, other things constant

isocost line Line identifying all combinations of capital and labor the firm can hire for a given total cost

isoquant A curve that shows all the technologically efficient combinations of two resources, such as labor and capital, that produce a certain amount of output

L

labor The physical and mental effort used to produce goods and services

labor force Those 16 years of age and older who are either working or looking for work

labor force participation rate The labor force as a percentage of the adult population

labor productivity Output per unit of labor; measured as real GDP divided by the hours of labor employed to produce that output

labor union A group of workers who organize to improve their terms of employment

lagging economic indicators Variables that follow, or trail, changes in overall economic activity; examples include the interest rate and the average duration of unemployment

law of comparative advantage The individual, firm, region, or country with the lowest opportunity cost of producing a particular good should specialize in that good

law of demand The quantity of a good demanded during a given period relates inversely to its price, other things constant

law of diminishing marginal returns As more of a variable resource is added to a given amount of a fixed resource, marginal product eventually declines and could become negative

law of diminishing marginal utility The more of a good a person consumes per period, the smaller the increase in total utility from consuming one more unit, other things constant

law of increasing opportunity cost To produce each additional increment of a good, a successively larger increment of an alternative good must be sacrificed if the economy's resources are already being used efficiently

law of supply The quantity of a good supplied during a given period is usually directly related to its price, other things constant

leading economic indicators Variables that predict, or *lead to,* a recession or recovery; examples include consumer confidence, stock market prices, business investment, and big-ticket purchases, such as automobiles and homes

leakage Any diversion of income from the domestic spending stream; includes saving, taxes, and imports

legal tender U.S. currency that constitutes a valid and legal offer of payment of debt

leisure Time spent on nonwork activities

liability Anything that is owed to another individual or institution

life-cycle model of consumption and saving Young people borrow, middle agers pay off debts and save, and older people draw down their savings; on average net savings over a lifetime is small

linear demand curve A straight-line demand curve; such a demand curve has a constant slope but usually has a varying price elasticity

liquidity A measure of the ease with which an asset can be converted into money without a significant loss of value

loanable funds market The market in which savers (suppliers of loanable funds) and borrowers (demanders of loanable funds) come together to determine the market interest rate and the quantity of loanable funds exchanged

long run In microeconomics, a period during which all resources under the firm's control are variable; in macroeconomics, a period during which wage contracts and resource price agreements can be renegotiated; there are no surprises about the economy's actual price level

long-run aggregate supply (LRAS) curve A vertical line at the economy's potential output; aggregate supply when there are no surprises about the price level and all resource contracts can be renegotiated

long-run average cost curve A curve that indicates the lowest average cost of production at each rate of output when the size, or scale, of the firm varies; also called the planning curve

long-run equilibrium The price level and real GDP that occurs when (1) the actual price level equals the expected price level, (2) real GDP supplied equals potential output, and (3) real GDP supplied equals real GDP demanded

long-run industry supply curve A curve that shows the relationship between price and quantity supplied by the industry once firms adjust fully to any change in market demand

long-run Phillips curve A vertical line drawn at the economy's natural rate of unemployment that traces equilibrium points that can occur when workers and employers have the time to adjust fully to any unexpected change in aggregate demand

Lorenz curve A curve showing the percentage of total income received by a given percentage of recipients whose incomes are arrayed from smallest to largest

M

M1 The narrowest measure of the money supply, consisting of currency and coins held by the nonbanking public, checkable deposits, and traveler's checks

M2 A money aggregate consisting of M1 plus savings deposits, small-denomination time deposits, and money market mutual funds

M3 A money aggregate consisting of M2 plus large-denomination time deposits

macroeconomics The study of the economic behavior of entire economies

managed float system An exchange rate system that combines features of freely floating rates with sporadic intervention by central banks

marginal Incremental, additional, or extra; used to describe a change in an economic variable

marginal cost The change in total cost resulting from a one-unit change in output; the change in total cost divided by the change in output, or $MC = \Delta TC/\Delta q$

marginal product The change in total product that occurs when the use of a particular resource increases by one unit, all other resources constant

marginal propensity to consume (MPC) The fraction of a change in income that is spent on consumption; the change in consumption divided by the change in income that caused it

marginal propensity to save (MPS) The fraction of a change in income that is saved; the change in saving divided by the change in income that caused it

marginal rate of return on investment The marginal revenue product of capital expressed as a percentage of its marginal cost

marginal rate of substitution (MRS) A measure of how much of one good a consumer would give up to get one more unit of another good, while remaining equally satisfied

marginal rate of technical substitution (MRTS) The rate at which one resource, such as labor, can substitute for another, such as capital, without affecting total output

marginal resource cost The change in total cost when an additional unit of a resource is hired, other things constant

marginal revenue The change in total revenue from selling an additional unit; in perfect competition, marginal revenue is also the market price

marginal revenue product The change in total revenue when an additional unit of a resource is hired, other things constant

marginal social benefit The sum of the marginal private benefit and the marginal external benefit of production or consumption

marginal social cost The sum of the marginal private cost and the marginal external cost of production or consumption

marginal tax rate The percentage of each additional dollar of income that goes to the tax

marginal utility The change in total utility derived from a one-unit change in consumption of a good

marginal valuation The dollar value of the marginal utility derived from consuming each additional unit of a good

market A set of arrangements through which buyers and sellers carry out exchange at mutually agreeable terms

market demand Sum of the individual demands of all consumers in the market

market failure A condition that arises when the unregulated operation of markets yields socially undesirable results

market power The ability of a firm to raise its price without losing all its customers to rival firms

market structure Important features of a market, such as the number of firms, product uniformity across firms, firms' ease of entry and exit, and forms of competition

market supply The sum of individual supplies of all producers in the market

market work Time sold as labor

means-tested program A program in which, to be eligible, an individual's income and assets must not exceed specified levels

median income The middle income when all incomes are ranked from smallest to largest

median voter model Under certain conditions, the preferences of the median, or middle, voter will dominate other preferences

median wage The middle wage when wages of all workers are ranked from lowest to highest

mediator An impartial observer who helps resolve differences between union and management

Medicaid An in-kind transfer program that provides medical care for poor people; by far the most costly welfare program

Medicare Social insurance program providing health insurance for short-term medical care to older Americans, regardless of income

medium of exchange Anything that facilitates trade by being generally accepted by all parties in payment for goods or services

mercantilism The incorrect theory that a nation's economic goal should be to accumulate precious metals in the public treasury; this theory prompted trade barriers to reduce imports, but other countries retaliated, reducing trade and the gains from specialization

merchandise trade balance The value of a country's exported goods minus the value of its imported goods during a given period

microeconomics The study of the economic behavior in particular markets, such as that for computers or unskilled labor

minimum efficient scale The lowest rate of output at which a firm takes full advantage of economies of scale

mixed system An economic system characterized by the private ownership of some resources and the public ownership of other resources; some markets are unregulated and others are regulated

monetary policy Regulation of the money supply to influence economy-wide activity such as inflation, employment, and economic growth

money Anything that is generally accepted in exchange for goods and services

money aggregates Measures of the economy's money supply

money income The number of dollars a person receives per period, such as $400 per week

money market mutual fund A collection of short-term interest-earning assets purchased with funds collected from many shareholders

money multiplier The multiple by which the money supply increases as a result of an increase in fresh reserves in the banking system

monopolistic competition A market structure with many firms selling products that are substitutes but different enough that each firm's demand curve slopes downward; firm entry is relatively easy

monopoly A sole producer of a product for which there are no close substitutes

moral hazard A situation in which one party, as a result of a contract, has an incentive to alter their behavior in a way that harms the other party to the contract

movement along a demand curve Change in quantity demanded resulting from a change in the price of the good, other things constant

movement along a supply curve Change in quantity supplied resulting from a change in the price of the good, other things constant

N

national debt The net accumulation of federal budget deficits

national income All income earned by American-owned resources, whether located in the United States or abroad

natural monopoly One firm that can serve the entire market at a lower per-unit cost than can two or more firms

natural rate hypothesis The natural rate of unemployment is largely independent of the stimulus provided by monetary or fiscal policy

natural rate of unemployment The unemployment rate when the economy produces its potential output

natural resources So-called gifts of nature used to produce goods and services; includes renewable and exhaustible resources

negative, or inverse, relation Occurs when two variables move in opposite directions; when one increases, the other decreases

net domestic product Gross domestic product minus depreciation

net export function The relationship between net exports and the economy's income, other things constant

net exports The value of a country's exports minus the value of its imports

net taxes (NT) Taxes minus transfer payments

net unilateral transfers The unilateral transfers (gifts and grants) received from abroad by residents of a country minus the unilateral transfers sent abroad

net wealth The value of a assets minus liabilities

net worth Assets minus liabilities

nominal GDP GDP based on prices prevailing at the time of the transaction; current-dollar GDP

nominal interest rate The interest rate expressed in current dollars as a percentage of the amount loaned; the interest rate on the loan agreement

nominal wage The wage measured in current dollars; the dollar amount on a paycheck

nonmarket work Time spent getting an education or producing goods and services for personal consumption

normal good A good, such as new clothes, for which demand increases, or shifts rightward, as consumer incomes rise

normal profit The accounting profit earned when all resources earn their opportunity cost

normative economic statement A statement that represents an opinion, which cannot be proved or disproved

O

oligopoly A market structure characterized by a few firms whose behavior is interdependent

open-access good A good that is rival in consumption but nonexclusive, such as ocean fish

open-market operations Purchases and sales of government securities by the Federal Reserve in an effort to influence the money supply

open-market purchase The purchase of U.S. government bonds by the Fed to increase the money supply

open-market sale The sale of U.S. government bonds by the Fed to reduce the money supply

opportunity cost The value of the best alternative forgone when an item or activity is chosen

origin On a graph depicting two-dimensional space, the zero point; the point of departure

other-things-constant assumption The assumption, when focusing on the relation among key economic variables, that other variables remain unchanged

outsourcing A firm buys inputs from outside suppliers

P

partnership A firm with multiple owners who share the firm's profits and bear unlimited liability for the firm's debts

patent A legal barrier to entry that grants its holder the exclusive right to sell a product for 20 years from the date the patent application is filed

payoff matrix In game theory, a table listing the payoffs that each player can expect based on the actions of the other player

per se illegal In antitrust law, business practices that are deemed illegal regardless of their economic rationale or their consequences

perfect competition A market structure with many fully informed buyers and sellers of a standardized product and no obstacles to entry or exit of firms in the long run

perfectly discriminating monopolist A monopolist who charges a different price for each unit sold; also called the monopolist's dream

perfectly elastic demand curve A horizontal line reflecting a situation in which any price increase reduces quantity demanded to zero; the elasticity has an absolute value of infinity

perfectly elastic supply curve A horizontal line reflecting a situation in which any price decrease drops the quantity supplied to zero; the elasticity value is infinity

perfectly inelastic demand curve A vertical line reflecting a situation in which any price change has no effect on the quantity demanded; the elasticity value equals zero

perfectly inelastic supply curve A vertical line reflecting a situation in which a price change has no effect on the quantity supplied; the elasticity value is zero

permanent income Income that individuals expect to receive on average over the long term

personal income The amount of before-tax income received by households; national income less income earned but not received plus income received but not earned

per-worker production function The relationship between the amount of capital per worker in the economy and average output per worker

Phillips curve A curve showing possible combinations of the inflation rate and the unemployment rate

physical capital Manufactured items used to produce goods and services; includes new plants and new equipment

planned investment The amount of investment that firms plan to undertake during a year

political business cycles Economic fluctuations that result when discretionary policy is manipulated for political gain

populist legislation Legislation with widespread benefits but concentrated costs

pork-barrel spending Special-interest legislation with narrow geographical benefits but funded by all taxpayers

positive economic statement A statement that can be proved or disproved by reference to facts

positive rate of time preference Consumers value present consumption more than future consumption

positive, or direct, relation Occurs when two variables increase or decrease together; the two variables move in the same direction

potential output The economy's maximum sustainable output, given the supply of resources, technology, and production incentives; the output level when there are no surprises about the price level

predatory pricing Pricing tactics employed by a dominant firm to drive competitors out of business, such as temporarily selling below marginal cost or dropping the price only in certain markets

present value The value today of income to be received in the future

price ceiling A maximum legal price above which a good or service cannot be sold; to have an impact, a price ceiling must be set below the equilibrium price

price discrimination Increasing profit by charging different groups of consumers different prices when the price differences are not justified by differences in production costs

price elasticity formula Percentage change in quantity demanded divided by the percentage change in price; the average quantity and the average price are used as bases for computing percentage changes in quantity and in price

price elasticity of demand Measures how responsive quantity demanded is to a price change; the percentage change in quantity demanded divided by the percentage change in price

price elasticity of supply A measure of the responsiveness of quantity supplied to a price change; the percentage change in quantity supplied divided by the percentage change in price

price floor A minimum legal price below which a good or service cannot be sold; to have an impact, a price floor must be set above the equilibrium price

price index A number that shows the average price of goods; changes in a price index over time show changes in the economy's average price level

price leader A firm whose price is adopted by other firms in the industry

price level A composite measure reflecting the prices of all goods and services in the economy relative to prices in a base year

price maker A firm that must find the profit-maximizing price when the demand curve for its output slopes downward

price taker A firm that faces a given market price and whose quantity supplied has no effect on that price; a perfectly competitive firm

prime rate The interest rate lenders charge their most trustworthy business borrowers

principal A person or firm who hires an agent to act on behalf of that person or firm

principal-agent problem The agent's objectives differ from those of the principal's, and one side can pursue hidden actions

prisoner's dilemma A game that shows why players have difficulty cooperating even though they would benefit from cooperation

private good A good that is both rival in consumption and exclusive, such as pizza

private property rights An owner's right to use, rent, or sell resources or property

producer surplus A bonus for producers in the short run; the amount by which total revenue from production exceeds variable cost

product market A market in which a good or service is bought and sold

production function The relationship between the amount of resources employed and a firm's total product

production possibilities frontier (PPF) A curve showing alternative combinations of goods that can be produced when available resources are used fully and efficiently; a boundary between inefficient and unattainable combinations

productive efficiency The condition that exists when market output is produced using the least-cost combination of inputs; minimum average cost in the long run

productivity The ratio of a specific measure of output, such as real GDP, to a specific measure of input, such as labor; in this case productivity measures real GDP per hour of labor

profit The reward for entrepreneurial ability; the revenue from sales minus the cost of resources used by the entrepreneur

progressive taxation The tax as a percentage of income increases as income increases

proportional taxation The tax as a percentage of income remains constant as income increases; also called a flat tax

public good A good that, once produced, is available for all to consume, regardless of who pays and who doesn't; such a good is nonrival and nonexclusive, such as national defense

public utilities Government-owned or government-regulated monopolies

purchasing power parity (PPP) theory The idea that the exchange rate between two countries will adjust in the long run to reflect price-level differences between the countries

pure capitalism An economic system characterized by the private ownership of resources and the use of prices to coordinate economic activity in unregulated markets

pure command system An economic system characterized by the public ownership of resources and centralized planning

Q

quantity demanded The amount demanded at a particular price, as reflected by a point on a given demand curve

quantity supplied The amount offered for sale at a particular price, as reflected by a point on a given supply curve

quantity theory of money If the velocity of money is stable, or at least predictable, changes in the money supply have predictable effects on nominal GDP

quasi-public good A good that is nonrival in consumption but exclusive, such as cable TV

quota A legal limit on the quantity of a particular product that can be imported or exported

R

rational expectations A school of thought that argues people form expectations based on all available information, including the likely future actions of government policy makers

rational ignorance A stance adopted by voters when they find that the cost of understanding and voting on a particular issue exceeds the benefit expected from doing so

real GDP per capita Real GDP divided by the population; the best measure of an economy's standard of living

real gross domestic product (real GDP) The economy's aggregate output measured in dollars of constant purchasing power

real income Income measured in terms of the goods and services it can buy

real interest rate The interest rate expressed in dollars of constant purchasing power as a percentage of the amount loaned; the nominal interest rate minus the inflation rate

real wage The wage measured in dollars of constant purchasing power; the wage measured in terms of the quantity of goods and services it will buy

recession A decline in the economy's total output lasting at least two consecutive quarters, or six months; an economic contraction

recognition lag The time needed to identify a macroeconomic problem and assess its seriousness

recycling The process of converting waste products into reusable material

regressive taxation The tax as a percentage of income decreases as income increases

relevant resources Resources used to produce the good in question

renewable resource A resource that regenerates itself and so can be used indefinitely if used conservatively, such as a properly managed forest

rent Payment to resource owners for the use of their natural resources

rent seeking Activities undertaken by individuals or firms to influence public policy in a way that will increase their incomes

representative money Bank notes that exchange for a specific commodity, such as gold

required reserve ratio The ratio of reserves to deposits that banks are obligated by regulation to hold

required reserves The dollar amount of reserves a bank is obligated by regulation to hold

reserves Funds that banks use to satisfy the cash demands of their customers and the reserve requirements of the Fed; reserves consist of cash held by banks plus deposits at the Fed

residential construction Building new homes or dwelling places

resource complements Resources that enhance one another's productivity; an increase in the price of one resource decreases the demand for the other

resource market A market in which a resource is bought and sold

resource substitutes Resources that substitute in production; an increase in the price of one resource increases the demand for the other

resources The inputs, or factors of production, used to produce the goods and services that people want; resources consist of labor, capital, natural resources, and entrepreneurial ability

retained earnings After-tax corporate profit reinvested in the firm rather than paid to stockholders as dividends

right-to-work states States where workers in unionized companies do not have to join the union or pay union dues

rule of reason Before ruling on the legality of certain business practices, a court examines why they were undertaken and what effect they have on market competition

rules of the game The formal and informal institutions that promote economic activity; the laws, customs, conventions, and other institutional elements that determine transaction costs and thereby affect people's incentive to undertake production and exchange

S

saving function The relationship between saving and income, other things constant

savings deposits Deposits that earn interest but have no specific maturity date

scarcity Occurs when the amount people desire exceeds the amount available at a zero price

screening The process used by employers to select the most qualified workers based on readily observable characteristics, such as a job applicant's level of education and course grades

seasonal unemployment Unemployment caused by seasonal changes in the demand for certain kinds of labor

secondary effects Unintended consequences of economic actions that may develop slowly over time as people react to events

seigniorage The difference between the face value of money and the cost of supplying it; the "profit" from issuing money

service An activity used to satisfy human wants

Sherman Antitrust Act of 1890 First national legislation in the world against monopoly; prohibited trusts, restraint of trade, and monopolization, but the law was vague and, by itself, ineffective

shift of a demand curve Movement of a demand curve right or left resulting from a change in one of the determinants of demand other than the price of the good

shift of a supply curve Movement of a supply curve left or right resulting from a change in one of the determinants of supply other than the price of the good

short run In microeconomics, a period during which at least one of a firm's resources is fixed; in macroeconomics, a period during which some resource prices, especially those for labor, are fixed by explicit or implicit agreements

shortage At a given price, the amount by which quantity demanded exceeds quantity supplied; a shortage usually forces the price up

short-run aggregate supply (SRAS) curve A curve that shows a direct relationship between the price level and real GDP supplied in the short run, other things constant

short-run equilibrium The price level and real GDP that occur when the aggregate demand curve intersects the short-run aggregate supply curve

short-run firm supply curve A curve that shows the quantity a firm supplies at each price in the short run; in perfect competition, that portion of a firm's marginal cost curve that intersects and rises above the low point on its average variable cost curve

short-run industry supply curve A curve that indicates the quantity supplied by the industry at each price in the short run; in perfect competition, the horizontal sum of each firm's short-run supply curve

short-run Phillips curve Based on an expected inflation rate, a curve that reflects an inverse relationship between the inflation rate and the unemployment rate

signaling Using a proxy measure to communicate information about unobservable characteristics; the signal is more effective if more-productive workers find it easier to send than do less-productive workers

simple money multiplier The reciprocal of the required reserve ratio, or $1/r$; the maximum multiple of fresh reserves by which the money supply can increase

simple spending multiplier The ratio of a change in real GDP demanded to the initial change in spending that brought it about; the numerical value of the simple spending multiplier is $1/(1 - MPC)$; called "simple" because only consumption varies with income

simple tax multiplier The ratio of a change in real GDP demanded to the initial change in autonomous net taxes that brought it about; the numerical value of the simple tax multiplier is $-MPC/(1 - MPC)$

slope of a line A measure of how much the vertical variable changes for a given increase in the horizontal variable; the vertical change between two points divided by the horizontal increase

social insurance Government programs designed to help make up for lost income of people who worked but are now retired, unemployed, or unable to work because of disability or work-related injury

social regulation Government regulations aimed at improving health and safety

Social Security Supplements retirement income to those with a record of contributing to the program during their working years; by far the largest government redistribution program

social welfare The overall well-being of people in the economy; maximized when the marginal cost of production equals the marginal benefit to consumers

sole proprietorship A firm with a single owner who has the right to all profits and who bears unlimited liability for the firm's debts

special-interest legislation Legislation with concentrated benefits but widespread costs

specialization of labor Focusing work effort on a particular product or a single task

speculator Someone who buys or sells foreign exchange in hopes of profiting from fluctuations in the exchange rate over time

stagflation A contraction, or *stag*nation, of a nation's output accompanied by in*flation* in the price level

stock variable A variable that measures something at a particular point in time, such as the amount of money you have with you right now

store of value Anything that retains its purchasing power over time

strategy In game theory, the operational plan pursued by a player

strike A union's attempt to withhold labor from a firm to stop production

structural unemployment Unemployment because (1) the skills in demand do not match those of the unemployed, or (2) the unemployed do not live where the jobs are

substitutes Goods, such as Coke and Pepsi, that are related in such a way that an increase in the price of one shifts the demand for the other rightward

substitution effect of a price change When the price of a good falls, consumers substitute that good for other goods, which become relatively more expensive

substitution effect of a wage increase A higher wage encourages more work because other activities now have a higher opportunity cost

sunk cost A cost that has already been incurred in the past, cannot be recovered, and thus is irrelevant for present and future economic decisions

Supplemental Security Income (SSI) An income assistance program that provides cash transfers to the elderly poor and the disabled; a uniform federal payment is supplemented by transfers that vary across states

supply A relation between the price of a good and the quantity that producers are willing and able to sell during a given period, other things constant

supply curve A curve showing the relation between price of a good and the quantity supplied during a given period, other things constant

supply of loanable funds The relationship between the market interest rate and the quantity of loanable funds supplied, other things constant

supply shocks Unexpected events that affect aggregate supply, sometimes only temporarily

supply-side economics Macroeconomic policy that focuses on a rightward shift of the aggregate supply curve through tax cuts or other changes that increase production incentives

surplus At a given price, the amount by which quantity supplied exceeds quantity demanded; a surplus usually forces the price down

T

tangent A straight line that touches a curve at a point but does not cut or cross the curve; used to measure the slope of a curve at a point

tariff A tax on imports

tastes Consumer preferences; likes and dislikes in consumption; assumed to be constant along a given demand curve

tax incidence The distribution of tax burden among taxpayers; who ultimately pays the tax

technologically efficient Produces the maximum possible output given the combination of resources employed; that same output could not be produced with fewer resources

Temporary Assistance for Needy Families (TANF) An income assistance program funded largely by the federal government but run by the states to provide cash transfer payments to poor families with dependent children

term structure of interest rates The relationship between the duration of a loan and the interest rate charged; typically interest rates increase with the duration of the loan

terms of trade How much of one good exchanges for a unit of another good

thrift institutions, or thrifts Savings banks and credit unions; depository institutions that historically lent money to households

time deposits Deposits that earn a fixed rate of interest if held for the specified period, which can range from several months to several years; also called certificates of deposit

time-inconsistency problem When policy makers have an incentive to announce one policy to influence expectations but then pursue a different policy once those expectations have been formed and acted on

tit-for-tat In game theory, a strategy in repeated games when a player in one round of the game mimics the other player's behavior in the previous round; an optimal strategy for encouraging the other player to cooperate

token money Money whose face value exceeds its cost of production

total cost The sum of fixed cost and variable cost, or $TC = FC + VC$

total product The total output produced by a firm

total revenue Price multiplied by the quantity demanded at that price

total utility The total satisfaction a consumer derives from consumption; it could refer to either the total utility of consuming a particular good or the total utility from all consumption

traditional public-goods legislation Legislation that involves widespread costs and widespread benefits—nearly everyone pays and nearly everyone benefits

transaction costs The costs of time and information required to carry out market exchange

transfer payments Cash or in-kind benefits given to individuals as outright grants from the government

trust Any firm or group of firms that tries to monopolize a market

tying contract A seller of one good requires a buyer to purchase other goods as part of the deal

U

U.S. official poverty level Benchmark level of income computed by the federal government to track poverty over time; initially based on three times the cost of a nutritionally adequate diet

underemployment Workers are overqualified for their jobs or work fewer hours than they would prefer

underground economy An expression used to describe market activity that goes unreported either because it is illegal or because those involved want to evade taxes

undifferentiated oligopoly An oligopoly that sells a commodity, or a product that does not differ across suppliers, such as an ingot of steel or a barrel of oil

unemployment benefits Cash transfers for those who lose their jobs and actively seek employment

unemployment rate The number unemployed as a percentage of the labor force

unit of account A common unit for measuring the value of each good or service

unit-elastic demand The percentage change in quantity demanded equals the percentage change in price; the resulting price elasticity has an absolute value of 1.0

unit-elastic demand curve Everywhere along the demand curve, the percentage change in price causes an equal but offsetting percentage change in quantity demanded, so total revenue remains the same; the elasticity has an absolute value of 1.0

unit-elastic supply The percentage change in quantity supplied equals the percentage change in price; the resulting price elasticity of supply equals 1.0

unit-elastic supply curve A percentage change in price causes an identical percentage change in quantity supplied; depicted by a supply curve that is a straight line from the origin; the elasticity value equals 1.0

Uruguay Round The most recently concluded multilateral trade negotiation under GATT; this 1994 agreement cut tariffs, formed the World Trade Organization (WTO), and will eventually eliminate quotas

utility The satisfaction or sense of well-being received from consumption

V

value added The difference at each stage of production between the selling price of a product and the cost of intermediate goods purchased from other firms

variable A measure, such as price or quantity, that can take on different values

variable resource Any resource that can be varied in the short run to increase or decrease production

variable technology Occurs when the amount of externality generated at a given rate of output can be reduced by altering the production process

velocity of money The average number of times per year each dollar is used to purchase final goods and services

vertical axis Line on a graph that begins at the origin and goes up and down; sometimes called the y axis

vertical integration The expansion of a firm into stages of production earlier or later than those in which it specializes, such as a steel maker that also mines iron ore

vertical merger A merger in which one firm combines with another from which it had purchased inputs or to which it had sold output

W

wages Payment to resource owners for their labor

winner's curse The plight of the winning bidder who overestimates an asset's true value

winner-take-all labor markets Markets in which a few key employees critical to the overall success of an enterprise are richly rewarded

world price The price at which a good is traded on the world market; determined by the world supply and world demand for the good

World Trade Organization (WTO) The legal and institutional foundation of the multilateral trading system that succeeded GATT in 1995